POOLEYS FLIGHT GUIDE
UNITED KINGDOM
2001

Compiled with the assistance of
THE CIVIL AVIATION AUTHORITY

Editors
Robert Pooley
Roy Patel
Consultant Editor
William Ryall

For Julian

POOLEYS FLIGHT EQUIPMENT LIMITED,
ELSTREE AERODROME, ELSTREE, HERTS. WD6 3AW
Tel/Fax: (+44) 020 8207 0171 - Editorial
E-Mail: Editor@pooleys.com

See page iii for other telephone numbers

ISBN

0 902037 96 X Loose Leaf
0 902037 86 2 Bound Volume
0 902037 91 9 Spiral Bound

Pooleys Flight Equipment Ltd
Elstree Aerodrome
Elstree
Hertfordshire
WD6 3AW
England
Fax 020 8953 5219

CONTENTS

INDEX TO UNITED KINGDOM AERODROMES

Aerodrome	Page

Aerodrome	Page

POOLEYS FLIGHT GUIDE
AIRNOTES
AN 1- 01.   14 February 2001

U.K FLIGHT INFORMATION REGIONS

xvi   Belfast (Aldergrove) Approach frequency changed to 124·90.

SERVICES TO AIRCRAFT OUTSIDE CONTROLLED AIRSPACE

17   Sub paragraph (e), line 3 - amend 5000 ft to 3000 ft.

LOWER AIRSPACE RADAR SERVICE (LARS)

21/22   London/Luton withdrawn.

NORTHERN OFF-ROUTE CO-ORDINATION AREA (NORCA)

25   Sub paragraph 1.1 - amend Airway B4/B1 to Airway B4/ L975.
Sub paragraph 2.2 (a) - amend Airway B1 to Airway L975.
27   Amend references to B1/UB1 to read L975/UL975.
28   Amend Airway B1 to L975.

DACS and DAAIS

35   **D207** Holbeach   Hours of activity: Sep-Apr, Tue & Thu changed to 1800-2300 and as notified.
D307 Donna Nook   Hours of activity: Sep-Apr, Tue & Thu changed to 1730-2300 and as notified.
37   **D708** Rosehearty   Danger Area withdrawn.

NAVIGATIONAL AIDS

38   Add: **Ballykelly** TACAN 'BKL' 109·10 N55 03·65 W007 00·80.
Campbeltown NDB 'CBL' 380·0 15 nm range N55 26·13 W005 41·10.
39   **Fife/Glenrothes** NDB 'GO' withdrawn.
40   Add **Leeming** TACAN 'LEE' 112·60 N54 17·80 W001 32·20.
41   **Newcastle** NDB 'NEW' co-ordinates revised to N55 03·02 W001 38·57.
NDB 'WZ' co-ordinates revised to N55 00·40 W001 48·42.
42   **Shoreham** NDB 'SHM' co-ordinates revised to N50 50·13 W000 17·72.
DME 'SRH' co-ordinates revised to N50 50·17 W000 17·62.
Swansea DME 'SWZ' withdrawn.
Talla   NDB 'TLA' withdrawn.
43   **Vallafield** TACAN 'VFD' withdrawn.

AERODROME OPERATING MINIMA

57   **Gloucestershire** Rwy 09 NDB(L) 'GST'/DME 'GOS' minima revised to OCH 520, DH/MDH 720.

Rwy 27 SRA (0·5 nm termination range) minima revised to OCH 520, DH/MDH 720.
60   **Londonderry/Eglinton** Rwy 26 ILS/DME 'I EGT' minima revised to OCH 280, DH/MDH 500.

60   **Manchester**   Minima revised to:

Rwy	Approach Aid	OCH (ft)	DH/MDH (ft)
06R	ILS/DME 'I MC' or 'MCT'	135	500
06R	LLZ/DME 'I MC' or 'MCT'	320	600
06R	VOR/DME 'MCT' or 'I MC'	420	620
06L	ILS/DME 'I MM' or 'MCT'	146	500
06L	LLZ /DME 'I MM' or 'MCT'	370	600
06L	VOR/DME 'MCT' or 'I MM'	430	630
06L	NDB(L) 'MCH'/DME 'I MM' or 'MCT'	430	630
24R	ILS/DME 'I NN' or 'MCT'	142	500
24R	LLZ /DME 'I NN' or 'MCT'	300	600
24R	VOR/DME 'MCT' or 'I NN'	390	600
24R	NDB(L) 'MCH'/DME 'I NN' or 'MCT'	390	600
24L	VOR/DME 'MCT' or 'IMC'	410	610

AERODROMES

96   **BAGBY (Thirsk)**   Rwy 24 downslope revised to 2·5%
      Op hrs: 0830-SS (Services 0930-1900, closed Tue 1700-1930).
      Landing Fee: Free with fuel uplift.
      MATZ clearance to be obtained from Topcliffe.
      Catering: Sat and Sun hours changed to 1000-1600.

102   **BELFAST (Aldergrove)** Com/Nav: RAD freq 120·0 withdrawn.

104   VRPs:
      Ballymena: Amend HB 325°M to HB 324°M.
      Cluntoe: Amend BEL 265° to BEL 264° and OY 262°M to OY 261°M.
      Portadown: Amend all references to DUB R002 to DUB R001.

109   **BELFAST (City)** VRPs :
      Comber: Amend BEL 119°/18 nm to BEL 118°/18 nm and IOM R317 to IOM R316.
      Groomsport: Amend TRN R223 to TRN R224 and all references to IOM R328 to IOM R327.
      Saintfield: Amend all references to IOM R309 to IOM R 308.
      Whitehead: Amend all references to IOM R328 to IOM R327.

115   **BENBECULA** Tel: Aerodrome and Met information available on 01870-604818.

132   **BOURNEMOUTH** VRPs:
      Tarrant Rushton (Disused A/D): Amend SAM R261/28 nm to SAM R261/29 nm.

149   **CAERNARFON**   Rwy 20 LDA revised to 1040.

153   **CAMPBELTOWN** Com/Nav: New facility - NDB 'CBL' 380·0 (On A/D).

164   **CHILBOLTON (Stonefield Park)** Hangarage: Available to de-rigged microlights only.
      Maintenance: Available by arrangement.
      Remarks - Helicopters are not permitted.
      Taxis: Tel - delete 0589-292801.

175   **COVENTRY** Rwy 17/35 - Runway length changed to 708 m and Declared Distances to:
      Rwy 17 TORA 482, LDA 708. Rwy 35 TORA 708, LDA 482.

187   **DAVIDSTOW MOOR** Fax changed to: 01288-361402.

195   **DUNDEE** Sun op hrs changed to 0900-2100.

204   **EAST MIDLANDS** e-mail changed to: atsm@eastmidlandsairport.com

210   **EDINBURGH** Com/Nav: ATIS frequency 132·075 changed to 123·90.
      Holds - New Holds M6 and M5 established Rwy 12 threshold area.

229   **EXETER** Com/Nav: New facility - ATIS 119·325 introduced into service.

230   **FADMOOR (Moors National Park)** Fuel: 100LL - amend 60p to 70p.
      Tel: Mobile changed to 07989- 383 562.

236   **FARNBOROUGH** Com/Nav: New facility - ATIS 128·40 introduced into service.
      Rwy 11/29 closed as runway, and designated as Twy B.

237   **FARNBOROUGH** Rwy 11/29 closed.
      Remarks - Airport operated by TAG Aviation, Farnborough Airport, Farnborough, Hampshire
      GU14 6XA.

240	**FENLAND** Com/Nav: AFIS available by arrangement Sat and Sun.
	Fuel: Jet A1 not available.
	Tel: delete 01945-582891 Aerodrome Licencee.
241	**FIFE AIRPORT (Glenrothes)** Com/Nav: NDB 'GO' withdrawn.
267	**HENSTRIDGE** Op hrs: WINTER: PPR. 0900-1700 or SS if earlier/later.
	SUMMER: Mon-Sat 0900-1900, Sun 0900-1800.
275	**HUMBERSIDE** Op hrs: Sun-Fri 0630-2015; Sat 0630-2000.
277	**INVERNESS** Sun Winter op hrs changed to 0815-2200.
	Remarks - All international flights (including CI and Eire) and all domestic flights over 2729 kg
	MAUW must organise a handling agent.
294	**KIRKWALL** Sat op hrs changed to 0800-1715.
305	**LEEDS BRADFORD CTR/CTA Chart:** Amend Airway B1 to L975.
307	**LEEMING** Com/Nav: New facility - TACAN 'LEE' 112·60 (on A/D).
316	**LIVERPOOL** Holding Points - Hold V redesignated Hold V1. Hold V2 established north of it.
	Hold B only available to aircraft with a MTWA of 5700 kg or less.
321	**LONDON (City Airport)** Op hrs: Mon-Fri 0630-2155 PPR 2155-2230; Sat 0700-1230 PPR
	0630-0700 & 1230-1300; Sun 1230-2155 PPR 2155-2230.
327	**LONDON (Heathrow)** Rwy 23 LDA changed to 1962.
337	**LONDON (Stansted)** Com/Nav: Delivery frequency 125·55 changed to 121·95.
344	**LYDD** Rwy 04/22 - Declared Distances revised to: Rwy 04/22 TORA/LDA 1505;
	Rwy 22 TORA 1505, LDA 1468.
359	**MANCHESTER CTR/CTA Chart:** Amend Airway B1 to L975.
361	**MANCHESTER (Barton)** Remarks - Twins not accepted unless in emergency. Aircraft over
	1500 kg must apply in writing to aerodrome manager.
384	**NORTHAMPTON (Sywell)** Rwy 03/21 lighting - LITAS replaced by APAPI (4°) LH
	Landing Fee: Microlights £8.00; Singles, fixed & rotary – £10.00; Twins £18.00; All inc of VAT.
	Special rates for Circuit training.
386	**NORTHOLT** Remarks - Approaches to Rwy 07 offset by 30° to the left of the centreline until
	4 nm from touchdown in order to deconflict with Heathrow traffic patterns.
	High visibility clothing required on the apron areas.
397	**ODIHAM** Tel: Exts changed to Ext 7295 ATC, Ext 7254 Ops.
416	**PLYMOUTH City Airport** ARP changed to N50 25·37 W004 06·35.
417	**PLYMOUTH City Airport** ARP changed to N50 25·37 W004 06·35.
	Rwy 24 LDA revised to 710.
	Rwy 13/31- Declared Distances revised to: Rwy 13 TORA 1109, LDA 1027;
	Rwy 31 TORA 1102, LDA 1045.
422/23	**PRESTWICK** Aerodrome elevation changed to 65 ft amsl.
442	**SHEFFIELD CITY** Op hrs: PPR. Mon-Fri 0735-1930; Sat 1100-1215; Sun 1800-2000.
443	**SHEFFIELD CITY** Noise Abatement Procedures: Aircraft on visual approaches and circuit
	training height raised to 2000 ft aal.
	Add new line - Departures Rwy 28 must climb on runway heading until passing 1500 ft aal.
452	**SHOREHAM** A/G Stn op hrs changed to Mon-Sat 0800-0830 PPR.
454	**SHUTTLEWORTH (Old Warden)** Aerodrome closed until 1 May 2001 due to new runway
	construction.
457	**SLEAP** Rwy 05/23 width increased to 46 m.
458	**SOUTHAMPTON** Amend Osprey Hangar to Signature Hangar.
459	**SOUTHAMPTON** Sat and Sun Op hrs changed to - Sat 0630-1900 PPR 2130-2200;
	Sun 0930-2130 PPR 2130-2200.
	Hangarage/Maintenance: delete Osprey Aviation Ltd insert Signature Aircraft Engineering,
	Tel: 023-8048 3700; Fax: 023-8065 1897.
	Remarks - Handling Agencies: delete Osprey Aviation Ltd insert Signature Flight Support (Full
	FBO facilities), Tel: 023-8061 6600 (24 hrs); Fax: 023-8062 9684; Freq: 130·375;
	e-mail: eghi@signatureflight.co.uk
460	**SOUTHAMPTON VRPs:**
	Bishops Waltham: Amend SAM 095°/5nm to SAM 094°/5 nm, and EAS R095°M to EAS
	R094°M.
	Calshot: Amend BIA 088°M to BIA 087°M.
	Totton: Amend EAS 252°M to EAS 251°M.

| 465 | **SOUTHEND** Remarks - GA visitors are encouraged to wear high visibility clothing when airside. |

465   **SOUTHEND** Remarks - GA visitors are encouraged to wear high visibility clothing when airside.

Helicopter circuits normally parallel to the fixed wing runway in use and flown at 500 ft or 1000 ft as instructed by ATC.

473   **STORNOWAY** Op hrs - WINTER: Mon-Fri 0800-1730; Sat 0800-1500 and by arrangement.

513   **WICK** Tel: ATIS available on 01955-605428.

517   **WOODVALE** Op hrs: PPR by telephone. 0800-1800.

GOVERNMENT AERODROMES

561   **SCAMPTON** ARP changed to N53 18·46 W000 33·05.

HELICOPTER SITES

571   New Site:

H52a   COCKERMOUTH   N54 37·86 W003 22·21   308 ft AMSL

2 nm SW of Cockermouth   DCS 115·20 196 5·9

Concrete area NE end of the Hangar.

Remarks: Operated by M. Sport Ltd, Dovenby Hall, Dovenby, Cockermouth, Cumbria. CA13 0PN. Strictly PPR. Call Carlisle APP 123·60 for FIS.

Warnings: High lamp post near the Tennis court. Military low-level aircraft cross the area at all times of the day and night.

Fuel: Jet A1 by arrangement.   Tel: 01900-828 888. Fax: 01900-823823

                                     e.mail: nosment@m-sport.co.uk

578   New Site:

H89a   HATFIELD (Bush Hall Hotel)   N51 45·00 W000 12·00   207 ft AMSL

2 nm NNE of Hatfield (disused airfield)

Grass pad adjacent to the Hotel car park. 'H' displayed.

Remarks: Operated by Bush Hall Hotel, Mill Green, Hatfield, Herts. AL9 5NT.

Fuel: Nil.   Tel: 01707-271 251. Fax: 01707- 272 289.

578   **H90 HAYES (Heliport)** Remarks - Heliport operated by McAlpine Aviation Services Ltd.

599   **LONDON (Westland Heliport)** Name changed to LONDON Heliport.

HANG GLIDING and PARASCENDING WINCH/AUTO-TOW LAUNCH SITES

621   New Sites:

Bloreheath Farm, Almington,Shropshire N52 54·58 W002 26·40 Op ht 800 ft agl, Site Elev 300 ft amsl.

Cockle Park, Northumberland N55 12·23 W001 40·30 Op ht 2000 ft agl, Site Elev 248 ft amsl.

621   Hamble, Hamps - site withdrawn.

622   Wheaton Aston, Staffs - site withdrawn.

AVIATION ADDRESSES

639   Add: Beagle Pup Club, c/o 20 Primrose Close, Flitwick, Bedford MK45 1PJ.

Tel: 01525- 751 587. e-mail: pabbott@avnet.co.uk

640   Flying Farmers Association (FFA) - New Hon Secretary:

Paul Stephens, Moor Farm, West Heslerton, Malton, N Yorks. YO17 8RU.

Tel: 01944-738 281. Fax: 01944-738 240.

e-mail: gbsdg@farmline.com   Web: http://members.farmline.com/flyfarm

POOLEYS FLIGHT GUIDE

Elstree Aerodrome, Herts WD6 3AW.

Editorial Tel: 020 8207 0171. Fax: 020 8953 2512

E-mail: editor@pooleys.com

Distribution/Subscription Tel: 020 8207 3749. Fax: 020 8953 2512

E-mail: shop@pooleys.com

AMENDMENT

AN 2-01. 17 May 2001

Pages to be removed	Pages to be inserted
71/72......Metfax/Airmet.....................1 Dec 00	71/72 ....Metfax/Airmet....................17 May 01
73/74......Airmet.................................1 Dec 00	73/74 ....Airmet ....17 May 01
155/156..Cardiff ....1 Dec 00	155/156 ...Cardiff ....17 May 01
171/172..Compton Abbas ....1 Dec 00	171/172 ...Compton Abbas ....17 May 01
191/192..Denham/Derby...................1 Dec 00	191/192 ...Denham/Derby..................17 May 01
389/390..Northolt/North Ronaldsay...1 Dec 00	389/389a . Northolt ....17 May 01
	389b/390 .North Moor/North Ronaldsay 17 May 01

AIRNOTES

Airnotes provide a comprehensive listing of all changes applicable to the current Flight Guide, with the exception of those already incorporated in replacement pages. Changes notified since the last issue of Airnotes are identified by a 'bullet' in the left-hand margin.

To obviate the necessity of incorporating lengthy manuscript amendments, It is suggested that pages which are subject to amendment be suitably annotated, and then refer to the Airnotes, as required, for details of the changes.

Where extensive changes occur on any one page a revised page is issued.

POOLEYS FLIGHT GUIDE
AIRNOTES
AN 2- 01.   17 May 2001

● Denotes change since last Airnote.

U.K FLIGHT INFORMATION REGIONS

xvi   Belfast (Aldergrove) Approach frequency changed to 124·90.

SERVICES TO AIRCRAFT OUTSIDE CONTROLLED AIRSPACE

17   Sub paragraph (e), line 3 - amend 5000 ft to 3000 ft.

LOWER AIRSPACE RADAR SERVICE (LARS)

● **21/22**   LARS now also available from:
  Bournemouth on 119·625, 0730-2100, radius 30 nm.
  Southend on 128·95, 0900-1800, radius 25 nm.
● **21/22**   Humberside freq 124·67 changed to 119·125
  21/22   London/Luton withdrawn.

NORTHERN OFF-ROUTE CO-ORDINATION AREA (NORCA)

25   Sub paragraph 1.1 - amend Airway B4/B1 to Airway B4/ L975.
  Sub paragraph 2.2 (a) - amend Airway B1 to Airway L975.
27   Amend references to B1/UB1 to read L975/UL975.
28   Amend Airway B1 to L975.

DACS and DAAIS

● **35**   **D207** Holbeach Hours of activity: Sep-Apr, Tue & Thu changed to 1700-2200 and as
  notified.
● **35**   **D307** Donna Nook Hours of activity: Sep-Apr, Tue & Thu changed to 1630-2200 and as
  notified.
● **37**   **D703** Tain Hours of activity: Mon 0900-1700, Tue-Thu 0900-2200, Fri 0900-1400 as notified.
  37   **D708** Rosehearty Danger Area withdrawn.

NAVIGATIONAL AIDS

38   Add: **Ballykelly** TACAN 'BKL' 109·10 N55 03·65 W007 00·80.
         Campbeltown NDB 'CBL' 380·0 15 nm range N55 26·13 W005 41·10.
● **39**   **Coventry** NDB 'CT' amend co-ordinates to N52 24·65 W001 24·35.
●   **Cranfield** NDB 'CIT' co-ordinates revised to N52 07·82 W000 33·42.
● **39**   **Enniskillen** NDB 'EKN' co-ordinates revised to N54 23·65 W007 38·60.
         DME 'ENN' co-ordinates revised to N54 23·92 W007 39·22.
39   **Fife/Glenrothes** NDB 'GO' withdrawn.
40   Add **Leeming** TACAN 'LEE' 112·60 N54 17·80 W001 32·20.
41   **Newcastle** NDB 'NEW' co-ordinates revised to N55 03·02 W001 38·57.
         NDB 'WZ' co-ordinates revised to N55 00·40 W001 48·42.
42   **Shoreham** NDB 'SHM' co-ordinates revised to N50 50·13 W000 17·72.
         DME 'SRH' co-ordinates revised to N50 50·17 W000 17·62.
         Swansea DME 'SWZ' withdrawn.
         Talla NDB 'TLA' withdrawn.
43   **Vallafield** TACAN 'VFD' withdrawn.

AERODROME OPERATING MINIMA

● 55 **Bristol** Minima revised to:

Rwy	Approach Aid	OCH (ft)	DH/MDH (ft)
09	ILS/DME 'I BON'	145	500
09	LLZ/DME 'I BON'	300	600
09	NDB(L) 'BRI'/DME 'I BON'	320	600
09	NDB(L) 'BRI' (No DME)	390	600
09	SRA (2 nm termination range,1nm MAPt)	300	600
27	ILS/DME 'I BTS'	159	500
27	LLZ/DME 'I BTS'	310	600
27	NDB(L) 'BRI'/DME 'I BTS'	360	600
27	NDB(L) 'BRI' (No DME)	590	790
27	SRA (2 nm termination range)	540	740

57 **Gloucestershire** Rwy 09 NDB(L) 'GST'/DME 'GOS' minima revised to OCH 520, DH/MDH 720.
Rwy 27 SRA (0·5 nm termination range) minima revised to OCH 520, DH/MDH 720.

60 **Londonderry/Eglinton** Rwy 26 ILS/DME 'I EGT' minima revised to OCH 280, DH/MDH 500.

60 **Manchester** Minima revised to:

Rwy	Approach Aid	OCH (ft)	DH/MDH (ft)
06R	ILS/DME 'I MC' or 'MCT'	135	500
06R	LLZ/DME 'I MC' or 'MCT'	320	600
06R	VOR/DME 'MCT' or 'I MC'	420	620
06L	ILS/DME 'I MM' or 'MCT'	146	500
06L	LLZ /DME 'I MM' or 'MCT'	370	600
06L	VOR/DME 'MCT' or 'I MM'	430	630
06L	NDB(L) 'MCH'/DME 'I MM' or 'MCT'	430	630
24R	ILS/DME 'I NN' or 'MCT'	142	500
24R	LLZ /DME 'I NN' or 'MCT'	300	600
24R	VOR/DME 'MCT' or 'I NN'	390	600
24R	NDB(L) 'MCH'/DME 'I NN' or 'MCT'	390	600
24L	VOR/DME 'MCT' or 'IMC'	410	610

● 61 **Prestwick** Add: Rwy 21 SRA (2 nm termination range) OCH 760, DH/MDA 960.

AERODROMES

● 84 **ABERDEEN (Dyce)** Com/Nav: APP/RAD/VDF freq 120·40 changed to 119·05

96 **BAGBY (Thirsk)** Rwy 24 downslope revised to 2·5%
Op hrs: 0830-SS (Services 0930-1900, closed Tue 1700-1930).
Landing Fee: Free with fuel uplift.
MATZ clearance to be obtained from Topcliffe.
Catering: Sat and Sun hours changed to 1000-1600.

102 **BELFAST (Aldergrove)** Com/Nav: RAD freq 120·00 withdrawn.
● GND 121·75 operating hrs changed to Summer/Winter 0800-1730.

104 VRPs:
Ballymena: Amend HB 325°M to HB 324°M.
Cluntoe: Amend BEL 265° to BEL 264° and OY 262°M to OY 261°M.
Portadown: Amend all references to DUB R002 to DUB R001.

109 **BELFAST (City)** VRPs :
Comber: Amend BEL 119°/18 nm to BEL 118°/18 nm and IOM R317 to IOM R316.
Groomsport: Amend TRN R223 to TRN R224 and all references to IOM R328 to IOM R327.
Saintfield: Amend all references to IOM R309 to IOM R 308.
Whitehead: Amend all references to IOM R328 to IOM R327.

•	113	**BEMBRIDGE (Isle of Wight)** Rwy 30 LDA (Day) revised to 751.

- **113 BEMBRIDGE (Isle of Wight)** Rwy 30 LDA (Day) revised to 751.
  Op hrs: 0830-1700 daily, Sat & Sun 0900-1600 (WINTER), 0900-1800 (SUMMER).
  Landing Fee: Singles £10 to £15; Twins £20 to £25; incl of VAT. Touch and Go 50%.
  Remarks - Aerodrome operated by B.N. Group Ltd.
  Car Hire - Delete Avis, insert South Wight Rentals Tel: 01983-864263,
  U Drive Tel: 0800-0926545.

  115 BENBECULA Tel: Aerodrome and Met information available on 01870-604818.

- **122 BIRMINGHAM INTL** Twy Y withdrawn. Twy Z redesignated Twy Y.
  Hold Z redesignated Hold Y1. Hold Y2 established just NE of it on the redesignated Twy Y.

- **127 BLACKPOOL** Rwy 13 LDA revised to 924.

  132 BOURNEMOUTH VRPs:
  Tarrant Rushton (Disused A/D): Amend SAM R261/28 nm to SAM R261/29 nm.

- **149 CAERNARFON** Rwy 02/20 & Rwy 08/26 - Declared Distances revised to:
  Rwy 02 TORA 1076, LDA 925; Rwy 20 TORA 925, LDA 1040.
  Rwy 08 TORA/LDA 880; Rwy 26 TORA 880, LDA 820.

- **151 CAMBRIDGE** Remarks - Third Party Insurance cover requirement raised to £1,000,000.

  153 CAMPBELTOWN Com/Nav: New facility - NDB 'CBL' 380·0 (On A/D).

- **162 CHICHESTER (Goodwood)** Op hrs: PPR by telephone recommended. Summer: 0900-1800.
  Winter: Nov-Jan 0900-1600, Feb-Mar 0900-1700.
  Remarks - All aircraft must have Third Party Insurance cover of not less than £500,000.
  When relief Rwy 14L/32R in use, the thresholds will be marked with black and white prismatic
  markers.

  164 CHILBOLTON (Stonefield Park) Hangarage: Available to de-rigged microlights only.
  Maintenance: Available by arrangement.
  Remarks - Helicopters are not permitted.
  Taxis: Tel - delete 0589-292801.

- **173 COSFORD** New Runways: 06L/24R 1028m Grass (local acft ops); 06R/24L 1085m Grass
  (glider ops) ; 18L/36R 849m Grass (local acft ops); 18R/36L 849m Grass (glider ops).
  Tel: Amend to: 01902-377582/377030.

  175 COVENTRY Rwy 17/35 - Runway length changed to 708 m and Declared Distances to:
  Rwy 17 TORA 482, LDA 708. Rwy 35 TORA 708, LDA 482.

  187 DAVIDSTOW MOOR Fax changed to: 01288-361402.

  195 DUNDEE Sun op hrs changed to 0900-2100.

  204 EAST MIDLANDS e-mail changed to: atsm@eastmidlandsairport.com

  210 EDINBURGH Com/Nav: ATIS frequency 132·075 changed to 123·90.
  Holds - New Holds M6 and M5 established Rwy 12 threshold area.

- Com/Nav: New facility - GND 121·75 available Mon-Fri 0700-2000, Sat & Sun 0900-1900.

- **211 EDINBURGH** Rwy 06/24 - add: Take-off from intersection with Hold B1 - TORA 1889. Rwy 24
  Take-off from intersection with Hold C1 - TORA 1889.

- Remarks - Handling Agents: add Comet Handling, Tel: 0131-344 3172, Fax: 0131-333 2255.

- **223 ENNISKILLEN (St. Angelo)** Rwy 33 TORA revised to 1327 and LDA to 1004.

  229 EXETER Com/Nav: New facility - ATIS 119·325 introduced into service.

  230 FADMOOR (Moors National Park) Fuel: 100LL - amend 60p to 70p.
  Tel: Mobile changed to 07989- 383 562.

- **231 FAIR ISLE** Com/Nav: Delete Sumburgh APP 123·15, insert Sumburgh RAD 131·30.

  236 FARNBOROUGH Com/Nav: New facility - ATIS 128·40 introduced into service.
  Rwy 11/29 closed as runway, and designated as Twy B.

  237 FARNBOROUGH Rwy 11/29 closed.
  Remarks - Airport operated by TAG Aviation, Farnborough Airport, Farnborough, Hampshire
  GU14 6XA.

  240 FENLAND Com/Nav: AFIS available by arrangement Sat and Sun.
  Fuel: Jet A1 not available.
  Tel: delete 01945-582891 Aerodrome Licencee.

  241 FIFE AIRPORT (Glenrothes) Com/Nav: NDB 'GO' withdrawn.

- **242 FILTON** Com/Nav: ILS/DME Rwy 09 - amend LLZ to 094°M, and Rwy 27 LLZ to 274°M
  Remarks - Circuit height increased to: Jet/Turbo Prop - 2000 ft QFE, 2200 QNH;
  All others - 1500 ft QFE, 1700 ft QNH.

- **256** **GLOUCESTERSHIRE** Rwy 09/27- Declared Distances revised to: Rwy 09 TORA 1277, LDA 1159. Rwy 27 TORA 1319, LDA 1007.
  267 **HENSTRIDGE** Op hrs: WINTER: PPR. 0900-1700 or SS if earlier/later.
- SUMMER: Mon-Sat 0900-1900 - PPR for arrivals after 1800, Sun 0900-1800.
- Landing Fee: Singles/Twins £7.00; Microlights & Gyros £3.50.
  275 **HUMBERSIDE** Op hrs: Sun-Fri 0630-2015; Sat 0630-2000.
- Com/Nav: APP/RAD and LARS freq 124·675 changed to 119·125.
- **276** **INSCH** Com/Nav: Aberdeen APP- delete 120·40, insert 119·05.
  277 **INVERNESS** Sun Winter op hrs changed to 0815-2200.
  Remarks - All international flights (including CI and Eire) and all domestic flights over 2730 kg MAUW must organise a handling agent.
- Handling Agents: Execair Aviation Services Tel: 01667-461122, Fax: 01667- 461133; British Airways Tel: 01667-462280, Fax: 01667-462840 and Servisair Tel: 01667-461030, Fax: 01667-461006.
- **287** **JERSEY** Remarks - GA aircraft with MAUW of less than 3 tonnes will normally be parked at Jersey Aero Club on the grass. The Aero Club will provide customs, immigration, handling and collection of landing fees. Aircraft with a MAUW of 3 tonnes or more will normally be parked at Aviation Beauport.
  294 **KIRKWALL** Sat op hrs changed to 0800-1715.
  305 **LEEDS BRADFORD** CTR/CTA Chart: Amend Airway B1 to L975.
  307 **LEEMING** Com/Nav: New facility - TACAN 'LEE' 112·60 (on A/D).
- **309** **LEICESTER** Landing Fee: Singles £10.00, Twins £20.00, incl VAT. Weekends only - all landing fees free with fuel uplift of 50 litres or more.
  316 **LIVERPOOL** Holding Points - Hold V redesignated Hold V1. Hold V2 established north of it. Hold B only available to aircraft with a MTWA of 5700 kg or less.
- **317** **LIVERPOOL** Landing Fee: Amend £17.45 to £17.87.
  Twy A from Hold A3 to Rwy 27 threshold restricted to aircraft with less than 52 m wingspan.
  Tel: Delete 0151-288 4302 Flight Planning, insert 0151-288 4151 Apron Control.
- **319** **LIVERPOOL** VRPs: Kirkby - Amend WAL R065/10 nm to WAL R065/11 nm;
  Seaforth - Amend WAL R046/5 NM to WAL R046/6 nm;
  Stretton Aerodrome - Amend MCT R271/9 nm to MCT R271/10 nm.
- **321** **LONDON (City Airport)** Op hrs: Mon-Fri 0645-2145, Sat 0645-1230, Sun 1230-2145.
- **322** **LONDON (Gatwick)** Following taxiways redesignated: 3 to K, 4 to L, 5 to N, 6 to P, 7 to Q, 8 to R, 9 to S and 10 to T.
- **323** **LONDON (Gatwick)** Com/Nav: GND 121·80 op hrs changed to 0500-2359.
  327 **LONDON (Heathrow)** Rwy 23 LDA changed to 1962.
- **331** **LONDON (Luton)** Remarks - Handling Agents: Amend Magec Aviation to Signature Flight Support, Tel: 01582-724182.
  Tel/Fax: ATC changed to 01582-395029.
  Tel: Add: 01582-395525 Ops; 01582-395257 Airport Duty Officer.
  Fax: ATC changed 01582-395309. Add: 01582-395257 Airport Duty Officer.
  337 **LONDON (Stansted)** Com/Nav: Delivery frequency 125·55 changed to 121·95.
- **341a** **LONDONDERRY (Eglinton)** Op hrs: Strictly PPR by phone. Mon-Fri 0715-2115, Sat 0715-1645, Sun 1230-2115.
  344 **LYDD** Rwy 04/22 - Declared Distances revised to: Rwy 04/22 TORA/LDA 1505; Rwy 22 TORA 1505, LDA 1468.
- **349** **MANCHESTER AIRPORT** Twys T and S changed to: Twy T changed to Rwy S. Twy T now commences at Hold T1 and ends at the Starter Extension Rwy 24L.
  359 **MANCHESTER** CTR/CTA Chart: Amend Airway B1 to L975.
  361 **MANCHESTER (Barton)** Remarks - Twins not accepted unless in emergency. Aircraft over 1500 kg must apply in writing to aerodrome manager.
- **365** **MANSTON** Remarks - Rwy 08 is the preferred departure runway when there is a tailwind component of 5 kt or less.
  GA aircraft under 4 tonnes PPR from TG Aviation, Tel: 01843-823656, Fax: 01843- 822024.
  384 **NORTHAMPTON (Sywell)** Rwy 03/21 lighting - LITAS replaced by APAPI (4°) LH
  Landing Fee: Microlights £8.00; Singles, fixed & rotary – £10.00; Twins £18.00; All inc of VAT.
  Special rates for Circuit training.

386	**NORTHOLT** Remarks - Approaches to Rwy 07 offset by 30° to the left of the centreline until 4 nm from touchdown in order to deconflict with Heathrow traffic patterns. High visibility clothing required on the apron areas.
397	**ODIHAM** Tel: Exts changed to Ext 7295 ATC, Ext 7254 Ops.
● 411	**PERTH (Scone)** Rwy 10/28 - Rwy lighting installed. Op hrs: PPR. WINTER: 0900-1700 - daylight hrs only. SUMMER: 0900-1900 & by arrangement.
416	**PLYMOUTH City Airport** ARP changed to N50 25·37 W004 06·35.
●	Rwy 06/24 - New Holding point D established 34m from runway centre line on the taxiway to the main Hangar.
417	**PLYMOUTH City Airport** ARP changed to N50 25·37 W004 06·35. Rwy 24 LDA revised to 710. Rwy 13/31- Declared Distances revised to: Rwy 13 TORA 1109, LDA 1027; Rwy 31 TORA 1102, LDA 1045.
●	Rwy 24 Approach lighting withdrawn.
422	**PRESTWICK** Aerodrome elevation changed to 65 ft amsl.
●	Com/Nav: ILS/DME Rwy 13 - amend LLZ to 127°M, and Rwy 31 LLZ to 307°M.
423	**PRESTWICK** Aerodrome elevation changed to 65 ft amsl.
● 431	**ROCHESTER** Rwy 16/34 - Rwy 16 LDA revised to 798, and Rwy 34 TORA revised to 963. Remarks - Pilot Shop available in the Clubhouse. Restaurant: Refreshments/cafe meals. Visitors welcome.
442	**SHEFFIELD CITY** Op hrs: PPR. Mon-Fri 0735-1930; Sat 1100-1215; Sun 1800-2000. Rwy 10/28 - Declared Distances revised to: Rwy 10 and 28 TORA/LDA 1211.
443	**SHEFFIELD CITY** Noise Abatement Procedures: Aircraft on visual approaches and circuit training height raised to 2000 ft aal. Add new line - Departures Rwy 28 must climb on runway heading until passing 1500 ft aal.
452	**SHOREHAM** Com/Nav: A/G Stn op hrs changed to Mon-Sat 0800-0830 PPR.
● 454	**SHUTTLEWORTH (Old Warden)** Remarks - Caution: add - High sided vehicles often use the College Road; approach to Rwy 21 is over a public road. Exercise extreme caution. Circuits at 800 ft, RH on Rwy 03, LH on Rwy 21. Add: e-mail: collection@shuttleworth.org.
457	**SLEAP** Rwy 05/23 width increased to 46 m.
458	**SOUTHAMPTON** Amend Osprey Hangar to Signature Hangar.
●	Com/Nav: New facility - GND 121·775 introduced into service.
459	**SOUTHAMPTON** Sat and Sun Op hrs changed to - Sat 0630-1900 PPR 2130-2200; Sun 0930-2130 PPR 2130-2200. Hangarage/Maintenance: delete Osprey Aviation Ltd insert Signature Aircraft Engineering, Tel: 023-8048 3700; Fax: 023-8065 1897. Remarks - Handling Agencies: delete Osprey Aviation Ltd insert Signature Flight Support (Full FBO facilities), Tel: 023-8061 6600 (24 hrs); Fax: 023-8062 9684; Freq: 130·375; e-mail: eghi@signatureflight.co.uk
460	**SOUTHAMPTON VRPs:** Bishops Waltham: Amend SAM 095°/5nm to SAM 094°/5 nm, and EAS R095°M to EAS R094°M. Calshot: Amend BIA 088°M to BIA 087°M. Totton: Amend EAS 252°M to EAS 251°M.
● 463	**SOUTH CAVE (Mount Airy)** Com/Nav: Humberside APP- delete 124·675, insert 119·125.
● 464	**SOUTHEND** Com/Nav: RAD - add new freq 128·95 (LARS), 125·05 (when directed).
465	**SOUTHEND** Remarks - GA visitors are encouraged to wear high visibility clothing when airside. Helicopter circuits normally parallel to the fixed wing runway in use and flown at 500 ft or 1000 ft as instructed by ATC.
● 468	**STAPLEFORD** Rwy 04R - 50x44 Starter Extension added; Rwy 22L - 23x48 Starter Extension added.
● 473	**STORNOWAY** Op hrs: Mon-Fri 0800-1730; Sats 0800-1600 - until 09 Jun; 0800-1700 16 Jun -1 Sep; 0800-1600 8 Sept - 22 Sept; 0800 -1500 29 Sept - 27 Oct. Sun Closed.
● 478	**SUMBURGH** Com/Nav: Delete APP and RAD, insert RAD Sumburgh Radar 131·30, 123·15 (123·15 stand-by freq as directed).

- **481** **SWANSEA** Tel/Fax: Fax changed to - 01792-207550.
- **492** **TIREE** Op hrs: Sat changed to 0930-1100.
- **499** **VALLEY** Com/Nav: New facility - ATIS 120·725 introduced into service.
- **510** **WHALSAY** Com/Nav: Delete Sumburgh APP 123·15, insert Sumburgh RAD 131·30.
-   **513** **WICK** Tel: ATIS available on 01955-605428.
- **515** **WOLVERHAMPTON** Remarks - Rwy 16 departures - To avoid overflying Highgate Farm situated left of the extended centreline, all aircraft are to maintain the runway track until abeam the Highgate Farm before turning into the fixed wing circuit pattern or on route as required.
-   **517** **WOODVALE** Op hrs: PPR by telephone. 0800-1800.
- **522** **YEOVIL (Westland)** Op hrs: Except PHs - Mon-Thu 0900-1630, Fri 0900-1530. PPR.

CONTINENTAL SECTION

- **531** **CALAIS - DUNKIRK** Com/Nav: Amend Lille APP/FIS freq 120·37 to 120·27.
- **532** **DINARD (Pleurtuit-St.-Malo)** Twys A, B and C redesignated as Twy S, N and L.
- **536** **LE TOUQUET** Com/Nav: Amend Lille APP freq 120·37 to 120·27. GND 125·30 withdrawn.

GOVERNMENT AERODROMES

- **558** **BOSCOMBE DOWN** Com/Nav: ILS Rwy 23 - amend LLZ to 234M°.
- **560** **MARHAM** Remarks - Inbound aircraft are to contact App at 25 nm.
-   **561** **SCAMPTON** ARP changed to N53 18·46 W000 33·05.

HELICOPTER SITES

- **569** **H38 CARDIFF/Tremorfa Foreshore Heliport** Remarks - Radio: Information also available from Veritair on 129·90, c/s Veritair Centre.
-   **571** New Site:

H52a COCKERMOUTH	N54 37·86 W003 22·21	308 ft AMSL
2 nm SW of Cockermouth		DCS 115·20 196 5·9

  Concrete area NE end of the Hangar.
  Remarks: Operated by M. Sport Ltd, Dovenby Hall, Dovenby, Cockermouth, Cumbria. CA13 0PN. Strictly PPR. Call Carlisle APP 123·60 for FIS.
  Warnings: High lamp post near the Tennis court. Military low-level aircraft cross the area at all times of the day and night.

Fuel: Jet A1 by arrangement.	**Tel:** 01900-828 888. **Fax:** 01900-823823
	e.mail: nosment@m-sport.co.uk

-   **578** New Site:

H89a HATFIELD (Bush Hall Hotel)	N51 45·00 W000 12·00	207 ft AMSL

  2 nm NNE of Hatfield (disused airfield)
  Grass pad adjacent to the Hotel car park. 'H' displayed.
  Remarks: Operated by Bush Hall Hotel, Mill Green, Hatfield, Herts. AL9 5NT.

Fuel: Nil.	**Tel:** 01707-271 251. **Fax:** 01707- 272 289.

-   **578** **H90 HAYES (Heliport)** Remarks - Heliport operated by McAlpine Aviation Services Ltd.
- **587** **H145 PENZANCE (Heliport)** Add ICAO location Indicator - EGHK. ARP co-ordinates changed to N50 07·68 W005 31·10. Elev changed to 14 ft AMSL. Op hrs: SUMMER: Mon-Sat 0800-1930. WINTER: Mon-Sat 0900-1800.
- **593** **H178 TRESCO (Heliport)** ARP co-ordinates changed to N49 56·73 W006 19·88. Elev changed to 20 ft AMSL.
- **597** **ABERDEEN (Culter Helipad)** Com/Nav: Aberdeen APP - delete 120·40, insert 119·05
-   **599** **LONDON (Westland Heliport)** Name changed to LONDON Heliport.

GLIDER LAUNCHING SITES

- **617** New Site: Llantysilio (W) N53 03·00 W003 13·00 Op ht 2000 ft agl, Site Elev 1120 ft amsl.

HANG GLIDING and PARASCENDING WINCH/AUTO-TOW LAUNCH SITES

621 New Sites:
Bloreheath Farm, Almington,Shropshire N52 54·58 W002 26·40   Op ht 800 ft agl,
Site Elev 300 ft amsl.
Cockle Park, Northumberland   N55 12·23 W001 40·30   Op ht 2000 ft agl,
Site Elev 248 ft amsl.
Hamble, Hamps - site withdrawn.

622 Wheaton Aston, Staffs - site withdrawn.

THE PREVENTION OF TERRORISM (TEMPORARY PROVISIONS) ACT

● **629** Requirements for Civil Helicopters: RUC - Tel Ext 22430 changed to 33607.

AVIATION ADDRESSES

639 Add: Beagle Pup Club, c/o 20 Primrose Close, Flitwick, Bedford MK45 1PJ.
Tel: 01525- 751 587. e-mail: pabbott@avnet.co.uk

640 Flying Farmers Association (FFA) - New Hon Secretary:
Paul Stephens, Moor Farm, West Heslerton, Malton, N Yorks. YO17 8RU.
Tel: 01944-738 281. Fax: 01944-738 240.
e-mail: gbsdg@farmline.com   Web: http://members.farmline.com/flyfarm

• Denotes change since last Airnote.

U.K FLIGHT INFORMATION REGIONS

xvi   Belfast (Aldergrove) Approach frequency changed to 124·90.

SERVICES TO AIRCRAFT OUTSIDE CONTROLLED AIRSPACE

17   Sub paragraph (e), line 3 - amend 5000 ft to 3000 ft.

LOWER AIRSPACE RADAR SERVICE (LARS)

21/22   LARS now also available from:
Bournemouth on 119·625, 0730-2100, radius 30 nm.
Southend on 128·95, 0900-1800, radius 25 nm.

21/22   Humberside freq 124·67 changed to 119·125

21/22   London/Luton withdrawn.

NORTHERN OFF-ROUTE CO-ORDINATION AREA (NORCA)

25   Sub paragraph 1.1 - amend Airway B4/B1 to Airway B4/ L975.
Sub paragraph 2.2 (a) - amend Airway B1 to Airway L975.

27   Amend references to B1/UB1 to read L975/UL975.

28   Amend Airway B1 to L975.

• **28**   Danger Area EG D303 withdrawn.

DACS and DAAIS

• **33**   **D044** Lydd Ranges   Hours of activity: H24.

• **34**   **D141** Hythe Ranges   Hours of activity: H24.

35   **D207** Holbeach Hours of activity: Sep-Apr, Tue & Thu changed to 1700-2200 and as notified.

35   **D307** Donna Nook Hours of activity: Sep-Apr, Tue & Thu changed to 1630-2200 and as notified.

37   **D703** Tain Hours of activity: Mon 0900-1700, Tue-Thu 0900-2200, Fri 0900-1400 as notified.

37   **D708** Rosehearty   Danger Area withdrawn.

NAVIGATIONAL AIDS

38   Add: **Ballykelly** TACAN 'BKL' 109·10 N55 03·65 W007 00·80.
        Campbeltown NDB 'CBL' 380·0 15 nm range N55 26·13 W005 41·10.

39   **Coventry** NDB 'CT' amend co-ordinates to N52 24·65 W001 24·35.
Cranfield NDB 'CIT' co-ordinates revised to N52 07·82 W000 33·42.

39   **Enniskillen** NDB 'EKN' co-ordinates revised to N54 23·65 W007 38·60.
DME 'ENN' co-ordinates revised to N54 23·92 W007 39·22.

• **39**   **Exeter** NDB 'EX' range increased to 25 nm.

39   **Fife/Glenrothes** NDB 'GO' withdrawn.

40   Add **Leeming** TACAN 'LEE' 112·60 N54 17·80 W001 32·20.

• **40**   **Liverpool** Aerodrome renamed LIVERPOOL/John Lennon Airport.

41   **Newcastle** NDB 'NEW' co-ordinates revised to N55 03·02 W001 38·57.
NDB 'WZ' co-ordinates revised to N55 00·40 W001 48·42.

42   **Shoreham** NDB 'SHM' co-ordinates revised to N50 50·13 W000 17·72.
DME 'SRH' co-ordinates revised to N50 50·17 W000 17·62.

42   **Swansea** DME 'SWZ' withdrawn.
     Talla NDB 'TLA' withdrawn.
43   **Vallafield** TACAN 'VFD' withdrawn.
• 43   **Wolverhampton** New facility: DME 'WOL' 108·60 N52 30·95 W002 15·72.

AERODROME VISUAL REFERENCE POINTS (VRPs)

• 47   **GLASGOW** ARP changed to N55 52·32 W004 25·98.
• 49   **LIVERPOOL** Aerodrome renamed LIVERPOOL/John Lennon Airport.
• 50   **PLYMOUTH City Airport** ARP changed to N50 25·37 W004 06·35.

AERODROME OPERATING MINIMA

55   **Bristol** Minima revised to:

Rwy	Approach Aid	OCH (ft)	DH/MDH (ft)
09	ILS/DME 'I BON'	145	500
09	LLZ/DME 'I BON'	300	600
09	NDB(L) 'BRI'/DME 'I BON'	320	600
09	NDB(L) 'BRI' (No DME)	390	600
09	SRA (2 nm termination range,1nm MAPt)	300	600
27	ILS/DME 'I BTS'	159	500
27	LLZ/DME 'I BTS'	310	600
27	NDB(L) 'BRI'/DME 'I BTS'	360	600
27	NDB(L) 'BRI' (No DME)	590	790
27	SRA (2 nm termination range)	540	740

57   **Gloucestershire** Rwy 09 NDB(L) 'GST'/DME 'GOS' minima revised to OCH 520,
     DH/MDH 720.
     Rwy 27 SRA (0·5 nm termination range) minima revised to OCH 520, DH/MDH 720.
• 59   **Liverpool** Aerodrome renamed LIVERPOOL/John Lennon Airport.
60   **Londonderry/Eglinton** Rwy 26 ILS/DME 'I EGT' minima revised to OCH 280, DH/MDH 500.
60   **Manchester** Minima revised to:

Rwy	Approach Aid	OCH (ft)	DH/MDH (ft)
06R	ILS/DME 'I MC' or 'MCT'	135	500
06R	LLZ/DME 'I MC' or 'MCT'	320	600
06R	VOR/DME 'MCT' or 'I MC'	420	620
06L	ILS/DME 'I MM' or 'MCT'	146	500
06L	LLZ /DME 'I MM' or 'MCT'	370	600
06L	VOR/DME 'MCT' or 'I MM'	430	630
06L	NDB(L) 'MCH'/DME 'I MM' or 'MCT'	430	630
24R	ILS/DME 'I NN' or 'MCT'	142	500
24R	LLZ /DME 'I NN' or 'MCT'	300	600
24R	VOR/DME 'MCT' or 'I NN'	390	600
24R	NDB(L) 'MCH'/DME 'I NN' or 'MCT'	390	600
24L	VOR/DME 'MCT' or 'IMC'	410	610

61   **Prestwick** Add: Rwy 21 SRA (2 nm termination range) OCH 760, DH/MDA 960.

AERODROMES

84   **ABERDEEN (Dyce)** Com/Nav: APP/RAD/VDF freq 120·40 changed to 119·05
96   **BAGBY (Thirsk)** Rwy 24 downslope revised to 2·5%
     Op hrs: 0830-SS (Services 0930-1900, closed Tue 1700-1930).
     Landing Fee: Free with fuel uplift.
     MATZ clearance to be obtained from Topcliffe.
     Catering: Sat and Sun hours changed to 1000-1600.
102 **BELFAST (Aldergrove)** Com/Nav: RAD freq 120·00 withdrawn.
     GND 121·75 operating hrs changed to Summer/Winter 0800-1730.

104	**BELFAST (Aldergrove)** VRPs:

104 **BELFAST (Aldergrove)** VRPs:
Ballymena: Amend HB 325°M to HB 324°M.
Cluntoe: Amend BEL 265° to BEL 264° and OY 262°M to OY 261°M.
Portadown: Amend all references to DUB R002 to DUB R001.

109 **BELFAST (City)** VRPs :
Comber: Amend BEL 119°/18 nm to BEL 118°/18 nm and IOM R317 to IOM R316.
Groomsport: Amend TRN R223 to TRN R224 and all references to IOM R328 to IOM R327.
Saintfield: Amend all references to IOM R309 to IOM R 308.
Whitehead: Amend all references to IOM R328 to IOM R327.

113 **BEMBRIDGE (Isle of Wight)** Rwy 30 LDA (Day) revised to 751.
Landing Fee: Singles £10 to £15; Twins £20 to £25; incl of VAT. Touch and Go 50%.
Remarks - Aerodrome operated by B.N. Group Ltd.
Car Hire: Delete Avis, insert South Wight Rentals Tel: 01983-864263,
U Drive Tel: 0800-0926545.
• Op hrs: Mon-Thu 0830-1630, Fri 0830-1145. Other times by request.

115 **BENBECULA** Tel: Aerodrome and Met information available on 01870-604818.

122 **BIRMINGHAM INTL** Twy Y withdrawn. Twy Z redesignated Twy Y.
Hold Z redesignated Hold Y1. Hold Y2 established just NE of it on the redesignated Twy Y.

127 **BLACKPOOL** Rwy 13 LDA revised to 924.

132 **BOURNEMOUTH** VRPs:
Tarrant Rushton (Disused A/D): Amend SAM R261/28 nm to SAM R261/29 nm.

149 **CAERNARFON** Rwy 02/20 & Rwy 08/26 - Declared Distances revised to:
Rwy 02 TORA 1076, LDA 925; Rwy 20 TORA 925, LDA 1040.
Rwy 08 TORA/LDA 880; Rwy 26 TORA 880, LDA 820.

151 **CAMBRIDGE** Remarks - Third Party Insurance cover requirement raised to £1,000,000.
• Rwy 05 LDA reduced to 1635 m.

153 **CAMPBELTOWN** Com/Nav: New facility - NDB 'CBL' 380·0 (On A/D).

162 **CHICHESTER (Goodwood)** Op hrs: PPR by telephone recommended. Summer: 0900-1800.
Winter: Nov-Jan 0900-1600, Feb-Mar 0900-1700.
Remarks - All aircraft must have Third Party Insurance cover of not less than £500,000.
When relief Rwy 14L/32R in use, the thresholds will be marked with black and white prismatic
markers.

164 **CHILBOLTON (Stonefield Park)** Hangarage: Available to de-rigged microlights only.
Maintenance: Available by arrangement.
Remarks - Helicopters are not permitted.
Taxis: Tel - delete 0589-292801.

173 **COSFORD** New Runways: 06L/24R 1028m Grass (local acft ops); 06R/24L 1085m Grass
(glider ops) ; 18L/36R 849m Grass (local acft ops); 18R/36L 849m Grass (glider ops).
Tel: Amend to: 01902-377582/377030.

175 **COVENTRY** Rwy 17/35 - Runway length changed to 708 m and Declared Distances to:
Rwy 17 TORA 482, LDA 708. Rwy 35 TORA 708, LDA 482.

187 **DAVIDSTOW MOOR** Fax changed to: 01288-361402.

• 190 **DENHAM** Op hrs: PPR by telephone. 0900-1730 or SS daily, and by arrangement.

195 **DUNDEE** Sun op hrs changed to 0900-2100.

• 201 **EARLS COLNE** Rwy 06/24 - Runway width increased to 30 m.

• 203 **EAST MIDLANDS** Com/Nav: APP/VDF freq 119·65 changed to 134·175. RAD remains on
119·65.

204 **EAST MIDLANDS** e-mail changed to: atsm@eastmidlandsairport.com

210 **EDINBURGH** Com/Nav: New facility - GND 121·75 available Mon-Fri 0700-2000, Sat & Sun
0900-1900.
Holds - New Holds M6 and M5 established Rwy 12 threshold area.
• Com/Nav: ATIS frequency 123·90 changed to 131·35.

211 **EDINBURGH** Rwy 06/24 - add: Take-off from intersection with Hold B1 - TORA 1889. Rwy 24
Take-off from intersection with Hold C1 - TORA 1889.
Remarks - Handling Agents: add Comet Handling, Tel: 0131-344 3172, Fax: 0131-333 2255.

223 **ENNISKILLEN (St. Angelo)** Rwy 33 TORA revised to 1327 and LDA to 1004.

229 **EXETER** Com/Nav: New facility - ATIS 119·325 introduced into service.

230	**FADMOOR (Moors National Park)** Fuel: 100LL - amend 60p to 70p.
	Tel: Mobile changed to 07989- 383 562.
231	**FAIR ISLE** Com/Nav: Delete Sumburgh APP 123·15, insert Sumburgh RAD 131·30.
236	**FARNBOROUGH** Com/Nav: New facility - ATIS 128·40 introduced into service.
	Rwy 11/29 closed as runway, and designated as Twy B.
•	Com/Nav: RAD c/s Talkdown 130·05 withdrawn.
237	**FARNBOROUGH** Rwy 11/29 closed.
	Remarks - Airport operated by TAG Aviation, Farnborough Airport, Farnborough, Hampshire
	GU14 6XA.
240	**FENLAND** Com/Nav: AFIS available by arrangement Sat and Sun.
	Fuel: Jet A1 not available.
	Tel: delete 01945-582891 Aerodrome Licencee.
•	Rwy 18/36 - Dimensions revised to 594 x 30m, and Declared Distances to:
	Rwy 18 TORA 594, LDA 512. Rwy 36 TORA 594, LDA 591.
241	**FIFE AIRPORT (Glenrothes)** Com/Nav: NDB 'GO' withdrawn.
242	**FILTON** Com/Nav: ILS/DME Rwy 09 - amend LLZ to 094°M, and Rwy 27 LLZ to 274°M
	Remarks - Circuit height increased to: Jet/Turbo Prop - 2000 ft QFE, 2200 QNH;
	All others - 1500 ft QFE, 1700 ft QNH.
• 248/49	**GLASGOW** ARP changed to N55 52·32 W004 25·98.
256	**GLOUCESTERSHIRE** Rwy 09/27- Declared Distances revised to: Rwy 09 TORA 1277,
	LDA 1159. Rwy 27 TORA 1319, LDA 1007.
•	Southern taxiway withdrawn.
267	**HENSTRIDGE** Op hrs: Winter: PPR. 0900-1700 or SS if earlier/later.
	Summer: Mon-Sat 0900-1900 - PPR for arrivals after 1800, Sun 0900-1800.
	Landing Fee: Singles/Twins £7.00; Microlights & Gyros £3.50.
275	**HUMBERSIDE** Op hrs: Sun-Fri 0630-2015; Sat 0630-2000.
	Com/Nav: APP/RAD and LARS freq 124·675 changed to 119·125.
276	**INSCH** Com/Nav: Aberdeen APP- delete 120·40, insert 119·05.
277	**INVERNESS** Sun Winter op hrs changed to 0815-2200.
	Remarks - All international flights (including CI and Eire) and all domestic flights over 2730 kg
	MAUW must organise a handling agent.
	Handling Agents: Execair Aviation Services Tel: 01667-461122, Fax: 01667- 461133;
	British Airways Tel: 01667-462280, Fax: 01667-462840 and Servisair Tel: 01667-461030,
	Fax: 01667-461006.
287	**JERSEY** Remarks - GA aircraft with MAUW of less than 3 tonnes will normally be parked at
	Jersey Aero Club on the grass. The Aero Club will provide customs, immigration, handling and
	collection of landing fees. Aircraft with a MAUW of 3 tonnes or more will normally be parked at
	Aviation Beauport.
294	**KIRKWALL** Sat op hrs changed to 0800-1715.
305	**LEEDS BRADFORD CTR/CTA Chart:** Amend Airway B1 to L975.
307	**LEEMING** Com/Nav: New facility - TACAN 'LEE' 112·60 (on A/D).
309	**LEICESTER** Landing Fee: Singles £10.00, Twins £20.00, incl VAT. Weekends only - all
	landing fees free with fuel uplift of 50 litres or more.
316	**LIVERPOOL** Holding Points - Hold V redesignated Hold V1. Hold V2 established north of it.
	Hold B only available to aircraft with a MTWA of 5700 kg or less.
•	Aerodrome renamed LIVERPOOL/John Lennon Airport.
•	Holds A8, A9 and A10 withdrawn. Hold Y3 moved to position of the old Hold A8.
317	**LIVERPOOL** Landing Fee: Amend £17.45 to £17.87.
	Twy A from Hold A3 to Rwy 27 threshold restricted to aircraft with less than 52 m wingspan.
	Tel: Delete 0151-288 4302 Flight Planning, insert 0151-288 4151 Apron Control.
•	Aerodrome renamed LIVERPOOL/John Lennon Airport.
• 318	**LIVERPOOL** Aerodrome renamed LIVERPOOL/John Lennon Airport.
319	**LIVERPOOL** VRPs: Kirkby - Amend WAL R065/10 nm to WAL R065/11 nm;
	Seaforth - Amend WAL R046/5 NM to WAL R046/6 nm;
	Stretton Aerodrome - Amend MCT R271/9 nm to MCT R271/10 nm.
•	Aerodrome renamed LIVERPOOL/John Lennon Airport.
321	**LONDON (City Airport)** Op hrs: Mon-Fri 0645-2145, Sat 0645-1230, Sun 1230-2145.
322	**LONDON (Gatwick)** Following taxiways redesignated: 3 to K, 4 to L, 5 to N, 6 to P, 7 to Q,

8 to R, 9 to S and 10 to T.

323   **LONDON (Gatwick)** Com/Nav: GND 121·80 op hrs changed to 0500-2359.

327   **LONDON (Heathrow)** Rwy 23 LDA changed to 1962.

331   **LONDON (Luton)** Remarks - Handling Agents: Amend Magec Aviation to Signature Flight Support, Tel: 01582-724182.
Tel/Fax: Tel: ATC changed to 01582-395029.
Tel: Add: 01582-395525 Ops; 01582-395257 Airport Duty Officer.
Fax: ATC changed 01582-395309. Add: 01582-395257 Airport Duty Officer.

337   **LONDON (Stansted)** Com/Nav: Delivery frequency 125·55 changed to 121·95.

● **341**   **LONDONDERRY (Eglinton)** Rwy 03/21 redesignated Rwy 02/20.
Twys F and J withdrawn.

341a   **LONDONDERRY (Eglinton)** Op hrs: Strictly PPR by telephone. Mon-Fri 0715-2115, Sat 0715-1645, Sun 1230-2115.

●   Rwy 03/21 redesignated Rwy 02/20.

344   **LYDD** Rwy 04/22 - Declared Distances revised to: Rwy 04/22 TORA/LDA 1505; Rwy 22 TORA 1505, LDA 1468.

349   **MANCHESTER AIRPORT** Twys T and S changed to: Twy T changed to Rwy S. Twy T now commences at Hold T1 and ends at the Starter Extension Rwy 24L.

359   **MANCHESTER CTR/CTA Chart:** Amend Airway B1 to L975.

361   **MANCHESTER (Barton)** Remarks - Twins not accepted unless in emergency. Aircraft over 1500 kg must apply in writing to aerodrome manager.

365   **MANSTON** Remarks - Rwy 28 is the preferred departure runway when there is a tailwind component of 5 kt or less.
GA aircraft under 4 tonnes PPR from TG Aviation, Tel: 01843-823656, Fax: 01843- 822024.

384   **NORTHAMPTON (Sywell)** Rwy 03/21 lighting - LITAS replaced by APAPI (4°) LH
Landing Fee: Microlights £8.00; Singles, fixed & rotary – £10.00; Twins £18.00; All inc of VAT. Special rates for Circuit training.

386   **NORTHOLT** Com/Nav: Add RAD c/s Talkdown 125·875. Ops 132·65.
Remarks - Approaches to Rwy 07 offset by 30° to the left of the centreline until 4 nm from touchdown in order to deconflict with Heathrow traffic patterns.
High visibility clothing required on the apron areas.

397   **ODIHAM** Tel: Exts changed to Ext 7295 ATC, Ext 7254 Ops.

●   Com/Nav: Amend Farnborough/Odiham APP 125·25 to Farnborough RAD 125·25 (M); Odiham APP/RAD 131·30.

● **405**   **OXFORD (Kidlington)** Op hrs: PPR. Mon-Thu 0730-2100, Fri 0730-2030, Sat 0830-1700, Sun & PHS 0900-1700.
Remarks - Aerodrome now operated by Oxford Aviation Services.

411   **PERTH (Scone)** Op hrs: PPR. WINTER: 0900-1700 - daylight hrs only. SUMMER: 0900-1900 & by arrangement.

●   Rwy 10/28 redesignated Rwy 09/27, and now has runway lights.

●   Tel/Fax: Fax number changed to 01738-553170.

416   **PLYMOUTH City Airport** ARP changed to N50 25·37 W004 06·35.
Rwy 06/24 - New Holding point D established 34m from runway centre line on the taxiway to the main Hangar.

417   **PLYMOUTH City Airport** ARP changed to N50 25·37 W004 06·35.
Rwy 24 LDA revised to 710.
Rwy 13/31- Declared Distances revised to: Rwy 13 TORA 1109, LDA 1027;
Rwy 31 TORA 1102, LDA 1045.
Rwy 24 Approach lighting withdrawn.

423   **PRESTWICK** Aerodrome elevation changed to 65 ft amsl.

●   Landing Fee: Amend £6.80 to £7.00.

431   **ROCHESTER** Rwy 16/34 - Rwy 16 LDA revised to 798, and Rwy 34 TORA revised to 963.
Remarks - Pilot Shop available in the Clubhouse.
Restaurant: Refreshments/cafe meals. Visitors welcome.

● **433**   **ST. MAWGAN** Com/Nav: ILS Rwy 31 - amend LLZ to 305°M.

442   **SHEFFIELD CITY** Op hrs: PPR. Mon-Fri 0735-1930; Sat 1100-1215; Sun 1800-2000.
Rwy 10/28 - Declared Distances revised to: Rwy 10 and 28 TORA/LDA 1211.

443	**SHEFFIELD CITY** Noise Abatement Procedures: Aircraft on visual approaches and circuit training height raised to 2000 ft aal.

443   **SHEFFIELD CITY** Noise Abatement Procedures: Aircraft on visual approaches and circuit training height raised to 2000 ft aal.
Add new line - Departures Rwy 28 must climb on runway heading until passing 1500 ft aal.

● 445   **SHERBURN IN ELMET** Rwy 01/19 - Dimensions revised to 585 x 18m, and Declared Distances to: Rwy 01 TORA/LDA 553. Rwy 19 TORA 553, LDA 521.
Rwy 06/24 - Dimensions revised to 793 x 18m, and Declared Distances to:
Rwy 06 TORA 723, LDA 676. Rwy 24 TORA 696, LDA 703.
Airfield diagram - amend NDB SLB 323·0 to NDB SBL 323·0.

452   **SHOREHAM** Com/Nav: A/G Stn op hrs changed to Mon-Sat 0800-0830 PPR.
●   Helipad 1 withdrawn.

454   **SHUTTLEWORTH (Old Warden)** Remarks - Caution: add - High sided vehicles often use the College Road; approach to Rwy 21 is over a public road. Exercise extreme caution.
Circuits at 800 ft, RH on Rwy 03, LH on Rwy 21.
Add: e-mail: collection@shuttleworth.org.

● 455   **SILVERSTONE** Aerodrome now operated by Octogon Motorsports.

457   **SLEAP** Rwy 05/23 width increased to 46 m.

458   **SOUTHAMPTON** Amend Osprey Hangar to Signature Hangar.
Com/Nav: New facility - GND 121·775 introduced into service.

459   **SOUTHAMPTON** Sat and Sun Op hrs changed to - Sat 0630-1900 PPR 2130-2200;
Sun 0930-2130 PPR 2130-2200.
Hangarage/Maintenance: delete Osprey Aviation Ltd insert Signature Aircraft Engineering, Tel: 023-8048 3700; Fax: 023-8065 1897.
Remarks - Handling Agencies: delete Osprey Aviation Ltd insert Signature Flight Support (Full FBO facilities), Tel: 023-8061 6600 (24 hrs); Fax: 023-8062 9684; Freq: 130·375;
e-mail: eghi@signatureflight.co.uk

460   **SOUTHAMPTON VRPs:**
Bishops Waltham: Amend SAM 095°/5nm to SAM 094°/5 nm, and EAS R095°M to EAS R094°M.
Calshot: Amend BIA 088°M to BIA 087°M.
Totton: Amend EAS 252°M to EAS 251°M.

463   **SOUTH CAVE (Mount Airy)** Com/Nav: Humberside APP- delete 124·675, insert 119·125.

464   **SOUTHEND** Com/Nav: RAD - add new freq 128·95 (LARS), 125·05 (when directed).

465   **SOUTHEND** Remarks - GA visitors are encouraged to wear high visibility clothing when airside.
Helicopter circuits normally parallel to the fixed wing runway in use and flown at 500 ft or 1000 ft as instructed by ATC.

468   **STAPLEFORD** Rwy 04R - 50x44 Starter Extension added; Rwy 22L - 23x48 Starter Extension added.

● 473   **STORNOWAY** Op hrs: Until 01 Sept 0800-1700, 08 Sept - 22 Sept 0800-1600,
29 Sept - 27 Oct 0800-1500. Sun Closed.

478   **SUMBURGH** Com/Nav: Delete APP and RAD, insert RAD Sumburgh Radar 131·30, 123·15 (123·15 stand-by freq as directed).

481   **SWANSEA** Tel/Fax: Fax changed to - 01792-207550.

● 485   **TEESSIDE** Op hrs: H24, but PPR 2200-0600 from Duty Officer Tel 01325- 331008.

● 490   **THRUXTON** ARP changed to N51 12·63 W001 36·00.
Aerodrome Elevation changed to 319 ft AMSL.

499   **VALLEY** Com/Nav: New facility - ATIS 120·725 introduced into service.

● 502   **WARTON** Remarks - Amend Operator to BAE Systems.

510   **WHALSAY** Com/Nav: Delete Sumburgh APP 123·15, insert Sumburgh RAD 131·30.

513   **WICK** Tel: ATIS available on 01955-605428.

515   **WOLVERHAMPTON** Remarks - Rwy 16 departures - To avoid overflying Highgate Farm situated left of the extended centreline, all aircraft are to maintain the runway track until abeam the Highgate Farm before turning into the fixed wing circuit pattern or on route as required.
●   Com/Nav: New facility - DME 'WOL' 108·60 (On A/D) introduced into service.

517   **WOODVALE** Op hrs: PPR by telephone. 0800-1800.

522   **YEOVIL (Westland)** Op hrs: Except PHs - Mon-Thu 0900-1630, Fri 0900-1530. PPR.

CONTINENTAL SECTION

531	**CALAIS - DUNKIRK** Com/Nav: Amend Lille APP/FIS freq 120·37 to 120·27.
532	**DINARD (Pleurtuit-St.-Malo)** Twys A, B and C redesignated as Twy S, N and L.
536	**LE TOUQUET** Com/Nav: Amend Lille APP freq 120·37 to 120·27. GND 125·30 withdrawn.
•	Op hrs: 0900-2000. O/T commercial flights only on request to LFATYDYX before 1700.

GOVERNMENT AERODROMES

558	**BOSCOMBE DOWN** Com/Nav: ILS Rwy 23 - amend LLZ to 234M°.
• 558	**CHIVENOR** Op hrs: Strictly PPR (24 hrs). Civilian aircraft not accepted.
• 558	**COLERNE** Com/Nav: TWR 122·10 changed to APP/TWR 120·075.
561	**SCAMPTON** ARP changed to N53 18·46 W000 33·05.

HELICOPTER SITES

• 564	**H6 ASHBOURNE (Rodsley)** Remarks - amend to: Operated by Richard McLachlan, French Horn Cottage, Rodsley, Ashbourne, Derby DE6 3AL. Visiting helicopters welcome on prior permission (to move cattle and electric fence) and at at pilot's own risk. Helipad marked and Windsock displayed next to small orchard at top of field. Please approach from NE and do not overfly the village.
	Warning: Delete Power lines warning, as they are now buried.
569	**H38 CARDIFF/Tremorfa Foreshore Heliport** Remarks - Radio: Information also available from Veritair on 129·90, c/s Veritair Centre.

571	New Site:

H52a COCKERMOUTH   N54 37·86 W003 22·21   308 ft AMSL
2 nm SW of Cockermouth   DCS 115·20 196 5·9
Concrete area NE end of the Hangar.
Remarks: Operated by M. Sport Ltd, Dovenby Hall, Dovenby, Cockermouth, Cumbria. CA13 0PN. Strictly PPR. Call Carlisle APP 123·60 for FIS.
Warnings: High lamp post near the Tennis court. Military low-level aircraft cross the area at all times of the day and night.
Fuel: Jet A1 by arrangement.   **Tel:** 01900-828 888. **Fax:** 01900-823823
    e-mail: nosment@m-sport.co.uk

578	New Site:

H89a HATFIELD (Bush Hall Hotel)   N51 45·00 W000 12·00   207 ft AMSL
2 nm NNE of Hatfield (disused airfield)
Grass pad adjacent to the Hotel car park. 'H' displayed.
Remarks: Operated by Bush Hall Hotel, Mill Green, Hatfield, Herts. AL9 5NT.
Fuel: Nil.   **Tel:** 01707-271 251. **Fax:** 01707- 272 289.

578	**H90 HAYES (Heliport)** Remarks - Heliport operated by McAlpine Aviation Services Ltd.
587	**H145 PENZANCE (Heliport)** Add ICAO location Indicator - EGHK.
	ARP co-ordinates changed to N50 07·68 W005 31·10. Elev changed to 14 ft AMSL.
	Op hrs: SUMMER: Mon-Sat 0800-1930. WINTER: Mon-Sat 0900-1800.
593	**H178 TRESCO (Heliport)** ARP co-ordinates changed to N49 56·73 W006 19·88.
	Elev changed to 20 ft AMSL.
597	**ABERDEEN (Culter Helipad)** Com/Nav: Aberdeen APP - delete 120·40, insert 119·05
599	**LONDON (Westland Heliport)** Name changed to LONDON Heliport.

GLIDER LAUNCHING SITES

• 616	Aberporth, Dyfed - site withdrawn.
617	New Site: Llantysilio (W) N53 03·00 W003 13·00 Op ht 2000 ft agl, Site Elev 1120 ft amsl.
• 618	New Site: Swansea Airport (W) N51 36·32 W004 04·07 Op ht 1500 ft agl,
	Site Elev 299 ft amsl.

HANG GLIDING and PARASCENDING WINCH/AUTO-TOW LAUNCH SITES

621	New Sites:
	Bloreheath Farm, Almington,Shropshire N52 54·58 W002 26·40 Op ht 800 ft agl,
	Site Elev 300 ft amsl.
	Cockle Park, Northumberland N55 12·23 W001 40·30 Op ht 2000 ft agl,
	Site Elev 248 ft amsl.
621	Hamble, Hamps - site withdrawn.
● 621	New Sites:
	Brown Wardle, Lancs N53 39·87 W002 09·35 Op ht 2000 agl, Site Elev 1312 ft amsl.
	Chirk, Shropshire N52 56·83 W003 02·87 Op ht 1200agl, Site Elev 430 ft amsl.
622	Wheaton Aston, Staffs - site withdrawn.
● 622	New Sites:
	Trehayne Vean, Cornwall N50 18·40 W004 59·98 Op ht 2000 ft agl, Site Elev 300 ft amsl.
	Upfield Farm, Gwent N51 33·13 W002 53·73 Op ht 2000 ft agl, Site Elev 20 ft amsl.

THE PREVENTION OF TERRORISM (TEMPORARY PROVISIONS) ACT

629	Requirements for Civil Helicopters: RUC - Tel Ext 22430 changed to 33607.

GOVERNMENT AERODROMES - TELEPHONE NUMBERS

● 633	Leconfield - changed to: 01904- 665460.

ICAO LOCATION INDICATORS - DECODE

● 635	EGGP Liverpool Airport - Aerodrome renamed Liverpool/John Lennon Airport.

AVIATION ADDRESSES

639	Add: Beagle Pup Club, c/o 20 Primrose Close, Flitwick, Bedford MK45 1PJ.
	Tel: 01525- 751 587. e-mail: pabbott@avnet.co.uk
● 639	British Air Line Pilots Association (BALPA) - Amend Tel & Fax to: Tel: 020-8476 4000,
	Fax: 020-8476 4077.
640	Flying Farmers Association (FFA) - New Hon Secretary:
	Paul Stephens, Moor Farm, West Heslerton, Malton, N Yorks. YO17 8RU.
	Tel: 01944-738 281. Fax: 01944-738 240.
	e-mail: gbsdg@farmline.com Web: http://members.farmline.com/flyfarm
● 641	Guild of Air Pilots and Air Navigators (GAPAN) - Amend address & Tel/Fax to:
	Cobham House, 9 Warwick Court, London WC1R 5DJ. Tel: 020-7404 4032,
	Fax: 020-7404 4035. e-mail: gapan@gapan.org Web: www.gapan.org

My grateful thanks to the many aerodrome operators/owners who have given so much help and indeed, without this help, the Guide would be impracticable. Also my thanks to A.I.S., Heathrow, always a staunch ally in the compilation of this Guide, and of course to the Officer Commanding 1. AIDU, RAF, Northolt.

R.J.P.

AERODROME FACILITY DIRECTORY
GENERAL

It should be appreciated that aerodrome information is subject to change at short notice and the information in this Guide is only correct to the date given on the title page. Regular updating of this information is effected by the issue of amendment lists (Airnotes) and the Guide is **revised annually**.

Geographical co-ordinates: Latitude and Longitude are expressed in terms of the World Geodetic Survey 1984 (WGS 84) reference datum, and are shown in Degrees, Minutes and decimals of a Minute.

Navigational Aids A quick reference aid to aerodrome location in relation to appropriate radio navigation aids is given at the top of each aerodrome entry, expressed as follows: OTR 113·90 357 26·5 — OTR (Facility identification), 113·90 (Facility frequency), 357 (VOR Radial/Magnetic Bearing) 26·5 (Distance in nautical miles from facility to aerodrome).

Note 1. Where the range/bearing is shown in a lighter type face it indicates that range/bearing information is not obtainable from that facility e.g. NDB or TACAN.

Note 2. Navigational Aids located on, or within the immediate vicinity of the aerodrome are also listed under the Communication/Navigation section.

Lighting Aerodrome lighting facilities are shown as follows: Ap – Approach, Thr – Threshold; Rwy – Runway and RCL – Runway centre-line, are shown separately for each runway. Approach Slope Indicators are shown appropriate to each runway as: PAPI, APAPI, VASIS and LITAS . A standard setting of 3° is assumed and the setting angle will be quoted only when there is a significant divergence from the standard. Aerodrome and Identification Beacons are given followed by colour and identification characteristics as follows: ABn Wh/Gn, IBn 'MR' Red.

Operating Hours All times quoted throughout the Guide are in **Local Time,** unless otherwise stated when the suffix Z is used to denote UTC.
Consult NOTAMs for up-to-date operating hours.
The symbol ¢ is used to denote 'By arrangement'.
Where PPR (Prior Permission Required) is stated, then please telephone the Operator and obtain permission to use the aerodrome.

Note: Outside of published scheduled operating hours, aerodrome operators may levy surcharges for the use of the aerodrome and its services.

Landing Fees Current fees are quoted, where appropriate, under the aerodrome entry. For a comprehensive listing of charges, supplements, surcharges and rebates, reference should be made to the aerodrome authority. Also see page xviii

AERODROME OPERATORS

(a) BAA plc

BAA operate London/Gatwick, Heathrow, Stansted and Southampton as subsidiary companies. The conditions of Use and Scale of Charges can be obtained from the Finance Departments.

BAA plc	Tel: 020-7834 9449. Fax: 020-7932 6699
Heathrow Airport Limited	Tel: 020-8745 7970. Fax: 020-8745 7832
Gatwick Airport Limited	Tel: 01293-503 249. Fax: 01293-504 700

BAA plc continued

BAA plc continued

Southampton Intl. Airport Ltd   Tel: 023-8062 9600. Fax: 023-8062 9300

Stansted Airport Limited   Tel: 01279-662 382. Fax: 01279-662 974

(b) Scottish Airports Ltd

Scottish Airports Ltd operate Aberdeen, Edinburgh and Glasgow Airports.
The Conditions of Use and Scale of Charges can be obtained from the Finance
Departments.

Scottish Airports Ltd	Tel: 0141-887 1111. Fax: 0141-887 1669
Aberdeen Airport Ltd	Tel: 01224-722 331. Fax: 01224-725 724
Edinburgh Airport Ltd	Tel: 0131-333 1000. Fax: 0131-335 3181
Glasgow Airport Ltd	Tel: 0141-887 1111. Fax: 0141-848 4586

(c) Highlands and Islands Airports Ltd (HIAL)

HIAL operate Barra, Benbecula, Campbeltown, Inverness, Islay, Kirkwall,
Stornoway, Sumburgh, Tiree and Wick.
The Conditions of Use and Scale of Charges can be obtained from the Finance
Department.

Highlands and Islands Airports Ltd   Tel: 01667-462 445.   Fax: 01667-462 579

(d) Other Civil Aerodrome Operators

Contact the individual aerodrome operators for the conditions of Use and Scale
of Charges.

(e) Ministry Of Defence (Government Aerodromes)

The Ministry of Defence is responsible for RAF Aerodromes, RN Stations and
other Government Aerodromes.
The Conditions of Use and Scale of Charges can be obtained from:

Ministry of Defence, CS (CTS) 1a, RAF High Wycombe.

Tel: 01494-461 461 Ext 7234. Fax: 01494-497 227

Customs Availability at aerodromes is annotated. Designated and Concession
Airports are listed at pages 80/81.
Customs and Immigration Regulations to and from UK are shown at page 78.

Meteorological Services – See page 66

Fuel Always a wise precaution to check the availability, since its availability may not
always coincide with the stated operating hours of the aerodrome.

VFR Charts Where specific routeing is notified for VFR flights to/from aerodromes
within Controlled Airspace, a VFR Chart is provided on the page/s following the
aerodrome entry. All bearings/headings quoted on these charts are in degrees
magnetic.

Abbreviations All abbreviations used in this Flight Guide are listed at the back of
the Guide.

LEGEND
AERODROME and VISUAL APP/DEP CHARTS

Runway - Aspalt / Concrete

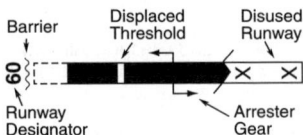

Barrier

Displaced Threshold

Disused Runway

Runway Designator

Arrester Gear

Runway - Grass

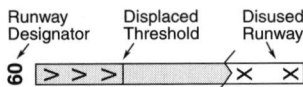

Runway Designator

Displaced Threshold

Disused Runway

Taxiway

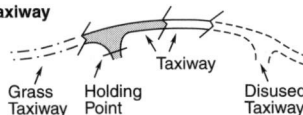

Taxiway

Grass Taxiway

Holding Point

Disused Taxiway

✦ Aerodrome Ident/Beacons

⊟ Signals Square   ☀ Floodlights

C Reporting Office   ◈ Castle

Windsock (Unlit)   Windsock (Lit)

Obstacle (Lit)   Obstacle (Unlit)

Ⓗ Heli Landing Pad   Ⓗ Heli Aiming Point

H⟩ Heli Route   ☒ Heli Hold

Tumulus   ✕ Runway(s)

Bridge

Parachute Dropping Zone   Gliding

Holding Pattern   Aerodrome Building

⊡ DME   VOR/DME

VOR   ⊙ NAVAID (as specified)

NDB   NDB/DME

VORTAC   TACAN

X Windmill   Heli Parking Pads

T.V. Mast   Lighthouse

⊕ Visual Reference Point

○ Private Airfield

Civil Aerodrome

◎ Military Aerodrome

▲ Reporting Point

⊗ Disused or Abandoned Aerodrome

Robert Pooley ©

1 DEC 00

xiv

LEGEND
AERODROME and VISUAL APP/DEP CHARTS

 Built-up Areas

 Glasshouses

 Wooded Area

 Shingle

 Marshland

 Pebble Beach

 Water Feature

 Exclusive Areas

 Danger/Restricted Area

 ATZ

 Prohibited Area

 MATZ

Power Cables

Aerodrome Boundary

Fence

River

Offset Rwy Approach Track

 Motorway — M25   Road — A40

Minor Road   Railway

Cutting

Embankment

 Class 'A' Airspace

Class 'B' Airspace

Class 'C' Airspace

 Class 'D' Airspace

Class 'E' Airspace

FIR Boundary

1 DEC 00

U.K. FLIGHT INFORMATION REGIONS

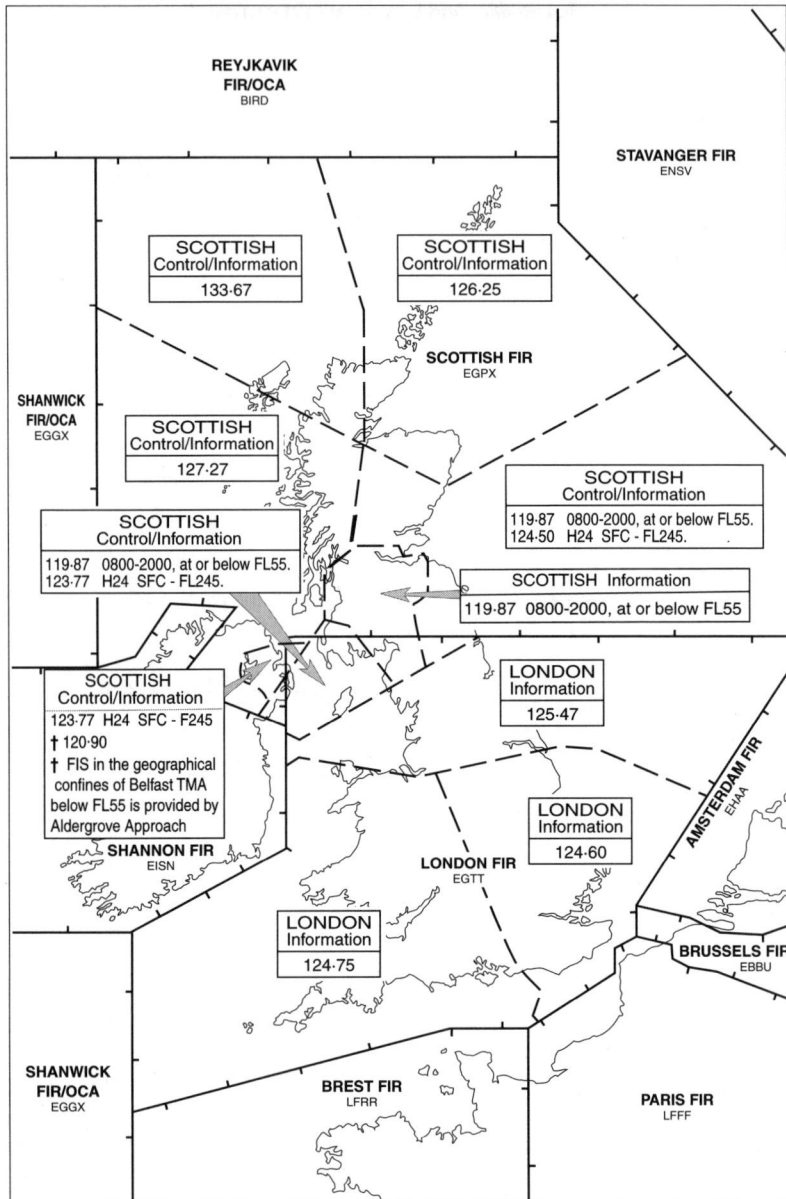

REYJKAVIK
FIR/OCA
BIRD

STAVANGER FIR
ENSV

SCOTTISH
Control/Information
133·67

SCOTTISH
Control/Information
126·25

SCOTTISH FIR
EGPX

SHANWICK
FIR/OCA
EGGX

SCOTTISH
Control/Information
127·27

SCOTTISH
Control/Information
119·87 0800-2000, at or below FL55.
124·50 H24 SFC - FL245.

SCOTTISH
Control/Information
119·87 0800-2000, at or below FL55.
123·77 H24 SFC - FL245.

SCOTTISH Information
119·87 0800-2000, at or below FL55

LONDON
Information
125·47

SCOTTISH
Control/Information
123·77 H24 SFC - F245
† 120·90
† FIS in the geographical
  confines of Belfast TMA
  below FL55 is provided by
  Aldergrove Approach

AMSTERDAM FIR
EHAA

SHANNON FIR
EISN

LONDON
Information
124·60

LONDON FIR
EGTT

BRUSSELS FIR
EBBU

LONDON
Information
124·75

SHANWICK
FIR/OCA
EGGX

BREST FIR
LFRR

PARIS FIR
LFFF

See Notes on the opposite page.

1 DEC 00

U.K. FLIGHT INFORMATION REGIONS

Notes

1. FIS boundaries do not coincide with FIR boundaries.

2. All times shown are local.

3. Scottish FIR

   (a) Call sign 'Scottish Control' will be used when Control or Advisory Service is being provided. Otherwise call sign 'Scottish Information' will be used.

   (b) Aircraft in the Shetland area experiencing difficulty with Scottish FIR may call Sumburgh Approach on 123·15 during its hours of operation.

   (c) Traffic flying within or beneath the Scottish TMA requiring FIS should call Scottish Information.

4. London FIR

   Limited service frequencies, consult NOTAMs.

DIVERSION AERODROMES

Following aerodromes have been awarded the AOPA Air Safety Certificate in recognition of accepting the CAA's CAP 667 9.2(c) recommendation. These aerodrome operators will waive the charges for genuine emergency or precautionary diversion landings for private GA aircraft.

Aberporth	Fife/Glenrothes	Peterborough/Conington
Alderney	Finmere	Peterborough/Sibson
Andrewsfield	Fowlmere	Plymouth
Ashcroft	Full Sutton	Popham
Audley End	Gigha Island	Redhill
Bagby	Glenforsa/Mull	Retford Gamston
Barra	Great Massingham	Rochester
Barrow/Walney Island	Guernsey	Sanday
Belfast City	Hanley (Hanley William)	Sandtoft
Belle Vue	Haverfordwest	Seething
Bembridge	Henstridge	Sherburn-in-Elmet
Benbecula	Hawarden	Shipdham
Beverley	Hinton-in-the-Hedges	Shobdon
Blackbushe	Inverness	Shoreham
Bodmin	Islay	Shuttleworth
Bourn	Isles of Scilly	Sleap
Bournemouth	Jersey	Southampton
Breighton	Kemble	Southend
Brimpton	Kingsmuir	Stapleford
Brough	Kirkwall	Stornoway
Bruntingthorpe	Lamb Holm	Stornsay
Caernarfon	Lands End	Sturgate
Cambridge	Langar	Sumburgh
Campbeltown	Lasham	Swansea
Chalgrove	Lashenden/Headcorn	Tatenhill
Charterhall	Lee-on-Solent	Thruxton
Chichester/Goodwood	Leicester	Tiree
Clacton	Little Gransden	Top Farm
Compton Abbas	Londonderry/Eglinton	Truro
Coventry	Ludham	Turweston
Cranfield	Lydd	Walton Wood
Cromer	Manchester/Barton	Warton
Cumbernauld	Manchester/Woodford	Wellsbourne Mountford
Davidstow Moor	Manston	Welshpool
Denham	Netherthorpe	Westray
Derby	Newcastle	White Waltham
Dornoch	Newquay (St Mawgan)	West Freugh
Duxford	Newtownards	Wick
Eaglescott	North Ronaldsay	Wombleton
East Midlands	North Weald	Wycombe Air Park/Booker
Eday	Northampton Sywell	Yeovil
Elmsett	Nottingham	York Rufforth
Elstree	Oaksey Park	
Enniskillen/St Angelo	Old Sarum	
Enstone	Oxford/Kidlington	
Fair Isle	Panshanger	
Fairoaks	Papa Westray	
Farway Common	Pembrey	
Fenland	Perth	

CLASSIFICATION OF
UNITED KINGDOM AIRSPACE

C O N T R O L L E D   A I R S P A C E

Class A — Airways (except where they pass through a TMA, CTA, or CTR of lower status),
Channel Islands CTR/CTA
Cotswold CTA
London TMA
London CTR
Shanwick Oceanic CTA
Manchester TMA,
Daventry CTA
Worthing CTA

Class B — Upper Airspace Control Area - London and Scottish UIRs between FL245-FL660 (includes Hebrides UTA)

Class C — Not yet allocated, held for possible use at a later date.

Class D —

Aberdeen CTR/CTA	Leeds Bradford CTR/CTA
Alderney CTR	Liverpool CTR
Belfast CTR	London/City CTR
Belfast/City CTR/CTA	London/Gatwick CTR/CTA
Birmingham CTR/CTA	London/Luton CTR/CTA
Bournemouth CTR	London/Stansted CTR/CTA
Bristol CTR/CTA	Lyneham CTR/CTA
Brize Norton CTR	Manchester CTR/CTA
Cardiff CTR/CTA	Newcastle CTR/CTA
East Midlands CTR/CTA	Scottish TMA
Edinburgh CTR	Solent CTA
Glasgow CTR	Southampton CTR
Guernsey CTR	Strangford CTA
Isle of Man CTR/CTA	Sumburgh CTR/CTA
Jersey CTR	Teesside CTR/CTA

Class E — Belfast TMA
Scottish TMA
Teesside CTR

Class F — Advisory Routes. Note: Although Advisory Routes are depicted only as a centreline on UK Aeronautical Charts, they are deemed to be 10 nm wide.

Class G — 'Open' Flight Information Region (FIR).

Aerodrome Traffic Zones (ATZs) — are not allocated a specific class of airspace as they adopt the class of airspace within which they are located. Flights within ATZs are subject to the specific provisions of Rule 39 of the Rules of the Air Regulations 1996. Where the requirements of a particular class of airspace are more stringent than Rule 39 then these must be complied with. Thus, in Class G airspace Rule 39 will apply but in Class A airspace the requirements of Class A take precedence. The more stringent requirements of a particular class of airspace will always encompass the requirements of Rule 39. **ATZs at Goverment Aerodromes**— It should be noted that the vast majority of these ATZs are active H24, as annotated under the particular aerodrome entry.

Flight Plan and Air Traffic Control Clearance

A flight plan and ATC clearance is required for all IFR flights in controlled airspace and for VFR flights in Class B and D airspace. This need not be construed as the compilation and submission of the Flight Plan Form CA 48/RAF F2919 though in some circumstances, particularly for IFR flights, this could be advantageous. A flight plan is a means of providing sufficient particulars of flight to an ATC Unit to enable that unit to issue an ATC clearance which will permit flight in the particular airspace subject to any instructions contained in the clearance. This requirement will be met by contacting the ATC Unit on the appropriate frequency giving details of the aircraft's position, level and proposed track and requesting clearance to enter the Controlled Airspace.

UK ATS AIRSPACE CLASSIFICATIONS

Airspace	Separation	Services	VMC Minima	Speed Limit	Radio	ATC Clearance
Class A (IFR)	All aircraft	ATC service	Not applicable	N/A	Required	Required
(VFR)	Not Permitted (see exceptions at page 12)					
Class B (IFR)	All aircraft	ATC service	N/A	N/A	Required	Required
(VFR)	All aircraft	ATC service	FL100 and above: *Vis 8km and clear of cloud* Below FL100: *Currently not applicable.*	N/A	Required	Required
Class C	Not allocated					
Class D (IFR)	IFR from IFR	ATC service including traffic info about VFR flights (and traffic avoidance advice on request)	Not applicable	250 kt below FL100	Required	Required
(VFR)	Not provided	ATC service — traffic information on all other flights	FL100 and above: *Vis 8 km, 1500 m and 1000 ft from cloud.* Below FL100: *Vis 5 km, 1500 m and 1000 ft from cloud.* **Or, at 140 kt or less, at or below 3000 ft amsl:** †*Vis 5 km, clear of cloud and in sight of surface.*	250 kt below FL100	Required	Required
Class E (IFR)	IFR from IFR	ATC service and traffic information about VFR traffic as far as practical.	Not applicable	250 kt below FL100	Required	Required
(VFR)	Not provided	Traffic information as far as practical	FL100 and above: *Vis 8 km, 1500 m and 1000 ft from cloud.* Below FL100: *Vis 5 km, 1500 m and 1000 ft from cloud.* **Or, at 140 kt or less, at or below 3000 ft amsl:** †*Vis 5 km, clear of cloud and in sight of surface.*	250 kt below FL100	Not required	Not required

Airspace	Separation	Services	VMC Minima	Speed Limit	Radio	ATC Clearance
Class E (IFR)	IFR from IFR (participating IFR traffic)	Air traffic advisory service. Flight information service.	Not applicable	250 kt below FL100	Not required	Not required
(VFR)	Not provided (See Note)	Flight information service. (See Note)	FL100 and above: *Vis 8 km, 1500 m and 1000 ft from cloud.* Below FL100: *Vis 5 km. 1500 m and 1000 ft from cloud;* **or** At or below 3000 ft amsl: *Vis 5 km*, clear of cloud and in sight of surface.*	250 kt below FL100	Not required	Not required
Class G (IFR)	Not provided (See Note)	Flight information service. (See Note)	Not applicable	250 kt below FL100	Not required	Not required
(VFR)	Not provided (See Note)	Flight information service (See Note)	FL100 and above: *Vis 8 km, 1500 m and 1000 ft from cloud.* Below FL100: *Vis 5 km. 1500 m and 1000 ft from cloud;* **or** below 3000 ft amsl: *Vis 5 km*, clear of cloud and in sight of surface.*	250 kt below FL100	Not required	Not required

Speed limitations do not apply to military aircraft.

* At speeds of 140 kt IAS or less the minimum flight visibility is 1500 m. Helicopters may operate in less than 1500 m at a speed which having regard to the visibility is reasonable.

† Helicopters may fly VFR in Class D & E Controlled Airspace below 3,000' — clear of cloud and in sight of surface

Note: The Separation and Services provisions shown above are the minimum required to meet ICAO Standards and Recommended Practices and may be supplemented when practicable. In particular, in Class F and Class G a Radar Advisory Service (RAS) and a Radar Information Service (RIS) are often available from ATS Units. Pilots are urged to make use of these services, details of which are published at page 16 and in Aeronautical Information Circulars (AICs).

UK CRITERIA FOR VFR FLIGHT

At and above FL100

Class B Airspace   − Vis 8 km, clear of cloud;

Class D, E, F, G Airspace   − Vis 8 km, 1500 m and 1000 ft from cloud.

Below FL100

Class D, E, F & G Airspace   − Vis 5 km, 1500 m and 1000 ft from cloud;

or,

At or below 3000 ft amsl.

Class D and E Airspace   − Vis 5 km, 1500 m and 1000 ft from cloud;

At 140 k or less   − Vis 5 km, clear of cloud and sight of surface;

Helicopters   − Clear of cloud and in sight of surface.

Class F and G Airspace   − Vis 5 km, clear of cloud and in sight of surface;

At 140 kt or less   − Vis 1500 m clear of cloud and in sight of surface;

but,

Helicopters may operate in flight visibilities of less than 1500 m at a speed, which having regard to visibility, is reasonable.

PRIVILEGES of a PPL and BCPL

In accordance with the Air Navigation Order the privileges of a PPL and BCPL permit the holder to operate within the following limitations:

PPL/BCPL without IMC /Instrument Weather Rating

- Minimum flight visibility 3 km in Uncontrolled Airspace;
- Remain in sight of surface at all times;
- Minimum visibility 10 km and in sight of surface on an SVFR clearance in a CTR.
- Flight in circumstances which require compliance with IFR not permitted.

PPL/BCPL with IMC /Instrument Weather Rating

- Minimum flight visibility 3 km and in sight of surface on a SVFR clearance in a CTR;
- Minimum visibility below cloud 1800 m for any take-off or landing;
- Flight in circumstances which require compliance with IFR not permitted in Controlled Airspace other than Class D and E.

SPECIAL VFR FLIGHT (SVFR)

1. Clearance for SVFR flight in the UK is an authorization by ATC for a pilot to fly within a Control Zone although he is unable to comply with IFR. *In exceptional circumstances, requests for SVFR flight may be granted for aircraft with an all-up-weight exceeding 5700 kg and capable of flight under IFR.* SVFR clearance is only granted when traffic conditions permit it to take place without hindrance to the normal IFR flights, but for aircraft using certain notified lanes, routes and local flying areas see paragraph 2. Without prejudice to existing weather limitations on SVFR flights at specific aerodromes (as detailed in the aerodromes directory) ATC will not issue a SVFR clearance to any fixed-wing aircraft intending to depart from an aerodrome within a Control Zone, when the official meteorological report indicates that the visibility is 1800 m or less and/or the cloud ceiling is less than 600 ft.

2. Aircraft using the access lanes and local flying areas notified for **Denham**, **White Waltham** and **Fairoaks** in the **London CTR** and any temporary Special Access Lanes which may be notified from time to time will be considered as SVFR flights and compliance with the procedures published for the relevant airspace will be accepted as compliance with ATC clearance. Separate requests should not be made nor will separate clearances be given. Separation between aircraft which are using such airspace cannot be given, and pilots are responsible for providing their own separation from other aircraft in the relevant airspace.

3. When operating on a SVFR clearance, the pilot must comply with ATC instructions and remain at all times in flight conditions which enable him to determine his flight path and to keep clear of obstacles. Therefore, it is implicit in all SVFR clearances that the aircraft remains clear of cloud and in sight of the surface. It may be necessary for ATC purposes to impose a height limitation on a SVFR clearance which will require the pilot to fly either at or not above a specific level.

4. A full flight plan, Form CA48/RAF2919, is not required for SVFR flight but ATC must be given brief details of the call sign, aircraft type and pilots intentions. These details may be passed either by RTF or, at busy aerodromes, through the Flight Clearance Office. A full flight plan must be filed if the pilot wishes the destination aerodrome to be notified of the flight.

5. Requests for SVFR clearance to enter a Control Zone, or to transit a Control Zone, may be made to the ATC authority whilst airborne. Aircraft departing from aerodromes adjacent to a Control Zone boundary and wishing to enter may obtain SVFR clearance either prior to take-off by telephone or by RTF when airborne. In any case, all such requests must specify the ETA for the selected entry point and must be made 5 to10 minutes beforehand.

6. ATC will provide standard separation between all SVFR flights and between such flights and other aircraft under IFR. However, pilots with a SVFR clearance should note that they cannot be given separation from aircraft flying in the lanes, routes and local flying areas detailed in paragraph 2; nor from aircraft flying in any temporary Special Access Lanes which may be notified from time to time.

7. A SVFR clearance within a Control Zone does not absolve the pilot from the responsibility for avoiding an Aerodrome Traffic Zone unless prior permission to penetrate the ATZ has been obtained from the relevant ATC Unit.

Continued on next page

SPECIAL VFR FLIGHT (SVFR) - Cont'd

8. Because SVFR flights are made at the lower levels, it is important for pilots to realise that a SVFR clearance does not absolve them from the need to comply with the relevant low flying restrictions of Rule 5 of the Rules of the Air Regulations 1996 (other than the 1500 ft rule where the clearance permits flight below that height). In particular, it does not absolve pilots from the requirement that an aircraft, other than a helicopter, flying over congested areas must fly at such a height as would enable it to clear the area and alight without danger to persons or property on the ground in the event of an engine failure and that a helicopter, whether flying over a congested area or not, must fly at such a height as would enable it to alight without danger to persons or property on the ground in the event of an engine failure. In addition there are special rules applicable to flight by helicopters over London - see Non- IFR Helicopter Flights in the London CTR and London City CTR page.

CHANNEL ISLANDS CTR/CTA

Within the operating hours of the Channel Islands CTR/CTA all flights are subject to the regulations applicable to Class 'A' Controlled Airspace — see page 2.
Outside operating hours the area which lies within the Brest FIR becomes Class E Airspace under the control of Brest ACC; the area which lies within the UK FIR becomes Class G (uncontrolled airspace)

1. Special VFR Clearance in the Channel Islands Control Zone (CTR)

A flight plan must be filled for all Special VFR flights in the Channel Islands CTR.

The aircraft must be equipped with the appropriate transponder equipment.

Special VFR clearances for flights within the CTR may be requested and will be given whenever traffic conditions permit. These flights are subject to the general conditions laid down for Special VFR Flights.

The use of special VFR clearances is intended to be limited to light aircraft which cannot comply with full IFR requirements and wish to proceed to or from an aerodrome within the CTR or to transit the CTR at the lower levels.

Special VFR clearance to operate within the Channel Islands CTR, for the purpose of proceeding to or from an aerodrome within the CTR, will not be granted to aircraft if the reported visibility is less than 3 km or the reported cloud ceiling is less than 600 ft at the aerodrome concerned.

Aircraft may be given a radar service whilst within the Channel Islands CTR if, due to the traffic situation, ATC considers it advisable. It will be the responsibility of the pilot to remain at all times clear of cloud and in sight of the surface. Pilots must inform the Radar Controller if compliance with the above entails a change of heading or height.

Special VFR flights may be subject to delay when they cannot be fitted readily into the main traffic flow. Pilots should, therefore, always ensure that they have adequate fuel reserves and are to divert to another aerodrome if necessary.

Pilots are to note that flying is not permitted at a height of less than 2000 ft above ground level within three nautical miles of N4925·77 W00221·75 in the Island of Sark (EG R095) except with the permission of the States Board of Administration or by Guernsey ATC as necessary.

2. Guernsey/Alderney VFR Lane

A VFR lane is established in Class 'D' Airspace for use by traffic routeing between Guernsey and Alderney. The lane is 5 nm either side of a line joining Guernsey and Alderney Airports, maximum altitude 2000', and its use is subject to ATC clearance.

The following minimum weather conditions must exist at **both** airports for VFR clearance to be given:

Visibility: 10 km
Cloud ceiling: 1500 ft.

3. Procedures Outside the Channel Islands Control Zone

Radar Advisory Service or Radar Information Service will not be given to aircraft flying outside the Channel Islands CTR.

Traffic information will not normally be given to aircraft operating outside the Channel Islands CTR due to traffic intensity in adjacent areas. Pilots are reminded that aircraft in transit to or from the CTR may not be flying in accordance with the Quadrantal/Semi-circular rule.

Traffic information will not normally be given to aircraft operating outside the Channel Islands CTR due to traffic intensity in adjacent areas. Pilots are reminded that aircraft in transit to or from the CTR may not be flying in accordance with the Quadrantal/Semi-circular rule.

A bi-directional Recommended VFR Route between the Channel Islands CTR and the Solent CTA is aligned in UK Airspace on a track between the 'MP' NDB on the Cherbourg Peninsula and Southampton VOR (' SAM '). South of the Isle of Wight the Route may be used up to FL100 and all traffic flying above 3000 ft amsl (irrespective of the flight rules being observed) is advised to maintain an altitude appropriate to the magnetic track in order that opposite direction conflictions may be minimised. The Route penetrates Royal Navy Danger Area EG D036. The Route may not be available during EG D036 scheduled hours or at other times promulgated by NOTAM. Flights wishing to use the Route during EG D036 scheduled hours can request a Danger Area Crossing Service from Plymouth Military. See DACS/ DAAIS pages for frequency, operating hours and pre-flight information telephone contact number. Pilots are advised to call as early and as high as practicable (but south of N51 10·00) to facilitate availability of the route. Subject to unit workload, a radar service may be offered to flights in the sea area west of EG D036 if Danger Area activities preclude flight along the VFR Recommended Route itself. The activity status may also be confirmed through Southampton or Jersey ATSUs or London Information.

Arriving flights will be given the appropriate reporting point for onward routeing into the CTR. This is not an ATC clearance to use this route. Aircraft must obtain onward clearance from the appropriate reporting point.

The base of Airway November Eight Six Six (N866) between the Solent CTA and the Channel Islands CTR is FL35. In order that the class G Airspace beneath the Airway is not constricted during periods of low pressure, the actual base of the Airway will always remain above 3000 ft amsl, thus guaranteeing the airspace up to this altitude for General Aviation traffic.

4. Flight Plans
All flights inbound to Guernsey and Alderney and overflfying the Channel Islands up to FL195 must ensure that flight plans are addressed to the Channel Island Control Zone – EGJJZRZX.

5. Flights within the local circuit area of the Aerodromes within the Zone
Exemption from the requirements of IFR will be granted to flights which remain within the local circuit area of aerodromes within the Zones.

6. ALDERNEY, GUERNSEY & JERSEY CONTROL ZONES
Unless otherwise authorised by the appropriate ATC unit at the relevant aerodrome, flights within the Alderney, Guernsey and Jersey CTRs are subject to the following:

(a) Contact the controlling ATC unit on the appropriate frequency before entering the airspace giving position, level and intended track;
(b) Obtain permission from the appropriate ATC unit for the flight;
(c) Listen out on the appropriate frequency;
(d) Obey all instructions from the appropriate ATC unit.

CHANNEL ISLANDS

Special VFR Routes

Aircraft operating in accordance with Special VFR will normally be cleared on one of the following special routes:

Destination or Departure Point	Associated French Route		Route Reporting Point
Jersey Airport	No 1	Dinard – Jersey	Minquiers
	No 6	Cherbourg – Jersey	Cap de Flamanville
	No 7	St Germain – Jersey	St Germain
	No 8	Granville – Jersey	East of Iles Chausey or Granville
	No 9	Ile de Brehat – Jersey	Ile de Brehat
Guernsey Airport	No 2	Dinard – Guernsey	West of Minquiers
	No 5	Cherbourg – Guernsey	Cap de Flamanville
	No 10	Ile de Brehat – Guernsey	Ile de Brehat
Alderney Airport	No 4	Cherbourg – Alderney	Cap de la Hague

Visual Reference Points (VRPs)

Name	Position	VOR/DME FIX		
		Jersey (JSY)	Guernsey (GUR)	Dinard (DIN)
Alderney (NDB)	N49 42·53 W002 11·98	352°/30 nm	048°/23 nm	–
Cap de Flamanville	N49 31·00 W001 53·00	023°/19 nm	084°/28 nm	–
Cap de la Hague	N49 43·00 W001 56·00	012°/30 nm	061°/31 nm	–
Carteret Lighthouse	N49 22·00 W001 48·00	051°/13 nm	101°/32 nm	–
Casquets Lighthouse	N49 43·00 W002 22·00	341°/32 nm	033°/19 nm	–
Corbiere Lighthouse	N49 11·00 W002 15·00	258°/8 nm	142°/21 nm	353°/36 nm
East of Iles Chausey	N48 53·00 W001 39·00	146°/26 nm	135°/50 nm	047°/25 nm
Granville	N48 50·00 W001 39·00	150°/28 nm	138°/52 nm	053°/23 nm
Ile de Brehat	N48 51·00 W003 00·00	243°/44 nm	208°/39 nm	297°/40 nm
Minquiers	N48 57·00 W002 08·00	196°/17 nm	152°/35 nm	358°/22 nm
North East Point	N49 30·42 W002 30·52	317°/25 nm	045°/6 nm	–
South East Corner	N49 10·00 W002 02·00	176°/3 nm	130°/28 nm	008°/35 nm
St Germain	N49 14·00 W001 38·00	091°/16 nm	111°/40 nm	028°/43 nm
West of Minquiers	N48 57·00 W002 18·00	215°/19 nm	161°/32 nm	342°/23 nm

Communications Procedures

General. Pilots of aircraft wishing to operate in the Channel Islands CTR via the special routeings detailed above are reminded that Airspace to the north of N50° (the London FIR) is subject to London ACC, and Airspace to the east, south and west (the Brest FIR) is subject to Brest ACC and that it is the responsibility of pilots to acquaint themselves with the requirements of the respective UK and French authorities.

Departures. Pilots of departing aircraft must acquaint themselves with the appropriate departure routes.

Intentionally Blank

FLIGHTS CROSSING AIRWAYS

Note: All airways are Class A airspace — compliance with IFR is mandatory.

1. Flights Crossing Airways in IFR

1.1 Aircraft may, without ATC clearance, fly at right-angles across the base of an en-route section of an Airway where the lower limit is defined as a Flight Level.

1.2. Pilots wishing to cross an Airway are required to file a flight plan either before departure or when airborne, and to request crossing clearance when at least 10 mins from the intended crossing point.

1.3. To obtain crossing clearance make the initial call giving *aircraft ident* and request crossing . . . . . *Airway* at. . . . . . .*position.* When instructed by ATC the following flight details should be passed:

      (a) Aircraft Ident & Type   (d) Position of crossing
      (b) Position & heading   (e) Requested crossing level
      (c) Level & flight conditions (f) Estimated time of crossing

1.4. Requests for joining clearance of Airways for which the Controlling Authorities are London, Scottish or Manchester Control should be obtained as follows:
    (a) From the ATSU with which the aircraft is already in communication; or
    (b) from the appropriate FIR Controller (if different from (a));
       or, if it is not possible to obtain any form of clearance from (a) or (b), then
    (c) on the published frequency of the Airway Controlling Authority.

1.5. Unless otherwise requested by ATC, aircraft crossing Airways will remain in communication with the FIR Controller and, after obtaining clearance, will report when the aircraft is at the Airway boundary as follows:

. . . . . *(ident)* – Crossing. . . . .*(Awy).* . . . . .*(position).* . . . . .*(time)* – at. . . . . *(level).*

1.6. Except where otherwise authorised by ATC, aircraft are required to cross the Airway by the shortest route (normally, at right angles) and to be in level flight at the cleared flight level on entering the Airway.

2. Airways Crossings or Penetrations in VMC

2.1. Powered Aircraft – Airways Crossings

2.2 Aircraft may, without ATC clearance, fly at right-angles across the base of an en-route section of an Airway where the lower limit is defined as a Flight Level.

2.3 Powered aircraft may cross an Airway in VMC by day without compliance with the full IFR requirements in relation to the aircraft equipment provided that the pilot holds a valid Instrument Rating and that clearance is obtained from the appropriate ACC. This clearance must be obtained by RT (normally on the FIR frequency); The request for clearance and a crossing report should be made as shown in paras 1.3 and 1.5.

3. Powered Aircraft – Other Penetrations

3.1 Other flights in VMC, for example photographic survey flights, may also do so without compliance with the full IFR requirements, provided that:
   (a) Prior arrangements are made with the appropriate ACC;
   (b) specific ATC clearance is obtained for individual flights;
   (c) the aircraft can communicate by RT on the appropriate Airways frequency.

4. Procedures for Military Aircraft

4.1 These procedures apply to military aircraft in all weather conditions.
4.2 Military aircraft flying along Airways will conform to the normal Airways procedures.
4.3 Military aircraft crossing Airways will do so either:
   (a) Under the control of an approved ATC Radar Unit; or
   (b) under a positive ATC clearance.
4.4 In an emergency, where neither a radar nor a procedural crossing can be obtained, an Airway may be crossed at an intermediate 500 ft level. The intermediate 500 ft levels referred to are flight levels of whole thousands plus 500 ft.

BOSCOMBE DOWN
ADVISORY RADIO AREA (ARA)

The objectives of the ARA are as follows:

(a) Providing pilots in the ARA with information, if required, about any limited manoeuvrability test flights from Boscombe Down;

(b) Highlighting the position of limited manoeuvrability test flights to controllers of adjacent ATSUs;

(c) Providing controllers, if requested, and pilots the opportunity to plan detours clear of test flight activity;

(d) Enhancing flight safety.

Vertical limits of the area are FL 50 to FL 245.

Hours of operation: Monday to Friday 0930 to 1730 (local)

Test flight activity often requires the pilots to fly profiles which limit their ability to manoeuvre their aircraft in compliance with the Rules of the Air. Such flights will receive a radar service from Boscombe Down or the London Radar Special Tasks Cell.

Pilots entering the area are strongly advised to call the most appropriate ATSU from among those listed below to obtain information on test flight activity:

Boscombe Down	126·700	London Radar	135·150
Bournemouth	119·625	Lyneham	123·400
Bristol	128·550	Middle Wallop	126·700
Brize Norton	134·300	Plymouth	133·550
Cardiff	125·850	Southampton	120·225
Exeter	128·150	Yeovilton	127·350
Filton	122·725		

See chart on the opposite page

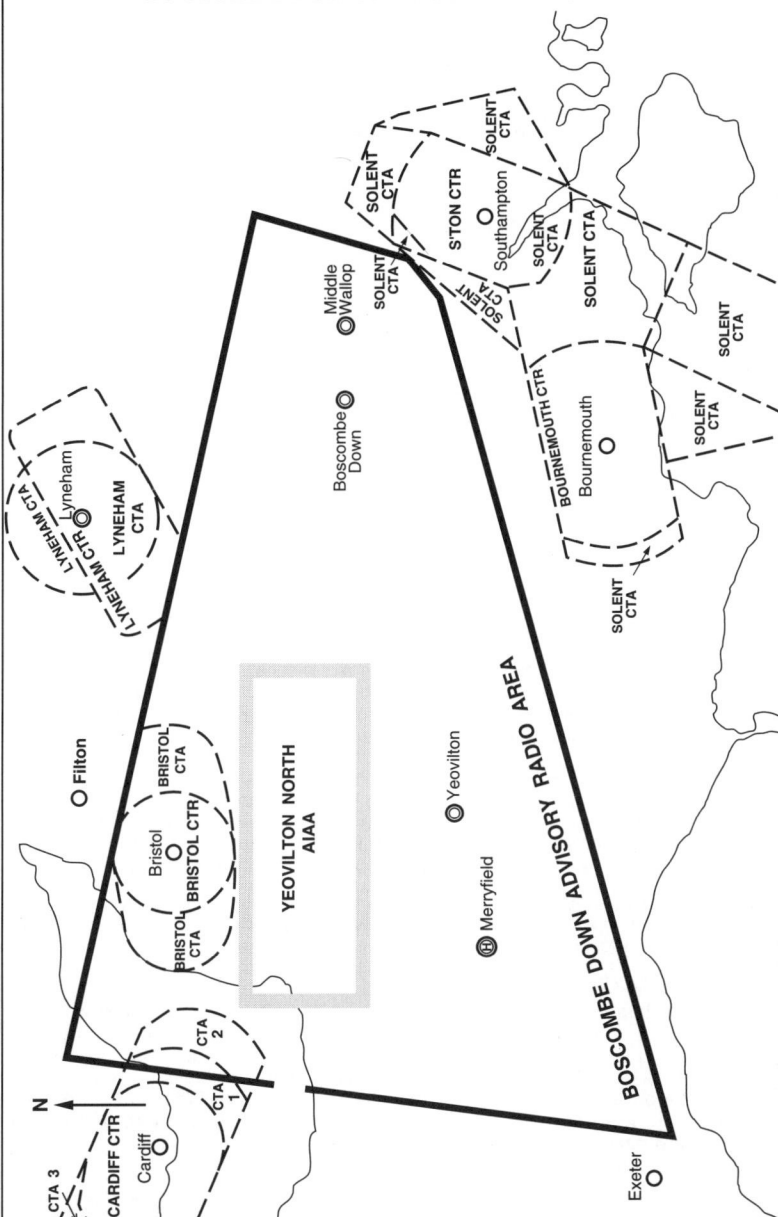

BOSCOMBE DOWN ADVISORY RADIO AREA

Robert Pooley ©

15

1 DEC 00

SERVICES TO AIRCRAFT OUTSIDE CONTROLLED AIRSPACE

1.   Introduction

1.1   The following information has been condensed from authoritive documents and is intended to give an outline of the type and range of Air Traffic Services available to aircraft operating outside controlled airspace in the UK Flight Information Region (FIR), which has become known as the 'Open' FIR.

2   Range of Services

2.1   The range of services available from civil and military ATSUs is listed below. Detailed information about the individual services can be found elsewhere in this Guide, in the UK AIP, RAF En-Route Supplement – British Isles and North Atlantic (BINA), and AICs.

Description of Service

Lower Airspace Radar Service (LARS) – page 20.

Military Middle Airspace Radar Service – page 23.

Military Aerodrome Traffic Zone (MATS) – page 29.
Penetration Service

Danger Area Crossing Service (DACS) and
Danger Area Activity Information Service (DAAIS) – page 32.

VHF Aeronautical Emergency Service – (Note 1).

Helicopter Radar Advisory Service -
Northern and Southern North Sea (Note 2).

Note 1: Applicable to Controlled and Uncontrolled Airspace.

Note 2: Dedicated radar services to helicopters operating over the North Sea (outside the scope of this article).

2.2   The published information on the range of services is intended to help the pilot to select the ATSU most likely to be able to meet his requirements during a particular stage of flight. If conditions permit, the controller at the selected ATSU will establish a specific type of service at the request of the pilot.

3   Types of Service

3.1   Four specific types of service are provided by controllers operating within the broad range of services available from ATSUs. Two of these are supported by radar — **Radar Advisory Service** and **Radar Information Service**. The other, non-radar, types of service are **Flight Information Service** and **Procedural Service**.

3.2   Whether provided by a civil or military controller, the type of service will be in the standard form described in the following paragraphs. Availability will be dependent upon controller workload at the time of the request.

4   Radar Services

4.1 **Radar Advisory Service (RAS).** RAS is an air traffic radar service in which the controller will provide advice necessary to maintain prescribed separation between aircraft participating in the advisory service in which he will pass to the pilot the bearing, distance and, if know, level of conflicting non-participating traffic, together with advice on action necessary to resolve the confliction. Where time does not permit this procedure to be adopted, the controller will pass advice on avoiding action followed by information on the conflicting traffic.
Under a RAS the following conditions apply:

Continued on opposite page

(a) The service will be only be provided to flights under IFR irrespective of meteorological conditions;

(b) Controllers will expect the pilot to accept vectors or level allocations which may require flight in IMC. **Pilots not qualified to fly in IMC should accept a RAS only where compliance with ATC advice permits the flight to be continued in VMC;**

(c) There is no legal requirement for a pilot flying outside Controlled Airspace, to comply with instructions because of the advisory nature of the service. However, a pilot who chooses not to comply with advisory avoiding action must inform the controller. The pilot will then become responsible for initiating any avoiding action that may subsequently prove necessary;

(d) The pilot must advise the controller before changing heading or level;

(e) The avoiding instructions which a controller may pass to resolve a confliction with non-participating traffic will, where possible, be aimed at achieving separation which is not less than 5 nm or 5000 ft, except when specified otherwise by the regulating authority. However, it is recognised that in the event of the sudden appearance of unknown traffic, and when unknown traffic make unpredictable changes in flight path, it is not always possible to achieve these minima;

(f) Information on conflicting traffic will be passed until the confliction is resolved;

(g) The pilot remains responsible for terrain clearance, although ATSUs providing a RAS will set a level or levels below which a RAS will be refused or terminated.

4.2 Radar Information Service (RIS).

RIS is an air traffic radar service in which the controller will only provide traffic information; he will inform the pilot of the bearing, distance and, if known, the level of the conflicting traffic. No avoiding action will be offered. **The pilot is wholly responsible for maintaining separation from other aircraft whether or not the controller has passed traffic information.** Under a RIS, the following conditions apply:

(a) The service may be requested under any flight rules or meteorological conditions;

(b) The controller will only update details of conflicting traffic after the initial warning at the pilot's request, or if the controller considers that the conflicting traffic continues to constitute a definite hazard;

(c) The controller may provide radar vectors for the purpose of tactical planning or at the request of the pilot. However, vectors will not be provided to maintain separation from other aircraft, which remains the responsibility of the pilot. There is no requirement for a pilot to accept vectors;

(d) The pilot must advise the controller before changing level, level band, or route;

(e) RIS may be offered when the provision of RAS is impracticable;

(f) Request for a RIS to be changed to a RAS will accepted subject to the controller's workload; prescribed separation will be applied as soon as practicable. If a RAS cannot be provided, the controller will continue to offer a RIS.

(g) For manoeuvring flights which involve frequent changes of heading or flight level, RIS may be requested by the pilot or offered by the controller. Information on conflicting traffic will be passed with reference to cardinal points. The pilot must indicate the level band within which he wishes to operate and is responsible for selecting the manoeuvring area, but may request the controller's assistance in finding a suitable location. The controller may suggest re-positioning on his own initiative, but the pilot is not bound to comply;

continued overleaf

(h) The pilot remains responsible for terrain clearance. ATSUs providing a RIS will set a level or levels below which vectors will not be provided, except when specified otherwise by the regulating authority.

4.3 Establishing a Service.

In order to establish a radar service the pilot and controller must reach an 'accord'. When requesting a radar service the pilot must state the flight rules under which he is operating and whether he requires a RAS or a RIS. If the controller is able to offer a service, he will attempt to identify the aircraft. When he is satisfied that he has positively identified the aircraft, the controller will confirm the type of service he is about to provide, and the pilot must give a read-back of the service. **The identification procedure does not imply that a radar service is being provided and the pilot must not assume that he is in receipt of a RAS or a RIS until the controller has made a positive statement to that effect.** If the controller is unable to provide a service he will inform the pilot.

4.3.1 Should the pilot fail to specify the type of service required, the controller will ask the pilot which service he requires before endeavouring to provide any service.

4.3.2 If, for any reason, the controller is unable to continue to provide the agreed type of service he will inform the pilot that the service is terminated. Where possible the controller will offer an alternative service and if the offer is accepted he will re-state the type. Similarly, the pilot should inform the controller when a radar service is no longer required.

4.3.3 London Control – Requests for RAS or RIS

4.3.3.1 To avoid excessive RTF conversations on the frequencies used by 'London Control', pilots who intend to request such a service from 'London Control' are to make their initial request on the FIS frequency ('London Information') appropriate to their geographical position. The FIS controller will co-ordinate with the appropriate Radar Sector and subsequently inform the pilot whether or not a RAS or RIS can be provided and, if so on what frequency.

4.3.3.2 Pilots should note that no RAS or RIS will be available on any London Control Frequency below FL70. In any case a serviceable transponder will be pr-requisite for either service.

4.4 RT Procedures.

A pilot requiring a radar service should establish radio contact with the appropriate ATSU on the notified frequency. The pilot should then pass the following information:

(a) Call sign and type of aircraft;

(b) Estimated position;

(c) Heading;

(d) Level (or level and band for traffic wishing to carry out general handling);

(e) Intention (next reporting/turning point, destination etc);

(f) Type of service required (RAS or RIS).

4.5 Limitations of Service.

Outside Controlled Airspace any radar service may be limited. If a radar controller considers that he cannot maintain a full radar service he will warn the pilot of the nature of the limitations that may affect the service being provided. Thereafter, the pilot is expected to take the stated limitation into account in his general airmanship.

continued on opposite page

In particular, warning of the limitation will be given to the pilot in the following circumstances:

(a) When the aircraft is close to the lateral or vertical limits of solid radar cover;

(b) When the aircraft is close to areas of permanent echoes or weather returns;

(c) When the aircraft is in or approaching areas of high traffic density;

(d) When the controller considers that the performance of his radar is suspect;

(e) When the controller is providing a service using SSR data only.

4.6 Successive Approaches.

If successive approaches to an aerodrome are required for training purposes etc, the pilot will be informed of the type of service on the first approach only.

4.7 Radar Handovers.

To maintain continuity of service during radar handovers, controllers will advise each other on the type of service being provided and the receiving controller will confirm the type of service with the pilot when radio contact has been made.

5 Non-Radar Services
5.1 Flight Information Service (FIS).

An FIS is provided by all ATSUs within the limits of available information. A specific FIS is provided day and night in each of the FIRs by the London Air Traffic Control Centre (LATCC) and the Scottish Air Traffic Control Centre (ScATCC). The controllers providing this service have no access to radar derived information.

5.1.1 At the discretion of the controller, warning or proximity hazards may be issued to pilots when there is evidence that aircraft are, or might be, in dangerous proximity to each other. However, the controller cannot assume responsibility for the accuracy or completeness of such warnings because:

(a) Position reports passed by pilots may be inaccurate;

(b) Many civil and military aircraft fly on a multiplicity of tracks and levels without communicating with ATSUs.

5.2 Procedural Service.

Procedural service is a non-radar air traffic service in which the prescribed standard separation minima based on reported levels and position, are applied between participating aircraft. The service may be provided in the following circumstances:

(a) For the separation of aircraft in holding patterns;

(b) For participating aircraft operating on Advisory Routes;

(c) When it is impracticable to provide a radar service due to radar non-availability, radar overhead dark areas, permanent echoes, clutter etc;

(d) When an ATSU is providing an approach control service to participating IFR traffic without the use of radar.

6 Entering Controlled Airspace

6.1   The receipt of any of the types of service described above does not carry an implied permission to fly in Controlled Airspace. Clearance to enter Controlled Airspace is the responsibility of the pilot and whilst ATSU controllers may assist, if workload permits, pilots must be prepared to obtain a clearance from the appropriate controlling authority independently.

LOWER AIRSPACE RADAR SERVICE (LARS)

Availability of Service

The service is available to all aircraft flying outside Controlled Airspace up to and including FL95, within the limits of radar/radio cover. The service will be provided within approximately 30 nm of each participating ATS unit. Unless a participating ATS unit is H24, the service will normally be available between 0800 and 1700 Mondays to Fridays. However, as some participating units may remain open to serve evening, night or week-end flying, pilots are recommended to call for the service irrespective of the published hours of ATS. If no reply is received after three consecutive calls, it should be assumed that the service is not available. Information on the operation of aerodromes outside the published hours may be obtained by telephone from the appropriate Military Air Traffic Control Centre:–

North of N54 30 ScATCC (Mil) Prestwick 01292–479800 Ext. 6703/4.

South of N54 30 LATCC (Mil) West Drayton 01895-426150.

LARS will not be normally be available at non-H24 stations at weekends and during public holidays.

Pilots intending to operate above FL95 may be advised to contact an appropriate ATCRU and request a RAS or RIS. However, as VHF frequencies at Military ATCRUs are not continuously monitored, unless in use, civil pilots may ask controllers to arrange a frequency on which to call the appropriate Unit.

Description of Service

The service provided will be Radar Advisory Service (RAS) or Radar Information Service (RIS) as described at page 16.

Request for RIS to be upgraded to RAS will be accepted subject to the controllers workload and standard separation will be applied as soon as practicable. If a RAS cannot be provided the controller will continue to offer a RIS.

Outside regulated airspace any radar service may be limited. If a radar contoller considers that he cannot maintain a full radar service he will warn the pilot of the nature of the limitations which may affect the service being provided, thereafter the pilot is expected to take the stated limitations into account in his general airmanship. In particular, warning of the limitations will be given to the pilot in the following circumstances:

(a) When the aircraft is close to the lateral or vertical limits of solid radar cover;

(b) when the aircraft is close to areas of permanent echoes or weather returns;

(c) when the aircraft is operating in areas of high traffic density;

(d) when the controller considers the performance of his radar suspect;

(e) when the controller is using SSR only.

In areas of high traffic density, controllers may have to limit RAS to the extent that standard separation from all traffic cannot be maintained and advisory avoiding action cannot be given. In these circumstances, pilots will be so advised. However, standard separation will be applied between participating traffic.

Emergency Service. In emergency, pilots will be given all possible assistance.

ATS Units Participating in the Lower Airspace Radar Service

Unit	Frequency	Service Radius (nm)	Op Hrs	Remarks
Boscombe Down	126·70	30	P	Note 1
Bristol	128·55	30	H24	Note 2
Brize Norton	134·30	60	H24	
Cardiff	125·85	40	P	
Coltishall	125·90	40	P	
Coningsby	120·80	30	P	
Cottesmore	130·20	30	P	
Culdrose	134·05	30	P	
Exeter	128·15	30	P	
Farnborough	125·25	30	P	Note 3
Filton	122·72	30	P	Note 2
Humberside	124·67	30	P	
Leeming	127·75	30	P	
Leuchars	126·50	40	H24	
Linton-on-Ouse	129·15	30	P	
London/Luton	129·55	30	H24	Note 4
Lossiemouth	119·35	40	P	Note 5
Manston	126·35	30	P	
Marham	124·15	30	P	
Newcastle	124·37	40	H24	
Plymouth Military	121·25/124·15	40	P	Note 6
St. Mawgan	126·50	30	P	
Shawbury	120·77	40	P	
Teesside	118·85	40	H24	
Valley	134·35	40	P	
Waddington	127·35	30	H24	
Warton	129·525	40	P	
Yeovilton	127·35	30	P	

P = Published times, normally 0800–1700 local time, Mondays to Fridays.

Notes:

1 Service not available at weekends and Public Holidays.

2 Filton 0800-1800 Mon-Fri, other times service available from Bristol. North of River Avon service will be provided by Filton. South of River Avon service will be provided by Bristol.

3 Available 0800-2000.

4 Minimum altitude for service between 25 and 30 nm is 3000 ft.

5 Mon-Fri during Inverness A/D notified hours, Lossiemouth also provide a radar service to aircraft operating to/from Inverness A/D. Pilots should contact Lossiemouth Radar. Availability of service at other times will be promulgated by NOTAM.

6 Plymouth Military also provide LARS in the Portland Area. Pilots operating East of the western edge of Airway A25 should call Plymouth Mil on 124·15, and those operating West of the western edge of A25 should call Plymouth Mil on 121·25.

Radar Coverage Diagram overleaf.

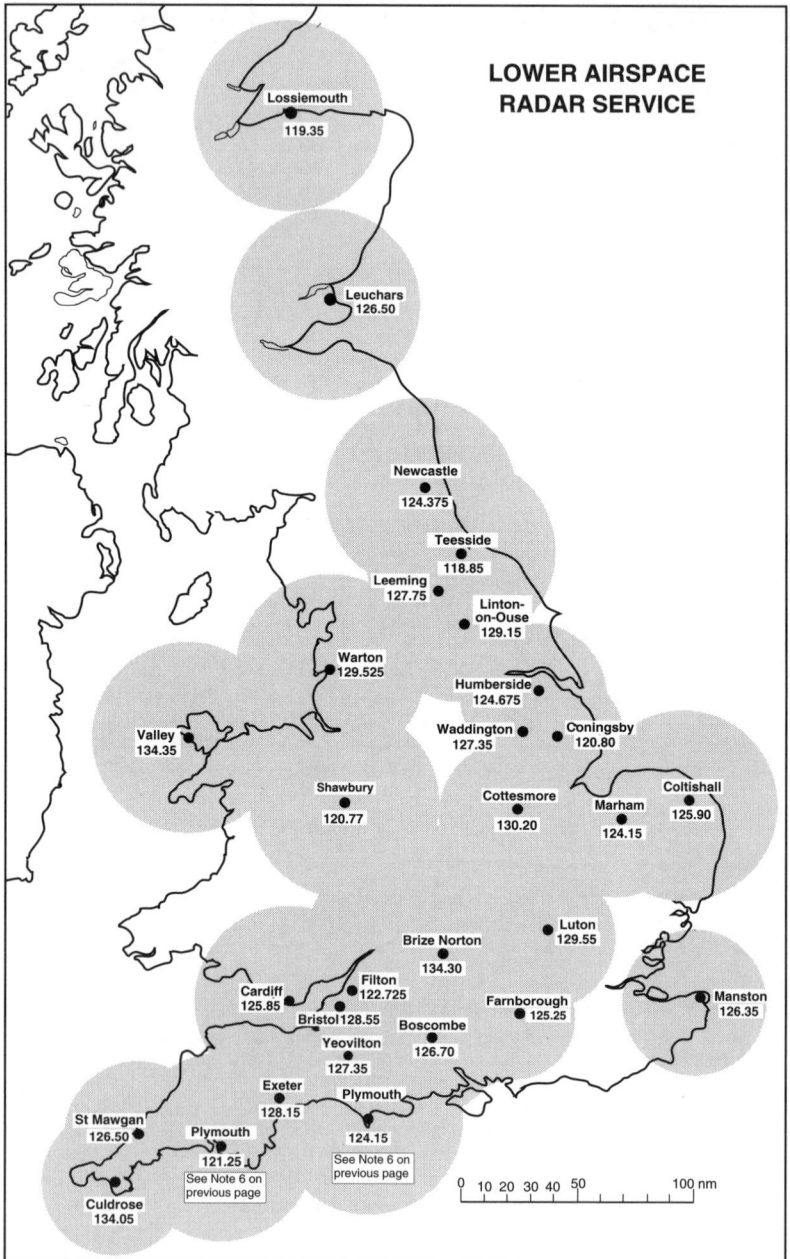

LOWER AIRSPACE RADAR SERVICE

Lossiemouth
119.35

Leuchars
126.50

Newcastle
124.375

Teesside
118.85

Leeming
127.75

Linton-
on-Ouse
129.15

Warton
129.525

Humberside
124.675

Valley
134.35

Waddington
127.35

Coningsby
120.80

Shawbury
120.77

Cottesmore
130.20

Marham
124.15

Coltishall
125.90

Luton
129.55

Brize Norton
134.30

Cardiff
125.85

Filton
122.725

Farnborough
125.25

Manston
126.35

Bristol 128.55

Boscombe
126.70

Yeovilton
127.35

Exeter
128.15

Plymouth
124.15

St Mawgan
126.50

Plymouth
121.25

See Note 6 on
previous page

See Note 6 on
previous page

Culdrose
134.05

0 10 20 30 40 50   100 nm

Military Middle Airspace Radar Service

1. Availability of Service

This service is available to all aircraft flying outside Controlled Airspace in the UK FIR except for flight along advisory routes, for flight within the Northern Off-Route Co-ordination Area (NORCA) and for flight within the Sumburgh FISA. It is available from FL100 to FL240. This service is subject to Unit capacity.

The military Units providing this service together with their boundaries and a table giving their hours of operation, the RTF frequency and a telephone number for pre-flight contact, is shown opposite.

Participating aircraft must be equipped with a serviceable transponder.

2. Type of Service

The service provided will be a Radar Advisory Service or Radar Information Service (see page 16).

3. Procedures

In order to comply with the requirements of the FPPS at LATCC (Mil) captains of aircraft requiring a radar service in the Upper, Middle or Lower Airspace within the London Radar area of responsibility are to pre-notify their intended flight details to LATCC (Mil) by one of the following methods:

(a) Pre-flight Notification - Flight Plans. As the preferred method of notification flight plans (F2919/CA48) should be submitted as far in advance of ETD as possible and in any case not less than 30 minutes before service is required. The LATCC (Mil) signals address — EGWDZQZX must be included on the flight plan. When appropriate these additions to the standard flight plan format must also be included:

(i) Item 18. The point and the time at which a radar service is required to commence;

(ii) Item 15. The point of entry into the area and the point of exit.

Note. Item 15. If a flight is planned to enter any Controlled Airspace (CAS) within the London Military area of responsibility and a service is required before joining or after leaving CAS, both parts of the route may be entered in Item 15 of the same flight plan. In this case both IFPS — EGZYIFPS and LATCC (Mil) — EGWDZQZX must appear as addressees.

(b) Pre-Flight Notification - Military Prenote. When it has not been possible to file a flight plan, as sub paragraph (a), relevant details of the intended flight should be telephoned by the pilot or by his aerodrome operations or ATC to LATCC (Mil), Main Flight Plan Reception Section, (ATOTN Telephone Ext 6710) at least 15 minutes before service is required. Flight details should be passed in this order:

(i)   Call sign;

(ii)   number of aircraft (if more than 1) and aircraft type(s);

(iii)   position and time at which service is required to commence;

(iv)   speed and flight level at commencement of service;

(v)   route (including any required speed or level changes);

(vi)   position of leaving the delineated area (if applicable), and

(vii) destination (ICAO Location Indicator).

(c) In-Flight Notification (Air Filing). Exceptionally, when neither form of pre-flight notification has been made the flight details listed in sub-paragraph (b) above, may be notified in flight (Air Filed) by radio to:

(i) ATCRU: Airfile with the ATCRU, currently providing a service for onward transmission by them to LATCC (Mil) at least 15 minutes in advance of service being required

(ii) London Radar: Request radar service by calling London Radar on the appropriate (ICF), at least 5 minutes before service is required passing the details listed in sub-paragraph (b) above.

4. Changes to Flight Details

(a) Pre-Flight Notification. Changes to pre-flight notifications are to be passed to LATCC (Mil) as soon as possible by:

(i)   Amended flight plan if time permits (as in paragraph 3 (a) (ii)); otherwise

(ii) by telephone (as in paragraph 3 (b)).

(b) In-Flight Notification (Air Filing). By RT as soon as possible (as in paragraph 3 (c)).

See diagram overleaf.

MILITARY MIDDLE AIRSPACE RADAR SERVICE

UNIT	OP HRS	ICF FREQUENCY	TELEPHONE
London Radar (London Mil)	H24	135·275 135·15	01895-426464
Scottish Mil	H24	134·30	01292-479800 Ext 6020

1 DEC 00

NORTHERN OFF-ROUTE CO-ORDINATION AREA (NORCA)

1   Northern Off-Route Co-ordination Area (NORCA)

1.1   The NORCA is a portion of Class G Airspace nominally 10 nm wide with its longitudinal centre-line aligned on the direct track between POL VOR and NEW VOR. There are three segments, as defined below, delineated by Reporting Points GASKO and TILNI. The vertical limits between the Airway B4/B1 boundaries and GASKO is FL 150-FL 245, with a fillet bounded by a line 5 nm north of centre-line GASKO-RIBEL. Between GASKO and TILNI, FL100 -FL190 and between TILNI and the Newcastle CTR/CTA boundary, FL 60-FL 150. See also chart at page 28.

Lateral Limits	Vertical Limits	Controlling Authority
N54 14·38 W002 05·73 - N54 12·58 W001 48·97 - N53 48·22 W001 56·55 - N53 49·08 W002 01·25 - N53 53·70 W002 06·92 - N54 08·40 W002 17·02 - N54 14.38 W002 05·73 **(Note)**	FL 245 ⎯⎯⎯ FL 150	See paragraph 1.4
N54 53·48 W001 53·55 - N54 57·93 W001 34·48 - N54 31·95 W001 42·85 - N54 33·75 W001 59·75 - N54 53·48 W001 53·55.	FL 190 ⎯⎯⎯ FL 100	
N54 33·75 W001 59·75 - N54 31·95 W001 42·85 - N54 12·58 W001 48·97 - N54 14·38 W002 05·73 - N54 33·75 W001 59·75.	FL 150 ⎯⎯⎯ FL 60	

Note: The NORCA does not include airspace between FL 95 and FL 245 within Airway B4.

1.2   The MOD has agreed that military aircraft which require to enter the NO RCA will obtain an ATC service from nominated military ATCRUs. Civil IFR/VFR flights are advised to contact Pennine Radar if they intend to enter the NORCA (see para 1.4).

1.3   The NORCA is H24. Within the NORCA, Pennine Radar will endeavour, subject to controller workload, to provide a RAS to all GAT flights. If necessary the service may be downgraded to RIS.

1.4   Pennine Radar, located at the Manchester Area Control Centre, hours of service are 0700-2100 Local daily, on frequency 128·675, callsign 'Pennine Radar'. Outside the hours of Pennine Radar, an air traffic service is provided by London Radar.

2   Pennine Radar Area of Responsibility

2.1   The NORCA.

2.2   Pennine Radar is also responsible for providing Air Traffic Services Outside Controlled Airspace (ATSOCA) within the following areas subject to controller workload and radar cover:

   (a)   Beneath Airways A2 and B4, north to a line drawn between DCS VOR and NEW VOR, where this line meets N55, continuing east along N55 to the 0° meridian thence south along the meridian to N5430, east to 01 E thence south to a point 5 nm northeast of the base of UL602, along the eastern edge of the base of UL602 to the northern edge of Airway B1 (DOGGA) thence west coincident with the northern edge of B1 to the Manchester TMA;

   (b)   Excluding that portion of the Newcastle CTR/CTA south of N55, the Teesside CTR/CTA and all Danger Areas. (Pennine Radar provide a DAAIS, on 128·675 for D407/D407A (Warcop));

2.3   Vertical limits between FL 55 and FL 245. RAS shall not be provided below 5000 ft Regional Pressure Setting (RPS). Exceptionally a RIS may be provided below 5000 ft, however, radar vectors will not be provided.

2.4   Radar services east of 1°E provided only at controller's discretion when workload permits as this area is normally outside the displayed radar range.

2.5   Other ATSUs providing a radar service, within the Pennine Area of Responsibility, are:

(a) Lower Airspace Radar Service (LARS) areas of Warton, Teesside, Newcastle, Leeming, Linton-on-Ouse, Humberside;

(b) Anglia Radar Area of Responsibility (ENR 6-1-15-3).

Note: Pilots operating within the airspace of a LARS Unit are to contact the relevant Unit initially in accordance with procedures detailed at ENR 1-6-4-1.

2.6   During the promulgated hours of operation, Pennine radar may provide a RAS, RIS or FIS when controller workload and radar cover permits.

2.7   For the purposes of effecting transfer of traffic between Pennine Radar and Humberside Approach, a Reporting Point is established at Leconfield, defined as N53 52·55 W000 26·40 ('OTR' VOR/DME fix 317°/16 nm) to be used at FL40 and above.

3. Routes

3.1   Recommended routes as shown on the opposite page, are provided for the main Civil traffic flows. They are based on fixed navigational facilities and are designed to assist pilots in avoiding Danger Areas and the intense military flying activity in the Vale of York.

3.2   Pilots of aircraft destined for Newcastle or Teesside and intending to penetrate the NORCA from the southwest should, where practicable, plan to join the recommended Radar Advisory Service Routes at either GASKO or TILNI as appropriate.

3.3   Pilots of aircraft entering the NORCA from the south via AWY A1 should leave Controlled Airspace at the Pole Hill VOR.

4. Procedures

4.1   Pilots of aircraft intending to fly within the NORCA during its promulgated hours should:

(a) If in communication with an ATC Unit, contact Scottish Control or Pennine Radar when advised;

(b) if flying in the FIR and not in communication with an ATS Unit, pass flight details and an estimate for the NORCA boundary to Scottish Control or Pennine Radar and, if appropriate, an ETA for GASKO or TILNI..

5. Radio Communication

5.1   Pilots receiving a service who wish to leave the frequency temporarily (for example to listen to VOLMET), and as a result will be unable to maintain two-way communication, must inform the Controlling Authority of their intention to leave the frequency and also of their return to it.

5.2   If radio communication is lost, attempts should be made to establish contact with either Newcastle, Teesside, London, Manchester or Scottish Control as appropriate to the planned route.

5.3   If complete radio failure occurs, pilots should follow the standard radio failure procedure detailed at ENR 1-1-3-2/7.

6. Radar Failure

6.1   In the event of temporary radar failure, a Flight Information Service will be available on the NORCA frequency until the radar is restored.

6.2   In the event of protracted radar failure, pilots will be advised of the appropriate ATC Unit to contact.

7. Meteorological Information

7.1   Aerodrome weather reports will not normally be given on the radar service frequency; however, weather broadcasts are available from VOLMET.

NORCA – Recommended Routes

To/Via	From/Via	FL	Route	Remarks
A25	NITON	Below 195	NITON - A25 - REXAM - WAL - POL	
A25	NITON	At 200 to 240	NITON - Y98 - POL	
A25/UA25	NITON	Requesting 250 or above	NITON - UY98 - NOKIN - Y98 - POL	
Newcastle	POL VOR		POL - GASKO - TILNI - NEW VOR	
Teesside	POL VOR		POL - GASKO - TD NDB	
South to join Airways	Newcastle	Above 185	TILNI - GASKO - RIBEL - CROFT	See A1, A25/UN862 below. See Note 1.
South to join Airways	Newcastle	Below 185	TILINI - GASKO - POL VOR	See A1, A25/UN862 below. See Note 1.
South to join Airways	Teesside	Above 185	GASKO - RIBEL - CROFT	See A1, A25/UN862 below. See Note 1.
South to join Airways	Teesside	Below 185	GASKO - POL VOR	See A1, A25/UN862 below. See Note 1.
A1	Newcastle/Teesside	Above 185	CROFT - BARTN - A1	
A1	Newcastle/Teesside	Below 185	POL VOR - BARTN - A1	
A25	Newcastle/Teesside	At 190	RIBEL - CROFT - WAL - A25	
A25	Newcastle/Teesside	At 180 or below	POL - WAL - A25	
A25	Newcastle/Teesside	At 200 to 240	RIBEL - Y99 -NOKIN - Y98 - NITON - A25	
A25/UN862	Newcastle/Teesside	Requesting 250 or above	RIBEL - UY99 -NOKIN - UN862	
B1/UB1	Newcastle/Teesside	175 and above	RIBEL - CROFT - WAL - B1/UB1	
B1/UB1	Newcastle/Teesside	Below 175	POL - WAL - B1/UB1	

Note 1: Traffic inbound to the Manchester TMA from Newcastle and Teesside at all levels will route SETEL - ROSUN.

Note 2: Traffic inbound to London Heathrow, London Luton, London Stansted, Northolt and ALKIN arrivals are to route via MCT - WCO.

NORTHERN OFF-ROUTE CO-ORDINATION AREA (NORCA)

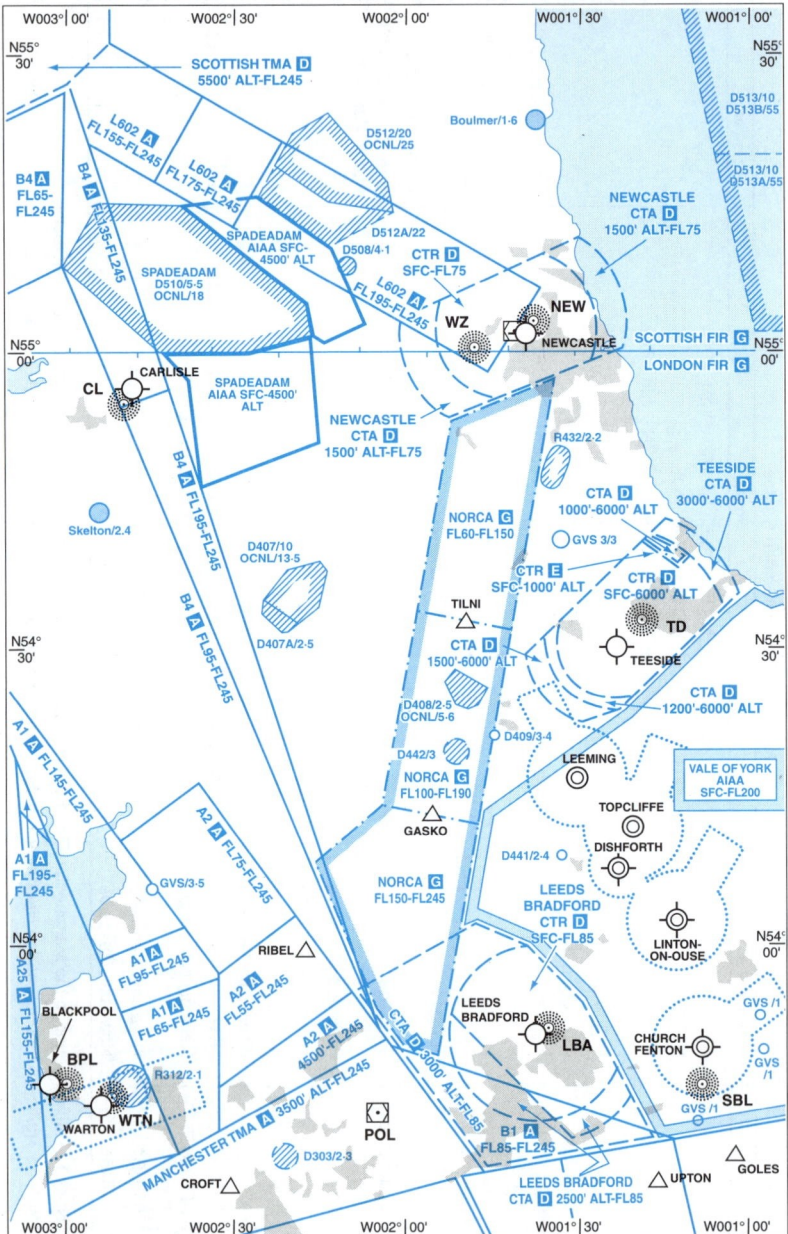

W003° 00'   W002° 30'   W002° 00'   W001° 30'   W001° 00'

N55° 30'

SCOTTISH TMA D
5500' ALT-FL245

L602 A
FL155-FL245

L602 A
FL175-FL245

B4 A FL235-FL245

B4 A
FL65-FL245

SPADEADAM
AIAA SFC-
4500' ALT

SPADEADAM
D510/5-5
OCNL/18

D512/20
OCNL/25

Boulmer/1-6

D512A/22

D508/4-1

L602 A
FL195-FL245

CTR D
SFC-FL75

WZ

NEW
NEWCASTLE

NEWCASTLE
CTA D
1500' ALT-FL75

D513/10
D513B/55

D513/10
D513A/55

SCOTTISH FIR G
LONDON FIR G

N55° 00'

N55° 00'

CL
CARLISLE

SPADEADAM
AIAA SFC-4500'
ALT

B4 A FL195-FL245

Skelton/2.4

NEWCASTLE
CTA D
1500' ALT-FL75

R432/2-2

NORCA G
FL60-FL150

GVS 3/3

CTA D
1000'-6000' ALT

CTR E
SFC-1000' ALT

TEESIDE
CTA D
3000'-6000' ALT

CTR D
SFC-6000' ALT

TD
TEESIDE

D407/10
OCNL/13-5

D407A/2-5

B4 A FL95-FL245

TILNI

CTA D
1500'-6000' ALT

CTA D
1200'-6000' ALT

N54° 30'

N54° 30'

A1 A FL145-FL245

A2 A FL75-FL245

A1 A
FL195-
FL245

GVS/3-5

D408/2-5
OCNL/5-6

D442/3

NORCA G
FL100-FL190

GASKO

D409/3-4

LEEMING

TOPCLIFFE

DISHFORTH

VALE OF YORK
AIAA
SFC-FL200

D441/2-4

N54° 00'

A25 A FL155-FL245

RIBEL

A1 A
FL95-FL245

A2 A
FL55-FL245

NORCA G
FL150-FL245

LEEDS
BRADFORD
CTR D
SFC-FL85

LINTON-
ON-OUSE

N54° 00'

BLACKPOOL

BPL

WARTON
WTN

R312/2-1

A1 A
FL65-FL245

A2 A
FL75-FL245

A2 A FL245-FL245

CTA D 3000' ALT-FL85

POL

CROFT

D303/2-3

LEEDS
BRADFORD

LBA

B1 A
FL85-FL245

CHURCH
FENTON

SBL

GVS /1

GVS
/1

GVS /1

MANCHESTER TMA A 3500' ALT-FL245

LEEDS BRADFORD
CTA D 2500' ALT-FL85

UPTON

GOLES

W003° 00'   W002° 30'   W002° 00'   W001° 30'   W001° 00'

MILITARY AERODROME TRAFFIC ZONES
(MATZ)

Military Aerodrome Traffic Zones (MATZ) are established at the locations listed overleaf. The purpose of a MATZ is to provide a volume of airspace within which increased protection may be given to aircraft in the critical stages of circuit, approach and climb-out. Normally these zones comprise:–

(a) The airspace within 5 nm radius of the mid-point of the longest Runway extending from the surface to 3000ft aal.

(b) The airspace within a 'stub' (or at some aerodromes 2 stubs) projected from the above airspace having a length of 5 nm along its centre-line, aligned with a selected final approach path, and a width of 4 nm (2 nm either side of the centre-line), extending from 1000ft aal to 3000ft aal.

The dimensions of the zone and associated stub(s) may vary. Often, two or more neighbouring MATZ are amalgamated with one of the aerodromes being designated as the controlling authority for the combined zone. In these instances , the upper limit is measured from the higher or highest aerodrome forming part of the combined zone.

An ATZ (Aerodrome Traffic Zone as defined in the Air Navigation Order currently in force) exists within a MATZ. Although civil recognition of a MATZ is not mandatory, pilots are to comply with the current Rules of the Air Regulations in respect of the ATZ. The notified hours of operation of an ATZ may vary from the notified hours of watch of a MATZ.

It should be noted that the majority of ATZs at military aerodromes are active H24, as annotated under the particular aerodrome entry.

MATZ Penetration procedures for Civil Aircraft

A MATZ Penetration Service is available from the controlling aerodromes listed opposite for the provision of increased protection for VHF RTF equipped civil aircraft. Pilots wishing to penetrate a MATZ are requested to observe the following procedures:–

(a) When 15 nm or 5 mins flying time from the zone boundary, establish radio contact with the controlling aerodrome on the appropriate frequency, and request MATZ penetration.   '............ (controlling A/D), this is .... (aircraft callsign), request MATZ penetration'.

(b) When asked for flight details, pass the following information:–
Callsign, Aircraft type, Position, Heading, Altitude, Intentions (eg destination).

(c) Comply with any instructions issued by the controller.

(d) Maintain a listening watch on the allocated frequency until the aircraft is clear of the MATZ.

(e) Advise the controller when clear of the MATZ.

Flight conditions are not required unless requested by the controller.

Whenever possible, a Radar Advisory Service or Radar Information Service will be given but when radar separation cannot be applied, vertical separation of at least 500 ft between known traffic will be applied.

The altimeter setting for use within a MATZ will be the aerodrome QFE, except for the following:

• Within the Odiham MATZ the transit pressure setting will be the Farnborough QNH;

• Within the Warton MATZ the altimeter setting will be the Warton QNH;

• Within the Lakenheath/ Mildenhall MATZ the altimeter setting will be the Lakenheath QNH.

Full details of Military Aerodrome Traffic Zones are given in the UK AIP ENR 2-2-4-1

MILITARY AERODROME TRAFFIC ZONES (MATZ)

MATZ	Mid Point of the Longest Runway	Controlling Aerodrome	Frequency to be used
Barkston Heath *1 *2	N52 57·80 W000 33·62	Cranwell	119·37
Benson	N51 36·98 W001 05·75	Benson	120·90
Boscombe Down	N51 09·12 W001 45·07	Boscombe Down	126·70
Church Fenton	N53 50·07 W001 11·72	Church Fenton	126·50
Coltishall	N52 45·30 E001 21·45	Coltishall	125·90
Coningsby	N53 05·58 W000 09·97	Coningsby	120·80
Cottesmore	N52 44·15 W000 38·93	Cottesmore	130·20
Cranwell	N53 01·80 W000 29·57	Cranwell	119·37
Culdrose	N50 05·13 W005 15·25	Culdrose	134·05
Dishforth *1	N54 08·23 W001 25·22	Leeming	127·75
Fairford *3	N51 41·02 W001 47·40	Brize Norton	134·30
Honnington *3	N52 20·55 E000 46·38	Lakenheath	128·90
Kinloss	N57 38·97 W003 33·63	Lossiemouth	119·35
Lakenheath *4 *5	N52 24·55 E000 33·67	Lakenheath	128·90
Leeming	N54 17·55 W001 32·12	Leeming	127·75
Leuchars	N56 22·48 W002 51·67	Leuchars	126·50
Linton-on-Ouse	N54 02·97 W001 15·22	Linton-on-Ouse	129·15
Lossiemouth	N57 42·42 W003 20·25	Lossiemouth	119·35
Marham	N52 38·90 E000 33·03	Marham	124·15
Merryfield *1	N50 57·78 W002 56·22	Yeovilton	127·35
Middle Wallop *6	N51 08·37 W001 34·12	Boscombe Down	126·70
Mildenhall *7 *8	N52 21·70 E000 29·18	Lakenheath	128·90
Mona	N53 15·55 W004 22·45	Valley	134·35
Odiham	N51 14·05 W000 56·57	Farnborough	125·25
Predanack	N50 00·10 W005 13·92	Culdrose	134·05
St. Mawgan	N50 26·43 W004 59·72	St. Mawgan	126·50
Scampton *9	N53 18·47 E000 33·05	Waddington	127·35
Sculthorpe *3	N52 50·75 E000 45·95	Marham	124·15
Shawbury	N52 47·62 W002 40·07	Shawbury	120·77
Ternhill	N52 52·42 W002 31·92	Shawbury	120·77
Topcliffe	N54 12·33 W001 22·92	Leeming	127·75
Valley	N53 14·83 W004 32·02	Valley	134·35
Waddington	N53 09·97 W000 31·43	Waddington	127·35
Warton *10	N53 44·70 W002 53·03	Warton	129·52
Wattisham	N52 07·63 E000 57·35	Wattisham	125·80
West Freugh	N54 51·27 W004 56·37	West Freugh	130·05
Wittering	N52 36·75 W000 28·60	Cottesmore	130·20
Yeovilton	N51 00·48 W002 38·75	Yeovilton	127·35

Notes:

* 1   MATZ 3 nm radius.
* 2   Barkston Heath stub extends from ground level to 3000 ft aal.

Notes continued on opposite page

MILITARY AERODROME TRAFFIC ZONES
(MATZ)

Notes (continued)

* **3** These aerodromes are opened on very limited occasions when advised by NOTAM or Supplement.

* **4** Non-standard North Easterly stub SFC to 3000 ft.

* **5** Helicopters tasked to operate in EG D208 are required to call Lakenheath ATC to notify entry to EG D208 prior to penetrating the CMATZ.
No restrictions will be imposed on helicopters which operate within that portion of their north-easterly stub which is also within the lateral limits of EG D208, provided that the aircraft remain at or below 800 ft amsl.

* **6** Non-standard reference point aligned with common radar touchdown point.

* **7** Non-standard extension to both stubs - 5 nm South of extended centre-lines.

* **8** Non-standard demarcation of the 5 nm circles which are joined by a straight line at their most Easterly points.

* **9** **Warning:** 5 nm radius portion of MATZ co-incident with Restricted Area R313.

* **10** Non-standard MATZ with the following dimensions:

    Lateral: A rectangle of airspace, 20 nm x 6 nm. The major axis is centred on the ARP, aligned with the major runway headings 071° (T)/ 251° (T) and off-set 1 nm to the south.

    Vertical: The portion of the rectangle contained within the part circle radius 5 nm centred on the ARP extends from the surface to 3000 ft aal. The remainder extends from 1000 ft aal to 3000 ft aal.

    Warning: The northern sector of the ATZ is not wholly contained within the MATZ.

DANGER AREA CROSSING SERVICE (DACS) AND
DANGER AREA ACTIVITY INFORMATION SERVICE (DAAIS)

Identification & Name	Hours of activity (LOCAL)	DACS/DAAIS
D001 Trevose Head	Mon-Thu 0800-2359; Fri 0800-1800.	DACS: St. Mawgan App 126·50 O/T DAAIS : London Information 124·75.
D003/004 Plymouth	Mon-Thu 0800-2359; Fri 0800-1600 and as notified	DACS: Plymouth Military 121·25 O/T London Information 124·75. Pre-flight information from Plymouth Ops 01752-557550.
D006 Falmouth Bay	Mon-Thu 0800-2359; Fri 0800-1600 and as notified	DACS: Culdrose App 134·05 O/T DAAIS London Information 124·75. Pre-flight information from Culdrose Ops 01326-552201.
D006A Falmouth Bay	Mon-Thu 0800-2359; Fri 0800-1600 and as notified	DACS: Plymouth Military 121·25 O/T London Information 124·75. Pre-flight information from Culdrose Ops 01326-552201.
D007 Fowey Inner	Mon-Thu 0800-2359; Fri 0800-1600 and as notified	DACS: Plymouth Military 121·25 O/T London Information 124·75. Pre-flight info from St. Mawgan Ops 01637-872201 Ext 2045/6.
D007A/007B Fowey	Mon-Thu 0800-2359; Fri 0800-1600 and as notified	DACS: Plymouth Military 121·25 O/T London Information 124·75. Pre-flight information from Plymouth Ops 01752-557550.
D008/008A/008B Plymouth	Mon-Thu 0800-2359; Fri 0800-1600 and as notified	DACS: Plymouth Military 121·25 O/T London Information 124·75. Pre-flight information from Plymouth Ops 01752-557550.
D009/009A Wembury	Mon-Thu 0800-2359; Fri 0800-1600 and as notified	DACS: Plymouth Military 121·25 O/T London Information 124·75. Pre-flight information from Plymouth Ops 01752-557550.
D012/013/014 Lyme Bay	Mon-Thu 0800-2359: Fri 0800-1600 and as notified	DACS: Plymouth Military 124·15. O/T London Information 124·75. Pre-flight information from Plymouth Ops 01752-557550.

Identification & Name	Hours of activity (LOCAL)	DACS/DAAIS
D015 Bovington	When notified	DAAIS: Bournemouth Tower 125·60
D017 Portland	Mon-Thu 0800-2359; Fri 0800-1600 and as notified	DACS: Plymouth Military 124·15.
		O/T London Information 124·75. Pre-flight
		information from Plymouth Ops 01752-557550.
021/023 Portland	Mon-Thu 0800-2359; Fri 0800-1600 and as notified	DACS: As for D017
D026 Lulworth	Mon-Fri 0800-2359 and as notified	DAAIS: London Information 124·75. Pre-flight
		information from Plymouth Ops 01752-557550.
D031 Portland	Mon-Thu 0800-2359; Fri 0800-1600 and as notified	DACS: As for D017
D036 Portsmouth	Mon-Thu 0800-1700; Fri 0800-1400 and as notified	DACS: Plymouth Military 124·15
		Note: Contact Plymouth Mil south of N51 10·00.
		O/T London Information 124·75. Pre-flight
		information from Plymouth Ops 01752-557550.
D037 Portsmouth	Mon-Fri 1000-1800 and as notified	DAAIS: London Info 124·75 or 124·60
D038/039/040 Portsmouth	Mon-Fri 0800-1800 and as notified	DAAIS: London Info 124·75 or 124·60
D044 Lydd Ranges	0800-2359 and as notified	DAAIS: London Info 124·75 or 124·60
		DAAIS: Lydd Information 120·70
		O/T London Information 124·60
D060 Browndown	When notified	DAAIS: Solent App 120·225
D061 Woodbury Common	When notified	DAAIS: Exeter App 128·15
D110 A & B Braunton Burrows	When notified	DAAIS: London Information 124·75
D112 Hartland North & South	Mon-Fri 0800-1800	DACS: London Information 124·75
D113 Castle Martin (W)	Mon-Fri 0800-2359 and as notified	DAAIS: London Information 124·75
D114 Castle Martin (E)	When firing Mon-Fri	DAAIS: London Information 124·75
D115A/115B Manorbier	Mon-Fri 0830-1700 and as notified	DAAIS: London Information 124·75
D117 Pendine	Mon-Fri 0800-1800 and as notified	DAAIS: Pembrey Range 122·75
	No firings on Public Holidays	O/T London Information 124·75
D118 Pembrey	Mon-Thu 0900-1700; Fri 0900-1400 and as notified	DAAIS: Pembrey Range 122·75
D119 Bridgewater Bay	When notified	DAAIS: Yeovilton App 127·35
		O/T London Information 124·75

Identification & Name	Hours of activity (LOCAL)	DACS/DAAIS
D121 St. Thomas' Head	H24	DAAIS: Bristol App 128·55
		O/T London Information 124·75
D123 Imber	H24	DACS: Salisbury Operations 122·75
		O/T DAAIS may be avail via ATIS 122·75. Pre-flight information from 01980-674710 or 674730.
D124 Lavington	When notified	DACS: As for D123
D125 Larkhill	H24	DACS: As for D123
D126 Bulford	H24	DACS: As for D123
D127 Porton	H24	DAAIS: Boscombe Down Zone 126·70
		O/T London Information 124·75
D128 Everleigh	H24	DACS: As for D123
D129 Weston-on-the-Green	H24	DAAIS: Brize Radar 134·30
D130 Longmoor	H24	DAAIS: Farnborough App 125·25
		O/T London Information 124·60.
		Pre-flight information from AIS Heathrow 020-8745 3451.
D131 Hankley Common	When notified	DAAIS: Farnborough App 125·25
		O/T London Information 124·60.
D132 Ash Ranges	When notified	DAAIS: As for D131
D133/133A Pirbright	0800-2359 and when notified	DAAIS: As for D131
D136 Shoeburyness	When notified Mon-Fri 0800-1800	DAAIS: Southend App 128·95
		O/T London Information 124·60.
D138/138A Shoeburyness	Mon-Fri 0600-1800 and as notified	DAAIS: As for D136
D138B Shoeburyness	When notified as for D138.	DAAIS: As for D136
D141 Hythe Ranges	0800-2359 and as notified	DAAIS: Lydd Information 120·70
		O/T London Information 124·60.
D145 Hullavington	When notified	DAAIS: Lyneham Zone 123·40.

Identification & Name	Hours of activity (LOCAL)	DACS/DAAIS
D146 Yantlet	When notified 0800-1700	DAAIS: Southend App 128·95
D201/201A Aberporth	Mon-Fri 0800-2300 and as notified	DACS: Aberporth Control 133·50, Info 122·15 or London Military 135·15
D201B Aberporth	When notified	DACS: As for D201
D202 Llanbedr	Mon-Fri 0800-2300 and as notified	DACS: Llanbedr Radar 122·50
D207 Holbeach	Mon-Thu 0900-1700; Fri 0900-1200; Sep-Apr: Tue & Thur 1800-2200 and as notified.	DAAIS: London Information 124·60
D208 Stanford	H24	DAAIS: Lakenheath Zone 128·90
D213 Kineton	When notified	DAAIS: Coventry ATIS 126·05
D215 North Luffenham	When notified	DAAIS: Cottesmore App 130·20
D304 Upper Hulme	When notified 0800-1800, and occasionally up to 2100 Oct to Mar.	DAAIS: Manchester App 119·40
D307 Donna Nook	Mon-Thu 0900-1630; Fri 0900-1500; Sep-Apr: Tue & Thu 1800-2200 and as notified.	DAAIS: Donna Nook Range 122·75
D308 Wainfleet	Mon & Wed 1300-2300; Tue & Thu 0900-1700; Fri 0900-1500 and as notified	DAAIS: Wainfleet Range 122·75
D314 Harpur Hill	Mon-Fri 0800-1900	DAAIS: Manchester App 119·40
D316/317 Neatishead	Mon-Fri SR-SS and as notified	DACS: London Radar 135·275. Pre-flight info from RAF Neatishead 01692-633445.
D402A Luce Bay (N)	Mon-Thu 0800-2230, Fri 0800-1630 and as notified	DACS: West Freugh App 130·05 or Scottish Information 119·87
D402B Luce Bay (N)	When notified	DACS: As for D402A
D402C Luce Bay (N)	Mon-Fri 0730-1520	DACS: West Freugh App 130·05
D403 Luce Bay	Mon-Thu 0900-2230, Fri 0900-1630 and as notified	DACS: As for D402A
D403A Luce Bay	H24	DACS: West Freugh App 130·05
D405 Kirkcudbright	Mon-Fri 0800-2359 and as notified	DACS: West Freugh App 130·05 A/D op hrs or Kirkcudbright Range 122·10 – 0800-1630.

Robert Pooley ©

Identification & Name	Hours of activity (LOCAL)	DACS/DAAIS
D405A Kirkcudbright.	Mon-Fri 0800-2359.	DACS: As for D405
D406 Eskmeals.	Sep - Mar: Mon-Fri 0800-1700	DAAIS: London Information 125·47
	Apr - Aug: Mon-Fri 0800-2000 and as notified.	
D406B Eskmeals	When notified.	DAAIS: London Information 125·47
D406C Eskmeals.	When notified.	DACS: Eskmeals Range 122·75
D407 Warcop.	0900-1700 daily.	DAAIS Pennine Radar 128·67
D407A Warcop.	Tue, Wed, Thu and Sat 1800-0200.	DAAIS Pennine Radar 128·67
D408 Feldom.	Tue-Sun 0830-1630 and as notified	DAAIS: Leeming App 127·75
		O/T London Information 125·47.
D409 Catterick	When notified.	DAAIS: Leeming App 127·75
		O/T London Information 125·47.
D411 Portpatrick Wigtownshire.	Mon-Fri 0800-1630 and as notified.	DACS: West Freugh App 130·05
		O/T DAAIS: Scottish Information 119·875.
D412 Staxton.	When notified Mon-Fri 0830-1630	DAAIS: London Information 125·47
D441 Ellington Banks	When notified Mon-Sat 0900-1700	DAAIS: Linton App 129·15.
D508 Ridsdale.	Mon-Fri 0800-1700 and as notified.	DACS: Newcastle App 124·37. Pre-flight
		information from Newcastle ATC 0191-2860966
		Ext 3251.
D509 Campbelton	When notified.	DAAIS: West Freugh App 130·05
		O/T Scottish Information 119·87.
D510 Spadeadam.	Mon-Thu 09-1700, Fri 09-1600 and as notified	DAAIS: Newcastle App 124·37 or
		Carlisle Twr 123·60
		DACS: Spadeadam 122·10
D512 Otterburn.	H24.	DAAIS: Scottish Information 119·87
D512A Otterburn.	When notified.	DAAIS: Scottish Information 119·87
D513 Druridge Bay	When notified Mon-Fri 0830-1630	DAAIS: Scottish Information 119·87
D513A/B Druridge Bay.	When notified.	DAAIS: Scottish Information 119·87
D604 Barry Buddon.	H24.	DAAIS: Leuchars App 126·50

Identification & Name	Hours of activity (LOCAL)	DACS/DAAIS
D607 Firth of Forth (Middle)	When notified	DAAIS: Scottish Information 119·87
D608 Firth of Forth (Outer)	When notified	DAAIS: Scottish Information 119·87
D609 St. Andrews	H24	DAAIS: Scottish Information 119·87
D701 Hebrides	Mon-Fri 1000-1800 and as notified	DAAIS: Scottish Information 127·27
D701A/701B/701C/701D Hebrides	When notified	DAAIS: Scottish Information 127·27
D701E Hebrides	When notified Mon-Fri 1630-SS and Sat 1300-SS	DAAIS: Scottish Information 127·27
D702 Fort George	0800-1600 daily and as notified	DAAIS: Inverness Twr 122·60, O/T Scottish Information 126·25
D703 Tain Range	Mon & Thu 0900-1700, Tue & Wed 0900-2359 Fri 0900-1230 and as notified.	DAAIS: Tain Range 122·75
D708 Rosehearty	Mon-Fri 0900-1700; May-Aug: Tue & Wed 2100-2259 and as notified.	DAAIS: Rosehearty Range 122·75
D710 Raasay	When notified Mon-Sat SR-SS	DAAIS: Scottish Information 127·27
D801/802 Cape Wrath (NW) & (SE)	When notified	DAAIS: Scottish Information 126·25
D803 Garvie Island	When notified Mon-Fri 0800-1800	DAAIS: Scottish Information 126·25
D807 Moray Firth	Mon-Fri 0700-2359 and as notified	DAAIS: Lossiemouth Departures 119·35
D809(N) Moray Firth (North)	When notified	DAAIS: Scottish Information 126·25
D809(C) Moray Firth (Central)	When notified	DAAIS: Scottish Information 126·25
D809(S) Moray Firth (South)	When notified	DAAIS: Scottish Information 126·25

NAVIGATIONAL AIDS in UK.

Details of runway approach aids such as ILS, ILS/DME and LLZ are given under the appropriate aerodrome entry in the Aerodrome Directory.

Station	Facility	Ident.	Freq.	Range nm.	Co-ordinates
Aberdeen	NDB	ATF	348·0	25	N57 04·65 W002 06·35
Aberdeen	NDB	AQ	336·0	15	N57 08·30 W002 24·28
Aberdeen	VOR/DME	ADN	114·30		N57 18·63 W002 16·03
Aberporth	NDB	AP	370·5	20	N52 06·98 W004 33·59
Alderney	NDB	ALD	383·0	30	N49 42·53 W002 11·98
Barkway	VOR/DME	BKY	116·25		N51 59·38 E000 03·72
Barra	NDB	BRR	316·0	15	N57 01·53 E007 26·93
Barrow (Walney Is.)	NDB	WL	385·0	15	N54 07·53 W003 15·78
Barrow (Walney Is.)	DME	WL	109·40		N54 07·63 W003 15·90
Belfast	VOR/DME	BEL	117·20	54	N54 39·67 W006 13·80
Belfast (Aldergrove)	NDB	OY	332·0	15	N54 41·57 W006 05·12
Belfast (City)	NDB	HB	420·0	15	N54 36·93 W005 52·92
Bembridge IOW	NDB	IW	426·0	15	N50 40·82 W001 06·27
Benbecula	VOR/DME	BEN	113·95		N57 28·68 W007 21·92
Benbecula	DME	BCL	108·15		N57 28·50 W007 22·22
Berry Head	VOR/DME	BHD	112·05		N50 23·92 W003 29·62
Biggin	VOR/DME	BIG	115·10		N51 19·85 E000 02·08
Birmingham	NDB	BHX	406·0	25	N52 27·27 W001 45·15
Blackbushe	NDB	BLK	328·0	15	N51 19·40 W000 50·68
Blackbushe	DME	BLC	116·20		N51 19·40 W000 50·70
Blackpool	NDB	BPL	420·0	15	N53 46·37 W003 01·67
Boscombe Down	TACAN	BDN	108·20		N51 08·93 W001 45·15
Bourn	NDB	BOU	391·5	15	N52 12·65 W000 02·73
Bournemouth	NDB	BIA	339·0	15	N50 46·67 W001 50·55
Bovingdon	VOR/DME	BNN	113·75		N51 43·57 W000 32·98
Brecon	VOR/DME	BCN	117·45		N51 43·53 W003 15·78
Bristol Airport	NDB	BRI	380·0	25	N51 22·83 W002 42·97
Brize Norton	TACAN	BZN	111·90		N51 44·89 W001 36·21
Brize Norton	NDB	BZ	386·0	10	N51 44·95 W001 36·09
Brookmans Park	VOR/DME	BPK	117·50		N51 44·98 W000 06·40
Brough	NDB	BV	372·0	15	N53 43·52 W000 34·88
Burnham	NDB	BUR	421·0		N51 31·13 W000 40·63
Caernarfon	NDB	CAE	320·0	15	N53 06·00 W004 20·40
Cambridge	NDB	CAM	332·5	15	N52 12·65 E000 10·97
Cardiff	NDB	CDF	388·5	20	N51 23·60 W003 20·30

Station	Facility	Ident.	Freq.	Range nm.	Co-ordinates
Carlisle	NDB	CL	328·0	20	N54 56·42 W002 48·33
Carlisle	DME	CO	110·70		N54 56·40 W002 48·32
Carnane (IOM)	NDB	CAR	366·5	25	N54 08·47 W004 29·50
Chiltern	NDB	CHT	277·0	25	N51 37·38 W000 31·12
Clacton	VOR/DME	CLN	114·55		N51 50·92 E001 08·85
Coltishall	TACAN	CSL	116·50		N52 44·41 E001 21·02
Compton	VOR/DME	CPT	114·35		N51 29·50 W001 13·18
Compton Abbas	NDB	COM	349·5		N50 57·98 W002 09·22
Coningsby	TACAN	CGY	111·10		N53 05·46 W000 10·13
Cottesmore	TACAN	CTM	112·30		N52 44·12 W000 39·04
Coventry	NDB	CT	363·5	20	N52 4·65 W001 24·35
Cranfield	NDB	CIT	850·0	15	N52 07·78 W000 33·42
Cranfield	VOR	CFD	116·50		N52 04·45 W000 36·65
Cranwell	NDB	CWL	423·0	25	N53 01·58 W000 29·34
Cranwell	TACAN	CWZ	117·40		N53 01·78 W000 29·12
Cumbernauld	NDB	CBN	374·0	25	N55 58·53 W003 58·48
Cumberland	DME	CBN	117·55		N55 58·53 W003 58·47
Daventry	VOR/DME	DTY	116·40		N52 10·82 W001 06·83
Dean Cross	VOR/DME	DCS	115·20		N54 43·32 W003 20·43
Detling	VOR/DME	DET	117·30		N51 18·23 E000 35·83
Dover	VOR/DME	DVR	114·95		N51 09·75 E001 21·55
Dundee	NDB	DND	394·0	25	N56 27·30 W003 06·90
East Midlands	NDB	EME	353·5	20	N52 49·97 W001 11·67
East Midlands	NDB	EMW	393·0	10	N52 49·72 W001 27·27
Edinburgh	NDB	EDN	341·0	35	N55 58·72 W00317·13
Edinburgh	NDB	UW	368·0	25	N55 54·32 W003 30·15
Enniskillen	NDB	EKN	357·5	15	N54 23·58 W007 38·67
Enniskillen	DME	ENN	116·75		N54 23·93 W007 39·22
Epsom	NDB	EPM	316·0	25	N51 19·17 W000 22·32
Exeter	NDB	EX	337·0	15	N50 45·13 W003 17·70
Fairford	TACAN	FFA	111·50		N51 40·81 W001 47·86
Fairoaks	NDB	FOS	348·0	08	N51 20·78 W000 33·83
Fairoaks	DME	FRK	109·85		N51 20·78 W000 33·83
Fenland	NDB	FNL	401·0	15	N52 44·50 W000 01·65
Fife/Glenrothes	NDB	GO	402·0	15	N56 10·95 W003 13·20
Filton	NDB	OF	325·0	25	N51 31·32 W002 35·42
Gamston	VOR/DME	GAM	112·80		N53 16·88 W000 56·83
Glasgow	VOR/DME	GOW	115·40		N55 52·23 W004 26·75

Station	Facility	Ident.	Freq.	Range nm.	Co-ordinates
Glasgow	NDB	AC	325·0	25	N55 48·85 W004 32·57
Glasgow	NDB	GLG	350·0	45	N55 55·47 W004 20·17
Gloucestershire	NDB	GST	331·0	25	N51 53·52 W002 10·07
Gloucestershire	DME	GOS	115·55		N51 53·53 W002 10·08
Goodwood	VOR/DME	GWC	114·75		N50 51·32 W000 45·40
Gt Yarmouth (N.Denes)	NDB	ND	417·0	10	N52 38·12 E001 43·62
Guernsey	NDB	GRB	361·0	30	N49 26·05 W002 37·95
Guernsey	VOR/DME	GUR	109·40		N49 26·22 W002 36·23
Haverfordwest	NDB	HAV	328·0	10	N51 49·93 W004 58·10
Haverfordwest	DME	HDW	116·75	10	N51 49·93 W004 58·18
Hawarden	NDB	HAW	340·0	25	N53 10·75 W002 58·77
Henton	NDB	HEN	433·5	30	N51 45·58 W000 47·42
Honiley	VOR/DME	HON	113·65		N52 21·40 W001 39·82
Humberside	NDB	KIM	365·0	15	N53 34·43 W000 21·22
Inverness (Dalcross)	VOR/DME	INS	109·20		N57 32·55 W004 02·50
Islay	NDB	LAY	395·0	30	N55 40·97 W006 14·97
Islay	DME	ISY	109·95		N55 40·98 W006 14·97
Isle of Man	NDB	RWY	359·0	20	N54 04·85 W004 37·37
Isle of Man	VOR/DME	IOM	112·20		N54 04·02 W004 45·82
Jersey	VOR/DME	JSY	112·20		N49 13·27 W002 02·77
Jersey	NDB	JW	329·0	25	N49 12·35 W002 13·20
Kinloss	NDB	KS	370·0	20	N57 39·03 W003 35·23
Kinloss	TACAN	KSS	109·80		N57 39·56 W003 32·11
Kirkwall †	VOR/DME	KWL	108·60		N58 57·58 W002 53·63
† Operates as TVOR during ATC hours, range 25 nm at 10,000 ft.					
Kirkwall	NDB	KW	395·0	40	N58 57·58 W002 54·70
Lakenheath	TACAN	LKH	110·20		N52 24·39 E000 32·48
Lambourne	VOR/DME	LAM	115·60		N51 38·77 E000 09·10
Lands End	VOR/DME	LND	114·20		N50 08·18 W005 38·22
Lashenden (Headcorn)	NDB	LSH	340·0	15	N51 09·28 E000 38·88
Leeds Bradford	NDB	LBA	402·5	25	N53 51·90 W001 39·17
Leicester	NDB	LE	383·5	10	N52 36·38 W001 02·10
Lerwick	NDB	TL	376·0		N60 11·30 W001 14·78
Leuchars	TACAN	LUK	110·50		N56 22·36 W002 51·82
Lichfield	NDB	LIC	545·0	50	N52 44·80 W001 43·17
Linton-on-Ouse	TACAN	LOO	109·00		N54 03·02 W001 14·94
Liverpool	NDB	LPL	349·5	25	N53 20·38 W002 43·50
London	VOR/DME	LON	113·60		N51 29·23 W000 28·00

Station	Facility	Ident.	Freq.	Range nm.	Co-ordinates
London City	NDB	LCY	322·0	10	N51 30·27 E000 07·00
London (Gatwick)	NDB	GY	365·0	15	N51 07·83 W000 18·95
London (Gatwick)	NDB	GE	338·0	15	N51 09·87 W000 04·15
London (Heathrow)	NDB	HRW	424·0	20	N51 28·73 W000 27·57
London (Luton)	NDB	LUT	345·0	20	N51 53·68 W000 15·15
Londonderry (Eglinton)	NDB	EGT	328·5	25	N55 02·73 W007 09·30
London (Stansted)	NDB	SSD	429·0	20	N51 53·68 E000 14·70
Lundy Island	NDB	LS	296·5		N51 09·73 W004 39·37
Lydd	DME	LDY	108·15		N50 57·52 E000 56·35
Lydd	NDB	LYX	397·0	15	N50 58·33 E000 57·32
Lydd	VOR/DME	LYD	114·05		N50 59·98 E000 52·72
Lyneham	TACAN	LYE	109·8		N51 30·44 W001 59·53
Lyneham	NDB	LA	282·0	40	N51 30·50 W002 00·35
Machrihanish	VOR/DME	MAC	116·00		N55 25·80 W005 39·02
Manchester	NDB	MCH	428·0	15	N53 21·20 W00216·38
Manchester	VOR/DME	MCT	113·55		N53 21·42 W002 15·73
Manchester/Barton	NDB	BAE	325·0	10	N53 28·15 W002 23·32
Manchester/Woodford	NDB	WFD	380·0	15	N53 20·25 W002 09·50
Manston	NDB	MTN	347·0	20	N51 20·63 E001 20·78
Marham	TACAN	MAM	108·70		N52 38·49 E000 33·18
Mayfield	VOR/DME	MAY	117·9		N51 01·03 E000 06·97
Midhurst	VOR/DME	MID	114·0		N51 03·23 W000 37·50
Mildenhall	TACAN	MLD	115·90		N52 21·80 E000 29·29
Newcastle	VOR/DME	NEW	114·25		N55 02·30 W001 41·82
Newcastle	NDB	NEW	352·0	40	N55 03·03 W001 38·90
Newcastle	NDB	WZ	416·0	10	N55 00·40 W001 48·43
New Galloway	NDB	NGY	399·0	35	N55 10·65 W004 10·12
Northampton (Sywell)	NDB	NN	378·5	15	N52 17·95 W000 47·82
Norwich	NDB	NH	371·5	20	N52 40·58 E001 23·08
Norwich	NDB	NWI	342·5	20	N52 40·65 E001 17·48
Nottingham	NDB	NOT	430·0	10	N52 55·30 W001 04·77
Ockham	VOR/DME	OCK	115·30		N51 18·30 W000 26·83
Odiham	TACAN	ODH	109·60		N51 13·97 W000 56·90
Ottringham	VOR/DME	OTR	113·90		N53 41·90 W000 06·22
Oxford (Kidlington)	NDB	OX	367·5	25	N51 49·95 W001 19·40
Oxford (Kidlington)	DME	OX	117·70		N51 49·95 W001 19·37
Penzance Heliport	NDB	PH	333·0	15	N50 07·70 W005 31·07
Perth	VOR	PTH	110·40		N56 26·55 W003 22·12
Plymouth	NDB	PY	396·5	20	N50 25·40 W004 06·73

Station	Facility	Ident.	Freq.	Range nm.	Co-ordinates
Pole Hill	VOR/DME	POL	112·10		N53 44·63 W002 06·20
Prestwick	NDB	PIK	355·0	30	N55 30·37 W004 34·63
Prestwick	NDB	PW	426·0	30	N55 32·67 W004 40·90
Redhill	NDB	RDL	343·0	10	N51 12·97 W000 08·33
Rochester	NDB	RCH	369·0	10	N51 21·23 E000 30·22
Ronaldsway	NDB	RWY	359·0	25	N54 05·17 W004 36·52
St. Abbs	VOR/DME	SAB	112·50		N55 54·45 W002 12·38
St.Athan	TACAN	SAT	114·80		N51 24·38 W003 26·09
St. Mawgan	TACAN	SMG	112·60		N50 26·07 W005 01·82
St. Mawgan	NDB	SM	356·5		N50 26·88 W004 59·67
Scatsta	NDB	SS	315·5	25	N60 27·62 W001 12·92
Scilly Is. (St. Mary's)	NDB	STM	321·0	15	N49 54·85 W006 17·47
Scotstownhead	NDB	SHD	383·0	80	N57 33·55 W001 49·03
Seaford	VOR/DME	SFD	117·00		N50 45·63 E000 07·32
Shawbury	DVOR/DME	SWB	116·80		N52 47·88 W002 39·75
Sheffield	NDB	SMF	333·0		N53 23·57 W001 22·98
Sherburn-in-Elmet	NDB	SBL	323·0	10	N53 47·37 W001 12·50
Shobdon	NDB	SH	426·0	20	N52 14·68 W002 52·55
Shoreham	NDB	SHM	332·0	10	N50 50·13 W000 17·73
Shoreham	DME	SRH	109·95		N50 50·17 W000 17·60
Sleap	NDB	SLP	382·0	10	N52 50·02 W002 46·07
Southampton	VOR/DME	SAM	113·35		N50 57·32 W001 20·70
Southampton	NDB	EAS	391·5	15	N50 57·30 W001 21·37
Southend	NDB	SND	362·5	20	N51 34·58 E000 42·02
Stornoway	VOR/DME	STN	115·10		N58 12·42 W006 10·98
Stornoway	NDB	SAY	431·0		N58 12·85 W006 19·57
Stornoway	DME	ISV	110·90		N58 12·80 W006 19·60
Strumble	VOR/DME	STU	113·10		N51 59·68 W005 02·42
Sturgate	NDB	SG	358·0		N53 22·87 W000 41·12
Sumburgh	NDB	SBH	351·0	75	N59 52·95 W001 17·68
Sumburgh	VOR/DME	SUM	117·35		N59 52·73 W001 17·20
Swansea	NDB	SWN	320·5	15	N51 36·13 W004 03·95
Swansea	DME	SWZ	109·20		N51 36·22 W004 03·92
Talla	NDB	TLA	363·0	25	N55 30·17 W003 25·83
Talla	VOR/DME	TLA	113·80		N55 29·95 W003 21·17
Tatenhill	NDB	TNL	327·0	10	N52 48·88 W001 46·00
Teesside	NDB	TD	347·5	25	N54 33·62 W001 20·00
Tiree	VOR/DME	TIR	117·70		N56 29·60 W006 52·53
Topcliffe	TACAN	TOP	113·70		N54 12·34 W001 22·71

Station	Facility	Ident.	Freq.	Range nm.	Co-ordinates
Trent	VOR/DME	TNT	115·70		N53 03·23 W001 40·20
Turnberry	VOR/DME	TRN	117·50		N55 18·80 W004 47·03
Vallafield	TACAN	VFD	114·90		N60 44·98 W000 55·77
Valley	TACAN	VYL	108·40		N53 15·45 W004 32·65
Waddington	TACAN	WAD	117·10		N53 09·92 W000 31·62
Wallasey	VOR/DME	WAL	114·10		N53 23·52 W003 08·07
Warton	TACAN	WTN	113·20		N53 44·42 W002 53·56
Warton	NDB	WTN	337·0	15	N53 45·10 W002 51·13
Wattisham	TACAN	WTM	109·00		N52 07·31 E000 56·42
Welshpool	NDB	WPL	323·0	10	N52 37·80 W003 09·23
Welshpool	DME	WPL	115·95		N52 37·78 W003 09·23
Westcott	NDB	WCO	335·0	30	N51 51·18 W000 57·75
West Freugh	NDB	WFR	339·0	25	N54 51·65 W004 56·42
Whitegate	NDB	WHI	368·5	25	N53 11·10 W002 37·38
Wick	NDB	WIK	344·0	30	N58 26·80 W003 03·78
Wick	VOR/DME	WIK	113·60		N58 27·53 W003 06·02
Wittering	TACAN	WIT	117·60		N52 36·48 W000 29·92
Wolverhampton	NDB	WBA	356·0	10	N52 31·05 W002 15·68
Woodley	NDB	WOD	352·0	25	N51 27·17 W000 52·73
Yeovil	NDB	YVL	343·0	20	N50 56·48 W002 39·87
Yeovil	DME	YVL	109·05		N50 56·45 W002 39·23
Yeovilton	TACAN	VLN	111·00		N51 00·30 W002 38·32

Intentionally Blank

Aerodrome	VRP	Position	
ABERDEEN/DYCE	BANCHORY	N57 03·00	W002 30·10
EGPD	INSCH	N57 20·57	W002 36·85
N57 12·25 W002 12·02	MELDRUM T.V. MAST	N57 23·20	W002 24·00
	PETERHEAD	N57 30·42	W001 46·60
	STONEHAVEN	N56 57·75	W002 12·60
	TURRIFF	N57 32·32	W002 27·60
ALDERNEY	ALDERNEY NDB	N49 42·53	W002 11·98
EGJA	CAP DE LA HAGUE	N49 43·00	W001 56·00
N49 42·37 W002 12·88	CASQUETS LIGHTHOUSE	N49 43·00	W002 22·00
BELFAST/ALDERGROVE	BALLYMENA	N54 51·80	W006 16·40
EGAA	CLUNTOE (DISUSED A/D)	N54 37·23	W006 32·03
N54 39·45 W006 12·93	DIVIS	N54 36·45	W006 00·57
	GLENGORMLEY M2/J4	N54 40·83	W005 58·90
	LARNE	N54 51·20	W005 49·52
	PORTADOWN	N54 25·50	W006 26·85
	TOOME (DISUSED A/D)	N54 45·47	W006 29·67
BELFAST/CITY	COMBER	N54 33·05	W005 44·75
EGAC	GROOMSPORT	N54 40·50	W005 37·08
N54 37·08 W005 52·35	SAINTFIELD	N54 27·62	W005 49·97
	WHITEHEAD	N54 45·17	W005 42·57
BENBECULA	LOCHMADDY PIER	N57 35·77	W007 09·40
EGPL	MONACH ISLANS LIGHTHOUSE	N57 31·57	W007 41·67
N57 28·65 W007 21·98			
BIGGIN HILL	SEVENOAKS	N51 16·60	E000 10·90
EGKB			
N51 19·85 E000 01·95			
BLACKPOOL	FLEETWOOD (GOLF COURSE)	N53 55·13	W003 02·72
EGNH	INSKIP (DISUSED A/D)	N53 49·63	W002 50·05
N53 46·30 W003 01·72	KIRKHAM	N53 46·95	W002 52·28
	MARSHSIDE	N53 41·78	W002 58·23
	POULTON (RAILWAY STATION)	N53 50·90	W002 59·42
BOURNEMOUTH	HENGISTBURY HEAD	N50 42·72	W001 44·93
EGHH	SANDBANKS	N50 41·00	W001 56·83
N50 46·80 W001 50·55	STONEY CROSS (DISUSED A/D)	N50 54·70	W001 39·42
	TARRANT RUSHTON (DISUSED A/D)	N50 51·00	W002 04·70

Aerodrome	VRP	Position
BRISTOL EGGD N51 22·97 W002 43·15	BATH CHEDDAR RESERVOIR CHEW VALLEY CHURCHILL CLEVEDON EAST NAILSEA HANHAM PORTISHEAD RADSTOCK WESTON-SUPER-MARE	N51 22·70 W002 21·42 N51 16·78 W002 48·08 N51 19·50 W002 35·70 N51 20·00 W002 47·60 N51 26·35 W002 51·08 N51 25·80 W002 44·10 N51 26·93 W002 30·95 N51 29·70 W002 46·42 N51 17·53 W002 26·92 N51 20·70 W002 58·33
BRIZE NORTON EGVN N51 45·00 W001 35·02	BAMPTON BURFORD CHARLBURY FARINGDON FARMOOR RESERVOIR LECHLADE NORTHLEACH ROUNDABOUT	N51 43·50 W001 32·80 N51 48·40 W001 38·20 N51 52·30 W001 28·90 N51 39·30 W001 35·20 N51 45·20 W001 21·40 N51 41·60 W001 41·40 N51 50·25 W001 50·15
CARDIFF EGFF N51 23·80 W003 20·60	CARDIFF DOCKS COWBRIDGE FLAT HOLM LIGHTHOUSE M4 JUNCTION 36 (SERVICES) MINEHEAD NASH POINT LIGHTHOUSE NASH SOUTH ST HILARY T.V. MAST WENVOE T.V. MAST	N51 27·40 W003 09·10 N51 27·60 W003 26·23 N51 22·55 W003 07·13 N51 31·93 W003 34·40 N51 12·35 W003 28·50 N51 24·08 W003 33·33 N51 22·88 W003 33·45 N51 27·45 W003 24·18 N51 27·60 W003 16·95
CARLISLE EGNC N54 56·25 W002 48·55	GRETNA HALTWHISTLE PENRITH WIGTON	N54 59·73 W003 04·05 N54 58·13 W002 27·73 N54 39·87 W002 45·02 N54 49·48 W003 09·67
COVENTRY EGBE N52 22·18 W001 28·78	BITTESWELL (DISUSED A/D) CEMENT WORKS DRAYCOTT WATER NUNEATON (DISUSED A/D)	N52 27·47 W001 14·78 N52 16·35 W001 23·07 N52 19·57 W001 19·58 N52 33·90 W001 26·88
CRANFIELD EGTC N52 04·33 W000 37·00	OLNEY TOWN STEWARTBY BRICKWORKS WOBURN TOWN	N52 09·20 W000 42·10 N52 04·40 W000 31·05 N51 59·40 W000 37·15
DENHAM EGLD N51 35·32 W000 30·78	MAPLE CROSS ST. GILES	N51 37·77 W000 30·25 N51 38·03 W000 34·02
DUNDEE EGPN N56 27·15 W003 01·55	BROUGHTY CASTLE	N56 27·75 W002 52·18

Aerodrome	VRP	Position
EAST MIDLANDS	BOTTESFORD	N52 57·88 W000 46·90
EGNX	CHURCH BROUGHTON	N52 53·17 W001 41·90
N52 49·87 W001 19·60	MARKFIELD (M1 JUNCTION 22)	N52 41·73 W001 17·55
	MEASHAM (M42 JUNC 11)	N52 41·33 W001 32·88
	MELTON MOWBRAY	N52 44·37 W000 53·57
	TROWELL (M1 SERVICE)	N52 57·70 W001 16·05
EDINBURGH	ARTHURS SEAT	N55˙56·63 W003 09·70
EGPH	BATHGATE	N55 54·17 W003 38·42
N55 57·15 W003 21·77	COBBINSHAW RESERVOIR	N55 48·47 W003 34·00
	DALKEITH	N55 53·60 W003 04·10
	FORTH ROAD BRIDGE, NORTH TOWER	N56 00·37 W003 24·23
	HILLEND SKI SLOPE	N55 53·30 W003 12·50
	KELTY	N56 08·08 W003 23·25
	KIRKCALDY HARBOUR	N56 06·83 W003 09·00
	KIRKLISTON	N55 57·33 W003 24·18
	KIRKNEWTON	N55 53·25 W003 25·08
	MUSSELBURGH	N55 56·83 W003 02·42
	PENICUIK	N55 49·92· W003 13·42
	PHILPSTOUN(M9 JUNCTION 2)	N55 58·90 W003 30·72
	POLMONT	N55 59·33 W003 41·00
	WEST LINTON	N55 45·17 W003 21·45
EXETER	AXMINSTER	N50 46·90 W002 59·90
EGTE	CREDITON	N50 47·43 W003 39·08
N50 44·07 W003 24·83	CULLOMPTON	N50 51·47 W003 23·63
	EXMOUTH	N50 37·48 W003 24·13
	TOPSHAM	N50 41·38 W003 28·82
FARNBOROUGH	ALTON	N51 09·12 W000 57·97
EGLF	BAGSHOT	N51 20·95 W000 41·95
N51 16·55 W000 46·56	FARNBOROUGH RAILWAY STATION	N51 17·78 W000 45·30
	GUILDFORD	N51 14·37 W000 35·10
	HOOK	N51 16·77 W000 57·72
FILTON	OLD SEVERN BRIDGE	N51 36·67 W002 38·62
EGTG	M5 BRIDGE OVER RIVER AVON	N51 29·33 W002 41·58
N51 31·17 W002 35·45	THORNBURY	N51 36·67 W002 31·10
GLASGOW	ALEXANDRIA	N55 59·33 W004 34·58
EGPF	ARDMORE POINT	N55 58·28 W004 41·95
N55 52·32 W004 26·00	BAILLIESTON	N55 51·17 W004 05·37
	BARRHEAD	N55 48·00 W004 23·50
	BISHOPTON	N55 54·13 W004 30·10
	DUMBARTON	N55 56·67 W004 34·10
	EAST KILBRIDE	N55 45·83 W004 10·33
	ERSKINE BRIDGE	N55 55·22 W004 27·77
	GREENOCK	N55 56·83 W004 45·08
	INVERKIP POWER STATION	N55 53·90 W004 53·20
	KILMACOLM	N55 53·67 W004 37·65
	KILMARNOCK	N55 36·75 W004 29·90
	KINGSTON BRIDGE	N55 51·37 W004 16·18

Aerodrome	VRP	Position
GUERNSEY EGJB N49 26·10 W002 36·12	CAP DE FLAMANVILLE ILE DE BREHAT NORTH EAST POINT WEST OF MINQUIERS	N49 31·00 W001 53·00 N48 51·00 W003 00·00 N49 30·42 W002 30·52 N48 57·00 W002 18·00
HUMBERSIDE EGNJ N53 34·52 W000 21·08	IMMINGHAM DOCKS NORTH TOWER HUMBER BRIDGE CAISTOR BRIGG LACEBY CROSSROADS ELSHAM WOLDS	N53 37·70 W000 11·60 N53 42·85 W000 27·03 N53 29·77 W000 19·10 N53 33·20 W000 29·20 N53 32·12 W000 10·82 N53 36·52 W000 25·68
INVERNESS EGPE N57 32·40 W004 03·00	INVERGORDON LOCHINDORB TOMATIN DORES DINGWALL	N57 41·53 W004 10·05 N57 24·17 W003 42·95 N57 20·03 W003 59·50 N57 22·92 W004 19·92 N57 35·97 W004 25·88
ISLAY EGPI N55 40·92 W006 15·40	MULL OF OA NORTH COAST PORT ELLEN RHINNS POINT	N55 35·50 W006 20·30 N55 56·00 W006 09·90 N55 38·00 W006 11·40 N55 40·40 W006 29·10
ISLE OF MAN EGNS N54 05·00 W004 37·45	LAXEY PEEL	N54 13·75 W004 24·10 N54 13·33 W004 41·50
JERSEY EGJJ N49 12·48 W002 11·73	CAP DE FLAMANVILLE CARTERET LIGHTHOUSE CORBIERE LIGHTHOUSE EAST OF ILES CHAUSEY GRANVILLE ILE DE BREHAT MINQUIERS ST GERMAIN SOUTH EAST CORNER	N49 31·00 W001 53·00 N49 22·00 W001 48·00 N49 11·00 W002 15·00 N48 53·00 W001 39·00 N48 50·00 W001 39·00 N48 51·00 W003 00·00 N48 57·00 W002 08·00 N49 14·00 W001 38·00 N49 10·00 W002 02·00
KIRKWALL EGPA N58 57·47 W002 54·32	FOOT LAMB HOLM ISLAND STROMBERRY	N59 01·72 W002 48·38 N58 53·23 W002 53·60 N59 01·82 W002 56·02
LEEDS BRADFORD EGNM N53 51·95 W001 39·63	DEWSBURY (DBY) ECCUP RESERVOIR (ECP) HARROGATE (HGT) KEIGHLEY (KLY)	N53 41·50 W001 38·10 N53 52·27 W001 32·60 N53 59·50 W001 31·60 N53 52·00 W001 54·60

Aerodrome	VRP	Position
LIVERPOOL EGGP N53 20·02 W002 50·98	AINTREE RACECOURSE BURTONWOOD CHESTER KIRKBY NESTON OULTON PARK SEAFORTH STRETTON AERODROME	N53 28·60 W002 56·58 N53 25·00 W002 38·28 N53 11·70 W002 50·68 N53 28·80 W002 52·90 N53 17·50 W003 03·60 N53 10·57 W002 36·80 N53 27·68 W003 02·08 N53 20·77 W002 31·58
LONDON GATWICK EGKK N51 08·88 W000 11·42	BILLINGSHURST DORKING GUILDFORD HANDCROSS HAYWARDS HEATH TUNBRIDGE WELLS	N51 00·90 W000 27·00 N51 13·62 W000 20·10 N51 14·37 W000 35·10 N51 03·17 W000 12·13 N51 00·45 W000 05·77 N51 08·00 E000 15·90
LONDON LUTON EGGW N51 52·47 W000 22·10	HEMEL HYDE PIRTON	N51 45·37 W000 24·97 N51 50·65 W000 21·97 N51 58·30 W000 19·90
LONDON STANSTED EGSS N51 53·10 E000 14·10	AUDLEY END RAILWAY STATION BRAINTREE CHELMSFORD DIAMOND HANGAR EPPING GREAT DUNMOW HAVERHILL NORTH END OF HANGAR 4 NUTHAMPSTEAD A/D PUCKERIDGE A10/A120 INT WARE	N52 00·25 E000 12·42 N51 52·70 E000 33·23 N51 44·00 E000 28·40 N51 52·67 E000 14·15 N51 42·00 E000 06·67 N51 52·30 E000 21·75 N52 04·95 E000 26·07 N51 53·32 E000 13·53 N51 59·40 E000 03·72 N51 53·10 E000 00·27 N51 48·70 W000 01·60
LONDONDERRY EGAE N55 02·57 W007 09·67	BUNCRANA COLERAINE DUNGIVEN MOVILLE NEW BUILDINGS	N55 08·00 W007 27·40 N55 07·90 W006 40·30 N54 55·70 W006 55·50 N55 11·40 W007 02·40 N54 57·50 W007 21·50
LYNEHAM EGDL N51 30·31 W001 59·60	AVEBURY BLAKEHILL FARM CALNE CHIPPENHAM CLYFFE PYPARD DEVIZES JUNCTION 15 (M4 MOTORWAY) JUNCTION 16 (M4 MOTORWAY) JUNCTION 17 (M4 MOTORWAY) MALMESBURY MARLBOROUGH MELKSHAM SOUTH MARSTON WROUGHTON	N51 25·68 W001 51·28 N51 37·00 W001 53·10 N51 26·20 W002 00·30 N51 27·60 W002 07·40 N51 29·40 W001 53·70 N51 20·80 W001 59·30 N51 31·60 W001 43·48 N51 32·70 W001 51·25 N51 30·88 W002 07·30 N51 35·10 W002 06·20 N51 25·20 W001 43·70 N51 22·50 W002 08·30 N51 35·40 W001 44·10 N51 30·55 W001 47·98

Aerodrome	VRP	Position
MANCHESTER	ALDERLEY EDGE HILL	N53 17·72 W002 12·73
EGCC	BARTON AERODROME	N53 28·27 W002 23·42
53 21·22 W002 16·50	BUXTON	N53 15·35 W001 54·77
	CARRINGTON	N53 25·70 W002 24·47
	CONGLETON	N53 09·90 W002 10·85
	HILLTOP	N53 20·50 W002 10·45
	JODRELL BANK	N53 14·18 W002 18·55
	ROSTHERNE	N53 21·23 W002 23·12
	SALE WATER PARK	N53 26·00 W002 18·17
	SANDBACH	N53 09·00 W002 23·62
	STRETTON AERODROME	N53 20·77 W002 31·58
	SWINTON INTERCHANGE	N53 31·40 W002 21·60
	THELWELL VIADUCT	N53 23·43 W002 30·42
	WARBURTON GREEN	N53 21·50 W002 18·90
NEWCASTLE	BLAYDON	N54 58·10 W001 41·62
EGNT	BLYTH POWER STATION	N55 08·50 W001 31·50
N55 02·25 W001 41·50	BOLAM LAKE	N55 07·88 W001 52·47
	DURHAM	N54 46·43 W001 34·60
	HEXHAM	N54 58·25 W002 06·17
	MORPETH RAILWAY STATION	N55 09·75 W001 40·97
	OUSTON (DISUSED A/D)	N55 01·50 W001 52·52
	STAGSHAW MASTS	N55 02·00 W002 01·42
	TYNE BRIDGES	N54 58·05 W001 36·42
OLD SARUM	ALDERBURY	N51 02·90 W001 43·90
EGLS		
N51 05·93 W001 47·05		
PLYMOUTH	AVON ESTUARY	N50 17·00 W003 53·00
EGHD	IVY BRIDGE	N50 23·08 W003 55·10
N50 25·36 W004 06·35	SALTASH	N50 24·07 W004 13·07
	YELVERTON	N50 29·07 W004 04·15
PRESTWICK	CULZEAN BAY/CASTLE	N55 22·17 W004 46·08
EGPK	CUMNOCK	N55 27·33 W004 15·45
N55 30·47 W004 35·20	HEADS OF AYR	N55 25·97 W004 42·78
	IRVINE HARBOUR	N55 36·50 W004 40·90
	KILMARNOCK	N55 36·75 W004 29·90
	PLADDA	N55 25·58 W005 07·07
	WEST KILBRIDE	N55 41·13 W004 52·08
REDHILL	GODSTONE (JUNC A25/B2236)	N51 14·83 W000 04·02
EGKR	GODSTONE RAILWAY STATION	N51 13·08 W000 03·07
N51 12·82 W000 08·32	JUNC 7 M25/JUNC 8 M23	N51 15·83 W000 07·68
	REIGATE RAILWAY STATION	N51 14·52 W000 12·25
SCATSTA	BRAE	N60 23·82 W001 21·23
EGPM	FUGLA	N60 26·95 W001 19·43
N60 25·97 W001 17·77	HILLSWICK	N60 28·55 W001 29·32
	VOE	N60 21·00 W001 15·97

Aerodrome	VRP	Position	
SCILLY ISLES EGHE N49 54·80 W006 17·52	PENDEEN LIGHTHOUSE ST MARTINS HEAD	N50 09·88 N49 58·05	W005 40·30 W006 15·95
SHEFFIELD CITY EGSY N53 23·65 W001 23·32	BARNSLEY RAILWAY STN CHESTERFIELD RAILWAY STN OLD COATS (CROSSROADS) REDMIRES RESERVOIR	N53 33·27 N53 14·25 N53 23·52 N53 21·92	W001 28·65 W001 25·22 W001 07·12 W001 36·42
SHOREHAM EGKA N50 50·13 W000 17·83	BRIGHTON MARINA LEWES INTERSECTION A27T/A26 LITTLEHAMPTON WASHINGTON INTERSECT A24/A283	N50 48·65 N50 51·87 N50 48·77 N50 54·57	W000 06·05 W000 01·45 W000 32·78 W000 24·47
SOUTHAMPTON EGHI N50 57·02 W001 21·40	BISHOPS WALTHAM CALSHOT ROMSEY TOTTON	N50 57·28 N50 49·07 N50 59·45 N50 55·20	W001 12·58 W001 19·75 W001 29·75 W001 29·33
SOUTHEND EGMC N51 34·28 E000 41·73	BILLERICAY MALDON SHEERNESS SOUTH WOODHAM FERRERS ST MARYS MARSH	N51 38·00 N51 43·70 N51 26·50 N51 39·00 N51 28·50	E000 25·00 E000 41·00 E000 44·90 E000 37·00 E000 36·00
SUMBURGH EGPB N59 52·73 W001 17·73	BODAM MOUSA	N59 55·10 N60 00·00	W001 16·10 W001 09·60
TEESSIDE EGNV N54 30·55 W001 25·77	HARTLEPOOL MOTORWAY JUNCTION A1(M)/A66(M) NORTHALLERTON REDCAR RACECOURSE SEDGEFIELD RACECOURSE STOKESLEY	N54 41·00 N54 30·00 N54 20·33 N54 36·43 N54 38·75 N54 28·18	W001 12·83 W001 37·60 W001 25·92 W001 03·85 W001 28·10 W001 11·68
WARTON EGNO N53 44·70 W002 53·03	BLACKBURN FORMBY POINT GARSTANG M6 JUNCTION 26/M58	N53 44·85 N53 33·12 N53 54·38 N53 32·07	W002 28·78 W003 06·32 W002 46·55 W002 41·87
WICK EGPC N58 27·40 W003 05·85	CASTLETOWN A/D (DISUSED) DUNCANSBY HEAD LIGHTHOUSE KEISS VILLAGE LOCH WATTEN LYBSTER VILLAGE THRUMSTER MASTS	N58 35·12 N58 38·60 N58 32·00 N58 29·00 N58 18·00 N58 23·58	W003 21·02 W003 01·50 W003 07·40 W003 20·10 W003 17·10 W003 07·43

RECOMMENDED AERODROME OPERATING MINIMA FOR PILOTS WITH AN IMC/INSTRUMENT WEATHER RATING

GENERAL

The detail given in the Tables applies to pilots with an IMC/Instrument Weather Rating. Pilots with Instrument Ratings should refer to the UK Air Pilot for the recommended aerodromes operating minima applicable to their qualification. All pilots should be thoroughly familiar with the principles governing the three elements of the Aerodrome Operating Minima described in the UK Air Pilot.

It should be noted that pilots who do not hold a valid instrument rating, IMC rating or Instrument Weather rating are prohibited from flying an Instrument Approach in cloud.

In setting out recommended operating minima, it is a basic assumption that the pilot has received training, is in current practice, and that the aircraft is suitably equipped for the type of approach. Common sense and the best interests of safety must deter a pilot from attempting a type of approach with which he is not conversant. If he is trained but not in current practice, at the very least it would be prudent to add a substantial increment to the recommended minima, or better still, have a dual check before risking the need to carry out such an approach in poor weather.

The minima to be used will be derived from the ATC clearance given and the privileges of the pilot's licence and rating.

It should be noted that the recommended minima passed by ATC at the commencement of an instrument approach will be appropriate to the Instrument Rated pilot and should not be confused with the minima to be used, as quoted in the following Tables.

OBSTACLE CLEARANCE HEIGHT (OCH)

The OCH is the lowest height above the elevation of the relevant runway threshold or above the aerodrome elevation, used in establishing compliance with the appropriate obstacle clearance criteria.

DECISION HEIGHT/MINIMUM DESCENT HEIGHT

Decision Height (DH) — The height in a precision approach at which a missed approach must be initiated if the required visual reference to continue the approach has not been established.

Minimum Descent Height (MDH) — The height in a non-precision approach below which descent may not be made without the required visual reference.

The Decision Heights/Minimum Descent Heights listed at Table 1 are derived from those shown in the UK Air Pilot but revised specifically for the IMC/Instrument Weather Rating.

Note. The Decision Heights, for precision approaches, published in Table 1 include a standard 50 ft Altimeter Pressure Error Correction (PEC).

The following increments as recommended for IMC/Instrument Weather rated pilots have been applied for Table 1:

- **Precision Approach — plus 200 feet with a minimum of 500 feet.**

- **Non-Precision Approach — plus 200 feet with a minimum of 600 feet.**

RVR/METEOROLOGICAL VISIBILITY

No individual runway visual range (RVR) or meteorological visibility value is given for the listed instrument approach procedures, as for the IMC/ Instrument Weather rated pilots, a minimum visibility of 1800 m for take-off and landing is prescribed under the Air Navigation Order.

TAKE-OFF MINIMA

In addition to the 1800 m RVR/Meteorological Visibility, pilots should make sure that conditions are such that, following take-off, a safe transition can be made from visual to instrument flight before entering cloud. An absolute minimum cloud ceiling of 600 feet is recommended. This includes a very small provision for engine failure after take-off, for both single and twin engined aeroplanes.

VISUAL MANOEUVRING AFTER AN INSTRUMENT APPROACH

At Table 2 are listed the recommended Visual Manoeuvring (Circling) heights for use following an instrument approach. Derived from the UK Air Pilot, this figure should be used by both Instrument and IMC/ Instrument Weather rated pilots.

AERODROME WITHOUT PUBLISHED INSTRUMENT APPROACH PROCEDURES

To land at civil aerodromes for which no approach procedures are listed in the UK Air Pilot, either, a descent below cloud should be made away from the aerodrome either visually or using a navigation aid, followed by a visual approach to the aerodrome, or, descend using an IAP for a nearby aerodrome and then transit to the destination aerodrome in accordance with VFR and Low Flying Rules. The minimum height to which a descent may be made is governed by the Instrument Flight Rules for flight outside Controlled Airspace, namely 1,000 feet above the highest obstacle within 5 nautical miles of the aircraft. If a safe descent to visual contact conditions, with a minimum in flight visibility of 1800 m , cannot be made, a diversion should be made to a suitable aerodrome with a published instrument approach procedure.

Determination of Minima at Military Aerodromes
in UK Territorial Airspace

For military aerodromes, a Procedure Minimum for each IAP is shown on the RAF Approach Chart in a table of Aircraft Categories (CAT); the words 'Procedure Minimum' are not shown. The Procedure Minimum shown in bold print is a minimum height (minimum with QFE set on the altimeter, the equivalent of OCH), with the minimum altitude shown in light print beside to the left; the increments applicable to IMC/Instrument Weather rated pilots as described on previous page, should be applied to this figure.

The Procedure Minimum (minimum altitude) will also be passed by ATC who will request the pilots DA or MDA.

WARNING
COMMENCING AN INSTRUMENT APPROACH

PILOTS SHOULD NEVER COMMENCE OR CONTINUE AN APPROACH WHERE THE CLOUD CEILING IS REPORTED TO BE AT OR BELOW THE DECISION HEIGHT OR THE REPORTED RVR/VISIBILITY IS BELOW THE VALUE REQUIRED. THEREFORE A FLIGHT SHOULD NOT BE PLANNED TO TERMINATE IN CONDITIONS BELOW THE RELEVANT MINIMA.

SHOULD THE DESTINATION WEATHER DETERIORATE BELOW MINIMA AFTER DEPARTURE, A DIVERSION TO A SUITABLE PLANNED ALTERNATE SHOULD BE MADE FORTHWITH.

TABLE 1

RECOMMENDED AERODROME OPERATING MINIMA - NON PUBLIC TRANSPORT FLIGHTS BY AIRCRAFT

For landing, the minimum visibility should be at least 1800 metres.

Note: The tabulated OCHs have been calculated using Aircraft Category A, for other aircraft categories, the OCHs can be found in UK Air Pilot. The Decision Heights, for precision approaches, quoted below include a standard 50 ft Altimeter Pressure Error Correction (PEC).

Aerodrome	Rwy	Approach Aid	OCH (feet)	DH/MDH (feet)
Aberdeen/Dyce	16	ILS/DME 'IAX'/'ADN'	151	500
	16	LLZ/DME 'IAX'/'ADN'	490	690
	16	SRA (2 nm termination range)	830	1030
	16	VOR/DME 'ADN'	660	860
	34	ILS/DME 'I ABD'/'ADN'	152	500
	34	LLZ/DME 'I ABD'/'ADN'	460	660
	34	NDB(L) 'ATF'	910	1110
	34	SRA (2 nm termination range)	680	880
Alderney	08	NDB 'ALD'	390	600
	26	NDB 'ALD'	380	600
Belfast/Aldergrove	07	VOR/ DME 'BEL'	350	600
	07	VDF	560	600
	07	SRA (2 nm termination range, 1 nm MAPt)	350	600
	17	ILS/DME 'IFT'	162	500
	17	LLZ/DME 'IFT'	270	600
	17	VOR /DME 'BEL'	370	600
	17	VOR 'BEL'	420	620
	17	SRA (2 nm termination range, 1nm MAPt)	350	600
	25	ILS/DME 'IAG' (also without DME)	136	500
	25	LLZ/DME 'IAG'	400	600
	25	VOR /DME 'BEL'	400	600
	25	NDB(L) '0Y'	530	730
	25	SRA (2 nm termination range)	650	750
	35	VOR /DME 'BEL'	450	650
	35	SRA (2 nm termination range, 1 nm MAPt)	430	630
Belfast City	04	LLZ/DME 'HBD'	480	680
	04	NDB(L) 'HB'/DME 'HBD'	620	820
	04	NDB(L) 'HB'	1000	1200
	22	ILS/DME 'I BFH'	280	530
	22	LLZ/DME 'I BFH'	450	650
	22	NDB(L) 'HB'/DME 'I BFH'	750	950
	22	NDB(L) 'HB'	980	1180
	22	NDB(L) 'HB'/VOR 'BEL'	750	950
Benbecula	06	VOR /DME 'BEN'	300	600
	06	VOR 'BEN'/DME 'BCL'	300	600
	06	VOR 'BEN'	350	600
	24	VOR/DME 'BEN'	300	600
	24	VOR 'BEN'/DME 'BCL'	300	600
Biggin Hill	21	ILS/DME 'I BGH'	280	530
	21	LLZ/DME 'I BGH'	300	600
	21	VOR/DME 'BIG'	350	600

Aerodrome	Rwy	Approach Aid	OCH (feet)	DH/MDH (feet)
Birmingham	06	SRA (2 nm termination range)	700	900
	15	ILS/DME 'I BIR'	163	500
	15	LLZ/DME 'I BIR'	410	610
	15	NDB(L) 'BHX'/DME 'I BIR'	470	670
	15	SRA (2 nm termination range, 1nm MAPt)	510	710
	24	SRA (2 nm termination range)	700	900
	33	ILS/DME 'I BM'	162	500
	33	LLZ/DME 'I BM'	420	620
	33	NDB(L) 'BHX'/DME 'I BM'	470	670
	33	SRA (2 nm termination range, 1nm MAPt)	470	670
Blackpool	10	NDB(L) 'BPL'/ DME 'BPL'	420	620
	10	NDB(L) 'BPL'	470	670
	10	SRA (2 nm termination range, 1nm MAPt)	480	680
	28	ILS/DME 'I BPL'	135	500
	28	LLZ/DME 'I BPL'	350	600
	28	NDB(L) 'BPL'/DME 'I BPL'	450	650
	28	NDB(L) 'BPL'	500	700
	28	SRA (2 nm termination range, 1nm MAPt)	500	700
Bournemouth	08	ILS/DME 'I BMH'	170	500
	08	LLZ/DME 'I BMH'	340	600
	08	LLZ 'I BMH'	650	850
	08	NDB(L) 'BIA'/DME 'I BMH'	400	600
	08	NDB(L) 'BIA'	650	850
	08	SRA (2 nm termination range, 1nm MAPt)	420	620
	26	ILS/DME 'I BH'	180	500
	26	LLZ/DME 'I BH'	330	600
	26	LLZ 'I BH'	620	820
	26	NDB(L) 'BIA'/DME 'I BH'	420	620
	26	NDB(L) 'BIA'	620	820
	26	SRA (2 nm termination range, 1nm MAPt)	500	700
Bristol	09	ILS/DME 'I BON'	155	500
	09	LLZ/DME 'I BON'	260	600
	09	NDB(L) 'BRI'/DME 'I BON'	300	600
	09	NDB(L) 'BRI'	340	600
	09	SRA (2 nm termination range,1nm MAPt)	350	600
	27	ILS/DME 'I BTS'	176	500
	27	LLZ/DME 'I BTS'	340	600
	27	NDB(L) 'BRI'/DME 'I BTS'	340	600
	27	NDB(L) 'BRI'	570	770
	27	SRA (2 nm termination range,1nm MAPt)	350	600
Cambridge	05	NDB(L) 'CAM'/DME 'I CMG'	450	650
	05	NDB(L) 'CAM'	580	780
	05	VDF	640	840
	05	SRA (0·5 nm termination range)	300	600
	05	SRA (2 nm termination range)	600	800
	23	ILS/DME ' ICMG'	168	500
	23	LLZ/DME ' ICMG'	350	600
	23	NDB(L) 'CAM'/DME 'I CMG"	350	600
	23	NDB (L) 'CAM'	540	740
	23	VDF	540	740
	23	SRA (0·5 nm termination range)	330	600
	23	SRA (2 nm termination range)	600	800

Aerodrome	Rwy	Approach Aid	OCH (feet)	DH/MDH (feet)
Cardiff	12	ILS/DME 'CDF'	137	500
	12	LLZ/DME 'CDF'	310	600
	12	NDB(L)/DME 'CDF'	420	620
	12	SRA (2 nm termination range,1nm MAPt)	480	680
	30	ILS/DME 'CWA' (also without DME)	155	500
	30	LLZ/DME 'CWA'	310	600
	30	LLZ 'CWA'	360	600
	30	NDB(L) 'CDF'/DME 'CWA'	330	600
	30	NDB(L) 'CDF'	380	600
	30	VDF	420	620
	30	SRA (2 nm termination range,1nm MAPt)	350	600
Carlisle	07	NDB(L) 'CL'/DME 'CO'	400	600
	07	NDB(L) 'CL'/DME 'CO' Direct Arrivals	400	600
	07	NDB(L) 'CL'	450	650
	25	NDB(L) 'CL' /DME 'CO'	300	600
	25	NDB(L) 'CL' /DME 'CO' Direct Arrivals	300	600
Coventry	05	ILS/DME 'I CTY'	220	500
	05	LLZ/DME 'I CTY'	380	600
	05	NDB (L) 'CT'/DME 'I CTY'	420	620
	05	SRA (1nm termination range)	350	600
	05	SRA (2 nm termination range)	650	850
	23	ILS 'I CT'	166	500
	23	LLZ 'I CT'	370	600
	23	NDB(L) 'CT'	410	610
	23	SRA (1nm termination range)	370	600
	23	SRA (2 nm termination range)	650	850
Cranfield	22	ILS 'I-CR'	136	500
	22	LLZ 'I-CR'	300	600
	22	VOR 'CFD'	350	600
	22	NDB(L) 'CIT'	340	600
	22	VDF	400	600
Dundee	10	ILS/DME 'DDE'	280	530
	10	LLZ/DME 'DDE'	360	600
	10	LLZ 'DDE'	500	700
	10	NDB(L) 'DND'/DME 'DDE'	560	760
East Midlands	09	ILS/DME 'I EMW' (also without DME)	180	500
	09	LLZ/DME 'I EMW' (also without DME)	400	600
	09	NDB(L) 'EMW'/DME 'I EMW' (also without DME)	400	600
	09	SRA (2 nm termination range, 1 nm MAPt)	400	600
	27	ILS/DME 'I EME' (also without DME)	160	500
	27	LLZ/DME 'I EME' (also without DME)	430	630
	27	NDB(L) 'EME'/DME 'I EME' (also without DME)	430	630
	27	SRA (2 nm termination range, 1 nm MAPt)	430	630
Edinburgh	06	ILS/DME 'I VG'	160	500
	06	LLZ/DME 'I VG'	550	750
	06	LLZ 'I VG'	720	920
	06	NDB(L) 'UW'/DME 'I VG'	600	800
	06	NDB(L) 'UW'	720	920
	06	SRA Vectored AD APP (4 nm termination range)	1250	1450
	12	SRA (2 nm termination range)	650	850
	24	ILS/DME 'I TH'	*Edinburgh continued*	

Aerodrome	Approach Aid	OCH (feet)	DH/MDH (feet)
Edinburgh (cont'd)	24.........LLZ/DME 'I TH'	460	660
	24.........ILS 'I TH'	160	500
	24.........LLZ 'I TH'	460	660
	24.........NDB(L) 'EDN'/DME 'I TH' (also without DME)	550	750
	24.........SRA (2 nm termination range)	600	800
	30.........SRA Vectored AD APP (4 nm termination range)	1600	1800
Exeter	08.........ILS/DME 'IET'	135	500
	08.........LLZ/DME 'IET'	250	600
	08.........SRA (1 nm termination range)	360	600
	08.........SRA (2 nm termination range)	600	800
	26.........ILS/DME 'I-XR' (also without DME)	135	500
	26.........LLZ/DME 'I-XR' (also without DME)	500	700
	26.........LLZ 'I-XR' with Radar fix	500	700
	26.........LLZ 'I-XR' without Radar fix	780	980
	26.........NDB(L) 'EX'	780	980
	26.........SRA (1 nm termination range)	480	680
	26.........SRA (2 nm termination range)	720	920
	A/D App 004°M VDF	830	1030
Farnborough	07.........PAR	270	500
	07.........PAR (Azimuth only)	450	650
	07.........SRA (2 nm termination range)	730	930
	25.........PAR	270	500
	25.........PAR (Azimuth only)	360	600
	25.........LLZ/DME 'I FNB'	360	600
	25.........SRA (2 nm termination range)	480	680
Filton	09.........ILS/DME 'I BRF'	280	530
	09.........LLZ/DME 'I BRF'	390	600
	09.........NDB(L) 'OF'/DME 'I BRF'	450	650
	09.........SRA (2 nm termination range)	600	800
	27.........ILS/DME 'I FB'	290	540
	27.........LLZ/DME 'I FB'	430	630
	27.........NDB(L) 'OF'/DME 'I FB'	500	700
	27.........SRA (2 nm termination range)	600	800
Glasgow	05.........ILS/DME 'I UU' (also without DME)	160	500
	05.........LLZ/DME 'I UU'	400	600
	05.........VOR/DME 'GOW'	450	650
	05.........NDB(L) 'AC'	900	1100
	05.........SRA (2 nm termination range, 1 nm MAPt)	1040	1240
	10.........SRA (2 nm termination range)	450	650
	23.........ILS/DME 'I OO'	160	500
	23.........LLZ/DME 'I OO'	440	640
	23.........VOR/DME 'GOW'	440	640
	23.........NDB(L) 'GLG'/DME 'I OO'/'GOW' (also without DME)	680	880
	23.........SRA (2 nm termination range, 1 nm MAPt)	650	850
	28.........SRA (2 nm termination range)	650	850
Gloucestershire	A/D App NDB(L) 'GST' App Dir 115°M	750	950
	09.........NDB(L) 'GST'/DME 'GOS'	350	600
	09.........SRA (0·5 nm termination range)	310	600
	09.........SRA (2 nm termination range)	600	800
	27.........NDB(L) 'GST'/DME 'GOS'	420	620
	27.........SRA (0·5 nm termination range)	330	600
	27.........SRA (2 nm termination range)	700	900

Aerodrome	Rwy	Approach Aid	OCH (feet)	DH/MDH (feet)
Great Yarmouth (North Denes) Helicopters only	10	NDB(L) 'ND' Aircraft Cat H	430	630
	28	NDB(L) 'ND' Aircraft Cat H	370	600
Guernsey	09	ILS 'I UY'/DME 'GUR'	280	530
	09	LLZ 'I UY'/DME 'GUR'	330	600
	09	LLZ 'I UY'	380	600
	09	NDB(L) 'GRB'/DME 'GUR'	330	600
	09	NDB(L) 'GRB'	380	600
	09	VOR/DME 'GUR'	330	600
	09	VOR 'GUR'	380	600
	09	VDF	380	600
	09	SRA (2 nm termination range, 1 nm MAPt)	280	600
	27	ILS 'I GH'/DME 'GUR'	280	530
	27	LLZ 'I GH'/DME 'GUR'	330	600
	27	LLZ 'I GH'	380	600
	27	NDB(L) 'GRB'/DME 'GUR'	330	600
	27	NDB(L) 'GRB'	380	600
	27	VOR/DME 'GUR'	330	600
	27	VOR 'GUR'	380	600
	27	VDF	410	610
	27	SRA (2 nm termination range, 1nm MAPt)	360	600
Hawarden	05	NDB(L) 'HAW'/ DME 'I HDN'	800	1000
	05	SRA (1 nm termination range)	690	890
	23	ILS/DME 'I HDN'	300	500
	23	LLZ/DME 'I HDN'	300	600
	23	NDB(L) 'HAW'/ DME 'I HDN'	300	600
	23	NDB(L) 'HAW'	440	640
	23	SRA (1 nm termination range)	350	600
	A/D	NDB(L) 'HAW'/DME 'I HDN' 314° to A/D	900	1100
	A/D	NDB)L) 'HAW' 314° to A/D	1000	1200
	A/D	SRA 318° to A/D	900	1100
Humberside	03	NDB(L) 'KIM'/ DME 'I-HS' (also without DME)	450	650
	03	SRA (1 nm termination range)	450	650
	03	SRA (2 nm termination range, 1nm MAPt)	470	670
	21	ILS/DME 'I-HS'	150	500
	21	LLZ/DME 'I-HS'	370	600
	21	LLZ 'I-HS'	440	640
	21	NDB(L) 'KIM'/DME 'I-HS'	390	600
	21	NDB(L) 'KIM'	640	840
	21	SRA (2 nm termination range, 1nm MAPt)	420	620
Inverness	06	VOR/DME 'INS'	400	600
	24	VOR/DME 'INS'	350	600
	24	VOR 'INS'/Marker	400	600
	24	VOR 'INS'/ Without Marker	750	950

Aerodrome	Rwy	Approach Aid	OCH (feet)	DH/MDH (feet)
Isle of Man (Ronaldsway)	03	SRA (2 nm termination range)	600	800
	08	VOR/DME 'IOM'	450	650
	08	NDB(L) 'RWY'/DME 'I RY'	420	620
	08	SRA (2 nm termination range, 1 nm MAPt)	420	620
	26	ILS/DME 'I RY' (also without DME)	136	500
	26	LLZ/DME 'I RY'	400	600
	26	NDB(L) 'RWY'/DME 'I RY'	550	750
	26	NDB(L) 'RWY'	600	800
	26	SRA (2 nm termination range)	600	800
Jersey	09	ILS/DME 'I JJ'	139	500
	09	LLZ /DME 'I JJ'	310	600
	09	LLZ 'I JJ'	360	600
	09	NDB(L) 'JW'/DME 'I JJ'	310	600
	09	NDB(L) 'JW'	360	600
	27	ILS/DME 'I DD'/VOR 'JSY'	156	500
	27	LLZ /DME 'I DD'/VOR 'JSY'	350	600
	27	LLZ 'I DD'	480	680
	27	NDB(L) 'JW'/DME 'JSY'	400	600
	27	NDB(L) 'JW'	480	680
	27	VOR/DME 'JSY'	390	600
	27	VOR 'JSY'	480	680
Kirkwall	09	NDB(L) 'KW'/DME 'KWL'	600	800
	09	VOR/DME 'KWL'	600	800
	24	NDB(L) 'KW'/DME 'KWL'	460	660
	24	NDB(L)'KW'	510	710
	27	VOR/DME 'KWL'	440	640
	27	VOR 'KWL'	550	750
	27	NDB(L) 'KW'/DME 'KWL'	440	640
	27	NDB(L) 'KW'	550	750
Leeds Bradford	14	ILS 'I LBF'/DME 'LBF' (also without DME)	171	500
	14	LLZ 'I LBF'/DME 'LBF'	360	600
	14	NDB(L) 'LBA'/DME 'LBF'	460	660
	14	NDB(L) 'LBA'	600	800
	14	NDB(L) 'LBA' (Alternative Timed Procedure)	970	1170
	14	SRA (1 nm termination range)	510	710
	14	SRA (2 nm termination range)	600	800
	28	SRA (2 nm termination range)	600	800
	32	ILS 'I LF'/DME 'LF' (also without DME)	170	500
	32	LLZ 'I LF'/DME 'LF'	330	600
	32	NDB(L) 'LBA'/DME 'LF'	330	600
	32	NDB(L) 'LBA'	480	680
	32	NDB(L) 'LBA' (Alternative Timed Procedure)	480	680
	32	SRA (1 nm termination range)	330	600
	32	SRA (2 nm termination range)	600	800
Liverpool	09	LLZ/DME 'LVR'	320	600
	09	SRA (2 nm termination range, 1 nm MAPt)	450	650
	27	ILS/DME 'I LQ' (also without DME)	160	500
	27	LLZ /DME 'I LQ'	330	600
	27	NDB(L) 'LPL'/DME 'I LQ' (also without DME)	500	700
	27	SRA (2 nm termination range, 1 nm MAPt)	420	620
Aerodrome	**Rwy**	**Approach Aid**	**OCH**	**DH/MDH**

			(feet)	(feet)
London/ Gatwick	08R	ILS/DME 'IGG'	140	500
	08R	LLZ/DME 'IGG'	520	720
	08R	NDB(L) 'GY'/DME 'IGG'	520	720
	08R	NDB(L) 'GY'	560	760
	08R	SRA (2 nm termination range, 1 nm MAPt)	520	720
	08L	SRA (2 nm termination range)	650	850
	26L	ILS/DME 'I WW'	152	500
	26L	LLZ/DME 'I WW'	500	700
	26L	SRA (2 nm termination range, 1 nm MAPt)	400	600
	26R	SRA (2 nm termination range)	650	850
London/ Luton	08	ILS/DME 'I LTN'	142	500
	08	LLZ/DME 'I LTN'	350	600
	08	SRA (2 nm termination range, 1 nm MAPt)	440	640
	26	ILS/DME 'I LJ'	146	500
	26	LLZ/DME 'I LJ'	330	600
	26	NDB(L) 'LUT'	380	600
	26	SRA (2 nm termination range, 1 nm MAPt)	410	610
London/ Stansted	05	ILS/DME 'I SED'	157	500
	05	LLZ/DME 'I SED'	350	600
	05	SRA (2 nm termination range)	650	850
	23	ILS/DME 'I SX'	157	500
	23	LLZ/DME 'I SX'	410	610
	23	SRA (2 nm termination range)	650	850
Londonderry/Eglinton	08	NDB(L)/DME 'EGT'	500	700
	26	ILS/DME 'I EGT'	280	530
	26	LLZ/DME 'I EGT'	350	600
	26	NDB(L)/DME 'EGT'	450	650
	26	NDB(L) 'EGT'	600	800
Manchester	06L	ILS/DME 'I MM' or 'MCT'	160	500
	06L	LLZ /DME 'I MM' or 'MCT'	360	600
	06L	VOR/DME 'MCT' or 'I MM'	420	620
	06L	NDB(L) 'MCH'/DME 'I MM' or 'MCT'	420	620
	24R	ILS/DME 'I NN' or 'MCT'	150	500
	24R	LLZ /DME 'I NN' or 'MCT'	320	600
	24R	VOR/DME 'MCT' or 'I NN'	380	600
	24R	NDB(L) 'MCH'/DME 'I NN' or 'MCT'	380	600
Manchester Woodford	07	NDB(L) 'WFD'/DME 'I WU'	400	600
	07	SRA (2 nm termination range)	670	870
	25	ILS/DME 'I WU'	400	500
	25	LLZ/DME 'I WU'	600	800
	25	NDB(L) 'WFD'/DME 'I WU'	670	870
	25	SRA (2 nm termination range)	830	1030
Manston	10	NDB(L) 'MTN'/DME 'I MSN'	320	600
	10	NDB(L) 'MTN'	400	600
	10	SRA (2 nm termination range)	690	890
	28	ILS /DME 'I MSN'	143	500
	28	LLZ/DME 'I MSN'	280	600
	28	NDB(L) 'MTN'/DME 'I MSN'	390	600
	28	NDB(L) 'MTN'	440	640
	28	SRA (2 nm termination range)	690	890
Aerodrome	**Rwy**	**Approach Aid**	**OCH**	**DH/MDH**

			(feet)	(feet)
Newcastle	07	ILS/DME 'I NC' (also without DME)	173	500
	07	LLZ/DME 'I NC'	400	600
	07	LLZ 'I NC'	550	750
	07	NDB(L) 'WZ'/DME 'I NC'	420	620
	07	NDB 'WZ'	550	750
	07	VOR/DME 'NEW'	430	630
	07	SRA (1 nm termination range)	430	630
	07	SRA (2 nm termination range, 1 nm MAPt)	430	630
	25	ILS/DME 'I NWC' (also without DME)	160	500
	25	LLZ/DME 'I NWC' (also without DME)	320	600
	25	NDB(L) 'NEW'/DME 'I NWC' (also without DME)	340	600
	25	VOR/DME 'NEW'	320	600
	25	SRA (1 nm termination range)	320	600
	25	SRA (2 nm termination range, 1 nm MAPt)	320	600
Norwich	04	SRA (2 nm termination range)	900	1100
	09	NDB(L) 'NWI'/DME 'INH'	310	600
	09	NDB(L) 'NWI'	360	600
	09	SRA (1 nm termination range)	310	600
	09	SRA (2 nm termination range)	650	850
	22	SRA (2 nm termination range)	850	1050
	27	ILS/DME 'I-NH' (also without DME)	170	500
	27	LLZ/DME 'I-NH'	320	600
	27	NDB(L) 'NH'/DME 'INH' (also without DME)	310	600
	27	SRA (1 nm termination range)	310	600
	27	SRA (2 nm termination range)	650	850
Oxford/Kidlington	02	NDB(L) 'OX'/DME 'OX'	420	620
	09	NDB(L) 'OX'/DME 'OX' or Marker K (also without DME)	520	720
	09	NDB(L) 'OX' No Marker	950	1150
	20	NDB(L) 'OX'/DME 'OX'	500	700
Plymouth	13	NDB(L) 'PY'	910	1110
	31	ILS 'I PLY'/DME 'PLY'	157	500
	31	LLZ 'I PLY'/DME 'PLY'	270	600
	31	ILS 'I PLY'	300	550
	31	LLZ 'I PLY'	480	680
	31	NDB(L) 'PY'/DME 'PLY'	300	600
	31	NDB(L) 'PY'	540	740
	31	VDF	590	790
Prestwick	13	ILS/DME 'I PP'	180	500
	13	LLZ/DME 'I PP'	360	600
	13	NDB(L)/DME 'PW' (Also without DME)	460	660
	13	SRA (2 nm termination range, 1 nm MAPt)	440	640
	21	NDB(L)/DME 'PIK'	580	780
	21	NDB(L) 'PIK'	800	1000
	31	ILS/DME 'I KK'	170	500
	31	LLZ /DME 'I KK'	440	640
	31	NDB(L)/DME 'PIK'	510	710
	31	SRA (2 nm termination range, 1 nm MAPt)	680	880
Scatsta	24	NDB(L) 'SS'	720	920
	24	SRA (0·5 nm termination range)	520	720
Aerodrome	**Rwy**	**Approach Aid**	**OCH**	**DH/MDH**

Aerodrome	Rwy	Approach Aid	OCH (feet)	DH/MDH (feet)
Scilly Isles/St. Mary's	27	NDB(L) 'STM'	400	600
	33	NDB(L) 'STM'	400	600
Sheffield City	10	NDB(L) 'SMF'/DME 'I SFH'	390	600
	28	ILS/DME 'I SFH'	200	500
	28	LLZ/DME 'I SFH'	450	650
	28	LLZ 'I SFH'	730	930
	28	NDB(L) 'SMF'/DME 'I SFH'	450	650
	28	NDB(L) 'SMF'	730	930
Shoreham	03	NDB(L) 'SHM'/DME 'SRH'	450	650
	03	NDB(L) 'SHM'	550	750
	03	VDF	850	1050
	21	NDB(L) 'SHM'/DME 'SRH'	690	890
Southampton	02	VOR/DME 'SAM'	500	700
	02	VOR 'SAM'	660	860
	02	NDB(L) 'EAS'/DME 'ISN'	500	700
	02	SRA (2 nm termination range, 1 nm MAPt)	500	700
	20	ILS/DME ' I SN' (also without DME)	280	530
	20	LLZ/DME ' I SN' or DME 'SAM'	350	600
	20	VOR/DME 'SAM'	470	670
	20	VOR 'SAM'	610	810
	20	NDB(L) 'EAS'/DME 'ISN' or DME 'SAM'	470	670
	20	SRA (2 nm termination range, 1 nm MAPt)	490	690
Southend	06	NDB(L) 'SND'/DME 'I ND'	470	670
	06	NDB(L) 'SND'	630	830
	06	SRA (2 nm termination range)	600	800
	24	ILS/DME 'I ND'	280	530
	24	LLZ/DME 'I ND'	350	600
	24	LLZ 'I ND'	400	600
	24	SRA (2 nm termination range)	600	800
	A/D App NDB(L) 'SND'/DME 'IND' 230°M		550	750
	NDB(L) 'SND' 230°M		610	810
Stornoway	18	NDB(L) 'SAY'/DME 'ISV'	400	600
	36	NDB(L) 'SAY'/DME 'ISV'	410	610
	A/D App 285°M VOR 'STN'		550	750
Sumburgh	09	NDB(L) 'SBH'/LLZ/DME 'SUB'	300	600
	09	LLZ/DME 'SUB'/VOR 'SUM'	300	600
	09	VOR/DME 'SUM' (also without DME)	820	1020
	15	VOR/DME 'SUM'	700	900
	27	ILS/DME 'I-SG'/VOR 'SUM'	250	500
	27	LLZ/DME 'I-SG'/VOR 'SUM'	310	600
	27	VOR/DME 'SUM'	460	660
	27	VOR 'SUM'	570	770
	27	NDB(L) 'SBH'/ILS/DME 'I SG'	250	500
	27	NDB(L) 'SBH'/LLZ/DME 'I SG'	310	600
	A/D App 005°M VOR/DME 'SUM'		700	900
Swansea	04	NDB(L) 'SWN'/DME 'SWZ'	350	600
	04	NDB(L) 'SWN'	600	800
	04	VDF 045°	650	850
	22	NDB(L) 'SWN'/DME 'SWZ'	480	680
	22	NDB(L) 'SWN'	1000	1200

Aerodrome	Rwy	Approach Aid	OCH (feet)	DH/MDH (feet)
Teesside	05	ILS/DME 'I TSE'	145	500
	05	LLZ/DME 'I TSE'	320	600
	05	NDB(L) 'TD'/DME 'I TSE'	360	600
	05	SRA (1 nm termination range)	360	600
	05	SRA (2 nm termination range)	650	850
	23	ILS/DME 'I TD' (also without DME)	140	500
	23	LLZ/DME 'I TD'	420	620
	23	NDB(L) 'TD'	420	620
	23	NDB(L) 'TD'/DME 'I TD'	390	600
	23	SRA (1 nm termination range)	420	620
	23	SRA (2 nm termination range)	650	850
Wick	13	VOR 'WIK'/DME 'WIK'	320	600
	13	VOR 'WIK'	740	940
	13	NDB(L) 'WIK'/DME 'WIK'	350	600
	13	NDB(L) 'WIK'	740	940
	26	VOR 'WIK'/DME 'WIK' (also without DME)	400	600
	31	VOR 'WIK'/DME 'WIK'	330	600
	31	VOR 'WIK'	380	600
	31	NDB(L) 'WIK'/DME 'WIK' (also without DME)	300	600
Yeovil	10	NDB(L) 'YVL'/DME 'YVL'	540	740
	10	NDB(L) 'YVL'	660	860
	10	SRA (0·5 nm termination range)	520	720
	10	SRA (2 nm termination range)	580	780
	28	NDB(L) 'YVL'/DME 'YVL'	470	670
	28	NDB(L) 'YVL'	730	930
	28	SRA (0·5 nm termination range)	470	670
	28	SRA (2 nm termination range)	540	740

TABLE 2
RECOMMENDED MINIMUM VISUAL MANOEUVRING (CIRCLING) HEIGHTS AT AERODROMES FOLLOWING AN INSTRUMENT APPROACH BY AIRCRAFT IN CATEGORY A ONLY.

Note. For other aircraft categoties, please refer to UK Air Pilot.

Aerodrome	OCH (ft) aal
Aberdeen/Dyce	850
North of Rwy 16/34	700
Alderney	400
Belfast/Aldergrove	500
Belfast City	1010
Benbecula	690
Biggin Hill	750
Birmingham	600
Blackpool	550
South of Rwy 10/28	400
Bournemouth	550
Bristol	570
Cambridge	600
Cardiff	600
Carlisle	450
Coventry	600
Cranfield	400
Dundee	960
South of Rwy 10/28	410
East Midlands	500
Edinburgh	600
Exeter	600
North of Rwy 08/26	500
Filton	500
Glasgow	700
Gloucestershire	820
Sector clockwise from Rwy 04 to Rwy 27	650
Guernsey	450
Hawarden	900
Sector 320° M clockwise to 230° M	500
Humberside	530
Inverness	650
Northwest of Rwy 06/24	600
Sector 150° M clockwise to 050° M	700
Isle of Man (Ronaldsway)	600
Islay	1050
Jersey	500

Aerodrome	OCH (ft) aal
Kirkwall	600
Leeds Bradford	600
Liverpool	500
London/Gatwick	600
London/Luton	560
London/Stansted	570
Londonderry/Eglinton	950
Sector North of Rwy 08/26	650
Manchester	450
Manchester (Woodford)	670
Manston	500
Sector South of Rwy 10/28	450
Newcastle	500
Norwich	450
Oxford/Kidlington	520
Plymouth	460
Prestwick	850
Southwest of Rwy 13/31	550
Scatsta	1050
North of Rwy 06/24	700
Scilly Isles/St Mary's	590
South of Rwy 09/27	400
Sheffield City	600
Shoreham	1100
South of Rwy 07/25	750
Southampton	630
Southend	550
Stornoway	550
East of Rwy 18/36	450
Sumburgh	700
Swansea	520
Teesside	480
Wick	400
Yeovil	600

METEOROLOGICAL SERVICES

Types of Service Provided

1 Pre-flight Briefing

1.1 The primary method of meteorological briefing for flight crew in the UK is by self-briefing, using information and documentation routinely displayed in aerodrome briefing areas. Alternatively Flight crew and operators may obtain information direct by using the Met Office's PC Service MIST (Meteorological Information Self-briefing Terminal), the Fax services jointly provided by the Met Office and the CAA, and the CAA's Automated METAR and TAF telephone service.

1.2 Where this primary method is not available, or is inadequate for the intended flight, Special Forecasts, as described in paragraph 6, may be provided.

1.3 When necessary, the personal advice of a forecaster, or other meteorological information, can be obtained from the designated Forecast Office for the departure aerodrome. Pilots should contact the nearest Forecast Office providing a service to civil aviation (as listed at page 77). For other aerodromes, the nearest Forecast Office should be contacted, except in the case of departures from military or government aerodromes where a forecaster or briefing service is provided for civil aviation departures from that aerodrome. **Forecaster advice or other information for safety related clarification/amplification will only be given from a Forecast Office on the understanding that full use has already been made of all meteorological briefing material available at the departure aerodrome or, where appropriate, by telephone recording. Forecaster clarification/amplification of conditions is not provided for flights departing from locations outside UK.**

1.4 Forecast Offices and self-briefing facilities are under no obligation to prepare briefing documentation packages.

2. Meteorological Charts

2.1 Meteorological charts are available via facsimile from two automated services, Broadcast Fax and METFAX. Broadcast Fax is a routine broadcast service available to users requiring a minimum number of charts each week. METFAX is a dial up premium rate facsimile service for users who have a varying requirement for charts.

2.2 Charts routinely transmitted over the Broadcast Fax network include:
- (a) Low and medium level flights within the UK and Near Continent;
- (b) Medium and high level flights to Europe and the Mediterranean;
- (c) High level flights to North America;
- (d) High level flights to the Middle/Far East;
- (e) High level flights to Africa.

2.3 Additional charts which are not routinely available may be obtained on request from Bracknell National Meteorological Centre.

2.4 Details of the charts available from METFAX are given on the METFAX index page (dial 09060-700 501), and as listed at page 70.

3 Broadcast Text Meteorological Information

3.1 Aerodrome Meteorological Reports (METAR), Aerodrome Forecasts (TAF) and warnings of weather significant to flight safety (SIGMET) including Volcanic Activity Reports are broadcast by teleprinter throughout the UK and internationally in text form. This information is distributed within the UK through dedicated communication channels (OPMET 1, 2 and 3) by AFTN and by autotelex.

3.2 Short term Landing Forecasts valid for two hours (TREND) may be added to METARs issued by those aerodromes so designated.

3.3 Information on runway state is added to the METAR when weather conditions so require and continues until these conditions have ceased.

3.4 Special Aerodrome Meteorological Reports are issued for operational use locally when conditions change through specified limits (see AIP GEN 3-5-19) Selected Special Reports (SPECI) are defined as Special Reports disseminated beyond the aerodrome of origin; civil aerodromes in the UK do not normally make Selected Special Reports. Aerodromes reporting only a SYNOP will not normally provide Special Reports to the Air Traffic Service Unit.

3.5 In general TAFs are provided only for those aerodromes where official meteorological observations are made and recent reports are available. For other aerodromes, Local Area Forecasts can be made by arrangement with Met Authority. Amended TAFs or Local Area Forecasts are issued when forecast conditions change significantly. (AIP GEN 3-5-19).

3.6 Description of the formats and codes used for METAR, SPECI, TREND, TAF and the METAR Runway State Group can be found in the AIP GEN 3-5-19.

3.7 Area Forecasts for the AIRMET service (see para 4) are broadcast in text form by teleprinter. Amended Area Forecasts are issued when forecast conditions change significantly, see AIP GEN 3-5-19.

4 AIRMET Service

4.1 AIRMET is a general aviation weather briefing service. The basic service consists of ten routine Forecasts, in plain language, covering the UK and near Continent and a comprehensive selection of TAFs and METARs for aerodromes in the UK and the near Continent. Information is provided in spoken form at dictation speed via the public telephone network and in text form via the AFTN, Telex and facsimile.

4.2 The AIRMET Forecast telephone service is intended for use by pilots who do not have access to meteorological information disseminated by Fax or to the AIRMET Forecasts disseminated in text form by teleprinter. It is provided in a standard format to facilitate transcription on to a Pilots Proforma (see para 4.6). Area of coverage of the ten Regional Forecasts is shown at page 76 this is also depicted in map form on the Proforma. AIRMET Forecasts are obtainable from the telephone numbers listed below, usually in recorded form but at night from the designated Forecast Offices.

For Area forecast between 0530-2300, dial 09068-7713 plus the AIRMET Code for the desired Forecast area.

AIRMET Code	Forecast Area
40	Southern Region
41	Northen region
42	Scottish Region
43	UK Weather
44	UK Upper Winds
45	UK Update and Outlook
46	Southwest England
47	Southeast England
48	Cross-Channel
49	Central England

For Area Forecast between 2300 and 0530 plus consultation for amplification of all forecasts call:

Bracknell 01344-856 267. Manchester 0161-429 0927. Glasgow 0141-221 6116

4.4 The forecasts will reflect the contents of SIGMETs which are current at the time of issue or amendments of the forecasts. Safety related amplification of an AIRMET forecast may be obtained from a forecaster by telephoning one of the three main forecast offices as listed at the foot of preceding page. Callers must confirm that they have received a current AIRMET forecast on contacting the forecast office, otherwise no additional forecast information will be given.

4.5 Special Forecasts in accordance with paragraph 6.6 are not provided for flights within the coverage of AIRMET Forecasts. For flights which extend beyond the area of coverage, Special Forecasts will be available on request from selected forecast offices providing a service to civil aviation.

4.6 A copy of the Pilots Proforma is a prerequisite to making optimum use of AIRMET. Supplies of the Proforma may be obtained, free of charge, on request to:

The Technical Secretary
Aircraft Owners and Pilots Association
50a Cambridge Street
LONDON SW1V 4QQ

provided a stamped, self-addressed A4 size envelope is included with the request. Photocopying of the Proforma is permitted. An AIRMET explanatory leaflet, "Users Notes", is also available on the same terms.

4.7 Automated METAR and TAF Telephone Service

4.7.1 An Automated METAR and TAF Service (page 72), giving METARs and TAFs for the UK, near Continent and Eire is available on 0881-800 400. 'GET MET', a pocket sized booklet is available (sae required) from CAA Safety Promotion Section, Aviation House, Gatwick, W. Sussex RH6 0YR or the MET Authority.

4.8 JERSEY AIRMET (Available from UK)

4.8.1 The States of Jersey Meteorological Office provides a 50 nm radius Channel Islands Low Level telephone recorded forecast service called JERSEY AIRMET, with a format very similar to the UK AIRMET. Amplification or clarification of the current JERSEY AIRMET forecast may be obtained, following receipt of the recording, by consulting the Forecast Office at Jersey Airport. Telephone calls to JERSEY AIRMET and the Forecast Office are charged at a premium rate and are not available outside the Channel Islands and UK. The appropriate telephone numbers are shown at page 77

5   METFAX Services

5.1 Meteorological pre-flight briefing information, in addition to that specified in paragraph 2.4 is available from the joint Met Office/CAA Broadcast Fax and METFAX Services. METAR and TAF bulletins (see para 3) and Area Forecasts (see para 4) are available on a 24 hour service. The METFAX service also includes planning forecasts, Satellite images and tephigrams (temperature-height-cross sections), the complete schedule can be found on the index page (dial 09060-700 501).

6. Special Forecasts and Specialized Information

6.1 For departures where the standard pre-flight meteorological self-briefing material cannot be obtained or is inadequate for the intended flight, a Special Forecast may be issued on request to the appropriate Forecast Office for a specific period for a designated route, or an area which includes the route. Normally a Special Flight Forecast will be supplied from the last UK departure point to the first transit aerodrome outside the coverage of standard documentation, at which point pilots should re-brief. However by prior arrangement, a forecast may be prepared for other legs, provided initial ETD to final ETA does not exceed 6 hours and no stops longer than 60 minutes are planned.

6.1.1 The usual method of issuing Special Flight Forecasts is by AFTN,Telex and Fax to the aerodrome of departure, but if the Flight Briefing Unit is not so equipped or will not be open, pilots may telephone the Forecasting Office for a dictation of the forecast. Similarly, Aerodrome Forecasts and reports for the destination and up to four alternates will be provided with the forecast, if not otherwise available.

6.2 Forecast Offices normally require prior notification for Special Forecasts as follows:

(a) For flights up to 500 nm, at least two hours before the time of collection;
(b) for flights of over 500 nm, at least four hours before the time of collection.

6.2.1 Request for Special Forecasts must include details of the route, the period of the flight and where appropriate the ETD/ETA of each leg, the height to be flown and the time at which the forecast is required. Ideally a forecast should be collected no earlier than 90 minutes before departure.

6.2.2 It is in the interest of all concerned that the maximum possible period of notice is given. The Forecast Office will give priority to emergencies, in-flight forecast and to forecast requirements which have been properly notified. Other requests could be delayed at busy periods and might not comprise full forecasts. A Forecast collected a long time in advance of departure will be less specific and might be less accurate than one prepared nearer departure time.

6.3 Forecast Offices providing Special Forecasts are shown at page 77. They are not provided for flights returning to UK.

6.4 Take-off Forecasts containing information on expected conditions over the runway complex in respect of surface wind, temperature and pressure can be made available from Forecast Offices. Prior notification is not normally required.

6.5 Meteorological information for specialized aviation use, as defined below, is not included in the AIRMET service or given as Special Forecasts but arrangements can be made for its provision on prior request:

(a) To enable glider, hang glider, microlight and balloon organizations to obtain surface wind and temperature, lee-wave, QNH and thermal activity forecasts;
(b) to provide meteorological information for special aviation events for which routine forecasts are not adequate;
(c) to provide helicopter operators in off-shore areas with forecast winds and temperatures at 1000 ft amsl, information on airframe icing, and sea state and temperature.

6.6 Appropriate forecasts for (a) and (b) above will be made available up to twice in any 24 hour period. For (a), the initial request should be made to the nearest forecasting office designated as providing service 'C' in the Table at page 77, at least 2 hours in advance of the forecast being required. For (b) and (c), application must be made to the Meterological Authority (AIP GEN 3-5-1 paragraph 2) for approval, giving at least 6 weeks notice of the requirement. The application must specify the nature of the aviation activity, the location(s) involved, the meteorological information required and the associated time periods. If appropriate an AFTN, Telex or Facsimile address should also be included. Applicants will be advised of the time at which the information will be available and of the means of collection/delivery.

6.7 Additional Meteorological Services

6.7.1 When specialist, non-standard, aviation meteorological services additional to those given above are required (eg forecaster briefings for aerial photography, test flying, crop spraying and for outlooks for over a day ahead), they may be obtained on a repayment basis by prior arrangement with the Meteorological Office. Enquiries should be directed to The Met Office, Manager Civil Aviation Branch, London Road, Bracknell, RG12 2SZ or to one of the Weather Centres listed at page 77

7. The Dial-Up Service - MetFax

7.1 The MetFax service enables users with access to most types of facsimile equipment support polling to obtain pre-flight Met information, for flight within the UK and to the near continent, from an automated dial-up facsimile system.

7.1.2 MetFax is a premium rate telephone service.

7.2 Requirements for Fax Machine to Receive The Dial-up Service - MetFax

7.2.1 In general the fax machine must be set to POLL RECEIVE mode, without documents in the feeder, before dialling one of the product access numbers. If the machine has a handset, however, it may be sufficient to pick up the handset, dial one of the product access numbers, and press the START button after the service message.

7.2.2 Some fax machines will automatically go into POLL RECEIVE mode if a product access number is dialled from the keypad and the START button is pressed.

7.2.3 If the access methods described above do not work, the fax machine instruction book should be consulted for details of how to POLL from another fax machine. The POLL facility is usually selected from a menu, mode, poll or function key on the fax machine.

7.2.4 Some PC fax Software/hardware is incompatible with Metfax. In general, use POLL RECEIVE facility if this is available, otherwise dial Metfax from a telephone in parallel with the fax modem and select MANUAL RECEIVE when the tone is heard.

7.2.5 In the event of difficulties, users may obtain advice by giving their name, fax and telephone number, make and details of their fax machine, and details of the problem, to the MetFax Helpline staff — Tel: 08700-750075; Fax: 08700-750076.

7.3 The information currently available from the MetFax Service is:

Fax Number	Product Description
09060-700 501	Index page

Note 1. THE INDEX PAGE CONTAINS LATEST DETAILS OF THE WHOLE RANGE OF DIAL-UP FAX PRODUCTS AVAILABLE TO THE PILOT.

Note 2. UPDATE TIME (UT) AND VALIDITY TIME (VT) IS SHOWN ON ALL PRODUCTS. (All times UTC)

Fax Number	Product Description
09060-700 502	Surface Analysis chart / Surface T+24 Forecast chart
09060-700 503	F215 UK Low Level Weather chart / F214 UK Spot Wind chart
09060-700 504	Surface T+48, T+72, +96, +120 Forecast chart / 3 day planning text (South England)
09060-700 544	Surface T+48, T+72 +96, +120 Forecast chart / 3 day planning text (North England)
09060-700 505	Explanatory notes for F215
09060-700 506	4 Tephigrams temperature/height chart

Fax Number	Product Description

SATELLITE PICTURES

09060-700-538 ......Guide to Satellite Images
09060-700-537 ......Satellite Picture (Visible & Infrared)
09060-700-539 ......Satellite Picture (Infrared)

EUROPEAN

09060-700-541 ......RAFC European FL100-450 Sig. Weather chart
　　　　　　　　　　F614 European Med-High Spot Wind chart
09060-700-542 ......F415 European Low Level Weather chart
　　　　　　　　　　F414 European Low Level Spot Wind chart

AIRMET

09060-700-510 ......Airmet Index Page
09060-700-507 ......Regional Airmet South text
09060-700-508 ......Regional Airmet North text
09060-700-509 ......Regional Airmet Scottish text
09060-700-511 ......Airmet UK Weather text
09060-700-512 ......Airmet UK Upper Winds text
09060-700-513 ......Airmet UK Update and Outlook text
09060-700-514 ......Airmet area South West England text
09060-700-515 ......Airmet area South East England text
09060-700-516 ......Airmet area Central England text
09060-700-517 ......Airmet area Cross Channel text

METAR BULLETINS

09060-700-520 ......TAF & METAR Index Page
09060-700-521 ......METAR 1 - S England, S Wales, Channel Islands
09060-700-522 ......METAR 2 - SE England, E Anglia, Midlands, Wales
09060-700-523 ......METAR 3 - N England, Scotland, Ireland
09060-700-524 ......METAR 4 - SE England, Channel Islands, France
09060-700-525 ......METAR 5 - Europe

TAF BULLETINS

09060-700-530 ......TAF 18 hour Bulletin
09060-700-531 ......TAF 1 - S England, S Wales, Channel Islands
09060-700-532 ......TAF 2 - SE England, Midlands, E Anglia, Wales
09060-700-533 ......TAF 3 - N England, Scotland, Ireland
09060-700-534 ......TAF 4 - SE England, Channel Islands, France
09060-700-535 ......TAF 5 - Europe

8. AUTOMATED METAR AND TAF SERVICE

8.1 The AIRMET automated METAR and TAF telephone service enables users to dial a single telephone number and obtain the latest METARs and TAFs for a comprehensive selection of UK aerodromes and some near continental ones, using a menu of 3 – figure code numbers for the aerodromes.

8.1.2 Calls are charged at 50p per minute (34p per minute off peak) including VAT.

8.1.3 The Aerodrome Weather Message order:

    (a) The latest METAR for the aerodrome;

    (b) The current 9 hour TAF (if provided for the aerodrome);

    (c) The current 18 hour or 24 hour TAF (if provided for the aerodrome).

8.1.4 The aerodromes in the Menu are listed starting below.

8.1.5 The service is only available through telephones which have a means of tone dialling.

8.2 Use of the Quick Keys on the Telephone Keypad

- Press the * key followed by the 3-digit aerodrome code number.
- Press the **0** key once to pause the current read-out, and once again to restart.
- Press the **#** key to stop the current read-out and obtain further options as follows:

        Press the **1** key to enter another aerodrome code;

        Press the **2** key to replay the message;

        Press the **3** key for Menu of aerodrome options;

        Press the **4** key to exit.

8.2.1 The voice output of the AIRMET system is automated in a similar way to that used for the UK VOLMET broadcasts.

8.2.2 The METAR and TAF service is obtained on telephone number:

09063 800 400

CODE NUMBER	ICAO IDENT	AERODROME	TIMES (LOCAL) BETWEEN WHICH OBSERVATIONS ARE MADE	METAR	9 HR FORECAST	18 HR FORECAST
		UK CIVIL AERODROMES				
222	EGPD	ABERDEEN	06-2200	•	•	•
224	EGJA	ALDERNEY	08-1900	•	•	
228	EGAA	BELFAST/ALDERGROVE	H24	•	•	•
232	EGAC	BELFAST/CITY	06-2200	•	•	
234	EGPL	BENBECULA (No METAR Sat &Sun)	08-1600	•	•	
236	EGKB	BIGGIN HILL	08-2000	•	•	
238	EGBB	BIRMINGHAM	H24	•	•	•
242	EGNH	BLACKPOOL	07-2100	•	•	
246	EGHH	BOURNEMOUTH	07-2100	•	•	
252	EGGD	BRISTOL	H24	•	•	•
256	EGSC	CAMBRIDGE	07-1900	•	•	
366	EGEC	CAMPBELTOWN (No METAR Sat/Sun)	H24	•	•	

CODE NUMBER	ICAO IDENT	AERODROME	TIMES (LOCAL) BETWEEN WHICH OBSERVATIONS ARE MADE	METAR	9 HR FORECAST	18 HR FORECAST
		09063 800 400				
258	EGFF	CARDIFF	H24	•	•	•
262	EGNC	CARLISLE (No METAR Sat &Sun)	09-1700	•	•	
266	EGBE	COVENTRY	H24	•	•	
268	EGTC	CRANFIELD	08-1800	•	•	
274	EGNX	EAST MIDLANDS	H24	•	•	•
276	EGPH	EDINBURGH	H24	•	•	•
278	EGTE	EXETER	07-0100	•	•	
282	EGLF	FARNBOROUGH	07-1900	•	•	
286	EGPF	GLASGOW	H24	•	•	•
288	EGBJ	GLOUCESTERSHIRE	09-1800	•	•	
292	EGJB	GUERNSEY	04-2100	•	•	
296	EGNJ	HUMBERSIDE	06-2100	•	•	
298	EGPE	INVERNESS	07-2100	•	•	
322	EGNS	ISLE OF MAN	H24	•	•	
324	EGJJ	JERSEY	04-2100	•	•	
328	EGPA	KIRKWALL (No METAR Sun)	06-1800	•	•	
334	EGNM	LEEDS BRADFORD	H24	•	•	
342	EGGP	LIVERPOOL	H24	•	•	•
344	EGLC	LONDON/CITY	07-2000	•	•	
346	EGKK	LONDON/GATWICK	H24	•	•	•
348	EGLL	LONDON/HEATHROW	H24	•	•	•
352	EGSS	LONDON/STANSTED	H24	•	•	•
354	EGAE	LONDONDERRY	06-1700	•	•	
358	EGGW	LONDON/LUTON	H24	•	•	•
362	EGMD	LYDD	09-1600	•	•	
368	EGCC	MANCHESTER	H24	•	•	•
372	EGMH	MANSTON	H24	•	•	
376	EGNT	NEWCASTLE	H24	•	•	•
378	EGSH	NORWICH	H24	•	•	
386	EGHD	PLYMOUTH	07-1900	•	•	
388	EGPK	PRESTWICK	H24	•	•	•
394	EGPM	SCATSTA (No METAR Sat &Sun)	08-1600	•	•	
396	EGHE	SCILLY/ST MARY'S (No METAR Sun)	08-1700	•	•	
410	EGSY	SHEFFIELD CITY	07-2100	•	•	
422	EGKA	SHOREHAM	08-1800	•	•	
424	EGHI	SOUTHAMPTON	06-2000	•	•	
426	EGMC	SOUTHEND	H24	•	•	
428	EGPO	STORNOWAY (No METAR Sun)	07-1600	•	•	•
432	EGPB	SUMBURGH	06-2200	•	•	
434	EGFH	SWANSEA (No METAR Sun)	09-1700	•	•	
436	EGNV	TEESSIDE	07-2200	•	•	
438	EGPU	TIREE (No METAR Sun)	10,11 & 1200	•	•	
452	EGPC	WICK (No METAR Sun)	07-2100	•	•	

CODE NUMBER	ICAO IDENT	AERODROME	TIMES (LOCAL) BETWEEN WHICH OBSERVATIONS ARE MADE	METAR	9 HR FORECAST	18 HR FORECAST
		09063 800 400				
		UK MILITARY AERODROMES				
244	EGDM	BOSCOMBE DOWN (No METAR Sat/Sun)	H24	•	•	
254	EGVN	BRIZE NORTON	H24	•		• 24 Hr
272	EGDR	CULDROSE	H24	•	•	
326	EGQK	KINLOSS	H24	•		•
336	EGXE	LEEMING	H24	•	•	
338	EGQL	LEUCHARS	H24	•		•
356	EGQS	LOSSIEMOUTH (No METAR Sat &Sun)	H24		•	•
364	EGDL	LYNEHAM	H24	•		•
374	EGYM	MARHAM (No METAR Sat &Sun)	H24	•	•	
382	EGVO	ODIHAM	H24	•	•	
392	EGDG	ST MAWGAN	H24	•		•
398	EGOS	SHAWBURY	H24	•		•
444	EGOV	VALLEY	H24	•		•
446	EGXW	WADDINGTON	H24	•		•
448	EGUW	WATTISHAM	H24	•	•	
454	EGXT	WITTERING	H24	•	•	
456	EGDY	YEOVILTON	H24	•	•	
		CONTINENTAL and IRISH AERODROMES				
522	EHAM	AMSTERDAM		•	•	•
524	LFOB	BEAUVAIS		•	•	
526	LFRB	BREST		•	•	
528	EBBR	BRUSSELS		•	•	•
532	LFRK	CAEN		•	•	
534	LFAC	CALAIS		•	•	
536	LFRC	CHERBOURG		•	•	
538	EICK	CORK		•	•	
542	LFRG	DEAUVILLE		•	•	
544	LFRD	DINARD		•	•	
546	EIDW	DUBLIN		•	•	•
548	LFRM	LE MANS		•	•	
552	LFAT	LE TOUQUET		•	•	
554	LFQQ	LILLE		•	•	•
556	ELLX	LUXEMBOURG		•	•	•
562	EBOS	OSTEND		•	•	•
564	LFPG	PARIS/Charles De Gaulle		•	•	•
566	LFPB	PARIS/Le Bourget		•	•	•
568	LFPO	PARIS/ORLY		•	•	•
572	LFRN	RENNES		•	•	
574	LFSR	REIMS		•	•	
576	EHRD	ROTTERDAM		•	•	•
578	EINN	SHANNON		•	•	•
582	LFPN	TOUSSUS LE NOBLE		•	•	

VOICE WEATHER BROADCASTS (VOLMET)
(H24 continuous)

LONDON VOLMET (Main)   **135·375**

Amsterdam, Brussels, Dublin, Glasgow, LONDON/Gatwick, LONDON/Heathrow, LONDON/Stansted, Manchester, PARIS/Charles de Gaulle.

LONDON VOLMET (South)   **128·60**

Birmingham, Bournemouth, Bristol, Cardiff, Jersey, LONDON/Luton, Norwich, Southampton, Southend.

LONDON VOLMET (North)   **126·60**

Blackpool, East Midlands, Isle of Man, Leeds/Bradford, Liverpool, LONDON/Gatwick, Manchester, Newcastle, Teesside.

SCOTTISH VOLMET   **125·725**

Aberdeen, BELFAST/Aldergrove, Edinburgh, Glasgow, Inverness, LONDON/Heathrow, Prestwick, Stornoway, Sumburgh.

Contents :

1. Half hourly reports (METAR).

2. The elements of each report broadcast in the following order:

      a. Surface wind
      b. Visibility (or CAVOK)
      c. RVR if applicable
      d. Weather
      e. Cloud (or CAVOK)
      f. Temperature
      g. Dewpoint
      h. QNH
      i Recent Weather if applicable
      j. Windshear if applicable
      k. TREND if applicable
      l. Runway Contamination Warning if applicable

3. Non-essential words such as 'surface wind', 'visibility' etc are not spoken.

4. Except for 'SNOCLO', the Runway State Group is not broadcast.

Remarks: The spoken word 'SNOCLO' will be added to the end of the aerodrome report when that aerodrome is unusable for take-offs and landings due to heavy snow on runways or runway snow clearance.

AIRMET AREAS AND BOUNDARIES

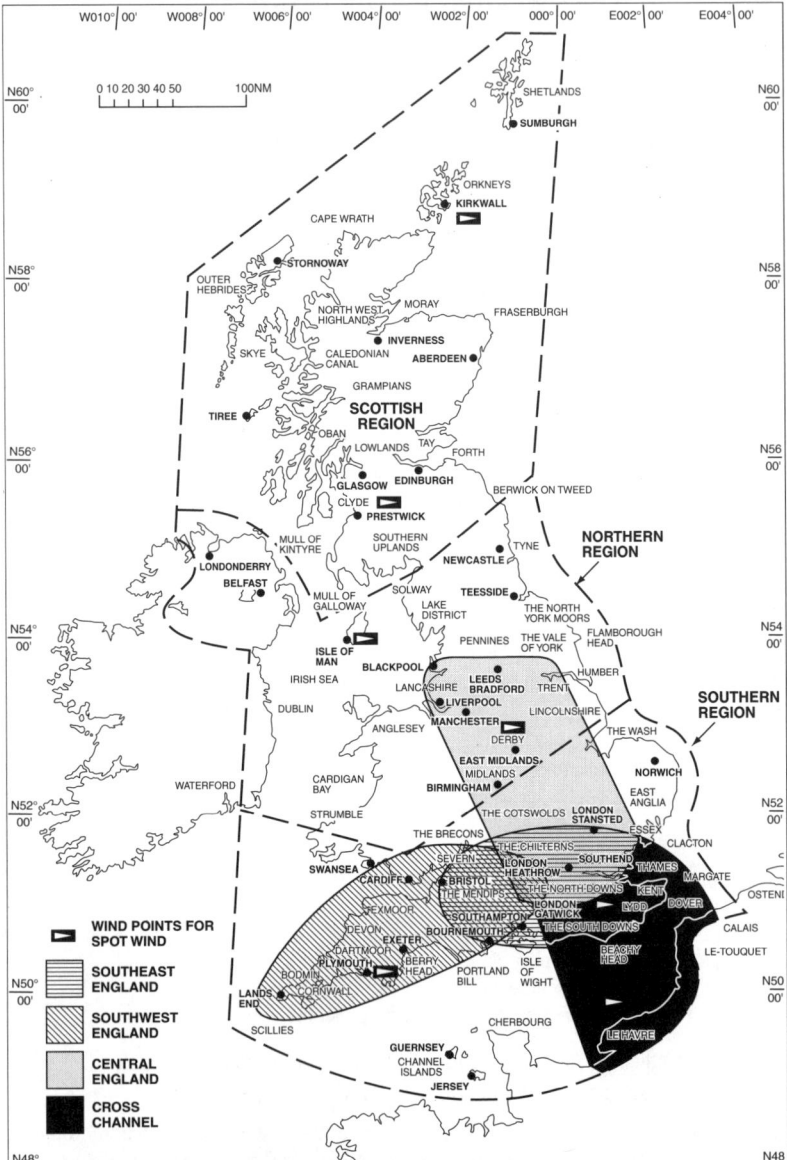

WIND POINTS FOR SPOT WIND

SOUTHEAST ENGLAND

SOUTHWEST ENGLAND

CENTRAL ENGLAND

CROSS CHANNEL

The place names shown on the map will be used by forecasters to locate the position of fronts and other weather features.

1 DEC 00

FORECAST OFFICES PROVIDING A SERVICE TO CIVIL AVIATION

Forecast Office	Telephone No.	Services Available	AFTN	Remarks
Aberdeen Weather Centre	0122-421 1842	A, B, C	–	Note 1
BELFAST/Aldergrove Airport	028-9442 3275	A, B, C, D	EGAAYMYX	Note 2
Birmingham Weather Centre	0121–717 0580	A, B	EGROYMYX	
Bracknell National Meteorological Centre	01344–856 267	A, B, C, D, E	EGRRYMYX	
Cardiff Weather Centre	029–2039 0492	A, B	EGRGYMYX	
Glasgow Weather Centre	0141–221 6116	A, B, C, D	EGRAYMYX	
Isle of Man Airport	01624-821 641	A, B, C	EGNSYMYX	Note 3
Jersey Airport	01534-49229	A, B, C	EGJJYMYX	Note 4
JERSEY AIRMET	0696-60033	–	–	Note 4
Leeds Weather Centre	01132-457 687	A, B	EGRYMYX	
Manchester Weather Centre	0161–429 0927	A, B, C, D	EGRCYMYX	
Newcastle Weather Centre	0191-232 4245	A	EGRTYMYX	
Sella Ness	0180-624 2069	A	–	Note 5

Services Available:

A   Provision of TAF, warnings and take-off data for assigned principal aerodromes. Amplification /clarification of these aerodrome forecasts and warnings only.

B   Dictation of TAFs and METARs unobtainable from the automated services (usually limited to four aerodromes).

C   Amplification/clarification of AIRMET Region/Area Forecasts and Metforms 214/215, and requests for Special Forecasts, including specialised supplementary information for Ballooning/Gliding.

D   Dictation of AIRMET amendments and Regional Forecasts.

E   Amplification /clarification and amendments for Metforms 414/415 and EUR Charts.

Note 1.   Aberdeen services B and C available only to North Sea operators.
Note 2.   Belfast services B, C and D available only to departures from within Northern Ireland.
Note 3.   Isle of Man services B and C available only to departures from within the isle of Man.
Note 4.   Jersey services B and C available only to departures from the Channel Islands. JERSEY AIRMET available 0600-2200, and only to callers in the Channel Islands and UK.
Note 5.   Operational hours 0600-1800; outside these hours Glasgow Weather Centre provides service.

1 DEC 00

CUSTOMS AND IMMIGRATION REGULATIONS TO AND FROM THE UK

IMMIGRATION

Flying <u>within</u> and outside of the European Union (EU)

Prior to departing for the UK, **it is essential** you contact the destination Immigration Service to arrange clearance on arrival.

You will be asked for Flight Plan details and passenger information; full names, dates of birth, and nationalities. Customs offices may pass on the relevant information to the Immigration Service on your behalf, but you should check on this.

Notification is not required from flights originating from the Republic of Ireland, Northern Ireland or any of the Islands - (Common Travel Area). Notification for such flights are covered under the requirements of the Prevention of Terrorism legislation.

CUSTOMS

Flying within the European Union (EU)

Inbound to the UK

1. At a **Designated Customs & Excise Airport**, i.e Southampton, Coventry (see list at page 80), you may arrive without prior notification to Customs. However, you will be required to complete a general aviation report (formerly known as a general declaration), on arrival.

2. At a **Concession Airport**, i.e Thruxton, Old Sarum (see list at page 81), you must notify Customs at least 4 (four) hours prior to landing.

3. At **private airfields and helipads** you must notify Customs at least 4 (four) hours prior to landing.

Notification for flights stated at paragraph 2 and 3 above, should be made to the Duty Officers of the responsible Collection Co-ordination Unit by telephone or fax. See map at page 83

Note: 1. You must declare to customs any birds, animals, and any prohibited or restricted goods on board.

Note: 2. See the Immigration requirement above.

Outbound from the UK

No Customs or immigration clearance required for departure. However, you will be required to complete a general aviation report (formerly known as a general declaration) prior to departure.

Flying outside the European Union (EU)

Inbound to the UK

1. You must land at a Customs and Excise airport, or if you are a UK, EU or EEA passport holder you may land at any aerodrome holding a Customs concession. At least 24 hours prior notice is required by local Customs Office.
The full list of the Member States of the EU and EEA are shown overleaf.

2. You must declare to customs any birds, animals, prohibited or restricted goods, duty - free stores on board and goods in excess of your duty - free allowance.

The above arrangements generally apply, but in certain areas you may be instructed to notify Immigration and Customs *separately* of all passengers of any nationality arriving from outside the UK.

Continued

CUSTOMS REGULATIONS TO AND FROM THE UK (Cont'd)

Outbound from the UK

If you are eligible to use a concession aerodrome, you *must* notify Customs at least 24 hours notice and are advised to notify Immigration well in advance. Check Customs Office for details.

There is no need for prior notification at permanent Customs and Excise airports.

Note: Unlike the UK, other EU countries still require first landings to be made at a designated Customs aerodrome.

The **Channel Islands** are not within the EU, but they do form part of the Common Travel Area. You can fly from them to any Customs concession aerodrome even if you are a non - EU passport holder.

Temporary Importation within EU Countries

There are no formalities, providing tax on the aircraft has been accounted for in a member state of the EU.

Temporary Importation outside EU Countries

You can temporarily import your aircraft free of VAT if you are a non - EU resident and you intend to re - export the aircraft from the Community when you next leave the EU, or when it has been in the Community for a total of 6 months in any 12 month period, whichever comes first.

Customs and Immigration Officers may still meet your aircraft on arrival, ask a few questions and still have the right to board your aircraft for checks. **Anybody may be stopped.**

Note. The above arrangements do not effect the requirements under the Prevention of Terrorism legislation.

Member States of European Union (EU)

Austria	Luxembourg
Belgium	Portugal
Denmark	Spain (not the Canary Islands for Customs
Finland	allowance purposes)
France	Sweden
Germany	The Irish Republic
Greece	The Netherlands
Italy	United Kingdom

Member States of European Economic Area (EEA)

Iceland
Norway
Liechtenstein

DESIGNATED CUSTOMS & EXCISE AIRPORTS

Aberdeen
Belfast/Aldergrove
Biggin Hill
Birmingham
Blackpool
Bournemouth
Bristol Airport
Cambridge
Cardiff
Coventry
East Midlands
Edinburgh
Exeter
Glasgow
Humberside
ISLE OF MAN/ Ronaldsway
Leeds Bradford
Liverpool
LONDON/City
LONDON/Gatwick
LONDON/Heathrow
LONDON/Luton
LONDON/Stansted
Lydd
Manchester Intl
Manston
Newcastle
Norwich
Plymouth
Prestwick
Sheffield
Shoreham
Southampton
Southend
Sumburgh
Teesside

Non-Customs and Excise Airports which have a concession for flights to and from EU and certain non-EU countries

Andrewsfield
Barrow/Walney Island
Bembridge
Beverley/Linley Hill
Blackbushe
Bodmin
RAF Brize Norton
Bourn
Caernarfon
Chalgrove
Chichester/Goodwood
Clacton
Compton Abbas
Cranfield
Crowfield
Cumbernauld
Denham
Doncaster
Dundee
Dunkeswell
Duxford
Eaglescott
Earls Come
Elstree
DRA Farnborough
Fenland
Filton
Halfpenny Green
Haverfordwest
Hawarden
Isle of Wight/Sandown
Lands End/St. Just
Lasham
Lashenden|Headcorn
Leicester
Little Gransden
Llanbedr
RAF Lyneham
Manchester/Barton
RAF Mona
Netherthorpe
Newtownards

Northampton/Sywell
Nottingham
RAF Northolt
Old Sarum
Oxford|Kidlington
Perranporth
Perth/Scone
Peterborough|Conington
Peterborough/Sibson
Redhill
Retford/Gamston
Rochester
RAF St. Mawgan (Newquay)
Sandtoft
Scilly Ises/St Marys
Seething
Sherburn-in-Elmet
Shipdham
Shobdon
Sleap
Stapleford
Sturgate
Swansea
Thruxton
RAF Valley
Warton
Wellesbourne Mountford
Welshpool
White Waltham
Wycombe Air Park/Booker
Yeovil/Westland

Intentionally Blank

H.M. CUSTOMS & EXCISE

The telephone and fax numbers listed are for notifying Customs of Aircraft movements

CCU (Collection Co-Ordination Units)

Collection	Telephone	Fax
Anglia	01473 - 235704	01473 - 255001
Central England	0121 - 7829704	0121 - 7822437
Eastern England	0115 - 9712377	0115 - 9712291
London Airports	020 - 89103800	020 - 89103741
London Central	020 - 78653544	020 - 78653575
South London & Thames	01474 - 537115	01474 - 335069
North West	0161 - 9126977	0161 - 9126986
Northern England	01482 - 782107	01482 - 702413
Northern Ireland	01232 - 358251	01232 - 743332
Scotland	0141 - 8879369	0141 - 8481639
South East England	01304 - 224251	01304 - 210017
Southern England	01752 - 234600	01752 - 234603
Thames Valley	01189 - 644200	01189 - 644208
Wales, West & Borders	029 - 20767000	029 - 20767001

If you are in doubt as to which Collection your airfield belongs to or for any general advice on general Aviation matters please contact the General Aviation Centre of Operational Expertise on 023 -80701811 or Fax: 023 - 80702966

N57 12·25 W002 12·02	**ABERDEEN (Dyce)**	215 ft AMSL
5 nm NW of Aberdeen.		**ADN 114·30 168 6·7**

APP 120·40.   TWR 118·10.   GND 121·70.   RAD 120·40, 128·30,121·25,134·10.

VDF 120·40, 128·30, 121·25, 118·10.   ATIS 121·85 & 114·30.

NDB 'ATF' 348·0 (344°/7·5 nm to A/D).

ILS/DME Rwy 16 (164°M) I-AX 109·90.   ILS/DME Rwy 34 (344°M) I-ABD 109·90.

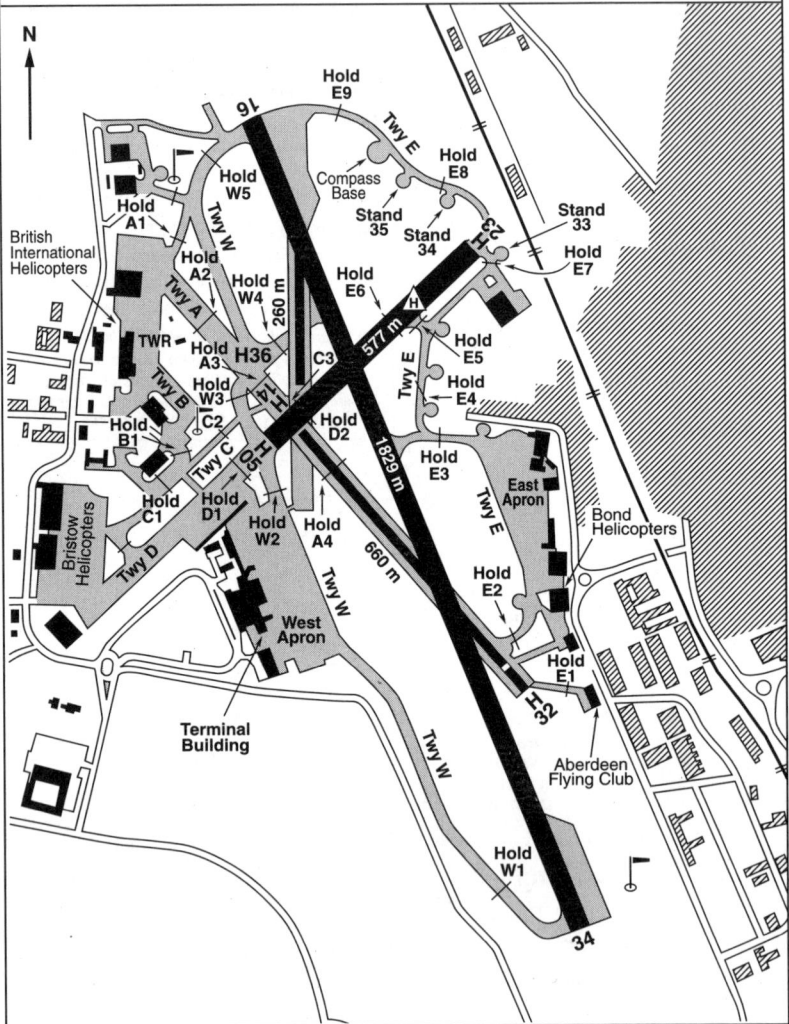

ABERDEEN (Dyce)

Rwy	Dim(m)	Surface	TORA(m)	LDA(m)	Lighting
16/34	1829x46	Asphalt	16-1829	16-1829	Ap Thr Rwy RCL PAPI
			34-1829	34-1829	Ap Thr Rwy RCL PAPI
36H	260x23	Asphalt	Helicopters only		Nil
05H/23H	577x46	Asphalt	Helicopters only		23 Thr Rwy CHAPI 6°
14H/32H	660x23	Asphalt	Helicopters only		Nil

Op hrs: Mon-Sat 0620-2150, Sun 0645-2150 (2150-2230 by arrangement).

Landing Fee: BAA Rates | **Customs:** Available

Hangarage: ¢ 01224 -723441 **Maintenance:** Limited **Met:** H24. 0141-221-6116

Remarks: Operated by Aberdeen Airport Ltd. Flights within the Aberdeen CTR/CTA are subject to the regulations applicable to Class 'D' controlled airspace — see page 2 and chart overleaf.

Non radio aircraft PPR. Training flights with PPR from the MD, Aberdeen Airport.

Handling Services: Business and General Aviation aircraft must have a Handling agent appointed prior to arrival/departure. Handling Agencies:

        Servisair   Tel: 01224-723357, Fax: 01224-728146, Radio 130·60.
        Caledonian Tel: 01224-770222, Fax: 01224-770012, Radio 130·625.
        Execair   Tel: 01224-723636, Fax: 01224-725458.

Helicopter, Loganair and Air Ambulance flights may take place outside published hours.

Warnings: Moderate/severe turbulence and windshear may be experienced on approaches to all runways when the 1000 ft wind exceeds 15 kt from sector 200° through west to 320°.

TV masts 1290 ft amsl 12·5 nm to NW, and 443ft aal (648 ft amsl) 146°T/2·9 nm.

Restaurant: Full restaurant service available.

Car Hire: Europcar 01224-770770. Avis 01224-722282. Hertz 01224-7223

Fuel: 100LL, Jet A1. S Diners, Multi Service	**Tel:** 01224-722331 BAA, 723714 ATC. **Fax:** 01224-727177 Admin, 727176 ATC.

ABERDEEN CTR/CTA VISUAL REFERENCE POINTS

VRP	VOR/NDB	VOR/DME FIX
Banchory N57 03·00 W002 30·10	ADN R212 ATF 268°M	ADN R212°/17 nm.
Insch N57 20·57 W002 36·85	ADN R286 AQ 337°M	ADN R286°/11 nm.
Meldrum TV Mast N57 23·20 W002 24·00	ADN R322 AQ 006°M	ADN R322°/6 nm.
Peterhead N57 30·42 W001 46·60	ADN R059 SHD 163°M	ADN R059°/20 nm.
Stonehaven N56 57·75 W002 12·60	ADN R181 ATF 212°M	ADN R181°/21 nm.
Turriff N57 32·32 W002 27·60	ADN R341 SHD 273°M	ADN R341°/15 nm.

Aberdeen CTR/CTA Chart & Helicopter Flights in the CTR – Pages 86-88.

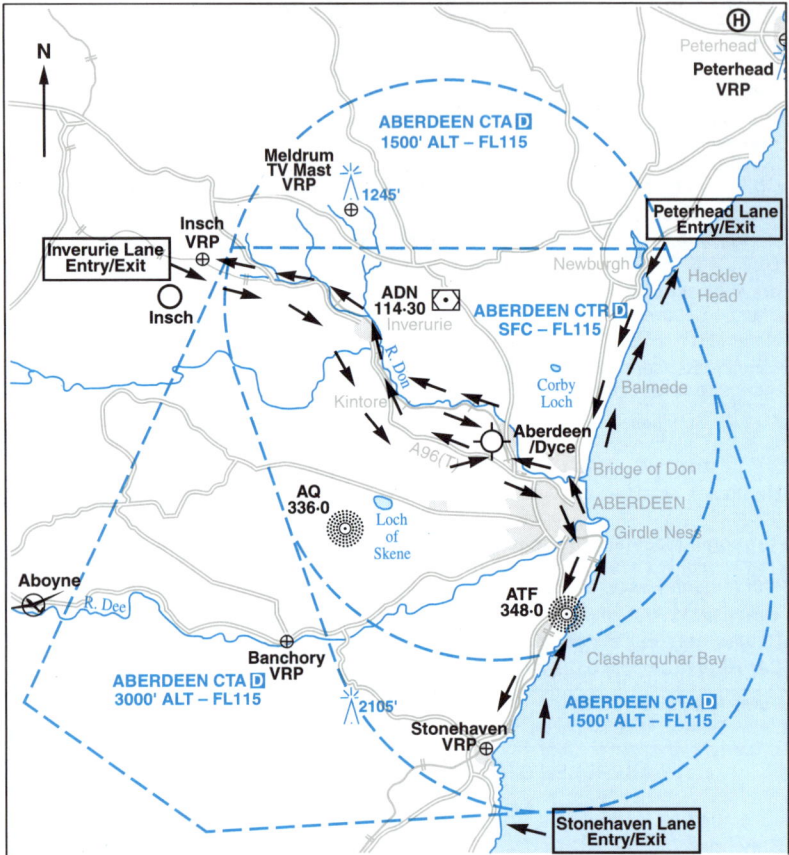

N

(H)
Peterhead
**Peterhead
VRP**

ABERDEEN CTA D
1500' ALT – FL115

Meldrum
TV Mast ☀
VRP
⊕ **1245'**

**Peterhead Lane
Entry/Exit**

**Insch
VRP**

**Inverurie Lane
Entry/Exit**
⊕

Newburgh

Hackley
Head

○
Insch

**ADN
114·30** ⊡
Inverurie

ABERDEEN CTR D
SFC – FL115

R. Don

Kintore

Corby
Loch

Balmede

A96()

○ **Aberdeen
/Dyce**

**AQ
336·0**
Loch
of
Skene

Bridge of Don

ABERDEEN

Girdle Ness

Aboyne
✕ R. Dee

**ATF
348·0** ⊙

Banchory
⊕ **VRP**

Clashfarquhar Bay

ABERDEEN CTA D
3000' ALT – FL115

☀ **2105'**

**Stonehaven
VRP** ⊕

ABERDEEN CTA D
1500' ALT – FL115

**Stonehaven Lane
Entry/Exit**

Flights within the Aberdeen CTR/CTA are subject to the regulations applicable to Class 'D' controlled airspace — see page 2.

Entry/Exit Lanes Peterhead Lane, Stonehaven Lane and Inverurie Lane. All lanes are 3 nm wide. The entry/exit lanes have been established to permit the operation of aircraft to and from Aberdeen/Dyce Airport subject to the rules governing VFR flight in Class D controlled airspace and under the following conditions:

1. Clearance must be obtained from Aberdeen ATC before entering the lane; non-radio aircraft must obtain clearance prior to take-off.

2. Aircraft must remain clear of cloud and in sight of surface, not above 2,000 ft. (Aberdeen QNH) and in flight visibility of not less than 3 km.

3. An a/c using a lane shall keep the centre line on its left unless otherwise instructed by ATC.

4. Pilots are responsible for mantaining adequate clearance from the ground or other obstructions

5. Model aircraft flying at 'Haremoss', N57 05·25 W002 09·20, approximately 1·5 nm NW of Portlethen up to 400 ft agl, daily during daylight hours.

Note: Aircraft using the Inverurie Lane will be required to route via the A96 Highway between Aberdeen Airport and Kintore when departing Rwy 16 or arriving Rwy 34.

HELICOPTER FLIGHTS IN THE ABERDEEN CTR 1 DEC 00

1 General

1.1 In the Aberdeen CTR, helicopter flights will normally be required to follow the defined routes agreed to in these procedures and to fly at or below a specified altitude.

1.2 The helicopter routes described below have been specially selected in order to provide maximum safety in avoiding most built up areas. It is the pilot's duty to ensure that the performance of his aircraft is adequate to permit safe flight along the routes and for compliance with the relevant regulations.

2 Procedures for Flights along Helicopter Routes

2.1 Flights in the Aberdeen CTR, other than H6 (See Note after table of Routes) are not to be operated unless helicopters can remain in a flight visibility of at least 3 km, except when routeing over, taking-off from, or landing at ABERDEEN/Dyce Airport, when the reported visibility at Aberdeen must be at least 2 km. Helicopters must remain clear of cloud and in sight of the surface.

2.2 Altimeter setting will be ABERDEEN/Dyce Airport QNH.

2.3   Maximum altitudes (normally 1500 ft outbound and 2500 ft inbound) are shown in the Table of Routes. Special VFR clearances will be issued in the form 'not above . . . . ft'.
These altitudes are for ATC separation purposes and procedures.

2.4 Where a route is defined by a line feature, a helicopter shall keep the centre-line on its left unless otherwise instructed by ATC for separation purposes. In these circumstances ATC will pass traffic information to the traffic concerned.

2.5 In periods of heavy traffic or poor visibility, helicopters joining from or leaving to the east on Routes H1/H4 may be routed via River Don (Route H6) rather than via Balmedie. This route may also be used for helicopters routeing to and from the south.

2.6 On all routes in order to minimize noise nuisance, pilots should maintain the maximum altitude compatible with their ATC clearance and with the prevailing cloud conditions.

3 Holding

3.1 Helicopters may be required to hold at specified geographical locations.

Robert Pooley ©

87

4   Table of Routes

4.1 Routes are listed in departure order. Arrival routes are reversed except for those helicopters making Instrument Approaches on ILS or Radar.

DESIGNATION	ROUTE	MAX ALT (ft)
H1	Departure 16 - left turn out - Far Burn (north of Stoneywood) - Grandhome Moss - Corsehill - B977 - Balmedie.	2500
H2	Departure 34 - straight ahead - Kirkton - Corsehill - B977 - Balmedie.	2500
H3	Departure 23 - right turn out - Kirkton - Corsehill - B977 - Balmedie.	2500
H4	Departure 05 - turn left on to a northerly heading as soon as possible - remain west of the A947 until intercepting the River Don. At the Don turn right - Corsehill - B977 - Balmedie.	2500
H5	Kirkton - Inverness/Aberdeen railway line - northwest.	2500
H6	Far Burn/Stoneywood Gap - River Don - Bridge of Don.	As directed by ATC

Note: H6 is the designated low visibility/bad weather route and will be used in accordance with the operators' operating minima. Helicopters using the route in poor visibility will be expected to fly over the river unless otherwise instructed by ATC.

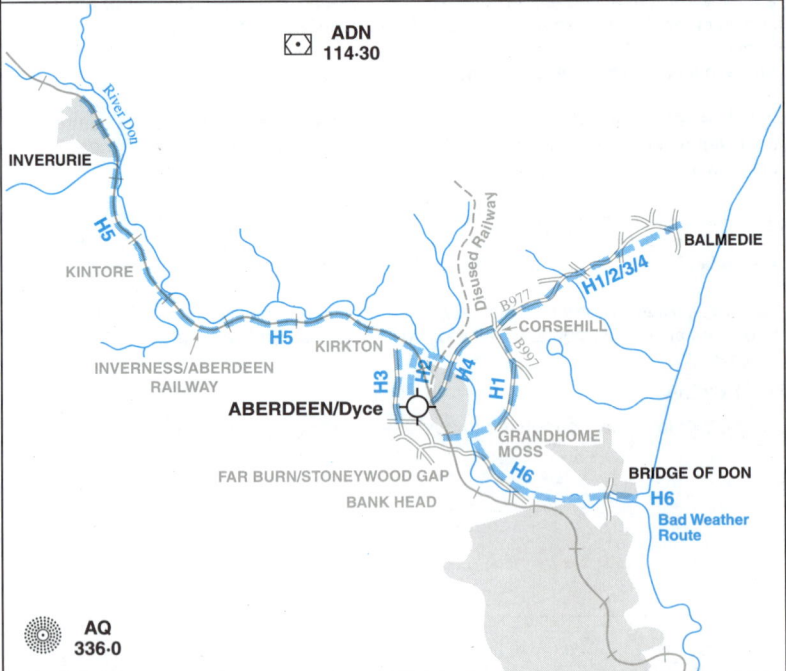

N52 06·75 W004 33·33	**ABERPORTH**	425 ft AMSL
4nm ENE of Cardigan.		STU 113·10 076 19
		BCN 117·45 303 53

c/s Aberporth Information. 122·15 AFIS.
NDB 'AP' 370·5 (on A/D).

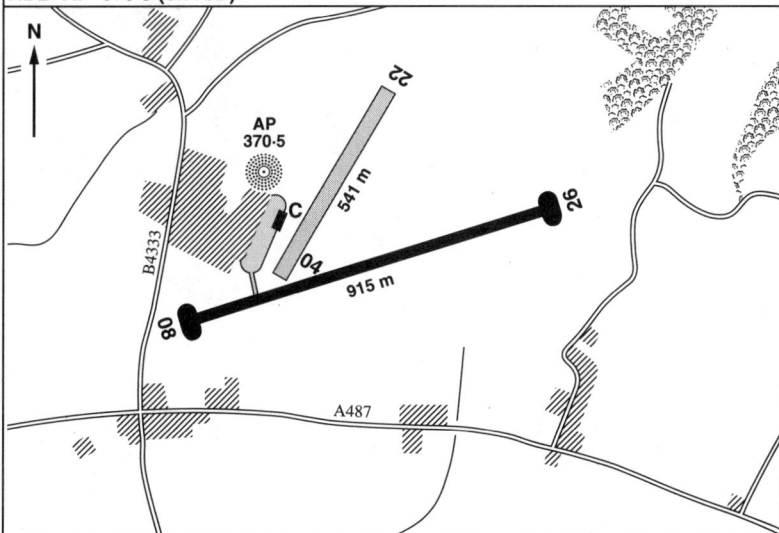

Rwy	Dim(m)	Surface	TORA(m)	LDA(m)	Lighting
08/26	915x23	Asphalt	08-915	08-915	Portable electric
			26-915	26-915	Rwy lighting available
04/22	541x32	Grass	04-541	04-541	with Prior Notice.
			22-541	22-541	

Op hrs: PPR. 24 hrs. Mon-Fri 0830-1600 (except PHs). Other times by arrangement.

Landing Fee: MoD Rates	**Customs:** Nil.
Hangarage: Limited.	**Maintenance:** Nil.

Remarks: Operated by DERA Aberporth, Cardigan, Ceredigion SA43 2BU.
PPR. Initial approach not below 3200ft. (QFE) unless in visual contact with surface.
Circuits RH on Rwys 04 & 08; LH on 22 & 26.

Aerodrome is located just inside the Southern boundary of Danger Area D201.

Except for aircraft already in receipt of prior permission, ATC Services may be
withdrawn during published Op hrs and 3 hrs notice will be required to re-activate.
Helicopter activity outside normal Op hrs; Air Traffic Services not always provided.

Glider flying outside of op hrs and at weekends, plus on occasions during weekdays.

Mast 191 ft aal, 616 ft amsl. 318°T/0·7 nm.

Restaurant: Facilities available locally.

Car Hire/Taxi: Arranged through ATC.

Fuel: 100LL, Jet A1 with FSII.	**Tel:**	01239-813090
	Tel/Fax:	01239-813090

Robert Pooley ©

EGJA		1 DEC 00
N49 42·37 W002 12·88	**ALDERNEY**	291 ft AMSL
1nm SW of St Annes		**GUR 109·40 048 22**
		JSY 112·20 352 30

Jersey Zone 125·20. Guernsey APP 128·65. Alderney TWR 125·35.
NDB 'ALD' 383·0 (265°M/0·37nm to Thr 26).

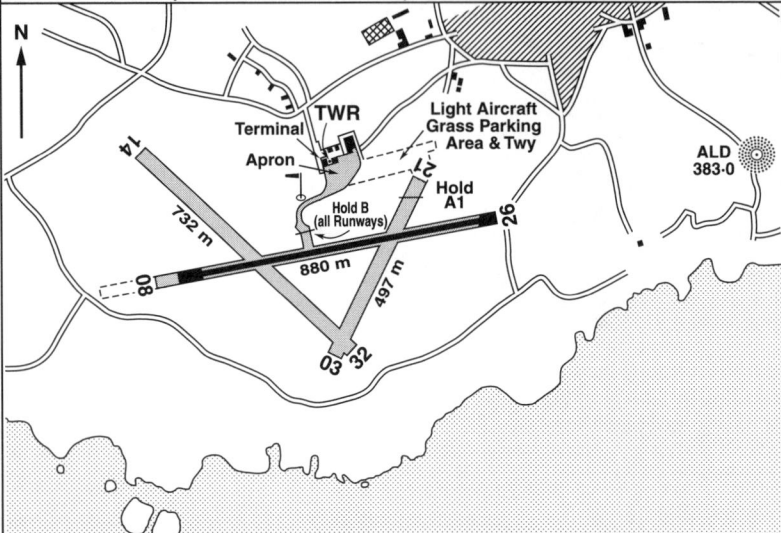

N

TWR
Terminal
Apron
Light Aircraft Grass Parking Area & Twy
ALD 383·0
14
732 m
21
Hold B (all Runways)
Hold A1
26
880 m
497 m
08
03 32

Rwy	Dim(m)	Surface	TORA(m)	LDA(m)	Lighting
03/21	497x37	Grass	03-497	03-497	Nil.
			21-497	21-497	Nil.
14/32	732x37	Grass	14/32-732	14/32-732	Thr* Rwy*
# 08/26	880x23	Asphalt/	08-880	08-880	Ap Thr Rwy APAPI 3°
		Grass	26-880	26-880	Ap Thr Rwy APAPI 3°

830x18m Asphalt and 50m Grass at western end.   * Portable Electric

Op hrs: SUMMER: Mon-Thu 0740-1830, Fri-Sun 0740-1930.
WINTER: Mon-Sat 0740-1830, Sun 0855-1830. Circuit and Instrument Training PPR.

Landing Fee: Reduced Rates - Private aircraft under 3000 kg: Singles £6, Twins £12 , includes 5 days free parking. In first instance Tel: 01481-237766 or Fax: 01481-239595.

Hangarage: Limited.	**Maintenance:** Nil.	**Customs:** Available.

Remarks: Use governed by regulations applicable to Channel Islands CTR (Class 'A' Airspace) and Alderney CTR (Class 'D') — see chart overleaf. Aircraft must be able to maintain R/T communication with Jersey Zone, Guernsey App and Alderney TWR. Circuits at 700 ft QFE; LH on 03, 32 & 26; RH on 14, 21 & 08. Exercise caution because of turbulence caused by nearby cliffs. Rwy surfaces are undulating. Grass Rwys marked by inset concrete blocks. Main Twy and apron are Bitmac. Grass Twy and light a/c parking area connects apron to Rwy 21 thld and is also used as twy route from other runways to apron. Aircraft must carry Third Party Insurance cover of not less than £500,000.
High visibility clothing to be worn by aircrew whilst airside.

Caution: Animals grazing in fields on final approach to Rwys 03 & 32; low boundary fence with orange/white markers. Bird hazard.

Fuel: 100LL	**Tel:** 01481-822851 ATC, 238957 ATIS.
	Fax: 01481-822352.

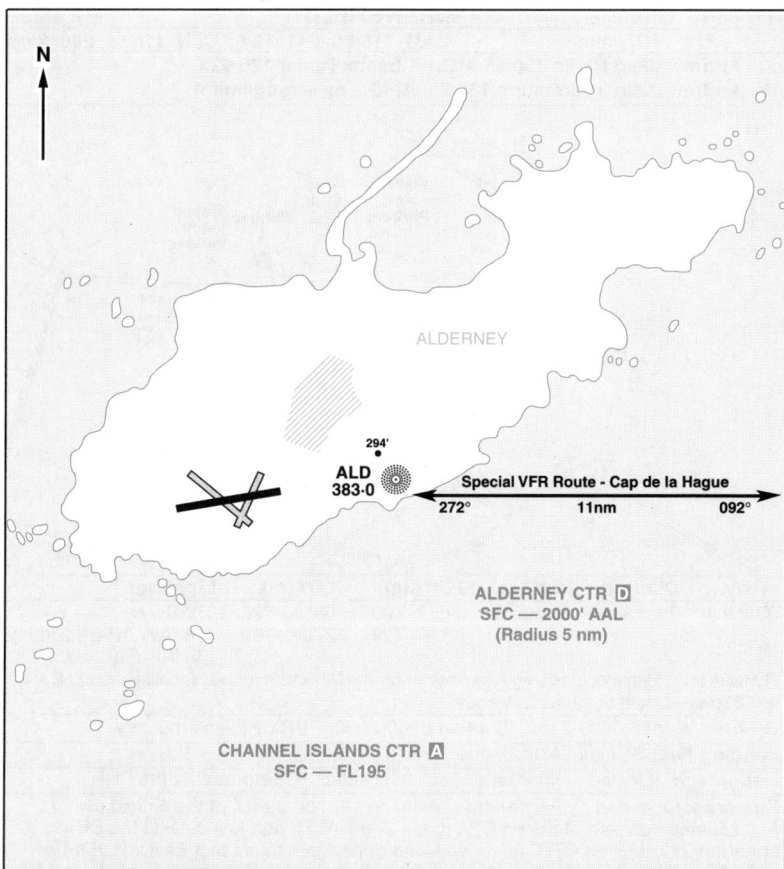

N

ALDERNEY

294'

ALD
383·0

Special VFR Route - Cap de la Hague
272°   11nm   092°

ALDERNEY CTR [D]
SFC — 2000' AAL
(Radius 5 nm)

CHANNEL ISLANDS CTR [A]
SFC — FL195

Channel Islands CTR (Class 'A') and Alderney CTR (Class 'D') procedures are outlined at pages 8 to 11.
Flights between Alderney and Guernsey may take place without compliance with IFR requirements, subject to the following conditions:
(a) Clearance must be obtained from Guernsey Approach Control.
(b) Aircraft to remain below cloud and in sight of surface, not above 2,000 ft.

Special VFR Route 4. Alderney – Cap de la Hague.
Subject to following conditions:
(a) Special VFR Clearance must be obtained from Jersey Zone before entering the Channel Islands CTR.
(b) Aircraft shall remain at least 1500 m horizontally and 1,000 ft. vertically clear of cloud and in flight visibility of at least 5 km (for Instrument/IMC Rating visibility not less than 3 km).
Note. SSR Mode A 4096 Codes mandatory for SVFR flights within the Channel Islands CTR.

N51 53·70 E000 26·95	**ANDREWSFIELD**	286 ft AMSL

4 nm WNW of Braintree   **LAM 115·60 041 18·6. CLN 114·55 280 25·8**

c/s Andrewsfield Radio 130·55 A/G.   Essex Radar 120·625.
c/s Andrewsfield Information 130·55 AFIS – by arrangement.

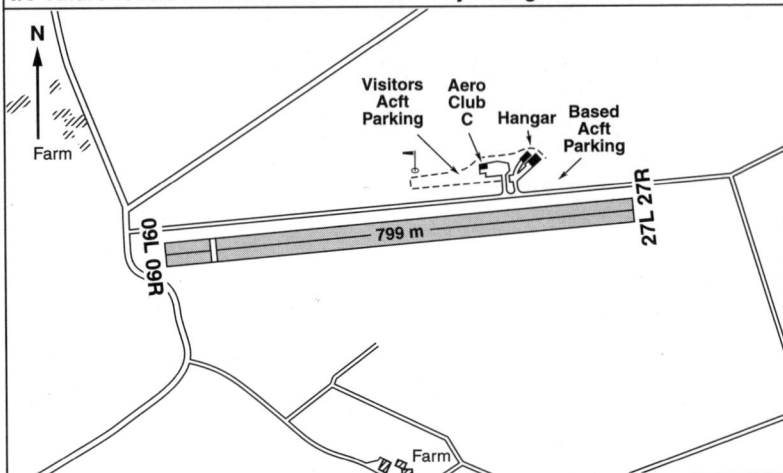

Rwy	Dim(m)	Surface	TORA(m)	LDA(m)	Lighting
09/27L/R	799x36	Grass	09L/R -799 27L/R -799	09L/R -720 27L/R -799	Thr Rwy. Thr Rwy APAPI 3°(LH) IBn 'AF' Gn

Runway is divided along its length into two separate 799x18m runways, designators L & R are displayed short of the runway ends.

Op hrs: WINTER 0830-2100; SUMMER 0900-2000. PPR by telephone only.

Landing Fee: Singles £4.00; Twins £6.00

Hangarage: Limited.   **Maintenance:** Available.   **Customs:** 24 hrs PNR

Remarks: Operated by Andrewsfield Aviation Ltd., on behalf of the airfield owners. A/D situated beneath Stansted CTA (base 2000' ALT), and just outside the SE boundary of Stansted CTR. All arrivals and departures to contact Essex Radar on 120·625, and contact must be established with Andrewsfield before entering the LFA.

Flights without reference to Stansted ATC may be made within the Local Flying Area (LFA) which extends from surface to 1500' QNH within a radius of 2 nm from the centre of the aerodrome, subject to the following restrictions:
* Remain clear of cloud, in sight of surface and with a flight visibility of at least 3 km;
* Not above 1500' QNH, 1214' QFE.
* Non radio aircraft PPR, pilots must obtain briefing by telephone.

Noise Abatement Procedures in force. Obtain brief before departure.

Circuits RH at 700 ft aal. Microlights at 500' inside normal circuit pattern.

Avoid overflying villages in vicinity of airfield.

Aerodrome not available at night for public transport flights.

Visiting aircraft are to park in the area adjacent to the windsock.

Restaurant: Hot and cold food available.   **Car Hire & Taxis:** By arrangement.

Fuel: 100LL.	**Tel:** 01371-856744. **Fax:** 01371-856500.

N53 09·82 W002 34·17	**ASHCROFT**	150 ft AMSL

2 nm SW of Winsford	WAL 114·10 132 24·3
	WHI 368·5 132 2·2

Ashcroft Radio 122·525 (not always manned)

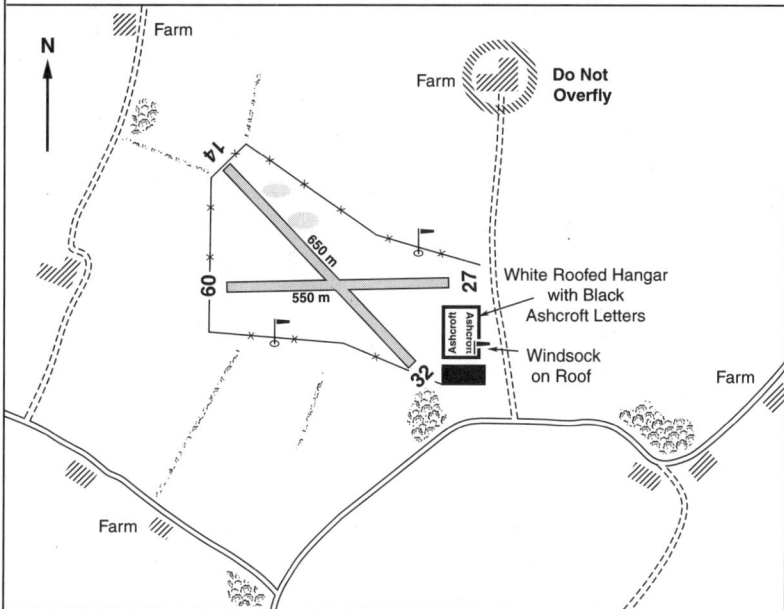

N

Farm

Farm

Do Not
Overfly

14

650 m

60

27

550 m

White Roofed Hangar
with Black
Ashcroft Letters

Ashcroft

Windsock
on Roof

Farm

32

Farm

Farm

Rwy	Dim(m)	Surface	TORA(m)	LDA(m)	Lighting
09/27	550x12	Grass	Unlicensed		Nil
14/32	650x12	Grass	Unlicensed		Nil

Op hrs: PPR. SR–SS.

Landing Fee: £5.00.	**Customs:** Nil.
Hangarage: Limited.	**Maintenance:** Nil.

Remarks: Operated by Steve Billington, Ashcroft Farm, Darnhall, Winsford, Cheshire CW7 4DQ. Strictly PPR.
Airfield situated beneath Manchester CTA (Base 2500' ALT).
Light aircraft welcome on prior permission and at pilot's own risk.
Essential no flying on north side of airfield. Overnight parking at owner's risk.
No multiple circuits or joyrides.
Avoid overflying local habitation especially farm buildings.

Warning: Runways are marked by white crosses when unusable due to waterlogging, mainly during winter months.

Accommodation: Boot & Slipper Tel: 01270-73238
Taxis: Ace Cars Tel: 01606-862149.

Fuel: Nil.	**Tel/Fax:** 01270-528697.

Robert Pooley ©

N52 00·52 E000 13·57	**AUDLEY END**	283 ft AMSL
1nm SW of Saffron Walden	BPK 117·50 043 20. LAM 115·60 011 22	
	BKY 116·25 083 6·2	

No Radio. Essex Radar 120·625.

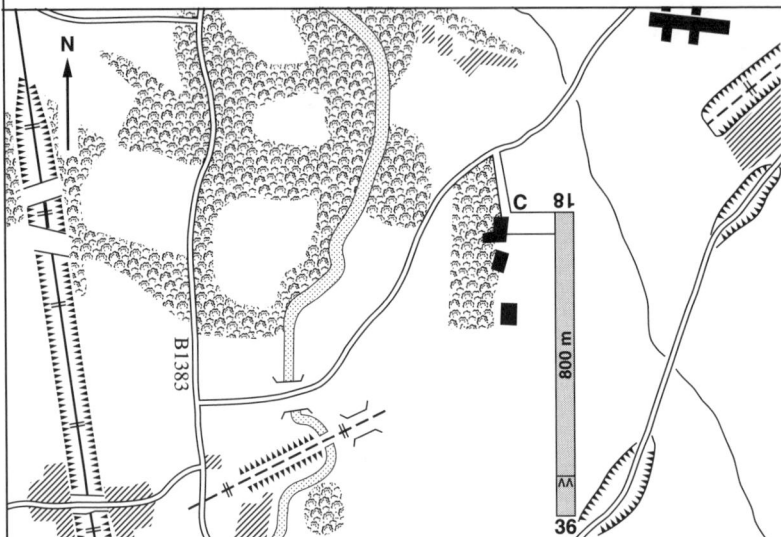

Rwy	Dim(m)	Surface	TORA(m)	LDA(m)	Lighting
18/36	800x30	Grass	18-700	18-800	Nil.
			36-800	36-700	Nil.

Advisory declared distances.

Op hrs: PPR. SR-SS.

Landing Fee: PRIVATE – Singles £5.00. Twins £10.00.
COMMERCIAL – Singles & Twins £10.00.
PARKING – All parking £5.00 per night by prior arrangement.

Hangarage: Nil.	**Maintenance:** Nil.	**Customs:** Nil.

Remarks: Operated by Audley Development Ltd.,The Estate Office, Bruncketts
Ambo, Saffron Walden, Essex CB11 4JL. An unlicensed aerodrome.
All circuit traffic to avoid overflying Saffron Walden.
Aerodrome situated beneath the Stansted CTA (base 2500') and on the NW
boundary of the Stansted CTR, contact Essex Radar 120·625.

All visiting pilots to report to the Control Point at the green hangar.

Restaurant: Available in Saffron Walden

Car Hire: Available in Saffron Walden

Fuel: Nil.	**Tel:** 01799-541354/541956 **Fax:** 01799-542134 e-mail: AEE@farming.co.uk

N51 32·98 W002 17·92	**BADMINTON**	495 ft AMSL

3·5nm ENE of Chipping Sodbury.	**BCN 117·45 110 37·5.**	**BZN 111·90 – 28**
		BZ 386·0 250 –

c/s Badminton Radio 123·175 A/G
Lyneham APP 123·40 or 118·425. Filton APP 122·725.

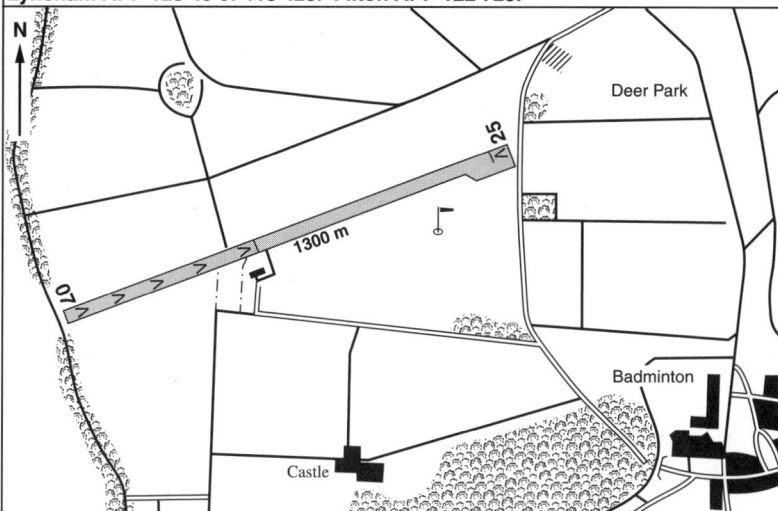

Rwy	Dim(m)	Surface	TORA(m)	LDA(m)	Lighting
07/25	1300x27	Grass	07-850	07-800	Thr Rwy APAPI 4°
			25-800	25-1250	Ap Thr Rwy APAPI 4°

Advisory declared distances.

Op hrs: PPR.

Landing Fee: None.	**Customs:** Nil.

Hangarage: Nil.	**Maintenance:** Nil.

Remarks: Operated by The Duke of Beaufort, Badminton Aerodrome, Badminton, South Gloucestershire GL9 1DD. Unlicensed aerodrome.

Strictly PPR, all movements must be recorded.

Care must be taken August to March when runway may be fenced against stock. Displaced threshold on Rwy 07 (as marked) although light aircraft may use new western extension.

Circuits LH on 07, RH on 25.

Caution: On final approach to Rwy 25 ensure adequate clearance on crossing public road just short of runway threshold.

Fuel: 100LL.	**Tel:** 01454-218333.
	01249-783158 Weekends.

Robert Pooley ©

N54 12·67 W001 17·40	**BAGBY (Thirsk)**	160 ft AMSL
2 nm SE of Thirsk.		**POL 112·10 051 40**
3 nm E of RAF Topcliffe.		**NEW 114·25 169 52**

Leeming Zone 127·75. Topcliffe App 125·00. Linton Zone 129·15.
Bagby Radio 123·25 A/G (not always manned).

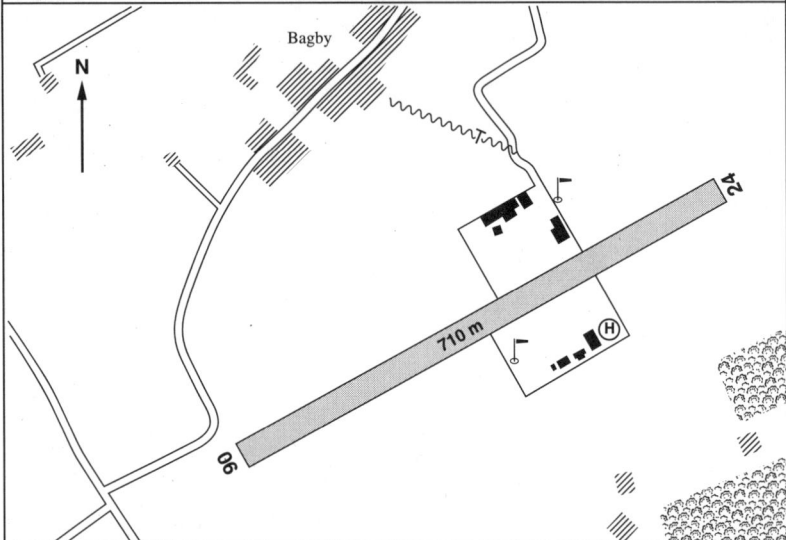

Rwy	Dim(m)	Surface	TORA(m)	LDA(m)	Lighting
06/24	710x20	Grass	Unlicensed		Rwy *

Note: Rwy 24 has a 3% downslope.

* Electric Rwy Lighting by prior arrangement.

Op hrs: 0800-SS (Services 0930-1900, closed Tue 1700-1930)   **Customs:** Nil

Landing Fee: Private Nil; Commercial £5. (free with fuel uplift); Large Helis £10.

Hangarage: Limited.   **Maintenance:** M3. G. Fox Engineering Tel: 01845-597707

Remarks: Operated by J.M. Dundon, Milford, Bagby, Thirsk, N. Yorks YO7 2PH.

Unlicensed airfield situated within Leeming/Topcliffe CMATZ, obtain MATZ clearance from Leeming. All pilots are to comply with Special Departure Procedures, details of which will be issued on arrival.

Circuits at 800 ft, LH on 24, RH on 06, **avoid overflying the village of Bagby**.

Non radio aircraft — please obtain a telephone briefing.

Catering - Mon-Fri 1200-1400; Sat 0930-1600; Sun 0930-1600.

Aviation oils from clubhouse.

Pilot supplies from Bagby Aviation, Tel: 01845-597536.

Fuel: 100LL, Jet A1.	**Tel:** 01845-597385 Airfield. Mobile 07774-680186 **Fax:** 01845-597747 Office. e-mail: bagbyair@aol.com Website: http://www.bagbyairfield.freeserve.co.uk

N57 01·62 W007 26·25	**BARRA**	Sea Level

Foreshore of Traigh Mhor, Island of Barra.	**TIR 117·70 339 37**
	BEN 114·40 195 27·5

Barra Information 118·075 AFIS.   NDB 'BRR' 316·0 (On A/D).

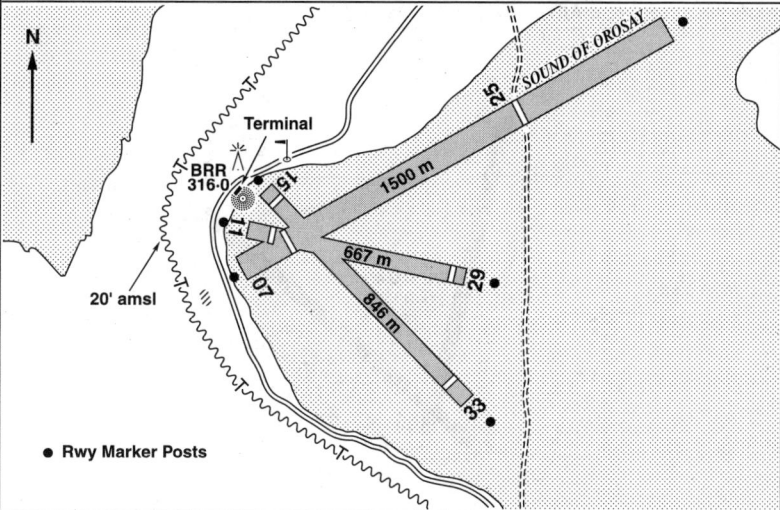

20' amsl

● Rwy Marker Posts

Rwy	Dim(m)	Surface	TORA(m)	LDA(m)	Lighting
† 07/25	1500x60	Sand	07-700	07-700	Nil.
			25-700	25-700	Nil.
11/29	667x46	Sand	11-667	11-617	Nil.
			29-667	29-597	Nil.
15/33	846x46	Sand	15-846	15-796	Nil.
			33-846	33-776	Nil.

Op hrs: Strictly PPR. Airfield hours variable daily due tides.

Landing Fee: £10.90 for aircraft up to 2700 kg AUW, VFR & booked in advance.

Hangarage: Nil.	**Maintenance:** Nil.	**Customs:** Nil.

Remarks: Operated by Highlands & Islands Airport Ltd. Aerodrome PPR.
The obstacle clearance surfaces associated with a Code 2 runway are infringed at both ends of Rwy 07/25. The minima of **3 km and 1000 ft** aal must be strictly adhered to. Pilots must be able to see and avoid obstacles on take-off and landing.
PPR essential, in order to obtain information on surface conditions.
† The thresholds of Rwy 07/25 will be marked by black/white tri-boxes on the landward side of each threshold during operating hours when runway in use .

Warnings:
- The landing and take-off areas may be considerably ridged by hard sand and contain pools of standing water, presenting potential hazards to aircraft.
- The bearing strength, braking action and contamination of the beach is unknown, variable and unpredictable.
- Downdraughts may be experienced at the western end of Rwy 07/25 with strong winds from the west through south.
- High ground 1260 ft aal, 225°T/3·5 nm.

Fuel: Nil.	**Tel:** 01871-890212 PPR
	Fax: 01871-890220

N54 07·87 W003 15·82	**BARROW (Walney Island)**	47 ft AMSL

1·5 nm NW of Barrow-in-Furness	**WAL 114·10 001 44·5**
	DCS 115·20 183 35·7

c/s Walney Information 123·20 AFIS.
NDB 'WL' 385·0 (On A/D).   DME 'WL' 109·40 (On A/D).

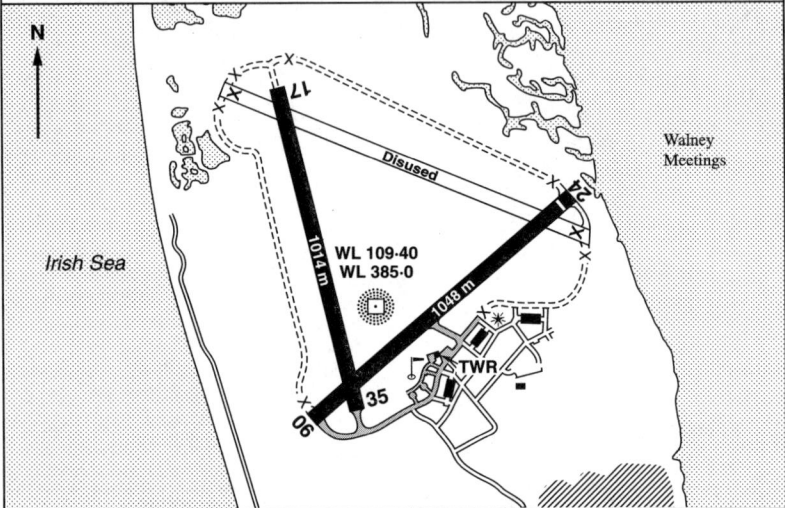

Rwy	Dim(m)	Surface	TORA(m)	LDA(m)	Lighting
06/24	1048x46	Asphalt	(06-1020)	(06-1020)	Thr Rwy APAPI 4° LH
			(24-1014)	(24-966)	Thr Rwy APAPI 3·5° LH
17/35	1014x46	Asphalt	(17-1014)	(17-1014)	Thr Rwy APAPI 4° RH
			(35-1014)	(35-1014)	Thr Rwy APAPI 3° LH
					ABn Wh

Op hrs: Strictly PPR.	**Customs:** Nil.

Landing Fee: £5.00 per 0·5 tonne up to 3 tonnes. £10.00 per tonne over 3 tonnes.

Maintenance: Nil.	**Hangarage:** Nil.	**Met:** 0161-499-5033

Remarks: Operated by BAe Systems (Marine) Ltd. PPR.

Non radio aircraft not accepted. Unlicensed aerodrome.

Airfield closed to all traffic except for the home based aircraft and gliders, at weekends, PHs and at other notified periods. Landings absolutely prohibited when airfield is closed.

Restaurant: Nil

Car Hire: Avis   Tel: 01229-829555
              Hertz Tel: 01229-836666

Fuel: Jet A1.	**Tel:** 01229-470087 or 471407.
	Fax: 01229-470619
	Telex: 65350.

| N52 26·12 E001 37·07 | **BECCLES** | 80 ft AMSL |

2 nm SE of Beccles, 5 nm SW of Lowestoft.

c/s Beccles Radio 134·60 A/G.

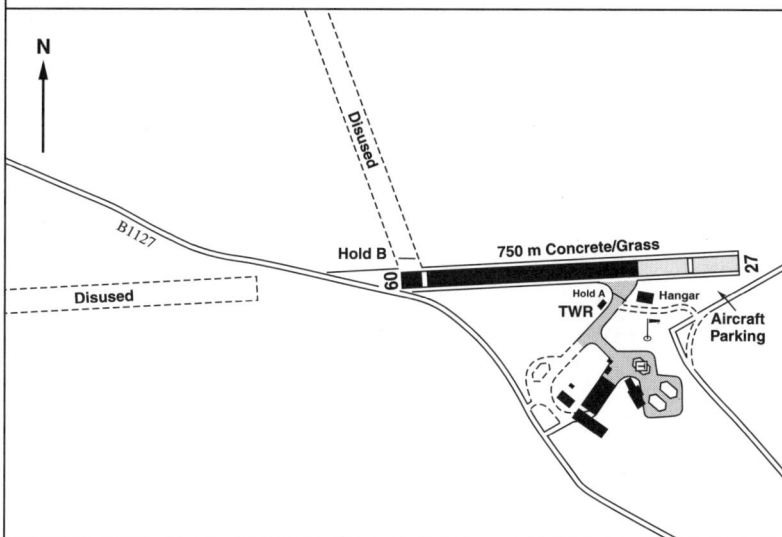

Rwy	Dim(m)	Surface	TORA(m)	LDA(m)	Lighting
09/27	750x18	Concrete/ Grass	09-663 27-695	09-663 27-626	Nil Nil

Op hrs: 0900-SS and by arrangement.

Landing Fee: Singles £5, Twins/Small Helicopters £10.

Customs: 24 hrs PNR.   **Hangarage:** Available.

Maintenance: Available.

Remarks: Operated by Rainair (Beccles) Ltd., Beccles Airport, Beccles, Suffolk NR34 7TE. Licensed aerodrome.

Fixed wing and Helicopters welcome.

Circuits at 1000 ft QFE, RH on Rwy 09, LH on Rwy 27.

Avoid overflying local villages.

Caution: Disused runway west of the airfield used for Sunday Market.

Restaurant: Available.

Car Hire/Taxis: By arrangement.

Flying Training, aircraft hire and Winter hangarage available.

| **Fuel:** 100LL | **Tel:** 07767-827172.
Fax: 01502-711376 or 475157. |

Intentionally Blank

| N52 08·60 W000 24·37 | **BEDFORD (Castle Mill)** | 70 ft AMSL |

| 2 nm ENE of Bedford | DTY 116·40 100   26 |
| | BNN 113·75 017 25·5 |

No Radio.   FIS — London Information 124·60.

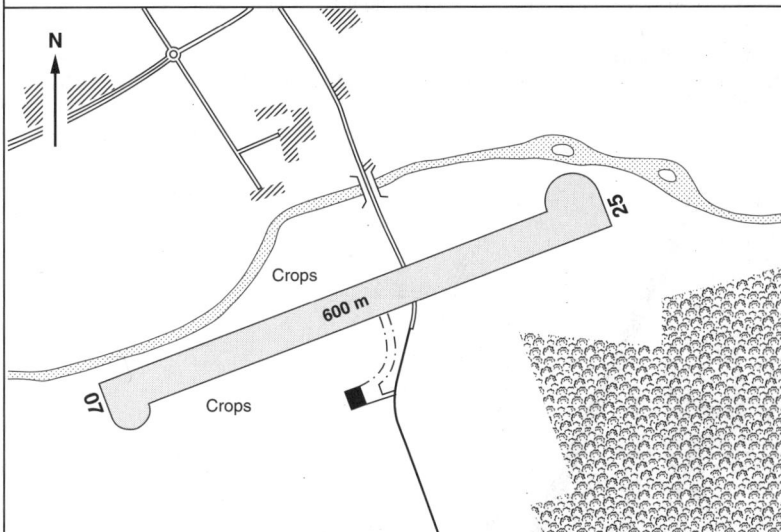

Rwy	Dim(m)	Surface	TORA(m)	LDA(m)	Lighting
07/25	600x18	Grass	Unlicensed		Nil.

Op hrs: PPR. SR-SS.

| **Landing Fee:** Private aircraft no charge. | **Customs:** Nil. |
| **Hangarage:** Limited. | **Maintenance:** Nil. |

Remarks: Operated by Millair Services Limited. Unlicensed aerodrome which may be available to visiting aircraft on 48hrs PPR.

Liable to flooding in winter.

Aerodrome situated 1nm North of Danger Area D206.

Power cables running ESE–WNW 0·5 nm to the NE.

Radio Mast 140' aal, 210' amsl 290°/0·8 nm.

Restaurant: Nil

Car Hire: Progress Ford. Tel: 01234-358391

| **Fuel:** Nil. | **Tel:** 01234-262441 |
| | **Fax:** 01234-273357 |

N5439·45 W00612·95   **BELFAST (Aldergrove)**   268 ft AMSL

3·5nm S of Antrim.
11·5nm NW of Belfast.

c/s Aldergrove. APP 124·90.   TWR 118·30.   GND 121·75 - 08-1700 Summer only.
RAD 120·90, 120·00 (as directed).   VDF 124·90.   ATIS 128·20.
VOR/DME 'BEL' 117·20 (On A/D).
NDB 'OY' 332·0 (253°M/4·3nm to Thr 25)
ILS/DME Rwy 25 (253°M) I-AG 109·90.   ILS/DME Rwy 17 (170°M) I-FT 110·90

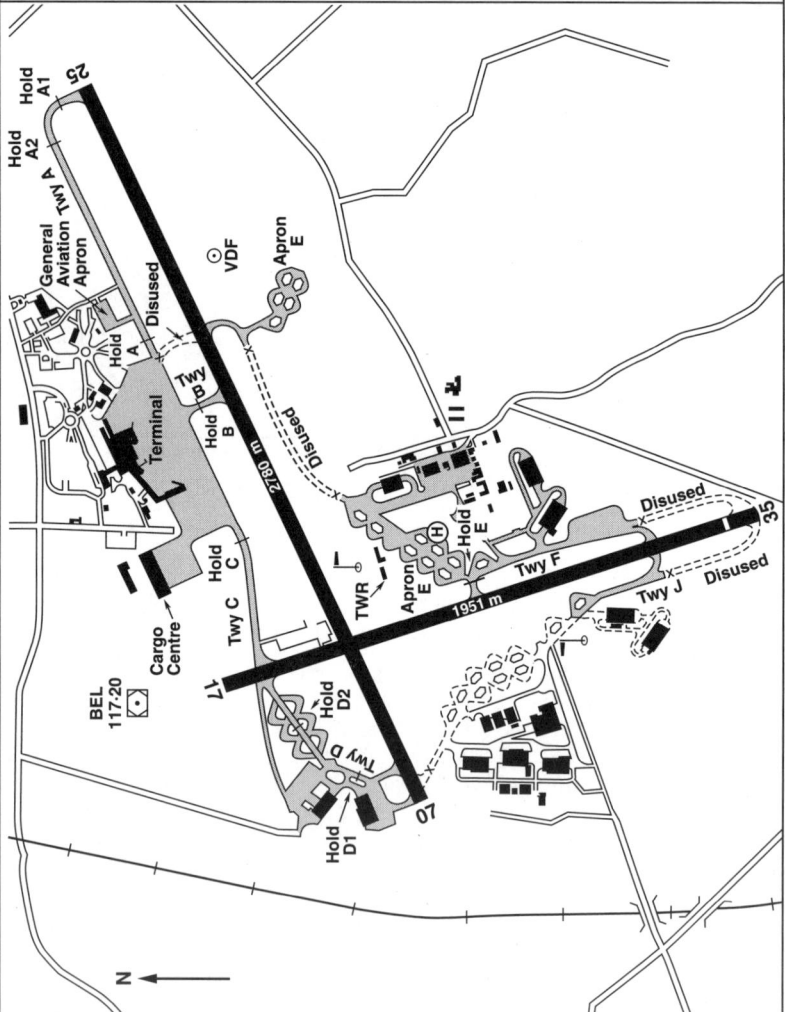

| N54 39·45 W006 12·95 | **BELFAST (Aldergrove)** | | | | 268 ft AMSL |

3·5nm S of Antrim, 11·5nm NW of Belfast

Rwy	Dim(m)	Surface	TORA(m)	LDA(m)	Lighting
07/25	2780x45	Asphalt	07-2780	07-2780	Ap Thr Rwy RCL PAPI 3°
			25-2780	25-2780	Ap Thr Rwy RCL PAPI 3°
17/35	1951x45	Asphalt	17-1799	17-1799	Ap Thr Rwy PAPI 3°
			35-1891	35-1799	Ap Thr Rwy PAPI 3°

Op hrs: H24.

Landing Fee: Minimum charge £12.75 & £8.16 per tonne up to 15 tonnes.

| **Customs:** Available. | **Met:** H24. 028 942 3275 |
| **Hangarage:** Nil. | **Maintenance:** Limited. |

Remarks: Operated by Belfast International Airport Ltd. Within the Belfast CTR/ CTA the Class 'D' Controlled Airspace regulations apply — see pages 8 to 10.
Visual Reference Points (VRPs) are listed overleaf.
VAD/VRP Chart for the Belfast TMA is at page 105. Non radio aircraft PPR.
Severe bird hazard during autumn and winter months, pilots will be advised by ATC.
Circuits variable at discretion of ATC.
Low-level helicopter operations south of Rwy 25, but will remain at least 250 m from that runway unless further cleared by ATC.
All aircraft using Belfast International Airport are to carry third insurance cover of not less than £500,000.

International GA Flights:
(1) Arriving aircraft will be parked for examination on the GA Apron Customs Examination Station, Stand 12 area or as directed.
(2) Aircraft Commanders are required by law to present their aircraft and contents for Police inspection on arrival and before departure.

Aircraft below 2000 kg AUW will park, normally self-manoeuvring, on the GA Apron or as directed.

Ground Handling facilities available from: Executive Jet Centre operate 0800-2000 local daily and by prior arrangement, Tel: 028- 9442 2646 ,
Fax: 028- 9442 2640.

Aldergrove Flight Training Centre (AFTC) operate 0900-2000 local daily and by prior arrangement, Tel: 028- 9442 3747, Fax: 028- 9442 3777.

Warning: The attention of pilots is drawn to the existence of LANGFORD LODGE unlicensed aerodrome with crossed runways 08/26 and 03/21, situated 3 nm SW of ALDERGROVE, very close to Rwy 07 centre line of app to Rwy 07. When Rwy 07 is in use, pilots making apps to this runway should exercise due caution to ensure they have identified the correct aerodrome.

Model aircraft flying at Nutts Corner, a disused airfield 3 nm SW of Aldergrove, up to 400 ft agl.

Restaurant: Bar and Buffet, Hotel on site.

Car Hire: Avis, Budget, Europcar, Hertz, McCausland and National available at Terminal Building.

Fuel: 100LL 09-1700 daily, Jet A1. H24. Fuelling from Simon Aviation.

Tel: 028-9448 4313 Duty Ops Officer H24.
      028-9448 4281 NATS ATC/FBU.
Fax: 028-9442 3883 Airport Duty Officer.

VRP	VOR/VOR	VOR/NDB	VOR/DME FIX
Ballymena N54 51·80 W006 16·40	BEL R360 MAC R220	BEL R360 HB 325°M	BEL 360°/12 nm
Cluntoe (Disused Aerodrome) N54 37·23 W006 32·03	BEL R264 MAC R220	MAC R220 OY 262°M	BEL 265°/11 nm
Divis N54 36·45 W006 00·57	BEL R119 DUB R015	BEL R119 HB 270°M	BEL 119°/8 nm
Glengormley (M2 Junc 4) N54 40·83 W005 58·90	BEL R089 TRN R234	BEL R089 HB 325°M	BEL 089°M/9 nm
Larne N54 51·20 W005 49·52	BEL R057 MAC R198	MAC R197 OY 050°M	BEL 057°/18 nm
Portadown N54 25·50 W006 26·85	BEL R215 DUB R002	DUB R002 OY 225°M	BEL 215°/16 nm
Toome (Disused Aerodrome) N54 45·47 W006 29·67	BEL R309 MAC R223	MAC R223 OY 292°M	BEL 309°/11 nm

N

A42

A42

River Bann

Ballymena VRP ⊕ Ballymena

A36

River Main

A26

Toome
Toome VRP ⊕

Toome

A6

BELFAST CTR **D**
SFC – FL105

Six Mile Water

A6

A6

Antrim

P435/2·5

A6

River Ballinderry

Lough Neagh

BEL 117·20

Belfast Aldergrove

OY 332·0

Cluntoe VRP ⊕

Cluntoe

Langford Lodge

Belfast Nutts-Corner ⊗

A52

BELFAST TMA-1 **E**
2000' * – FL105
*or 700' agl if higher

B3 **D** FL45 – FL245

A30

P414/2

Lisburn

River Bann

R431/2

Maghaberry ⊗

A3

P420/2

Long Ke

M1

BE

M1

A1

M12

River Logan

Lurgan

Dromore

Portadown
Portadown VRP ⊕

A3

Intentionally Blank

Larne VRP

Larne

BELFAST TMA-2 **E**
3500' ALT - FL105

STRANGFORD
CTA-3 **D**
FL105 - FL180

BELFAST TMA-1 **E**
2000' * - FL105
*or 700' agl if higher

Whitehead

Whitehead VRP

BELFAST/City CTA-2 **D**
1500' - 2000' ALT

SCOTTISH FIR

LONDON FIR

Ballyclare

Carrickfergus

engormley VRP

A2

Newtown Abbey

Groomsport VRP

Donaghadee

R421/2

Bangor

A48

HB
420·0

Belfast City

BELFAST/City CTR
SFC - 2000' ALT

Newtownards

Newtownards

FL55 - FL245

P600 **D**
(minimum ALT 5000')

STRANGFORD
CTA-2 **D**
3500' ALT - FL245

ivis
RP

Belfast

BELFAST/City CTA-3 **D**
2000' - 3500' ALT

Comber VRP

A20

Ballyhalbert

A24

BELFAST/City CTA-1 **D**
00' - 2000' ALT

A23

B3 **D** FL45 - FL245

Saintfield VRP

A22

A7

A20

Strangford Lough

Kirkistown

BELFAST TMA-2 **E**
3500' ALT - FL105

A21

A7

A2

STRANGFORD
CTA-3 **D**

BELFAST TMA, BELFAST CTR/CTA
and VRPs

Intentionally Blank

N54 37·08 W005 52·35	**BELFAST (City)**	15 ft AMSL

1·5nm E of Belfast City Centre.   **BEL 117·20 110 12·7**

c/s Belfast.   APP 130·85.   TWR 130·75.   RAD 134·80.   ATIS 136·625.
City Handling Radio 129·75.   NDB 'HB' 420·0 (on A/D).
ILS/DME Rwy 22 (222°M) I-BFH 108·10.   LLZ/DME Rwy 04 (042°M) HBD 108·10.

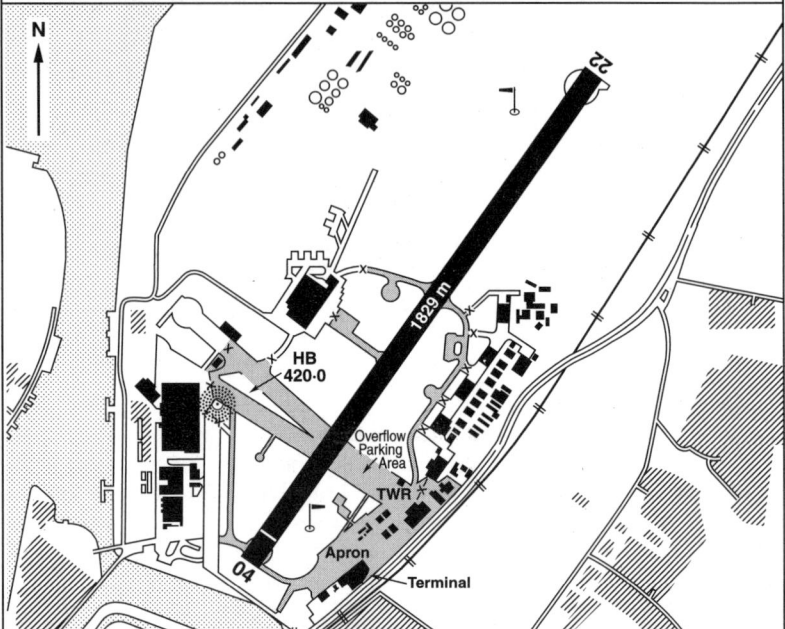

Rwy	Dim(m)	Surface	TORA(m)	LDA(m)	Lighting
04/22	1829x61	Concrete	04-1829 22-1767	04-1737 22-1767	Ap Thr Rwy PAPI 3° Ap Thr Rwy PAPI 3°

Op hrs: Mon-Sat 0630-2130, Sun 0815-2130.

Landing Fee: £4.10 per 500 kg up to 2 tonnes plus Nav fee £8.20 per tonne.

Hangarage: Limited.	**Maintenance:** Nil.

Met: H24 028-942 3275.	**Customs:** Non EU 24 PNR.

Remarks: Operated by Belfast City Airport. Within the Belfast City CTR/CTA the
Class 'D' Controlled Airspace regulations apply — see pages 2 and 6.
Belfast TMA, CTR/CTA and VRPs chart is at page 105.
Non-radio aircraft prohibited. Circuits LH on 04, RH on 22.
Rwy 22 is the preferred landing runway. Rwy 04 is the preferred departure runway.
TV masts, 1740' aal,1755 ft amsl 251°/5·2 nm, and 1683' aal, 1698' amsl 260°/4·8nm.

Noise Abatement Procedures and VRPs are listed opposite.
Restaurant: Licensed Snack Bar in Departure Lounge.

Taxi: Airport Taxi Rank.   **Car Hire:** Available – 6 outlets .

Fuel: 100LL, Jet A1. BP.	**Tel:** 028-9045 4871 ATC. 028-9045 8578 Handling. **Fax:** 028-9073 1557 ATC. 028-9045 9198 Admin.

BELFAST(City)
Noise Abatement Procedures and VRPs

Noise Abatement Procedures:

Arrivals Rwy 04:
VFR traffic maintain altitude 1500 ft before establishing on the final approach track at 5 nm.

Arrivals Rwy 22:
VFR traffic establish on the 7 DME arc (I BFH) and coast out not below altitude 2500 ft before establishing on the final approach track at 5 nm.

Aircraft with a MTWA of less than 13,000 kg (excluding jets), when downwind left hand 04 are exempt from the above restriction if the flight path avoids residential areas.

Departures Rwy 04:
Propeller aircraft categorised as 'light' – Early left turn onto 037°M and climb to altitude 1500 ft before commencing turn, and then as per the ATC clearance.

Propeller aircraft categorised as 'small' or 'medium' – Early left turn onto 037°M and climb to altitude 2000 ft before commencing turn, and then as per the ATC clearance.

Departures Rwy 22:
Propeller aircraft 13,000 kg or less – Climb on runway heading to altitude 1500 ft before turning, then as per the ATC clearance.

Propeller aircraft above 13,000 kg – Climb on runway heading to altitude 2000 ft before turning, and then as per the ATC clearance.

Visual Reference Points (VRPs)

VRP	VOR/VOR	VOR/NDB	VOR/DME FIX
Comber N54 33·05 W005 44·75	TRN R223 IOM R317	TRN R223 HB 136° M	BEL 119° 18 nm
Groomsport N54 40·50 W005 37·08	TRN R223 IOM R328	IOM R328 HB 075°M	BEL 094° 21 nm
Saintfield N54 27·62 W005 49·97	TRN R222 IOM R309	IOM R309 HB 176°M	BEL 138°/18 nm
Whitehead N54 45·17 W00542·57	TRN R230 IOM R328	IOM R328 HB 043°M	BEL 080°/19 nm

See Belfast TMA, CTR/CTA and VRPs chart at page 105.

N55 06·00 W006 58·05	**BELLARENA**	15 ft AMSL
5 nm N of Limavady		**BEL 117·2 327 37**
10 nm W of Coleraine		**MAC 116·0 255 47**

Bellarena Radio 130·10 A/G (During gliding ops).

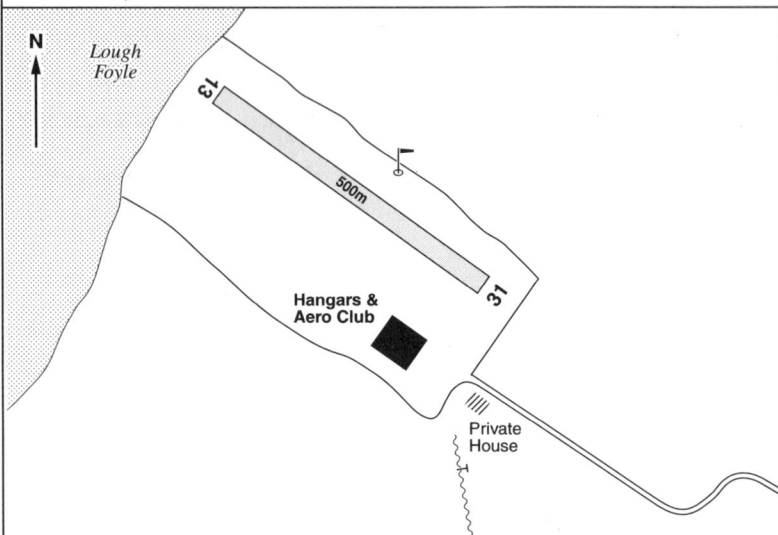

Rwy	Dim(m)	Surface	TORA(m)	LDA(m)	Lighting
E/W	500	Grass	Unlicensed		Nil
or 13/31	500	Grass	Unlicensed		Nil

Op hrs: PPR. SR–SS.

Landing Fee: Nil.	**Customs:** Nil.
Hangarage: By arrangement	**Maintenance:** Nil.

Met: 028-942 3275.

Remarks: Unlicensed Private site operated by Ulster Gliding Club.
Avoid low flying due to intensive gliding activity.

Caution: High ground 1260' amsl, 2 nm East of site.

Restaurant: 3 miles

Accommodation: Available nearby.

Taxi: 028-7775 0561/0489

Fuel: 100LL - Check availability.	**Tel:** 028-7775 0301 weekends (Club) **Fax:** 028-7776 63321.

| N50 58·48 W004 05·40 | **BELLE VUE** | 675 ft AMSL |

2·5 nm NE of Great Torrington
6 nm SSW of Barnstaple

BCN 117·45 220 54
BHD 112·05 330 41

c/s Belle Vue Radio 123·575 A/G.

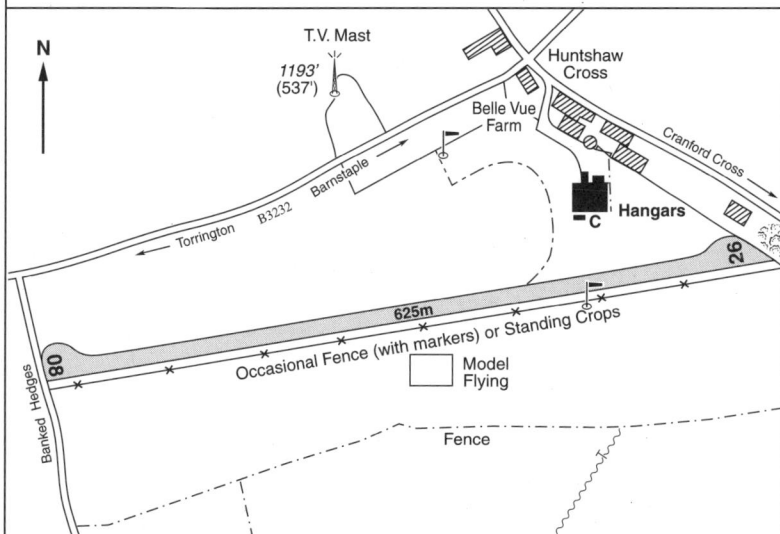

Rwy	Dim(m)	Surface	TORA(m)	LDA(m)	Lighting
08/26	625x15	Grass	Unlicensed		Nil

Op hrs: PPR. Mon-Sat 0800-2100 or SS whichever earlier.
Sun and PHs 0900-1800 (take-off) - 2100 (landing) or SS whichever earlier.

| **Landing Fee:** £3.00. | **Customs:** 01752- 235600 |
| **Hangarage:** Limited. | **Maintenance:** Nil |

Remarks: Operated by The Wingnuts Flying Club, Belle Vue Airfield. Yarnscombe, Barnstaple, North Devon EX31 3ND.
Due planning restrictions no Helicopters accepted or Microlights with a cruise speed of less than 45 kts.

Circuits at 1000 ft aal. Standard overhead joins at 2000 ft aal.

Avoid overflying nearby villages and settlements (PPR includes briefing of sensitive areas).

Warning: Beware of the Television Mast 537 ft agl, 1193 ft amsl, 300 metres due north, within the circuit.
Modellers occasionally operate to south of runway. Call blind if radio not manned.

Restaurant: Refreshments available.

Accommodation: Available locally on request.

Taxis: By arrangement.

| **Fuel:** Mogas by arrangement | **Tel:** 01805-623113. Mobile 07971-278984 |

Robert Pooley ©

Intentionally Blank

112

| N50 40·68 W001 06·55 | **BEMBRIDGE (Isle of Wight)** | 55 ft AMSL |

| 2·3 nm NE of Sandown | SAM 113·35 157 19 |
| | MID 114·00 224 29 |

c/s Bembridge Radio 123·25 A/G.
NDB 'IW' 426·0 (On A/D). Nav. only

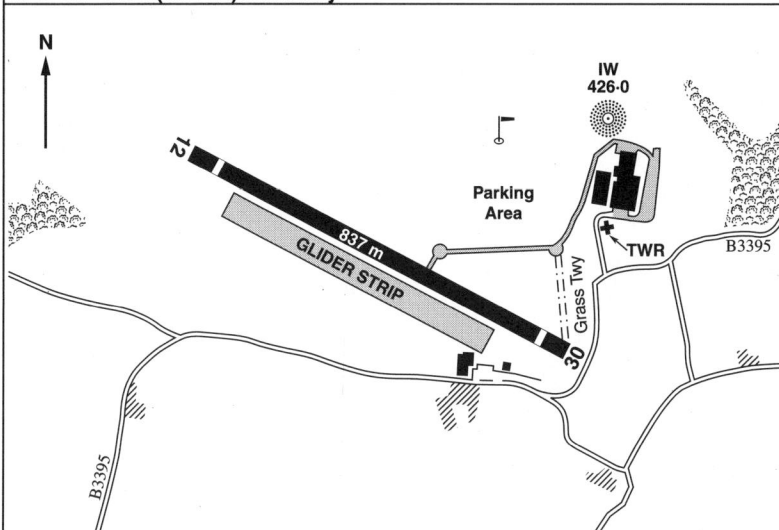

Rwy	Dim(m)	Surface	TORA(m)	LDA(m)	Lighting
12/30	837x23	Concrete	12-837	12-837	Thr Rwy APAPI 4°
			30-837	30-775 (Day)	Thr Rwy APAPI 4°
				30-699 (Night)	

Op hrs: Aerodrome closed to all visiting aircraft.

Landing Fee: Aerodrome closed to all visiting aircraft.

Hangarage: Nil. **Maintenance:** Nil. **Customs:** 24 hrs PNR.

Remarks: Non radio aircraft not accepted.
Circuits RH on Rwy 30, LH on Rwy 12. When gliders are operating, joining a/c are to position to overfly the A/D at 1500' QFE on the Rwy QDM. When overhead the upwind end of the runway, turn left or right (as appropriate) to level at circuit height 1000' QFE on crosswind leg prior to turning downwind. Glider circuits opposite direction to powered a/c.
Landing prohibited when Tower is not manned.
Grass taxiway to threshold Rwy 30.
High Ground 345' aal, 400' amsl 270°/2 nm.
Trees and rising ground within the approach sector to Rwy 30.
Aerotow gliding activity during and outside published Op hrs.

Restaurant: Propeller Inn Tel: 01983-873611

Car Hire: Avis Tel: 01983-615522   **Taxis:** Ralph's Taxis Tel: 01983-811666.

| **Fuel:** 100LL, Jet A1 | **Tel:** 01983-873331 TWR; 871538 Admin. |
| | **Fax:** 01983-871566. |

Robert Pooley ©

N57 28·65 W007 21·98	**BENBECULA**	19 ft AMSL

West side of Isle of Benbecula.	TIR 117·70 354 61
	STN 115·10 230 58

c/s 'Benbecula', APP/TWR/FIS * 119·20.
VOR/DME 'BEN' 113·95 (On A/D). DME 'BCL' 108·10 (on A/D).
  * FIS may be provided outside op hrs for Ambulance and SAR Flights only.

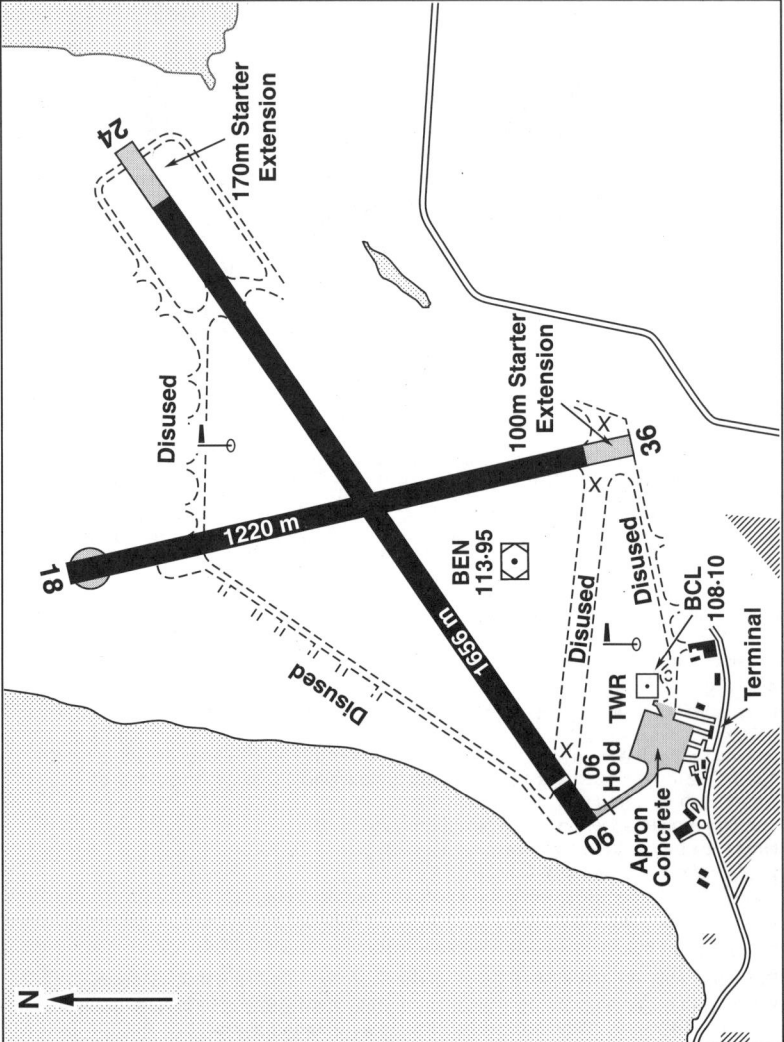

N57 28·65 W007 21·98   **BENBECULA**   19 ft AMSL

Rwy	Dim(m)	Surface	TORA(m)	LDA(m)	Lighting
06/24	1656x46	Bitumen	06-1656 24-1506 *	06-1534 24-1506	Ap Thr Rwy PAPI 3° Ap Thr Rwy PAPI 3°
18/36	1220x46	Bitumen	18-1220 36-1220 *	18-1220 36-1220	† On request † On request

* Additional 170 m starter extension available O/R for Rwy 24, and 100 m for Rwy 36.

† Low intensity battery edge lights available on request for Air Ambulance and SAR Operations only.

Op hrs: PPR 3 Hrs . Mon-Fri 0900-1600, Sat 1100-1230, Sun closed.

Landing Fee: Highlands & Islands Rates.

Customs: By arrangement, 48 hrs PNR.   **Met:** 0141-221-6116.

Hangarage: Nil.   **Maintenance:** Nil.

Remarks: Operated by Highlands & Islands Airports Ltd., Benbecula Aerodrome, Balivanich, Western Isles HS7 5LA.

Prior permission required for all movements.

Intensive military activity in the vicinity.

All taxiways are closed except for the SW portion between Runway 06 threshold and the apron.

Grass areas soft and unsafe. Use marked taxiways only.
Helicopter landing area as directed by TWR.

Danger Areas D701/A/B/C/D and E may be active outside of aerodrome/ATC hours.

Visual Reference Points:

Lochmaddy Pier N57 35·77 W007 09·40.
Monach Islands Lighthouse N57 31·57 W007 41·67.

Restaurant: Light refreshments available.

Car Hire: Tel: 01870-602191

Fuel: Ltd 100LL and Jet A1- by arrangement with Loganair. Tel: 01870-603147. Fax: 01870-602714.	**Tel:** 01870-602051 Admin. **Fax:** 01870-602278 Admin. **Fax:** 01870-604826 ATC.

N51 36·98 W001 05·75	**BENSON**	226 ft AMSL

11nm SE of Oxford.	CPT 114·35 037 8·8
	BNN 113·75 257 21·5

c/s **Benson Zone 120·90.** LARS – Brize Radar 134·30
ILS Rwy 19 (192°M) 'BO' 108·50.

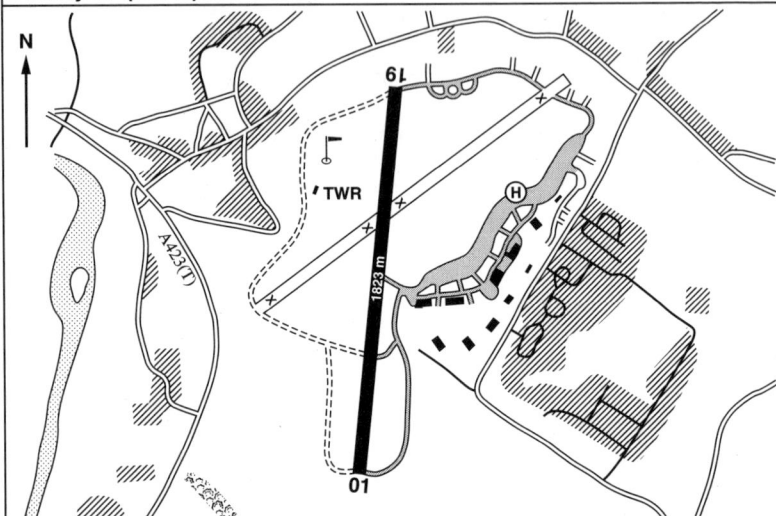

Rwy	Dim(m)	Surface	TORA(m)	LDA(m)	Lighting
01/19	1823x46	Asphalt/	01-1823	01-1823	Ap Thr Rwy PAPI
		Concrete	19-1823	19-1823	Ap Thr Rwy PAPI
					IBn 'BO' Red

Op hrs: PPR. Mon-Fri 0800-1730. O/T HO.	**Note: ATZ active H24**
Landing Fee: MoD (RAF) Rates.	**Customs:** Nil.
Hangarage: Nil.	**Maintenance:** Nil.

Remarks: RAF Aerodrome. PPR for civil aircraft.

Visiting aircraft PPR through Ops, Ext 7555/7272.

VFR arrivals below 3000 ft are to contact Benson Zone at least 5 nm before MATZ boundary.

Possible light aircraft activity evenings and Sat, Sun & PHs. Fixed wing and helicopter activity outside published Op hrs. Landing lights to be switched on for visual circuits or when within 3 nm on instrument approach.

Pilots are to avoid overflying WALLINGFORD and the villages of BENSON and EWELME.

Circuits at 1000' QFE. RH on Rwy 01. Locally based aircraft give late final calls.

Pilots must report personally to operations after landing and before take-off.

Caution: Intensive Helicopter and initial pilot training activity within the MATZ and on the aerodrome.

Fuel: Avgas, Avtur.	**Tel:** 01491-837766 Ext 7555 or 7272 Ops.

N53 53·92 W000 21·72	**BEVERLEY (Linley Hill)**	3 ft AMSL
4 nm NNE of Beverley.		**OTR 113·90 329 15**

c/s Beverley Radio 123·05 A/G.

Rwy	Dim(m)	Surface	TORA(m)	LDA(m)	Lighting
12/30	720x30	Grass	12-720	12-639	Nil.
			30-720	30-720	Nil.

Op hrs: PPR. 0900-SS.

Landing Fee: Singles £5.00; Twins £10.00.	**Customs:** 24 hrs PNR
Hangarage: By arrangement.	**Maintenance:** Nil.

Remarks: Operated by Hull Aero Club. Linley Hill Aerodrome, Leven, North Humberside HU11 5LT. Licensed aerodrome available on prior permission, not licensed for public transport. Non radio aircraft not accepted.
Circuits at 1000' aal; LH on 12, RH on 30. Normal join 1500' overhead. No right base join for Rwy 12 due to proximity of power cables. Avoid overflying LEVEN village, 1·5 nm east of aerodrome. Aircraft departing Rwy 12 must turn left before reaching Leven village. No right turns due to possibility of confliction with SAR helicopter activity.
Warnings: (a) RAF Leconfield is located 3·25 nm SW of the aerodrome. No special procedures are required but SAR helicopters, normally in contact with Beverley Radio, may fly through the ATZ at short notice.
(b) Power cable 100' aal crosses approach to Rwy 12, 850 m from threshold. Pilots should ensure that they have visual contact with the cable before starting their final approach.
(c) There is a dyke 30 m before Rwy 30 threshold marked with red/white warning markings. A further dyke runs parallel to Rwy 30 on the right hand side, 23 m from runway edge.
(d) Telephone Mast, 79 ft amsl on centreline Rwy 30, 1300 m from touchdown. Mast 775' aal, 778' amsl, 235°/7·5 nm.

Fuel: 100LL.	**Tel & Fax:** 01964-544994.

	BIGGIN HILL	600 ft AMSL
N51 19·85 E000 01·95		
5·5 nm ESE of Croydon	**DET 117·30 278 21. OCK 115·30 090 18**	
12 nm SE of London	**LON 113·60 122 21**	

c/s Biggin. APP 129·40. TWR 134·80 Weekends only. **VDF 129·40,134·80. ATIS 121·875.**
Thames Radar 132·70 (Inbound IFR flights requiring a radar service)
VOR/DME 'BIG' 115·10 (On A/D).   ILS /DME Rwy 21 (209°M) I-BGH 109·35.

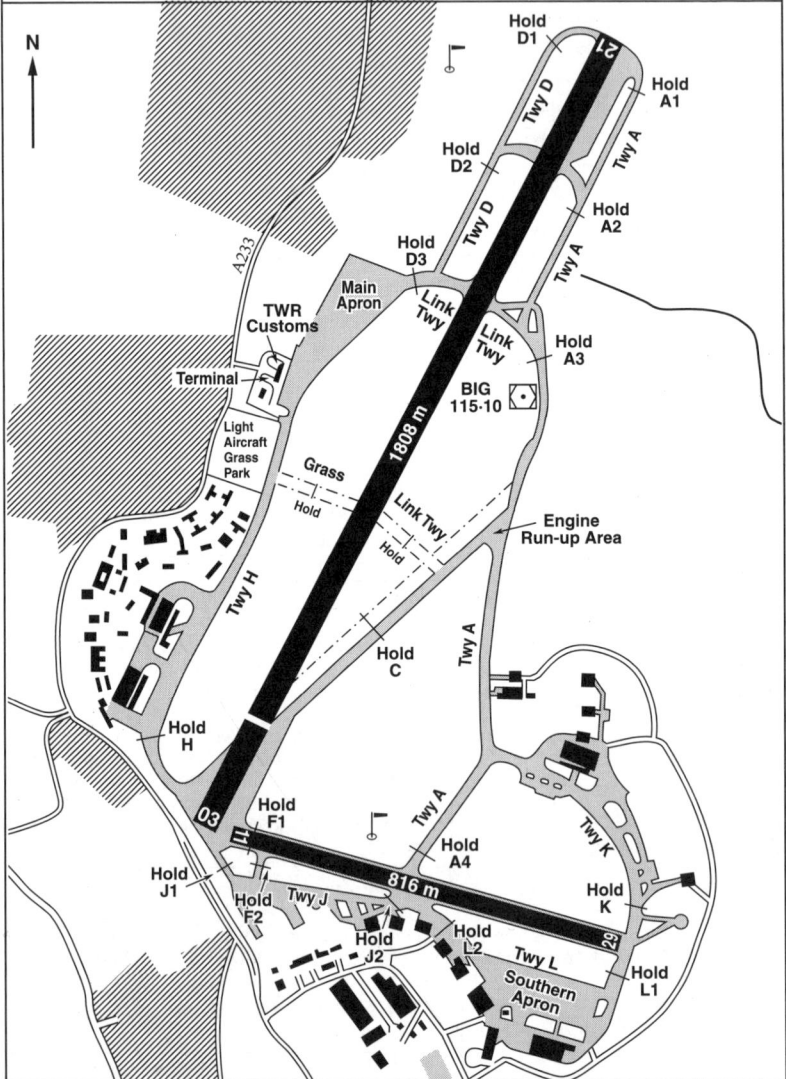

N

Hold D1
Hold A1
Twy D
Twy A
Hold D2
Twy D
Hold A2
Twy A
Hold D3
Main Apron
Link Twy
Link Twy
Hold A3
TWR Customs
BIG 115·10
Terminal
Light Aircraft Grass Park
1808 m
Grass
Hold
Link Twy
Engine Run-up Area
Hold
Twy A
Twy H
Hold C
Hold H
Hold F1
Twy A
Hold J1
Hold A4
Twy K
Hold F2
Twy J
Hold K
816 m
Hold J2
Hold L2
Twy L
Hold L1
Southern Apron
A233
03
21
03
21

Robert Pooley ©

118

Rwy	Dim(m)	Surface	TORA(m)	LDA(m)	Lighting
03/21	1808x46	Asphalt	03-1778	03-1558	Thr Rwy PAPI 4°
			03-1050 From Grass link taxiway.		
			21-1678	21-1678	Ap Thr Rwy PAPI 3°
11/29	816x24	Asphalt	11-816	11-816	Nil
			29-816	29-816	Nil

Op hrs: Mon-Fri 0730-2100, Sat, Sun, & Public Holidays 09-2000. O/T ¢.

Landing Fees: Up to 800 kg £14.80; 800–1700 kg £17.50; 1701–2500 kg £27.30; 2501–3500 kg £38.60; 3501–4500 kg £56.65; 4501–6000 kg £79.70; 6001–7000 kg £102.55; 7001–8000 kg £117.20. All rates exclude VAT.
Visiting Helicopters: Minimum charge £38.60 up to 3500 kg.
Out of hours, Handling, Apron, International and other charges on application.

Parking: First 2 hrs free, then per day: Up to 800 kg £5.50; 801-1700 kg £6.90; 1701–2500 kg £8.30.

ILS and VOR Training: Up to 3500 kg £16.00; 3500–7000 kg £26.00 per approach.

Customs: As Op hrs, Tel: 01959-575747.   **Bonded Store:** Tel: 01959-576212.

Hangarage & Maintenance: Biggin Hill Operations Tel: 01959-576404.

Met: Biggin Hill 01959-574677. Bracknell CFO 01344-856267.

Remarks: Operated by Regional Airports Ltd., Biggin Hill Airport, Kent. TN16 3BN.
Not available to non-radio aircraft. Microlight flying is prohibited at this airport.
Noise Preferential Routings applicable to jet and turbine aircraft available on request.
Due to the close proximity of residential areas the running of APUs on the West Apron is limited to a maximum of 30 minutes.
Airport Rules and Conditions of Use are available on request from the operator.

Circuit Procedures

Circuits LH on 03 and 11; RH on 21 and 29. Circuit height 1000' QFE, 1600' QNH.
Aircraft taking-off, 'going around' or making 'touch and go' landings are to remain at or below 500' QFE until the upwind end of the runway has been passed, when a left or right turn (as appropriate) should be initiated. Aircraft joining or re-joining the circuit for landing are to fly across the upwind end of the runway in use at 1000' QFE at 90° to the runway heading, a left or right turn (as appropriate) should be made onto the downwind leg.

VFR Departure Routes – See overleaf and page 121

Helicopter Operations: PPR — Tel: 01959-574677.
Helicopter Arrivals – Follow the fixed wing circuit pattern unless otherwise as directed by ATC.
Helicopter Departures – As instructed by ATC.
General – Avoid overflying Biggin Hill village to the South, Downe village on the NE boundary and the residential area on the NW boundary.

Restaurant: Restaurant and Refreshments always available.

Aircraft Handling: Biggin Operations Tel. 01959-574679.

Aircraft Cleaning: Biggin Hill Executive Aircraft Handling Tel. 01959-574679.

Fuel: 100LL, Jet A1. (01959-574737). Most Debit Cards, also, Visa, Diners, Mastercard, Amex and Multi-Service.	**Tel:** 01959-574677 ATC; 571111 Admin **Fax:** 01959-576404 Ops **Telex:** 957045 BIGGIN G **AFTN:** EGKBZPZX

Rwy 03

Departures to East, South and Northeast:

Straight ahead for 1·5 nm, then right turn.
Caution: Look out for aircraft joining deadside 03/21 at altitude 1600 ft. Avoid Farnborough and Downe.

Departures to North and West:

Straight ahead for 1 nm, then turn left. Avoid built up areas.

Rwy 21

Departures to East, South and Northeast:

Avoid built up areas. Keep School and Silos on left hand side. Straight ahead for 2 nm, then left turn.

Departures to West and North:

Straight ahead for 1 nm, then turn right. Keep school on left hand side.

Rwy 11

Departures All Directions:

Straight ahead for 1 nm, then left or right on to track. Avoid Cudham, Downe, Biggin Hill.

Caution: If turning to West or South, look out for aircraft joining deadside 11/29 at altitude 1600 ft.

Rwy 29

Departures to South and East:

Straight ahead for 1 nm, then left turn. Keep Silos on left hand side.
Caution: Look out for aircraft joining deadside 11/29 at altitude 1600 ft.

Departures to North and Northeast:

Straight ahead for 1 nm, then right turn. Avoid Leaves Green.

Departures to West:

Straight ahead for 1 nm, then turn on to track.

See Chart on the opposite page

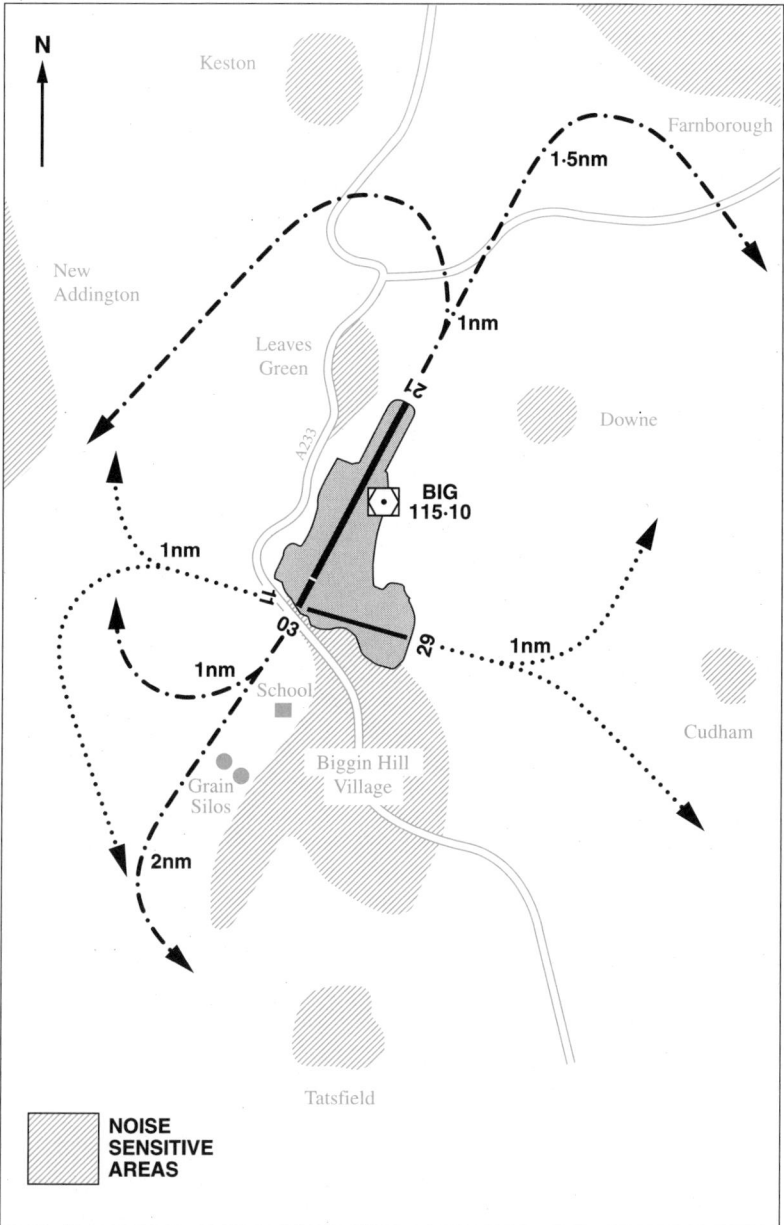

N

Keston

Farnborough

1·5nm

New
Addington

1nm

Leaves
Green

21

A233

Downe

BIG
115·10

1nm

11

03

29

1nm

1nm

School

1nm

Cudham

Grain
Silos

Biggin Hill
Village

2nm

Tatsfield

NOISE
SENSITIVE
AREAS

Robert Pooley ©

121

EGBB

BIRMINGHAM INTL

N52 27·23 W001 44·88

325 ft AMSL

5·5nm ESE of Birmingham

HON	113·65	338	6·6
DTY	116·40	311	28·5

APP/RAD/VDF 118·05. TWR 118·30. GND 121·80. ATIS 126·275.
RAD 131·325 as directed.   NDB 'BHX' 406·0 (On A/D).
ILS/DME Rwy 33 (330°M) I-BM 110·10. ILS/DME Rwy 15 (150°M) I-BIR 110·10.

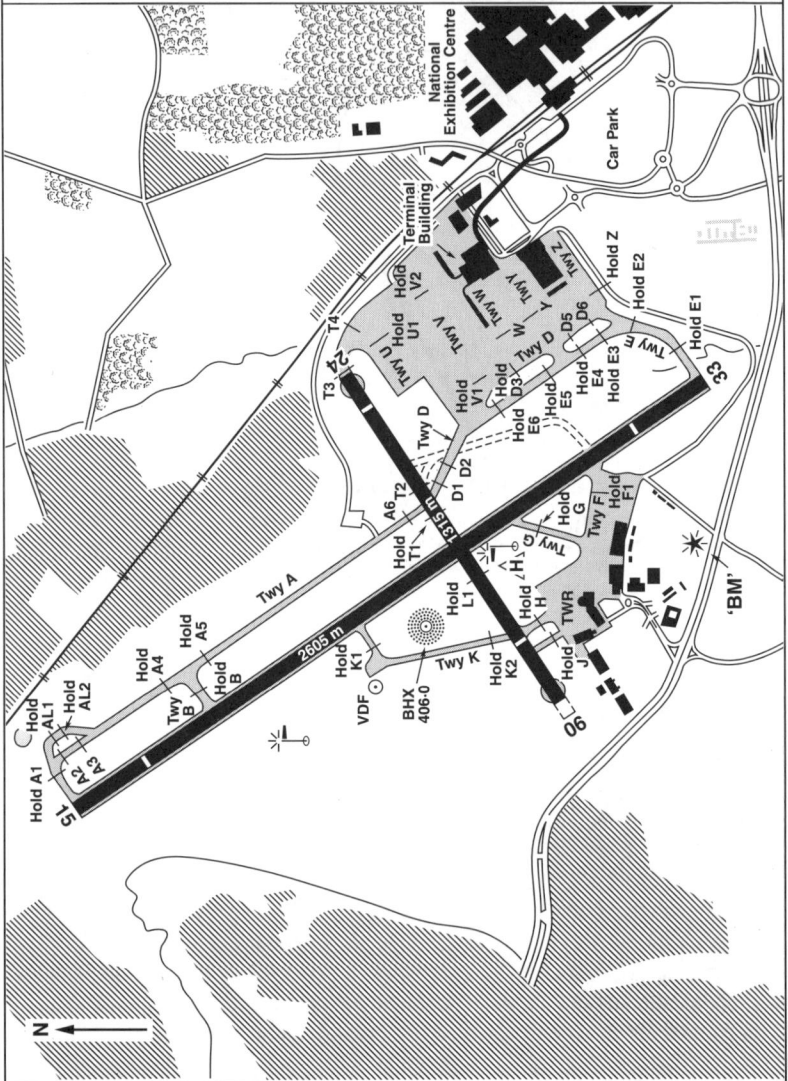

Rwy	Dim(m)	Surface	TORA(m)	LDA(m)	Lighting
06/24	1315x30	Asphalt	06-1260	06-1025	APAPI 3·5°
			24-1315	24-1188	PAPI 3·5°
15/33	2605x46	Asphalt	15-2575	15-2279	Ap Thr Rwy RCL PAPI 3°
			33-2600	33-2304	Ap Thr Rwy RCL PAPI 3°
					IBn 'BM' Gn

Op hrs: H24.

Met: H24.0121-717-0580.	**Customs:** Available

Landing Fees: £9.71 per tonne or part. For departures between 2300 to 1000 hrs and 1600 to 1900 hrs, a minimum charge equivalent to 10 tonnes MTWA will apply.

Hangarage: Limited.	**Maintenance:** Available.

Remarks: Operated by Birmingham International Airport Ltd. Flights within the Birmingham CTR/CTA are governed by regulations applicable to Class 'D' Controlled Airspace — see pages 2 and 6. Clearance for Special VFR flights below 1500 ft ALT will not be given in sector 240°T to 360°T within the CTR.

Non radio aircraft and training flights strictly PPR.

Training aircraft must climb straight ahead to 1000 ft QFE before turning unless otherwise instructed.

Visual Circuits Approaches: Propeller driven aircraft MTWA 5700 kg or less, the minimum height for joining the final approach track is 1000 ft QFE for all approaches. For other category aircraft, the minimum height is 1500 ft QFE, except for right hand visual circuits to Rwy 33 when the minimum height for joining the final approach track will be 900 ft QFE.

Circuit height for GA aircraft 1000 ft, circuit direction as instructed by ATC.

A Ground Movement Control (GMC) operates 0700-2100 local on 121·80.

Within the Manoeuvring Area, pilots will be cleared under GMC. ATC instructions will normally specify taxi route to be followed. Requests for taxying or towing clearance to GMC should state their location in the initial call.

Mandatory Handling for all Business and GA Aircraft. Handling agencies are:

Execair	Tel: 0121-782 1999	Fax: 0121-782 1899;
Midland Airport Services	Tel: 0121-767 7715	Fax: 0121-782 0530;
Servisair	Tel: 0121-767 7772	Fax: 0121-782 7766;
British Airways	Tel: 0121-767 7518	Fax: 0121-767 7590;
Groundstar	Tel: 0121-767 7996	Fax: 0121-767 7849.

Marshalling mandatory for all parking on the Western Apron.

Restaurant: Full restaurant service available.

Car Hire: Hertz, 0121-782-5158. Avis, 0121-742-6183. Europcar, 0121-742-6507.

Fuel: 100LL, Jet A1. Multi Service.	**Tel:** 0121-767 5511 Airport 0121-780 0906 ATC 0121-767 7139/7153 Ops Duty Mgr. 0121-780 0907 FBU 0121-782 2486 ATIS **Fax:** 0121-782 8802 Airport 0121-780 0917 ATC

Robert Pooley ©

N51 19·43 W000 50·85	**BLACKBUSHE**	329 ft AMSL

2 nm W of Camberley	OCK 115·30 279 15·0. CPT 114·35 131 17·2

c/s Blackbushe Information/Radio. 122·30 AFIS/A/G. Farnborough RAD 125·25.
Air Hanson Ops 130·37. NDB 'BLK' 328·0 (on A/D). DME 'BLC' 116·20 (on A/D)

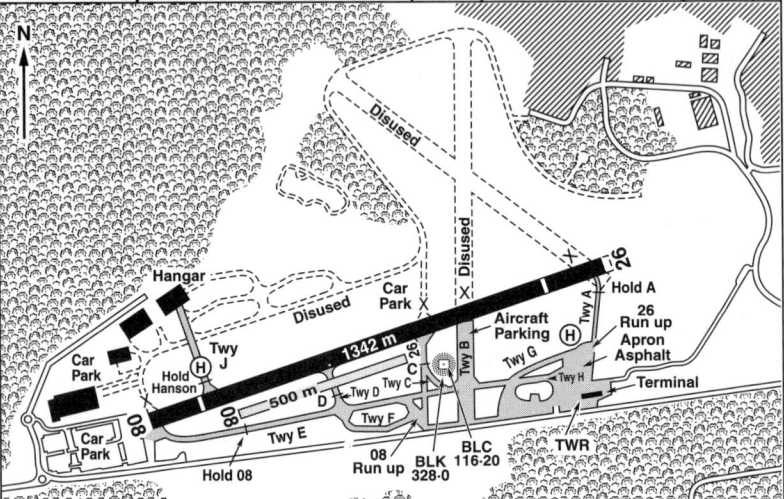

Rwy	Dim(m)	Surface	TORA(m)	LDA(m)	Lighting
08/26	1342x46	Asphalt	08-1237	08-1102	Thr Rwy PAPI 3°
			26-1237	26-1065	Thr Rwy PAPI 3°
08/26	500x18	Grass	08-500	08-500	Nil
			26-500	26-500	Nil
				Helipad	CHAPI 5°
					ABn Wh

Op hrs: 0800-1800 daily (0700-0800 & 1800-2200 PNR).

Landing Fee: Singles from £14.89 plus VAT (discount for fuel uplift and club aircraft).

Customs: EC - 4 hrs PNR; others 24hrs PNR.

Hangarage: Limited (Air Hanson).   **Maintenance:** On request

Remarks: Operated by Blackbushe Airport Ltd. Visiting aircraft welcome. Prior permission by telephone or radio. The Eastern limit of the licensed area is indicated by standard boundary markers. Radar assistance may be available from ATC Farnborough to aircraft in IMC on 125·25. Circuits LH on 26, RH on 08; SE aircraft at 800', twins & executive aircraft at 1200'. At night the circuit height is 1000' for all a/c.
PAPI signals for Rwys 08 & 26 are visible to the South of extended centrelines and should not be used until the aircraft is aligned with the runway. Visual Arr/Dep should at all times avoid the following Exclusion Areas: HARTLEY WINTNEY, YATELEY, EVERSLEY, HAZELEY, MATTINGLEY AND BRAMSHILL— see Area Chart opposite.
Note:
• A/D often active outside published Op hrs; call AFIS on 122·30 at all times.
• Pilots are responsible for their passengers whilst airside. High visibility clothing required.
• A/D not licensed on some Public Holidays.Check with Tower what services are available.
Restaurant: Club restaurant facilties available plus the 'Auctioneer' fully licensed restaurant in the BCA Auctions Complex.
Car Hire: Europcar Tel: 01483-757007.

Fuel: 100LL, Jet A1	**Tel:** 01252-873338 Twr. 879449 Admin.
Diners, Access, VISA, AMEX , Multi-Service.	01252-890089 Air Hanson

Robert Pooley ©

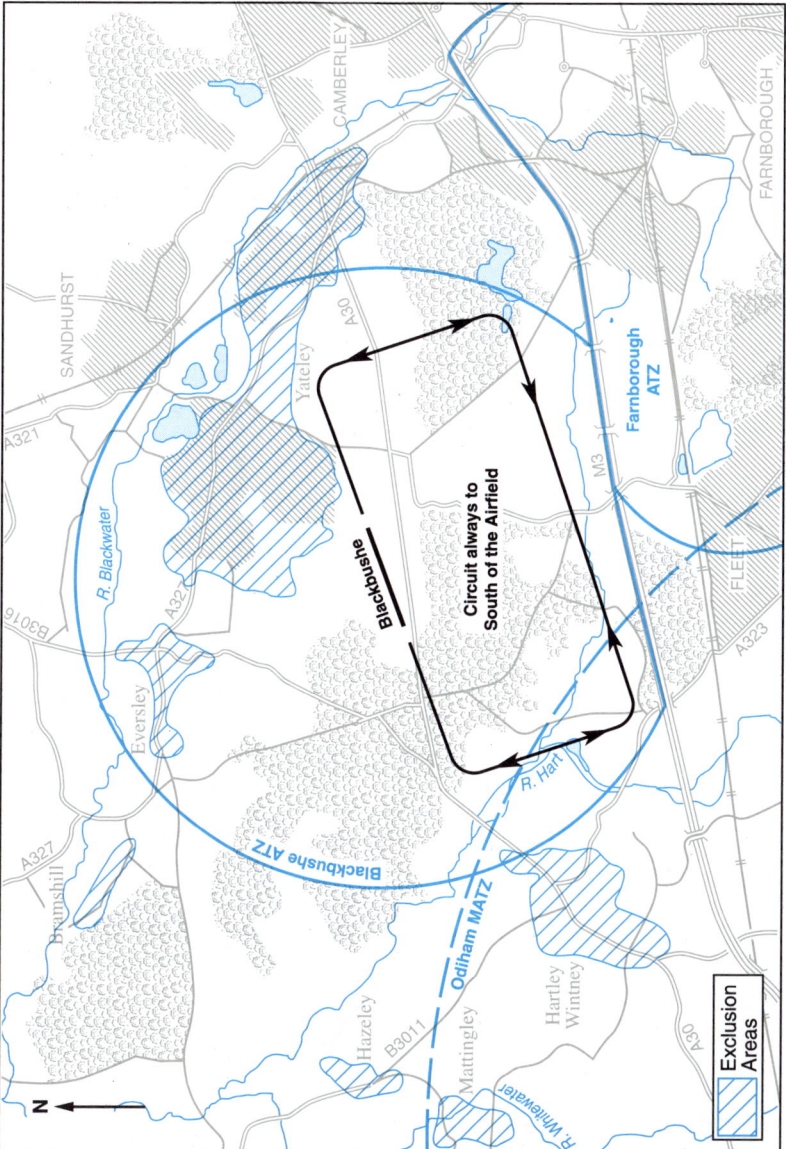

CAMBERLEY

FARNBOROUGH

SANDHURST

A30

Yateley

Farnborough
ATZ

A321

M3

A321

R. Blackwater

Blackbushe

Circuit always to
South of the Airfield

FLEET

B3016

A323

Eversley

R. Hart

A327

Blackbushe ATZ

Bramshill

Odiham MATZ

Hazeley

Hartley
Wintney

A30

B3011

Mattingley

R. Whitewater

N

Exclusion Areas (shown in broad cross hatch) to be avoided at all times. All circuits
to the South of runway, as shown above, at 800 ft QFE for light aircraft and training aircraft; at
1200 ft for twins and executive aircraft.
Note proximity of **Farnborough ATZ** and **Odiham MATZ**.

Exclusion
Areas

125

N53 46·30 W003 01·72 **BLACKPOOL** 34 ft AMSL

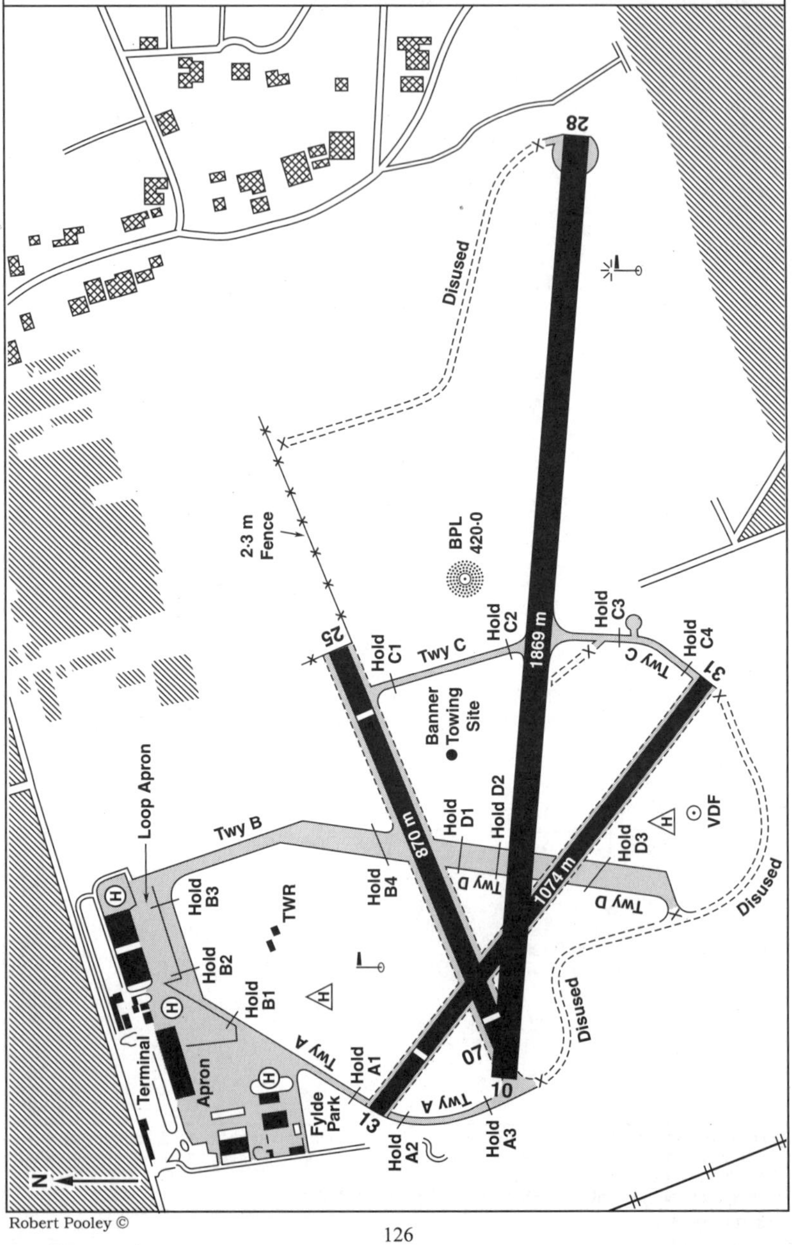

28
Disused
2·3 m
Fence
BPL
420·0
25
Hold
C1
Twy C
Hold
C2
1869 m
Hold
C3
Twy C
Hold
C4
31
Banner
Towing
Site
Loop Apron
Twy B
Hold
B4
870 m
Hold
D1
Hold D2
Twy D
1074 m
Hold
D3
VDF
Twy D
Disused
Hold
B3
TWR
Hold
B2
Hold
B1
Twy A
Hold
A1
07
10
Twy A
Disused
Terminal
Apron
Fylde
Park
13
Hold
A2
Hold
A3
N

Robert Pooley ©

| N53 46·30 W003 01·72 | **BLACKPOOL** | 34 ft AMSL |

2·6 nm SSE of Blackpool   **WAL 114·10 015 23·1. MCT 113·55 318 37·2**

APP 119·95. TWR 118·40. RAD 119·95. VDF 118·40. 119·95. ATIS 121·75.
NDB 'BPL' 420·0 (On A/D). ILS/DME Rwy 28 (281°M) I-BPL 108·15.

Rwy	Dim(m)	Surface	TORA(m)	LDA(m)	Lighting
10/28	1869x46	Asphalt	10-1869	10-1869	Ap Thr Rwy PAPI 3°
			28-1869	28-1869	Ap Thr Rwy PAPI 3°
13/31	1074x23	Asphalt	13-1074	13-934	Thr Rwy APAPI 4°
			31-1074	31-1074	Thr Rwy APAPI 3·25°
07/25	870x30	Asphalt	07-760	07-730	Nil
			25-820	25-760	Nil

Op hrs: 0700-2100 daily.   **Met:** H24. 0161-429-0927   **Customs:** 24hrs PNR.

Landing Fee: Under 500 kg £6.00; 501–1000 kg £12.00; 1001–1500 kg £18.00;
1501– 2000 kg £24.00; 2001–2500 kg £30.00; 2501-5000 kg – 20% discount on
standard landing fees. All charges incl VAT and cash on the day. Min invoice £35.25.

Hangarage: Limited.   **Maintenance:** Fixed wing (limited), and light helicopters.

Remarks: Operated by Blackpool Airport Ltd.   Aircraft using Blackpool Airport are to
carry third party insurance cover of not less than £1,000,000.
Non-radio aircraft PPR. Landing on grass areas by fixed wing aircraft is prohibited.
A light aircraft parking area known as 'Fylde Park' is situated on the grass area North
of Rwy 13 undershoot.
All instrument and VFR training to be booked through ATC; the filing of a flight plan
does not constitute a booking to carry out training. All departures must be booked out
with ATC by telephone.

Circuits: RH on 25, 28 and 31; LH on 07, 10 and 13.

VFR Flights
VFR Reference Points:
South — MARSHSIDE; **SE —** WARTON A/D; **East —** KIRKHAM; **ENE —** INSKIP;
NE — POULTON; **North —** FLEETWOOD. Pilots must be prepared to route clear of
Instrument approaches to Rwy 10/28 when so instructed by ATC.
All VFR arrivals must always contact Warton LARS 129·525 in the first instance.
Pilots must be prepared to route via VRP as instructed by ATC.

Helicopter Operations
Two helicopter aiming points marked with an 'H' (depicted opposite) are located:
(1) **H North**—140 m west of ATC Tower;
(2) **H South**—75 m east end of disused Rwy 20.

Parking: The helicopter parking stands known as 'Blackpool Park' are marked on the
paved surface immediately to the south of main apron for visiting helicopters;
Air taxying on the main apron is not permitted except with the approval of ATC and
under the guidance of a marshaller.

Fuel: 100LL not available to helicopters without wheels for ground handling.

Arr/Dep Routes: Helicopters arriving and departing VFR, in addition to routing via
the published VFR Reporting Points, may be asked to route via the following
positions: St Annes Pier – 185°T/1·5 nm;   Gasometers – 037°T/1·8 nm;
Blackpool Tower – 338°T/2·6 nm

Restaurant: Restaurant, Bar and Club facilities available.

Taxi: Blacktax (Freephone in Terminal).

| **Fuel:** 100LL (Helis- see Heli Ops above), | **Tel:** 01253-343434 Airport. Ext 8212 ATC |
| Jet A1.   Diners, Multi Service | **Fax:** 01253-405009; 402004 ATC. |

N50 29·98 W004 39·95	**BODMIN**	625 ft AMSL
3·5 nm NE of Bodmin	LND 114·20 067 43·0. BHD 112·05 284 45·3	
	SMG 112·60 081 14·3	

c/s Bodmin Radio. 122·70 A/G.
(If radio unmanned please transmit normal circuit calls)

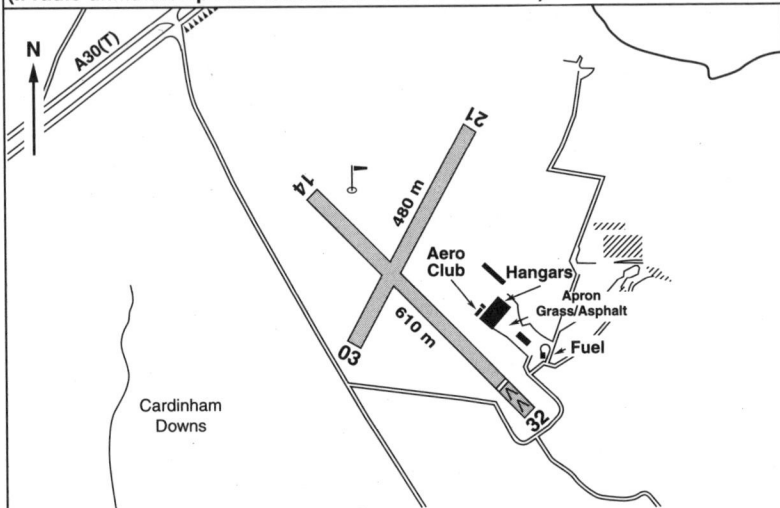

Rwy	Dim(m)	Surface	TORA(m)	LDA(m)	Lighting
14/32	610x18	Grass	14-598	14-598	Nil.
			32-610	32-540	Nil.
03/21	480x18	Grass	03-480	03-480	Nil.
			21-480	21-480	Nil.

Op hrs: PPR. Winter: 0830-1730 or SS. Summer: 0830-1930,and by arrangement.

Landing Fee: Singles £6.00. Twins £8.00. All Commercial Flights £15.00.

Hangarage: £5 per night.   **Maintenance:** Available.   **Customs:** 24 hrs PNR.

Remarks: Licensed airfield operated by Cornwall Flying Club Ltd. Strictly PPR by telephone. No night flying. Runways delineated by centreline marking. Rwys 32 and 03 LH circuit and Rwys 14 and 21 RH circuit; both at 800 ft. Intensive flying training. Inform St. Mawgan App 126·50, crossing W00420.

Warning: In strong wind conditions windshear and turbulence may be encountered on the approaches to all runways. Downdraught effect and sudden changes in surface wind velocity are possible in light wind conditions in summer months due to the effect of sea breezes from both coasts.

Down gradient on Rwys 14 and 21.

Exercise extreme caution taxiing to apron and refuelling area; centre-line to obstruction restricted to 8 m at the minimum semi-width of the taxiway.

Large vehicles use the road passing through the undershoot area to Rwy 03. The road is within 40m of the marked threshold on the runway extended centreline.

High Ground 385' aal, 1010' amsl 048°/3·8 nm, and 267' aal, 892' amsl 070°/1·8 nm.

Pilot's Shop; Bar; Good Food available.   **Car Hire:** 01208- 72354 or 73000.

Fuel: 100LL.	**Tel:** 01208- 821419/821711.
	Fax: 01208- 821711.

BOURN

N52 12·62 W000 02·57		225 ft AMSL
7nm W of Cambridge.	BPK 117·50 010 28.	BKY 116·25 349 14·0
		CFD 116·50 074 22·5

c/s Bourn Radio 129·80 A/G. NDB 'BOU' 391·5 (on A/D).

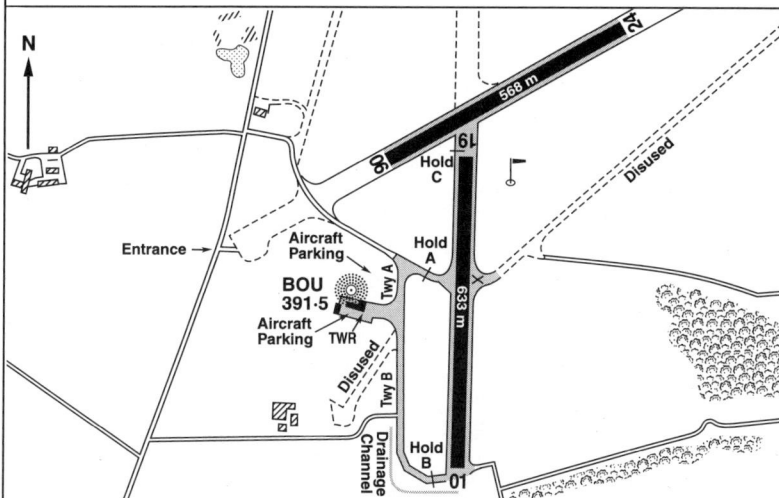

Rwy	Dim(m)	Surface	TORA(m)	LDA(m)	Lighting
01/19	633x18	Asphalt	01-633	01-633	Nil.
			19-633	19-633	Nil.
06/24	568x18	Asphalt	06-568	06-568	Nil
			24-568	24-568	Nil

Op hrs: PPR. Winter: 0930-1700 or SS. Summer: 0930-1800. O/T by arrangement.

Landing Fees: Singles £5.00. Multi £10.00. Micros & Ultras £1.00. (Any exotic, interesting, historic or unusual flying machines FREE if a 'fly-by' is given).

Hangarage: Nil. Parking limited.   **Maintenance:** Nil.   **Customs:** 24 hrs PNR.

Remarks: Operated by Rural Flying Corps. PPR. Licensed aerodrome located on Southern part of disused airfield. Not licensed for public transport passenger flights. A/D subject to closure at short notice for activities of a non-aviation nature, hence PPR essential. Rwy 01/19 gradient UP South to North. Culvert (orange/white markers) across undershoot Rwy 01 and ditch adjacent to S edge of Western loop taxiway. No engine run-up/power checks on the taxiway South of the visiting A/c park. Variable circuits, at 1,000ft. AAL, climb to 700ft. before turning cross-wind.
On departure climb straight ahead to 1,000ft. AAL before proceeding on course.
Caution: Gliding takes place at Gransden Lodge 3 nm SW of airfield, winch launch up to 3000 ft.

Note: A/D closed for Rwy Maintenance on all Bank Holiday Mondays.

Restaurant: Friendly cup of coffee/tea always available.

Car Hire: By arrangement, Cambridge (15 mins)

Fuel: Not available to visitors.	**Tel/Fax:** 01954-719602.

EGHH

1 DEC 00

N50 46·80 W001 50·55   **BOURNEMOUTH (Hurn)**   36 ft AMSL

3·5nm NNE of Bournemouth.   SAM 113·35 245 21·5

c/s Bournemouth. APP/RAD 119·625. TWR 125·60. GND 121·70. Dep ATIS 121·95.
NDB 'BIA' 339·0 (On A/D)
ILS/DME Rwy 08 (079°M) I-BMH 110·50. ILS/DME Rwy 26 (259°M) I-BH 110·50.

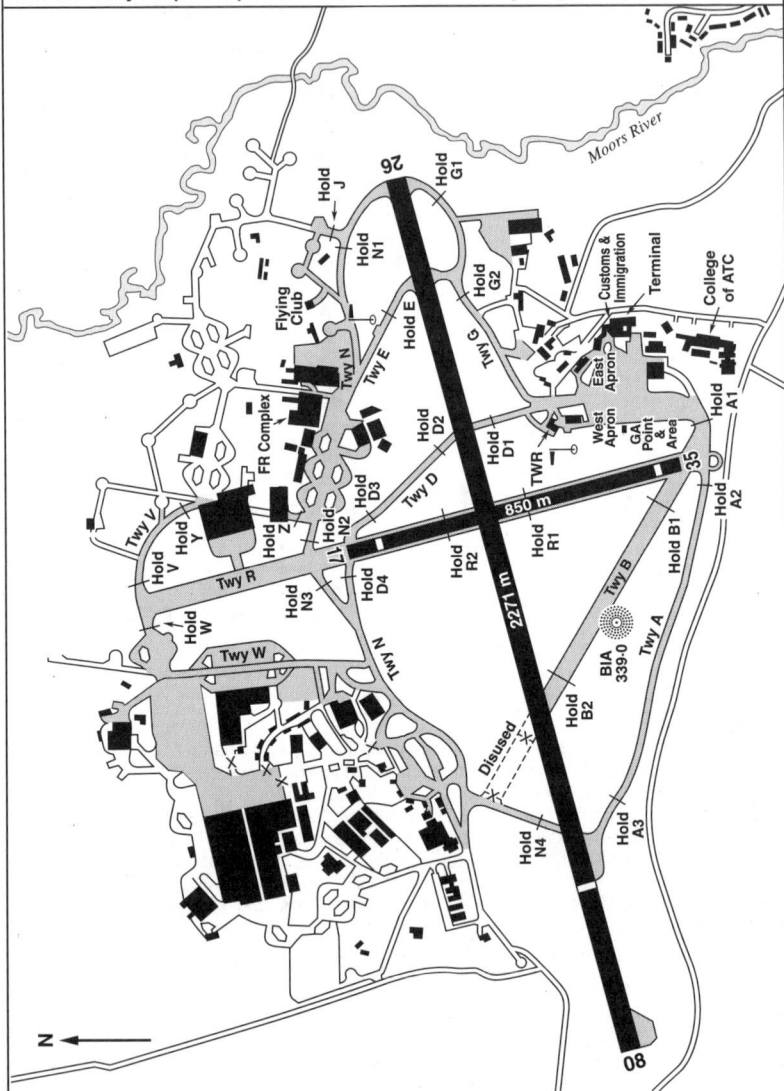

Robert Pooley ©

130

N50 46·80 W001 50·55 | | | **BOURNEMOUTH** | | 36 ft AMSL

Rwy	Dim(m)	Surface	TORA(m)	LDA(m)	Lighting
08/26	2271x46	Asphalt	08-2271	08-1838	Ap Thr Rwy PAPI
			26-2026 *	26-1970	Ap Thr Rwy PAPI
17/35	850x23	Asphalt	17-800	17-750	APAPI 3°
			35-750	35-800	APAPI 3°

* 2211 available on request, only three such departures permitted 0730-0900 and 16-1800.

Op hrs: 0630-2130 daily. O/T by arrangement. **Customs:** Available.

Landing Fees: Inclusive of navigational service charge. £14.50 per tonne MTWA or part thereof. Discount for 'cash on the day' available for aircraft up to 3.5 tonnes MTWA.
Parking Fees: First 2 hrs free, Rates per period of 24 hrs or part thereof: Not over 10 tonnes £10 flat rate; 10-20 tonnes £20 flat rate; over 20 tonnes £1 per tonne or part of. + VAT.

Hangarage: Available. **Maintenance:** Available. **Met:** H24. 01344-856267

Remarks: Operated by Bournemouth Intl. Airport Ltd. Non-radio aircraft strictly PPR. Within the Bournemouth CTR & Solent CTA, the Class 'D' Controlled Airspace regulations apply — see page 2. Visual Reference Points (VRPs) are listed below, also see CTR/CTA & VRPs Chart for Solent CTA at page 461.
Training flights subject to prior permission. Pilots using the west apron for parking are, after parking, to wait at the GA Point until transport to the main Terminal is available. They are also required to book in and out at the Operations Centre.
High visibility yellow clothing required on the airside areas.

Booking Out: Pilots should 'Book-out' by reporting to the Flight Clearance office in the Operations Centre, or by telephoning their details to the Flight Clearance office on telephone number 364152. The payment of landing fees at the Information Desk does not constitute a 'Book-out'. Because of the heavy R/T loading, pilots who attempt to 'Book-out' on the R/T may face extensive delays.

Handling: All aircraft carrying passengers for hire or reward, or carrying 5 or more passengers, or with a MTWA of 3 metric tonnes or greater that utilise the eastern or western apron and/or the terminal facilities are required to be handled by a handling agent approved by the airport authority. The airport's appointed handling agent is Servisair Plc Tel: 01202-364 252, Fax: 01202-364 253.

Ground Movements: All aircraft with a MTWA of 3 tonnes or greater intending to park on the eastern or western apron are to be under positive marshaller guidance prior to leaving the apron taxilane.

Circuit height: All aircraft less than 5700 kg AUW – 1000 ft aal;
All other aircraft and Jets – 1500 ft aal;
Circuit height after 2000 hrs local – 1500 ft aal for all aircraft.

Duty/Tax Free stores available 0900-1700 and on request

Restaurant: Self-Service Buffet & Bar facilities Tel: 01202-364160.

Car Hire: Freephones within main terminal for Hertz and Europcar.

Taxis: Airport licensed cabs stand at Taxi rank located outside Arrivals Hall.

VRPs are listed overleaf

Fuel: 100LL, Jet A1. Shell 01202-575037. ESSO 01202-594000.	**Tel:** 01202-364150 ATC/FBU 01202- 364170 Ops. **Fax:** 01202-364119 Admin; 364179 Ops. **Telex:** 41345.

BOURNEMOUTH

VISUAL REFERENCE POINTS (VRPs)

VRPs	VOR/NDB	VOR/DME
Hengistbury Head N50 42·72 W001 44·93	SAM R230 BIA 142°M	SAM R230/21nm
Sandbanks N50 41·00 W001 56·83	No suitable VOR/NDB	SAM R239/28nm
Stoney Cross (Disused A/D) N50 54·70 W001 39·42	SAM R262 BIA 045°M	SAM R262/12nm
Tarrant Rushton (Disused A/D) N50 51·00 W002 04·70	SAM R261 BIA 300°M	SAM R261/28nm

See VAD/VRP Chart for Solent CTA, Southampton CTR and Bournemouth CTR page 461.

N53 48·12 W000 54·85	**BREIGHTON**	20 ft AMSL
5·5 nm ENE of Selby		OTR 113·90 289 29·4
		GAM 112·80 008 31·2

Breighton Radio 129·80 A/G.

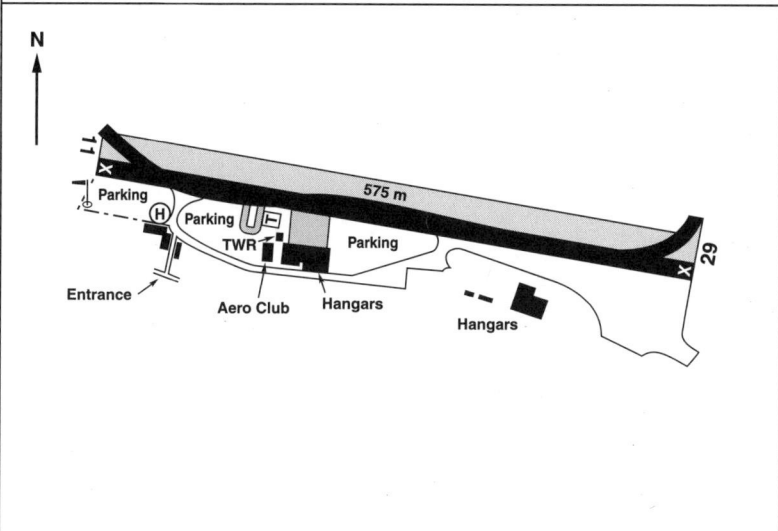

Rwy	Dim(m)	Surface	TORA(m)	LDA(m)	Lighting
11/29	575x30	Grass	Unlicensed		Nil

Op hrs: PPR. Mon-Fri 0830-1700; Sat & Sun 1000-SS.

Landing Fee: Nil.	**Customs:** Nil
Hangarage: Nil	**Maintenance:** M5.

Remarks: Operated by The Real Aeroplane Company Ltd.
Unlicensed aerodrome situated at SW corner of disused military airfield.
Home of Vintage and Classic aircraft.
Visiting aircraft, including non radio, welcome on prior permission and at pilot's own risk.
Circuits at 700' aal, LH on 29, RH on 11. Live side join required due to frequent aerobatic activity on north side of runway centreline.
Vintage & Classic aircraft especially welcome.

Caution: Power cables on western approach. Special rules apply on display days.

Refreshments & food at weekends.   Camping and Caravan space available.

Pub accommodation: 01757-630070.

Fuel: 100LL, Jet A1.	**Tel:** 01757-289065

Intentionally Blank

N51 23·03 W001 10·35	**BRIMPTON (Wasing Lower Farm)**	210 ft AMSL

5·5 nm ESE of Newbury	**SAM** 113·35 018 27.	**MID** 114·00 318 29
		CPT 114·35 168 6

c/s Brimpton Radio 135·125 A/G.

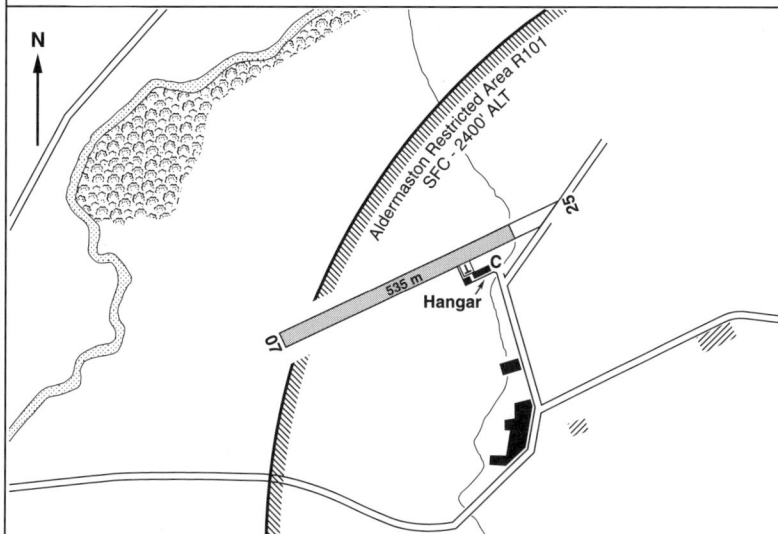

Rwy	Dim(m)	Surface	TORA(m)	LDA(m)	Lighting
07/25	535x25	Grass	Unlicensed		Nil

Additional 100 m available for take-off Rwy 25.

Op hrs: Strictly PPR by telephone, Alan House Tel: 01635-863433, 0836-775557.

Landing Fee: Singles £4.00; Twins £6.00.

Maintenance: Limited. **Hangarage:** Nil. **Customs:** Nil.

Remarks: Operated by Alan House Esq, Sylmar Aviation & Services Ltd., Kennet House, 77-79 Bath Road, Thatcham, Berks RG18 3BD. Unlicensed airfield. Strictly PPR, aircraft landing without PPR will incur a doubled landing fee.

Warning: Airfield is situated just within the NW edge of the Aldermaston Restricted Area - R101, and operates under a Special Exemption.
All approaches to the airfield must be from the North. Flying South of the airfield below 2400 ft agl prohibited.

Circuits at 800ft QFE, LH on Rwy 07, RH on Rwy 25.

Avoid overflying the villages of Brimpton, Aldermaston, Woolhampton and all local habitation close to the circuit.

Restaurant: Light snacks available in the clubhouse.

Taxis: Tadley Taxis 01734-816600.

Fuel: Nil	Tel: 01635-863433 Operator
	01635-866088 Sylmar Aviation
	0118-971 3822 Club, when manned

N51 22·97 W002 43·15	**BRISTOL AIRPORT**	622 ft AMSL

7 nm SW of Bristol.	**BCN 117·45 141 29**

c/s Bristol. APP 128·55. TWR 133·85. RAD 124·35 (when directed).
VDF 128·55. ATIS 126·025.
NDB 'BRI' 380·0 (On A/D).
ILS/DME Rwy 09 (093°M) I-BON 110·15. ILS/DME Rwy 27 (273°M) I-BTS 110·15.

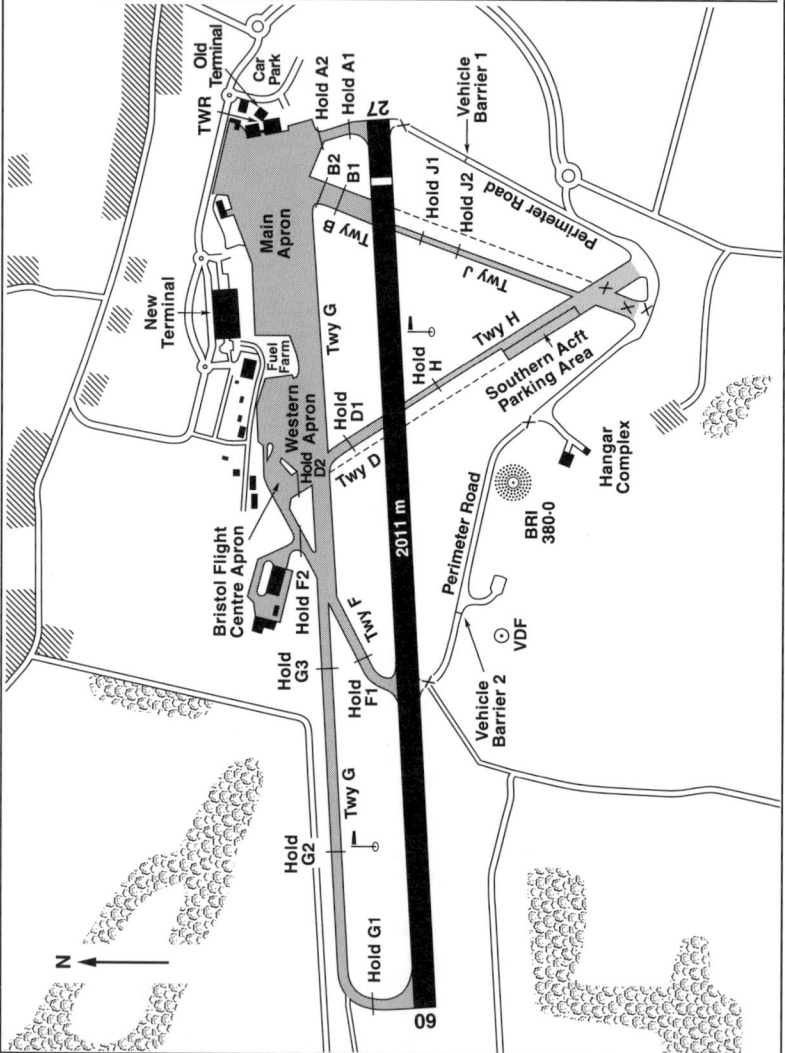

Old Terminal
Car Park
TWR
Hold A2
Hold A1
27
Vehicle Barrier 1
Hold J1
Hold J2
Perimeter Road
B2
B1
Twy B
Main Apron
Hold J2
Twy J
New Terminal
Fuel Farm
Twy G
Twy H
Hold H
Southern Acft Parking Area
Western Apron
Hold D2
Hold D1
Twy D
2011 m
Perimeter Road
Hangar Complex
BRI 380·0
Bristol Flight Centre Apron
Hold F2
Twy F
Hold G3
Hold F1
VDF
Vehicle Barrier 2
Hold G2
Twy G
N
Hold G1
09

N51 22·97 W002 43·15	**BRISTOL AIRPORT**			622 ft AMSL	

7nm SW of Bristol.				BCN 117·45 141 29	
Rwy	**Dim(m)**	**Surface**	**TORA(m)**	**LDA(m)**	**Lighting**
09/27	2011x46	Asphalt	09-2011	09-1938	Ap Thr Rwy RCL PAPI 3°
			27-2011	27-1876	Ap Thr Rwy RCL PAPI 3°

Op hrs: H24. Night Surcharge for all landings between 2200-0700.

Landing Fee: £6.75 per 500 kg up to 3000 kg, thereafter £3.25 per 1000 kg.

Hangarage: Limited.   **Maintenance:** Available.   **Customs:** Available.

Remarks: Operated by Bristol Airport Plc, Bristol Airport, Bristol BS48 3DY.

Flights within the Bristol CTR/CTA are governed by the regulations applicable to Class 'D' Controlled Airspace—see page 2.

VRPs are listed overleaf and Bristol/Cardiff CTRs/CTAs chart is at page 139.

Non- radio aircraft not accepted.

Instrument and circuit training strictly by prior permission.

Helicopter circuits at 700 ft QFE above the grass areas south of Rwy 09/27.

Aircraft using Bristol Airport are to carry third party insurance cover of not less than £500,000.

Mandatory handling for all aircraft. Handling Agents:

    Servisair Tel: 01275-472776, Fax: 01275-474514, and

    Bristol Flying Centre Tel: 01275- 474501, Fax: 01275-474851. - Handling surcharge applicable 2200-0700.

Fuel: 100LL available 0800-2000. Surcharge applies outside of these hours. 100LL for visiting aircraft only available from the Bristol Flying Centre.

Marshalling to stands and start-up procedure for all aircraft on Western and the Main aprons is under the guidance of the apron marshaller, following clearance from Aerodrome Control. GA aircraft will normally self park and start up on the Western apron and be handled by Clifton Operations, Freq 130·62. GA aircraft booking out can only be done via the Bristol Flight Centre.

Taxiway F closed to all aircraft above MTWA 25000 kg.

WARNINGS: Most grass areas unsuitable for aircraft parking.

Hot air balloon activity takes place in VMC and daylight hrs from Ashton Court, 4·5 nm NE of the aerodrome and downwind of the site.

Glider and hang glider activity along the Mendip hills to the south of the aerodrome.

Caution: Possible windshear/turbulence especially if wind is strong south easterly (using Rwy 09) or strong westerly (using Rwy 27).

Noise Abatement Procedures for Light Aircraft Operations: See overleaf

Restaurant: Restaurant, Refreshments and Club facilities available
                 Duty-Free Shop and 24 hour (airside) bar.

Car Hire: G. Davis 0117-922111. Avis 0117-9292123. Hertz 0117-9874441.

Fuel: 100LL - See Remarks above. Jet A1. Diners, Multi Service, Access, Visa, Amex.	**Tel:** 01275-474444 **Fax:** 01275-474800 **Fax:** 01275-474482 ATC

**Noise Abatement Procedures for Light Aircraft Operations and
Visual Reference Points (VRPs)**

Noise Abatement Procedures for Light Aircraft Operations:

Rwy 09:

Practice engine failures after take-off not permitted.

Circuits normally RH, but ATC may require non-standard circuit direction.

Avoid overflying Felton village whenever possible.

Aircraft requiring to turn left should climb ahead to 1 nm DME before commencing the left turn.

Rwy 27:

Arrange flight so as to minimise noise nuisance, and avoid manoeuvres which will attract attention to the aircraft.

Circuits normally LH.

Landing aircraft should maintain a descent path not lower than indicated by PAPI. Flying Instructors demonstrating visual and flapless approaches should aim for the aiming point markings which are 450m from displaced thld. The runway designator markings or displaced thld markings should not be used as aiming points.

────────────────────

Visual Reference Points (VRPs)

VRP	BRISTOL DME	VOR/NDB	VOR/DME
Bath N51 22·70 W002 21·42	13 nm	BCN R126 LA 244°M	BCN 126°/40 nm
Cheddar Reservoir N51 16·78 W002 48·08	7 nm	BCN R152 BRI 212°M	BCN 152°/32 nm
Chew Valley N51 19·50 W002 35·70	5 nm	BCN R139 BRI 130°M	BCN 139°/35 nm
Churchill N51 20·00 W002 47·60	4 nm	BCN R148 BRI 230°M	BCN 148°/29 nm
Clevedon N51 26·35 W002 51·08	6 nm	BCN R143 LA 267°M	BCN 143°/23 nm
East Nailsea N51 25·80 W002 44·10	2 nm	BCN R137° BRI 352°M	BCN 137°/26 nm
Hanham N51 26·93 W002 30·95	8 nm	BCN R125 BRI 066°M	BCN 125°/32 nm
Portishead N51 29·70 W002 46·42	6 nm	BCN R132 BRI 348°M	BCN 132°/23 nm
Radstock N51 17·53 W002 26·92	11 nm	BCN R135 LA 236°M	BCN 135°/40 nm
Weston-Super-Mare N51 20·70 W002 58·33	9 nm	BCN R159 BRI 262°M	BCN 159°/25 nm

Note. Aircraft entering the Bristol CTR/CTA via Portishead, Radstock or Cheddar VRPs may be required to hold at East Nailsea, Churchill or Chew Valley VRPs as appropriate.

CTR/CTA and VRPs Chart opposite

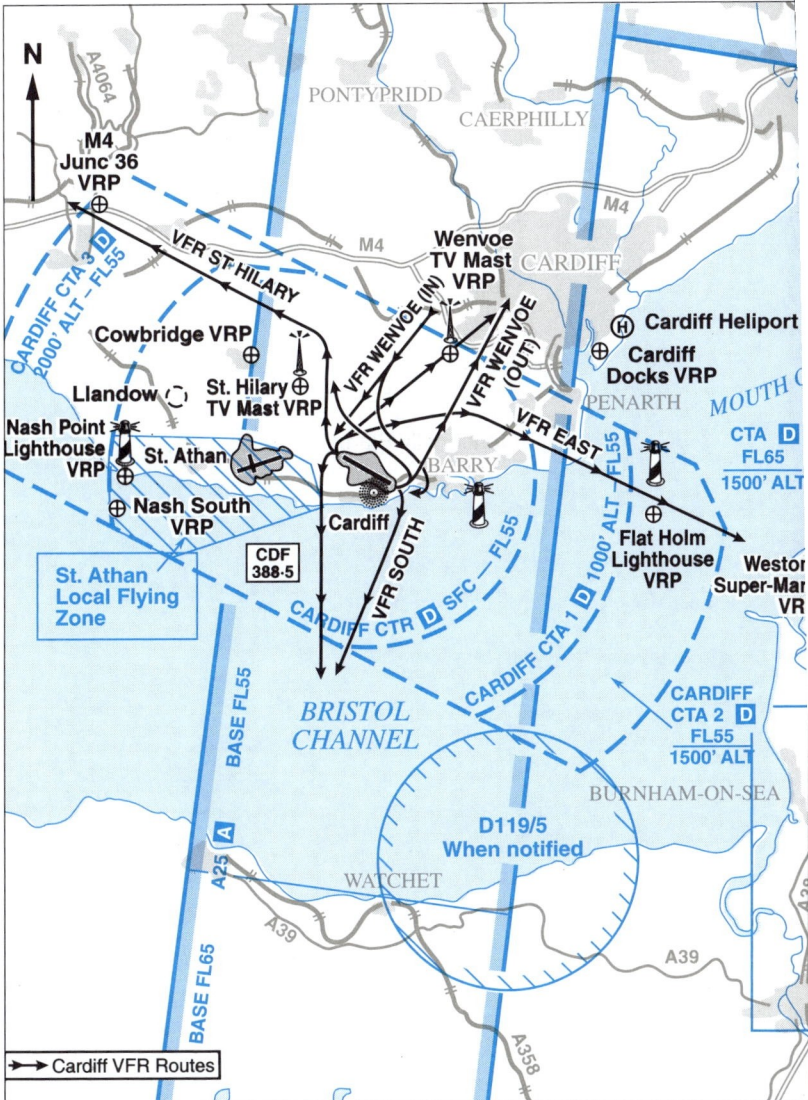

N

M4
Junc 36
VRP

A4064

PONTYPRIDD

CAERPHILLY

M4

M4

CARDIFF

VFR ST HILARY

CARDIFF CTA 3 D 2000' ALT – FL55

Cowbridge VRP

Wenvoe
TV Mast
VRP

VFR WENVOE (IN)

VFR WENVOE (OUT)

(H) Cardiff Heliport

Cardiff
Docks VRP

PENARTH

MOUTH (

Llandow

St. Hilary
TV Mast VRP

VFR EAST

CTA D
FL65
1500' ALT

Nash Point
Lighthouse
VRP

St. Athan

BARRY

Nash South
VRP

Cardiff

VFR SOUTH

CARDIFF CTR D SFC – FL55

CARDIFF CTA 1 D 1000' ALT – FL55

Flat Holm
Lighthouse
VRP

Weston
Super-Mar
VR

St. Athan
Local Flying
Zone

CDF
388·5

CARDIFF
CTA 2 D
FL55
1500' ALT

BASE FL55

BRISTOL
CHANNEL

D119/5
When notified

BURNHAM-ON-SEA

A25 A

WATCHET

A39

BASE FL65

A39

A358

→ Cardiff VFR Routes

Robert Pooley ©

Intentionally Blank

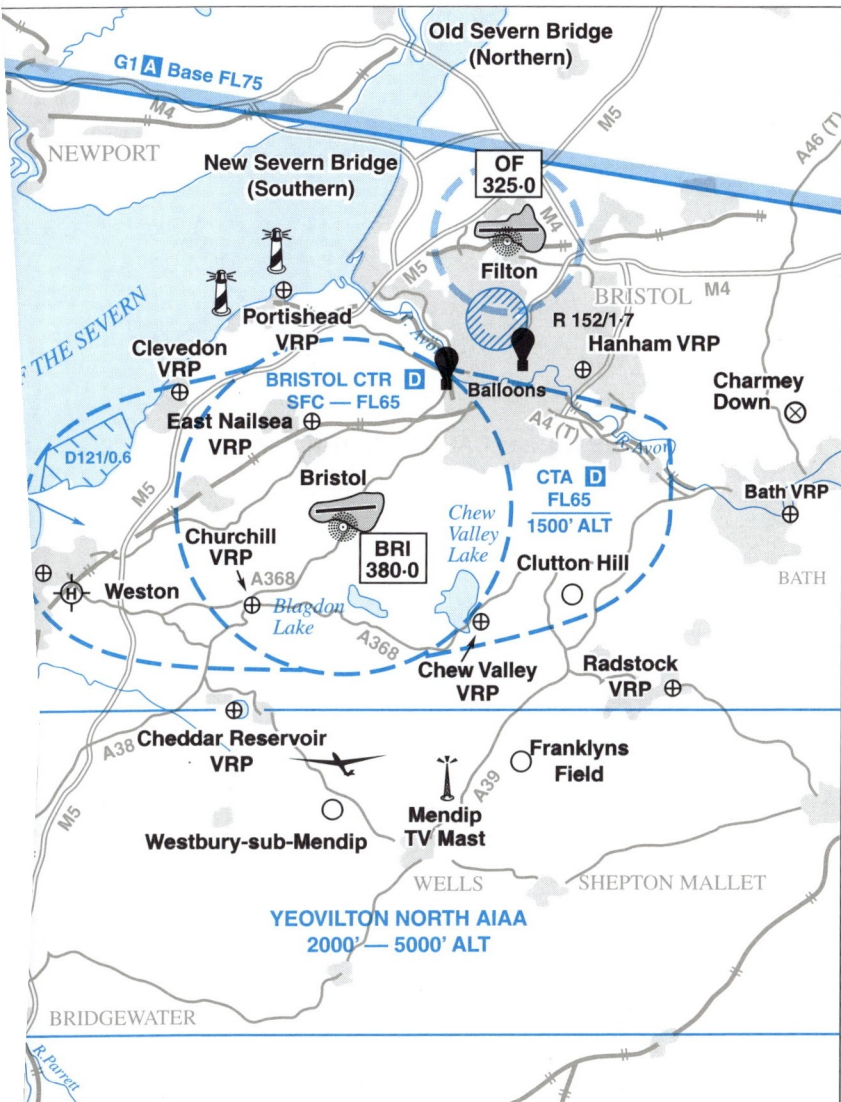

G1 **A** Base FL75

NEWPORT

Old Severn Bridge
(Northern)

New Severn Bridge
(Southern)

OF
325·0

Filton

BRISTOL M4

Portishead
VRP

R 152/1·7

Hanham VRP

Clevedon
VRP

BRISTOL CTR **D**
SFC — FL65

Balloons

Charmey
Down

East Nailsea
VRP

D121/0·6

Bristol

CTA **D**
FL65
1500' ALT

Bath VRP

Chew
Valley
Lake

Churchill
VRP

BRI
380·0

Clutton Hill

BATH

Weston

Blagdon
Lake

A368

A368

Chew Valley
VRP

Radstock
VRP

Cheddar Reservoir
VRP

A38

Franklyns
Field

A39

Westbury-sub-Mendip

Mendip
TV Mast

WELLS

SHEPTON MALLET

YEOVILTON NORTH AIAA
2000'— 5000' ALT

BRIDGEWATER

R Parret

1 DEC 00

BRISTOL and CARDIFF CTRs/CTAs
VFR Routes and VRPs

N51 45·00 W001 35·02	**BRIZE NORTON**	288 ft AMSL

12nm W of Oxford.	CPT 114·35 324 20·5
	DTY 116·40 219 31·0

Brize Radar 134·30 (LARS).   **ZONE 119·0** (Zone Transits).   **APP 127·25.**
TWR 123·72.   GND 121·725.   VDF 119·00, 121·725, 134·30.   Ops 130·075.
TACAN 'BZN' 111·90 (On A/D).   **NDB 'BZ' 386·0** (On A/D).
ILS Rwy 08 (078°M) **BZA 111·90.   ILS Rwy 26** (258°M) **BZB 111·90.**

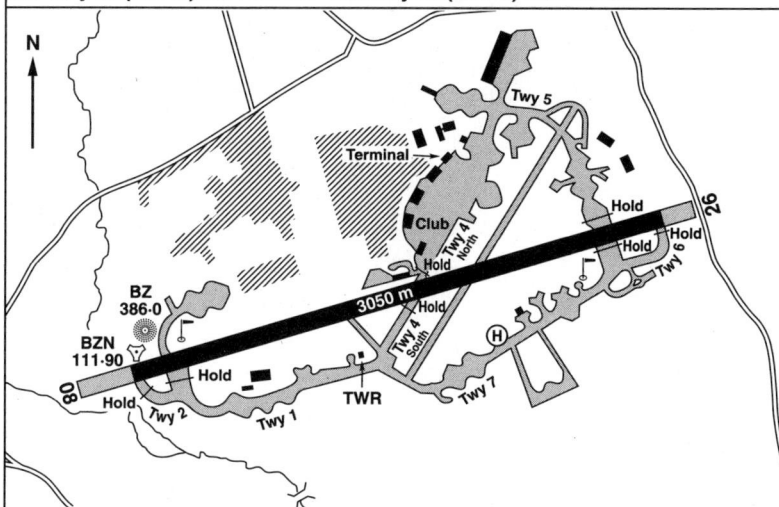

Rwy	Dim(m)	Surface	TORA(m)	LDA(m)	Lighting
08/26	3050x55	Asphalt	08-3050	08-3050	Ap Thr Rwy RCL PAPI 3°
			26-3050	26-3050	Ap Thr Rwy RCL PAPI 3°

Op hrs: HO. 24 hrs PPR. Visiting acft accepted 0800 hrs-1700 hrs Mon-Fri only.
CTR active H24.

Landing Fee: MoD(RAF) Rates.   **Hangarage/Maintenance:** Nil.   **Customs:** H24.

Remarks: Royal Air Force Aerodrome. Flights within the Brize Norton CTR are governed by the regulations applicable to the Class 'D' Controlled Airspace – see page 2.

Light aircraft will normally be required to enter or leave the Brize Norton CTR via the Burford or Faringdon VRPs. Arriving aircraft are to proceed at 1000' QFE directly from the VRPs as directed by Brize Tower.

Circuits as directed, circuit height 1500' QFE, light aircraft 1000' QFE, avoid Cotswold Wildlife Park, Shilton and Witney.

Free-fall parachuting SR-SS at short notice or by NOTAM.

ILS frequency paired DME indicates ranges to TACAN and not to threshold.

Visual Transit Flights and VRPs - see overleaf;   VRP Chart – see page 143.

Fuel: Jet A1. (100LL only by prior arrangement with Brize Norton Flying Club Ltd, Tel 01993-845886).	**Tel:** 01993-842551 Ext 7551 Ops., Ext 7433 – Private and Charter aircraft. ATIS 01993-842551 Ext 8818

VFR Transit Flights

Clearance to transit through the Control Zone may include routeing and/or altitude restrictions to enable VFR flights to be integrated with other traffic. Pilots should anticipate routeing and/or holding instructions via the VRPs listed below. Exceptionally, radar vectoring of VFR flights may be necessary for the effective integration of traffic.

Pilots are reminded of the requirement to remain in VMC at all times and to comply with the relevant parts of the Low Flying Rules. **Pilots must advise ATC if any time they are unable to comply with the instructions issued.**

Visual Reference Points

VRP	VOR/VOR	VOR/NDB	VOR/DME FIX
Bampton N51 43·50 W001 32·80	CPT R324 DTY R215	CPT R324 BZ 129°M	CPT 324°/19 nm
Burford N51 48·40 W001 38·20	CPT R325 DTY R225	CPT R325 BZ 344°M	CPT 325°/24 nm
Charlbury N51 52·30 W001 28·90	CPT R341 DTY R221	CPT R341 BZ 035°M	CPT 341°/25 nm
Faringdon N51 39·30 W001 35·20	CPT R310 DTY R214	CPT R310 BZ 179°M	CPT 310°/17 nm
Farmoor Reservoir N51 45·20 W001 21·40	CPT R347 DTY R204	CPT R347 BZ 093°M	CPT 347°/17 nm
Lechlade N51 41·60 W00 141·40	CPT R309 DTY R221	CPT R309 BZ 229°M	CPT 309°/21 NM
Northleach Roundabout N51 50·25 W001 50·15	CPT R317 DTY R237	CPT R317 BZ 306°M	CPT 317°/31 nm

CTR/VRPs Chart opposite

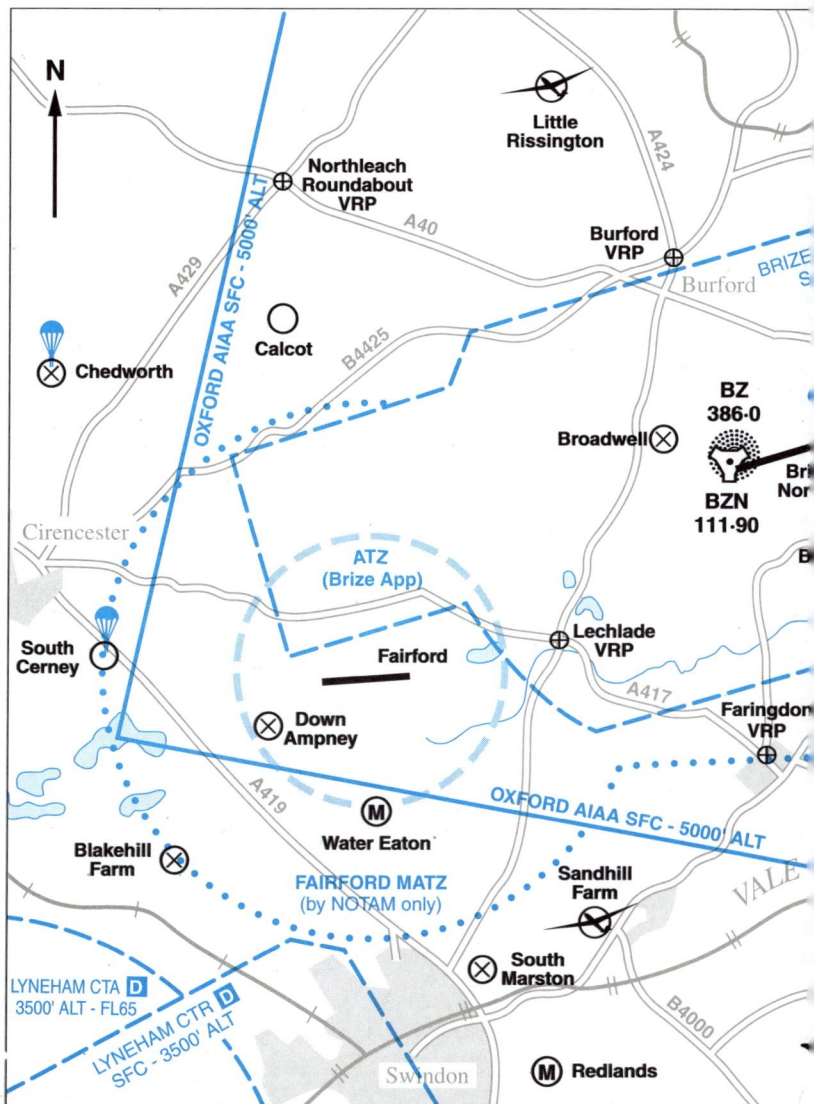

BRIZE
CTR an

N

Little
Rissington

Northleach
Roundabout
VRP

A40

A424

Burford
VRP

BRIZE
S

Burford

OXFORD AIAA SFC - 5000 ALT

A429

Calcot

B4425

Chedworth

BZ
386·0

Broadwell

Bri
Nor

BZN
111·90

Cirencester

ATZ
(Brize App)

Lechlade
VRP

A417

Faringdon
VRP

Fairford

South
Cerney

Down
Ampney

OXFORD AIAA SFC - 5000' ALT

(M) Water Eaton

Blakehill
Farm

FAIRFORD MATZ
(by NOTAM only)

Sandhill
Farm

VALE

South
Marston

B4000

LYNEHAM CTA D
3500' ALT - FL65

LYNEHAM CTR D
SFC - 3500' ALT

Swindon

(M) Redlands

Robert Pooley ©

Intentionally Blank

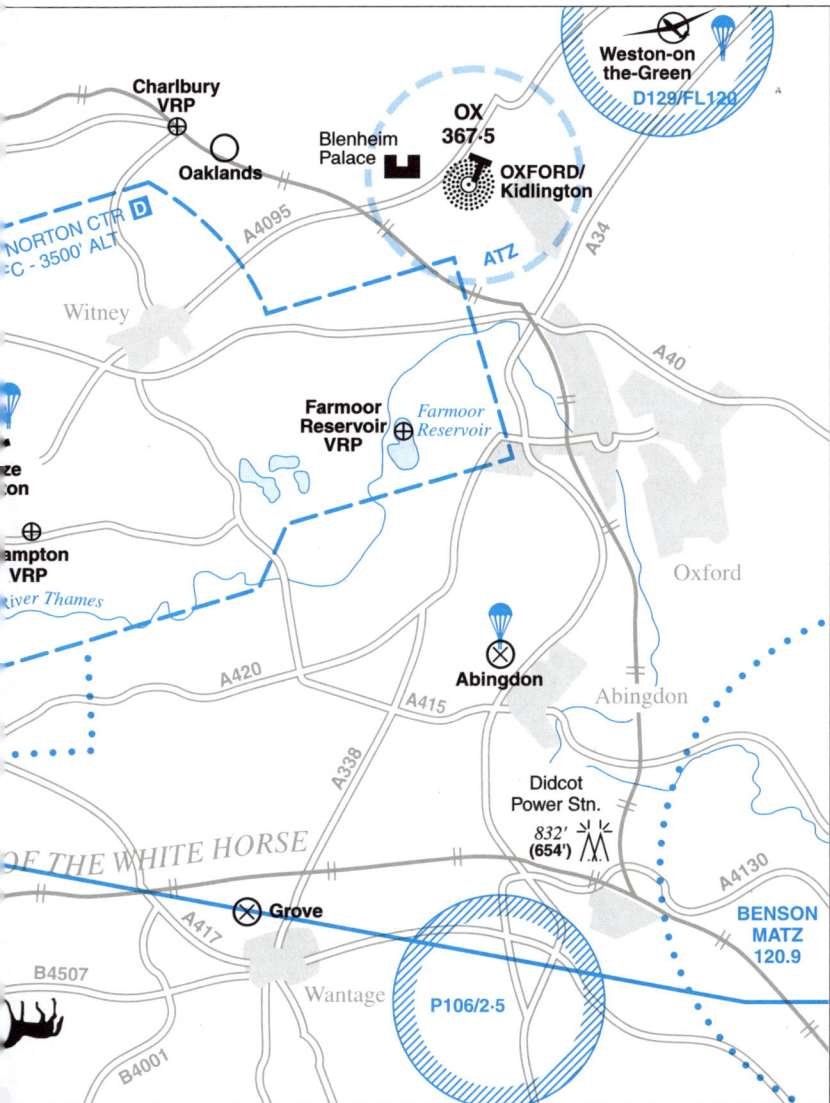

Charlbury
VRP

Oaklands

Blenheim
Palace

OX
367·5

OXFORD/
Kidlington

Weston-on
the-Green

D129/FL120

NORTON CTR **D**
FC - 3500' ALT

A4095

ATZ

A34

Witney

A40

Farmoor
Reservoir
VRP

*Farmoor
Reservoir*

ze
on

ampton
VRP

River Thames

Oxford

A420

A415

Abingdon

Abingdon

A338

Didcot
Power Stn.

832'
(654')

OF THE WHITE HORSE

A4130

BENSON
MATZ
120.9

Grove

A417

B4507

Wantage

P106/2·5

B4001

1 DEC 00

BRIZE NORTON
CTR and VRPs

N53 43·18 W000 33·98	**BROUGH**	12 ft AMSL

8 nm W of Hull	GAM 112·80 032 29·6
	OTR 113·90 280 16·7

Brough Radio 130·55 A/G.
NDB 'BV' 372·0 (To be used as Nav Aid only).

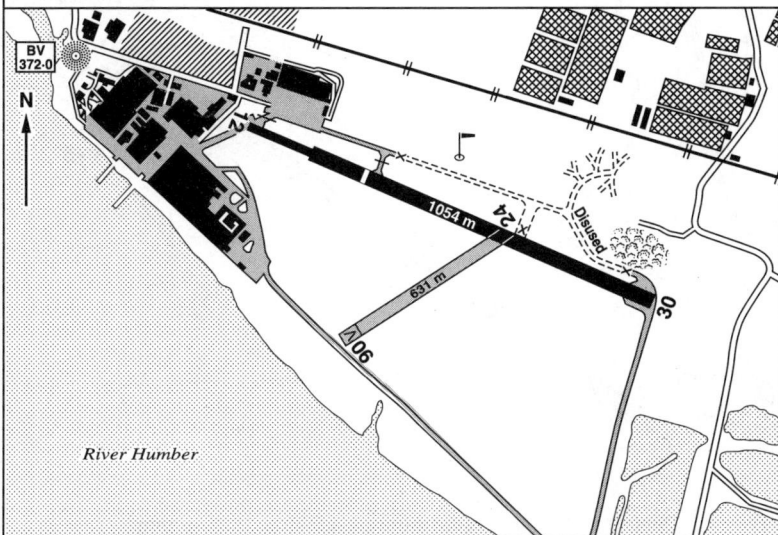

Rwy	Dim(m)	Surface	TORA(m)	LDA(m)	Lighting
06/24	631x18	Grass	06-631	06-571	Nil
			24-631	24-631	Nil
12/30	1054x30	† Asphalt	12 Unlicensed		Nil.
			30 Unlicensed		Nil.

† With Friction Course 192x18 m.

Remarks: Operated by BAe Systems Ltd, Brough, East Riding of Yorkshire HU15 1EQ.

Airfield closed to visiting aircraft. Facilities on care and maintenance.

Limited usage by Company aircraft.

Fuel: Nil.	**Tel:** 01482-666900.

N52 29·22 W001 07·83	**BRUNTINGTHORPE**	467 ft AMSL

6 nm S of Leicester.

DTY 116·40 003 18·4
HON 113·65 074 21

c/s Bruntingthorpe Radio 122·825 A/G - by arrangement.

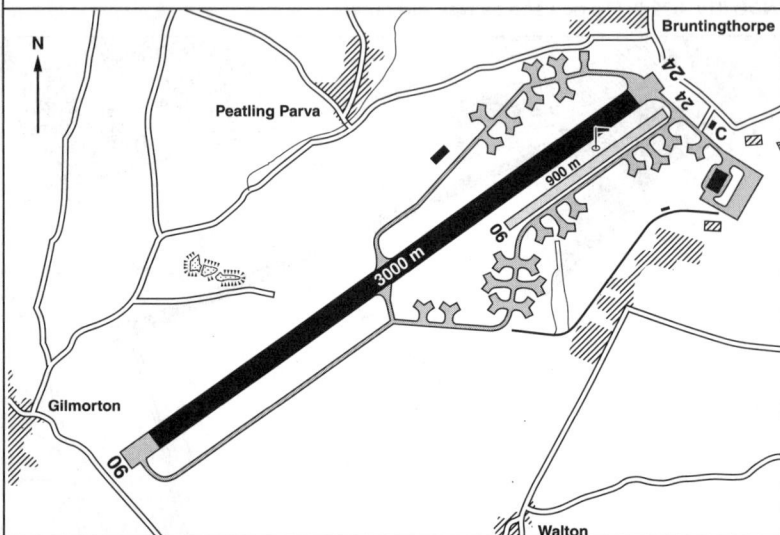

Rwy	Dim(m)	Surface	TORA(m)	LDA(m)	Lighting
06/24	3000x60	Asphalt	(06-2630	06-2630)	Nil
			(24-2630	24-2630)	Nil
06/24	900x25	Grass	Unlicensed		Nil
Advisory declared distances					

Op hrs: PPR.

Landing Fee: On application.   **Customs:** PNR.

Hangarage: Limited.   **Maintenance:** Nil.

Remarks: Operated by C. Walton Ltd., Bruntingthorpe, Nr Lutterworth, Leicester LE17 5QS, as an unlicensed aerodrome.

The aerodrome is used intensively by the Motor Industry for vehicle proving.

Visiting aircraft strictly by prior permission.

Extensive long term parking/storage facilities available for large aircraft etc.

Customs clearance available for civil aircraft over 8000 kg MTWA providing minimum stay of 30 days.

Fuel: Nil.	**Tel:** 0116 247 8030/40
	0116 247 8494 Security, 24 hrs.
	Fax: 0116 247 8031

N55 45·00 W005 03·00	**BUTE**	50 ft AMSL
1 nm W of Kilchattan Bay.		GOW 115·40 256 21·8
		TRN 117·50 347 27·6

No Radio.

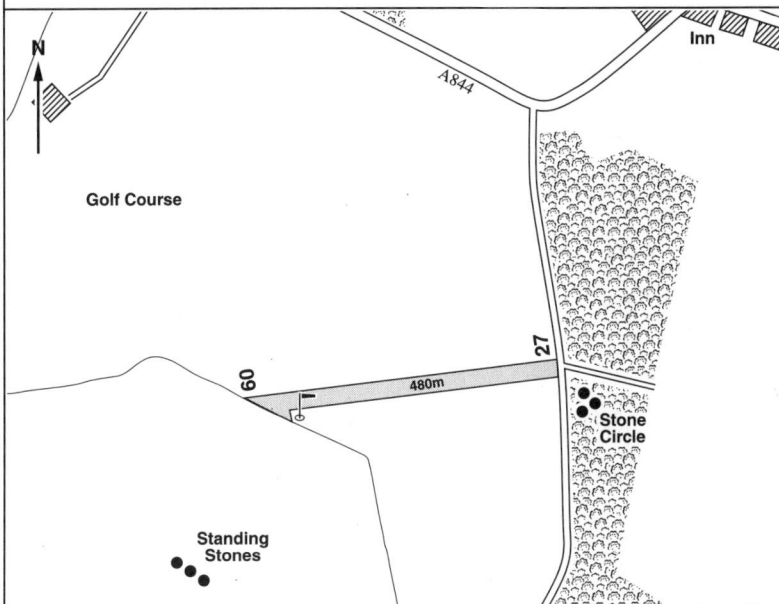

Rwy	Dim(m)	Surface	TORA(m)	LDA(m)	Lighting
09/27	480x23	Grass	Unlicensed		* Rwy Thr

Rwy 27 slopes down 1%.

* For Loganair Air Ambulance aircraft only.

Op hrs: Day light hours only. PPR.

Landing Fee: Nil.

Hangarage: Nil	**Maintenance:** Nil	**Customs:** Nil

Remarks: Operated by Bute Estate Ltd.,Estate Office, High Street, Rothesay, Isle of Bute PA20 9AX. Unlicensed airfield available during day light hours only.
PPR and at pilot's own risk.
All circuits to the North.
Caution when taxying due to runway edge and threshold lights.
Warnings: Trees border the final approach to Rwy 27. High ground to South East.

Restaurant: Inn nearby.

Taxis/Car Hire: Nil

Fuel: Nil.	**Tel:** 01700-502627 - Mon-Fri 0900-1700. **Fax:** 01700-502353.

Intentionally Blank

N53 06·25 W004 20·43		**CAERNARFON**			Sea Level
3·5nm SW of Caernarfon.				**WAL 114·10 255 46**	

c/s Caernarfon Radio. 122·25 A/G. NDB 'CAE' 320·0 (On A/D).
Valley APP 134·35. Llanbedr APP 122·50.

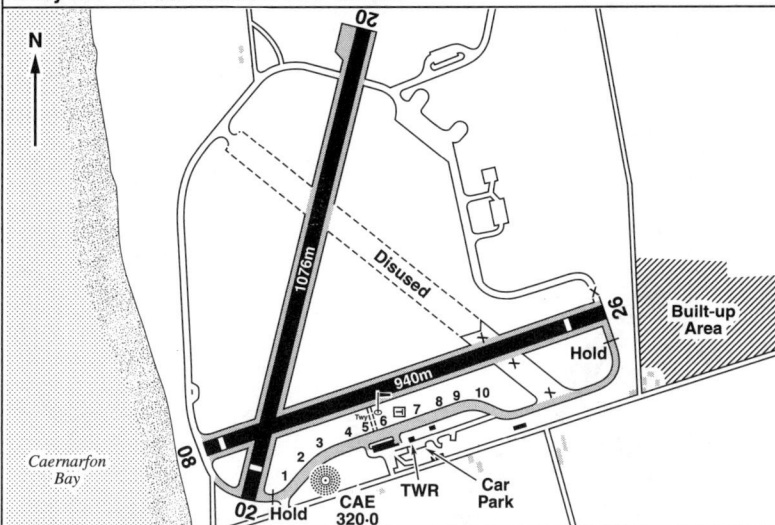

Rwy	Dim(m)	Surface	TORA(m)	LDA(m)	Lighting
02/20	1076x23	Asphalt	02-1076	02-1000	Nil
			20-1000	20-1076	Nil
08/26	940x23	Asphalt	08-920	08-885	Nil
			26-910	26-820	Nil
					IBn 'CN' Gn

Op hrs: Winter: 0900-1630; Summer 0900-1900; or by arrangement.

Landing Fee: Private from £10.00, others on application.

Customs: If required then 24 hrs PNR.

Hangarage: Limited.   **Maintenance:** CAMCO Tel: 01286-830782

Remarks: Operated by Caernarfon Air Park. Aerodrome is in the vicinity of Valley MATZ, and inbound aircraft should call Valley on 134·35 (aircraft inbound from the south should call Llanbedr on 122·50). Outbound aircraft call Valley on departure. Aircraft should transit the Menai Straits below 1500'.
Overhead joins at 1300 ft for 800 ft circuits, LH on 08 and 20, RH on 02 and 26.
All aircraft movements restricted to paved surfaces, grass areas are generally unsuitable, other than grass taxiway adjacent to windsock.

Noise Abatement Procedures: Helicopters must not overfly any caravan site within the ATZ below 1000 ft QFE.

TV Mast 1983' amsl 157°/5 nm. High ground beyond 6 nm SE of aerodrome rising to 3559' amsl.

Restaurant: Fully licensed. Tel: 01286-831600, and Coffee Shop.

Taxi: Tel: 01286-676091 (Visa, Access,Amex, Mastercard, Delta & Switch).

Fuel: 100LL, Jet A1.	**Tel:** 01286-830800; 830475 Flying Club.
	Fax: 01286-830280

Robert Pooley ©

1·5 nm E of Cambridge.   BKY 116·25 023 13·5. BPK 117·50 026 29
                                                    CLN 114·55 305 42

c/s Cambridge APP 123·60. TWR 122·20. RAD 124·975. VDF/Hmr. 123·60.
c/s Magnet Air 130·175.   NDB 'CAM' 332·50 (on A/D).
ILS/DME Rwy 23 (233°) 'I CMG' 111·30 .

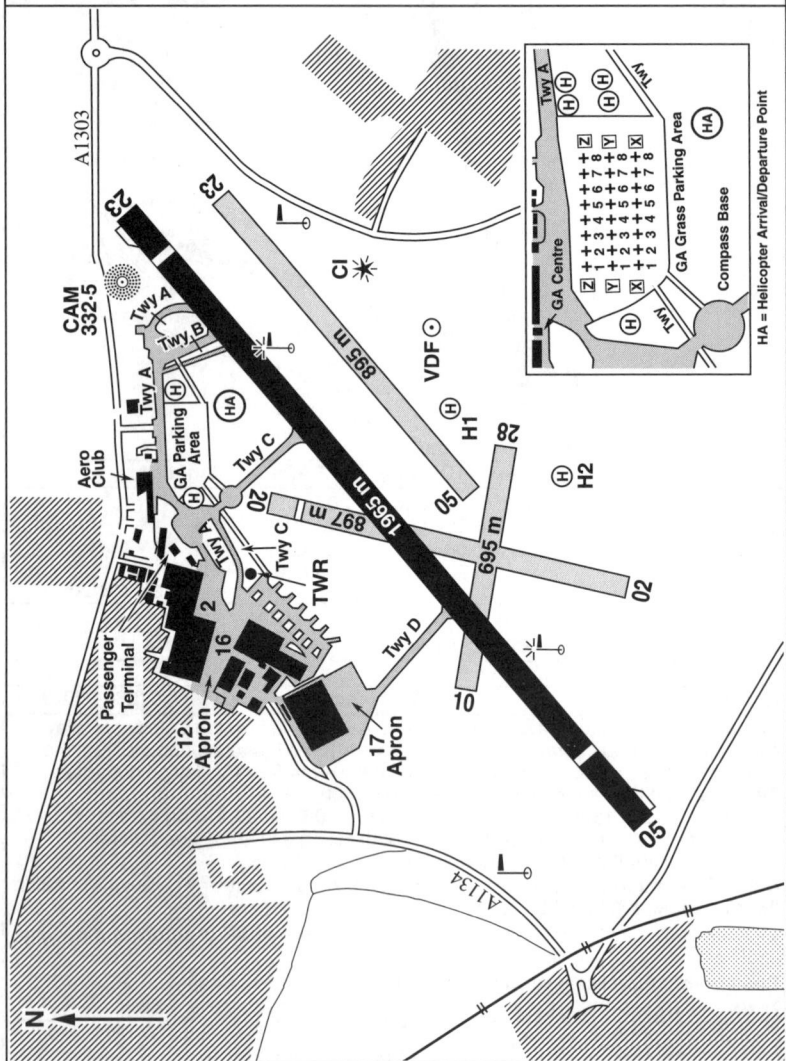

HA = Helicopter Arrival/Departure Point

N52 12·30 E000 10·50			**CAMBRIDGE**		50 ft AMSL
Rwy	**Dim(m)**	**Surface**	**TORA(m)**	**LDA(m)**	**Lighting**
05/23	1965x46	Asphalt	05-1852 23-1893	05-1668 23-1748	Thr Rwy PAPI 3° Ap Thr Rwy PAPI 3°
02/20	897x35	Grass	02-808 20-897	02-897 20-808	Nil Nil
05/23	895x35	Grass	05/23-895	05/23-895	Nil
10/28	695x35	Grass	10/28-695	10/28-695	Nil
					IBn 'CI' Gn

Op hrs: 0900-1800 daily.	**Customs:** Available.
Landing Fee: On application **Hangarage:** Limited.	**Maintenance:** Available.

Remarks: Operated by Marshall Aerospace, The Airport, Cambridge CB5 8RX.

Non radio aircraft not accepted. Microlights prohibited.

Aircraft must carry Third Party Insurance of not less than £500,000.

Light aircraft will be directed to the grass parking area in front of No 1 Hangar.

Parking is on a grid of three rows marked X,Y, Z and numbered 1-8 from west to east.

Runway control signals may be received from an orange and white caravan.

Aircraft taxying on grass areas are to keep to cut grass taxiways. The long grass areas are not inspected and are unfit for manoeuvring.

Go-around Procedure Rwy 05/23 Grass: Parallel runway operations may be in progress on Rwys 05/23 main and 05/23 grass. Subject to ATC instructions, aircraft going round from approaches to 05/23 grass must not fly north of the 05/23 grass centre-line.

High visibility clothing required when airside.

Noise Abatement Procedures in force - See UK AIP.

Avoid flying below 2000 ft (Cambridge QNH) within 3 nm of Cambridge City unless landing or taking off at Cambridge Airport.

Circuits at 1000 ft, LH on 20, 23 & 28; RH on 02, 05 & 10. Helicopters at 700 ft QFE.

Helicopters joins via one of three VRPs: "N'- Small lake/reservior 0·25 nm NE of Horningsea, 'E'- Plantation just south of A14 and 'S' - Golf course.

The preferred landing runway is Rwy 23. Aircraft approaching asphalt Rwy 05/23 visually are to follow a descent path from at least 1000 ft that is no lower than the normal approach path indicated by the PAPI.

The preferred take-off runway is Rwy 05. Aircraft requiring a left turn after take-off on Rwy 05 are to maintain runway hdg until at least 2000' aal. Aircraft requiring a right turn after take-off on Rwy 23 are to maintain runway hdg until at least 2000' aal.

Handling Agents: Magnet Air Services. Tel: 01223-293621.

Restaurant: Full restaurant service 1230-1400 Mon-Fri only.
                Vending machine at weekends.

Car Hire: Tel: 01223-373498, 01223-414600, 01223-365365

Fuel: 100LL: 0800 -1800; Jet A1/FSII: Mon-Fri 0800-1630, Sat, Sun & PHs by arrangement. Multi-Service & most other Credit Cards.	**Tel:** 01223-293737 ATC. 01223-373737 Switchboard. **Fax:** 01223-373502 ATC

Intentionally Blank

N55 26·23 W005 41·18	**CAMPBELTOWN**	44 ft AMSL

3 nm WNW of Campbeltown.   **TRN 117·50 292 32**

c/s Campbeltown Information 125·90 AFIS.

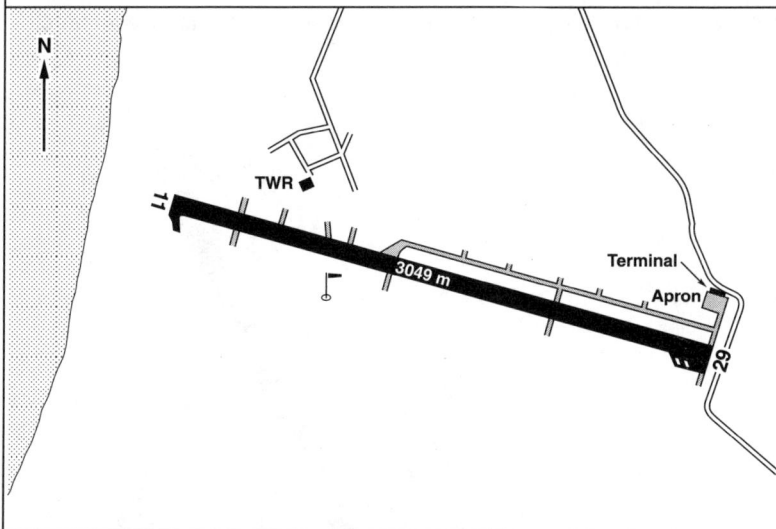

Rwy	Dim(m)	Surface	TORA(m)	LDA(m)	Lighting
11/29	3049x46	Concrete/ Asphalt	11-2899 29-2899	11-2727 29-2497	Ap Thr Rwy PAPI 3° Ap Thr Rwy PAPI 3°

Op hrs: PPR. Mon-Fri 0930-1730 and by arrangement.

Landing Fee: Highlands & Islands Rates.	**Customs:** Nil
Hangarage: Nil	**Maintenance:** Nil

Remarks: Operated by Highlands and Island Airport Ltd., Campbeltown Aerodrome, Campbeltown, Argyll PA28 6NU. All flights PPR.

Non-radio aircraft not accepted.

No ground signals.

Caution: • Bird activity may be seasonally high.
  • High ground, 1159 ft amsl 135°T/4 nm and 1465 ft amsl 230°T/5 nm.

Fuel: 100LL by arrangement or within 45 min request Tel: 01586-552372.	**Tel:** 01586-553797 AFIS **Fax:** 01586-552620 AFIS

Robert Pooley ©

153

EGFF

N5123·80 W00320·60

8.5 nm SW of Cardiff.

CARDIFF

1 DEC 00

220 ft AMSL

BCN 117·45 195 20

c/s Cardiff. APP/VDF 125·85. TWR 125·00. RAD 125·85, 124.10. ATIS 119·475.
NDB 'CDF' 388·50 (On A/D)
ILS/DME Rwy 12(122°M) I-CDF 110·70. ILS/DME Rwy 30(302°M) I-CWA 110·70.

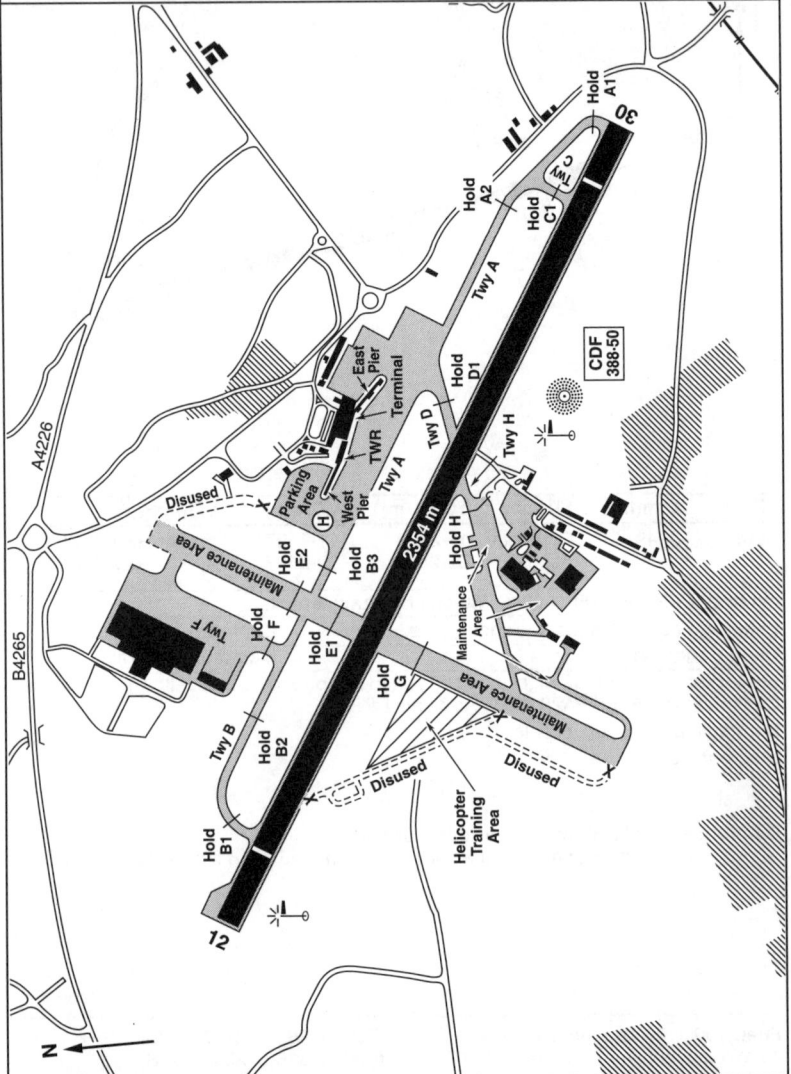

Robert Pooley ©

154

Rwy	Dim(m)	Surface	TORA(m)	LDA(m)	Lighting

N5123·80 W00320·60   **CARDIFF**   220ft AMSL

Rwy	Dim(m)	Surface	TORA(m)	LDA(m)	Lighting
12/30	2354x46	Asphalt	12-2354	12-2134	Ap Thr Rwy PAPI 3°
			30-2354	30-2201	Ap Thr Rwy PAPI 3°

Op hrs: H24.

Landing Fee: Up to 1000 kg £13.02; 1001–1500 kg £15.51; 1501–2000 kg £18.15; 2001–2500 kg £20.78; 2501–3000 kg £23.36; 3001-4000 £36.29 + VAT.
Parking: £13.40 + VAT all weights. First 12 hours free.

Customs: Available.

Hangarage: Limited   **Maintenance:** Light aircraft 01446-710106.

Remarks: Operated by Cardiff International Airport Ltd, Cardiff International Airport, Rhoose, Barry, South Glamorgan CF62 3BD.

Flights within the Cardiff CTR/CTA are governed by the regulations applicable to Class 'D' Controlled Airspace — see pages 2 and 6.

VRPs are listed overleaf and shown on the Bristol/Cardiff CTR/CTA and VRP Chart at page 139. VFR Routes - See pages 139 and 157.

PPR to non-radio aircraft.

Due to proximity of St. Athan aerodrome (3 nm W) overhead joining will not normally be approved.

Rwy 30 RH circuits unless otherwise directed by ATC.

Handling agent for GA aircraft - Cardiff Aeronautical Services, Tel: 01446-719719.

Warnings: Expect turbulence on final approach to Rwy 30 in strong West to South Westerly winds, and on final to Rwy 12 in strong East to North Easterly winds.

Single engined aircraft should avoid overflying the Chemical Complex at Barry.

TV Mast 992' aal 1212' amsl 035°/4·5 nm and 944' aal 1164' amsl 331°/4·2 nm.

R.A.F. St Athan is located just 3 nm west of Cardiff Airport. Fast jets operate in their circuit VFR. Glider flying takes place at weekends. Cardiff ATC will advice whether St. Athan is active.

Restaurant: Restaurant and refreshments available in Terminal Building, also restaurant available 0900-1700 local at Cardiff Wales Flying Club.

Car Hire: Hertz/Europcar 01446-711705.

Airport Travel Shop: 01446-711777.

Flying Training available from Cardiff Aero Flying School Ltd - Tel: 01446-711987.

Fuel: 100LL- Normally 0900-1800, but also available H24 with Surcharge Tel: 01446-711987. Jet A1 - Air BP - 0600-2245 Tel: 01446-710281. Diners. Multi Service.	**Tel:** 01446-712562 ATC 01446-711111 Airport 029-2039 0492 MET **Fax:** 01446-711838 ATC 01446-711675 Airport

CARDIFF CTR/CTA
VISUAL REFERENCE POINTS (VRPs)

VRP	NDB/DME	VOR/DME FIX
Cardiff Docks N51 27·40 W003 09·10	CDF 065° M *CWA/CDF DME 8 nm	BCN 172°/17 nm
Cowbridge N51 27·60 W003 26·23	CDF 321°M *CWA/CDF DME 5nm	BCN 206°/17 nm
Flat Holm Lighthouse N51 22·55 W003 07·13	CDF 101° M *CWA/CDF DME 8 nm	BCN 171°/22 nm
Minehead N51 12·35 W003 28·50	CDF 208° M *CWA/CDF DME 12 nm	BCN 199°/32 nm
M4 Junction 36 (Services) (North of Bridgend) N51 31·93 W003 34·40	CDF 318°M *CWA/CDF DME 11 nm	BCN 229°/16 nm
Nash Point Lighthouse N51 24·08 W003 33·33	CDF 278°M *CWA/CDF DME 8 nm	BCN 214°/22 nm
Nash South (on St. Athan C/L, 1 nm S of Nash Point) N51 22·88 W003 33·45	CDF 270° M *CWA/CDF DME 8 nm	BCN 212°/23 nm
St Hilary TV Mast † N51 27·45 W003 24·18	CDF 332°M *CWA/CDF DME 4nm	BCN 202°/17 nm
Wenvoe TV Mast †† N51 27·60 W003 16·95	CDF 032°M *CWA/CDF DME 5 nm	BCN 187°/16 nm

* DME frequency-paired with ILS gives zero range indication with respect to the threshold of the runway with which it is associated ie., range to A/D is approximate.

† Pilots should exercise caution when routeing via this VRP, due to the nature of this lighted Air Navigation Obstacle height 745 ft agl,. 1161 ft amsl.

†† Pilots should exercise caution when routeing via this VRP, due to the nature of this lighted Air Navigation Obstacle height 787 ft agl, 1212 ft amsl.

**See CTA/CTR and VRP Chart for Bristol/Cardiff at page 139
and VFR routes opposite page**

VFR Flights and Routes to/from Cardiff

VFR clearance in the Cardiff CTR will be given for flights operating in VMC. Pilots are reminded of the requirements to remain in VMC at all times and to comply with the relevant parts of the Low Flying Rules, and must advise ATC if at any time they are unable to comply with the clearance instructions issued.

Standard Outbound Visual Routes

Route Designator	Exit Point	Rwy	Route	Maximum Altitude
VFR St.Hillary	Bridgend	12/30	Route north of St.Hillary TV Mast and leave the CTR to the west via Bridgend.	1500 ft
VFR East	NE Flat Holm Lighthouse	12/30	Route north of Barry, then north of Flat Holm Island, leaving the CTR to the east.	1500 ft
VFR South	N Minehead	12/30	Route towards Minehead and leave the CTR to the south.	1500 ft
VFR Wenvoe	W Cardiff Docks	12/30	Route towards and to the east of the Wenvoe TV Mast and leave the CTR to the northeast.	1500 ft

Standard Inbound Visual Routes

Route Designator	Entry Point	Rwy	Route	Maximum Altitude
VFR Wenvoe	NE CTR	12/30	At the CTR boundary, route towards and to the west of the Wenvoe TV Mast, then as directed by 'Cardiff Tower'.	1500 ft

Remarks: Aircraft may be held at the Wenvoe VRP.

Route Designator	Entry Point	Rwy	Route	Maximum Altitude
VFR (Followed by approppriate VRP designator)	All other Inbound VFR Routes	12/30	The words 'VFR' followed by one of Cardiff's notified VRPs will mean: to route from CTR boundary towards the nominated VRP.	1500 ft

Remarks: Aircraft may be held at the appropriate VRP.

N54 56·25 W002 48·55	**CARLISLE**	190 ft AMSL
5 nm ENE of Carlisle	DCS 115·20 062 22·5. TLA 113·80 158 38·5	
	NEW 114·25 268 39·0	

c/s Carlisle. APP/TWR/VDF 123·60.   A/G c/s Radio 123·60 Sat & Sun Only.
NDB 'CL' 328·0 (On A/D). DME 'CO' 110·70 (Co-located with NDB)

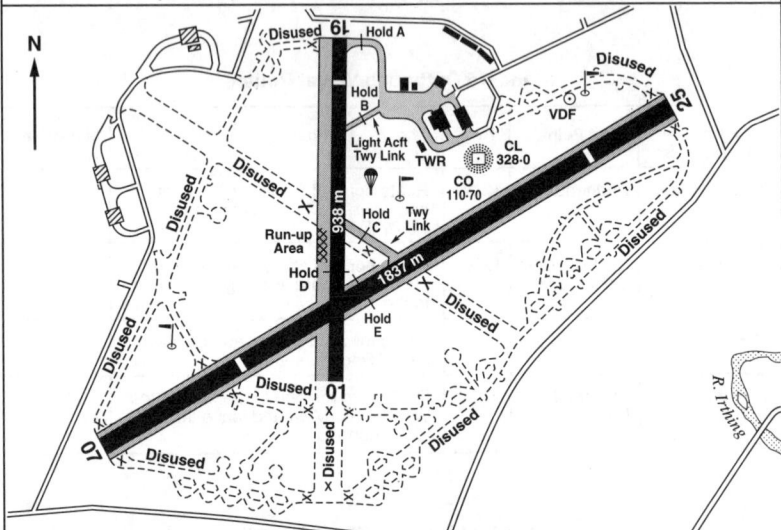

Rwy	Dim(m)	Surface	TORA(m)	LDA(m)	Lighting
01/19	938x23	Asphalt	01-803	01-803	Nil.
			19-938	19-809	Nil.
07/25	1837x30	Asphalt	07-1659	07-1321	† Thr Rwy PAPI 3·5°
			25-1714	25-1469	† Ap Thr Rwy PAPI 3·25°

† The ends of TORA/ED/LDA on Rwys 07 & 25 are shown by RED edge lights only.
The red lights across the runways mark the end of usable pavement.

Op hrs: Mon-Fri 0830-1900; Sat, Sun & PHs 0900-1700 PPR.

Landing Fee: £7.50 per half tonne + VAT. (Discounts may apply).

Hangarage: Ltd. **Maintenance:** Available 01228-573001. **Customs:** 24 hrs PNR.

Remarks: Operated by the Carlisle City Council. PPR to multi-engined aircraft and to all aircraft at weekends and PHs. Non radio aircraft strictly PPR.
Variable circuits.
Danger Area D510 — 5 nm NE of aerodrome. DAAIS available from Carlisle App.
Free-fall Parachuting on aerodrome Mon-Fri evenings, and on Sat and Sun during daylight hours.

VRPs: Gretna N54 59·73 W003 04·05, Haltwhistle N54 58·13 W002 27·73, Penrith N54 39·87 W002 45·02, Wigton N54 49·48 W003 09·67.
High ground to the SE of A/D between 7 and 10 nm rising to 1847' aal, 2037' amsl.

Restaurant: Refreshments available. **Car Hire:** By arrangement with Reception.

Fuel: 100LL, Jet A1. ¢	Tel: 01228-573629 (ATC). 573641 (Switchboard).
	Fax: 01228-573310. Telex: 64476.

N51 40·57 W001 04·85	**CHALGROVE**	241 ft. AMSL
8 nm SE of Oxford.		BNN 113·75 265 20·2. CPT 114·35 029 12·5

c/s Chalgrove Radio 125·40 A/G. Benson APP 120·90.

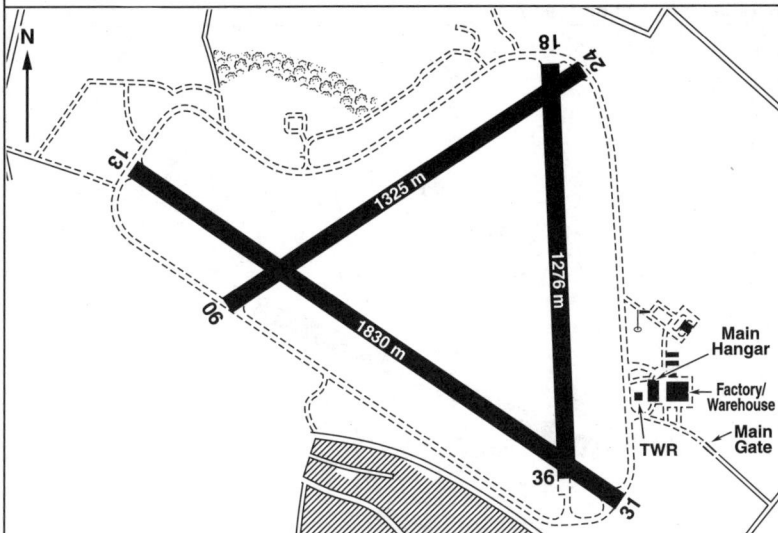

Rwy	Dim(m)	Surface	TORA(m)	LDA(m)	Lighting
06/24	1325x46	Asphalt	06-1289	06-1289	Rwy
			24-1289	24-1289	Rwy
13/31	1830x46	Asphalt	13-1801	13-1801	Rwy
			31-1801	31-1801	Thr Rwy
18/36	1276x46	Asphalt	18-1270	18-1270	Ap Rwy
			36-1270	36-1224	Rwy

Op hrs: Strictly PPR by Telephone. Mon-Thu 0830-1630, Fri 0830-1230.

Landing Fee: On application.	**Customs:** By arrangement.
Hangarage: Nil	**Maintenance:** Nil.

Remarks: Operated by Martin-Baker Aircraft Company Ltd, Chalgrove Airfield, Oxford OX44 7RJ. Licensed for day use only for company operations. Visitors by special arrangements only. Airfield situated within Benson MATZ, contact Benson APP for MATZ crossing service, and for landing/departures at Chalgrove.

Movements on all grass areas prohibited due obstructions.

To avoid noise over Chalgrove village, departures from Rwy 18 not permitted.

Overflight of hangar and buildings prohibited below 1000 ft agl.

Circuits at 1000 ft to the north. No circuits Rwy 36.

Warnings: Ejection seat inflight tests from Meteor aircraft take place up to 1000 ft agl/450 kt. Parachute drop tests also conducted from helicopters up to 5500 ft agl.

Fuel: Jet A1.	**Tel:** 01865-892200. **Fax:** 01865-892214.

Robert Pooley ©

N55 42·43 W002 22·63	**CHARTERHALL**	350 ft AMSL
4·5 nm SSW of Duns.		SAB 112·50 213 13·3
		TLA 113·80 077 35·5

No Radio.
Scottish Information 119·875.

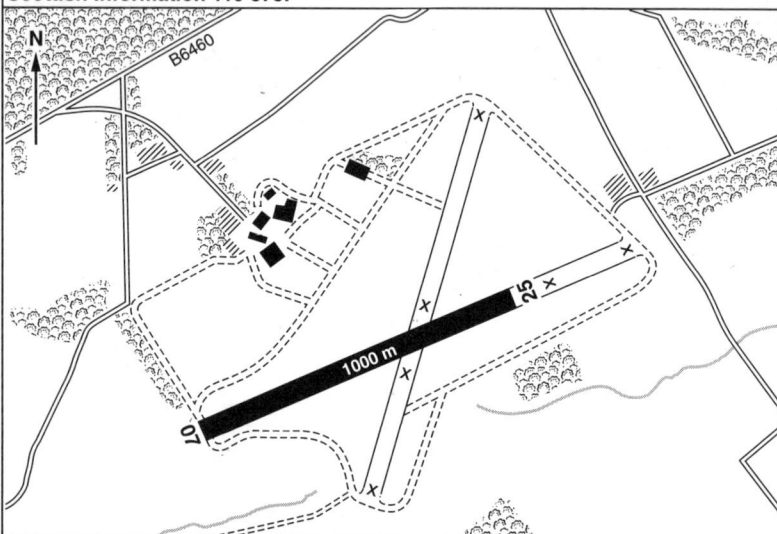

Rwy	Dim(m)	Surface	TORA(m)	LDA(m)	Lighting
07/25	1000x46	Asphalt	Unlicensed		Nil

Runway surface rough.

Op hrs: PPR. SR–SS.

Landing Fee: £10.00	**Customs:** Nil
Hangarage: Nil	**Maintenance:** Nil

Remarks: Operated by A.R. Trotter Esq., Charterhall, Duns, Berwickshire.
Light aircraft accepted on prior permission and at pilot's own risk.
Circuits at 1000' aal; RH on 07, LH on 25.
Microlight activity on airfield.

Warnings.

- Airfield used for farming — always check runway for stock which may encroach onto the runway.
- Care must be taken to identify a fence which crosses the eastern end of the runway.

Taxi: Robertson Tel: 01361-882340.

Fuel: Nil	**Tel:** 01890-840301 **Fax:** 01890-840651

N52 29·12 E000 05·43	**CHATTERIS**	57 ft AMSL
3·5 nm S of March		BKY 116·25 006 30

c/s Chatteris Radio 129·90 A/G - manned only during parachuting operations.

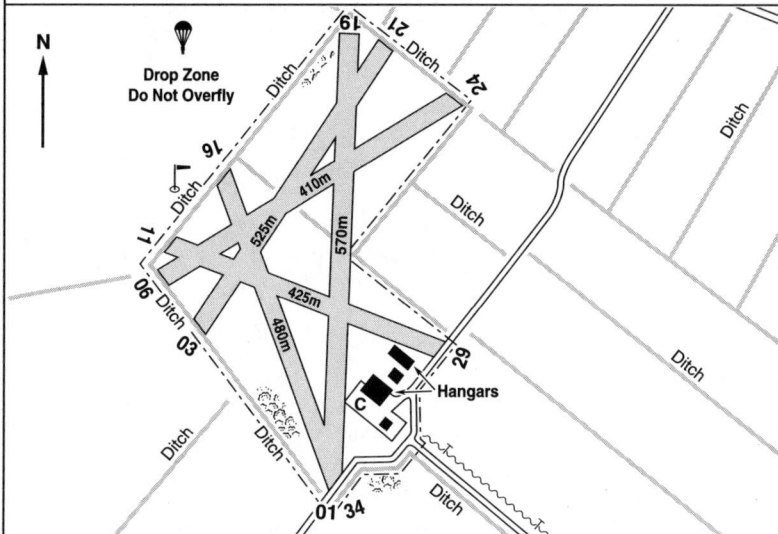

Rwy	Dim(m)	Surface	TORA(m)	LDA(m)	Lighting
01/19	570x11	Grass	Unlicensed		Nil
03/21	525x11	Grass	Unlicensed		Nil
06/24	410x11	Grass	Unlicensed		Nil
† 11/29	425x11	Grass	Unlicensed		Nil
† 16/34	480x11	Grass	Unlicensed		Nil

† Runways 11/29 and 16/34 are for microlight use only.

Op hrs: Strictly PPR – see Remarks.

Hangarage: Available.	**Maintenance:** Nil	**Customs:** Nil

Remarks: Operated by Chatteris Leisure Ltd, Chatteris Airfield, Lower Mount Pleasant Farm, Stonea, Nr. March, Cambs PE15 0EA. Unlicensed airfield. Strictly PPR due to intensive parachute operations up to FL150. Drop Zone is adjacent and to North of airfield.
Microlights operate from dawn to dusk.
Circuits at 700' aal, LH on Rwys 21 and 24; RH on Rwys 03 and 06.

Warning: Do not overfly the Drop Zone at any time.

Please use noise abatement techniques applicable to your aircraft type, do not overfly villages.

Restaurant: Restaurant and licensed Bar 0800-2000 Thu to Sun.

Accommodation: On site Tel: 01473-829982.   **Taxis:** Tel: 01354-658083.

Fuel: (100LL - emergency only)	**Tel:** 01354-740810 Airfield/Para Centre. 01473-829982 Out of hours. **Fax:** 01354-740406. e-mail: chatpara@AOL.com

N50 51·55 W000 45·55   **CHICHESTER (Goodwood)**   100 ft AMSL

1·5nm NNE of Chichester.   **MID 114·00 209 12·7**
                                                     SAM 113·35 109 22·8

c/s **Goodwood Information 122·45 AFIS.**
VOR/DME 'GWC' 114·75 (On A/D).   LARS – Dunsfold APP 135·175 (Mon-Fri).

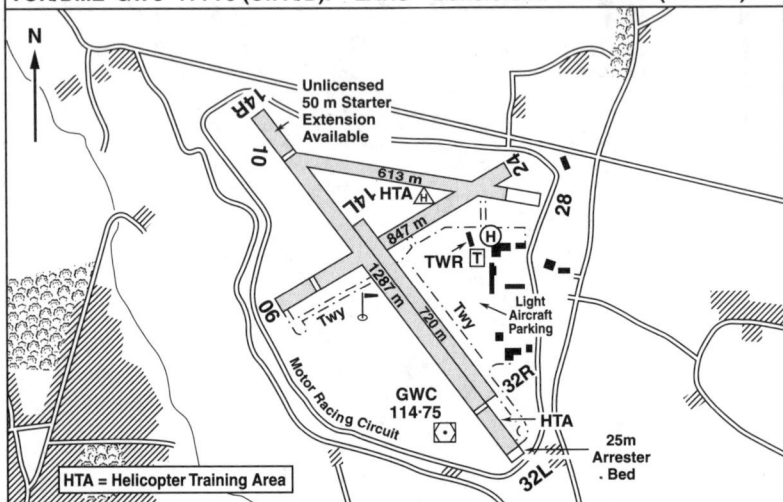

HTA = Helicopter Training Area

Rwy	Dim(m)	Surface	TORA(m)	LDA(m)	Lighting
14R/32L	1287x46	Grass	14-1242	14-1072	Thr Rwy APAPI 3° LH
			32-1213	32-1040	Thr Rwy APAPI 3° LH
14L/32R	720x30	Grass	14-720	14-720	Nil
			32-720	32-720	Nil
06/24	847x46	Grass	06-847	06-708	Nil
			24-837	24-837	Nil
10/28	613x36	Grass	10/28-613	10/28-613	Nil
					ABn Wh/Gn

Op hrs: SUMMER: 09-1800. WINTER: 1Oct-30 Nov 09-1700; 1 Dec-31 Jan 09-1600; 1 Feb-31 Mar 0900-1700 or earlier by NOTAM.

Landing Fee: Singles £11.55 + VAT. Others on application.

Customs: Non EU Deps; EU and non EU Arrs - 3hrs PNR via ATS.

Hangarage: Available. **Maintenance:** Available Tel: 01243-781934. Fax: 780312.

Remarks: Operated by Goodwood Road Racing Co. Ltd.
Strictly PPR *by telephone* before depature. Circuits as directed by ATS.
Noise Abatement procedures in operation – See page opposite.
Rwy 14L/32R available 1 November to 31 March only.
The motor racing track on the airfield perimeter is in constant use during daylight hours. It is not to be used for the taxying of aircraft at any time.

Car Hire: 01243-782403 or 789136.

Restaurant: Cafe in the Flying Club: Bar, Food –0930 until airfield closing.

Fuel: 100LL, Jet A1.	**Tel:** 01243-755061 ATS, **Fax:** 755062 ATS
Access & Barclaycard.	01243- 755060 (Admin) **Fax:** 755065 (Admin)

Noise Abatement Procedures

Circuit heights: Fixed-wing 1200 ft; Helicopters 900 ft or as directed by ATS.

Circuit directions: Rwys 06,10 and 14L/14R – Left Hand.
Rwys 24, 28 and 32L/32R – Right Hand.
Note: Rwy 14L/32R **in use** 1 Nov to 31 Mar only.

Runway 06
Take-off: No restrictions.
Landing: No low approaches over the built up-areas in the undershoot.

Runway 24
Take-off: As soon as practicable after departure, turn right to avoid built up area. Maintain track until reaching or passing circuit height. No practice engine failures after take-off until west of A286 road.
Landing: No restrictions.

Runway 14L/14R
Take-off: Turn left 10° as soon as practicable after departure to avoid overflying the school and houses under the climb out path. No practice engine failures after take-off until well clear of the school and houses.
Landing: No low approaches over East Lavant village. Light aircraft should aim to touch down beyond the intersection of runways 10 and 14.

Runway 32L/32R
Take-off: Turn right 20° as soon as practicable after departure to avoid East Lavant village. Maintain that heading until well beyond the village. No practice engine failures after take-oft until well beyond the village.
Landing: No restrictions.

Runway 10
Take-off: No restrictions.
Landing: No restrictions.

Runway 28
Take-off: Maintain runway heading until clear of Lavant village.
Landing: No restrictions.

Helicopter
Helicopters are to avoid routeing over Chichester, Westerton and Summersdale. Helicopters are not permitted to join the circuit below 700 ft QFE unless weather dictates a lower height.

N51 08·13 W001 25·28	**CHILBOLTON (Stonefield Park)**	292 ft AMSL

5 nm SSE of Andover.	SAM 113·35 349 11·5
	MID 114·0 284 30·6

No Radio. Boscombe Down APP 126·70 (MATZ).

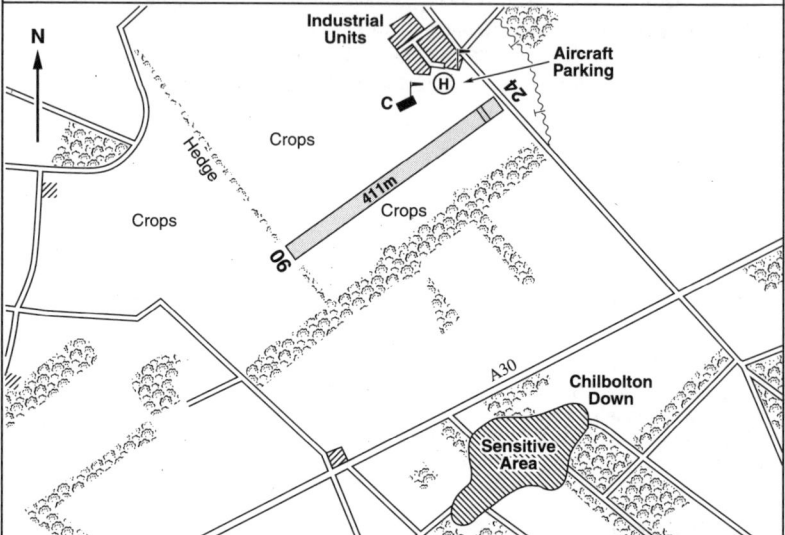

Rwy	Dim(m)	Surface	TORA(m)	LDA(m)	Lighting
06/24	411x18	Grass	Unlicensed		Nil

Rwy 24 gradient 2% UP.

Op hrs: 0800-2100 daily. PPR by telephone.

Landing Fee: £3.00	**Customs:** Nil
Hangarage: By arrangement	**Maintenance:** Nil

Remarks: A commercial/Club unlicensed airfield operated by Stonefield Park and Chilbolton Flying Club. Airfield situated under the Middle Wallop MATZ stub. Contact Boscombe Down App 126·70 for Boscombe Down/Middle Wallop CMATZ clearance. Visitors welcome on prior telephone briefing of noise sensitive areas.

Intense low-level military helicopter traffic in the area.

Preferred approach to the airfield is from the south and east.

Circuit height 600' aal. All circuits to the south of the airfield due to noise sensitive areas. Light aircraft should make large circuit south of the A30 avoiding Chilbolton Down. Microlights may make a tight circuit strictly north of the A30.

All aircraft are to avoid overflying Chilbolton village and the Radar Dish to the NNW.

All flights must be logged in the Flight Log in the control Caravan. Landing fees should be put in a sealed envelope and left in the locked box by the Flight Log.

Warning: Power cables 24 ft high cross final approach to Rwy 24.

Restaurant: Abbot's Mitre in village.   **Accommodation:** B&B at the Rectory.

Taxis: 01264-810258, 01264-359000, 0589-292801.

Fuel: Nil.	**Tel:** 01276-691563 PPR – Mr Colin Marsh

N52 57·00 W003 03·00	**CHIRK**	448 ft. AMSL
1 nm E of Chirk.		WAL 114·10 179 27·5

c/s Chirk Radio 129·825 A/G. Shawbury Radar 120·775 LARS

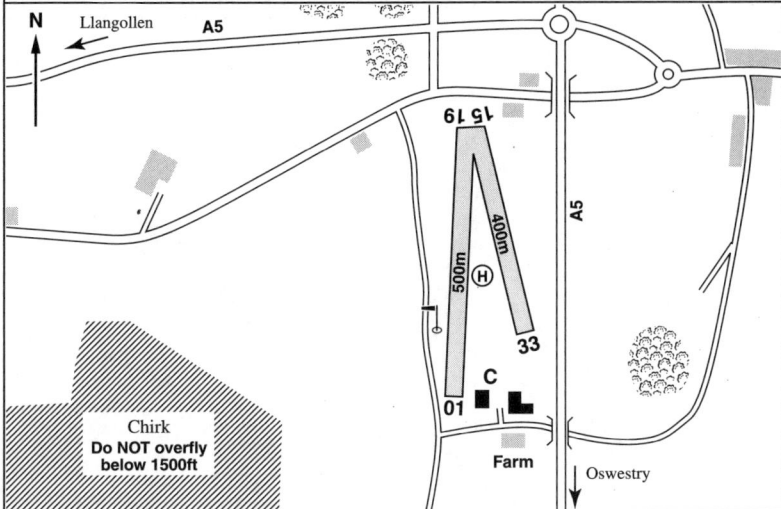

Rwy	Dim(m)	Surface	TORA(m)	LDA(m)	Lighting
01/19	500x20	Grass	Unlicensed		Nil
15/33	400x20	Grass	Unlicensed		Nil

Caution: Severe downslope towards last 300m of Rwy 01.

Op hrs: PPR.

Landing Fee: Nil	**Customs:** Nil
Hangarage: Nil	**Maintenance:** Nil

Remarks: Operated by MR. R. Everitt, 3 School Lane, St Martins, Shorpshire.
An unlicensed microlight airfield. STOL aircraft welcome at pilot's own risk.
Airfield easily identifiable by a white concrete 'H' in the centre of the airfield.
Circuits at 600 ft QFE, LH on Rwys 15 and 19, RH on Rwys 01 and 33.
Do not overfly the noise sensitive area west of the airfield below 1500 ft .

Warning: Sheep may be grazing if there is no microlight activity.

Restaurant: Cafe on the airfield open Mon to Fri.

Fuel: Nil	**Tel:** 01691-774137.

N53 50·06 W001 11·73	**CHURCH FENTON**	29 ft AMSL

4 nm SE of Tadcaster.	OTR 113·90 287 39·5
	POL 112·10 087 32·5

c/s Fenton. APP 126·50 (MATZ). TWR/GND 122·10 - On request.
ILS Rwy 24 (236°M) 'CF' 109·30 (LLZ offset 3°, Rwy QFU 239°).

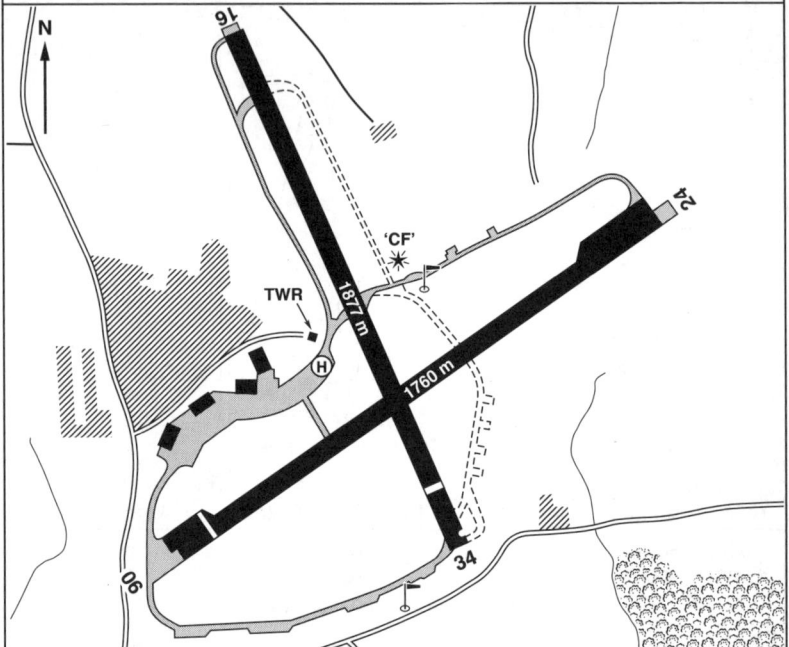

Rwy	Dim(m)	Surface	TORA(m)	LDA(m)	Lighting
06/24	1877x46	Asphalt/	06-1712	06-1712	Ap Thr Rwy PAPI 3°
		Concrete	24-1829	24-1829	Ap Thr Rwy PAPI 3°
16/34	1666x46	Asphalt/	16-1666	16-1666	Thr Rwy PAPI 3°
		Concrete	34-1666	34-1466	Thr Rwy PAPI 3°
					IBn 'CF' Red

Op hrs: PPR. Mon-Thu 0830-1715; Fri 0830-1700; Sat & Sun 0830-1700.
ATZ active H24 Mon-Thu, 0700-2359 Fri-Sun.

Landing Fee: MoD(RAF) Rates.	**Customs:** Nil.
Hangarage: Nil.	**Maintenance:** Nil.

Remarks: RAF Aerodrome. Satellite aerodrome of RAF Linton-on-Ouse.
A public road crosses final approach to Rwys 06 & 34.
Visual circuits at 1000 ft.
Civil aerodrome at Sherburn-in-Elmet 3 nm to SW.

Caution: Full obstacle clearance criteria not met on approach to Rwy 06.

Fuel: 100LL, Avtur.	**Tel:** 01347-848261 Ext 7491/2 Linton-on-Ouse
By arrangement with Linton-on-Ouse	

N51 47·12 E001 07·73	**CLACTON**	35 ft AMSL
2 nm W of Clacton.		**CLN 114·55 193 04**

c/s Clacton Radio 135·40 A/G. Clacton VOR/DME 'CLN' 114·55.

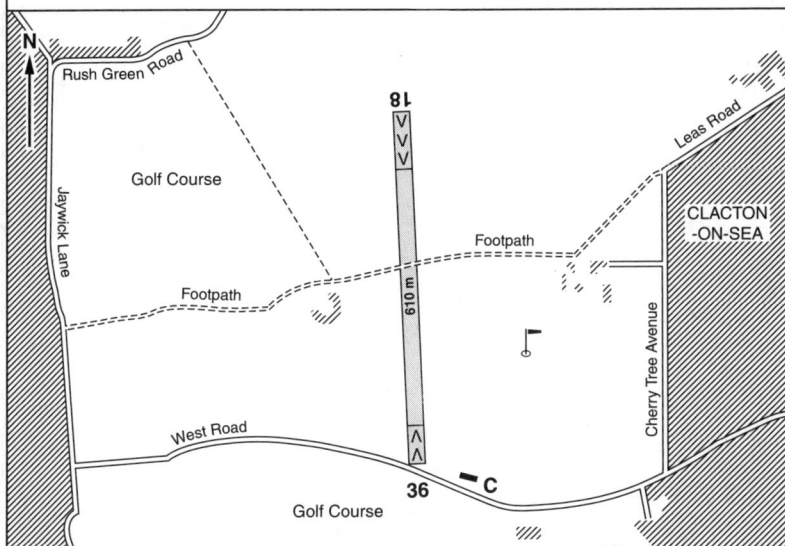

Rwy	Dim(m)	Surface	TORA(m)	LDA(m)	Lighting
18/36	610x18	Grass	18-596	18-502	Nil
			36-600	36-542	Nil

Note: Rwy 18/36 QDM markings appear before the Displaced Threshold markings.

Op hrs: PPR by telephone essential. WINTER: 1000-1600 or SS daily.
SUMMER: 0830-2030 or SS daily.

Landing Fees: Singles £5.00; Twins £10.00.

Hangarage: Nil.	**Maintenance:** Available.	**Customs:** 24 hrs PNR.

Remarks: Operated by Clacton Aero Club Ltd. Visiting aircraft, including non radio aircraft, welcome on prior permission at pilot's own risk.
Telephone briefing necessary prior to visit.
Airfield not available to helicopters or microlights.
No overhead joins. Pilots are requested to join on the downwind leg and are to avoid overflying the village west of the airfield.

Warning: There is a line of lamp posts 16 ft agl on the public road crossing the final approach to Rwy 36 just before the aerodrome boundary.
Power cables 86 ft agl 118 ft amsl 360°/2 nm, running N–S.

Beach is five minutes walk from airfield.

Restaurant: Refreshments available.

Taxi: 01255-220050

Fuel: Nil.	**Tel:** 01255-424671
	Fax: 01255-475364

| N53 18·28 W001 25·83 | **COAL ASTON** | 720 ft AMSL |

5 nm S of Sheffield.

| TNT | 115·70 | 036 | 17·3 |
| GAM | 112·80 | 280 | 17·4 |

No Radio.
FIS – London Information 124·60

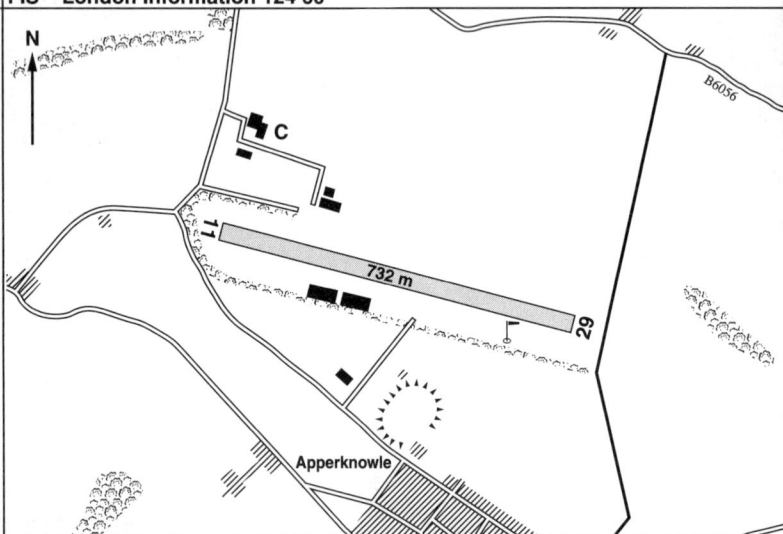

Rwy	Dim(m)	Surface	TORA(m)	LDA(m)	Lighting
11/29	732x20	Grass	Unlicensed		Nil

Gradient 1·6 % UP on Rwy 11.

Op hrs: † Strictly PPR. SR-SS

| **Landing Fee:** On application. | **Customs:** Nil. |
| **Hangarage:** Nil. | **Maintenance:** Nil. |

Remarks: Operated by Mr. W. H. Valle. Bentley Farm, Summerley, Apperknowle, Sheffield. Unlicensed airfield.

† Private and Business aircraft welcome on prior permission and at pilot's own risk.

| **Fuel:** Nil. | **Tel:** 01246-412305 |

Robert Pooley ©

N56 03·42 W006 14·53	**COLONSAY (Machrins)**	35 ft. AMSL

West side of Colonsay Island.

TIR 117·70 151 34
MAC 116·00 340 43

No Radio. Recommend contact Tiree Information 122·70.

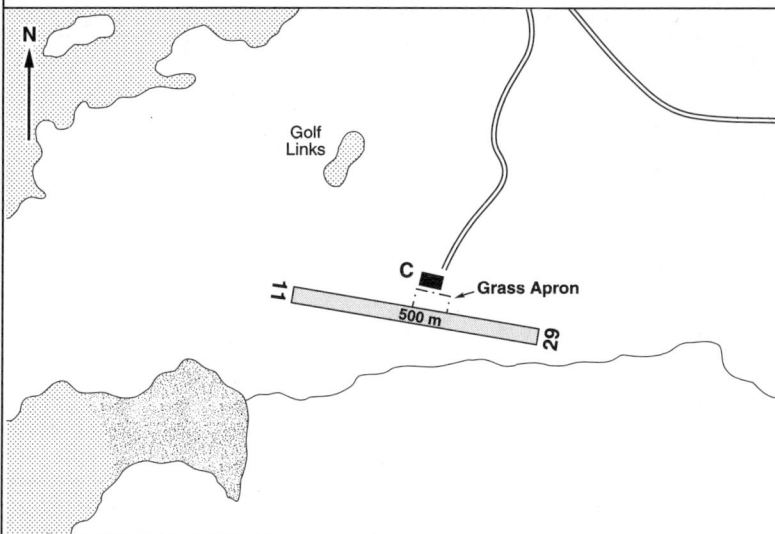

Golf Links

C

Grass Apron

11

500 m

29

Rwy	Dim(m)	Surface	TORA(m)	LDA(m)	Lighting
11/29	500x30	Grass	Unlicensed		Nil.

Op hrs: PPR. SR–SS.

Landing Fee: £15.00	**Customs:** Nil.
Hangarage: Nil.	**Maintenance:** Nil.

Remarks: Unlicensed airfield operated by Colonsay Estate.

Visiting light aircraft accepted on prior permission and at pilot's own risk.

Airfield is primarily for air ambulance use.

Application for permission in writing to include acceptance of own risk and proof of third party insurance to: Alex Howard, Colonsay House, Isle of Colonsay, Argyll, PA61 7YU.

Avoid overflying bird sanctuaries which extend along the coast to the north of airfield.

Caution: Eastern end of runway liable to waterlogging after heavy rainfall. Possible presence of sheep on the runway.

Fuel: Nil	**Tel :** 01951-200211 **Fax:** 01951-200369

Robert Pooley ©

N52 45·30 E001 21·44   **COLTISHALL**   66 ft AMSL

7·5nm NNE of Norwich.   **CLN 114·55 011 55. NH 371·5 348 4·8**

Coltishall Zone 125·90*.   TWR 122·10.   TACAN 'CSL' 116·50 (On A/D)
ILS Rwy 22 (223°M) 'CS' 111·50, Rwy QFU 220°.
* Also frequency for Southern North Sea Radar Advisory, FIS & Alerting Service.

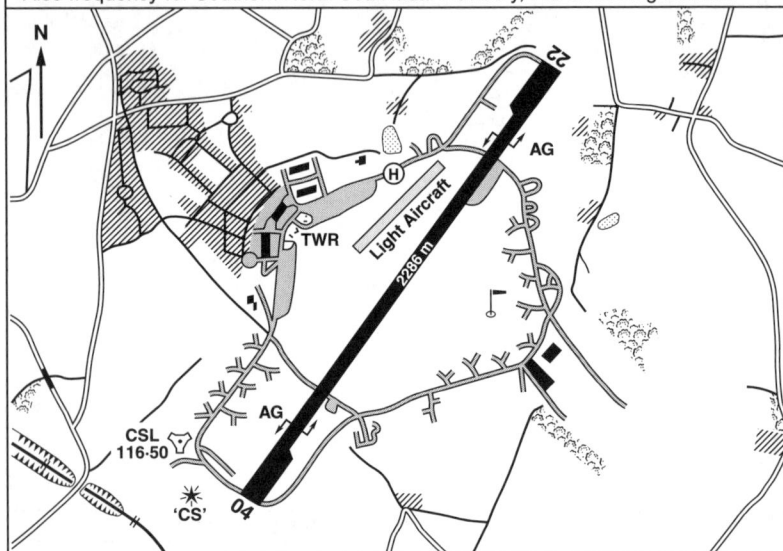

Rwy	Dim(m)	Surface	TORA(m)	LDA(m)	Lighting
04/22	2286x46	Asphalt	04-2286	04-2286	Ap Thr Rwy PAPI
			22-2286	22-2286	Ap Thr Rwy PAPI
					IBn 'CS' Red

Op hrs: PPR. (24 hrs). Mon-Thu 0830-1730, Fri 0830-1700.   **ATZ active H24.**

Landing Fee: MoD(RAF) Rates	**Customs:** Nil.
Hangarage: Nil.	**Maintenance:** Nil.

Remarks: RAF Aerodrome. Strictly PPR.

Norwich Airport is at 5 nm to SW.

The undershoot area for Rwy 04 at Norwich Airport is marked 'NORWICH' and Rwy 04 at Coltishall is marked 'CS'.

Holding pattern for Norwich NDB is 4·5 nm to SSE.

Arrester gear 396m from each end of runway.

Flying Club operations outside of nornal aerodrome operating hours.

Fuel: Avtur - By arrangement.   **Tel:** 01603-737361 Ext 7205/7543

Robert Pooley ©

N50 58·05 W002 09·22	**COMPTON ABBAS**	810 ft AMSL
3 nm S of Shaftesbury.		**SAM 113·35 277 30·5**

c/s Compton Radio 122·70 A/G. Radar Service available Mon-Fri from Boscombe Down 126·70, or Yeovilton 127·35.   NDB 'COM' 349·5 (On A/D).

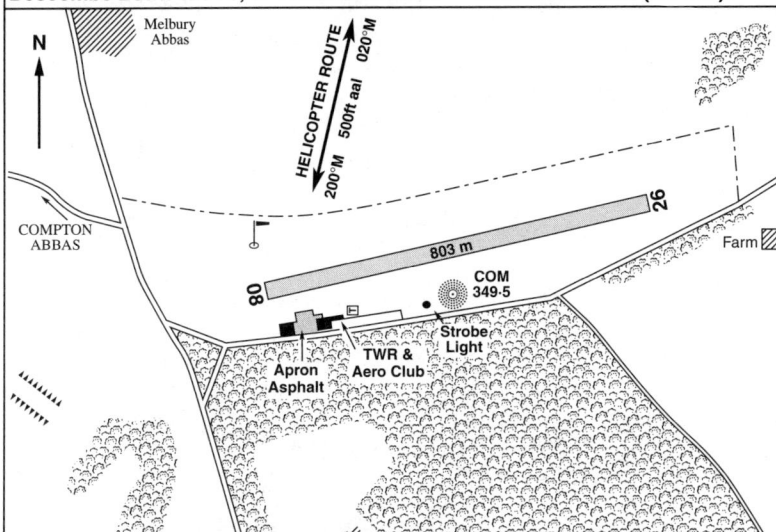

Rwy	Dim(m)	Surface	TORA(m)	LDA(m)	Lighting
08/26	803x30	Grass	08-803	08-803	Nil.
			26-803	26-803	Nil.

Op hrs: 0900-SS daily.

Landing Fee: £7.50	**Customs:** 24hrs PNR.
Hangarage: Available.	**Maintenance :** Available

Remarks: Operated by Compton Abbas Airfield Ltd, Ashmore, Salisbury, Wilts SP5 5AP

Circuits at 800 ft aal – LH on Rwy 08, RH on Rwy 26.

A high intensity white flashing strobe light operates continuously during airfield operational hours.

Due to the visual screening effect of tall trees to the south of the airfield, it is recommended that first time visitors approach from a northerly direction, i.e Shaftesbury – Comton Abbas is 150°M/ 3 nm.

Noise Abatement Procedures - See overleaf.

Warning: Due to trees on the southern boundary, expect turbulance and windshear on approachs to Rwy 08 and 26 with southerly winds.

Restaurant & Bar: Highly acclaimed restaurant and bar open all year. Group fly-ins and corporate days catered for.

Taxis: Readily available.

Fuel: 100LL. Cash, cheque and most credit cards accepted.	**Tel:** 01747-811767 **Fax:** 01747-811161

Robert Pooley ©

COMPTON ABBAS
Noise Abatement Procedures

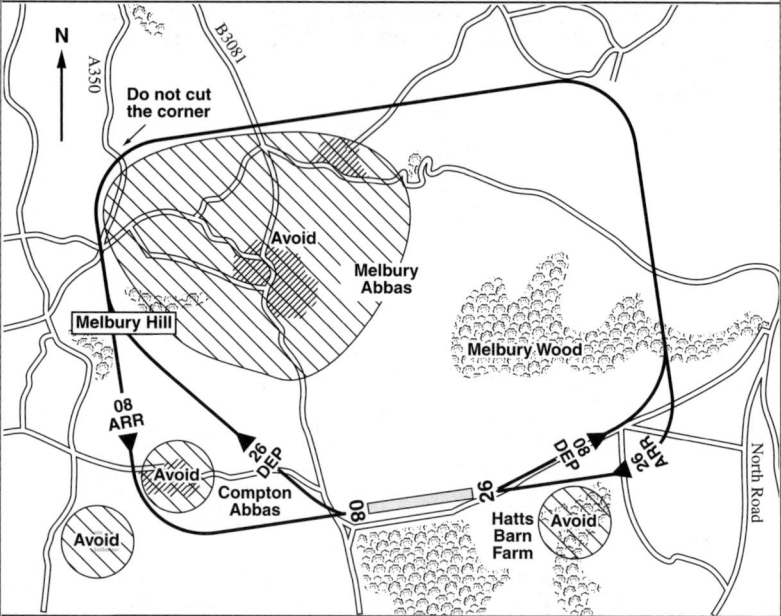

The airfield operates in an area of outstanding natural beauty, and to maintain the existing good relationship with the community, please observe good airmanship and avoid overflying hamlets and villages in close proximity to the airfield.

Arrivals:

Rwy 08 - A normal approach, but please avoid getting low on fianl approach or using excessive power settings when overflying Compton Village.

Rwy 26 - A normal approach.

Departures:

Rwy 08 - As soon as practicable, on passing the end of the runway, turn left in order to avoid overflying Hatts Barn Farmhouse.

Rwy 26 - As soon as practicable, on passing the end of the runway, turn right in order to cross the top of the Melbury Hill. Avoid overflying any part of Compton Abbas village.

N52 38·40 W002 18·33	**COSFORD**	272 ft AMSL
7 nm NW of Wolverhampton.		HON 113·65 312 29
		TNT 115·70 229 34

c/s Cosford App.   **APP 135·875.**   **TWR/GND 121·95.**

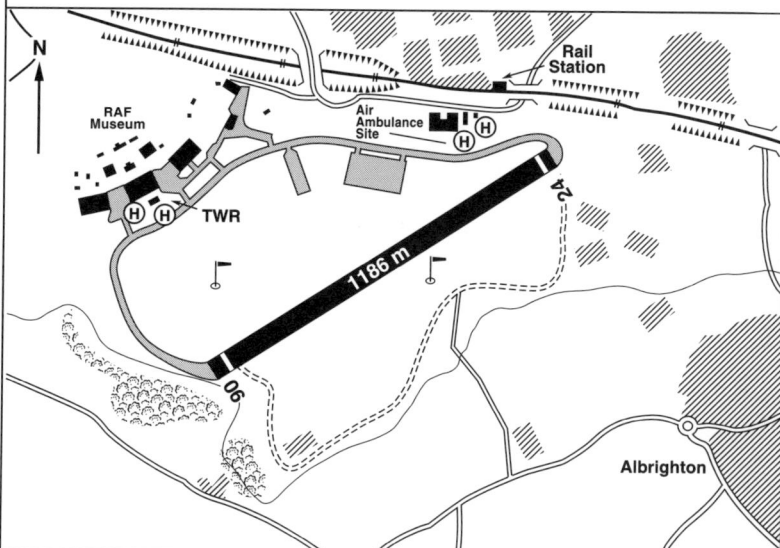

Rwy	Dim(m)	Surface	TORA(m)	LDA(m)	Lighting
06/24	1186x46	Asphalt	06-1185	06-1141	Nil.
			24-1185	24-1141	Nil.

Op hrs: PPR 24hs. HO.	**ATZ active H24.**
Landing Fee: MoD(RAF) Rates	**Customs:** Nil.
Hangarage: Nil.	**Maintenance:** Nil.

Remarks: RAF Aerodrome. Ab initio pilot training.

No civil aircraft accepted Sat and Sun.

Aerodrome may close at indeterminate times.

All aircraft should contact Cosford Approach prior to ATZ entry.

Glider flying and aero-tows during daylight hours.

Up to 12 light aircraft may be operating at any one time.

Avoid overflying Albrighton village 1 nm SE.

Air Ambulance helicopter operations H24.

Caution:
- Railway embankment 20ft aal., 275m before Rwy 24 Thr.
- Ravine, 60 ft deep, 91m before Rwy 06 Thr.
- Full obstacle clearance not met on approach to all runways.

Fuel: Nil.	**Tel:** 01902-377582 Ext 7582/7055.
	Fax: 01902-377143

N52 22·18 W001 28·78	**COVENTRY**	281 ft AMSL
3 nm SSE of Coventry.	HON 113·65 090 6·8. DTY 116·40 316 17·5	

c/s Coventry. **APP** 119·25. **TWR** 119·25, 124·80. **GND** 121·70 (When directed).
VDF 122·00, 119·25, 124·80. **RAD** 122·00. **ATIS** 126·05.
NDB 'CT' 363·50 (231°M/3·25 nm to Thr Rwy 23).
ILS/DME Rwy 05 (051°M) I-CTY 109·75.   **ILS/DME Rwy 23** (231°M) I-CT 109·75.

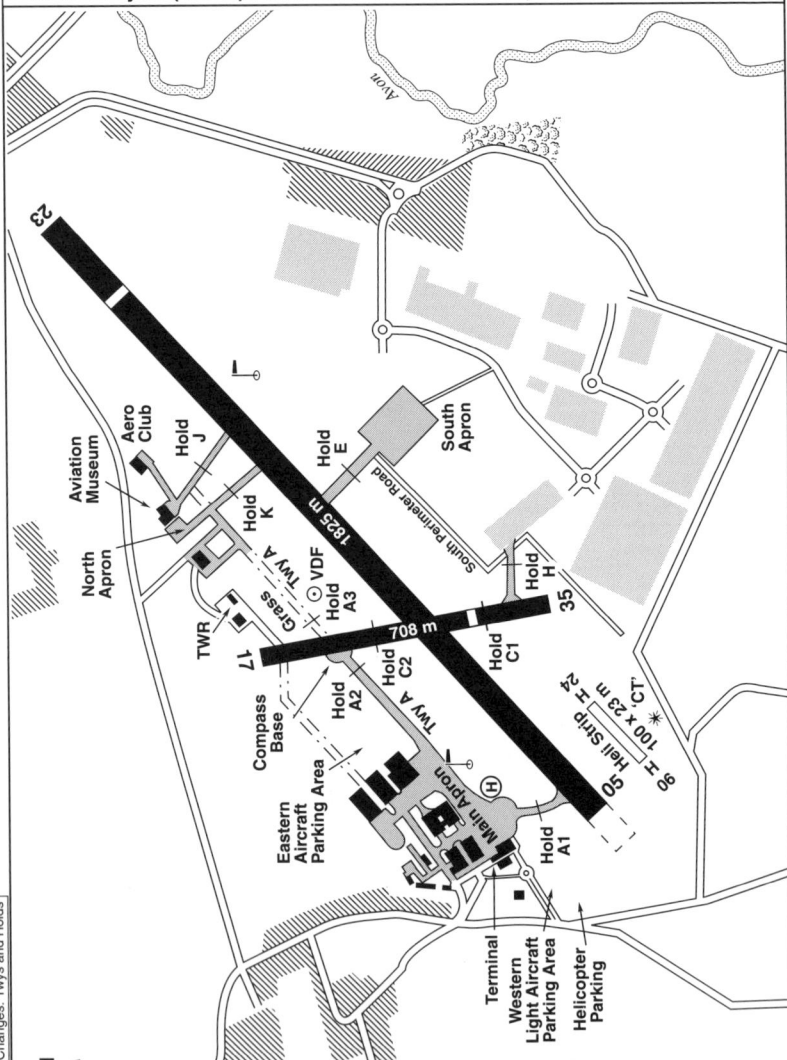

Changes: Twys and Holds

COVENTRY			281 ft AMSL		

N52 22·18 W001 28·78

3 nm SSE of Coventry.   **HON 113·65 090   6·8.   DTY 116·40 316 17·5**

Rwy	Dim (m)	Surface	TORA(m)	LDA(m)	Lighting
05/23	1825x46	Asphalt	05-1615	05-1795	Ap Thr Rwy PAPI †
			23-1825 *	23-1615	Ap Thr Rwy PAPI
FATO 06/24	100x23	Grass	Helicopter Strip		Nil
17/35	712x30	Asphalt	17-486	17-712	Nil
			35-712	35-486	Nil IBn 'CT' Gn

† Rwy 23 - PAPI 5·5° for training purpose only. PPR. Black and white marker boards
  displayed when in use.

* Rwy 23 TORA includes 210 m block paved starter extension.

Op hrs: Mon 0630-2359; Tue-Fri H24; Sat 0000-2000; Sun 0830-2100.
(PPR 2000-0700 Mon-Fri), and by arrangement.

Landing Fee: Up to 3000 kg £7.75 per 500 kg; thereafter £14.50 per tonne. Visiting
private/club below 1500 kg £10.00, if paid before departure.

Hangarage: Available.   **Maintenance:** Available.

Customs: PNR 1600 previous day.

Remarks: Operated by West Midlands International Airport Ltd.
Aerodrome situated below Birmingham CTA (1500' ALT – FL45) Class 'D' Airspace
— see page 2. Visual Reference Points – See Chart at page 177.

Non radio aircraft PPR. All Training flights by prior booking with ATC.

Microlights (500 kg AUW) restricted operations - PPR from ATC.

Pilots are required to 'book out' from the Flight Briefing Room, telephone ATC, or by
R/T if traffic permits.

Circuits RH on 05 and 35, LH on 17 and 23.

Circuit height: 1000' aal;

Helicopter circuits at 700' aal, landing area as directed by ATC.

Danger Area Activity Information Service (DAAIS) for D213, Kineton, available on
Coventry ATIS.

Noise Preferential Routeings:

Dep Rwy 05 - Climb on track to 'CT', then turn on track or as instructed by ATC.
Training aircraft in the circuit: As above, then complete the right turn crosswind.

Dep Rwy 23 - Southerly Deps: Climb straight ahead to 500' aal, then turn left onto
track 200°M, on reaching 1000' aal, turn onto track or as instructed by ATC.

Dep Rwy 23 - Northerly Deps: Climb straight ahead to 500' aal, then turn left onto
track 215°M. After intercepting HON RADIAL 115° (HON DME 5·5), turn on track or
as instructed by ATC.

Training aircraft in the circuit: As 'Southerly Deps', but continue on track 200°M, then
complete the left turn downwind.

Mast 1188 ft amsl 10nm to E.

Restaurant: Licensed Buffet and Cafeteria in Terminal Building.

Car Hire: Hertz, Godfrey Davis (Europcar), Talbot Rental and Avis through local
(Coventry City) Offices.

Taxi: Allen's 024-7655 5555.

Fuel: 100LL, Jet A1. Access, Visa, American Express,Diners, Multi-Service	**Tel:** 024-7630 1717 Admin. **Fax:** 024-7630 6008 Airport. 024-7663 9451 ATC.

Intentionally Blank

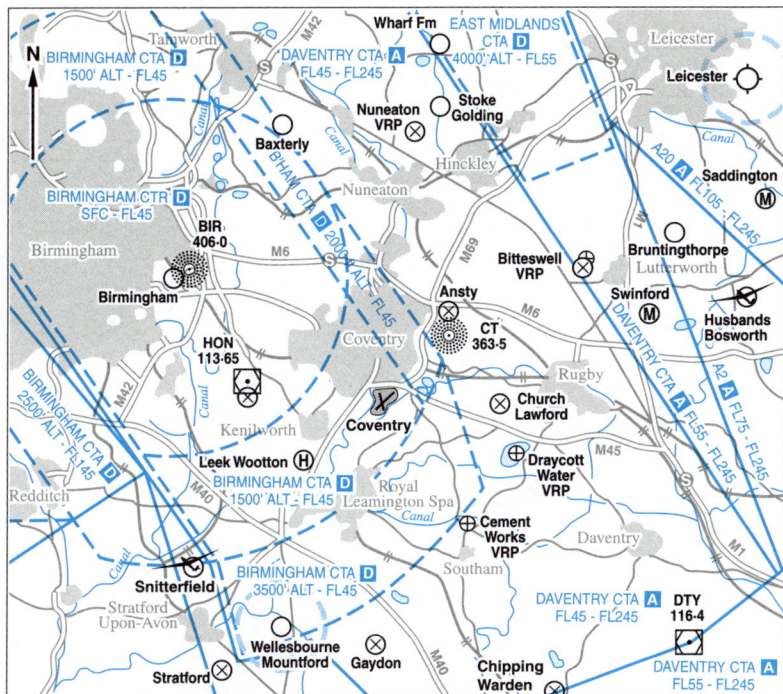

Bitteswell (Disused A/D)	N52 27·47	W001 14·78
Cement Works	N52 16·35	W001 23·07
Draycott Water	N52 19·57	W001 19·58
Nuneaton (Disused A/D)	N52 33·90	W001 26·88

N52 04·33 W000 37·00

364 ft AMSL

7 nm SW of Bedford.
6 nm E of Milton Keynes.

DTY 116·40 115 19·4
BNN 113·75 358 20·8

c/s Cranfield. APP 122·85. TWR 134·925. Dep ATIS 121·875.
VDF 122·85. VOR 'CFD' 116·50 (On A/D).
NDB 'CIT' 850 (216°M/3·7 nm to A/D).
ILS Rwy 22 (216°M) I-CR 108·90.

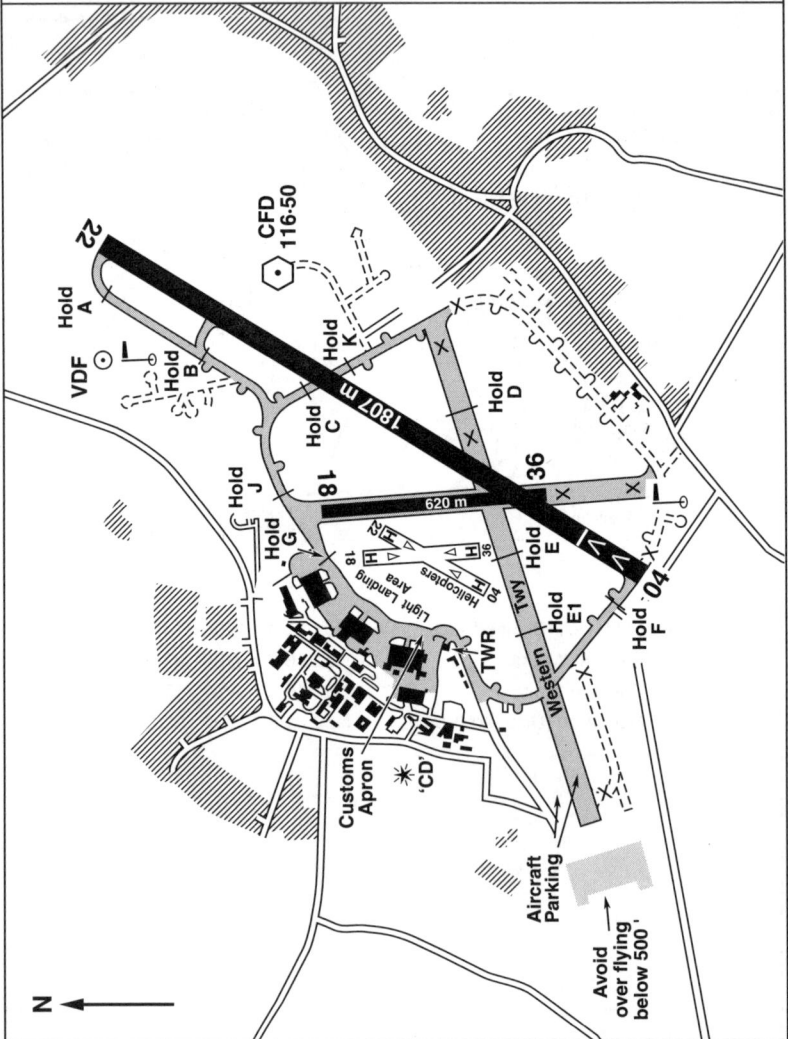

Robert Pooley ©

178

N52 04·33 W000 37·00		**CRANFIELD**			364 ft AMSL
Rwy	**Dim(m)**	**Surface**	**TORA(m)**	**LDA(m)**	**Lighting**
04/22	1807x46	Asphalt	04-1807 22-1680	04-1602 22-1680	Nil. Ap Thr Rwy PAPI 3°
18/36	620x18	Asphalt	18-620 36-620	18-620 36-620	Nil Nil
Only Rwy 22 licensed for night use.					IBn 'CD' Gn

Op hrs: Mon-Fri 0830-1900; Sat, Sun & PHs 0900-1800. O/T ¢.

Landing Fees: On Application.   **Customs:** 4 hrs PNR.

Hangarage: Limited.   **Maintenance:** Available - Various Organisations.

Remarks: Operated by Cranfield University, Cranfield, Bedford MK43 0AL.

Strictly PPR to non-radio aircraft and any aircraft requiring Instrument Approach Training or non-based aircraft requiring Circuit training.

No deadside due to Helicopter circuits on all runways.

Circuits: Day – Fixed wing 800' QFE, Rotary 1000' QFE.
          Night – Fixed wing and Rotary 1200' QFE.

All VFR traffic should join circuit via VRPs:

Stewartby Brickworks N5204·40 W000 31·05 , Woburn N51 59·40 W000 37·15 or Olney Town N52 09·20 W000 42·10 Rwy 04, 18 and 36 only.

Avoid overflying all buildings and structures located up to 1500 m west of disused runway intersection below 500' aal.

Caution: Due to drainage ditches, all fixed wing aircraft entering/exiting the grass area via the northern taxiway between threshold of Rwy 18 and ATC are to use the concrete entry/exit points.

Helicopter Operations - see overleaf.

Restaurant: Cafe Pacific. Licensed Restaurant & Bar, Mon-Fri 0800-1800 L, Wed and Thu 0800-2100 L, Sat and Sun 0900-1600 L. Tel: 01234-754611.

Car Hire: Budget Tel: 01908-373111. Hertz Tel: 01908-374492.
            AVIS Tel: 01908-588760.

Taxi: JT Cars Tel: 01234-750005. Village Private Hire Tel: 01234-765252.

Fuel: 100LL, Jet A1. Diners, Access,Visa, Mastercard, Eurocard, American Express.	**Tel:** 01234-754761 ATC, **Fax:** 754785 **Tel:** 01234-754784 Admin, **Fax:** 751805 **Tel:** 01234-750661 Handling, **Fax:**751731

Robert Pooley ©

Helicopter Operations

Aerodrome Elevation: 364 ft.   FATO Elevation: 358 ft
Helicopter Grass Landing Areas: 04/22 300 x 23m; 18/36 300 x 23m.
Helicopter Circuits: LH on 04 & 36; RH on 18 & 22 unless otherwise advised by ATC.
Circuit Height: Day - 1000 ft QFE; Night 1200 ft QFE.

1. Helicopters operations take place on the grass area to the north west of the main runway intersection.
2. Helicopters must request start up clearance.
4. Helicopters arriving/departing will be expected to use the FATO parallel to the runway in use, unless otherwise advised.
5. Each FATO is marked with two aiming points. Helicopters are to land on the approach end aiming point unless otherwise advised.
6. Helicopters may operate for quick stop/hover practice on the grass light landing area, remaining clear of the FATO, with the permission of the ATC.
7. FATOs are licensed for day use only.

N53 01·82 W000 28·99	**CRANWELL**	218 ft AMSL
9 nm NE of Grantham.		**GAM 112·80 137 22·8**

Cranwell APP 119·375. TWR 122·10. ATIS 135·675. NDB 'CWL' 423·0 (On A/D).
TACAN 'CWZ' 117·40 (On A/D). ILS Rwy 27 (267°M) 'CW' 109·70.

Rwy	Dim(m)	Surface	TORA(m)	LDA(m)	Lighting
09/27	2082x46	Asphalt/	09-2082	09-1918	Ap Thr Rwy PAPI
		Concrete	27-2082	27-1989	Ap Thr Rwy PAPI
01/19	1464x46	Asphalt/	01/19-1464	01/19-1464	Thr Rwy PAPI
		Concrete			ABn Wh. IBn 'CW' Red
		CRANWELL NORTH			
07/25	1100	Grass	07-1100	07-963	Nil
			25-1100	25-1100	Nil

Op hrs: PPR from Ext 7377. Mon-Fri 0745-1700.	**ATZ active H24.**
Landing Fee: MoD(RAF) Rates.	**Customs:** Nil.
Hangarage: Nil.	**Maintenance:** Nil.

Remarks: RAF Aerodrome. PPR.Flying Training School. Visiting aircraft are allotted arrival slot times which must be adhered to. Contact APP at least 5 nm before the Cranwell/Barkston Heath MATZ.
Light aircraft operate outside of normal operating hours and use 119·375 A/G.

CRANWELL NORTH is a grass airfield normally used for glider operations, Mon-Fri 1700-SS and at weekends, and use 129·975. It is located immediately north of RAF Cranwell domestic site.
All powered aircraft must use the main Cranwell aerodrome.

Fuel: 100LL, Avtur. ¢.	**Tel:** 01400-261201 Ext 7377.

Robert Pooley ©

N52 54·17 E001 19·72	**CROMER (Northrepps)**	150 ft AMSL
2 nm SE of Cromer.		**NH 371·5 355** 13·7
		CSL 116·5 359 **9·5**

Coltishall Zone 125·90. Norwich APP 119·35. Anglia Radar 125·275
Cromer Micro 129·825 A/G.   Marine NDB 'CM' 313·5 (158°M/1·9 nm to A/D)

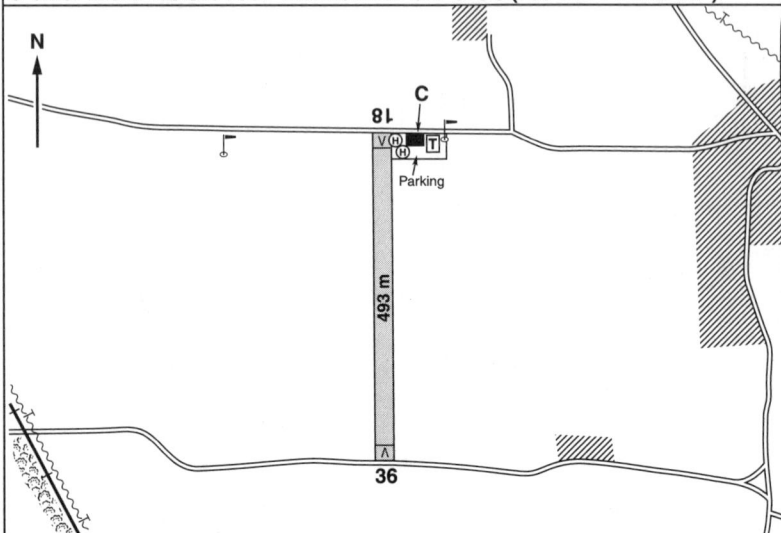

Rwy	Dim(m)	Surface	TORA(m)	LDA(m)	Lighting
18/36	493x23	Grass	Unlicensed		Nil
Rwy 36 gradient 1·8% UP.					

Op hrs: PPR. SR–SS.

Landing Fee: Aircraft £4.00, Microlights £2.00.	**Customs:** PNR
Hangarage: Nil	**Maintenance:** Nil

Remarks: Operated by C. Gurney Esq., Heath Cottage, Northrepps, Cromer. Norfolk.
NR27 9LB. Unlicensed airfield. Light aircraft and helicopters welcome on prior
permission and at pilot's own risk. Circuits at 600' aal, LH on 36, RH on 18.
Several Helicopter Main Routes (1500' – FL60) run NW/SE to the North of airfield,
HMR 7 crossing the Northern boundary of the airfield.
Intensive military and civil low level flying in the area seven days a week.
All aircraft should contact Coltishall Zone during their hours of operation, otherwise
Norwich App. LARS available from Coltishall. FIS and Alerting Service available from
Coltishall or Anglia Radar.
Departures — Normally restricted to Rwy 18 only, depending on aircraft take-off
capability, surface wind, ambient temperature and runway conditions.
Microlight activity 7 days a week. Occasional Crop spraying, Banner towing and
Model flying (weekdays only).

Accommodation: Hotel/Free house Restaurant within 5 mins walk,
Tel: 01263-579691 or Tourist Office 01263-512497.

Taxis: Blue Star 01263-512645. A1 Cabs 01263-513371. Bike/Car Hire on request.

Fuel: MOGAS	**Tel:** 01263-513015 or 07860-466484
100LL by arrangement.	**Fax:** 01263 515516

Robert Pooley ©

N52 10·27 E001 06·67	**CROWFIELD**	201 ft AMSL

4 nm ESE of Stowmarket.	CLN 114·55 001 19·5
	BKY 116·25 078 40·2

Crowfield Radio 122·775 A/G.
Wattisham APP 125·80.   Lakenheath 128·90.

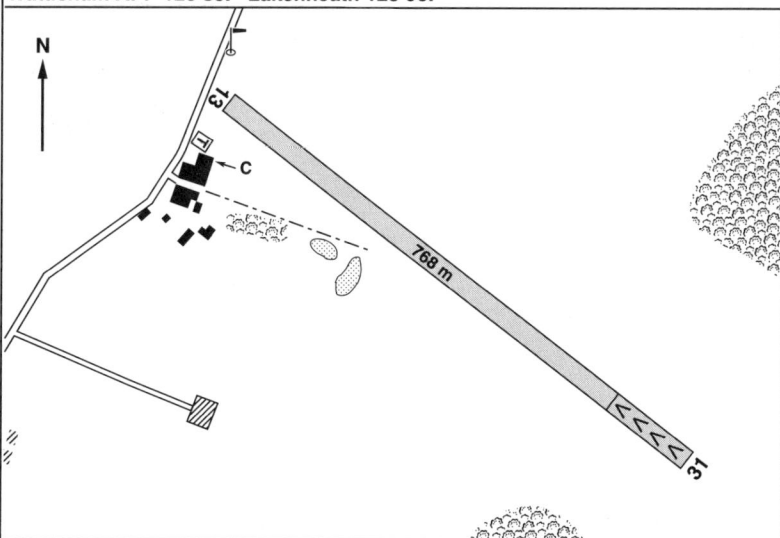

Rwy	Dim(m)	Surface	TORA(m)	LDA(m)	Lighting
13/31	768x27	Grass	13-741	13-741	Nil.
			31-768	31-644	Nil.

Op hrs: **PPR.** Winter: 0900-1800 or SS daily. Summer: 0800-2000 daily.

Landing Fees: Visitors £5.00

Hangarage/Parking: Available.   **Maintenance:** Nil.   **Customs:** 24 hrs PNR.

Remarks: Operated by Mr. A. C. Williamson. Private airfield.
Airfield situated within Wattisham MATZ. Circuits at 800' aal, directions variable.
Due to Discontinuance Order imposed by the Mid Suffolk District Council, the
following Restrictions apply: No Twins; No aircraft over 180 HP or 1200kg; No Single
seaters; No Gliders, Microlites or Helicopters. Not more than 20 movements in any
one day.

Arrival Procedure Pilots approaching Crowfield must call Wattisham App 125·80.

Departure Procedure Unless otherwise instructed by Wattisham, initial departure not
above 800' and maintain this height while within 5 nm of Crowfield. Contact
Wattisham App 125·80 as soon as possible after take-off.

Noise Abatement.
Departing Rwy 13 — Track 140°M initially to avoid farm on NE side of extended
centreline. Do not turn crosswind until east of farm.
Departing Rwy 31 — Maintain Rwy heading until main road West of airfield.
Radio Mast 1027' aal 1217' amsl 360°/3·9 nm.

Fuel: 100LL.	**Tel:** 01449-711017, 711524 outside Op hrs.
	Fax: 01449-711054.

N52 42·53 W000 08·57	**CROWLAND (Spalding)**	10 ft AMSL
4nm S of Spalding	GAM 112·80 145 45.	WJ 406·0 069 13·7
(On Spalding/Crowland Road).		WIT 117·60 069 14·1

Cottesmore APP 130·20 (MATZ/LARS).
Crowland Radio 130·10 or 130·40 A/G (Glider operations).

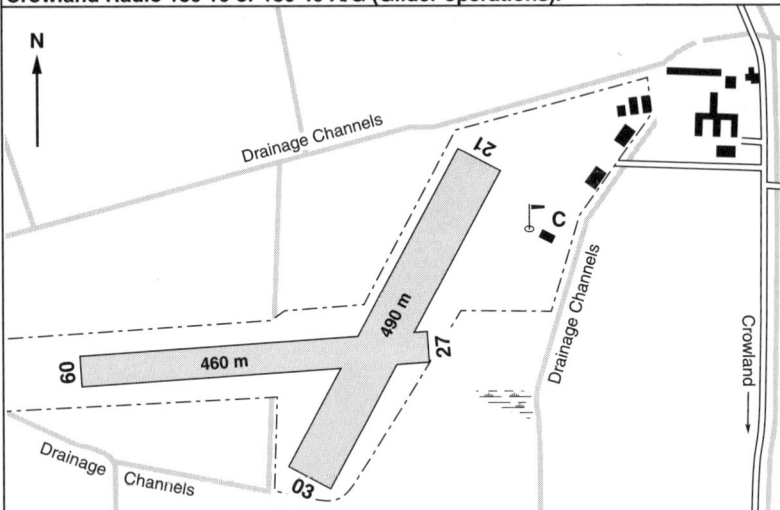

Rwy	Dim(m)	Surface	TORA(m)	LDA(m)	Lighting
03/21	490x60	Grass	Unlicensed		Nil
09/27	460x45	Grass	Unlicensed		Nil

Op hrs: PPR. SR-SS daily.

Landing Fee: No charge.	**Customs:** Nil.
Hangarage: Nil.	**Maintenance:** Nil.

Remarks: Operated by Peterborough and Spalding Gliding Club, Crowland Airfield, Crowland, Lincs.

Visiting aircraft welcome. Strictly prior permission only, at pilot's own risk. Good approaches.

Frequent aero-tow glider flying.

Circuits at 800 ft (QFE), powered aircraft LH, gliders RH.

RAF Wittering MATZ Panhandle begins 5 nm WSW of Crowland. Intensive military low-flying activity Mon-Fri in the vicinity of Crowland.

Mast 200 ft agl, situated 1 nm South of Crowland.

Restaurant: Club facilities

Accommodation: The Dun Cow, Barrier Bane, Cowbit, Nr Spalding, Lincs, PE12 6AL. Tel: 01406 - 380543.

Fuel: Nil.	**Tel:** 01933-274198 CFI.
	01733-210463 Airfield (Weekends).

N50 05·17 W005 15·34	**CULDROSE**	267 ft AMSL
1 nm SE of Helston.	**LND 114·20 109 15. SM**	**356·5 212** 23·9
	SMG 112·60 210 **22·8**	

c/s Culdrose. APP 134·05. TWR 122·10.

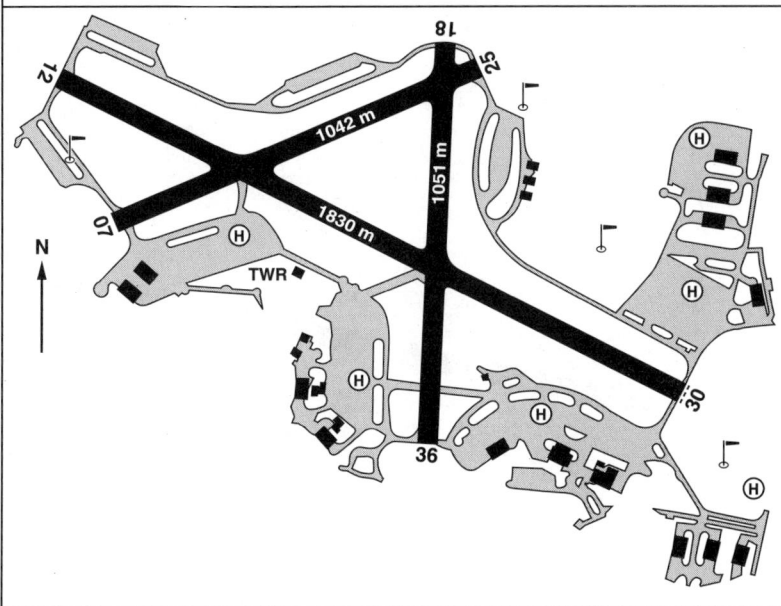

Rwy	Dim(m)	Surface	TORA(m)	LDA(m)	Lighting
07/25	1042x46	Asphalt	07-1028	07-1028	Ap Rwy PAPI
			25-1028	25-1028	Ap Rwy PAPI
12/30	1830x46	Asphalt	12-1830	12-1830	Ap Rwy PAPI
			30-1830	30-1830	Ap Rwy PAPI
18/36	1051x46	Asphalt	18-1051	18-1051	Ap Rwy PAPI
			36-1051	36-1051	Ap Rwy PAPI
					IBn 'CU' Red

Op hrs: 24 hrs PPR. Mon-Thur 0830-1700 or SS, Fri 0830-1400 or SS. **ATZ active H24.**

Landing Fee: MoD(Navy) Rates.	**Customs:** ¢.
Hangarage: Nil.	**Maintenance:** Nil.

Remarks: RN Aerodrome. Civil aircraft PPR.
Inbound aircraft to contact Culdrose APP at 20 nm. Radar recovery mandatory.
High intensity helicopter operations in the area.
No 'deadside', helicopter circuits left and right of runway in use.
More than one runway may be in use simultaneously.
Glider activity evenings Mon-Fri and SR-SS Sat. & Sun.

Fuel: 100LL, Avtur. ¢.	**Tel:** 01326-574121 Ext 2415 ATC.
	PPR from Air Ops Ext 2620.

Robert Pooley ©

N55 58·50 W003 58·38	**CUMBERNAULD**	350 ft AMSL

16 nm NE of Glasgow.	GOW 115·40 076 17
	TLA 113·80 331 35·5

c/s Cumbernauld Radio 120·60 A/G. WINTER: 0900-1700. SUMMER: 0900-2000.

If no contact, make standard calls and proceed with caution.

NDB 'CBN' 374·0 (On A/D).   DME 'CBN' 117·55 (On A/D).

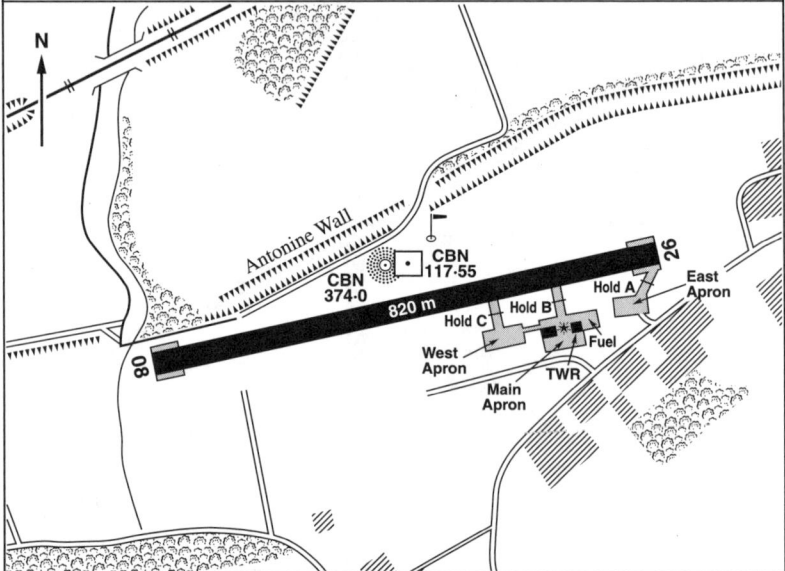

Rwy	Dim(m)	Surface	TORA(m)	LDA(m)	Lighting
08/26	820x23	Asphalt	08-820	08-820	Thr Rwy APAPI 4°(LH)
			26-820	26-820	Ap Thr Rwy APAPI 3°(LH)
					ABn Wh

Op hrs: Strictly PPR.

Landing Fees: Up to 2730 kg - Single £15; Twin up to 3000 kg - £37.50, incl of VAT.

Customs: 24 hrs PNR.

Hangarage: Available.	**Maintenance:** Available.	**Met.** 0141-221 6116

Remarks: Operated by Cumbernauld Airport Ltd, Cumbernauld Airport, 2/6 Duncan McIntosh Rd, Cumbernauld G68 0HH. PPR. The aerodrome is situated beneath the Scottish TMA (2500' ALT– FL60) Class 'E' Controlled Airspace. In IMC suitably equipped aircraft may let down at Edinburgh and proceed to Cumbernauld VFR. Circuits at 1000 ' QFE, LH on Rwy 08, RH on Rwy 26. Standard overhead joins at 2000' QFE.

High Ground 1153' aal 1503' amsl 300°/4 nm.
Chimney 103' aal 435' amsl 102°/0·4 nm.

Restaurant: Beverages and Snacks available.

Car Hire: By arrangement.

Fuel: 100LL, Jet A1.	**Tel:** 01236-722100 Airfield; 722822 ATC.
	Fax: 01236- 781646.

N50 38·25 W004 37·13	**DAVIDSTOW MOOR**	970 ft AMSL
3 nm ENE of Camelford		BHD 112·05 295 44·8

No Radio.
St. Mawgan APP 126·50.

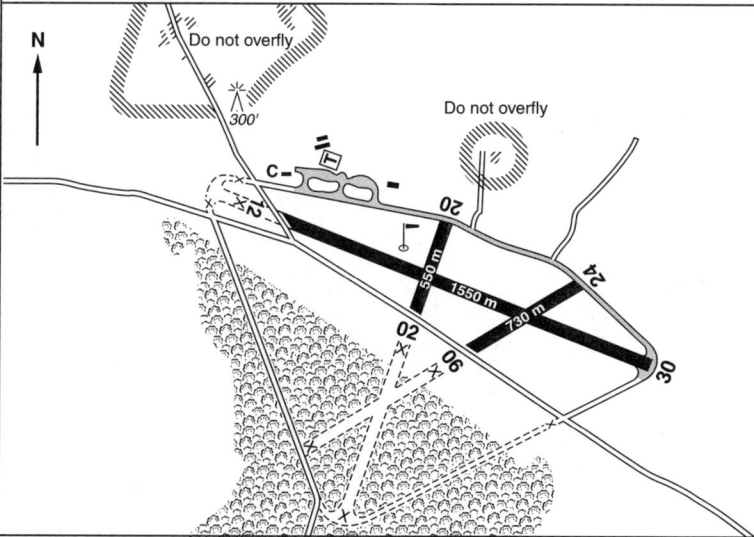

Rwy	Dim(m)	Surface	TORA(m)	LDA(m)	Lighting
02/20	550x46	Concrete	Unlicensed		Nil.
06/24	730x46	Concrete	Unlicensed		Nil.
12/30	1550x46	Concrete	Unlicensed		Nil.

Op hrs: Strictly PPR, 0900-1900.

Landing Fee: On Application.	**Customs:** Nil.
Hangarage: Limited for Microlights.	**Maintenance:** Microlights.

Remarks: Operated by The Moorland Flying Club. Ex military airfield on unfenced moorland. The airfield is bisected by a class 'C' road running SE/NW.

Only runways to the NE of the road are available for use.

Deep drain holes are hidden in the grass beside the runways.

Intense microlight activity, circuit height 500'.

Windsock displayed when flying in progress.

Do not overfly Chicken farm approximately 1 nm east of the airfield boundary.

Gliding at weekends.

Occasional high level parachuting. Therefore PPR **must** be obtained.

Beware of livestock and tourists on runways.

Accommodation: Nearby Hotels.

Taxis: Available.

Fuel: MOGAS & Two Stroke only.	**Tel:** 01840-261517 **Fax:** 01840-213844 e-mail: mfc@avnet.co.uk

Robert Pooley ©

N50 52·73 E000 09·38	**DEANLAND (Lewes)**	65 ft AMSL

6 nm E of Lewes.	**SFD 117·00 014 7·5**
	LYD 114·05 259 28·5

Deanland Radio 129·725 A/G (not always manned but normal circuit calls must be made).

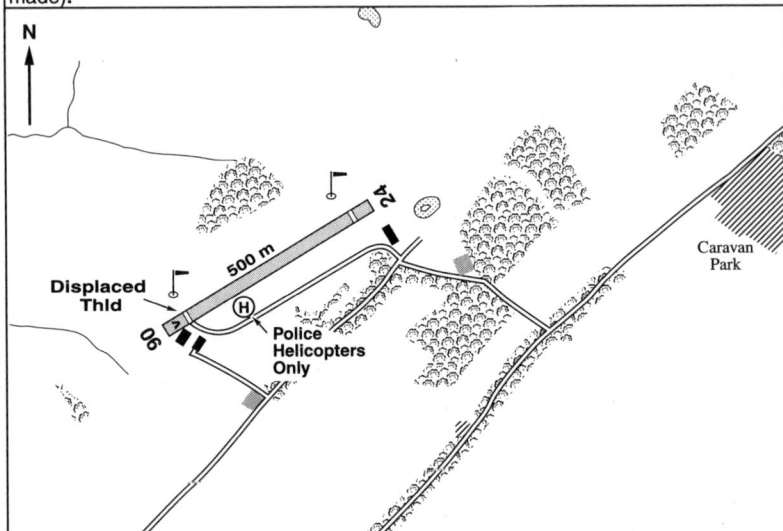

Rwy	Dim(m)	Surface	TORA(m)	LDA(m)	Lighting
06/24	500x27	Grass	Unlicensed		Rwy

Op hrs: PPR. SR–SS   **Customs:** Nil.

Landing Fee: £3 minimum donation to 'World wide fund for Nature' at Control Point. Parking £3 per night.

Hangarage: Nil. Tiedowns available.   **Maintenance:** M3.

Remarks: Operated by Messrs Brook & Price.

Caution: Do not mistake Ringmer, a private gliding site located 2 nm to the NW or a private airfield 2 nm to SW for Deanland (Lewes).

Single engined aircraft only. Strictly No microlights of any type.

Fill in details in movements book at the Control Point.

Avoid overflying Ripe village, the caravan park and local houses, particularly the two to the North of the airfield with large lakes.

Circuits at 1000' aal., LH on 06, RH on 24.

Arr – Large circuits with minimum of 1·5 nm final maintaining extended centreline.

Dep – After take-off maintain runway heading for 1·5 nm before turning on track.

Taxis: 01323-811337.

Fuel: Nil.	**Tel:** 01323-811 410 Airfield.
	07785-316 368. 01293-429 802.
	01273-400 768. 01903-774 379
	Fax: 01293-429 836.
	e-mail: david@gatwick-group.co.uk

N52 30·37 W000 35·35	**DEENETHORPE**	328 ft AMSL

4 nm E of Corby	DTY 116·40 051 27
	CFD 116·50 007 26

Cottesmore APP 130·20.
Deenethorpe Radio 127·575 A/G - By arrangement.

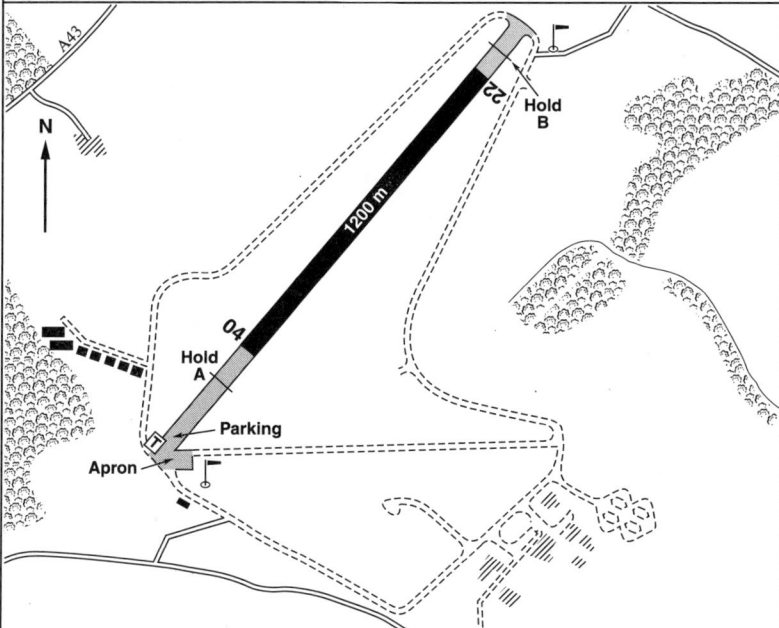

Rwy	Dim(m)	Surface	TORA(m)	LDA(m)	Lighting
04/22	1200x43	Asphalt	Unlicensed		Nil

Op hrs: PPR.

Landing Fee: On application.

Hangarage: Nil.	**Maintenance:** Nil.	**Customs:** 3 hrs PNR

Remarks: Operated by Mr. A.P.I. Campbell, Estates Office, Deene Park, Corby, NN17 3 EW. PPR by telephone. Unlicensed aerodrome.
Aerodrome located just outside Witterng MATZ – contact Cottesmore App 130·20.
Circuits LH at 1000' aal.
Parking area forms part of undershoot to Rwy 04 — do not land short.
'DT' displayed on roof near signals square. All taxiways disused.
Microlights also operate from the aerodrome.
Avoid overflying the Deene Park 1 nm NNW of airfield.
Aircraft using Deenethorpe must carry Third party and public liability Insurance cover to at least £500,000 in respect of any one incident.

Caution: LYVEDEN Gliding Site 3 nm to SE — cable launched up to 2,000 ft.

Accommodation/Taxis: Available.

Fuel: Nil.	**Tel:** 01780-450361 - Operator. **Fax:** 01780-450282

Robert Pooley ©

N51 35·32 W000 30·78	**DENHAM**	249 ft AMSL
7·5nm N of Heathrow Airport.	BNN 113·75 177 8·4. LON 113·60 349 6·3	
c/s Denham Information/Radio 130·725 AFIS/A/G.		

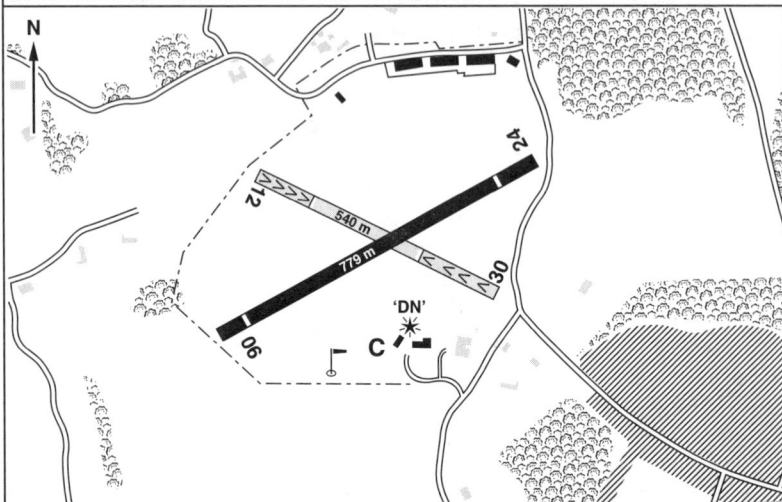

Rwy	Dim(m)	Surface	TORA(m)	LDA(m)	Lighting
06/24	779x18	Asphalt	06-737	06-701	Thr Rwy APAPI 4·5°†
			24-727	24-675	Thr Rwy APAPI 4·5°
12/30	540x18	Grass	12-439	12-428	Nil.
			30-540	30-380	Nil.
					IBn 'DN' Gn

Op hrs: PPR. 0900-1730 or SS daily, & ¢.

Landing Fee: Up to 1000 kg £9.50 per tonne; 1001–1500 kg £14; 1501–2000 kg £19; 2001–3000 kg £28; 3001–4000 kg £37, 4001–5000 kg £46 - All inclusive of VAT.

Customs: EU — forms only required; Non EU — PNR.

Hangarage: By arrangement.   **Maintenance:** Available.

Remarks: Operated by Bickerton's Aerodromes Ltd. PPR. A/D situated within the London CTR (Class 'A' Controlled Airspace), see opposite page for procedures within Denham Local Flying Area. Non-radio aircraft not accepted.

Variable circuits, maximum 750' QFE.

Power cables 120' aal, 369' amsl, 270°/0·6 nm, running NS.
Public road crosses final approach to Rwy 24, 100 m from threshold.

Rwy 12/30 is not to be used for solo training flights.

All aircraft using Denham are required to have a valid third party liability insurance cover of not less than £1 million pounds.

† APAPIs on Rwy 06 are visible to the left of extended centreline where normal obstacle clearance is not guaranteed. Ignore signals until aligned with runway.

Restaurant: Restaurant facilities closed Mons, visitors welcome. Tel: 01895-834241.

Taxis: Cabline Tel: 01895-270001.   **Car Hire:** Avis Tel: 0645-123456

Fuel: 100LL, Jet A1.	**Tel:** 01895-832161 Admin. 01895-833236 Twr.
	Fax: 01895-833486. Ansaphone 01895-835161

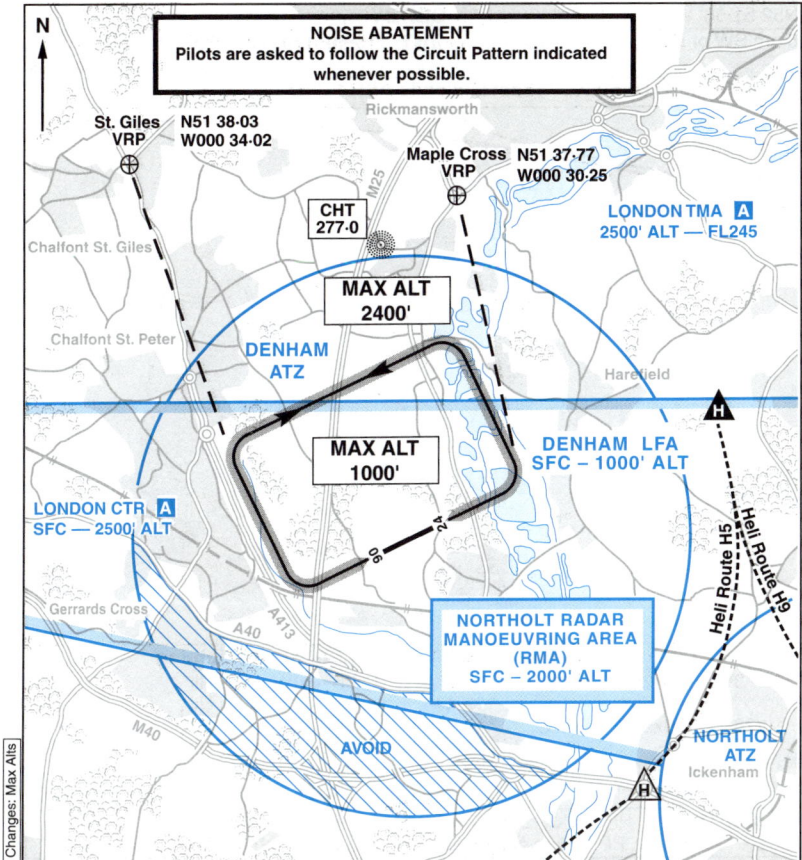

NOISE ABATEMENT
Pilots are asked to follow the Circuit Pattern indicated whenever possible.

St. Giles VRP N51 38·03 W000 34·02

Maple Cross VRP N51 37·77 W000 30·25

CHT 277·0

LONDON TMA A 2500' ALT — FL245

MAX ALT 2400'

DENHAM ATZ

MAX ALT 1000'

DENHAM LFA SFC – 1000' ALT

LONDON CTR A SFC — 2500' ALT

Heli Route H5 Heli Route H9

NORTHOLT RADAR MANOEUVRING AREA (RMA) SFC – 2000' ALT

AVOID

NORTHOLT ATZ Ickenham

Changes: Max Alts

Procedures: There is no overhead joining procedure. Circuit joining will be made directly to base leg, via Chalfont St. Giles for Rwy 06 and via Maple Cross for Rwy 24. Inbound aircraft must establish radio contact with Denham Radio at 10 nm range and then report at the VRP. Aircraft must be below 2500 ft QNH under the London TMA, and at or below 1000 ft QNH within the London CTR.

Within the Denham Local Flying Area (LFA), flights without compliance with IFR requirements may take place subject to the following conditions:

1. Aircraft to remain below cloud and in sight of surface.

2. Maximum altitude 1000 ft QNH, with a minimum flight visibility of 3 km.

3. The area to the South of the A40 is to be avoided at all times.

Note: Pilots of aircraft flying in the LFA are responsible for providing their own separation. Joing aircraft should give way to circuit traffic.

Northolt traffic in the Northolt Radar Manoeuvring Area (RMA) will cross Denham ATZ not below 1500 ft QNH but may be below this altitude in the Northolt ATZ which extends to within 0·1 nm of the edge of Denham ATZ at its closest point. Aircraft wishing to make use of the Northolt RMA when en route to or from Denham are to contact Northolt on 126·45 .

Robert Pooley ©

N52 51·58 W001 37·05	**DERBY**	175 ft AMSL
6 nm SW of Derby	**TNT 115·70 175 12.**	**HON 113·65 010 30**
		DTY 116·40 343 45

Derby Radio 118·35 A/G.   **East Midlands APP 119·65.**

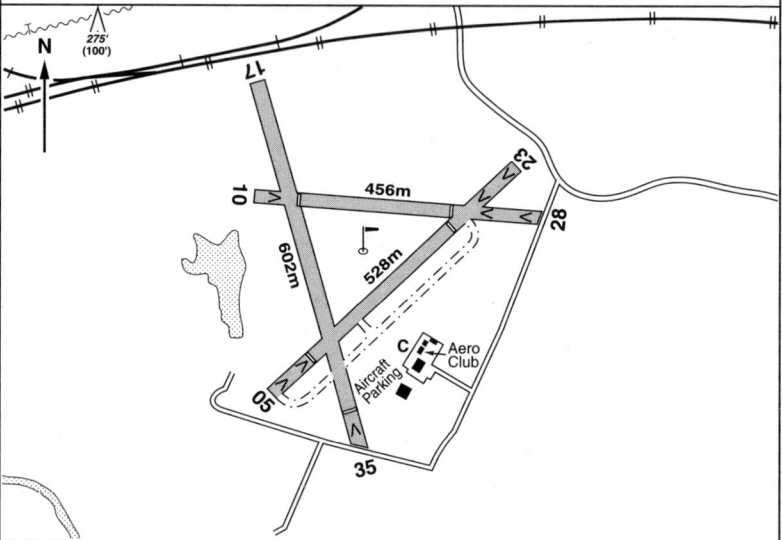

Rwy	Dim(m)	Surface	TORA(m)	LDA(m)	Lighting
05/23	528x20	Grass	05-356	05-430	Nil
			23-445	23-341	Nil
10/28	456x20	Grass	10-276	10-315	Nil
			28-300	28-291	Nil
17/35	602x20	Grass	17-513 (Take-off only)		Nil
			(Landing Only) 35-528		Nil

Op hrs: WINTER: PPR. Mon-Sat 0900-SS, Sun & PHs 0930-SS.
   SUMMER: PPR. Mon-Sat 0900-1700, Sun & PHs 0930-1700.

Landing Fee: £5.   **Customs:** Nil.   **Hangarage:** Ltd.   **Maintenance:** Available

Remarks: Operated by Derby Aero Club. Licensed aerodrome situated beneath East Midlands CTA (1500' – FL55). Special procedures applicable to all flights must be obtained by telephone from Derby Aero Club when arranging prior permission.
Non radio aircraft **not** accepted. Aerodrome not licensed for public transport flights.
Circuits: LH on 05 & 10; RH on 23 & 28, all at 1000' aal; LH on 17, RH on 35, both at 800' aal. No runway designators. Displaced landing thresholds marked by black/white or red/white wing bars. Avoid overflying local villages.
No overhead joins due to proximity of East Midlands CTA (base 1500').
Caution: Power cables 100' aal immediately North of A/D. An early 'Go around' decision vital in the event of missed approach to Rwy 35. Power cables 30' aal on approach to Rwy 28. Possible turbulence from trees on final approach to Rwy 23. These trees also shield aircraft low on final approach from those at the 23 hold.
Chimney 100' aal, 275' amsl, 010°/800 m.

Restaurant: Club facilities.   **Taxi/ Car Hire:** By arrangement.

Fuel: 100LL	**Tel:**01283-733803 **Fax:** 01283-734829

N54 08·23 W001 25·22	**DISHFORTH**	117 ft AMSL
3·5nm E of Ripon.		**POL 112·10 052 33**
		LBA 402·5 033 18

Topcliffe APP 125·00. Dishforth TWR 122·10 (O/R). A/G 130·10 Gliders.
Leeming c/s Zone Radar 127·75 – For Leeming/Topcliffe/Disforth CMATZ.

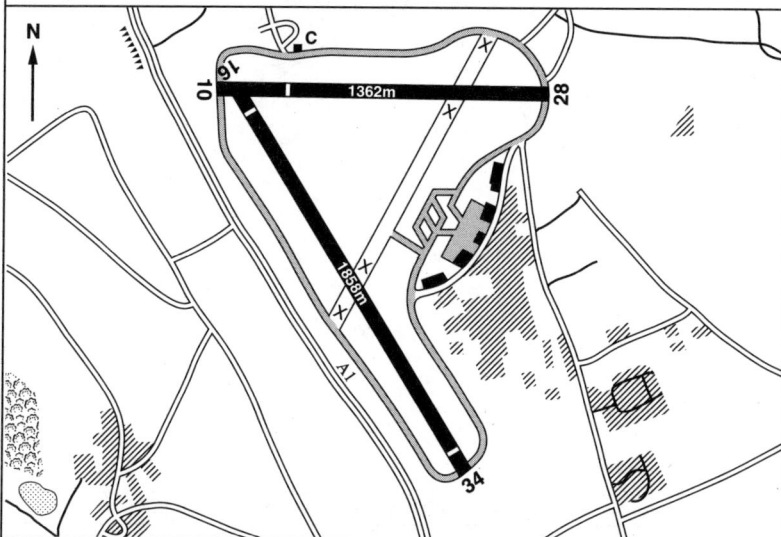

Rwy	Dim(m)	Surface	TORA(m)	LDA(m)	Lighting
16/34	1858x46	Asphalt	16-1858	16-1716	Ap Rwy PAPI
			34-1858	34-1782	Ap Rwy PAPI
10/28	1362x46	Asphalt	10-1362	10-936	PAPI
			28-1362	28-1362	PAPI

Op hrs: PPR. Mon-Fri 0830-1700.	ATZ active H24
Landing Fee: MoD (ARMY) Rates.	Customs: Nil.
Hangarage: Nil.	Maintenance: Nil.

Remarks: RAF/Army Aerodrome. Satelite aerodrome of Linton-on-Ouse. PPR for fixed wing and civilian, Tel: 01748-874633. All inbound/outbound Flight Plans to include EGXEZGZX and EGXUYWYO in the addresses.
Circuits: LH on Rwy 28 and 34; RH on Rwy 10 and 16.
Circuit height for light aircraft 1000' aal.
High intensity military flying during operating hours. Glider flying and aerotows at weekends throughout the year, and evenings during the summer.
Helicopter operations may take place when ATC not manned.
Aircraft in visual circuits to avoid overflying the town of Borougbridge, the Kirby Hill village and airfield domestic area.

Pilots are advised to contact Leeming Zone 127·75 before entering the area.

Fuel: Nil.	Tel: 01748-874633 Fixed wing and civilian. 01748-874561/2 AAC Helicopters

Robert Pooley ©

N57 52·33 W004 01·58	**DORNOCH**	3 ft AMSL
On S edge of Town.	**INS 109·20 009 20.**	**KS 370·0 321 19·4**
		KSS 109·80 317 20·2

No Radio. Recommend contact Lossiemouth APP 119·35.

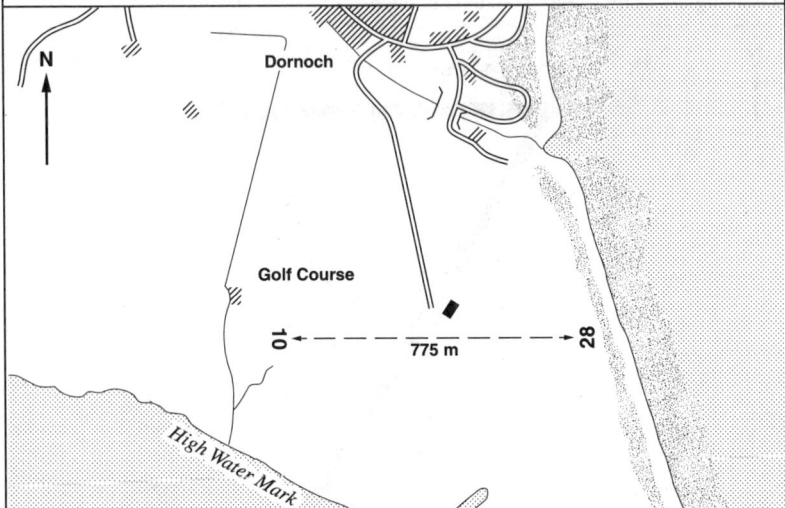

Rwy	Dim(m)	Surface	TORA(m)	LDA(m)	Lighting
10/28	775x23	Grass	Unlicensed		Nil.

Op hrs: By arrangement, daylight hours only.

Landing Fee: Highland Council Rates. **Customs:** Nil.

Hangarage: Nil. **Maintenance:** Nil.

Remarks: Operated by The Highland Council Roads and Transport Services, Sutherland. Unlicensed. Light aircraft accepted by arrangement and at pilot's own risk. Care must be taken. Windsock by arrangement. Good grass surface.

Aerodrome situated within Danger Area D703, DAAIS from Tain Range on 122·75. Pilots must obtain clearance to enter the Danger Area prior to arrival and departure.

An Entry/Exit lane is situated between Embo (N5756 W00401) and aerodrome from ground level up to 1,000 ALT.

Restaurant: Nil.

Car Hire: Available through Mr. H.A. Mackay, Tel: 01862-810162.

Fuel: Nil.	**Tel:** 01408-623400 Roads & Transport Mgr.
	01862-810491 Area Manager.
	Fax: 01408-621118 Roads & Transport Mgr.

N56 27·15 W003 01·55	**DUNDEE**	17 ft AMSL

0·5 nm S of Dundee,	**LUK** 110·5 319 **7·3**
on N bank of River Tay.	**LU** 330·0 319 7·3

c/s Dundee. APP/TWR 122·90.
NDB 'DND' 394·00 (102°M/2·63 nm to Thr 10).
ILS/DME Rwy 10 (096°M) 'DDE' 108·10.

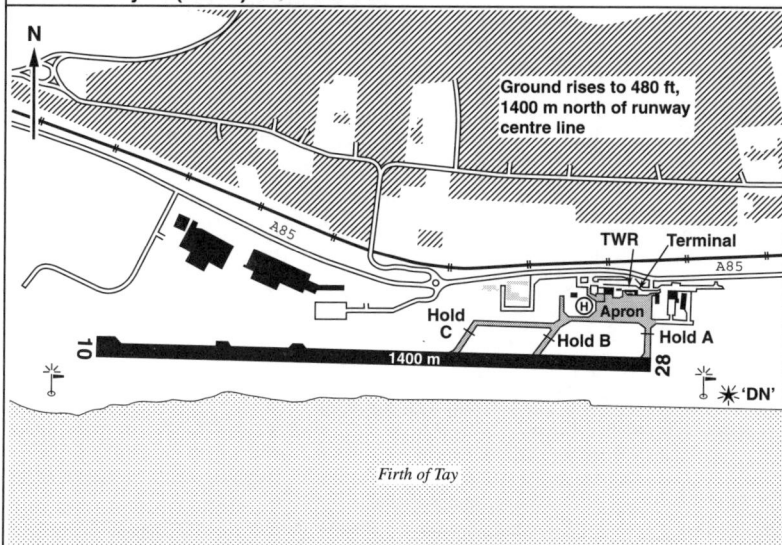

Rwy	Dim(m)	Surface	TORA(m)	LDA(m)	Lighting
10/28	1400x30	Asphalt	10-1319	10-1400	Ap Thr Rwy PAPI 3°
			28-1319	28-1400	Rwy PAPI 3·25°
					I Bn 'DN' Gn

Op hrs: Mon-Fri 0600-2100, Sat 0800-1600, Sun 1100-2100.

Landing Fee: Singles £6.81 cash or credit card on the day, others £9.70 per tonne or part thereof plus VAT. Minimum credit invoice £35.00

Hangarage: Limited.   **Maintenance:** Available - JAR 45.   **Customs:** 24 hrs PNR

Remarks: Operated by Dundee City Council. Non-radio aircraft PPR.
Training flights strictly PPR. RH circuits Rwy 10, LH circuits Rwy 28.
Aerodrome is the vicinity of Leuchars MATZ.
Local flights to the North of the aerodrome below 2000' amsl are not permitted.
Aircraft departing to the North are to climb straight ahead to 2000 ft before turning.
Avoid overflying Nine-Wells Hospital 306°T/1·2 nm.

Warnings. Moderate bird hazard throughout the year and may be severe in Autumn.
Twy C is 10 m wide and is restricted to aircraft with weight of 5700 kg or less.

Visual Reference Point (VRP) - Broughty Castle N56 27·75 W002 52·18.

Restaurant: Drinks and food dispensers in lounge. 'Tom Cobleigh' restaurant 200 m from Terminal Building.   **Car Hire:** Agencies in city.

Fuel: 100LL, Jet A1. Mulit-Service	**Tel:** 01382-662200 Airport. **Fax:** 01382-641263

Robert Pooley ©

Intentionally Blank

N50 51·60 W003 14·08	**DUNKESWELL**	850 ft AMSL

14 nm NE of Exeter.	BHD 112·05 026 29·5
	VLN 111·00 255 24·0

c/s Dunkeswell Radio 123·475 A/G.

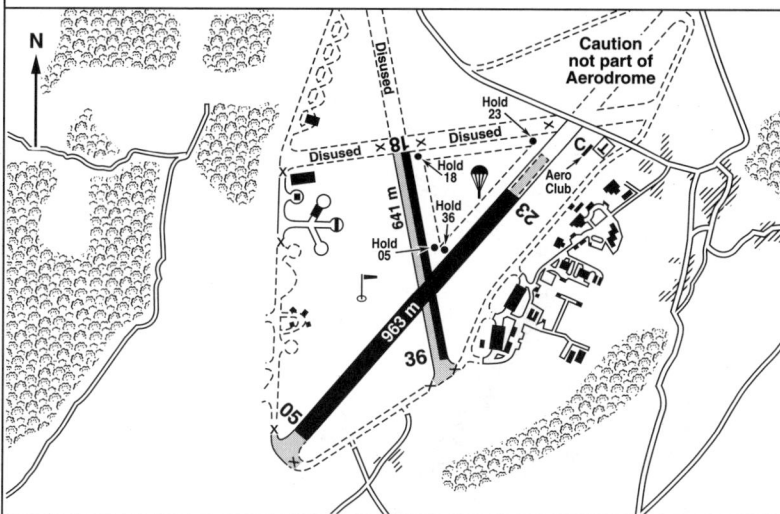

Rwy	Dim(m)	Surface	TORA(m)	LDA(m)	Lighting
05/23	963x46	Asphalt	05-963	05-963	Goosenecks for
			23-963†	23-963	emergency use only.
18/36	641x20	Asphalt	18-641	18-641	
			36-641	36-641	

† Additional 150x30m starter extension available on request.

Op hrs: 0900-1800 (1900 Summer) or SS+30 whichever earlier

Landing Fee: Singles £6.38 +VAT; Twins 3.50 per 0·5 tonne +VAT.

Hangarage: Limited.	**Maintenance:** Available.	**Customs:** 24 hrs PNR

Remarks: Operated by Air Westward Co. Ltd. Strictly PPR. No regular surface traffic control. Avoid glider site at North Hill 1·5 nm WSW of aerodrome.
Circuits at 800' aal, LH on18 and 23, RH on 05 and 36.
Cautionary look-out for low flying military aircraft on E/W headings approximately 5 nm North of airfield. Maintain special lookout for gliders in local area.
Grass Landing Strips available on request (unlicensed).
The old perimeter tracks are unsuitable for use as taxiways, use established taxyways/runways only.

Caution: Outside the NE boundary of the aerodrome and separated from it by a public road is a large paved area. It is not part of the aerodrome. Pilots should positively identify the displaced landing threshold to Rwy 23 before committing the aircraft to final approach.

Free-fall parachuting from up to FL150, normally during daylight hours.

Restaurant: Club facilities and refreshments at the aircentre.

Fuel: 100LL.	**Tel:** 01404-891271/891643 Airfield.
	Fax: 01404-891024.

N52 05·45 E000 07·92	**DUXFORD**	124 ft AMSL

8 nm S of Cambridge.	**BKY 116·25 029 6·4. BPK 117·50 028 22·1**
	LAM 115·60 003 26·5

c/s Duxford Information 122·075 AFIS.

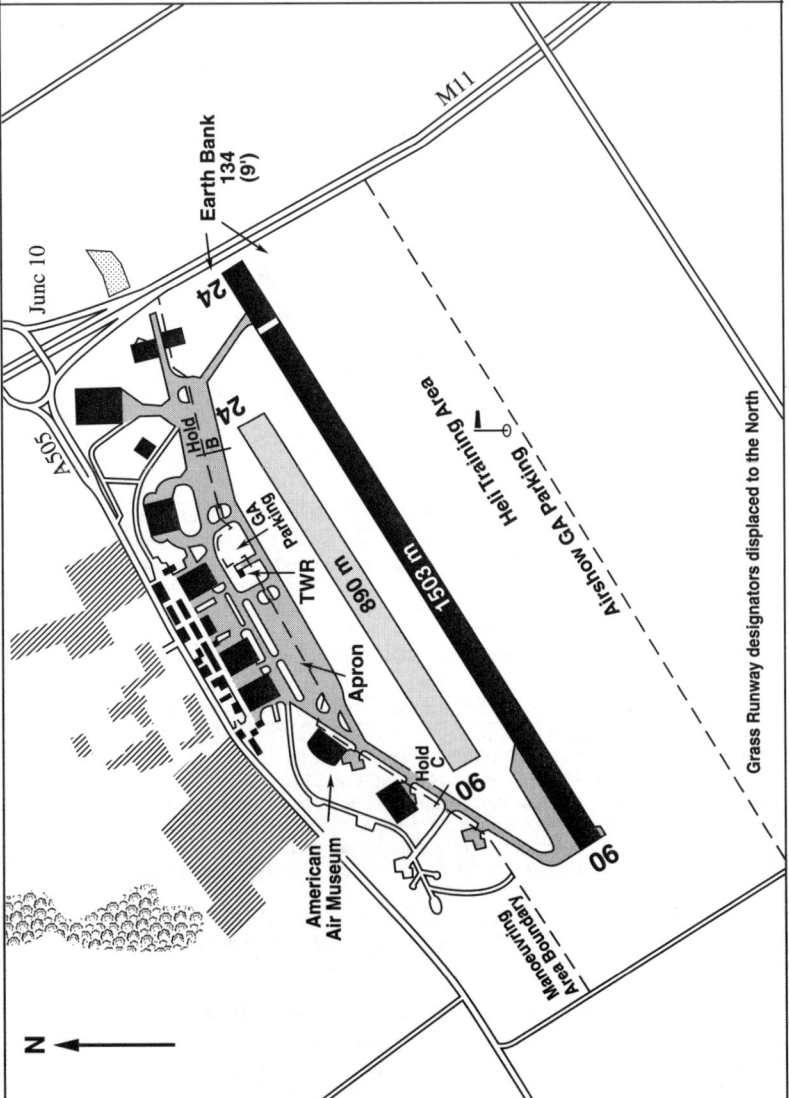

M11

Earth Bank
134 (9')

Junc 10

24

A505

Hold B

24

GA parking

TWR

890 m

1503 m

Heli Training Area

Airshow GA parking

Grass Runway designators displaced to the North

Apron

Hold C

06

06

American Air Museum

Manoeuvring Area Boundary

Z ←

| N52 05·45 E000 07·92 | **DUXFORD** | | | | 124 ft AMSL |

Rwy	Dim(m)	Surface	TORA(m)	LDA(m)	Lighting
06/24	1503x45	Asphalt/	06-1353	06-1353	Nil
		Concrete	24-1453	24-1353	Nil
06/24	890x53	Grass	06-890	06-890	Nil
			24-890	24-890	Nil

Op hrs: Nov to Mid March – PPR by phone. 1000-1600 daily.
Mid Mar to Nov – PPR. 1000-1800 or SS (which ever is earlier) daily.

Landing Fee: Singles £13.50; Twins £17.00. Special landing fees apply for Airshows.
Special reductions for Club Rallies, Outings and Training X-Country Flights

| **Hangarage:** Nil. | **Maintenance:** Nil. | **Customs:** 12 hrs PNR |

Remarks: Administered by the Cambridge County Council/Imperial War Museum. Licensed aerodrome. Check Rescue/Fire service availability prior to flight.

Aerodrome PPR during Winter period, but R/T calls may be initiated 5 minutes away by pilots who have visited previously. Circuits LH on Rwy 24, RH on Rwy 06 for visitors.

Fowlmere and Duxford ATZs overlap. Circuit patterns are mutually agreed between the two aerodromes so it is essential that pilots obtain a briefing from Duxford before departure (inbound or outbound).

Special Rules apply for Event Day - see relevant AIC.

Caution: High performance aircraft often join via 'run and break' manoeuvre. GA aircraft are to join overhead at 1500 ft QFE before turning and descending downwind to a circuit height of 1000 ft QFE.

Caution using taxiways, max wingspan 23 m.

Simultaneous runway operations not authorised.

Inbound routes to avoid infringements of Controlled Airspace around Stansted:

1. Inbounds from the south to pass west of Stansted:
   Route LAM VOR – BPK VOR – BKY VOR – Duxford A/D.
2. Inbounds from the south to pass east of Stansted:
   Route Chelmsford VRP – Braintree VRP – Haverhill VRP – Duxford A/D.
3. Inbounds from the east:
   Route CLN VOR – Haverhill VRP – Duxford A/D.

Notes: For above VRPs – See London (Stansted) CTR/CTA and VRPs chart.
Avoid Wethersfield glider site - op height 2000 ft agl, and Linton Zoo - E of Duxford by 5 nm up tp 2500 ft.

Noise Abatement Procedures: Avoid overflying the nearby villages of DUXFORD, THRIPLOW, WHITTLESFORD and the chemical works of DUXFORD and WHITTLESFORD. Arriving traffic for Rwy 24 position for 2 nm final.

Traffic departing Rwy 06 maintain runway heading for 2 nm before turning.

Visitors are not to wander on the manoeuvring area, but to report to the Tower as soon as possible.

All aircraft landing at Duxford require a minimum of £500,000 third party/legal liability insurance.

| **Restaurant:** Available. | **Car Hire:** Will Hire, Tel: 01223-414600. |
| **Taxi:** Mastercab, Tel: 01223-566654. | Sawston Taxis 01223-833838. |

Fuel: 100LL (1000-1600 only).	**Tel:** 01223-833376 AFIS.
Jet A1	**Fax:** 01223-833376 AFIS.
	E-mail: airtraffic@iwm.org.uk **Web:** www.iwm.org.uk

N50 55·72 W003 59·37	**EAGLESCOTT**	655 ft AMSL
6 nm ESE of Torrington.		**BHD 112·05 337 37**
10nm SSE of Barnstaple.		**CVR 111·60 153 11**

Eaglescott Radio 123·00 A/G

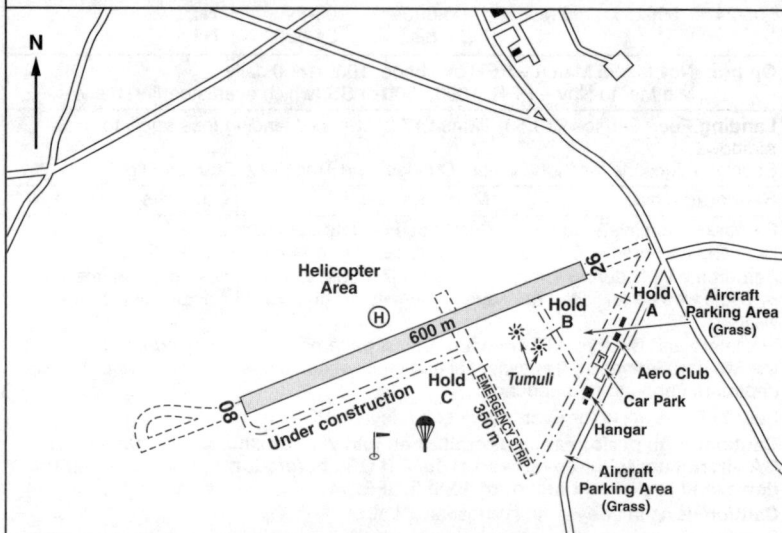

Rwy	Dim(m)	Surface	TORA(m)	LDA(m)	Lighting
08/26	600x18	Grass	08-600	08-600*	Nil.
			26-600	26-600*	Nil.

*115 m over-run on Rwy 08; 180 m over-run on Rwy 26.

Op hrs: PPR. 0800-2100 or SS whichever earlier.

Landing Fee: Singles £3 one landing or £5 all day. Twins £7.50. Helis £5.

Customs: 24 hrs PNR or Southwest Area Customs, Tel: 01752-235600.

Hangarage: Limited, for fabric aircraft only.   **Maintenance:** Nil

Remarks: Operated by Devon Airsports Ltd. Eaglescott Airfield, Burrington, Umberleigh, N. Devon. EX37 9LH. Non radio aircraft must obtain prior permission before departure. Gliding activity by aerotow using the area to the right of the runway in use. Use by rotary wing aircraft restricted to the area indicated above.
Standard overhead joins. Parachuting up to FL150.
Circuits LH at 800', home based gliders and microlights RH.
Runway slopes down E to W (downslope on 26) slightly.
Avoid overflying local habitation.
Occasionally Model aircraft flying on south side of the Emergency strip.
Radio mast 538' agl, 1193' amsl, 308°/5·2nm.
Four Radar Aerials 75'aal 730' amsl 060°/550 m.

Flying ,Gliding tuition , Parachute courses and Microlight training available.

Refreshments: Tea/Coffee available. **Accommodation/Taxis:** Available locally on request.

Fuel: 100LL, MOGAS.	**Tel:** 01769-520 404 - after 11 am. 07850- 640 268 - Microlight Training

N51 54·83 E000 40·97	**EARLS COLNE**	225 ft AMSL
3 nm SE of Halstead.	BKY 116·25 105 23·5. CLN 114·55 287 17·7	
	LAM 115·60 054 25·5	

c/s Earls Colne Radio 122·425 A/G.

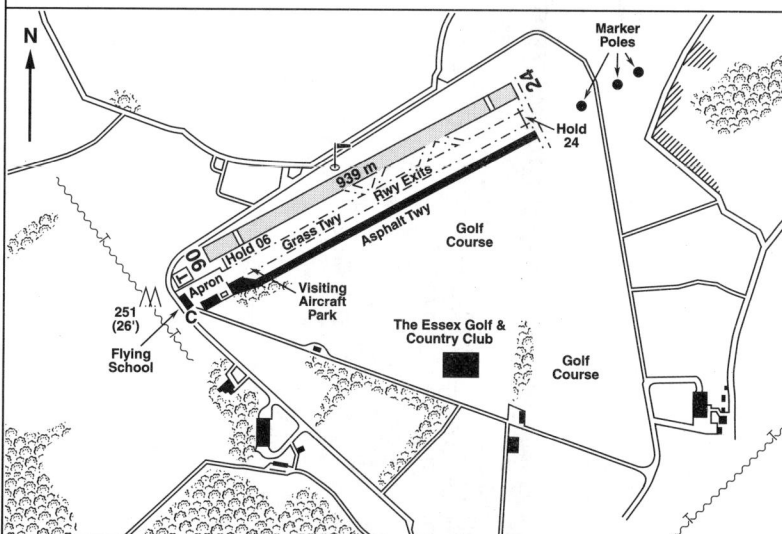

Rwy	Dim(m)	Surface	TORA(m)	LDA(m)	Lighting
06/24	939x18	Grass	06-866	06-767	Nil.
			24-840	24-767	Nil.

Op hrs: WINTER: 09-1800 or SS daily, & ¢.   SUMMER: 09-1800 daily, & ¢.

Landing Fee: Singles £10.00; Twins & Helis £13.00.   **Customs:** 4 hrs PNR

Hangarage: Nil.   **Maintenance:** By arrangement Tel: 01787-224988.

Remarks: Operated by Bulldog Aviation Ltd., Earls Colne Airfield, Earls Colne, Essex. Airfield licensed for Training and Private Flights.

During Winter and early Spring, grass taxiway is redesignated as runway. Pilots are to check before departure as to the runway status.

Non radio aircraft may be accepted on PPR.

Standard overhead join, circuits at 1000 ft. RH on Rwy 06, LH on Rwy 24.

Avoid overflying Earls Colne village.

Departures Rwy 06 –Keep left of marker poles and climb to 500' agl before turning.

Departures Rwy 24 –Maintain runway centre-line and climb to 700' agl before turning.

Caution: Power cables 26 ft aal cross final approach to Rwy 06 at 300m from thld.

Golf and Country Club facilities available to visiting aircraft on pay as you use basis. Booking recommended.

Flying Tuition and Aircraft Hire: Details from Anglian Flight Centre Ltd.

Accommodation: Available locally.   **Taxi:** By arrangement.

Fuel: 100LL.	**Tel/Fax:** 01787-223943 ATC
	Tel: 01787-223676 AFC Flying School

EGNX

1 DEC 00

N52 49·87 W001 19·68

EAST MIDLANDS

306 ft AMSL

7 nm SE of Derby.

TNT **115·70** 143 18. GAM **112·80** 212 30

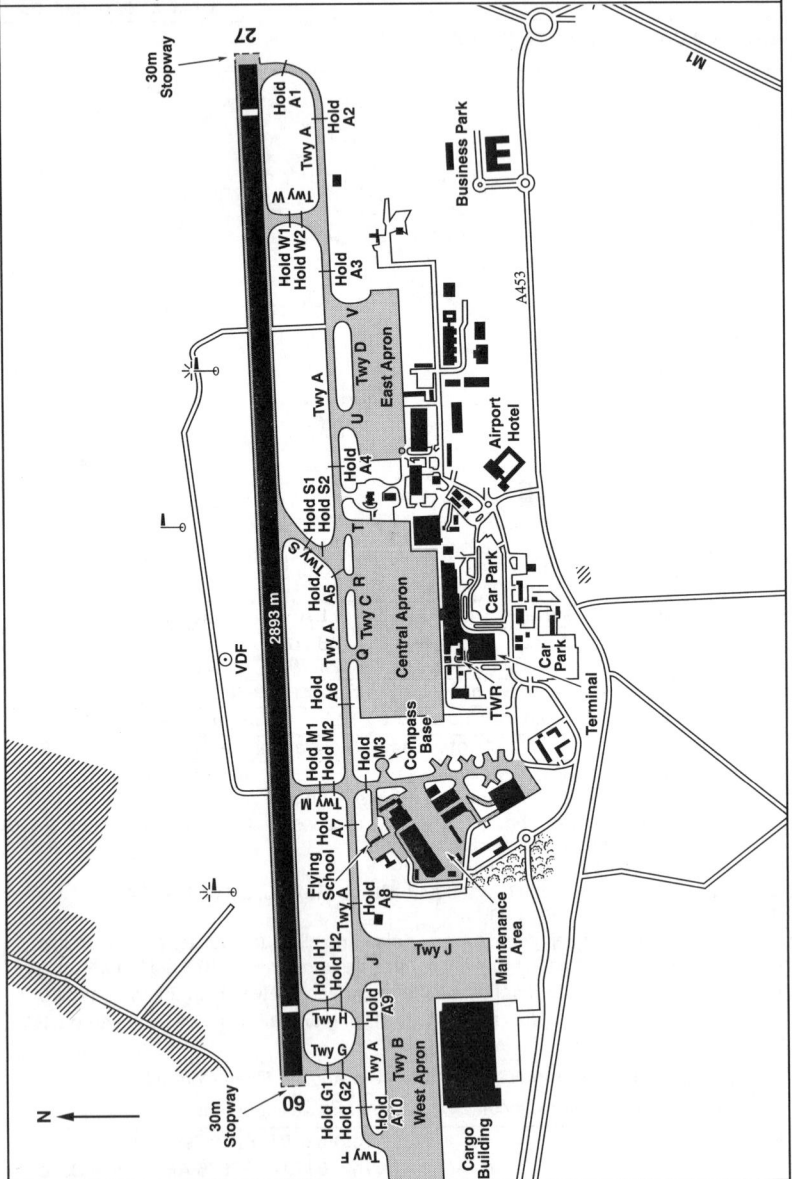

27

30m Stopway

Hold A1

Hold A2

Twy A

Business Park

Twy W

Hold W1
Hold W2

Hold A3

Twy V

Twy D

East Apron

Twy A

Twy U

Hold A4

Airport Hotel

Hold S1
Hold S2

A453

Twy T

Twy S

Hold A5

Twy A

Twy R

Twy Q

Central Apron

2893 m

VDF

Hold A6

Car Park

Car Park

Hold M1
Hold M2

TWR

Hold M3

Compass Base

Terminal

Twy W

Flying School

Hold A7

Twy A

Hold A8

Maintenance Area

Hold H1
Hold H2

Twy J

Twy J

Twy H

Hold A9

Twy G

Twy A

Twy B

West Apron

Hold G1
Hold G2

09

30m Stopway

Hold A10

Cargo Building

Twy F

N

Robert Pooley ©

N52 49·87 W001 19·68	**EAST MIDLANDS**	306 ft AMSL

APP/RAD 119·65.   **TWR** 124·00.   **GND** 121·90 (as directed)

VDF 119·65.   **Arr ATIS** 128·225.

Lctr 'EME' 353·50 (272°M/ 4·1 nm to Thr 27).

ILS/DME Rwy 27 (272°M) I-EME 109·35.

Lctr 'EMW' 393·0 (092°M/ 3·9 to Thr 09).

ILS/DME Rwy 09 (092°M) I-EMW 109·35.

Rwy	Dim(m)	Surface	TORA(m)	LDA(m)	Lighting
09/27	2893x46	Asphalt	09-2893†	09-2713	Ap Thr Rwy RCL PAPI 3°
			27-2893†	27-2763	Ap Thr Rwy RCL PAPI 3°

† Take-off:

Rwy 09 - Take-off from abeam Holding Point H1 - TORA 2713m.

Rwy 09 - Take-off from abeam Holding Point M1 - TORA 2080m.

Rwy 27 - Take-off from abeam Holding Point W1 - TORA 2463m.

Rwy 27 - Take-off from abeam Holding Point S1 - TORA 1583m.

Op hrs: H24.   **Customs:** H24.

Landing Fee: £10.90 per tonne MTOW or part.
Under 2 tonnes: £0.01 per kg (provided payment is made to designated handling agent prior to departure - cash, cheque or credit card).
Parking: £0.25 per tonne or part, per hour or part. First 2 hours free.

Hangarage: Limited.   **Maintenance:** By arrangement.

Remarks: Operated by East Midlands International Airport Ltd., East Midlands Airport, Castle Donington, Derby DE74 2SA.

Flights within the East Midlands CTR/CTA are governed by the regulations applicable to Class 'D' Controlled Airspace — see pages 2 and 6.

VFR Helicopter Arrivals/Departures and Entry/Exit Lanes - See page 205.

Visual Reference Points (VRPs) are listed at page 206 . Also see CTR/CTA, Entry/Exit Lanes and VRPs Chart at page 207.

Non radio aircraft strictly PPR. Variable circuits.

Pilots should avoid making their final turn on approach to Rwy 27 over Kegworth village.

Handling —A nominated handling agent is mandatory for all aircraft using the main apron. Full handling services are available from the following companies:
British Midland Tel: 01332-852204, Fax: 01332-811416.
Execair East Midlands Ltd   Tel: 01332-811179, Fax: 01332-811139.
Servisair (Passenger and Cargo)   Tel: 01332-812278, Fax: 01332-811904.
DHL (Cargo only) Tel: 01332-850323, Fax: 01332-811889.

Continued overleaf

Remarks continued:

Warnings: Magnetic Interference – large fluctuations to heading indications of magnetic compasses may be experienced in the vicinity of Holding Point W1 and on the runway, north of Hold W1. Carry out any pre take-off check of Direction Indicator against magnetic compass elsewhere.

In Spring and Autumn bird concentrations may be present on all areas under agricultural use on approaches to Rwy 09/27.

A pyrotechnic factory is sited approximately 3 nm north of aerodrome. Rockets, carrying flares of up to 150000 candela deployed on parachutes, may be tested up to 1000 ft agl, 1100 ft amsl, by day and night.

A flare stack is sited at Chellaston. The stack is 36 ft agl, 266 ft amsl and the flare is 20 ft in length.

Restaurant: Restaurant and Refreshments available.

Car Hire: National Tel: 01332- 382251.   Kenning Tel: 01332- 810621.
Avis Tel: 01332- 811403.   Hertz Tel: 01332-811726.

Fuel: 100LL, Jet A1. S. Multi Service	**Tel:** 01332-852852. **Fax:** 01332-850393 General. **Fax:** 01332-852823 ATC, **Fax:** 0891-517567 Airport MET Info. **E-mail:** atsm@eastmidsairport.demon.co.uk

VFR Arrival Procedures

Helicopters are to approach from the north or the south, remaining clear of the approach and take-off areas of Rwy 09/27 not below 500 ft QFE or at a height/altitude assigned by ATC. Do not overfly the villages of Castle Donington to the north or Diseworth to the south.

Arrivals from the north are to obtain clearance to cross Rwy 09/27 prior to crossing the aerodrome boundary and, on crossing the boundary are to descend towards to the allocated stand on the apron, avoiding overflight of equipment and occupied stands.

Arrivals from the south are to join on close-in right base for Rwy 09 or close-in left base for Rwy 27, or as directed by ATC. Descend along the runway or other safe path parallel to and south of the runway, as directed by ATC. Ground or air taxi to the parking areas as instructed by ATC and following the taxiways.

VFR Departure Procedures

Depart as cleared by ATC. Obtain clearance to cross Rwy 09/27 and crossings are to be made at right angles to the runway. Helicopters departing to the south are to ground or air taxi to Rwy 09 or 27 and, then on ATC departure clearance, are to climb along and above the appropriate runway to 500 ft initially, turning south only when clear of all airport buildings.

On reaching the airport boundary, pilots are to comply with ATC instructions regarding heading/route and height/altitude.

Entry/Exit Lanes

To permit aircraft to operate to/from East Midlands Airport in IMC but not under IFR the LONG EATON and SHEPSHED Entry/Exit lanes (3 nm wide) have been established for use, subject to the following conditions:

  (a) Use of the lanes is subject to SVFR clearance being obtained from East Midlands ATC.
  (b) Aircraft using the lanes must remain clear of cloud and in sight of the surface, not above 2000 ft (East Midlands QNH) and in a flight visibility of not less than 4 km.
  (c) All aircraft using a lane shall keep the centreline on its left, unless otherwise instructed.
  (d) Pilots of aircraft are responsible for maintaining adequate clearance from the ground or other obstacles.

In order to expedite the arrival and departure of light aircraft in VMC, use of these lanes by such aircraft operating under VFR is also recommended. Use of these lanes for this purpose, irrespective of prevailing weather conditions, remains subject to clearance being obtained from East Midlands ATC.

VRP	VOR/VOR	VOR/NDB	VOR/DME
Bottesford N52 57·88 W000 46·90 **(See Note 2)**	TNT R103° HON R045° DTY R018°	TNT R103° EME 066°M	TNT 103°/33 nm GAM 167°/20 nm
Church Broughton N52 53·17 W001 41·90 **(See Note 1)**	TNT R190° HON R002° DTY R338°	TNT R190° EME 284°M EMW 295°M	TNT 190°/10 nm
Markfield (M1 Motorway Junction 22) N52 41·73 W001 17·55 **(See Note 1)**	TNT R152° HON R037° DTY R352°	DTY R352° EME 207°M	HON 037°/24 nm DTY 352°/32 nm
Measham (M42 Motorway Junction 11) N52 41·33 W001 32·88 **(See Note 1)**	TNT R173° HON R016° DTY R337°	HON R016° EME 240°M	HON 016°/20 nm DTY 337°/34 nm
Melton Mowbray N52 44·37 W000 53·57 **(See Note 3)**	TNT R128° HON R054° DTY R018°	HON R054° DTY R018° EME 121°M	HON 054°/36 nm DTY 018°/35 nm
Trowell (M1 Motorway Service Area) N52 57·70 W001 16·05	TNT R115° HON R025° DTY R357°	TNT R115° EME 345°M EMW 044°M	TNT 115°/16 nm GAM 215°/22 nm

Note 1: Below 2500 ft ALT.

Note 2: Pilots routeing via Bottesford should avoid overflying the area around Langar aerodrome, which is designated as an area of intense parachuting activity.

Note 3: Pilots routeing via Melton Mowbray are advised of the proximity of the TV Mast at Waltham on the Wold which rises to 1487 ft amsl.

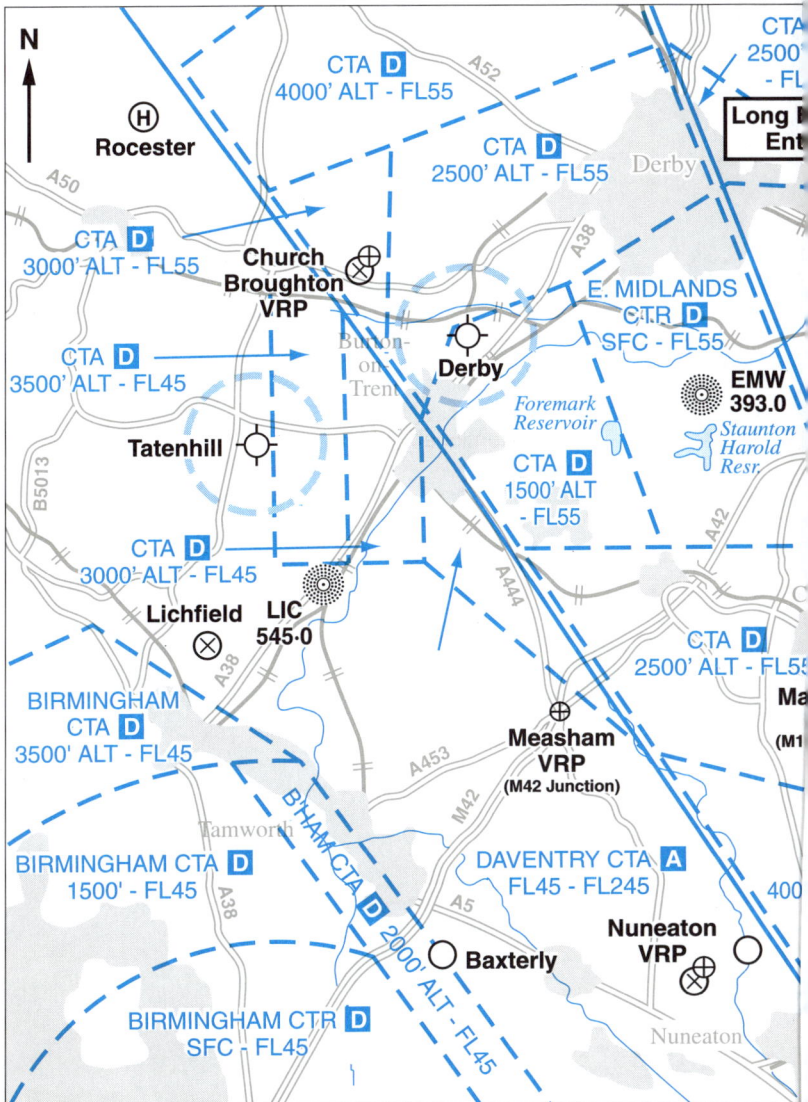

N

CTA **D**
4000' ALT - FL55

A52

CTA **D**
2500...
- FL

Long ...
Ent...

CTA **D**
2500' ALT - FL55

Derby

(H)
Rocester

A50

CTA **D**
3000' ALT - FL55

Church
Broughton
VRP

E. MIDLANDS
CTR D
SFC - FL55

A38

CTA **D**
3500' ALT - FL45

Burton-
on-
Trent

Derby

Foremark
Reservoir

EMW
393.0

Staunton
Harold
Resr.

B5013

Tatenhill

CTA **D**
1500' ALT
- FL55

A42

CTA **D**
3000' ALT - FL45

Lichfield
⊗

LIC
545·0

A444

CTA **D**
2500' ALT - FL55

Ma...

(M1...

BIRMINGHAM
CTA D
3500' ALT - FL45

A38

Measham
VRP
(M42 Junction)

A453

M42

Tamworth

B'HAM CTA D

BIRMINGHAM CTA D
1500' - FL45

A38

2000' ALT - FL45

A5

DAVENTRY CTA A
FL45 - FL245

Nuneaton
VRP

400...

○ **Baxterly**

BIRMINGHAM CTR D
SFC - FL45

Nuneaton

Robert Pooley ©

Intentionally Blank

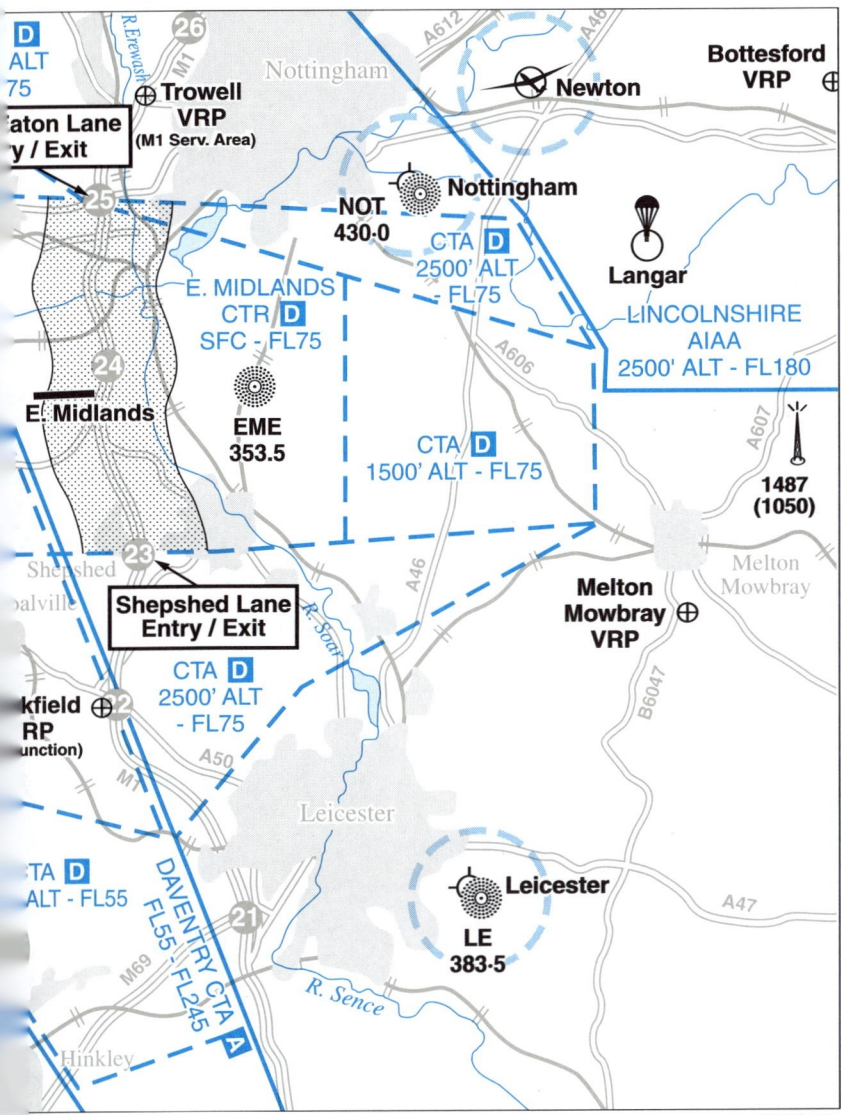

D
ALT
75

Trowell VRP
(M1 Serv. Area)

aton Lane
y / Exit

Nottingham

R.Erewash

26

25

A612

A46

Newton

Bottesford VRP

NOT
430·0

Nottingham

E. MIDLANDS
CTR **D**
SFC - FL75

CTA **D**
2500' ALT
- FL75

Langar

LINCOLNSHIRE
AIAA
2500' ALT - FL180

A606

24

E. Midlands

EME
353.5

CTA **D**
1500' ALT - FL75

A607

1487
(1050)

23

Shepshed
alville

**Shepshed Lane
Entry / Exit**

R. Soar

A46

**Melton
Mowbray VRP**

Melton
Mowbray

B6047

CTA **D**
2500' ALT
- FL75

kfield
RP
unction)

A50

2

M1

Leicester

Leicester

A47

TA **D**
ALT - FL55

DAVENTRY CTA
FL55 - FL245

21

M69

R. Sence

LE
383·5

A

Hinkley

1 DEC 00

EAST MIDLANDS CTR/CTA
ENTRY/EXIT LANES and VRPs

EDAY

N59 11·48 W002 46·43		10 ft AMSL
On Isle of Eday.		**WIK 113·60 021 45**
		WIZ 113·60 021 45

No Radio. Recommend contact Kirkwall APP 118·30.

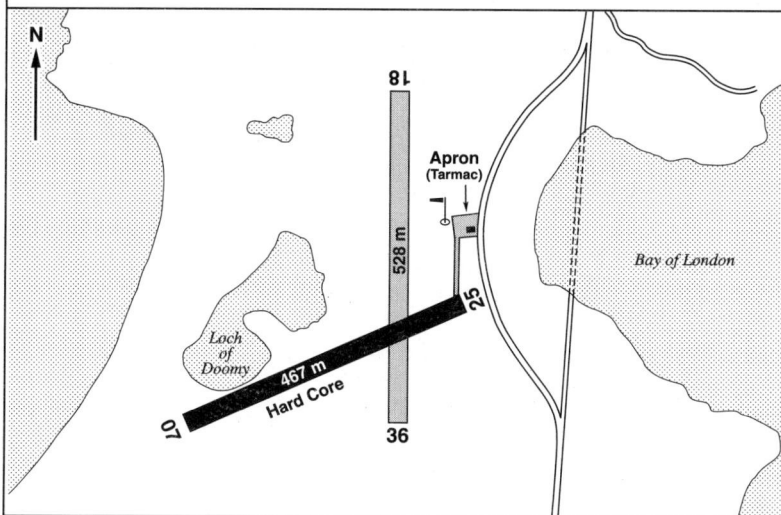

Rwy	Dim(m)	Surface	TORA(m)	LDA(m)	Lighting
18/36	528x30	Grass	18-518	18-518	* Portable APAPI 4·5°
			36-518	36-518	* Portable APAPI 4·5°
07/25	467x18	Hard Core	07-462	07-452	Nil.
			25-457	25-452	Nil.
					ABn Wh

* available on request.

Op hrs: PPR. Aerodrome available daylight hours only.

Landing Fee: Nil. If Fire cover is provided then £17.24 + VAT.

Hangarage: Nil.	**Maintenance:** Nil.	**Customs:** Nil.

Remarks: Operated by Orkney Islands Council, School Place, Kirkwall, Orkney KW15 1 NY. PPR. Licensed aerodrome - day use only.
Visiting aircraft accepted on prior permission and at pilot's own risk. In first instance, contact Orkney Islands Council.
Rwy 18/36 may become soft and waterlogged after periods of continuous rainfall.
High ground 324' aal 334' amsl 191°/2·4 nm.
Scheduled services operate usually on a wednesday.

Warning: Rwy 07/25 - Graded Hard Core runway generally unsuitable for light aircraft with low ground /propeller clearance due to unstabilised surface.

Accommodation/Restaurant: B & B and self catering available, contact The Tourist Board.   **Car Hire:** 01857-622 256.

Fuel: Nil.	**Tel:** 01856-873535 Ext 2305 Council for PPR.
	Fax: 01856-876094 - Council.

Robert Pooley ©

EDINBURGH

N55 57·15 W003 21·77	135 ft AMSL

5 nm W of Edinburgh.

TLA	113·80	007	27
GOW	115·40	091	36

c/s Edinburgh. **APP** 121·20, 130·40 (for gliders transiting the CTR). **VDF** 118·70.
TWR 118·70. **GND** 121·75. **RAD** 121·20. **ATIS** (Arr/Dep) 132·075 c/s Information.
NDB 'EDN' 341 (245°M/2·8nm to Thr 24). **NDB** 'UW' 368 (065°M/4·5nm to Thr 06).
ILS/DME Rwy 06 (065°M) I-VG 108·90. **ILS/DME** Rwy 24 (245°M) I-TH 108·90.

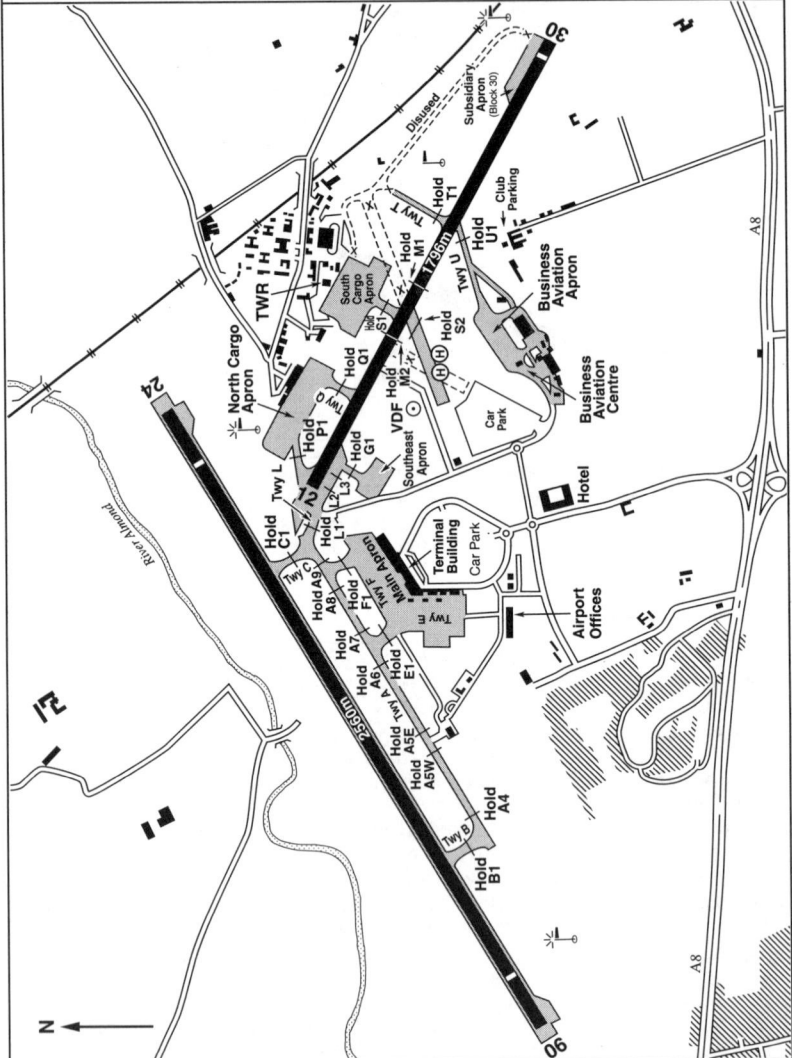

					135 ft AMSL

N55 57·15 W003 21·77 **EDINBURGH**

Rwy	Dim(m)	Surface	TORA(m)	LDA(m)	Lighting
06/24	2560x46	Asphalt	06-2560	06-2347	Ap Thr Rwy PAPI 3°
			24-2560	24-2347	Ap Thr Rwy PAPI 3°
12/30*	1796x46	Asphalt	12-1796	12-1796	Ap Thr Rwy PAPI 3°
			30-1796	30-1734	Ap Thr Rwy PAPI 3·5°

* Rwy 12/30 visual runway only.

Op hrs: H24.

Landing Fee: BAA Rates.   **Customs:** Available.

Hangarage: Limited.   **Maintenance:** Limited.

Remarks: Operated by Edinburgh Airport Ltd, (EAL). Flights within Edinburgh CTR/CTA are governed by the regulations applicable to Class 'D' Controlled Airspace see pages 2 and 6.

Edinburgh CTR Entry/Exit Lanes and VRPs – see pages 212 and 213.

Non radio aircraft PPR from ATC. All flights are subject to the approval of the MD and PPR from Airport Co-ordination Ltd, Tel: 0121-767 7519, Fax: 0121 767 7036.

All aircraft operators must make prior arrangements with a handling agent for ground handling of all flights. Due to limited parking space, all aircraft are PPR with their handling agent. Handling agents: Execair Tel: 0131-317 7447, Fax: 0131-317 7484, and Servisair Tel: 0131-344 3111, Fax: 0131-333 4066.

GA aircraft requiring HM Customs may be initially directed to the passenger apron. Passengers will be taken to the main passenger Terminal for clearance by their handling agent. Aircraft may then taxi to the Business Aviation Centre apron once necessary formalities have been completed. GA aircraft not requiring Customs inspection may taxi directly to the Business Aviation Centre apron.

For visual approaches to Rwy 06/24 the following limitations apply:

• Propeller driven aircraft whose MTWA does not exceed 5700 kg will not join the final approach to either runway below 1000' aal.

• All approaches to Rwy 24 by aircraft with an MTWA in excess of 5700 kg are to be made from a position not less than 5 nm DME on the runway extended centre-line. Aircraft approaching this point from a southerly direction are not to descend below 2000' QFE until after crossing the Firth of Forth coastline northbound. Aircraft approaching Rwy 06 are to join the extended runway centre-line at a height of not less than 1500'.

Warning: Bird hazard. Large Bird population around the airport.

Restaurant: Restaurant and refreshments available.

Car Hire: Hertz 0131-333 1019. Avis 0131-333 1866.

Fuel: 100LL, Jet A1.	**Tel:** 0131-333 1000 EAL
	0131-344 3139 Airfield Ops
	0131-339 7950 Met
	0131-317 7638 ATC Watch Manager
	Fax: 0131-335 3181 EAL
	0131-333 3159 Airfield Ops
	0131-317 7126 ATC

Entry/Exit Lanes (see also chart opposite)
To permit aircraft to operate to and from Edinburgh in IMC but not under IFR the following entry/exit lanes have been established for use, under the conditions stated, as follows:

(a) (i)**Polmont Lane** — 3nm wide, centre-line M9 Motorway from Grangemouth (near Western boundary of Edinburgh CTR) eastwards , via the Polmont Roundabout, Linlithgow Loch and Philpstoun to a point at which it crosses the Edinburgh ATZ;

   (ii)   **Kelty Lane** — 3nm wide, centre-line M90 Motorway extending from Kelty (near Northern boundary of Edinburgh CTR) southwards, across the Forth Road Bridge, to a point at which it crosses the Edinburgh ATZ.

(b) Clearance must be obtained from Edinburgh ATC, irrespective of prevailing weather conditions, before entering the lane. For non-radio aircraft, clearance is to be obtained prior to take-off.

(c) Aircraft using the lanes must remain clear of cloud and in sight of the surface, not above 2000 ft (Edinburgh QNH) and in flight visibility of not less than 3 km.

(d) An aircraft using a lane shall keep the centre-line on its left, unless otherwise instructed by ATC for separation purposes.

(e) Pilots of aircraft are responsible for maintaining adequate clearance from the ground or other obstacles.

VISUAL REFERENCE POINTS

VRP	VOR/VOR	VOR/NDB	VOR/DME
Arthur's Seat N55 56·63 W003 09·70	GOW R090 TLA R019	TLA R019 EDN 123°M	SAB 280°/32 nm
Bathgate N55 54·17 W003 38·42	TLA R344 GOW R092	TLA R344 EDN 255°M	GOW 092°/27 nm
Cobbinshaw Reservoir N55 48·47 W003 34·00	TLA R345 GOW R103	TLA R345 EDN 229°M	TLA 345°/19 nm
Dalkeith N55 53·60 W003 04·10	TLA R028 SAB R274	TLA R028 EDN 131°M	TLA 028°/26 nm
Forth Road Bridge North Tower N56 00·37 W003 24·23	GOW R083 TLA R003	PTH R189 EDN 299°M	SAB 284°/41 NM
Hillend Ski Slope N55 53·30 W00312·50	TLA R018 SAB R274	SAB R274 EDN 160°M	TLA 018°/24 nm
Kelty N56 08·08 W003 23·25	TLA R004 SAB R295	SAB R295 EDN 346°M	GOW 072°/39 nm
Kirkcaldy Harbour N56 06·83 W003 09·00	TLA R016 SAB R297	SAB R297 EDN 035°M	GOW 077°/46 nm
Kirkliston N55 57·33 W003 24·18	GOW R087 TLA R002	GOW R 087 EDN 257°M	GOW 087°/35 NM
Kirknewtown N55 53·25 W003 25·08	GOW R094 TLA R360	GOW R094 EDN 225°M	GOW 094°/35 nm
Musselburgh N55 56·83 W003 02·42	TLA R027 SAB R281	TLA R027 EDN 109°M	TLA 027°/29nm
Penicuik N55 49·92 W003 13·42	GOW R099 TLA R018	GOW R099 EDN 173°M	GOW 099°/41 nm
Philipstoun (M9, Junc 2) N55 58·90 W003 30·72	GOW R084 TLA R355	GOW R084 UW 227°M	GOW 084°/32 nm
Polmont N55 59·33 W003 41·00	TLA R345 SAB R282	TLA R345 EDN 279°M	GOW 080°/27nm
West Linton N55 45·17 W003 21·45	TLA R005 SAB R262	SAB R262 EDN 196°M	TLA 005°/15 nm

See Edinburgh CTR chart opposite

N

River Forth

OCHIL HILLS

M9

SCOTTISH TMA
D 6000' ALT - FL245
E 4000' - 6000' ALT

Alloa

Stirling

M9

Dunfirmline

Rosyth

M80

M876

KILSYTH HILLS

Grangemouth

Bo'ness

R603/2

Falkirk

Cumbernauld

Polmont VRP
Entry / Exit

Philpstoun
VRP

Linlithgow

M9

Kirklist
VRP

M73

SCOTTISH TMA
D 6000' ALT - FL245
E *2500' - 6000' ALT

GVS / 3·7

EDINBURGH CTR D
SFC - 6000' ALT

Bathgate
VRP

UW
368·0

Kirk

M8

Airdrie

Hillend
Reservoir

Armadale

Livingston

Baillieston
VRP

Roughrig
Reservoir

M8

Whitburn

SCOTTISH TMA **D**
6000' ALT - FL245

M74

R504/2·8

SCOTTISH TMA
D 6000' ALT - FL245
E *1500' - 6000' ALT

Cobbinshaw
Reservoir

Motherwell

Cobbinshaw
Reservoir VRP

Hamilton

West Water
Reservoir

M74

River Clyde

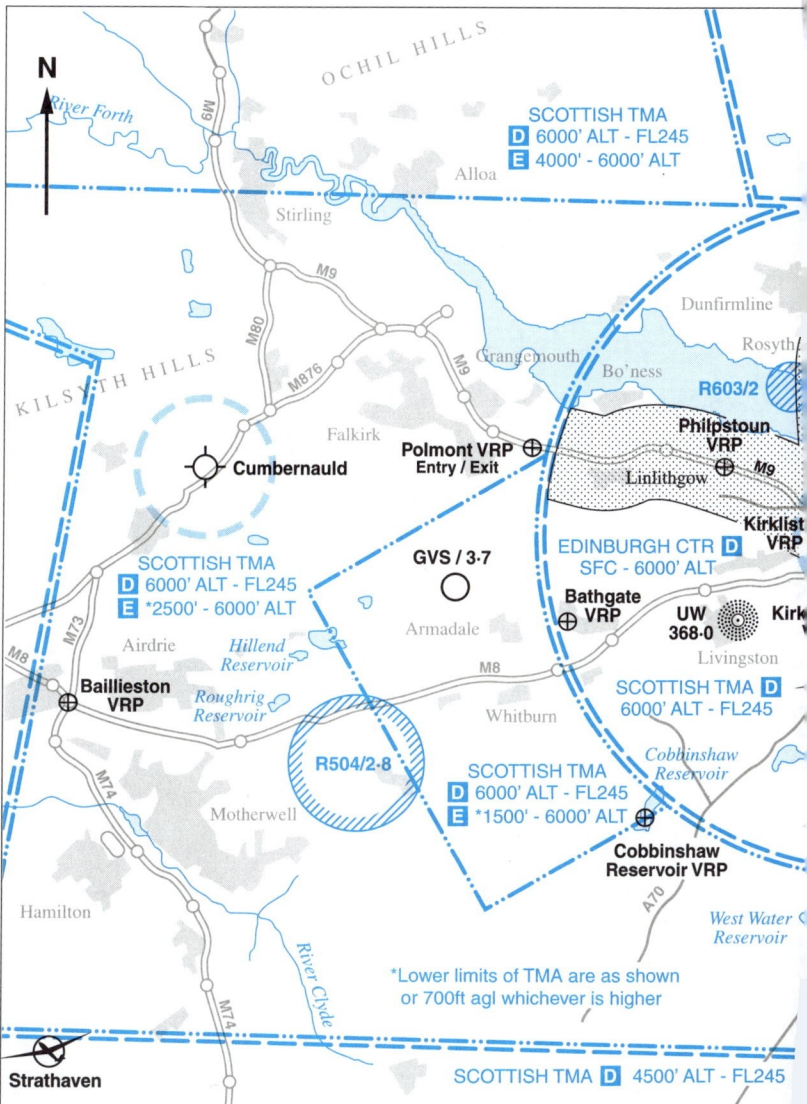

*Lower limits of TMA are as shown
or 700ft agl whichever is higher

A70

Strathaven

SCOTTISH TMA **D** 4500' ALT - FL245

Robert Pooley ©

Intentionally Blank

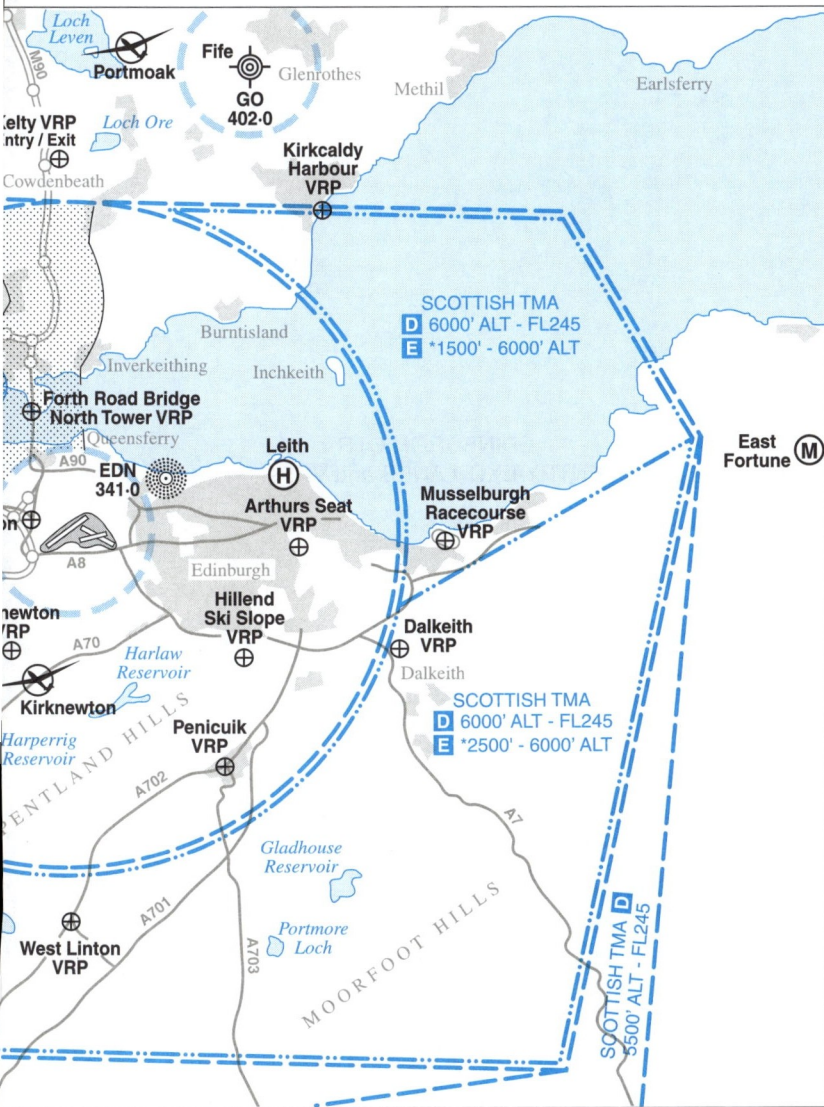

Loch Leven

Portmoak

Fife

GO 402·0

Glenrothes

Methil

Earlsferry

Celty VRP
ntry / Exit

Loch Ore

Cowdenbeath

Kirkcaldy
Harbour
VRP

SCOTTISH TMA
D 6000' ALT - FL245
E *1500' - 6000' ALT

Burntisland

Inverkeithing

Inchkeith

Forth Road Bridge
North Tower VRP

Queensferry

EDN
341·0

Leith
(H)

Arthurs Seat
VRP

Musselburgh
Racecourse
VRP

East
Fortune (M)

A90

A8

Edinburgh

newton
RP

A70

Hillend
Ski Slope
VRP

Dalkeith
VRP

Dalkeith

Harlaw
Reservoir

Kirknewton

SCOTTISH TMA
D 6000' ALT - FL245
E *2500' - 6000' ALT

Harperrig
Reservoir

Penicuik
VRP

ENTLAND HILLS

A702

A7

Gladhouse
Reservoir

West Linton
VRP

A701

Portmore
Loch

A703

MOORFOOT HILLS

SCOTTISH TMA
D 5500' ALT - FL245

1 DEC 00

EDINBURGH CTR
ENTRY/EXIT LANES and VRPs

N52 04·53 E000 58·68	**ELMSETT**	226 ft AMSL
3 nm S of Wattisham airfield, 6 nm WNW of Ipswich.		CLN 114·55 338 15

c/s Elmsett Radio 130·90 A/G.   Wattisham App 125·80

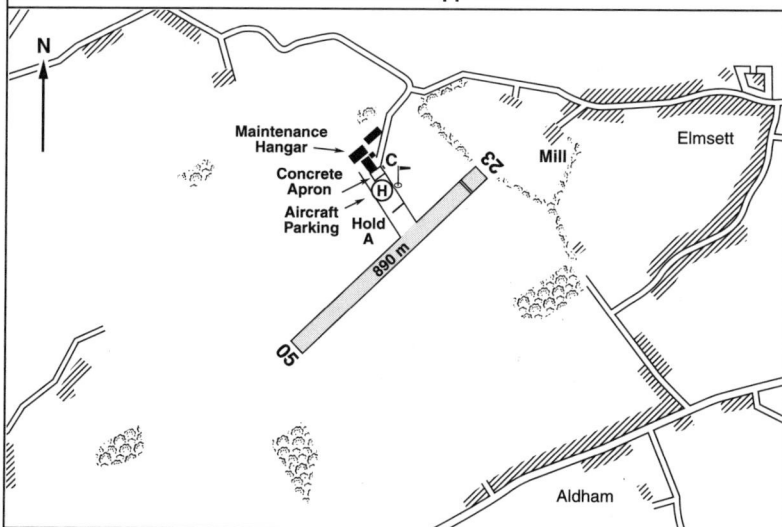

Rwy	Dim(m)	Surface	TORA(m)	LDA(m)	Lighting
05/23	890x26	Grass	05-799	05-799	Thr Rwy
			23-799	23-775	Thr Rwy

Rwy 05 slopes up 1.8%.

Op hrs: 0900-1700 daily. **PPR by Telephone.**

Landing Fee: Singles £10.00 AUW; Twins £15.00 AUW. All inclusive of VAT.

Hangarage: Ltd, parking available. **Maintenance:** Aero Anglia.   **Customs:** PNR.

Remarks: Operated by Mr.T. D. Gray, Poplar Aviation Ltd, Poplar Hall, Elmsett, Ipswich, Suffolk. IP7 6LN. Due to restrictions, airfield is normally unlicensed.
Elmsett ATZ is situated within Wattisham MATZ.

Arrival Procedures: Contact Wattisham App 125·80 when at least 15 nm from Wattisham and obtain clearance. If unable contact Wattisham, pilots should:
- Route not above 800' agl via Raydon disused airfield or Copdock Junction of A12 and A14 roads.
- Remain VFR at or below 800' agl within the Wattisham MATZ/Elmsett ATZ.

Departure Procedures:
- Contact Wattisham App 125·80 before departure and if unsuccessful as soon as possible after departure and always before climbing above 800 ft agl.
- If no contact with Wattisham, then route not above 800' agl via Raydon disused airfield or Copdock Junction of A12 and A14 roads.

Noise Abatement Procedures: See page 217.

Final power checks to be carried out at Holding Point Alpha only.

Warning: Helicopters may overfly the aerodrome at 1500 ' agl.

Fuel: 100LL	**Tel:** 01473-824116. **Fax:** 01473-822896.
	E- mail: poplartoys@aol.com

Robert Pooley ©

Intentionally Blank

ELMSETT
Noise Abatement Procedures

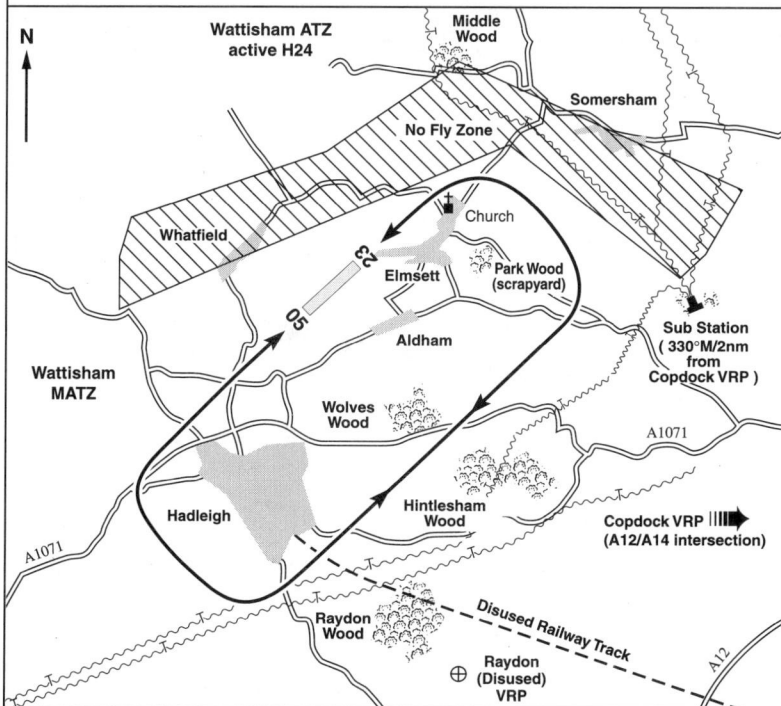

Circuits: 800 ft QFE, RH on Rwy 05, LH on Rwy 23.
Please keep to the circuit pattern shown above, and avoid the No Fly Zone between Wattisham and Elmsett ATZs.

Rwy 05 RH:

On departure, maintain runway track until well past the Church to avoid houses and farms to the NE of Elmsett;

Turn from crosswind onto downwind well after Park Wood (scrapyard);

On downwind, track south of Hadleigh, and turn onto base when clear of town;

Turn onto finals just NW of Hadleigh.

Rwy 23 LH:

On departure, maintain runway track until past Hadleigh,

On downwind leg, track S of Hadleigh, parallel to runway, between Wolves and Hintlesham Woods;

Turn 0·5 nm before power lines which run parallel to base leg;

On base leg, aim to the left of Middle Wood avoiding No Fly Zone;

Turn onto final as late as possible to avoid houses and farms to NE of of Elmsett.

N51 39·35 W000 19·55	**ELSTREE**	334 ft AMSL
2·5 nm E of Watford.	**BPK 117·50 240 9·9. BNN 113·75 122 9·4**	
North side of Hilfield Park Reservoir.	**LAM 115·60 276 17·8**	

c/s Elstree Radio/Information £122·40. A/G / AFIS.   AFIS Fri-Sun 0800-SS.

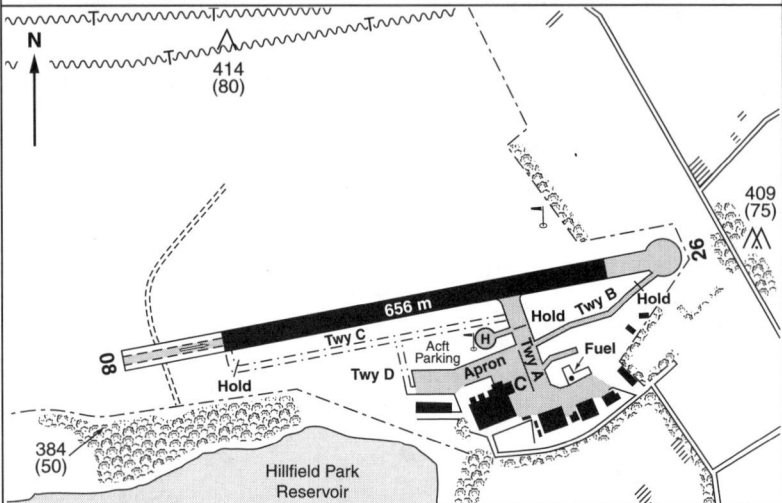

Rwy	Dim(m)	Surface	TORA(m)	LDA(m)	Lighting
08/26	* 656x30	Asphalt	08-656	08-656	Rwy
			26-656	26-656	Rwy LITAS 4·5°
					IBn 'EL' Gn/ABn Wh

*174 x 18m pavement beyond west end of runway is not maintained..

128m paved area at E end not available for take-off or landing.

Op hrs: 0900-SS daily & ¢.

Landing Fee: Up to 1360 kg £17.02, then £6.38 for each additional 450 kg, plus VAT.
50% reduction for cash payment.

Hangarage: Available.   **Maintenance:** Available.   **Customs:** PNR.

Remarks: Remarks: Operated by Montclare Shipping Co. Ltd. PPR.
Northern boundary of London CTR is 3 nm S of airfield. Normal operations are confined to the area between marked thresholds. Variable circuits.
Terms and conditions of use of aerodrome are displayed at the aerodrome, and are available on request from the operators.
Fixed Wing Noise Abatement Procedures - see pages 220 and 221
Helicopter Arr/Dep Routes – see Chart on the opposite page.
Warning: Distance between taxyway centreline and parked aircraft can be as little as 8 m, taxy with extreme caution.
Circuits may extend up to 1 nm north of the ATZ.

Restaurant: Licensed restaurant.   **Car Hire:** Godfrey Davis. Tel: 020-8565 7272.
Pooleys Pilot Shop: Tel: 020-8207 3749. Fax: 020-8953 2512.

Fuel: 100LL, Jet A1.	**Tel:** 020-8953 7480 Tower/Admin; 3502 Hangar
Services Diners Card.	**Fax:** 020-8207 3691.

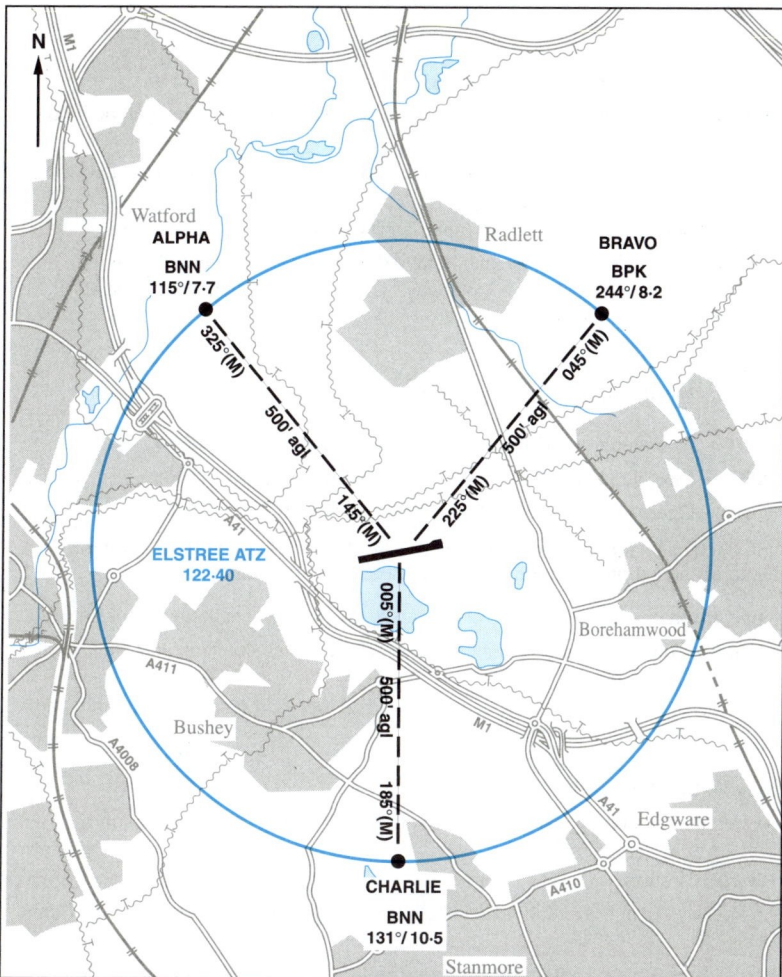

ELSTREE AREA
HELICOPTER ARR/DEP ROUTES

1 DEC 00

N

Watford
ALPHA

BNN
115°/7·7

Radlett

BRAVO

BPK
244°/8·2

325°(M)

045°(M)

500' agl

500' agl

145°(M)

225°(M)

ELSTREE ATZ
122·40

005°(M)

Borehamwood

500' agl

Bushey

185°(M)

M1

Edgware

CHARLIE

BNN
131°/10·5

Stanmore

All helicopter arrivals and departures via ALPHA, BRAVO or CHARLIE at 500' agl.

Establish contact with Elstree Radio 122·40 before reaching ATZ boundary.

Pilots should check with the Aerodrome Operator prior to flight.

Note: Only Robinson R22's operated by Cabair Group are permitted to carry out circuit training. Circuit height 750' QFE or below to the north of aerodrome.

Robert Pooley ©

ELSTREE
Noise Abatement and Circuit Patterns

Approaches:

- Overhead joins are discouraged;
- Make straight-ins from 5 nm out crossing ATZ boundary (2 nm out) at 1300 ft QNH;
- Circuit traffic should give way to the straight-in traffic by extending downwind or going around;
- Report at 5 nm and at 2nm (approaching "Tall Building" for Rwy 26);
- Alternatively for Rwy 26, join from M25 Motorway on extended base leg, Report when leaving the Motorway " On extended right base for Rwy 26". Give way to circuit traffic.

Circuits:

Rwy 26 - North circuits. There are three:

OUT - Operated from 0900 - 1000, 1200 - 1300 and 1500 - 1600.

MID - Operated from 1000 - 1100, 1300 - 1400 and 1600 - 1700.

IN - Operated from 1100 - 1200, 1400 - 1500 and 1700 - 1800.

In each case, turn right after take-off and fly close to Motorway until close to intersection, then turn north towards Wallhall University and:

In Circuit - Turn right short of University and fly over southern part of Radlett.

Mid Circuit - Turn slightly right short of University and continue until short of Sewage Works, then fly over centre of Radlett.

Out Circuit - Continue until over the Sewage Works, then fly over northern part of Radlett.

Rwy 26 South Circuit:

As per the chart on opposite page. Aircraft **MUST** fly south of Bentley Priory.

Rwy 08 Circuits:

As for Rwy 26, but reversed, except both north and south circuits extend over Bushey to give straight-in finals.

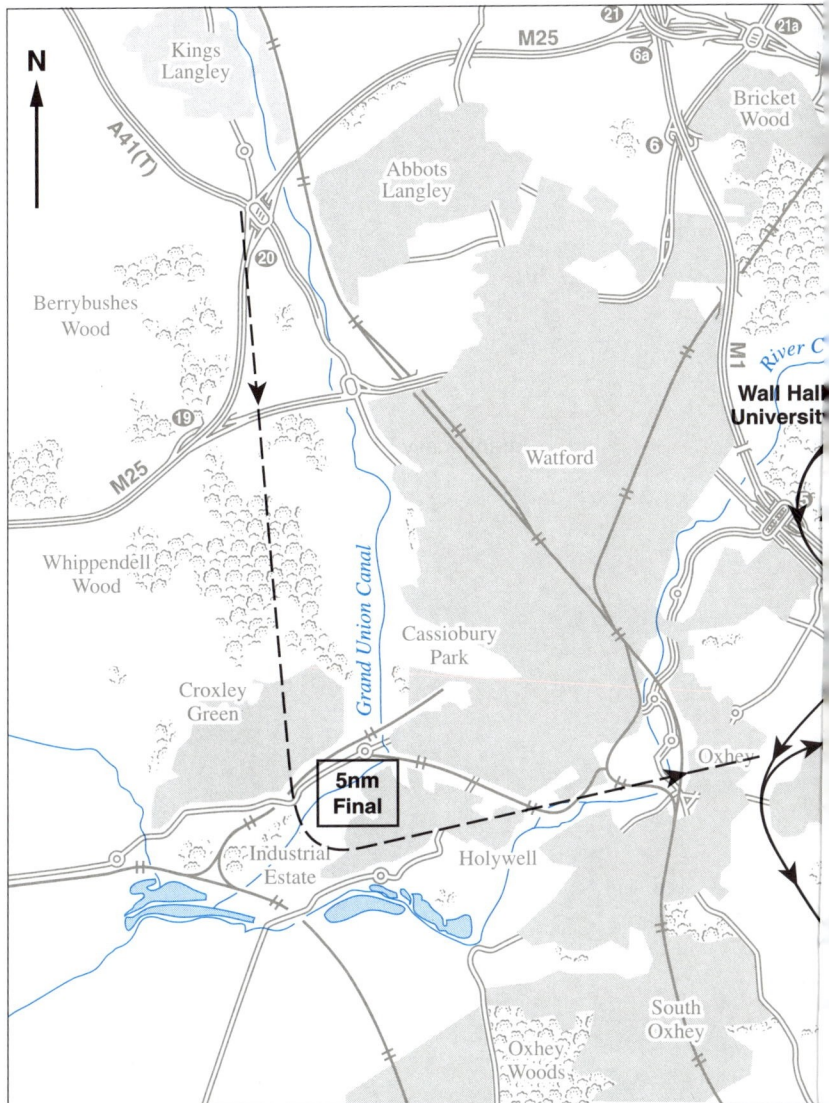

ELSTREE FIXED WING
and CIRCUIT

N

Kings Langley

M25

21

6a

21a

A41(T)

Bricket Wood

6

Abbots Langley

20

Berrybushes Wood

M1

River C

Wall Hall University

19

M25

Watford

5

Whippendell Wood

Grand Union Canal

Cassiobury Park

Croxley Green

Oxhey

5nm Final

Industrial Estate

Holywell

South Oxhey

Oxhey Woods

Robert Pooley ©

Intentionally Blank

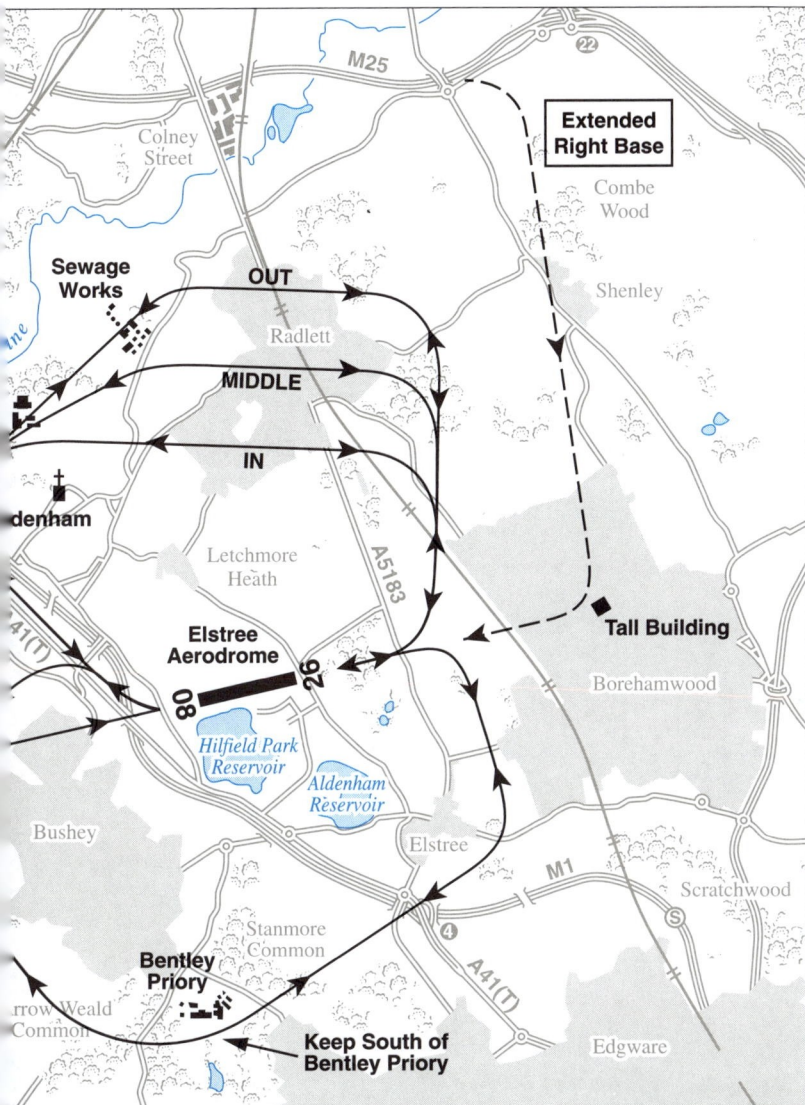

M25

22

Colney
Street

Extended
Right Base

Combe
Wood

Sewage
Works

OUT

Shenley

Radlett

MIDDLE

IN

denham

Letchmore
Heath

A5183

Tall Building

Elstree
Aerodrome

26

Borehamwood

80

41(T)

Hilfield Park
Reservoir

Aldenham
Reservoir

Bushey

Elstree

M1

Scratchwood

Stanmore
Common

4

A41(T)

S

Bentley
Priory

rrow Weald
Common

Keep South of
Bentley Priory

Edgware

1 DEC 00

ELSTREE FIXED WING NOISE ABATEMENT
and CIRCUIT PATTERNS

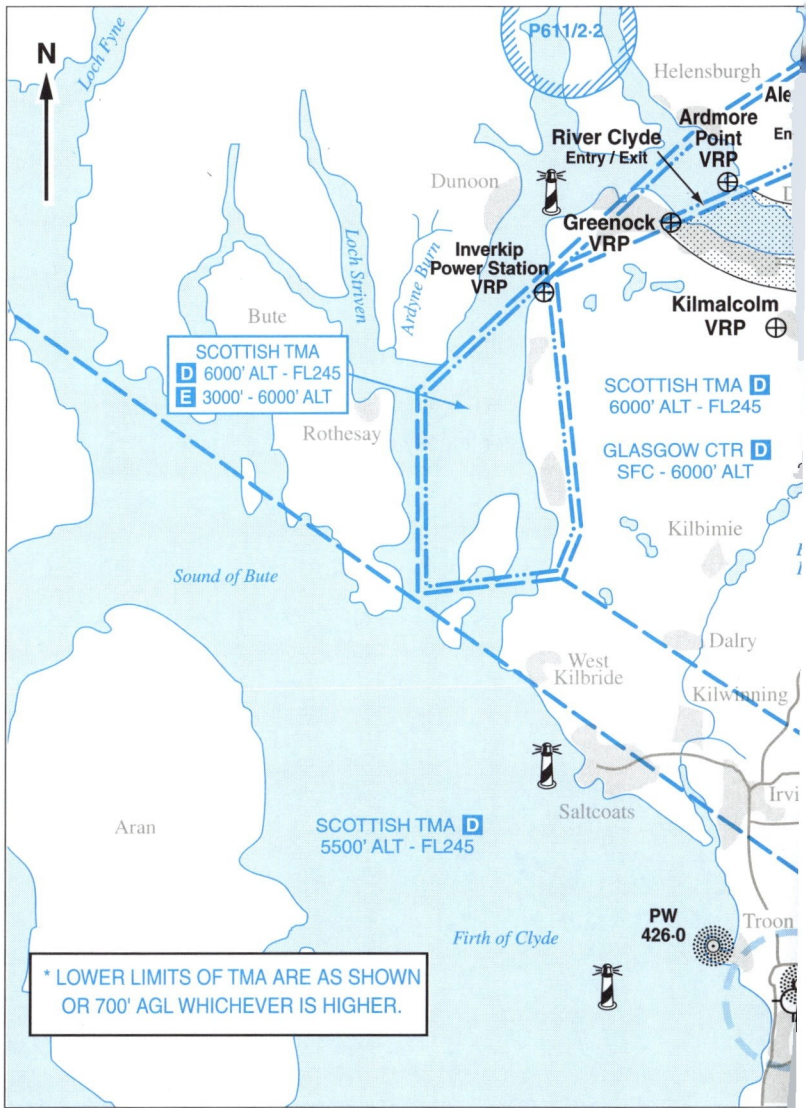

N

P611/2·2

Helensburgh

Ale

Ardmore
Point
VRP

En

River Clyde
Entry / Exit

Dunoon

Greenock ⊕
VRP

Inverkip
Power Station
VRP ⊕

Kilmalcolm
VRP ⊕

Bute

SCOTTISH TMA
D 6000' ALT - FL245
E 3000' - 6000' ALT

SCOTTISH TMA D
6000' ALT - FL245

Rothesay

GLASGOW CTR D
SFC - 6000' ALT

Kilbimie

Sound of Bute

Dalry

West
Kilbride

Kilwinning

Aran

SCOTTISH TMA D
5500' ALT - FL245

Saltcoats

Irvi

PW
426·0

Troon

Firth of Clyde

* LOWER LIMITS OF TMA ARE AS SHOWN
OR 700' AGL WHICHEVER IS HIGHER.

Intentionally Blank

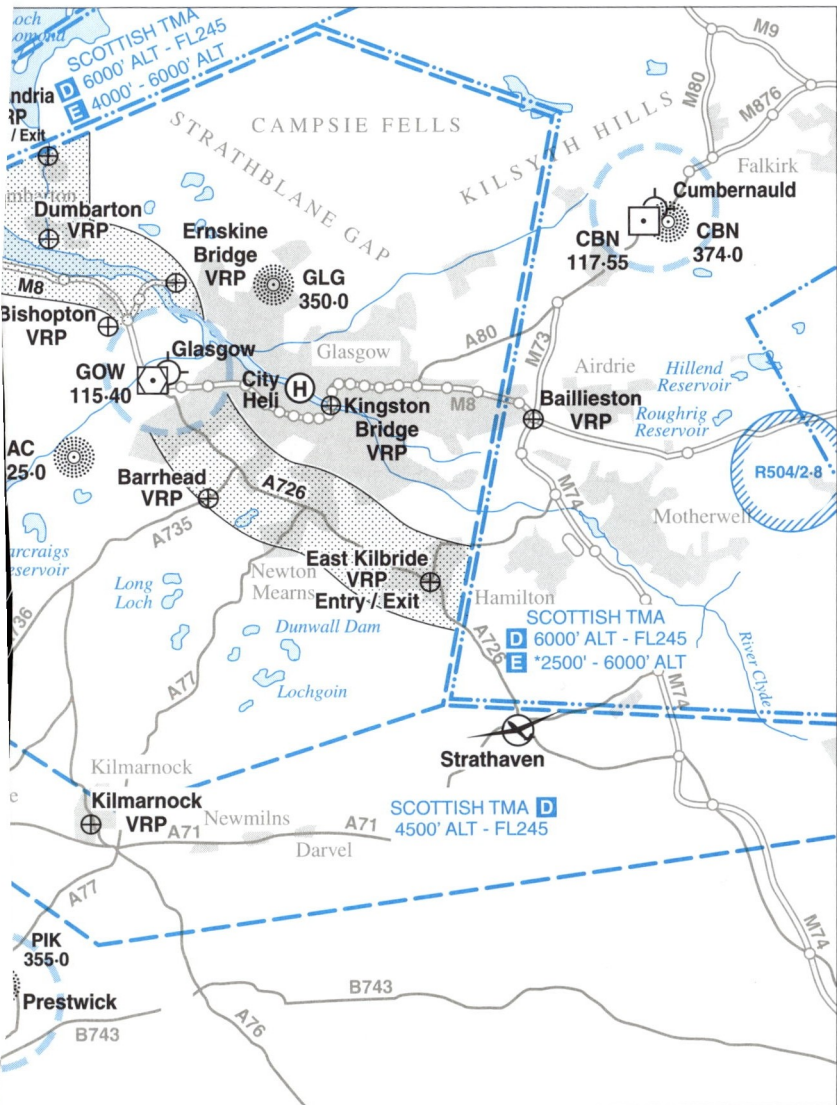

SCOTTISH TMA
D 6000' ALT - FL245
E 4000' - 6000' ALT

CAMPSIE FELLS

STRATHBLANE GAP

KILSYTH HILLS

M9

M80

M876

Falkirk

Cumbernauld

CBN
117·55

**CBN
374·0**

ndria
RP
/ Exit

**Dumbarton
VRP**

**Ernskine
Bridge
VRP**

GLG
350·0

M8

**Bishopton
VRP**

Glasgow

Glasgow

A80

M73

Airdrie

*Hillend
Reservoir*

GOW
115·40

**City
Heli**

(H)

**Kingston
Bridge
VRP**

M8

**Baillieston
VRP**

*Roughrig
Reservoir*

AC
25·0

**Barrhead
VRP**

A726

Motherwell

R504/2·8

A735

*urcraigs
eservoir*

**East Kilbride
VRP
Entry / Exit**

Newton
Mearns

*Long
Loch*

Hamilton

Dunwall Dam

A726

M74

SCOTTISH TMA
D 6000' ALT - FL245
E *2500' - 6000' ALT

A77

Lochgoin

River Clyde

Kilmarnock

Strathaven

**Kilmarnock
VRP** A71

Newmilns

A71

SCOTTISH TMA **D**
4500' ALT - FL245

M74

Darvel

A77

**PIK
355·0**

B743

Prestwick

B743

A76

M74

GLASGOW CONTROL ZONE
ENTRY/EXIT LANES and VRPs

N54 23·93 W007 39·10	**ENNISKILLEN (St. Angelo)**	155 ft AMSL
3 nm N of Enniskillen.		**BEL 117·20 261 52**

c/s St. Angelo Radio. 123·20 FIS.
NDB 'EKN' 357·50 (On A/D).   DME 'ENN' 116·75 (On A/D).

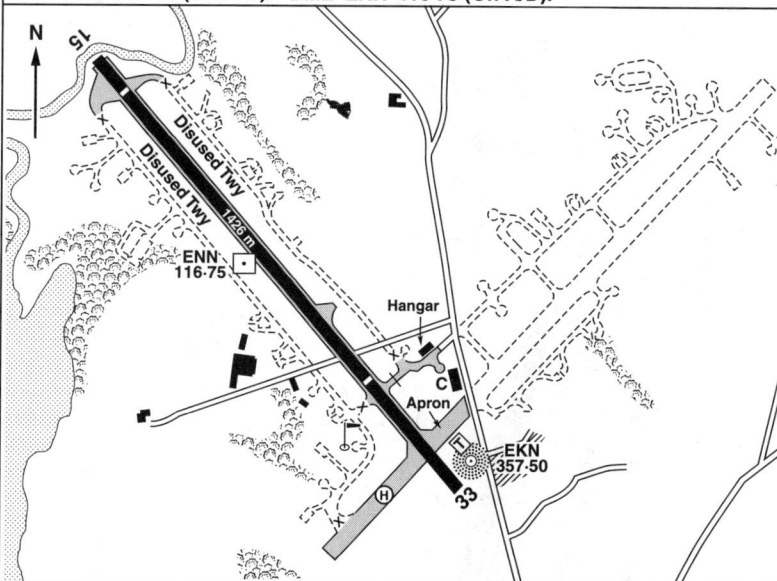

Rwy	Dim(m)	Surface	TORA(m)	LDA(m)	Lighting
15/33	1426x30	Asphalt	15-1236	15-1286	PAPI 3·5°
			33-1326	33-979	* PAPI 4·5°

* PAPI signals visible to the SW of the extended centre line where clearance not
  guaranteed. Use only when aircraft aligned with the runway.

Op hrs: PPR. Tue-Sun 0900-1700 & ¢.

Landing Fee: PRIVATE Singles £5; Twins £10. COMMERCIAL £23.50. Including VAT.

Hangarage: Limited.   **Maintenance:** Nil.   **Customs:** 028-9035 8255

Remarks: Operated by St. Angelo Aviation Ltd. Fermanagh District Council,
Enniskillen Airport, Trory, Enniskillen, Co. Fermanagh, Northern Ireland. PPR.
Aerodrome not available to non-radio aircraft except on prior permission.
Circuits RH on 15, LH on 33.
Flights to and from aerodromes outside Northern Ireland must have security
clearance from Duty Inspector Force Information. Tel: 028-9065 0222.
High ground 516' aal 671' amsl 277°/3·4 nm, running NW/SE.

Restaurant: Nil.

Car Hire: M & N Motors Tel: 028-6632 2727.

Fuel: 100LL, Jet A1	**Tel/Fax:** 028-6632 2771.

N51 55·77 W001 25·92	**ENSTONE**	550 ft AMSL

4·5nm E of Chipping Norton.	DTY 116·40 223 19·1
	HON 113·65 169 26·5

c/s Enstone Radio 129·875 A/G - Managed by Oxfordshire Sport Flying Club.

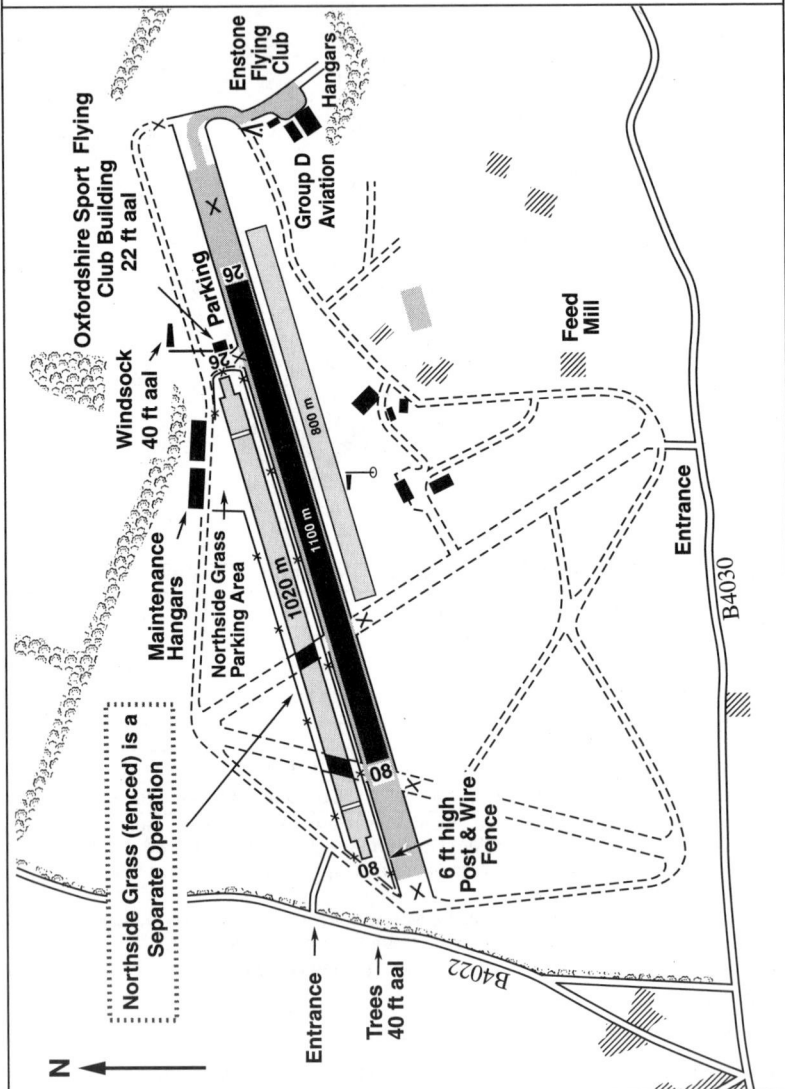

Enstone Flying Club

Hangars

Group D Aviation

Oxfordshire Sport Flying Club Building 22 ft aal

Parking

26

Windsock 40 ft aal

92

800 m

Feed Mill

Maintenance Hangars

Northside Grass Parking Area

1100 m

1020 m

Entrance

B4030

08

6 ft high Post & Wire Fence

08

Northside Grass (fenced) is a Separate Operation

N

Entrance

Trees 40 ft aal

B4022

Rwy	Dim(m)	Surface	TORA(m)	LDA(m)	Lighting
		ENSTONE			550 ft AMSL

N51 55·77 W001 25·92

Rwy	Dim(m)	Surface	TORA(m)	LDA(m)	Lighting
08/26	1100x40	Asphalt	Unlicensed		Nil
08/26	800x40	Grass	Unlicensed		Nil

Northside Grass Operation:

Rwy	Dim(m)	Surface	TORA(m)	LDA(m)	Lighting
08/26	1020x18	Grass	Unlicensed		Nil

Displaced Thresholds marked by Yellow/Orange marker boards.

Op hrs: PPR.

Landing Fee: Singles £6.50; Twins £13.00. Also See Remarks.

Customs: By arrangement

Hangarage: Limited. **Maintenance:** Available.

Remarks: Operated by Oxfordshire Sport Flying Ltd., Enstone Aerodrome, Church Enstone, Oxon OX7 4NP. Unlicensed aerodrome. PPR, Tel: 01608-677208.
Motor Gliders, light aircraft and Microlights operate from the aerodrome.
Microlights PPR from Group D Aviation, Tel: 01608-678741, 07860-864445. Landing fees by arrangement.

Northside Grass Strip (N51 55·88 W001 25·94) - A separate operation, it is operated by The Maintenance Facility. For additional landing information, Tel: 01608-683625 or 07768-478173.
No landing fees, but all movements at pilot's own risk. All approaches to the Northside Grass must be straight, no curved approaches permitted. Advise 'Landing Northside Grass' if using R/T.

Asphalt Rwy 08/26 - No arrivals/departures before 0800. No departures after 1930 or SS whichever earlier.

Avoid overflying the noise sensitive villages of GREAT TEW, LITTLE TEW, SANDFORD ST. MARTIN, ENSTONE AND CHURCH ENSTONE.

Circuits:
Powered aircraft to the North of the airfield. Group A aircraft at 800' aal, Motor Gliders and Microlights at 600' aal.

Warnings:
Windsock, 40 ft aal, adjacent to the Oxfordshire Sport Flying Club building.
6 ft high post and wire fence on the northern edge of the asphalt runway.
Trees 40 ft high on approach to Rwy 08.
Radio mast 120' aal 670' amsl at SE corner of aerodrome.
Intensive parachuting takes place at EG D129 - 'Weston-on-the-Green'.

Restaurant: Snacks, Tea/coffee available on the airfield.
Crown Inn in nearby village, Tel: 01608-677262.

Accommodation: Swan Lodge, Tel: 01608-678736; Crown Inn, Tel: 01608-677262.

Taxis: Ambassador, Tel: 01608-644015. Charlbury Taxis, Tel: 01608-810501.

Car Hire: Target Car Rental, Tel: 01295- 265 432.

Fuel: 100LL.	**Tel:** 01608-677208 Oxfordshire Sport Flying Club. 01608-678204 Enstone Flying Club. 01608-678741 Group D Aviation (Microlights). 01608-683625 North Side Grass.

Robert Pooley ©

Intentionally Blank

N55 16·90 W001 42·65	**ESHOTT**	197 ft AMSL

7 nm N of Morpeth.	**NEW 114·25 004 14·5**

**Eshott Radio 122·85 A/G – weekends only.   FIS — London Information 134·70.
Newcastle APP 124·375.**

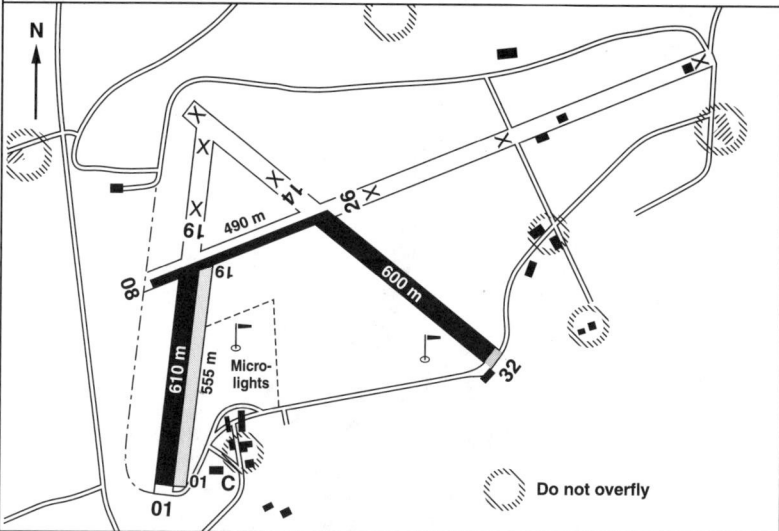

Rwy	Dim(m)	Surface	TORA(m)	LDA(m)	Lighting
01/19	610x45	Asphalt	Unlicensed		Nil
01/19	555x25	Grass	Unlicensed		Nil
08/26	490x40	Asphalt	Unlicensed		Nil
14/32	600x43	Asphalt	Unlicensed		Nil

Op hrs: PPR. 0900-1900 daylight hours only.

Landing Fee: £2.00.	**Customs:** Nil
Hangarage: Nil	**Maintenance:** Nil

Remarks: Operated by Eshott Airfield Ltd. Bockenfield, Felton, Northumberland.
NE65 9QJ. Unlicensed airfield. Visiting aircraft welcome on prior permission. Main
contact is Roger Rhodes.
Intense Microlight activity in the area, contact Newcastle Approach 124·375 for
information.
Asphalt area East of intersection 14/32 & 08/26 is a go-kart track and is not available
to aircraft. A fence runs along the East side Rwy 14/32 separating the aerodrome
from the go-kart track.
Circuits variable.
Avoid overflying FELTON village to the North and habitation in the immediate vicinity of
the airfield.

Restaurant: Airfield Cafe and Shop weekends. Local Bed & Breakfast.
Taxi: By arrangement

| **Fuel:** MOGAS - Local garage. | **Tel/Fax:** 01670-825427
Tel: 01670- 787881 Airfield. 07974-768148 |
|---|---|

Robert Pooley ©

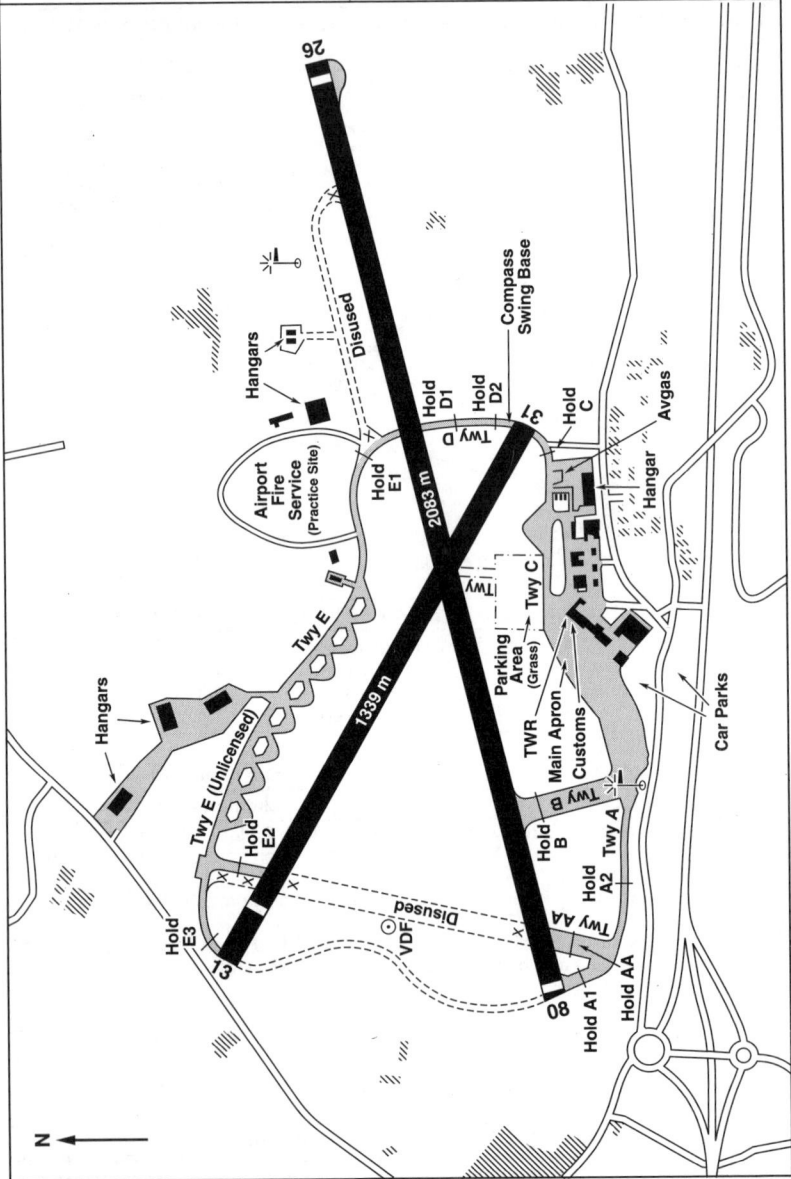

EGTE
EXETER

N50 44·07 W003 24·83

1 DEC 00

102 ft AMSL

4 nm NE of Exeter.

BHD 112·05 014 20·5

Robert Pooley ©

228

| N50 44·07   W003 24·83 | **EXETER** | 102 ft AMSL |

c/s Exeter. APP 128·15 (LARS). TWR 119·80. RAD 128·15, 119·05. VDF 128·15
NDB 'EX' 337·0 (261°M/4·1 nm to Thr 26).
ILS/DME Rwy 08 (081°M) I-ET 109·90.   ILS/DME Rwy 26 (261°M) I-XR 109·90.

Rwy	Dim(m)	Surface	TORA(m)	LDA(m)	Lighting
08/26	2083x46	Asphalt	08-2047	08-2037	Ap Thr Rwy PAPI 3°
			26-2073	26-2037	Ap Thr Rwy PAPI 3·5°
13/31	1339x46	Asphalt	13-1332	13-1196	Nil.
			31-1210	31-1210	Nil.

Op hrs: Mon 0700-2359; Tue-Fri 0001-0200, 0700-2359. (PPR before 0800 & after 1900 Mon-Fri).
*Sat 0001-0200, 0630 -2100 (PPR before 0800 & after 1700). *Sun 08-2359 (PPR before 0900 & after 1700). *Summer: Sat and Sun PPR before 0800 and after 2000.

| **Landing Fee:** £7.50 per 500 kg up to 3000 kg. | **Customs:** Available. |
| **Hangarage:** Very Limited. | **Maintenance:** Available. |

Remarks: Operated by Exeter & Devon Airport Ltd., Exeter Airport, Exeter, Devon EX5 2BD. Non-radio aircraft not accepted.

Training flights must book slots by telephone to ATC.

Unless otherwise required by an instrument approach procedure, or otherwise instructed by ATC, inbound aircraft shall maintain as high an altitude as practicable and shall maintain at least 1000' aal, until commencing descent on final approach.

Aircraft approaching without assistance from radar shall follow a descent path no lower than the normal approach path indicated by the PAPIs.

Wearing of high visibility clothing **mandatory** whilst on foot 'airside'. Suitable I.D. must be produced prior to entry to Restricted Zone.

Warnings:
Light aircraft pilots beware of elevated runway lights and PAPI Rwy 08/26.

With exception of twy B, all taxiways are only 15 m wide and thus not suitable for use by aircraft whose wheelbase exceeds 18 m and whose wheelspan is greater than 9 m. Taxiway B is 23 m wide and is suitable for use by all civil aircraft.

Public road crosses final approach for Rwy 13 (137 m from threshold).

Caution: Bird hazard.

Northern taxiway limited to light single and twin-engined aircraft not exceeding 15 m wingspan.

AVGAS 100LL : Only aircraft with a wing span not exceeding 15 m are permitted to use the Avgas installation. A maximum of two aircraft are permitted at any one time. Aircraft must call ATC prior to leaving the fuelling apron. No 100LL Bowser available.

Handling: By Exeter Airport Handling.

Restaurant: Bar/Buffet facilities available.

Accommodation: Hotels in the vicinity.

Car Hire: Europcar Tel: 01392-275398.

Fuel: 100LL, Jet A1. (see Remarks above) Diners, Multi Service, Visa & Access.	**Tel:** 01392-367433 Switchboard 01392-447433 Ops
	Fax: 01392-364593 Airport 01392- 366170 ATC 01392- 447422 Ops
	E- mail: exeterair@eclipse.co.uk

Robert Pooley ©

N54 18·52 W000 58·43	**FADMOOR (Moors National Park)**	780 ft AMSL

4·5 nm N of Wombleton.	OTR 113·90 325 48. POL 112·10 055 52
	GAM 112·80 005 61

Fadmoor Radio 123·22 A/G.

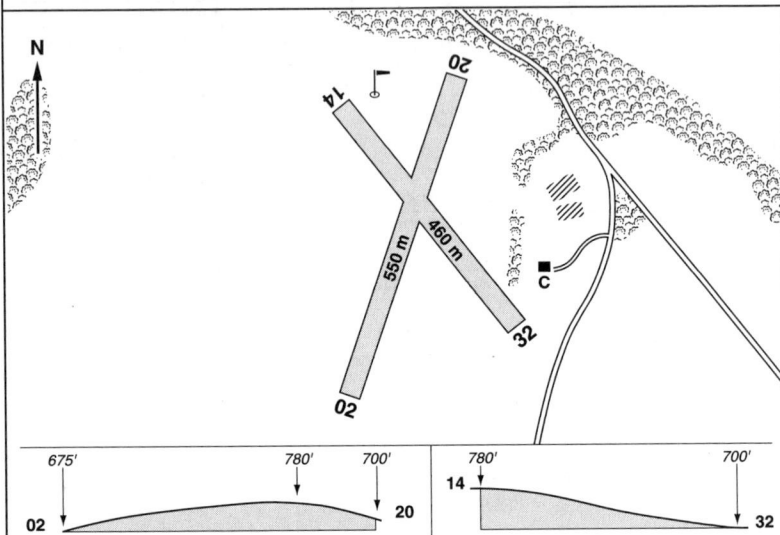

Rwy	Dim(m)	Surface	TORA(m)	LDA(m)	Lighting
02/20	550x27	Grass	02-550	02-550	Nil.
			20-550	20-550	Nil.
14/32	460x27	Grass	14-460	14-460	Nil.
			32-460	32-460	Rwy (on request)

Note: Runways 02 or 32 preferred for landing.

Op hrs: PPR. Mon-Sat SR-SS. Closed Sundays.

Landing Fee: Nil.	**Customs:** Nil.
Hangarage: Limited.	**Maintenance:** Nil.

Remarks: Operated by P.H. Johnson. Fadmoor, Kirkbymoorside, Yorks. YO62 7JH. Use of airfield restricted to aircraft operating on private or agricultural business. Airfield situated on crown of hill, on edge of escarpment, at southern edge of moorland. Ground slopes away from all thresholds.

Caution. All thresholds except Rwy 14 are uphill — as depicted above.
Beware of low flying military aircraft above and **below** airfield level.

Restaurant: Two excellent pubs 1 mile down the hill. Royal Oak Tel: 01751-31414, Plough Inn Tel: 01751-431515.

Accommodation: B&B and Holiday flat.   **Car Hire:** On request.

Fuel: 100LL (price 60p per litre + VAT. (Variable).	**Tel:** 01751-431171 Airfield. Mobile 07702-641732. **Fax:** 01751-432727.

N59 32·15 W001 37·68	**FAIR ISLE**	223 ft AMSL

Centre of Island.	**SUM 117·30 214 23**
	KWL 108·60 056 52

c/s Fair Isle Radio 118·025 A/G - Daylight hrs only and PPR.
Sumburgh APP 123·15.

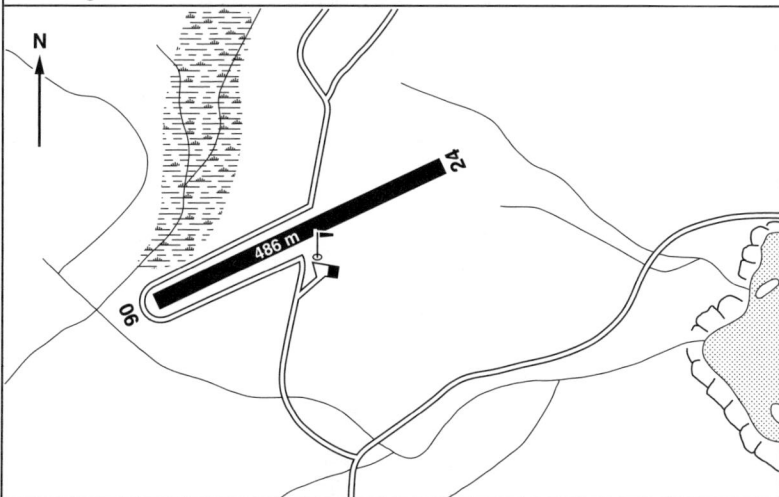

Rwy	Dim(m)	Surface	TORA(m)	LDA(m)	Lighting
06/24	486x22	Gravel	06-486 24-486	06-486 24-486	Goosenecks in emergency.

Op hrs: PPR.

Landing Fee: Light Singles £10.00 plus VAT. Others on application.

Hangarage: Nil.	**Maintenance:** Nil.	**Customs:** Nil.

Remarks: Operated by National Trust for Scotland, Abertarff House, Church Street, Inverness. Aircraft should not fly low over islands or cliffs. Runway is banked above surrounding land and is subject to turbulence with Westerly winds. Ground falls away very steeply approx 30m from each runway end. Rwy surface prone to moss growth and may be slippery in patches, particularly when wet. Windsock displayed.

For permission to land contact Mr. Dave Wheeler, to whom the landing fee is payable.

Visiting aircraft welcome at pilot's own risk. 150 ft. mast E side of Ward Hill.

Fire cover available with at least half an hour's prior notice.

Circuits RH on Rwy 06, LH on Rwy 24.

Warning: Bird hazard especially May to Aug. Highest area of risk is to aircraft on final approach to Rwy 06.

Restaurant: Food and Accommodation at the Fair Isle Observatory Trust, East of airfield. Tel: 01595-760258.

Car Hire: J. Stout. Tel: 01595-760222.

Fuel: Nil.	**Tel:** 01595-760224.
	Fax: 01595-760252.

Robert Pooley ©

N51 20·88 W000 33·53	**FAIROAKS**	80 ft AMSL

2 nm N of Woking	OCK 115·30 307 05
8 nm SW of LONDON/Heathrow Airport	LON 113·60 207 09

c/s Fairoaks Information/Radio 123·425 AFIS/AG.
Farnborough Radar 125·25.
NDB 'FOS' 348·0 (On A/D).   DME 'FRK' 109·85 (On A/D).

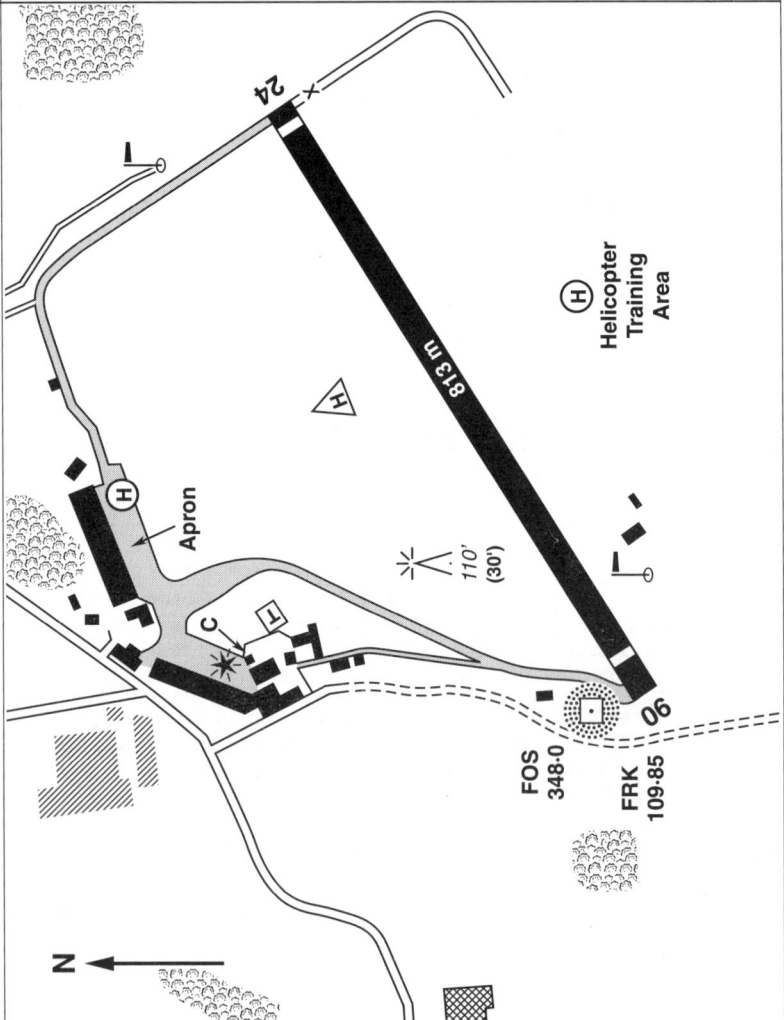

Helicopter Training Area

813 m

Apron

24

06

110' (30')

C

FOS 348·0

FRK 109·85

N

N51 20·88 W000 33·53 **FAIROAKS** 80 ft AMSL

Rwy	Dim(m)	Surface	TORA(m)	LDA(m)	Lighting
06/24	813x27	Asphalt	06-800	06-747	Thr Rwy APAPI 3·5°
			24-813	24-800	Thr Rwy APAPI 3·5°
					ABn Wh.

Op hrs: Mon-Fri 0800-1800, Sat 0800-1800, Sun & PHs 1000-1800. (Other times within 0700-2200 daily by arrangement).

Landing Fee: Up to 1000 kg £11.06, 1001-1500 kg £12.77 All + VAT. Other fees on request.

Customs: EU 4 hrs PNR, Non EU 24 hrs PNR (but less if agreed by an appropriate officer).

Hangarage: Limited, overnight only.

Maintenance: CAA approved M3 & B1 01276-857441. **Avionics:** 01276-857444.

Remarks: Operated by Fairoaks Airport Ltd., Chobham, Woking, Surrey, GU24 8HX.
Aerodrome in London CTR (Class 'A'), see Area Chart page 235.
Non-radio aircraft not accepted. No microlights. No Balloons. No Parachuting.
Variable circuits. Helicopter training.
First time visitors are requested a obtain a telephone briefing from the Tower.
Aerodrome often active outside published Op hrs, call AFIS on 123·425 at all times.
Pilots are responsible for their passengers whilst airside. No mobile phones airside.
Grass areas subject to waterlogging in winter.

Taxying – pilots are advised to exercise extreme caution when taxying through the apron/parking areas due to reduced wing tip clearances.

Noise Abatement Procedure:
Pilots are to avoid overflying the properties in the North East corner of the airfield below 1000 ft QFE.

IMC Arrivals:
Farnborough Radar may, after co-ordination with Fairoaks, provide a RIS to inbound aircraft, positioning them overhead Knaphill at 1300ft QNH with advisory headings and ranges to overhead Fairoaks. Such aircraft will not be cleared for descent below 1000ft QFE.

Restaurant: 'Prop Coffee Shop' offers Lunches, refreshments and In-Flight Catering, Tel: 01276-485897.

Car Hire: Moores Car Rental 01276-857557.

Taxis: Chobham Cars 01276-855151. Boomerang Taxis 01483-714062

Flying Training: Fixed wing 01276-858075. Helicopters 01276-857471

Fuel: 100LL, Jet A1. Diners,Visa, Amex, Switch and Master Card.	**Tel:** 01276-857300 Tower. 01276-857700 Admin. **Fax:** 01276-856898 Tower **Telex:** 859033 FKSATC.

Intentionally Blank

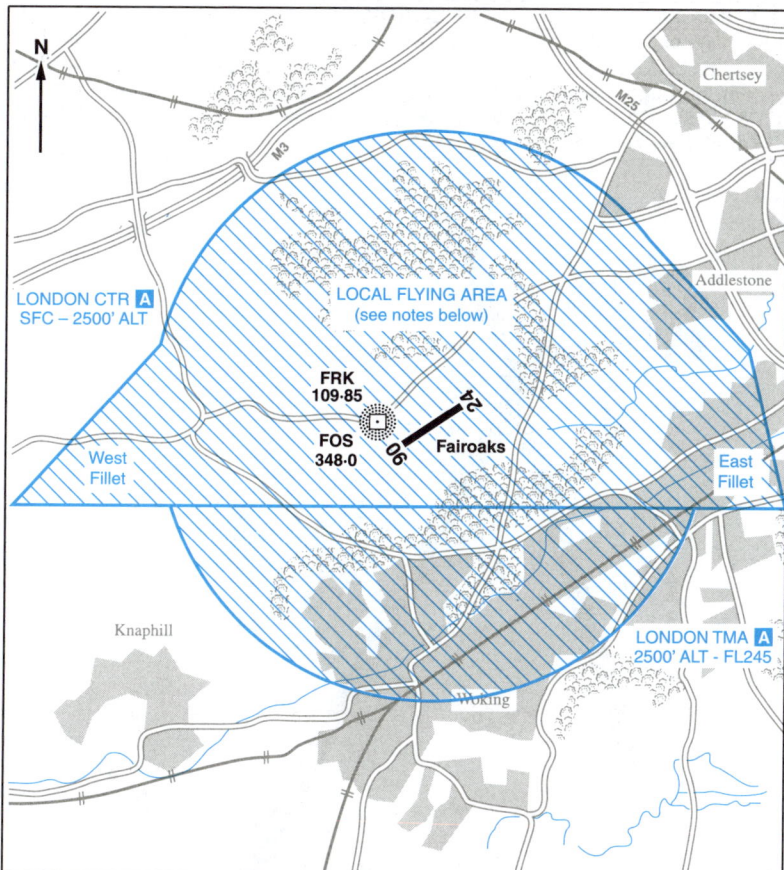

N

Chertsey

M25

M3

Addlestone

LONDON CTR **A**
SFC – 2500' ALT

LOCAL FLYING AREA
(see notes below)

FRK
109·85

FOS
348·0

24

90

Fairoaks

West
Fillet

East
Fillet

Knaphill

LONDON TMA **A**
2500' ALT - FL245

Woking

Within the ATZ/Local flying area and fillets to the east and west, as shown above, flights without compliance with IFR requirements may take place subject to the following conditions:

(a) Aircraft to remain below cloud and within sight of ground, in a flight visibility of not less than 3 km.

(b) Maximum altitudes: 800 ft. QNH when Rwy 23 is in use for take-offs at London/Heathrow, otherwise 1,500 ft. QNH.

Note 1. Pilots of aircraft flying in the local flying area are responsible for providing their own separation from other aircraft operating in the relevant airspace.

Note 2. ATC LONDON/Heathrow will advise Fairoaks when Rwy 23 is in use for take-offs.

Note 3. Aircraft may approach Fairoaks from the southern quadrant, between the western and the eastern fillets, but must remain west of the M25 motorway.

Aircraft operating on a SVFR clearance in the London CTR inbound to Fairoaks must not assume clearance has been issued to penetrate the Fairoaks ATZ. Pilots must obtain prior permission from Fairoaks by R/T. Heathrow Approach will, whenever possible, permit an aircraft to leave the frequency temporarily to obtain such clearance. If this is not possible, aircraft must leave the Zone clear of the ATZ and route to Fairoaks from a southerly direction.

Robert Pooley ©

N51 16·55 W000 46·58   **FARNBOROUGH**   237 ft AMSL

1 nm NNW of Aldershot.	OCK 115·30 271 12·4. MID 114·00 348 14·3
	CPT 114·35 133 20·9

c/s Farnborough Radar 134·35. RAD (LARS) 125·25. RAD c/s Talkdown 130·05
TWR 122·50.   VDF 134·35, 125·25, 122·50.   Ops 130·375 c/s Farnborough Exec.
LLZ/DME Rwy 25 (246°M) 'I-FNB' 111·55

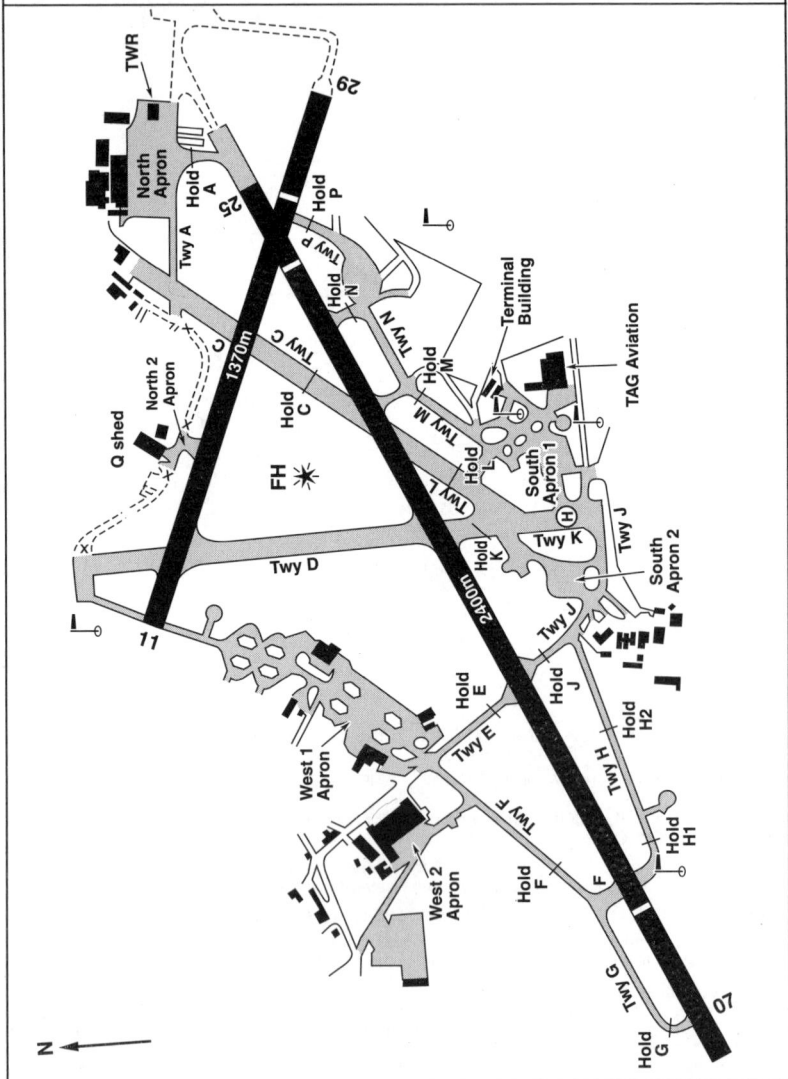

Robert Pooley ©

N51 16·55 W000 46·58   **FARNBOROUGH**   237 ft AMSL

Rwy	Dim(m)	Surface	TORA(m)	LDA(m)	Lighting
07/25*	2400x46	Concrete/ Asphalt	07-2400 25-2400	07-2080 25-2074	Ap Thr Rwy PAPI 3·5° Ap Thr Rwy PAPI 3·5°
11/29	1370x46	Asphalt	11-1370 29-1370	11-1370 29-1110	Thr Rwy PAPI 3·5° Thr Rwy PAPI 3·5° I Bn 'FH' Red

* Rwy 07/25 friction surface – no tight turns on asphalt section.

Op hrs: Mon-Fri 07-2200 ; Sat, Sun & PHs 08-2000 & ¢.   **ATZ active H24.**
Airfield may close after 2000 and before 2200 on weekdays.

Landing Fee: Singles & SE Helis £30. Twin Helis £50. Twin Piston up to 5000 kg £60. (Includes all airfield related costs, passenger & baggage handling, customs, immigration & Special branch plus 4 hrs parking). Aircraft above 5000kg contact TAG for rates. .

Hangarage: Available   **Customs:** Available.

Maintenance: Farnborough Aviation Services, Tel: 01252-372400.

Remarks: Operated by COMAX (on behalf of MoD), Control Tower Building, Farnborough Airport, Farnborough, Hampshire GU14 6TD.
Prior permission from TAG Aviation, Tel: 01252-524440.
Radar sequencing mandatory in IMC.
Inbound pilots are requested to notify ATC of their landing datum (ie QFE or QNH) on first contact.
Circuit at 1000ft QFE (2730 kg or less), 1500ft QFE (over 2730 kg).
Aircraft on MOD business obtain PPR from ATC by 1300 on previous day. Other aircraft must notify TAG as early as possible. Ops 130·375 c/s Farnborough Exec. Where no flight plan is filed, pilots must book in or out with ATC or TAG by telephone.

Noise Abatement
Aircraft are to be operated in a manner likely to cause the least disturbance in the areas surrounding the aerodrome.

All departures are to use the best rate of climb to initial clearance level and thereafter at least 500 ft per minute at a power settings which will ensure progressively decreasing noise levels at points on the ground under the flight path.

All jet aircraft and other aircraft above 5700 kg MTWA departing from Rwy 25 and requiring a right turn out must delay the turn until above 1800 ft QNH or 2·5 DME from I-FNB whichever is sooner. All other departures as per UK AIP (Civil). Pilots of aircraft shall not descend below 1000 ft agl until established on the final approach path and thereafter shall follow a descent path which will not result in aircraft being lower than the defined approach path of 3·5°.

Warnings:

(a) ATZ active H24. Helicopter activity takes place outside normal Op hrs and at weekends and public holidays during periods when ATC are not operating.

(b) Danger Areas D132, D133 and D133A are within 3 nm to the east of A/D.

(c) Traffic carrying out instrument approaches to Rwy 28 at ODIHAM will pass approx 2·5 nm S of Farnborough aerodrome at 1900ft QNH or lower.

VRPs: Alton N51 09·12 W000 57·97; Bagshot N51 20·95 W000 41·95; Farnborough Railway Stn N51 17·78 W000 45·30; Guildford N51 14·37 W00035·10; Hook N51 16·77 W000 57·72.

Helicopter Procedures – See overleaf.

Fuel: 100LL, Jet A1. Multi-Service	**Tel:** 01252-524440 PPR. 01252-526017 ATC **Fax:** 01252-518771 TAG. 01252-526024 ATC **Telex:** 858981. FNBAPT

HELICOPTER PROCEDURES

Aerodrome Elevation: 237 ft.   Arr/Dep Point Elevation: 227 ft.
Helicopter Arrival/Departure Point is on taxiway 'K' (disused Rwy 36) abeam the west gate of the South Apron.

Civil helicopters will be handled by TAG Aviation on South Apron.
PPR by telephone (01252-524440) or call Farnborough Exec on 130·375

1. ARRIVAL PROCEDURES

1.1 **IFR** — LLZ/DME to Rwy 25 or PAR or SRA to Rwy 07 or 25, then ground/air taxi to the west gate of South Apron

1.2 **VFR**

1.2.1 **From the West:** Follow the Basingstoke - Woking railway line to intercept Rwy 11 extended centreline. On crossing Rwy 11 threshold, turn right along taxiway 'D' (disused Rwy 18) towards the arrival point. Do not cross Rwy 07/25 until cleared by ATC.

1.2.2 **From the North and Bagshot:** Aim for the north end of taxiway 'D' (disused Rwy 18), then as for 1.2.1 above.

1.2.3 **From the South:** Follow taxiway 'K' (disused Rwy 36) centreline to the arrival point.

2. DEPARTURE PROCEDURES

2.1 **IFR**

2.1.1 Departures will normally be carried out from the departure point on taxiway 'K' abeam West Gate, however, Rwy 07/25 must be used when Low Visibility Procedures are in operation (visibility less than 2500 m), departing from the intersection Rwy 07/25 and taxiway 'K'.

2.1.2 ATC will allocate a transponder code, along with an assigned heading and altitude, which will ensure separation from known or conflicting traffic. Radar Advisory Service (RAS) or Radar Information Service (RIS) will be provided by Farnborough Approach.

2.2 **VFR**

2.2.1 Departures will normally be carried out from the departure point on taxiway 'K', however, either Rwy 07/25 or Rwy 11/29 may be used on request.

2.2.2 ATC will allocate a transponder code. Outbound routeing will be as required, but it is recommended that notified VRP's and line features are used until clear of the Farnborough/Odiham/ Blackbushe area. RIS or Flight Information Service will be provided by Farnborough Approach.

Note:
1. Helicopters are to be operated in accordance with the BHAB Code of Conduct at all times.
2. Special procedures, as notified by NOTAM, will be in force during SBAC Air Shows.

N50 44·28 W003 10·83	**FARWAY COMMON**	771 ft AMSL
9 nm E of Exeter Airport		**BHD 112·05 036 23·7**
4 nm NE of Sidmouth		

No Radio

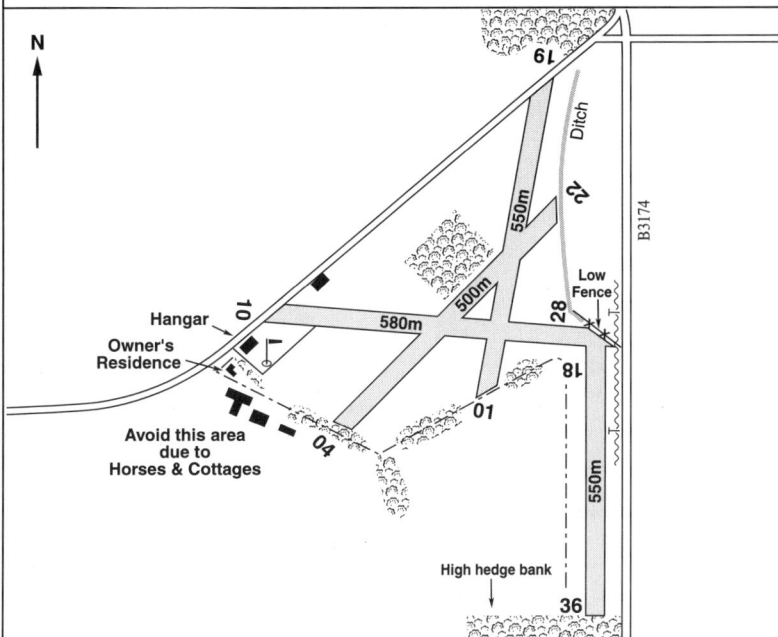

N

19

Ditch

22

B3174

550m

500m

580m

10

Hangar

Owner's
Residence

Low
Fence

28

18

01

04

**Avoid this area
due to
Horses & Cottages**

550m

High hedge bank

36

Rwy	Dim(m)	Surface	TORA(m)	LDA(m)	Lighting
01/19	550x12	Grass	Unlicensed		Nil
04/22	500x12	Grass	Unlicensed		Nil
10/28	580x16	Grass	Unlicensed		Nil
18/36	550x16	Grass	Unlicensed		Nil

Runways 01, 18 and 28 have downslopes.

Op hrs: PPR.

Hangarage: Nil	**Maintenance:** Nil	**Customs:** Nil

Remarks: Operated by Jean and Terry Case, Moorlands Farm, Sidbury, Sidmouth, Devon EX10 0QW. Unlicensed airfield.

Caution: Sheep may be grazing. Avoid overflying area to south west.

Restaurant/Accommodation: Hotels and B&B available locally.

Taxis: By arrangement.

Fuel: Nil	**Tel/Fax:** 01395-597535.

	FENLAND	
N52 44·35 W00001·78		8 ft AMSL
6 nm SE of Spalding.		**BKY 116·25 001 45**
		GAM 112·80 140 46

c/s Fenland Radio 122·925 A/G. c/s Information 122·925 AFIS (Weekends).
NDB 'FNL' 401·0 (On A/D. Nav. only).

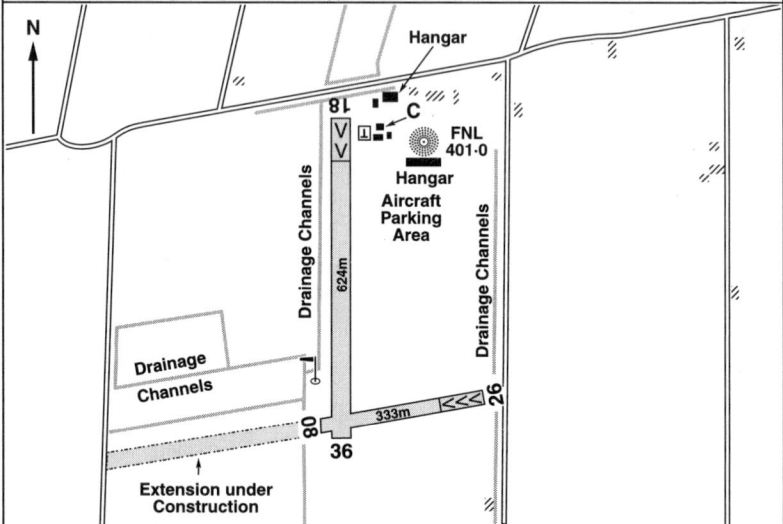

Rwy	Dim(m)	Surface	TORA(m)	LDA(m)	Lighting
18/36	624x40	Grass	18-624	18-536	† Thr Rwy LITAS 4·5°
			36-624	36-624	† Thr Rwy LITAS 3·75°
08/26	333x18	Grass	08-333	08-333	Nil.
			26-333	26-244	Nil.
† Lighting available on prior notice.					IBn 'FE' Gn.

Op hrs: 0900–Dusk daily, and by arrangement.

Landing Fee: Free where reciprocal arrangement exists, otherwise £5.

Hangarage: Ltd.   **Maintenance:** Available. 01406-540255.   **Customs:** 24 hrs PNR.

Remarks: Aerodrome operated by Fenland Aero Club. Flying Instruction by Fenland
Flying School and Helicentre. Fenland PFA Strut Base.
Avoid overflying village to ENE of aerodrome.
PPR at night and to non radio aircraft. Visitors welcome.
Circuits at 1000 ft aal, LH on Rwy 18, 36 and 26, RH on Rwy 08.
Use of Rwy 08/26 by aircraft required to use a licensed aerodrome is not permitted
without specific permission from the CFI of Fenland Flying School, until new
extension is available.

Warnings: Inset lighting on Rwy 18/36. Aircraft movements confined to marked grass
runways & taxiways. Displaced thresholds on Rwys 18 and 26 due to public roads.

Restaurant: Licensed restaurant Tue to Sun (closed Mon), Tel: 01406-540330.

Car Hire: Available on airfield by arrangement with the Restaurant staff.

Fuel: 100LL, Jet A1.	**Tel/Fax:** 01406-540461 Flying School.
	Tel: 01406-540115 Helicentre; 540330 Clubhouse/ATC
	Tel: 01945-582891 Aerodrome Licencee, Mr P. Coulten

FENLAND
Noise Abatement

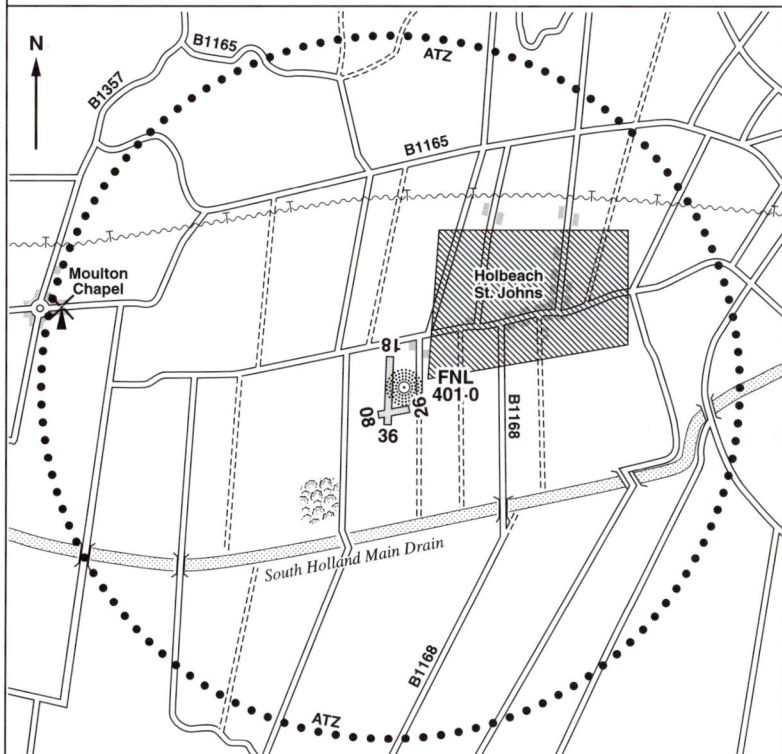

Noise Abatement:

Do not overfly the shaded area indicated above.

Circuits at 1000 ft aal, LH on Rwy 18, 36 and 26, RH on Rwy 08.

When Rwy 18 left hand is in use, the downwind leg for this runway must be wide to the east of the area indicated.

At times, the circuit direction for Rwy 18 may be changed to right hand. Pilots will be advised on initial call and the appropriate signal will be displayed within the Signal Square.

Intentionally Blank

N56 11·00 W003 13·22	**FIFE AIRPORT (Glenrothes)**	399 ft AMSL

2 nm W of town centre.   **TLA 113·80 013 41·5**
  SAB 112·50 303 38

c/s Fife Radio 130·45 A/G, (not continuously manned).
NDB 'GO' 402·0 (On A/D).

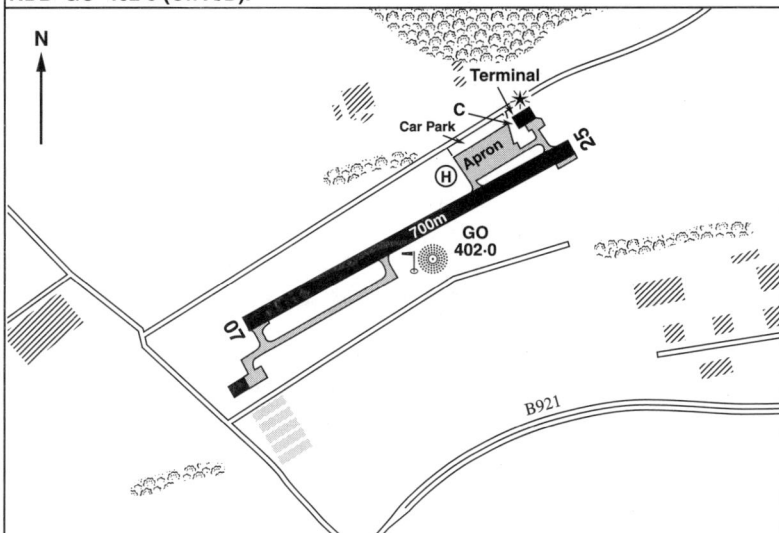

Rwy	Dim(m)	Surface	TORA(m)	LDA(m)	Lighting
07/25	700x18	Asphalt	07-700	07-700	Thr Rwy APAPI 4°
			25-700	25-700	Thr Rwy APAPI 4·25°
					A Bn Wh

Op hrs: PPR. WINTER: 0900-1700. SUMMER: Mon-Sat 0830-1800, Sun 0930-1800.

Landing Fee: Singles £8, Twins £16, incl VAT.
Landing fee waived if equivalent amount spent in restaurant.

Hangarage: Ltd, SE £8, Twins £ POA.   **Maintenance:** Nil.   **Customs:** Nil.

Remarks: Operated by Tayside Aviation Ltd, Fife Airport, Glenrothes, Fife. KY6 2SL. Airport Manager Bob Malcolm. All movements PPR. Pilots wishing to use the Airport after 1800 must phone prior to flight for PPR and check availability of Fire/Ops cover. Circuits LH on 25, RH on 07. Pilots should avoid overflying the housing estate to the East of the airfield on approach to Rwy 25 and, on take-off from Rwy 07 when a right turn should be made on reaching 300' aal.
On take-off from Rwy 25, climb straight ahead until West of Kinglassie village before turning left into circuit. On Rwy 07, extend downwind leg to turn base leg on West side of Kinglassie village.
In IMC, suitably equipped aircraft may let down at Edinburgh and proceed to Fife VFR.
High ground 1113' aal 1512' amsl 318°/4 nm.

Restaurant: Licensed restaurant. **Car Hire & Accommodation:** By arrangement.

Fuel: 100LL	**Tel:** 01592-753792
	Fax: 01592-612812

Robert Pooley ©

N51 31·17 W002 35·45   **FILTON**   226 ft AMSL

4 nm N of Bristol   BCN 117·45 122 28

APP/RAD c/s Filton App 122·725.   TWR 132·35.   RAD c/s Director 124·95, 127·975 (as directed).   VDF 122·725.   NDB 'OF' 325·0 (On A/D). ILS/DME Rwy 09 (095°M) I-BRF 110·55.   ILS/DME Rwy 27 (275°M) I-FB 110·55.

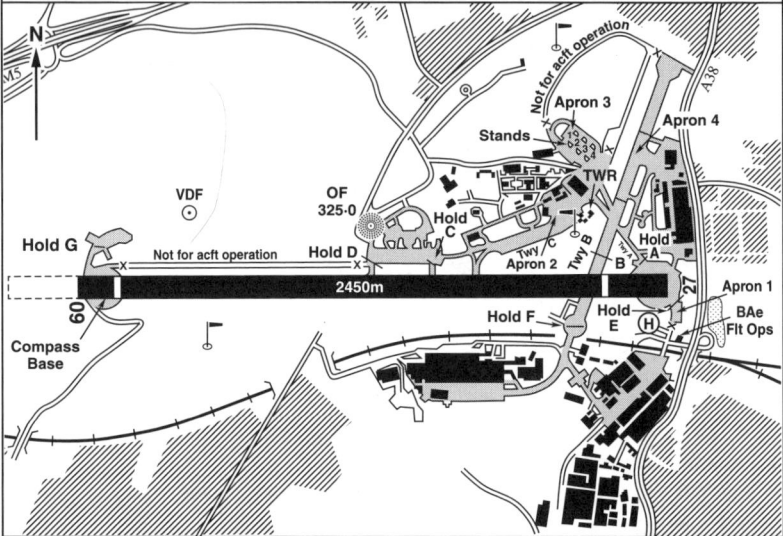

Rwy	Dim(m)	Surface	TORA(m)	LDA(m)	Lighting
09/27	2450x91	Concrete	09-2300	09-2125	Ap Thr Rwy RCL PAPI 3°
			27-2300	27-2060	Ap Thr Rwy RCL PAPI 3°

Op hrs: PPR. Mon 0700-2030; Tue-Fri 0645-2030; Sat 0900-1700; Sun 1000-1800.

Landing Fee: £13.95 per tonne (discounts for training movements).

Hangarage: 3900 sq ft.   **Maintenance:** By arrangement.   **Customs:** 24 hrs PNR.

Remarks: Operated by BAE Systems Ltd. Aircraft on approach to Rwy 27 are to cross the road not below 100 ft agl. Avoid overflying built up areas and the aircraft Assemly Hall on south side of aerodrome.

Aircraft must carry third party insurance cover of not less than £500,000.

Noise Abatement Procedures in force. Subject to ATC operations at the time, departing aircraft will be offered Rwy 27, and arrivals Rwy 09 whenever possible, along with the surface wind and runway status.

Circuits: Rwy 09 LH, 27 RH. Circuit height: Jet/Turbo Prop – 1500' QFE, 1700' QNH; All others –1000' QFE, 1200'QNH.

Pilots must request start clearance and have a marshaller in attendance.

Warnings: Not all taxiways are available for use. Remain within the marked manoeuvring areas.

Rwy 09/27 subject to slow clearance of standing water after heavy rain.

VRPs: Old Severn Bridge, M5 Bridge over River Avon and Thornbury.

Car Hire: Hertz Tel: 0117-9793101.

Fuel: 100LL, Jet A1. | **Tel:** 01179-699094 Ops **Fax:** 01179-362474 Ops

N51 59·12 W001 03·38	**FINMERE (Bucks)**	405 ft AMSL
2·5 nm WSW of Buckingham.		DTY 116·40 174 12
		BNN 113·75 314 24

No Radio.

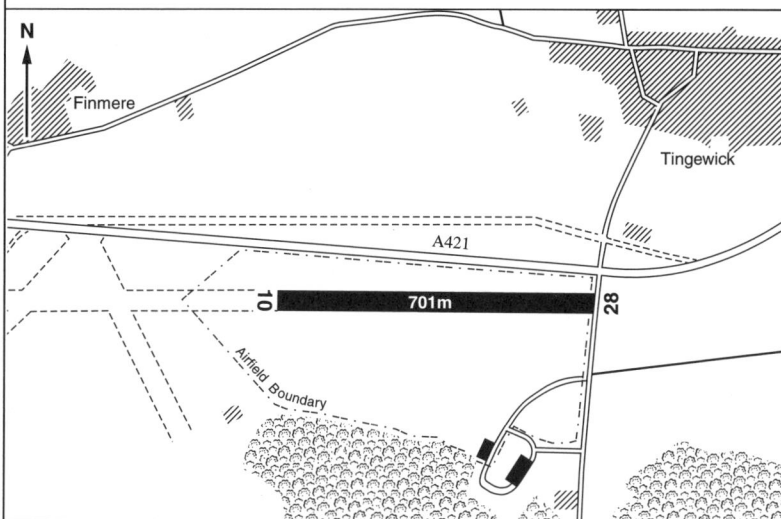

Rwy	Dim(m)	Surface	TORA(m)	LDA(m)	Lighting
10/28	701x46m	Asphalt	10-701	10-701	Nil.
			28-701	28-701	Nil.

Op hrs: PPR.

Landing Fee: Nil.	**Customs:** Nil.
Hangarage: Nil.	**Maintenance:** Nil.

Remarks: Owned and operated by Mrs. P. J. Knapton. 23 Gorrell Close, Tingewick, Bucks MK18 4PL. Unlicensed aerodrome.
Used by Vintage Aircraft Club on occasions as published in Aviation magazines. At all other times aerodrome is unattended and used by resident aircraft only.
Visiting light aircraft on prior permision at pilot's own risk.
Runway surface best at east end of runway.
Circuits LH on 28, RH on 10, avoid overflying Tingewick and Finmere villages, Sunday market to West of runway and dwellings to SSW.
Book in and out in the movements book at East end of the runway.

Caution:
- Power cables to South and West of runway.
- Barbed wire and netting fence along South side of runway.
- Only one runway usable and may be in use for HGV training and by model aircraft. One low level circuit should be made prior to final approach in order to permit lorries and model aircraft to clear the runway.
- Main road immediately north of runway.

Fuel: Nil.	**Tel:** 01280-848 589.

Robert Pooley ©

N5441·30 W00127·85	**FISHBURN**	377 ft AMSL

2·3 nm NNW of Sedgefield, Co. Durham.   **NEW 114·25 166 22·6**
2·5 nm N of Sedgefield Racecourse.

c/s Fishburn Radio 118·275.   Teesside APP 118·85.

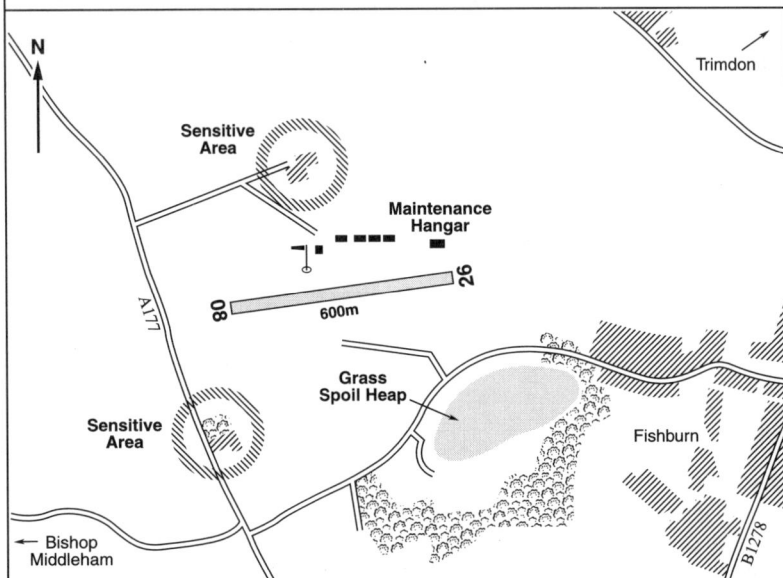

Rwy	Dim(m)	Surface	TORA(m)	LDA(m)	Lighting
08/26	600 x 30	Grass	Unlicensed		Nil

Runway Gradient — 1·6% UPSLOPE on Rwy 26

Op hrs: PPR. 0800-2030 daily.

Landing Fee: Singles £2; Twins £5. No landing fee with fuel uplift of 40 litres or more.

Hangarage: By arrangement   **Maintenance:** Emergency only   **Customs:** PNR

Remarks: Unlicensed airfield operated by Mrs. Beryl Morgan. Home base of Skyshaw Aerobatics – Mr. Peter Metcalfe, Tel: 01642-676115, Fax: 01642-640610.
Airfield situated 3 nm from the NNW boundary of Teesside CTR/CTA, contact Teesside App 118·85. Visiting fixed wing and light helicopters welcome with PPR.
Circuits at 800' aal, LH on 08, RH on 26. Join circuit only from the North, no deadside.
Avoid overflying the villages of TRIMDON, FISHBURN and BISHOP MIDDLEHAM, and the noise sensitive areas shown above.
Note: Private Landing Strip 1 nm to the North.

Aircraft Spares and Oils: Durham Aviation Co. Tel: 01207-521199.

Restaurant: Light refreshments available.

Accommodation: 2 miles to south of airfield.   **Taxi:** Ron's 01740-621862.

Fuel:100LL - at competitive price.	**Tel:** 0191-3770137 Airfield 0191-3720213 or 3770448 Operator **Fax:** 01642-640610 Skyshaw Aeros

N52 04·65 E000 03·70	**FOWLMERE**	124 ft AMSL
3·5nm NE of Royston.		**BKY 116·25 004 5·3**

c/s Fowlmere Radio 120·925 A/G.   Duxford Information 122·075 AFIS.
Essex Radar 120·625.

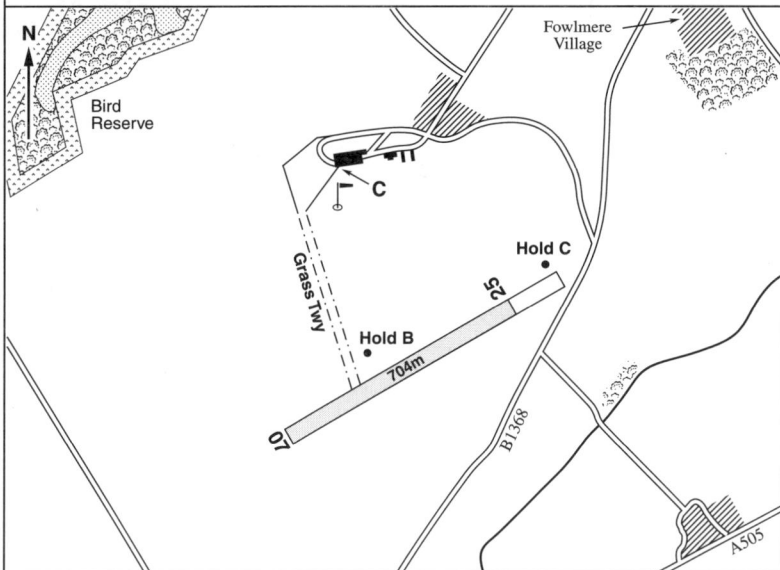

N

Fowlmere Village

Bird Reserve

C

Hold C

Grass Twy

25

Hold B

704m

07

B1368

A505

Rwy	Dim(m)	Surface	TORA(m)	LDA(m)	Lighting
07/25	*704x30	Grass	704	704	Nil.

* Additional 150 m of unmarked, unlicensed runway available for take-off on Rwy 25.

Op hrs: PPR essential, closed Mondays.

Landing Fee: Singles £10.00 inclusive of VAT.

Hangarage: Nil.	**Maintenance:** M 3.	**Customs:** 4 hrs PNR.

Remarks: Operated by Modern Air, Self-Fly Aircraft Rental, Fowlmere Aerodrome, Herts. SG8 7SJ. Visitors must obtain prior permission and Briefing before departure.

No Helicopters or Microlights.

Licensed airfield situated 2·5 nm WSW of Duxford A/D. Fowlmere and Duxford ATZs overlap, during the coincidental hours of operation of the two aerodromes the ATZs are merged to form a Combined ATZ (CATZ). Aerodrome Flight Information for the CATZ is provided by Duxford AFIS.

Northern boundary of Stansted CTA (Class 'D') 3 nm to S of airfield.

No overhead joins. No deadside. Circuits at 800 ft aal. LH on 07, RH on 25.

Mast 851ft amsl 4 nm SSW of airfield. Avoid overflying RSPB Bird Reserve 700 m NW of airfield and the village of FOWLMERE just to the N of airfield.
Public road crosses final approach to Rwy 25, avoid low approaches to this runway; displaced threshold on 25.

Taxis: Tel: 01223-837773.

Fuel: 100LL by arrangement. No Credit Cards taken.	**Tel:** 01763-208281/208141/208316/208349 01223-833376 Duxford ATC **Fax:** 01763-208861/208842

EGNU 1 DEC 00

| N53 58·83 W000 51·85 | **FULL SUTTON** | 86 ft AMSL |

7 nm E of York.
Centre of R315

POL 112·10 077 46. **OTR** 113·90 305 32
GAM 112·80 010 42

Full Sutton Radio 132·32 A/G. *Radio use Mandatory.*

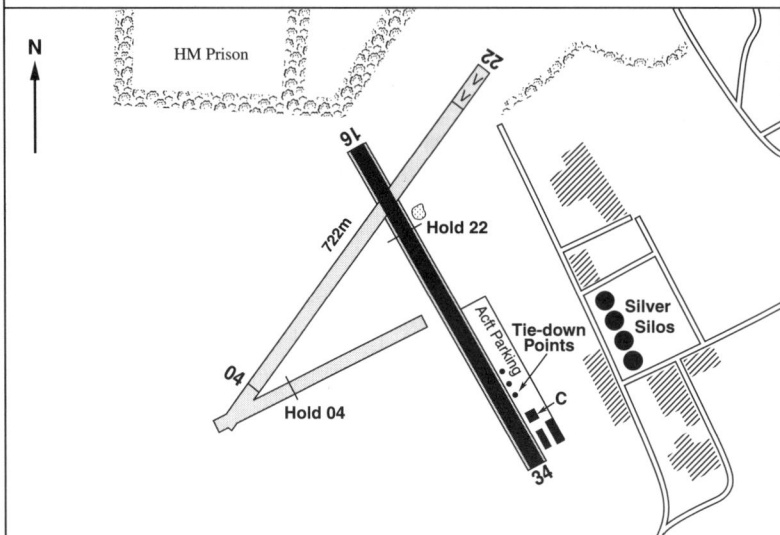

Rwy	Dim(m)	Surface	TORA(m)	LDA(m)	Lighting
04/22	722x20	Grass	04-772	04-772	Nil.
			22-772	22-693	Nil.
†16/34	700x25	Asphalt	Unlicensed		

† Primarily used as a taxiway, use as a Rwys only with PPR from A/D Manager.

Op hrs: PPR. 0900-1700 daily.

Landing Fee: £5.00 Singles, £10.00 Twins.

Hangarage/ Maintenance: Available.

Remarks: Operated by Full Sutton Flying Centre Ltd.
PPR Mandatory due to Prison avoidance flying Procedures.
Aerodrome not available for Public Transport flights required to use a licensed aerodrome.
Circuits at 800' QFE, RH on 04, LH on 22.
Overflying of nearby Prison is strictly forbidden. Offenders will be videod and prosecuted by the Prison authorities and Police.

Intensive gliding takes place at Pocklington aerodrome located 4 nm to the south east of the aerodrome.

Caution: Power cables cross the approach to Rwy 22.

| **Fuel:** 100LL - by arrangement | **Tel:** 01759-372717/ Club 373277.
Fax: 01759-372991. |

Robert Pooley ©

246

N55 39·20 W005 45·47	**GIGHA ISLAND**	46 ft AMSL
1·5 nm S of village.		**MAC 116·00 001** 13·0

No Radio.

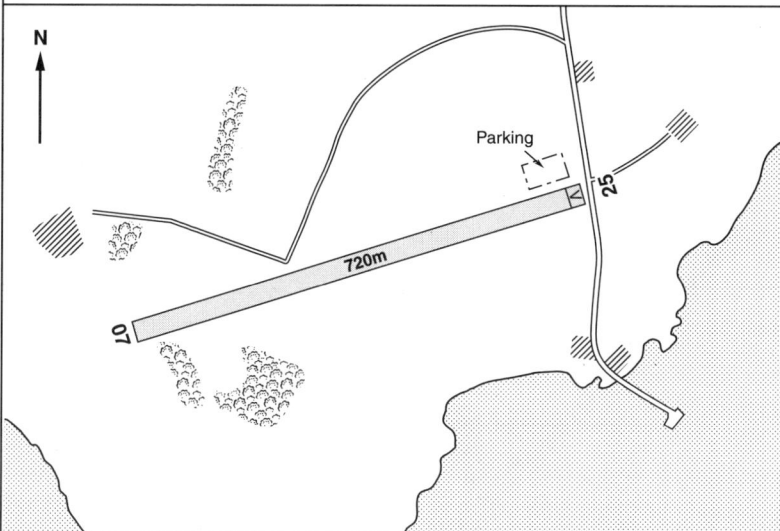

Rwy	Dim(m)	Surface	TORA(m)	LDA(m)	Lighting
07/25	720x60	Grass	Unlicensed		Nil.

Op hrs: PPR. SR–SS.

Landing Fee: Single: £15.00, Twins £25.00; £5.00 discount if staying overnight at Gigha Hotel. Special discount for Clubs.

Customs: Nil.

Hangarage: Nil. Tie-downs available N side of 25 Thr. **Maintenance:** Nil.

Remarks: Operated by Holt Leisure Parks Ltd., Achamore House, Isle of Gigha, Argyll. PA41 7AD.
Visiting aircraft welcome on prior permission.
Avoid overflying the village on Sundays between 1200 and 1300 hrs.

Fuel: MOGAS.	**Tel:** 01583- 505 254. **Fax:** 01583- 505 244.

N55 52·32 W004 26·00 **GLASGOW** 26 ft AMSL

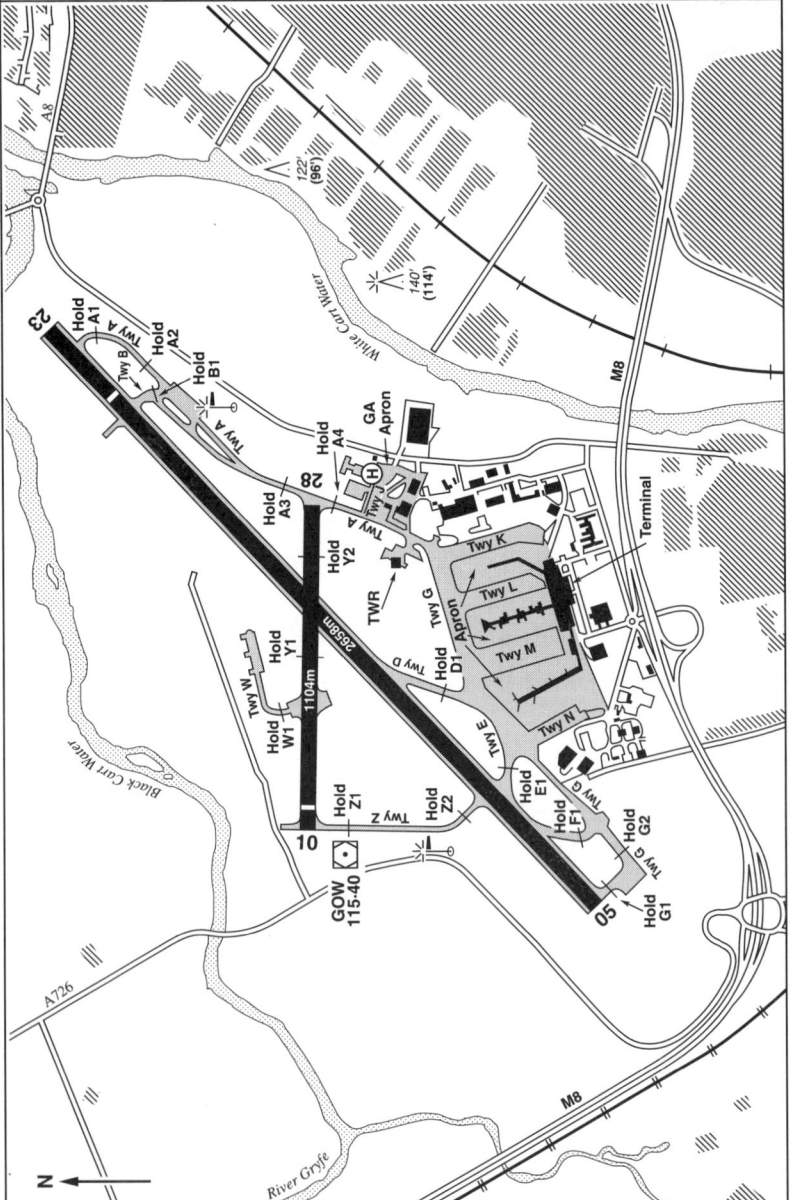

122' (96')

140' (114')

White Cart Water

A8

M8

Hold A1
Twy B
Hold A2
Twy A
Hold B1
Hold A4
GA Apron
Twy A
Hold A3
28
Hold Y2
Twy A
TWR
Twy G
Twy K
Twy L
Apron
D1
Twy D
Twy M
Terminal
23

Twy W
Hold Y1
Hold W1
2658m
1104m
Twy E
Twy N
Hold Z1
Twy Z
Hold Z2
Hold E1
Twy F
Twy G
Hold F1
Hold G2
10
GOW 115·40
05
Hold G1
Twy G

Black Cart Water

River Gryfe

A726

M8

Z ←

N55 52·32 W004 26·00	**GLASGOW**	26 ft AMSL
6 nm W of Glasgow.		**TRN 117·50 027 35·6**

c/s Glasgow. APP 119·10. TWR 118·80. GMC 121·70. RAD 119·10, 119·30, 121·30.
ATIS 129·575 (0620-0020). VOR/DME 'GOW' 115·40 (On A/D).
NDB 'GLG' 350 (233°M/4 nm to Thr 23).   NDB 'AC' 325 (053°M/4·3 nm to Thr 05).
ILS/DME Rwy 05 (053°M) I-UU 110·10.   ILS/DME Rwy 23 (233°M) I-OO 110·10.

Rwy	Dim(m)	Surface	TORA(m)	LDA(m)	Lighting
05/23	2658x46	Asphalt	05-2658	05-2658	Ap Thr Rwy RCL PAPI
			23-2658	23-2353	Ap Thr Rwy RCL PAPI
10/28	1104x46	Asphalt	10-1104	10-1042	Thr Rwy PAPI 3°*
			28-1104	28-1104	Thr Rwy PAPI 3°*

* Lighting for Rwy 10/28 available at 30 mins prior notice.

Op hrs: H24

Landing Fee: BAA Rates.	**Customs:** H24
Hangarage: Nil. **Maintenance:** Available.	**Met:** H24. 0141-221-6116

Remarks: Operated by Glasgow Airport Ltd., Glasgow Airport, Paisley, Strathclyde PA3 2ST.

Use governed by the regulations applicable to Class D and E Controlled Airspace within the Glasgow CTR (D) and the Scottish TMA (D/E) – see page 2.

Microlight Operations – see page 251.

Visual Reference Points (VRPs) are listed at page 252.

CTR and Entry/Exit Lanes – see overleaf and chart at page 253.

All pleasure, training and non business GA traffic is subject to prior notification to ATC, the filing of a flight plan does not constitute permission to use Glasgow Airport.

Visiting General Aviation (GA) aircraft including International arrivals will be parked on the GA Area via taxiway Juliet.

All operators must make prior arrangements with a handling agent for ground handling.

Handling for GA aircraft is provided by Execair Aviation on 122·35 or telephone 0141-887-8348; Fax: 0141-887-9099. Execair Aviation accept all major credit cards for handling/fuel.

Visiting helicopters will join and route to parking area as directed by ATC.

Warninig: Bird hazard. Large Bird population around the airport. Swans active September/October to March/April.

Restaurant: Restaurant and Refreshments available.

Car Hire: Avis. Tel: 0141 887-2261. Hertz. Tel: 0141 887-1111, Ext. 4244.
                Swan National. Tel: 0141-887-1111, Ext. 4285.

Fuel: 100LL, Jet A1. S. Diners. Multi Service.	**Tel:** 0141-887 1111 Airport.
	0141-840 8029 ATC.
	0141-840 8000 NATS Ltd.
	0141-848 4141 Airfield Ops.
	0141-887 7449 ATIS.
	Fax: 0141-848 4354 Airport.
	0141-840 8011 NATS Ltd.

Robert Pooley ©

1. VFR Flights

1.1 VFR flights in the CTR will be given routeing instructions and/or altitude restrictions in order to integrate VFR flights with other traffic.

1.2 Routeing will normally be via the Visual Reference Points or the Entry/Exit lanes detailed below.

1.3 Pilots are reminded of the requirement to remain in VMC at all times and to comply with the relevant parts of the Low Flying Rules, and must advise ATC if at any time they are unable to comply with the instructions issued.

1.4 **Helicopters:** Whenever possible helicopter flights in the Glasgow CTR will be cleared on direct routeings under VFR (or, when requested at night, on SVFR clearance in accordance with the procedures for Special VFR flights).

2. Special VFR (SVFR) Clearance

2.1 Clearance may be requested for SVFR flight in IMC or at night within the Glasgow CTR and will be given whenever the traffic situation permits. Such flights are subject to the general conditions laid down for SVFR flights at page 6.

2.2 SVFR clearance will include routeing and maximum altitude instructions and may not necessarily be confined to the Entry/Exit Lanes detailed below.

2.3 PPL holders are reminded of the visibility requirements for SVFR flights as laid down in Schedule 8 of the ANO and the specified minimum visibility of 3 km for SVFR flights within the Glasgow CTR, which may require them to request routeing via the Entry/Exit Lanes.

2.4 SVFR clearance will not normally be granted for flights operating in VMC or for flights by aircraft exceeding 5700 kg MTWA.

3. Entry/Exit Lanes

3.1 To permit aircraft to operate to and from Glasgow Airport in IMC but not under VFR, entry/exit lanes have been established for use, as depicted on the chart opposite.

3.2 Use of these lanes is subject to the following conditions:

(a) Clearance must be obtained from Glasgow ATC and the carriage of Glasgow Approach Control frequency is mandatory.

(b) Aircraft using the lanes must remain clear of cloud and in sight of surface, not above 3,000 ft. (Glasgow QNH) and in flight visibility of not less than 3 km.

(c) An aircraft using a lane shall keep the centre-line on its left unless otherwise instructed by ATC, (it should be noted that the centre-line of the Clyde Lane is the middle of the River Clyde).

(d) Aircraft using the lanes when visibility at Glasgow Airport is better than 4 km may be instructed by ATC to fly:
   (i)   between Glasgow Airport and Greenock/Ardmore Point; north of the north bank or south of the south bank of the Clyde; or
   (ii) between Glasgow Airport and Loch Lomond (Alexandria); north of the Clyde/east of the Leven or south of Clyde/west of the Leven;
   (iii) between Glasgow Airport and East Kilbride, north of the A726 or south of the A726.

(e) Pilots of aircraft are responsible for maintaining adequate clearance from the ground or other obstacles.

3.3 Additionally, to permit the effective integration of traffic, flights operating in VMC and under VFR may be required by ATC to follow these routes as detailed at para 1.

Hang Gliding and Paragliding

a. By arrangement with Glasgow ATC, hang gliding takes place up to 2500 ft amsl (and occasionally, up to 3000 ft amsl with ATC permission) within the Glasgow Control Zone from various sites on the Campsie Fells/Kilsyth Hills to the northeast and inland from Largs to the west.

b. The Campsie Fells sites lie in close proximity to the Rwy 23 Final Approach Track to Glasgow Airport at ranges between 10 and 13 miles.

c. Paragliding takes place up to 1500 ft amsl from a site encompassing Ballageich Hill (N55 43· 32 W004 20·33) and Bennan Hill (N55 43·57 W004 21·30) approximately 10 nm south-southeast of Glasgow Airport.

d. Pilots of VFR flights are responsible for maintaining their own separation for hang gliders and paragliding. The sites are shown on aeronautical charts. **Traffic Information will not be passed by ATC.**

Microlight Operations

Only 3 axis microlight aircraft will be permitted to enter, leave or transit the CTR. To obtain permission to enter the CTR, such aircraft must meet the following criteria:

a. Two way VHF Radio is carried;

b. Operated by day in VMC;

c. Microlight aircraft must remain at least 4 nm fro Rwy 05/23 centre-line or, if crossing the centre-line, must remain at or below 1000 ft Glasgow QNH and cross the centre-line at a range of not less than 7 nm.

VRP	VOR/VOR	VOR/NDB	VOR/DME
Alexandria N55 59·33 W004 34·58	GOW R334 TRN R016	TRN R016 GLG 302°M	GOW 334°/8 nm TRN 016°/41 nm
Ardmore Point N55 58·28 W004 41·95	GOW R312 TRN R010	GOW R312 GLG 290°M	GOW 312°/10 nm
Baillieston N55 51·17 W004 05·37	TLA R317 GOW R101	TLA R317 AC 087°M	GOW 101°/12 nm
Barrhead N55 48·00 W004 23·50	TRN R031 TLA R303	TLA R303 GLG 200°M	GOW 163°/5 nm TRN 031°/32 nm
Bishopton N55 54·13 W004 30·10	GOW R322 TRN R021	GOW R322 GLG 263°M	GOW 322°/3 nm
Dumbarton N55 56·67 W004 34·10	GOW R323 TRN R017	GOW R323 GLG 285°M	GOW 323°/6 nm TRN 017°/39 nm
East Kilbride N55 45·83 W004 10·33	TRN R044 TLA R306	TRN R044 GLG156°M	GOW 131°/11 nm
Erskine Bridge N55 55·22 W004 27·77	GOW R355 TRN R023	GOW R355 GLG 273°M	GOW 355°/3 nm
Greenock N55 56·83 W004 45·08	GOW R300 TRN R008	TRN R008 GLG 282°M	GOW 300°/11 nm
Inverkip Power Sta. N55 53·90 W004 53·20	GOW R283 TRN R001	TRN R001 GLG 272°M	GOW 283°/15 nm
Kilmacolm N55 53·67 W004 37·65	TRN R015 GOW R289	TRN R015 GLG 266°M	GOW 289°/6 nm TRN 015°/35 nm
Kilmarnock N55 36·75 W004 29·90	GOW R193 TRN R035	GOW R193 NGY 343°M	GOW 193°/16 nm
Kingston Bridge N55 51·37 W004 16·18	GOW R104 TRN R034	GOW R104 GLG 157°M	GOW 104°/6 nm TRN 034°/37 nm

See Glasgow CTR and VAD/VRP Chart on opposite page.

GLASGOW CONTROL ZONE
ENTRY/EXIT LANES and VRPs

1 DEC 00

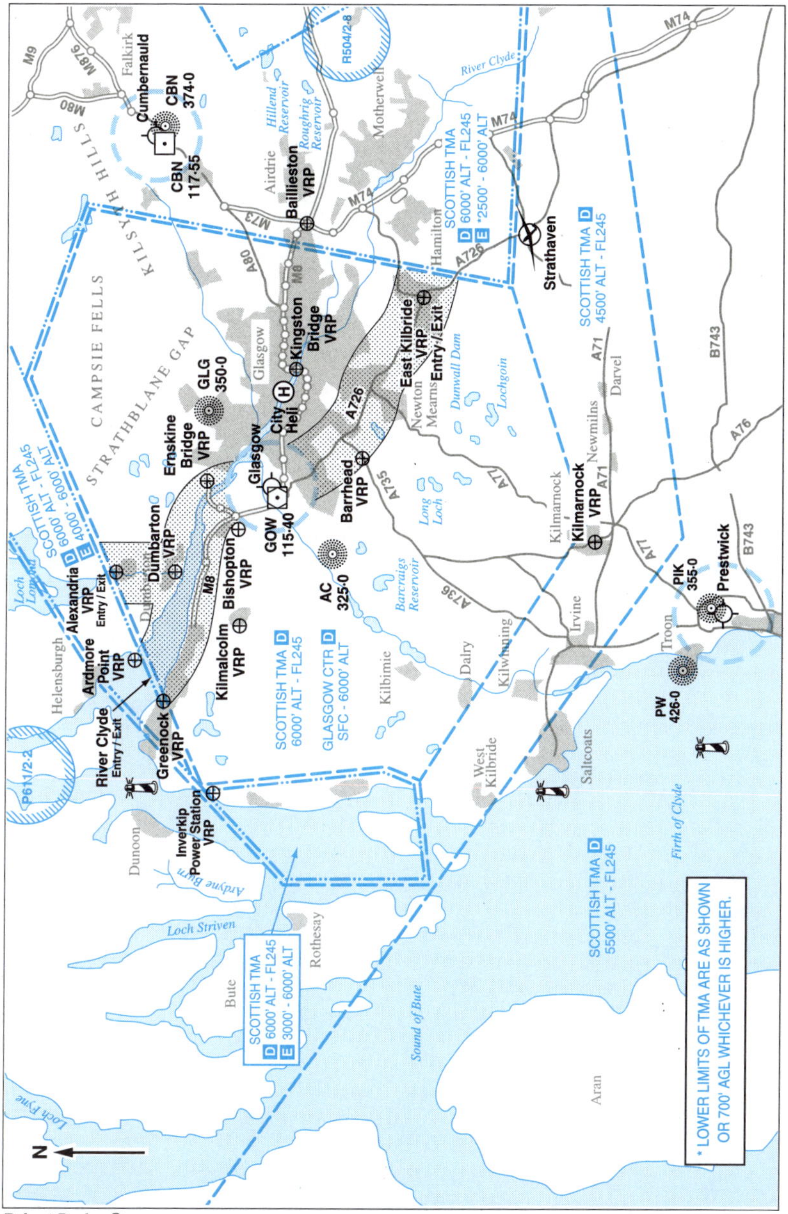

Robert Pooley ©

Intentionally Blank

N56 31·05 W005 54·85	**GLENFORSA (Mull)**	15 ft AMSL
1nm E of Salen, on Isle of Mull.		**TIR 117·70 096 32**

c/s Glenforsa Radio 129·825 A/G - Not always manned.

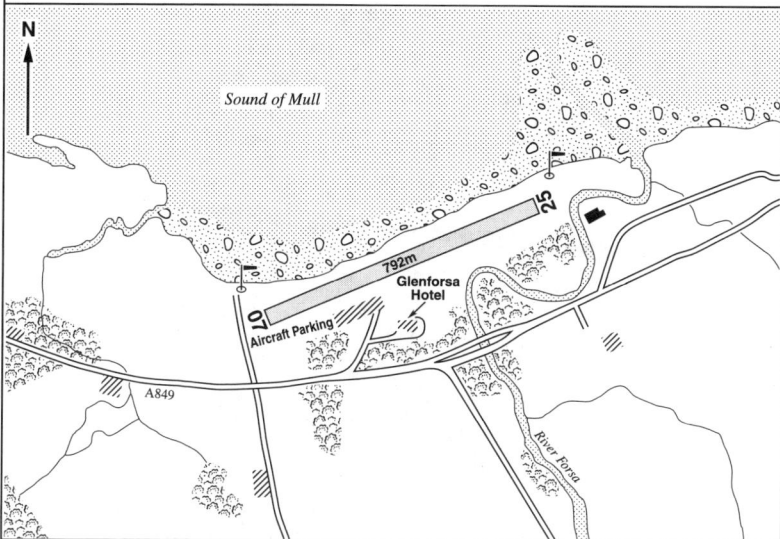

Rwy	Dim(m)	Surface	TORA(m)	LDA(m)	Lighting
† 07/25	792x46	Grass	Unlicensed		Nil

† **Warning:** Concrete runway designators still show 08/26.
Use South side of runway only, due to poor drainage.

Op hrs: 24 hrs PPR essential 1 Oct-30 Apr, when sheep may be grazing.

Landing Fee: Private: Singles £8, Microlights £4.75, Twins £12. All inclusive of VAT.
Commercial: £4.75 per half tonne + VAT.

Hangarage: Nil.	**Maintenance:** Nil.	**Customs:** Nil.

Remarks: Operated by Argyll and Bute Council. Unlicensed airfield. Ideally PPR from local representative D. S. Howitt, Airfield Bungalow, Glenforsa, Mull PA72 6JN. Tel: 01680-300402 for information on airfield conditions and *advisory* weather actuals.

Livestock on runway weekdays Oct to Apr. Airfield clear of livestock every weekend except for the months of Oct and Apr when PPR is required. No sheep on airfield from May to Sept.

Restaurant: Glenforsa Hotel adjacent to strip, meals/accommodation;

Car Hire: Available by arrangement, Tel: 01680-300402

Fuel: 100LL – PNR to James Knight 01680-812475 Jet A1 - Paul Keegan, Connel Aerodrome 01631-710384.	**Tel:** 01680-300402 Airfield. 01631-562125 Council.

N51 53·65 W002 10·03	**GLOUCESTERSHIRE**	95 ft AMSL

3·5 nm W of Cheltenham.   **HON 113·65 220 33·3   BCN 117·45 082 41·8**

c/s Gloster. **APP 125·65. TWR 122·90 . RAD 120·975** (as directed). **VDF 125·65.**

ATIS 127·475. NDB 'GST' 331·0 (On A/D) - see Remarks. **DME 'GOS' 115·55** (On A/D).

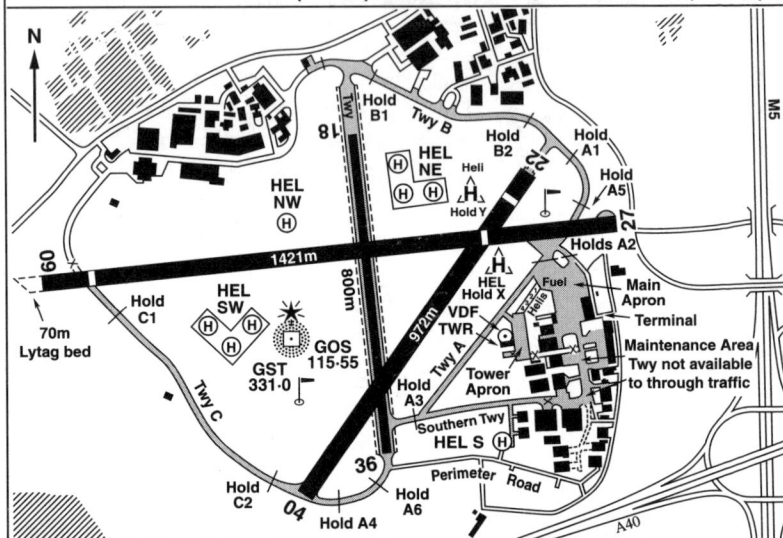

Rwy	Dim(m)	Surface	TORA(m)	LDA(m)	Lighting
04/22	972x41	Asphalt	04-972	04-972	APAPI 4·5°
			22-972	22-895	APAPI 3·5°
09/27	1421x37	Asphalt	09-1279	09-1161	Ap Thr Rwy PAPI 3°
			27-1345	27-1027	Ap Thr Rwy PAPI 3·5°
18/36	800x18	Asphalt	18/36-800	18/36 -800	Nil.
					IBn 'GO' Gn

STOL PAPIs on Rwys 09 & 27 set at 5·3° Right hand side.

Op hrs: Mon-Fri 0830-1930 all year, Sat and Sun 0900-1800 Winter, 09-1930 Summer.

Landing Fees: Min £12 inc VAT. Half price for single engines with fuel uplift.

Hangarage: Available.   **Maintenance:** Available.   **Customs:** 24 hrs PNR.

Remarks: Operated by Gloucestershire Airport Ltd., Cheltenham, Glos. GL51 6SR. Non-radio aircraft not accepted. Permission to use the A/D outside scheduled hours must be obtained from ATC when the surcharge involved will be advised. Circuits are variable.
Aerodrome is PPR for Instrument training, Tel 01452-857700 Ext 229.
Jet aircraft only Departures Rwy 09 - climb on runway heading to 1500' QFE before turning.
All Departures Rwy 27 - execute a 10° right turn immediately on crossing the upwind end of the runway. A subsequent left turn on track may be made after passing 700 ft QFE.
All Departures Rwy 18 – make a 20° left turn as soon practicable.
Warning NDB/L 'GST' Interference may occur within 5 nm of Droitwich and some ADFs may show occasional bearing fluctuations on approach to Rwy 27.
Restaurant: Refreshments and Club facilities available.

Car Hire: Hertz Tel: 01452-854477. Thrifty Car Rental Tel: 01452-383866

Taxi: Tel: 01242-222333 (Cheltenham). Tel: 01452-523523 (Gloucester).

Fuel: 100LL, Jet A1. S.	**Tel:** 01452-857700 Ext 223 ATC/Briefing,
Diners, Visa, Multi Service	Ext 227 Admin. **Fax:** 01452-715174.

N52 46·73 E000 40·35	**GREAT MASSINGHAM**	295 ft AMSL
10 nm E of Kings Lynn		BKY 116·25 029 52.
		DH 342·50 289 19

No Radio.
Marham APP 124·15.

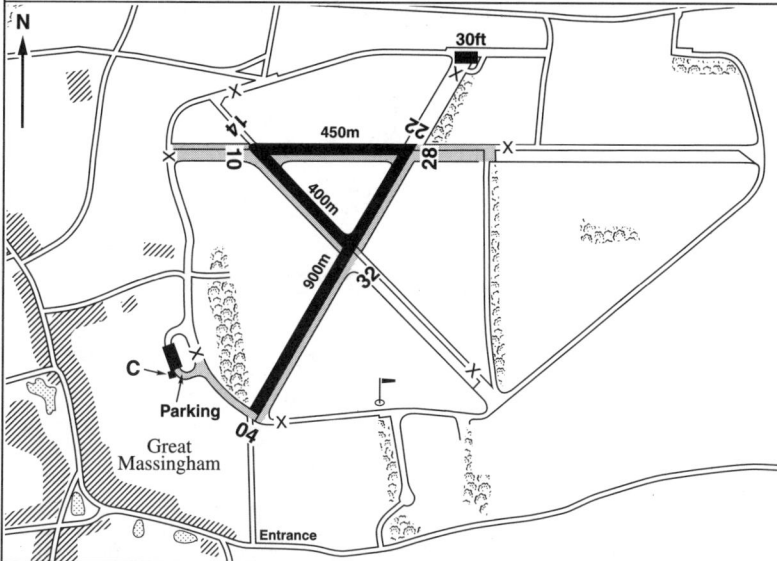

Rwy	Dim(m)	Surface	TORA(m)	LDA(m)	Lighting
04/22	900x20	Concrete	Unlicensed		Rwy †
10/28	450x20	Concrete	Unlicensed		Nil.
14/32	400x15	Concrete	Unlicensed		Rwy †

† Available by arrangement and with specific approval of the aerodrome operator.

Op hrs: PPR. SR–SS

Landing Fee: Contributions to GA Awareness Campaign - Singles £5; Twins £10.

Hangarage: Limited.   **Maintenance:** Nil.   **Customs:** Nil.

Remarks: Reactivated WW2 airfield operated by O.C. Brun Esq. Strictly PPR.
Unlicensed airfield situated 2 nm north of Marham MATZ. Radio contact with Marham
App 124·15 mandatory when Marham is active, due to proximity to Marham military
aerodrome. Non radio aircraft prohibited. No signals square.
Agricultural operations may temporarily block runways.
Avoid overflying the village of Great Massingham.
Aircraft parking next to hangar at SW corner of airfield.
No training flights permitted.
Visiting pilots are requested to complete the movements book in the Control Hut
adjacent to hangar, and must read the posted instructions regarding Marham MATZ.

Warning: Beware of children and dogs on peri-track (a public footpath).

Taxis: 01553-772616 or 692121 and 01485-520938

Fuel: Nil.	**Tel:** 01485-520257 or 520234.
	Fax: 01485-520234.

Robert Pooley ©

N49 26·10 W002 36·12	**GUERNSEY**	336 ft AMSL
2·5 nm WSW of St. Peter Port.		**JSY 112·20 306 25·2**

c/s Guernsey. APP 128·65. TWR 119·95. GND 121·80 - Jul-Sept Sat & Sun 0930-1800
RAD 118·90, 124·50. VDF 128·65, 124·50. ATIS on VOR 'GUR' 109·40
NDB 'GRB' 361·0 (093°M/1·08nm to Thr 09). VOR/DME 'GUR' 109·40 (On A/D).
ILS Rwy 09 (093°M) I-UY 108·10.   ILS Rwy 27 (273°M) I-GH 108·10.

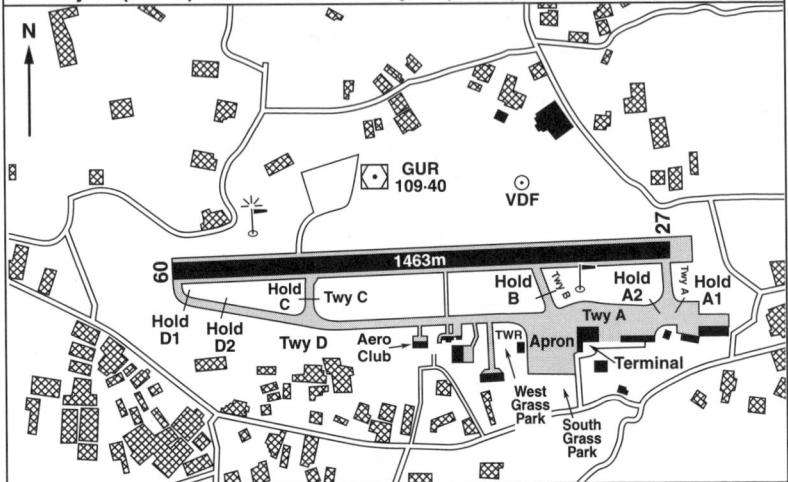

Rwy	Dim(m)	Surface	TORA(m)	LDA(m)	Lighting
09/27	1463x45	Asphalt	09-1453	09-1453	Ap Thr Rwy RCL PAPI 3°
			27-1463	27-1453	Ap Thr Rwy RCL PAPI 3°

Op hrs: 0615-2100 daily.

Landing Fee: Reduced Rates - Private aircraft under 3000 kg: Singles £6, Twins £12 , includes 5 days free parking. In first instance Tel: 01481-237766 or Fax: 01481-239595.

Hangarage: Nil.	**Maintenance:** Available	**Customs:** As Op hrs

Remarks: Operated by States of Guernsey. Use governed by regulations applicable to Channel Islands CTR (Class 'A') and Guernsey CTR (Class 'D')—see chart opposite and pages 8 to 11. Aircraft must carry Third Party Insurance cover of not less than £500,000. Circuit height 700 ft aal. Light aircraft parking area South and West of Control Tower.

All customs and Special Branch clearance to be carried out in the FBU located below Control Tower, on arrival. Aircrew must wear high visibility clothing whilst airside. Aircrew must escort passengers at all times whilst airside.

Avoid overflying hospital (3·2nm ENE of A/D) below 1000ft agl.
SFVR/VFR Flights - Take-off: Aircraft at or below 1000 ft QNH, continue straight ahead until clear of the coastline before turning on course.

Warnings: Flight below 2000ft aal not permitted within EG-R95 (Island of Sark) radius 3 nm centred on N49 25·77 W002 21·75.
Model aircraft flying at CHOUET headland (N49 30·35 W002 32·78) up to 400' amsl.

Restaurant: Refreshments available.	**Car Hire:** Available.

Fuel: 100LL, Jet A1. S. Carnet. Multi Service.	**Tel:** 01481-237766 General 01481-238957 ATIS **Fax:** 01481-239440 ATC/FBU

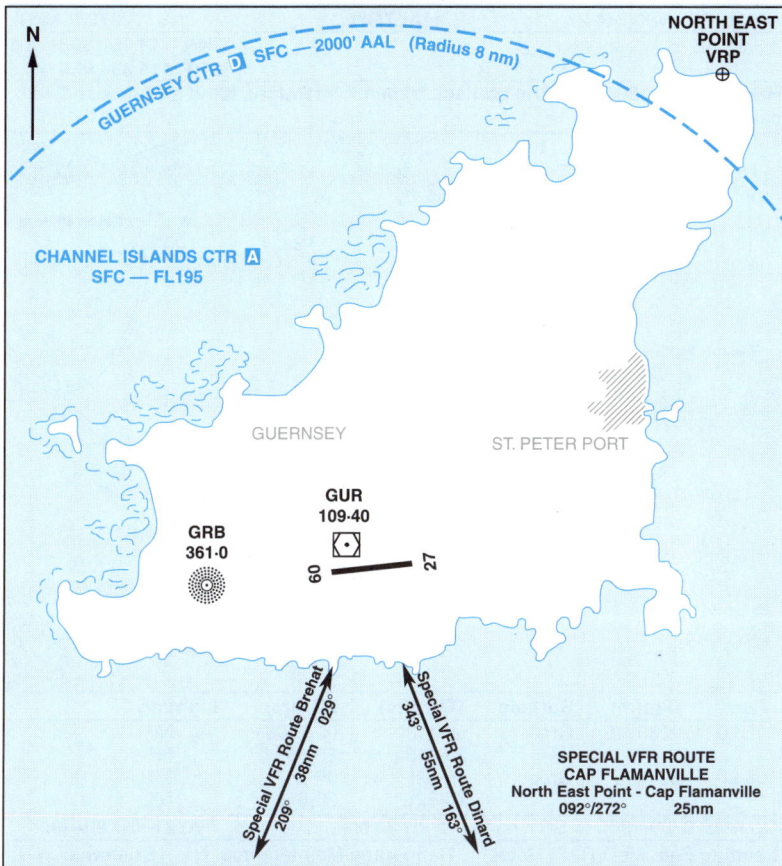

N

GUERNSEY CTR Ⓓ SFC — 2000' AAL (Radius 8 nm)

**NORTH EAST
POINT
VRP**

**CHANNEL ISLANDS CTR Ⓐ
SFC — FL195**

GUERNSEY

ST. PETER PORT

**GUR
109·40**

**GRB
361·0**

60   27

Special VFR Route Brehat
029°
38nm
209°

Special VFR Route Dinard
343°
55nm
163°

**SPECIAL VFR ROUTE
CAP FLAMANVILLE
North East Point - Cap Flamanville
092°/272°   25nm**

Procedures applicable to the Channel Islands CTR (Class 'A') and Guernsey CTR (Class 'D') are outlined at pages 8 to 11.

Flights between Guernsey and Alderney may take place without compliance with IFR requirements, subject to the following conditions:

(a) Clearance must be obtained from Guernsey Approach Control.

(b) Aircraft to remain below cloud and in sight of surface, not above 2,000 ft.

Special VFR Routes

No. 2 Guernsey – Dinard, **No. 5** Guernsey – Cap Flamanville (via NE Point) and **No.10** Guernsey – Brehat are subject to the following conditions:

(a) Special VFR Clearance must be obtained from Jersey Zone before entering the Channel Islands CTR

(b) Aircraft shall remain at least 1500 m horizontally and 1,000 ft. vertically clear of cloud and in flight visibility of not less than 5 km (for Instrument/IMC Rating visibility not less than 3 km).

Note. SSR Mode A 4096 Codes mandatory for SVFR flights within Channel Is CTR.

Government Aerodrome	**EGWN**	1 DEC 00
N51 47·55 W000 44·27	**HALTON**	370 ft AMSL
3·5nm SE of Aylesbury.		**BNN** 113·75 305 8·0
		CPT 114·35 050 25·5

Halton Radio 130·425 (If no contact, transmit intentions blind and proceed with caution)

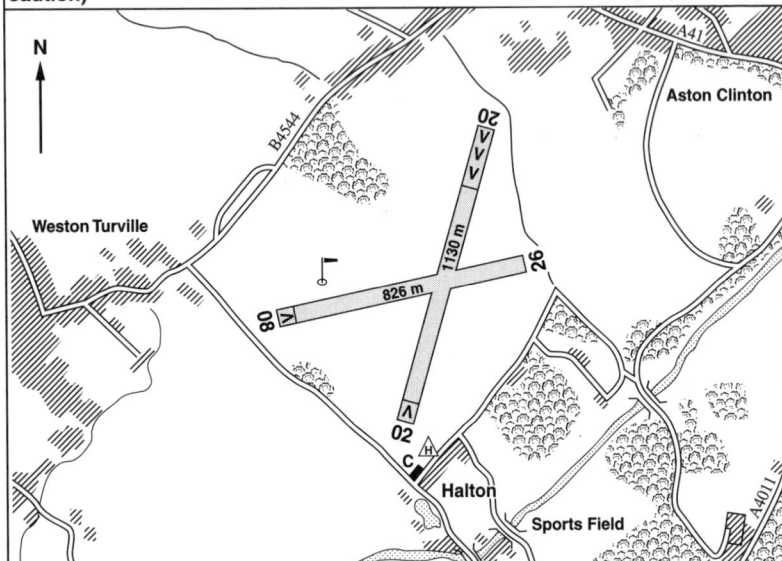

Rwy	Dim(m)	Surface	TORA(m)	LDA(m)	Lighting
02/20	1130x45	Grass	02-1130	02-1100	Nil.
			20-1130	20-840	Nil.
08/26	826x45	Grass	08-826	08-762	Nil.
			26-826	26-826	Nil.

Op hrs: 0700-1900 or SS if earlier, PPR 24 hrs.	**ATZ active SR–SS.**

Landing Fee: MoD(RAF) Rates.   **Hangarage/Maintenance:** Nil.   **Customs:** Nil.

Remarks: Operator Royal Air Force. A/D situated 1·5 nm W of Luton CTA (2500 - 3500ft). Runways marked with white sidelines. Intensive light aircraft, microlight, motor glider, and winch launched gliding from airfield especially at weekends.
Mirror circuits with no deadside, gliders to SE and powered to NW. Circuits height 1000' aal. Extensive soaring from ridge 1·5 nm to SE upto 2500'.

Inbound aircraft should be prepared to route via VRPs at 1500' agl.

VRPs: Lakes 060°M/ 2·5 nm for Rwys 20 and 26.
   Terrick Village 230°M/ 2·5 nm for Rwys 02 and 08.

Visiting pilots to receive arrival brief by telephone before departure.
Noise reduction routes to be followed on departure for all rwys except Rwy 08.
Mast 200ft agl /1053ft amsl 127°/2·3 nm.

Helicopter operators from/to Aston Clinton (Bell Inn) helipad co-ordinate arrivals by telephone and call Halton Radio before entering Halton ATZ and prior to lifting for departure.

Fuel: Nil.	**Tel:** 01296-623535 Ext 6367 PPR 0830-1700 Mon-Fri, Other times Ext 6211. 01296-622697 Flying Club.

Robert Pooley ©

N52 17·98 W002 28·22	**HANLEY (Hanley William)**	645 ft AMSL

12 nm NW of Worcester
5 nm ESE of Tenbury Wells

HON 113·65 269 30
BCN 117·45 045 45·3

No Radio.

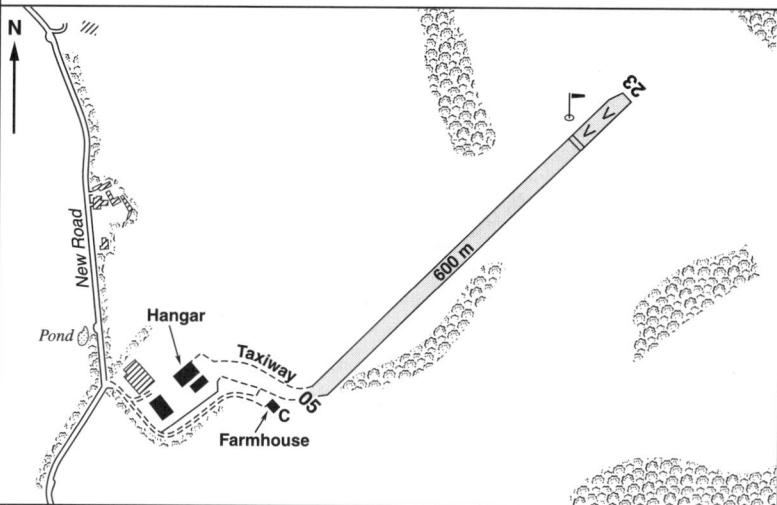

Rwy	Dim(m)	Surface	TORA(m)	LDA(m)	Lighting
05/23	600x30	Grass	Unlicensed		Nil

Caution: Landing threshold Rwy 23 displaced by 100 m due 18% upslope.

Op hrs: PPR. 0900-SS (28 Days). Telephone Briefing essential prior to visit.

Landing Fee: £5.00. | **Customs:** Nil

Hangarage: Nil. | **Maintenance:** Nil

Remarks: Operated by Geoff and Angela Bunyan, Hanley House Farm, Hanley William, Tenbury Wells, Worcs WR15 8QT. Unlicensed airfield.
Airfield is located atop a plateau, with a steep slope at the east end of the runway.
Two White Chevrons mark the displaced threshold.
Runway surface is very smooth, but gentle undulations present.
Considerate pilots welcome at own risk. Aircraft Third Party liability mandatory.
Circuits at 800 ft aal, generally left hand on both runways, but can be variable, clear instructions will be issued with the telephone brief.
Avoid overflying local houses. Maintain runway centre-line on approach/departure to minimise noise.
Warning: On final approach to Rwy 23 expect turbulence and wind shear in strong southerly winds.
Camping/overnight stay on request.
Resturant: Light refreshments on site.
Accommodation: The Fox Inn 01886-853219. Tally-Ho Inn 01886-853241
Taxis: Swan Cabs 01584-810310.   **Car Hire:** Dunley Service Stn. 01299-827867.

Fuel: Nil | **Tel/Fax:** 01886-853410.

Robert Pooley ©

N52 27·85 E001 18·65	**HARDWICK (Norwich)**	178 ft AMSL
12 nm S of Norwich		CLN 114·55 012 38
		BKY 116·25 061 54

No Radio.

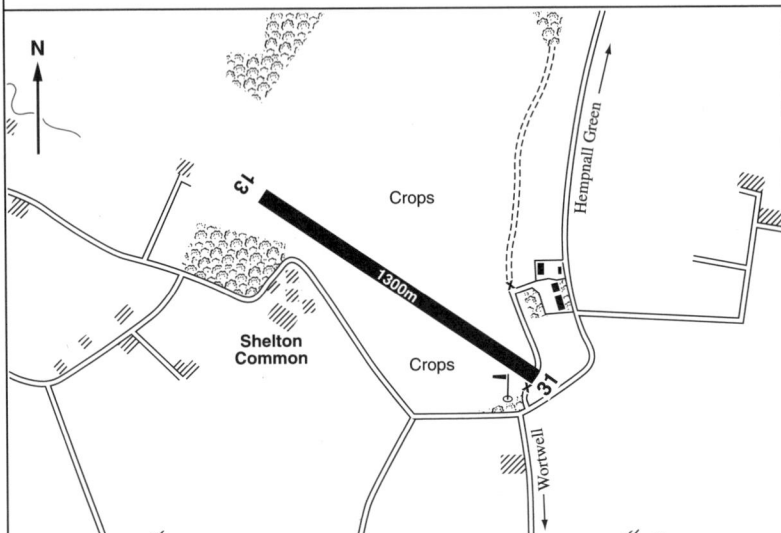

Rwy	Dim(m)	Surface	TORA(m)	LDA(m)	Lighting
13/31	1300x20	Concrete	Unlicensed		Nil

Op hrs: SR-SS. Prior permission essential by Telephone or Fax.

Landing Fee: Nil, but maintenance contribution appreciated. **Customs:** Nil

Hangarage: Limited. **Maintenance:** Fixed & Rotary Tel: 07887-652308.

Remarks: Operated by Hardwick Classic Aircraft. Unlicensed airfield.

Light aircraft welcome at pilot's own risk.

No Circuits. On go-around, clear the area and make new approach.

All aircraft are to avoid overflying local villages.

Aircraft parking and storage available on short or long term basis.

Noise Abatement:

Rwy 13 - Approach on 150°M. After take-off, turn onto 170°M as soon as practicable.

Rwy 31 - Approach on 330°M. After take-off, turn onto 330°M as soon as practicable.

Whenever possible, land on Rwy 13 and take-off on Rwy 31.

Warning: Beware of aircraft movements at Airfield Farm (0·5 nm ENE of thld Rwy 31) and Nut Tree Farm (1 nm WSW).

Taxis: By arrangement. *Aeroshop* Tel: 07802-727337.

Fuel: 100LL at weekends, and by arrangement Mon-Fri.	**Tel/Fax:** 01379-855374. 0802-611647. **Tel:** 01603-420640 Norwich ATIS. **E. mail:** wavian@msn.com

N51 50·02 W004 57·63	**HAVERFORDWEST**	152 ft AMSL

2 nm N of Haverfordwest.

STU	113·10	170	10
BCN	117·45	283	63

c/s Haverfordwest Radio 122·20 A/G.
NDB 'HAV' 328·0 (On A/D). DME 'HDW' 116·75 (On A/D)

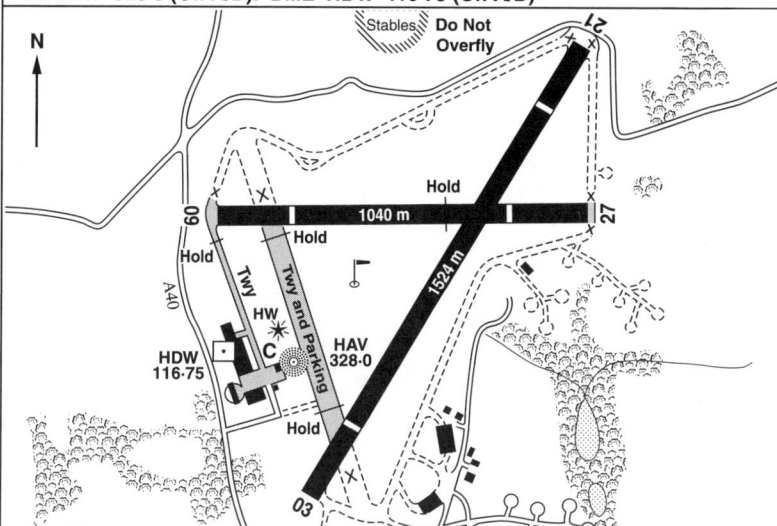

Rwy	Dim(m)	Surface	TORA(m)	LDA(m)	Lighting
03/21	1524x45	Asphalt	03-1269	03-1202	Thr Rwy APAPI 3·5°
			21-1262	21-1269	Thr Rwy APAPI 3·5°
09/27	1040x45	Asphalt	09-1040	09-800	Nil.
			27-1010	27-800	Nil.
					IBn 'HW' Gn.

Op hrs (Licensed) Mon-Fri 0915-1630, other times on request.

Landing Fee: £8.00 /tonne.	**Customs:** 24 hrs PNR.

Hangarage: On request.	**Maintenance:** M3 (JAR) – 01437-766 126.

Remarks: Owned and operated by Pembrokeshire County Council, Haverfordwest Aerodrome, Fishguard Road, Haverfordwest, Pembrokeshire SA62 4BN. PPR. Licensed aerodrome Monday to Friday. (And at other times by arrangement). The grass areas are unsuitable for aircraft movement. Rwy lighting on request. Microlights operate on the aerodrome using RH circuits. All other traffic LH circuits.

Avoid overflying the local Riding Stables to north of Rwy 09/27.

TV Mast 965' aal 1120' amsl 042°/4·8 nm.

Note. Outside published licensing times, Haverfordwest Flight Centre is available for general information and fuel sales Tel: 01437-760822.
Weekend visitors are very welcome to use the club's facilities.

Restaurant: Open 7 days a week.

Accommodation: Available near the airfield, Tel: 01437-763839 and excellent B & B in the locality.   **Car Hire:** Days Drive Tel: 01437-760860. **Taxi:** 01437-764822.

Fuel: 100LL, Jet A1.	**Tel:** 01437-765283 ATC (also 24 hr Ansaphone)
	Fax: 01437-769246 (also 24 hr)

Robert Pooley ©

N53 10·68 W002 58·67	**HAWARDEN**	35 ft AMSL
3·5 nm WSW of Chester.		**WAL 114·10 163 14**

c/s Hawarden. APP 123·35. TWR 124·95. RAD 130·25. VDF 123·35, 130·25.
NDB 'HAW' 340·0 (On A/D).   ILS/DME Rwy 23 (226°M) IHDN 110·35

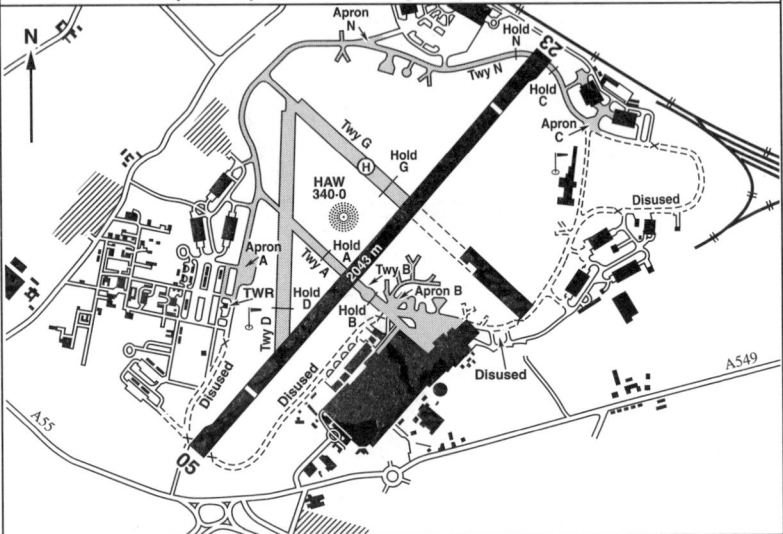

Rwy	Dim(m)	Surface	TORA(m)	LDA(m)	Lighting
05/23	2043x46	Asphalt/ Concrete	05-1963 23-2043	05-1663 23-1743	Ap Thr Rwy PAPI 3·5° RH Ap Thr Rwy PAPI 3° ABn Gn.

Op hrs: Mon-Fri 0800-1900, Sat & Sun 0930-1600.

Landing Fee: Less than 1500 kg £15 including VAT. Other landing fees on application.

Hangarage: Hawarden Air Services 01244-538568. **Maintenance:** Available. **Customs:** 24 hrs PNR

Remarks: Operated by BAE Systems Ltd, Airbus Division, Hawarden Airport,
Broughton, Chester, N Wales CH4 0DR. Strictly PPR.
Test flying outside promulgated hours. Aerodrome not available to non-radio aircraft.
Circuits at 1000' QFE, RH on Rwy 05, LH on Rwy 23.
Avoid overflying towns and villages below 1500'.
Aircraft over 3000 kg mandatory handling, Chester Handling Services, Apron 'N',
Tel: 01244-536853, Fax: 01244-537268.

Warnings: Reinforcing steel within the concrete pavement of Rwy 05/23 may cause
Compass deviation on stationary aircraft.
Glider flying at weekends, up to 3000' QFE at RAF Sealand, 3 nm NNW of A/D.
Chimney 561' aal 596' amsl 241°/3·4 nm.
High ground rising to 1848' amsl between 5 nm and 10 nm SW of aerodrome.
Restricted Area R311, 5 nm north of aerodrome.

Restaurant: Nil.   **Car Hire:** Avis Rent-a-car. Tel: (01244) 311463.

Fuel: 100LL (Apron N), Jet A1 By arrangement with Chester Handling.	**Tel:** 01244-522012 ATC; 522013 PPR. **Fax:** 01244-523035.

Robert Pooley ©

| N53 28·53 W002 37·30 | **HAYDOCK PARK (Newton-Le-Willows)** | 130 ft AMSL |

Haydock Park Racecourse.
4 nm NNW of Warrington.

WAL 114·10 082 19·2

Manchester APP 119·40.
Liverpool App 119·85.

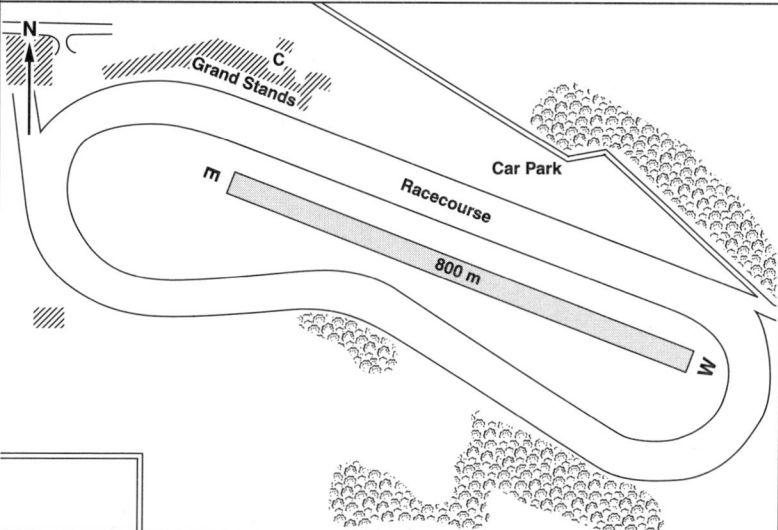

Rwy	Dim(m)	Surface	TORA(m)	LDA(m)	Lighting
E/W	800	Grass	Unlicensed		Nil.

Op hrs: PPR.

Landing Fee: Light aircraft £50.00 inc VAT non racedays.   **Customs:** Nil.

Hangarage: Nil. **Maintenance:** Limited helicopter servicing and fuel available on race days and by arrangement, contact Ground Zero Tel: 0161-799-6967

Remarks: Operated by The Haydock Park Racecourse Ltd. Newton-le-Willows, Merseyside, WA12 0HQ.

Airfield situated in the Special Low Level Route within the Manchester CTR — see Manchester TMA – VAD/VRP chart.

Unlicensed airfield primarily for use on racedays when all landings and take-offs are prohibited if horses are in sight.

Light aircraft may be accepted on non racedays on prior permission and at pilot's own risk.

Care should taken over rough ground, particularly at each end of runway.

Windsock displayed.

| **Fuel:** Heli fuel available on race days, others ¢ Tel: 0161-799-6967 | **Tel:** 01942-402624 (0900-1700 Mon-Fri). **Fax:** 01942-270879. |

Robert Pooley ©

N52 01·17 W000 18·10	**HENLOW**	170 ft AMSL
3 nm W of Stotfold		**BKY 116·25 282 13·5**
4 nm NW of Letchworth		**BNN 113·75 030 20**

c/s Henlow Radio 121.10 A/G. (If no contact, transmit intentions blind and proceed with caution)

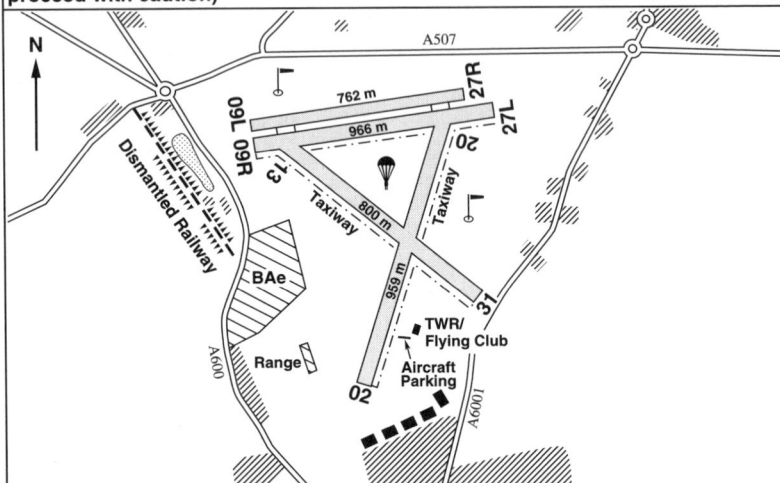

Rwy	Dim (m)	Surface	TORA(m)	LDA(m)	Lighting
02/20	959x46	Grass	02/20-959	02/20-959	Nil
09L/27R	762x23	Grass	09L/27R-762	09L/27R-762	Nil
09R/27L	966x46	Grass	09R/27L-966	09R/27R-966	Nil
13/31	800X46	Grass	13/31-800	13/31-800	Nil

Op hrs: 48 hrs PPR. 0830-SS daily.	**Customs:** Nil
Landing Fee: MoD (RAF) Rates	**Hangarage/Maintenance:** Nil

Remarks: Operator Royal Air Force. 48 hrs PPR from O.C. Flying or Station Duty Officer, and an arrival briefing from the Twr/club.
Airfield situated 3 nm north of Luton CTR/CTA.
Glider flying Sat and Sun throughout the year and also on some weekdays during the Summer. Grass areas poor in places, remain within the confines of the runways and taxiways. Runways marked with retroflective posts each side.
Avoid overflying BAe complex and the firing range.
Circuits when available, at 1000' QFE, all LH except Rwys 13 and 27 variable circuits.

Arrivals: Standard overhead joins, but when gliding in progress, pilots will be required to route via VRPs - Blue Lagoon (140°M/2·25 nm), Chicksands (300°M/2·5 nm) or the Water Tower (060°M/3·5 nm).

Departures: Rwy 02- Do not turn left before 700' ; Rwy 31- Turn 15° left at 300' on climbout. Other runways standard departures.

Free-fall parachuting may take place from 3500 ft amsl and exceptionally up to FL150.
Model aircraft flying on the airfield. Chimneys 365' amsl,135°/2200m from Twr.
Water Twr 115' agl, 250°/1·25 nm. Meppershall light aircraft strip 258°/2 nm.

Fuel: 100LL	**Tel:** 01462-851515 OC Flying; 851936 Flying Club

N50 59·30 W002 21·52	**HENSTRIDGE**	184 ft AMSL
5 nm SSE of Wincanton.	**SAM 113·35 278 38. BCN 117·45 149 56**	
7 nm ENE of Sherborne	**BHD 112·05 057 56**	

Henstridge Radio 130·25 A/G.   Yeovilton APP 127·35 (MATZ).

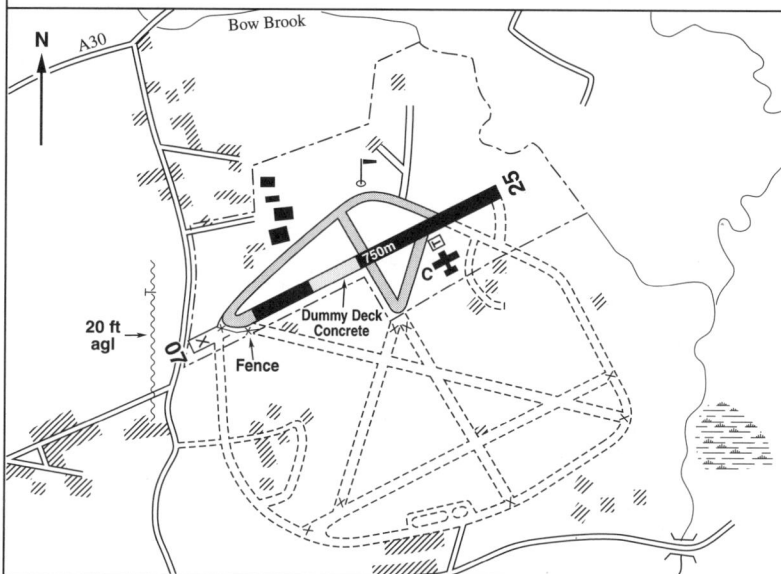

Rwy	Dim(m)	Surface	TORA(m)	LDA(m)	Lighting
07/25	750x26	Asphalt	Unlicensed		Nil

Op hrs: 0900-1800 or SS if earlier.
Earlier or later times by arrangement with Operations.

Landing Fee: Singles £7.00. Twins: £12.00; Microlights & Gyros £3.50.

Hangarage: Limited	**Maintenance:** Limited	**Customs:** PNR

Remarks: Operated by Henstridge Airfield Ltd., Henstridge Airfield, Henstridge, Somerset BA8 0TN. PPR by telephone if non-radio, otherwise call on radio.

Unlicensed airfield situated 1 nm SE of Yeovilton MATZ Stub.

Contact Yeovilton App prior to joining.

Of the five runways, only 07/25 is available for use - recognised by concrete 'Dummy Deck' in the middle.

Circuits at 800 ft aal, LH on Rwy 07, RH on Rwy 25.

Avoid overflying all nearby villages and dwellings.

Caution: Power cables 20 ft agl at 230m and a fence at 50m, from thld of Rwy 07.

Restaurant: Refreshments available.

Taxis/Car Hire/ Hotel/ B&B: By arrangement through Operations.

Fuel: 100LL, Jet A1.	**Tel:** 01963-364231. **Fax:** 01963-364232

N51 48·35 E000 20·53	**HIGH EASTER**	244 ft. AMSL
4 nm S of Great Dunmow.		LAM 115·60 041 11·8
		BPK 117·50 083 16·8

No Radio.
Essex Radar 120·625

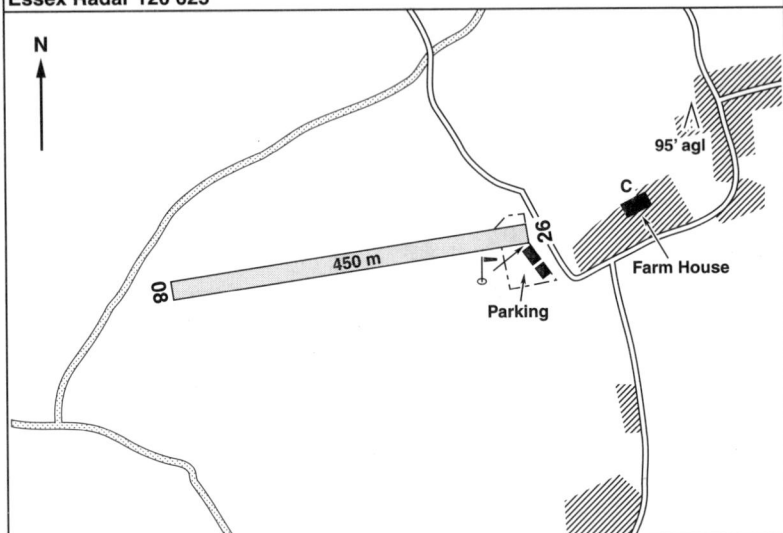

N

95' agl

C

Farm House

26

450 m

08

Parking

Rwy	Dim(m)	Surface	TORA(m)	LDA(m)	Lighting
08/26	450x21	Grass	Unlicensed		Nil.

Op hrs: Emergency Use Only. No visitors.

Landing Fee: On application.	**Customs:** Nil
Hangarage: Nil	**Maintenance:** Nil.

Remarks: Operated by Michael Luckin Esq. Bury Farm, High Easter, Chelmsford, Essex CM1 4QW.

Due to local objections, airfield available for Emergency use only. Regrettably, No Visitors.

Airfield situated beneath Stansted CTA (2000– 3500' ALT) Class 'D' Controlled Airspace. Contact Essex Radar 120·625.

Crop spraying base.

Occasional glider activity.

Circuits LH, avoid overflying village.

Church Tower 125' aal 369' amsl 080°/0·6 nm.

Fuel: Nil	**Tel:** 01245-231284

N52 01·75 W001 12·48	**HINTON-IN-THE-HEDGES**	505 ft. AMSL

2 nm W of Brackley.

DTY 116·40 206 9·7

c/s Hinton Radio 119·45 A/G.

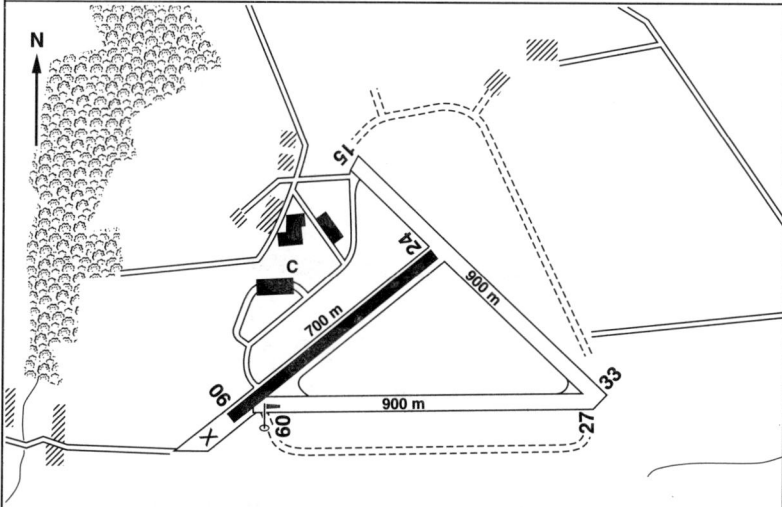

Rwy	Dim(m)	Surface	TORA(m)	LDA(m)	Lighting
06/24	700x18	Asphalt	Unlicensed		Nil.
† 09/27	900x45	Asphalt	Unlicensed		Nil.
† 15/33	900x45	Asphalt	Unlicensed		Nil.

† *Surface rough, loose grit and small stones. Not to be used for take-off; landings are permissible in strong crosswind conditions and in emergency.*

Op hrs: PPR. SR–SS.

Landing Fee: On application. **Customs:** Nil.

Hangarage: Limited. **Maintenance:** Holdcroft Aviation. 01295-810287. Fax: 812247

Remarks: Operated by Mr. R. B. Harrison, Walltree House Farm, Steane, Brackley, Northants. Visitors welcome on prior permission.
Circuits variable. Gliding and parachuting daily throughout the year.

Noise Abatement: Avoid overflying villages and habitation in vicinity of aerodrome.

Parachuting contact — Hinton Skydiving, Tel: 01295-812300, Fax: 01295-812400.

Pilot Flight Training — 01295-812775.
Group 'A' training, IMC (simulator available), Aircraft Hire. S.L.M.G. training,
Silver 'C' conversions. F.A.A. Bi-annuals and F.A.A. Instrument Ratings.

Accommodation: Walltree House Farm, (on airfield). 01295-811235

Taxi: P. J. Cars. Brackley. Tel: 01280-704330.

Fuel: 100LL.	**Tel:** 01295-811235 Airfield/Operator. 811056 Gliding Club **Fax:** 01295-811147

N52 20·56 E000 46·38	**HONINGTON**	174 ft. AMSL

3·8 nm SE of Thetford.
5·4 nm NE of Bury St Edmunds.

BKY 116·25 054 33·9
CLN 114·55 338 32·8

Zone c/s Lakenheath Radar/App 128·90. APP c/s Honington App 123·30.
TWR 122·10 (On request). ILS Rwy 27 (265°M) 'HT' 111·90.

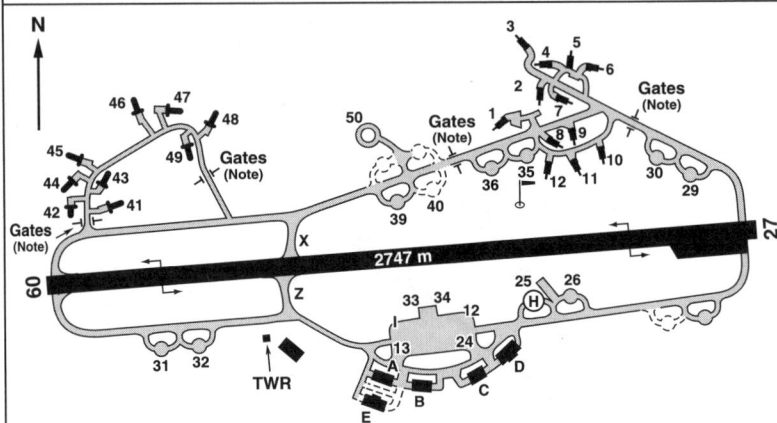

Note:
Gates - Use of these taxiways is restricted to aircraft having a wingspan of 75ft or less.

Rwy	Dim(m)	Surface	TORA(m)	LDA(m)	Lighting
09/27	2747x45	Asphalt	09-2747	09-2747	Ap Thr Rwy PAPI
			27-2747	27-2747	Ap Thr Rwy PAPI
					I Bn 'HT' Red

Op hrs: 24 hrs PPR.	ATZ Active H24.	
Landing Fee: MoD(RAF) Rates.		**Customs:** Nil
Hangarage: Nil		**Maintenance:** Nil.

Remarks: RAF Aerodrome. No permanent ATC staff, but ATZ active.
Civil aircraft accepted on 24 hours prior notice.
Both Arrester Gear Cables de-rigged.
Circuits at 1000 ft aal, LH on Rwy 09, RH on Rwy 27.

Fuel: Nil	**Tel:** 01359-269561 Ext 7571 PPR.
	Fax: 01359- 269561 Ext 7440.

Robert Pooley ©

N53 00·87 W001 13·10		264 ft AMSL
5 nm NNW of Nottingham.		**TNT** 115·70 104 16·5
		HON 113·65 028 42·7

c/s Hucknall Radio 130·80 A/G.

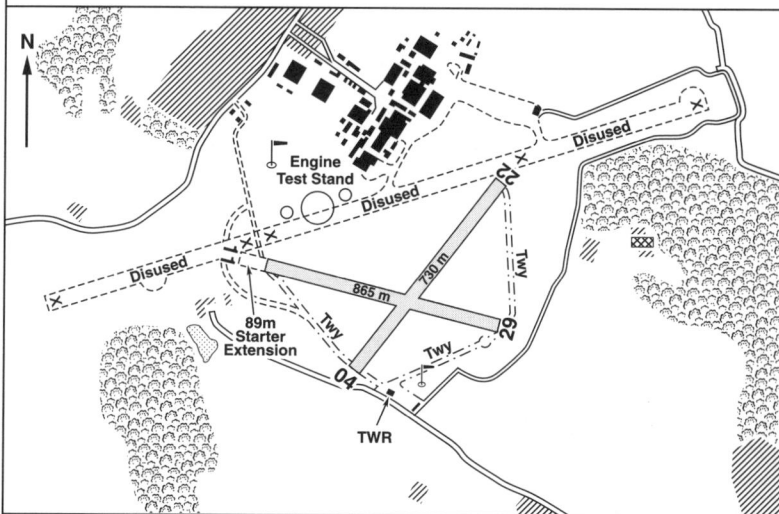

Rwy	Dim(m)	Surface	TORA(m)	LDA(m)	Lighting
04/22	730x23	Grass	04-730	04-730	Nil.
			22-730	22-730	Nil
11/29	776x25	Grass	11-865	11-776	Nil.
			29-776	29-776	Nil.

Op hrs: Sat & Sun only 1000-1800 or SS. PPR.

Landing Fee: On application.	**Customs:** Nil.
Hangarage: Nil.	**Maintenance:** Nil.

Remarks: Operated by Merlin Flying Club, Rolls Royce Ltd., Aero Division, Hucknall, Notts. NG15 6EU. Airfield closed to visiting aircraft Mon-Fri.

Airfield closed when Rolls Royce engine testing in operation.

Concrete Rwy 08/26 is disused.

Mast 249' aal 530' amsl. 280°/1·4 nm. Mast 249' aal 530' amsl. 275°/1·9 nm.

Chimney 154' aal 435'amsl 049°/1·8 nm. Mast 119' aal 400' amsl 026°/1·7 nm.

TV Masts 144' aal 425' amsl 076°/2·4 nm. Chimney 135' aal 416' amsl 349°/1·0 nm.

Car Hire: Godfrey Davis. Tel: 01602-42813.

Fuel: 100LL by prior arrangement with Merlin Flying Club.	**Tel:** 0115-9642539
	0115-633111 Rolls Royce

Robert Pooley ©

Intentionally Blank

N53 37·28 W001 49·72	**HUDDERSFIELD (Crosland Moor)**	825 ft. AMSL

1·5 nm SW of Huddersfield.	POL 112·10 133 12·2
	MCT 113·55 050 22·1

c/s Huddersfield Radio 122·20 A/G.

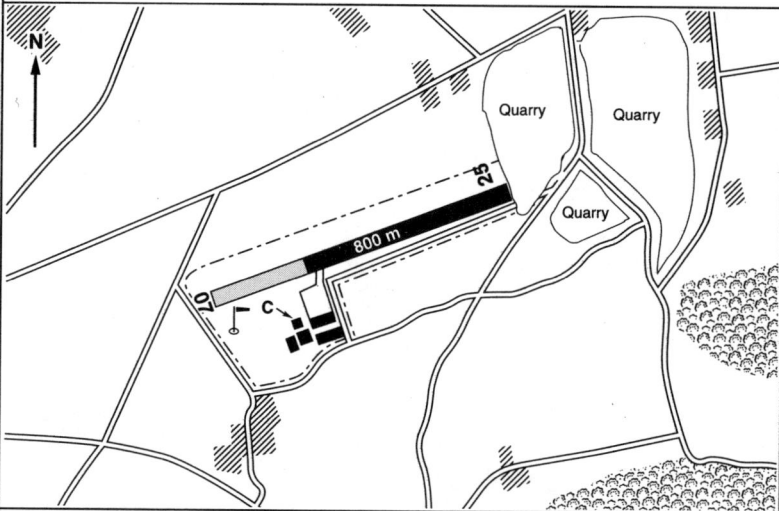

Rwy	Dim(m)	Surface	TORA(m)	LDA(m)	Lighting
07/25	800x22	*Asphalt/	07-800	07-800	Nil.
		Grass	25-800	25-800	Nil.
		* 550m asphalt, 250m grass.			

Runway gradient — 2·6% Down on Rwy 07, from start of asphalt.

Op hrs: PPR.	**Customs:** Nil.

Landing Fee: Singles £2.00, Twins £5.00. (Free to club aircraft).

Hangarage: Limited.	**Maintenance:** By arrangement.

Remarks: Unlicensed aerodrome operated by Huddersfield Outdoor Services Ltd. Use restricted to aircraft up to 2720 kg AUW. Non radio aircraft welcome on prior permission. Circuits left-hand at 1000' aal.

Emley Moor TV Mast (concrete) 1924ft. amsl 6 nm East.

Holme Moss TV Mast 2490ft. amsl 5 nm to South.

Radio masts 1614ft. amsl 2·5 nm to NW.

Avoid low flying over houses and hospital 0·5 nm from threshold of Rwy 25.

Whenever possible land and take-off on Rwy 25. When Rwy 25 is in use pilots are advised to land well beyond the threshold.

Restaurant: Refreshments available.

Car Hire: Godfrey Davis. Tel: 01484-22456.

Fuel: 100LL.	**Tel:** 01484-645784

Robert Pooley ©

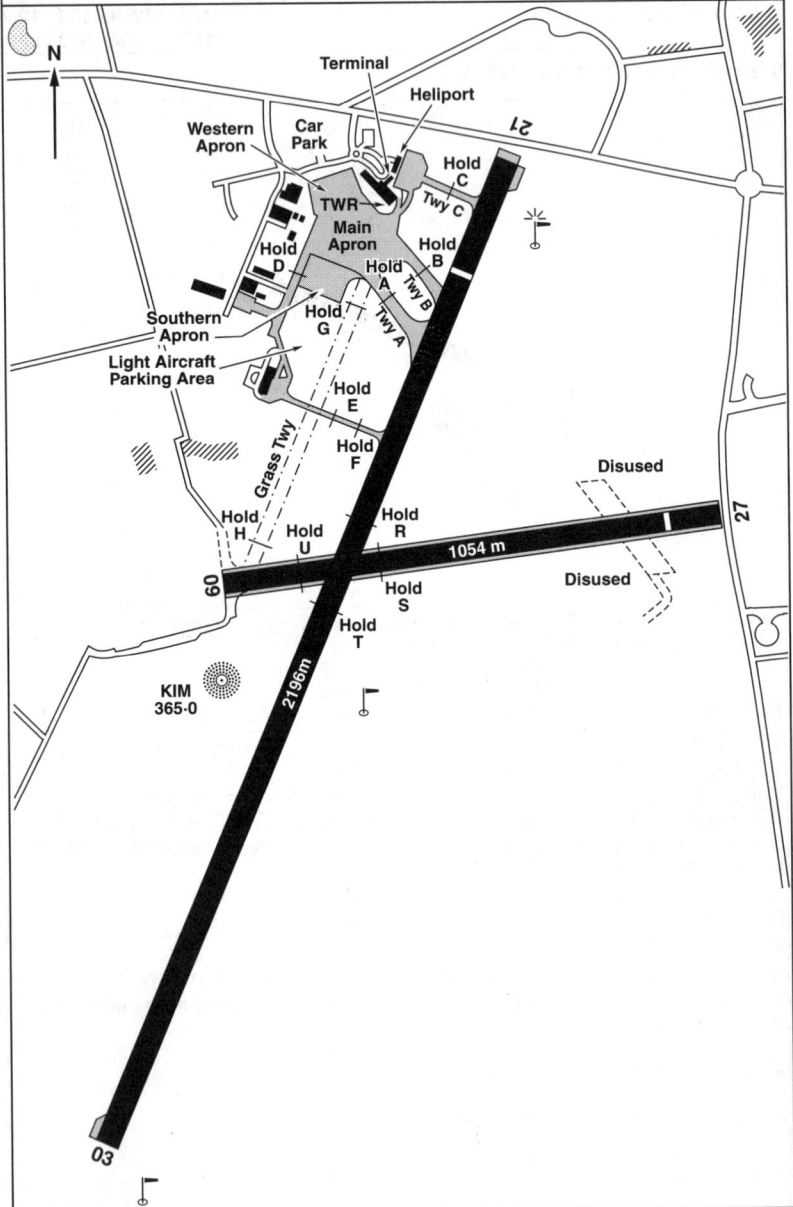

N

Terminal

Heliport

Western
Apron

Car
Park

21

Hold
C

TWR

Twy C

**Main
Apron**

Hold
D

Hold
B

Hold
A

Twy B

**Southern
Apron**

Hold
G

Twy A

**Light Aircraft
Parking Area**

Hold
E

Grass Twy

Hold
F

Disused

Hold
H

Hold
U

Hold
R

27

60

1054 m

Hold
S

Disused

Hold
T

2196m

**KIM
365·0**

03

Robert Pooley ©

274

| N53 34·47 W000 21·07 | **HUMBERSIDE INTL. AIRPORT** | 121 ft AMSL |

| 10 nm WNW of Grimsby. | OTR   113·90 236 11·3 |
| | GAM 112·80 056 27·8 |

c/s Humberside. **APP/RAD 124·675. LARS 124·675. RAD 123·15. TWR 118·55.**
ATIS 124·125. NDB 'KIM' 365·0 (On A/D).
ILS/DME Rwy 21 (207°M) I-HS 108·75.

Rwy	Dim(m)	Surface	TORA(m)	LDA(m)	Lighting
03/21	2196x45	Asphalt/	03-2070	03-2070	Thr Rwy RCL PAPI 3°
		Concrete	21-2196	21-1950	Ap Thr Rwy RCL PAPI 3°
09/27	1054x30	Asphalt	09-994	09-994	Nil.
			27-1034	27-920	Nil.

Op hrs: WINTER: Mon-Fri 0630-2015, Sat & Sun 0630-2000.
SUMMER: Mon-Sat 0630-2015, Sun 0630-2000. O/T by arrangement.

Landing Fee (*Pay on the Day*) : Up to 1500 kg £12, 1501-3000 kg £22. All + VAT.
Discount for various Training flights available by prior arrangement with ATC.

Hangarage: On request.   **Maintenance:** Available.   **Customs:** Aerodrome hours

Remarks: Operated by Humberside International Airport Ltd. Non-radio aircraft not
accepted. Jet aircraft RH circuits on Rwy 21. A trunk road crosses the N end of Rwy
03/21 and another road crosses the E end of Rwy 09/27.

The taxiway to the light aircraft parking area & maintenance area is routed through
the apron area and is marked with a single yellow centreline — taxy with caution.

Helicopters to land as instructed by ATC. Helicopters operating to and from main
apron are to avoid overflying buildings on southern edge of apron.

Aircraft must carry Third Party Insurance cover of not less than one million.

Aircrew are to wear high visibility jackets whilst on apron areas.

Warning: Light aircraft should be aware of the possible effects of rotor downwash
generated by large helicopters operating through the main apron area.

Caution: Parachuting takes place at Hibaldstow unlicensed aerodrome up to FL150.

Ground Handling: (Not mandatory).
Servisair Tel: 01652-688491. Fax: 01652-688060

VISUAL REFERENCE POINTS (VRPs):

Immingham Docks, North Tower Humber Bridge, Caistor, Brigg, Laceby Crossroads
and Elsham Wolds.

Restaurant: Fully licensed restaurant at Airport Terminal.

Car Hire: Avis Tel: 01652-680325. Europcar Tel: 01652-680338.
Hertz, Budget & National also serve the airport.

Fuel: 100LL, Jet A1. S.	**Tel:** 01652- 688456 Admin, 682022 ATC.
Tel: 01652-682044.	01652- 682020 Met.
Multi Service	**Fax:** 01652- 680524 Admin, 680244 ATC.

Robert Pooley ©

N57 18·62 W002 38·70	**INSCH**	500 ft. AMSL
2 nm SW of Insch.		**ADN 114·30 278 12**

Insch Radio 129·825 A/G.
Aberdeen APP 120·40.

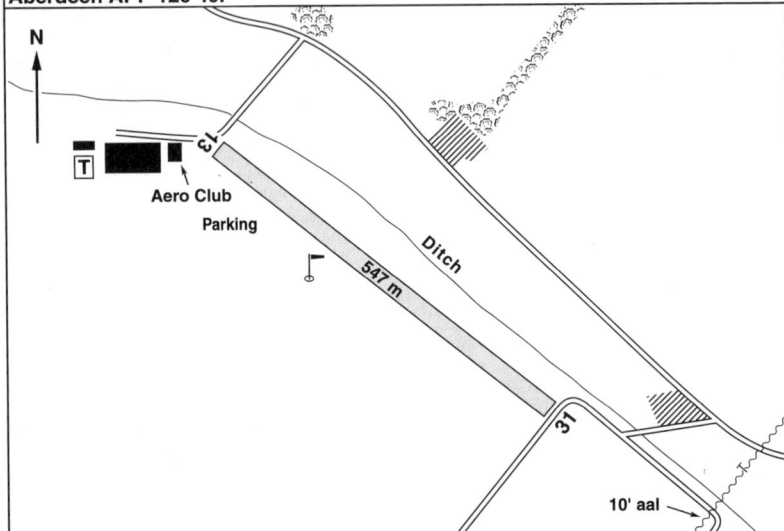

Rwy	Dim(m)	Surface	TORA(m)	LDA(m)	Lighting
13/31	547x18	Grass	Unlicensed		Nil

Op hrs: Strictly PPR.

Landing Fee: Donations gratefully received.	**Customs:** Nil
Hangarage: Nil	**Maintenance:** Nil

Remarks: Operated by Ken Wood Esq, Insch Aerodrome, Auchleven, Insch, Aberdeenshire AB5 6QB. PPR.

Unlicensed airfield situated 2 nm outside the NW boundary of Aberdeen CTR (Class 'D' Controlled Airspace — see page 2). Military aircraft avoiding the CTR tend to overfly the airfield; contact Aberdeen App 120·40 for traffic information.

Avoid overflying the village of AUCHLEVEN 0·5 nm East of airfield.

Warnings: High ground 1233' aal 1733' amsl 111°/3 nm.
Power cables 10' aal cross final approach to Rwy 31 at 174 metres from threshold.

Fuel: 100LL by arrangement.	**Tel:** 01464-820422 Operator. 820003 Airfield. 07831-412619 Mobile

N57 32·40 W004 03·00	**INVERNESS**	31 ft AMSL
7nm NE of Inverness.		**ADN 114·30 291 59·2**

APP/TWR/VDF 122·60. Lossiemouth Rad 119·35.   VOR/DME 'INS' 109·20 (On A/D).

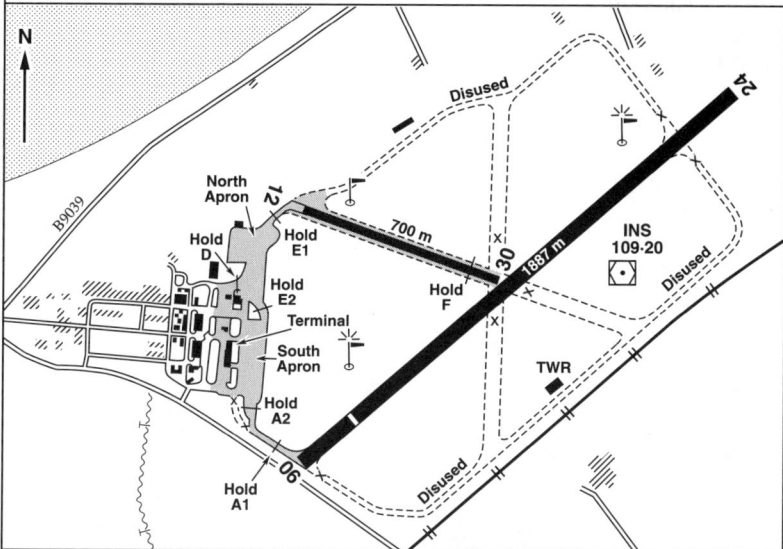

Rwy	Dim(m)	Surface	TORA(m)	LDA(m)	Lighting
06/24	1887x46	Asphalt	06-1887	06-1664	Ap Thr Rwy PAPI 3°
			24-1765	24-1765	Ap Thr Rwy PAPI 3°
12/30	700x18	Asphalt	12-700	12-700	Nil.
			30-700	30-700	Nil.

Op hrs: PPR. Winter: Mon-Fri 0645-2200, Sat 0645-1915, Sun 0745-2200.
Summer: 0645-2200 daily.

Landing Fee: Highlands & Islands Airports Rates.

Hangarage: Ltd ¢   **Maintenance:** Merlin Maintenance.   **Customs:** 24 hrs PNR

Remarks: Operated by Highlands & Islands Airports Ltd. All flights PPR. Inbound aircraft
Mon-Fri are requested to contact Lossiemouth Radar when 40 nm from Inverness.

Controlled surface traffic on road 81m from Rwy 06 threshold. Exercise caution taxiing to
Hangars 1 and 2 due to close proximity of adjacent security fence. Taxiway between northern
end of the South Apron and thld Rwy 12 available only to aircraft with wingspan up to, but not
including 36 m. Agricultural work takes place on the grass areas throught the year.

Hill 678' amsl 3·8 nm to ESE. High ground 1500' amsl 5 nm to south.
TV Masts 1074' amsl 5·6 nm to N, and 1495' amsl 8 nm to WNW.

Warning: Bird hazard due to the surrounding terrain and tidal mud flats adjacent to the A/D.
Deer hazard, particularly at dawn and dusk.

VRPs: Invergordon, Lochindorb, Tomatin, Dores and Dingwall.

Restaurant: Refreshments and bar.

Car Hire: Avis. Tel: 01667-462787. Hertz Tel: 01667-462652.

Fuel: Jet A1 - 01667-462360 Air BP	Tel: 01667-464000 PABX
100LL.- 01667-462664 Highland Airways.	01667-464293 ATC
	Fax: 01667-462586 ATC

Robert Pooley ©

N55 40·92 W006 15·40   **ISLAY**   54 ft AMSL

4·5 nm NNW of Port Ellen.   **MAC 116·00 316 23·7**

c/s Islay Information 123·15 AFIS.
NDB 'LAY' 395·0 (On A/D).
DME 'ISY' 109·95 (Co-located with NDB).

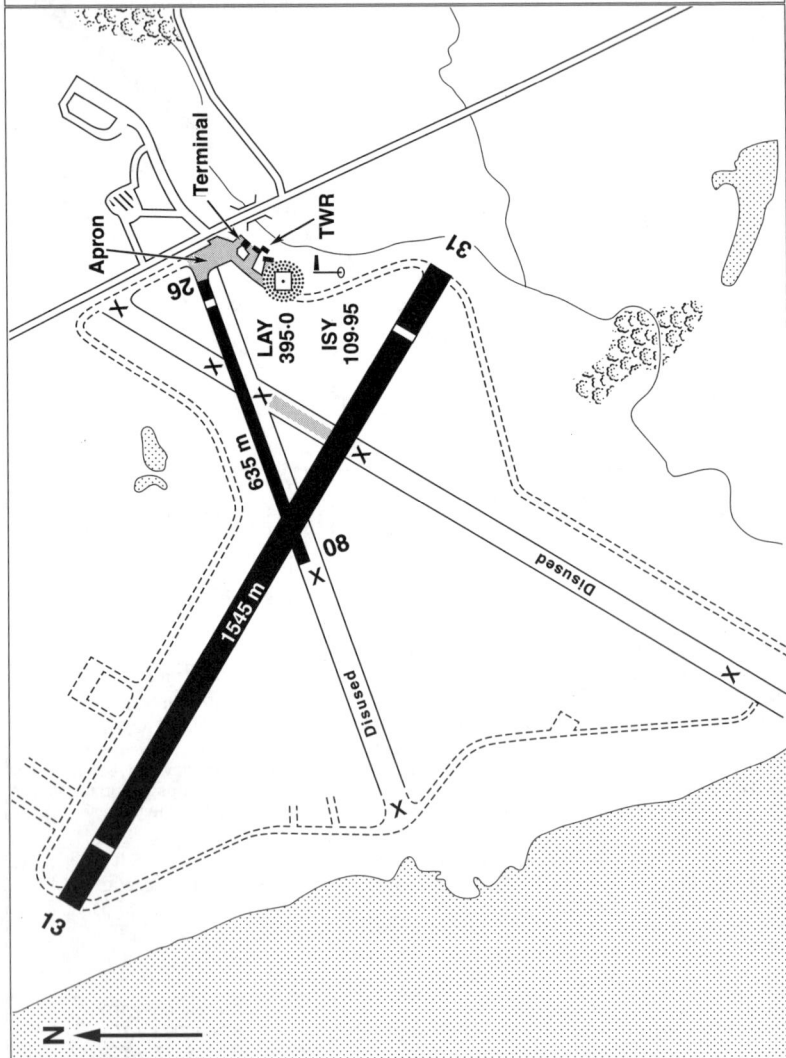

Robert Pooley ©

278

N55 40·92 W006 15·40		**ISLAY**			54 ft AMSL
Rwy	**Dim(m)**	**Surface**	**TORA(m)**	**LDA(m)**	**Lighting**
13/31	1545x46	Asphalt	13-1245†	13-1245	Ap Thr Rwy APAPI 3°
			31-1230†	31-1230	Thr Rwy APAPI 4°
08/26	635x18	Asphalt	08-635	08-635	Thr Rwy
			26-635	26-575	Thr Rwy

† 150 m unlit starter extension available by daylight only.

Op hrs: PPR. Winter/Summer: Mon-Fri 0945-1830; Sat 0945-1030. Closed Sun.

Landing Fee: H & I Rates. Private a/c up to 3000 kg £10.65 incl VAT.
Note: Pilots should confirm the conditions applicable when requesting prior permission.

Hangarage: Nil.   **Maintenance:** Nil.   **Customs:** Nil.

Remarks: Operated by Highlands & Islands Airports Ltd., Islay Airport, Glenegedale, Isle of Islay PA42 7AS. All flights 3 hrs PPR.

Pilots should only call 'Islay Information' when within 10 nm and below 3000 ft.

Rwy 26 has a displaced threshold due to uncontrolled public road. Aircraft should not land short of sterilization markings.

Helipad on apron at Rwy 26 threshold.

Perimeter track closed except for a section from the apron passing in front of the tower, used as a light aircraft park.

Jet training within 5 nm of the aerodrome. Traffic Information from AFIS.

Warnings: Increased number of deer can be found on the aerodrome, and large flocks of geese in the vicinity of the aerodrome during the months of October and March.

Mobile obstructions in undershoot Rwy 13, farm track east of Rwy 31 threshold and uncontrolled public track NE of Rwy 13/31 (outside Islay aerodrome boundary).

Hill rising to 1609' amsl to the East.

Grass areas soft and unsafe. Only marked taxiways to be used.

Visual Reference Points:

Mull of Oa	N55 35·50	W006 20·30
North Coast	N55 56·00	W006 09·90
Port Ellen	N55 38·00	W006 11·40
Rhinns Point	N55 40·40	W006 29·10

Accommodation: Glenegedale Guest House and Restaurant opposite the airport, Tel/Fax: 01496-302147.

Car Hire: 01496-810206, 810348 or 302300.

Fuel: Nil.	**Tel:** 01496-302361
	Fax: 01496-302096

Robert Pooley ©

N54 05·00 W004 37·43	**ISLE OF MAN**	55 ft AMSL
6 nm SW of Douglas.		IOM 112·20 084 4·9

c/s Ronaldsway. APP 120·85. TWR 118·90. RAD 120·85, 118·20*, 125·30*.
VDF/Hmr. 120·85, 118·90.   * When directed by ATC only.
NDB 'RWY' 359·0 (On A/D).
ILS/DME Rwy 08 I-RW 111·15.   ILS/DME Rwy 26 (264°M) I-RY 111·15.

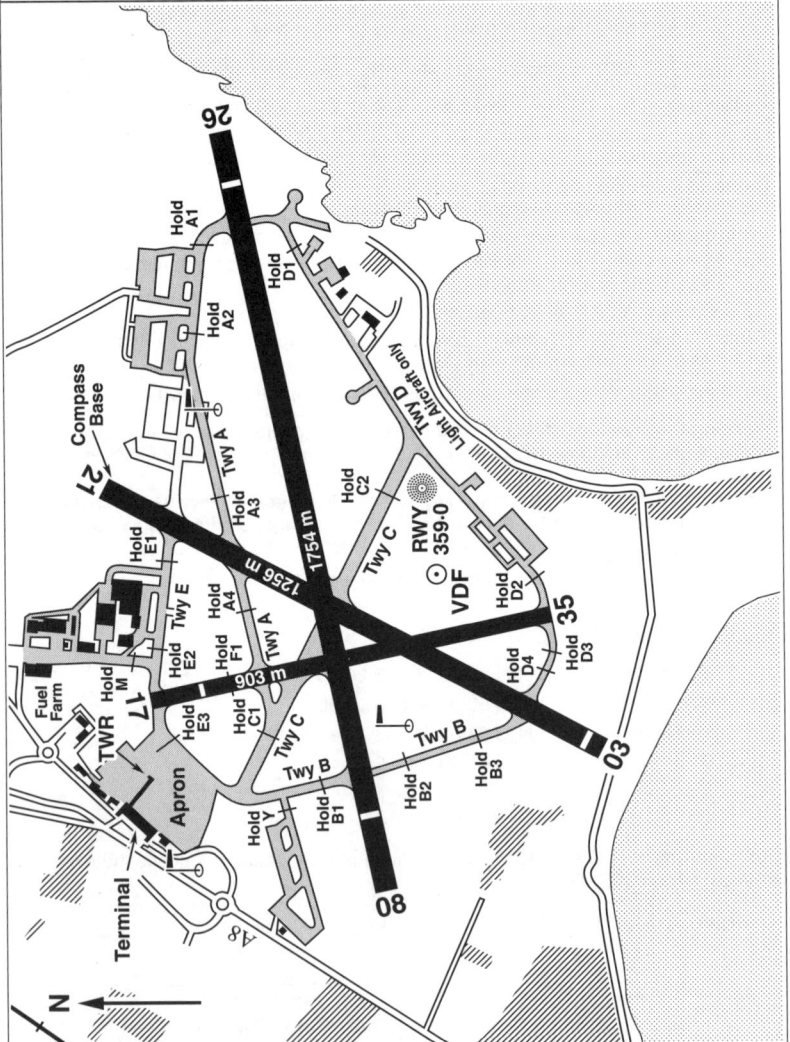

N54 05·00 W004 37·43			**ISLE OF MAN**		55 ft AMSL
Rwy	**Dim(m)**	**Surface**	**TORA(m)**	**LDA(m)**	**Lighting**
03/21	1256x46	Asphalt	03-1256	03-1226	Ap Thr Rwy PAPI 3°
			21-1226	21-1226	Ap Thr Rwy PAPI 3·5°RH
08/26	1754x46	Asphalt	08-1631	08-1463	Ap Thr Rwy RCL PAPI 3°
			26-1736	26-1613	Ap Thr Rwy RCL PAPI 3°
†17/35	903x27	Asphalt	17-903	17-787	Thr Rwy
			—	35-898	Thr Rwy

† Rwy 17/35 not available at night to any aircraft.

Rwy 35 available for landings only.

Op hrs: Mon-Sat 0615-2045, Sun 0700-2045. Other times by arrangement.

Landing Fee: Light Single £12.44, Small Twin £24.88. All inclusive of VAT, No Passenger Load Supplement for Private flights.

Customs: Available.

Hangarage: Limited.   **Maintenance:** Limited.

Remarks: Operated by The Isle of Man Government Department of Transport, Airports Division, Isle of Man Airport, Ballasalla, Isle of Man IM9 2AS.

Flights within the Isle of Man CTR/CTA are governed by the regulations applicable to Class 'D' Controlled Airspace see page 2.

Non-radio aircraft strictly PPR.

When approaching Rwy 08, all aircraft should intercept the extended centre-line at a minimum range of 1·5 nm and should not descend below the PAPI indicated approach slope of 3°.

Owing to high ground to the left of the approach for Rwy 21, pilots must establish on the runway extended centreline before descending on the PAPI glidepath.

Departures - Climb straight ahead to 500' (Jets 1000'). **Do not** commence any turns until having passed the aerodrome boundary.

Simulated engine failure on departure Rwy 26 not permitted.

Warning Windshear on short final Rwy 08 when wind from South East.

Restaurant: Restaurant and Refreshments available.

Car Hire: Available.

VRPs and Prevention of Terrorism Act 1990 – See overleaf

Fuel: 100LL, Jet A1. S. Multi Service	**Tel:** 01624-821600 Airport 01624-821625 FBU 01624-821642 MET **Fax:** 01624-821611 Airport 01624-821626 FBU 01624-821646 MET 01624-821627 ATC

Robert Pooley ©

ISLE OF MAN
Visual Reference Points (VRPs) and
Prevention of Terrorism Act 1990

Visual Reference Points

VRP	VOR/NDB	VOR/DME Fix
Laxey N54 13·75 W004 24·10	IOM R059	IOM 059°/16 nm
Peel N54 13·33 W004 41·50	IOM R022	IOM 022°/10 nm

Prevention of Terrorism (Temporary Provisions) Act 1990

Under the terms of this order pilots and passengers of Private or Charter aircraft who have come from or are going to Great Britain, the Republic of Ireland, Northern Ireland or the Channel Islands, must report immediately on arrival or immediately before departure to a Police Examining Officer in the arrivals area of the passenger terminal.

See page 629 for further details of Prevention of Terrorism Act, and Class 1 NOTAMN D0491/98.

Information in relation to flights to and from non-designated airfields in the Isle of Man and airfields within the Common Travel Area may be obtained from Police H.Q, Douglas, Tel: 01624-631212, Fax: 01624-631337.

N57 15·18 W005 49·67	**ISLE OF SKYE (Broadford)**	34 ft AMSL
3 nm E of Broadford.	BEN 114·40 114 51·6	
	STN 115·10 178 58·4	

No Radio.

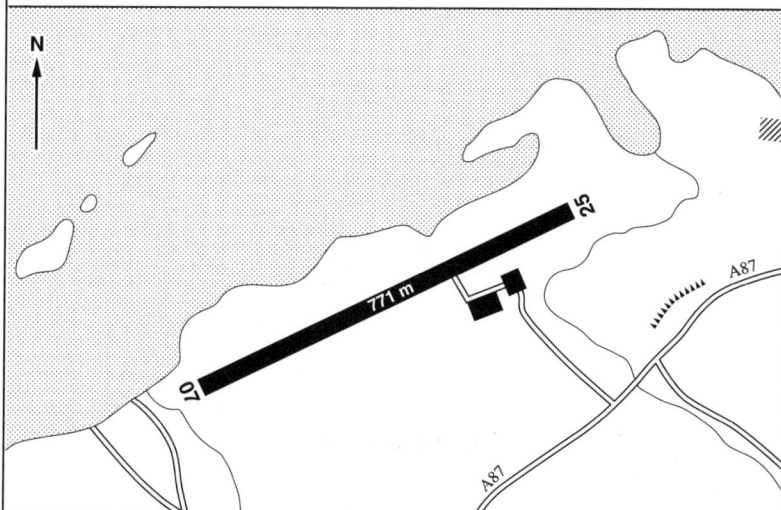

Rwy	Dim(m)	Surface	TORA(m)	LDA(m)	Lighting
07/25	771x23	Asphalt	Unlicensed		Nil, except in emergency.

Op hrs: PPR. (24hrs notice).

Landing Fee: Highland Council Rates.	**Customs:** Nil.
Hangarage: Nil	**Maintenance:** Nil.

Remarks: Unlicensed aerodrome operated by Highland Council, Transport Services. PPR.
High ground up to 2,400ft to E and W of aerodrome.

Area Roads & Transport Services Manager, Skye & Lochalsh Division, Portree, Isle of Skye — Tel: 01478-612727, Fax: 612255.

Restaurant: Nil

Car Hire: Nil.

Fuel: Nil.	**Tel:** 01463-702604 Council.
	01471-822202 Aerodrome.
	Fax: 01463-702606 Council.

Intentionally Blank

| N50 39·17 W001 10·92 | **ISLE OF WIGHT - SANDOWN** | 60 ft AMSL |

| 1 nm W of Sandown. | SAM 113·35 165 19·1 |
| | MID 114·00 226 31·6 |

c/s Sandown Radio 123·50 A/G.

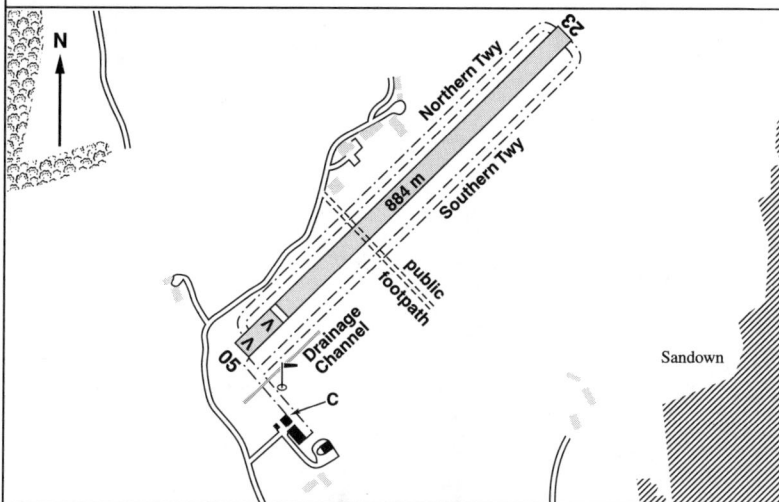

Rwy	Dim(m)	Surface	TORA(m)	LDA(m)	Lighting
05/23	884x40	Grass	05-884	05-775	Nil.
			23-884	23-884	Nil.

Location of landing thresholds emphasised by black/white wing bars.

Op hrs: Winter: 0900-SS or 1700. Summer: 0900-1800.

Landing Fee: Singles £8.00 incl VAT. Twins £14.00 incl VAT.

Customs: EU - Nil outbound. 3 hrs PNR inbound; C.I. 24 hrs PNR.

Hangarage: Usually available.   **Maintenance:** M3 available.

Remarks: Operated by Isle of Wight Airport Ltd. Non-radio aircraft PPR.
Visiting aircraft always welcome.
Circuits at 1000' aal, RH on Rwy 23, LH on 05. All aircraft please join from deadside.
Uncontrolled traffic on access road crossing SW approach to Rwy 05 at 90 m from threshold.
Public footpath crosses runway 300 m from Rwy 05 threshold.
Fixed wing/Helicopter PPL courses and Tailwheel conversion available from Specialist Flying School with accommodation on site, Tel: 01983-402402.
Fixed wing PPL courses also from Birnie Air Services Flying Training, 01983-408374.

Restaurant: Licensed Bar and Coffee Shop.

Car Hire: 01983-864263. Avis Tel: 01983- 615522. Wiltons Tel: 01983-864414.

Taxi: 01983-402641/403204.

| **Fuel:** 100LL. | **Tel:** 01983-405125. **Fax:** 01983-406117. |
| | **Telex:** 86841 |

Robert Pooley ©

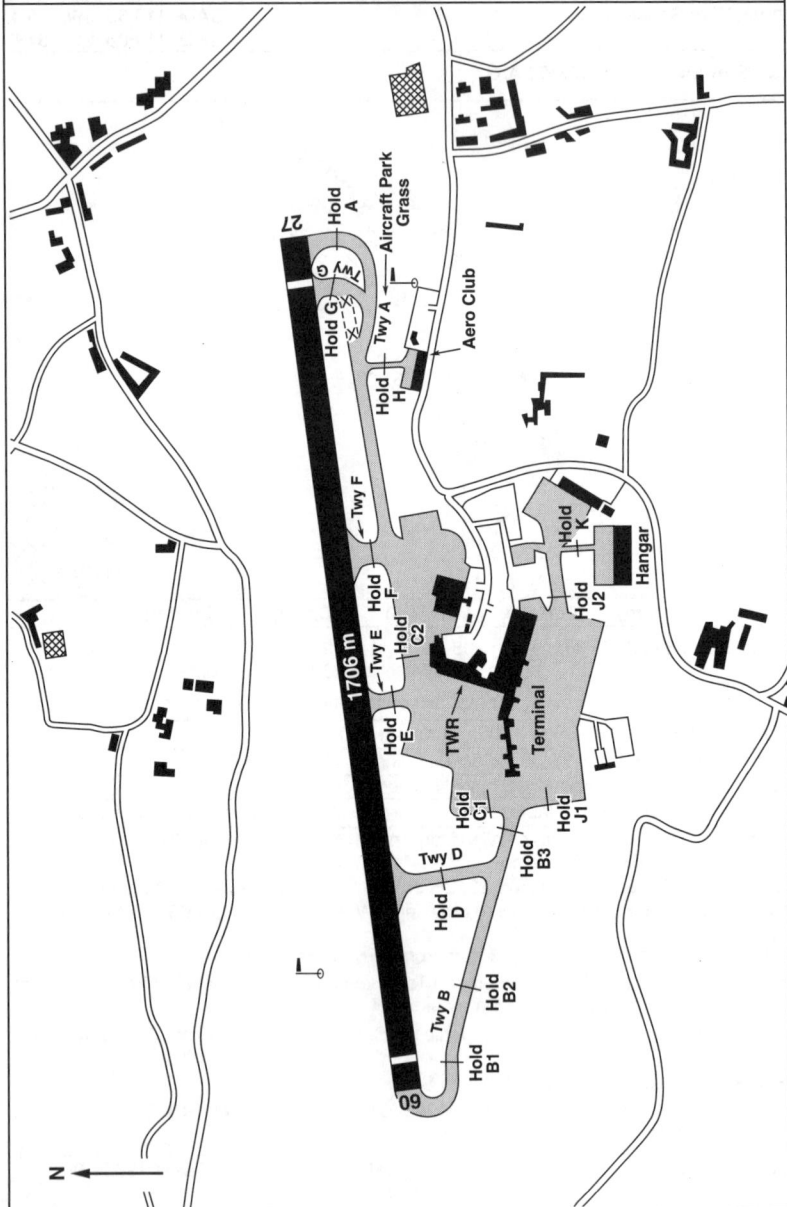

09

27

1706 m

Hold A

Twy G

Hold G

Twy A

Aircraft Park
Grass

Aero Club

Hold H

Twy F

Hold F

Twy E

Hold C2

Hold E

TWR

Terminal

Hold K

Hold J2

Hangar

Hold C1

Hold B3

Hold J1

Twy D

Hold D

Hold B2

Twy B

Hold B1

N

N49 12·48 W002 11·73	**JERSEY**	277 ft AMSL
4 nm WNW of St.Helier		**JSY 112·20 267 5·5**
		GUR 109·40 136 21

c/s Jersey. ZONE 125·20, 120·45.   APP 120·30, 118·55.   TWR 119·45.
GND 121·90. RAD 118·55, 125·20, 120·45, 120·30.
ATIS 129·725 and also on 'JSY' VOR 112·20.
NDB 'JW 329·0 (087°/0·5 nm to Thr 09).
ILS/DME Rwy 09 (087°M) I-JJ 110·90. ILS/DME Rwy 27 (267°M) I-DD 110·30.

Rwy	Dim (m)	Surface	TORA (m)	LDA (m)	Lighting
09/27	1706x46	Asphalt/	09-1706	09-1645	Ap Thr Rwy RCL PAPI
		Concrete	27-1645	27-1554	Ap Thr Rwy RCL PAPI

Op hrs: Winter: 0700-2100 daily. Summer: 0700-2130 daily.

Landing Fee: On application.

Hangarage: Nil.   **Maintenance:** Available.   **Customs:** As Op hrs.

Remarks: Operated by States of Jersey. Use governed by the regulations applicable to the Channel Islands CTR (Class 'A') and the Jersey CTR (Class 'D') – see pages 8 to 11 and Jersey CTR chart at page 289.

Commercial Operators not based at this airport are required to make prior arrangements for ground handling. Communications to : Airport Administration or Information Services with details of: Aircraft type, registration and operator, point of origin and destination, ETA and ETD Jersey and nominated handling agent.

Visiting light aircraft will be parked as directed by ATC. All occupants will be required to be transported to the Terminal Bldg by courtesy bus for Customs and Immigration processing. All occupants to remain with their aircraft until the courtesy bus arrives. Transport will be provided for departure purposes.

All visiting private aircraft landing fees and, if appropriate, handling fees will be collected by Aviation Beauport.

All aircraft must carry Third Party Insurance cover of not less than £500,000.

Circuits at 1000 ft aal, with the majority of the circuits carried out over the sea.

Warning: On final approach to Rwy 09, turbulance and variable wind conditions may be experienced due to terrain.

Noise Preferential Procedures for Propeller driven aircraft:

Rwy 09/27 Landings – Maintain at least 1000' aal until intercepting the ILS glidepath or PAPI indication and thereafter descend on the facility. If under 5700 kg and making a visual approach, land must not be overflown below 500' agl unil on final approach.

Rwy 09 Take-off – Climb straight ahead to a minimum of 500' aal before turning and climb as rapidly as is compatible with flight safety to not less than 1000' agl.

Rwy 27 Take-off – Climb to minimum 500' aal before turning on to a heading and avoid overflying land below 1000' aal.

Restaurant/ Car Hire: Available at the terminal.

Fuel: 100LL, Jet A1	**Tel:** 01534-492000 Admin.
Multi Service	01534-492226/492227 ATC Supervisor.
	Fax: 01534-492131 Admin, 492194 ATC/FBU

Intentionally Blank

N

JERSEY CTR D
SFC — 2000' ALT
(Radius 8nm)

No. 6
Special VFR Route Flamanville
039°
23nm
219°

JERSEY

No. 7
Special VFR Route St. Germain
272° 28nm 092°

JW
329·0

60

27

No. 9
Special VFR Route Brehat
061°
39nm
241°

ST. HELIER

358°

No. 1
Special VFR Route Dinard
38nm
178°

No. 8
Special VFR Route Granville
318° 32nm
138°

CHANNEL ISLANDS CTR A
SFC — FL195

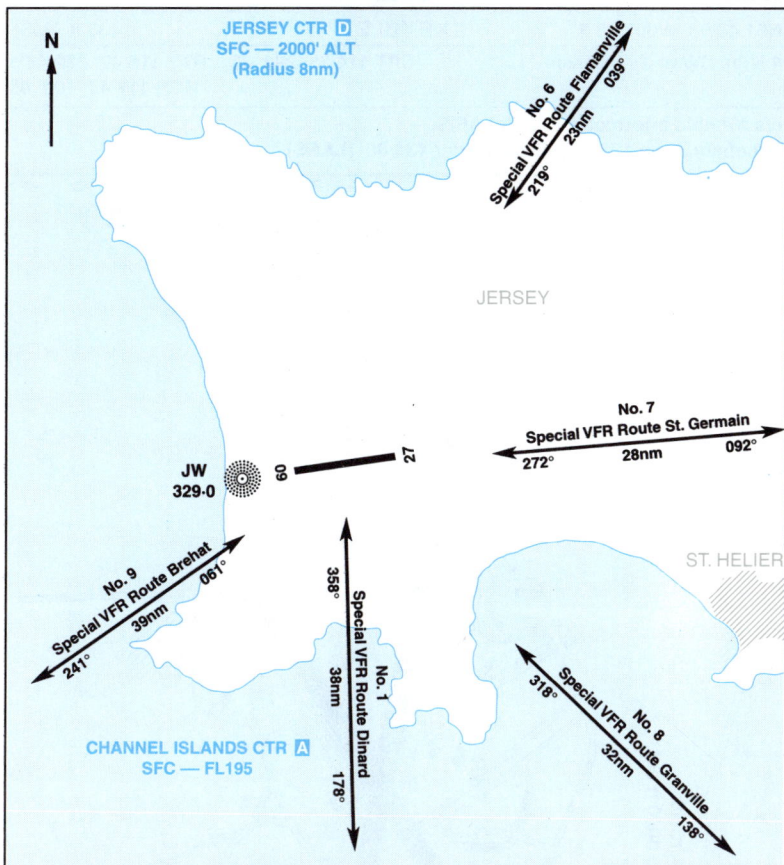

Procedures applicable to the Channel Islands CTR (Class 'A') and the Jersey CTR (Class 'D') are given at pages 8 to 11.

No. 1   Jersey – Dinard.
No. 6   Jersey – Cap de Flamanville.
No. 7   Jersey – St. Germain.
No. 8   Jersey – Granville.
No. 9   Jersey – Brehat.

Special VFR Clearance inbound must be obtained from Jersey Zone before reaching the CTR (Class A) boundary.

Note. SSR Mode A, 4096 Codes mandatory for SVFR flights within Channel Is CTR.

N51 40·08 W002 03·37

4·5 nm SW of Cirencester

CPT 114·35 294 33   DTY 116·40 232 46·5
BCN 117·45 100 45

c/s Kemble Information 118·90 AFIS.
Lyneham Zone 123·40.   Brize Radar 134·30 (LARS).

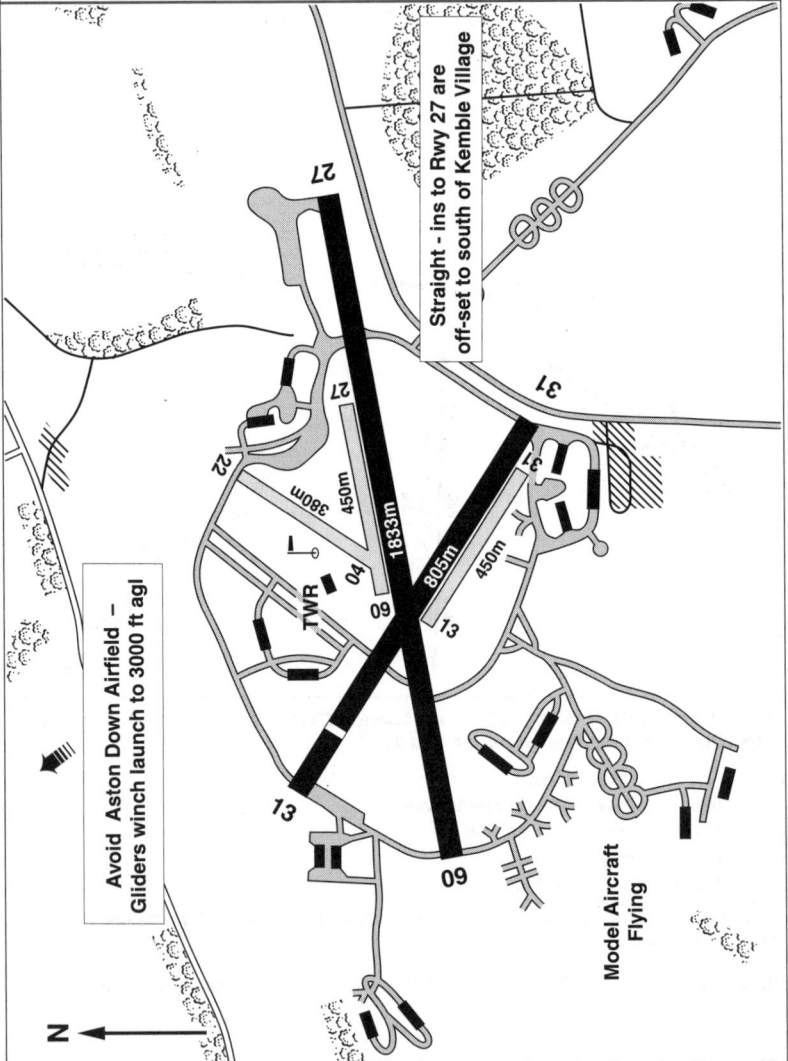

Straight - ins to Rwy 27 are off-set to south of Kemble Village

Avoid Aston Down Airfield – Gliders winch launch to 3000 ft agl

Model Aircraft Flying

27

27

22

31

31

04

09

13

13

09

380m

450m

1833m

805m

450m

TWR

N

N51 40·08 W002 03·37			**KEMBLE**		435 ft AMSL
Rwy	**Dim(m)**	**Surface**	**TORA(m)**	**LDA(m)**	**Lighting**
† 09/27	1833x46	Asphalt	Unlicensed		09 - Thr Rwy PAPI 27 - Thr Rwy
13/31	805x46	Asphalt	Unlicensed		Nil
04/22	380x20	Grass	Unlicensed		Nil
09/27	450X20	Grass	Unlicensed		Nil
13/31	450x20	Grass	Unlicensed		Nil

† No 180° turns on high friction runway surface.

Op hrs: PPR (Phone or Radio) SR - SS. Night flying Thursdays until 2000 hrs.

Landing Fee: Microlights £5. Singles £8; Light Twins & Helicopters £10.

Customs: By arrangement.

Hangarage: Available.   **Maintenance:** Available.

Remarks: Operated by Kemble Airfield Management Ltd.,The Control Tower, Kemble Airfield, Kemble, Cirencester, Glos. GL7 6BA.

Multi purpose use airfield.

Non-radio aircraft strictly PPR.

Keep a sharp look out for Microlights, Fast jet traffic, Paragliders and Model aircraft.

Circuit height 800 ft aal for Microlights, 1200 ft aal for light aircraft. Left Hand unless otherwise directed.

Inbound aircraft are to avoid approaching from NW sector due to Aston Down airfield (gliders winch launch to 3000 ft agl). *Pilots have often mistaken Aston Down for Kemble!* Also avoid South Cerney (parachuting) and maintain good look out for Oaksey Park traffic.

All visitors welcome. Arriving pilots to book in at the Tower coffee Bar and pay landing fees to Tower direct.

Noise Abatement Procedures:
Do **not** overfly **any** villages/housing in the proximity of the airfield whilst joining/flying the circuit. **Straight in approaches to Rwy 27 are off-set to the south of Kemble village to avoid overflying it.**

Helicopter Access Routes:
Arriving helicopters join circuit in use at 500 ft agl.

Caution: Turbulance on final approach to Rwy 27 with Northerly/Southerly winds above 10 kts. Runway liable to flooding in moderate/heavy rain.

Light aircraft available for Hire.

Accommodation: Mayfield House Hotel, Crudwell, Tel: 01666-577409.

Restaurant: Pilots' lounge & excellent catering facilities available in the Tower building.

Car Hire/Taxis: Station Taxis Tel: 01285-650850.

Fuel: 100LL, Jet A1/F34	**Tel/Fax:** 01285-771177 Tower/Ops.

Robert Pooley ©

N56 16·17 W002 45·05	**KINGSMUIR (Sorbie)**	387 ft AMSL

7·4 nm SSE of RAF Leuchars,
2·5 nm from MATZ Boundary.

TLA 113·80 030 50·5

Leuchars App 126·50.   129·90 A/G - Manned during parachuting operations only.

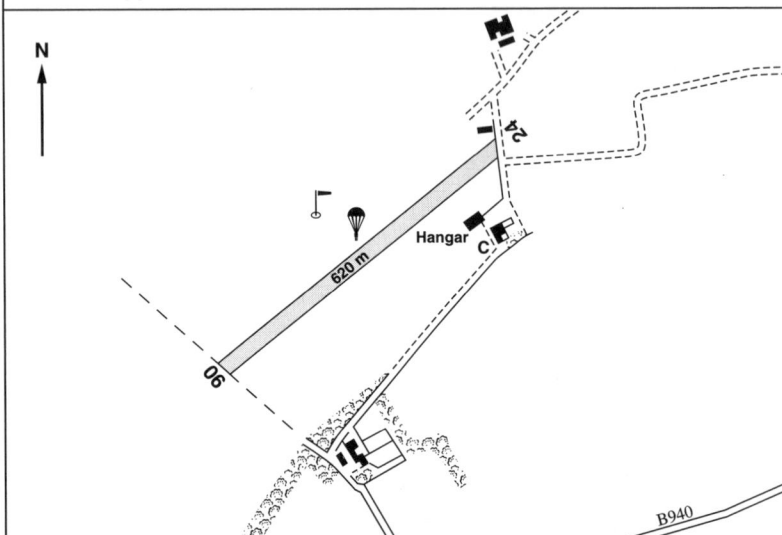

N

Hangar

620 m

06

24

B940

Rwy	Dim(m)	Surface	TORA(m)	LDA(m)	Lighting
06/24	620x25	Grass	Unlicensed		Nil

Op hrs: PPR, Tel: 01333-310619.

Landing Fee: Donations left to users discretion.	**Customs:** Nil
Hangarage: Nil.	**Maintenance:** Nil

Remarks: Operated by David and Violet Smith, Kingsmuir Farm, Strevithie,
St. Andrews, Fife KY16 8QQ.
Contact Leuchars App for traffic Information.
Overnight parking available at owner's risk.

Warning: Parachuting on the airfield from up to FL150.

Restaurant: Available at the Skydiving Centre.

Accommodation: B&B by arrangement.

Fuel: Mogas PPR	**Tel:** 01333-310619.

Robert Pooley ©

N54 53·00 W003 12·00	**KIRKBRIDE**	38 ft AMSL

9·5 nm W of Carlisle. **DCS 115·20 032 10·5**

Carlisle APP 123·60. c/s Kirkbride Radio 124·40. if no contact transmit intentions blind, and proceed with caution.

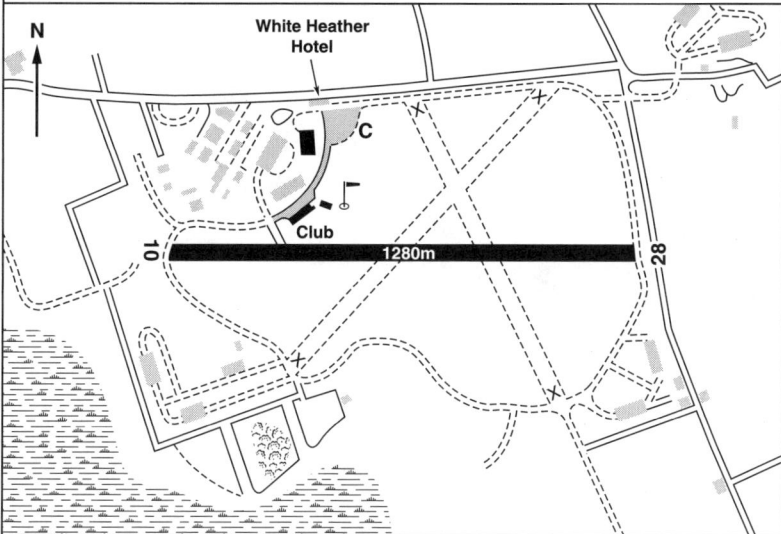

Rwy	Dim(m)	Surface	TORA(m)	LDA(m)	Lighting
10/28	1280x46	Asphalt	Unlicensed		Nil

Op hrs: PPR.

Landing Fee: Donations to club funds gratefully accepted. **Customs:** Nil.

Hangarage: Nil **Maintenance:** Nil.

Remarks: Operated by White Heather Hotel, Kirkbride, Cumbria. Unlicensed airfield. Visiting aircraft welcome at pilot's own risk.
All aircraft must carry third party insurance.

Warnings: Military low flying activity around the area during weekdays.
HGV traffic use centre section of the runway for crossing.

Restaurant: Available at the White Heather Hotel, but check availability and hours prior to flight.

Accommodation: Available at the White Heather Hotel.

Taxis: Nil.

Fuel: Nil. Nearest Airfield Carlisle	Tel: 01697-351373 Hotel for PPR. 01697-351006 Kirkbride Aero Club. 01697-342142 John Plaskett Co-ordinator Mobile 07710-672087 John Plaskett,

Robert Pooley ©

| N58 57·47 W002 54·32 | **KIRKWALL** | 50 ft. AMSL |

| 2·5 nm SE of Kirkwall. | **WIK 113·60 019 30·6** |

c/s Kirkwall. APP/TWR 118·30.
VOR/DME 'KWL' 108·60 (On A/D) NDB 'KW' 395·0 (On A/D)

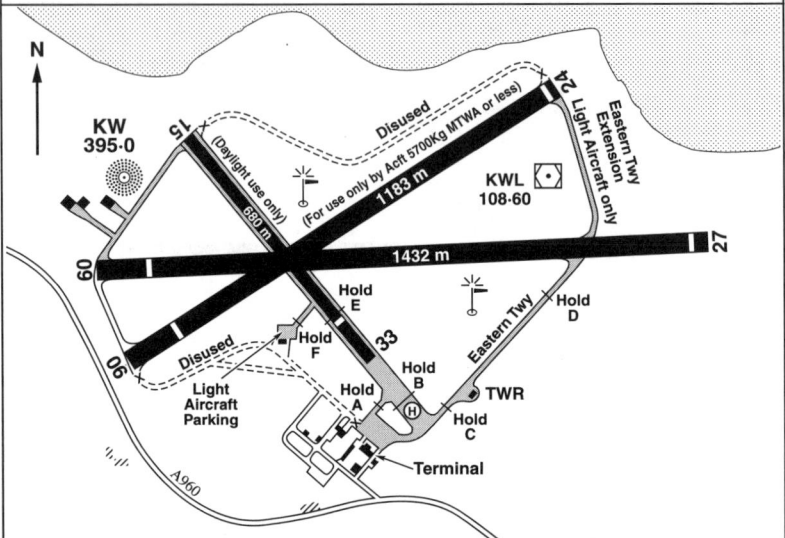

Rwy	Dim(m)	Surface	TORA(m)	LDA(m)	Lighting
§ 06/24	1183x46	Asphalt	06-1168	06-1031	Nil.
			24-1084	24-1078	PAPI 3°
09/27	1432x46	Asphalt	09-1400	09-1289	Thr Rwy PAPI 3·5°
			27-1365	27-1320	Ap Thr Rwy PAPI 3·25°
† 15/33	680x18	Asphalt	15-560	15-560	Nil.
			33-680	33-560	Nil.

§ Rwy 06/24 limited to aircraft up to 5700 kg MTWA. Rwy 06 — Down Gradient 0·7%
† Rwy 15/33 available for daylight use only. Rwy 15 — Down Gradient 2% over first 550 m.

Op hrs: PPR. Mon-Fri 0745-1845, Sat 0800-1645, Sun 0900-1100. O/T by arrangement.

Landing Fee: Highlands & Islands Rates.   **Customs:** PNR.

Hangarage: Limited. **Maintenance:** Available (Loganair). **Met:** H24. 01856-873802

Remarks: Operated by Highland & Island Airports Ltd. PPR to all flights. Height of landing area varies considerably, elevation at runway intersection is 35 ft amsl. All grass areas outside the strips are unserviceable owing to open drains and aerodrome is subject to water-logging.

A public road passes under the take-off and climb paths of Rwys 24 and 27. A height allowance of 15 ft to clear a vehicle on this road must be applied to performance calculations for departures from these runways.

Note. All taxiways are unlicensed except Eastern and Eastern Taxiway Extension.

Restaurant: Light Refreshments. **Car Hire:** W. R. Tullock. 01856-875500.

| **Fuel:** 100LL, Jet A1
Tel: 01856-872415 | **Tel:** 01856-872421 A/D. 01856- 886205 ATC.
Fax: 01856-875051 ATC; 871882 A/D Manager. |

N58 53·18 W002 53·60	**LAMB HOLM**	65 ft AMSL

Lamb Holm Island	KWL 108·60 190 4·5
	WIK 113·6 022 26

Lamb Holm Radio 129·825 A/G (Microlight operations).   **Kirkwall App/Twr 118·30**

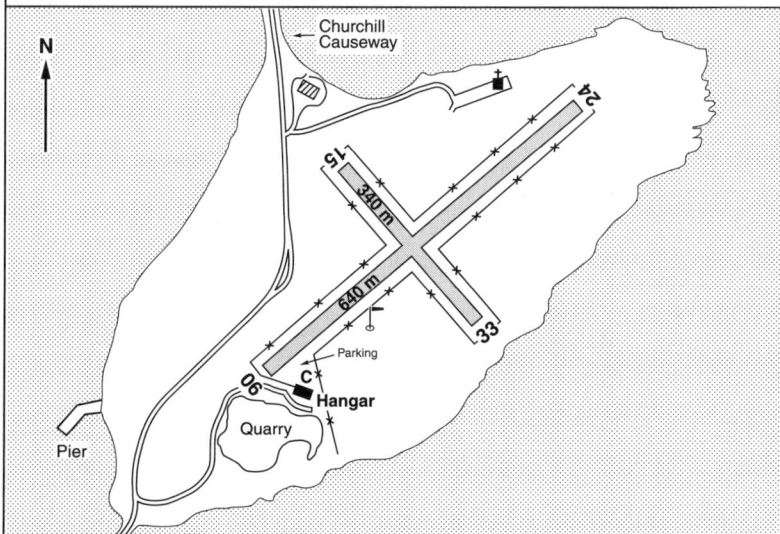

Rwy	Dim(m)	Surface	TORA(m)	LDA(m)	Lighting
06/24	640x18	Grass	Unlicensed		Nil
15/33	340x18	Grass	Unlicensed		Nil

Op hrs: Strictly PPR.

Landing Fee: Donations accepted.	**Customs:** Nil
Hangarage: Limited.	**Maintenance:** Nil

Remarks: Operated by Tom Sinclair, Tighsith, Holm, Orkney Islands, KW17 2RX.
Unlicensed airfield. All movements at pilot's own risk.
Rwy 15/33 has significant up slopes from both thresholds towards the centre and is only available when strong winds favour its use.
Circuits - LH on Rwys 24 and 33, RH on Rwys 06 and 15.

Warning: An electricity pole, 20 ft high, is located 125 metres from Rwy 15 threshold to the left of Rwy 15 final approach.
Avoid overflying St. Mary's village 1 nm NW of the airfield.

Accommodation/Restaurant: Commodore Motel Tel: 01856-781319.

Taxis/Mini Bus Hire: Andersons Tel: 01856-781237 day, 781267 evening.

Fuel: By arrangement	**Tel:** 07803- 088938.
	Tel/Fax: 01856-781310 Home.

N50 06·17 W005 40·23	**LANDS END (St. Just)**	401 ft AMSL

5 nm W of Penzance.	LND 114·20 221 2·4

c/s Lands End APP/TWR 130·70 – Mon to Sat Normal Op hrs.
c/s Radio 130·70 A/G – Sun and occasional lunch periods.

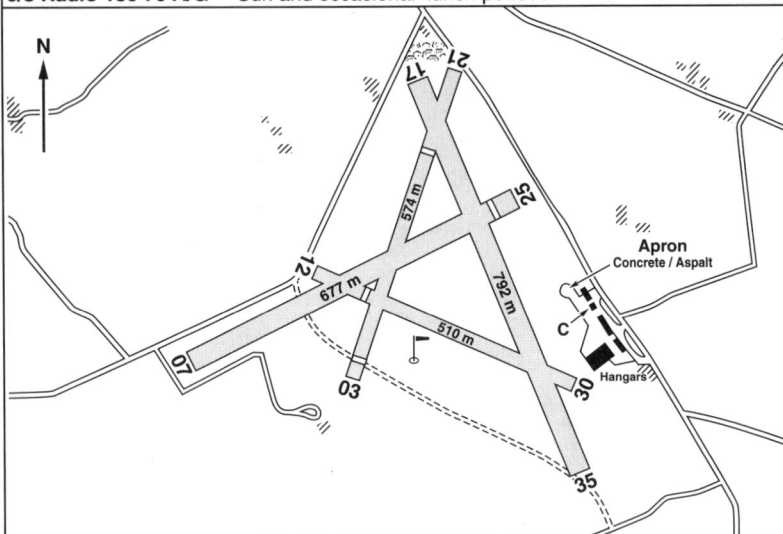

Rwy	Dim(m)	Surface	TORA(m)	LDA(m)	Lighting
17/35	792x36	Grass	17-792	17-707	Nil
			35-792	35-792	Nil
07/25	677x36	Grass	07-677	07-677	Nil
			25-677	25-630	Nil
12/30	510x18	Grass	12-479	12-417	Nil
			30-510	*—	Nil
03/21	574x18	Grass	03-574	03-544	Nil
			21-574	21-436	Nil
* Rwy 30 not licensed for landing for Public Transport.					A Bn Wh

Op hrs: PPR Mandatory by Telephone. WINTER: 0900-1700 or SS whichever earlier. SUMMER: Mon-Sat 0800-1700; Sun 0800-1600. Other times by arrangement.

Landing Fee: Private – SE £7.50, Twin £15. Commercial Twin £30.

Hangarage: £7.00 per night. **Maintenance:** Available. **Customs:** 24 hrs PNR

Remarks: Operated by Westward Airways (Land's End) Ltd. All aircraft PPR by telephone, Tel: 01736-788944 ATC. Whole grass area is maintained and usable. Some parts of the manoeuvring area are undulating. Western end of 03/21 runway slopes down. Rwys 07/25 & 17/35 are wide enough to allow differential use of each side of Rwy in order to conserve grass surfaces.
Pilots should anticipate being asked to land (left or right) in order to achieve this. Flashing Beacon on top of Tower during operational hours.
Caution: Soft ground, especially Rwy thresholds
Warning: Mast 286' aal., to the right of approach to Rwy 21, range 1 nm.
Restaurant: Restaurant and Club facilities. **Car Hire:** By arrangement.

Fuel: 100LL.	**Tel:** 01736-788944 ATC.
	01736-788771 Westward Airways.

N52 53·63 W000 54·27	**LANGAR**	109 ft AMSL

10 nm ESE of Nottingham	GAM 112·80 182 23
	TNT 115·70 116 29

Cottesmore APP 130·20. Langar Drop Zone 129·90.

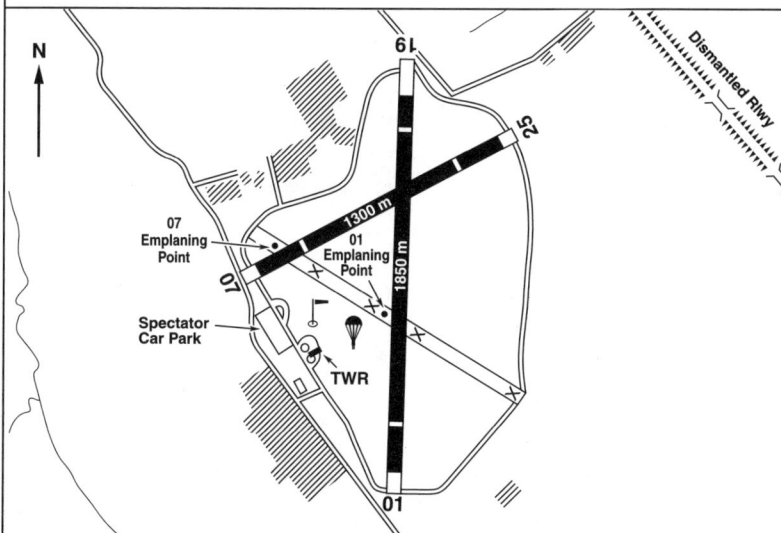

Rwy	Dim(m)	Surface	TORA(m)	LDA(m)	Lighting
01/19	1850x60	Asphalt	Unlicensed		Nil.
07/25	1300x60	Asphalt	Unlicensed		Nil.

Op hrs: PPR. SR–SS

Landing Fee: Singles £2.00; Twins £5.00. No charge if on BPS business.

Hangarage: Nil.   **Maintenance:** Nil.   **Customs:** Nil.

Remarks: Operated by British Parachute Schools. Aerodrome situated 3 nm NE of East Midlands CTA (Class 'D' Controlled Airspace) 2500' ALT– FL75.

Visiting aircraft welcome on prior permission. PPR is vital in order to obtain briefing on parachuting operations for the day.

Do not overfly the airfield — intensive para-dropping up to FL150 daily.

Circuits at 1000' aal; LH on 19 and 25, RH on 01 and 07.

Contact Langar at least 5 nm from airfield for joining information — normally a straight-in approach or base leg join.

Disused runway 13/31 is available as taxiway.

Restaurant: Available weekends.

Taxis: 01949-839000

Fuel: 100LL, Jet A1 Emergency supply only.	**Tel/Fax:** 01949-860878

Robert Pooley ©

N51 11·20 W001 01·92	**LASHAM**	618 ft AMSL
5 nm SE of Basingstoke.		SAM 113·35 045 18·2
		OCK 115·30 259 23·1

c/s Farnborough APP 125·25. For Odiham MATZ clearance.
c/s Lasham 129·90 Glider Operations

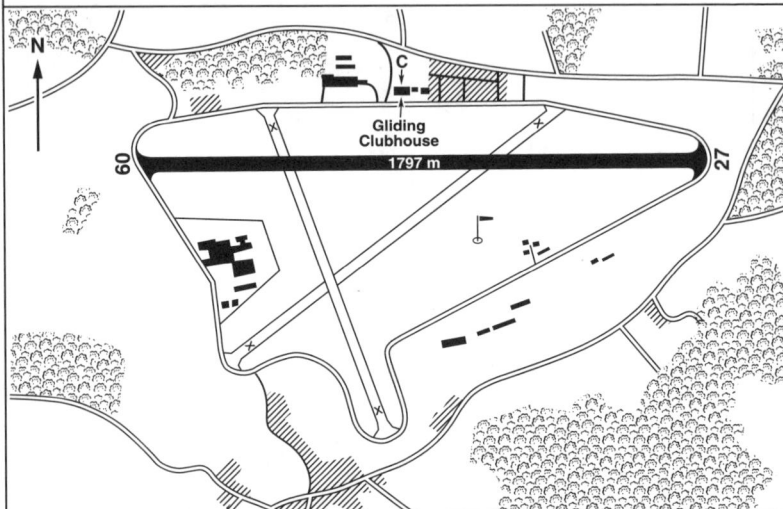

Gliding Clubhouse

60 | 1797 m | 27

Rwy	Dim(m)	Surface	TORA(m)	LDA(m)	Lighting
09/27	1797x40	Asphalt	Unlicensed		Nil.

Op hrs: PPR.

Landing Fee: Singles £10.00; Others £20 per tonne.   **Customs:** 24 hrs PNR.

Hangarage: Nil.   **Maintenance:** Nil.

Remarks: Gliding site operated by Lasham Gliding Society, Lasham Aerodrome, Nr. Alton, Hants. Powered aircraft may only visit by prior permission by telephone, during normal working hours, permission normally restricted to visits in connection with gliding and to pilots with gliding experience to Silver 'C' standard.
Light aircraft must use grass area North of main runway or centre triangle depending on runway in use.
Intensive glider operations every day with simultaneous RH and LH circuits by up to 20 gliders and tug aircraft, and danger of launch cables both on the ground and in the air up to 3000ft aal.
Visiting aircraft should call on 129·90 before joining.
Visiting pilots and passengers are required to become temporary members of the Society fully indemnifying the Society from all liability. No ATC.
Mast 251' aal 869' amsl 087°/2·8 nm.

Restaurant: Clubhouse facilities available.

Fuel: Nil.	**Tel:** 01256-384900.

N51 09·42 E000 38·50	**LASHENDEN (Headcorn)**	1 DEC 00

1 nm SE of Headcorn.	DET 117·30 173 9·0
	MAY 117·90 071 21·5

c/s Lashenden Radio 122·00 A/G.   NDB 'LSH' 340·0 (On A/D).

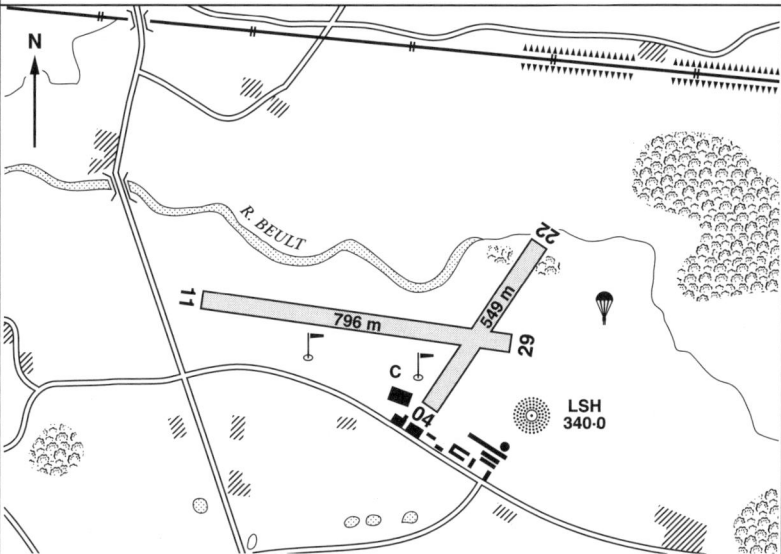

Rwy	Dim(m)	Surface	TORA(m)	LDA(m)	Lighting
11/29	796x30	Grass	11-796	11-796	Portable electric or
			29-796	29-796	Goosenecks - PNR.
04/22	549x30	Grass	Unlicensed		

Op hrs: 0900–SS, and by arrangement.

Landing Fee: £5.00	**Customs:** Available
Hangarage: Nil.	**Maintenance:** Available

Remarks: Operated by Mr. J. P. A. Freeman, Shenley Farms (Engineering) Ltd, Headcorn Aerodrome, Kent TN27 9HX. Licensed aerodrome. PPR. Aerodrome not licensed for night use.

Free-fall parachuting from up to FL150. Parachute DZ 300 m NE of Rwy 29 thld. Whilst parachuting in progress, no overhead joins, all aircraft to join downwind. Rotary wing aircraft are to obtain clearance prior to engaging rotors.

Circuits: Fixed Wing – at 1,000' aal, LH. Rotary – at 700 aal, LH on 11, RH on 29.

Aircraft departing Rwy 11/29 are to climb to 500 ft QFE before turning keeping clear of built-up areas. All aircraft are to avoid overflying local villages.

Caution: Taxi with care at all times due to undulating ground in some parts of the taxiway.

Restaurant: Available.   **Car Hire:** Available.

Fuel: 100LL, Jet A1(Business users only).	**Tel:** 01622-890226, 890236 night.
	Telex: 966127. **Fax:** 01622-890876

Intentionally Blank

N52 00·20 W002 28·58	**LEDBURY**	200 ft AMSL

3 nm SW of Ledbury.

BCN 117·45 066 33.   HON 113·65 241 37
GST 398·0 300 13.   GOS 115·55 300 13

No Radio.
Gloster APP/TWR 125·65.

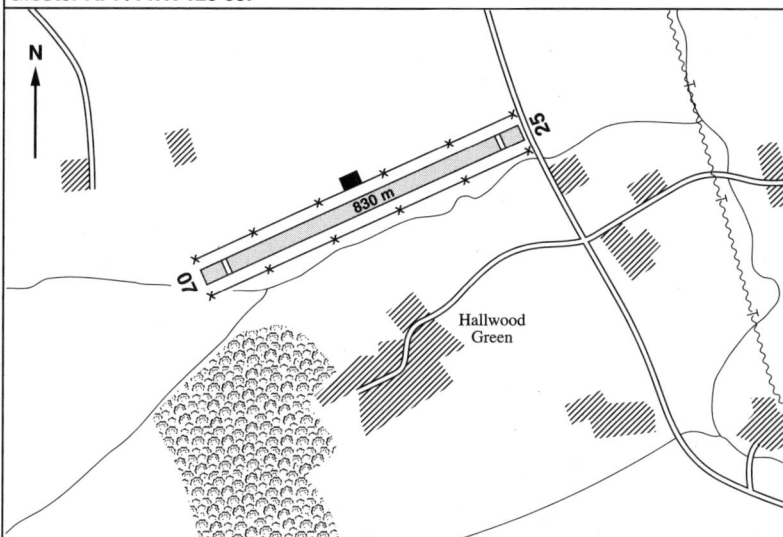

N

25

830 m

07

Hallwood
Green

Rwy	Dim(m)	Surface	TORA(m)	LDA(m)	Lighting
07/25	830x28	Grass	Unlicensed		Nil.

Op hrs: PPR. SR–SS.

Landing Fee: No charge.	**Customs:** Nil.
Hangarage: Nil.	**Maintenance:** Nil.

Remarks: Unlicensed airfield owned by the Bromesberrow Estate and operated by Velcourt Ltd. The Veldt House, Much Marcle, Ledbury, Herefordshire HR8 2LJ.

Light aircraft welcome at all times on prior permission and at pilot's own risk.

Circuits LH at 1000' aal. Windsock displayed on hangar roof.

Care must be taken. Trees on approach to Rwy 07.

Power cables cross final approach to Rwy 25 at 450 m from threshold.

TV Mast 1210' amsl 2 nm West of airfield.

Fuel: Nil.	**Tel:** 01531- 660207
	Fax: 01531- 660307
	Please call during Office hours.

Robert Pooley ©

N53 51·95 W001 39·63	**LEEDS BRADFORD**	682 ft AMSL
6 nm NW of Leeds.		**POL 112·10 071 17·5**

c/s Leeds.   APP 123·75 (all initial calls).   TWR 120·30.   RAD 121·05.
VDF/Hmr. 123·75.   ATIS (Arr) 118·025.
NDB 'LBA' 402·50 (On A/D).
ILS/DME Rwy 32 (323°M) I-LF 110·90.   ILS/DME Rwy 14 (143°M) I-LBF 110·90 .

| N53 51·95 W001 39·63 | **LEEDS BRADFORD** | | | | 682 ft AMSL |

Rwy	Dim(m)	Surface	TORA(m)	LDA(m)	Lighting
09/27	1100x37	Asphalt	09-1004	09-900 †	Thr Rwy
			27-1002	27-954	Thr Rwy PAPI 3°
14/32	2250x46	Concrete	14-2113	14-1802	Ap Thr Rwy RCL PAPI 3·5°
			32-2190	32-1916	Ap Thr Rwy RCL PAPI 3°

† Rwy 09 not available for night landings.

Op hrs: H24. PPR between 2300 and 0700.

Landing Fees: Up to 3 tonnes £6.59 per 0.5 tonne or part, over 3 tonnes £13.18 per tonne or part.

| **Hangarage:** Limited | **Maintenance:** Available. | **Customs:** Available |

Remarks: Operated by Leeds Bradford International Airport Ltd., Leeds Bradford International Airport, Leeds LS19 7TU.

Flights within the Leeds Bradford CTR/CTA are governed by the regulations applicable to Class 'D' Controlled Airspace — see page 2 and chart on page 305.

Non radio aircraft & Microlights not accepted.

Training Flights A booking slot system in operation— slots must be booked by application to ATC Tel. 0113-3913282. The filing of a flight plan does not constitute a booking to carry out intrument training.

Handling All Public Transport aircraft, GA multi-engined aircraft and GA aircraft must designate a handling agent in advance of any flight operating from the main North side apron.

Handling Agents: British Midland Tel: 0113-2508194
                  Servisair Tel: 0113-2503251
                  Nordic Aero Ltd Tel: 0113-2501401 (aircraft with 12 pax or less).

Due to capacity restrictions, all non-based aircraft are requested to co-ordinate parking arrangements with Multiflight, Tel: 0113-2387100.

Minimum Noise Routeings are in force for all jets and aircraft with MTWA in excess of 5700kg.
Aircraft must carry Third party Insurance cover of not less than two million pounds.

Warnings: Southern taxiway restricted to use by aircraft with a wing span of 17 m or less.
Bird hazard - Large flocks of Lapwings on and adjacent to the airfield.
Expect Windshear and turbulence when the surface wind is between 190° and 240° above 20 kt.

Restaurant: Restaurant, buffet and bar.

Car Hire: Avis. 0113-2503880. Hertz. 0113-2504811. Europcar 0113-2509066.

VRPs are listed overleaf.

| **Fuel:** 100LL - Multiflight Ltd. Jet A1 by BP/Conoco - Northside or Multiflight - Southside. | **Tel:** 0113-2509696 Airport. 0113-3913282 ATC. 0113-3913287 Flt Planning. **Fax:** 0113-2505426 Airport (09-1700 Mon-Fri) 01132508131 Flt Planning. |

LEEDS BRADFORD
VISUAL REFERENCE POINTS (VRPs)

VRP	VOR/DME FIX
Dewsbury (DBY) N53 41·50 W001 38·10	Pole Hill R105°/17 nm
Eccup Reservoir (ECP) N53 52·27 W001 32·60	Pole Hill R073°/21 nm
Harrogate (HGT) N53 59·50 W001 31·60	Pole Hill R058°/25 nm
Keighley (KLY) N53 52·00 W001 54·60	Pole Hill R048°/10 nm

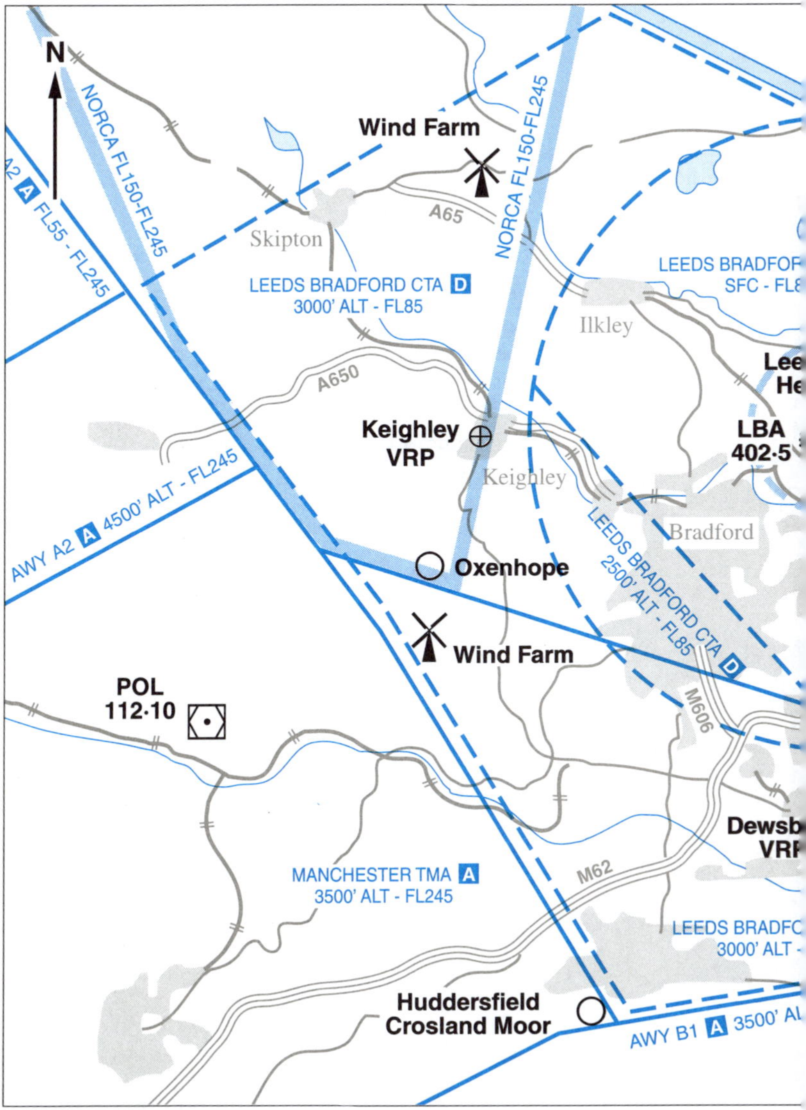

N

NORCA FL150-FL245

A2 **A** FL55 - FL245

Wind Farm

NORCA FL150-FL245

A65

Skipton

LEEDS BRADFORD CTA **D**
3000' ALT - FL85

LEEDS BRADFOR
SFC - FL8

Ilkley

A650

Keighley
VRP

Keighley

Lee
He

LBA
402·5

AWY A2 **A** 4500' ALT - FL245

○ **Oxenhope**

LEEDS BRADFORD CTA **D**
2500' ALT - FL85

Bradford

Wind Farm

POL
112·10

M606

**Dewsb
VRP**

MANCHESTER TMA **A**
3500' ALT - FL245

M62

LEEDS BRADFC
3000' ALT -

Huddersfield
Crosland Moor

AWY B1 **A** 3500' AL

Intentionally Blank

FORD CTR/CTA
VRPs

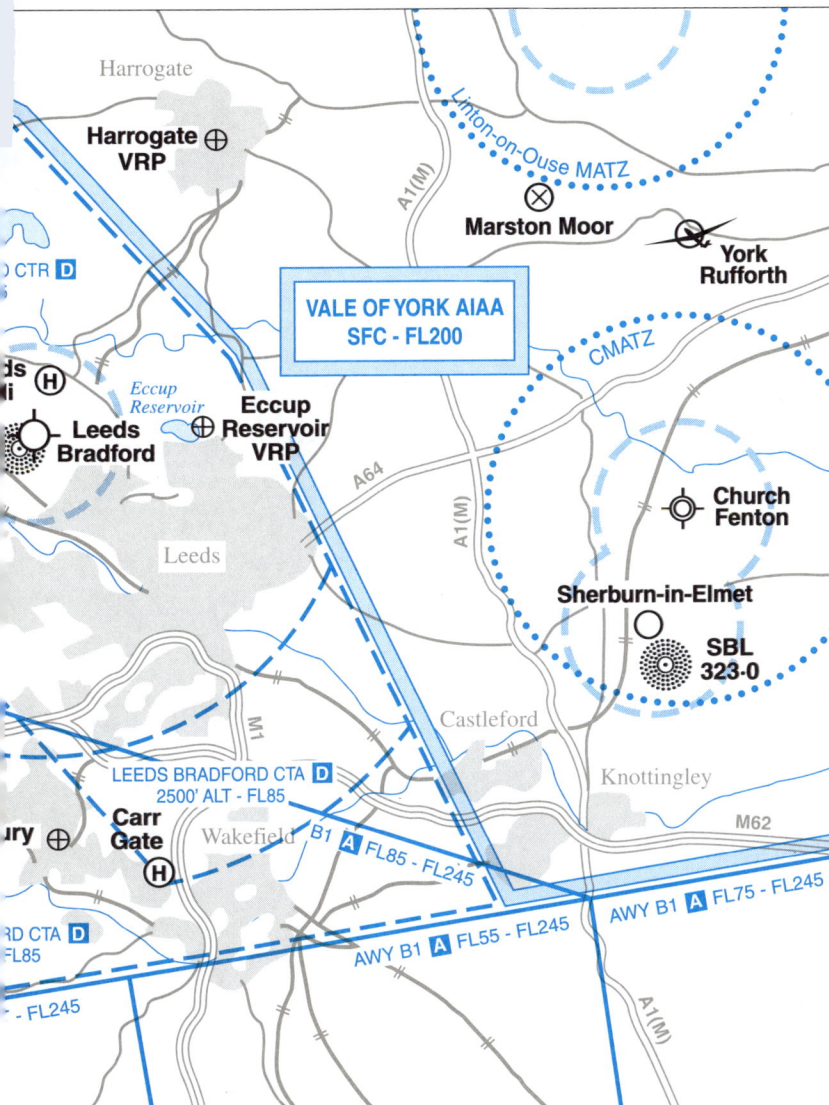

Harrogate

Harrogate VRP ⊕

A1(M)

Linton-on-Ouse MATZ

Marston Moor ⊗

York Rufforth

D CTR **D**

VALE OF YORK AIAA SFC - FL200

CMATZ

ds i ⊕

Leeds Bradford

Eccup Reservoir

Eccup Reservoir VRP ⊕

A64

A1(M)

Church Fenton

Leeds

Sherburn-in-Elmet ○

SBL 323·0

Castleford

M1

Knottingley

LEEDS BRADFORD CTA D
2500' ALT - FL85

M62

Carr Gate (H)

Wakefield

B1 **A** FL85 - FL245

ury ⊕

AWY B1 **A** FL75 - FL245

RD CTA **D**
FL85

AWY B1 **A** FL55 - FL245

A1(M)

- FL245

1 DEC 00

LEEDS BRADFORD CTR/CTA
and VRPs

Government A/D	**EGXE**	1 DEC 00
N54 17·54 W001 32·11	**LEEMING**	132 ft AMSL
7 nm SW of Northallerton.		POL 112·10 036 39
		NEW 114·25 179 45

c/s Zone Radar 127·75 (MATZ/LARS). TWR 120·50 (on request).
ILS Rwy 16 (161°M) 'LI' 110·30.   ATIS Tel: 01677-423041 Ext 7770.

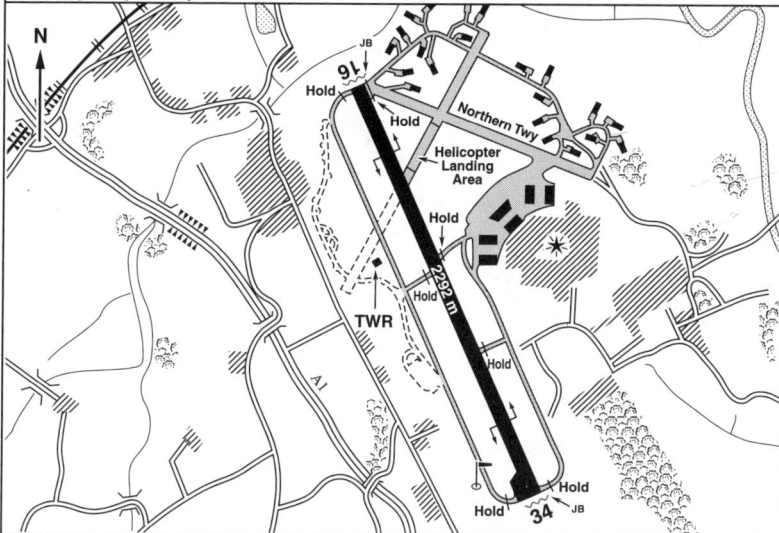

Rwy	Dim(m)	Surface	TORA(m)	LDA(m)	Lighting
16/34	2292x46	Asphalt	16-2292	16-2292	Ap Thr Rwy PAPI
			34-2292	34-2292	Ap Thr Rwy PAPI
					IBn 'LI' Red

Op hrs: PPR (24hrs)	**ATZ active H24**	
Landing Fee: MoD(RAF) Rates.		**Customs:** Nil.
Hangarage: Nil.		**Maintenance:** Nil.

Remarks: RAF Aerodrome, not normally available to civil aircraft. PPR.
High intensity fast jet operations. Station based fast jets have priority take-off; visiting aircraft may be required to break off radar/ILS approach to permit departures.
Arrester gear on Rwy 16/34.

Visual joins are to be at a minimum 1000 ft.

Circuits at 1000' QFE, RH on Rwy 34.

Aerodrome normally active at weekends.

Caution: Rwy 16 — with surface wind 210°– 250° and 10 – 25 kts, windshear may be encountered in the undershoot.

Glider activity outside Op hrs at RAF Dishforth and RAF Catterick at all levels.

Fuel: 100LL, Avtur.	**Tel:** 01677- 423041 Ext 2058/2059
	01677- 423041 Ext 7770 ATIS

N50 48·92 W001 12·42	**LEE-ON-SOLENT**	32 ft AMSL

2 nm NW of Gosport.	SAM 113·35 153 9·9
	MID 114·00 242 26

No Radio. Transit aircraft contact Fleetlands Twr 135·70, if no contact, transmit intentions blind "To all stations" on 135·70.

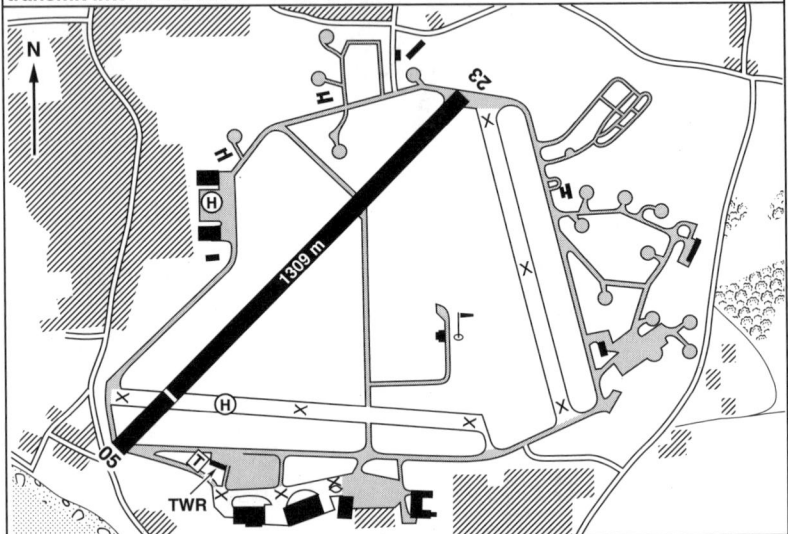

Rwy	Dim(m)	Surface	TORA(m)	LDA(m)	Lighting
05/23	1309x46	Asphalt	Unlicensed		Rwy

Op hrs: By arrangement.

Hangarage: Nil	Maintenance: Nil	Customs: Nil

Remarks: Operated by Hampshire Police Air Support Unit, Lee-on-Solent Airfield, Argus Gate, Broome Way, Lee-on-Solent, Hampshire PO14 9YA.
This unlicensed airfield is *strictly* PPR and is normally only available to civil aircraft in connection with Police operations or having business with Bristow Helicopters Ltd.
Operators are required to provide evidence of a minimum of £7,500,000 crown indemnity insurance before landing at this airfield.
Specific operating procedures apply to this airfield. Visiting pilots are required to obtain a comprehensive briefing either in writing or by phone before departing for Lee.

Warnings: Part of the airfield lies within the Fleetlands ATZ.
Police aircraft and helicopters and SAR helicopters operate H24.
Helicopter Test flying takes place.
Light aircraft and glider flying take place during daylight hours.
First 154m Rwy 05 sterile for landing.

Due to the Police and SAR operations and with the possibilty of intense gliding operations, pilots transiting the area are requested to avoid the airfield by 2 nm.

Fuel: Nil	Tel: 01705-551714
	Fax: 01705-553872

N52 36·47 W001 01·92   **LEICESTER**   469 ft AMSL

4 nm ESE of Leicester.	**HON 113·65 062 27·6** **DTY 116·40 010 25·8**

c/s Leicester Radio 122·125 A/G.
NDB 'LE' 383·50 (On A/D range 10 nm**).**

Changes: New Twy link by Control Twr

Rwy	Dim(m)	Surface	TORA(m)	LDA(m)	Lighting
04/22	490x18	Asphalt	04/22-490	04/22-490	Nil.
10/28	940x30	Asphalt	10/28-940	10/28-940	Thr Rwy APAPI 3·25°
15/33†	495x18	Asphalt	15/33-495	15/33-495	Nil.
06/24	335x30	Grass	06/24-335	06/24-335	Nil.
16/34	418x30	Grass	16/34-418	16/34-418	Nil.
					IBn 'LE' Gn

† Rwy 15/33 used for short term aircraft parking when not in use.

Op hrs: PPR. 0900-1700 daily, and by arrangement.

Landing Fees: Singles £8.50. Twins £25.00. incl VAT. Weekends only - all landing fees £6 incl VAT or free with fuel uplift of 30 litres or more.
Parking Fees: Singles £7.50 per day. Twins £12.50 per day. incl VAT.

Hangarage: Limited   **Maintenance:** Available   **Customs:** By arrangement.

Remarks: Operated by Leicestershire Aero Club Ltd, Leicester Airport, Gartree Rd, Leicester. LE2 2FG. Aircraft welcome outside the above hours, but telephone first. Variable circuits. Non-radio aircraft must obtain prior clearance.
Helicopters to join circuit not above 600ft.
Aircraft departing from Rwy 28 are to climb straight ahead to 1000' QFE before turning.

Restaurant: Club facilities and Bar meals - closed Mondays.
Taxis: ABC Taxis Tel: 0116-2555111. Oadby Express Taxis Tel: 0116-2710088.

Fuel: 100LL	**Tel:** 0116-259 2360/3484 **Fax:** 0116-259 2712

N60 11·53 W001 14·62	**LERWICK (Tingwall)**		43 ft AMSL

4·5 nm W of Lerwick.   **SUM 117·30 011 18·7**

c/s Tingwall Radio 122·60 A/G.
NDB 'TL' 376·0 (On A/D).

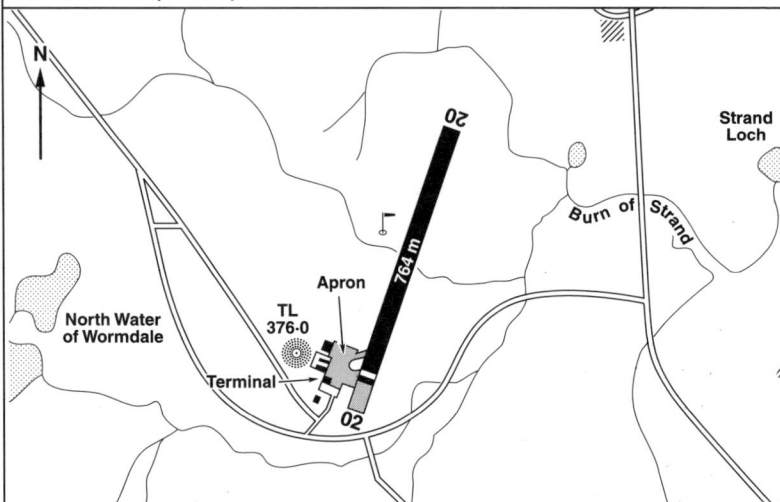

Rwy	Dim(m)	Surface	TORA(m)	LDA(m)	Lighting
02/20	764x18	Asphalt	02-764 20-764	02-744 20-764	Ap Thr Rwy APAPI 4° Thr Rwy APAPI 4°

Op hrs: PPR. Mon-Fri 0900-1700; Sat 1000-1200.

Landing Fees: Per 0·5 tonne or part:- up to 3 tonnes £4.20; 3 – 20 tonnes £8.40
Parking Fees: £1.50 per tonne or part thereof for each 24 hrs or part thereof.
Passenger Supplement: £1.90 per arriving passenger.
All fees subject to VAT at standard rate.

Hangarage: Nil   **Maintenance:** Nil   **Customs:** Nil

Remarks: Operated by the Infrastructure Services Department of the Shetland
Islands Council, Grantfield, Lerwick, Shetland ZE1 0NT. PPR.
Licensed aerodrome.

High ground 449 ft aal, 492 ft amsl, 1·25 nm to NW.

Fuel: 100LL	**Tel:** 01595-840306 Aerodrome. 01595-744866 Operator. **Fax:** 01595-744869 Operator.

N56 22·37 W002 52·11	**LEUCHARS (MEDA)**	38 ft AMSL
3·5 nm NW of St. Andrews.		SAB 112·50 328 35·7
		PTH 110·40 111 17·1

Leuchars RAD 126·50 (MATZ/LARS). TWR/GND 122·10. Director 123·30.
TACAN 'LUK' 110·50 (On A/D).
ILS Rwy 27 (268°M) 'LU' 108·70.

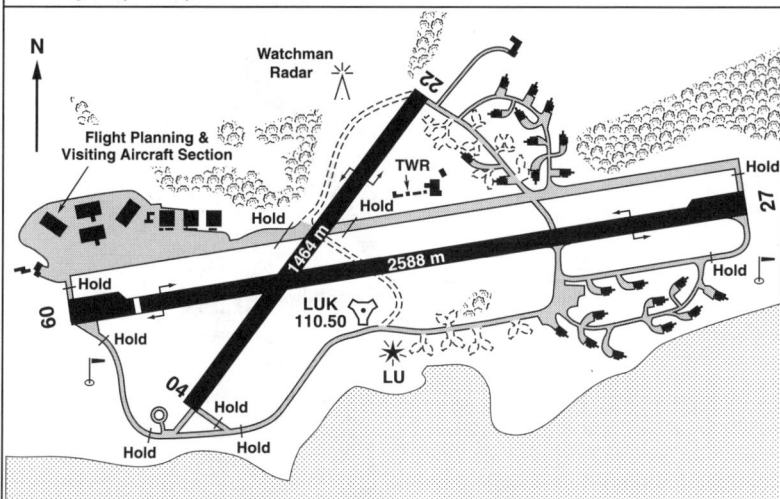

Rwy	Dim(m)	Surface	TORA(m)	LDA(m)	Lighting
09/27	2588x46	Asph/ Concrete	09-2588 27-2588	09-2318 27-2588	Ap Thr Rwy PAPI 3° Ap Thr Rwy PAPI 2·5°
04/22	1464x46	Asphalt	04-1464 22-1464	04-1464 22-1464	Thr Rwy PAPI 3° Ap Thr Rwy PAPI 3° IBn 'LU' Red

Op hrs: PPR (24 hrs)	**ATZ active H24**
Landing Fee: MoD(RAF) Rates.	**Customs:** Nil
Hangarage: Nil	**Maintenance:** Nil

Remarks: RAF Military Emergency Diversion Aerodrome, not normally available to civil aircraft.

Arrester gear Rwy 09/27 396 m from each end; Rwy 22 396 m from Rwy 22 threshold.

Caution: Between 2000 ft and 2500 ft north side of Rwy 27, there is a significant dip in the runway.

RADHAZ - Helicopters are not hover or taxi within the vicinity of the Watchman radar Tower (W of Rwy 22 thld) above 66 ft agl.

Increased bird hazard 30 minutes either side of sunset September-March.

Light aircraft/helicopter activity with non-standard circuits up to 800ft. **Caution:** Light aircraft go around on live side.

All aircraft are to avoid St Andrews (SE/3·5 nm) by 2000 ft/2 nm.

Fuel: 100LL, Avtur.	**Tel:** 01334-839471 Ext 2055
	01334-839471 Ext 7829 ATIS

N54 02·95 W001 15·17	**LINTON-ON-OUSE**	53 ft AMSL
9 nm NW of York.		**POL** 112·10 064 35·2
	·	**OTR** 113·90 303 45·8

Linton APP/Zone 129·15 (MATZ/LARS). TWR/GND 122·10. A/G 129·15 (Gliders) TACAN 'LOO' 109·00 (On A/D). ILS Rwy 04 (037°M) 'LOB' 110·70 (LLZ 037°, Rwy QFU 036°). ILS Rwy 22 (219°M) 'LOA' 110·70 (LLZ 219°, Rwy QFU 216°).

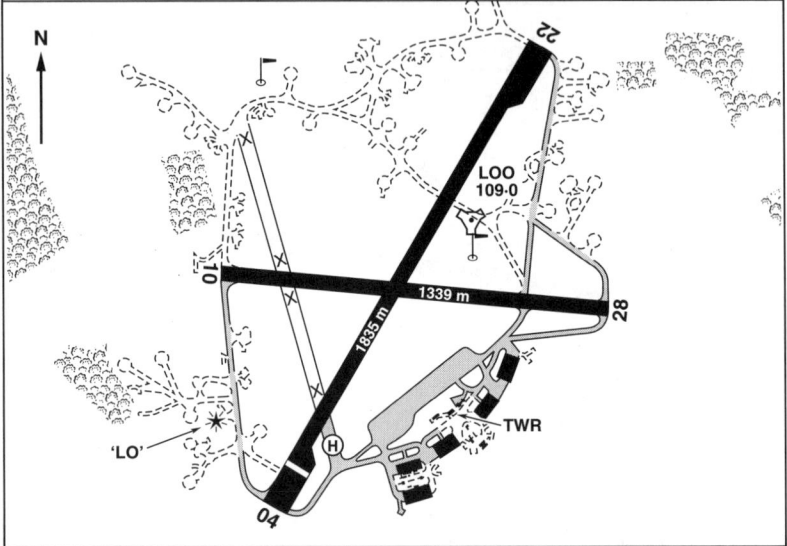

Rwy	Dim(m)	Surface	TORA(m)	LDA(m)	Lighting
04/22	1835x46	Asphalt	04-1835	04-1681	Ap Thr Rwy PAPI
			22-1835	22-1833	Ap Thr Rwy PAPI
10/28	1339x46	Asphalt	10-1339	10-1339	Thr Rwy PAPI
			28-1339	28-1339	Thr Rwy PAPI
					IBn 'LO' Red

Op hrs: PPR. Mon-Thu 0730-1715; Fri 0730-1700.
     ATZ active H24 Mon-Thu; 0700-2359 Fri-Sun.

Landing Fee: MoD(RAF) Rates	**Customs:** Nil
Hangarage: Nil	**Maintenance:** Nil

Remarks: RAF Aerodrome. High Intensity Flying Training School. Variable circuits, heights and direction, RH on 22 and 28.
Two runways may be in use at same time.

Glider activity evenings Mon-Fri, and HJ Sat. and Sun.

For MATZ penetration contact Linton Zone 129·15 at least 15 nm range.

Caution: Rwy 10 only available for landing in an emergency. Emergency aircraft are to exercise caution due to trees within the final approach area up to 143 ft amsl.

Fuel: 100LL (limited). Avtur. ¢.	**Tel:** 01347 848261 Ext 7511 ATC
	01347 848261 Ext 7491/2 Ops
	01347 848261 Ext 7467 ATIS

N52 10·00 W000 09·23	**LITTLE GRANSDEN**	250 ft AMSL
5 nm SE of St Neots.		**BKY 116·25 328 13**

Little Gransden Radio 130·85 A/G.

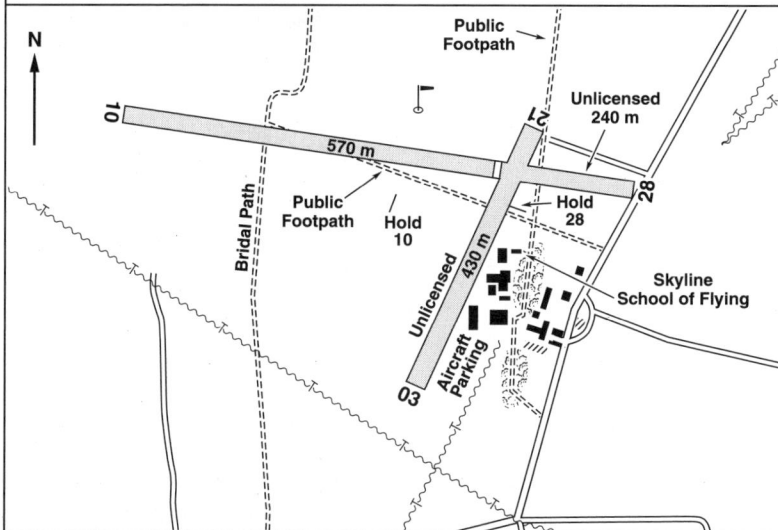

Rwy	Dim(m)	Surface	TORA(m)	LDA(m)	Lighting
10/28	570x18	Grass	10-810	10-570	Nil.
			28-810	28-570	Nil.
03/21	430x23	Grass	Unlicensed		Nil.

Op hrs: PPR. Mon-Sat 0830-1830, Sun and PHs 0900-1500.

Landing Fee: £5.00 (no charge with fuel uplift of 50 litres or more).

Hangarage: Available	**Maintenance:** Available	**Customs:** 24 hrs PNR.

Remarks: Licensed airfield operated by Skyline School of Flying Ltd. Not licensed for public transport flights. Available to aircraft of less than 1200 kg MTOW or 250 hp. Visiting aircraft welcome on prior telephone briefing of noise abatement procedures. No brief, **No** landing permission given. Non radio aircraft strictly PPR.
Circuits at 800' aal; LH on 03 and 28, RH on 10 and 21.
Joining Procedures: No dead-side. All aircraft to join downwind to the south 10/28 or west 03/21 of the aerodrome. Rwy 03/21 for experienced pilots only.
Power cables cross threshold of Rwys 03 and 10 at 150m out.
A Public bridleway crosses Rwy 10/28.
Pilots operating aircraft equipped with constant speed propellers should, at the safest opportunity, set cruise climb configuration to reduce noise.
Avoid overflying the GRANSDENS, GAMLINGAY, HATLEY ESTATE AND WARESLEY.
Gransden Lodge Gliding Aerodrome is 1·4 nm to the NE, cables up to 3000', do not overfly.
Mast 722' aal 972' amsl 244°/4·2 nm.
Car Hire: Budget 01223-323838.   **Taxis:** Derek's 01767-260430.
Local B & B: Mrs Cox 01767-677365, Mrs Bygraves 01767-677459.

Fuel: 100LL.	**Tel/Fax:** 01767-651950 Skyline School of Flying Ltd.
	Fax: 01767-651157 A/D Owner/ Hangar.

N52 51·65 E000 54·57	**LITTLE SNORING**	196 ft AMSL
3 nm NE of Fakenham.	**CLN 114·55 357 61.**	**OTR 113·90 149 62**
		NH 371·50 30 20·4

c/s Little Snoring Radio 118·125 – Not always manned.
Recommend contact Marham APP 124·15 on weekdays.

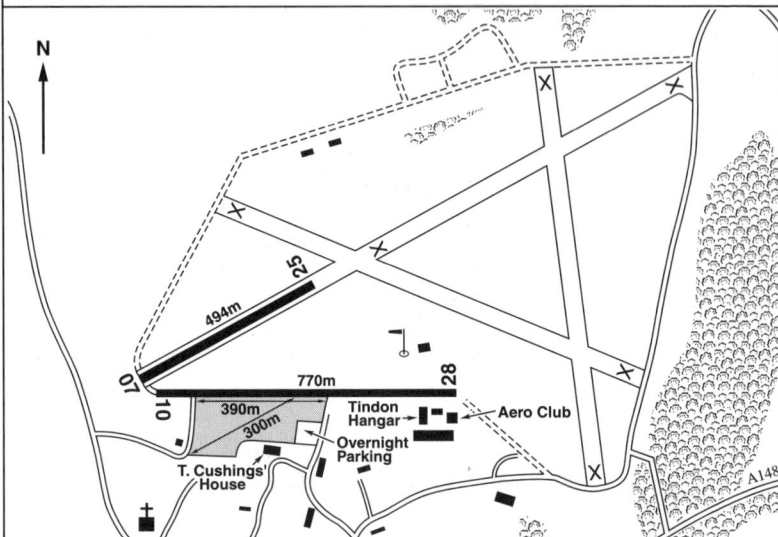

Rwy	Dim(m)	Surface	TORA(m)	LDA(m)	Lighting
10/28	770x16	Asphalt/Concrete	Unlicensed		Nil.
07/25	494x23	Asphalt/Concrete	Unlicensed		Nil.

Grass Landing Area depicted above is for use by tail-wheel aeroplanes only.

Op hrs: SR–SS

Landing Fee: Donations for maintenance in box provided near club house please.

Hangarage: Nil   **Maintenance:** Tindon Engineering Ltd   **Customs:** Nil

Remarks: Operated by McAully Flying Group. PPR.
Visiting aircraft welcomed at owner's risk only.
Land and take-off on runways only.
Circuits LH at 800 ft aal.

Restaurant: Nil.

Taxi: Courtesy Cabs Tel: 01328-855500

Fuel: 100LL - weekdays 09 -1700.	**Tel:** 01328-878470 (Mr. T. Cushing)
Available from Tindon Engineering Ltd only.	01328-878809 (Tindon Engineering Ltd)

N52 14·57 W000 21·85	**LITTLE STAUGHTON**	225 ft AMSL
4 nm WNW of St. Neots.		CFD 116·50 047 14
		BKY 116·25 320 22

c/s Little Staughton Radio 123·925 A/G. – Not always manned, make 'Blind' calls.

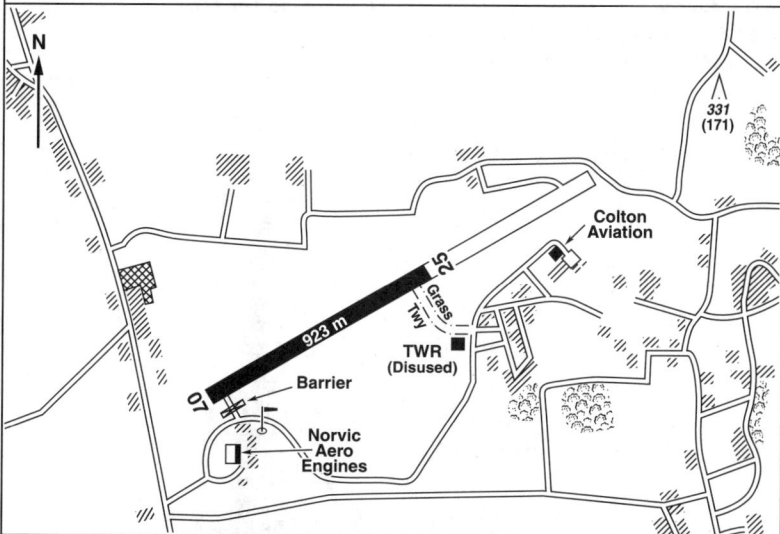

Rwy	Dim(m)	Surface	TORA(m)	LDA(m)	Lighting
07/25	923x46	Asphalt	Unlicensed		Nil

500m starter extension available for take-off on Rwy 25.

Op hrs: PPR. SUMMER: 0900-2000 daily. WINTER: 0900-SS daily.

Landing Fee: Singles £5. Multis £10. No charge if in for maintenance.

Hangarage: Limited	**Maintenance:** Available	**Customs:** 24 hrs PNR

Remarks: Operated by Colton Aviation Limited (Maintenance and Aircraft Painting/Trimming). Aerodrome available on prior permission.

Circuits RH on 07, LH on 25.

Visiting aircraft should proceed to Colton Aviation.

Warnings: Mast, 171 ft agl., 331 ft amsl, 1200m from threshold on approach to Rwy 25.

Taxiway leads to the asphalt perimeter road which is also used by motor vehicles.

Restaurant: Pub in village.

Car Hire: National, Bedford - 7 miles, Tel: 01234-269565.
Anglian, St. Neots 01480-72232.

Fuel: 100LL	**Tel:** 01234-376775 or 376705
	Fax: 01234-376544

Robert Pooley ©

N53 20·02 W002 50·98	**LIVERPOOL**	81 ft AMSL
6·5 nm SE of Liverpool.		MCT 113·55 273 21
		WAL 114·10 115 11

c/s Liverpool   APP 119·85.   TWR 118·10.   RAD 119·85, 118·45 (as directed).
ATIS 124·325.   NDB 'LPL' 349·5 (271°M/3·88nm to Thr 27).
ILS/DME Rwy 27 (271°M) I-LQ 111·75.
LLZ/DME Rwy 09 (091°M) LVR 111·75.

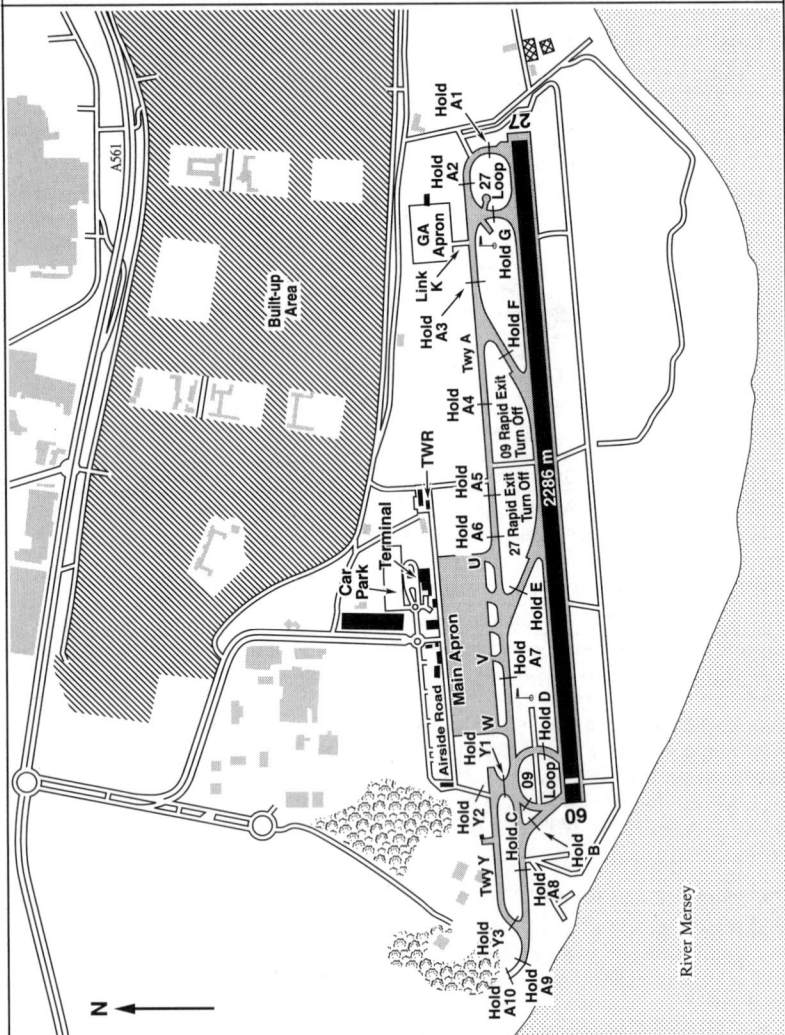

Robert Pooley ©

N53 20·02 W002 50·98			**LIVERPOOL**		81 ft AMSL
Rwy	**Dim(m)**	**Surface**	**TORA(m)**	**LDA(m)**	**Lighting**
09/27	2286x46	Asphalt	09-2286	09-2225	Ap Thr Rwy RCL PAPI 3°
			27-2286	27-2286	Ap Thr Rwy RCL PAPI 3°

Op hrs: H24.	**Customs:** Available

Landing Fee: Single engined fixed wing aircraft up to 2 tonnes (inc 24 hrs parking), fee paid at time of landing: £17.45 + VAT.

Hangarage and Maintenance:
Keenair (North West) Ltd. 0151-427-3275/7449. Telex: 629131.

Remarks: Operated by Liverpool Airport Plc.
Flights within Manchester CTR/CTA and Liverpool CTR are governed by the regulations applicable to Class 'D' Controlled Airspace — see page 2.
Note: Manchester TMA (base 3500' ALT) is Class 'A' Controlled Airspace.

Noise Abatement Procedures and Helicopter Operations – see overleaf.

Liverpool Entry/Exit Lanes, VRPs – see page 319 and page 359 for VAD/VRPs Chart for Manchester CTR.

Aerodrome is PPR for non-radio aircraft and for aircraft not based at Liverpool. PPR through a Handling Agent. ATC will not grant permission. Mandatory handling for all visiting or non-based aircraft.

Pilots are to 'book out' by telephoning details to ATC. 'Booking out' by radio will not be accepted.

All training flights PPR from ATC and are subject to availability of training slots.

Variable circuits. Overhead joins not available. Join circuit as instructed by ATC.

High visibility clothing mandatory on the apron area.

All aircraft are to enter the apron through taxiway Victor.

Aircraft repositioning on the apron must do so under Marshaller's guidance.

GA Apron is not part of the licensed aerodrome, limited to aircraft of 5700 kg or less.

All aircraft of less than 5700 kg not requiring Customs and/or Immigration can expect parking on the GA apron.

Holding point Golf available to aircraft with a MTWA of 5700 kg or less. Not available at night or in Low Visibility Procedures.

Handling Agents:

Liverpool Aviation Services Ltd, Tel: 0151-486 6161, Fax: 0151-486 5151,
Radio: c/s LAS Liverpool 131·75.

Reed Aviation, Tel: 0151-448 0826, Fax: 0151-448 0852,
Radio: c/s Reed Liverpool 122·35.

Servisair, Tel: 0151-486 5421, Fax: 0151-448 1427,
Radio: c/s Servisair Liverpool 130·60.

Warnings: Positively identify runway in use before committing to landing.
Beware of the Restricted Area R311, 5 nm SW of aerodrome.

Exercise caution when leaving the main apron not to enter the rapid exit turn-off when taxiing to Rwy 09 or 27.

Restaurant: Airport Restaurant and refreshments available.
Car Hire: Hertz. Tel: 0151-427 5131. Europcar. Tel: 0151-448 0020.

Fuel: 100LL, Jet A1.

Tel: 0151-288 4300 ATC. 0151-288 4000 Administration.
      0151-288 4302 Flight Planning.
Fax: 0151-288 4610 Flt Plans. 0151-288 4004 Admin. 0151-288 4603 Apron Control

Noise Abatement Procedures and Helicopter Operations

Noise Abatement Procedures:

Arrivals: Inbound aircraft, other than light aircraft flying under VFR or SVFR shall maintain at least 1500 ft aal unil cleared to descend for landing. Aircraft approaching without assistance from ILS or radar must not fly lower than the ILS glidepath.

Departures: Rwy 27 – All aircraft of more than 5730 kg MTWA shall climb straight ahead to 1000 ft aal before turning.

Rwy 09 – Initial turn onto outbound heading shall be commenced as soon as practicable, but not below 500 ft aal and not before passing the end of the runway.

Helicopter Operations

Arrivals: ATC will either select the appropriate threshold or instruct the helicopter to make an approach to the runway. if instructed to approach the runway, the helicopter is to turn on to a final approach and arrange the descent to flare to ground or hover taxiing speed in the fixed wing runway touchdown zone.

Parallel Taxiway Arrivals: Approach to the parallel taxiway is permitted only when:

a. The runway is closed, and;

b. The helicopter is operating on a VFR clearance and;

c. There are no aircraft, vehicles or personnel on the taxiway.

Departures: These will be made from the runway, Aiming Points or parallel taxiway as selected by ATC.

Parallel Taxiway Departures: Helicopter departures from the parallel taxiway may be permitted by ATC subject to the following conditions:

a. The helicopter is operating on a VFR clearance;

b. No other aircraft or vehicle is operating on that portion of the parallel taxiway or its associated holdIng points ahead of the helicopter's departure point;

c. No other aircraft has been cleared to land or take-off or exercise a 'go-around' from the runway. The helicopter will be permitted to depart once the landing aircraft has completed its landing run and has slowed to taxiing speed. Pilots must ensure that they do not overfly the previously landed traffic on or exiting the runway.

> Departures from the parallel taxiway will not be given in a direction opposing that of the operational runway. Timed vortex wake separations will be applied as if departing from the runway.

Taxiing: Hover (or ground taxiing if applicable) is required to/from the parking area via designated taxiways.

Training: Helicopter training is only permitted to/from the runway. Helicopters flying circuits to the runway must, as far as possible, arrange their circuits to reflect these being flown by fixed wing aircraft. Pilots must inform ATC if periods in excess of 30 seconds are required on the runway between touchdown and departures.

Local Flying Area and Entry/Exit Lanes

Flights without compliance with IFR requirements may take place within the Liverpool Local Flying Area and the Neston and Mersey Entry/Exit Lanes, subject to the following conditions:

- Prior clearance must be obtained from Liverpool ATC;
- Aircraft to remain below cloud and in sight of surface;
- Maximum altitude 1500 ft, Liverpool QNH;
- Minimum flight visibility of not less than 3 km.

Note: SVFR clearances will not be issued to fixed wing aircraft wishing to depart Liverpool if the reported weather conditions are: Visibility 1800m or less, or the cloud ceiling is less than 600 ft.

LIVERPOOL CTR / MANCHESTER CTA
VISUAL REFERENCE POINTS

VRP	VOR/VOR	VOR/NDB	VOR/DME FIX
Aintree Racecourse N53 28·60 W002 56·58	WAL R058 MCT R291	MCT R291 WHI 332°M	WAL R058/9 nm
Burtonwood N53 25·00 W002 38·28	WAL R090 POL R229	WAL R090 WHI 002°M	WAL R090/18 nm MCT 290/14 nm
Chester N53 11·70 W002 50·68	WAL R144 MCT R250	WAL R144 WHI 279°M	WAL R144/16 nm MCT 250/23 nm
Kirkby N53 28·80 W002 52·90	WAL R065 MCT R293	MCT R293 WHI 337°M	WAL R065/10 nm MCT 293/23 nm
Neston N53 17·50 W003 03·60	WAL R161 MCT R267	WAL R161 WHI 297°M	WAL R161/7 nm MCT R267/29 nm
Oulton Park N53 10·57 W002 36·80	MCT R234 WAL R129	MCT R234 LPL 162°M	WAL R1291/23 nm MCT R234/17 nm
Seaforth N53 27·68 W003 02·08	MCT R288 WAL R046	MCT R288 WHI 323° M	WAL R046/5 nm
Stretton Aerodrome N53 20·77 W002 31·58	WAL R102 POL R217	MCT R271 WHI 024°M	WAL R102/22 nm MCT R271/9 nm

See also VAD/VRP Chart for Manchester CTR at page 359.

Intentionally Blank

N51 30·32 E000 03·27	**LONDON (City Airport)**	17 ft AMSL

6 nm E of the City of London.	**LAM** 115·60 208 9·5
	BIG 115·10 009 10·5

City APP/Thames Radar 132·70. City TWR 118·075, 118·40. City Radar 128·025.
NDB 'LCY' 322·0 (On A/D). ILS/DME Rwy 10 (097°M) LST 111·15 (5·5° GP).
ILS/DME Rwy 28 (277°M) LSR 111·15 (5·5° GP).   **ATIS 136·35**

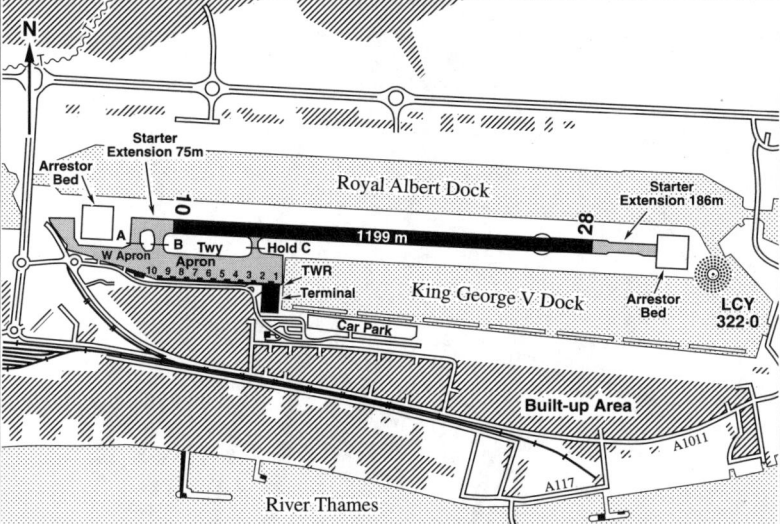

Rwy	Dim(m)	Surface	TORA(m)	LDA(m)	Lighting
10/28	1199x30	Concrete	10-1199	10-1199	Ap Thr Rwy PAPI 5·5°
			28-1199	28-1199	Ap Thr Rwy PAPI 5·5°

Op hrs: Mon-Fri 0630-2230, Sat 0630-1230, Sun 1230-2230, PHs 0900-2230.

Landing Fee: On application	**Customs:** Available
Hangarage: Nil	**Maintenance:** Limited

Remarks: Operated by London City Airport Limited. PPR. Flights within the London City CTR are subject to the regulations applicable to Class 'D' Controlled Airspace — see page 2. The controlling authority for the CTR is Thames Radar on 132·70.
Non radio aircraft not accepted. Use of the airport by helicopters and flights for recreation not permitted. Training flights not normally permitted.
To minimise noise disturbance aircraft should use runway starter extensions and climb straight ahead to a minimum of 1000 ft aal. before turning on track, unless otherwise instructed by ATC.
Aircraft approaching without assistance from ILS shall follow a descent path which will ensure that the aircraft will at no time descend below the approach path that would be followed by an aircraft using the ILS glide path.

Restaurant: Buffet Bar.

Fuel: 100LL, Jet A1.	**Tel:** 020-7646 0205 ATC. 020-7646 0241 Ops.
	Fax: 020-7511 1040 Admin. 020-7511 0248 Ops.

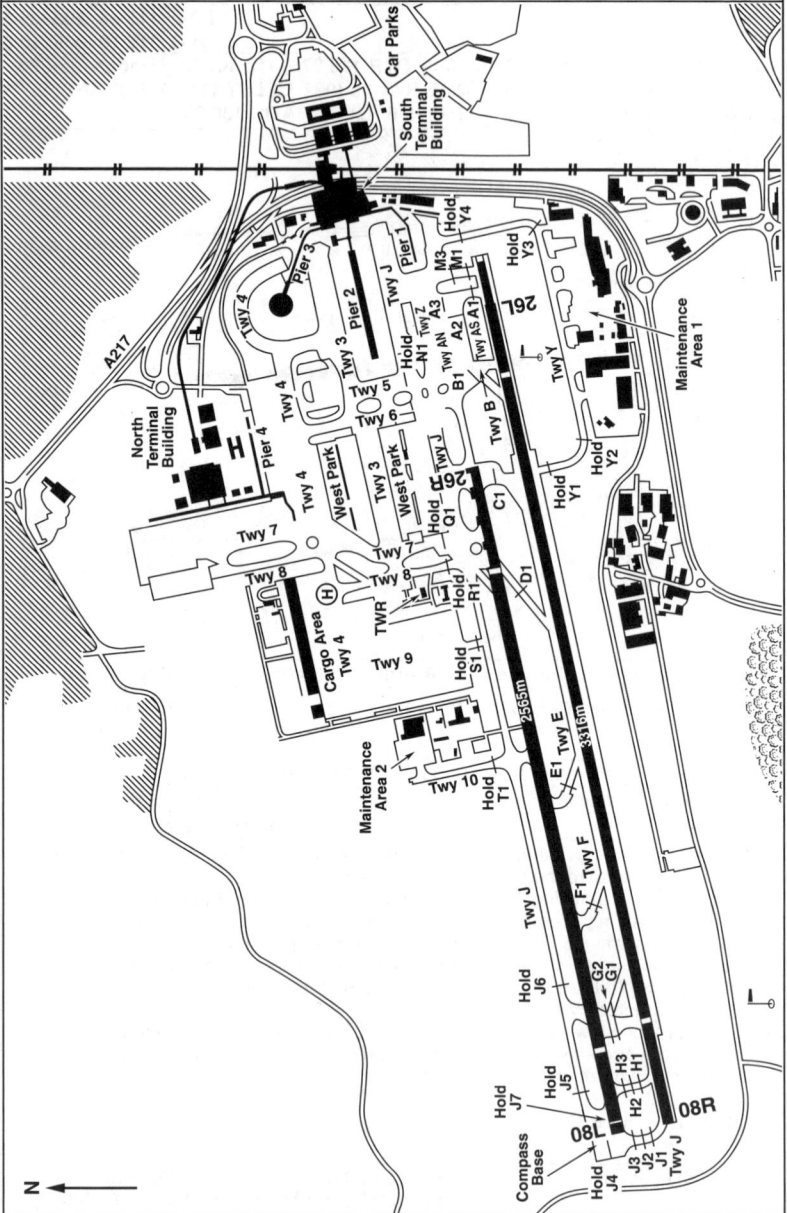

Car Parks

South Terminal Building

Pier 1

Pier 2

Pier 3

Twy 4

A217

Twy J

Hold Y4

Hold Y3

M3
M1

26L

Hold Y4

N1 Twy Z

Twy AN A3
A2

Twy AS A1

B1

Hold
Twy Y

Maintenance Area 1

North Terminal Building

Pier 4

Twy 4

Twy 5

Twy 6

Twy B

Hold Y2

Twy 4

West Park

Twy 3

West Park

26R

Hold
Q1

C1

Hold Y1

Twy 7

Twy 7

D1

Twy 8

Twy 8

R1

TWR

S1

Hold

Cargo Area
Twy 4

(H)

Twy 9

Maintenance Area 2

Twy 10

Hold T1

2565m

E1 Twy E

3315m

F1 Twy F

Twy J

Hold J6

G2
G1

Hold J5

H3
H2
H1

Hold J7

08L

08R

Compass Base

Hold J4

J3
J2
J1
Twy J

Z ←

N51 08·88 W000 11·42	**LONDON (Gatwick)**	196 ft AMSL

5 nm S of Redhill.	**OCK 115·30 138 13·2**
	BIG 115·10 223 13·6

APP c/s Director 126·825. TWR 124·225. RAD As directed.

GND 121·80 0530-2330

Delivery 121·95 0630-2200, initial call for departing aircraft, other times call GND.

ATIS Gatwick Information **136·525.**

NDB 'GY' 365 (082°/4·23 nm to Thr 08R/L).

NDB 'GE' 338 (262°/3·95nm to Thr 26L/R).

ILS/DME Rwy 08R (082°M) I-GG 110·90.

ILS/DME Rwy 26L (262°M) I-WW 110·90.

Rwy	Dim(m)	Surface	TORA(m)	LDA(m)	Lighting
08R/26L	3316x46	Asph/Con	08R-3159	08R-2766	Ap Thr Rwy PAPI 3°
			26L-3255	26L-2831	Ap Thr Rwy PAPI 3°
#08L/26R	2565x45	Asph/Con	08L-2565	08L-2243	Ap Thr Rwy PAPI 3°
			26R-2565	26R-2148	Ap Thr Rwy PAPI 3°

#Rwy 08L/26R is a non-instrument runway and will only be used when 08R/26L is not available. At no time are the two runways used simultaneously.

Op hrs: H24.

Landing Fees: BAA Plc Airports Rates	**Customs:** H24.

Hangarage: Limited	**Maintenance:** Available	**Met:** H24. 01344-856267

Remarks: Operated by Gatwick Airport Ltd. Flights within Gatwick CTR/CTA are subject to the regulations applicable to Class 'D' Controlled Airspace —see pages 2 and 6.

Use by Executive and Private aircraft is subject to the following conditions:

PPR (Mandatory Requirement not more than 10 days and not less than 24 hrs before intended movement).

Operators must notify the following details of each flight in advance either to Airport Co-ordination Ltd (office hrs) or (to their nominated handling agent who will obtain the PPR). Tel: 01293- 569233, Fax: 01293-516709, or at all other times to Apron Control, Tel: 01293-503089, AFTN: EGKKYDYX. Fax: 01293-505149.

1. Aircraft type, registration and operator.

2. Point of origin and destination.

3. Date/time of ETA and ETD Gatwick.

4. Nominated Handling Agent (Mandatory for domestic and international flights).

Operators are advised that their requested slot time may not always be available and the nearest available slot time will be offered by Apron Control.

Helicopter Facilities: A helicopter alighting pad is situated at the junction of the northern end of Taxiway 8 and Taxiway 4 (day use only).

Car Hire: Godfrey Davis 01293-31062. Hertz 01293-30555. Avis 01293-29721.

VRPs are listed overleaf

Fuel: Jet A1. Carnets. BP Diners, Multi-Service	**Tel:** 01293-535353 Airport; 575278 NATS Ltd 01293-575278/575280 FBU. **Fax:**01293-505093 Airport; 575204 NATS

LONDON (Gatwick)
VISUAL REFERENCE POINTS (VRPs)

VOR	VOR/VOR	VOR/NDB	VOR/DME
Billingshurst N51 00·87 W000 27·00	MID R113 GWC R054	MID R113 Gatwick GY 220°M	MID 113°/7 nm
Dorking N51 13·62 W000 20·10	BIG R249 LON R166	BIG R249 Gatwick GY 356°M	BIG 249°/15 nm LON 166°/16 nm
Guildford N51 14·37 W000 35·10	MID R012 BIG R261	MID R012 Gatwick GY 306°M	MID 012°/11 nm
Handcross N51 03·17 W000 12·13	MID R094 SFD R328	MID R094 Gatwick GE 220°M	MID 094°/16 nm MAY 284°/12 nm
Haywards Heath N51 00·45 W000 05·77	MID R102 SFD R334	MID R102 Gatwick GE 189°M	MID 102°/20 nm MAY 269°/8 nm
Tunbridge Wells N51 08·00 E000 15·90	BIG R147 DET R234	BIG R147 Gatwick GE 101°M	BIG 147°/15 nm MAY 042°/9 nm

GATWICK CONTROL ZONE

The regulations applicable to Class 'D' Controlled Airspace are given at
pages 2- 6.

Special VFR Flights
Special VFR clearances for flights within the Gatwick CTR may be requested and
will be given whenever traffic conditions permit. These flights will be subject to the
general conditions laid down for Special VFR flights and will normally only be
given to aircraft which carry RTF including the appropriate frequencies.

The use of Special VFR clearances is intended to be confined to the following
types of flight:
(a) Light aircraft which cannot comply with full IFR requirements and wish to
proceed to or from Gatwick Airport.
(b) Light aircraft which cannot comply with full IFR requirements and wish to transit
the Gatwick CTR.

Special VFR clearances to operate within the Gatwick CTR for the purpose of
proceeding to/from the Airport will not be granted to fixed wing aircraft if the
reported visibility at the Airport is less than 3 km or the reported cloud ceiling less
than 1,000 ft.

Aircraft may be given a radar service whilst within the Zone if, due to the traffic
situation, ATC considers it advisable. It will remain the responsibility of the pilot to
maintain flight conditions which will enable him to determine his flight path and to
keep clear of obstacles, and to ensure that he is able to comply with the relevant
low flying restrictions of Rule 5 of the Rules of the Air Regulations 1996, with
particular regard to Rule 5(1) (a) (i). Pilots must inform the Radar Controller if
compliance entails a change of heading or height.

Special VFR flights may be subject to delay. Pilots should, therefore, always
ensure that they have adequate fuel reserves for diversion to another aerodrome if
necessary.

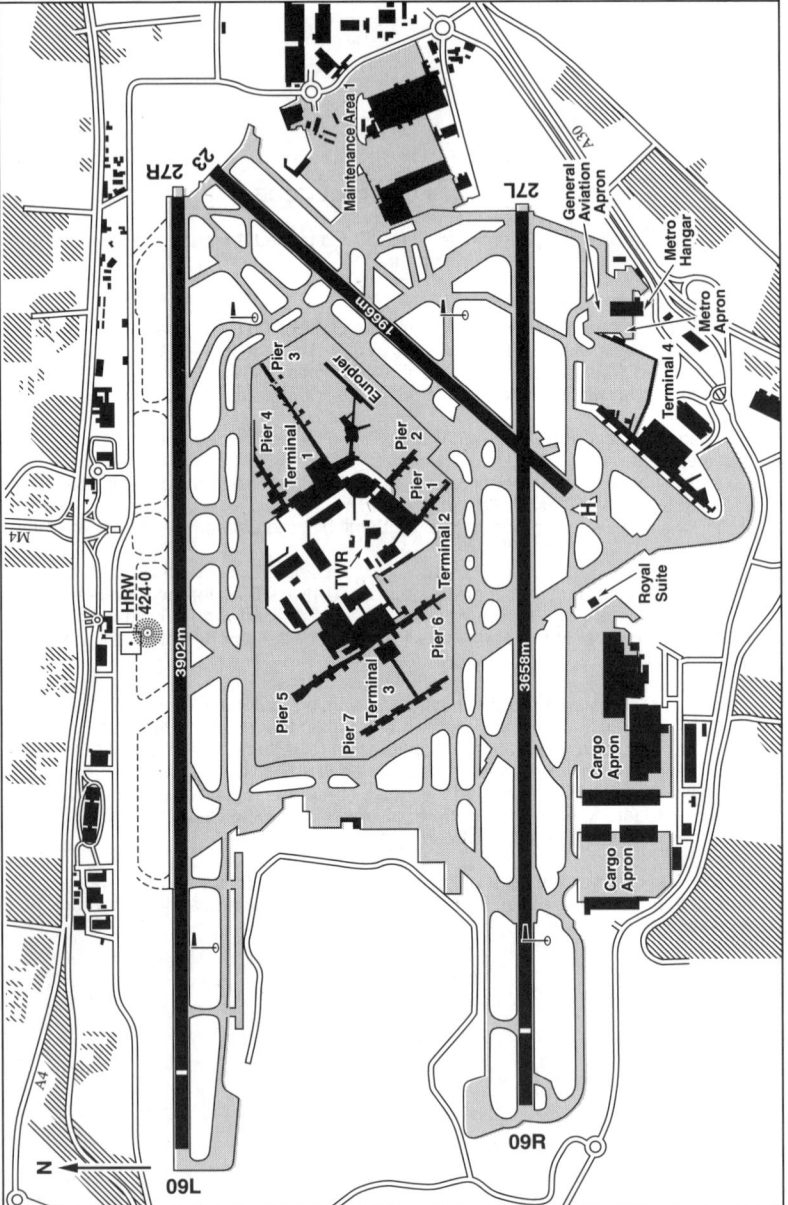

LONDON (Heathrow)

N51 28·65 W000 27·68

80 ft AMSL

Maintenance Area 1

27R 23

27L

General Aviation Apron

A30

Metro Hangar

Metro Apron

1·96m

Europier

Pier 3

Pier 4

Terminal 1

Pier 2

Pier 1

Terminal 4

Terminal 2

TWR

H1

Pier 6

Royal Suite

Pier 5

Pier 7

Terminal 3

3902m

3658m

Cargo Apron

Cargo Apron

HRW 424·0

M4

A4

N

09L

09R

Robert Pooley ©

| N51 28·65 W000 27·68 | **LONDON (Heathrow)** | 80 ft AMSL |

12 nm W of London.

**c/s Heathrow Director. APP 119·725, #134·975, #120·40, TWR 118·50, 118·70.
GND 121·90, 121·975*. RAD 119·90, #125·625. Arr ATIS 123·90, also VORs BNN
113·75, BIG 115·10, OCK 115·30 & LAM 115·60   DEP ATIS 121·85   # As directed.
* Departing aircraft to make initial call 'Heathrow Delivery' on this frequency.
Special VFR and Heli flights within London CTR: 0700-2030 – Heathrow APP
119·90; 0630-0700 and 2030-2200 – Thames Radar 132·70; outside these times –
Heathrow Director 119·725.**

Rwy	Dim(m)	Surface	TORA(m)	LDA(m)	Lighting
23 †	1966x45	Concrete	1183	1966	Ap Thr Rwy PAPI 3°
09L/27R	3902x45	Concrete/ Asphalt	09L-3902	09L-3597	Ap Thr Rwy RCL PAPI 3°
			27R-3902	27R-3902	Ap Thr Rwy RCL PAPI 3°
			27R-3492 – Short take-off from Block 18.		
09R/27L	3658x45	Asphalt	09R-3658	09R-3353	Ap Thr Rwy RCL PAPI 3°
			09R-2919 – Short take-off from Block 79.		
			27L-3658	27L-3658	Ap Thr Rwy RCL PAPI 3°
			27L-3218 – Short take-off from Block 86.		

† Take-offs permitted only by propeller driven a/c up to 24 tonnes MTOW & PPR.

| **Op hrs:** H24 | **Customs:** H24 |

Landing Fee: BAA Plc Airports Rates

| **Hangarage:** By arrangement | **Maintenance:** By arrangement |

Remarks: Operated by London (Heathrow) Airport. Use governed by regulations
applicable to London CTR (Class 'A' Controlled Airspace — see page 2).
The airport may be used by non-scheduled commercial and executive aircraft subject
to special conditions as listed overleaf. Light single and twin engined aircraft will not
be permitted to use the airport.

Restaurant: Restaurant and refreshments available.

Car Hire: Hertz. Tel: 020-8542 6688. Avis. Tel: 020-8897 9321.

| **Fuel:** Jet A1. BP., Mobil. Diners, Multi Service | **Tel:** 020-8759-4321 HAL. 020-8745-3328 NATS. **Fax:** 020-8745-4290 HAL. 020-8745-3491/2 NATS/FBU **Telex:** 934892 HAL, 22807 NATS. |

NAVIGATIONAL AIDS

VOR/DME 'LON' 113·60 Ch 83X N51 29·23 W000 28·00.

Lctr 'HRW' 424·0 N5128·73 W00027·57.

Rwy 09L   ILS/DME I-AA 110·30 Ch 40X.

Rwy 09R   ILS/DME I-BB 109·50 Ch 32X.

Rwy 27L   ILS/DME I-LL 109·50 Ch 32X.

Rwy 27R   ILS/DME I-RR 110·30 Ch 40X.

Rwy 23   DME 'HHT' 110·70 N5128·43 W00026·02.

LONDON (Heathrow)

Use of LONDON/Heathrow by General and Business Aviation Aircraft.

Availability.
Availability, H24, provided that prior permission and a clearance number is obtained from the Managing Director, Heathrow Airport Limited.

Operators of General and Business aviation aircraft may only operate in the peak during any operating season if they obtain permission to do so from the airport operator as well as a slot in advance of each movement also from the airport operator. In practice, permission to operate in the peak will be deemed to have been granted under the terms of the Traffic Distribution Rule (copies available from Manager Heathrow Operations Centre, Heathrow Airport Ltd), if a slot for each movement in the peak is granted. Operators who operate at any time may operate the movement provided that the aircraft departs or arrives as the case may be within thirty minutes before or after the time of the slot.

Those who fail to operate within the permitted time period or who operate in the peak without having first obtained permission and a slot from the airport operator, are liable to be prohibited from operating in the peak thereafter, unless the airport operator is satisfied that the movement amounted to an emergency or other circumstances beyond the control of the operator or the commander of the aircraft. This permission will not be given for flights for recreational, charity and record breaking purposes. Light single and twin engine aircraft will not be permitted to use the airport

Applications for prior permission must be made not more than 10 days and not less than 24 hours before the proposed flight and should be addressed to:
The Manager, Airport Co-ordination Ltd, by telephone 020-8759 4871, or 020-8759 2995; or by telex 934892 LHR. Ltd.

These applications must contain the following information:
(a)　Aircraft owner/operator
(b)　Aircraft type, registration
(c)　Point of origin and/or destination
(d)　ETA and ETD Heathrow
(e)　Number of passengers
(f)　A handling agent (Airline Operator or Handling Agent based at Heathrow) is essential for all flights including helicopter movements.

LONDON/Heathrow — Helicopter Operations — see page 613

Intentionally Blank

EGGW   1 DEC 00

N51 52·47 W000 22·10   **LONDON (Luton)**   525 ft AMSL

1·5 nm E of Luton.   BPK 117·50 313 12·4
                        BNN 113·75 041 11·2

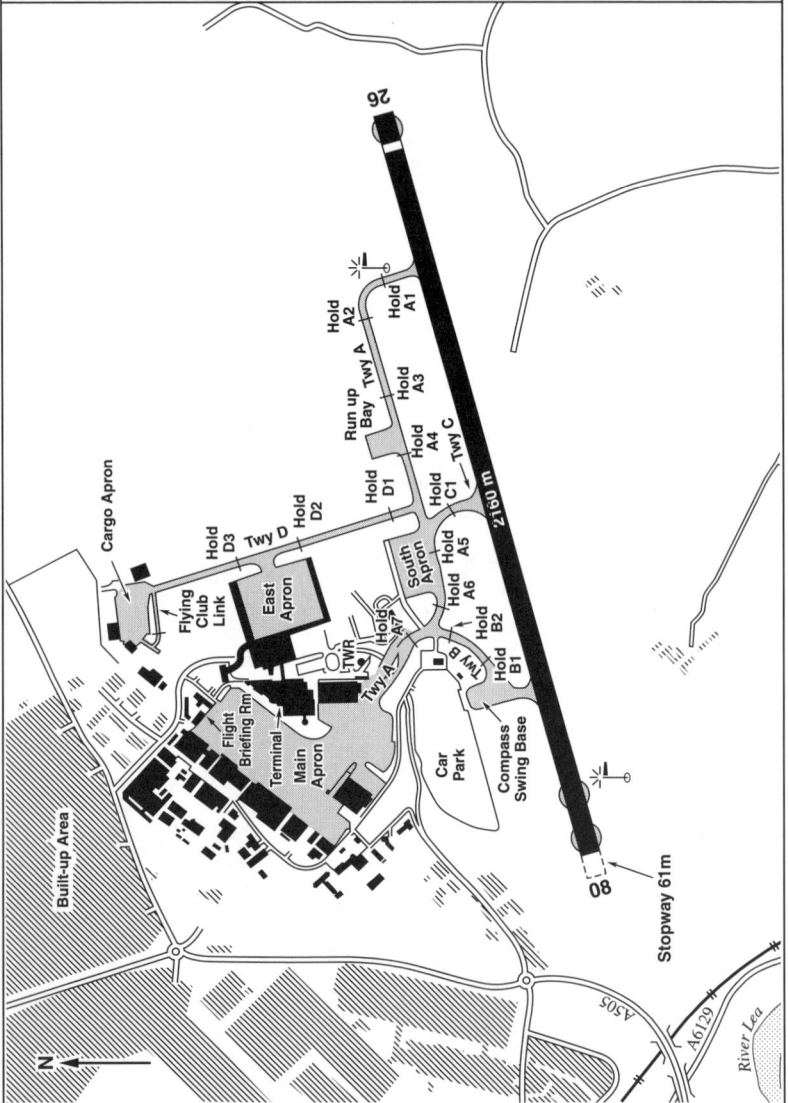

Robert Pooley ©

330

N51 52·47 W000 22·10	**LONDON (Luton)**	526 ft AMSL
1·5 nm E of Luton.		BPK 117·50 313 12·4
		BNN 113·75 042 11·2

c/s Luton. APP/RAD/VDF 129·55, 128·75, 126·725.
TWR/VDF 132·55.   GND 121·75 (0630 - 2300).
ATIS 120·575 c/s Arr/Dep Info.
NDB 'LUT' 345·0 (259°M/3·94 nm to Thr 26).
ILS/DME Rwy 08 (079°M) I-LTN 109·15.
ILS/DME Rwy 26 (259°M) I-LJ 109·15.

Rwy	Dim(m)	Surface	TORA(m)	LDA(m)	Lighting
08/26	2160x46	Asphalt	08-2160†	08-2160	Ap Thr Rwy RCL PAPI
			26-2160†	26-2075	Ap Thr Rwy RCL PAPI

† Take-off: Rwy 08 from intersection with Twy B – TORA 1685 m
             Rwy 08 from intersection with Twy C – TORA 1135 m
             Rwy 26 from intersection with Twy C – TORA 1055 m
             Rwy 26 from intersection with Twy A – TORA 1765 m

Op hrs: H24. PPR.	**Customs:** H24

Landing Fee: On application. Apron parking payable by the hour after 2 hours.

Hangarage: Nil	**Maintenance:** Available	**Met:** H24. 01344-856267.

Remarks: Operated by London Luton Airport Operations Ltd., Percival House,
Percival Way, Luton, Beds LU2 9LY.
Flights within the Luton CTR/CTA are governed by the regulations applicable to Class
'D' Controlled Airspace – see pages 2 and 6.
SVFR/VFR Flights, Entry/Exit Lanes and VRPs – see overleaf.
Luton CTR/CTA Chart - see page 333.
Non-Radio aircraft prohibited.
Airport available only to qualified pilots.

Non-scheduled commercial executive and private aircraft are subject to PPR.

To assist parking arrangements, details of each flight must be notified in advance to
ATC Watch Manager.

All General Aviation traffic using the main apron must use a handling agent.
Handling Agents: Air Foyle 01582-488410.   Allied Signals 01582-402040,
Metro Aviation 01582-738322. Magec Aviation 01582-724182,
Reed Aviation 01582-700900 and Servisair 01582-618603.

Restaurant: KFC, Sabarro Pizza, Granary Self-Service and Club facilities.

Car Hire: Avis. Tel: 01582-736537.   Europcar Tel: 01582-413438.
              Alamo. Tel: 01582-486414.

Fuel: Jet A1, 100LL.	**Tel:** 01582-395000 Switchboard.
Diners. Multi Service.	01582-395455 ATC.
	0906-4744474 ATIS.
	Fax: 01582-395499 ATC.

LONDON (Luton)

Special VFR and VFR Flights

Clearance for Special VFR and VFR flights may be requested and will be given whenever the traffic situation permits.

Entry/Exit Lanes

Entry/Exit Lanes are established to permit aircraft to operate to and from LONDON (Luton) Airport in IMC but not under IFR. North Lane via PIRTON VRP, South Lane via HEMEL VRP and HYDE VRP. Both lanes are 1·5 nm wide and use of the lanes is subject to the following conditions:

(a) Special VFR clearance must be obtained from Luton ATC.

(b) Aircraft using the lanes are to remain clear of cloud and in sight of the surface, not above 1500 ft (Luton QNH).

(c) Minimum flight visibility of 3 km.

(d) Pilots are responsible for their own separation from other aircraft and are also responsible for maintaining adequate ground clearance.

Visual Reference Points (VRPs)

VRP	BPK VOR/DME	BNN VOR/DME	LUT NDB
Hemel N5145·37 W00024·97	276°/12 nm	074°/5 nm	220°M
Hyde N5150·65 W00021·97	304°/11 nm	047°/10 nm	238°M
Pirton N51 58·30 W00019·90	332°/16 nm	032°/17 nm	331°M

LONDON (Luton) CTR/CTA Chart opposite

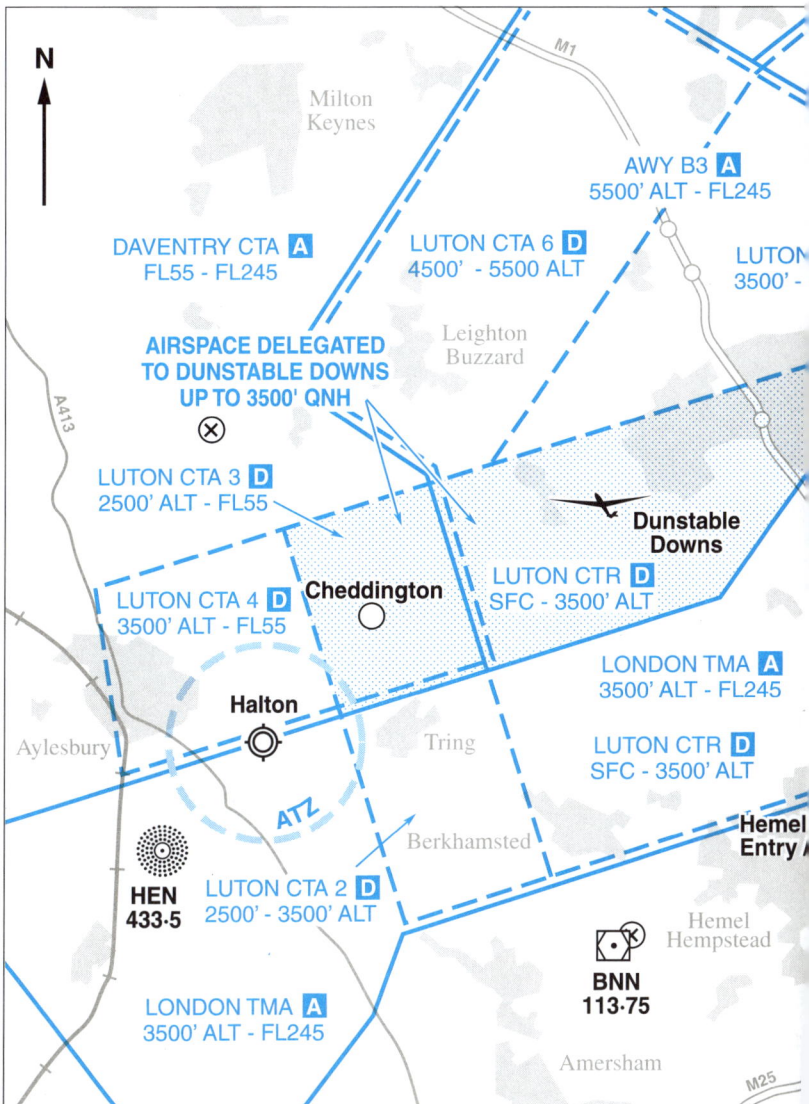

N

M1

Milton Keynes

AWY B3 **A**
5500' ALT - FL245

DAVENTRY CTA **A**
FL55 - FL245

LUTON CTA 6 **D**
4500' - 5500 ALT

LUTON
3500' -

Leighton Buzzard

AIRSPACE DELEGATED
TO DUNSTABLE DOWNS
UP TO 3500' QNH
⊗

A413

LUTON CTA 3 **D**
2500' ALT - FL55

Dunstable
Downs

LUTON CTA 4 **D**
3500' ALT - FL55

Cheddington
○

LUTON CTR **D**
SFC - 3500' ALT

Halton
◎

LONDON TMA **A**
3500' ALT - FL245

Aylesbury

Tring

LUTON CTR **D**
SFC - 3500' ALT

ATZ

Berkhamsted

Hemel
Entry

HEN
433·5

LUTON CTA 2 **D**
2500' - 3500' ALT

Hemel
Hempstead

⊡⊗

BNN
113·75

LONDON TMA **A**
3500' ALT - FL245

Amersham

M25

Robert Pooley ©

Intentionally Blank

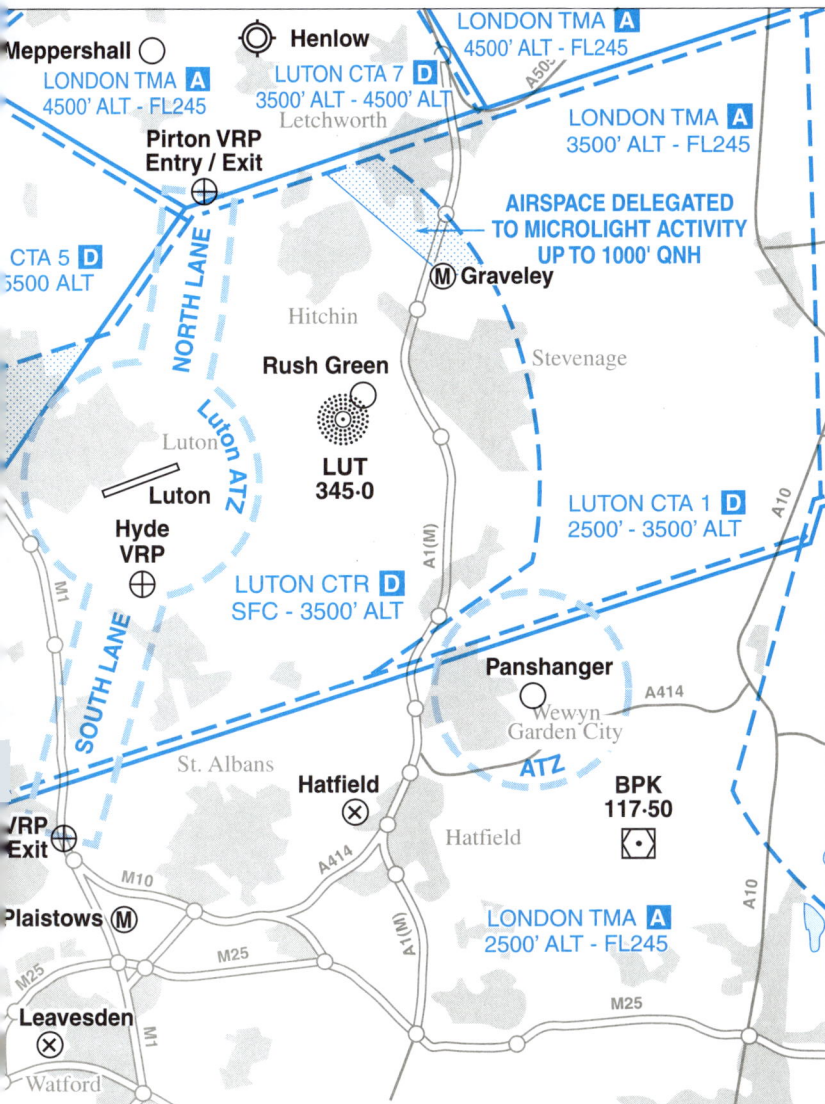

Meppershall ○

LONDON TMA **A**
4500' ALT - FL245

Henlow

LUTON CTA 7 **D**
3500' ALT - 4500' ALT
Letchworth

LONDON TMA **A**
4500' ALT - FL245

LONDON TMA **A**
3500' ALT - FL245

Pirton VRP
Entry / Exit

NORTH LANE

CTA 5 **D**
5500 ALT

M Graveley

AIRSPACE DELEGATED
TO MICROLIGHT ACTIVITY
UP TO 1000' QNH

Hitchin

Rush Green

Stevenage

Luton ATZ

Luton

LUT
345·0

Luton

LUTON CTA 1 **D**
2500' - 3500' ALT

A10

Hyde
VRP

LUTON CTR **D**
SFC - 3500' ALT

A1(M)

SOUTH LANE

Panshanger

A414

Welwyn
Garden City

ATZ

BPK
117·50

St. Albans

Hatfield

Hatfield

M1

VRP
Exit

M10

A414

A1(M)

LONDON TMA **A**
2500' ALT - FL245

A10

Plaistows **M**

M25

M25

Leavesden

M25

M1

Watford

LONDON (Luton) CTR/CTA
ENTRY/EXIT LANES and VRPs

Intentionally Blank

2·5 nm ENE of Bishops Stortford.   **LAM 115·60 017 14·5.   BPK 117·50 064 15**
                                   BKY 116·25 144 9·5

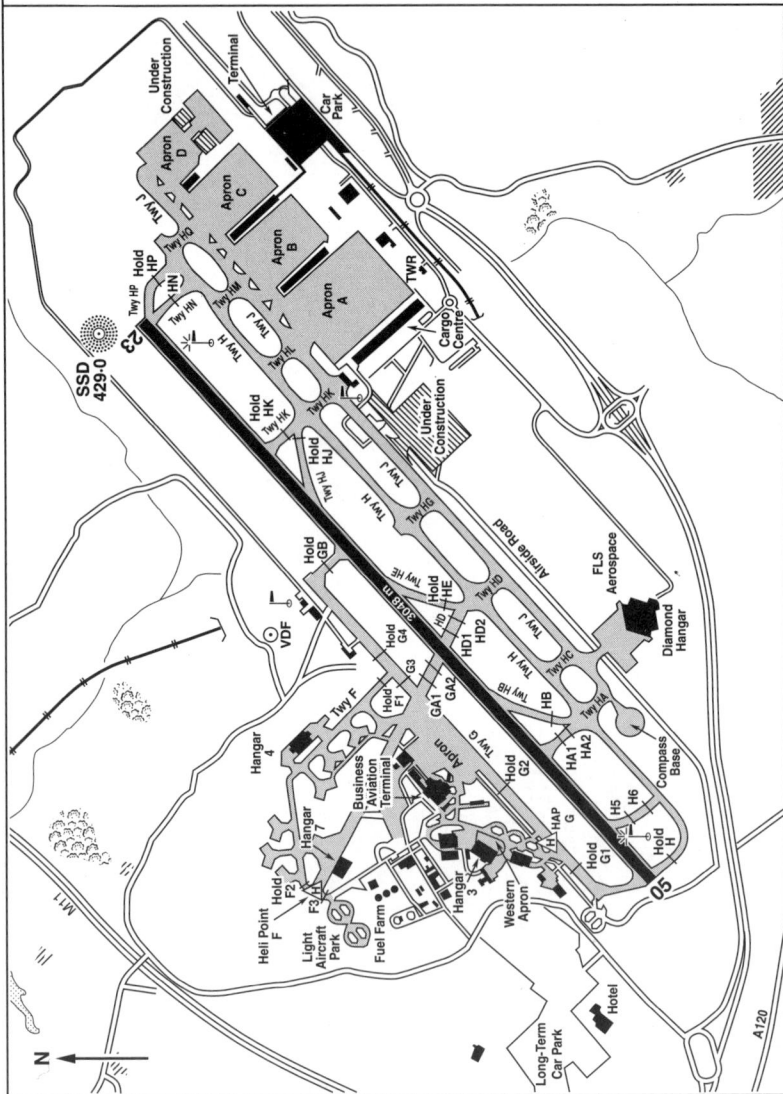

| N51 53·10 E000 14·10 | **LONDON (Stansted)** | 348 ft AMSL |

APP c/s Essex Radar **120·625.**   **TWR 123·80, 125·55** (as directed).
GND 121·725. GMP c/s Delivery **125·55. RAD** c/s Stansted Director **126·95** (as directed)
ATIS 127·175.   NDB 'SSD' 429·0 (On A/D).
ILS/DME Rwy 23 (227°M) **I-SX 110·50.   ILS/DME Rwy 05** (047°M) **I-SED 110·50.**

Rwy	Dim(m)	Surface	TORA(m)	LDA(m)	Lighting
05/23	3048x46	Asphalt	05-3048	05-3048	Ap Thr Rwy RCL PAPI 3°
			23-3048	23-3048	Ap Thr Rwy RCL PAPI 3

Op hrs: H24	**Customs:** H24
Landing Fee: BAA plc Airports Rates.	**Met:** H24. 01344-856267
Hangarage: By arrangement	**Maintenance:** Available

Remarks: Operated by Stansted Airport Ltd. Flights within the Stansted CTR/CTA are subject to the regulations applicable to Class 'D' Controlled Airspace — see pages 2 and 6. CTR/CTA and VRPs Chart is at page 339.

Prior permission (PPR) of not less than 4 hours required before intended flight.

Fixed wing aircraft departing or arriving are required to obtain a runway slot from Airport Co-ordination Ltd (ACL), Tel: 020-8759 5472, Fax: 020-8759 2995.

The use of the Airport for training purposes is subject to slot allocation from ACL, Tel: 020-8759 5472 and prior permission from ATC, Tel: 01279-669328.

Aerodrome is not available to non-radio aircraft.

Extensive instrument flying training takes place in the vicinity of airport.

Visual Reference Points (VRPs) are listed overleaf.

RH circuit on Rwy 05. Training aircraft in the circuit should not descend below 2000' QNH downwind. Avoid overlying Great Dunmow and Takeley.

Pilots of non-commercial (GA) flights arriving from abroad are required to report to the Customs at the Designated Customs Clearance Office in the Business Aviation Terminal.

Ground Handling: Use of a Handling agent is mandatory. Handling service for all executive and private aircraft can be obtained from:

    Metro Business Aviation Ltd, Tel: 01279-680167, Fax: 01279-681367.
    Inflite Ltd, Tel: 01279-680736, Fax: 01279-680104.
    Universal Aviation (UK) Ltd, Tel: 01279-680349, Fax: 01279-680372.

The Business Aviation Terminal is open 0600-2200 local daily, other times by prior arrangement with the operator (Metro Business Aviation Ltd). Customs and Immigration routinely available at the Business Aviation Terminal between 0730-2130 local daily.

Helicopter aiming point F is situated at western end of Twy F and is indicated by 'H'. The aiming point is lit and available 0700-2300 (L) for VFR/SVFR operations only. Helicopters may arrive or depart from the aiming point and air or ground taxi as directed by ATC. In exceptional circumstances, ATC may use Heli Point G situated at western end of Twy G for tactical positioning.

Restaurant: Terminal Building.

Taxi/Car Hire: Available at the Terminal.

Fuel: Jet A1	**Tel:** 01279-669 328 ATC
Diners. Multi Service.	01279-680 500 Airport Admin.
	Fax: 01279-662 066 Airport Admin.

Robert Pooley ©

VRP	VOR/VOR	VOR/DME FIX
Audley End Rly Sta. N52 00·25 E000 12·42	BKY R084 LAM R009	BKY 084°/5 nm
Braintree N51 52·70 E000 33·23	BKY R113 LAM R050	LAM 050°/20 nm
Chelmsford N51 44·00 E00028·40	BKY R138 LAM R070	LAM 070°/13 nm
Epping N51 42·00 E000 06·67	BKY R177 BNN R097	BNN 097°/25nm
Great Dunmow N51 52·30 E000 21·75	BKY R126 LAM R033	BKY 126°/13 nm
Haverhill N52 04·95 E000 26·07	BKY R071 LAM R025	LAM 025°/28 nm
Nuthampstead N51 59·40 E000 03·72	BKY VOR On site	LAM 354°/21 nm
Puckeridge A10/A120 N51 53·10 E000 00·27	BKY R200 LAM R343	BKY 202°/7 nm
Ware N51 48·70 W000 01·60	BKY R200 LAM R330	LAM 330°/12nm

Additional VRPs for Helicopters:

From the North: North end of Hangar 4 (N51 53·32 E00013·53).

From the South: Diamond Hangar (clear of the airside road)
(N51 52·67 E000 14·15).

Helicopters positioning from the VRPs to either the Helicopter Aiming Point or the runway shall maintain at least 500 ft agl until aligned with the let down point.

Note 1. In order to reduce conflict with IFR traffic, SVFR arrivals and departures will normally be cleared not above 1500 ft ALT via the following routes:

- Audley End Railway Station VRP via M11 Motorway;
- Great Dunmow VRP via A120 Trunk road;
- Puckeridge VRP via A120 Trunk road avoiding Bishops Stortford;
- Nuthampsted VRP.

Note 2. VFR flights inbound to and transitting the Stansted CTR/CTA should contact Essex Radar at least 5 mins prior to the CTR/CTA boundary. Do not enter the CTR/CTA unless clearance has been given. Anticipate clearance with reference to the VRPs listed above.

In order to reduce conflict with IFR traffic, VFR arrivals and departures will normally be cleared not above 1500 ft ALT via the routes detailed as above for SFVR flights.

Beware of busy minor aerodromes and ATZs in close proximity of Stansted CTR/CTA.

LONDON TMA 9 **A** 5500' ALT - FL245

N

Duxford

ATZ

LON
3500'

Fowlmere

ATZ

LONDON TMA 6 **A**
4500' ALT - FL245

A505

LO
35
Saffr
Wald

Roystone

Audley
End

Audley End
Rly Station
VRP

LUTON CTA 7 **D**
3500' - 4500' ALT

Letchworth

Nuthampstead
VRP

BKY
116·25

SVFR/VFR

LONDON TMA 3 **A**
3500' ALT - FL245

STANSTED CTA 4 **D**
2500' - 3500' ALT

LONDON TMA 3 **A**
3500' ALT - FL245

M Graveley

Buntingford

Rush Green

Stevenage

LUTON CTA 1 **D**
2500' - 3500' ALT

LUT
345·0

Puckeridge
VRP

A120

SVFR/VFR

Bishops
Stortford

A10

A1184

LUTON CTR **D**
SFC - 3500' ALT

A1(M)

ATZ

Sawbridgeworth

LONDO
3500' A

M11

Panshanger

Ware
VRP

Hunsdon
M

A414

A414

BPK
117·50

LONDON TMA 1 **A**
2500' ALT - FL245

Harlow

Hatfield

A10

STANSTED CTA 2 **D**
1500' - 2500' ALT

North
Weald

Chi
O

LONDON TMA 1 **A**
2500' ALT - FL245

A1

M25

Epping
VRP

LONDON T
2500' ALT -

ATZ

M25

Routes notified for Rule 5. Flight permitted below 1500' but
not below 800' above highest fixed obstacle beneath route.

LAM
115·60 Stapleford

Robert Pooley ©

Intentionally Blank

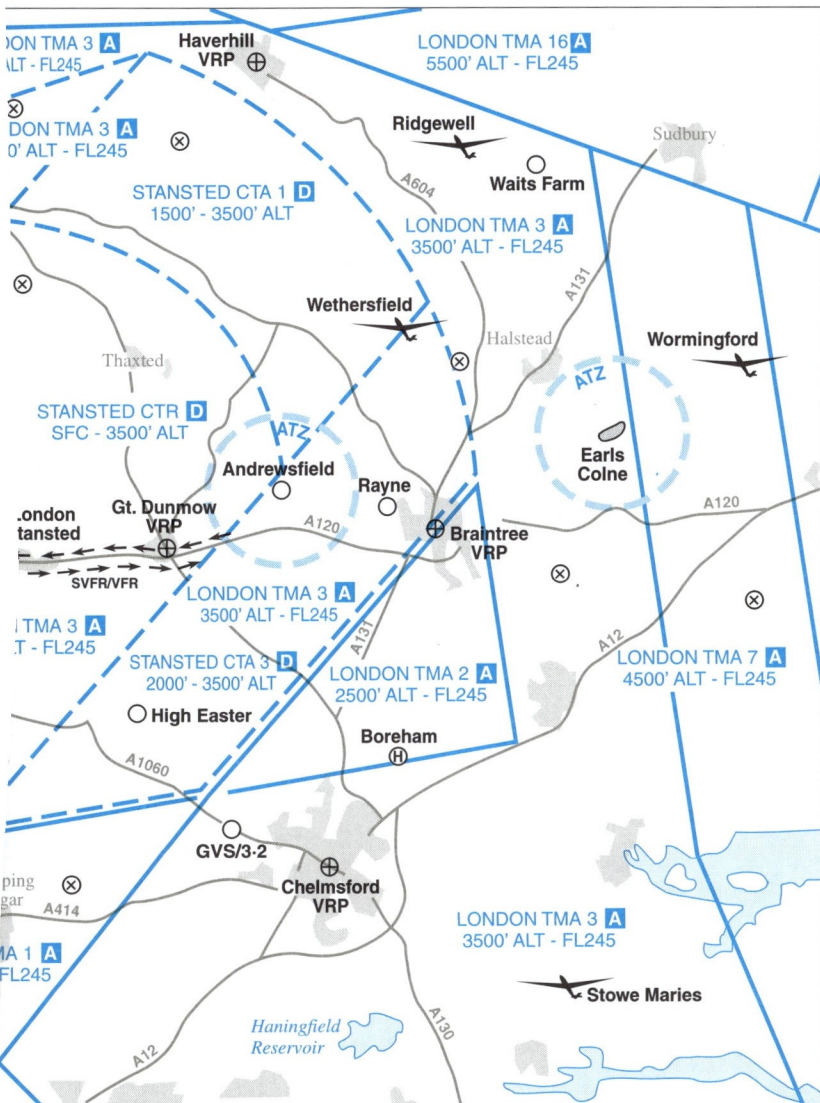

LONDON TMA 3 **A**
LT - FL245

Haverhill VRP ⊕

LONDON TMA 16 **A**
5500' ALT - FL245

DON TMA 3 **A**
0' ALT - FL245

⊗

Ridgewell ✈

Sudbury

A604

Waits Farm ○

STANSTED CTA 1 **D**
1500' - 3500' ALT

LONDON TMA 3 **A**
3500' ALT - FL245

⊗

A131

Wethersfield ✈

Thaxted

Halstead

Wormingford ✈

⊗

ATZ

STANSTED CTR **D**
SFC - 3500' ALT

ATZ

Earls Colne

Andrewsfield ○

Rayne ○

A120

.ondon tansted

Gt. Dunmow VRP ⊕

A120

⊕ **Braintree VRP**

⊗

⊗

SVFR/VFR

A12

LONDON TMA 3 **A**
3500' ALT - FL245

A131

| TMA 3 **A**
.T - FL245

STANSTED CTA 3 **D**
2000' - 3500' ALT

LONDON TMA 3 **A**
3500' ALT - FL245

LONDON TMA 2 **A**
2500' ALT - FL245

LONDON TMA 7 **A**
4500' ALT - FL245

○ **High Easter**

Boreham
Ⓗ

A1060

GVS/3·2 ○

⊕ **Chelmsford VRP**

ping
ar ⊗

A414

MA 1 **A**
FL245

LONDON TMA 3 **A**
3500' ALT - FL245

✈ **Stowe Maries**

A130

A12

Haningfield Reservoir

LONDON (Stansted) CTR/CTA
and VRPs

| N55 02·57 W007 09·67 | **LONDONDERRY (Eglinton)** | 22 ft AMSL |

| 7 nm ENE of Londonderry. | BEL 117·20 314 39. |
| | MAC 116·00 253 55 |

c/s Eglinton. APP/VDF 123·625. TWR 134·15.
NDB 'EGT' 328·50 (on A/D).
ILS/DME Rwy 26 (262°M) I EGT 108·30.

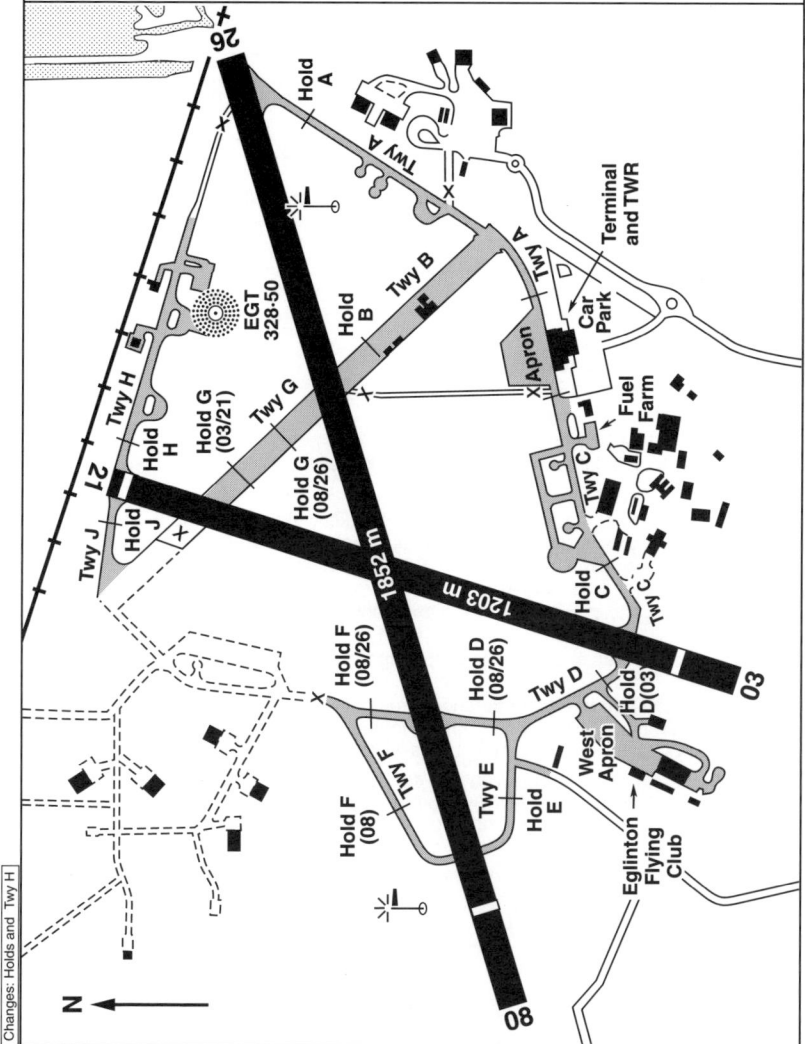

Changes: Holds and Twy H

Robert Pooley ©

341

N55 02·57 W007 09·67	**LONDONDERRY (Eglinton)**				22 ft AMSL

Rwy	Dim(m)	Surface	TORA(m)	LDA(m)	Lighting
08/26	1852x45	Asphalt	08-1762 26-1817	08-1640 26-1817	Thr Rwy RCL PAPI 3° Apt† Thr Rwy RCL PAPI 3°
03/21	1203x45	Asphalt	03-1203 21-1203	03-1086 21-1191	Thr Rwy PAPI 4° Thr Rwy APAPI 4° Abn/Wh

† Strobe Approach lights extend over water and reflections of lighting may be seen.

Op hrs: Strictly PPR by phone. Mon-Fri 0700-2015, Sat 0700-1545, Sun 1230-2115.

Landing Fees: Commercial £6.35/tonne; private SE £7.22, Twins £14.44; plus VAT.

Hangarage: Avialable.   **Maintenance:** Ltd.

Customs: 24 hrs PNR.

Remarks: Operated by Derry City Council, City of Derry Airport, Airport Road,
Co Londonderry BT47 3PY. Non-radio aircraft PPR.
Aircraft departing/arriving from/to destinations outside of Northern Ireland are required
to use the main terminal building for Customs, Immigration and Special Branch, as
appropriate.
Aircraft must have third party liability insurance cover in the sum of £1,000,000.
High visibility clothing mandatory for all ramp activities.
In calm wind conditions, Rwy 08 is the preferred departure runway and Rwy 26 is the
preferred arrival runway.

Circuit directions and height:
Rwys 03 and 21 - 1200 ft aal;
Rwy 08 - 1000 ft for LH and 1200 ft for RH;
Rwy 26 - 1200 ft for LH and 1000 ft for RH.
At night, the circuit heights will be raised to 1500 ft aal.

Warnings:
Pilots are reminded of the close proximity of Ballykelly airfield 5 nm ENE of this
aerodrome. Ballykelly is close to the extended centreline to Rwy 26 and runway
lighting may be displayed there. Positively identify Londonderry/Eglinton before
committing the aircraft to landing.
Large congregations of sea-birds in the approach area to Rwy 26 (take-off area for
Rwy 08).
Single engined aircraft should avoid overflying factory complex 2·5 nm W of airfield
below 1500 ft.
A railway passes through the undershoot area of Rwy 26. Aircraft not permitted to
land on Rwy 26 or depart Rwy 08 from 5 minutes before the train until the train has
passed. Expect delays of up to 10 minutes where movements conflict with trains.

VRPs: Buncrana - N55 08·00 W007 27·40; Coleraine - N55 07·90 W006 40·30;
Dungiven - N54 55·70 W006 55·50; Moville - N5511·40 W007 02·40 and
New Buildings - N54 57·50 W007 21·50.

Car Hire: Avis Tel: 028-7181 1708. Ford Tel: 028-7136 0420.

Taxi: Available at the Terminal.

Fuel: 100LL, Jet A1.	**Tel:** 028-7181 0784 Terminal Switchboard. 028-7181 0784 Ext 208 Ops/Ground Handling. 028-7181 1099 ATC. **Fax:** 028-7181 2152 ATC. 028-7181 1426 Admin/Ops/Handling.

Intentionally Blank

4 nm N of Elgin.	ADN 114·30 312 42
	INS 109·20 074 25

c/s Lossie. RAD 119·35 (MATZ/LARS). TWR 118·20 (As directed).
ILS Rwy 23 (231°M) 'LM' 111·10. ATIS Tel: 0134-381 2121 Ext 7666.

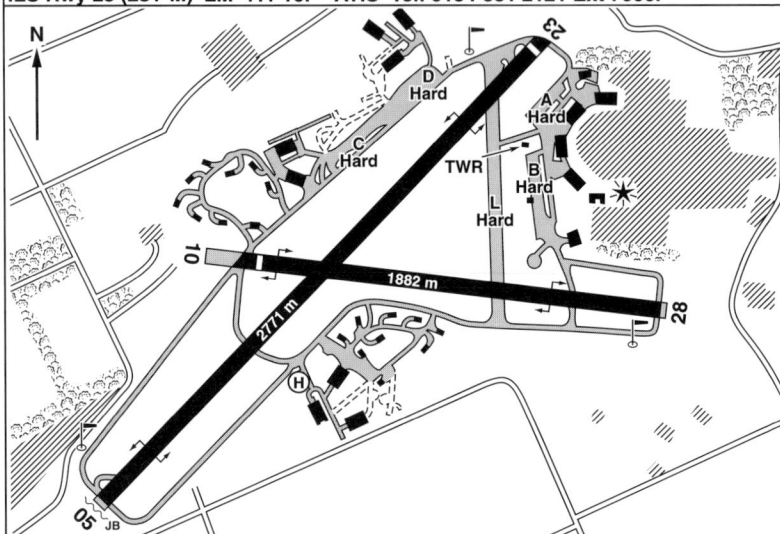

Rwy	Dim(m)	Surface	TORA(m)	LDA(m)	Lighting
05/23	2771x45	Asphalt/	05-2771	05-2771	Ap Thr Rwy PAPI
		Concrete	23-2771	23-2678	Ap Thr Rwy PAPI
10/28	1882x45	Asphalt/	10-1849	10-1751	Ap Thr Rwy PAPI
		Concrete	28-1849	28-1849	Ap Thr Rwy PAPI
					IBn 'LM' Red

Op hrs: PPR.   **ATZ active H24.**

Landing Fee: MoD(RAF) Rates   **Customs:** Nil

Hangarage: Nil   **Maintenance:** Nil

Remarks: RAF Aerodrome, not normally available to civil aircraft.
Lossiemouth/Kinloss Area of Intense Air Activity.

Visual joins not below 1000 ft.

Avoid overflying Elgin, Lossiemouth Town and Gordonstoun School.

Aerial Farm (lit) 230ft amsl at Milltown 125°T/4 nm from aerodrome.

Arrester gear 425m from Rwy 23 and 28 threshold, 395m from Rwy 05 threshold, and
162m from Rwy 10 threshold.

Fuel: 100LL. Avtur - by arrangement.	**Tel:** 0134 381-2121 Ext 2051

N52 43·10 E001 33·07	**LUDHAM**	50 ft AMSL

10 nm ENE of Norwich Airport.

CLN 114·55 020 54·5
NH 371·5 072 6·6

No Radio. Recommend contact Norwich App 119·35.

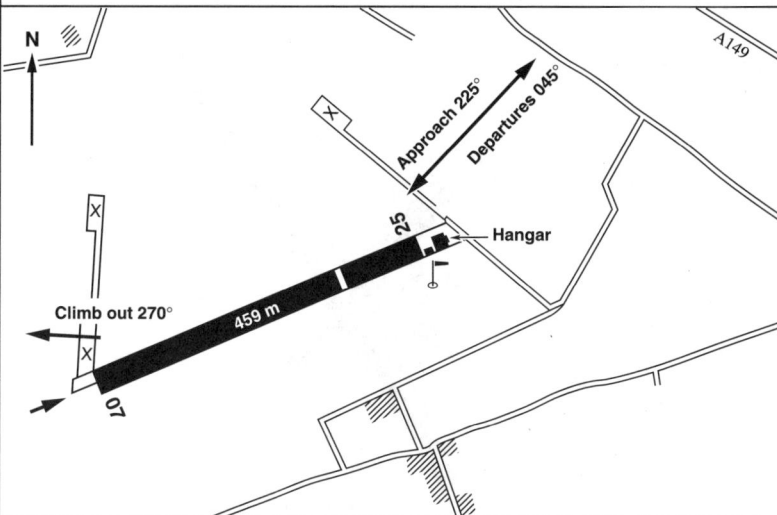

N

Approach 225°   Departures 045°

A149

X

25   ■— Hangar

Climb out 270°   459 m

X

07

Rwy	Dim(m)	Surface	TORA(m)	LDA(m)	Lighting
07/25	549x46	Concrete	(07-420	07-450)	Nil.
			(25-549	25-420)	Nil.

Advisory declared distances.

Op hrs: PPR.

Landing Fee: £5.00.   **Customs:** Nil

Hangarage: Nil   **Maintenance:** Nil

Remarks: Operated by Ludham Aerodrome. PPR.

Unlicensed airfield situated 2·5 nm E of Coltishall MATZ and on the western edge of the BACTON – NORTH DENES Helicopter Corridor (500-1500ft. ALT).

Hangar at eastern end of runway necessitating an angled approach to Rwy 25.

Circuits LH on 07, RH on 25, at 1000 ft aal. Do not overfly villages.

Noise Abatement: Arrival and Departure Headings as above.

Fuel: Nil

Tel: 01692- 630886 Tony Foyster.
Tel/Fax: 01603- 721032 Ivan Smith.

N50 57·37 E000 56·35	**LYDD**		12 ft AMSL
1·2 nm E of Lydd.		LYD 114·05 144 3·5	
		DVR 114·95 236 20·2	

c/s Lydd Information 120·70 AFIS & DAAIS for EG D044.
DME 'LDY' 108·15.   NDB 'LYX' 397·0 (217°M/1·17 nm to A/D)

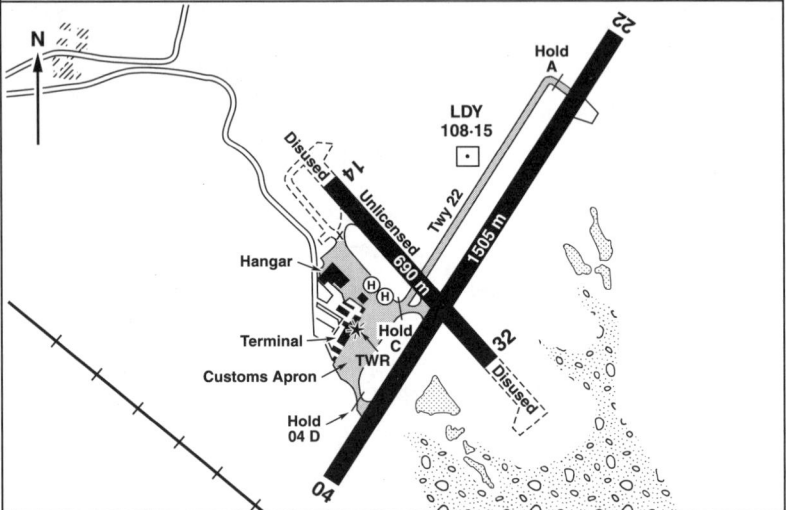

Rwy	Dim(m)	Surface	TORA(m)	LDA(m)	Lighting	
04/22	1504x37	Asphalt	04-1468	04-1468	Ap Thr Rwy PAPI 3°	
			22-1504	22-1468	Ap Thr Rwy PAPI 3·5°	
14/32	690x35	Asphalt	Unlicensed		Nil.	ABn Wh

Op hrs: Sun-Thu 0900-1730,   Fri, Sat 0900-1900.

Landing Fee: 1.3 p per kg MAUW. Training 25% discount. Further discounts for multiple training. Parking by arrangement. All charges subject to VAT.

Hangarage: By arrangement.   **Maintenance:** JAR approved available. **Customs:** As Op hrs

Remarks: Operated by Lydd Airport Group Ltd. Non-radio aircraft and Microlights PPR.
Take-offs: Rwy 04 - Climb straight ahead to 1000 ft, or crossing the coast, whichever is sooner, before turning right or left as advised by ATSU.
Rwy 22 - Climb straight ahead to 800 ft before turning left or right as advised by ATSU.
Landings: Rwy 04 and 22 - All inbound aircraft unless otherwise advised by ATSU should maintain an altitude of at least 800 ft until commencing on final approach.

Joining procedure for VFR traffic: Overhead at 1500 QNH, descending to join downwind leg at circuit height 1000 ft QFE. Dead-side joins not permitted due to poor visibility from the visual Tower.
Circuits : RH on Rwys 04 and 32, LH on 14 and 22.
NE Hard taxiway is open to light single engined aircraft, in VMC daylight hours only. Taxi with caution as taxiway is only 6 m wide and uneven at edges.
All Rwy 22 departures will carry out power checks as directed by ATSU.
Avoid overflying Dungeness Power Station (2·5 nm SE of A/D) below 2000 ft.
Restaurant: Available.   **Car Hire/Taxis:** By arrangement.

Fuel: 100LL, Jet A1.	**Tel:** 01797-322417 ATC, 322411 Admin.
All cards accepted	**Fax:** 01797-321964 ATC; 322419 Admin/Flt Briefing.

Robert Pooley ©

N51 30·31 W001 59·60	**LYNEHAM (MEDA)**	513 ft AMSL

8 nm WSW of Swindon.

CPT 114·35 277 29
SAM 113·35 329 41

Lyneham APP 118·425. RADAR c/s Zone 123·40. RADAR c/s Director 118·425.
Brize Radar 134·30. TWR 119·225. GND 129·475.
NDB 'LA' 282·0 (On A/D). TACAN 'LYE' 109·80 (On A/D).
ILS Rwy 24 (248°M) 'LA' 109·70 (Rwy QFU 245°).

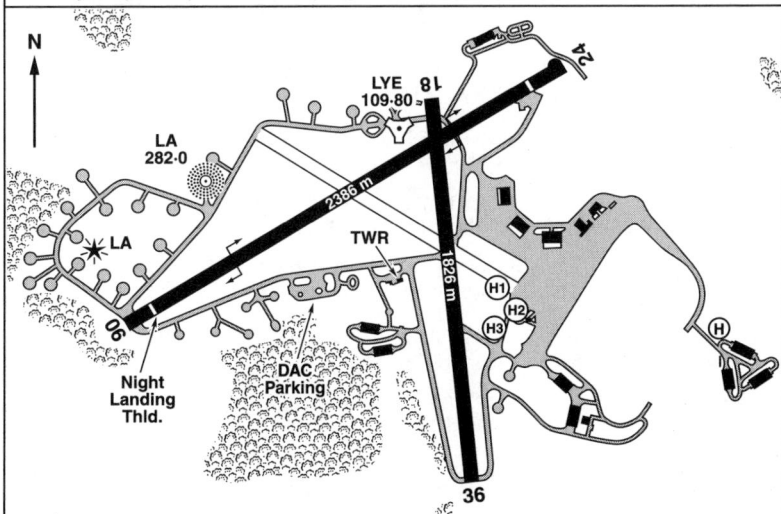

Rwy	Dim(m)	Surface	TORA(m)	LDA(m)	Lighting
06/24	2386x46	Concrete/ Asphalt	06-2386	06-2386(D) 06-2234(N)	Ap Thr Rwy PAPI
			24-2386	24-2204	Ap Thr Rwy PAPI
18/36	1826x46	Asphalt	18-1826	18-1826	Ap Thr Rwy PAPI
			36-1826	36-1826	Ap Thr Rwy PAPI

Op hrs: H24. PPR 24 hrs notice .	**ATZ active H24**
Landing Fee: MoD(RAF) Rates	**Customs:** 24 hrs PNR
Hangarage: Nil	**Maintenance:** Nil

Remarks: RAF Emergency Diversion Aerodrome. Flights within the Lyneham CTR/CTA are subject to the regulations applicable to Class 'D' Controlled Airspace - see page 2. VRPs are listed overleaf and CTR/VRPs Chart is at page 347 .
Aerodrome may be used by private aircraft subject to 24hrs prior notice, and by charter aircraft by special arrangement.
Aircraft requiring to transit the CTR/CTA are to call Zone.
Ground rises sharply from 300ft below A/D level to Rwy 06 Thr. No night-stop facilities for visiting aircraft.
Flight Plans required at Operations at least 2 hours before ETD.
Warning: Heavy bird concentration in the area at dawn and dusk.
Car Hire: Thrifty, Tel: 01793-422644.

Fuel: 100LL (72 hrs PNR). Avtur - PNR	**Tel:** 01249-890381 Ext 6214 01249-890381 Ext 7308 ATIS

Robert Pooley ©

VFR flights requesting clearance to transit through the Control Zone/Area may be given routeing and/or altitude restrictions in order to enable VFR flights to be integrated with other traffic. Pilots should anticipate routeing and/or holding instructions via the Visual Reference Points shown below.

VRP	VOR/VOR	VOR/NDB	VOR/DME
Avebury N51 25·68 W001 51·28	CPT R265 SAM R330	CPT R265 LA 135°M	CPT 265°/24 nm
Blakehill Farm N51 37·00 W00 153·10	CPT R293 SAM R337	CPT R293 LA 039°M	CPT 293°/26 nm
Calne N51 26·20 W002 00·30	CPT R268 SAM R324	CPT R268 LA 184°M	CPT 268°/30 nm
Chippenham N51 27·60 W002 07·40	CPT R273 SAM R321	CPT R273 LA 241°M	CPT 273°/34 nm
Clyffe Pypard N51 29·40 W001 53·70	CPT R274 SAM R332	CPT R274 LA 109°M	CPT274°/25 nm
Devizes N51 20·80 W001 59·30	CPT R258 SAM R319	CPT R258 LA 181°M	CPT 258°/30 nm
Junction 15 (M4) N51 31·60 W001 43·48	CPT R281 SAM R342	CPT R281 LA 089°M	CPT R281°/19 nm
Junction 16 (M4) N51 32·70 W001 51·25	CPT R282 SAM R336	CPT R282 LA 073°M	CPT R282°/24 nm
Junction 17 (M4) N51 30·88 W002 07·30	CPT R277 SAM R324	CPT R277 LA 280°M	CPT 277°/34 nm
Malmesbury N51 35·10 W002 06·20	CPT R284 SAM R328	CPT R284 LA 327°M	CPT 284°/33 nm
Marlborough N51 25·20 W001 43·70	CPT R262 SAM R337	CPT R262 LA 121°M	CPT 262°/19 nm
Melksham N51 22·50 W002 08·30	CPT R263 SAM R315	SAM R315 LA 216°M	CPT 263°/35 nm
South Marston N51 35·40 W001 44·10	CPT R292 SAM R343	CPT R292 LA 069°M	CPT 292°/20 nm
Wroughton N51 30·55 W001 47·98	CPT R277 SAM R337	SAM R337 LA 094°M	CPT 277°/22 nm

Notes: 1. Caution advised when routeing via the M4 Motorway due to the lighted obstacle, 500' agl, (1200' amsl) at Membury.

  2. Intense microlight and hang-gliding activity over the high ground to the south of the Lyneham Control Zone.

See CTR/CTA and VRPs Chart opposite

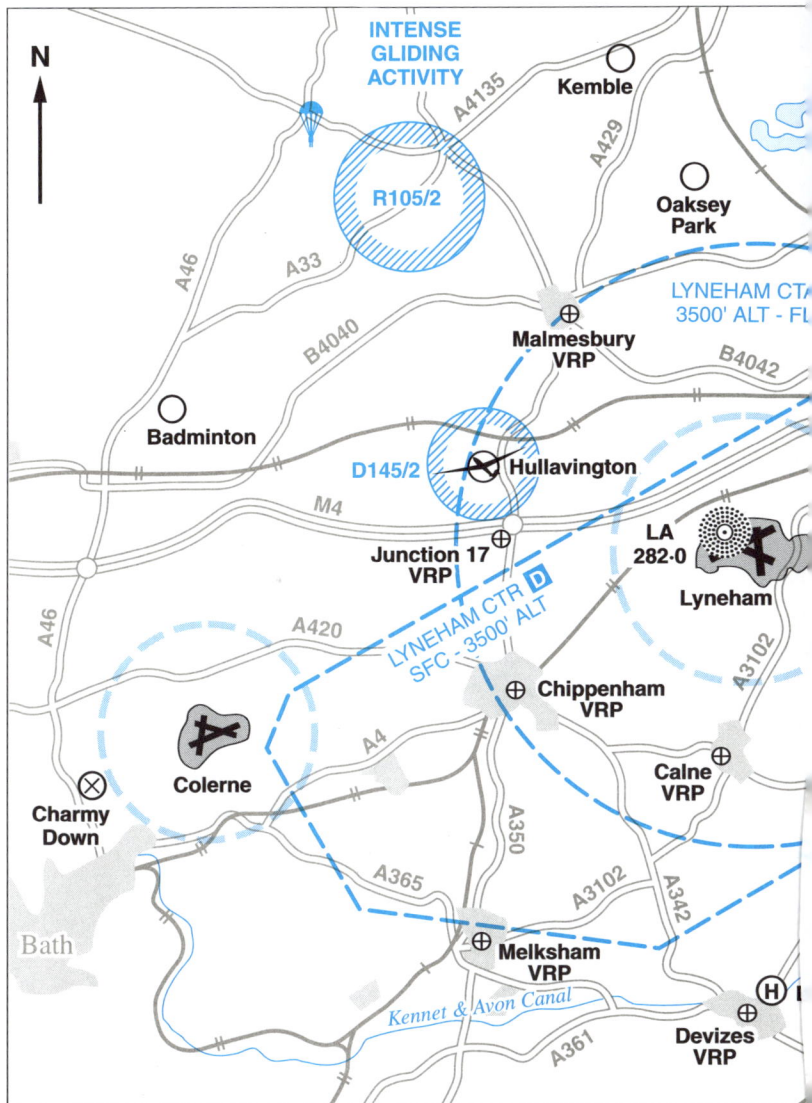

N

INTENSE
GLIDING
ACTIVITY

A4135

Kemble

A429

Oaksey
Park

R105/2

A46

A33

LYNEHAM CT
3500' ALT - FL

B4040

Malmesbury
VRP

B4042

Badminton

D145/2

Hullavington

M4

LA
282·0

Junction 17
VRP

Lyneham

A46

A420

LYNEHAM CTR D
SFC - 3500' ALT

A3102

Chippenham
VRP

A4

Calne
VRP

Colerne

A350

Charmy
Down

A365

A3102

A342

Melksham
VRP

(H)

Kennet & Avon Canal

Devizes
VRP

A361

Robert Pooley ©

Intentionally Blank

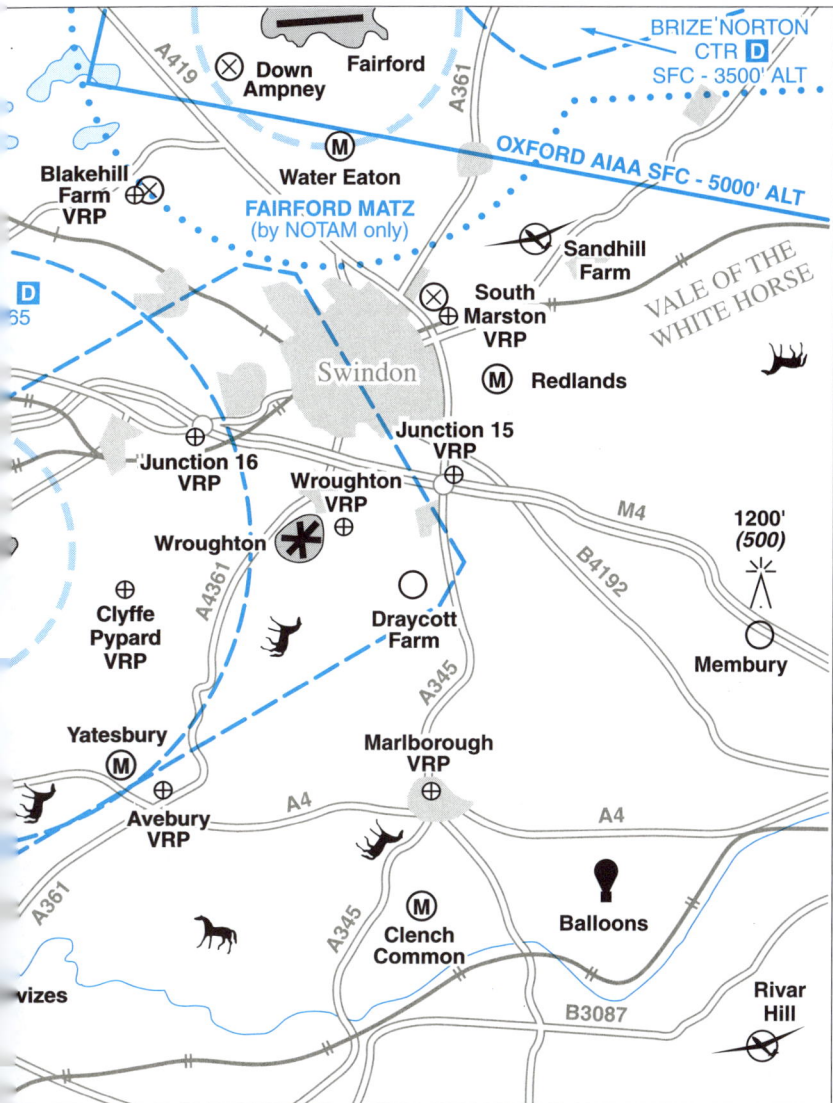

BRIZE NORTON
CTR **D**
SFC - 3500' ALT

A419

Down
Ampney

Fairford

A361

M

Water Eaton

OXFORD AIAA SFC - 5000' ALT

Blakehill
Farm
VRP

FAIRFORD MATZ
(by NOTAM only)

Sandhill
Farm

VALE OF THE
WHITE HORSE

D
65

South
Marston
VRP

Swindon

Redlands

Junction 15
VRP

Junction 16
VRP

Wroughton
VRP

M4

1200'
(500)

Wroughton

B4192

Clyffe
Pypard
VRP

A4361

Draycott
Farm

A345

Membury

Yatesbury

Marlborough
VRP

M

Avebury
VRP

A4

A4

A361

A345

Clench
Common

Balloons

vizes

B3087

Rivar
Hill

LYNEHAM CTA/CTR
and VRPs

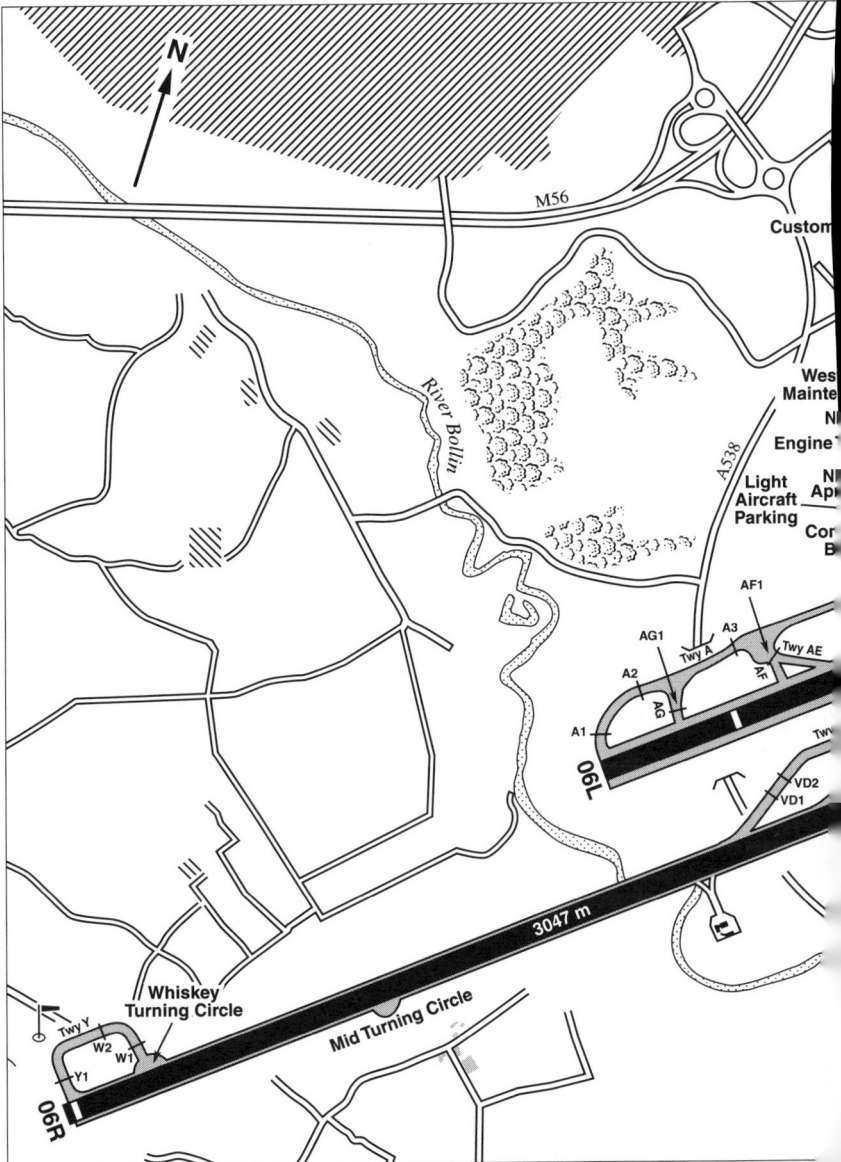

N

M56

Custom

River Bollin

Wes
Mainte

N
Engine

Light   N
Aircraft   Ap
Parking

Cor
B

AF1

AG1   A3
Twy A   Twy AE

A2   AF

AG

A1

06L

VD2
VD1

Twy

3047 m

Whiskey
Turning Circle   Mid Turning Circle

Twy Y
W2 W1
Y1

06R

A538

Robert Pooley ©

Intentionally Blank

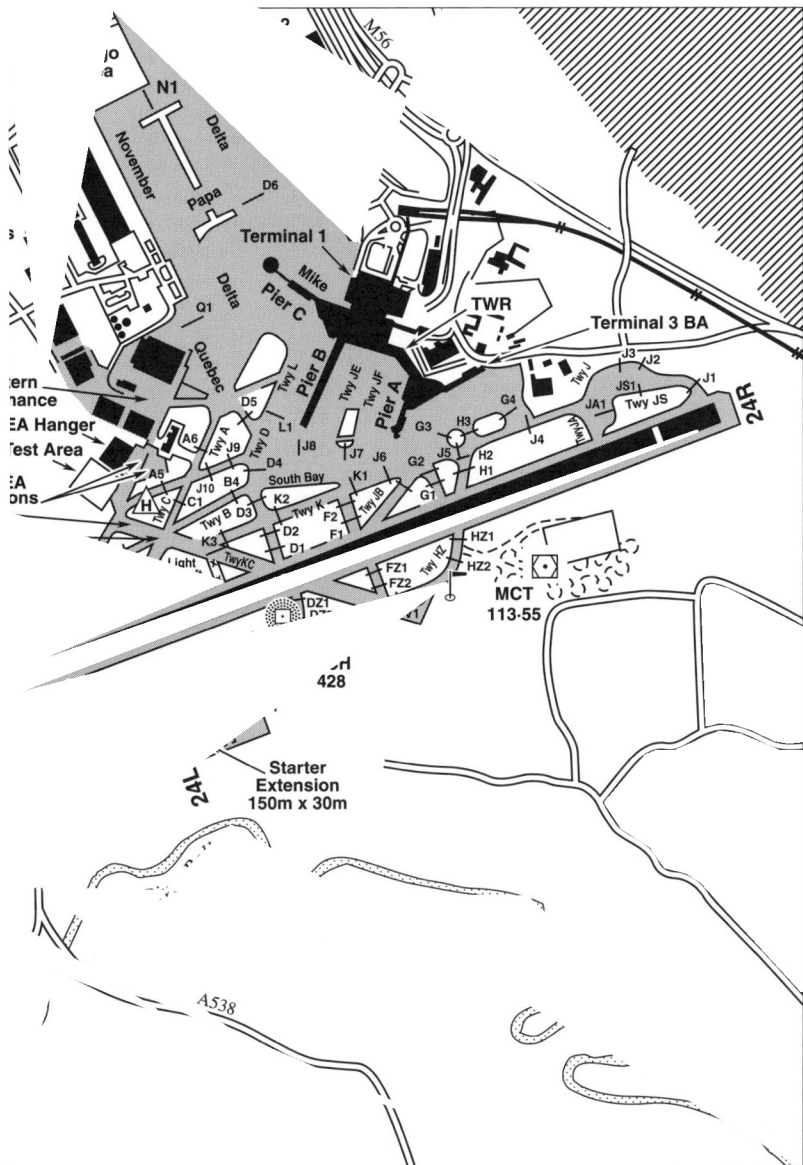

N1

Delta

November

Papa

D6

Terminal 1

Mike

TWR

Terminal 3 BA

Pier C

M56

J3 J2

Delta

Q1

J1

Quebec

Pier B

Twy JE

Twy JF

Twy J

JS1

Twy JS

JA1

ern
nance

D5

Pier A

G4

J4

24R

EA Hanger
est Area

A6

Twy A

L1

J8

G3

H3

G2

H2

J5

G1

H1

EA
ns

A5

J9

Twy D

D4

J7

J6

K1

C1

J10

B4

South Bay

K2

Twy B

D3

Twy K

F2

Twy JB

H

D2

F1

K3

D1

Light

Twy KC

FZ1

Twy JZ

HZ1

HZ2

FZ2

MCT
113·55

DZ1

428

Starter
Extension
150m x 30m

24L

A538

14 FEB 01

MANCHESTER AIRPORT

N53 21·22 W002 16·50	**MANCHESTER AIRPORT**	257 ft AMSL
7·5 nm SW of Manchester.		**POL 112·10 201 24·2**

APP 119·40 (c/s Radar), 118·575 (c/s Arrival, as directed by ATC).
RAD (c/s Director) 119·40, 121·35 (as directed by ATC). TWR 118·625.
GND 121·85.
Delivery 121·70 (Initial call for departing aircraft during Op hrs 0630-2200 (L), Other times call 'Ground').
Arrival ATIS 128·175;   Departure ATIS 121·975
NDB 'MCH' 428·0 (On A/D).
VOR/DME 'MCT' 113·55 (On A/D).
ILS/DME Rwy 06L (056°M) I MM 109·50.
ILS/DME Rwy 24R (236°M) I NN 109·50.
ILS/DME Rwy 06R (056°M) I MC 111·55.

Rwy	Dim(m)	Surface	TORA(m)	LDA(m)	Lighting
06L/24R	3048x46	Concrete/ Asphalt	06L-3048 24R-3048	06L-2622 24R-2865	Ap Thr Rwy RCL PAPI 3° Ap Thr Rwy RCL PAPI 3°
06R/24L	3047x46	Concrete/ Asphalt	06R-3047 24L -3047	06R-2864 24L-2864	Ap Thr Rwy RCL PAPI 3° Ap Thr Rwy RCL PAPI 3°

Op hrs: H24

Landing Fee: On application.	**Customs:** H24
Hangarage: Limited.	**Maintenance:** Limited.

Remarks: Operated by Manchester Airport PLC, Manchester Airport, Manchester. M90 1QX.

Flights within the Manchester CTR/ CTA are subject to the regulations applicable to Class 'D' Controlled Airspace — see pages 2 and 6. **Note:** Manchester TMA (base 3500' ALT) is Class 'A' Airspace.

See SVFR Flights and Special Low Level Route at page 353 and the routes at page 354.

VRPs are listed at page 358 and VAD/VRPs Chart is at page 359.

High visibility clothing mandatory on the apron areas.

Use by General and Business Aviation aircraft is subject to prior permission.

Filing of a Flight Plan does not constitute PPR.

Prior permission applications should be addressed as follows:

All request for Slots during office hours - Airport Co-ordination Ltd (ACL), Tel: 0161-489 2583/2422. Fax: 0161- 489 2470.

Slots outside office hours - Manchester Airport Plc, Airfield Operations, Tel: 0161-489 3657. Fax: 0161-489 2889.

Applications must include:– Aircraft Owner/Operator; Aircraft Type and registration; Flight number (if applicable); Requested time of arrival and departure at Manchester and nominated Handling Agent at Manchester.

Runway Operations:

Westerly runway Ops – Landing traffic will use Rwy 24R and departures Rwy 24L;

Easterly runway Ops – Landing traffic will use Rwy 06R and departures Rwy 06L.

Pilots requiring departure from an intermediate Link must inform ATC prior to taxying.

Rwy 24R arrivals – Link F and D are not available as runway exits.

continued overleaf

Remarks Continued

A nominated Handling Agent is **Mandatory** for all flights.

EASTERN AIRWAYS - Mon-Fri 0700-2000; Sat,Sun 0800-1200. Tel: 0161-436 2055, Fax: 0161-499-1890. Company freq 122·35.

NORTHERN EXECUTIVE AVIATION - Mon-Fri 0700-2000. Tel: 0161-436-6666, Fax: 0161-436-3450. Company freq 130·65.

Other handling agents are: British Airways, GHI, Servisair, Globe Ground and Ringway Handling.

Warning: Flocks of up to 100 racing pigeons may cross the airfield below 100 ft during the racing season April-September.

Restaurant: Airport restaurant and light refreshments H24.

Car Hire: Available at the Terminal.

Fuel: 100LL, Jet A1 Diners, Multi Service	**Tel:** 0161-489 3000 Airport. 0161-499 5320 ATC. 0161-499 5502 Flight Briefing Unit (FBU). 0161-489 3331 Ops Duty Manager. 0161-499 2324 ATIS. **Fax:** 0161-489-2889 Ops. 0161-499 5504 FBU.

Manchester VFR and Special VFR Flights

SVFR clearance for flights within the CTR may be requested and will be given whenever traffic conditions permit. These flights are subject to the general conditions for SVFR flight (see page 6) and will normally be given only to helicopters or aeroplanes other than microlights equipped with RT and the appropriate frequencies.

The use of SVFR clearances is intended to be confined to light aircraft below 5700 kg MTWA which cannot comply with full IFR requirements and wish to proceed to or from an aerodrome within the Zone or wish to transit the Zone at the lower levels.

SVFR clearances to operate within the Manchester CTR will not be granted to fixed wing aircraft when:

(a) Proceeding inbound to Manchester Airport, if the reported meteorological conditions at the airport are 2800 m or less visibility and/or cloud ceiling of less than 1000 ft; or

(b) Outbound from Manchester Airport, if the reported meteorological conditions at the airport are 1800 m or less visibility and/or cloud ceiling of less than 600 ft.

VFR clearance in the Control Zone will be given for flights operating in VMC. Routeing instructions and/or altitude restrictions may be specified in order to integrate VFR flights with other traffic. Pilots are reminded of the requirement to remain in VMC at all times and to comply with the relevant parts of the Low Flying Rules, and must advise ATC if at any time they are unable to comply with the clearance instructions issued.

Special Low Level Route

The Special Low Level Route is 4 nm in width. Within the Low Level Route, helicopters or aeroplanes may fly without individual ATC clearance subject to the following:

    a.   Aircraft to remain clear of cloud and in sight of the ground

    b.   Maximum altitude of 1250 ft, Manchester QNH. Manchester QNH available from ATIS.

    c.   Minimum flight visibilty of 4 km.

    d.   They are transitting through the CTR or proceeding directly to or from an aerodrome in the CTR.

Pilots are advised that the Special Low Level Route is not aligned on the M6 Motorway or on any railway line, and these should not therefore, be used as a navigational line feature for transit throughout the route. However, to the NW and SE of the route, stubs are aligned on the M6 and the Crewe - Winsford railway line to enable pilots to access the route accurately.

Note: Pilots using the Low Level Route are responsible for providing their own separation from other aircraft operating within the Low Level Route airspace at all times.

See CTR/CTA and Entry/Exit Lanes Chart at page 359

MANCHESTER VFR and SVFR ROUTES
VFR and Special VFR Routes to/from Manchester Airport

To integrate VFR and Special VFR flights to/from Manchester Airport with the normal flow of IFR traffic, a number of Standard Routes are established along which ATC VFR and Special VFR clearances will be issued subject to the conditions specified at page 353. These routes are defined by prominent ground features (eg Motorways) and are detailed below.

In order to reduce RTF congestion of Clearance Delivery freqs, the standard outbound Visual Routes are allocated Route Designators. Pilots are to ensure that they are familiar with the route alignment and altitude restrictions prior to departure.

The routes below are depicted on the Manchester CTR Chart at page 359. Visual Reference Points (VRPs) are at page 358.

Standard Outbound Visual Routes

Exit Point	Rwy	Route Designator	Route	Max Alt (QNH)	Remarks
Thelwall	06L/06R	Thelwall 1 Visual	Cross M56 Motorway. Route north of M56 to Thelwall Viaduct VRP, thence via the Low Level Route.	1250 ft	1. Avoid overflying Lymm. 2. Inbound traffic operates south of M56 for Rwy 06L and 06R. 3. **Warning:** Traffic in Low Level Route is unknown to ATC. Traffic information will not be passed.
Congleton	24L/24R	Congleton 3 Visual	Left turn towards Alderley Edge Hill VRP. Route west, then south of Alderley Edge Hill and join the Woodford Entry/Exit Lane at Prestbury Station. Keep the railway line on the left and leave the CTR via Congleton VRP.	2500 ft Notes 1 2 and 6	1. Maximum altitudes 1500 ft between Manchester and the northern edge of Macclesfield, 2500 ft south of the northern edge of Macclesfield to the CTR boundary. 2. **Warning:** High ground to east of the Entry/Exit Lane. 3. The Entry/Exit Lane may be under Woodford or Manchester control. *Notes continued on opposite page*

MANCHESTER VFR and SVFR ROUTES

Standard Outbound Visual Routes

Exit Point	Rwy	Route Designator	Route	Max Alt (QNH)	Remarks
Congleton – Notes continued					4. Aircraft may be routed direct from Manchester to Prestbury Station, or via Woodford. 5. Aircraft must not leave the confines of the Entry/Exit Lane without prior co-ordination with ATC. 6. **Caution:** Alderley Edge 650 ft amsl.

Standard Inbound Visual Routes

Entry Point	Rwy	Route	Max Alt (QNH)	Remarks
Stretton	06L/06R	From Stretton Aerodrome VRP, route via M56 Motorway, keeping the Motorway on the left. Join left base Rwy 06L/06R.	1250 ft	1. Outbound traffic operates north of M56. 2. Aircraft may be held at Stretton VRP or Rostherne VRP.
Congleton	24L/24R	From CTR Boundary east of Congleton VRP, route via the Woodford Entry/Exit Lane (keeping railway line on left) to Woodford aerodrome. Join left base for Rwy 24L/24R.	2500 ft Notes 1 and 5	1. Maximum altitudes 2500 ft between CTR Boundary and the northern edge of Macclesfield, 1500 ft north of Macclesfield ATZ to the Woodford ATZ Southern Boundary.

Notes continued overleaf

Standard Inbound Visual Routes

Entry Point	Rwy	Route	Max Alt (QNH)	Remarks
Congleton – Notes continued				2. Aircraft may be held at Hilltop VRP(open area 1nm NW of Woodford A/D factory). Pilots must hold by visual reference to ensure that the holding pattern does not deviate to the north, which would come into conflict with Rwy 24R final instrument approach, particularly in a southerly wind.
				3. When Rwy 24L is in use as the landing runway, Hilltop VRP will not be used. VFR inbound can expect to hold overhead Woodford aerodrome.
				4. The Entry/Exit Lane may be under the control of Woodford Twr or Manchester App. Pilots should contact Woodford Twr 120·70. If no contact, then Manchester App 119·40.
				5. **Warning:** High ground to the east of the Entry/Exit Lane.
				6. Aircraft must not leave the confines of the Entry/Exit Lane without prior co-ordination with ATC.
				7. Aircraft experiencing a radio failure **inbound** to Manchester whilst in the Woodford Entry/Exit Lane, or holding at Hilltop, are to carry out the Radio Communication Failure procedure detailed at ENR 1.2.2 para 2.9.

Intentionally Blank

VRP	VOR/VOR	VOR/NDB	VOR/DME
Alderley Edge Hill N53 17·72 W002 12·73	MCT R159 WAL R105	MCT R159 WHI 070°M	MCT R159°/4 nm
Barton Aerodrome N53 28·27 W002 23·42	MCT R331 POL R217	MCT R331 WHI 031°M	MCT R331°/8 nm
Buxton N53 15·35 W001 54·77	MCT R120 POL R172	MCT R120 WHI 085°M	MCT R120°/14 nm
Congleton N53 09·90 W002 10·85	MCT R175 TNT R294	MCT R175 WHI 099°M	MCT 175°/12 nm TNT 294°/20 nm
Hilltop N53 20·50 W002 10·45	MCT R111 TNT R318	MCT R111 WHI 064°M	MCT111°/3 nm TNT 318°/25 nm
Jodrell Bank N53 14·18 W002 18·55	MCT R198 WAL R112	MCT R198 WHI 079°M	MCT R198°/7 nm
Rostherne N53 21·23 W002 23·12	MCT R272 POL R208	MCT R272 WHI 045°M	MCT R272°/4 nm
Sale Water Park N53 26·00 W002 18·17	MCT R347 POL R206	MCT R347 WHI 042°M	MCT R347°/5 nm
Stretton Aerodrome N53 20·77 W002 31·58	POL R217 WAL R102	MCT R271 WHI 024°M	MCT R271°/10 nm WAL R102°/22 nm
Swinton Interchange N53 31·40 W002 21·60	POL R220 MCT R346	MCT R346 WHI 029°M	MCT R346°/11 nm
Thelwall Viaduct N53 23·43 W002 30·35	MCT R288 POL R219	MCT R288 WHI 023°M	MCT R288°/9 nm

VAD/VRP Chart for Manchester CTR opposite .

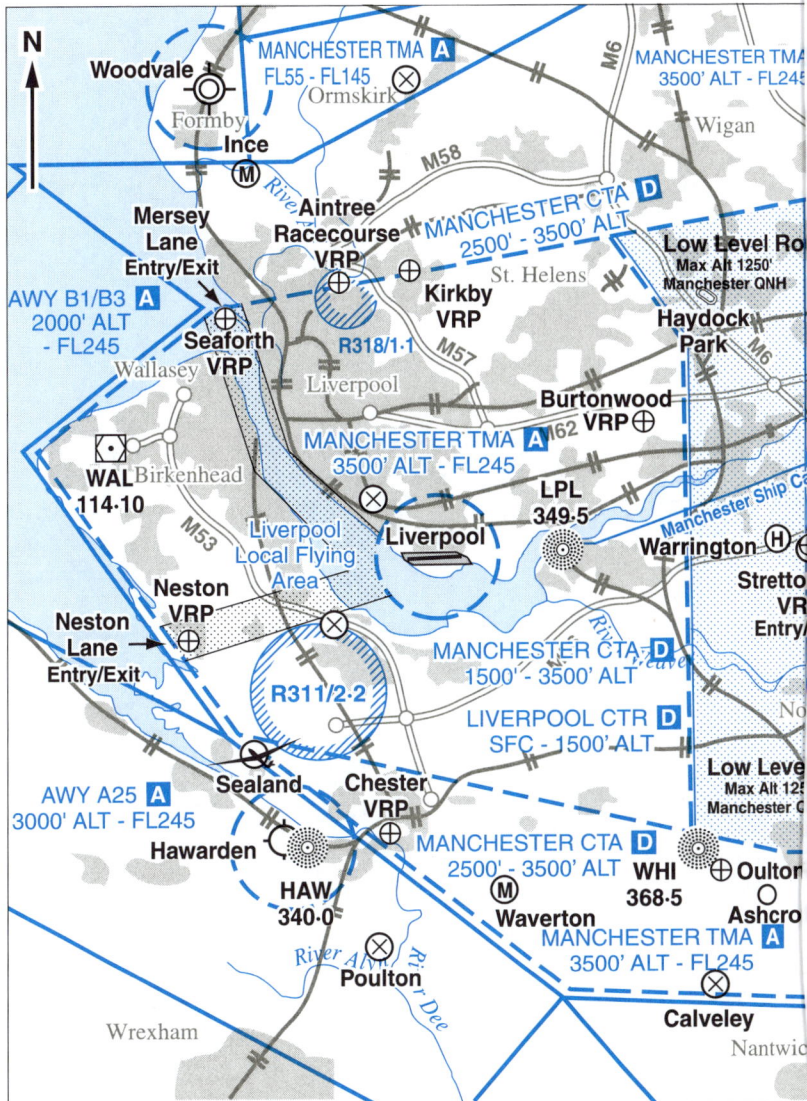

N

Woodvale

MANCHESTER TMA A
FL55 - FL145 ⊗
Ormskirk

M6

MANCHESTER TMA
3500' ALT - FL245

Wigan

Formby

Ince M

River

MANCHESTER TMA A
3500' ALT - FL245

**Mersey
Lane
Entry/Exit**

**Aintree
Racecourse
VRP**

M58

MANCHESTER CTA D
2500' - 3500' ALT

St. Helens

Low Level Ro
Max Alt 1250'
Manchester QNH

AWY B1/B3 A
2000' ALT
- FL245

**Seaforth
VRP**

Wallasey

**Kirkby
VRP**

R318/1·1 M57

**Haydock
Park** M6

Liverpool

WAL Birkenhead
114·10

M53

**Burtonwood
VRP** ⊕

162

MANCHESTER TMA A
3500' ALT - FL245

**LPL
349·5**

**Liverpool
Local Flying
Area**

⊗ Liverpool

Manchester Ship Ca

Warrington H

**Stretto
VR
Entry**

**Neston
VRP**

**Neston
Lane
Entry/Exit**

⊗

R311/2·2

MANCHESTER CTA D
1500' - 3500' ALT

River weaver

LIVERPOOL CTR D
SFC - 1500' ALT

No

**Low Leve
Max Alt 125
Manchester Q**

AWY A25 A
3000' ALT - FL245

Sealand

**Chester
VRP**

MANCHESTER CTA D
2500' - 3500' ALT

**WHI
368·5** ⊕ **Oulton**

Hawarden

**HAW
340·0**

M
Waverton

Ashcro

Poulton

Wrexham

River Al

River Dee

MANCHESTER TMA A
3500' ALT - FL245 ⊗

Calveley

Nantwic

Robert Pooley ©

Intentionally Blank

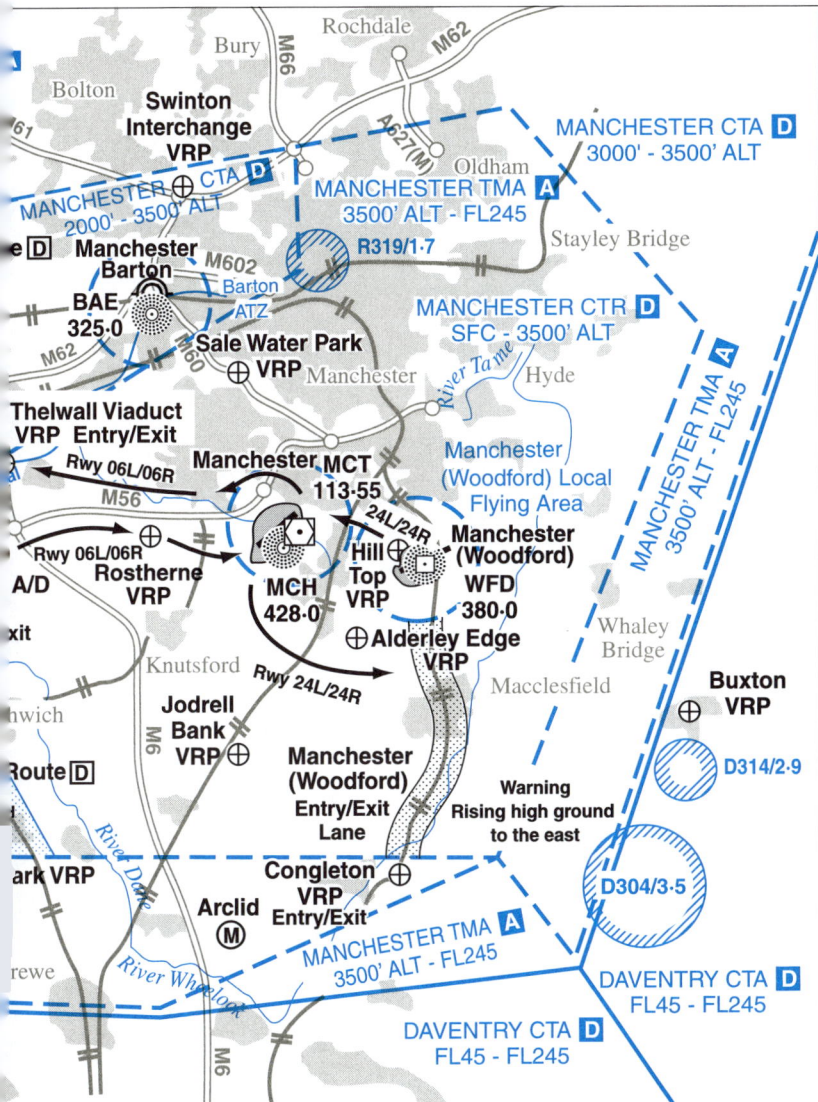

Rochdale

Bury

M62

M66

Bolton

Swinton
Interchange
VRP

Oldham

MANCHESTER CTA **D**
3000' - 3500' ALT

161

MANCHESTER CTA **D**
2000' - 3500' ALT

A627(M)

MANCHESTER TMA **A**
3500' ALT - FL245

Stayley Bridge

R319/1·7

e **D** Manchester
Barton

M602

Barton
ATZ

MANCHESTER CTR **D**
SFC - 3500' ALT

BAE
325·0

M62

M60

Sale Water Park
⊕ VRP

Manchester

River Tame

Hyde

MANCHESTER TMA **A**
3500' ALT - FL245

Thelwall Viaduct
VRP Entry/Exit

Rwy 06L/06R

M56

Manchester MCT
113·55

Manchester
(Woodford) Local
Flying Area

Rwy 06L/06R

⊕
Rostherne
VRP

A/D

xit

MCH
428·0

24L/24R

Hill
Top
VRP

Manchester
(Woodford)

WFD
380·0

Whaley
Bridge

⊕ Alderley Edge
VRP

Macclesfield

Buxton
VRP
⊕

Knutsford

Rwy 24L/24R

D314/2·9

hwich

Jodrell
Bank
VRP ⊕

M6

Manchester
(Woodford)
Entry/Exit
Lane

Warning
Rising high ground
to the east

D304/3·5

Route **D**

River Dane

ark VRP

Congleton
VRP
Entry/Exit ⊕

Arclid
Ⓜ

MANCHESTER TMA **A**
3500' ALT - FL245

DAVENTRY CTA **D**
FL45 - FL245

rewe

River Wheelock

M6

DAVENTRY CTA **D**
FL45 - FL245

1 DEC 00

MANCHESTER CTR/CTA
ENTRY/EXIT LANES, LOW LEVEL ROUTES and VRPs
LIVERPOOL CTR

N53 28·28 W002 23·35	**MANCHESTER (Barton)**	73 ft AMSL

5 nm W of Manchester.	MCT 113·55 332 8·2. POL 112·10 218 19·3

c/s Barton Information/Radio 122·70 AFIS/ A/G. A/G by arrangement.
NDB 'BAE' 325·0 (On A/D).

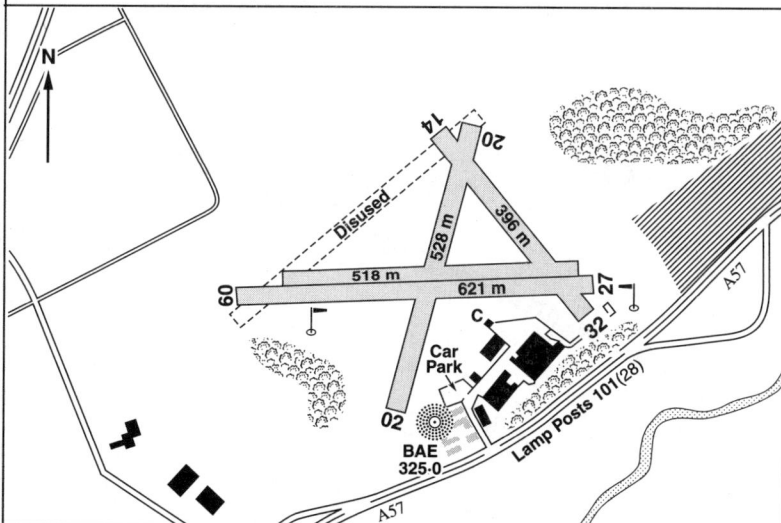

Rwy	Dim(m)	Surface	TORA(m)	LDA(m)	Lighting
02/20	528x33	Grass	02/20-528	02/20-528	Nil
09/27N	518x18	Grass	09/27-518	09/27-518	Nil
09/27S	621x33	Grass	09/27-621	09/27-621	Nil
14/32	396x33	Grass	14/32-396	14/32-396	Nil

Op hrs: PPR. 0900–SS daily. **Customs:** 24 hrs PNR. **Met:** H24. 0161-429 0927

Landing Fees: PRIVATE: £5.00; Rotary £5.00.
COMMERCIAL: SE £20; Rotary SE £20, Twins £40.
PARKING: PRIVATE £3.00/night. COMMERCIAL £5.00/night. All fees subject to VAT.

Hangarage: Limited   **Maintenance:** Light Planes (Lancashire) Ltd. 0161-707 8644.

Remarks: Operated by Lancashire Aero Club. Aerodrome within Manchester CTR —
see Manchester CTR/CTA Chart at page 359.
PPR for instructions on special aerodrome procedures. Aircraft over 1500 kg **must**
have PPR.
In nil wind conditions, pilots should land and take off to the west.
Over head joins at 1500 ft Manchester QNH.
Circuits at 800' Barton QFE, RH on Rwys 14, 20 and 27.
Helicopter circuits inside the fixed wing circuit at 500'.
Airfield situated close to Trafford Park Industrial area. Avoid overflying cemetery on
NE boundary of aerodrome.

Warnings: Power cables 1 nm to W. 35 ft high lamp standards on road SE of A/D.

Fuel: 100LL, Jet A1.	**Tel:** 0161-787 7326 Admin/ATC. **Fax:** 0161 787 8782.

N53 20·28 W002 08·93 | **MANCHESTER WOODFORD** | 298 ft AMSL

5 nm NNW of Macclesfield.

MCT 113·55 112 4·2
POL 112·10 191 24·5

c/s Woodford. APP/TWR 120·70.
NDB 'WFD' 380·0 (On A/D)   ILS/DME Rwy 25 (252°M) I-WU 109·15.

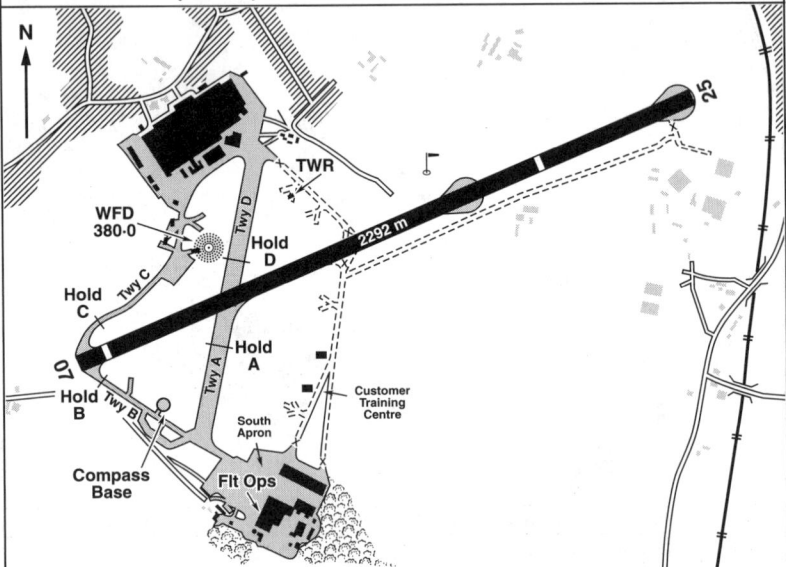

Rwy	Dim(m)	Surface	TORA(m)	LDA(m)	Lighting
07/25	2292x46	Asphalt	07-2167	07-2061	Thr Rwy PAPI 3°
			25-2217	25-1671	Thr Rwy PAPI 3·6°†
					IBn 'WF' Gn

† Additional set of PAPI are solely for test flying purposes.

Op hrs: PPR. SUMMER: Sun-Fri 08-2000, Sat 10-1600. WINTER: Sun-Fri 08-2000, Sat 09-1600

Landing Fee: Visiting aircraft not accepted

Hangarage: Nil.   **Maintenance:** Nil.   **Customs:** Nil.

Remarks: Operated by BAE Systems, Manchester Woodford Aerodrome, Chester Road, Woodford, Cheshire SK7 1QR. Aerodrome situated within the Manchester CTR. Flights within the CTR are governed by the regulations applicable to Class 'D' Controlled Airspace – see pages 2 to 6.

Aerodrome currently only available to BAE Systems aircraft. Visiting aircraft not accepted.

Local Flying Area and Entry/Exit Lanes - See opposite page.

Non standard runway markings are for test flying purposes only.

Fuel: Jet A1 by arrangement.

Tel: 0161-439 3383 ATC
0161 -955 4040 Flt Ops
Fax: 0161-955 3316 ATC

Robert Pooley ©

Local Flying - Within a local flying area of 1.5 nm radius, centred on the aeroodrome, VFR and Special VFR flights may take place subject to clearance from, and such conditions as may be specified by, by Manchester APP.

Manchester Woodford Entry/Exit Lane – An Entry/Exit Lane is established, 1 nm wide, aligned on the Congleton - Macclesfield - Poynton railway line from the boundary of the Manchester Woodford LFA to the southern boundary of the Manchester CTR. VFR and SVFR flights may take place within the Entry/Exit Lane subject to clearance from Manchester ATC and compliance with the following conditions:

(a) Aircraft using the Lane must remain clear of cloud and in sight of the ground.

(b) Maximum altitude of 1500 ft QNH when north of Macclesfield and maximum 2500 ft QNH when over or south of Macclesfield.

(c) Minimum flight visibilty of 3 km.

(d) Pilots must keep the centre-line (the railway line) on the left unless otherwise instructed by ATC.

(e) Pilots are responsible for maintaining adequate clearance from the ground and obstacles, and are warned of high ground to the east of the Entry/Exit Lane.

(f) Aircraft must not leave the confines of the Lane without prior co-ordination with ATC.

(g) Manchester Woodford bound aircraft experiencing a radio failure whilst in the Lane are to carry out Communication Failure Procedure as detailed at ENR 1.1.2 para 2.9.

Note: The Entry/Exit Lane may be under the control of Manchester Woodford or Manchester APP. Pilots should initially contact Woodford Twr 120·70. If no contact, then should contact Manchester App 119·40.

See CTR/CTA and Entry/Exit Lanes Chart for Manchester at page 359

Intentionally Blank

| N51 20·53 E001 20·77 | **MANSTON** | 178 ft AMSL |

2·5 nm W of Ramsgate.

| | **DVR 114·95 001 10·8** |
| | **DET 117·30 090 28·2** |

Manston APP 126·35, 119·925.   RAD 126·35, 129·45 (Director).   TWR 119·925.
NDB 'MTN' 347·0 (On A/D).
ILS/DME Rwy 28 (284°M) I MSN 111·75.

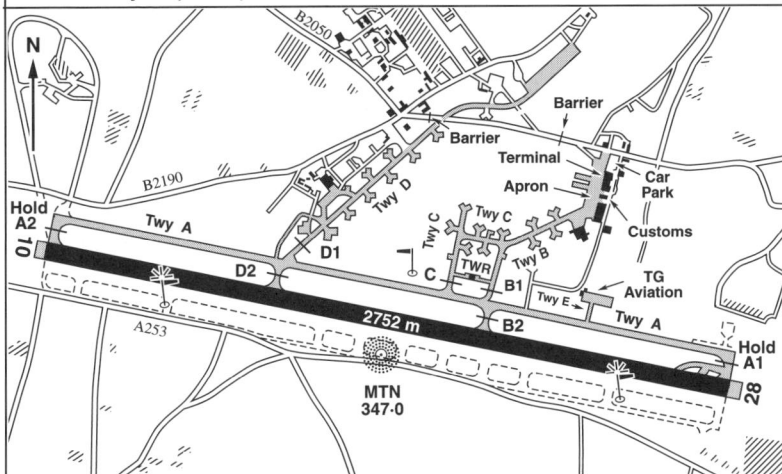

Rwy	Dim(m)	Surface	TORA(m)	LDA(m)	Lighting
10/28	2752x61	Asphalt/	10-2752	10-2752	Ap Thr Rwy PAPI
		Concrete	28-2752	28-2752	Ap Thr Rwy PAPI

Op hrs: PPR. 0800-2000. Other times by arrangement.

Landing Fee: On application.   **Customs:** PPR

Hangarage/Maintenance: Limited.   Jet Support Centre Tel: 01843-823661.
G.A (under 4 Tonnes) – T.G. Aviation 0830-1700 Tel: 01843-823656. O/T call Ops.

Remarks: Operated by London Manston Airport, PO Box 500, Manston, Kent
CT12 5BP.

Sterile areas on the sides of Rwy 10/28 are not to be used for taxiing of aircraft.

Pilots intending to transit between Twy A and B, C or D taxiways are warned that they
are narrow, have sharp turns at the junctions and steep gradients.

Aircraft must carry Third Party Insurance cover of not less than £500,000.

All aircraft should state their location in the initial call.

High visibility clothing mandatory airside.

Caution: Turbulence may be encountered on short final to Rwy 28 when wind is
northwesterly or southerly.

Restaurant: Restaurant and refreshments available.

Taxis: Ramsgate Cars Tel: 01843-581333. Sun Cars Tel: 01843-228822.

Car Hire: Spain's Car Hire Tel: 01843-592149.

| **Fuel:** 100LL - T.G. Aviation 01843-823656.
Jet A1 | **Tel:** 01843- 823600 Airport Ops
Fax: 01843- 821386 Airport Ops |

N51 08·96 W001 34·22	**MIDDLE WALLOP**	297 ft AMSL
5 nm SW of Andover.	**SAM 113·35 329 14·5. CPT 114·35 216 25**	

c/s Wallop. TWR 118·275.
Boscombe Zone 126·70 - For CMATZ Penetration.

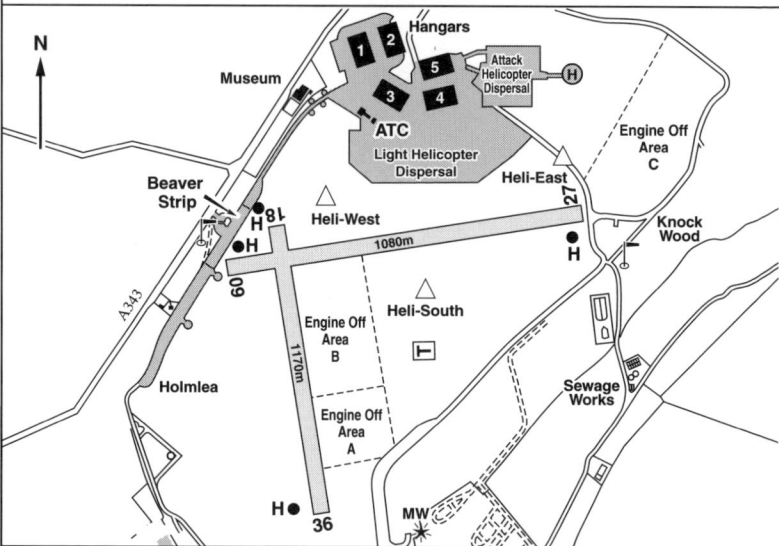

Rwy	Dim(m)	Surface	TORA(m)	LDA(m)	Lighting
09/27	1080x45	Grass	09-1150	09-1380	Ap Rwy (Portable)
			27-1080	27-1200	Rwy (Portable)
18/36	1170x45	Grass	18-1400	18-1370	Rwy (Portable)
			36-1170	36-1400	Rwy (Portable)
					IBn 'MW' Red

Op hrs: Strictly PPR (at least 24 hrs notice) from Deputy CFI.   **ATZ active H24.**

Landing Fee: MoD(Army) Rates.   **Customs:** Nil

Hangarage: Nil   **Maintenance:** Nil

Remarks: Operated by British Army. Flying Training School. Very intensive circuit and instrument flying training by rotary and fixed wing aircraft to radius of 20 nm.

In addition to PPR from Deputy CFI - Tel: 01980-674229, intending visitors must have 'Telephone Brief' from DATCO i/c immediately prior to departure for Middle Wallop.

Frequent night flying. Airfield very undulating.

Helicopters arrive/depart via Heli-west, Heli-east and Heli-south.

Helicopters departing/arriving on Rwy 09/27 will pass beneath the fixed wing circuit.

Helicopter Engine Off Landing (EOL) circuit will operate in opposite direction to fixed wing circuit. EOL Area A will be active on Rwy 09/27 and Area C on Rwy 18/36.

Visiting aircraft may be held clear of the ATZ to allow military training to be completed.

Parascending weekends and Public Holidays.

Fuel: 100LL & Jet A1- by arrangement.	**Tel:** 01980-674380 ATC.

N53 15·53 W004 22·38	**MONA**	202 ft AMSL

2 nm W of Llangefni.

WAL 114·10 266 45
IOM 112·20 170 50·5

c/s Valley Radar 134·35 (MATZ/LARS).
Mona Radio 122·00 A/G - Available evenings in Summer and Weekends only.

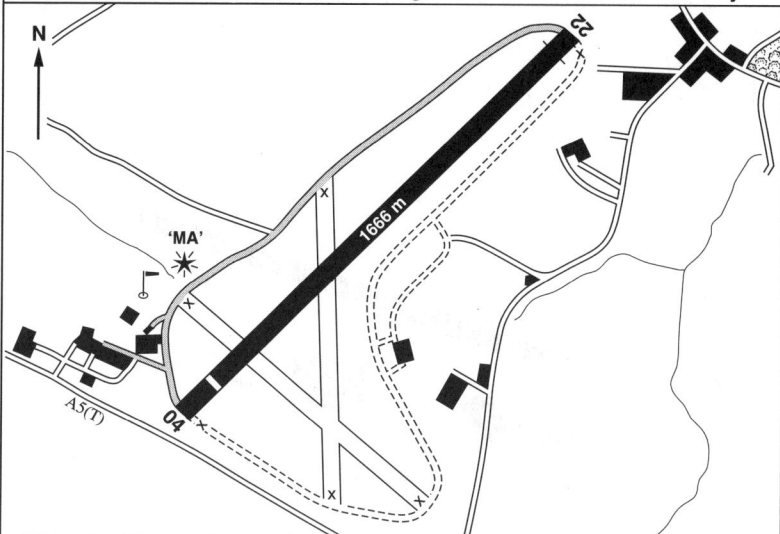

Rwy	Dim(m)	Surface	TORA(m)	LDA(m)	Lighting
04/22	1666x46	Asphalt	04-1579	04-1524	ApThr Rwy PAPI 3°
			22-1579	22-1579	ApThr Rwy PAPI 3·5° RHS
					IBn 'MA' Red

Op hrs: RAF: Mon-Thu 0800-1800, Fri 0800-1730.
Flying Club: WINTER : Sat-Sun 0900-1800.
SUMMER: Mon-Fri 1900-Dusk; Sat-Sun 0900-1800.

Landing Fee: MoD(RAF) Rates	**Customs:** 24 hrs PNR
Hangarage: Limited	**Maintenance:** Nil

Remarks: Relief aerodrome for RAF Valley Mon-Fri. CMATZ controlled by Valley.
Aerodrome operated by Mona Flying Club at weekends.

PPR from OC Ops RAF Valley; weekends PPR from the Mona Flying Club.

RH circuits on Rwy 04.

Fuel: Nil.	**Tel:** Mona Flying Club. 01407-720581 (weekends)
	RAF Valley 01407-762241 Ext 7291.

N54 59·17 W006 38·65	**MOVENIS**	180 ft AMSL
4 nm E of Garvagh.		**BEL 117·20 333 24·4**

c/s Movenis Radio 129·90 A/G.

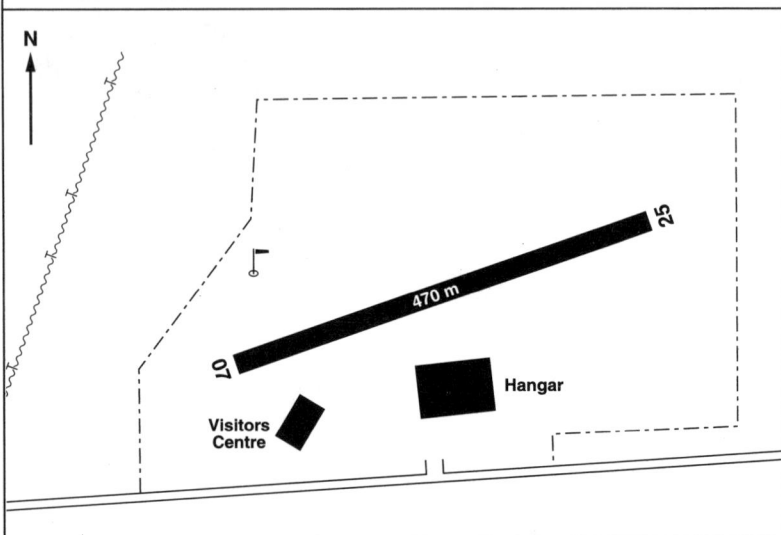

N

25

470 m

07

Hangar

Visitors Centre

Rwy	Dim(m)	Surface	TORA(m)	LDA(m)	Lighting
07/25	470x12	Asphalt	Unlicensed		Nil.

Op hrs: PPR. SR–SS.

Landing Fee: Nil   **Customs:** Nil

Hangarage: By arrangement   **Maintenance:** By arrangement

Met: 028-9442 2339.

Remarks: Operated by Wild Geese Sky-Diving Centre, 116 Carrowreagh Road, Garvagh, Coleraine, Co. Londonderry BT51 5LQ. Unlicensed airfield.

Intensive Parachuting 7 days a week, with increased activity at Weekends and Public Holidays.

Strictly PPR, contact club for briefing.

Inbound aircraft to call on 129·90 at least 10 minutes prior to reaching the airfield.

Restaurant: Buffet available.

Accommodation: Available.

Fuel: Nil.	**Tel:** 028-2955 8609
	Fax: 028-2955 7050
	E-Mail: parachute@wildgeese.demon.co.uk

N55 01·38 W006 35·45	**MULLAGHMORE**	33 ft AMSL
4 nm SW of Ballymoney.		**BEL 117·20 337 25**

c/s Mullaghmore Radio 122·30 A/G.

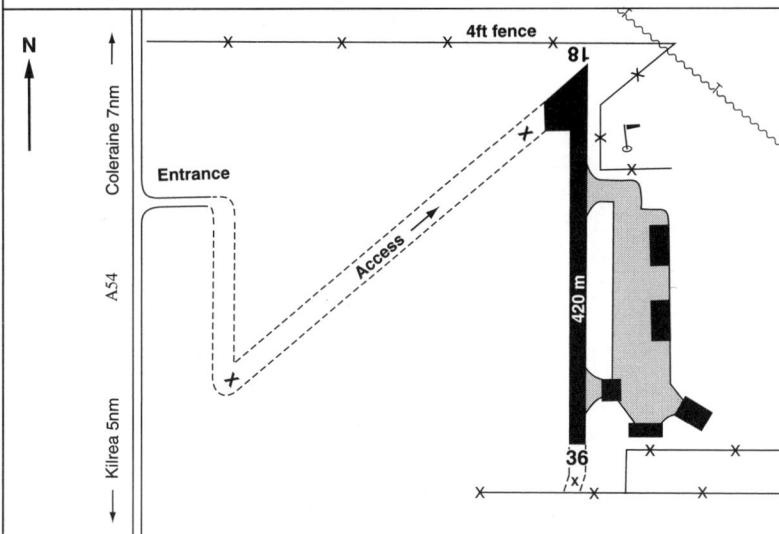

Rwy	Dim(m)	Surface	TORA(m)	LDA(m)	Lighting
18/36	420x10	Asphalt	Unlicensed		Nil.

Op hrs: PPR. SR–SS.

Landing Fee: On application	**Customs:** Nil
Hangarage: By arrangement	**Maintenance:** Microlights only.
Met: 028-9442 2339	**AIS:** 028-9442 2152.

Remarks: Operated by Microflight Ireland Ltd., 67 Main Street, Portrush, N. Ireland.
Unlicensed airfield.
Microlight Circuits at 500 ft aal to east of the airfield.
Sea Plane docking facilities on river Bann to the east of the airfield. Call for details.

Accommodation/Restaurant: Brown Trout, 0·5 mile away, Tel: 028-7086 8209.

Taxi: Tel: 0800-654321.   **Car Hire:** Avis Tel: 028-7034 3654.

Fuel: Mogas – Petrol Station 0·5 mile.	**Tel:** 028-7086 8002 Airfield. 028-7082 3793 Office. **Fax:** 028-7082 4625 Office.

Robert Pooley ©

N53 19·02 W001 11·77	**NETHERTHORPE**	250 ft AMSL
2 nm WNW of Worksop.		**POL 112·10 134 41·3**
		GAM 112·80 289 9·2

c/s Netherthorpe Radio 123·275 A/G. Sheffield City App 128·525 (Traffic Information)

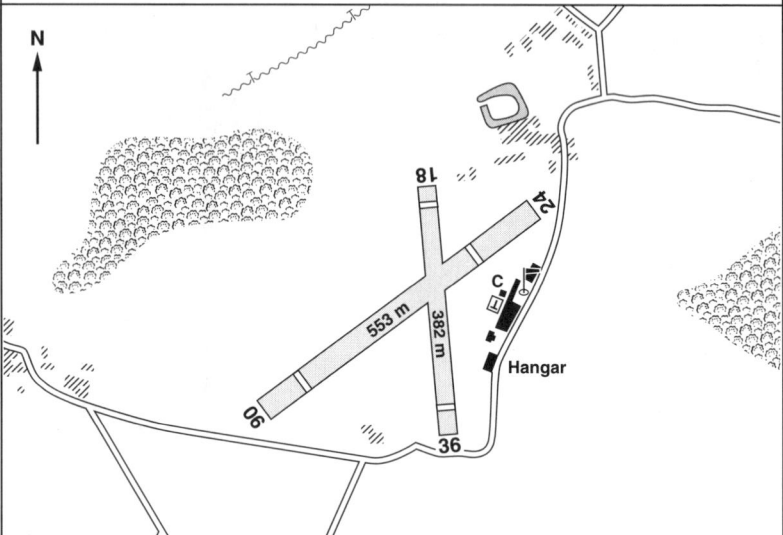

Rwy	Dim(m)	Surface	TORA(m)	LDA(m)	Lighting
06/24	553x36	Grass	06-476	06-407	Nil
			24-490	24-370	Nil
18/36	382x18	Grass	18-382	18-357	Nil.
			36-382	36-309	Nil.
Rwy 06 Gradient 1·9% DOWN.					

Op hrs: PPR. 0915–SS+30, and by arrangement.

Landing Fee: SE Private/Club £5.00 (except reciprocal "no fee" arrangement and PFA aircraft). Commercial: Fixed Wing and Rotary £10.00. Plus VAT.

Hangarage: Ltd   **Maintenance:** Tel: 01909-481802.   **Customs:** By arrangement

Remarks: Operated by Sheffield Aero Club. Strictly PPR by telephone. PPR may be refused to certain aircraft types and inexperienced pilots are to phone for advise.
Traffic inbound from the north or west should contact Sheffield City App 128·525 for traffic information.
Circuits at 800 ft — LH on Rwys 18 and 24, RH on Rwys 06 and 36.
Avoid overflying all farm buildings adjacent to extended centre-lines of runways. Keep clear of village of Thorpe Salvin, 1 nm NW of aerodrome. Do not overfly Shireoaks on left base for Rwy 24, and Whitwell on downwind Rwy 06/24.

Caution: Rwys 06, 24 and 36 have displaced thresholds due to the proximity of public roads. Any pilot whose approach would result in being below 20 ft crossing the road must initiate an immediate missed approach.

Fuel: 100LL by arrangement.	**Tel:** 01909-475233 Airfield, 473428 Club
Most major Credit cards accepted.	**Fax:** 01909- 532413

N51 23·65 W001 18·87	**NEWBURY RACECOURSE**	250 ft AMSL
0·5 nm E of Newbury		CPT 114·35 216 6·9

No Radio. Brize Radar 134·30. Boscombe APP 126·70.

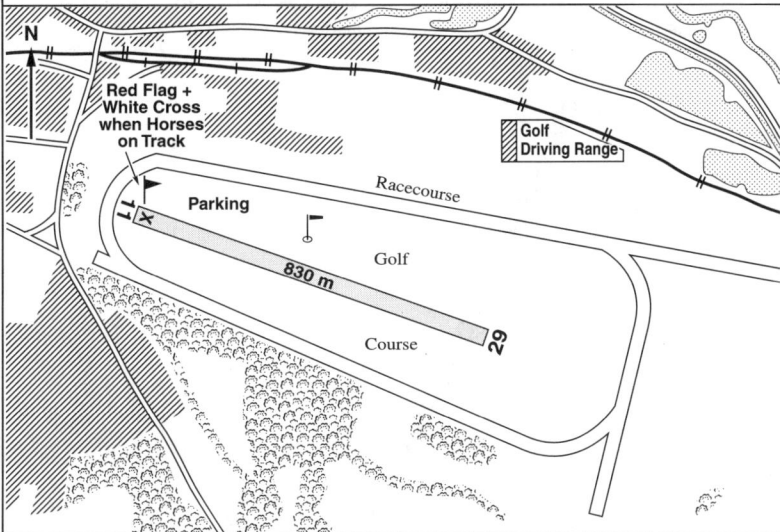

N

Red Flag +
White Cross
when Horses
on Track

Golf
Driving Range

Racecourse

Parking

11

830 m

Golf

Course

29

Rwy	Dim(m)	Surface	TORA(m)	LDA(m)	Lighting
11/29	830x30	Grass	Unlicensed		Nil.

Rwy 11 — take-off only.   Rwy 29 — landing only.

Op hrs: Race days only. PPR.

Landing Fee: Donations to the Groundsmans' Fund much appreciated (box in racecourse office)

Hangarage: Nil.   **Maintenance:** Nil   **Customs:** Nil.

Remarks: Operated by Newbury Racecourse PLC. Newbury, Berkshire, RG14 7NZ. The airfield is available on **race days only** and is strictly for the convenience of everyone involved in horse racing (including spectators) and is not available for use for any other purpose.

Comprehensive briefing notes for pilots are available on request.

The landing strip is sited in the centre of a Golf course. There will be no golf played on race days, but pilots must always exercise extreme caution.

Recommend contact Brize Radar 134·30 or Boscombe App 126·70.

All circuits to the North of runway. All take-offs on Rwy 11; all landings on Rwy 29. The Red Flag and White Cross indicates horses on the track, when all aircraft movements are banned and engines must be shut down. The signal for landing is a White T. Movements are strictly controlled 30 minutes before the first race to 30 minutes after the last race. Pilots should book in and out at the racecourse office.

Warnings: Tall trees 600 m E of Rwy 29 Thr. Tall tree 200 m West of Rwy 11 Thr. 4 ft plastic running rail 20 m from Rwy 29 Thr.

Fuel: Nil.	**Tel:** 01635-40015 Racecourse Office
	01386-853300 Capt. A. J. Biltcliffe (Advisor)

Robert Pooley ©

N55 02·25   W001 41·50   **NEWCASTLE**   266 ft AMSL

APP/RAD 124·375.   TWR 119·70.   RAD 118·50.   ATIS 114·25 (VOR)
VDF 124·375, 119·70, 118·50.   [Samson Ops 130·65]
VOR/DME 'NEW' 114·25 (On A/D).
NDB 'NEW' 352·0 (250°M/1·2 nm to Thr 25).   **NDB 'WZ' 416·0** (070°M/3·9 nm to Thr 07).
† ILS/DME Rwy 07 (070°M) **I-NC 111·50.   ILS/DME Rwy 25** (250°M) **I-NWC 111·50.**

† Rwy 07 GP not to be used at a range of greater than 8·5 nm from Thr.

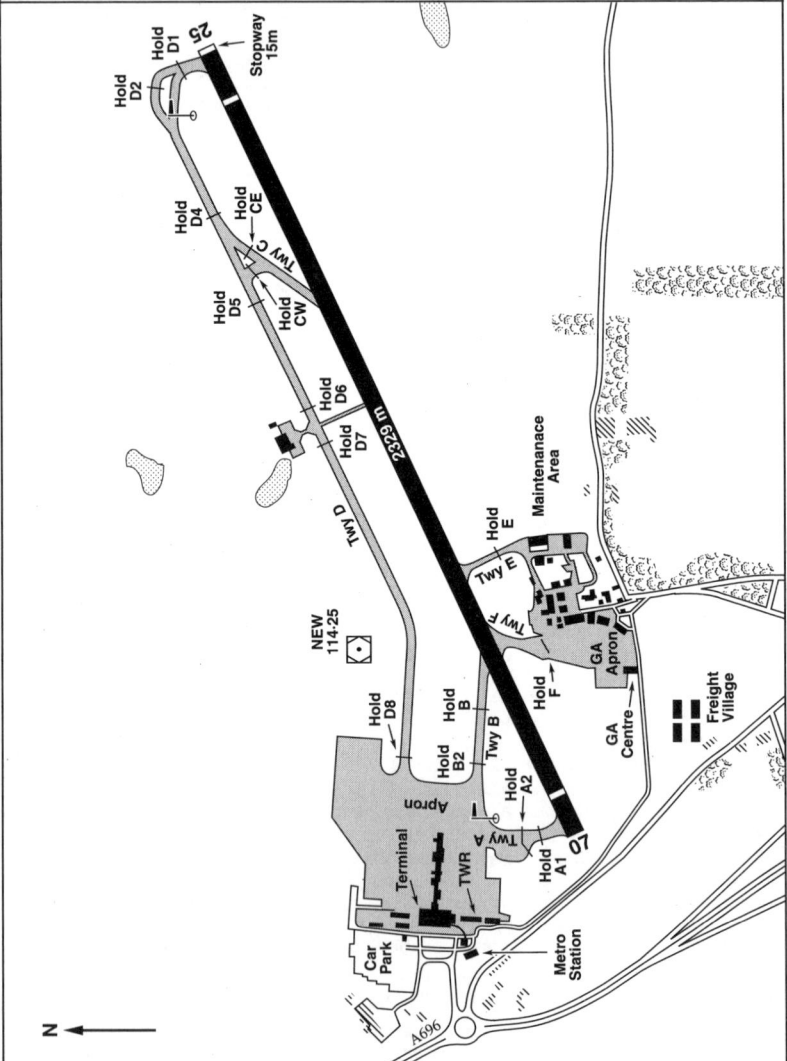

Robert Pooley ©

| N55 02·25 W001 41·50 | **NEWCASTLE** | 266 ft AMSL |

5 nm NW of Newcastle-upon-Tyne.

Rwy	Dim(m)	Surface	TORA(m)	LDA(m)	Lighting
07/25	2329x46	Asphalt	07-2329 25-2262	07-2209 25-2125	Ap Thr Rwy RCL PAPI (RH) Ap Thr Rwy RCL PAPI (LH) IBn 'NE' Gn

Op hrs: H24.

Landing Fee: Up to 3000 kg £6.34 per 500 kg or part;
Over 3000 kg £12.68 per tonne or part.

Hangarage: Limited.   **Customs:** Available.

Maintenance: M3 available at GA Terminal. 0191-214 4111

Remarks: Operated by Newcastle International Airport Limited, Newcastle Airport, Woolsington, Newcastle-Upon-Tyne NE13 8BZ.

Flights within the Newcastle CTR/CTA are subject to the regulations applicable to Class 'D' Controlled Airspace — see pages 2 and 6.

Visual Reference Points (VRPs) are listed overleaf.

CTA/CTR and VRPs Chart is at page 375.

Non-radio aircraft PPR.

Training flights may only take place by prior arrangement with ATC and only within the following times (local): Mon-Sat 0730-2300, Sun 1000-2300.

Variable circuits.

Gliding at Currock Hill 8 nm SW of Newcastle Airport from dawn to dusk; ATC will advise when active.

All aircraft are required to carry valid third party liability insurance cover of at least 1 million pounds.

High visibility clothing mandatory on the aprons.

Booking Out – Details should be passed by telephone, RT calls may result in delays.

Ground Handling:

All General Aviation aircraft are required to nominate a handling agent. Failure to do so will result in the provision of a security escort for which a charge will be levied.

The exceptions to the above are:

1. Ferry flights which have been agreed in writing by the Managing Director and for which only fuel is required;
2. Crew-only positioning flights but, for aircraft wishing to park on the main apron, a security charge will be levied;
3. Newcastle based operators. It will be the captain's responsibility to present to the Control Authorities any non-EC national as well as any other person required to be presented in accordance with current UK regulations.

Handling on the main apron is provided by Northeast Aviation and Servisair.
The General Aviation Centre on the South side is operated by Samson Aviation, 0800-2000 (local) and by arrangement, Freq 130·65, c/s 'Samson Operations'.
Noise Preferential Routes & Procedures in force.
Helicopter operations as directed by ATC.

continued overleaf

Remarks continued:

Visual Reference Points

VRP	VOR/DME
Blydon N54 58.10 W001 41.62	NEW R183/4 nm
Blyth Power Station N55 08.50 W001 31.50	NEW R049/9 nm
Bolam Lake N55 07·88 W001 52·47	NEW R317/8 nm
Durham N54 46.43 W001 34.60	NEW R170/16 nm
Hexham N54 58.25 W002 06.17	NEW R259/14 nm
Morpeth Rly Station N55 09.75 W001 40.97	NEW R009/7 nm
Ouston (Disused AD) N55 01.50 W001 52.52	NEW R267/6 nm
Stagshaw Masts N55 02.00 W002 01.42	NEW R273/11 nm
Tyne Bridges N54 58.05 W001 36.42	NEW R148/5 nm

Restaurant: Restaurant and Club facilities available.

Car Hire: Hertz. Tel: 0191-286 72500. Avis. Tel: 0191-286 0815.
Godfrey Davis. Tel: 01632-610772.

Fuel:

100LL & Jet A1 – Samson Aviation Ltd, Tel: 0191-214 4111/4114.
Jet A1 – Air BP & CONOCO. Tel: 0191-286 0966 Ext 4290, or 0191-286 2252.
　　　Fax: 0191-271 3002.

Tel:　0191-286 0966 Switchboard.　0191-214 3244 ATC Supervisor.
Fax:　0191-271 6080 Airport Authority. 0191-271 4742 ATC.

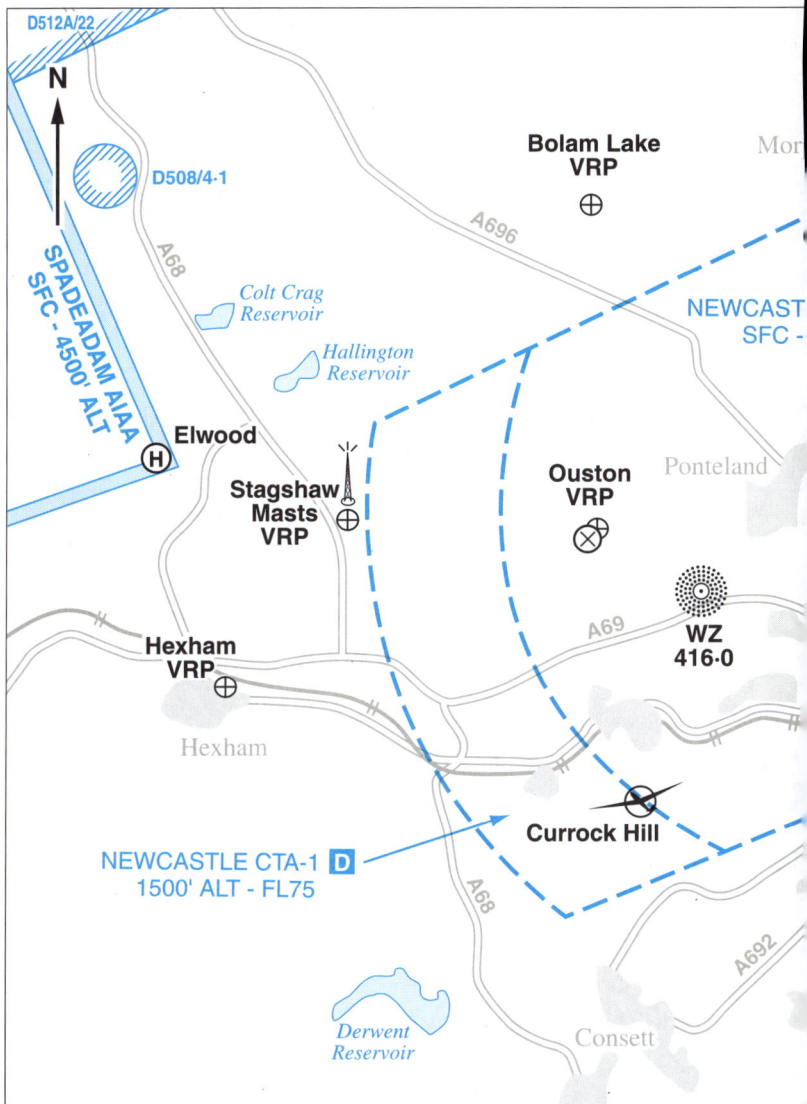

D512A/22

N

D508/4·1

Bolam Lake VRP
⊕

Mor

A696

NEWCAST
SFC -

Colt Crag Reservoir

SPADEADAM AIAA SFC - 4500' ALT

Hallington Reservoir

Elwood
Ⓗ

Stagshaw Masts VRP
⊕

Ouston VRP
⊗

Ponteland

A68

WZ 416·0

Hexham VRP
⊕

A69

Hexham

NEWCASTLE CTA-1 **D**
1500' ALT - FL75

⊗
Currock Hill

A68

A692

Derwent Reservoir

Consett

Robert Pooley ©

Intentionally Blank

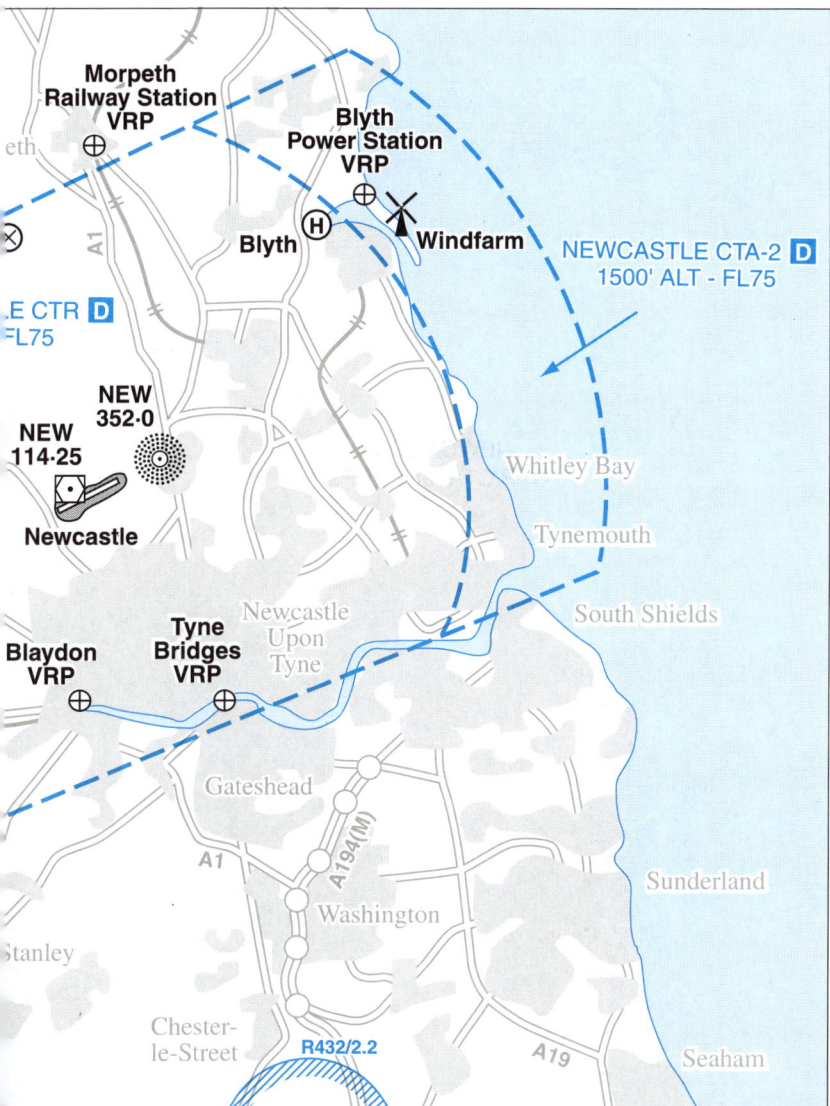

Morpeth
Railway Station
VRP

eth

⊗

A1

Blyth
Power Station
VRP

Ⓗ Blyth

Windfarm

NEWCASTLE CTA-2 Ⓓ
1500' ALT - FL75

E CTR Ⓓ
FL75

NEW
352·0

NEW
114·25

Newcastle

Whitley Bay

Tynemouth

South Shields

Tyne
Bridges
VRP

Newcastle
Upon
Tyne

Blaydon
VRP

Gateshead

A1

A194(M)

Washington

Sunderland

Stanley

Chester-
le-Street

R432/2.2

A19

Seaham

1 DEC 00

NEWCASTLE
CTR/CTA and VRPs

Intentionally Blank

N52 14·52 E000 22·23	**NEWMARKET HEATH**	100 ft AMSL
1·5 nm W of Newmarket.		BKY 116·25 042 19 CLN 114·55 314 37

No Radio. Lakenheath 128·90 (MATZ).
Cambridge App 123·60.

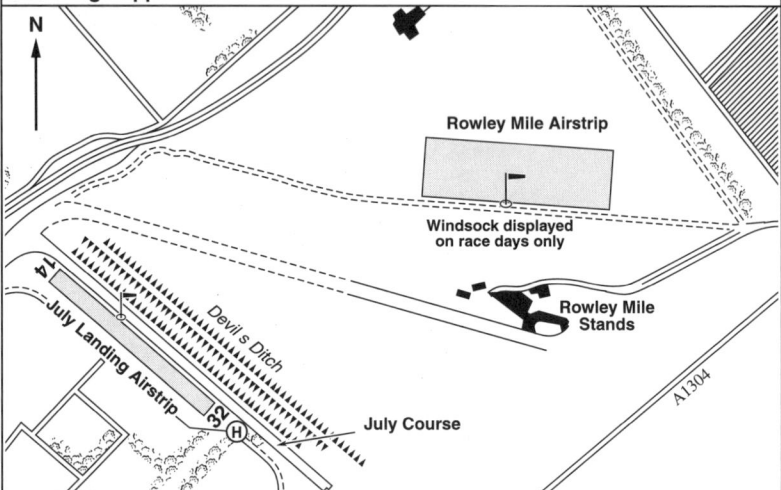

Rwy	Dim(m)	Surface	TORA(m)	LDA(m)	Lighting
Rowley Mile Strip:					
	800x 274	Grass	Unlicenced		Nil.
July Course Strip:					
14/32	914x70	Grass	Unlicenced		Nil.

Op hrs: PPR. Race Days 1200-1800 only.	**Customs:** Nil

Landing Fee: £20.00 + VAT non Race days. Nil on Race days.

Remarks: Operated by the Jockey Club Estates Ltd. Unlicensed airfield comprising two separate landing strips, the Rowley Mile Airstrip to the north of the Rowley Mile Racecourse and the July Airstrip adjacent to the July Racecourse. All landings and take-offs are at the pilot's own risk. Further details from the Jockey Club Estates Ltd.

Rowley Mile Airstrip

Available to light aircraft between 1200 and 1800 hrs **only when racing is on the Rowley Mile Course**. Prior permission must be obtained from Newmarket Racecourses Trust Ltd, Tel: 01638-662762 on race days; 01638-663482 if telephoning in advance.

Except with the express permission of the Racecourse Manager, pilots will not be permitted to land or take-off between half an hour before the first race and half an hour after the last race. Permission will only be given provided horses have not left the Parade ring and are not on the Racecourse itself.

July Airstrip — see opposite page.

Restaurant: Refreshments on the racecourse on race days only.

Car Hire: Godfrey Davis. Tel: 01223-48198/9.　　Marshall Hire: Tel: 01223-62211.

Taxi: Newtax Tel: 01638-561561. Style Cars Tel: 01638-662226.

Fuel: Nil.	**Tel:** Jockey Club Estates Ltd. Tel: 01638-664151 Newmarket Racecourses Trust Tel: 01638-663482

Robert Pooley ©

NEWMARKET HEATH

Rwy14/32 (July Airstrip) availability as follows:

1. **Race Days** — A detailed briefing sheet is available from either Newmarket Racecourses Trust or the Jockey Club Estates Ltd and pilots should be aware of its contents prior to arrival at the airfield.

All landings are to be made using Runway 14; Rwy 32 must be used for take-off.

Except with the express permission of the Racecourse Manager, pilots will not be permitted to take off or land between half an hour before the first race and half an hour after the last race. Permission will only be given provided horses have not left the parade ring and are not on the racecourse itself.

All landings and take offs are banned when either a large yellow or white cross is displayed at the Southern end of the strip.
Tel: 01638-662752 race days only.

2. **Other Days** — permission to land and take off is required from:
Jockey Club Estates Ltd, 101 High Street, Newmarket, Suffolk, CB8 8JL.
Tel: 01638-664151.

Intentionally Blank

Intentionally Blank

| N54 34·87 W005 41·52 | **NEWTOWNARDS** | 9 ft AMSL |

| 8·5 nm E of Belfast. | BEL 117·20 112 19 |
| | IOM 112·20 321 45 |

c/s Newtownards Radio 123·50 A/G.

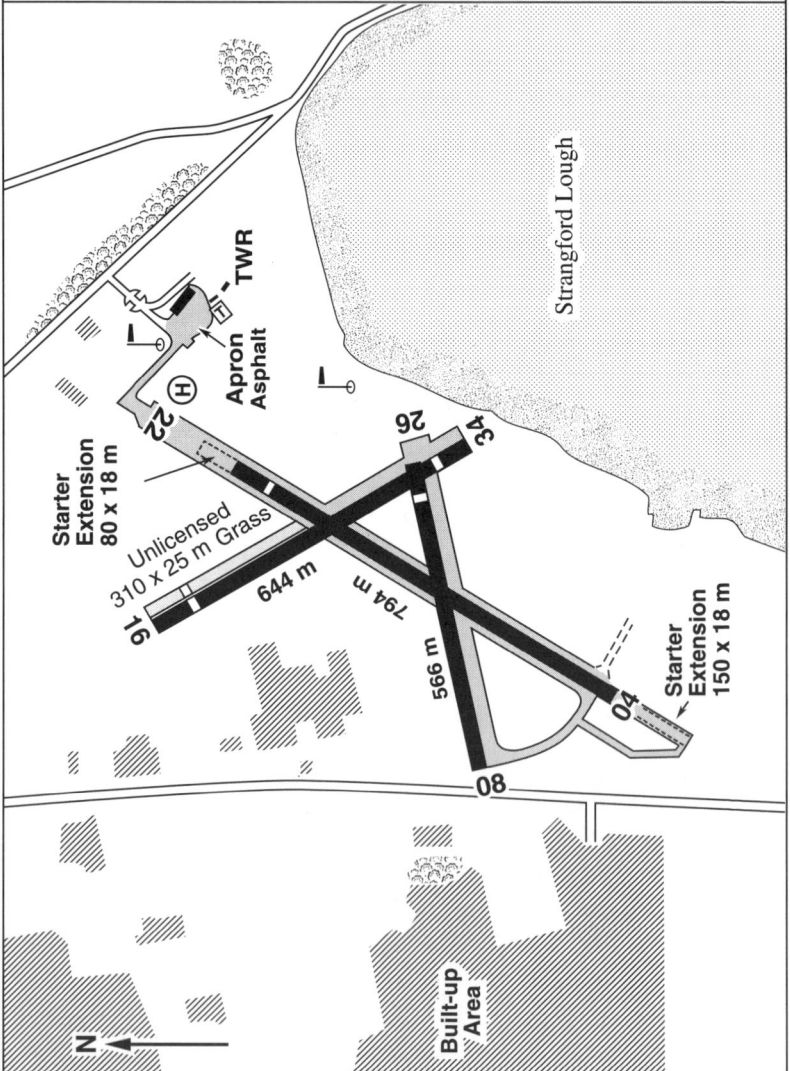

Strangford Lough

TWR

Apron Asphalt

Ⓗ

22

Starter Extension 80 x 18 m

Unlicensed 310 x 25 m Grass

16

644 m

26

34

794 m

566 m

04

Starter Extension 150 x 18 m

08

Built-up Area

N

Robert Pooley ©

N54 34·87 W005 41·52		**NEWTOWNARDS**			9 ft AMSL
Rwy	**Dim(m)**	**Surface**	**TORA(m)**	**LDA(m)**	**Lighting**
04/22	794x18	Asphalt	04-794 22-794	04-794 22-720	Thr Rwy APAPI 4·5° Thr Rwy APAPI 4·5°
† 08/26	566x18	Asphalt	08-566 ———	——— 26-566	Nil. Nil.
16/34	644x18	Asphalt	16-566 34-559	16-533 34-566	Nil. Nil.
					ABn Wh/Gn.

† Rwy 08 Take-offs only. Rwy 26 Landings only.

Op hrs: PPR. 0900-1730 daily.

Landing Fee: Singles £10, Twins £25. Incl of VAT.   **Customs:** 24 hrs PNR

Hangarage: Limited   **Maintenance:** Available on request

Remarks: Operated by Ulster Flying Club, Ards Aerodrome, Portaferry Road, Newtownards, Co. Down, BT23 8SG, Ireland. PPR.

Visiting aircraft welcome.

Not a 'Designated airfield' under the Prevention of Terrorism Act. Inbound and outbound flights must obtain prior approval from Duty Inspector Force Information Tel: 028-9065 0222.

Aerodrome unlicensed for aircraft exceeding 2,730 kg, and for public transport passenger flights.

Some areas between the runways may be under cultivation.

Rwy 08/26 not available to solo students.

Circuits at 1000 ft aal. Microlights at 700 ft aal. RH on Rwy 04, LH on Rwys 16, 22 and 34. Rwy 26 not available for circuits.

Warnings: Mast 126' aal 135' amsl. on approach to Rwy 16, 0·5 nm from 16 Thr.

Floodlighting standards 53' aal, 62' amsl, surround the football ground situated right of extended centreline on final approach to Rwy 22.

Hill 696' aal, 705 amsl 314°/2·8 nm.

Tower 582' aal, 591' amsl 267°/0·9 nm.

Chimney 82' aal, 91' amsl 358°/0·5 nm.

Power cables on high ground rising to 232' aal, 241' amsl on Rwy 22 approach 0·5 nm from runway.

There is high ground and a lighted obstruction that infringes the protected surface of the 26 climb-out. There are near-in lamp standards on the Comber Road that may present an obstruction in the event of a late decision to commence a missed approach. Turbulence may be experienced during a missed approach.

Restaurant: Licensed, Lunches & evening meals daily.

Car Hire: 028-9127 0942

Fuel: 100LL, Jet A1 by arrangement.	**Tel:** 028-9181 3327. **Fax:** 028-9181 4575.

N52 18·32 W000 47·57	**NORTHAMPTON (Sywell)**	429 ft AMSL

5 nm NE of Northampton.   **DTY** 116·40 063 14
HON 113·65 101 32

c/s Sywell Information. 122·70. AFIS.
NDB 'NN' 378·50 (030°M/0·2nm to Thr 03) Nav. only.

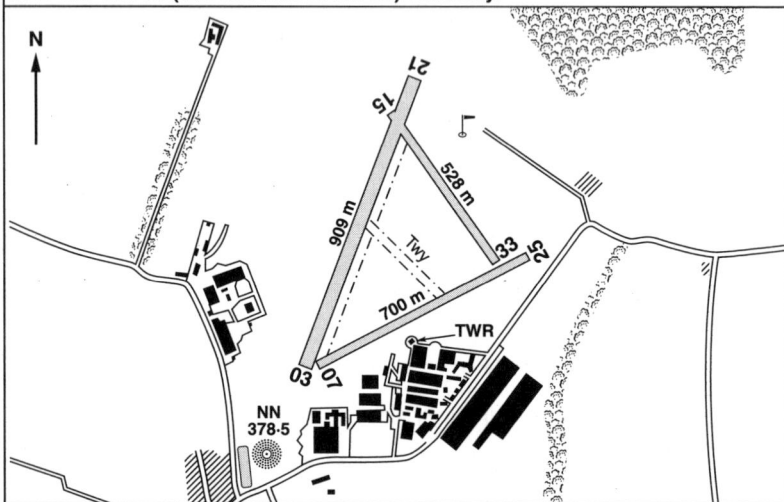

Rwy	Dim(m)	Surface	TORA(m)	LDA(m)	Lighting
03/21	909x30	Grass	03-909	03-909	Thr Rwy LITAS 4°(LH)
			21-909	21-909	Thr Rwy LITAS 4°(LH)
15/33	528x18	Grass	15-528	15-528	Nil.
			33-528	33-528	Nil.
07/25	700x18	Grass	07-700	07-700	Nil.
			25-700	25-700	Nil.
					IBn 'NN' Gn

Op hrs: WINTER: 09-1700 or SS daily (Whichever earlier)
SUMMER: Mon-Fri 0900-1900 or SS; Sat & Sun 0900-1800 or SS (Whichever earlier)

Landing Fee: Singles, fixed & rotary – £9.00; Twins £16.00; Microlights £7.00 —
All inc of VAT.   Special rates for Circuit training.

Hangarage: Available   **Maintenance:** Available   **Customs:** PNR.

Remarks: Operated by Sywell Aerodrome Ltd, Sywell, Northampton NN6 0BT. PPR.
Caution, public road runs along SE, S and SW boundaries.

Fixed wing circuits at 1000 ft aal; LH on 03, 15 & 25, RH on 07, 21 & 33.
Helicopter circuits at 700 ft in opposite direction to fixed wing.

Southern edge of Rwy 03/21 and northern edge of Rwy 15/33 are marked by a
number of 2 metre square white ground markers for helicopter operations; fixed wing
pilots should disregard.

Restaurant: Restaurant, Refreshments and Hotel (45 bedrooms), with
aircraft parking adjacent.

Fuel: 100LL, Jet A1 (AL48).	**Tel:** 01604- 644917 AFIS.
Diners Card, Visa, Mastercard,	01604- 491112 - Admin. 642111 Hotel.
Switch and Delta	**Fax:** 01604- 499210 AFIS.

N53 30·27 E000 03·73	**NORTH COATES**	17 ft. AMSL

6 nm SE Grimsby.	OTR 113·90 158 13
	GAM 112·80 075 38

North Coates Radio 120·15 A/G.
Donna Nook Range 122·75 A/G.

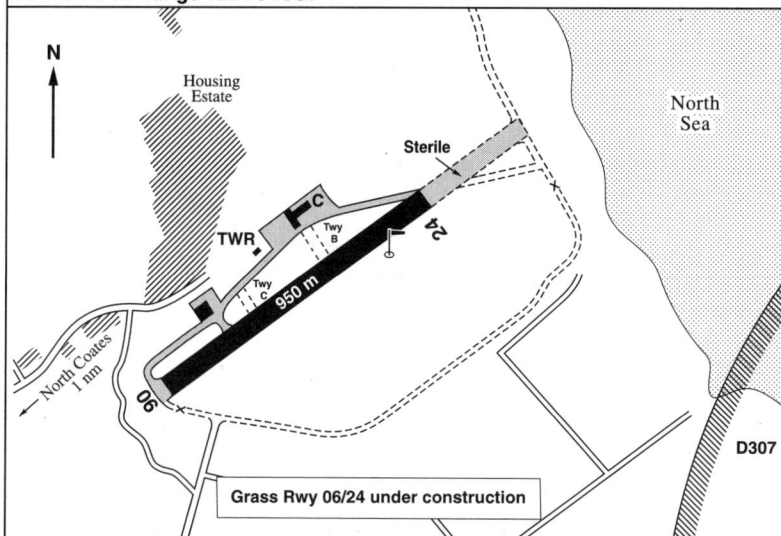

Grass Rwy 06/24 under construction

Rwy	Dim(m)	Surface	TORA(m)	LDA(m)	Lighting
06/24	950x45	Concrete	Unlicensed		Nil

Op hrs: PPR. Mon-Sun.

Landing Fee: £5. Microlights - £2.50	**Customs:** 24 hrs PNR

Hangarage: Available	**Maintenance:** Limited

Remarks: Operated by North Coates Flying Club Ltd. Unlicensed aerodrome.
Visiting aircraft welcome on prior permission and at pilot's own risk.
Inbound traffic must call Donna Nook Range on 122·75 at least 5 mins or 15 nm from
North Coates to ascertain range activity status.

Approach North Coates from the West or South West and, if notified that Donna Nook
Northerly pattern is active, descend to be at 500 ft (Donna Nook QFE) when within
2 nm of North Coates Airfield. Advise Donna Nook Range by radio when landing
complete.

Circuits normally at 1000' aal, LH on 06, RH on 24, opposite circuits at weekends
when the Range is closed.

Avoid overflying the village of North Coates and the housing estate on NW side of the
airfield.

DAAIS: Telephone RAF Donna Nook 01507-358716 Ext 130.

Restaurant: Refreshments and snacks.	**Car Hire/Taxis:** By arrangement

Fuel: 100LL.	Tel: 01472-388850 Flying Club Weekends
	and Evenings.
	01472-500144 Chairman - Evenings only.

N51 33·18   W000 25·09   **NORTHOLT**   124 ft AMSL

2 nm ENE of Uxbridge.   **BNN 113·75 160 11·5. LON 113·60 029 4·3**

Northolt APP 126·45. RAD c/s Director 130·35. TWR 120·675. Dep 120·325.
Brize/ Benson - Frequency as directed. **Essex Radar 120·625. ATIS 125·125.**
ILS/DME Rwy25 (254°M) 'I NHT' 108·55.

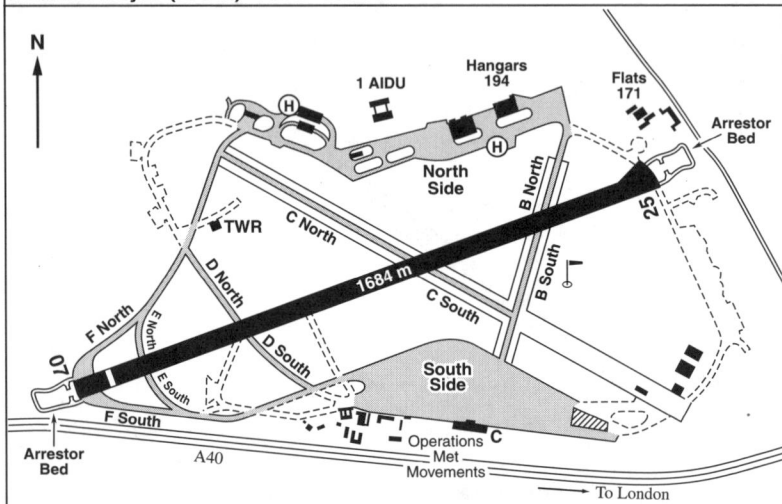

Rwy	Dim(m)	Surface	TORA(m)	LDA(m)	Lighting
07/25	1684x46	Asphalt	07-1684	07-1592	Ap Thr Rwy PAPI 3°
			25-1684	25-1684	Ap Thr Rwy PAPI 3·5°
					IBn 'NO' Red

Op hrs: 0800-2000 daily. (All civil aircraft 24 hrs PPR.). **Note:** Between 08 -2000 Sat & Sun civil aircraft will only be accepted when the aerodrome is planned to be open for military movements.

Landing Fee: MoD(RAF) Rates   **Customs:** 24 hrs PNR

Hangarage: Nil   **Maintenance:** Nil

Remarks: RAF Aerodrome. British Civil aircraft PPR from Ops Ext 4233. Civilian movements restricted to 28 per day. Single-engined aircraft accepted only under exceptional circumstances and are subject to the restrictions for SVFR flight in the London CTR. Except when operating under SVFR, pilots must hold a valid Instrument Rating. All procedures are flown on Northolt QNH.

Visual circuits at 1000' QNH, LH on Rwy 07, RH on Rwy 25.

A ground/safety crew must be in position at the aircraft before any engine start will be approved. Initial call on 120·675 for start and ATC clearance.

Noise abatement procedures:
Minimum ground running. Min ht 70 ft for crossing A/D bndy on take-off. Mandatory climb of at least 500 ft/min at power settings which will ensure progressively decreasing noise levels. Take off, overshoot and missed app on Rwy 07/25, climb to 700 ft (QNH) before turning. Aircraft on Radar App shall not descend below 1500 ft (QNH) before intercepting glidepath. Aircraft on visual approach shall follow a descent path not lower than PAPI approach path.

Warnings and Flight Procedures – See opposite and the following page.

Fuel: Avtur by arrangement. Jet A1   **Tel:** 020-8845 2300 Ext. 4233

Warnings

(a) Soft Ground arrester beds are provided to stop aircraft in the event of an overrun on either runway as detailed below:

(i) The bed for overrun on Rwy 07 is 90 m long and is disposed symmetrically about the extended runway centreline in a gentle hour glass shape being 70 m wide at its narrowest point. The bed starts 45 m beyond the end of the centre of the paved surface.

(ii) The bed for overrun on Rwy 25 is also 90 m long with a basic shape as for Rwy 07 but with a truncated top left hand corner as viewed from the runway. It is 70 m wide in the centre decreasing to 50 m at its narrowest point at the top. The bed starts 25 m beyond the end of the centre of the paved surface.

(b) Denham is 4 nm Northwest of Northolt, circuit altitude 1000 ft. SVFR departures from Northolt are to remain clear of the Denham ATZ.

(c) Moderate turbulence and windshear may be experienced on approach to Rwy 25 when there is a strong North-westerly wind.

(d) Starling roost active at dawn and dusk, October to March, 0·5 nm East of Rwy 25 threshold.

Flight Procedures

(a) Runway selection at Northolt is related to that at Heathrow. It may be necessary to operate with a tail wind component.

(b) When Rwy 23 at Heathrow is in use for approaches, non airways arrivals requiring an instrument approach to Rwy 25 at Northolt are not permitted. If the cloud base is 1200 ft or better and the visibility is 6 km or better, radar vectored visual approaches to Rwy 25 may be made under the control of Northolt, with the agreement of Heathrow Approach Control, providing the following conditions are observed:

(i)   The pilot must be familiar with Northolt Aerodrome;

(ii)   the aircraft must remain within 1·5 nm of the Northolt aerodrome boundary;

(iii) the circuit must not be flown above 1000 ft (QNH).

(c) If Northolt Radar is not available, the Romeo and Charlie Non-Airways arrival procedures will be suspended and all approaches are to be via airways excepting under the following procedure. When the cloudbase is greater than 2000 ft and the visibility is 10 km or greater, approaches made from the Princes Risborough area under a Radar Information Service provided by London Military Radar to a freelane. The freelane will be established 2 nm either side of the OCK VOR RDL 005° or BNN VOR RDL 160° (in the event of OCK VOR unserviceability) from Northolt northbound to the London CTR boundary from ground level up to 2000 ft on the London QNH. The following conditions apply:

(i)   The pilot must be familiar with Northolt Aerodrome;

(ii)   The aircraft must be authorised by Northolt to make a visual approach to the aerodrome before entering the London CTR via the freelane.

(d) The high traffic density in the local area may mean pilots using non airways arrival/departure procedures are given a limited radar service in which standard separation may not be achieved.

(e) All IFR procedures are flown on the LONDON QNH unless otherwise specified. Landing datum is the Northolt QNH. Northolt QFE is available on request.

(f) A minimum glidepath of 3·5° is mandatory for all instrument approaches to Rwy 25.

(g) Departing aircraft are to make their initial call on 120·675 for start and ATC clearance.

(h) Simulated and practice asymmetric approaches and landings are not permitted.

Aircraft Inbound to Northolt

(i)   The standard routes for aircraft inbound to Northolt are the same as those for London Heathrow.

(ii)   Inbound aircraft, after the clearance limit, will be radar vectored and issued with descent clearance by Heathrow Director. Where possible aircraft will be instructed to contact Northolt Radar at least 10 nm before touch-down.

(iii) London TMA speed restrictions apply to inbound flights

Radar Manoeuvring Area (RMA)

(i)   The RMA is the northern portion of the London CTR, with boundaries defined as follows:

From the Northolt ARP, on alignment of 283°(T) to the CTR Boundary;
From the Northolt ARP, on alignment of 084°(T) to the CTR Boundary;
The northern Boundary of the CTR between these lines.

(ii)   The vertical extent of the RMA is 2000 ft QNH. In order to facilitate expedition, vertical separation between aircraft flying in the RMA under the control of Northolt ATC may be reduced to 500 ft. The pilots concerned will be advised of this reduction in separation.

Non-Airways Arrival Procedures

(a) **Romeo Route:** At least 5 mins before abeam Princes Risborough, pilots not receiving a service from an adjacent radar unit are to:
  (i)   Contact Brize/Benson, or
  (ii)   Contact Northolt App, and proceed as directed.

(b) **Charlie Route:** At least 5 mins before the eastern boundary of the LONDON/Stansted CTA or Barkway VOR BKY, pilots not receiving a radar service from an adjacent radar unit are to call Essex Radar. Aircraft will then be vectored as necessary through or around London/Stansted Airspace to join the Charlie Route. Transfer will be effected to Northolt Director before the London CTR Boundary.

Non-Airways Arrival Routes

ROUTE	ROUTEING (incl. NOISE PREFERENTIAL ROUTEING)	ALTITUDE
ROMEO	From **BIG VOR** R310 DME 40 maintain **BIG VOR** R310 to London CTR BDY (**BIG** DME 29). Within London CTR routeing will be as directed by Northolt ATC.	As directed Max 2000' within London CTR
CHARLIE	From **BKY VOR** maintain **BKY VOR** R205 to London CTR BDY (**BKY** DME 26). Then as directed by Northolt ATC.	

Charlie Route Closure

When Rwy 23 is in use at Heathrow, the part of the RMA east of the Northolt ATZ is closed. Inbound traffic from the east may expect re-routeing to the north of the London CTR. The following special restrictions will apply:

When Rwy 23 at Heathrow is in use for approaches, an instrument approach to Rwy 25 at Northolt by non-airways arrivals will not be permitted.

Non-Airways Departure Procedures

(a) Follow published Romeo or Charlie Routes, or as directed;

(b) Departing aircraft will initially be controlled by Northolt Departures/Approach. Transfer to Essex Radar or Brize/Benson as appropriate will be effected when clear of the London CTR;

(c) Expect climb to 2400 ft ALT when clear of London CTR, except when London Stansted is using Rwy 05 for approaches when limitations to 2000 ft within London Stansted CTA may be anticipated.

NORTHOLT

Non-Airways Departure Routes — Rwy 07

ROUTE	ROUTEING (incl. NOISE PREFERENTIAL ROUTEING)	ALTITUDE
ROMEO	Climb straight ahead to 700' Northolt QNH, then turn left onto track 280°M climbing to 2000'. Intercept and follow **BIG VOR** R310 to **BIG** DME 40, or as directed.	2000' within London CTR. Expect further climb to 2400' when clear of London CTR.
CHARLIE	Climb straight ahead to 2000' to intercept **BKY VOR** R205. Then as directed.	

Non-Airways Departure Routes — Rwy 25

ROUTE	ROUTEING (incl. NOISE PREFERENTIAL ROUTEING)	ALTITUDE
ROMEO	Climb straight ahead to 700' Northolt QNH, then turn right to intercept and follow **BIG VOR** R310 climbing to 2000'. Maintain **BIG VOR** R310 to **BIG** DME 40, or as directed.	2000' within London CTR. Expect further climb to 2400' when clear of London CTR.
CHARLIE	Climb straight ahead to 700' Northolt QNH. Then turn right onto track 085°M climbing to 2000'. Intercept **BKY VOR** R205 to **BKY VOR**. Then as directed.	

Communication Failure on Non-Airways Arrival/Departure Routes

(a) Inbound

(i)   If complete communication failure occurs at any stage of the approach then continue a visual approach to land at Northolt if able to do so. Observe route maximum altitudes to remain clear of the London TMA.

(ii) If complete communication failure occurs and a visual approach is not possible, proceed as follows:

(1) INTERMEDIATE APPROACH: Leave or avoid Controlled Airspace by the shortest route, proceed avoiding areas of high traffic density to land at a suitable aerodrome;

(2) FINAL APPROACH: Continue to overhead Northolt not above 1500' QNH, turn north to hold at Chiltern NDB, climbing to 2000' QNH. If unable to establish communication in the hold, leave the hold, avoid Controlled Airspace and areas of high traffic density and proceed to land at a suitable aerodrome.

(b) Outbound

If complete communication failure occurs when established outbound on a published route, leave or avoid Controlled Airspace using the published route, maintaining the last assigned altitude until clear. When clear, continue, avoiding further penetration of Controlled Airspace and areas of high traffic density, and land at a suitable aerodrome.

Special Warning — Use of London ACC (Mil) Radar:
Due to the performance of the radar at low level (weather returns and permanent echoes) the facilities available below 3000 ft (QNH) are limited to navigational assistance and warning of the presence of other aircraft that can be seen. Full anti-collision protection is not provided.

Intentionally Blank

N53 32·09 W000 40·85	**NORTH MOOR**	22 ft AMSL

3·5 nm SSW of Scunthorpe.	OTR 113·90 249 23 GAM 112·80 034 17·8

c/s North Moor Radio 119·275 A/G.   c/s Humberside Radar 119·125 LARS.

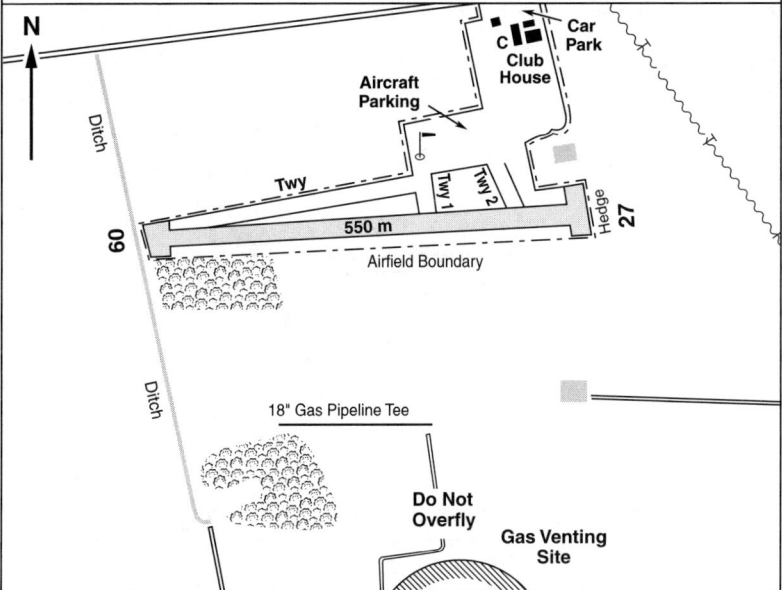

Rwy	Dim(m)	Surface	TORA(m)	LDA(m)	Lighting
09/27	550x20	Grass	Unlicensed		Nil.

Op hrs: PPR by Telephone. 0730-1930 or SS whichever earlier.

Landing Fee: £4.00.	**Customs:** Nil.

Hangarage: Nil. Tie downs available.	**Maintenance:** Nil.

Remarks: Operated by E.W. & A. Chapman, North Moor Aero Club, Low Hill Farm, Messingham, Scunthorpe, North Lincolnshire DN17 3PS.
Fixed wing aircraft only not above 2300 kg. Visitors welcome at pilot's own risk.
Circuit directions variable, height 1000 ft aal. Wide circuits must be flown.
Distance to go markers, to the airfield boundary are positioned at 200 m and 400 m.
Warnings: Do not overfly the Gas Venting Site (GVS) located 450m south of the airfield boundary.
Power cables cross final approach to Rwy 27, 270 m from threshold.
A 16 ft deep ditch runs across the airfied boundary at Rwy 09, marked by orange and white markers.
Avoid overflying the village of Messingham 1nm to the east of the airfield.
Accommodation/Restaurant: B & B, pub lunches/bar meals available in Messingham.
Taxis: By arrangement with the airfield operator.

Fuel: Nil.	**Tel:** 01724-846165 or **Tel/Fax:** 01724-851244

Changes: New Entry

Robert Pooley ©

N59 22·12 W002 26·12	**NORTH RONALDSAY**	40 ft AMSL

28 nm NNE of Kirkwall Airport.	SUM 117·30 236 46·4
	KWL 108·60 038 28·3

No Radio. Recommend contact Kirkwall APP 118·30.

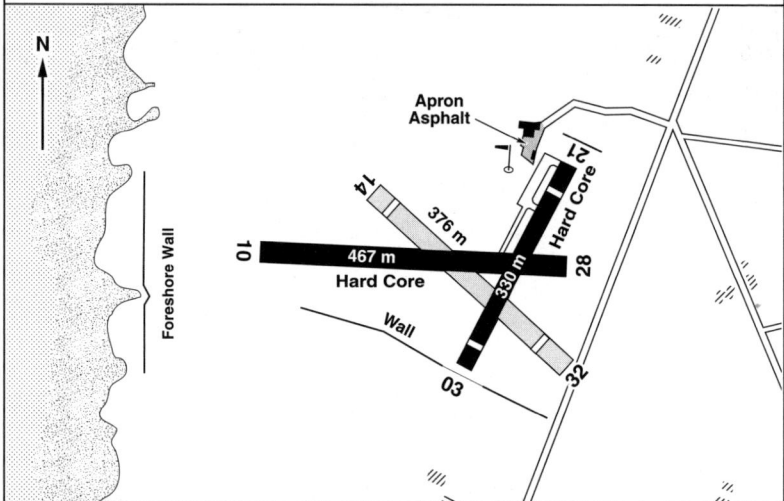

Rwy	Dim(m)	Surface	TORA(m)	LDA(m)	Lighting
10/28	467x18	Hard Core	10-467	10-467	Nil.
			28-467	28-467	Nil
14/32	376x30	Grass	14-336	14-323	Nil.
			32-326	32-306	Nil.
03/21	330x18	Hard Core	03-311	03-276	Nil.
			21-314	21-274	Nil.

Op hrs: PPR.

Landing Fee: Nil. If Fire cover is provided then £17.24 + VAT.

Hangarage: Nil	**Maintenance:** Nil	**Customs:** Nil

Remarks: Licensed aerodrome (day use only) operated by Orkney Islands Council, School Place, Kirkwall, Orkney KW15 1NY.

Visiting aircraft accepted on prior permission and at pilot's own risk. In first instance, contact Orkney Islands Council, Tel: 01856-873535 Ext 2305.

Scheduled services operate Monday to Saturday.

Warning: Rwy 03/21 and 10/28 - Graded Hard Core runways generally unsuitable for light aircraft with low ground /propeller clearance due to unstabilised surface.

Accommodation/Restaurant: B & B and self catering available, contact The Tourist Board.

Car Hire: 018573-244. Meals can also be provided.

Fuel: Mogas.	**Tel:** 01856-873535 Council
	Fax: 01856-876094

N51 43·30 E000 09·25	321 ft AMSL

3·5 nm SE of Harlow.

| LAM | 115·60 | 006 | 4·5 |
| BPK | 117·50 | 105 | 9·8 |

c/s **North Weald Radio** 123·525 A/G.
Company Freq: 130·175 c/s **Aceair North Weald.**

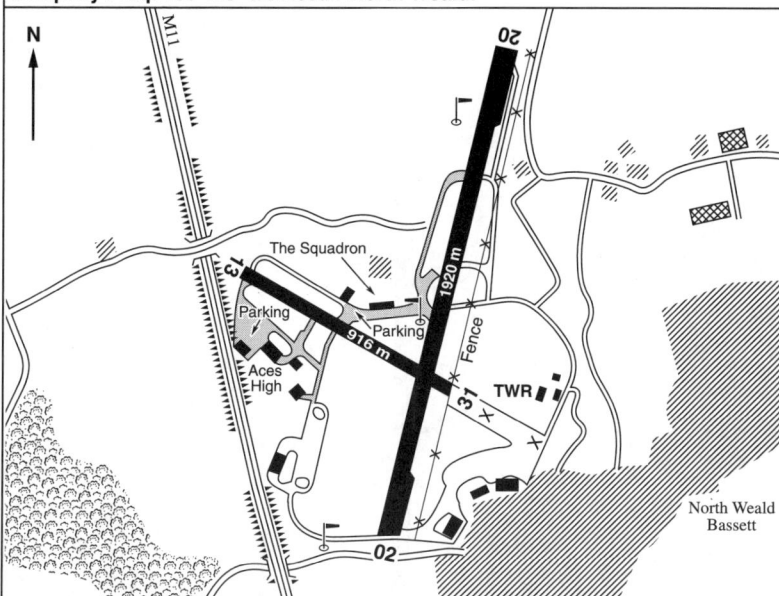

Rwy	Dim(m)	Surface	TORA(m)	LDA(m)	Lighting
02/20	1920x45	Asphalt	Unlicensed		Nil.
13/31	916x45	Asphalt	Unlicensed		Nil.

Op hrs: PPR 0900-1900 or SS.

Landing Fee: Nil.	**Customs:** 24 hrs PNR

Hangarage: Available	**Maintenance:** Available. M3/JR 145

Remarks: Operated by Epping Forest District Council. Unlicensed A/D situated beneath Stansted CTA (1500'—2500' ALT), London TMA base 2500' ALT. Contact must be established with Essex Radar 120·625 before entering Controlled Airspace. Use of the airfield is entirely at the pilot's/operator's own risk.
Rwy 13/31 to be used only when strong winds preclude the use of Rwy 02/20.
Rwy 13/31 is also closed on Saturdays for landings.
Limited Gliding, parascending and model aircraft activity on airfield.

"The Squadron" open to visiting Pilots and Crew. Restaurant & Bar available.
Aces High Hangar and apron available for storage and parking, up to B727.

Fuel: 100LL, Jet A1.	**Tel:** 01992-524740 ATC. **Fax:** 01992-524074. 01992-564200 Gate House. 01992-524510 Squadron. **Fax:** 01992-522238. 01992-522949 Aces High Hangar.

Robert Pooley ©

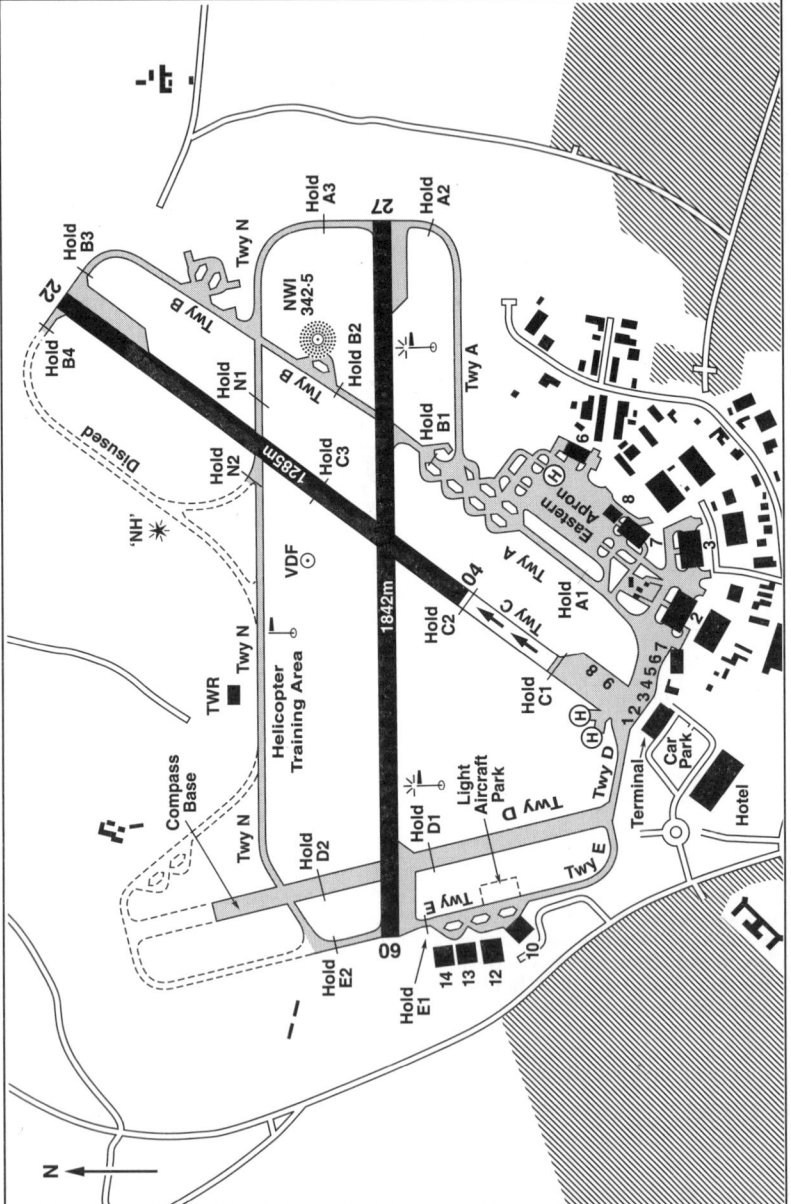

N52 40·55 E001 16·97   **NORWICH**   117 ft AMSL

Hold A3

Hold A2

27

Twy N

Hold B3

22

Hold B4

NWI
342·5

Hold B2

Twy A

Twy B

Hold N1

Twy B

Disused

Hold N2

Hold C3

1285m

'NH'

Hold B1

Eastern Apron

VDF

Twy A

04

Hold A1

Twy C

Hold C2

1842m

Helicopter
Training Area

TWR

Twy N

Hold C1

Twy D

Terminal

Car Park

Hotel

Compass Base

Twy N

Hold D2

Hold D1

Light Aircraft Park

Twy D

Twy E

09

Twy E

Hold E2

Hold E1

14 13 12

10

1 2 3 4 5 6 7

N

N52 40·55 E001 16·97	**NORWICH**	117 ft AMSL
2·8 nm N of Norwich City Centre.		CLN 114·55 010 50
		CSL 116·50 214 4·5

c/s Norwich. APP 119·35. TWR 124·25. RAD 119·35, 128·325.
ATIS 128·625.
NDB 'NH' 371·5(273°M/3·2nm to Thr 27). NDB 'NWI' 342·5 (on A/D).
ILS/DME Rwy 27 (273°M) I-NH 110·90.

Rwy	Dim(m)	Surface	TORA(m)	LDA(m)	Lighting
09/27	1842x45	Asphalt/	09-1841	09-1841	Ap Thr Rwy RCL PAPI
		Concrete	27-1841	27-1841	Ap Thr Rwy RCL PAPI
† 04/22	1285x45	Asphalt/	04-1266	04-1266	Thr Rwy PAPI 4°
		Concrete	22-1266	22-1266	Thr Rwy PAPI 3·75°

† Rwy 04/22 available only when crosswind precludes the use of Rwy 09/27.
  Rwy 04 — 305m starter extension available on request.

Op hrs. Sun-Fri 0630-2230, Sat 0630-2000. Other times by arrangement.

Landing Fees: Up to 1 tonne £14.12, thereafter £7.06 per half tonne. Discount on cash payment.

Hangarage: Nil   **Maintenance:** Available   **Customs:** Available

Remarks: Operated by Norwich Airport Ltd., Norwich NR6 6JA.
PPR to non-radio aircraft.

All aircraft must contact APP at least 10 minutes before ETA. RAF Coltishall situated 5 nm to NE, generate high intensity military jet traffic, early information on aircraft approaching Norwich is vital for co-ordination of traffic.

Light aircraft and microlights operate from Felthorpe aerodrome (3 nm NW), occasionally throughout the year with increased activity during the summer months.

All aircraft operating for hire or reward from/to Norwich will be required to be handled by Norwich Airport Ltd, Tel: 01603-420645, Fax: 01603-487523.

Aircraft must carry Third Party Insurance cover of not less than one million pounds.

Variable circuits. Joining circuit overhead not normally available.

Booking out details to be passed by telephone. Calls on RTF may result in delays.

On departures from any runway, aircraft in excess of 5700 kg are to climb straight ahead to 1000 ft aal before turning, unless instructed otherwise by ATC.
Aircraft of less than 5700 kg will climb to 500 ft aal before turning.

Restaurant: Available in the Terminal.

Car Hire: Avis Tel: 01603-416710/416719. Eurocar Tel: 01603-400280.
Hertz 01602-404010.

Fuel: 100LL, Jet A1.
Diners Card, Multi-Service
	Tel: 01603-411923 Admin; 420641 ATC
	    01603-420653 Information Desk
	    01603- 420640 ATIS
	Fax: 01603-487523 Admin; 01603-420667 ATC.

Robert Pooley ©

N52 55·20 W001 04·75	**NOTTINGHAM**	138 ft AMSL

3 nm SE of Nottingham.	TNT 115·70 116 22·8
	GAM 112·80 198 22·2

c/s Nottingham Radio 122·80 A/G. East Midlands APP 119·65.
NDB 'NOT' 430·0 (On A/D).

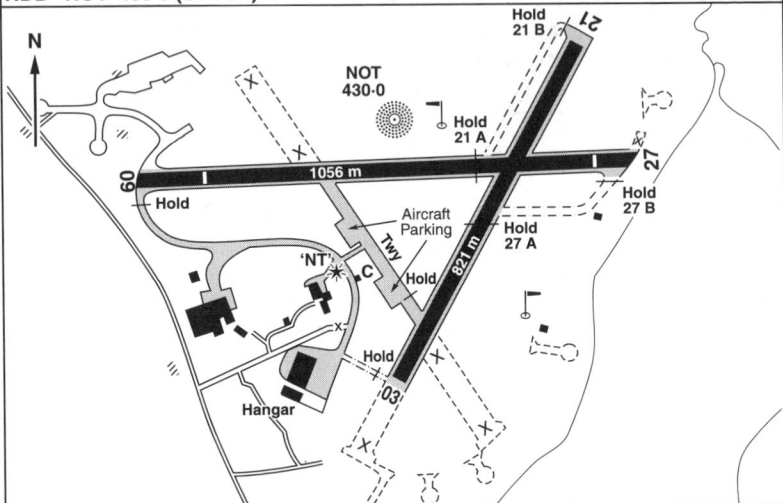

Rwy	Dim(m)	Surface	TORA(m)	LDA(m)	Lighting
03/21	821x23	Asphalt/	03-821	03-821	Nil.
		Concrete	21-821	21-821	Nil.
09/27	1056x30	Asphalt/	09-989(D)	09-837(D)	Thr Rwy LITAS 3·5°
		Concrete	09-837(N)	09-837(N)	
			27-975(D)	27-929(D)	Thr Rwy LITAS 3·75°
			27-837(N)	27-837(N)	
					IBn 'NT' Gn

Grass area in centre triangle available on request (unlicensed)

Op hrs: Winter. Mon-Sat 0900-1700, Sun 1000-1700.
     Summer. Mon-Fri 0900-1800, Sat 0900-1900, Sun 1000-1900; & ¢.

Landing Fees: Light singles £10. (half price weekends). Twins up to 3300 lbs £14.00,
     up to 7700 lbs £28.00, over 7700 lbs £39.00 (all inclusive of VAT).

Hangarage: Available	**Maintenance:** Available	**Customs:** PNR 24 hrs

Remarks: Operated by Truman Aviation Ltd. Non-radio aircraft strictly PPR. A/D
situated on the northern edge of East Midlands CTA (Class 'D'), contact East
Midlands Approach 119·65 for CTA transit and traffic information.
Circuit height 800 ft (QFE). The section of paved surface between the runways is a
taxiway and parking area. This aerodrome caters particularly for Executive and
Private aircraft both fixed and rotary wing.
Chimney 205' aal 343' amsl 285°/1·4 nm.

City centre 3 miles. Ring road 1 mile. Bus service to the city. Good taxi services.

Restaurant: Facilities available.

Fuel: 100LL, Jet A1.	**Tel:** 0115-9811327 ATC. 9815050 Sales.
Diners, Visa, Access or Cash	**Fax:** 0115-9811444

N51 37·93 W002 00·88	**OAKSEY PARK**	250 ft AMSL

5 nm SSE of Cirencester.	CPT 114·35 290 31
	HON 113·65 204 45

c/s Oaksey Radio 122·775 A/G. Lyneham Zone 123·40
Brize Radar 134·30.

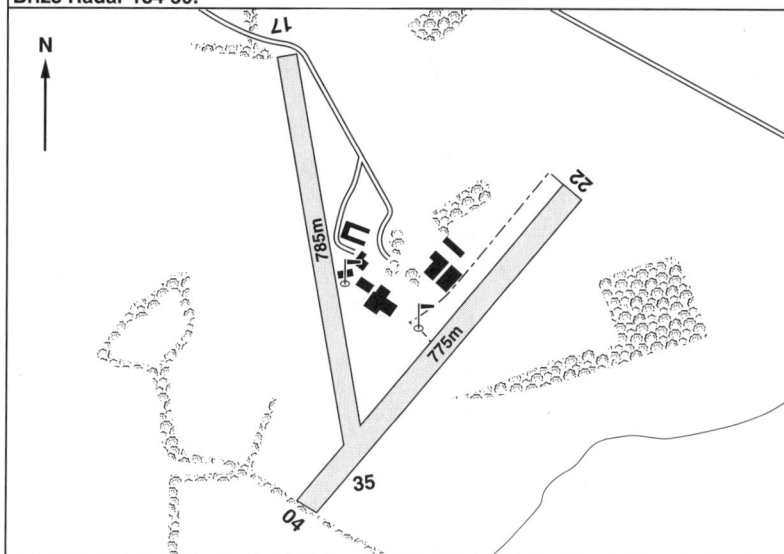

Rwy	Dim(m)	Surface	TORA(m)	LDA(m)	Lighting
04/22	775x30	Grass	Unlicensed		Nil
*17/35	785x20	Grass	Unlicensed		Nil

* Rwy 17 restricted to take-off only and Rwy 35 restricted to landing only, except when flight safety may be compromised.

Op hrs: PPR. SR–SS

Landing Fee: Singles £5.00; Twins & Helicopters £10.00. + VAT.

Hangarage: Limited	**Maintenance:** Limited

Remarks: Operated by Mr. M. Woodhouse. Oaksey Park, Oaksey, Malmesbury, Wilts. SN16 9SD. Unlicensed airfield.
Visiting aircraft welcome on prior permission and at pilot's own risk.
Circuits at 1000 ft (QNH), LH on 22 RH on 04 & 35 unless otherwise advised.
Standard circuit joining and departure procedures must be obeyed at all times.
Aircraft movements restricted to the mown manoeuvring areas.
Airfield may be unusable at times during winter months due to waterlogging.

Noise Sensitive Areas Avoid overflying the following villages: OAKSEY (N side of airfield); EASTCOURT (W side of airfield); HANKERTON (1·2 nm SW of airfield) and UPPER MINETY (1·2 nm SE of airfield). Avoid overflight of local habitation as much as possible.

Restaurant: Pubs in Oaksey village. **Taxis:** 01285-650850.

Fuel: 100LL	**Tel:** 01666-577152 Airfield. 577130 Operator.
	Fax: 01666-577169.

Robert Pooley ©

N56 27·81 W005 23·98	**OBAN (North Connel)**	20 ft AMSL
3·5nm NE of Oban.		**TIR 117·70 101 48.8**

c/s Oban Radio 118·05 A/G.
NDB 'CNL' 404·0 (On A/D) − Operates intermittently.

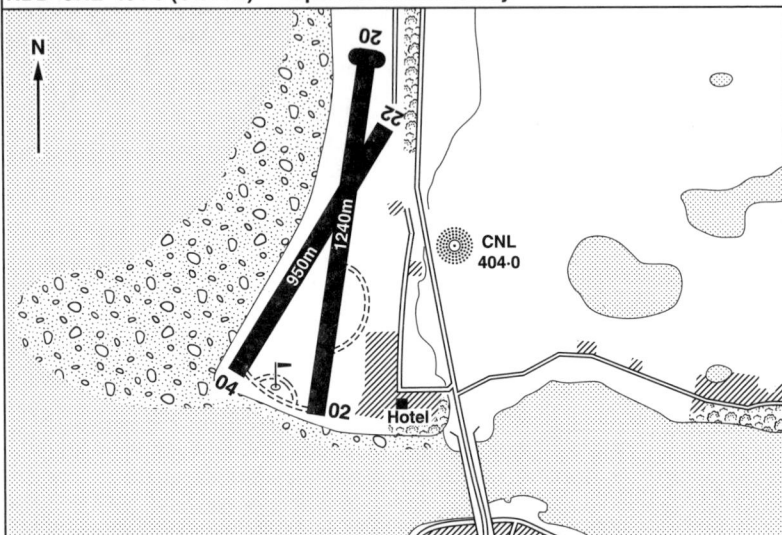

Rwy	Dim(m)	Surface	TORA(m)	LDA(m)	Lighting
02/20	1240x30	Asphalt	Unlicensed		Nil.
04/22	950x30	Asphalt	Unlicensed		Nil.

Op hrs: PPR by Phone or Radio. SR–SS. **Customs:** By arrangement.

Landing Fee: Private Singles £8.00, Twins £12.00 inclusive of VAT
Public Transport £4.90 per 500 kg AUW + VAT.

Hangarage: Nil. **Maintenance:** Nil

Remarks: Unlicensed aerodrome operated by Argyll and Bute Council. PPR.
All aircraft welcome at pilot's own risk. Runway 02/20 condition fair.

Circuits: Powered aircraft preferably to west, gliders usually to east.
    Microlight operate circuits at 500' to west of runway.

Cable launched gliding occasionally on Sundays. A double cross signal displayed
north of the northern end of Rwy 04/22 when gliding in progress.
Helicopter Landing - Rwy 22 threshold only.
High ground 990' aal 1010' amsl 1 nm to N and NNE.

Restaurant: Lochnell Arms Hotel nearby, Tel: 01631-710408.
Car Hire: At the Airport 01631-710 888. Bike hire available.
Taxis: 01631-562834. 01631-563784.

Fuel: 100LL, Jet A1. Available H24. c/s Total Oban 129·75 - Company Freq.	**Tel/Fax:** 01631-710384/710888 PPR 07770-620988. 01631-720215 Out of hours E-mail: info@obanairport.co.uk

N51 14·05 W000 56·57		ODIHAM	405 ft AMSL
8 nm SW of Aldershot.		**MID 114·00 316 16**	
		OCK 115·30 262 19	

Farnborough/Odiham APP 125·25. RAD 125·25. Odiham TWR 122·10 (O/R).
FIS Information 122·10 (O/R).   TACAN 'ODH' 109·60 (On A/D).
ILS Rwy 28 (QFU 277°M, LLZ 274°M) 'I ODH' 108·95 - **Caution:** There are no
markers, radar or DME mandatory.

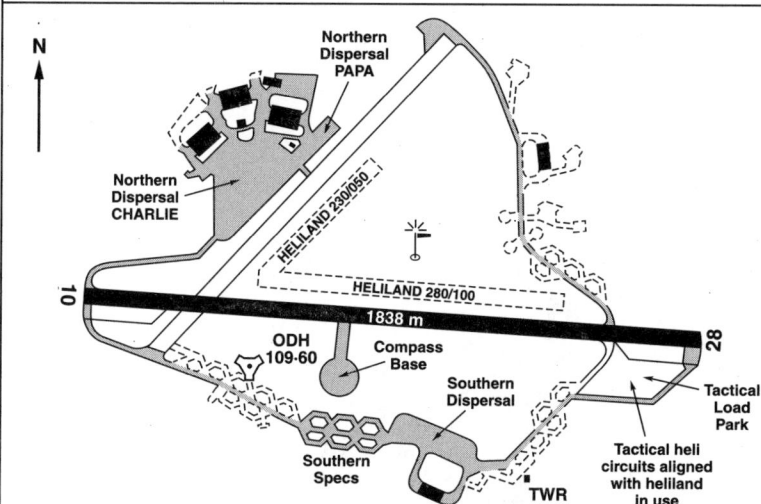

Rwy	Dim(m)	Surface	TORA(m)	LDA(m)	Lighting
10/28	1838x45	Asphalt	10-1838	10-1836	Ap Thr Rwy PAPI
			28-1838	28-1838	Ap Thr Rwy PAPI
					IBn 'OI' Red

Op hrs: PPR. Mon-Fri 0800-1700.	**ATZ active H24**
Landing Fee: MoD(RAF) Rates	**Customs:** Nil
Hangarage: Nil	**Maintenance:** Nil

Remarks: RAF Aerodrome. Intensive helicopter operations.
MATZ controlled by Farnborough App 125·25, transit pressure setting
London/Farnborough QNH.

Visiting inbound helicopters if flying VFR below 2000 ft London/Farnborough QNH,
are to call Odiham Information before 10 nm with details of which cardinal sector they
wish to recover from. Aircraft are to remain outside the MATZ boundary until given
clearance and height to fly to join the visual circuit.

All IFR arrivals or any aircraft inbound to Odiham above 2000 ft London/Farnborough
QNH are to call Odiham Radar.

Variable helicopter circuits. No deadside. Fixed wing circuits to South of Runway.

Glider flying Sat,Sun and during Summer 1700 till dusk Mon, Tue and Fri.

Fuel: Avtur ¢	**Tel:** 01256-702134 Ext 7295.

12 nm SW of Norwich City

BKY 116·25 054 47·5
CLN 114·55 358 39·2

c/s **Buckenham Radio 124·40 A/G.**

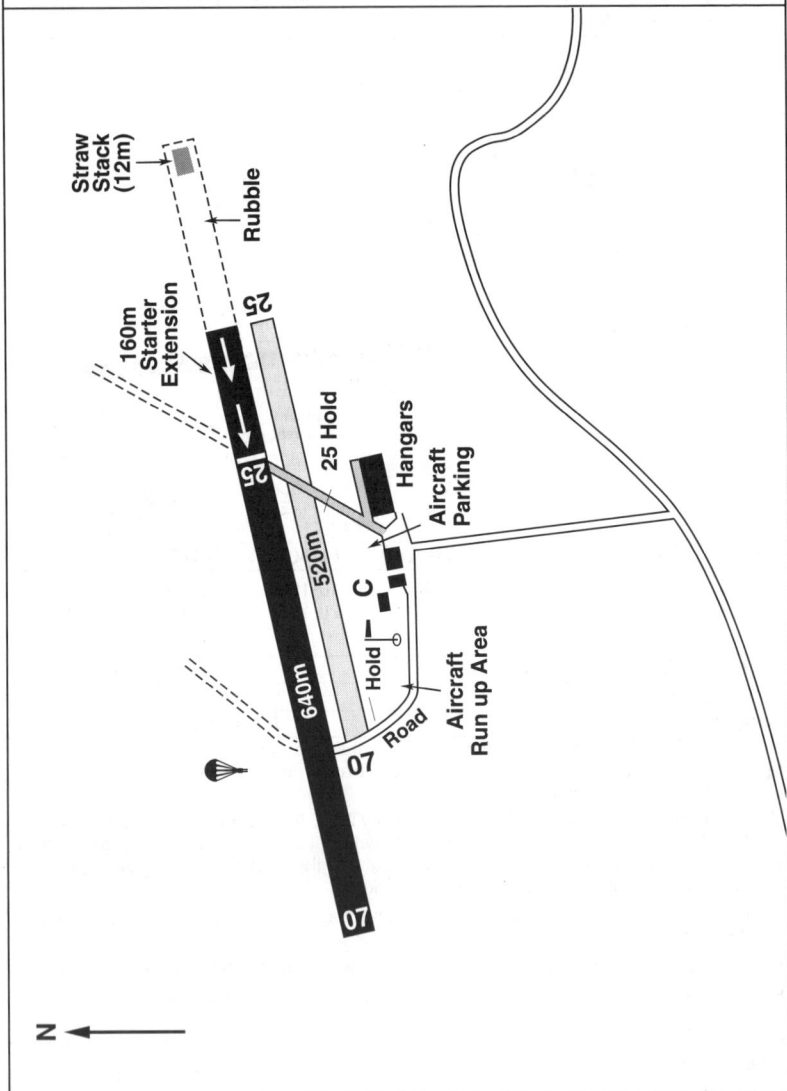

Straw
Stack
(12m)

Rubble

160m
Starter
Extension

25

25

25 Hold

Hangars

Aircraft
Parking

520m

C

Hold

Aircraft
Run up Area

640m

07 Road

07

N ←

| N52 29·83 E001 03·06 | | **OLD BUCKENHAM** | | | 185 ft AMSL |

Rwy	Dim(m)	Surface	TORA(m)	LDA(m)	Lighting
07/25	800x18	Asphalt	07-640	07-640	Nil
			25-800	25-640	Nil
Rwy 07 has 2% up slope.					
07/25	520x28	Grass	Unlicensed		Nil

Op hrs: WINTER: 0900-SS daily, and by arrangement.

SUMMER: Mon-Sat & PHs 0900-1800, Sun 1000-1800, and by arrangement.

Landing Fee: Light singles £6.00.	**Customs:** By arrangement
Hangarage: Available	**Maintenance:** Nil.

Remarks: An ex-home base of the USAAF 453rd Bomb Group. The airfield now has newly constructed runway and hangars, and is operated by Touchdown Aero Centre Ltd, Old Buckenham Airfield, Abbey Road, Old Buckenham, Norfolk NR17 1PU.

Licensed airfield. Non-radio aircraft PPR.

Microlights and Helicopters prohibited (Local authority regulation).

Arrivals: No overhead joins;

Rwy 07 joins from the west - join at 2 nm south of Snetterton Heath;

Avoid straight-in-approaches if visual circuit is active.

Departures: Rwy 07 - Maintain runway heading until reaching 1500 ft aal;

Rwy 25 - Turn onto track 270° and maintain until reaching the railway line South of Attleborough.

Circuits at 1000 ft aal, LH on Rwy 07, RH on Rwy 25.

Please avoid overflying the village of Old Buckenham (1 nm SSW of airfield) and the town of Attleborough (2 nm NW of airfield).

Warnings: Free-fall parachuting takes place Mon-Fri, HJ up to FL150.

Beware of the gliding site at Tibenham 5 nm to SE.

Tacolneston Radio mast, 735 ft amsl, 3 nm NE of the airfield.

Restaurant: Licensed Bar and Restaurant open 7 days.

Accommodation: Sherbourne Hotel, Tel: 01953-454363.

Taxis: A&G Cabs, Tel: 01953-453134. Andy Cabs, Tel: 01953-455566

Fuel: 100LL	**Tel:** 01953- 860806 **Fax:** 01953- 861212

N51 05·93 W001 47·05	**OLD SARUM**	285 ft AMSL
2 nm NNE of Salisbury.		SAM 113·35 302 18·7
		CPT 114·35 227 31·8

c/s Old Sarum Radio 123·20 A/G.
Boscombe App 126·70.

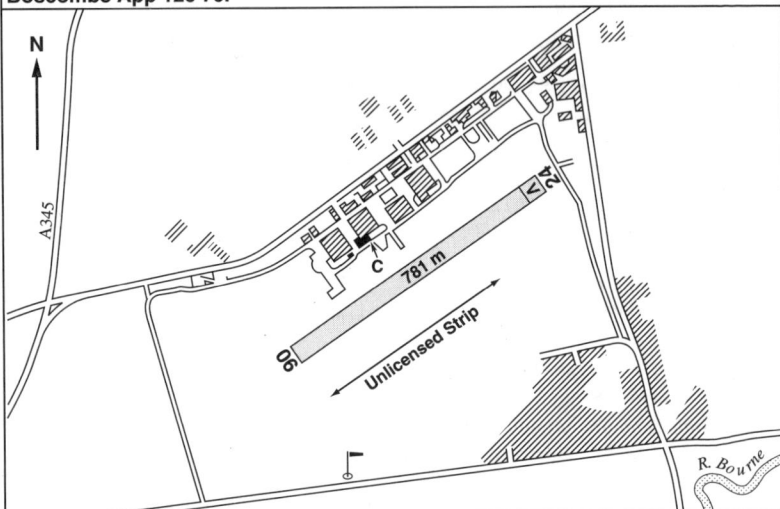

Rwy	Dim(m)	Surface	TORA(m)	LDA(m)	Lighting
06/24	781x50	Grass	06-781	06-781	Nil.
			24-781	24-731	Nil.

Op hrs. WINTER: 0830-1730 or SS (whichever earlier);
SUMMER: 0830-2000 or SS (whichever earlier) licensed to 1830.

Landing Fees: Singles £8.00, twins £16.00, microlights £5.00, (inclusive of VAT).

Hangarage: Available   **Maintenance:** Available   **Customs:** 24 hrs PNR.

Remarks: Operated by Old Sarum Flying Club. Licensed A/D situated within
Boscombe Down/Middle Wallop CMATZ, contact Boscombe Down App 126·70 before
CMATZ boundary. Danger Area D127, 2 nm NE of A/D.
Visiting aircraft PNR by radio, and at pilot's own risk. Non radio aircraft PPR.
High intensity low flying aircraft (fixed wing & helicopter) throughout the area.
Parallel unlicensed strip to South of marked runway
Note. Boscombe Down sometimes operate outside normal hours and a precautionary
call should be made to Boscombe App. During Boscombe Down hours of operation
non-radio aircraft may be accepted on prior permission.
Circuit Procedures:
Boscombe MATZ active   : Circuits to the South at 800' aal, Microlites at 600' aal.
Boscombe MATZ inactive : Circuits to the North at 800' aal, Microlites at 600' aal.
Avoid overflying Salisbury, local villages and habitation to the North and West of the
airfield. Cathedral 272' aal 557' amsl 191°/2 nm.
Restaurant: Home cooked menu. Licensed bar.   **Taxis/Car Hire:** Available.

See VAD Chart opposite.

Fuel: 100LL	**Tel:** 01722-322525 Ops. **Fax:** 01722-323702

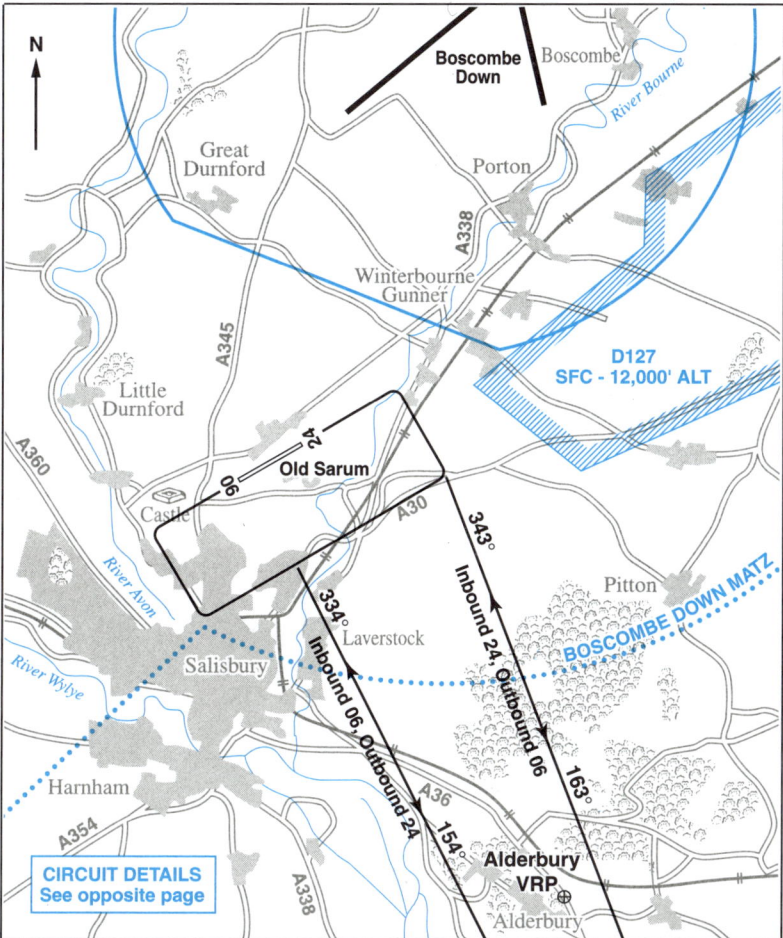

The Old Sarum ATZ is within the Boscombe Down MATZ.

Arrivals: Aircraft arriving at Old Sarum, when the MATZ is active, should contact Boscombe Down App 126·70 prior to entering the MATZ and should route abeam ALDERBURY VRP N51 02·90 W001 43·90 (4 nm SE of Salisbury), SAM 113·35 296 15·5, using tracks as shown according to runway in use at 800ft on Old Sarum QFE (1100ft QNH). Non radio aircraft should use the same routing.

Departures: Aircraft departing Old Sarum, when the MATZ is active, should route abeam ALDERBURY VRP N51 02·90 W001 43·90 (4 nm SE of Salisbury), SAM 113·35 296 15·5, not above 800ft aal, and contact Boscombe Down App 126·70 after departing the Old Sarum circuit.

When the MATZ is not active, standard overhead departures and circuit joins may be used.

Robert Pooley ©

Intentionally Blank

N52 42·83 W002 05·93	**OTHERTON**	340 ft AMSL
1 nm SE of Penkridge, Staffs		TNT 115·70 200 28
		HON 113·65 300 30

c/s Otherton Radio 129·82 A/G – Weekends and some weekdays .

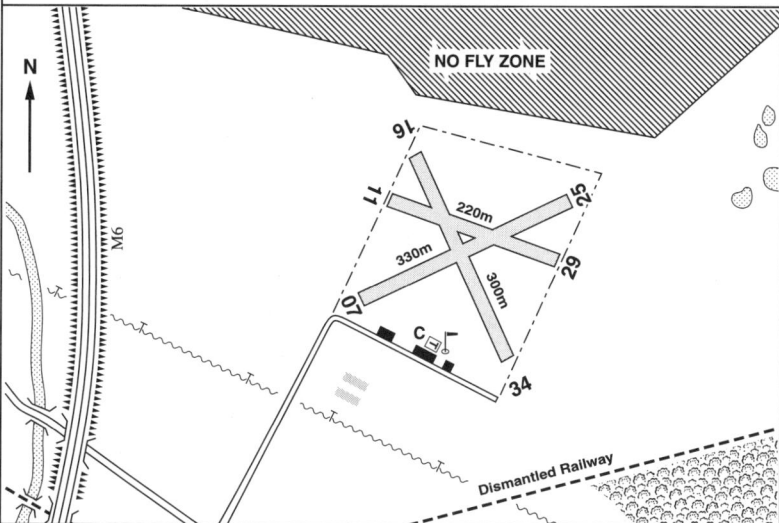

Rwy	Dim(m)	Surface	TORA(m)	LDA(m)	Lighting
07/25	330x15	Grass	Unlicensed		Nil
11/29	220x15	Grass	Unlicensed		Nil
16/34	300x15	Grass	Unlicensed		Nil

Rwy 07 has 2·5% upslope for first 80 m. **Rwy 25 has 2·5% downslope for last 80 m.**

Op hrs: PPR. Mon-Sat 0800-2000. Sun 0900-1700.

Landing Fee: Voluntary Donations accepted.

Hangarage: By arrangement   **Maintenance:** Nil   **Customs:** Nil

Remarks: Operated by Staffordshire Aero Club. Only small light aeroplanes can be accepted. Flying school operates 6 days a week, closed Mondays. North of the airfield is a declared no fly zone. Local and circuit traffic may be non-radio.
Arrivals: All arrivals are to be from the East or West only, straight in to the overhead from at least 2 nm out. Join overhead not below 1000 ft aal.
Circuits at 500 ft aal, RH on Rws 07, 11 and 16. Curved approach recommended on to Rwys 16R and 25L to avoid the no fly zone. Keep circuits fairly small.
Departures: Climb in overhead to minimum 1200 ft aal. Depart East or West, maintain heading until 2 nm from the airfield before turning on to course.
Do not overfly Penkridge town, the village or farm buildings to the North of the site, or Gailey lake wildlife reserve and the farm to the South.
Restaurant: Self service hot drinks available at the clubhouse most days.
Accommodation: The Bridge House Motel, Penkridge (1mile W), Tel: 01785-714426.
Taxis: Penkridge Cabs Tel: 01785-712589.

Fuel: Mogas only - by prior arrangement. Not available Mondays.	Tel: 07831-811783 Airfield. Tel: 07973- 940222 Briefings (Anytime) Tel/Fax: 01543-673075 Office.

Robert Pooley ©

N51 50·22 W001 19·20   **OXFORD (Kidlington)**   270 ft AMSL

6 nm NNW of Oxford.   CPT 114·35 355 21. DTY 116·40 206 22·1
                        BNN 113·75 288 29·3

c/s Oxford. APP 125·325. TWR/AFIS* 118·875 – AFIS* Sun and PHs.
GND 121·95.   VDF 125·325 (O/R).   Brize Radar 134·30 (LARS).
ATIS 136·225 - Not available Sun & PHs.
DME 'OX' 117·70 (On A/D).   NDB 'OX' 367·5 (On A/D).

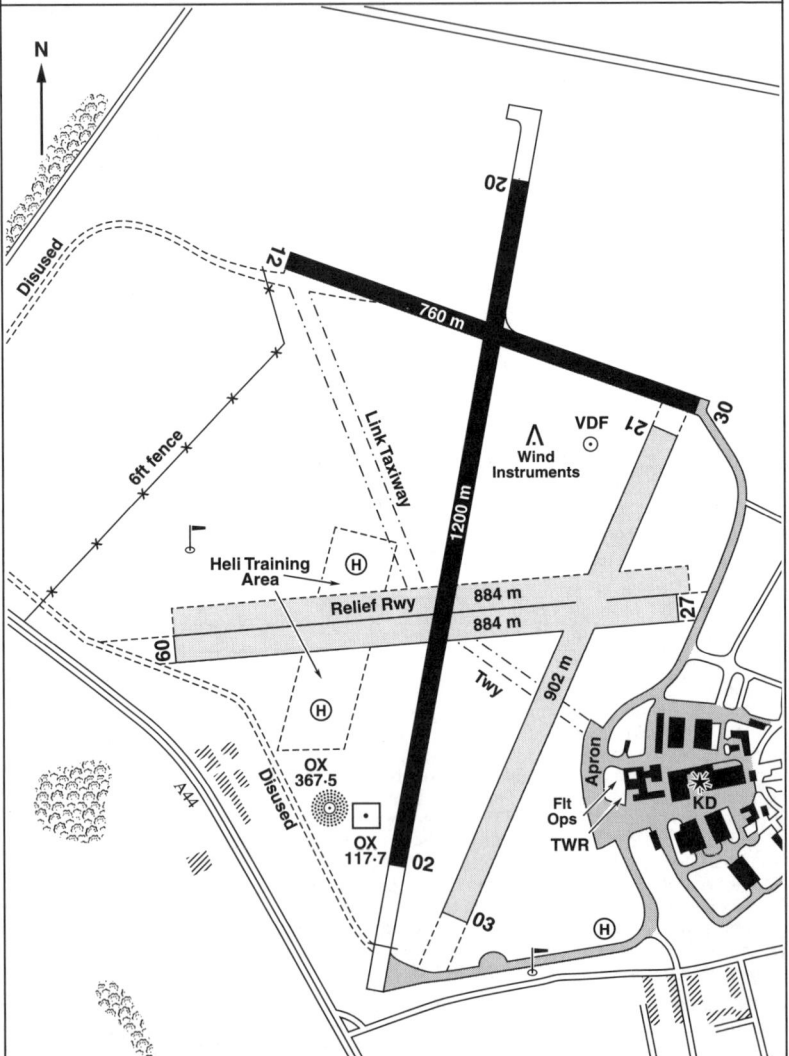

N

20

12

760 m

Disused

6ft fence

Link Taxiway

21

30

VDF

Wind Instruments

1200 m

Heli Training Area

(H)

Relief Rwy   884 m

884 m   27

60

Twy

902 m

(H)

Apron

Disused

OX 367·5

Flt Ops

TWR

KD

A44

OX 117·7

02

03

(H)

Robert Pooley ©   404

N51 50·22 W001 19·20	**OXFORD (Kidlington)**				270 ft AMSL
Rwy	**Dim(m)**	**Surface**	**TORA(m)**	**LDA(m)**	**Lighting**
02/20	1200x23	Asphalt	02-1200	02-1200	Ap Thr Rwy PAPI 3·5°
			20-1200	20-1200	Thr Rwy PAPI 3°
† 09/27	884x45	Grass	09-884	09-884	Rwy
			27-884	27-884	Thr Rwy APAPI 3°
12/30	760x28	Asphalt	12-760	12-760	Nil.
			30-760	30-760	Nil.
03/21	902x47	Grass	03- 902	03- 902	Nil.
			21- 902	21- 902	Nil.
					IBn 'KD' Gn

† Relief Rwy 09/27 parallel and adjacent to Rwy 09/27 on North side.
 Rwy 20 Gradient — 2·25% downslope over the last 200 m at the SW end.

Op hrs: PPR. Mon-Fri 0800-1730, Sat, Sun & PHs 0830-1700.
 Outside of Operating hours contact Operations.

Landing Fees: Private/Club: £12.50.
 Commercial: £6.00 per 0·5 tonne.

Customs: All inbound flights must be approved by Operations. Following Prior Notice required:

- All flights with EU Crew or pax - 6 hrs notice;
- All flights with non-EU Crew or pax - 12 hrs notice;
- All flights requiring Special Branch - 24 hrs notice, (36 hrs for weekends),
  Tel: 01865-844 267, Fax: 01865-841 807.

Hangarage: Limited   **Maintenance:** Available

Remarks: Licensed aerodrome operated by CSE Aviation Ltd., Oxford Airport, Kidlington, Oxford OX5 1RA. **Aerodrome is PPR by Telephone/Fax at all times.**

Grass Rwy Markings
- 09/27 by runway lighting by day and by night.
- 09/27 Relief Rwy by white corners and yellow reflective markers on North side.
- 03/21 White corners and yellow reflective markers indicate sideline.
- Rwy QDM displayed at threshold of all runways.

Warnings. Intensive circuit traffic. Helicopter training in designated areas on the aerodrome.

All aircraft are to avoid Weston-on-the Green Danger Area (D129).

Chimney 225' aal 495' amsl 027°/1·3 nm.

Taxiway from Rwy 02 threshold to Rwy 09 threshold is disused.

Flight and Noise Abatement Procedures   – see overleaf.

Restaurant: Restaurant or Refreshments.

Car Hire: Godfrey Davis. Tel: 01865-246373.   Target Car & Van Hire 01865-379691

Taxis: James Cars Tel: 01865-375742

Fuel: 100LL, Jet A1. Multiservice, Diners, Mastercard, Visa.	**Tel:** 01865- 844267 Ops - PPR 01865- 844272 ATC. **Fax:** 01865-841807.

Robert Pooley ©

Flight and Noise Abatement Procedures

Flight Procedures:

Circuit direction – Variable.

Fixed wing aircraft circuits at 1200 ft QFE (1500 ft QNH) to provide separation between fixed-wing and rotary-wing traffic.

Visiting pilots should familiarise themselves with Oxford's instrument arrival and departure routes. Instrument arrivals should contact Brize Norton ATC as soon as possible after leaving airways on 134·30 or as directed.

Pilots may be asked to use the Relief Rwy 09/27.

Noise Abatement Procedures:

Pilots are to avoid, where there is no overriding training or flight safety requirement, overflying local residential areas, including Blenheim Palace.

Departures Rwy 02 – Climb ahead to 750 ft QFE (1000 ft QNH) and 1·5 DME OX, before turning on course. Visual departures should endeavour to complete this turn before reaching the Mercury Satellite Station (at 1·5 nm). When turning right, pilots are to avoid overflying Shipton-on-Cherwell village.

Departures Rwy 20 – Climb ahead to 750 ft QFE (1000 ft QNH) or 1 DME OX, whichever is earlier, before turning right. Aircraft intending to turn left, climb ahead to 1.5 DME OX (IFR) or until south of Yarnton village (VFR), remaining clear, in all cases, of the Brize Norton CTR.

Departures from all other Rwys – Circuit and departing traffic must climb straight ahead to 750 ft QFE (1000 ft QNH) before turning on course.

Arrivals – Whenever possible, aricraft joining the circuit should, plan to join on base leg or via a straight-in approach, giving way to traffic already established in the circuit.

Noise Amelioration Scheme – Pilots are to familiarise themselves with the Oxford Aiport Noise Amelioration Scheme, a copy of which is held in Operations. This incorporates special Helicopter arrival and departure routes.

N51 48·15 W000 09·48	**PANSHANGER**	250 ft. AMSL

2·5 nm W of Hertford	**BPK 117·50 331 3·7. BNN 113·75 078 15·1**
	LAM 115·60 314 14·9

Panshanger Radio 120·25 A/G.

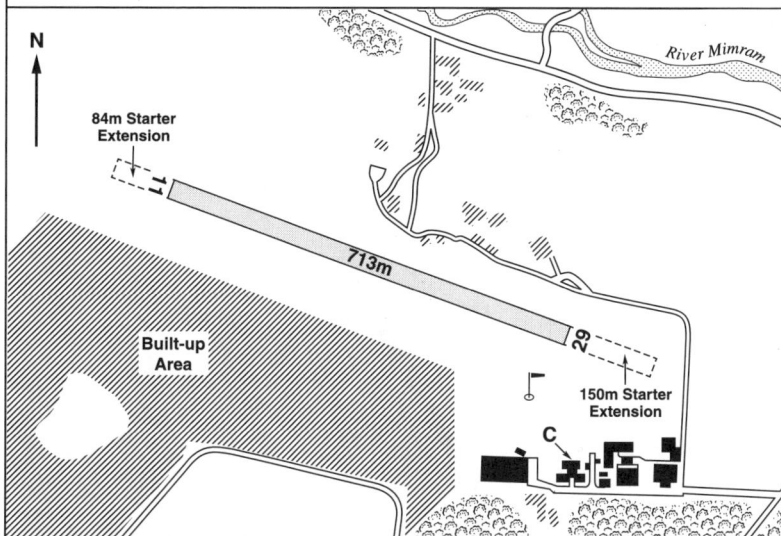

Rwy	Dim(m)	Surface	TORA(m)	LDA(m)	Lighting
11/29	713x26	Grass	11-797 *	11-713	Nil
			29-863 *	29-713	Nil

* Includes starter extensions - 84 m Rwy 11; 150 m Rwy 29.

Op hrs: PPR. 0900-SS daily & ¢.

Landing Fee: SE, ME, SEHeli £10; Commercial £25.   **Customs:** Nil

Hangarage: Nil.   **Maintenance:** Limited.

Remarks: Operated by Professional Flight Management Ltd, Panshanger Airfield, Cole Green, Hertford, Herts SG14 2 NH.

Licensed aerodrome. Visiting aircraft are required to obtain prior permission, and are welcome at their own risk.

Standard overhead joins. Circuits LH on 11, RH on 29, at 800' aal.

Rwy 29 Noise Abatement Routeing: After take-off, turn right to overfly the golf club house and on passing, turn to runway QDM until passing prominent white building (School). Turn right to fly to a square wood (approximately 0·5 nm), then turn downwind to fly between Tewin and Tewin Wood.

Mast 675' aal 925' amsl 190°/4·2 nm.

Restaurant: Snacks available at the aerodrome.

Taxis: A+A Tel: 01707-333 333.   **Car Hire:** Hertz Tel: 01707-331 433.

Fuel: 100LL	**Tel:** 01707-391791
	Fax: 01707-392792

Robert Pooley ©

N59 21·10 W002 54·02	**PAPA WESTRAY**	91 ft AMSL
23 nm N of Kirkwall Airport.		KWL 108·60 008 23·5
		WIK 113·60 013 54·0

No Radio. Recommend contact Kirkwall APP 118·30.

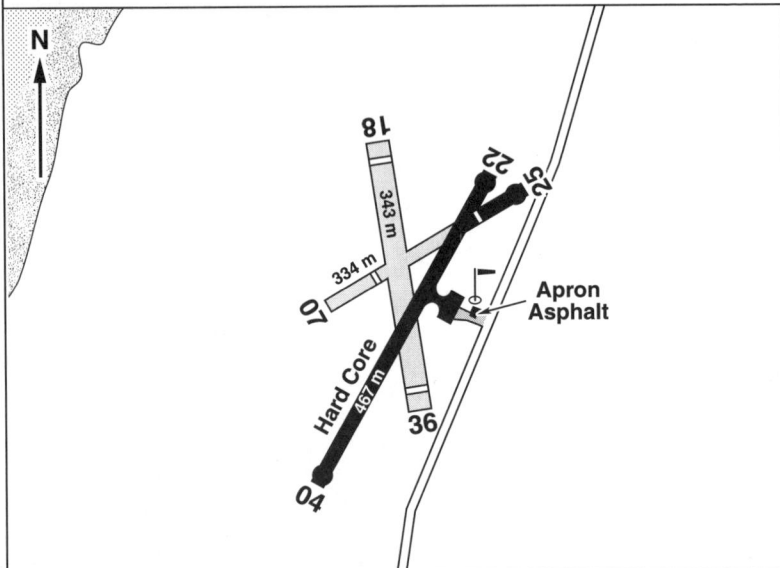

Rwy	Dim(m)	Surface	TORA(m)	LDA(m)	Lighting
04/22	467x18	Hard Core	04-467	04-467	Nil.
			22-467	22-467	Nil.
07/25	334x18	Grass/	07-292	07-250	Nil.
		Hard Core	25-292	25-250	Nil.
18/36	343x30	Grass	18-383	18-323	Nil.
			36-386	36-323	Nil.

Op hrs: PPR

Landing Fee: Nil. If fire cover is required then £17.24 + VAT.

Hangarage: Nil	**Maintenance:** Nil	**Customs:** Nil

Remarks: Licensed aerodrome (day use only) operated by Orkney Islands Council, School Place, Kirkwall, Orkney KW15 1NY. PPR.
Visiting aircraft accepted on prior permission and at pilot's own risk. In first instance, contact Orkney Islands Council, Tel: 01856-873535 Ext 2305.
Scheduled air services daily except Sundays.
Warning: Rwy 04/22 and stub Rwy 07/25 - Graded Hard Core runways generally unsuitable for light aircraft with low ground /propeller clearance due to unstabilised surface.
Accommodation/Restaurant: Contact the Tourist Board.
Car Hire: A. Davidson Tel: 01857- 644246.   J.Rendall Tel:01857-644229.

Fuel: Nil	**Tel:** 01856-873535 Council.
	Fax: 01856-876094 Council.

N51 42·83 W004 18·73	**PEMBREY**	18 ft AMSL

6 nm WNW of Llanelli.	STU 113·10 128 32
9 nm S of Carmarthen	BCN 117·45 274 39

c/s Pembrey Radio 124·40 A/G.
RAF Pembrey Range Control 122·75.

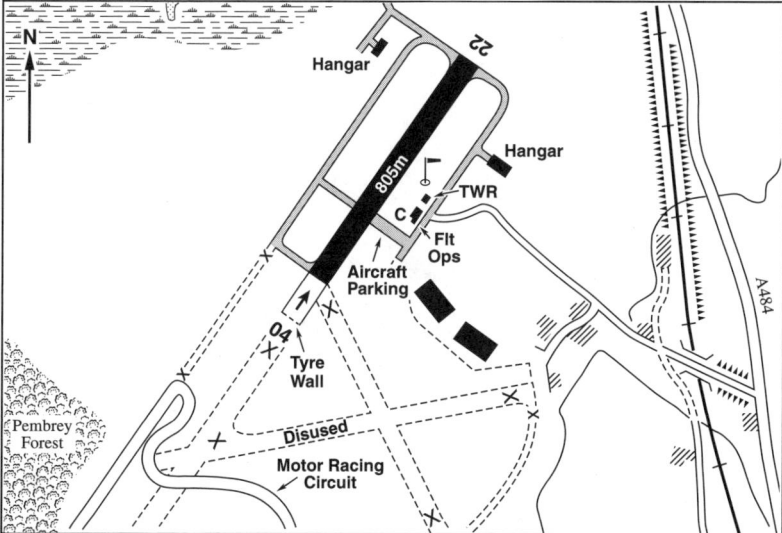

Rwy	Dim(m)	Surface	TORA(m)	LDA(m)	Lighting
04/22	805x30	Concrete	04-803	04-803	Nil
			22-803	22-803	Nil

Op hrs: PPR Mon-Fri. Prior permission not required Sat & Sun.

Landing Fee: Up to 1000kg £7.00; 1001-1500kg £12.00; 1501-2000kg £15.00; 2001-3000kg £22.00; 3001-4000kg £30.00. All plus VAT.

Customs: EC - Forms only required; Non EC - PNR.

Hangarage: By arrangement.   **Maintenance:** Available.

Remarks: Operated by Winston Thomas Esq, Pembrey Airport, Pembrey, Kidwelly, Carmarthenshire SA16 0HZ. Licensed airfield situated within Danger Area D118. The Danger Area is active Mon-Thu 0800 - 1700 and Fri 0800 -1400. Aircraft **must** call Range Control on 122·75 at 10 nm, and request clearance to enter during its active hours. **Clearance to enter is subject to the Danger Area activity, and pilots must be prepared to hold off when required to do so.**

Non radio aircraft not accepted. Variable circuits in operation.

Valid insurance cover to include third party and public liability required.

Restaurant: Available, visitors welcome.

Accommodation: Ashburnham Hotel Tel: 01554-834455,
Gwenllian Court Hotel Tel: 01554-890217 - Courtsey car available.

Taxis: Tel: 01554-890111.   **Car Hire:** Tel: 01554-755303.

Fuel: 100LL, Jet A1.	**Tel:** 01554-891534. **Fax:** 01554-891388
	Ansaphone outside hours.

N50 19·90 W005 10·65	**PERRANPORTH**	330 ft AMSL
6 nm SW of Newquay. 6 nm NW of Truro.		**LND 114·20 063 21·2**

c/s Perranporth Radio 119·75 A/G.   130·10 Glider ops.
St. Mawgan App 126·50 .   Culdrose App 134·05.

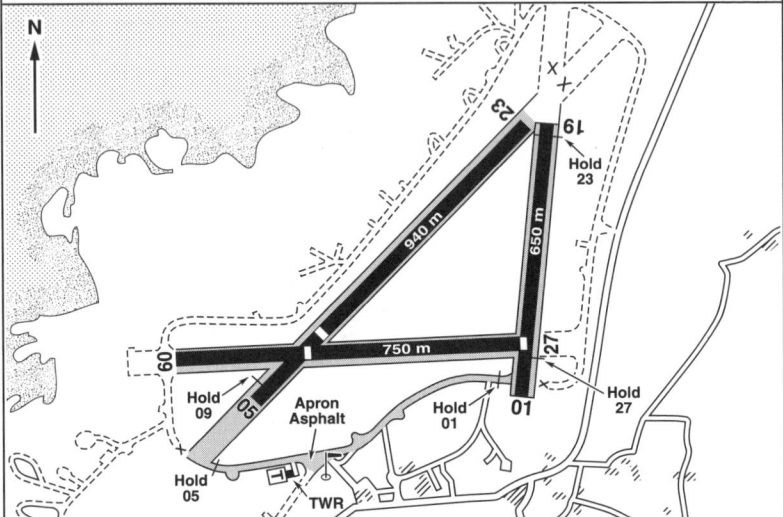

Rwy	Dim(m)	Surface	TORA(m)	LDA(m)	Lighting
05/23	940x23	Asphalt	05-940	05-799	Nil.
			23-799	23-799	Nil.
09/27	750x23	Asphalt	09/27-750	09/27-750	Nil.
01/19	650x23	Asphalt	01/19-650	01/19-650	Nil.

Op hrs: PPR. 0900-1730 or SS and by arrangement.

Landing Fee: Reasonable.   **Maintenance:** By arrangement.   **Customs:** PNR.

Remarks: Operated by Perranporth Airfield Company. Strictly PPR by telephone.
Circuits at 1000' QFE, LH on 01, 05 & 09, RH on 19, 23 & 27.
Avoid flying directly over St. Agnes, Perranporth & settlements to S of aerodrome. These
areas are particularly noise sensitive. After take-off, when practicable, reduce to climb
power and turn so as track out over the sea to at least 1500' QNH before proceeding on
course. For noise abatement, minimum power glide approaches, when practicable, would
be appreciated. Pilots arriving from the east should first contact St. Mawgan App. Aircraft
under control of RNAS Culdrose may operate in the Perranporth ATZ at 2000' QFE and
above, accordingly aircraft should not fly within the ATZ above 1500' QFE without
clearance from Culdrose ATC or via relay from Perranporth Radio.
Gliding activity on aerodrome. When gliding is in progress aircraft should fly wide circuits.
Warning: Rwy 27 - Expect wind shear and severe turbulence in strong winds.

Hotels: Rose-in-Vale Hotel Tel: 01872-552202.   Ponsmere Hotel Tel: 01872-572225.
Nampara Lodge Tel: 01872-572319.   **Tourist Information:** Tel: 01872-573368

Car Hire: By arrangement.   **Taxi:** Tel: 01872-572126; 01872-553795.

Fuel: 100LL	**Tel:** 01872-552266. **Fax:** 01872-552261 Website: www.perranporthairfield.co.uk

N56 26·35 W003 22·33	**PERTH (Scone)**			397 ft AMSL
3 nm NE of Perth.	**SAB 112·50 316 50·4.**		**LU**	**330·0 291** 17.6
	GOW 115·40 054 49·5.		**LUK 110·50**	291 **17·6**

c/s Perth Radio/Information 119·80 A/G or AFIS.

VOR 'PTH' 110·40 (On A/D).

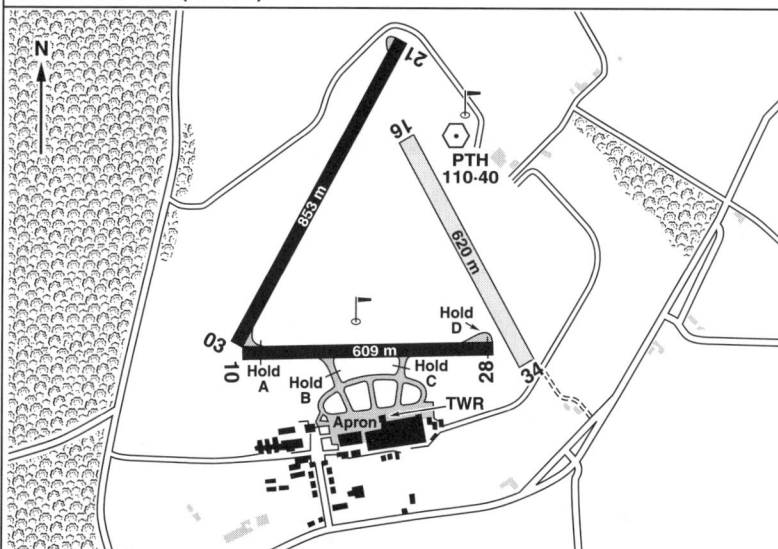

Rwy	Dim(m)	Surface	TORA(m)	LDA(m)	Lighting
03/21	853x27	Asphalt	03-853	03-853	Thr Rwy PAPI
			21-853	21-853	Thr Rwy PAPI
10/28	609x22	Asphalt	10-609	10-466	Nil
			28-466	28-609	Nil
16/34	620x36	Grass	16-620	16-620	Nil
			34-620	34-620	Nil

Op hrs: PPR.

Landing Fee: Private Singles & Helicopters £8, Twins £16 inclusive of VAT.

Hangarage: Available   **Maintenance:** Available, JAR 145   **Customs:** PNR

Remarks: Operated by Perth Airport 2000 Ltd. Licensed aerodrome.
All aircraft to join overhead.
When taking off from Rwy 28 there may be severe downdraughts and turbulence in
the vicinity of a line of trees which form an obstacle (70' agl) across the runway centre
line at 1050m beyond the start of TORA.
Circuits: RH on Rwys 21, 28 and 34; LH on 03, 10 and 16.
High ground running NE/SW, rising to 918' amsl within 2 nm, and 1236' amsl within
5 nm to the NE.

Restaurant: Available.

Car Hire: Europcar. Tel: 01738-636888. **Taxi:** Tel: 01738-636098.

Fuel: 100LL, Jet A1.	**Tel:** 01738-551631. **Fax:** 01738-553097
	E-mail: perthairport@merkensfry.co.uk

Robert Pooley ©

N52 28·08 W00015·07	**PETERBOROUGH (Conington)**	26 ft AMSL

6 nm S of Peterborough.

DTY 116·40 066 36
BKY 116·25 343 31

c/s Conington Radio 129·725 A/G.

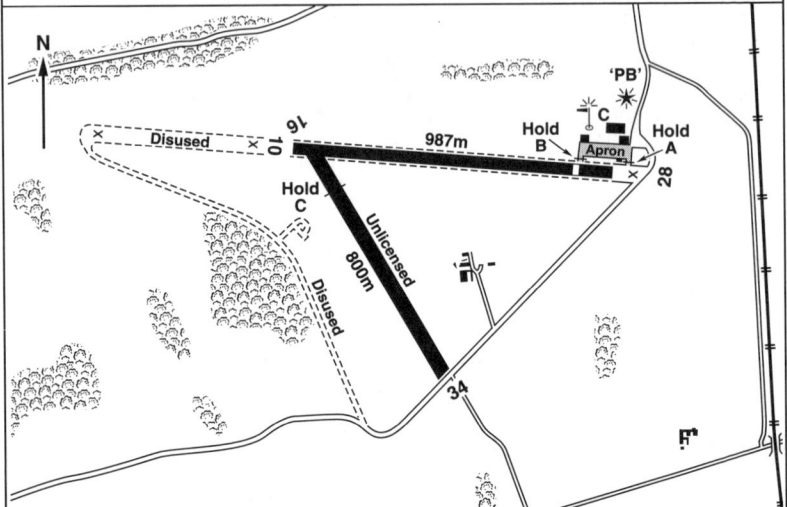

Rwy	Dim(m)	Surface	TORA(m)	LDA(m)	Lighting
10/28	987x23	Asphalt	10-957	10-957	Thr Rwy LITAS 3·25°
			28-987†	28-876*	Thr Rwy LITAS 3·25°
16/34	800x43	Concrete	Unlicensed		Nil.

† Plus 493m clearway.   * Plus 500m unlicensed.   IBn 'PB' Gn

Op hrs: WINTER. PPR. Mon-Fri 0830-1700, Sat & Sun 0900-1700, & ¢.
SUMMER. PPR. Mon-Fri 0830-1800, Sat & Sun 0900-1800, & ¢.

Landing Fee: Fixed Wing SE £10 Mon-Fri, £7 Sat/Sun - All incl VAT.   **Customs:** O/R

Hangarage: Ltd.   **Maintenance:** CAA & AOC JAR 145 Approved

Remarks: Owned and operated by Klingair Ltd. Non radio aircraft PPR.
Flying training by Aerolease Ltd, as Flying Club Conington, Tel: 01487-834161,
Fax: 01487-834246. Full ground support services available. Visitors welcome.

New purpose built Clubhouse/Coffee bar.

Circuit details: Height 1000 ft aal, Mon-Fri 0830-1700 (Local) all circuits to the South;
after 1700 (Local) and at weekends/PHs all circuits to the North.

Please avoid overflying villages to north and south of aerodrome.

Restaurant: Full club facilities with members licensed bar. Light snacks and hot
meals available 7 days a week.

Car Hire: On request.

Air Taxi service and self fly aircraft available.

Flying Training for PPL/IMC, Night and Twin Rating, Safety Course.

Fuel: 100LL, Jet A1.	**Tel:** 01487-832022
	01780-410576 Manager – outside Op hrs.

N52 33·35 W000 23·18	**PETERBOROUGH (Sibson)**	100 ft AMSL

6 nm W of Peterborough.	DTY 116·40 055 35.
	WIT 117·60 134 5·0

c/s Sibson Radio 122·30 Cottesmore APP/RAD 130·20 (MATZ & LARS)

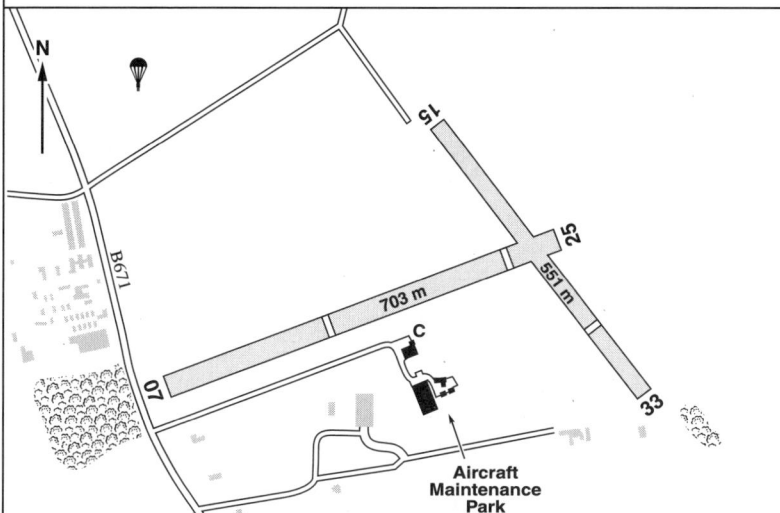

Rwy	Dim(m)	Surface	TORA(m)	LDA(m)	Lighting
07/25	703x30	Grass	07-703	07-411	Nil.
			25-703	25-613	Nil.
15/33	551x18	Grass	15-551	15-551	Thr Rwy APAPI 4°
			33-551	33-424	Thr Rwy APAPI 4°
					ABn Wh

Op hrs: 0800-1800 (and by arrangement). PPR by phone.

Landing Fee: Microlights £3.00; Singles £7.00; Twins £14.00. (Reciprocal arrangements excepted).

Hangarage: Phone. **Maintenance:** Available, CAA approved **Customs:** Phone.

Remarks: Operated by Walkbury Flying Club. Prior permission must be obtained before departure. Non-radio aircraft not accepted. Caution as power lines on Rwy 25 approach. Inbound aircraft to call Cottesmore Radar 130·20 when15 nm from Wittering. Circuit height 800 ft aal, LH on Rwy 25 and 15, RH on Rwy 07 and 33. No deadside and no overhead joining due to free-fall parachuting up to FL120. Avoid overflying Elton SW of the airfield.

Whilst parachuting is in progress:
- Transitting aircraft (fixed & rotary) may not penetrate the ATZ;
- Rotary wing aircraft may not operate in the ATZ.

Mast 586' aal 686' amsl 145°/2·1 nm.

Restaurant: Available Tue-Sun, Tel: 01832-280404.

Car Hire: AVIS Tel: 01733-349489. Hertz Tel: 01733- 893083.

Taxi: Tel: 01733-566661.

Fuel: 100LL	**Tel/Fax:** 01832-280289.

Intentionally Blank

N57 20·12 W005 40·32	**PLOCKTON**	80 ft AMSL

3·5 nm NE of Kyle of Lochalsh.

BEN 114·40 108 55·4
STN 115·10 172 54·8

c/s Plockton Radio 122·375 A/G.

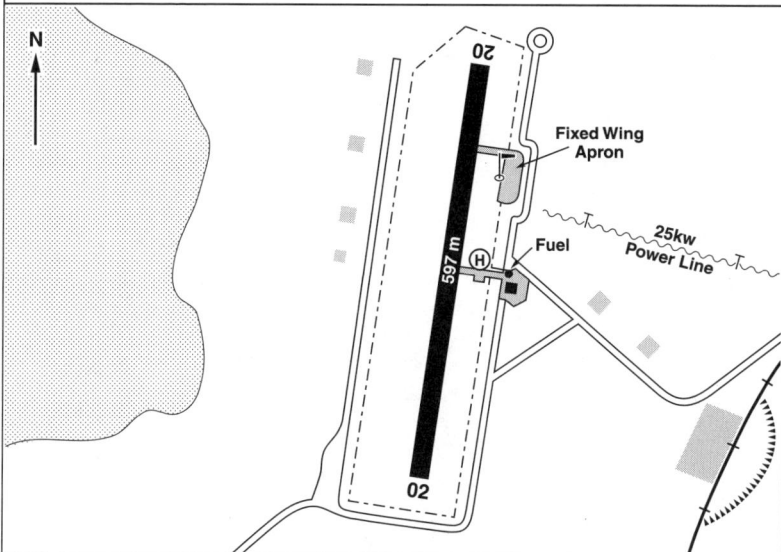

N

20

Fixed Wing Apron

25kw Power Line

597 m

(H)   **Fuel**

02

Rwy	Dim(m)	Surface	TORA(m)	LDA(m)	Lighting
02/20	597x23	Asphalt	Unlicensed		Nil.

Op hrs: 24hrs PPR.

Landing Fee: Highland Council Rates.	**Customs:** Nil
Hangarage: Available, contact PDG Helicopters Ltd.	**Maintenance:** Nil

Remarks: Airfield owned by Highland Council (HC). Unlicensed airfield. Visitors welcome.

Helicopter operations daily within a radius of 25 nm up to 2000 ft amsl. Helicopter pilots keep watch on 130·65.

Full office, workshop and changing room (with shower) facilities available for short term lets.

Camping on site.

Restaurant, Accommodation & Shops –10 mins walk.

Taxi: Kyle Taxi Tel: 01599-534323

Hotels: The Haven Tel: 01599-544223.   Plockton Hotel Tel: 01599-544274. Plockton Inn Tel: 01599-544222

Fuel: Jet A1. Available 24 hrs all year. PDG Helicopters Ltd.	**Tel:** 01599-534926 **Fax:** 01599-534926

| N50 25·36 W004 06·35 | **PLYMOUTH City Airport** | 485 ft AMSL |

| 3·5nm NNE of Plymouth. | **BHD 112·05 280 23·6** |

c/s Plymouth.   APP 133·55.   TWR 118·15.
VDF 133·55, 118·15.
NDB 'PY' 396·50 (On A/D).
ILS/DME Rwy 31(309°M) I–PLY 109·50. 3·5° GP

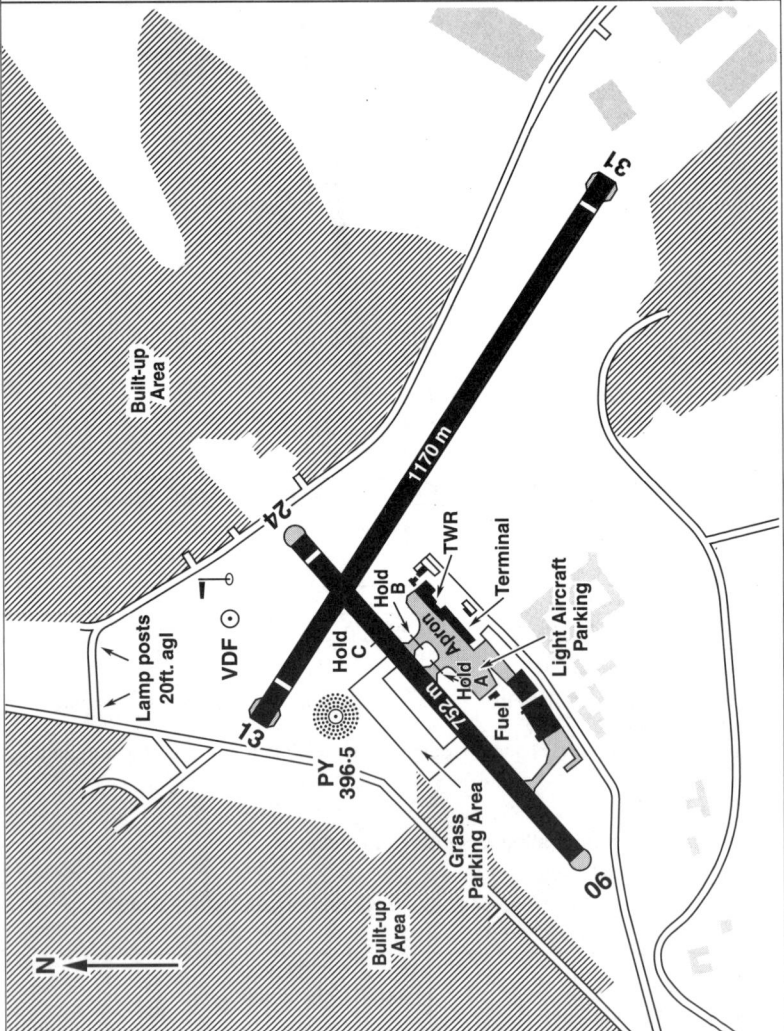

Built-up Area

31

1170 m

24

TWR

Terminal

Hold B

Hold C

Apron

Light Aircraft Parking

Hold A

VDF ⊙

Lamp posts 20ft. agl

13

752 m

Fuel

PY 396·5

Grass Parking Area

06

Built-up Area

N ◄

| N50 25·36 W004 06·35 | **PLYMOUTH City Airport** | 485 ft AMSL |

Rwy	Dim(m)	Surface	TORA(m)	LDA(m)	Lighting
06/24	752x26	Asphalt	06-752	06-752	Ap Thr Rwy APAPI 3·75°
			24-752	24-714	Ap Thr Rwy PAPI 3·5°
13/31	1170x30	Asphalt	13-1105	13-1038	APAPI 3·75° - See Note
			31-1100	31-1055	Ap Thr Rwy PAPI 3·5°

Note: PAPI 5·33° by prior arrangement only.   ABn Wh

Op hrs: 0630-2230 daily.

Use of aerodrome strictly **PPR** by telephone 01752-515341 during the following periods: Mon-Fri 2000-2230; Sat, Sun & PHs all day.

Landing Fee: £17.34 per tonne +VAT for aircraft MTWA over 2·5 tonnes. Out of hours surcharges apply to aircraft movements after 2000.

Customs: Available.

Hangarage/Maintenance: Plymouth Executive Ltd, Tel: 01752-786611.

Remarks: Operated by Plymouth City Airport Plc, Plymouth City Airport, Crownhill, Plymouth, Devon PL6 8BW.   Non-radio aircraft not accepted.

Aerodrome surface slopes down from the centre towards the boundaries, steep gradient at SW corner of aerodrome.

Availability of Rwy 06/24 limited. Contact ATC prior to departure if crosswinds likely to preclude the use of 13/31.

Circuits: LH on 06 & 13, RH on 24 & 31, or as directed.

Overload and long stay parking for light aircraft normally on the 'Grass Parking Area'. Marshallers not available.

Pilots using the grass light aircraft parking area, are after parking, to contact ATC using the telephone on the NE edge of the parking area to obtain permission for their passengers and themselves to use the pedestrian route across Rwy 06/24 delineated by green lines on the apron.

All aircraft must have a Third Party liability insurance cover of not less than one million pounds.

Signals for Rwy 06 are visible at night in an area North of extended centre-line where normal obstacle clearance is not guaranteed. Not to be used for approach slope guidance until aircraft is aligned with the runway.

Start-up clearance required.

Rescue and Police helicopter flights may take place at any time outside of aerodrome operating hours.

Warning: Windshear and turbulence in strong wind conditions. Downdraughts and sudden wind changes possible in light wind conditions.

TV mast 1889' aal, 2385' amsl, 028°/8·6. Chimney 76' aal, 561' amsl, 186°/950m.

VRPs: Avon Estuary, Ivy Bridge, Saltash and Yelverton.

Restaurant: Restaurant and refreshments available.

Car Hire: Hertz Tel: 01752-207206.

| **Fuel:** 100LL, Jet A1. Multi-Service | **Tel:** 01752-204090 A/D, 515341 ATC. **Fax:** 01752-770160 ATC/Airport Ops **Fax:** 01752-795590 Brymon Ops |

N53 55·52 W000 47·77	**POCKLINGTON**	87 ft AMSL

10 nm ESE of York.	OTR 113·90 304 28
	GAM 112·80 013 39

c/s Pocklington Base 129·975, 130·10 A/G (Glider operations).

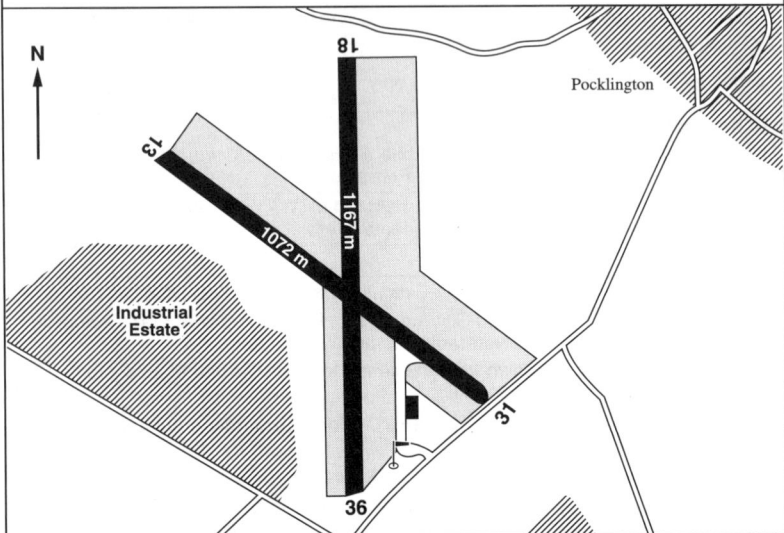

Rwy	Dim(m)	Surface	TORA(m)	LDA(m)	Lighting
13/31	1072x46	Asphalt	Unlicensed		Nil.
13/31	1072x110	Grass	Unlicensed		Nil.
18/36	1167x46	Asphalt	Unlicensed		Nil.
18/36	1167x130	Grass	Unlicensed		Nil.

Asphalt runways in poor condition but considered safe for landing & take-off.

Op hrs: SR–SS.

Landing Fee: Commercial £10.00; Private £5.00.	**Customs:** Nil.
Hangarage: Nil.	**Maintenance:** Nil.

Remarks: Unlicensed airfield operated by the Wolds Gliding Club Ltd.
Primary use for gliding. Visitors welcome. PPR if unfamiliar with gliding operations.
Joining Instructions
• Orbit the airfield at 1000' aal, keeping clear of glider traffic, to indicate intention to land. NEVER FLY OVERHEAD DUE TO CABLES. Land in same runway direction as in use by gliders. When approach and runway are suitably clear, land on asphalt or grass and backtrack to glider launch point.
• With no glider activity, land on any runway and taxy to hangar.

All grass areas are in good condition. Variable circuits.

Avoid overflying the villages of BARMBY MOOR (NW of aerodrome) and POCKLINGTON (NE of aerodrome).

KEEP A GOOD LOOK OUT FOR GLIDERS.

Fuel: 100LL.	**Tel:** 01759-303579

N51 11·67 W001 14·17	**POPHAM**	550 ft AMSL
6 nm SW of Basingstoke.		**SAM** 113·35 021 14·9
		CPT 114·35 188 17·8

c/s Popham Radio 129·80 A/G.

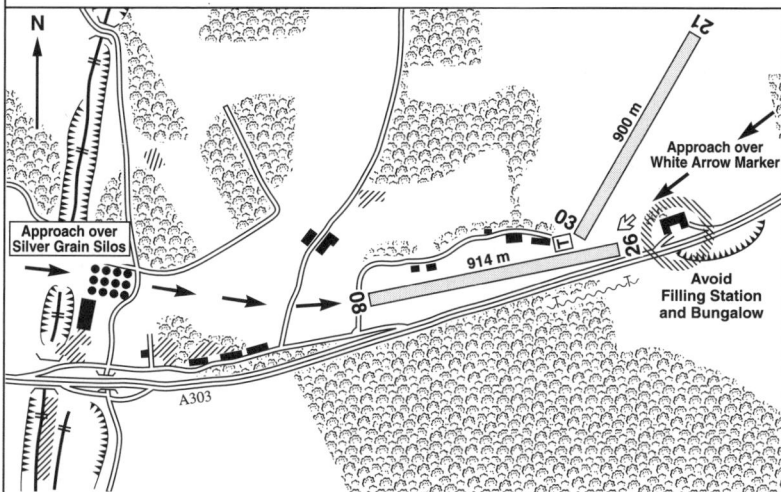

Rwy	Dim(m)	Surface	TORA(m)	LDA(m)	Lighting
08/26	914x25	Grass	Unlicensed		Nil.
† 03/21	900x25	Grass	Unlicensed		Nil.

† Restricted use. For operational dates check with airfield operator in advance.

Op hrs: 0830-1700. Non radio aircraft PPR.   **Customs:** Nil

Landing Fee: £5.00. Parking £4.00/night. Spitfire Flying Club members no charge.

Hangarage: Nil. Tie-downs available.   **Maintenance:** M3 - Tel: 01256-398372.

Remarks: Operated by Charles Church (Spitfires) Ltd, Popham Airfield,
Nr Winchester, Hants. SO21 3BD. Unlicensed airfield.
Any aircraft not exceeding 4500 lbs MAUW is welcome at pilot's own risk.

All circuits at 800 ft to the North. Permanent dead side to the south.

Approach to Rwy 26 marked with a large White arrow to avoid overflying filling station
and Bungalow at eastern end. *No touch and goes on Rwy 26.*

Approach to Rwy 08 over group of silver grain silos to avoid overflying houses at
western end. Observe ground signals at east end of clubroom building.

Water tower 60' aal 610' amsl in NW corner of A/D. Power cables 25' agl extend
westward from water tower and outside aerodrome boundary.
Trees up to 50' agl along aerodrome boundaries.

Fly-Ins generally second Sunday in each month.

Home of the Spitfire Flying Club.   Pilot's Shop in clubroom.

Restaurant: Light snacks available.

Fuel: 100LL. All grades of Oil.	**Tel:** 01256-397733. **Fax:** 01256-397114
(Cash or Cheques only)	**E-mail:** pophamairfield@aol.com
	Web: www.popham-airfield.co.uk

Intentionally Blank

N56 11·50 W003 19·55	**PORTMOAK (Kinross)**	360 ft. AMSL

3·7 nm ESE of Kinross. **GO** 402·0 283 3·5. **SAB** 112·50 302 41
0·5 nm E of Loch Leven. **PTH** 110·40 181 15. **GOW** 115·40 071 43

No Radio.
FIS Scottish Information 119·875.

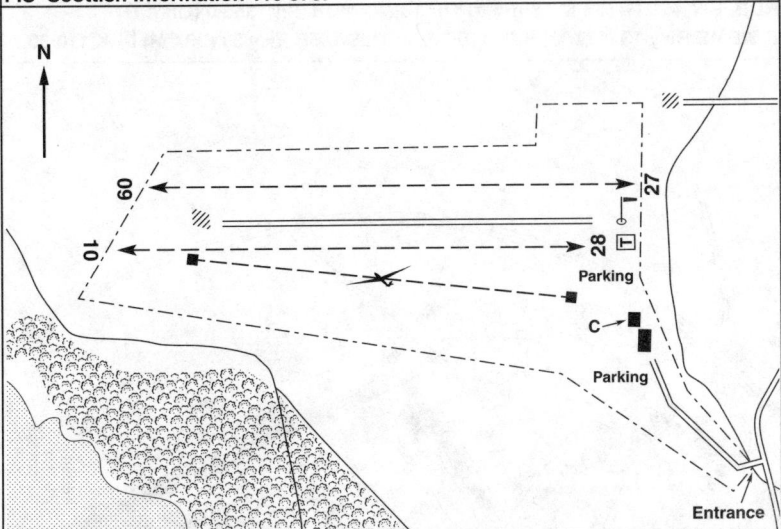

Rwy	Dim(m)	Surface	TORA(m)	LDA(m)	Lighting
09/27	700x15	Grass	Unlicensed		Nil.
10/28	900x15	Grass	Unlicensed		Nil.

Op hrs: PPR. SR–SS.

Landing Fee: £7.00.	**Customs:** Nil.
Hangarage: Nil.	**Maintenance:** Nil.

Remarks: Operated by Scottish Gliding Union, Portmoak Airfield, Scotlandwell, by Kinross KY13 9JJ, primarily for gliding purposes.

Intensive gliding activity.

Powered aircraft strictly PPR.

Circuits variable depending on glider activity.

Pilots of nose-wheel aircraft should exercise extreme caution.

Warning: Winch cables may lie across runways.

Fuel: Nil	**Tel:** 01592-840243 or 840543

N55 30·47 W004 35·20   **PRESTWICK**   65 ft AMSL

1 nm NE of Prestwick.   TRN 117·50 038 13·5
                                         GOW 115·40 200 22·3

APP/RAD 120·55. TWR 118·15.   ATIS c/s Information 127·125
NDB 'PW' 426·0 (134°M/2·9nm to Thr 13).   NDB 'PIK' 355·0 (On A/D)
ILS/DME Rwy 13 (127°M) I-PP 110·30.   ILS/DME Rwy 31 (307°M) I-KK 110·30.

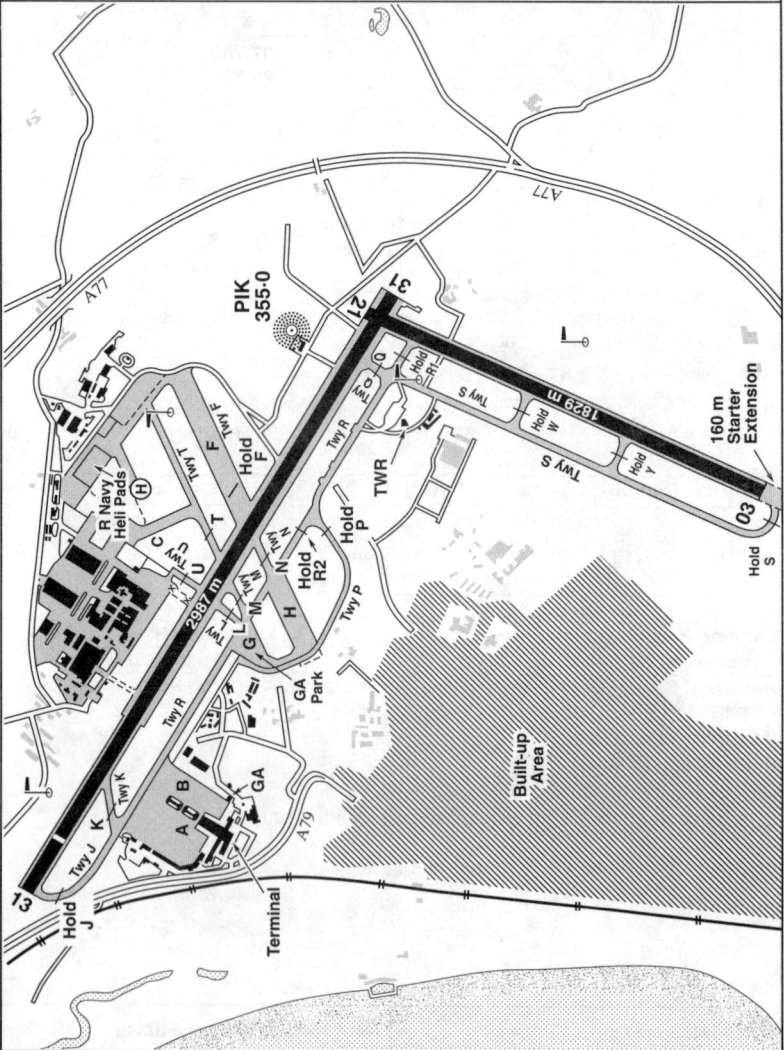

Rwy	Dim(m)	Surface	TORA(m)	LDA(m)	Lighting
			PRESTWICK		
13/31	2987x46	Concrete/	13-2987	13-2743	Ap Thr Rwy RCL PAPI 3°
		Asphalt	31-2987	31-2987	Ap Thr Rwy RCL PAPI 3·5°
03/21	1829x45	Asphalt	03-1829	03-1829	Thr Rwy PAPI 3°
			21-1829	21-1829	Ap Thr Rwy PAPI 3·5°

N55 30·47 W004 35·20   **PRESTWICK**   66 ft AMSL

Op hrs: H24.   **Customs:** As Op Hrs

Landing Fee: £6.80 per tonne or part thereof + VAT. Minimum charge £20.00 + VAT.
Concessionary landing fees for **private light aircaft only** - SE £10, Twins £15 + VAT, contact Prestwick Flight Centre Tel: 01292-476523. Free parking. 100LL available.

Hangarage: Ltd.   **Maintenance:** Corporate Jets plc, Tel: 01292-671990.

Met: H24. 0141-221-6116. H24. 01292-79800 Ext. 2617 (Prestwick Actuals only).

Remarks: Operated by Glasgow Prestwick International Airport (GPIA) Ltd, Aviation House, Prestwick, Scotland KA9 2PL.

Non based operators should make prior arrangements for ground handling of non-scheduled flights. All ground handling services are provided by GPIA Ltd.

Visitors to BAe Flight Training must PPR through Flt Ops by phone on 01292-671022 Ext 107/143. Aircraft should vacate runway at Twy Tango and call 'College Ops' on 123·65.

PPR all training aircraft. Pilots are to 'book out' by telephoning ATC.

Noise Preferential Procedures in force.

Aircraft operations in visibilities of 600 m or less are not permitted.

Twy links L and N are not used at night or in low visibility.

Only marked taxiways are to be used.

Taxiway route to/from Jetstream Aircraft, HMS Gannet and the Northside Flying Club is via Twy Tango (T).

Helicopter Operations: Civil helicopters would normally be allocated stand on the main Apron. Such helicopters are to operate to/from the main Aprons A/B by approaching to/from the main Rwy Block II or Taxiway Block 16 as directed by ATC. Helicopters may 'air' or 'ground' taxi between this area and the military parking circles. Due to the surface condition of Apron C, only marked designated taxiway routes must be used.

Warnings: Aircraft carrying out circuits on Runway 03/21 are warned of raising ground to the North East.

Bird Hazard assessed as 'moderate' but 'severe' during migratory periods. (Oct/Nov and Mar/Apr.

Mast 604 ft aal, 3·2 nm N of ARP.

Visual Reference Points (VRPs) are listed overleaf.

Restaurant: Terminal Building.

Car Hire: Hertz, 01292-511281. Avis, 01292-477218. Europcar, 01292-678198.

Fuel: 100LL, Jet A1. BP.
Multi Service. Diners.
	Tel: 01292-511107 ATC Ops
	     01292-511026 GPIA Handling.
	     01292-511000 Switchboard.
	Fax: 01292-475464 ATC; 511106 GPIA Ops.

PRESTWICK
VISUAL REFERENCE POINTS (VRPs)

VRP	VOR/VOR	VOR/NDB	VOR/DME
Culsean Bay/Castle N55 22·17 W004 46·08	TRN R016 GOW R208	TRN 016° Prestwick PE 247°M	TRN 016°/3·5 nm
Cumnock N55 27·33 W004 15·45	TRN R072 GOW R173	TRN R072 Glasgow GLG 182°M	TRN 072°/20 nm
Heads of Ayr N55 25·97 W0044 2·78	TLA R273 GOW R207	TRN R027 Prestwick PE 263°M	TRN 027°/8 nm
Irvine Harbour N55 36·50 W004 40·90	TRN R018 GOW R214	TRN R018 Prestwick PW 007°M	TRN 018°/18 nm
Kilmarnock N55 36·75 W004 29·90	TRN R036 TLA R288	TRN R036 New Galloway 344°M	TRN 036°/20 nm
Pladda N55 25·58 W005 07·07	GOW R228 TRN R309	GOW R228 New Galloway 304°M	TRN 309°/13 nm
West Kilbride N55 41·13 W004 52·08	GOW R240 TRN R002	GOW R240 Prestwick PE 321°M	GOW 240°/18 nm

N52 00·92 E001 00·25	**RAYDON WINGS**	170 ft AMSL

2·5 nm SE of Hadleigh, 4 nm SW of Ipswich.

BKY 116·25 090° 34·7
CLN 114·55 335° 11·3

No Radio.

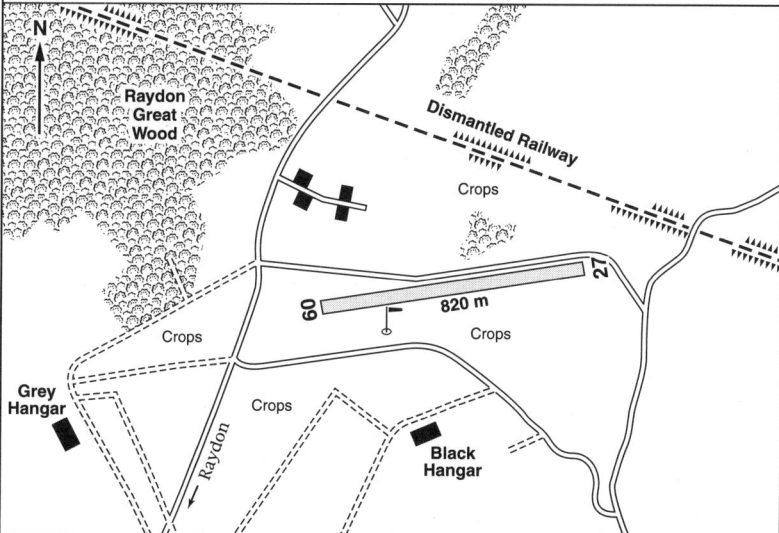

N

Raydon
Great
Wood

Dismantled Railway

Crops

Crops

820 m

60

27

Crops

Crops

Grey
Hangar

Raydon

Crops

Black
Hangar

Rwy	Dim(m)	Surface	TORA(m)	LDA(m)	Lighting
09/27	820x27	Grass	Unlicensed		Nil

Op hrs: Strictly PPR.

Landing Fee:	**Customs:** Nil.
Hangarage: Nil	**Maintenance:** Nil.

Remarks: Operated by Raydon Wings Ltd., Woodlands Hall, Raydon, Ipswich, Suffolk IP7 5QD. Unlicensed airfield.

Visiting aircraft strictly by prior permission only, and at pilot's own risk.

Aircraft should join the circuit from the south at 800 ft aal and depart to the south after take-off.

Circuits RH on Rwy 09, LH on Rwy 27. Curved approach to Rwy 27 is requested.

Warnings: Agricultural work could be taking place on the runway and approaches at any time.

Wattisham MATZ boundary lies 2·5 nm to the north of the airfield

Power lines run east to west 1nm to the north of the airfield.

Restaurant: Nil.	**Car Hire/Taxis:** Nil.

Fuel: Nil	**Tel:** 01473-827544. **Fax:** 01473-828992.

Robert Pooley ©

N51 12·82 W000 08·32 **REDHILL** 221 ft AMSL

1·5 nm SE of Redhill.

BIG 115·10 227 9·6.
OCK 115·30 120 12·8

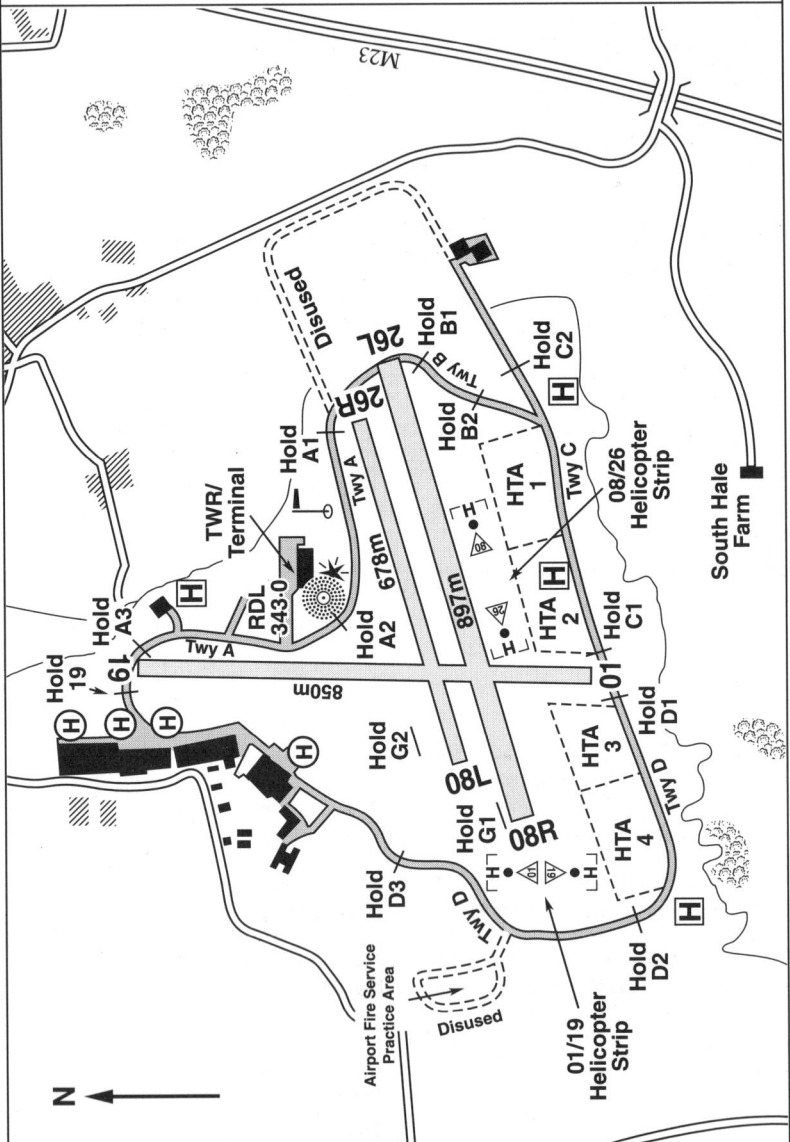

Z

M23

Disused

Hold B1

Hold C2

26L

26R

Twy B

Hold A1

Hold B2

Twy C

HTA 1

08/26 Helicopter Strip

South Hale Farm

TWR/ Terminal

Twy A

678m

897m

HTA 2

Hold C1

RDL 343·0

Hold A2

Twy A

Hold A3

Hold 19

850m

01

Hold D1

Hold G2

HTA 3

Twy D

Hold G1

08L

08R

HTA 4

Hold D3

Hold D2

Twy D

Airport Fire Service Practice Area

Disused

01/19 Helicopter Strip

| N51 12·82 W000 08·32 | **REDHILL** | 221 ft AMSL |

c/s Tower 119·60 TWR.

NDB 'RDL' 343·0 (On A/D) Nav Aid only.

Rwy	Dim(m)	Surface	TORA(m)	LDA(m)	Lighting
01/19	850x25	Grass	01-850	01-850	Nil
			19-850	19-699	Nil
08R/26L	897x30	Grass	08R-897	08R-897	Thr Rwy APAPI 4·25°
			26L-897	26L-897	Thr Rwy APAPI 3·5°
08L/26R	678x23	Grass	08L-678	08L-678	Nil
			26R-678	26R-678	Nil
					ABn Wh

Op hrs: PPR. SUMMER: 0900 - 2000 daily.   WINTER : 0900 - 1700 daily.

Customs: Inbound 4 hrs PNR.   **Landing Fee:** On application

Hangarage & Maintenance: London Helicopter Centres Tel: 01737-823514.

Remarks: Operated by Redhill Aerodrome Ltd., Terminal Building, Redhill Aerodrome, Surrey RH1 5YP. Licensed Aerodrome/Heliport. **PPR by telephone.**

Use of aerodrome by microlight aircraft restricted to aerodrome based aircraft only.

Flex wing microlights prohibited.

Intensive helicopter operations. **No deadside**, helicopters fly circuits on the opposite side of runway to fixed wing aircraft.

Unmarked taxiways should not be used without ATC permission.

Visual Reference Points (VRPs) – see below and Chart at page 429.

Circuit height: Fixed wing and Helicopters 1000' QFE.

Joining/Departure Procedures:

All aircraft must enter and leave ATZ via one of the following VRPs:

> Junction 7 M25/Junction 8 M23   N51 15·83 W000 07·68;
>
> Godstone (Junction of A25/B2236 roads) N51 14·83 W000 04·02;
>
> Reigate Railway Station N51 14·52 W000 12·25;
>
> Godstone Railway Station N51 13·08 W000 03·07.

Fixed-wing aircraft join at 1300 ft QFE. If required to join overhead - enter the ATZ on the runway QDM remaining within the fixed-wing circuit area (north of Rwy 08/26 or east of Rwy 01/19). When instructed, descend to circuit height and join the visual circuit pattern. Depart at 1500 ft QNH.

Helicopters join at 1000 ft QFE. When Rwy 01/19 is in use, helicopters joining from the east may be instructed to route from Godstone Station to the eastern aerodrome boundary at 500 ft QFE. Depart at 1200 ft QNH.

Noise Abatement: Always use best rate of climb. Avoid overflying South Nutfield village and the East Surrey Hospital.
Fixed-wing: After departure from Rwy 01,08 or 26, climb straight ahead to 1000 ft QNH before turning. After departure from Rwy 19, commence the left turn at 500 ft QNH.

Club Facilities: Redhill Flying Club.

| **Fuel:** 100LL. Jet A1
Visa, Masterrcard | **Tel:** 01737- 823377 Admin/ATC
         01737-823518 Fuel.
Fax: 01737-822110 Admin.   823640 ATC.
Website: www.redhillaerodrome.com |

Intentionally Blank

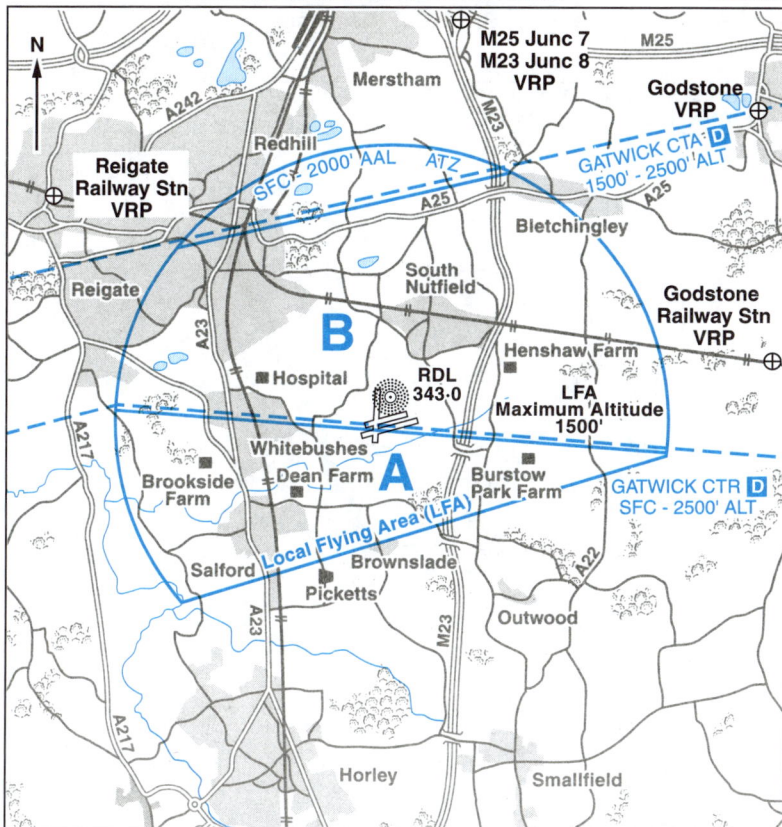

The southern half of Redhill Aerodrome lies within the Gatwick CTR and the northern half lies beneath the Gatwick CTA. During the hours of watch of Redhill ATC, flights, without reference to Gatwick ATC, may be made within the Redhill ATZ/ Local Flying Area subject to compliance with the following restrictions and procedures:

Within Gatwick CTR

Area 'A'
- Clear of cloud, in sight of surface, minimum visibility (fixed wing) 3 km.
- Max altitude 1500' QNH.
- Limits of circuit:
  - WEST   Redhill – Horley road (A23);
  - EAST   Outwood – Bletchingley road;
  - SOUTH   Picketts and Brownslade farms.

Area 'B'
- Max altitude 1500' QNH.

Note: All aircraft, including those that may be in radio contact with Gatwick ATC, must obtain clearance from Redhill ATC 5 mins prior to ETA.

Arr/Dep – Aircraft joining or leaving Redhill ATZ/Local Flying Area must do so north of the Gatwick CTR. Joining procedures are detailed at page 427.
Outbound aircraft will not normally be routed via a VRP being used by inbound aircraft.

Robert Pooley ©

N53 16·83 W000 57·08	**RETFORD (Gamston)**	87 ft AMSL
2 nm S of Retford.		OTR 113·90 236 39·1
		TNT 115·70 068 29·4

c/s Gamston Radio. 130·475. A/G.
VOR/DME 'GAM' 112·80 (On A/D).

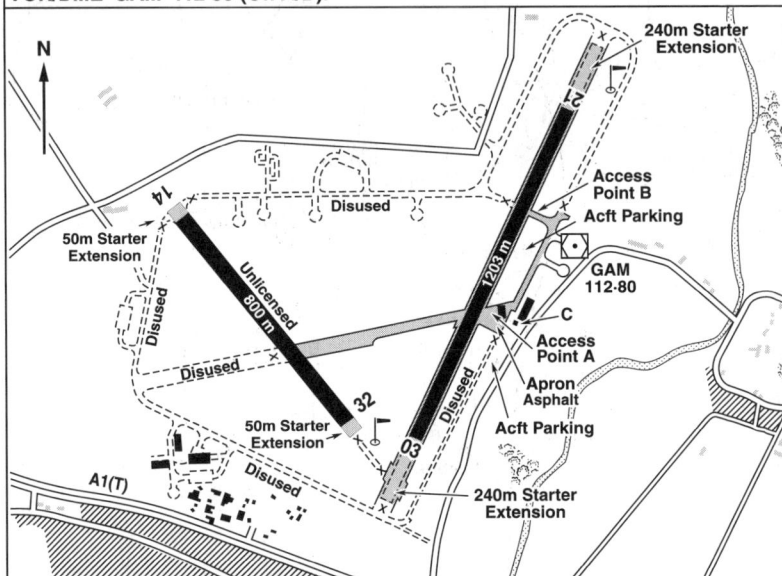

Rwy	Dim(m)	Surface	TORA(m)	LDA(m)	Lighting
03/21	1203x23	Asphalt	03-1203	03-1203	Thr Rwy PAPI 3·5°
			21-1203	21-1203	Thr Rwy PAPI 3°
14/32	800x18	Asphalt	unlicensed		Nil

Unlicensed starter extensions available on request.

Op hrs: Mon-Fri 0800-1800; Sat, Sun & PHs 0900-1800; & ¢.

Landing Fee: Singles: £8 inclusive VAT; Twins: £5 per half tonne, plus VAT.

Customs: Outbound No PNR; Inbound ETA, Names, Nationalities, DOB by Fax or Phone.

Hangarage: Limited　　　　　**Maintenance:** Available. M3. B1

Remarks: Operated by Gamston Aviation Ltd, Gamston Airport, Retford, Notts. DN22 0QL.
Visitors welcome on prior permission by telephone or by R/T.
Non radio aircraft accepted only by prior arrangement.
Glider launching on NW side of aerodrome at weekends and public holidays.
Mast 427' aal 518' amsl 178°/3·4 nm.

Restaurant: Light refreshments on airfield. Nearest restaurant 1·5 miles.

Car Hire: By arrangement.

Fuel: 100LL, Jet A1. Access, Diners, Visa & Multi Service.	Tel: 01777-838593/838594. 838521 Outside Op hrs Fax: 01777-838035 Web: www.gamstonairport.co.uk

Robert Pooley ©

N51 21·12 E000 30·20	**ROCHESTER**	436 ft AMSL

1·5 nm S of Rochester.

DET 117·30 315　4·6
BIG 115·10 090　17·6

c/s Rochester Information 122·25 AFIS
NDB 'RCH' 369·0 (On A/D)

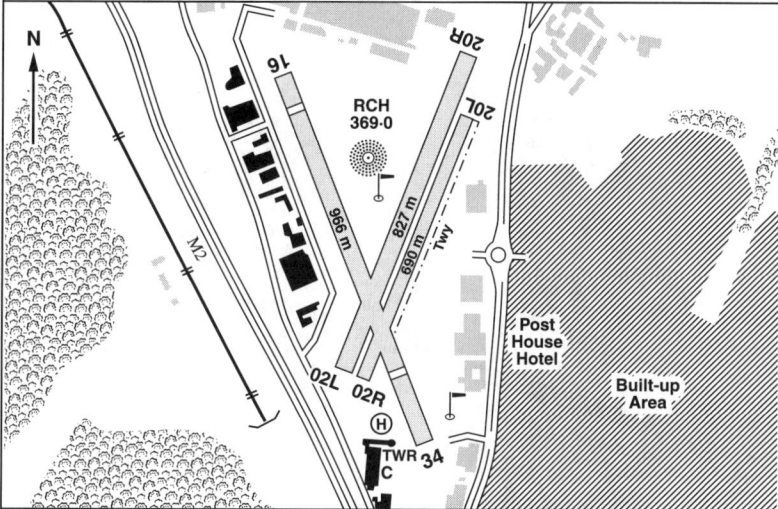

Rwy	Dim(m)	Surface	TORA(m)	LDA(m)	Lighting
02L/20R	827x32	Grass	02L-827	02L-826	Thr Rwy APAPI 4°
			20R-827	20R-827	Ap Thr Rwy APAPI 3·5°
02R/20L	690x21	Grass	02R-690 †	02R-690 †	Nil
			20L-690	20L-690	Nil
16/34	966x35	Grass	16-773	16-698	Nil
			34-966	34-773	Nil
† Additional 35m available on request.					ABn Wh

Op hrs: 0830-1830 daily.

Landing Fees: Singles £6.00. Twins £10.00; including VAT.
　　　　　　　Parking Fees: Singles £3.50, Twins £5.00; per night, incl. VAT.

Hangarage: Limited　　**Maintenance:** Available M3.　　**Customs:** 24 hrs PNR.

Remarks: Remarks: Operated by Rochester Airport plc, Rochester Airport, Chatham, Kent ME5 9SD. PPR. Circuits RH on Rwys 16 and 20, LH on Rwys 02 and 34.
Rwy 02R/20L is a relief runway and will only be used when 02L/20R undergoing maintenance. Simultaneous operations on the two parallel runways will not be permitted.
Taxy on prepared and marked areas only. A road used by vehicular traffic runs East/West immediately south of the take-off threshold Rwy 34.
Aircraft must have a valid third party liability insurance of at least £1million.
Masts 364' aal 800' amsl 153°/1·9 nm. Masts 312' aal 748' amsl 147°/1·7 nm.
Car Hire: Kenning Tel: 01634-845145. **Taxi:**　Tel: 01634-843601/222222.
Post House Hotel: At the A/D. Tel: 0870-400 9069, Fax: 01634-864 876.

Fuel: 100LL, Jet A1.	**Tel:** 01634-861378 ATC. 869968 Manager.
Visa, Mastercard, Switch.	**Fax:** 861682. **Telex:** 965209. **AFTN** EGTOZGZX

Robert Pooley ©

Government A/D	**EGDX**	1 DEC 00
N51 24·29 W003 26·15	**ST. ATHAN**	163 ft AMSL
3 nm W of Cardiff Airport.		**BCN 117·45 206 20**

Cardiff APP 125·85.   **St. Athan TWR 122·10 - on request**
ATIS 119·475 Cardiff Information.   **TACAN 'SAT' 114·80 (On A/D).**

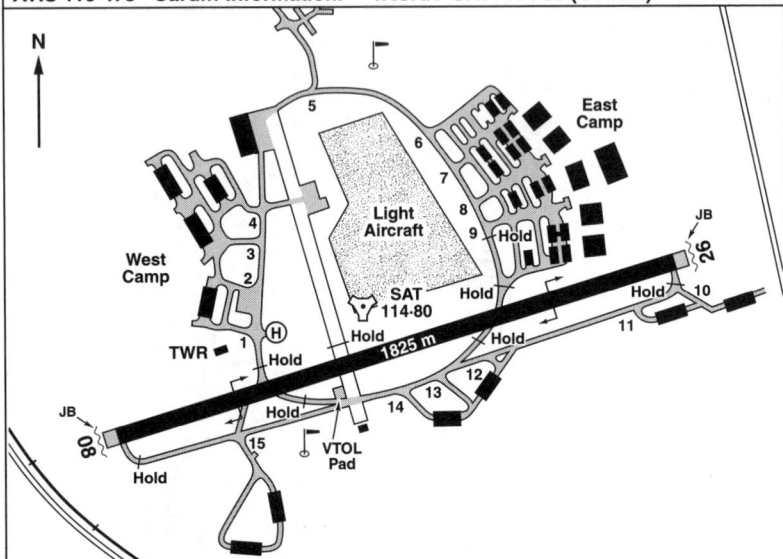

Rwy	Dim(m)	Surface	TORA(m)	LDA(m)	Lighting
08/26	1825x45	Asphalt	08-1825 26-1825	08-1825 26-1825	Thr Rwy PAPI 2·5° Ap Thr Rwy PAPI 2·5°

Op hrs: PPR.	**ATZ active H24**

Landing Fee: MoD(RAF) Rates	**Customs:** Nil.
Hangarage: Nil.	**Maintenance:** Nil

Remarks: RAF Aerodrome. Aerodrome situated within the Cardiff CTR/CTA where Class 'D' Airspace regulations apply — see page 2. Obtain ATC clearance from Cardiff Approach 5 mins before CTR boundary; normal join is a straight in approach to land only. Arresting Gear: Normal Ops - Approach cable down, overrun cable up. Circuits at 1000' QFE, RH on 08, LH on 26. No joining on dead-side.
Avoid overflying St. Athan village.
Locally based light aircraft give very late finals call.
Light aircraft landing area on North side of runway.
Light aircraft operate Sat and Sun 0900-1700.
Glider operations Sat and Sun SR—SS, and Wed evenings in summer months.
Caution: Wind shear on final approach to Rwy 26.
Railway line crosses final approach to Rwy 08, 282m from thld, and a road crosses the final approach to Rwy 26, 300m from the thld.

Fuel: 100LL, Jet A1.	**Tel:** 01446-798282 Ops.

N50 26·43 W004 59·72	**ST. MAWGAN**	390 ft AMSL
3·5 nm ENE of Newquay.		**LND 114·20 060 30·6**

c/s St. Mawgan.   RAD c/s Director 125·55.   RAD 126·50 (MATZ/LARS).
TWR 123·40.   NDB 'SM' 356·5 (on A/D).   ATIS Tel: 01637-872201 Ext 7854.
TACAN 'SMG' 112·60 (On A/D).   ILS Rwy 31 (307°M) 'SM' 108·70.

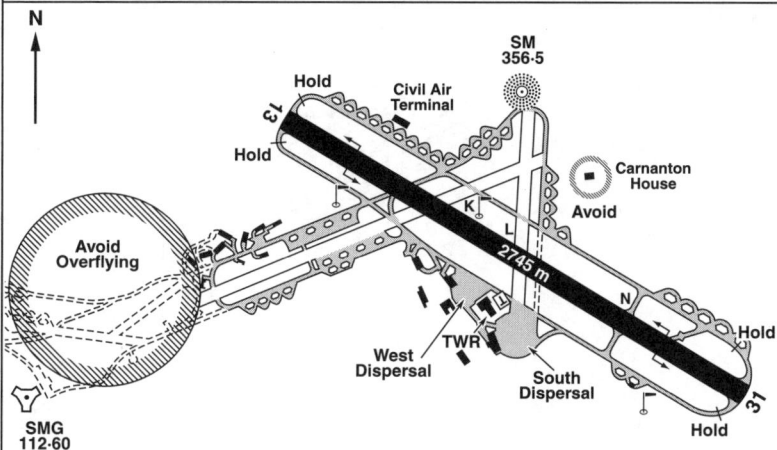

Rwy	Dim(m)	Surface	TORA(m)	LDA(m)	Lighting
13/31	2745x87	Asphalt/	13-2745	13-2745	Ap Thr Rwy PAPI 3°
		Conrete	31-2745	31-2745	Ap Thr Rwy PAPI 3°
For aircraft not cleared to trample arrester gear TORA/LDA are reduced as follows:					
			13-2230	13-2230	
			31-2325	31-2325	IBn 'SM' Red

Op hrs: Civil aircraft PPR from Brymon Airways, Tel: 01637-860551, Fax: 01637-860788
Newquay Airport operates 0730-2230 daily.   **ATZ active H24**

Landing Fee: Civil aircraft by arrangement with Brymon Airways.

Hangarage: Nil	**Maintenance:** Nil	**Customs:** 24 hrs PNR.

Remarks: RAF aerodrome. Non scheduled civil aircraft requiring to operate on Sat or Sun must request PPR before 1800 hrs Fri. Inbound aircraft to contact St. Mawgan Director at 20 nm. Radar approach may be mandatory.
Rwy QFE used for all apps. Airfield QNH may be used as a landing datum only O/R. Variable circuits at 1000' QFE, no deadside. Helicopters operate to within 100 m to the North of Rwy 13/31. Fixed wing circuits to South of runway.
Civil aircraft handled by Brymon Airways.
Civil users are to ensure that both inbound and outbound Flight Plans are sent to Stn Flight Plans – EGDGYWYO and ATC – EGDGZGZX.

Normal arrester gear operation: Approach cable down, overrun cable up.

Caution: Risk of Bird Strike.

Fuel: 100LL, Jet A1. Civil a/c by arrangement with Brymon Airways.	**Tel:** 01637-872201 Ext 2045/2046 RAF Ops 01637-872201 Ext 7224 Met.

N52 15·85 W000 29·08	**SACKVILLE FARM (Riseley)**	250 ft AMSL

2 nm N of disused Bedford/Thurleigh Aerodrome.	**DTY** 116·40 085 23·5
	BKY 116·25 313 26·0

No Radio.

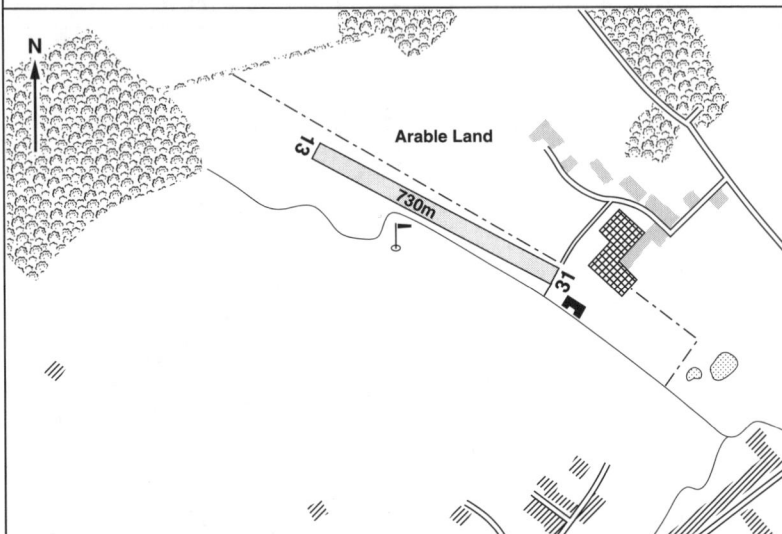

Rwy	Dim(m)	Surface	TORA(m)	LDA(m)	Lighting
13/31	730x23	Grass	Unlicensed		Nil

Op hrs: PPR. SR–SS.

Landing Fee: Nil.	**Customs:** Nil.
Hangarage: Nil	**Maintenance:** Nil.

Remarks: Operated by T. Wilkinson Esq., Sackville Lodge Farm, Riseley, Beds.
PPR essential as sheep/livestock may be grazing on strip.
Visiting aircraft welcome on prior permission and at pilot's own risk.
Pilots not familiar with the airfield should telephone for briefing.
Circuits LH on 13, RH on 31. Strip slopes UP at NW end.
Glider activity, cable launched and aerotows, at weekends.
Avoid overflying Riseley village 0·5 nm South of the airfield.

Fly in weekends (summertime) and try gliding !

Fuel: Nil.	**Tel:** 01234-708877 Airfield.
	Fax: 01234-708862

N59 15·02 W002 34·60	**SANDAY**	66 ft AMSL
20 nm NNE of Kirkwall Airport.		KWL 108·60 037 20 WIK 113·60 027 50

No Radio. Recommend contact Kirkwall APP 118·30.

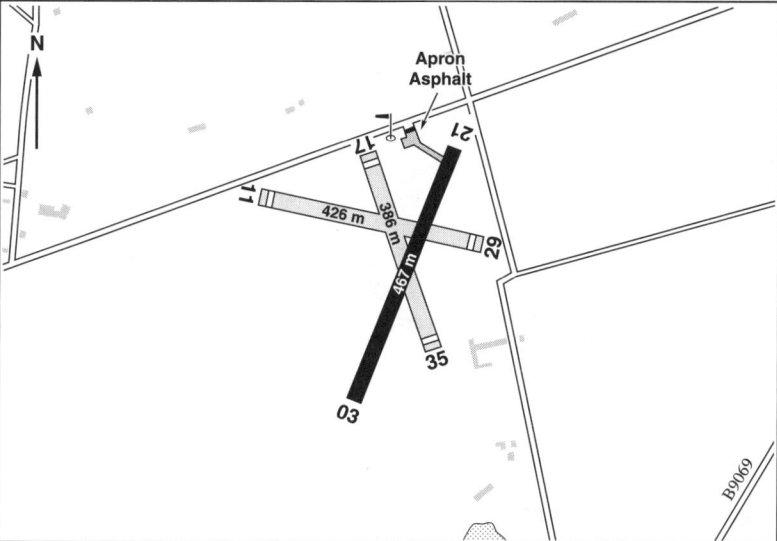

Rwy	Dim(m)	Surface	TORA(m)	LDA(m)	Lighting
03/21	467x18	Compacted Aggregate	03-467 21-467	03-467 21-467	Nil. Nil.
11/29	426x30	Grass	11-426 29-426	11-396 29-396	Nil. Nil.
17/35	386x30	Grass	17-378 35-378	17-366 35-366	Nil. Nil.

Op hrs: PPR. Aerodrome available daylight hours only.

Landing Fee: Nil. If fire cover is required, then £17.24 + VAT.

Hangarage: Nil   **Maintenance:** Nil   **Customs:** Nil

Remarks: Licensed aerodrome (day use only) operated by Orkney Islands Council, Dept of Technical Services, School Place, Kirkwall, Orkney KW15 1NY.

Visiting aircraft accepted on PPR and at pilot's own risk. In first instance, contact Orkney Islands Council, Tel: 01856-873535 Ext 2305.

Scheduled Air Service daily Mon-Sat.

Mast 343' aal 409' amsl 234°/2·7 nm.

Accommodation/Restaurant: Hotel and B&B available in nearby locality.

Car Hire: B. Flett, Quivals Garage Tel: Sanday 600418;
S. Thomson, Kettletoft Tel: Sanday 600321.

Fuel: Nil	**Tel:** 01856-873535 Council **Fax:** 01856-876094

Robert Pooley ©

N53 33·58 W000 51·50	**SANDTOFT**	11 ft AMSL

7 nm SW of Scunthorpe.

OTR 113·90 258 28·2
GAM 112·80 016 16·9

c/s Sandtoft Radio. 130·425. A/G. Waddington Radar 127·35 (LARS).
Humberside 124·67 (LARS).

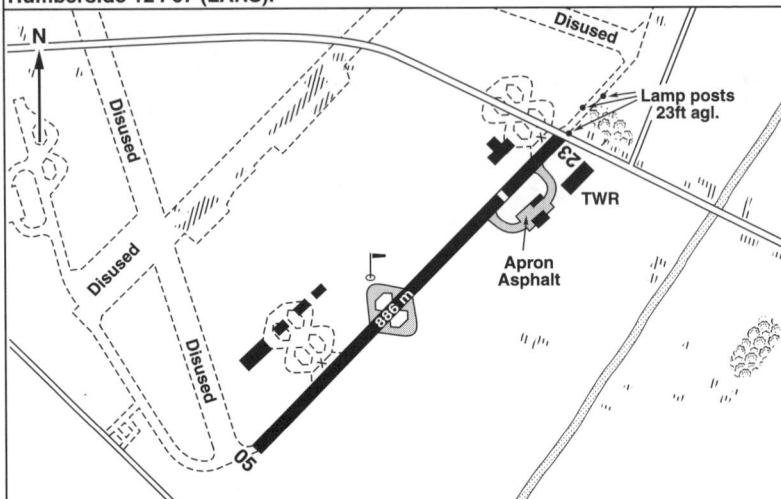

Rwy	Dim(m)	Surface	TORA(m)	LDA(m)	Lighting
05/23	886x18	Asphalt	05-786(D)	05-786(D)	Thr Rwy
			05-696(N)	05-696(N)	
			23-866(D)	23-696(D)	Thr Rwy APAPI 4°
			23-696(N)	23-696(N)	

(D) Day, (N) Night.

Op hrs: WINTER: 0900-SS; SUMMER: 0900-1800.   **Customs:** 24 hrs PNR.

Landing Fee: Singles £5.00, Twins & Helicopters £10.00 incl VAT. (No landing fee charged with fuel uplift of 100 litres or more).

Hangarage: Available; tie downs also available.   **Maintenance:** Nil

Remarks: Operated by Imperial Aviation (Sandtoft) Ltd. Visiting aircraft welcome. Non-radio aircraft subject to Prior Permission Only.

Local flying area NE of aerodrome clear of built-up areas.

Circuits at 1000' aal, LH on 05, RH on 23.

Avoid overflying the village of BELTON on the East perimeter of aerodrome.

Caution: Rwy 23 threshold displaced by 170 m due to lamp standards in the approach area.

Restaurant: Licensed Bar and Restaurant.

Car Hire: Godfrey Davis Europcar. Tel: 01724-840655 or 843239.

Fuel: 100LL, Jet A1.	**Tel:** 01427-873676 **Fax:** 01427-874656

N60 25·97 W001 17·77	**SCATSTA**	75 ft AMSL
17 nm N of Lerwick.		**SUM 117·30 007 33**

c/s Scatsta. APP/TWR 123·60. RAD 122·40.
NDB 'SS' 315·50 (241°M/ 2·7nm to Thr 24) – see Remarks.

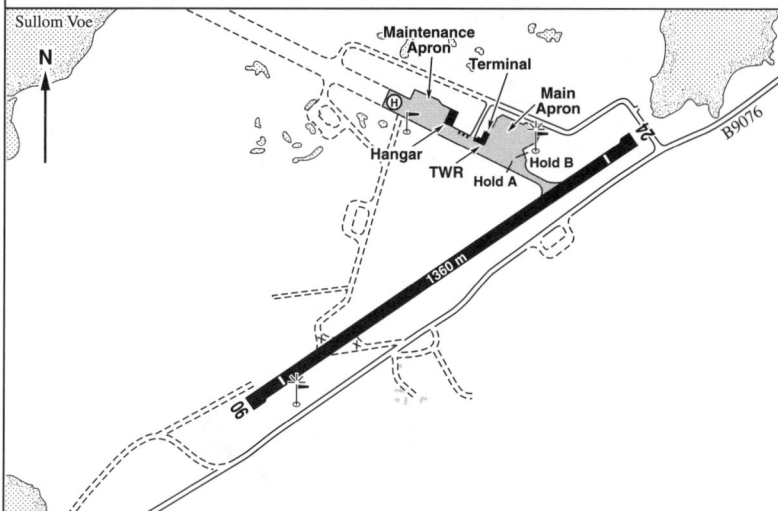

Rwy	Dim(m)	Surface	TORA(m)	LDA(m)	Lighting
06/24	1360x31	Asphalt	06-1253	06-1138	Ap Thr Rwy PAPI 4°
			24-1262	24-1168	Ap Thr Rwy PAPI 3·25°

Op hrs: PPR. Mon-Fri 0730-1730, Sat 0800-1400.

Landing Fee: On application	**Customs:** 24 hrs PNR
Hangarage: Nil	**Maintenance:** Nil

Remarks: Operated by Serco Aerospace Ltd, on behalf of BP Ltd., Scatsta Aerodrome, Brae, Shetland ZE2 9QP. Non-radio aircraft not accepted.

All circuits to the North. No flying over the Oil Terminal area. No training flights.

NDB 'SS' not to be used for holding, let down or approach unless ATC services are available.

Warnings: Pilots are warned that there is an area of bad ground within the south side of the strip near Rwy 06 threshold.

Taxiway south of the main apron has semi-width of only 6·6 m.

VRPs: Brae N60 23·82 W001 21·23; Fugla N60 26·95 W001 19·43;
Hillswick N60 28·55 W001 29·32 – Hillswick - Fugla - Scatsta A/D;
Voe N60 21·00 W001 15·97 – Voe - Brae - Scatsta A/D.

Restaurant: Nil.

Car Hire: Bolts Car Hire. Tel: Lerwick 692855.

Fuel: Jet A1. (2hrs PNR)	**Tel:** 01806- 242791. **Fax:** 01806-242110

N49 54·80 W006 17·52	**SCILLY ISLES (St. Mary's)**	116 ft AMSL
1 nm E of Hug Town.		**LND 114·20 249 28·6**

c/s Scillies. APP/TWR 123·15.   NDB 'STM' 321·0 (On A/D).

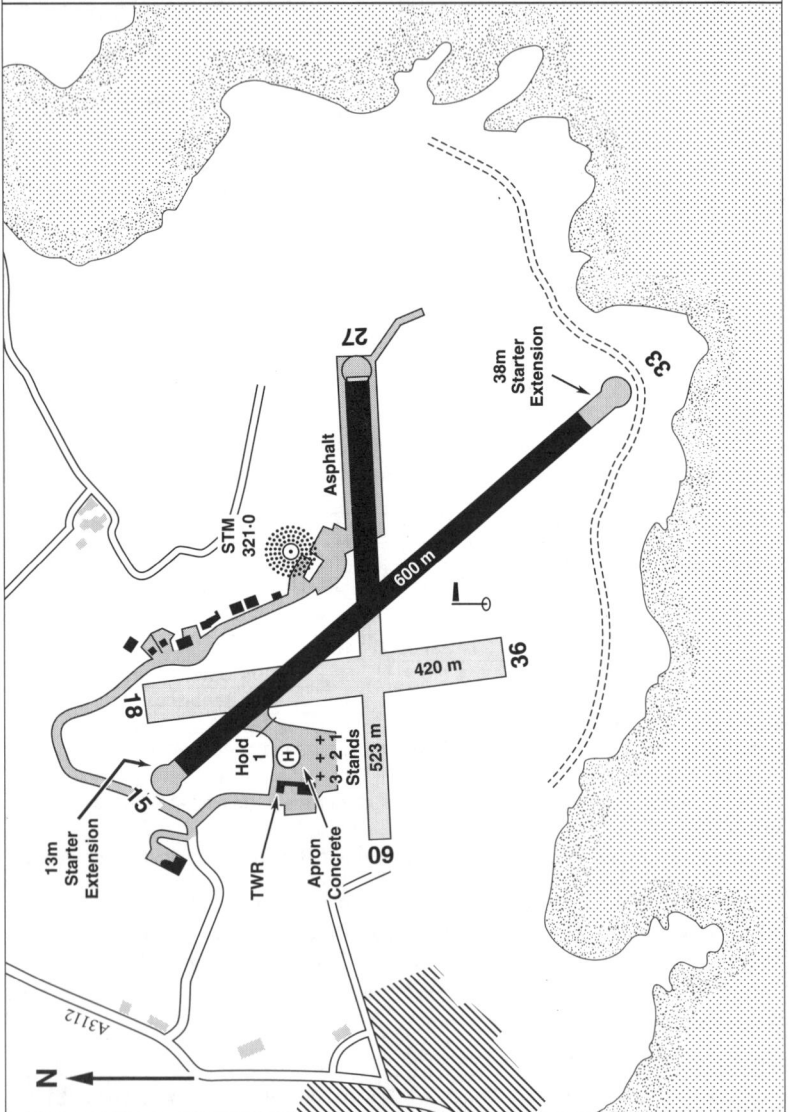

27

Asphalt

33

38m
Starter
Extension

STM
321·0

600 m

18

420 m

36

523 m

Hold
1

(H)

+ + +
3 - 2 - 1
+ + +
Stands

15

13m
Starter
Extension

TWR

Apron
Concrete

09

60

A3112

N

| N49 54·80 W006 17·52 | **SCILLY ISLES (St. Mary's)** | | | | 116 ft AMSL |

Rwy	Dim(m)	Surface	TORA(m)	LDA(m)	Lighting
09/27	523x18	Grass/ Asphalt *	09-523 27-523	09-523 27-523	Nil. Ap Thr Rwy
15/33	600x23	Asphalt	15-600 33-600	15-600 33-600	Thr Rwy APAPI 3·5°# Thr Rwy APAPI 3·5°

HELICOPTER RUNWAY

| 18/36 | 420x45 | Grass | 420 | 420 | Nil. |
| | | | | | IBn 'SC' Gn |

* 280m Asphalt at East end.

\# Visual glidepath signals for Rwy 15 are visible to the East of runway extended centreline where normal obstacle clearance is not guaranteed. They should only be used when aircraft is aligned with the runway.

Op hrs: Strictly PPR. **A/D Closed Sundays.**
WINTER: Mon-Fri 0830-1230 & 1330-1700, Sat 0830-1230 - during March, Sat hrs can be extended 08-1230 & 14-1700.   SUMMER: Mon-Sat 0730-1900.

Landing Fee: Single: £14.89, Twin: £21.70. Incusive of VAT.
Parking:
First 2 hrs free, then Singles £6.82 per day, Twins £9.00 per day. Incusive of VAT.

Customs: 6 hrs PNR.

| Hangarage Nil | **Maintenance:** Nil. |

Remarks: Operated by the Council of the Isles of Scilly, St. Mary's Airport, Isles of Scilly TR21 0NG.

Strictly PPR by telephone prior to flight.

Flight Plans optional.

Aerodrome is closed to aircraft on Sundays and pilots should not attempt to land.

Non radio airctaft not accepted.

Public transport operations are normally limited by the following aircraft types: Twin Otter (DH6), Islander (BN2) and Sikorsky S61 helicopter.

Pilots should exercise extreme caution when landing or taking-off as the aerodrome is severely hump-backed. The gradients increase to as much as 1 in 13 at runway ends.

A perimeter road runs around the Northern part of the aerodrome and traffic is liable to cross the approaches to Rwy 15.

Visual Reference Points:
Pendeen Lighthouse   N50 09·88 W005 40·30.
St. Martins Head   N49 58·05 W006 15·95.

Restaurant: Refreshments and Bar.
Accommodation: Tourist Information Centre Tel: 01720-422536, Fax: 01720-422049
Car Hire: By prior arrangement.

| Fuel: Nil | **Tel:** 01720-422677 Ext 232 ATC. **Fax:** 01720-422226. |

| N52 30·65 E001 25·03 | **SEETHING** | 130 ft AMSL |

| 9 nm SSE of Norwich. | **CLN 114·55 018 41** |

c/s Seething Radio 122·60 A/G.

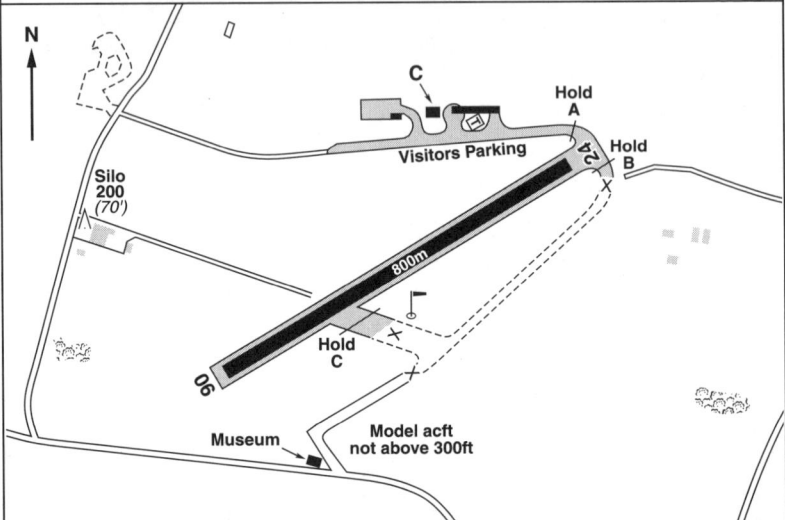

Rwy	Dim(m)	Surface	TORA(m)	LDA(m)	Lighting
06/24	800x18	Asphalt	Unlicensed		Thr Rwy

| **Op hrs:** PPR. 0900-SS daily. | **Customs:** Members only . |

Landing Fee: Business and training aircraft by arrangement. Pilots of private or club aircraft are asked to make a donation to the Group's Fund (unless a reciprocal arrangement exists). Please contact the Secretary.

| **Hangarage:** Nil | **Maintenance:** Nil |

Remarks: Unlicensed aerodrome owned by the Waveney Flying Group and operated by Wing Task 95 Ltd. Available to private and executive aircraft.
No landing 'T' displayed when airfield not manned.
Circuit height 1000 ft. aal; RH on Rwy 06, LH on Rwy 24.
Avoid overflying surrounding villages below 1000'.

Departures: Rwy 06 — Turn right 10° when passing over 24 threshold and climb to 500' before turning on course.
Rwy 24 — Climb straight ahead to 500' before turning on course.

Caution: Silo 70' aal 200' amsl (marked on plan). Part of disused short runway used by Motor Cycle School. Model Aircraft flying up to 300' agl on South side of southern perimeter track.

Warning: Width of taxyway between Hold 'A' and the reporting point is restricted, taxy with caution. Distance between taxyway centre-line and parked aircraft can be as little as 8 metres.

Museum: Open first Sunday each month from May to October. Tel: 01502-730905

Restaurant: Drinks only available. **Accommodation:** Bungay, Loddon Brooke & Sisland.

Car Hire: Willhire Tel: 01603-416410/1.   **Taxi:** Bungay 01986-893457..

| **Fuel:** 100LL. (Limited supplies). | **Tel/Fax:** 01508-550453 Airfield; 01508-550041(outside Op hrs) 01502-572420 Secretary (Home) |

N52 47·89   W002 40·08   **SHAWBURY**   249 ft AMSL

6 nm NNE of Shrewsbury.	MCT 113·55 210 36·6
	WAL 114·10 161 39·4

Shawbury Zone 120·775 (MATZ/LARS).   TWR 122·10 (On request).
ILS Rwy 18 (188°M) 'SY' 108·70 (Rwy QFU 185°). DVOR/DME 'SWB' 116·80 (on A/D)

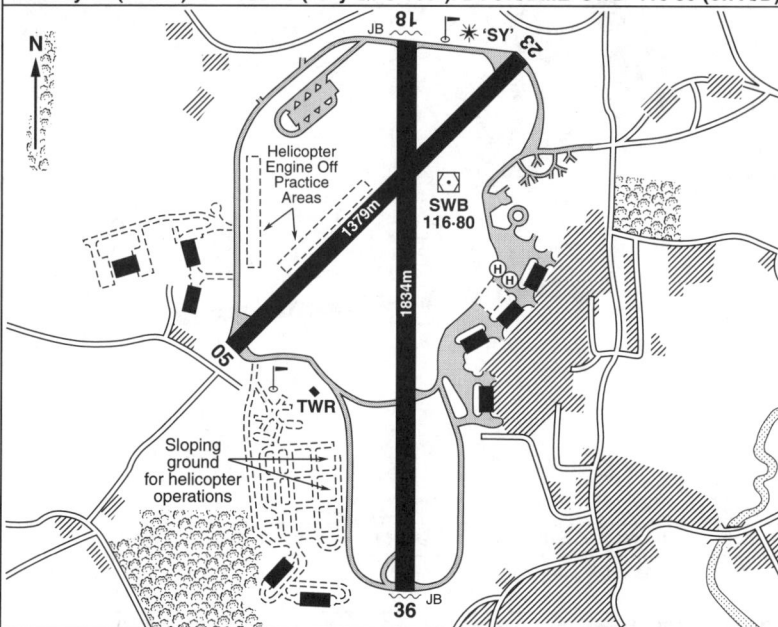

Rwy	Dim(m)	Surface	TORA(m)	LDA(m)	Lighting
18/36	1834x45	Asphalt/	18-1834	18-1834	Ap Thr Rwy PAPI
		Concrete	36-1834	36-1834	Ap Thr Rwy PAPI
05/23	1379x45	Asphalt/	05-1379	05-1379	Rwy Thr PAPI
		Concrete	23-1379	23-1379	Rwy Thr PAPI
					IBn 'SY' Red

Op hrs: PPR 24 hrs from Ops Ext. 7227.   Mon-Fri 0800-1700.   **ATZ active H24**

Landing Fee: MoD(RAF) Rates.   **Hangarage/Maintenance:** Nil   **Customs:** Nil

Remarks: RAF Aerodrome. Intensive helicopter operations within the Shawbury and Ternhill AIAA. Visitors contact Shawbury Zone at 20 nm for instrument or radar vectored visual approach.

All fixed wing aircraft are to carry out an instrument approach. However, subject to traffic and weather, a radar vectored visual straight in to land may be permitted, provided the pilot is visual and in line with the runway by 3 nm.

Go arounds to be made down the length of the runway.

Caution: Helicopters operate within 50 m of both sides of the runway in use.

Taxiway from Rwy 23 threshold to Rwy 36 link closed to fixed wing aircraft.

Fuel: 100LL. Avtur - by arrangement. 100LL not available to public.	**Tel:** 01939-250351 Ext 7227. ATIS - Ext 7574.

SHEFFIELD CITY

N53 23·65 W001 23·32		231 ft AMSL
3 nm ENE of Sheffield City.	GAM 112·80 296 17·9. TNT 115·70 030 23	

c/s Sheffield. APP/TWR 128·525. ATIS 121·70.
NDB 'SMF' 333·0 (On A/D). ILS/DME Rwy 28 (279°) I SFH 111·35 .

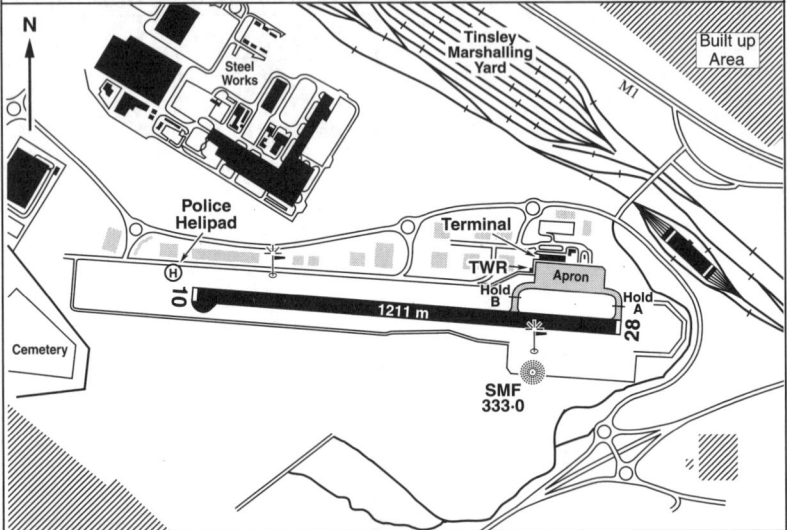

Rwy	Dim(m)	Surface	TORA(m)	LDA(m)	Lighting
10/28	1211x30	Asphalt	10-1199	10-1199	Ap Thr Rwy PAPI
			28-1199	28-1199	Ap Thr Rwy PAPI

Op hrs: PPR. Mon-Fri 0700-2030; Sat 0800-1430; Sun 1400-2030; PHs 0900-2030.

Landing Fee: £13 per metric tonne or part thereof.   **Customs:** Available

Hangarage: Nil   **Maintenance:** Nil   **Met:** 0114-201 5545.

Remarks: Operated by Sheffield City Airport Ltd, Europa Link, Sheffield S9 1XZ.
Aerodrome not available to single engine aircraft. Non radio aircraft prohibited.
Aircraft landing on Rwy 28 will have to back track the runway to the terminal area.
Training flights by prior approval and slot times must be adhered to.
VFR Helicopters must arrive/depart to/from the south via Tinsley Park Golf Course or
to/from the north via Tinsley Cooling Towers and east of the steel works.
Aircraft are to carry Third Party Insurance cover of not less than £1,000,000.
Aircraft handling facilities provided by Servisair Ltd, Tel: 0114-201 5331 for aircraft
with 20 seats or more. LEA Northern Ltd, Tel: 0114-201 5335 for aircraft with less
than 20 seats.

Warnings: High ground,141 ft aal, 0·32 nm to the south and parallel to the runway.
Steel works,101 ft aal, 0·24 nm to the north and parallel to the runway.

Restaurant: Buffet Bar.   **Accommodation:** Hotels in vicinity.

Taxis/Car Hire: Black Cabs - available on request at Terminal.

Noise Abatement Procedures and VRPs are listed on the opposite page.

Fuel: 100LL, Jet A1	Tel: 0114-201 1998 Switchboard Fax: 0114-201 1888 Admin; 5750 ATC

Robert Pooley ©

SHEFFIELD CITY
Noise Abatement Procedures and
Visual Reference Points (VRPs)

Noise Abatement Procedures

- Aircraft on visual approaches and circuit training must maintain 1500 ft aal until established on final approach.
- Pilots making visual approaches to Rwy 28 should avoid over flying the village of Laughton-en-le-Morthen, situated 6 nm on the extended centre-line and easily identifiable by its tall church spire.
- To reduce noise impact on the local community, aircraft should use the full limit of the runway for take-off.

Visual Reference Points (VRPs)

Barnsley Railway Station	N53 33·27 W001 28·65
Old Coats (Crossroads)	N53 23·52 W001 07·12
Chesterfield Railway Station	N53 14·25 W001 25·22
Redmires Reservoir	N53 21·92 W001 36·42

Intentionally Blank

	SHERBURN IN ELMET	
N53 47·28 W001 13·10		26 ft AMSL
5·5 nm W of Selby, Yorks.	POL 112·10 091 31·4. GAM 112·80 348 32	
	LBA 402·5 113 16	

c/s Sherburn Radio 122·60. Fenton APP 126·50. Linton APP 129·15.
NDB 'SBL' 323·0 (On A/D).

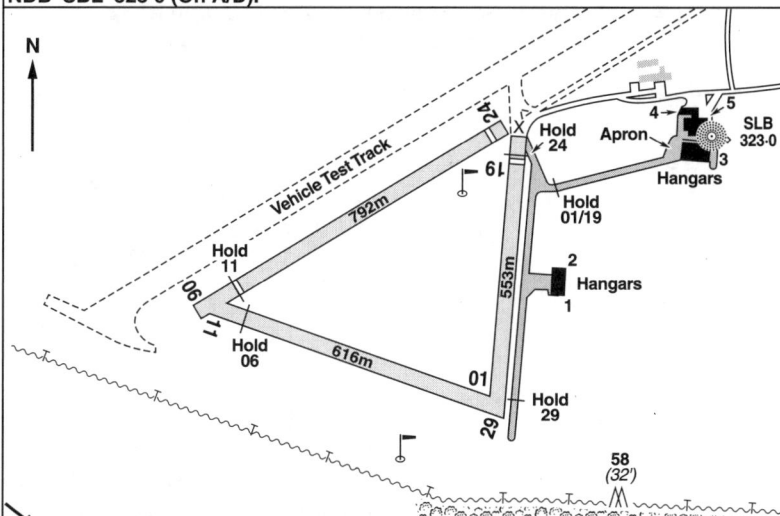

Rwy	Dim(m)	Surface	TORA(m)	LDA(m)	Lighting
01/19	553x18	Grass	01-553	01-553	Nil.
			19-553	19-520	Nil.
06/24	792x18	Grass	06-730	06-673	Nil.
			24-700	24-700	Nil.
11/29	616x18	Grass	11-616	11-616	Nil.
			19-616	19-616	Nil.

Op hrs: PPR. 0900-SS daily.

Landing Fee: SE £3.00; ME £6.00. No charge if in for maintenance or if fuel uplifted.

Hangarage: Limited   **Maintenance:** Available   **Customs:** 24 hrs PNR.

Remarks: Operated by Sherburn Aero Club Ltd. PPR. A/D situated within C. Fenton MATZ. Circuit height 1000 ft QFE, directions are variable, pilots will be informed of the direction on initial contact with Sherburn Radio.

Mandatory Noise Abatement Procedures — see overleaf and Page 447.

Inbound: Contact Fenton App 15 nm from MATZ boundary and enter MATZ at 1500ft. (Church Fenton QNH). If no contact with Fenton call Sherburn Radio or Linton App and advise.

Outbound: Contact Fenton App before leaving Sherburn circuit and depart MATZ below 1500ft. (QFE).

Caution: Power cables 32' aal cross final approach to Rwy 01, 258 m from Thr.

Note: Paved Rwy immediately N of grass runways is closed to aircraft and is used as a vehicle test track.

Restaurant: Club facilities open all day.

Car Hire: Godfrey Davis. Tel: 01904-20394. Hertz. Tel: 01532-35481.

Fuel: 100LL	**Tel:** 01977-682674. **Fax:** 01977-683699.

Robert Pooley ©

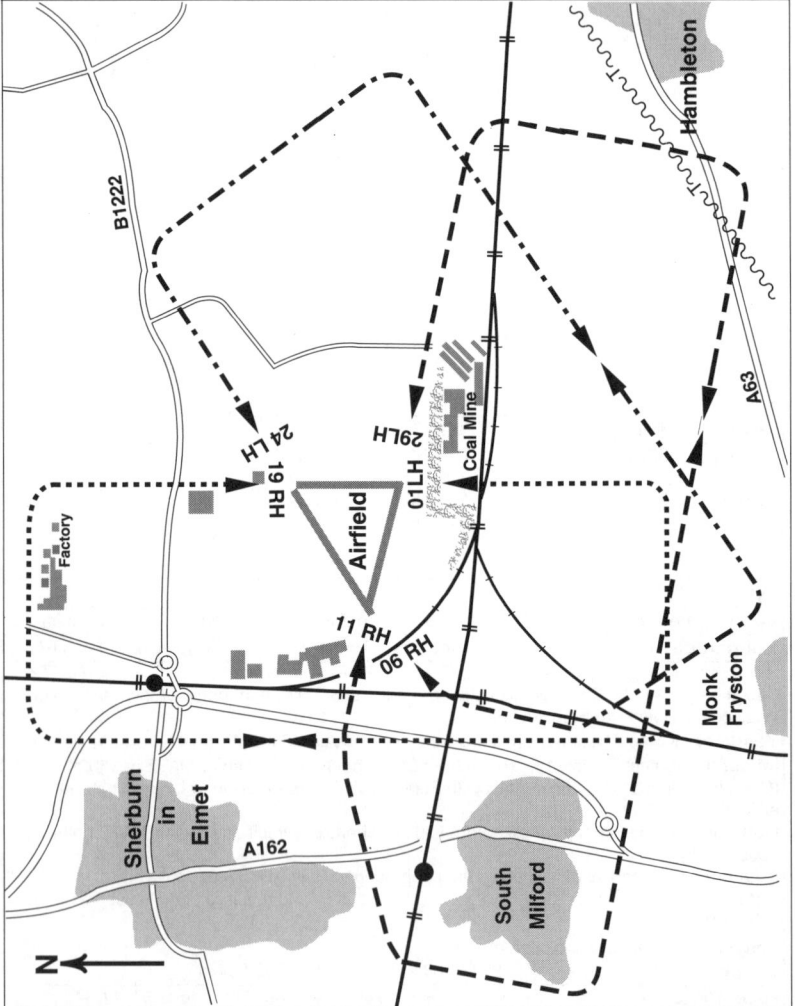

SHERBURN IN ELMET
MANDATORY NOISE ABATEMENT PROCEDURES

**Except in emergency, or as directed by Sherburn Radio,
the following procedures are to be adhered to.**

Hambleton

B1222

A63

24 LH

29LH

19 RH

01LH

Coal Mine

Airfield

11 RH

06 RH

Factory

Monk Fryston

Sherburn in Elmet

A162

South Milford

N

Robert Pooley ©

1 DEC 00

446

DEPARTURES

RWY 29 LH
TAKE-OFF – LEFT HAND CIRCUIT
Turn left approximately 30° to climb between the villages of **SOUTH MILFORD** and **SHERBURN**, then left to pass to the west of **SOUTH MILFORD** before turning **DOWNWIND**.

RWY 11 RH
TAKE-OFF – RIGHT HAND CIRCUIT
No restrictions.

RWY 01 LH
TAKE-OFF – LH CIRCUIT
Turn CROSSWIND early to keep clear of **CHURCH FENTON ATZ** to the north.
Note: Downwind leg to be east of **SHERBURN VILLAGE.**

RWY 19 RH
TAKE-OFF – RH CIRCUIT
Note: DOWNWIND leg to be east of **SHERBURN VILLAGE.**

RWY 24 LH
TAKE-OFF – LEFT HAND CIRCUIT
Turn left on to 200° and track along railway. Turn further left on to 150°, avod **MONK FRYSTON** on your right.

RWY 06 RH
TAKE-OFF – RIGHT HAND CIRCUIT
No restrictions.

Note: Do not depart to the North without first obtaining clearance from Church Fenton on 126·50 when they are active.

ARRIVALS

RWY 29 LH
LANDING – LEFT HAND CIRCUIT
Avoid **HAMBLETON** on base leg.

RWY 11 RH
LANDING – RIGHT HAND CIRCUIT
Turn base leg on western side of **SOUTH MILFORD.**

RWY 01LH/19RH
LANDING – Rwy 19 turn base leg early to keep clear of **CHURCH FENTON ATZ** to the north. Also when using 01LH or19RH, turn DOWNWIND early to keep to the east of **SHERBURN VILLAGE** (follow rail/road line).

RWY 06 RH
LANDING – RIGHT HAND CIRCUIT
Do not overfly **SOUTH MILFORD.**

RWY 24
LANDING – LEFT HAND CIRCUIT
Keep to the east of B1222.

NOTE.
1. Pilots are to avoid overflying the local villages when in traffic circuit.

2. Pilots flying aircraft with variable pitch propellers should always approach the airfield with RPM set to Minimum Cruise and only select 'MAX RPM' on final approach at 300' aal.

N52 44·13 W002 36·09	**SHERLOWE (High Ercall)**	210 ft AMSL

4·5 nm SE of Shawbury Aerodrome	**SWB 116·8 155 4·4**
5 nm NW of Telford	**HON 113·65 309 41·3**

c/s Sherlowe Radio 119·30 A/G - Not always manned.
Shawbury Zone 120·775 (LARS/MATZ)

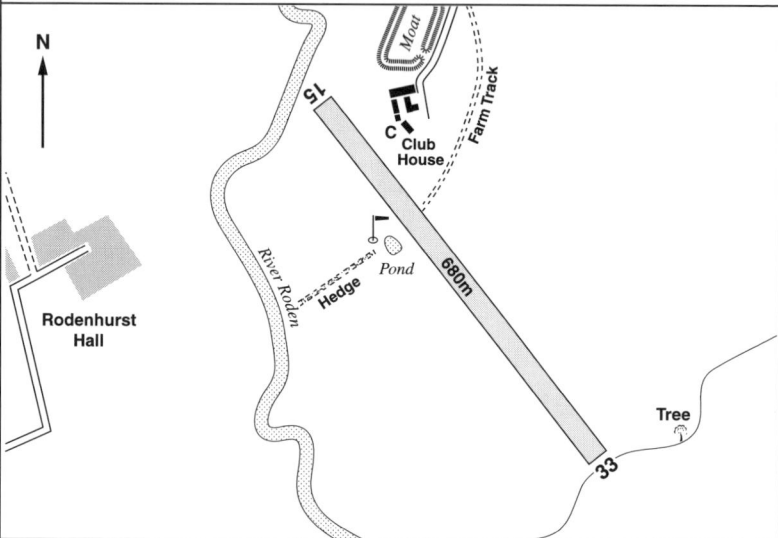

Rwy	Dim(m)	Surface	TORA(m)	LDA(m)	Lighting
15/33	680x25	Grass	Unlicensed		Nil.

Rwy 15 - last 450m has 3° downslope.   Rwy 33 - first 450m has 3° upslope.

Op hrs: Strictly PPR. SR-SS.

Landing Fee: Nil.	**Customs:** Nil.
Hangarage: Nil.	**Maintenance:** Nil.

Remarks: Unlicensed airfield operated by Mr. R.F. Pooler, Lower Grounds Farm, Sherlowe, High Ercall, Shropshire TF6 6LT. Strictly PPR.

Airfield situated within the Shawbury MATZ. Contact Shawbury Zone for MATZ clearance.

Circuits at 1000 ft aal.

Avoid overflying local villages and farms.

Restaurant: Snacks available in the club house.

Taxi/Car Hire: By arrangement.

Fuel: Nil.	**Tel:** 01952- 770189/ 01952- 770120.
	Mobile 07768- 333030.
	Fax: 01952- 770762.

N52 37·74 E000 55·78	**SHIPDHAM**	210 ft AMSL

4 nm S of East Dereham.	**NH** 371·5 264 16·8
13 nm W of Norwich Airport.	**CSL** 116·50 249 16·6

c/s Shipdham Radio 132·25 A/G - Weekends only

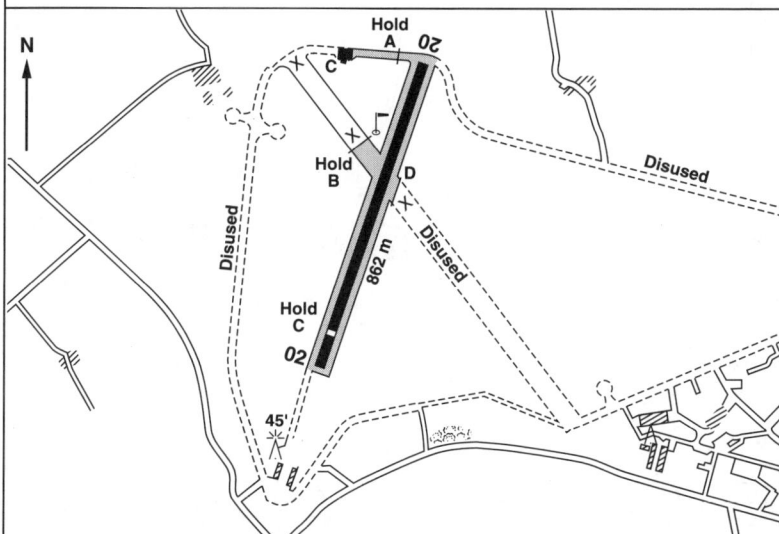

Rwy	Dim(m)	Surface	TORA(m)	LDA(m)	Lighting
02/20	862x18	Asphalt	(02-862	02-770)	Nil
			(20-770	20-770)	Nil
			(unlicensed)		

Op hrs: PPR. 0900-1800 or SS daily.

Landing Fee: £3.00.

Hangarage: Available **Maintenance:** Nil **Customs:** 24 hrs PNR.

Remarks: Unlicensed aerodrome operated by Shipdham Aero Club. PPR.

Visiting aircraft welcome but phone prior to departure.

Circuits at 1000 ft, RH on 02, LH on 20; standard joining procedure.

Avoid overflying Shipdham village.

Visiting aircraft to park as directed.

Radio Mast 105' aal 315' amsl 120°/0·5 nm.

Restaurant: Snacks available.

Taxis: By arrangement.

Fuel: 100LL	**Tel:** 01362- 820850 or
	01953-882187 / 851651 for information.
	01362-820709 Weekends.

N52 14·50 W002 52·88	**SHOBDON**	318 ft AMSL
6 nm W of Leominster.	**HON 113·65 267 45·5. BCN 117·45 030 33·9**	

c/s Shobdon Information/Radio 123·50. AFIS or A/G. AFIS Sat & Sun 10-1600 only.
NDB 'SH' 426·0 (On A/D) Nav. only.

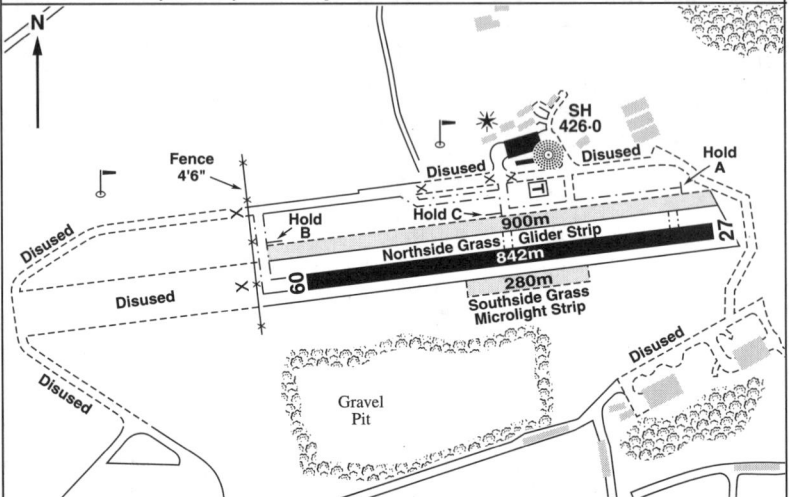

Rwy	Dim(m)	Surface	TORA(m)	LDA(m)	Lighting
09/27†	842x18	Asphalt	09-842	09-842	Thr Rwy
			27-842	27-842	Thr Rwy APAPI 3·5°
Northside	900x25	Grass	Unlicensed		Nil.
Southside	280x20	Grass	Unlicensed		Nil.
					ABn Wh

† Rwy 09 unlicensed for night use.

Op hrs: PPR. 0900-SS daily and Thur 0900-2100 (Winter). O/T by arrangement.

Landing Fee: Singles £7.00; Light twins £14.00.   **Customs:** 6 hrs PNR.

Hangarage: Limited, by arrangement.   **Maintenance:** M3. Tel: 01568- 709170.

Remarks: Operated by Herefordshire Aero Club Ltd, Shobdon Aerodrome, Leominister, Hereford HR6 9NR. Visitors welcome. PPR non radio aircraft.
Powered aircraft circuits LH on 27, RH on 09. Wide circuits (2nm) to S of EARDISLAND and PEMBRIDGE villages for conventional aircraft at 1000' aal. Land on asphalt runway.
Tight circuits for Helicopters at 800' aal and Microlights at 500' aal. Land Southside grass.
Glider circuits RH on 27, LH on 09. Intense activity at weekend. Land Northside grass.
Overhead Joins: Descend not below 1500' aal on deadside, further descent to circuit height when South of runway.

Mandatory Noise Abatement - See Chart opposite.

Warnings: Pilots landing at night should land as near as possible to the centre of the runway due to rough outer sections in many places.
Fence on undershoot Rwy 09. Fence and Power lines on undershoot
Rwy 27. High ground to North and West of aerodrome.

Restaurant: Club facilities.   On site camping and caravanning.

Car Hire: Watsons Car Hire 01568-612060.   **Taxi:** Markhams Tel: 01568-708208

Fuel: 100LL, Jet A1	Tel: 01568-708369. Fax: 01568-708935. Website: http://www.aeroclub.co.uk

Robert Pooley ©

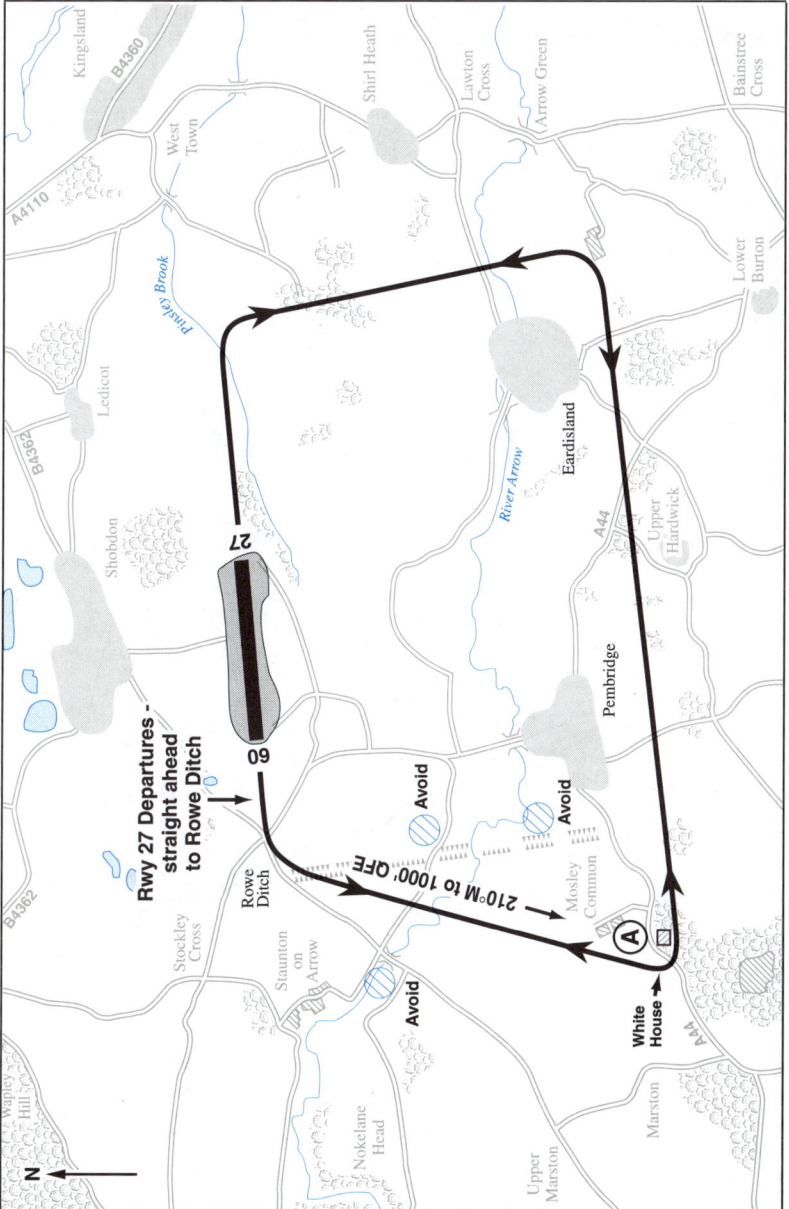

SHOBDON
NOISE ABATEMENT

1 DEC 00

Kingsland
B4360
West Town
A4110
Shirl Heath
Lawton Cross
Arrow Green
Bainstree Cross
Lower Burton
Pinsley Brook
Ledicot
B4362
Shobdon
River Arrow
Eardisland
A44
Upper Hardwick
Pembridge
27
09
Rwy 27 Departures - straight ahead to Rowe Ditch
Avoid
Avoid
Rowe Ditch
210°M to 1000' QFE
Mosley Common
Stockley Cross
Staunton on Arrow
B4362
Avoid
Nokelane Head
Upper Marston
Marston
A44
White House
A
N

Robert Pooley ©

451

N50 50·13 W000 17·83

1 nm W of Shoreham-by-Sea. SFD 117·00 291 16·4. MID 114·00 140 18·1

APP/TWR 123·15, (TWR 125·40 When Directed). **VDF 123·15. ATIS 132·40.
Shoreham Radio 123·15 A/G** (Mon-Sat 0800-0900 PPR).
NDB 'SHM' 332·0 (On A/D). DME 'SRH' 109·95 (On A/D).

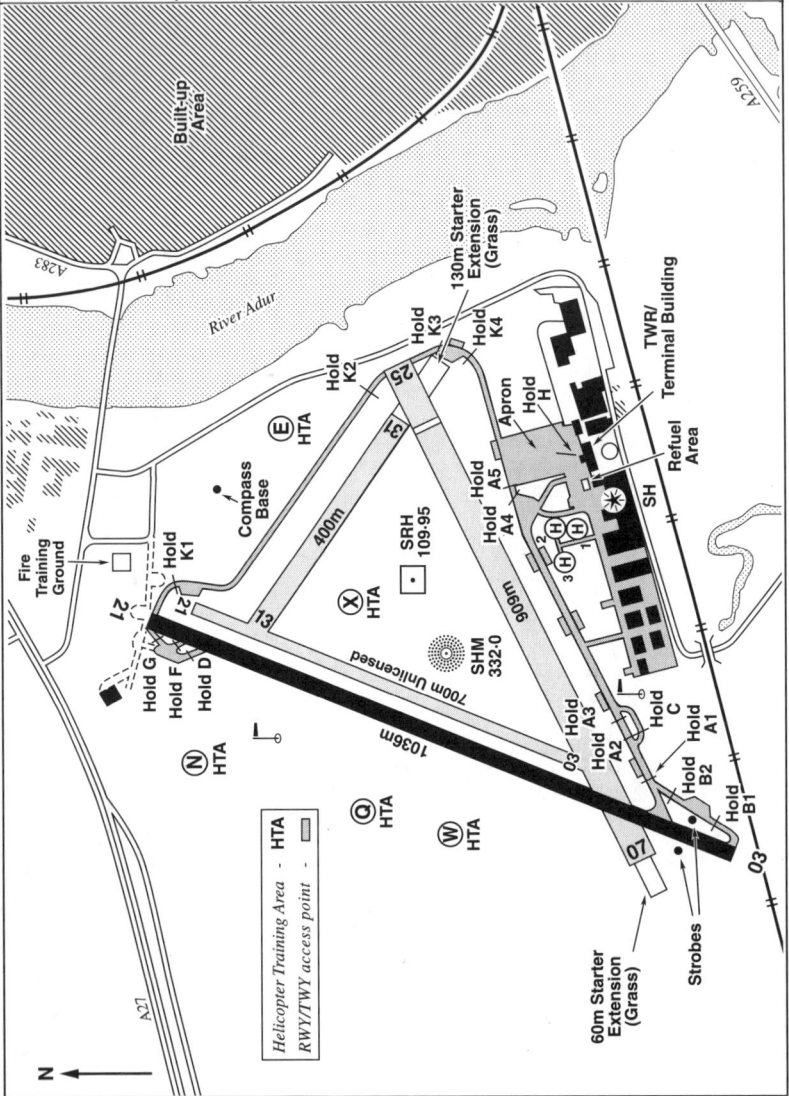

Built-up Area

A259

A283

River Adur

130m Starter Extension (Grass)

TWR/ Terminal Building

Hold K3
Hold K4
Hold K2
Hold H
Apron
Refuel Area

25

(E) HTA

31

Compass Base

Hold K1

400m

SRH 109·95

(X) HTA

Fire Training Ground

21

13

Hold G
Hold F
Hold D

909m

Hold A5
Hold A4

SH

(H) 1
(H) 2
(H) 3

SHM 332·0

700m Unlicensed

1036m

03

Hold A3
Hold A2

Hold C
Hold A1

Hold B2

Hold B1

(N) HTA

07

Hold G

03

(Q) HTA

(W) HTA

Helicopter Training Area - HTA
RWY/TWY access point -

60m Starter Extension (Grass)

Strobes

N ←

A27

Robert Pooley ©

452

N50 50·13 W000 17·83			**SHOREHAM**		7 ft AMSL
Rwy	**Dim(m)**	**Surface**	**TORA(m)**	**LDA(m)**	**Lighting**
03/21	1036x18	Asphalt	03-960	03-871	Thr Rwy PAPI 3·5°
			21-916	21-865	Thr Rwy PAPI 4·5°
03/21	700x18	Grass	Unlicensed		
07/25	909x50	Grass	07-877 †	07-877	Nil.
			25-909	25-794	Nil.
13/31	400x30	Grass	13-400	13-400	Nil.
			31-400 ††	31-400	Nil.

†	60 m starter extension available on PPR.	IBN 'SH' Gn.
††	128 m starter extension available on PPR.	

Op hrs: WINTER: Mon 08-1800, Tue-Sat 08-1900, Sun 0830-1800. (Mon-Sat 08-0830 PPR)
　　　　　SUMMER : Mon 08-2000, Tue-Sat 08-2000, Sun 0830-2000. (Mon-Sat 08-0830 PPR)

Landing Fees: Under 500 kg £12.00. 501 kg to 1.5 tonne £14.00, then £14.00 per additional tonne up to 6.5 tonne, inclusive of VAT.

Hangarage: Available.　　　　　　　　　**Maintenance:** Available.

Customs: PPR. Non EU Customs to be booked with ATC by 1600hrs (local) on preceding day.

Remarks: Operated by Brighton, Hove and Worthing Joint Municipal Airport Cmtte. NDB Training and non-radio aircraft PPR.

Joining: Unless otherwise instructed by ATC, aircraft joining the circuit will overfly the aerodrome at 2000 ft aal, when instructed descend to circuit height on the dead-side of the runway in use, and join the circuit by crossing the upwind end.
Aircraft on the crosswind leg are expected to position over the upwind end of the runway in use, and then fit into the visual circuit.

All circuits Left Hand; fixed wing at 1100 ft aal, helicopters at 600 ft aal.

Requests for use of alternative Grass Rwy due to crosswinds will be approved subject to traffic situation.

Visiting aircraft are to park on the grass parking area to the east of TWR/Terminal unless otherwise instructed by ATC.

Extensive helicopter training takes place on the airfield.

Practice EFATO permitted only on Rwys 03 and 31.

Helicopter Training Areas **E, N, Q, W, and X** are depicted on the opposite page.

Radio Failure Procedures:
Join overhead the airfield and fit into the traffic pattern, overfly the runway in use at 500' aal before positioning for landing. Standard light signals should be folowed.

Visual Reference Points (VRPs)
Brighton Marina	N50 48·65 W000 06·05;
Lewes Intersection A27T/A26	N50 51·87 W000 01·45;
Littlehampton	N50 48·77 W000 32·78;
Washington Intersection A24/A283	N50 54·57 W000 24·47.

Restaurant: Restaurant, Refreshments and Club facilities available.

Car Hire: 01273-441061 (Visitor Centre); Mobile 0585-707425

Taxis: Terminal building (forecourt). 01273-464646.

Fuel: 100LL, Jet A1. (Diners Card)	**Tel:** 01273-296900 A/D; 296888 ATC.
	Fax: 01273-296899.

N52 05·32 W000 19·10	**SHUTTLEWORTH (OLD WARDEN)**	110 ft AMSL

5 nm ESE of Bedford.	BNN 113·75 026 23·4
	BKY 116·25 298 15·2

c/s Shuttleworth Information/Radio 130·70 AFIS or A/G. (Display days or Special events).

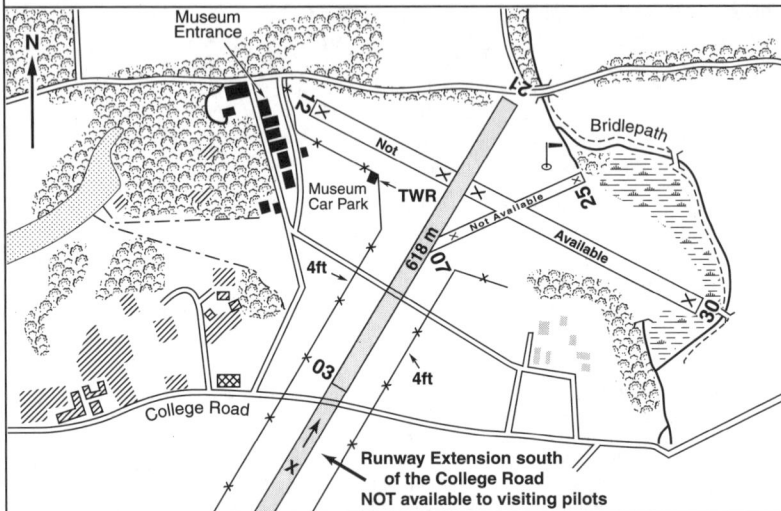

Museum Entrance
N
Bridlepath
Museum Car Park
TWR
618 m
Not Available
Available
4ft
03
4ft
College Road
Runway Extension south of the College Road NOT available to visiting pilots

Rwy	Dim(m)	Surface	TORA(m)	LDA(m)	Lighting
03/21	618	Grass	Unlicensed		Nil.

Note: Rwy 03 has marked downslope, the effective landing distance is reduced.

Op hrs: 0900-1700. **PPR ESSENTIAL** – £25 penalty payable if no prior permission.

Landing Fee: On application, includes admission to the Collection.

Hangarage: Nil	**Maintenance:** Nil	**Customs:** Nil

Remarks: Unlicensed Aerodrome, the home of the Shuttleworth Collection of flyable historic aeroplanes.
Rwys 07/25 and 12/30 not available. Visitors should avoid any conflicting movements when using Rwy 03/21. **Caution:** Rwy 03 starter extension **not available to visitors.**
Circuit height 800 ft, left hand.

Flying Days & Evenings: Parking limited, PPR should be made well in advance. Last landing 1300 days, 1730 evenings. Vacate Rwy 03/21 to the NW after landing. Departure will not be authorised until after the display. To expedite departures, do not back-track runways.
Look out for non radio aircraft and aircraft on display practice.

Safety: Local habitation, particularly within 1 nm, should not be overflown below 1500 ft. Full circuit (LH) must be flown at 800 ft (to allow aeromodellers to clear the landing area). Beware of sheep in the manoeuvring area in winter. Aircraft must be parked well clear of the end or sides of Rwy 12/30 at the NW end where manoeuvring space is restricted. Helicopters must land airside of spectator fence well clear of parked aircraft and NOT in Museum Car Park. Aerodrome closed during flight training and trials. Visiting pilots should monitor the signal square before joining the circuit.

Restaurant: Full facilities available until 1700 (1600 Nov–Mar)

Fuel: 100LL – (Flying display days only).	**Tel:** Normally: From 0900 hrs - 01767-627288.
	Flying Displays only: From 1000 days, 1530 evenings 627563

Robert Pooley ©

| | | **SILVERSTONE** | | | 508 ft. AMSL |

N52 04·28 W001 01·00 — **SILVERSTONE** — 508 ft. AMSL

4 nm S of Towcester. — **DTY 116·40 157 7·5. CFD 116·50 274 15**

c/s Silverstone Radio 121·075 A/G.
(ATC available during Grand Prix only - various call signs then in use).

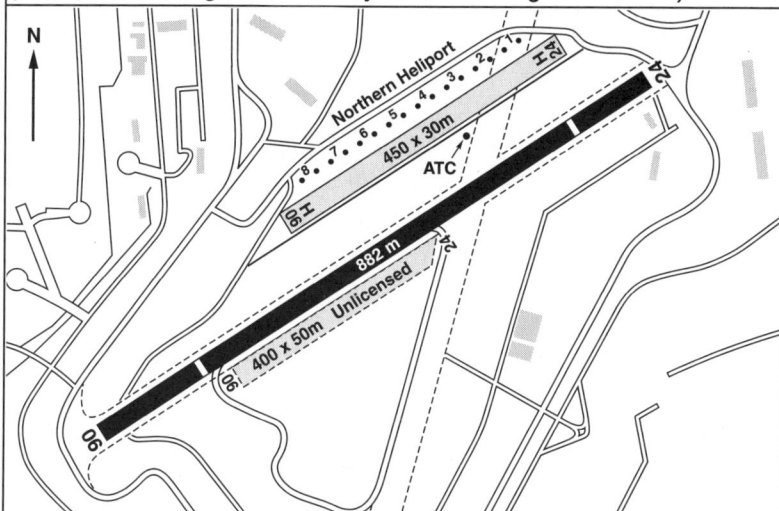

Rwy	Dim(m)	Surface	TORA(m)	LDA(m)	Lighting
06/24	882x23	Asphalt	06-842	06-722	Nil
			24-849	24-744	Nil

Op hrs: PPR.

Landing Fee: Nil. (Charges apply to watch Motor racing) — **Customs:** Nil

Hangarage: Nil — **Maintenance:** Nil.

Remarks: Operated by Silverstone Circuits Ltd., Silverstone, Nr. Towcester, Northants NN12 8TN. PPR from Aerodrome operations.

Licensed Aerodrome situated within Motor race circuit, available during limited, specific Motor race events for Fixed Wing and Rotary traffic. For 2001 event dates, call 01327-320247.

Visitors welcome.

Southern grass Rwy 06/24 unlicensed and unmarked.

Warning: Aerodrome not availble outside of specific race events - runways obstructed and used for Motor racing.

Fuel: Nil

Tel: 01327-320255 ATC
01327-320281 PPR - Aerodrome Ops
01327-857271 Switchboard

Intentionally Blank

EGCV

N52 50·03 W002 46·30	**SLEAP**	275 ft AMSL
10 nm N of Shrewsbury.	SWB 116·80 304 4·4.	WAL 114·10 165 36
		MCT 113·55 217 36·4

c/s Sleap Radio. 122·45 A/G. Shawbury App 120·775
NDB 'SLP' 382·0 (On A/D). Nav. only.

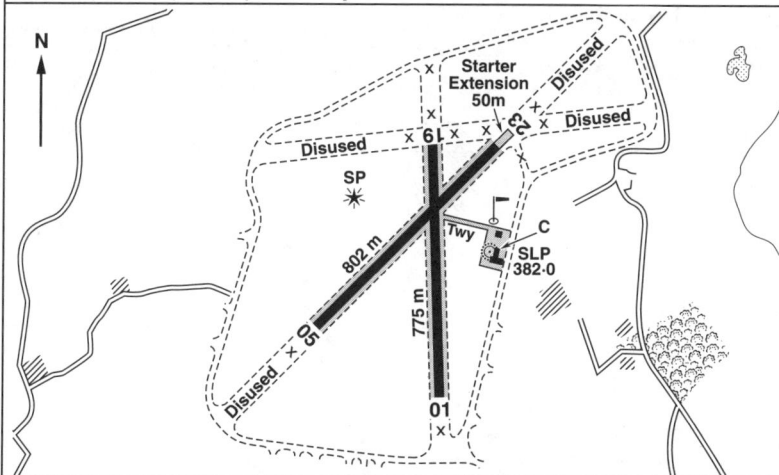

Rwy	Dim(m)	Surface	TORA(m)	LDA(m)	Lighting
05/23	802x23	Asphalt	05-802	05-802	Thr Rwy LITAS 3·5°
			23-802*	23-802	Thr Rwy LITAS 3·5°
01/19	775x18	Asphalt	01/19-775	01/19-775	Nil.
					IBN 'SP' Gn

*Additional 50 m starter extension available for take-off, during daylight hours only.

Op hrs: PPR. Sat-Wed 0930-1230 & 1300-1700 (- SS Winter); Thu-Fri 0930-1230 & 1300-2115.

Landing Fee: Singles £6.00. Twins £12.00.   **Customs:** PNR

Hangarage: Nil.   **Maintenance:** Available. 01939-290861

Remarks: Operated by Shropshire Aero Club Ltd., in conjunction with RAF Shawbury during weekdays. PPR. Airfield situated within Shawbury MATZ.
Following Procedures apply during weekdays only:
- Pilots must contact Shawbury App 120·775 for MATZ clearance.
- No deadside. Join over head centre line or downwind.
- Circuits at 1000' aal. Civil Fixed/Rotary traffic - LH; Military Rotary wing - RH.
- Beware of intensive military helicopter activity.
Standard overhead joins at 2000 ft QFE at all other times.
Airfield not available to helicopters requiring the use of a licensed airfield.
At weekends all circuits LH at 1000' aal. Frequent tug and glider activity, usually at weekends; gliders normally RH circuits. Limited long term aircraft parking available.

Warnings: No aircraft to be parked within the taxiway strip, taxy with caution and, if necessary, seek the assistance of a Marshaller.
The perimeter track is not available for aircraft use. Only available taxiway is apron to runway intersection.

Restaurant: 'Biggles Den', open daily.

Fuel: 100LL	**Tel:** 01939-232882 Ops.
	Fax: 01939-235058.

Robert Pooley ©

SOUTHAMPTON

N50 57·02 W001 21·40   44 ft AMSL

3·5 nm NNE of Southampton.   MID 114·00 262 28·3

Solent App 120·225.   Southampton App 128·85 as directed.
TWR 118·20.   RAD 128·85 as directed.   ATIS on 'SAM' VOR 113·35.
VOR/DME 'SAM' 113·35 (On A/D).   NDB 'EAS' 391·50 (On A/D).
ILS/DME Rwy 20 (204°M) I-SN 110·75.

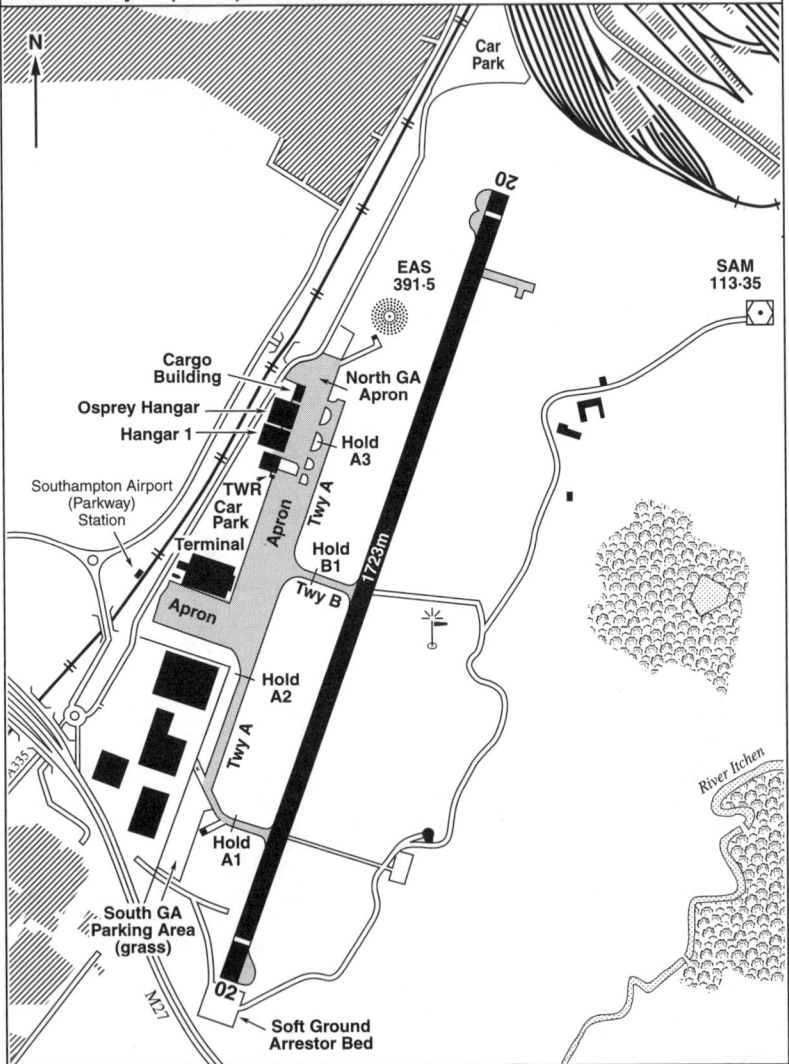

N

Car Park

20

EAS 391·5

SAM 113·35

Cargo Building

North GA Apron

Osprey Hangar

Hold A3

Hangar 1

Twy A

Southampton Airport (Parkway) Station

TWR Car Park

Apron

Terminal

Hold B1

Apron

Twy B

1723m

Hold A2

Twy A

River Itchen

A335

Hold A1

South GA Parking Area (grass)

M27

02

Soft Ground Arrestor Bed

Robert Pooley ©

N50 57·02 W001 21·40			**SOUTHAMPTON**		44 ft AMSL
Rwy	**Dim(m)**	**Surface**	**TORA(m)**	**LDA(m)**	**Lighting**
02/20	1723x37	Asphalt	02-1723	02-1650	Ap Thr Rwy RCL PAPI 3°
			20-1650	20-1605	Ap Thr Rwy RCL PAPI 3°
					A Bn Wh/Gn

Op hrs: Mon-Fri 0630-2130 PPR 2130-2200.
Sat 0630-2030 PPR 2030-2130.
Sun 0730-2030 PPR 2030-2130.

Landing Fee: On application. Discounts for private aircraft under 3 tonnes.

Customs: Aerodrome operating hours.

Hangarage and Maintenance: Available from Osprey Aviation Ltd, who also provide full FBO facilities. Tel: 023- 8061 6600.

Remarks: Operated by BAA Southampton International Airport Ltd., Southampton. SO18 2 NL.

Flights within Solent CTA, Southampton CTR and Bournemouth CTR are governed by the regulations applicable to Class 'D' Controlled Airspace – see page 2.

Visual Reference Points (VRPs) are overleaf.

See also Solent/Southampton/Bournemouth VAD/VRP Chart at page 461.

Non-radio aircraft not normally accepted.

BAe/HS 125 aircraft powered by RR Viper engines are prohibited, unless specific approval has been given. Request to Duty Manager, Tel: 023-8062 7113.

Handling Agencies: MAS (passengers only), Tel: 023-8062 7118.
Osprey Aviation Ltd, Tel 023-8062 9884.
AMI Cargo (cargo), Tel: 023-8062 7126.

Training flights are subject to approval from the aerodrome operator. Requests should be made to ATC Tel: 023-80627243.

Landing and taxying on grass area prohibited (except grass parking area).

Twy A south of the Apron restricted to aircraft with a wingspan of 40 m or less.

Noise Preferential Routes & Procedures are in force for all turbojets, all aircraft with MTOW of 5700 kg or greater and Pilatus Britton-Norman Trilanders.

Duty Free Shop available for private flight uplifts.

Southampton Parkway Station — 60 metres.

Restaurant: Cafeteria, licensed bar.

Car Hire/Taxi: Available at Terminal.

Fuel: 100LL, Jet A1. S. Diners Card, Multi-Service	**Tel:** 023-8062 9600 Admin. 023-8062 7113 Airport Duty Manager **Fax:** 023-8062 9300

Robert Pooley ©

Southampton
Visual Reference Points (VRPs)

Visual Reference Points

VRP	VOR/NDB	VOR/DME
Bishops Waltham N50 57·28 W001 12·58	SAM R094 EAS R095°M	SAM 095°/5 nm.
Calshot N50 49·07 W001 19·75	SAM R180 BIA 088°M	SAM 180°/8 nm.
Romsey N50 59·45 W001 29·75	SAM R295 EAS 296°M	SAM 295°/6 nm.
Totton N50 55·20 W001 29·33	SAM R253 EAS 252°M	SAM 253°/6 nm.

Note: VFR traffic requesting transit of the Southampton CTR routeing West-East or East-West can expect clearance subject to traffic as follows:

West Route: Bishops Waltham VRP – VOR SAM – Romsey VRP;
East Route: Romsey VRP – VOR SAM – Bishops Waltham VRP.

Transit will be subject to ATC clearance.

See Solent/Southampton/Bournemouth Chart opposite.

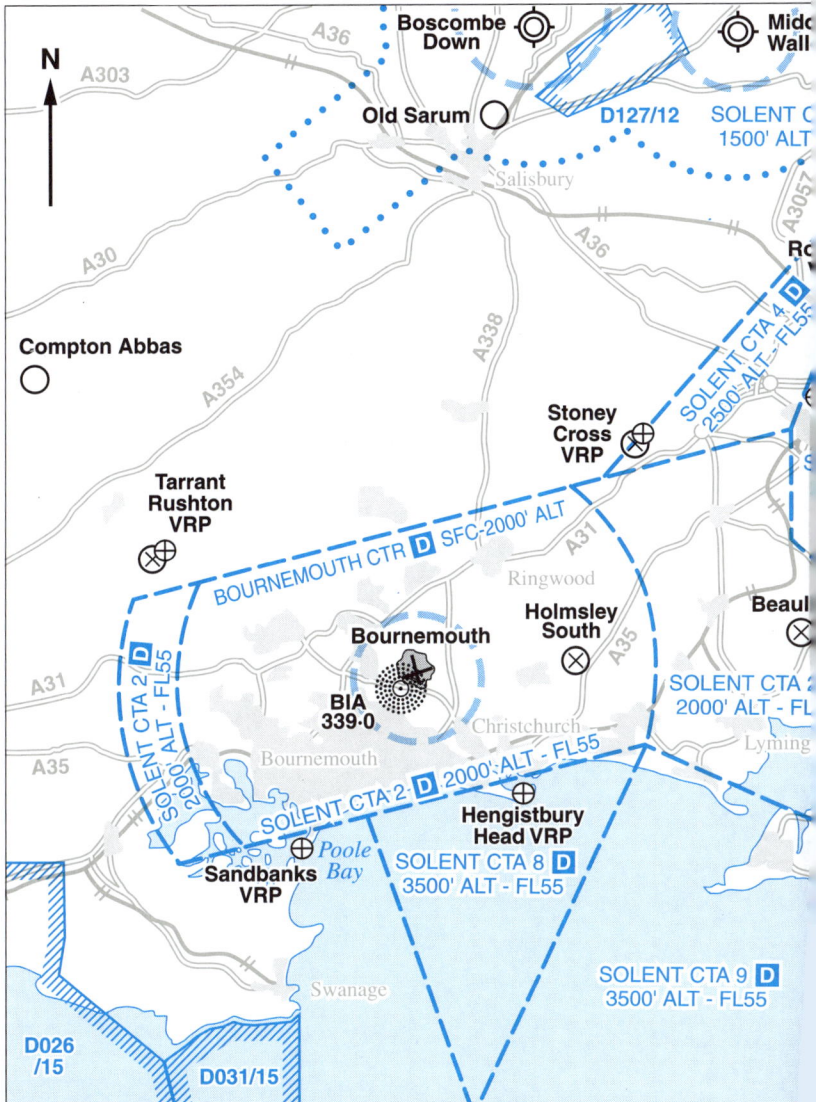

N

Boscombe
Down

Mid
Wall

A36

A303

Old Sarum

D127/12

SOLENT C
1500' ALT

Salisbury

A30

A36

A3057

Ro

A354

SOLENT CTA 4 D
2500' ALT - FL55

Compton Abbas

A338

Stoney
Cross
VRP

S

Tarrant
Rushton
VRP

BOURNEMOUTH CTR D SFC-2000' ALT

A31

Ringwood

Holmsley
South

A35

Beaul

SOLENT CTA 2 D
2000' ALT - FL55

A31

Bournemouth

BIA
339·0

Christchurch

SOLENT CTA 2
2000' ALT - FL

Lymin

A35

Bournemouth

SOLENT CTA 2 D 2000' ALT - FL55

Hengistbury
Head VRP

Poole
Bay

SOLENT CTA 8 D
3500' ALT - FL55

Sandbanks
VRP

Swanage

SOLENT CTA 9 D
3500' ALT - FL55

D026
/15

D031/15

Robert Pooley ©

Intentionally Blank

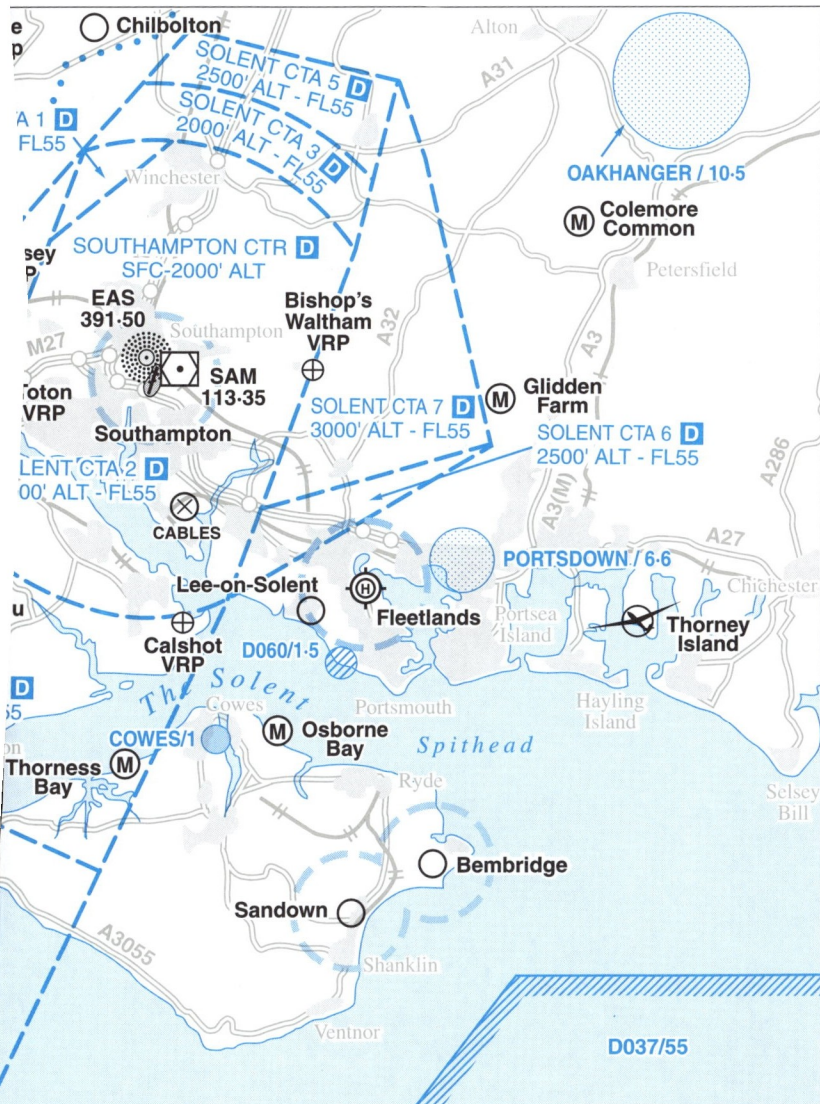

Chilbolton

Alton

A31

SOLENT CTA 5 **D**
2500' ALT - FL55

A 1 **D**
FL55

SOLENT CTA 3 **D**
2000' ALT - FL55

OAKHANGER / 10·5

Winchester

M Colemore
Common

Petersfield

SOUTHAMPTON CTR **D**
SFC-2000' ALT

sey

EAS
391·50

Southampton

M27

Bishop's
Waltham
VRP

A32

SAM
113·35

oton
VRP

Southampton

M Glidden
Farm

A3

SOLENT CTA 7 **D**
3000' ALT - FL55

SOLENT CTA 6 **D**
2500' ALT - FL55

A286

ENT CTA 2 **D**
00' ALT - FL55

A3(M)

A27

CABLES

PORTSDOWN / 6·6

Chichester

Lee-on-Solent

H

u

Fleetlands

Portsea
Island

Calshot
VRP

D060/1·5

Thorney
Island

D
5

The Solent

Cowes

Portsmouth

Hayling
Island

COWES/1

M Osborne
Bay

Spithead

Selsey
Bill

on

Thorness **M**
Bay

Ryde

Bembridge

Sandown

A3055

Shanklin

Ventnor

D037/55

SOLENT CTA
and SOUTHAMPTON & BOURNEMOUTH CTRs
and VRPS

N53 46·30 W000 34·62	**SOUTH CAVE (Mount Airy)**	500 ft. AMSL

9 nm WNW of Hull.
3 nm N of Brough A/D.

OTR 113·90 290 17·4
GAM 112·80 029 32·2

No Radio.

Humberside APP 124·675 (LARS). **Waddington APP 127·35** (LARS)

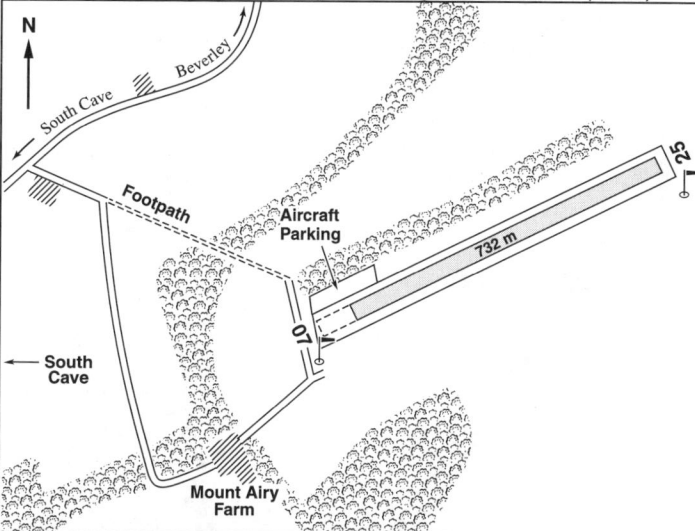

Rwy	Dim(m)	Surface	TORA(m)	LDA(m)	Lighting
07/25	732x20	Grass	Unlicensed		Nil

Runway Gradient 2·3% DOWN on Rwy 25

Op hrs: PPR. No take-offs before 0800 and after 2000 daily. Landings permissible.

Landing Fee: S.E. £3; Twins £5; Business £5.

Hangarage: Nil. **Maintenance:** Call-out and contact address available.

Remarks: Operated by Mr Neil May and wife Katie, Mount Airy Farm, South Cave, Nr. Hull HU15 2BD. Unlicensed airfield. Singles and light twins welcome on prior permission and at pilot's own risk. Join overhead (mid-runway) at 1500' aal, 2000' amsl. Circuits at 1,000 ' aal., RH on 07, LH or RH on 25.

Pilots of visiting aircraft should obtain briefing on landing and take-off procedures by by phone from the operator.

Warnings:
- Low flying military aircraft activity in the area;
- Public footpath crosses final approach to Rwy 07, 95 metres short of threshold;
- Radio Masts 150' aal on Rwy 25 approach 1300 m from threshold, 150 m North of extended centreline.

Avoid overflying the village of South Cave (western side of airfield) at all times.

Restaurant: Light refreshments available in South Cave (1·25 miles).

Taxi: Courtesy Car or Taxi usually available.

Fuel: 100LL.	**Tel:** 01430-422395 or 422973 Operator

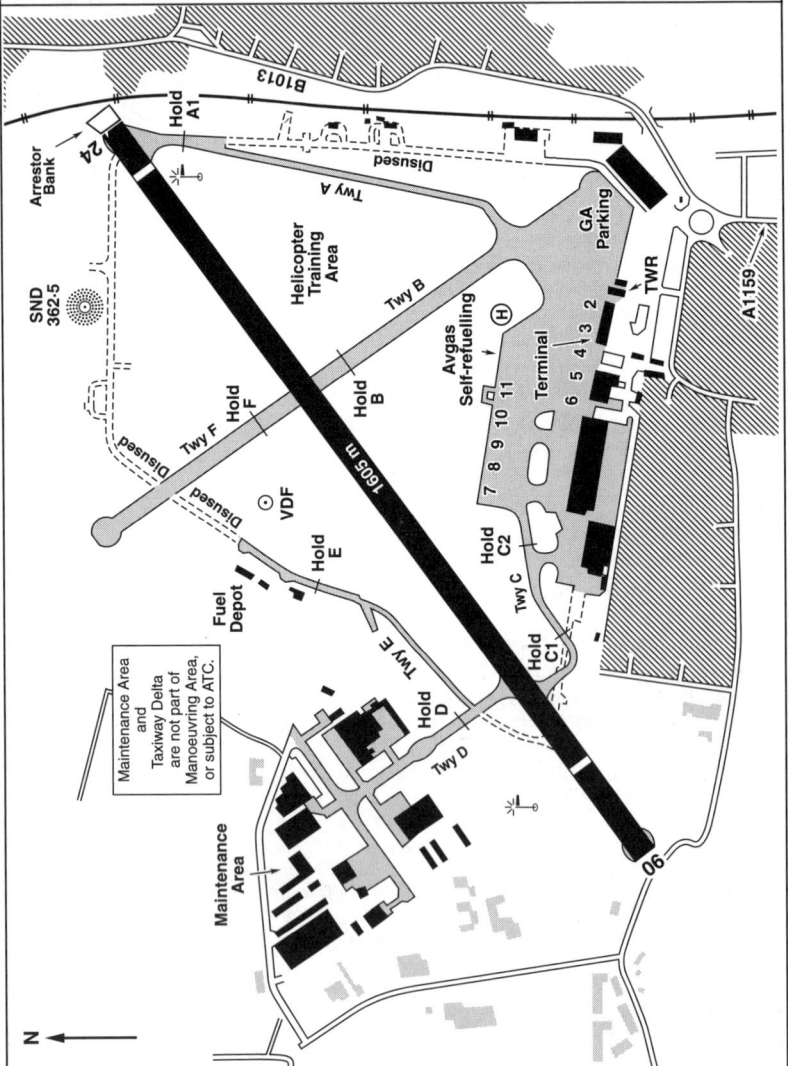

EGMC
1 DEC 00

SOUTHEND

N51 34·28 E000 41·73
49 ft AMSL

1·5 nm N of Southend.

DET 117·30 015 16·5. LAM 115·60 105 20·8

c/s Southend. APP 128·95. TWR 127·725. RAD 125·05.
VDF 128·95. Departure Info: 121·80 Dep ATIS.
NDB 'SND' 362·50 (On A/D).
ILS/DME Rwy 24 (237°M) I-ND 111·35

N51 34·28 E000 41·73			**SOUTHEND**		49 ft AMSL
Rwy	**Dim(m)**	**Surface**	**TORA(m)**	**LDA(m)**	**Lighting**
06/24	1605x37	Asphalt	06-1548 24-1545	06-1374 24-1454	Ap Thr Rwy PAPI 3°RH Ap Thr Rwy PAPI 3°LH ABn Wh

Op hrs: H24 (PPR 2200-0800)

Landing Fee: £13.50 /1000 kg plus VAT. Min charge £13.50 (Surcharge 2300-0600)

Hangarage: Available.   **Maintenance:** Available.   **Customs:** H24.

Remarks: Operated by London Southend Airport Co. Ltd.,Southend Airport, Southend-on-Sea, Essex SS2 6YF.

All training flights and non radio aircraft PPR.

When making a visual approach to either runway, all aircraft of 5·7 tonnes or more AUW should intercept the runway extended centreline at a minimum range of 2 nm from touchdown at a height not below the PAPI indicated approach slope of 3°.

A busy public road runs through the undershoot Rwy 06 close to the runway end, do not descend below the PAPI approach slope.

Handling Services provided by Southend Handling, Tel: 01702-608150, Fax: 01702-608128. Radio 131·40.

Circuit height 1000' aal, variable circuits as instructed by ATC.

On departure from either runway all propeller aircraft must climb straight ahead to at least 600' aal before turning.

On departure from Rwy 24 propeller aircraft requiring a left turn shall, after passing 600' aal, maintain a track of 190° to the north bank of the Thames, or until Detling DME 13 nm or less, before adopting normal navigation.

Jet aircraft departures — climb straight ahead to 1000' aal before turning.

Visual Reference Points (VRPs)

Billericay	N51 38·00 E000 25·00
Maldon	N51 43·70 E000 41·00
Sheerness	N51 26·50 E000 44·90
South Woodham Ferrers	N51 39·00 E000 37·00
St. Mary's Marsh	N51 28·50 E000 36·00

Restaurant: Coffee Shop, Fast food Restaurant.

Car Hire: Hertz 01245-350453,   Budget 01268-772774,   Avis 01702-480481, National 01268-530707, Enterprise 01702-522822, Europcar 01245-492919.

Fuel: 100LL, Jet A1. BP
Diners, Visa, Delta, Mastercard,Switch,
Air BP, UVAir, Multi-Service, World Fuel.
Duty Free Fuel available.
	Tel: 01702-608120 ATC
	   01702-608100 Airport
	Fax: 01702-608128 ATC
	   01702-608110 Airport

N53 38·72 W003 01·72	**SOUTHPORT (Birkdale Sands)**	4 ft AMSL

1 nm SW of Southport Pier	**POL 112·10 265 33·5**
	WAL 114·10 020 15·8

c/s Beach Ops 122·35 Radio A/G - Not always manned.
Warton APP 127·35 (MATZ). Woodvale APP 121·00.

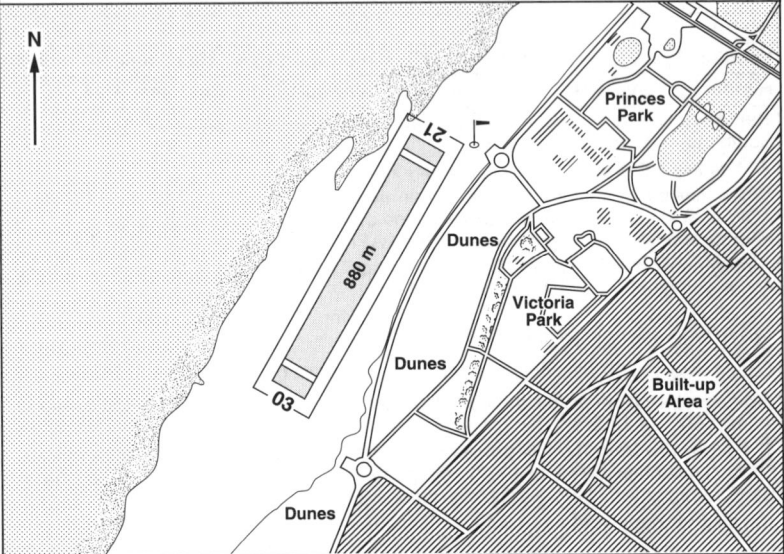

Rwy	Dim(m)	Surface	TORA(m)	LDA(m)	Lighting
03/21	880x110	Sand	03-880	03-820	Nil
			21-880	21-820	Nil

Op hrs: Available during Summer season, daylight hours only.

Landing Fee:

Hangarage: Nil	**Maintenance:** Nil	**Customs:** Nil

Remarks: Operated by Comed Aviation Ltd., Building 28, Blackpool Airport,
Blackpool, Lancs FY4 2QY. PPR. Availability subject to Tidal variation.
Contact with Warton Approach or Woodvale Approach recommended.

Fuel: Nil.	**Tel:** 01704-547811
	01253-349072
	Fax: 01253-349073

N52 33·97 W000 36·43	**SPANHOE**	340 ft AMSL
6 nm SW of RAF Wittering.	DTY 116·40 044 29. HON 113·65 077 41	
4 nm NE of Corby.	CFD 116·50 004 29·6	

No Radio. Cottesmore APP 130·20 MATZ/LARS

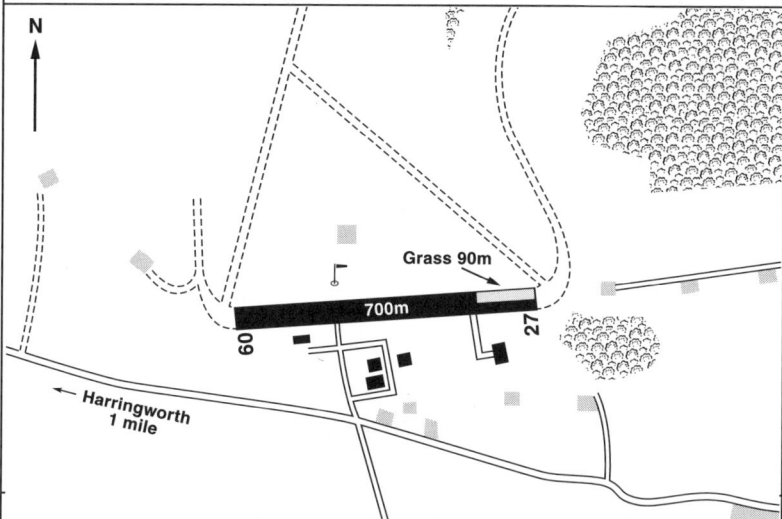

Grass 90m

700m

60

27

Harringworth
1 mile

N

Rwy	Dim(m)	Surface	TORA(m)	LDA(m)	Lighting
09/27	700x13	Concrete/ † Grass	Unlicensed		Rwy

† 90 m grass at east end.

Op hrs: Mon-Sat 0900-1700. Sun by PPR only.

Landing Fee: On applicatiom.

Hangarage: Available.	**Maintenance:** Available.	**Customs:** Nil.

Remarks: Operated by Windmill Aviation, Spanhoe Airfield, Laxton, Nr Corby, Northants NN17 3AT.
Unlicensed airfield situated within the Cottesmore/Wittering CMATZ.
Prominent Viaduct 2 nm west of the airfield.
Visiting pilots must telephone prior to departure.
Inbound aircraft must establish radio contact with Cottesmore App 130·20 before entering the CMATZ.

Restaurant: The White Swan, Tel: 01572-747543.

Accommodation: B&B and Hotel (White Swan) nearby.

Car Hire/Taxis: Corby Cars, Tel: 01536-6260033

Fuel: 100LL	**Tel/Fax:** 01780-450205.

Robert Pooley ©

| N51 39·15 E000 09·35 | **STAPLEFORD** | 185 ft AMSL |

4·5 nm N of Romford.

BPK 117·50 124 11·3.
BIG 115·10 017 20

c/s **Stapleford Radio 122·80 A/G.**
Aeromega Ops 122·05 (Heli Ops).
Stapleford Ops 130·62.
VOR/DME 'LAM' 115·60 (450 metres S of Thr 04).

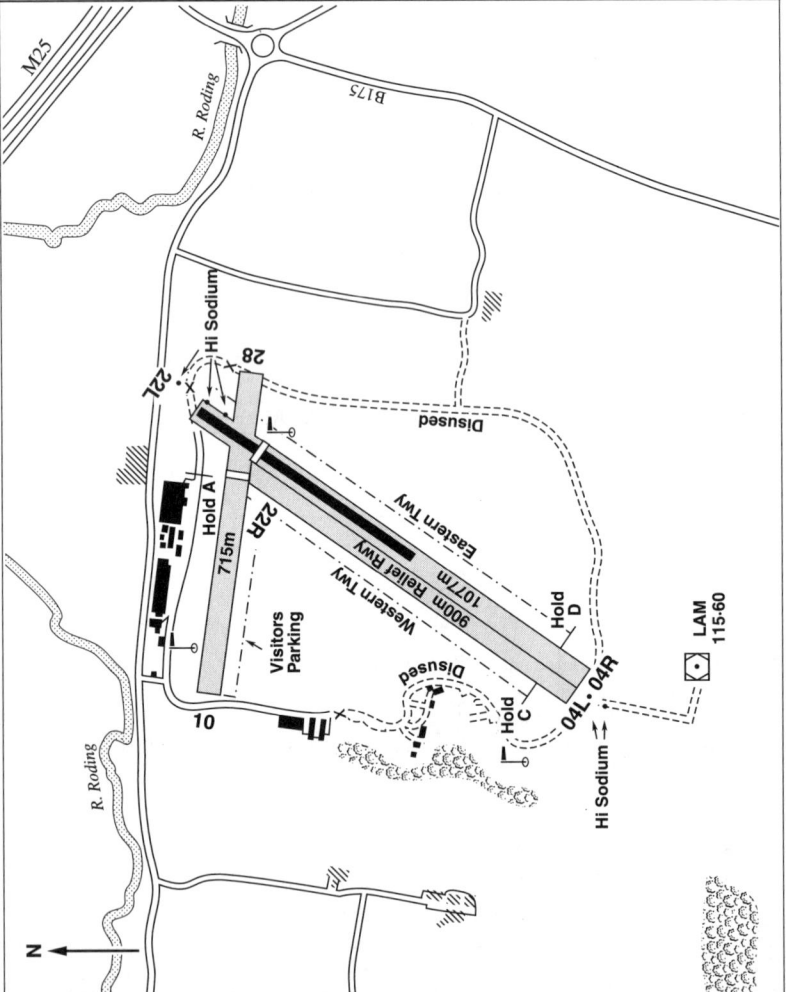

Robert Pooley ©

468

N51 39·15 E000 09·35	**STAPLEFORD**			185 ft AMSL

Rwy	Dim(m)	Surface	TORA(m)	LDA(m)	Lighting
04R/22L	1077x46	Grass/ Asphalt *	04-1077 (D) 04-900 (N) †22-1077 (D) 22-900 (N)	04-1077 (D) 04-900 (N) 22-900 (D) 22-900 (N)	Ap Thr Rwy LITAS 4·25° RH Ap Thr Rwy APAPI 4·25° LH
04L/22R	900x30	Grass	04-900 22-900	04-900 22-900	Nil. Nil.
10/28	715x46	Grass	10-500 28-715	10-698 28-500	Nil. Nil.

* Asphalt 600x18 m at NE end. **Note.** 600 m asphalt available for take-off, only 400 m available for landing due to displaced landing threshold.

† Rwy 22L - TORA 1150m available on request.   (D) = Day, (N) = Night.

Op hrs: 0830-SS. Strictly PPR.

Landing Fee: Singles £7.00, Twins and Helicopters £14.00. Inclusive of VAT.

Hangarage: Available.   **Customs:** 4 hrs PNR Inbound EU

Maintenance: Stapleford Maintenance, Tel: 01708-688449.

Remarks: Operated by The Herts and Essex Aero Club Ltd., Stapleford Aerodrome, Stapleford, Nr Romford, Essex RM4 1SJ. Managed by Stapleford Flight Centre.
Strictly PPR. Outside of published hours of operation, a minimum of 2 hours notice is required.
Night facilities 30 mins PNR before 1600 hrs.
High intensity traffic in circuit up to 2400 ft due to extensive training in IMC and VMC. Circuits LH at 1200' QNH.
Warnings: Do not land short of displaced thresholds on 22L and 22R.
Mast 295 ft aal 480' amsl 210°/1·2 nm (in line with Rwy 04/22 1nm from 04R thld).
Power cables running NW–SE 210 ft aal, 395 ft amsl 045°/1 nm.

Noise abatement procedures – Fixed Wing Aircraft:
Rwy 28 Departures – Maintain the runway heading until passing 1000 ft agl.
Rwy 22 Departures – Right turnout on request.
Pilots are requested to avoid overflying villages of ABRIDGE and LAMBOURNE below 1000 ft agl.

Helicopter Arrival/Departure Routes — see chart at page 471.

Handling – London Executive Aviation (LEA) provide handling facilities to business and commercial flights on request, Tel: 01708-688420.
Facilities include: Executive lounge, catering, transport, flight planning, Met briefing etc.

Restaurant: Refreshments available.

Taxis: 01992-814335.   **Car Hire:** Hertz, 01708-721882.

Fuel: 100LL. Jet A1 (Aeromega Helicopters) PNR on 122·05 or Tel: 020-8500 3030.	**Tel:** 01708-688380 **Fax:** 01708-688421 E-mail: sfc@enterprise.net

Intentionally Blank

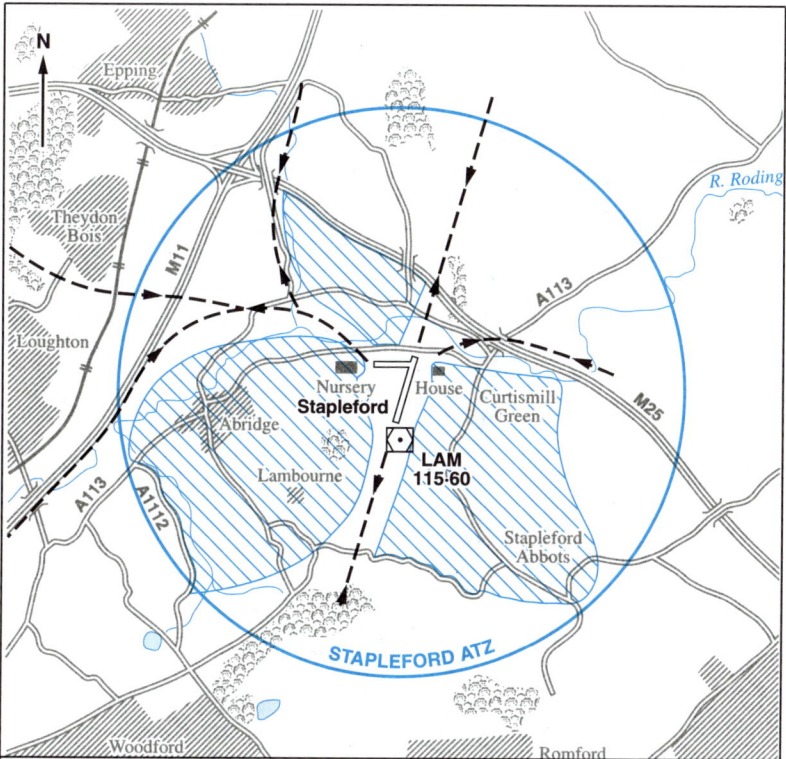

Initial contact — Stapleford Radio/Information 122·80.

Helicopter pilots should follow the routes shown above unless required to conform to the Stapleford fixed wing circuit pattern.

Operating height for helicopters within the ATZ is 500 ft agl.

Avoid overflying the shaded areas and the NURSERY and HOUSE at each end of Rwy 10/28.

Overflight of ABRIDGE, LAMBOURNE, CURTISMILL GREEN and STAPLEFORD ABBOTS is to be avoided at all times.

Aeromega Helipad – PPR

Jet A1 available on prior notice – Tel: 020-8500 3030 or call Aeromega Ops on 122·05.

N58 12·82 W006 19·73	**STORNOWAY**	26 ft AMSL
2 nm E of Stornoway.		**BEN 114·40 047 55**

c/s Stornoway APP/TWR 123·50. (AFIS 123·50 outside Op hrs by arrangement)
VOR/DME 'STN' 115·10 (284°M/5 nm to A/D).
Rwy 18 NDB 'SAY' 431·0 / DME 'ISV' 110·90 (FAT 179°).

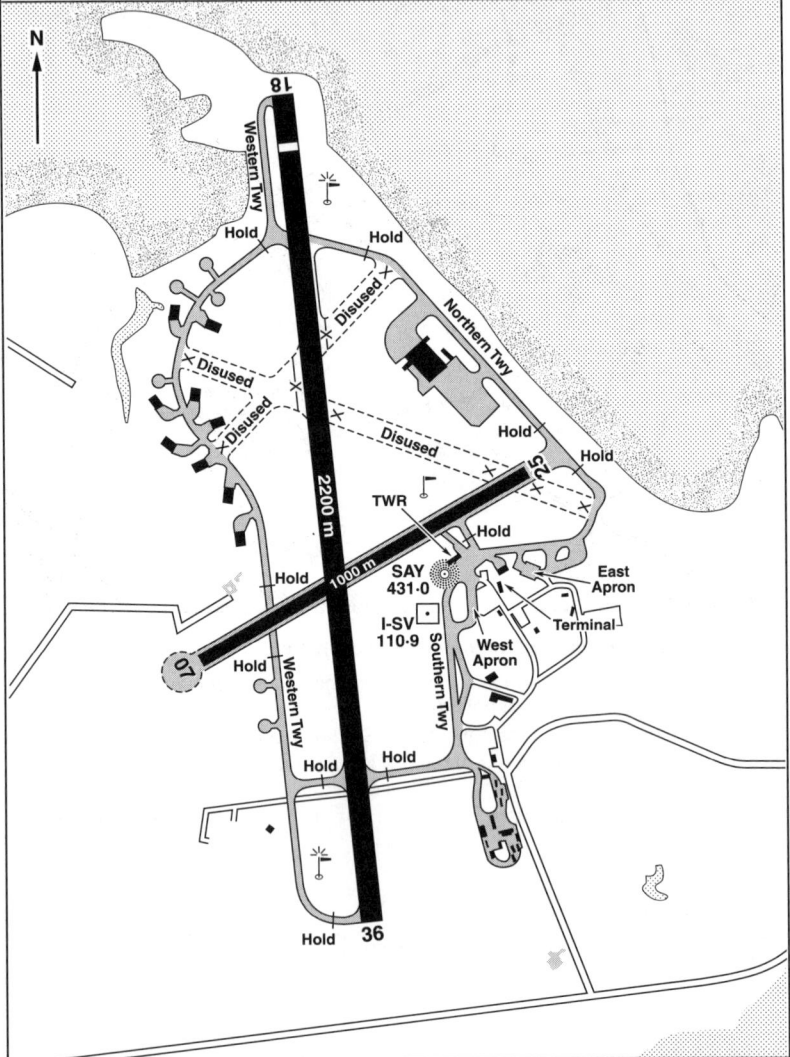

Robert Pooley ©

STORNOWAY

Rwy	Dim(m)	Surface	TORA(m)	LDA(m)	Lighting
18/36	2200x46	Asphalt	18-2200	18-2080	Ap Thr Rwy PAPI 3°
			36-2080	36-2080	# Ap Thr Rwy PAPI 3°
07/25	1000X23	Asphalt	07-1000	07-1000	Thr* Rwy* APAPI 4°
			25-1000	25-1000	Thr* Rwy* APAPI 3·5°
					ABn Wh/Gn

* Portable Electric.

Rwy 36 approach lights terminate 150 m short of threshold

Op hrs: PPR. WINTER: Mon-Fri 0815-1730, Sat 0815-1500, and by arrangement.
SUMMER: Mon-Fri 0830-1700; Sat 0830-1515, and by arrangement.

Landing Fee: Highlands & Islands Airports Rates.

Hangarage: Nil   **Maintenance:** Nil

Customs: Available by arrangement.

Remarks: Operated by Highlands & Islands Airports Ltd, Stornoway Aerodrome, Isle of Lewis HS2 0BN.

Use of aerodrome is subject to Prior Permission.

Take-offs by aircraft required to use a licensed aerodrome are not permitted in visibilities of 600 m or less, except in Emergency Air Ambulance Flights, when arrangements will be made to inspect and protect the runway in use.

Rwy 07/25 – Not available for night landings. It is available to aircraft exceeding 5700 kg MTWA only when crosswind on 18/36 exceeds 15 kts.

Rwy 36 – The 120 m asphalt runway (unlit) extending south beyond Rwy 36 threshold is not available for aircraft manoeuvring or as a starter extension.

Circuits: LH on Rwys 18 and 25, RH on Rwys 07 and 36.

Warnings:

A public road crosses the final approach to Rwy 36. The threshold is displaced accordingly and minimum approach angles of 3° (indicated by PAPI's) must be strictly adhered to when using this runway.

Only marked taxiways to be used. Grass areas soft and unsafe.

Width of the Northern and Southern taxiways on the east side of the aerodrome is 15 m.

All aircraft using the Eastern Apron will be marshalled. Exercise caution when manoeuvring due to the proximity of lighting pylons at the southern edge of the Eastern Apron.

No ground signals except light signals.

Severe downdraughts may be experienced on approachs.

Birds can be expected on all approaches.

Flocks of up to 400 geese present in fields to the west, mainly in December to March.

Coastguard SK61 helicopter operate from the aerodrome H24.

Restaurant: Refreshments.

Car Hire: Tel: 01851-702658; 01851-703026.

Fuel: 100LL, Jet A1. BP. PPR for large amounts. Diners, Amex, Access.	Tel: 01851-702256. 01851-702282 Met. Fax: 01851-703115. Telex: 75495.

N56 19·50 W003 44·92	**STRATHALLAN**	120 ft AMSL
2·5 nm NNW of Auchterarder.	GOW 115·40 048 36.	LU 330·0 272 29·8
		LUK 110·50 272 29·8

c/s Strathallan Radio 129·90 A/G.

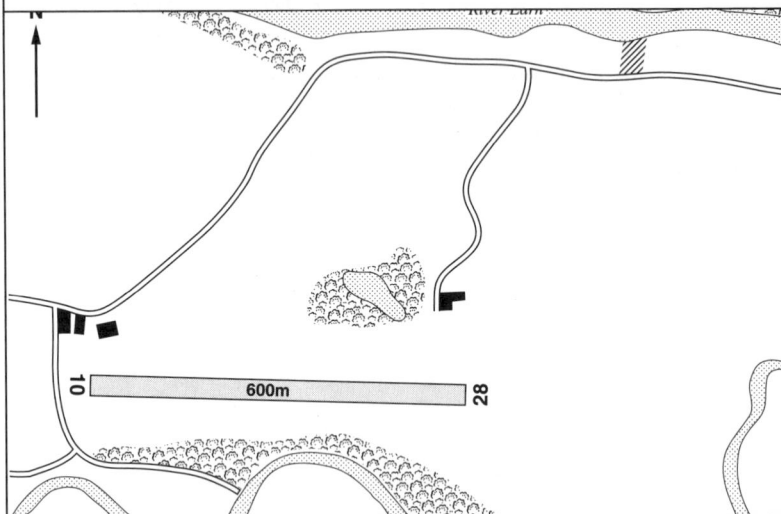

Rwy	Dim(m)	Surface	TORA(m)	LDA(m)	Lighting
10/28	600x30	Grass	Unlicensed		Nil.

Op hrs: Fri 1600-SS. Sat, Sun & PHs 0830-SS. Strictly PPR at all times.

Landing Fee: Not applicable.	**Customs:** Nil
Hangarage: Nil	**Maintenance:** Nil

Remarks: Operated by Scottish Parachute Club as an unlicensed aerodrome. Strictly PPR. Intensive free-fall parachuting from FL120 within a radius of 2·5 nm of the airfield.
Call Strathallan Radio on 129·90, if no response assume no parachuting but approach with caution. Do not overfly the aerodrome.
Non radio aircraft prohibited.
Call for start clearance on 129·90 before starting engines.
Windsock displayed.
High ground lying WNW–ESE 1225' aal 1345' amsl 121°/4 nm.
Trees to west and southwest of aerodrome. Possible sheep grazing.

Restaurant: Cafeteria 0900-2100 weekends only.

Car Hire: Nil.

Fuel: Nil	**Tel:** 01698-832462 weekdays
	01764-662572 weekends

Robert Pooley ©

N59 09·48 W002 38·48	**STRONSAY**	39 ft AMSL
14 nm NE of Kirkwall Airport.		**KWL 108·60 041 14·2**

No Radio. Recommend contact Kirkwall APP 118·30.

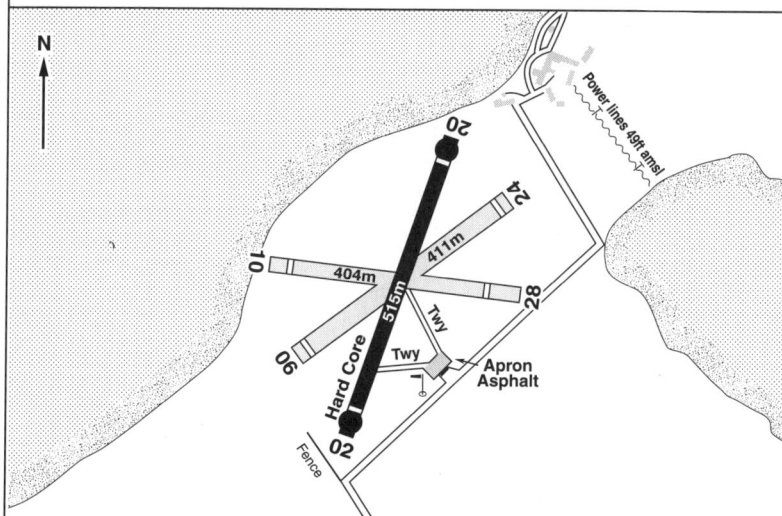

Rwy	Dim(m)	Surface	TORA(m)	LDA(m)	Lighting
02/20	515x18	Hard Core	02-495	02-480	Nil.
			20-515	20-478	Nil.
06/24	411x30	Grass	06-411	06-391	Nil.
			24-411	24-391	Nil.
10/28	404x18	Grass	10-360	10-340	Nil.
			28-384	28-340	Nil.

Op hrs: PPR. Day use only.

Landing Fee: Nil. If Fire cover is required, then fee is £17.74 + VAT.

Hangarage: Nil	**Maintenance:** Nil	**Customs:** Nil

Remarks: Licensed aerodrome (day use only) operated by the Orkney Islands Council, Dept of Technical Services, School Place, Kirkwall, Orkney KW15 1 NY.

Visiting aircraft accepted on prior permission only, and at pilot's own risk. In first instance, contact Orkney Islands Council, Tel: 01856-873535 Ext 2305.

Scheduled Air Services daily Monday - Saturday.

Warning: Rwy 02/20- Graded Hard Core runway generally unsuitable for light aircraft with low ground /propeller clearance due to unstabilised surface.

Accomodation/Restaurant: Hotel Tel: 01857-616213, and B&B on the island.

Car Hire: Tel: 01857-616335.

Fuel: Nil	**Tel:** 01856-873535 Council **Fax:** 01856-876094

Robert Pooley ©

N53 02·13 W000 41·20	**STUBTON PARK**	72 ft AMSL
2 nm SW of old Fulbeck Airfield	**GAM 112·80 152 17. TNT 115·70 097 35**	

Stubton Radio 119·425 A/G – Not always manned.
Waddington App 127·35. Cranwell App 119·375.

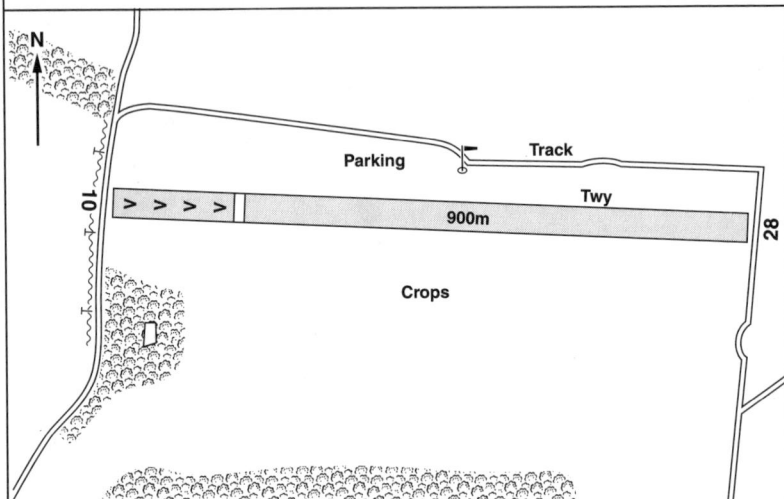

Parking
Track
Twy
900m
10
28
Crops

Rwy	Dim(m)	Surface	TORA(m)	LDA(m)	Lighting
10/28	900x30	Grass	Unlicensed		Nil.

Rwy 10 landing threshold displaced by 180 m.

Op hrs: PPR. All movements on prior permission by telephone.

Landing Fee: Singles £4.00; Twins £8.00.

Hangarage: Nil.	**Maintenance:** Nil.	**Customs:** EU 4 hrs PNR inbound.

Remarks: Operated by Stubton Park Aviation, Fenton Road, Stubton, Newark, Notts,
NG23 5DB. Unlicensed airfield is PPR, Tel: 01636-626223 – Mr. John Jeckelles.
Circuits at 800' aal, LH on 10, RH on 28; joining height 1000' aal.
Avoid overflying farms and villages in vicinity of airfield.
Arrivals
From the North — contact Waddington App on 127·35.
From the South — contact Cranwell App on 119·37 when at least 10 nm out.

Departures call Waddington or Cranwell, as appropriate, before climbing out of the
circuit.
Warnings:
 • Power cables and hedge on final approach to Rwy 10;
 • Hedge just short of threshold of Rwy 28;
 • Danger Area D305, 3 nm to the North;
 • Microlight strip, 2 nm to the South.

Restaurant: No restaurant facilities but a friendly cup of tea/coffee available.

Car Hire/Taxis: By arrangement.

Fuel: 100LL	**Tel:** 01636-626223 **Fax:** 01636-626639

N53 22·87 W000 41·12	**STURGATE**	58 ft AMSL
4 nm SE of Gainsborough.		OTR 113·90 233 28
		GAM 112·80 063 11

c/s Sturgate Radio 130·30 A/G. Waddington RAD 127·35 (LARS/MATZ).
NDB 'SG' 358·0 (On A/D)

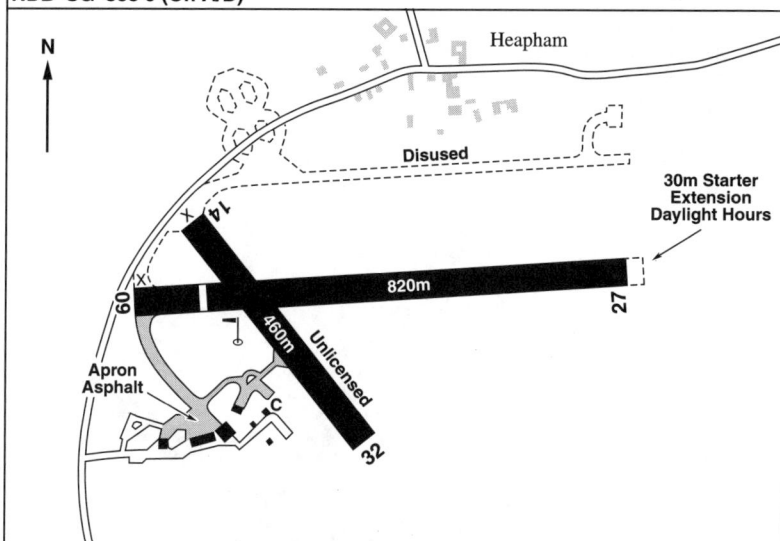

Rwy	Dim(m)	Surface	TORA(m)	LDA(m)	Lighting
09/27	820x46	Asphalt	09-805	09-705	Thr Rwy PAPI
			27-790*	27-790	Thr Rwy AVASIS
†14/32	460x46	Asphalt	Unlicensed		Nil.

* Additional 30m available during daylight hours.   IBn 'SG' Gn

† Eastern end of 14/32 ends abruptly in 2 ft drop at the white markers.

Op hrs: PPR. Winter 0900-1600, Summer 0900-1700; & ¢.

Landing Fee: Singles £5.00, Twins £15.00, incl VAT. **Customs**: By arrangement

Hangarage: Nil.   **Maintenance:** Available

Remarks: Operated by Eastern-Air Executive Ltd. Strictly PPR.
Aerodrome not licensed for public transport flights at weekends.

Eastern limit of both runways marked by a white line and row of crosses.

Public road crosses final approach to Rwy 09 just short of threshold.

Due to proximity of Waddington MATZ and R313 Scampton, aircraft should contact
Waddington App on 127·35 at least 10 nm from MATZ boundary.

Flight within the Aerodrome Traffic Zone limited to 1500 ft aal.

Variable circuits on Rwy 09/27.

Restaurant: Nil.

Taxi: By arrangement through Operations

Fuel: 100LL	**Tel:** 01427-838280 Mon-Fri. 838305 Sat & Sun.
	Fax: 01427-838416.

Robert Pooley ©

N59 52·73 W001 17·73 **SUMBURGH** 19 ft AMSL

1·5 nm NNW of Sumburgh Head. **KWL 108·60 049 74**

c/s Sumburgh. APP 123·15. TWR 118·25. ATIS 125·85.
RAD 123·15.
RAD 131·30 – North Sea Offshore Sector Radar Advisory Service.
NDB 'SBH' 351·0 (On A/D). VOR/DME 'SUM' 117·35 (On A/D).
LLZ/DME Rwy 09 (086°M) 'SUB' 108·50
ILS/DME Rwy 27 (266°M) 'I-SG' 108·50.

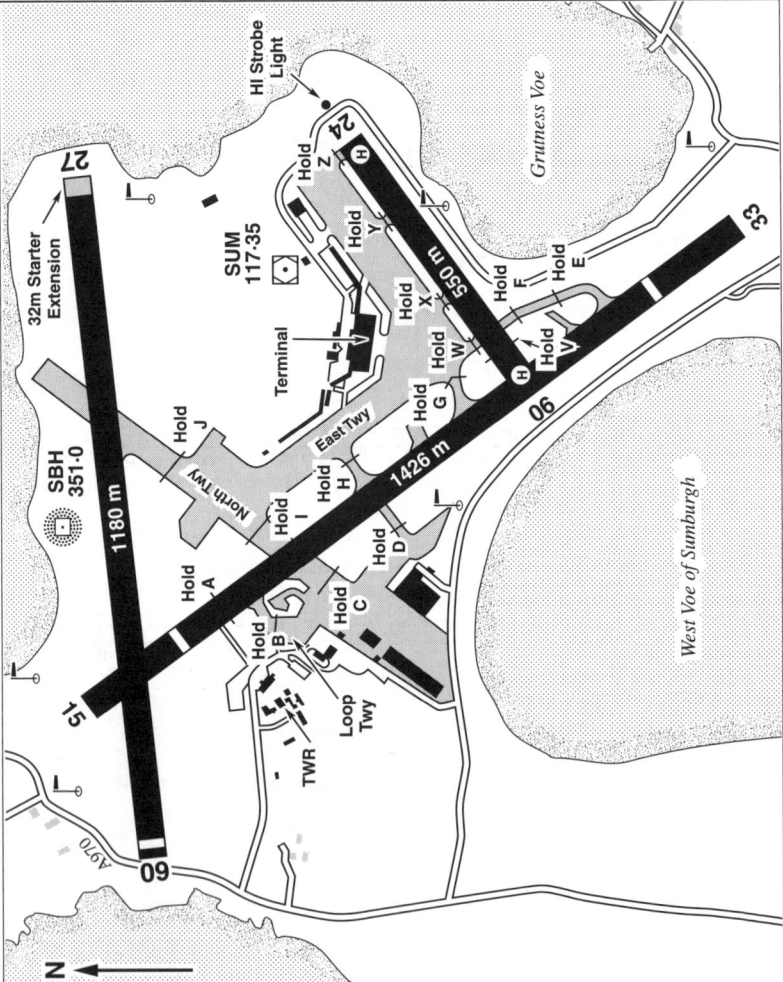

Robert Pooley ©

N59 52·73 W001 17·73			**SUMBURGH**		19 ft AMSL
Rwy	**Dim(m)**	**Surface**	**TORA(m)**	**LDA(m)**	**Lighting**
09/27	1180x46	Asphalt	09-1090	09-1083	Ap Thr Rwy PAPI 3°
			27-1123	27-1093	Ap Thr Rwy PAPI 3°
15/33	1426x46	Asphalt	15-1426	15-1239	Ap Thr Rwy APAPI 4°
			33-1426	33-1239	Ap Thr Rwy
06/24	550x45	Asphalt	Helicopter Runway		Ap Thr Rwy

Op hrs: Mon-Fri 0730-2030; Sat & Sun 0900-1730.
Request for extension of hours – HIAL, Tel: 01950-460654.

Landing Fee: Highlands & Islands Airports Rates.

Customs: see page 84

Hangarage: Nil   **Maintenance:** Limited

Remarks: Operated by Highlands & Islands Airports Ltd., Sumburgh Airport, Virkie Shetland ZE3 9JP.

Flights within Sumburgh CTR/CTA are subject to the regulations applicable to Class 'D' Controlled Airspace — see page 2.

Pilots not using a resident handling agent must ensure that all relevent airport documentation is completed upon initial arrival. Such documents may be obtained from security or HIAL administration staff.

Fixed wing aircraft requiring Customs clearance must park on stands 20 or 21.

No night landings by fixed wing aircraft on Rwy 15/33 except in emergency.

Night take-offs on 15/33 are subject to operators with procedures accepted by CAA.

Pilots using the northern taxiway should adhere to the marked centreline.
Departing aircraft should request start-up clearance on TWR frequency.

Warnings: During strong wind conditions, turbulence may be expected on approach to, or climb out from any runway.

Helicopter operations in support of North Sea oil rigs, SAR Helicopter and Air Ambulance flights may take place outside Operating hours.

Restaurant: Refreshments only.

Car Hire: Bolts Car Hire. Tel: 01950-60777.

Fuel: 100LL, Jet A1. BP. Multi Service	**Tel:** 01950-460654 HIAL. 01950-460173 ATC **Fax:** 01950-460218 HIAL 01950- 460718 ATC

Robert Pooley ©

N51 36·32 W004 04·07	**SWANSEA**	299 ft AMSL

5 nm WSW of Swansea.	BCN 117·45 263 31
	STU 113·10 130 43

Swansea Radio 119·70 A/G . VDF 119·70.
NDB 'SWN' 320·5 (On A/D).

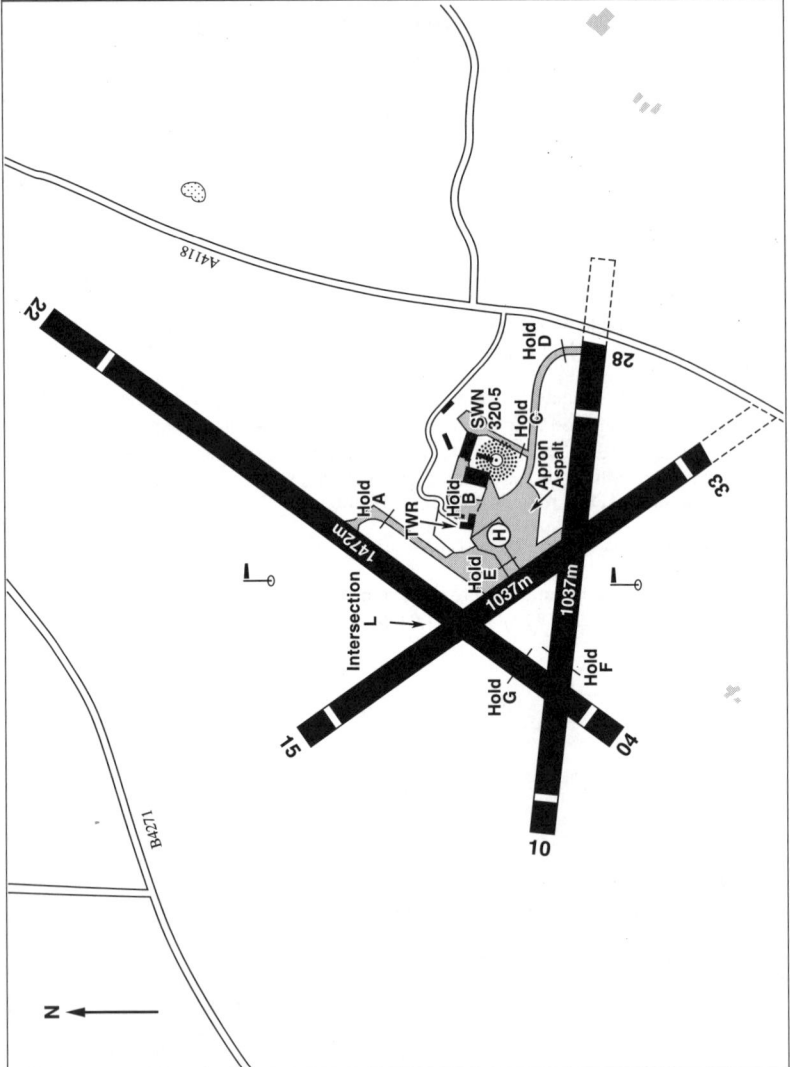

N51 36·32 W004 04·07		**SWANSEA**			299 ft AMSL
Rwy	**Dim(m)**	**Surface**	**TORA(m)**	**LDA(m)**	**Lighting**
04/22	1472x46	Concrete	04-1351	04-1351	Ap Thr Rwy APAPI 3°
			22-1352	22-1261	Ap Thr Rwy APAPI 3·25°
† 10/28	1037x46	Asphalt	10-896	10-896	Nil.
			28-940	28-827	Nil.
† 15/33	1037x46	Asphalt	15-904	15-904	Nil.
			33-909	33-849	Nil.
					IBn 'SX' Gn

† Not available to aircraft exceeding 5700 kg MTWA except in emergency.

Op hrs: Winter : 0900-1700, and by arrangement.
Summer: 0900-1800, and by arrangement.

Note: Aerodrome is frequently open outside of normal operating hours, pilots are invited to check by phone.

Landing Fee: Private: Singles £9.00, Twins £11.00.

Customs: 24 hours PNR.

Hangarage: Available.

Maintenance: By arrangement.

Remarks: Operated by Jaxx Landing Ltd., Swansea Aerodrome, Fairwood Common, Swansea SA2 7JU.
Non radio aircraft PPR.

Light aircraft experiencing radio failure in VMC are to carry out the standard overhead joining procedure for the runway in use.

Warnings: Unserviceable portions of runway short of the thresholds to Rwys 10 & 33 are marked by white crosses.
A public road passes close to the thresholds of Rwys 28 and 33; the road is marked by orange triangular markers on the side remote from the aerodrome and by orange and white circular markers on the aerodrome side.
Not all taxiways are available for use. Deviating from the marked manoeuvring area can be hazardous.

Prevention of Terrorism Act: Although not a designated airport, special branch clearance is available on 24 hours PNR.

Restaurant: Fully licensed restaurant, bar and cafe. Club facilities.

Car Hire (Not on site): Kennings 01792-781782; Hertz 01792-587391.

Taxi: 01792-456111.

Fuel: 100LL, Jet A1. Access, Visa and Switch.	**Tel:** 01792-204063 ATC. **Fax:** 01792-297923

Robert Pooley ©

N52 43·73 E000 57·65	**SWANTON MORLEY**	155 ft AMSL

13 nm WNW of Norwich.

CLN 114·55 357 53·3
NH 371·50 286 15·7

c/s Swanton Radio 123·50 A/G.

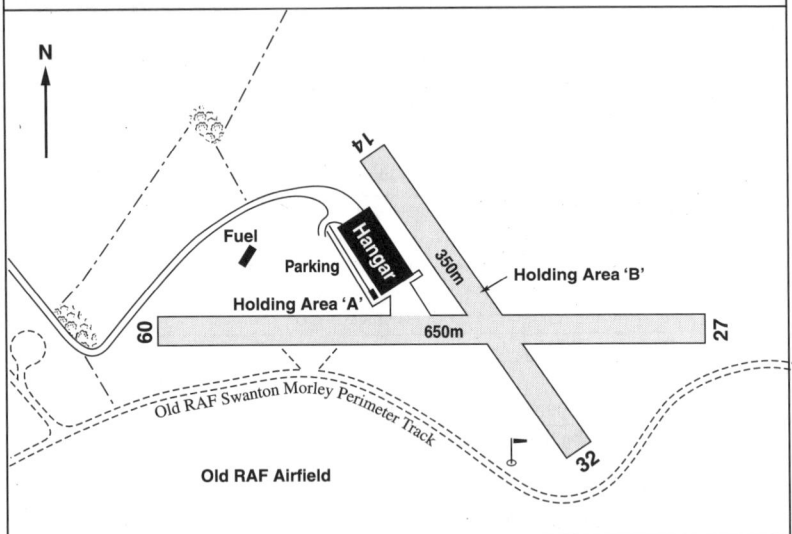

Rwy	Dim(m)	Surface	TORA(m)	LDA(m)	Lighting
09/27	650x45	Grass	Unlicensed		Nil.
14/32	350x45	Grass	Unlicensed		Nil.

Op hrs: By arrangement.	**Customs:** Nil

Landing Fee: £5.00

Hangarage: Available.	**Maintenance:** Available, M3.

Remarks: Operated by John Tyrrell Esq., Swanton Morley Airfield, Worthing, Dereham, Norfolk. NR20 5HR.

Circuits Rwy 09/27 to the South at 800' aal.

No overhead or deadside joins.

Pilots are requested to avoid overflying Worthing village, situated immediately to the north of the airfield.

Aviation Art gallery and Shop.

Restaurant: Snacks /refreshments and club facilities at weekends.

Taxi: By arrangement.

Fuel: 100LL.	**Tel:** 01362-638088 **Fax:** 01362-638505

N52 48·85 W001 45·67	**TATENHILL**	450 ft AMSL
5 nm W of Burton-on-Trent.		TNT 115·70 199 14·8
		HON 113·65 358 27·7

c/s Tatenhill Radio 124·075 A/G. NDB 'TNL' 327·0 (On A/D).

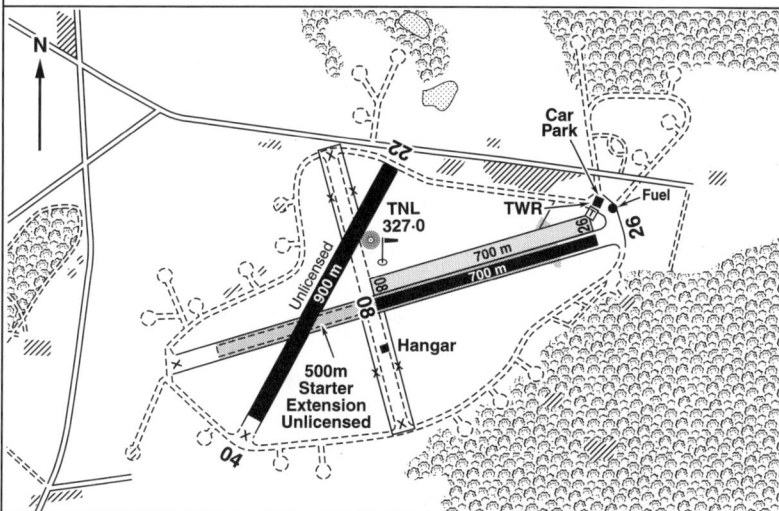

Rwy	Dim(m)	Surface	TORA(m)	LDA(m)	Lighting
08/26	700x28 †	Asphalt	08-700	08-700	Rwy *
			26-700	26-700	Rwy *
04/22 **	900x30	Asphalt	Unlicensed		Nil.
08/26	700x50	Grass	Unlicensed		Nil.

† An unlicensed 500 m starter extension available Rwy 08.

* Rwy lighting available by special arrangement only.

** 04/22 suitable for light aircraft only due to surface deterioration.

Op hrs: PPR. 0900-1700 daily. O/T by arrangement.

Landing Fee: Singles £7.00, Twins £15.00	**Customs:** 24 hours PNR.
Hangarage: Limited	**Maintenance:** M3 Approved

Remarks: Former RAF airfield operated by Tatenhill Aviation, Newborough Road, Needwood, Burton-on-Trent, Staffs. DE13 9PD. PPR. Licensed airfield.

Weight shift Microlights and Non-radio aircraft prohibited. Night flying by arrangement.

East Midlands CTA 6 nm to the East; Birmingham CTA 7 nm to the South, call East Midlands or Birmingham for traffic information before working Tatenhill Radio.

Circuits at 1000 ft aal, RH on 04, LH on 08, 22 and 26.

Caution: Low flying military aircraft in the area.
Gliding at Cross Hayes, 2 nm SW of the A/D. Winch launches up to 2000 ft agl.

Restaurant: Light refreshments available.	**Taxi:** By arrangement.

Fuel: 100LL. Jet A1 by arrangement.	**Tel:** 01283-575283
	Fax: 01283-575650

N54 30·55 W001 25·77	**TEESSIDE**	120 ft AMSL
4·7 nm SE of Darlington.		POL 112·10 033 52
		NEW 114·25 170 33

c/s Teesside. APP 118·85. TWR 119·80. RAD 118·85, 128·85. ATIS 136·20.
VDF 118·85, 119·80, 128·85.   NDB 'TD' 347·5 (232°M/3·93 nm to Thr 23).
ILS/DME Rwy 23 (232°M) I-TD 108·50. † ILS/DME Rwy 05 (052°M) I-TSE 108·50.
† **Warning:** ILS Rwy 05 — aircraft may receive incorrect OM indication at 10 nm from airport, this indication should be ignored.

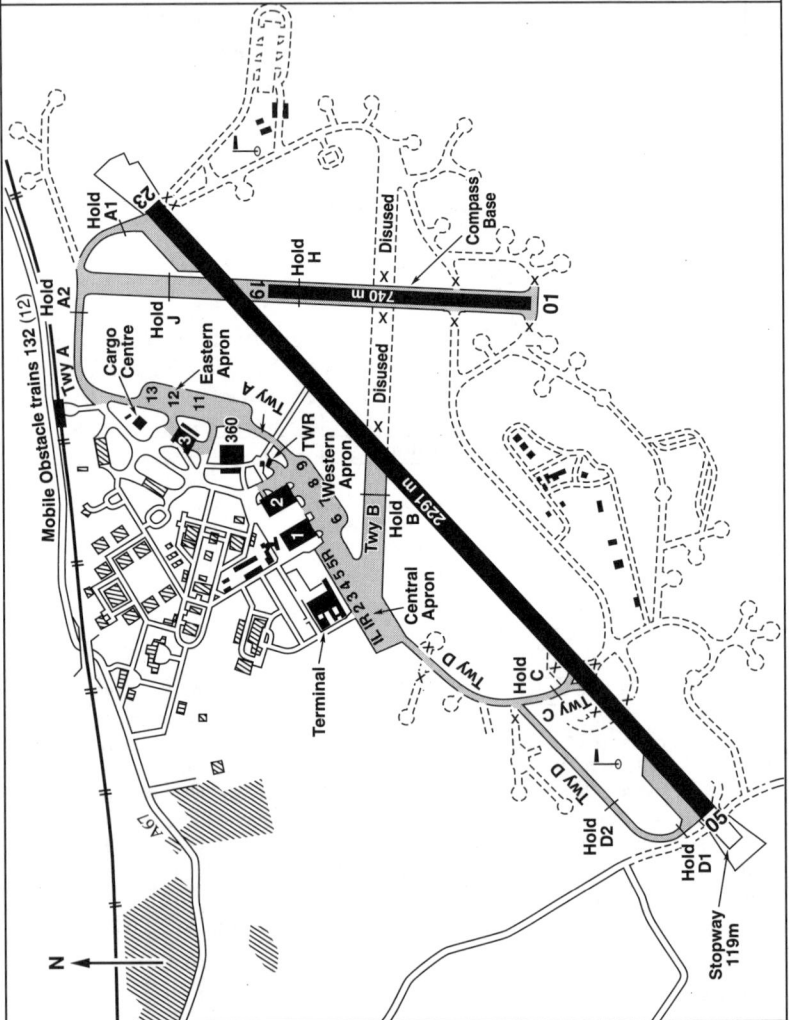

N54 30·55 W001 25·77	**TEESSIDE**	120 ft AMSL

4·7 nm SE of Darlington.	**POL 112·10 033 52**
	NEW 114·25 170 33

Rwy	Dim(m)	Surface	TORA(m)	LDA(m)	Lighting
05/23	2291x46	Asphalt	05-2291	05-2291	Ap Thr Rwy RCL PAPI 3°
			23-2291	23-2291	Ap Thr Rwy RCL PAPI 3°
* 01/19	740x18	Asphalt	01-740	01-740	Nil.
			19-740	19-740	Nil.

* Available by day only to Teesside based aircraft under 5700 kg MTWA.

Op hrs: H24.

Landing Fee: Up to 3 tonnes £6.55 per 0.5 tonne or part, and thereafter £13.10 per tonne or part + VAT. Reduced rate for training.

Hangarage: Available   **Maintenance:** Available.   **Customs:** Available.

Remarks: Operated by Teesside International Airport Ltd, Darlington, Co Durham DL2 1LU. Flights within Teesside CTR/CTA are subject to the regulations applicable to Class 'D' Controlled Airspace — see page 2.

VRPs are listed overleaf. See CTR/CTA and VRPs Chart at page 487.

Aerodrome not available to non-radio aircraft.

Training flights by prior permission via Duty Officer 01325-332811.

Circuits: Large aircraft at minimum 1500' aal, light aircraft at 1000' aal, direction variable.

Aircraft are to avoid overflying the villages of Middleton St George, Yarm and Eaglescliffe whenever practicable - See Chart at page 487.

Aircraft must carry third party liability insurance cover of at least £500,000.
Booking out details will not be accepted over the RTF.

Taxiway Alpha from Stand 9 on the west apron is available for use by aircraft up to 50,000 kg MTWA and aircraft with wingspans not exceeding 34m. All taxiways apart from the central taxiway are 15m wide. Aircraft requiring greater width must enter or vacate Rwy 05/23 via Hold B.

Hold C taxiway available for aircraft up to 50,000 kg. Pilots vacating the runway at Hold C must follow the lead off taxi guidance markings and not attempt to cut the corner. Hold C is closed during Low Visibility Procedures. ATC will advice when Hold C is available for use.

Access to Rwy 05/23 restricted to routeing via Holding Points A1, B, C and D1.

Warning: Deer hazard, please report any sightings to ATC.

VRPs are listed overleaf; CTR/CTA and VRPs chart is at page 487.

Accommodation: Hotels on airport - via Information Desk.

Restaurant: In Terminal and Flying Clubs.

Car Hire: Avis 01325-332091.   Hertz 01325-332600.   Europcar 01325-333329.

Taxis: On airport Taxi Rank or via Information Desk.

Fuel: 100LL, Jet A1.	**Tel:** 01325-332811.
Multi Service.	**Fax:** 01325-332810.

TEESSIDE

VISUAL REFERENCE POINTS (VRPs)

VRP	VOR/NDB	VOR/DME
Hartlepool N54 41·00 W001 12·83	NEW R147° TD 034°M	NEW R147°/27 nm
Motorway Junction **A1(M)/A66(M)** N54 30·00 W001 37·60	NEW R180° TD 255°M	NEW R180°/32 nm
Northallerton N54 20·33 W001 25·92	—	NEW R172°/43 nm
Redcar Racecourse N54 36·43 W001 03·85	NEW R144° TD 078°M	NEW R144°/34 nm
Sedgefield Racecourse N54 38·75 W001 28·10	—	NEW R166°/25 nm
Stokesley N54 28·18 W001 11·68	—	NEW R158°/38 nm

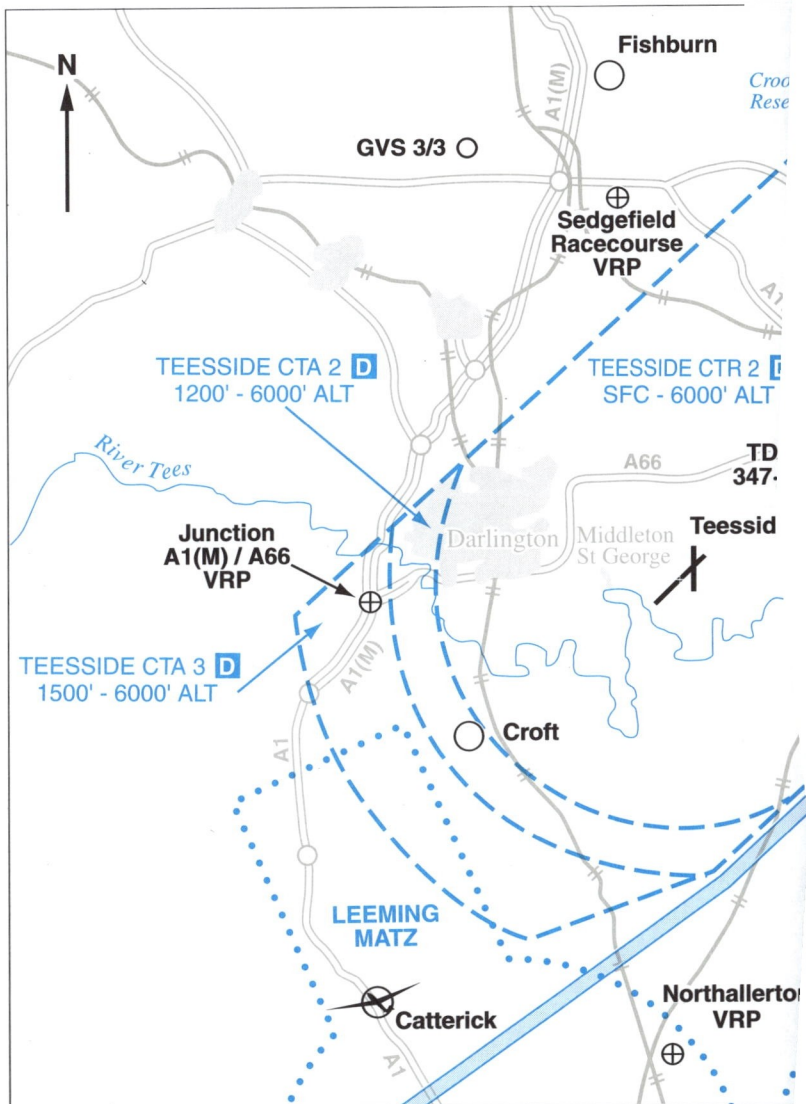

TEESSI[
an[

N

Fishburn

A1(M)

Cro[
Rese[

GVS 3/3 ○

⊕
Sedgefield
Racecourse
VRP

A1

TEESSIDE CTA 2 **D**
1200' - 6000' ALT

TEESSIDE CTR 2 **D**
SFC - 6000' ALT

River Tees

A66

TD
347·

Junction
A1(M) / A66
VRP

Darlington   Middleton
St George

Teessid

⊕

TEESSIDE CTA 3 **D**
1500' - 6000' ALT

A1(M)

A1

○ Croft

LEEMING
MATZ

A1

⊗ Catterick

Northallerto
VRP

⊕

Intentionally Blank

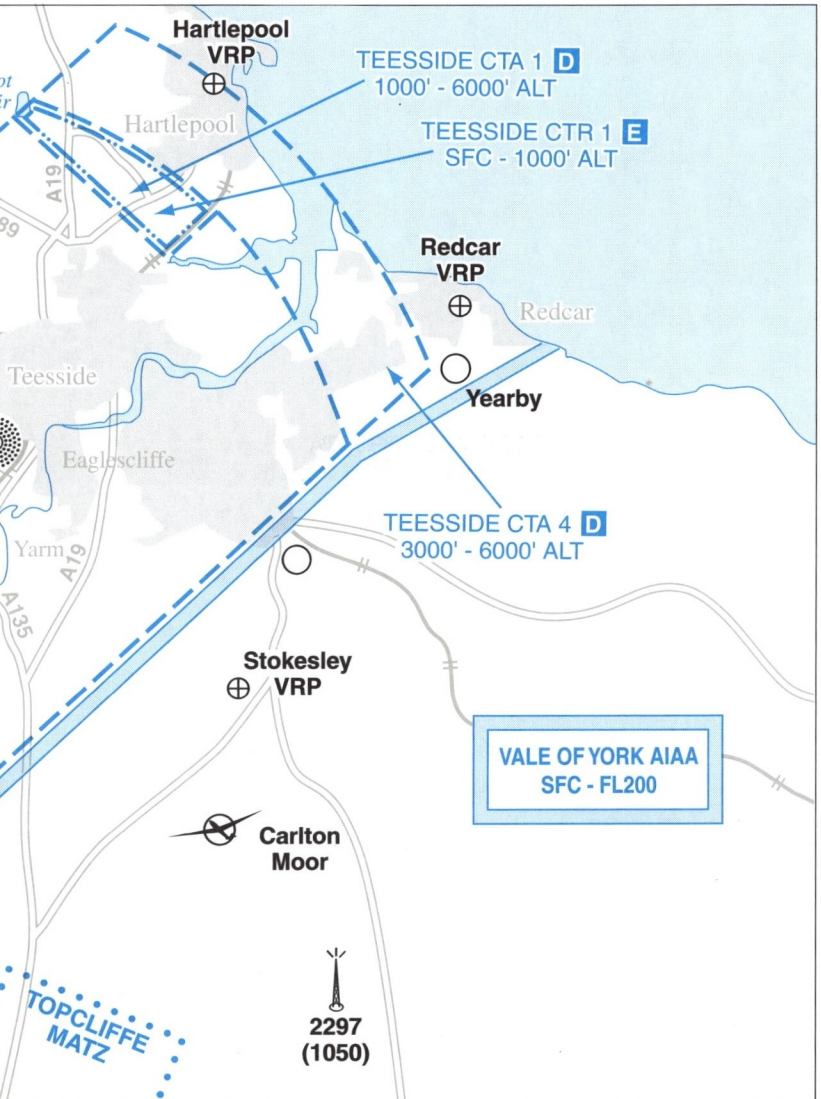

Hartlepool VRP

⊕

Hartlepool

A19

89

TEESSIDE CTA 1 D
1000' - 6000' ALT

TEESSIDE CTR 1 E
SFC - 1000' ALT

Redcar VRP

⊕

Redcar

Teesside

○ **Yearby**

Eaglescliffe

Yarm A19

A135

TEESSIDE CTA 4 D
3000' - 6000' ALT

○

Stokesley VRP
⊕

VALE OF YORK AIAA
SFC - FL200

⊗ **Carlton Moor**

TOPCLIFFE
MATZ

2297
(1050)

1 DEC 00

TEESSIDE CTR /CTA
and VRPs

Intentionally Blank

THRUXTON

N51 12·67 W001 35·82

330 ft AMSL

4·5 nm W of Andover.

SAM 113·35 333 18·1.
CPT 114·35 225 22·1

c/s Thruxton Radio 130·45 A/G.
Boscombe APP 126·70.

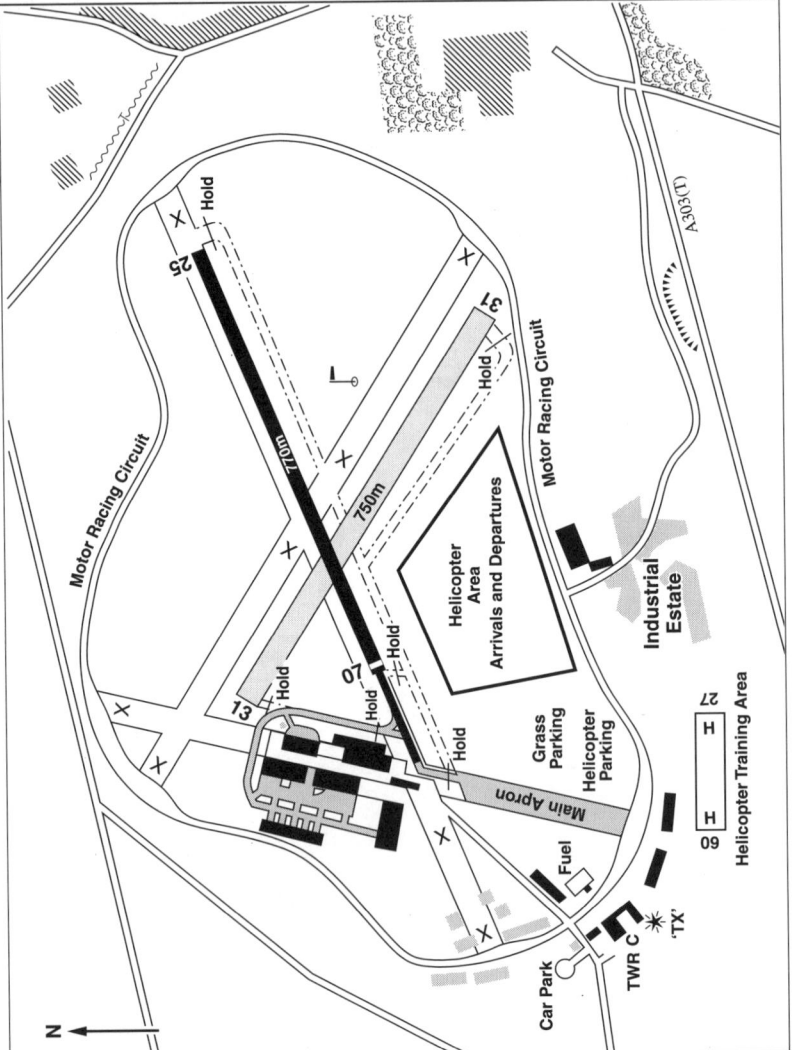

Hold

25

770m

Motor Racing Circuit

31

Hold

750m

Motor Racing Circuit

A303(T)

Helicopter Area
Arrivals and Departures

Industrial Estate

13

Hold

Hold

07

Hold

Hold

Main Apron

Grass Parking

Helicopter Parking

27

H

H

60

Helicopter Training Area

Fuel

TWR C

'TX'

Car Park

N

Robert Pooley ©

490

N51 12·63 W001 36·00		**THRUXTON**		319 ft AMSL	
Rwy	**Dim(m)**	**Surface**	**TORA(m)**	**LDA(m)**	**Lighting**
07/25	770x23	Asphalt	07-770 † 25-770	07-760 25-770 †	Thr Rwy APAPI 4° (LH) Thr Rwy APAPI 4° (LH)
13/31	750x31	Grass	13-750 31-750	13-750 31-750	Nil. Nil. IBn 'TX' Gn

† Plus unlicensed extension 220x7 m.

Op hrs: 0900-1700 (1 Apr-30 Sept 1700-1900 by arrangement)
0900-1700 (1 Oct- 31Mar).

Landing Fee: Singles £8.00. Twins – £15.00 and by arrangement. Landing fees exempt to all Students on qualifying cross-country flights. Landing fee concessions available on sufficient fuel uplift.

Customs: 24 hrs PNR.

Hangarage: Limited.   **Maintenance:** Available, Tel: 01264-771327.

Remarks: Operated by Western Air (Thruxton) Ltd., Thruxton Aerodrome, Nr Andover, Hampshire SP11 8PW. All movements on Race days PNR.
Non radio aircraft PPR. Microlights not permitted.

High visibility clothing recommended whilst airside.

No deadside on Rwy 07/25 due variable circuit directions.

Arrivals: Inbound aircraft call Boscombe Down App 126·70 before reaching CMATZ boundary. Boscombe ATC will ensure the aircraft inbound to Thruxton will be level at 1500 ft QNH (RPS) before free calling Thruxton Radio.

Departures: Outbound departing aircraft should free call Boscombe Down App before climbing above 800 ft Thruxton QFE or 1100 ft ALT or climb when clear from the CMATZ.

Westbound departures should obtain onward clearance from Boscombe Down App before leaving Thruxton ATZ.

Circuits: Normal circuit joining height is 1300 ft Thruxton QFE, with circuit height of 800 ft QFE. However, if Boscombe Down CMATZ is inactive, then the circuit joining height is 1500 ft Thruxton QFE, and the circuit height is 1000 ft QFE.

Circuit Directions:

Rwy 07- Fixed wing - LH, helicopters - RH; Rwy 25- Fixed wing - RH, helicopters - LH;
Rwy 13- Fixed wing and helicopters - RH;   Rwy 31- Fixed wing and helicopters - LH.
Aircraft vacating Rwy 07/25 must vacate to S, and Rwy 13/31 must vacate to the W.

When Boscombe/Middle Wallop CMATZ is active, non radio aircraft may route to/from Thruxton via Chilbolton (8nm SE of Thruxton) at 1000 ft aal on a track of 310°/130°M or via a point 1nm east of Ludgershall (010°M/3nm from Thruxton) at 1000 ft aal.

Aircraft should avoid overflying following villages:
Kimpton (N. boundary), Thruxton (E. boundary), Quarley (1 nm SSW) and
Fyfield (1 nm NE).

Caution: Power cables cross final approach to Rwy 25, 200m from threshold.
Avoid Danger Areas D123, D125, D125A, D126 and D127.
Intensive flying training at Middle Wallop 4 nm to the South.

Restaurant: Jackaroo, Tel: 01264-771322. **Car Hire:** Eurodollar Tel: 01264-338181

Fuel: 100LL, Jet A1. Cash, Cheque or Credit Cards	**Tel:** 01264-772352 or 772171 **Fax:** 01264-773913

N56 29·95 W006 52·15	**TIREE**	38 ft AMSL
2·5 nm NNE of Balemartin.		**BEN 114·40 174 61**

c/s Tiree Information 122·70 AFIS.
VOR/DME 'TIR' 117·70 (On A/D).

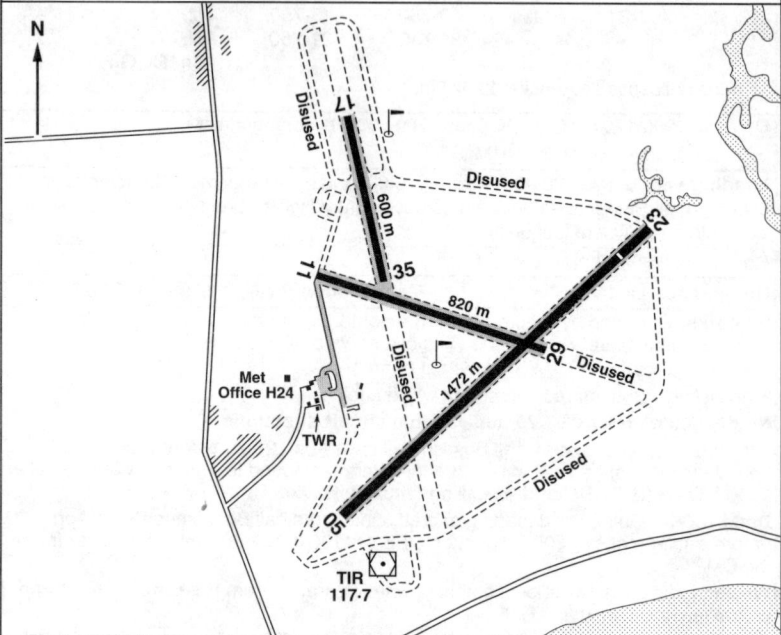

Rwy	Dim(m)	Surface	TORA(m)	LDA(m)	Lighting
05/23	1472x30	Asphalt	05-1402	05-1402	Rwy* APAPI 3°
			23-1402	23-1350	Rwy* APAPI 3°
11/29	820x19	Asphalt	11/29-820	11/29-820	Rwy*
17/35	600x18	Concrete	17/35-600	17/35-600	Rwy*
					* Portable Electric. ABn Wh

Op hrs: PPR. Mon-Fri 1000-1500, Sat 0930-1100. Closed Sundays .

Landing Fee: Highlands & Islands Airports Rates. - Cash £10.90 Special.

Hangarage: Nil	**Maintenance:** Nil	**Customs:** Nil

Remarks: Operated by Highlands & Islands Airports Ltd. Aerodrome PPR.
All taxiways are closed except between threshold of Rwy 11 and the parking apron.

Disused section of Rwy 17/35 is not available as taxiway. Unserviceable sections of runways are fenced off and marked with white crosses.

Warnings: Bird hazard - Large flocks of geese in the vicinity of the airfield between October and March. Hill 422' aal 530' amsl 215°/3·2 nm.

Guest House/Restaurant: Glassary Licensed Restaurant (approx 3 miles from A/D).

Car Hire: Tiree Motor Company. Maclennan Motors.	**Taxi:** 01879-220419/311.

Fuel: Nil	**Tel:** 01879-220 456 Airport **Fax:** 01879-220 714 Airport

Robert Pooley ©

N54 12·33 W001 22·93	**TOPCLIFFE**	92 ft AMSL

2·5 nm SW of Thirsk.

	POL 112·10 047 37·7
	NEW 114·25 173 51·2

APP/RAD 125·00.   **TWR 122·10.**   Leeming Zone 127·75 (CMATZ).
TACAN 'TOP' 113·70 (On A/D).

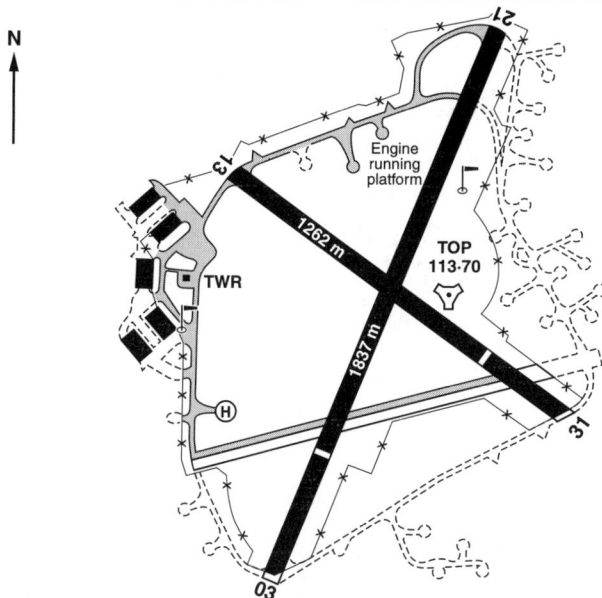

Rwy	Dim(m)	Surface	TORA(m)	LDA(m)	Lighting
03/21	1837x46	Asphalt	03-1814	03-1434	Ap Thr Rwy PAPI
			21-1814	21-1814	Ap Thr Rwy PAPI
13/31	1262x46	Asphalt	13-1242	13-1242	Thr Rwy PAPI
			31-1242	31-946	Thr Rwy PAPI

Op hrs: PPR. Mon-Thu 0800-1715, Fri 0800-1700.	**ATZ active H24**
Landing Fee: MoD(RAF) Rates	**Customs:** Nil
Hangarage: Nil	**Maintenance:** Nil

Remarks: RAF Aerodrome. Satellite aerodrome of RAF Linton-on-Ouse.
Leeming/Topcliffe and Dishforth CMATZ controlled by Leeming Zone 127·75.
All circuits to the West.
Helicopters route via West Tanfield, 270°/7·5 nm or Bagby 080°/3 nm.
Free-fall parachuting up to FL150, HJ, Sat, Sun & PHs, all aircraft are to contact A/G
Station on 129·90.

Fuel: Jet A1	**Tel:** 01347-848261 Ext 7491/2 Linton Ops
	01748-875376 Topcliffe Ops, 875340 ATC.

N52 07·45 W000 07·20	**TOP FARM**	200 ft AMSL
10 nm SW of Cambridge		**BKY 116·25 323 10·5**
5 nm NE of Biggleswade		**BNN 113·75 037 29**

No Radio.

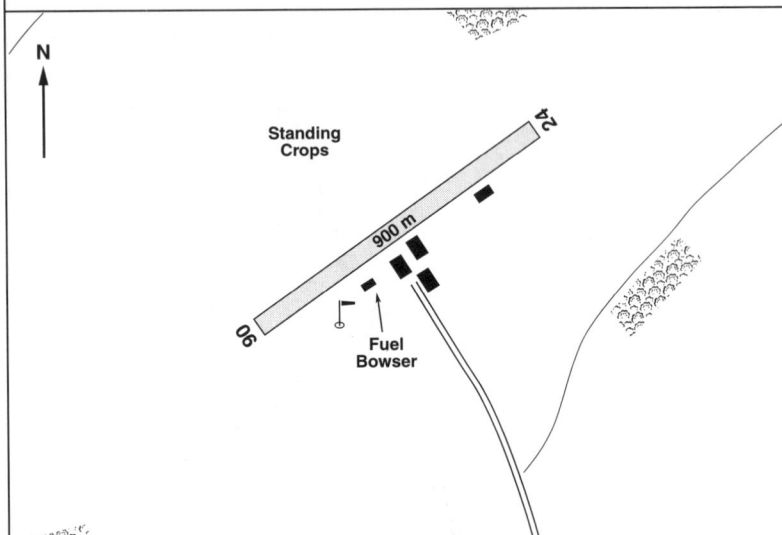

N

Standing Crops

24

900 m

06

Fuel Bowser

Rwy	Dim(m)	Surface	TORA(m)	LDA(m)	Lighting
06/24	700x24	Grass	Unlicensed		Nil

Op hrs: Strictly PPR - Restricted movements due planning constraints.

Landing Fee: £5.00.	**Customs:** Nil
Hangarage: Nil	**Maintenance:** Nil

Remarks: Operated by Mr. David Morris, Barmoor House, Top Farm, Croydon, Roystone, Herts, Herts SG8 0EQ.

Unlicensed airfield. Strictly PPR and at pilot's own risk.

Airfield is located in close proximity of Little Gransden's southern ATZ boundary.

Circuits to the south at 1000 ft aal. Avoid Farm house 1 nm east of the airfield and all local villages.

Sandy TV mast, 972 ft amsl, is 4·5 nm WNW.

Accommodation: By arrangement.

Taxis: Meltax Tel: 01763-244444.

Fuel: 100LL	**Tel/Fax:** 01767- 631377
	Mobile: 0411-197738.

N50 16·73 W005 08·97	400 ft AMSL	
3 nm WNW of Truro.	LND 114·20 072 20·6	
	BHD 112·05 270 63·8	

c/s Truro Radio 129·80 A/G (By arrangement)
Culdrose APP 134·05. St. Mawgan App 126·50

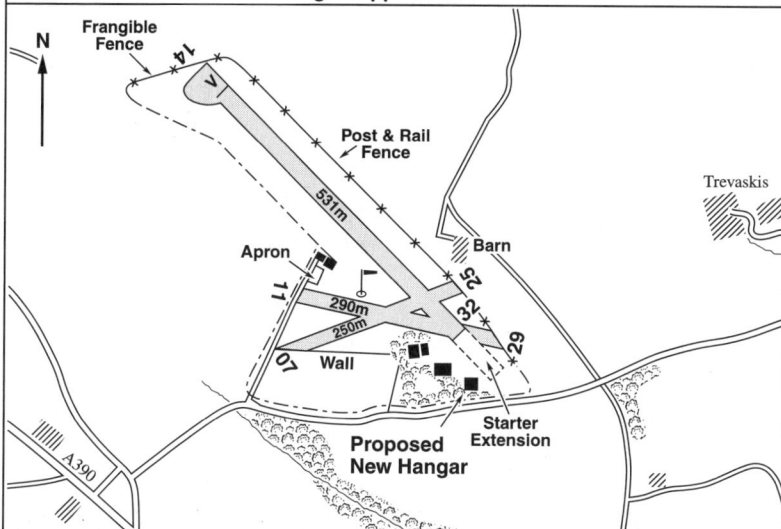

Rwy	Dim(m)	Surface	TORA(m)	LDA(m)	Lighting
07/25	250x12	Grass	Unlicensed		Nil
11/29	290x12	Grass	Unlicensed		Nil
14/32	531x18	Grass	Unlicensed		Nil

Rwy 07 – upslope 2%. Rwy 32 – 100 m Starter extention upslope 5·5% .

Op hrs: By arrangement with the Airfield Owner. 0700-2100 or SS, whichever earlier.

Landing Fee: On application. **Customs:** Nil

Hangarage: 2001 **Maintenance:** Nil.

Remarks: Operated by Philip Irish Esq (owner), Truro Airfield, Tregavethan, Truro. TR4 9EX. Airfield currently unlicensed due to lack of fire cover. Not available for Public Transport. Visitors welcome on prior permission and at pilot's own risk. Airfield is situated beneath RNAS Culdrose Area of Intense Air Activity (A) 1800–5800 ft; contact Culdrose App 134·05 for traffic information.

Inbound and outbound aircraft to and from the NE are requested to call St. Mawgan App on 126·50. All circuits left-hand. Aircraft departing Rwy 32 should maintain extended centreline for approx 0.75 nm; departing 14 likewise, but turn before reaching built-up area. In both cases avoid any deviations to the left for about 0.75 nm. Stone hedge on approachs to Rwys 07 & 11 and a fence on Rwys 25 & 29. Rwy 14 has a white frangible fence on approach. Rwy 32 — overall upslope of 1·8%. Rwys 07/25 and 11/29 are unmarked, use only after consulting the airfield owner.

Taxi: City Taxis 01872-73479 or 0800-318708. **Car Hire:** By arrangement with airfield owner.

Accommodation: Airfield owner will advise.

Fuel: 100LL. **Tel:** 01872-560488 Airfield owner.

TURWESTON   448 ft AMSL

N52 02·45 W001 05·73	
2 nm E of Brackley	DTY 116·40 182 8·4
	BNN 113·75 317 27·7

Turweston Radio 122·175 A/G.

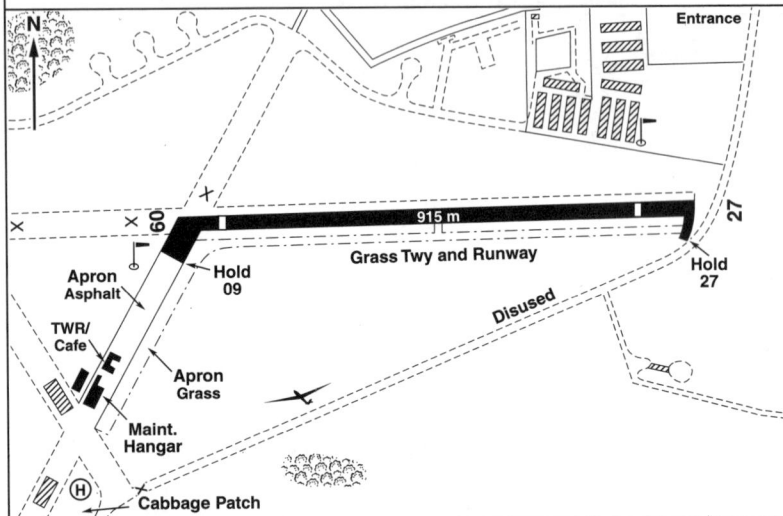

Rwy	Dim(m)	Surface	TORA(m)	LDA(m)	Lighting
09/27	915x18	Asphalt	09-800	09-800	Nil.
			27-800	27-800	Nil.

Op hrs: Mon-Fri 08-2000 or SS, Sat 09-1800 or SS, Sun 10-1800 or SS. Last Dep on Sun 1600

Landing Fee: SE £7.00,   Twins £10.00.   All inclusive of VAT.

Hangarage: Available.   **Customs:** Nil

Maintenance: AKKI Aviation Services Ltd, M3, JAR-145, Tel: 01280-706616.
Aircraft Resprays: Mick Allen – 01280-840661.

Remarks: Operated by Turweston Flight Centre Ltd. Turweston Aerodrome, Brackley, Northants. NN13 5YD. Licensed aerodrome. PPR by telephone.
Winch launched gliding at weekends and PHs, height 2000 ft agl. No deadside joins.

Circuit and Noise Abatement Procedures - See opposite page.

Warning: Intensive parachuting activity at D129 -Weston-on-the-Green, 8 nm SW of aerodrome, and also at Hinton-in-The-Hedges.
Radio Masts 232' aal 680' amsl 220°/3·5 nm. Power cables run NW/SE 1 nm W of A/D.
Introductory & Advanced Flight Training from Turweston Aero Club, Tel: 01280-701167.
Restaurant: McDeans   open 0800-1630, closed Mondays, Tel: 01280-841732/700123.

Fuel: 100LL.	**Tel:** 01280-705400 Twr.
	Tel: 01280-701167 Aero Club/School.
	Fax: 01280-840465 Aero Club/School.
	Fax: 01280-704647 Operator.
	Web: www.turweston.co.uk

TURWESTON
Noise Abatement Procedures

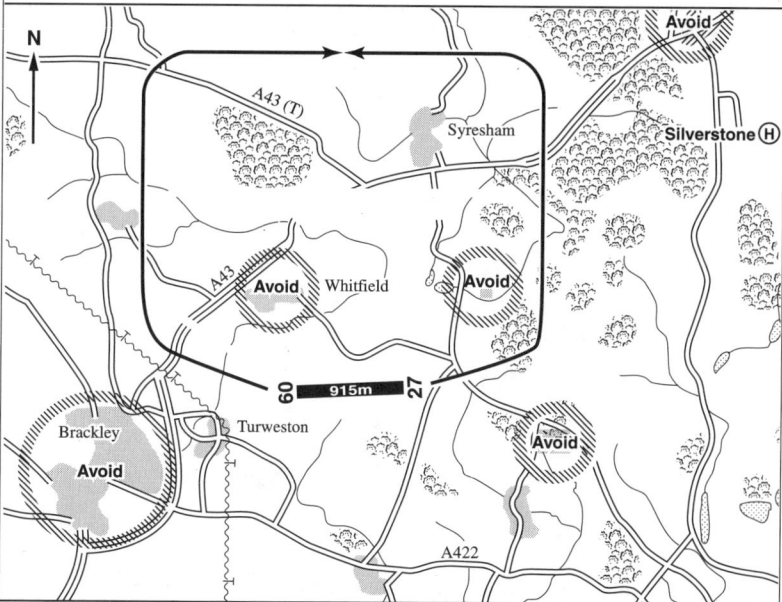

Circuits: Fixed wing circuits to the north at 1300' QFE (LH on 09, RH on 27). Gliders to the south of the runway.

Arrivals:

Rwy 09 – Fly the final approach leg to avoid the farmhouse located 1·1 nm West of threshold.

Rwy 27 – Fly the final approach leg to avoid the farmhouse located 0·5 nm East of threshold.

Departures:

Rwy 09 – After take-off, turn left 20° to avoid overflying farmhouse on extended centreline.

Rwy 27 – After take-off, turn right 20° to climb between BRACKLEY and WHITFIELD.

Avoid overflying local habitation and maintain circuit position on downwind legs to the North of A43.

Helicopter Arrivals:

Approach from the SE of the airfield to join at the boundary for the Cabbage patch.

Connecting service to Silverstone motor racing circuit available

N60 44·83 W000 51·23

UNST

62 ft AMSL

On the Isle of Unst (Shetland Islands)

SUM 117·30 021 53·6

c/s Unst/Radio Information 130·35 A/G / AFIS. AFIS by arrangement.

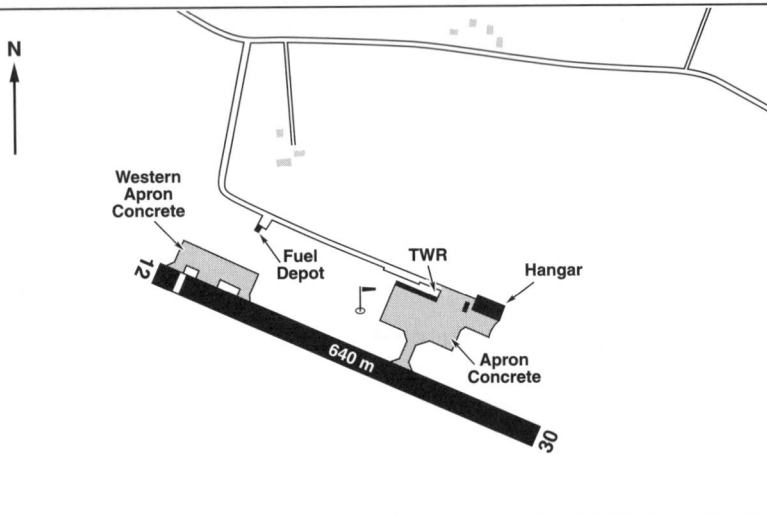

Rwy	Dim(m)	Surface	TORA(m)	LDA(m)	Lighting
12/30	640x28	Asphalt	12-640 30-610	12-610 30-610	Thr Rwy PAPI 4·5° Thr Rwy PAPI 4·5° I Bn 'UT' Gn

Op hrs: By arrangement.

Landing Fee: On application

Customs: By arrangement

Hangarage & Maintenance: Nil.

Remarks: Aerodrome operated by Shetland Islands Council, Grantfield, Lerwick, Shetland ZE1 0NT.

Aerodrome not available at night by flights required to use a licensed aerodrome.

Circuits at 1000 ft, LH on 12, RH on 30.

Frequent helicopter activity outside notified Op hrs.

Mast 430' aal 492' amsl 017°/1·9 nm. High ground 350' amsl 1 nm to south.

Accommodation: The Baltasound Hotel, Baltasound, Unst. Tel: 01957-81334

Taxis & Coaches: P & T Coaches, Baltasound, Unst. Tel: 01957-711666

Fuel: Nil.	**Tel:** 01957-711887 Airfield; 711541 ATC. 01595-744866 Council Office. **Fax:** 01957-711541.

| N53 14·89 W004 32·12 | **VALLEY** | 37 ft AMSL |

| 5 nm SE of Holyhead. | **IOM 112·20 178 50** |
| | **WAL 114·10 267 51** |

Valley RAD 134·35 (LARS & MATZ). **TWR 122·10.**
TACAN 'VYL' 108·40 (On A/D). ILS Rwy 14 (140°M) 'VY' 109·70. (Rwy QFU 137°).

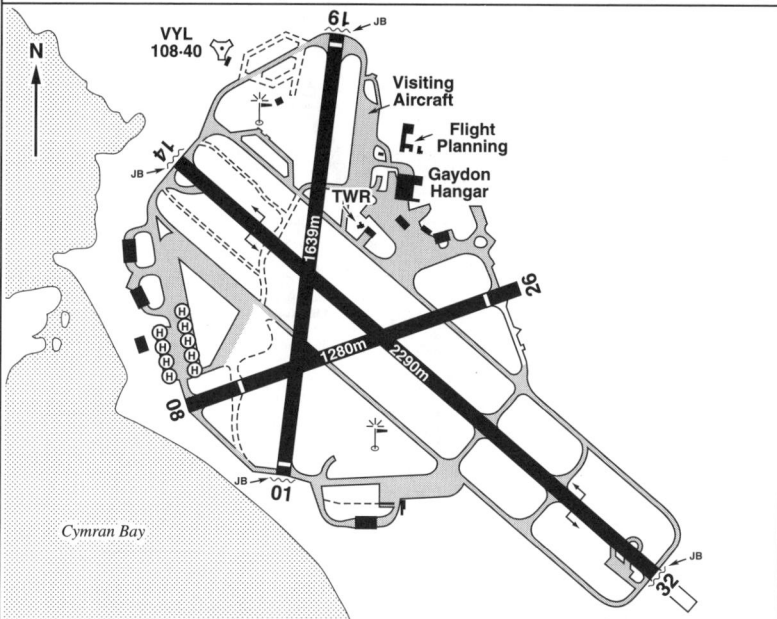

Rwy	Dim(m)	Surface	TORA(m)	LDA(m)	Lighting
14/32	2290x46	Asphalt	14-2290	14-2290	Ap Thr Rwy PAPI
			32-2290	32-2290	Ap Thr Rwy PAPI
01/19	1639x46	Asphalt	01-1572	01-1572	Thr Rwy PAPI
			19-1572	19-1572	Ap Thr Rwy PAPI
08/26	1280x46	Asphalt	08-1280	08-1066	Nil.
			26-1280	26-1158	Nil.
					IBn 'VY' Red

Op hrs: PPR	**ATZ active H24**
Landing Fee: MoD(RAF) Rates	**Customs:** 24 hrs PNR
Hangarage: Nil	**Maintenance:** Nil

Remarks: RAF Aerodrome. Flying Training School. High intensity fixed wing flying training in progress Mon-Fri, with regular helicopter movements within10 nm radius and possibility of simultaneous 'two runway' operations.

Arrester gear on Rwy 14/32 396 metres from each end.

Variable circuits, but RH on Rwys 19 and 32.

| **Fuel:** 100LL. Avtur. ¢. | **Tel:** 01407-762241 Ext 7299/7582 |

N53 09·97 W000 31·43	231 ft AMSL

| **WADDINGTON** | |

3·5 nm S of Lincoln.	OTR 113·90 210 35·3
	GAM 112·80 120 16·7

c/s Waddington Zone 127·35 (LARS/MATZ).   ATIS Tel: 01522-720271 Ext 7305.
TACAN 'WAD' 117·10 (on A/D). ILS Rwy 21 (208°M) 'WA' 110·50 (Rwy QFU 206°M).

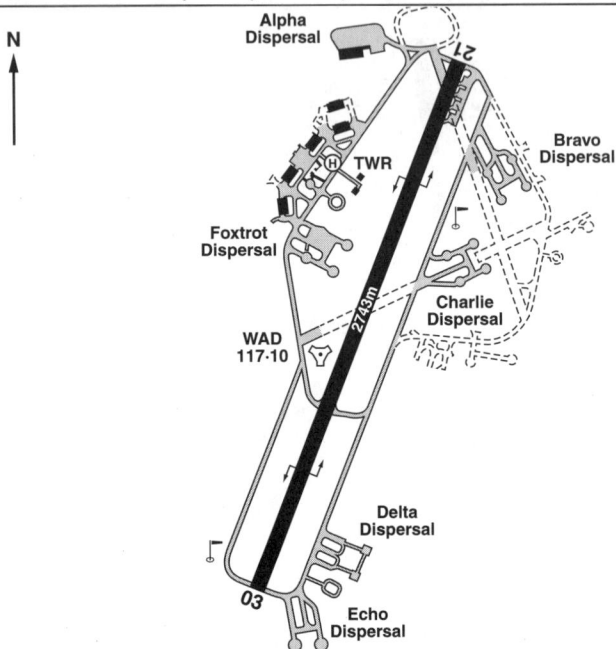

Rwy	Dim(m)	Surface	TORA(m)	LDA(m)	Lighting
03/21	2743x61	Asphalt	03-2743	03-2743	Ap Thr Rwy PAPI
			21-2743	21-2743	Ap Thr Rwy PAPI
					IBn 'WA' Red

Op hrs: PPR from Operations Ext 7301	**ATZ active H24**

Landing Fee: MoD(RAF)Rates	**Customs:** Nil.

Hangarage: Nil	**Maintenance:** Nil

Remarks: RAF Aerodrome, not normally available to civil aircraft.

Inbound aircraft to contact Waddington Zone at least 20 nm before MATZ boundary.

Public road crosses final approach to Rwy 21.

Arrester gear 610m from each end of runway.

Departures in sector 130°-220° not normally approved due Cranwell Operations.

Warning: Strong westerly winds can produce unexpected turbulance in final stages of approach to Rwy 21.

Fuel: 100LL, Avtur ¢.	**Tel:** 01522-720271 Ext 7451 - ATC.
	Ext 7301 - Ops.

1 DEC 00

N53 37·77 W001 15·55	**WALTON WOOD**	180 ft. AMSL
4·5 nm S of Pontefract.		GAM 112·80 338 24
		OTR 113·90 271 42

Walton Wood Radio 123·625 A/G.

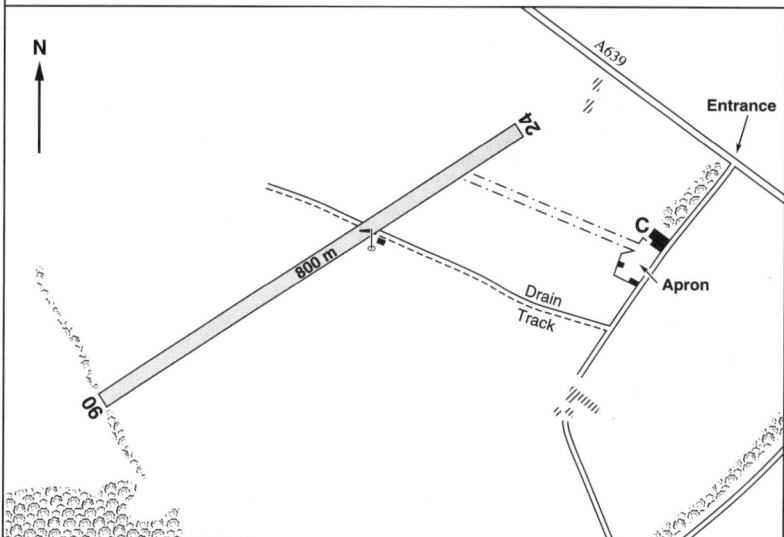

Rwy	Dim(m)	Surface	TORA(m)	LDA(m)	Lighting
06/24	800x16	Grass	Unlicensed		Nil

Op hrs: Strictly PPR. 0900-1800 or SS.

Landing Fee: On request. **Customs:** Nil

Hangarage: Limited **Maintenance:** Nil

Remarks: Operated by Heliscott Ltd, Walton Wood Airfield, Thorpe Audlin, Pontefract, W. Yorks, WF8 3HQ.
Unlicensed Airfield. Strictly PPR.
Airfield can be closed in Winter due to water logging.
Visiting aircraft welcome on prior permission and at pilot's own risk.
Circuits at 1000 ft aal, RH on 06, LH on 24.

Warnings: Power cables cross approach to Rwy 24.
Public footpath across the runway.

Taxi/Car Hire: By arrangement

Fuel: 100LL, Jet A1	**Tel:** 01977-621378
	Fax: 01977-620868

Robert Pooley ©

501

N53 44·70 W002 53·03	**WARTON**	54 ft AMSL

6 nm W of Preston.	**MCT 113·55 323 32**
	WAL 114·10 029 23

c/s Warton. APP/VDF/LARS 129·525. TWR 130·80. TACAN 'WTN' 113·20 (On A/D).
NDB 'WTN' 337·0 (258°M/0·6 nm to Thr Rwy 26). ILS/DME Rwy 26 'I WQ' 109·90.

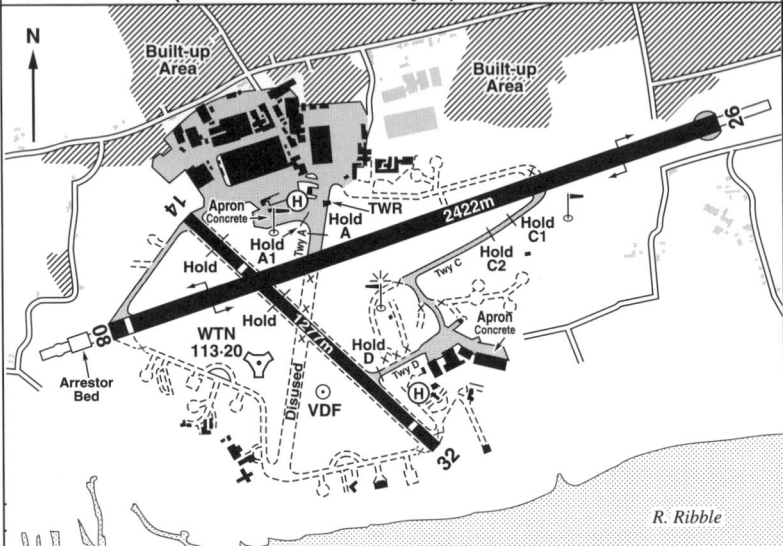

Rwy	Dim(m)	Surface	TORA(m)	LDA(m)	Lighting
08/26	2422x46	Asphalt	08-2422	08-2358	Ap Thr Rwy PAPI 2·83°
			26-2341	26-2341	Ap Thr Rwy PAPI 3°
14/32	1277x30	Asphalt	14-1051	14-891	Thr Rwy APAPI 3°
			32-969	32-861	Thr Rwy APAPI 3°

Op hrs: PPR. Mon-Fri 0730-1830	**ATZ active H24.**

Landing Fee: On application	**Customs:** By arrangement.
Hangarage: Nil	**Maintenance:** Nil

Remarks: Operated by British Aerospace, (Military Aircraft and Aerostructures)
Warton Aerodrome, Warton, Preston, Lancs PR4 1AX. PPR.
Not available to non radio aircraft. All circuits to the south of Rwy 08/26.

Red and white marker boards are positioned 35 m to the south of Rwy 08/26 for its
full length, 1000 ft apart.
Arrester gear on Rwy 08/26, 395m from end of full-width pavement. Cables are flush
with runway but pilots of light aircraft are advised to touch down after the cable housing.
To assist in identification of the threshold when visual manoeuvring (circling) 4 sodium
lights are visible on base leg and final approach (day only).

Marshaller must be present for all aircraft engine starts.
High visibility clothing must be worn on the apron at all times.

VRPs: Blackburn, Formby Point, Garstang and M6 Junction 26/M58.

Fuel: Jet A1.	**Tel:** 01772-633333 Switchboard.
	01772-852374 ATC. 852303 Civil Ops.
	Fax: 01772-634706.

N52 07·64 E000 57·36	**WATTISHAM**	284 ft AMSL
8·5 nm NW of Ipswich		**CLN 114·55 340 18·2**

Wattisham APP/RAD 125·80.   TWR 122·10.   RAD c/s Talkdown 123·30.
c/s Anglia Base/Wattisham Radio 125·80 A/G (Glider/SAR/Police ops outside A/D hrs).
TACAN 'WTM' 109·30 (On A/D).   ILS Rwy 23 (235°M) WT 111·10 (Rwy QFU 232°)

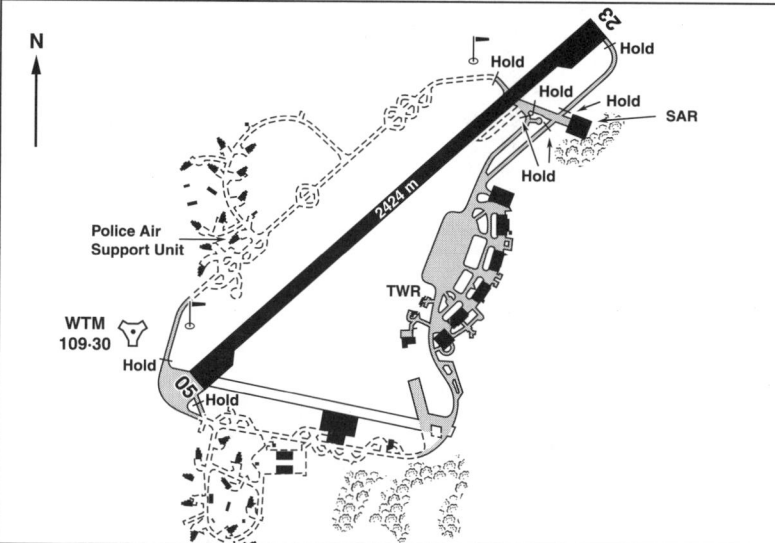

Rwy	Dim(m)	Surface	TORA(m)	LDA(m)	Lighting
05/23	2424x46	Asphalt	05-2424	05-2422	Ap Thr Rwy PAPI 3°
			23-2424	23-2283	Ap Thr Rwy PAPI 3°
					I Bn 'WT' Red

Op hrs: PPR. Mon-Fri 0800-1800. PPR through Ops.   **ATZ active H24.**
SAR and Police helicopter may scramble or recover at any time.

Landing Fee: Military (Army) Rates.   **Customs:** Nil

Remarks: Army Aerodrome. PPR through Operations.
Intensive helicopter activity. Variable circuits up to 1000' aal, no dead side.
Inbound aircraft to contact App at least 15 nm before MATZ boundary.
Telephone ATC Watch Supervisor for briefing prior to departure.
Glider and model aircraft flying outside of normal op hrs, especially at weekends.
Outside normal hours - Call App or Twr, if no reply, call A/G 'Wattisham Radio' for any
SAR activity status amd make blind calls inbound and outbound. If advised of glider
flying, call Glider A/G Station 'Anglia Base' and request gliders cease launching prior
to arrival and departure. Make blind calls as before.

Caution: 3 airfields in close proximity, Elmsett 3 nm S, Crowfield 3 nm NE and
Rattlesden 4 nm NW.
Possible Deer on airfield.   TV Mast 1234' amsl 9 nm NE of aerodrome.

Fuel: Avtur	**Tel:** 01449-728241/2 Ops/PPR; 728234 ATC

N52 11·53 W001 36·87   **WELLESBOURNE MOUNTFORD**   158 ft AMSL

3·5 nm E of Stratford-upon-Avon.

HON 113·65 175 10
DTY 116·40 278 18·5

c/s Wellesbourne Information 124·025 AFIS.

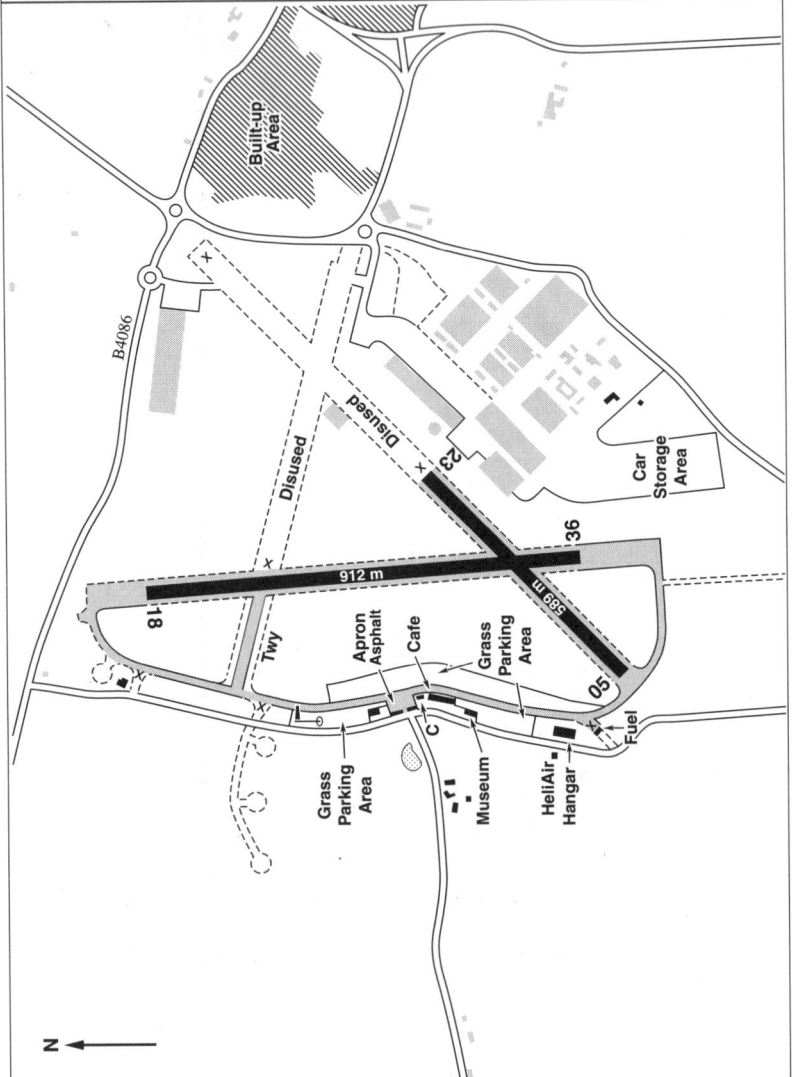

Built-up Area

B4086

Disused

Disused

23

36

912 m

689 m

18

05

Car Storage Area

Twy

Apron Asphalt

Cafe

Grass Parking Area

C

Museum

HeliAir Hangar

Fuel

Grass Parking Area

N ←

Robert Pooley ©

N52 11·53 W001 36·87		**WELLESBOURNE MOUNTFORD**			158 ft AMSL
Rwy	**Dim(m)**	**Surface**	**TORA(m)**	**LDA(m)**	**Lighting**
18/36	912x23	Asphalt	18-912 †	18-912	Thr Rwy APAPI 3°
			36-912 †	36-912	Thr Rwy APAPI 4·25°
05/23	589x18	Asphalt	05-589	05-589	Nil.
			23-589	23-589	Nil.
					ABn Gn

† Unlicensed starter extension: Rwy 18 -126 m; Rwy 36 - 178 m, available.

Op hrs: WINTER: Mon-Fri 0900-SS or 1730 whichever is earlier (up to 2000 by arrangement),   Sat & Sun 0900-1800.
SUMMER: 0900-1730, Sat, Sun & PHs 0800-2000 (Unlicensed 1730-2000).

Landing Fee: Singles £10.00, Twins £15.00. Helicopters £5.00.
Overnight Parking: £5.00.

Hangarage: Limited.   **Customs:** EU 4 hrs, non EU 24hrs PNR.

Maintenance: Wellesbourne Aircraft Maintenance, Tel: 01789-470978

Remarks: Operated by Radarmoor Ltd., Aviation House, Wellesbourne Aerodrome, Stratford-upon-Avon, Warwickshire CV35 9EU.

Aerodrome situated 3 nm from southern boundary of Birmingham CTA (base 1500') and below CTA (base 3500').

Radar assistance by Birmingham App on 118·05 is normally available in emergency.

Pilots are requested to contact Wellesbourne at least 10 minutes before ETA Wellesbourne.

Out of hours movements and refuelling by prior arrangement.

Non radio aircraft not accepted.

On Sat & PHs Rwy 05/23 will not be available.

Variable circuits at 1,000 ft (QFE). Flying over WELLESBOURNE village (1 nm E of A/D) strictly prohibited below 2000 ft.

Helicopter circuits West of runways at 800 ft QNH.

Areas between runways under cultivation. Taxi with extreme caution on grass areas.

Aircraft parking on grass section and disused runway 10/28, short stay by hangar.

Noise Abatement – Rwy 36 Departures: After departure, turn right onto a track of 030° to 1000 ft QFE before turning crosswind.

Do not fly over LOXLEY(1·5 nm SW) or CHARLECOTE (1 nm North) on departure.

Hill 262 ft aal, 1·8 nm SSW and 212 ft aal, 1·5 nm South.

Museum: Open Sundays and Public holidays.

Restaurant: Touchdown Inn, Tel: 01789-470575.

Hotel: Charlecote Pheasant (1 mile) 01789-470333.

Car Hire: Kendricks, Tel: 01789-842929.

Taxis: Run-a-bout Tel: 01789- 470062; Main Taxis Tel: 01789-414514.

Fuel: 100LL, Jet A1. Mastercard, Eurocard, Diners, Access, Visa	**Tel:** 01789-842007 Airfield. 01789-842000 Twr. **Fax:** 01789- 470465 Web: www.wellesbourneairfield.com

Robert Pooley ©

WELSHPOOL

N52 37·75 W003 09·15   233 ft AMSL

2 nm S of Welshpool.

WAL 114·10 188 46. HON 113·65 293 56·5
BCN 117·45 010 56. RNR 374·0 011 24

c/s Welshpool Radio 123·25

* NDB 'WPL' 323·0 (On A/D).   DME 'WPL' 115·95 (On A/D)

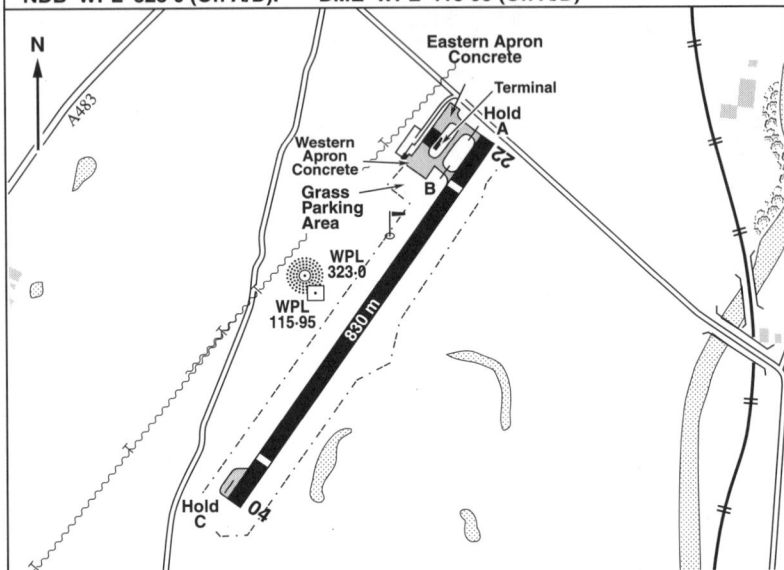

Rwy	Dim(m)	Surface	TORA(m)	LDA(m)	Lighting
04/22	830x18	Asphalt	04-812	04-722	† Rwy
			22-820	22-709	† Rwy

† Available only to specified home based operators.

Op hrs: PPR. 0900-1700 daily.

Landing Fee: Singles £7.00; Twins £12.00	Customs: 12 hrs PNR
Hangarage: Available	**Maintenance:** Available

Remarks: Operated by Pool Aviation Ltd. Montgomeryshire/Welshpool Aerodrome, Welshpool, Powys SY21 8SG.

Not available at night to aircraft required to use a licensed aerodrome.

No solo flying for the purpose of a licence shall take place when the visibility at the aerodrome is less than 8 km or the cloud base is less than 2500 ft aal.

The aerodrome is located in the River Severn Valley with high ground on each side of the valley. Pilots are advised not to descend below safety height until on the final approach after having positively identified the runway.

Circuits LH at 1500' aal.

* Warning NDB 'WPL' — Poor performance may be experienced due to terrain effect.

High Ground - 400' aal, 633' amsl 1600 m to W, and 250' aal, 483' amsl 1500 m to E.

Fuel: 100LL, Jet A1.	Tel: 01938-555062. Fax: 01938-555487

| N54 51·07 W004 56·87 | **WEST FREUGH** | 57 ft AMSL |

| 4 nm SE of Stranraer | **TRN** 117·50 199 28·3 |
| | **BEL** 117·20 084 45·8 |

West Freugh RAD/APP 130·05.   TWR 122·55.   RAD c/s Talkdown 130·725.
NDB 'WFR' 339·0 (On A/D).

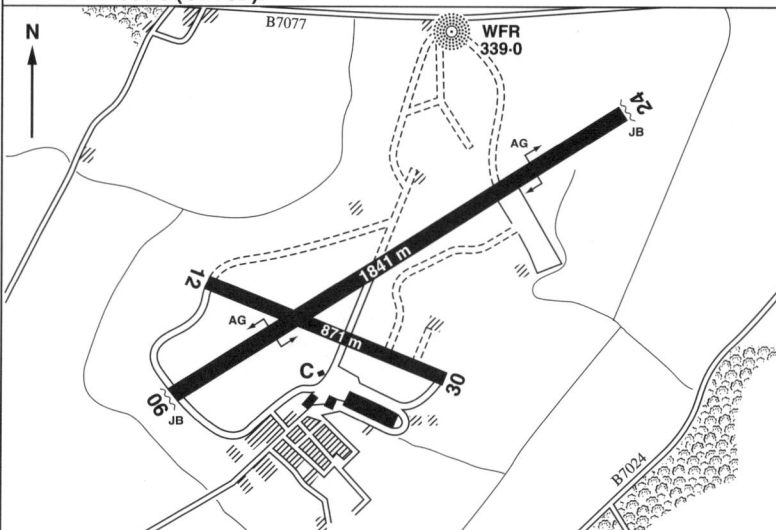

Rwy	Dim(m)	Surface	TORA(m)	LDA(m)	Lighting
06/24	1841x41	Asphalt/	06-1841	06-1841	Ap Thr PAPI 3·5°
		Concrete	24-1841	24-1841	Ap Thr PAPI 3·5°
12/30	871x23	Asphalt	12-871	12-871	Nil.
			30-871	30-871	Nil.

Op hrs: PPR 24 hrs. Mon-Thu 0845-1200 & 1300-1615 or SS if earlier;
Fri 0845-1200 & 1300-1545.   **ATZ H24**

| **Landing Fee:** On request. | **Customs:** On request. |

| **Hangarage:** By arrangement. | **Maintenance:** Nil |

Remarks: MoD (PE) Aerodrome. PPR – minimum of 24 hours notice preferred.
Movements accepted outside of operating hours subject to PPR.
Operating hours or ATC services subject to change at short notice.
Aerodrome is located within Danger Areas D402A/B/C and D403/403A, it is
therefore essential that inbound aircraft contact APP at 25 nm range.
Danger Area information available from ATC during ATC operating hours.
No movements to take place 0815-0845 Mon-Fri. No night flying facilities.
Avoid overflying Stranraer below 2000 ft.
All circuits to the north of runway at 1000 ft QFE.
Caution: Avoid overflying D403A at all times. Risk of bird strike.

| **Fuel:** 100LL - On request. | **Tel:** 01776-888792 PPR, 888791 ATC |
| Jet A1 - with PPR. | 01776-888800 Met. **Fax:** 01776-820600 |

N5113·83 W00243·42	**WESTBURY-SUB-MENDIP**	90 ft AMSL

3 nm WNW of Wells, Somerset. **BCN 117·45 152 36**
9 nm S of Bristol Airport.

No Radio. Bristol App 128·55 (LARS). Yeovilton App 127·35 (LARS).

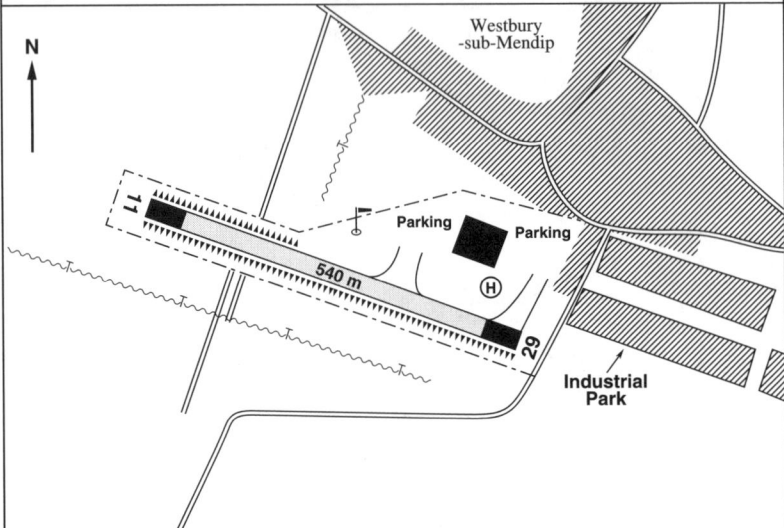

Rwy	Dim(m)	Surface	TORA(m)	LDA(m)	Lighting
11/29	540x20	Grass	Unlicensed		Nil.

Sharp DOWN gradient extending for 30 m at 120 m from Rwy 11 threshold.

Op hrs: PPR. SR–SS.

Landing Fee: On application.   **Customs:** Nil.   **Hangarage:** Nil.

Maintenance: Fixed & Rotary Wing (CAA Approved) by Somerset Helicopters Ltd.

Remarks: Operated by John Lloyd & Son, Westbury-sub-Mendip, Somerset.
Unlicensed airfield situated 4 nm south of Bristol CTR/CTA.
Landing strip is located on site of disused railway.
Light aircraft and helicopters welcome on prior permission and at pilot's own risk.
Circuits RH on 11, LH on 29.
Windsock displayed on north side near hangar.
Power cables on south side.

Car Hire & Accommodation: Available by arrangement.

Fuel: Nil.	**Tel:** 01749-870647

Robert Pooley ©

N59 21·07 W002 57·00	**WESTRAY**	29 ft AMSL

24 nm N of Kirkwall Airport.	WIK 113·60 013 53·7
	KWL 108·60 004 23·5

No Radio. Recommend contact Kirkwall APP 118·30.

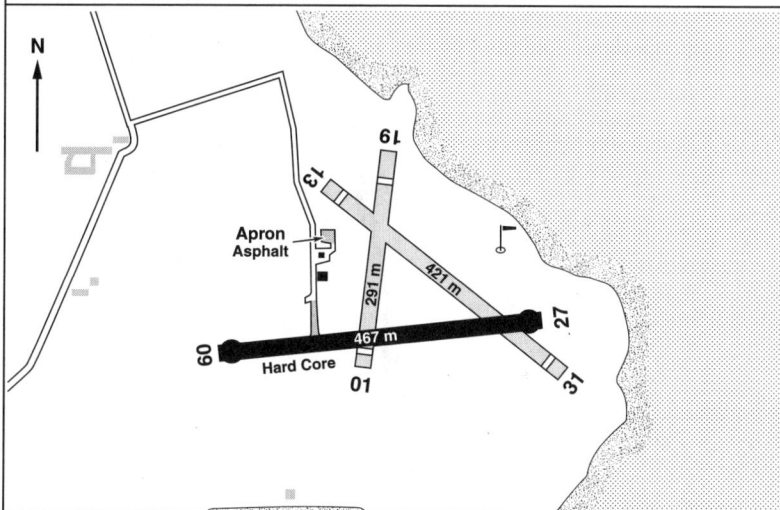

Rwy	Dim(m)	Surface	TORA(m)	LDA(m)	Lighting
09/27	467x18	Hard Core	09-467	09-467	Nil.
			27-467	27-467	Nil.
13/31	421x18	Grass	13-394	13-359	Nil.
			31-421	31-359	Nil.
01/19	291x18	Grass	01-261	01-235	Nil.
			19-291	19-218	Nil.

Op hrs: PPR

Landing Fee: Nil. If fire cover is required, then £17.24 + VAT. **Customs:** Nil

Hangarage: Nil **Maintenance:** Nil

Remarks: Licensed aerodrome (day use only) operated by Orkney Islands Council, School Place, Kirkwall, Orkney KW15 1NY.

Visiting aircraft accepted on prior permission and at pilot's own risk. In first instance, contact Orkney Islands Council, Tel: 01856-873535 Ext 2305.

Scheduled Air Services Monday to Saturday.

High ground 528' aal 557' amsl 202°/4 nm.

Warnings: Poor drainage, may be patches of mud and/or standing water after periods of heavy or continous rainfall on Rwy 01/19 and 13/31.

Rwy 09/27 - Graded Hard Core runway generally unsuitable for light aircraft with low ground /propeller clearance due to unstabilised surface.

Accommodation/Restaurant: B&B and Two Hotels, contact the Tourist Board.

Car Hire: Logi Tel: 01857-677220.

Fuel: Nil	**Tel:** 01856-873535 Council. **Fax:** 01856-876094 Council

Robert Pooley ©

N60 22·62 W000 55·53	**WHALSAY**	100 ft AMSL
Shetland Islands.		**SUM 117·35 027 32**

No Radio.
Contact Sumburgh APP 123·15.

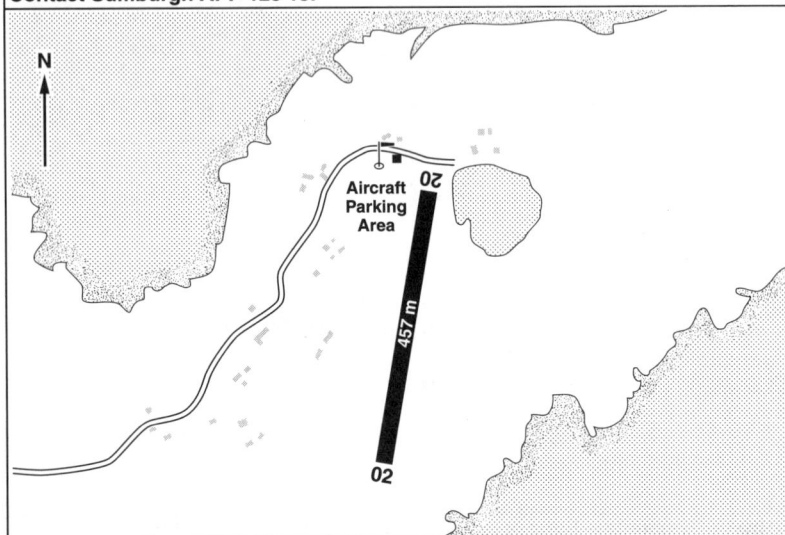

Rwy	Dim(m)	Surface	TORA(m)	LDA(m)	Lighting
02/20	457x18	Asphalt	Unlicensed		Nil

Op hrs: PPR. SR–SS.

Landing Fee: On application	**Customs:** Nil
Hangarage: Nil	**Maintenance:** Nil

Remarks: Operated by Whalsay Development Committee, Whalsay Aerodrome, Skaw, Whalsay, Shetland Islands.

Daylight hours only, subject to PPR

Hill 299' aal 399'amsl, 222°M/3·4 nm.

Fuel: Nil	**Tel:** 01806-566449.

N51 30·05 W000 46·47	**WHITE WALTHAM**	130 ft AMSL

2 nm SW of Maidenhead.	CPT 114·35 094 16·7. BNN 113·75 216 16
	LON 113·60 278 11·8. WOD 352·0 061 4·8

c/s Waltham Radio 122·60 A/G. Occasionally AFIS c/s Information.

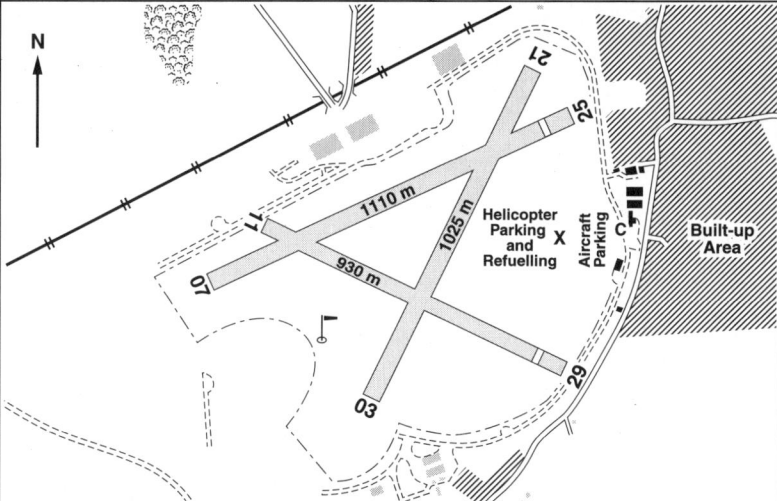

Rwy	Dim(m)	Surface	TORA(m)	LDA(m)	Lighting
03/21	1025x45	Grass	03-1025	03-1025	Nil.
			21-1025	21-1025	Nil.
07/25	1110x45	Grass	07-1110	07-1110	Nil.
			25-1110	25-1045	Nil.
11/29	930x30	Grass	11-930	11-930	Nil.
			29-930	29-867	Nil.

Op hrs: WINTER: 0800-SS+30.   SUMMER: 0800-2000, not licensed 2000-SS+30.

Landing Fee: Private: SE £7.50, Twin £15; Commercial: Single/Twin £25.   (Incl VAT)
Free with fuel uplift - SE 50 litres; Twin 100 litres. O/Night Parking SE £6; Twin £10. (Incl VAT)

Maintenance : JAR 145 available.   **Hangarage:** Limited   **Customs:** 4 hrs PNR.

Remarks: Operated by White Waltham Aerodrome Ltd. Non-radio aircraft require
telephone briefing from Operations prior to each flight. Helicopters 1hr PPR by phone.
Grass runways marked with centre-line marking and runway designators.
Circuits at 800' QFE, variable direction. Join overhead at 1300' QFE. No overhead
departures. No helicopter circuits/Hover practice.
Strict Noise Abatement in force, phone for details; avoid overflying residential areas
and local villages.
All aircraft using White Waltham airfield must carry third party insurance cover.
Caution. Vehicles use the perimeter track which bounds the manoeuvring area to the
north and east of the airfield. Public road runs NE/SW 40m from threshold of Rwy 29.
Reporting Points are shown on White Waltham Area Chart – see overleaf.
Restaurant: Licensed restaurant and Residential Club facilities available.
Car Hire & Taxis: Arranged by West London Aero Club.

Fuel: 100LL & Jet A1	**Tel:** 01628 - 823272/3/4. **Fax:** 01628 - 826070.
	Website: www.wlac.co.uk

Robert Pooley ©

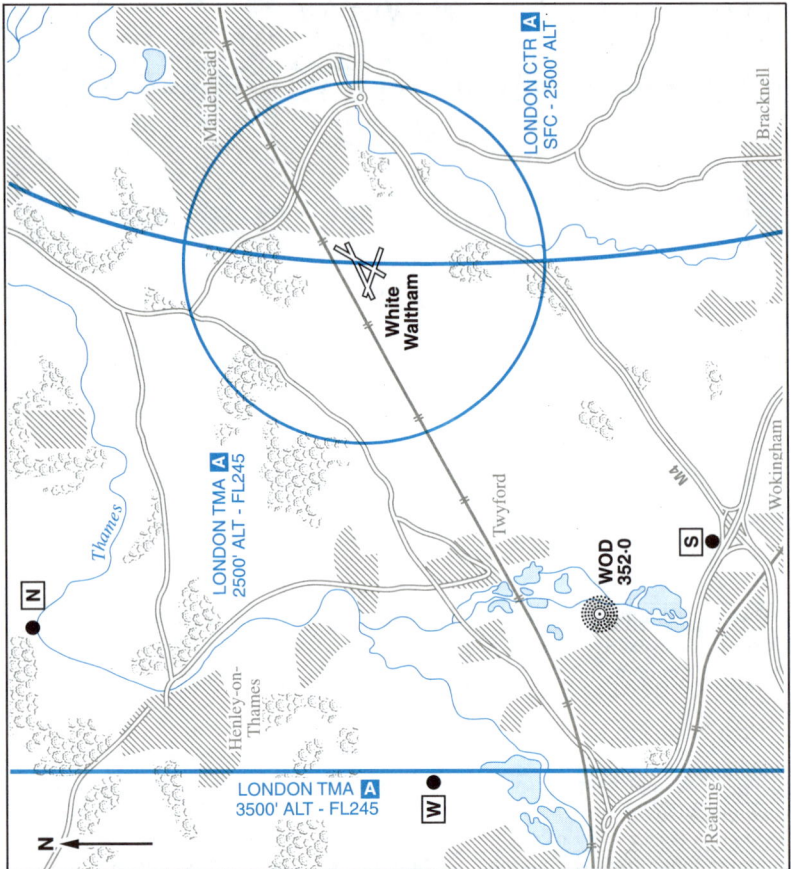

LONDON CTR Ⓐ
SFC - 2500' ALT

Maidenhead

Bracknell

White
Waltham

LONDON TMA Ⓐ
2500' ALT - FL245

Thames

Twyford

WOD
352-0

Ⓢ

M4

Wokingham

Ⓝ

Henley-on-
Thames

LONDON TMA Ⓐ
3500' ALT - FL245

Ⓦ

Reading

N ⟵

Although the eastern part of the ATZ lies within the London CTR, flights within the ATZ may take place without compliance with IFR requirements subject to the following conditions:

1. Aircraft to remain below cloud and in sight of the ground.

2. Maximum altitudes: 1,500 ft QNH, provided that aircraft can remain at least 500 ft below cloud; otherwise 1,000 ft QNH.

3. Minimum flight visibility 3 km.

Note. Pilots of aircraft flying in the local flying area are responsible for providing their own separation from other traffic operating in the relevant airspace.

Inbound aircraft are to report their position and altitude in relation to one of the following Reporting Points:

From North — **NOVEMBER** – bend in river north of HENLEY.

From West — **WHISKEY** – North of gravel pits by gasometers in READING.

From South — **SIERRA** – Motorway junction north of WOKINGHAM (M4/A329).

Robert Pooley ©

N58 27·40 W003 05·85 — 125 ft AMSL

1 nm N of Wick. — KWL 108·60 201 31

APP/TWR 119.70. NDB 'WIK' 344·0 (314°M/0·85 nm to Thr 31).
VOR/DME 'WIK' 113·60 (On A/D).

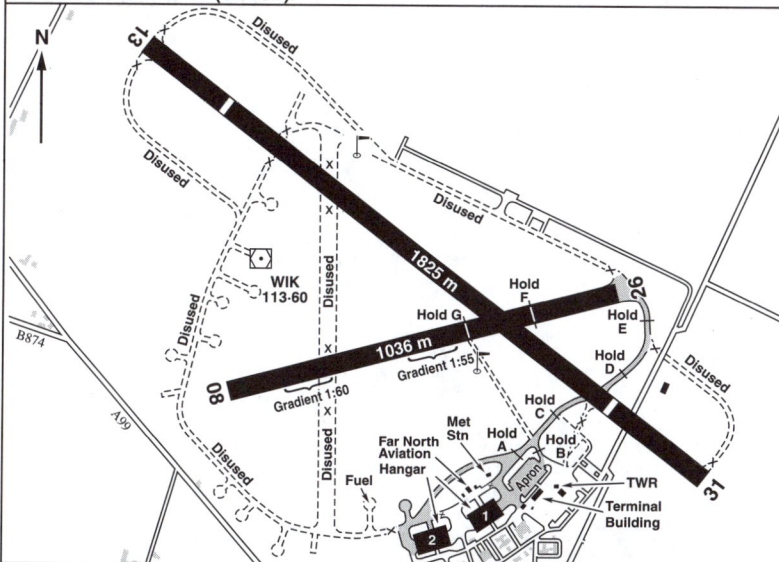

Rwy	Dim(m)	Surface	TORA(m)	LDA(m)	Lighting
08/26	1036x45	Asphalt	08-1036	08-1036	Thr Rwy * APAPI 4°
			26-1036	26-1036	Thr Rwy * APAPI 4°
13/31	1825x45	Asphalt	13-1740	13-1400	Ap Thr Rwy PAPI 3°
			31-1708	31-1398	Ap Thr Rwy PAPI 3°

Taxiway Blue Edge Lights from Rwy 13/31 to Apron — * Portable,15 min PNR

Op hrs: PPR. Mon-Fri 0745-1830, Sat 0900-1045 & 1115-1500.

Landing Fee: Highlands & Islands Airports Rates.

Hangarage: Through Far North Aviation. **Maintenance:** Nil **Customs:** On request

Remarks: Operated by Highlands & Islands Airports Ltd. Use of aerodrome PPR.

Warnings: Rwy 08/26 - variable UP gradient on Rwy 08 as shown on A/D plan above. No ground signals except light signals.

Deer hazard, particularly at dawn and dusk.

VRPs: Castletown Aerodrome (Disused), Duncansby Head Lighthouse, Keiss Village, Loch Watten, Lybster Village and Thrumster Masts.

Restaurant: Buffet facilities - Mon-Fri 0900-1700; Sat 1045-1315.

Accommodation/Taxis: By arrangement with Far North Aviation.

Car Hire: Practical Car Hire Tel: 01955-604125.

Fuel:100LL, Jet A1. Aval outside A/D hrs. (Far North Aviation) All major cards. — **Tel:** 01955-602215 HIAL A/D Operator / 01955-602201 Far North Aviation (H24) / **Fax:** 01955-604447 HIAL A/D Operator

Robert Pooley ©

N53 19·00 W000 20·98	**WICKENBY (Lincoln)**	63 ft AMSL

8 nm NE of Lincoln.	OTR 113·90 206 24·6
	GAM 112·80 090 21·5

c/s Wickenby Radio 122·45 A/G. Waddington Radar 127·35 (LARS/MATZ).

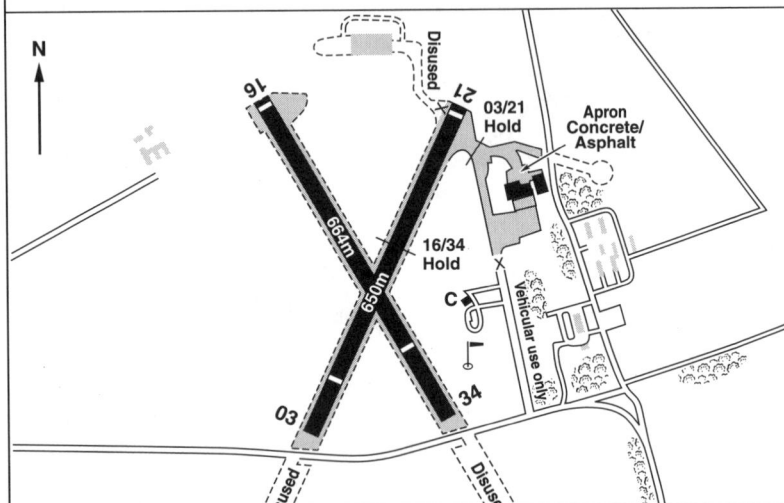

Rwy	Dim(m)	Surface	TORA(m)	LDA(m)	Lighting
03/21	650x18	Concrete	03-635	03-530	Nil.
			21-635	21-620	Thr Rwy LITAS 3·5°
16/34	664x18	Concrete	16-642	16-630	Nil.
			34-649	34-500	Nil.
					IBn 'WN' Gn

Op hrs: PPR. 0900 - SS. Night flying by arrangement.

Landing Fee: Singles £5.00 + VAT; Twins £10.00 + VAT.

Hangarage: Available.   **Customs:** May be available on request 24 hrs PNR.

Maintenance: Nil.

Remarks: Operated by Lincoln Aviation Ltd., The old Control Tower, Wickenby Airfield, Langworth, Lincoln LN3 5AX.

The runways in use are the two sections North of the public road running E/W across the aerodrome. HGVs cross Rwy 21 thld to far Hangar.

The runways to the south of the public road are not usable — see diagram above.

Inbound aircraft are requested to contact Waddington Radar 127·35.

Circuits at 1000 ft QFE, all left hand. Do not overfly local villages.

Flights within the ATZ above 1500 ft aal is subject to clearance from Waddington Radar 127·35.

High ground 134' aal 197' amsl 054°/3·6 nm.

Restaurant: Club facilities.

Car Hire: By arrangement with Lincoln Aviation Ltd.

Fuel: 100LL	**Tel/Fax:** 01673-885886

N52 31·05 W002 15·58	**WOLVERHAMPTON**	293 ft AMSL
5nm SE of Bridgnorth.		**HON 113·65 300 24**

c/s Wolverhampton Information 123·00 FIS.
NDB 'WBA' 356·0 (On A/D) Nav. only.

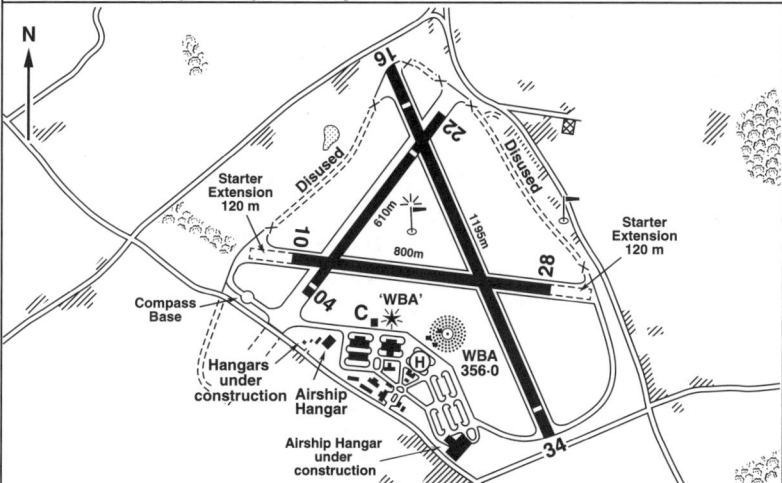

Rwy	Dim(m)	Surface	TORA(m)	LDA(m)	Lighting
04/22	610x18	Asphalt	04-610	04-610	Nil.
			22-610	22-550	Nil.
10/28	800x23	Asphalt	10-800	10-800	Thr Rwy APAPI 4°
			28-800	28-800	Thr Rwy APAPI 4°
16/34	1195x23	Asphalt	16-1104	16-1000	Rwy* LITAS 4·25°
			† 34-1082	34-1000	Rwy*

† Rwy 34 not licensed for night use.   * Portable lighting.   I Bn 'HG' Gn

Op hrs: PPR. 0900-1730 or SS and by arrangement.
Note: Surcharge will be levied against a/c landing out of hrs without prior permission.

Landing Fee: Singles £13/15 (£10/12 training flights); Twins £ POA (£25 training flights);
Helis £13 (free with fuel uplift). Fixed Wing half price landing fee with fuel uplift.

Customs: EU - 4hrs PNR; Non EU - 24 hrs PNR. Customs Information must be received during published hours by Fax.

Hangarage: Available.   **Maintenance:** Available.

Remarks: Operated by Bobbington Estates Ltd. Strictly PPR to all a/c. Jet a/c accepted.
Rwy 16/34 closed to all traffic on Bank Holidays, and also closed on Sats during Nov and Dec. On these days non radio a/c will not be accepted. A/D not available to microlight types. Night flying Tue/Thu until 2130, Nov, Dec & Jan.
Due helicopters operating right hand circuits at 800 ft QFE, joining aircraft are not to descend below1300 ft QFE on deadside.
Adjacent to control tower, taxiway semi-width restricted to 13 m on northside and 14·5 m on southside. Pilots are responsible for their passengers whilst airside.
A/D details also on Talking Pages – call Talking Pages FREE on 0800 600 900.

Restaurant: Club/Bar facilities with light refreshments, 09-1700 (until 2130 Night flying).

Car Hire: Avis   Tel/Fax: 01902- 25533.

Fuel: 100LL, Jet A1 with anti-icing. Pressure & Rotors running refuelling available.	Tel: 01384-221378 ATC; 221350 Admin. Fax: 01384-221514 ATC; 221328 Admin. Website: wolverhamptonbusinessairport.co.uk

Robert Pooley ©

N54 14·02 W000 58·13	**WOMBLETON**	120 ft AMSL

2·5 nm SW of Kirkbymoorside.   **NEW 114·25 152 55. OTR 113·90 316 45**

17 nm NNE York.   **POL 112·10 054 50**

No Radio. Recommend contact Leeming APP 127·75

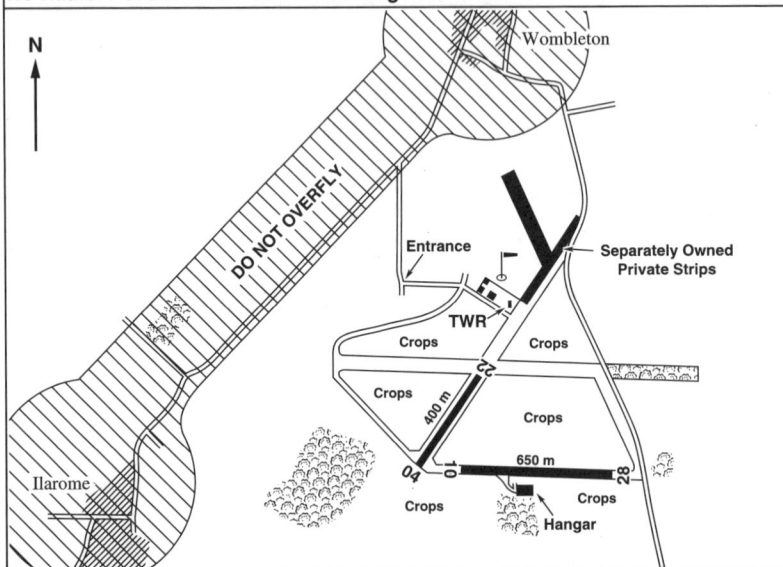

Rwy	Dim(m)	Surface	TORA(m)	LDA(m)	Lighting
04/22	400x10	Concrete	Unlicensed		Nil
10/28	650x15	Asphalt	Unlicensed		Nil

Op hrs: Strictly PPR.

Landing Fee: Private – Nil; Commercial on application.   **Customs:** Nil

Hangarage: Available   **Maintenance:** Limited

Remarks: Unlicensed airfield operated by Windsports Centre Ltd. Careful, noise conscious pilots very welcome on prior permission, at their own risk. Avoid overflying any habitation within 1 nm of the airfield and within the areas identified above.

Circuits at 1000', RH on 04 & 10; Microlights at 500', RH on 04 & 28.

The preferred runway is 10/28. Visiting aircraft park near Tower. Windsock on Tower. All pilots are required to enter their flight details in the airfield log.

Warnings:
- Some surfaces on the airfield are rough with the presence of loose stones.
- Vehicles, people, machinery, model aircraft and animals may be encountered.
- Aircraft may be operating from the two separately owned private airstrips on the northern side of the airfield.
- Kirkbymoorside Aerodrome 1·6 nm to the NE.
- 66 ft trees 200 m from threshold of Rwy 10.
- Farm, public road and 16 ft trees on approach to Rwy 28.

Fuel: Nil	**Tel/Fax:** 01751-432356.

Robert Pooley ©

N53 34·89 W003 03·33	**WOODVALE**	37 ft AMSL
4·5 nm SSW of Southport.		WAL 114·10 021 11·7
		MCT 113·55 302 31·4

Woodvale APP 121·00. TWR 119·75.

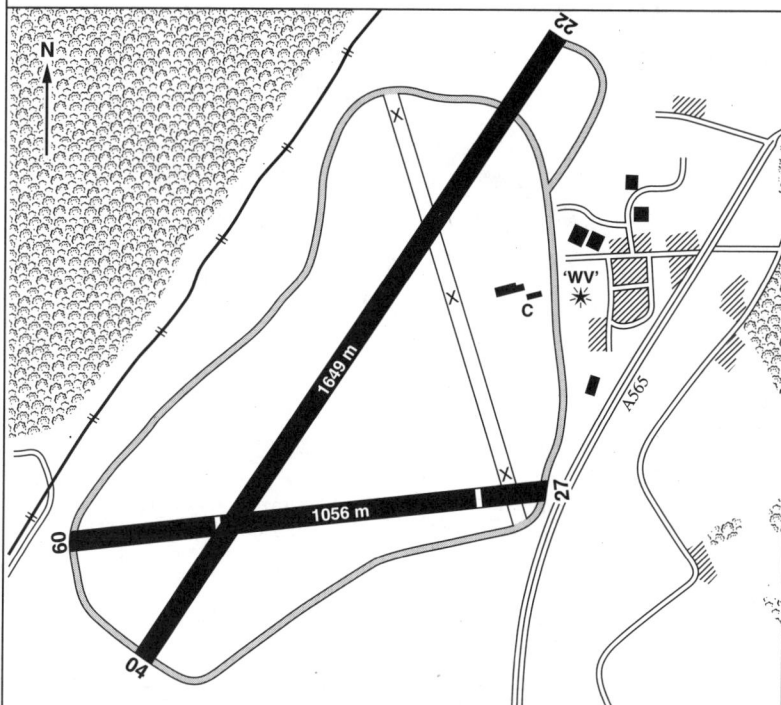

Rwy	Dim(m)	Surface	TORA(m)	LDA(m)	Lighting
04/22	1649x46	Asphalt	04-1649	04-1644	Nil
			22-1649	22-1644	Nil
09/27	1056x46	Asphalt	09-1056	09-710	Nil
			27-1056	27-918	Nil

Op hrs: PPR by telephone. Tue-Sun 0800-1800 or SS.

Landing Fee: MoD(RAF) Rates	**Customs:** Nil
Hangarage: Nil.	**Maintenance:** Nil.

Remarks: RAF Aerodrome operated by Serco Aerospace for the RAF. PPR by telephone.
Light aircraft activity outside published Op hrs. Police Helicopter activity H24.
Circuits at 800' QFE, LH on 04 and 09, RH on 22 and 27. Join at 1800'
Flight Plans to be sent by Fax to: 01704-834805.
Caution: Considerable risk of bird strike.

Fuel: Nil.	**Tel:**	01704-872287 Ext 7243.

Robert Pooley ©

517

| N51 36·70 W000 48·48 | **WYCOMBE AIR PARK (Booker)** | 520 ft AMSL |

2·5nm SW of High Wycombe.

BNN 113·75 239 11·8

CPT 114·35 070 17

c/s Wycombe. **TWR 126·55.**   **GND 121·775.**

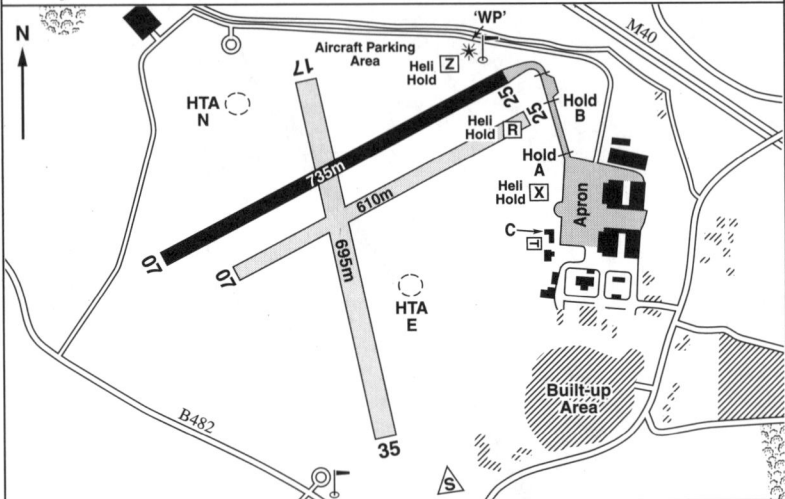

Rwy	Dim(m)	Surface	TORA(m)	LDA(m)	Lighting	
07/25	735x23	Asphalt	07-735	07-735	Thr Rwy LITAS 4°	
			25-735	25-735	Thr Rwy LITAS 4°	
07/25	610x23	Grass	07-610	07-610	Nil.	
			25-610	25-610	Nil.	
17/35	695x30	Grass	17-695	17-695	Nil.	
			35-695	35-695	Nil.	IBn 'WP' Gn

Op hrs: PPR. 0900-1730 daily, and ¢.

Landing Fee: Minimum charge £12.00 (incl VAT)   **Customs:** PNR

Hangarage: Limited   **Maintenance:** Fixed wing & helicopter available

Remarks: Operated by Airways Aero Associations Ltd. PPR essential.
Strict noise abatement procedures in force for all runways.
Caution. Intensive glider launching. Gliders will be flying a circuit opposite to that in use by powered aircraft. Variable circuits. Circuit Procedures - See pages 519/520.
Joining aircraft are to position to overfly the airfield at 1200 ft QFE, on the runway QDM. When overhead the midpoint of the runway in use, turn in the direction of the circuit and level at circuit height 1000 ft QFE on the crosswind leg prior to turning downwind.
Helicopter circuit 750 ft inside fixed wing circuit. Grass areas liable to waterlogging. Fixed wing Holds A & B, Heli Holds R, X & Z, Heli Aiming Point S, and Helicopter Training Areas (HTA) N & E as shown above.
Restaurant: Licensed Restaurant (7 days a week),Tel: 01494-525188.

Car Hire: National Tel: 01494-527853.

| **Fuel:** 100LL, Jet A1 by arrangement. | **Tel:** 01494-529 261 or 523 426.
Fax: 01494-461 237 Office.
Fax: 01494-438 657 ATC. |

WYCOMBE AIR PARK (Booker) – CIRCUIT PROCEDURES

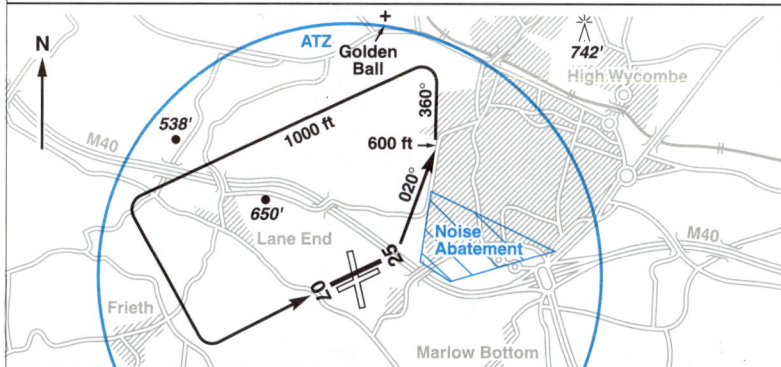

1. As soon **as Safely** possible, before reaching the M40 (e.g at the windsock), turn left to maintain a track of 020°M. Upon reaching 600' aal, turn crosswind to track 360°M and maintain to circuit height. **Warning:** Close proximity of helicopters during initial climb.
2. Practice Engine Failures after take-off are forbidden.
3. If remaining in the circuit, commence turn downwind to remain inside the ATZ following the published downwind track for 07/25. **Do not overfly Lane End or Frieth whilst on downwind leg.**
4. The **preferred base leg** is to **route between Lane End and Frieth (Track 160°M).** If extending the downwind leg (e.g for separation purposes, etc) is unavoidable, then the descent on base leg should be delayed commensurate with the distance out.
5. After landing, vacate right and taxy between the grass and hard runways, unless otherwise directed, as for Rwy 25 procedures. Do **not** roll to the end of Rwy 07 without permission.

Rwy 25 Hard – Right Hand Circuit

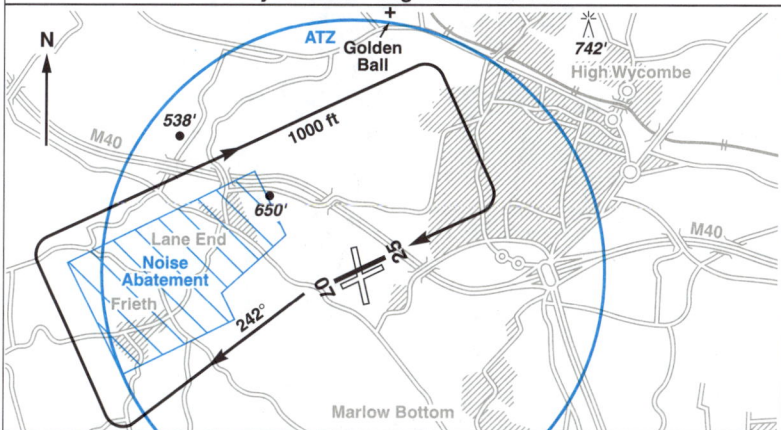

1. **Climb out** when clear of the airfield boundary - Track of 242°M until abeam Rockwell End.
2. **Crosswind -** Track 332°M towards the Stokenchurch Mast until abeam Fingest, then turn downwind or depart the circuit.
3. After landing, vacate left and taxy between the grass and the hard runways unless otherwise directed. Stop short of hard taxiway at hold **Bravo** and request permission to cross both the active 25 grass runway and the glider landing area.

Robert Pooley ©

519

1 DEC 00

WYCOMBE AIR PARK (Booker) – CIRCUIT PROCEDURES

Rwy 17 – Left Hand Circuit

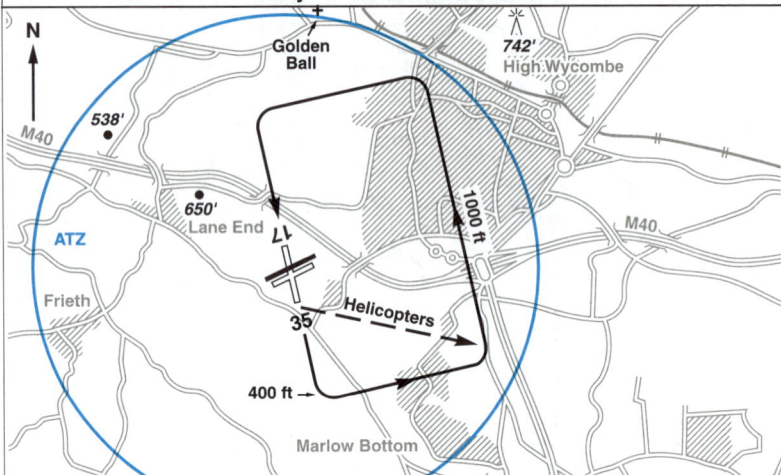

1. Turn crosswind at 400 ft aal.
2. **WARNING:** Close proximity of Helicopters during climbout.
3. After landing, vacate left and taxy parallel to Rwy 35 to intersect Rwy 07 grass.
Taxy down Rwy 07 Grass to intersect hard twy to the apron. (ATC may route aircraft direct).

Rwy 35 – Right Hand Circuit

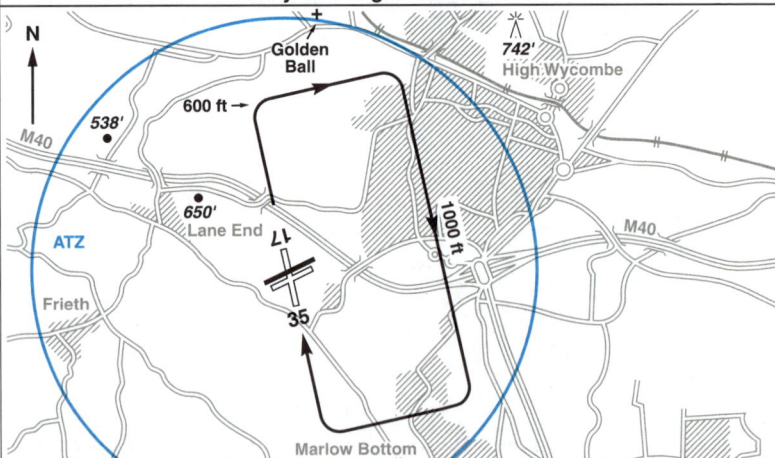

1. Turn crosswind at 600 ft aal.
2. After landing, vacate right and taxy parallel to Rwy 35 to intersect Rwy 07 grass. Taxy down 07 Grass to intersect hard taxiway to the apron. (ATC may route aircraft direct).

N52 21·43 W000 06·47	**WYTON**	135 ft. AMSL
3 nm NE of Huntingdon.	BKY 116·25 349 23. CFD 116·50 051 25·5	

Wyton APP 134·05. TWR/GND 122·10. VDF 134·05

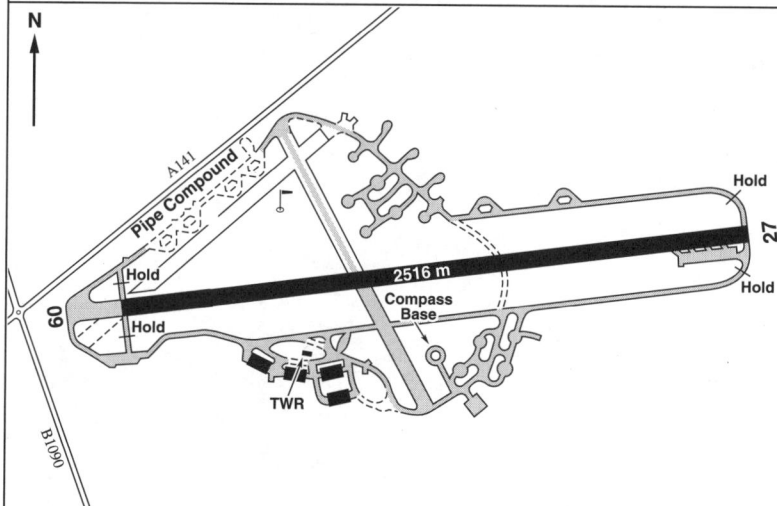

Rwy	Dim(m)	Surface	TORA(m)	LDA(m)	Lighting
09/27	2516x61	Asphalt	09-2516	09-2516	Nil
			27-2516	27-2516	Nil

Op hrs: Visiting aircraft strictly PPR through ATC. 0830-1700.

Landing Fee: MoD(RAF) Rates.	**Customs:** Nil
Hangarage: Nil	**Maintenance:** Nil.

Remarks: RAF Aerodrome. Ab initio pilot training.

Circuit height 1000 ft QFE, light aircraft at 800 ft QFE. RH on Rwy 09.
Aircraft in the visual circuit are to avoid overflying WOODHURST village (1·5 nm NE of Rwy 27 thld).

All aircraft are to avoid overflying HUNTINDON (3 nm SW) and the Raptor Foundation (IH 31, 2·75 nm on final approach to Rwy 27).

Displaced threshold on Rwy 27 used by light aircraft.

Caution: Turbulence may be encountered over the runway when wind speed greater than 15 kt from the South.
Clearance reduced to 17·5 m from taxiway centreline to fence south of Rwy 09 holding Point. Southern taxiway west of ATC available to light aircraft only.

Wyton Flying Club may monitor 134·05 outside of airfield operating hours.

Fuel: Nil	**Tel:** 01480- 52451 Ext 6426/6428.

Robert Pooley ©

N50 56·40 W002 39·52	**YEOVIL (Westland)**	207 ft AMSL

1 nm W of Yeovil.	BHD 112·05 050 45·5
	SAM 113·35 274 49·7

c/s Judwin.   APP 130·80.   TWR/A/G 125·40.   Yeovilton RAD 127·35 (LARS).
RAD 130·80 ¢.   NDB 'YVL' 343·0 (On A/D).   DME 'YVL' 109·05 (On A/D).

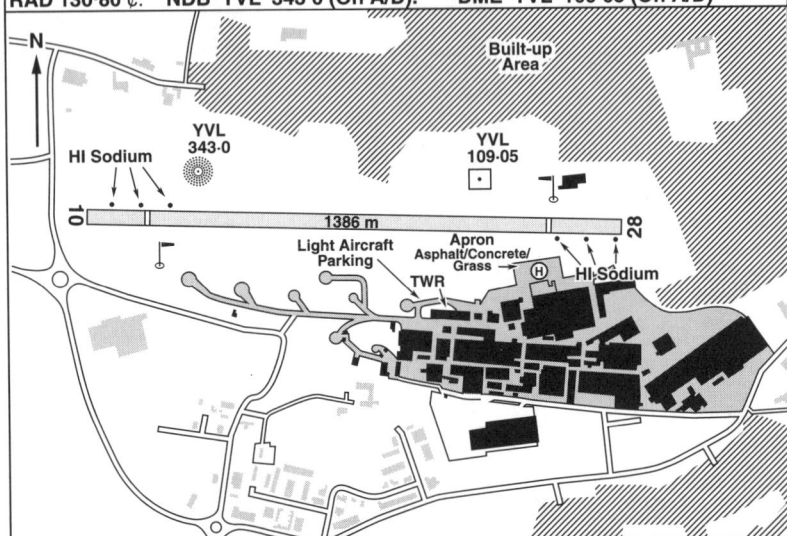

Rwy	Dim(m)	Surface	TORA(m)	LDA(m)	Lighting
10/28	1386x37	Grass	10-1376	10-1224	Apt† Rwy (Portable Elec).
			28-1321	28-1124	Apt† Rwy (Portable Elec).

† 3 sodium lights 90 m apart aligned with LH side of Rwy.   Heli apron edge lights.

Op hrs: PPR. Except PHs, 0800-1645 Mon-Thu; Fri 0800-1615. Aeromed & Police flights H24.

Landing Fee: Home Built/Classic and fuel stops no charge. Otherwise on request with PPR.

Hangarage: Nil	**Maintenance:** Nil	**Customs:** 48 hrs PNR.

Remarks: Operated by GKN Westland Helicopters Ltd, Yeovil, BA20 2YB.
Circuits at 1000 ft QFE to S of Rwy due to proximity to RNAS Yeovilton.
Visiting aircraft may be delayed due to helicopter test flying.
Light aircraft, helicopter and model aircraft flying outside notified Op hrs.

Warnings: ● Noticeable windshear on approach to Rwy 28.
   ● Airfield surface is convex with pronounced DOWN gradient to South at 10 Thr.
   ● Beware of bird concentrations. ● Houses adjacent to the N & E boundaries.
   ● High ground rising to 442' amsl, 2·5 nm to the SW with Radio mast 528' amsl.
   ● Trees on high ground up to 400' amsl within 1 nm to E.
   ● Aerial Mast 471' amsl 0·8 nm to NW.

Restaurant: Light refreshments available.   **Accommodation:** By arrangement.

Car Hire/Taxi: On request to ATC before or after landing. Booking via ATC to comply
with site security restrictions.

Fuel: Jet A1 - by arrangement.	**Tel:** 01935-475222.
	Fax: 01935-703055.

Robert Pooley ©

N51 00·56 W002 38·33	**YEOVILTON**
4 nm N of Yeovil.	BCN 117·45 156 48·5. BHD 112·05 047 49

75 ft AMSL

SAM 113·35 279 49

Yeovilton APP/RAD 127·35. TWR 122·10 O/R.
TACAN 'VLN' 111·00 (On A/D).

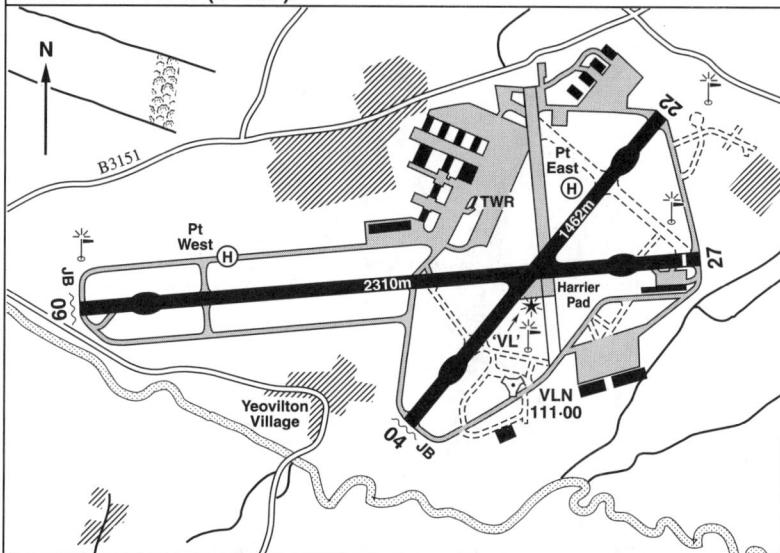

Rwy	Dim(m)	Surface	TORA(m)	LDA(m)	Lighting
09/27	2310x46	Concrete	09-2310	09-2310	Ap Thr Rwy PAPI 3°
			27-2310	27-2287	Ap Thr Rwy PAPI 3°
04/22	1462x46	Concrete	04-1462	04-1462	Ap Rwy
			22-1462	22-1462	Ap Rwy PAPI 3·25°
					IBn 'VL' Red

Op hrs: Mon-Thur 0830-1700, Fri 0830-1600. 24 hrs PPR from Ops. **ATZ active H24.**

Landing Fee: MoD Rates.	**Customs:** Nil
Hangarage: Nil	**Maintenance:** Nil

Remarks: Royal Naval Aerodrome. Not available to civil aircraft outside published operating hours. High intensity jet and helicopter activity.

Visiting aircraft contact App at 40 nm for jet or 20 nm piston.

Two runways may be in use at same time. Special Rules for helicopters.

Glider activity SR-SS and at weekends

Circuits: Fixed wing 1000' QFE; Helicopters 500' QFE.

Warning: Possible turbulance over first 600 ft of Rwy 27 due to inclined ramp left hand side of the threshold.

Due to an obstruction, the first 762 m of Rwy 09, the parallel taxiway, Heli Point West and final approach are not visible from the ATC Tower.

Intensive heli activity at Judwin (4 nm south) and Merryfield (12 nm west).

Fuel: Nil	**Tel:** 01935-840551 Ext 5497/8 PPR.

Robert Pooley ©

N53 56·85 W001 11·27	**YORK (Rufforth)**	65 ft AMSL

3 nm W of York.	**POL 112·10 076 35. GAM 112·80 354 41**
	OTR 113·90 297 41

c/s Rufforth Radio 129·975 A/G. (Gliding operations only).

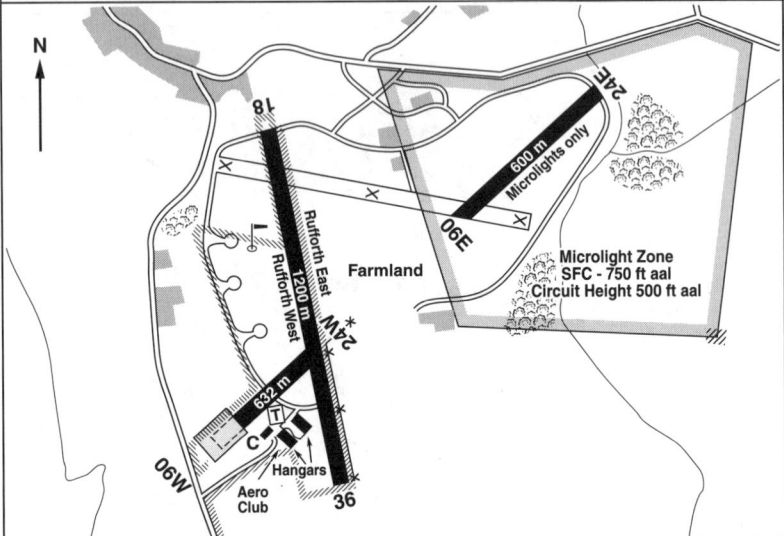

Rwy	Dim(m)	Surface	TORA(m)	LDA(m)	Lighting
RUFFORTH WEST					
18/36	1200x46	Asphalt	Unlicensed		Nil.
06W/24W	632x46	358 m Asphalt/274m Grass	Unlicensed		Nil.
RUFFORTH EAST					
06E/24E	600x46	Asphalt	Unlicensed		Nil.

Op hrs: Strictly PPR. Daylight only. **Hangarage/ Maintenance:** Nil. **Customs:** Nil.

Landing Fee: (WEST) S.E. £6.00; Twins £25 to £35 on size; Helis £6 to £35 on size.

Remarks: Aerodrome located between Church Fenton and Linton-on-Ouse MATZs.
Operated by York Gliding Centre. Pilots of visiting aircraft must maintain a good look out in the circuit area. No standard overhead joins due to glider activity.
Use of aerodrome is at pilot's own risk and the operators do not accept any liability for damage to visiting aircraft. Avoid overflying local villages and farms.

RUFFORTH WEST

Strictly PPR. Intense gliding. No O/H joins. Powered aircraft circuits: RH on 18, LH on 36, 06W & 24W variable. Aircraft landing Rwy 24W must avoid the microlight circuit. Beware gliders and powered aircraft on same circuit. Tug a/c operate variable circuits.

RUFFORTH EAST

Strictly PPR. Mainly microlight operations using Rwy 06E/24E; circuits at 500', RH on 06E, LH on 24E. No landing fees.

Fuel: 100LL (York Gliding Centre)	**Tel:** 01904-738694 York Gliding Centre
	01904-738877 Microlight Operations

Robert Pooley ©

CONTINENTAL SECTION

LOW LEVEL OPERATIONS BETWEEN UK AND FRANCE/BELGIUM

AIRSPACE REGULATIONS BELGIUM AND FRANCE

SELECTED BELGIAN AND FRENCH AERODROMES

Calais
Dinard
Granville
Le Chateau La Chassagne
Le Touquet
Ostend

Comprehensive coverage of Airfields in France - Pooleys Delage (published annualy), Belgium, Luxembourg and Netherlands is available in our range of Pooleys Flight Guides - Europe.

LOW LEVEL CROSS-CHANNEL OPERATIONS BETWEEN THE UK AND FRANCE/BELGIUM

1 Introduction
1.1 The required procedures for flights wishing to cross the English Channel between the UK and France/Belgium areas are as follows:

2 Flight Planning
2.1 Pilots undertaking Cross-Channel flights are reminded that a flight plan MUST be filed for all flights to or from the United Kingdom which will cross the United Kingdom/France/Belgium FIR boundary.

2.2 When filing the flight plan with the UK and French Authorities, pilots are to ensure that well defined significant points/features, at which the aircraft will cross the UK and FrenchlBelgium coastlines, are included in Item 18 (Other information)) of the flight plan form (eg Beachy Head, Berck sur Mer, Lydd, Boulogne, Dover, Cap Gris Nez, etc). This is for Search and Rescue purposes but will also assist ATC.

2.3 Pilots should plan their flights, where possible, at such altitudes which would enable radio contact to be maintained with the appropriate ATC Unit whilst the aircraft is transitting the Channel. In addition, the French Authorities have requested that aircraft fly at altitudes which will keep them within radar cover. The carriage of Secondary Surveillance Radar (SSR) equipment is recommended.

2.4 Position reports are required when crossing the coast outbound, inbound and when crossing the FIR boundary.

3 IFR Operations
3.1 Pilots undertaking Cross-Channel flights under IFR are reminded that normal IFR Rules apply particularly regarding altitudes and flight levels. Pilots are also reminded that the IMC rating is NOT recognised by the French Authorities.

4 General
4.1 In United Kingdom Airspace a bi-directional Recommended VFR Route between the Solent CTA and and the Channel Islands CTR routing towards the Cherbourg Peninsula is established (See AIP AD 2-EGJJ-3-1). All traffic using the route above 3,000 ft amsl are advised to maintain the appropriate quadrantal flight level irrespective of the flight rules being observed. Pilots flying above 3,000 ft amsl are reminded of the requirement to maintain an appropriate semi-circular level whilst within the French FIR.

4.2 When entering United Kingdom airspace from an adjacent region where the operation of transponders has not been required, pilots of suitably equipped aircraft should select Code 2000, Mode C.

London	EGTT	Reims	LFEE
Paris	LFFF	Brussels	EBBU
Brest	LFRR	Amsterdam	EHAA
Bordeaux	LFBB	Scottish	EGPX
Marseille	LFMM		

CROSS-CHANNEL CONTROLLING AUTHORITIES
AND FLIGHT INFORMATION SERVICE (FIS)

London FIS	London Information 124·60
FIS	Manston App 126·35 (LARS)
FIS	Lydd App 120·70
Calais TMA	Lille Information 120·37
Le Touquet TMA	Lille Information 120·37
Ostend TMA	Ostend App 120·60
Paris (North) FIS	Paris Information 125·70
Brussels FIS	Brussels Information 126·90

BELGIUM & LUXEMBOURG
ATS AIRSPACE CLASSIFICATIONS and VMC MINIMA

Airspace		Separation	Services	VMC Minima	Speed Limit	Radio	ATC Clearance
Class A	(IFR)	All aircraft	ATC service	Not applicable	N/A	Required	Required
	(VFR)			Not Permitted			
Class B	(IFR)	All aircraft	ATC Service	Not applicable	N/A	Required	Required
	(VFR)	All aircraft	ATC Service	Clear of cloud, *FL100 & above*: Vis 8 km *Below FL100*: Vis 5 km	N/A	Required	Required
Class C	(IFR)	VFR/IFR	ATC Service for IFR separation	Not applicable	250 k	Required	Required
	(VFR)	Not provided	VFR traffic info. (Traffic avoidance advice on request)	Vis 5 km, 1500 m and 1000 ft from cloud.	250 k	Required	Required
Class D	(IFR)	Not provided	Traffic information between IFR and VFR.(Traffic avoidance advice on request)	Not applicable	250 k	Required	Required
	(VFR)	Not provided	Traffic information between IFR and VFR flights. (Traffic avoidance advice on request)	Vis 5 km, 1500 m and 1000 ft from cloud.	250 k	Required	Required
Class G	(IFR)	Not provided	Flight information service.	Not applicable	N/A	Not required	Not required
	(VFR)	Not provided	Flight information service	Vis 5 km below FL100 and 8 km at or above FL100. *Above 3000' or 1000' SFC whichever higher*: 1500 m and 1000' from cloud. *At or below 3000'/1000' SFC, whichever higher:* Clear of cloud and in sight of surface, Vis 5 km * * See overleaf		Not required	Not required

1 DEC 00

* BELGIUM

Minimum flight visibility of 3000 m from SR-30 to SS+30 mins:
- for flights operating at 250 kts or less affording adequate time to avoid other traffic or obstacles;

Minimum flight visibility of 1500 m:
- for flights operating within a traffic circuit (local flights).
  Helicopters — Minimum flight visibility of 800 m
- when operating at a speed which affords adequate time and possibility of avoiding other traffic or obstacles.

* LUXEMBOURG

Minimum flight visibility of 1500 m from SR-30 to SS+30 mins:
- for flights operating at 140 kts or less giving adequate time to avoid other traffic or obstacles;
- when the probability of encountering other traffic is low (e.g. areas of low traffic density);
  Helicopters — Minimum flight visibility of 800 m
- at a speed which affords adequate time and possibility of avoiding other traffic or obstacles.

VFR LANDING/TAKE-OFF MINIMA

Except when a Special VFR clearance has been obtained from ATC, VFR flights shall not take-off or land from/at an aerodrome within a CTR or enter an ATZ or the traffic circuit when conditions are less than — **surface visibility of 5 km and a ceiling of 1500 ft.**

SPECIAL VFR (SVFR) — clearances for flights within control zones will be granted on request between SR - 30 and SS + 30 subject to the SVFR Minima as specified below. Separation is provided between all SVFR flights and also between them and IFR traffic.

- **SVFR Minima** — Visibility 1500 m, clear of cloud and in sight of surface.
- Helicopters 800 m, providing operating speed affords adequate time and possibility of avoiding other traffic or obstacles.

FLIGHT PLANS

A flight plan is mandatory:
- for all VFR flights within controlled airspace;
- for all flights crossing international borders, except civil VFR flights conducted between AACHEN (Merzbruck) in Germany and LIEGE (Bierset) or SPA (La Sauveniere).

Note. A pilot may submit a flight plan for any flight, and he is advised to do so if he intends to fly over sparsely populated areas, especially if his aircraft is not equipped with radio.

MINIMUM HEIGHT RULES

Aircraft must fly at sufficient height to enable the execution of an emergency landing without endangering people or property.

Except when necessary for take-off and landing, or except by specific permission, a VFR flight shall not be flown:

- at a height less than 1,000 ft above the highest obstacle within a radius of 600 m of the aircraft when flying over densely populated areas, large assemblies of people or industrial areas (nuclear power plants, factories etc);
- at a height less than 500 ft above the surface and at a distance less than 150 m from from any fixed or mobile artificial obstacle.

For helicopters in Belgium and for helicopters, microlights and lighter-than-air aircraft in Luxembourg the height and distance shall never be less than 50 m (150 ft)

NIGHT VFR

Belgium VFR at night (SS+30 to SR-30) in Belgian airspace is permitted only when specifically authorised by the Civil Aviation Authority, by the local authority responsible for the aerodrome and, if any, the ATS.

When authorised, VFR flights at night may operate:
- within a radius of 3 km of the ARP and continuously in sight of the TWR or its substitute;
- at or below 1000' SFC;
- surface visibility of 5 km with ceiling 1500 ft.

Luxembourg VFR flights at night may operate:
- within the CTR;
- within the TMA up to a maximum of FL70;
- in class G airspace up to a maximum of 2,000 ft.

TRANSPONDERS

The carriage of a serviceable transponder, Mode A/4096 codes or Mode C with automatic pressure altitude information is mandatory for all aircraft operating in:
- Class B airspace within Brussels FIR above 4500 ft;
- Brussels TMA/CTR

Exemption may be granted for a particular flight on request by telephone, prior to the flight, to Brussels FIC (02/753 83 57) or to ATCC Semmerzake (09/389 25 55), as appropriate.

Pilots operating non-controlled flights should select Mode A and C, code 7000 unless otherwise instructed.

USE OF MILITARY AERODROMES

Except in emergency, no civil aircraft should land at a military aerodrome, with the exception of BRUSSELS (Melsbroek) and LIEGE (Bierset), without the prior permission of the Belgian Air Staff.

The Air Force authorities can except no responsibility whatsoever for any civil aircraft carrying out an emergency landing at a military aerodrome.

The control towers at BEAUVECHAIN and KOKSIJDE can be called at any time, even outside normal Op hrs.

Runway and approach lighting will be made available at once by calling either:
- the particular aerodrome on the International Distress frequency 121·5 or 243·0, or
- by calling ACC BRUSSELS or UAC MAASTRICHT on any of the published frequencies.

FRENCH AIRSPACE
RULES & REGULATIONS

FLIGHT PLANS

A flight plan is required for:
- All IFR flights;
- VFR flights crossing the borders of Metropolitan France;
- VFR flights above maritime regions or inhospitable terrain;
- Night VFR flights

An 'abbreviated flight plan' may be filed **in the air** before entering class 'D' controlled airspace, traffic circuits of controlled aerodromes or before operating under Special VFR. Unless otherwise prescribed by the appropriate ATS authority, the closure of the abbreviated flight plan shall be made either in person on landing or by radio on leaving the controlled airspace.

Note 1. Estimated time of departure in the flight plan is the time at which the aircraft will be ready to leave the apron.

Note 2. It is a mandatory requirement that details of entry/exit to/from French airspace be notified in the flight plan; the point and time of crossing the boundary must be inserted in Section 18 of the flight plan.

VFR Landing/Take-Off Minima

Except when a Special VFR clearance has been obtained from ATC, VFR flights shall not take-off or land from/at an aerodrome within a CTR or enter the traffic circuit when conditions are less than:

Surface visibility 8 km, ceiling 1500 ft.

Special VFR Minima — each aerodrome which is located within a CTR has its own SVFR minima which can vary appreciably. The applicable SVFR minima is given under the particular aerodrome entry in the following pages.

Transponders

Transponders mode A or C are mandatory:
• within Class D Airspace (mode C recommended);
• above FL120 or 2,000' SFC (whichever is higher).

VFR Cruising Levels

VFR flights are required to fly at the following semi-circular cruising levels when operating above 3000' amsl or 1000' SFC (whichever higher).

Mag Track 000° – 179°: Flight Levels 35, 55, 75, and 95

Mag Track 180° – 359°: Flight Levels 45, 65, 85 and 105.

FRENCH AIRSPACE CLASSIFICATION

Only class 'A', 'D', 'E' and 'G' are implemented in France.

FIR up to FL115 (or 3,000' SFC whichever is higher):
• outside controlled airspace: class 'G'
• Within controlled airspace: class 'A', 'D' or 'E' according to airspace and activity.

FIR from FL 115 (or 3,000' SFC whichever is higher) up to FL195: class 'D'.

At and above FL195: class 'A'.

ATS AIRSPACE CLASSIFICATIONS and VMC MINIMA

Airspace	Separation	Services	VMC Minima	Speed Limit	Radio	ATC Clearance
Class A (IFR)	All aircraft	ATC service	Not applicable	N/A	Required	Required
(VFR)			**Not Permitted**			
Class B			Not Allocated			
Class C			Not Allocated			
Class D (IFR)	IFR/IFR	Traffic information IFR/VFR (Traffic avoidance advice on request)	Not applicable	N/A	Required	Required
(VFR)	Not provided	Traffic information VFR/IFR and VFR/ VFR flights. (Traffic avoidance advice on request)	Vis 8 km, 1500 m and 1000 ft from cloud.	N/A	Required	Required
Class E (IFR)	IFR/IFR	ATC service and traffic information about VFR traffic as far practical.	Not applicable	N/A	Required	Required
(VFR)	Not provided	Traffic information as far as practical	Vis 8 km, 1500 m and 1000 ft from cloud.	N/A	Not required	Not required
Class F			Not Allocated			
Class G (IFR)	Not provided	Flight information service.	Not applicable	N/A	Not required	Not required
(VFR)	Not provided	Flight information service	Vis 8 km, 1500 m and 1000 ft from cloud.		Not required	Not required

N50 57·65 E001 57·08	**CALAIS - DUNKIRK**	10 ft AMSL

3·8nm ENE of Calais.

DVR 114·95 121 25.   KOK 114·50 257 28
BNE 113·80 008 20.   ING 387·50 063 9

Lille APP 120·37.   Calais TWR 118·10 *.   FIS — Lille Information 120·37.
Lctr 'MK' 418·0 (244°/3·9 nm to Thr 24).   ILS Rwy 24 (244°) 'MK' 110·50.

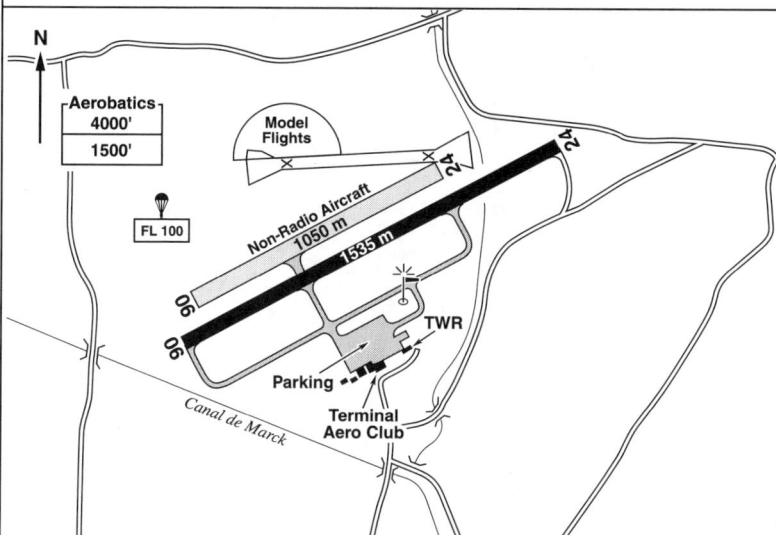

Rwy	Dim(m)	Surface	TORA(m)	LDA(m)	Lighting
06/24	1535x45	Asphalt	06 -1535	06 -1535	Thr Rwy
			24 -1535	24 -1535	Ap Thr Rwy
06/24	1050x60	Grass	06 -1050	06 -1050	Nil.
			24 -1050	24 -1050	Nil.

Op hrs: 0800-1900 daily. O/T (IFR only, except training flights):1900-2300, PPR before 1700hrs. 0600-0800 PPR preceding day before 1700 hrs.

Met/AIS: Lille (Lesquin).	**Customs:** Aerodrome hours.
Hangarage: Available	**Maintenance:** Nil.

Remarks: Flights within the Calais TMA are subject to the regulations applicable to Class 'E' Controlled Airspace — see page 518.
Special VFR flights are to contact Calais Twr (Lille App if above 2,000') before entering the Calais TMA.
Circuits at 1000 ft. aal; Asphalt Rwy, LH on 24, RH on 06; Grass Rwy, LH on 06, RH on 24. Non radio aircraft must use Grass Rwy. Aerodrome surface unusable outside Rwys & Twys. Demolition Area 1·2 nm NNW of A/D, radius 0·5 nm, SFC—1650 ft. Parachuting up to FL100 on north side of A/D.
Warning. Aerodrome susceptible to sudden unexpected sea-fog, diversion to a non coastal aerodrome should be pre-planned.
* TWR frequency outside Op hrs is Air/Air in French only.

Restaurant: Available.

Fuel: 100LL, Jet A1.	**Tel:** 03 21 00 11 00/01 ATS. 03 21 82 70 66 Operator **Fax:** 03 21 35 22 66 ATS

Robert Pooley ©

N48 35·27   W002 04·80   **DINARD (Pleurtuit-St.-Malo)**   211 ft AMSL

2·7nm SSW of Dinard.

Dinard APP. 120·15.   TWR 121·10.   VOR/DME 'DIN' 114·30 (On A/D).   ATIS 124·575
Lctr 'DR' 390·0 (354°/5·9 nm to Thr 35).   ILS Rwy 35 (354°M) 'DR' 110·75.

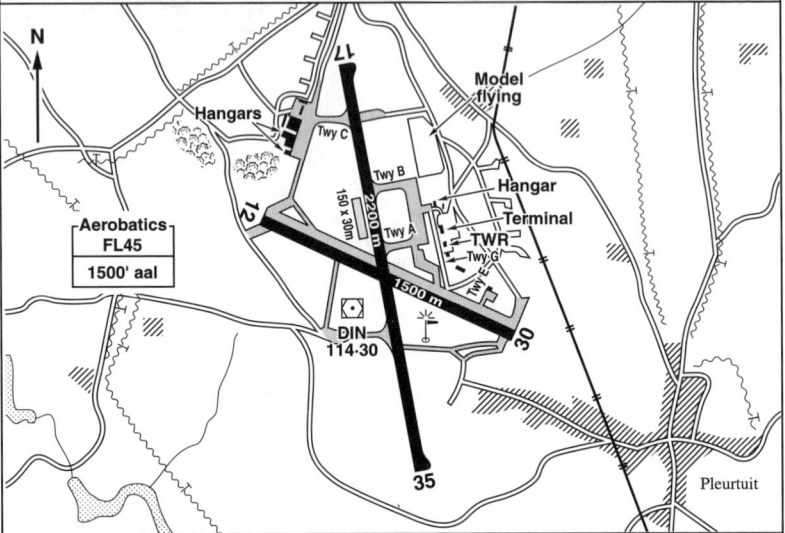

Rwy	Dim(m)	Surface	TORA(m)	LDA(m)	Lighting
12/30	1500x45	Asphalt	12 -1500	12 -1500	Nil.
			30 -1500	30 -1500	Nil.
17/35	2200x45	Asphalt	17 -2200	17 -2200	Thr Rwy
			35 -2200	35 -2200	Ap Thr Rwy

Op hrs: H24.

Met: On A/D Tel: 299 46 10 46.   **AIS:** Nantes-Atlantique.

Customs: 0730-2030; O/T on request 24 hrs on preceding workday.

Restaurant: Available.   **Hangarage:** Nil.   **Maintenance:** Available.

Remarks: Flights within the Dinard CTR/TMA are governed by the regulations
applicable to Class E Controlled Airspace — see page 518 and Arr/Dep Chart
opposite. Special VFR flights are to contact Dinard App before crossing the TMA
boundary. Non radio aircraft strictly PPR.
Circuits at 1000' aal., RH on Asphalt 30 & Grass 17 , LH on Asphalt 12, 17 & 35, and
Grass 35.
Instrument approaches to Rwy 35.
Aerodrome surface unusable outside Rwys & Twys.
Mandatory prior notification to Twr by telephone for SVFR flights .

Fuel: 100LL, Jet A1	**Tel:** 02 99 16 38 03 Aerodrome/ATS
	02 99 16 38 05 Operator
	Fax: 02 99 16 38 06

VISUAL APP/DEP CHART

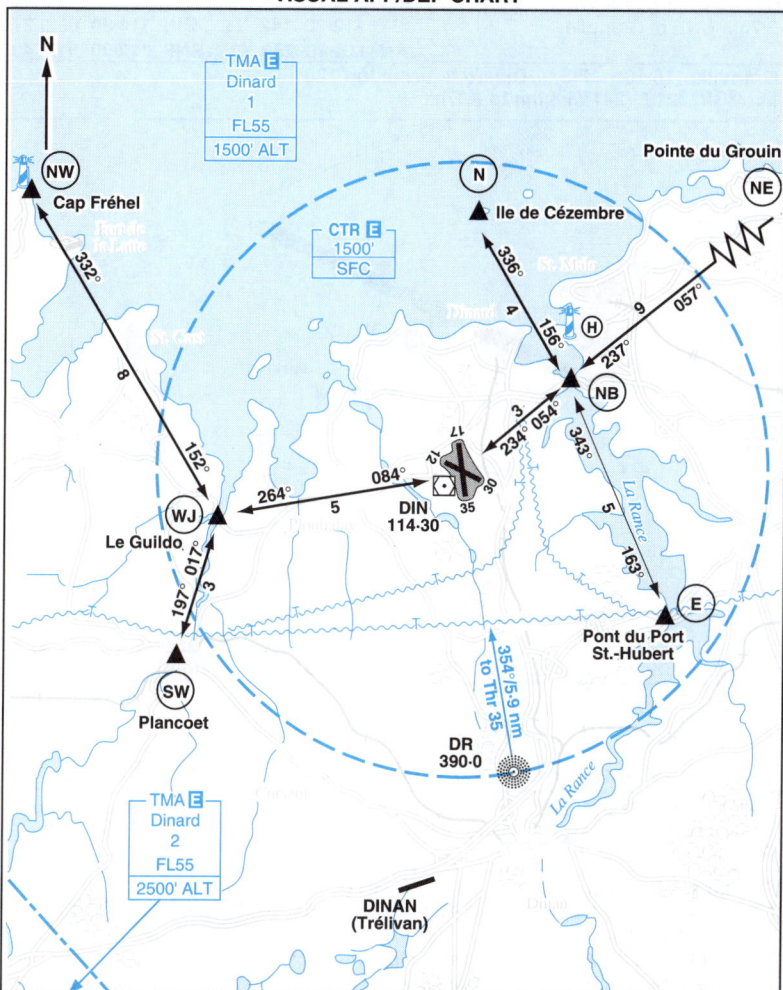

Arrival/Departure Routes shown above are mandatory for Special VFR flights and recommended for VFR Flights.

Special VFR Minima with IFR traffic

Fixed wing: Visibility 5000 m, ceiling 1000 ft.

Helicopters: Visibility 800 m, ceiling 500 ft.

GRANVILLE

N48 53·00 W00133·70		44 ft AMSL
2·7nm NNE of Granville.	JSY 112·20 142 28.	DIN 114·30 053 27
	CAN 115·40 253 47.	RNE 112·80 013 49

Granville 118·10.   FIS — Dinard Information 120·15.
Lctr 'GV' 321·0 (241°/3·8 nm to A/D)

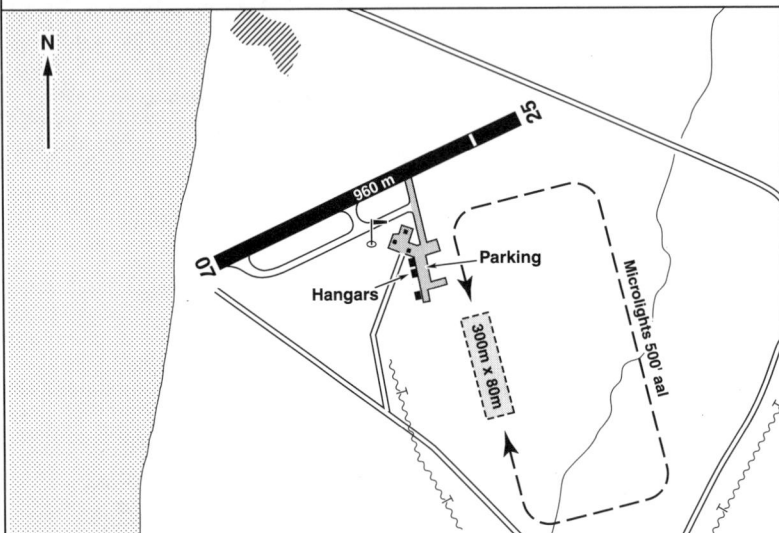

Rwy	Dim(m)	Surface	TORA(m)	LDA(m)	Lighting
07/25	960x30	Asphalt	07 -960	07 -960	Rwy
			25 -960	25 -825	Rwy

Op hrs: Daily 0900-1200 & 1400-1800 (Mon-Fri till 2200 O/R before 1600 hrs).

Met/AIS: Nantes Atlantique

Customs: On request preceding workday before 1800 hrs — Tel: 02 33 50 12 49.

Hangarage Nil.	**Maintenance:** Nil.

Remarks: Circuits at 1000' aal., LH on 25, RH on 07.
Microlights operate from N/S grass strip to the south of asphalt runway,
circuits at 500' aal.

Night VFR permissible on Asphalt Rwy, night circuits to the North.

Pilot Controlled Lighting (PCL) available on PPR before 1600LT on last work-day prior
to flight — Fax: 02 35 50 63 11.

Warning. Airfield susceptible to sudden unexpected sea-fog, the area can be covered
in a few minutes. Check with local MET office and pre-plan possible diversion to a
non-coastal airfield.

Restaurant: Available.

Fuel: 100LL.	**Tel:** 02 33 91 33 91 Operator
	02 33 50 24 24 Aero Club
	Fax: 02 33 50 63 11 Operator

N47 18·63 E004 49·18	**Le CHATEAU La CHASSAGNE**	1122 ft AMSL
9·7 nm W of Dijon.	**DIJ 113·50 282 11·6. ATN 114·90 039 37·8**	

c/s 'Checkpoint Charlie' A/G - Frequency will be given with PPR .

FIS – Reims Information 124·10.

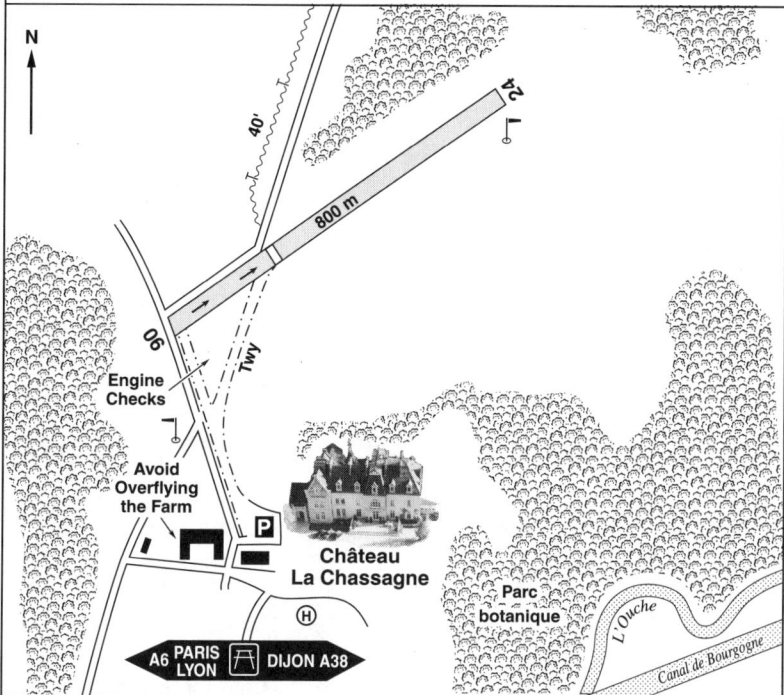

Rwy	Dim(m)	Surface	TORA(m)	LDA(m)	Lighting
06/24	800x50	Grass	Unlicensed		Nil

Op hrs: PPR by Fax: 0033-380 49 76 19. **Customs:** Dijon 03 80 67 67 67

Landing Fee: 65 FF or 10 Euro. **Hangarage/ Maintenance:** Nil

Remarks: Private airfield set in a 100 acre forest. Contact Flight Manager Marc Francis Bach, Hotel Château la Chassagne, F-21410 Pont-de-Pany, Dijon.

PPR. Airfield restricted to guests of the Château.

Minimum 250 hours as PIC for private pilots. Training Flights prohibited.

Circuit height 1000 ft agl, Rwy 06 LH, Rwy 24 RH.

Avoid overflying local villages.

Restaurant Formal dress required for the restaurant.

Taxis/Car Hire: By arrangement.

Fuel: Nil.	**Tel:** 0033 380 49 76 00 or 0033 380 97 21 10. **Fax:** 0033 380 49 76 19

N50 30·88 E001 37·65	**LE TOUQUET**	36 ft AMSL
1·5 nm ESE of Le Touquet.	DVR 114·95 168 40.	LYD 114·05 139 41
		BNE 113·80 241 12

Lille APP 120.375.   Le Touquet TWR 118·45.   GND 125·30.   ATIS 129·125.
Lctr 'LT' 358·0 (137°/1·08nm to Thr 14).   ILS Rwy 14 (137°) 'LT' 110·15.

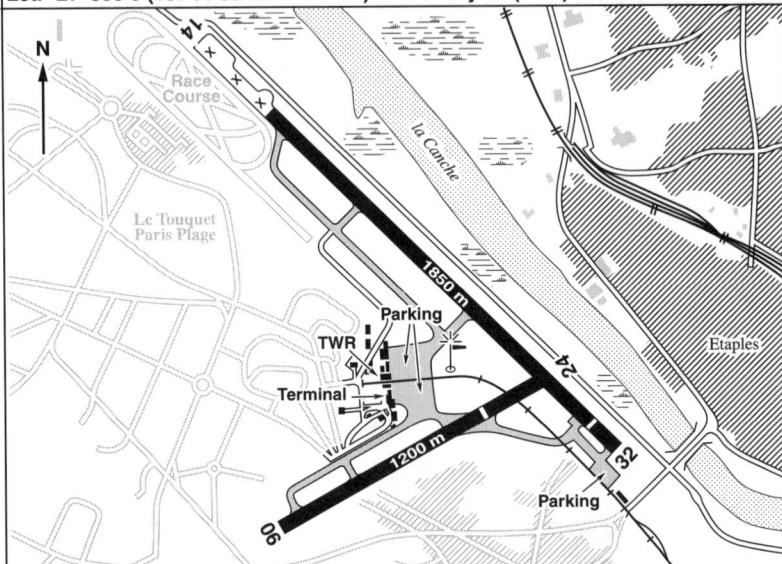

Rwy	Dim(m)	Surface	TORA(m)	LDA(m)	Lighting
06/24	1200x40	Asphalt	06 -1200	06 -1200	Nil.
			24 -1200	24 -900	Nil.
14/32	1850x40	Asphalt	14 -1850	14 -1850	Ap Thr Rwy
			32 -1850	32 -1700	Thr Rwy PAPI 3°

Op hrs: 0800-2000. O/T commercial flights only, on request to LFATYDYX before
1600 (Winter), 1700 (Summer).

Met: ATIS Tel: 03 21 05 51 26.	**AIS:** On Aerodrome.	**Customs:** As Op hrs.
Restaurant: Available.	**Hangarage:** Available.	**Maintenance:** Available.

Remarks: Flights within Le Touquet TMA/CTR are governed by the rules applicable
to Class 'E' controlled airspace — see page 518.
Special VFR flights are to contact Lille App for clearance before entering the TMA.
Circuits at 1000' aal., LH on 14 and 24, RH on 06 and 32.
Non radio aircraft PPR by telephone. SVFR not available to non radio aircraft.
In winds of less than 4 kt, use of Rwy 14 preferred.
Departures Call Le Touquet Ground 118·45 before starting engines.
Warning. Possibility of sudden unexpected sea-fog. Call aerodrome prior to
departure for local MET information. Advisable to pre-plan possible diversion to a non
coastal aerodrome.

Fuel: 100LL, Jet A1.	**Tel:** 03 21 05 00 66 ATC.
(Total credit card or cash).	03 21 05 03 99 Operator
	03 21 05 51 26 ATIS

Visual App/Dep Chart

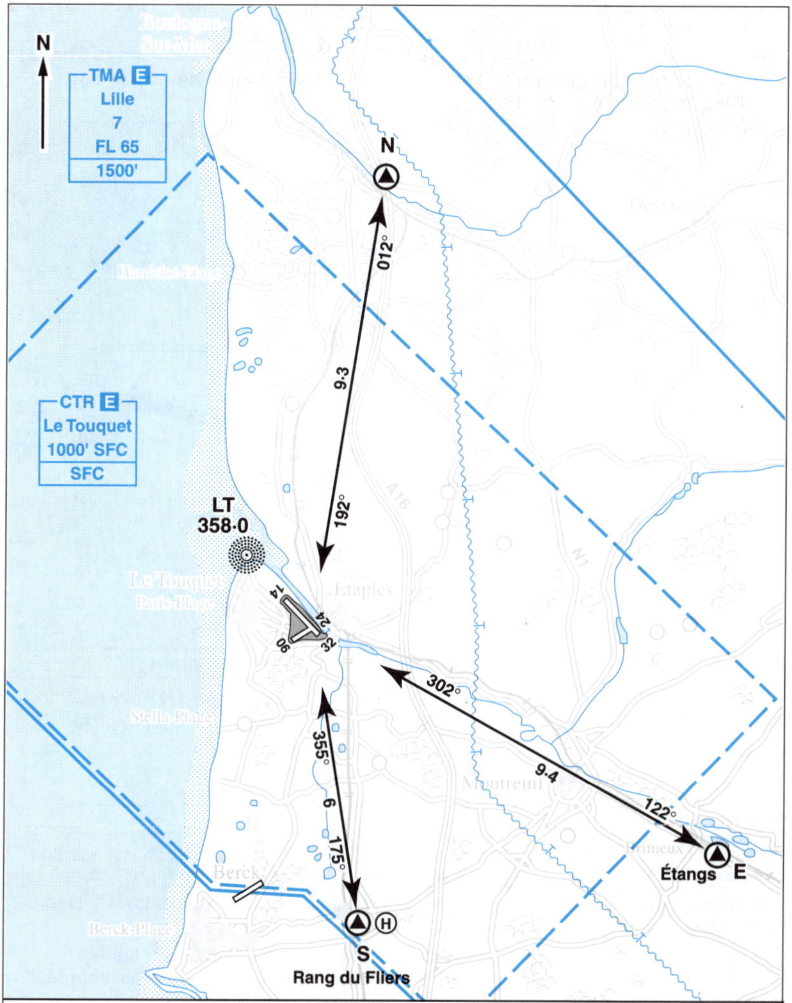
N
TMA E
Lille
7
FL 65
1500'
CTR E
Le Touquet
1000' SFC
SFC
LT
358·0
N
012°
9·3
192°
14
24
06
32
302°
9·4
122°
355°
6
175°
Étangs
E
S
Rang du Fliers

SVFR Minima with IFR traffic

Route N –	Fixed wing and Helicopters	Vis: 2,000 m
Route E –	Fixed wing	Vis: 1,500 m
	Helicopters	Vis: 800 m

APP 120·60. TWR 118·17. GND 121·90. NDB 'ONO' 399·5 (262°/4·37nm to Thr 26)
Lctr 'DD' 352·5 (082°/0·7 nm to Thr 08). Lctr 'OO' 375·0 (0·62 nm to Thr 26)
ILS Rwy 26 (259°) IOS 109·50.

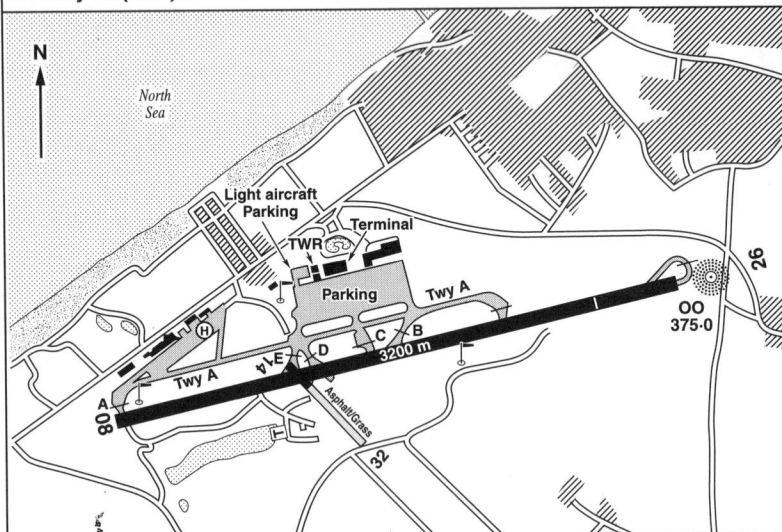

Rwy	⌀Dim(m)	Surface	TORA(m)	LDA(m)	Lighting
08/26	3200x45	Asphalt/	08 -3200	08 -3200	Ap Thr Rwy PAPI 3°
		Concrete	26 -3200	26 -2785	Ap Thr Rwy PAPI 3°
14/32	627x45	Asphalt/	14-627	14-627	Nil
		Grass	32-627	32-627	Nil

Op hrs: H24. Reporting Office 0630-2200 daily.

Met: On A/D. 059-551452 **AIS:** On A/D. **Customs:** 0600-2400 daily. O/T 2 hrs PNR

Restaurant: Available **Hangarage:** Nil. **Maintenance:** Limited.

Remarks: Use governed by the regulations applicable to Class C controlled airspace see pages 515/516 and the Area Chart opposite.

Aircraft approaching without ILS or radar assistance shall not descend below 1500' QNH before intercepting the PAPI approach slope nor fly below this approach slope thereafter.
Non radio aircraft accepted between 1 October and 30 April, on prior permission.

Twy C1 (SR-SS) and Apron 3 to be used only by aircraft up to 5700 kg.
Exit and departure from Apron 2 only via Twys B2, C2 and E2.

Fuel: 100LL, Jet A1.	**Tel:** 059-551411 Airport Fax: 513251
	Tel: 059-551490 ATC Fax: 512951
	Fax:059-551464 Self Briefing

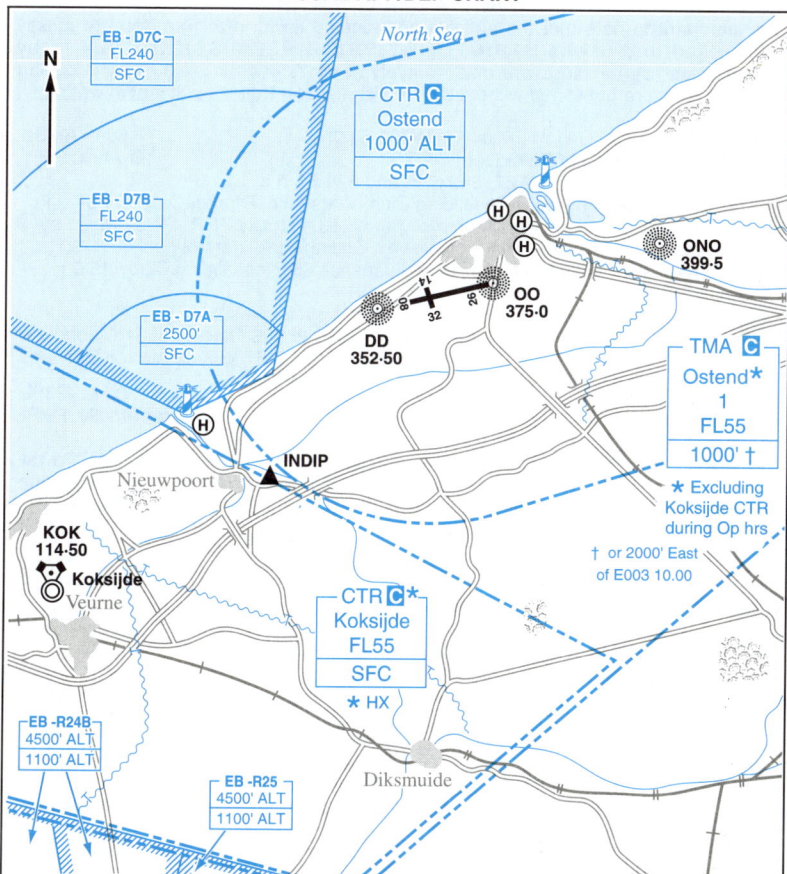

Contact Ostend App 10 mins before entering controlled airspace and request ATC clearance, giving position, level, heading and ETA for TMA boundary. Maintain listening watch and conform strictly to all ATC instructions.

SVFR Minima — Ceiling: 820 ft; Visibility: 2·5 Km.

Reporting Points for entering Ostend TMA:

1. **BRESKENS**	N51 24·00 E003 32·90	2. **AALTER**	N51 05·20 E003 32·90
3. **TORHOUT**	N51 04·00 E003 06·10	4. **DUNKIRK**	N51 02·00 E002 22·40

UNITED KINGDOM
PRIVATE AIRFIELDS/STRIPS

It is important to note that the airfields and landing fields in this section are mostly unlicensed and use is **STRICTLY BY PRIOR PERMISSION ONLY** or by arrangement (¢). Landings are made entirely at pilot's own risk. No extracts or part thereof may be re-published without the Publisher's and Editor's consent in writing.

1 ABOYNE   N57 04·52 W002 50·08   460 ft. AMSL
1 nm W of Aboyne. (N of River Dee)   **Op hrs:** PPR
Two parallel tarmac strips 09/27, 540x7 m and 520 x 5·5 m
Remarks: Operated by Deeside Gliding Club, Waterside, Dinnet. Only aircraft on Gliding Club business or for maintenance permitted – strictly PPR. Field grazed by cattle at times. Windsock N and S of runway. Gliding site – aerotow only.
Landing fee: Gliding Club Business or Maintenance £6; Non Gliding Club £15.00; Motor Gliders £4.
Accommodation: Hotels in Aboyne and Dinnet, both 2 miles.
Fuel: Nil.   **Tel:** 013398-85339 Office, 85354 Clubhouse
                                              013398-85236 Aboyne Aircraft Services

2 ALLENSMORE   N52 00·02 W002 50·08   300 ft. AMSL
4 nm SW of Hereford.   **Op hrs:** Strictly PPR.
Grass field N/S 550m.
Remarks: Operated by Willox Bridge, Allensmore, Hereford. Contact Mr. Powell. Prior permission advisable. Care must be taken due to animals grazing. Large letter 'A' on white background on hangar roof at N end of strip. **Taxi:** 01432-351238
Fuel: Nil   **Tel:** 0198121-570203

3 AVIEMORE (Feshie)   N57 06·14 W003 53·51   850 ft. AMSL
1·5 nm SE of Loch Insh.   O.S. Sheet 35/NH 855028
Grass strip 03/21 800 x 5 m. Rwy 03 has a slight downslope for about 1/3 strip length.
Remarks: Operated by Cairngorm Gliding Club, Feshie Airstrip, Blackmill Farm, Kincraig, Kingussie, Inverness-shire, PH21 1NG, for Miss Jane Williamson. PPR. Glider flying, winch and aerotows. Windsock displayed near the centre of the airfield to the west side of the strip. Parking available and sometimes hangarage.
Warning: Beware of steeply rising ground to 4000ft to East of the airfield.
Landing fee: £10.00.   **Radio:** c/s Feshie Base 130·10 A/G (not always manned).
Fuel: Nil.
Tel: 01540-651317 Club; If no reply 01540-661098, 01540-651246 Miss J. Williamson.

4 BANBURY (Shotteswell)   N52 06·27 W001 22·83   530 ft. AMSL
3 nm N of Banbury on A41.
Two grass strips 15/33, 853 m. 09/27, 400 m.
Remarks: Operated by F. Spencer, D.F.C. and Bar, Church Farm, Shotteswell. Light aircraft always welcome at pilot's own risk. Parking available.
Windsock displayed at North end. **Landing Fees:** Nil.
Fuel: Limited.   **Tel:** 01295-730275. **Fax:**738577.

5 BERWICK-ON-TWEED (Winfield)   N55 44·95 W002 09·82   170 ft. AMSL
6 nm W of Berwick
Tarmac runways 13/31, 900 x 46 m; 06/24, 800 x 46 m.
Remarks: Operated by M. Fleming & Sons, Winfield, Berwick-on-Tweed. Light aircraft are welcome at all times on PPR. Care must be taken. Windsock displayed. All runway thresholds are displaced, wire fence crosses threshold of runway 24.
Landing Fee: £5.00
Fuel: Nil.   **Tel:** 01890-870225/870247.

6 BOUGHTON   N52 35·52 E000 30·95   80 ft. AMSL
4 nm SSW of RAF Marham, Norfolk
Grass Strips 08/26, 520m, 16/34 415m.
Remarks: Operated by P. Coulten Esq, Oxborough Road, Boughton, Kings Lynn,
Norfolk. Site situated within RAF Marham MATZ. Contact Marham on 124·15 before
entry or take-off. Prior permission essential. Strips bordered by paddock fencing.
Windsock displayed.
Warning: Another Boughton airstrip 0·5 nm to South.
Fuel: Nil.   **Tel:** 01366-500315. 07771-552870

7 BRAINTREE (Rayne Hall Farm)   N51 53·25 E000 31·32   225 ft. AMSL
1·3 nm West of Braintree.   O.S. Sheet 167/735238.   **BKY 116·25 116 18**
Grass strip 09/27, 785 x 20m.
Remarks: Operated by D.S. McGregor Esq. PPR. Unlicensed airfield located
beneath Stansted CTA, base 2000 ft ALT., contact Essex Radar on 120·625.
Andrewsfield Airfield 2·7 nm to WNW. Visiting aircraft welcome at pilot's own risk.
Avoid overflying local villages.Windsock displayed.   **Landing Fee:** £4.00.
Radio: 130·775 A/G.
Fuel: Nil.   **Tel:** 01376-321899 Operator, 346217 Airfield. 0850-921961
                                                          Fax: 01376-321899

8 BRIDGNORTH (Ditton Priors)   N52 30·02 W002 34·12   690 ft. AMSL
6 nm WSW of Bridgnorth. 2 nm NE of spot height 1771ft amsl.
Grass strip (slightly undulating) 07/25, 500x16 m.
Remarks: Operated by W. E. Lowe, Ditton Farm, Ditton Priors, Bridgnorth,
Shropshire. Windsock. Growing crops surround strip. Trees close to South side of
runway at approx. half distance. Runway slopes uphill from East.
In light wind conditions land uphill and take-off downhill. Light aircraft welcome on
request and at pilot's own risk; care must be taken.
Fuel: Nil.   **Tel:** 01746-712240 or 712368

9 BROOKLANDS   N51 21·05 W000 28·20   50 ft. AMSL
1 nm SW of Weybridge.   **Op hrs:** Strictly PPR.
Asphalt Rwy 01/19 503 x 30m (displaced thresholds).
Remarks: Operated by Brooklands Museum Trust, Weybridge, Surrey. This
aerodrome is strictly PPR and is only available on an invitation basis only, and then
only on selected weekend days in conjunction with the Museum's activities.
Brooklands Radio in operation on flying days only.
Fuel: Nil.   **Tel:** 01932-857381. **Fax:** 01932-855465.

10 CARK (Grange-over-Sands)   N54 09·88 W002 57·62   20 ft. AMSL
7 nm S of Lake Windermere.
Asphalt Runway 06/24, 400 x 15m (200m over-run at each end).
Two other runways are disused.
Op hrs: PPR. Summer: 0900-1900. Winter: 0900-SS
Remarks: Operated by North West Parachute Centre. Cark Airfield, Moor Lane,
Flookburgh, Grange-over-Sands, Cumbria. Light aircraft are welcome on PPR and at
pilot's own risk. Non radio aircraft not accepted.
Inbound aircraft call Cark Radio on 129·90 A/G at 10 nm.
Avoid overflying local villages.
Circuits at 1000' aal, RH on 06, LH on 24; over sea to reduce noise.
Do not join overhead due to intensive Free Fall Parachuting. Parachutists exit aircraft
free-fall up to 10000 ft., parachutes deploy from 2200 ft down.
Landing Fees: Singles £5.00; Twins £10.00.
Fuel: Nil.
Tel: 01772-720848 Weekdays. 01539-558555 or 558672 Weekends.

11 CHALLOCK N51 12·50 E000 49·75 600 ft. AMSL
4 nm NNW of Ashford.
Unmarked grass strips NE/SW 800 m & N/S 800 m.
Remarks: Gliding site operated by Kent Gliding Club, Squids Gate, Challock,
Ashford, Kent TN25 4DR. PPR by telephone. Regular glider launching and aerotow.
Winch cables can extend up to 2600 ft amsl.
All approaches over trees and unmarked electricity cables run along NE side of
airfield.
Surface generally undulating and is particularly uneven in SW corner. Sheep may be
grazing when gliding is not in progress.
Fuel: Nil. **Tel:** 01233-740274

12 CLENCH COMMON N51 23·35 W001 43·88 620 ft. AMSL
2 nm SSW of Marlborough.
2 Grass strips, 05/23 360 x 20m, 16/34 380 x 20m.
Op Hrs: PPR. Mon-Sat 0800-2000; Sun 1000-1900.
Remarks: Operated by Graham J. Slater, Clench Common Airfield, Marlborough,
Wilts SN8 4NZ. Full time Microlight School. Suitable light aircraft welcome.
Upslope on first 150 metres of Rwy 34. Trees on approach to Rwy 05. Join overhead
at 1500' aal. Circuits at 500' aal, RH on Rwy 05 and 34; LH on Rwys 16 and 23.
Windsock near intersection of runways.
Radio: 129·82 A/G. **Landing Fees:** £3.00.
Restaurant: Tea/coffee available.
Fuel: MOGAS. **Tel:** 01672-515535. **Fax:** 01672-511574

COLEFORD — see EASTBACH FARM

13 COLL (Ballard) N56 35·92 W006 37·23 41 ft. AMSL
Island of Coll, Inner Hebrides.
Grass strip 11/29 434x18 m.
Remarks: Operated by Mr. A.C. Brodie. Coll/Ballard Aerodrome, Inner Hebrides,
Strathclyde Region, Scotland. The owner has no objection to the strip being used but
accepts no responsibility for its operation. Visiting aircraft are to contact Tiree
Information 122·70. Surface north of the runway is subject to flooding, manoeuvring
area restricted to the marked runway and the area adjacent to the hut on south side
of runway.
Fuel: Nil **Tel:** 0187-93367

14 CRAIL N56 16·08 W002 36·33
75 ft. AMSL
1 nm E of Crail, 7·5 nm S of St. Andrews.
4 Asphalt runways, all 1000 x 10 m. **Remarks:** Former Royal Naval air station 'HMS
Jackdaw' built in 1918. Now arguably one of the best preserved, abandoned airfields
in Scotland.
Operated by Mr W. J. Robertson, Crail Airfield Promotions, Balcomie Road, Crail,
Fife KY10 3XL. PPR essential. Car boot sales some Sundays in Summer months
and motor racing takes place on the airfield.
Fuel: Nil. **Tel:** 01333-450203. **Fax:** 01333-450112.

15 CURROCK HILL   N54 56·03 W001 50·73   800 ft AMSL
8 nm SW of Newcastle Airport.   O.S. Sheet 88/100599   **NEW 114·25 224 8·2**
Grass Strip 06/24 600 x 50m.
Op hrs: PPR. Sat, Sun & Wed 0900-SS,and by arrangement.
Remarks: Operated by Northumbria Gliding Club Ltd. Strictly PPR. Situated within
Newcastle CTR, obtain entry clearance from Newcastle APP 124·375.
Circuits: Powered aircraft to the South; gliders variable. Strip runs from windsock to
WSW, steep upslope to 24 threshold. Runway gradient —slight upslope on 24.
Caution: • Expect windshear on final approach to Rwy 24;
            • Glider launching by winch and aerotow, may be from separate points;
            • Sheep on field when gliding not in progress.
Landing Fees: Private £5.00, Commercial £10.00.   **Radio:** Currock Base 130·10.
Fuel: 100LL   **Tel:** 01207-561286

16 DEFFORD (Croft Farm)   N52 05·22 W002 08·22   69 ft. AMSL
0·5 nm SE of Disused Aerodrome.
Grass strip 09/27, 570 x 18m.
Remarks: Operated by Mr. C.H. Porter. The Croft Farm, Defford, Worcester. WR8 9BN
Visiting aircraft accepted on prior permission and at pilot's own risk.
Good clear appro- aches, strip marked, windsock displayed.
All circuits to S to avoid overflying radar site.
Landing Fees: Donations to Mission Aviation Fellowship gratefully accepted.
Radio: Defford Radio 119·10 A/G.
Fuel: Nil.   **Tel:** 01386-750400. Mobile 07767- 606172.

17 DONEMANA   N54 53·42 W007 17·55   340 ft. AMSL
10 nm S of Londonderry Eglinton. **Op hrs:** PPR. HJ.   **BEL 117·20 299 39**
Rwy: Paved runway 06/24 300 x 30 m.
Remarks: Unlicensed private airfield operated by Mr. Alfie Danton. Use of airfield is
at pilot's/owner's own risk. Prior briefing mandatory for first time users.
Taxi/Car Hire: By prior arrangement **Accommodation:** Available nearby.
Fuel: MOGAS (limited supplies)   **Tel/Fax:** 01504-398000

18 DUNSTABLE (Dunstable Downs)   N51 52·00 W000 32·90   500 ft. AMSL
1 nm S of Dunstable.
Grass Airfield
Remarks: Gliding site operated by the London Gliding Club, Dunstable Downs,
Tring Road, Dunstable, Beds. Situated within Luton CTR, contact Luton App 129·55.
Powered aircraft accepted on strict PPR by telephone.
Intensive gliding operations. Permission normally restricted to pilots with a gliding
standard of Silver 'C' or higher and who are on gliding business.
Strict lookout be kept by visiting pilots.
Sharply undulating field surface, very rough in places.
Landing information given on telephone contact. No landing fees.
Fuel: Nil.   **Tel:** 01582-663419

19 EASTBACH (Spence Airfield) (Coleford)   N51 50·00 W002 35·00   600 ft. AMSL
6 nm S of Ross-on-Wye, 6 nm NE of Monmouth.
Multiple grass strips NW/SE max 400 m.
Remarks: Operated by 'Spence Airfield' Associates, Acorn Cottage, Hangerberry,
Lydbrook, Glos GL17 9QG. Strictly PPR and at pilot's own risk.
Airfield situated on sloping ground and suitable for aircraft with short field
performance. Land only from North or South West. Please avoid large house to the
South of the field.
Sheep frequently on landing strips. Windsock displayed. No landing fees.
Fuel: MOGAS (on request).
Tel: Contact Bruce Morgan or Wendy Durrad on 01594-835435 (Day),
01594-860988 (evenings). **Fax:** 01594-861533.

20 EASTON MAUDIT   N52 12·77 W000 41·75   300 ft. AMSL
7 nm ESE of Northampton.
Grass strip 16/34, 604 x 23m.
Remarks: Operated by Tim Allebone, The Limes, Easton Maudit, Nr. Wellingborough,
Northants. Strictly PPR. Windsock displayed.
Rwy 16 is recommended in light winds as there is a pronounced downhill slope at the
Northern end of the field.
Avoid overflying the village and farmhouse half a mile south of strip
Caution: Power cables running N/S to the West of strip.
Fuel: Nil.   **Tel:** 01933-663225

21 EAST WINCH   N52 43·35 E000 31·90   49 ft. AMSL
4 nm SE of Kings Lynn.
Grass Strip 10/28, 850 x 16m.
Remarks: Operated by Scanrho Aviation, Hillington, Kings Lynn. PPR. Airfield
situated within Marham MATZ, contact Marham APP 124·15. (Tel: 01760-337261).
Circuits at 800 ft. LH on 10, RH on 28.
Crop spraying a/c operate from the airfield.
Fuel: Nil.   **Tel:** 01553-840396.

22 EGGESFORD   N50 52·13 W003 52·13   516 ft. AMSL
4 nm E of Winkleigh Airfield (disused).   **BHD 112·70 339 31·5**
Op hrs: PPR.
Grass strip 11/29, 630m (Gradient — upslope for first 200m at both ends)
Remarks: Operated by N. Skinner Esq., Trenchard, Eggesford, Chumleigh, Devon.
Light aircraft are welcome at pilot's own risk.
Approaches are good with low hedge at 29 Thld and gravel road at 11 Thld. Beware
of windshear on final approach to 29 when winds are southerly.
Windsock displayed.
Caution: Farm stock on airfield. Low flying military aircraft.
Fuel: 100LL.   **Tel:** Lapford 01363-83746. **Fax:** 01363-83972

23 ERROL   N56 24·30 W003 10·92   31 ft. AMSL
6 nm SW of Dundee Airport.   **PTH 110·40 117 6·5**
Asphalt runway 05/23, 700x46m (northern part of disused airfield).
Op hrs: SR–SS (closed Mon and Thur).
Remarks: Operated by Mr. L. Doe. Muirhouses Farm, Errol, Tayside.
Unlicensed aerodrome.
Strictly PPR. Contact Leuchars App 126·50 and Dundee App 122·90 and advise
intention to land at Errol.
Free-Fall Parachuting up to FL150.
Circuits at 900ft aal; LH on 23, RH on 05. Approach and climb-out on 05 and 23 on
extended centreline for at least 1nm to avoid overflying sensitive habitation.
Parking at NE end on perimeter track in front of farmhouse.
Visiting pilots are required to report to either Fife Parachuting Centre, Muirhouses
Farm or Harbour Sawmills Ltd (on disused Rwy 11).
Landing Fee: Singles £5, twins £10.
Fuel: Nil   **Tel:** 01821-642555/642333/642673. **Fax:** 01821-642825

24 FARTHING CORNER   N51 19·83   E000 36·07   420 ft. AMSL
4 nm S of Gillingham (300 m from Medway Services on M2).
Grass strip 06/24, 380x20 m.
Remarks: Operated by Stoneacre Boys Club, Stoneacre Farm, Matts Hill Road,
Sittingbourne, Kent ME9 7XA. Unlicensed airfield located 1 nm N of Detling VOR.
Use of airfield by prior permission essential.
Power cables run parallel to the strip, 80 m NW of boundary.
Avoid overflying farmhouse 400 m to the east of runway.
Final approach to Rwy 24 to be made between Farm House and threshold.
Warning: In light wind conditions severe windshear may be encountered on final
approach to Rwy 06.
Landing Fee: £2.00. Beverages available free.
Fuel: Nil.   **Tel:** 07880-748064.

25 FEARN (Fearn)   N57 45·48   W003 56·58   25 ft.AMSL
8 nm NE of Invergordon.   **Op hrs:** PPR.
Asphalt runway 11/29, 1097 x 46m.
Remarks: Operated by Mrs D. Sutherland. Tullich Farm, Fearn, Ross-shire,
IV20 1XW. PPR by telephone. Other runways obstructed by fences.
Light aircraft accepted by arrangement and at pilot's own risk.
Care must be taken. Airfield situated in Danger Area EGD 703, call Tain Range
122·75 for DAAIS.
Fuel: Nil.   **Tel:** 01862-832278

26 FELTHORPE   N52 42·35   E001 11·57   120 ft. AMSL
4 nm NNW of Norwich Airport.
Two grass runways 16/34, 436 x 28m. 05/23, 487 x 26m.
Remarks: Operated by Felthorpe Flying Group Ltd., Taverham Road, Felthorpe,
Norwich NR10 4DR. Group Secretary: Norman Dean, Valley View, Intwood Lane,
Swardeston, Norwich NR14 8EA.
Light aircraft are welcome at all times on PPR and at pilot's own risk.
Join overhead at 1000' QFE. Circuits at 500' QFE.
RH on Rwys 05 and 16, LH on Rwys 23 and 34. Aircraft should avoid overflying
Felthorpe village, also Taverham and Taverham Nursery to the South of the airfield.
Windsock and landing T displayed.
Radio: Felthorpe Radio 123·50 A/G. Norwich APP 119·35.
Landing Fees: Nil.
Hangarage: Limited.   **Restaurant:** Clubhouse amenities.
Fuel: By arrangement.   **Tel:** Airfield 01603-867691.
                                        Secretary 01508-571148, **Fax:** 01508-571142,
                                                  E-mail: ndean@iname.com.
                                                  Chairman 01603-755317.

27 FETLAR   N60 36·20   W000 52·45   270 ft. AMSL
Shetland Islands.
Rolled mortar strip 01/19, 481 x 18m.
Remarks: Operated by Fetlar Development Group, Fetlar, Shetland.
PPR. Unlicensed airfield.
Fuel: Nil.   **Tel:** 01957-733267

28 HITCHIN (Rush Green)   N51 54·18 W000 14·85   350 ft. AMSL
3 nm S of Hitchin.
Grass strip NNW/SSE 549m.
Remarks: Operated by Bowker Farm Services Ltd, Rush Green, Hitchin, Herts.
PPR. Light aircraft are welcome during normal working hours and at pilot's own risk.
Care must be taken, no aerodrome control. Contact Luton APP 129·55.
Limited hangarage. Servicing and repairs available.
Visitors requested to book-in at caravan
Radio: 122·35 O/R.
Fuel: 100LL.   **Tel:** 01438-355051 (Airfield). 01462-452295 (Office).

29 HOUGHAM   N53 00·37 W000 41·35   120 ft. AMSL
5 nm SE of Newark.
Grass runways 18/36, 402 x 20m Light Aircraft & Microlights.
                09/27, 120 x 20m Microlights only
Remarks. Operated by Hougham Flying Group. Unlicensed airfield. Light aircraft
and microlights welcome at all times at pilot's own risk. Western boundary of
Cranwell MATZ is 2 nm East of airfield. Circuits at 800ft aal; RH on 36, LH on 18.
Rwy 09/27 for use by microlights only with strong easterly/westerly winds.
Windsock E of Rwy 18/36. Avoid overflying farms and habitation in vicinity of airfield.
Caution: Railway embankment with overhead electrification 400 m N of 18 threshold
and telegraph wires 400 m S of 36 threshold. **Radio:** 129·825 by arrangement.
Fuel: Nil.
Tel: 0115-9613140 John Fairweather evenings, or 01400-250293 days & weekends,
ask for Mike or Connie Barnatt Millns.

30 HULL (Humbleton)   N53 47·83 W000 09·98   20 ft. AMSL
7 nm ENE of Hull centre.
Grass strip 08/26, 610 x 14m.
Remarks: Operated by C. R. Knapton Esq., Light aircraft welcome on PPR and at
pilot's own risk. Danger Area D306 1 nm to NE. Windsock on hangar at end of
taxiway, 200m North of rwy. No landing fees.
Fuel: Nil.   **Tel:** 01964-670242

31 HUNTINGDON (Kimbolton)   N52 19·00 W000 22·85   246 ft. AMSL
Kimbolton Airfield. 1 nm W of Grafham Water (large Reservoir).
2 grass strips * 14/32, 400 x 18 m; 10/28, 600 x 12 m.
Remarks: Operated by R. C. Convine, Yendis, Stow Longa, Hunts. Light aircraft are
welcome at pilot's own risk. Narrow strip. Visiting pilots fly over hangar; if no one
there, circle over Stow Longa to attract attention. Windsock displayed.
Caution: Gas Booster Station with tall mast on approach to Rwy 32.
Note: * Rwy 14/32 closed on the second Saturday and Sunday of each month due to
kart racing, use Rwy 10/28. No landing fees.
Fuel: Nil.   **Tel:** Huntingdon 01480-860300/727

32 HUSBANDS BOSWORTH   N52 26·43 W001 02·63   505 ft AMSL
8·5 nm NE of Rugby.   **Op hrs:** Daily May-Sept.
Grass strip E/W. Grass area only to be used.   W/Es only Oct-Apr.
Remarks: Operated by The Soaring Centre, Husbands Bosworth Airfield,
Lutterworth, Leics. LE17 6JJ. Ex-RAF airfield, now gliding site. Strictly PPR.
Care must be taken as landing area is North of road running East to West.
Fuel: Nil.   **Tel:** 01858-880521 Office

33 INNERLEITHEN (Glenormiston)   N55 37·42 W003 05·35   500 ft. AMSL
1 nm W of Innerleithen
Grass strip 13/31 515 x 15m
Remarks: Operated by J. G. Hogg (Owner). PPR from George Askew, Glenormiston,
Innerleithen, Peebleshire. Use is at pilot's own risk and prior permission is required.
The strip is flat, but the western end can be boggy.
Caution: Farm road and power lines to the West. Difficult approaches due to high
ground to N and S of the strip. Windsock only shown after PPR. Avoid overflying local
village. No landing fee.
Fuel: Nil.   **Tel:** 01896-830940; 07798-574245

34 KING'S LYNN (Tilney St. Lawrence)   N52 43·02 E000 18·90   10 ft. AMSL
4·5 nm SW of King's Lynn. 1·6 nm W of River Great Ouse.
Grass strip 16/34, 400 x 32m.
Remarks: Operated by J. Goodley & Sons Ltd., Hirdling House,
Tilney St. Lawrence. Strictly PPR. Aircraft accepted on prior permission and at pilot's
own risk. Pylons 200 ft. high 0·5 nm to the North. Windsock displayed.
No landing fee.
Fuel: Nil.   **Tel:** 01945-880237

35 KIRKCUDBRIGHT (Plunton)   N54 51·00 W004 09·05   250 ft. AMSL
5 nm W of Kirkcudbright.   **Op hrs:** PPR. SR-SS.
Grass strip 02/20, 459m
Remarks: Operated by William S. Sproat, Lennox Plunton Farm, Borgue,
Kirkcudbright. Use is entirely at visitor's risk and is strictly PPR as stock may have to
be moved. Boundary of runway marked. It is essential to adhere to these marks.
Windsock at East side of strip. Picketing facilities available.
Caution: Power cables 400m South of strip.
Fuel: Nil.   **Tel:** Borgue 870210.

36 LAMBLEY   N53 00·55 W001 03·48   300 ft. AMSL
4 nm NE of Nottingham, 7nm SW of Southwell.   **TNT 115·70 103 23**
Grass strip 08/26, 600 x 18m. TORA/LDA 500 m.   **Op hrs:** PPR. SR-SS.
Remarks: Operated by Mr. John Hardy, Jericho Farm, Green Lane, Lambley, Notts.
NG4 4QE. Strictly PPR. Use at pilots' own risk. Runway has markers on each side,
and the runway is liable to waterlogging in Winter.
Caution: Public road crosses approach to Rwy 08, and a fence on approach to
Rwy 26. Avoid overflying local villages and Lowdham Grange Cat 2 Prison.
Radio: c/s Lambley Radio 123·05 A/G - on request.
Restaurant: 800 yds in village.   **Taxi:** On request.
Fuel: Emergency only.   **Tel:** 0115-931 3530 (Home/Office);
                                                  0115-931 3639; 07768-726279

37 LANGHAM   N52 56·30 E000 57·38   120 ft. AMSL
9 nm W of Sheringham.
Two concrete runways 07/25, 1000 x 10m; 10/28, 700x15m (old taxiway)
Grass strip 02/20, 550x18m (SW end of disused airfield).
Remarks: Operated by H. Labouchere Esq. PPR. No circuits. Mast (lit) 98ft,
250m N of Rwy 25 threshold and very close to final approach on Rwy 20.
NE section of airfield is disused. Airfield not suitable for inexperienced pilots due to
obstructions.
Caution: Trees and Huts on approach to Rwy 28.
Maintenance: M3 approved.
Landing Fee: £10.
Fuel: Nil.   **Tel:** 01328-830003
                                                         Fax: 01328-830232

38 LONG MARSTON   N52 08·42   W001 45·22   154ft AMSL
3·5nm SW of Stratford-on-Avon.   **HON 113·65 200 14**
Asphalt Rwy 04/22, 800 x 50 m.   **Op hrs:** PPR. 0900–SS
Remarks: Operated by Long Marston Airfield Limited, Long Marston Airfield,
Stratford-upon-Avon, Warwickshire CV37 8RT. PPR. Gliding, Parachuting and
Microlight activity on airfield. Microlight training school operated by Freedom Sports
Aviation. Restaurant facilities available at weekends.
Fuel: Nil.   **Tel:** 01789-299229 PPR.
                  Aerolite Flight Training (Mobile) 07770-680195
     Freedom Sports Aviation   07802-728051/01283-716265 or 07710-229082.
                           E-mail: fsportavia@aol.com.

39 LONG STRATTON   N52 29·32   E001 12·90   172 ft. AMSL
11·5 nm SW of Norwich Airport   **CLN 114·55 008 38·5**
Grass Rwy 17/35, 800 x 20 m
Remarks: Operated by Cheqair Ltd. Unlicensed airfield. Strictly PPR. Visitors at
pilot's own risk on company business for Cheqair, SMC Aviation or Stratton Motor
Company. Fixed wing circuits - LH on Rwy 17, RH on Rwy 35.
Helicopters via Joining Gates. Pilots must receive a brief from Chief Pilot or Ops
personnel.
Avoid overflying local villages.
Warning: Tibenham airfield 3·5 nm to SW.
Maintenance: JAR 145.
Landing Fee: On application.
Radio: Cheqair Ops 122·95, if no reply make a "blind call" and proceed with caution.
Fuel: Jet A1 only.
Tel: 01508-531144. 530493 (outside hours) **Fax:** 01508-531670.

40 LOUTH (Stewton)   N53 21·52   E000 01·90   60 ft. AMSL
1·5 nm SE of Louth, Lincs.   **Op hrs:** PPR. SR-SS
Grass strip 06/24, 675 m. Width varies from 12 m at narrowest to 60 m.
Remarks: Operated by Douglas Electronic Industries Ltd., Louth, Lincs.
Strip lies between road and North side of disused Louth/Mablethorpe railway line.
Windsock usually displayed.
Light aircraft are welcome on PPR and at pilot's own risk.
Care must be taken – undulations in centre of strip.
Aid to location – strip lies midway between Louth town and disused Manby airfield.
Caution: Gliders operate from Manby up to 2,000 ft agl.
Fuel: Nil.   **Tel:** 01507-606128 for advice or transport.

41 LUNDY ISLAND   N51 10·20   W004 40·23   400 ft. AMSL
11 nm NW of Hartland Point (N. Devon).   **Op hrs:** PPR. SR-SS.
Grass Rwy NE/SW, 400 m.
Remarks: Operated by the Lundy Company, Lundy Island, Bristol Channel, Devon
EX39 2LY. Light aircraft accepted on prior notice, and at pilots own risk.
Lighthouse near airfield.
Caution: Runway surface rough and farm stock may be in the area. Prior notice is
essential as a fence has to be removed.
B & B and letting accommodation available.
Landing Fees: £10.00. £3.50 National Trust admission.
Fuel: Nil.   **Tel:** 01237-431831. **Fax:** 01237-431832

42 MILSON N52 21·68 W002 32·75 500 ft. AMSL
3 nm WSW of Cleobury Mortimer. **Op hrs:** PPR. Day only
Grass strip 17/35, 450 x 15m. Grass kept cut. O.S. Sheet 138/629738
Remarks: Operated by Mr. Hugh Thompson, Little Down Farm, Milson,
Kidderminster, Worcester. DY14 0BD.
Possibility of sheep on airstrip for short periods. Up-slope at Northern end.
Windsock displayed at East of strip.
Occasional military helicopter activity weekdays.
Helicopters to land/hover at northern end only using metal helicopter pad area if
possible.
Caution: High ground up to 1,750 ft amsl with Radar station on top, 3 nm NW of
strip.
Note: Landings are normally made from S on Rwy 35 which affords an unobstructed
approach. Use of airfield in strong East or Westerly winds not recommended.
No take-offs permitted on main airstrip 1400-1700 on Sundays during April-Sept,
(The two allowed Fly-ins not included).
Landing Fee: £2.00 for aircraft, £1.00 for Microlights.
Hangarage: Possible.
Fuel: Nil. **Tel:** 01584-890486, 07702-077996

43 NAYLAND N5158·00 E00051·00 180 ft. AMSL
5 nm NW of Colchester, 7 nm SE of Sudbury. **Op hrs:** PPR.
Grass strip 14/32 600 x 20m, marked with white markers.
Remarks: Operated by Mr. R. A. Harris and the Nayland Flying Group, Hill Farm,
Wiston, Nayland. CO6 4 NL. Visitors welcome, PPR by telephone, and at pilot's own
risk. Rwy 14/32 has a severe upslope to the NW.
Alternative unmarked landing directions available.
Circuits at 800' aal avoiding built-up areas in vicinity of the strip. Wattisham MATZ to
the NW. Sudbury Radio mast, 768 ' amsl, 541 ' agl, to the NW.
Tea/Coffee available. Windsock displayed.
Landing Fee: £2.00
Maintenance: Available, Tel: 01206-263178; 01206-230333.
Accommodation: Available nearby.
Taxi: Redding Taxis, Tel: 01206-262530.
Fuel:100LL.
Tel: 01206-262298 R.A. Harris; Mobile 07887-594355; 01206-263317 Club Room.

44 NUTHAMPSTEAD (Royston) N51 59·67 E000 04·12 460 ft. AMSL
4 nm SE of Royston, 8 nm NE of Buntingford. **VOR/DME 'BKY' 116·25 (On A/D).**
Grass strip 05/23, 700 x 35 m.
Op hrs: HJ.
Remarks: Operated by Nuthampstead Airfield Associates Ltd., Keffords, Barley,
Roystone, Herts SG8 8LB.
Ex-RAF aerodrome, the grass strip is where part of the old runway was removed, and
using the 23 end of this old runway. Windsock displayed.
Light aircraft are welcome at all times on PPR and at pilot's own risk.
Strip clearly marked and it is essential to land only within the markers.
There is a 120 ft mast adjacent to the office block due West of the 05 end.
Care must be taken as cars and farm tractors may be using the 6 m wide concrete
strips left from old runway. Transport can be arranged.
Fuel: Nil. **Tel:** 01763-848287
Fax: 01763-849616

45 NYMPSFIELD (Stroud)   N51 42·85 W002 17·02   700 ft. AMSL
3 nm SW of Stroud, on edge of Cotswold Escarpment.
Grass strip E/W 1,120 m.
Remarks: Gliding site operated by the Bristol & Gloucestershire Gliding Club.
Powered aircraft accepted strictly PPR by telephone on the day, gliding business
only. Intensive gliding operation including winch launching.
Field undulating and subject to strong turbulence and wind gradients in crosswinds.
Details of these and further hazards will be given by telephone if permission is
granted.
Landing Fee: £5.00
Fuel: 100LL.   **Tel:** Dursley 01453-860342

46 OAKLANDS FARM   N51 50·85 W00126·73   370 ft AMSL
5 nm W of Oxford (Kidlington) airfield.   **Op hrs:** PPR. SR-SS.
Grass strip 12/30, 400 x 12 m.
Remarks: Operated by Mr. Robert J. Stobo, Oaklands Farm, Stonesfield, Oxford.
OX8 8DW. Prior permission essential.
Power lines cross the approach to Rwy 12, approx 150 m from the threshold 12.
Rwy 30 threshold close to a minor road.
STOL aircraft welcome on prior permission and at pilots own risk.
Avoid overflying local villages. Windsock displayed.
Fuel: Nil.   **Tel:** 01993-891226

47 OSWESTRY (Knockin)   N52 48·35 W002 59·42   250 ft. AMSL
4·5 nm SE of Oswestry.
Grass field 10/28, 650m., along Northern edge of field.
Remarks: Operated by Mr. T.R. Jones, Sandford Hall, Oswestry, Shropshire
SY11 4EX.
Light aircraft PPR and at pilot's own risk.
Windsock displayed. No landing fee.
Fuel: Nil.
Tel: 01691-610888 (day); 01691-610206 (night); **Fax:** 01691-610144.

48 OXFORD (Weston-on-the-Green)   N51 52·82 W001 13·18   282 ft. AMSL
7 nm from Oxford. 4 nm NE of Oxford Airport (Kidlington).
Three grass strips 01/19, 690 m; 06/24, 830 m; 10/28 910 m.
Remarks: Gliding site operated by Oxford Gliding Club. Strictly PPR.
Permanent Danger Area (EGD 129). Circle radius 2 nm centred on the airfield is
military and RAFSPA dropping zone up to FL120., including free-fall parachuting.
Pilots should be aware that in the immediate vicinity military aircraft may fly pre-set
range patterns and an especially sharp lookout is required.
DAAIS is available from Brize Radar on 134·30.

The area should be avoided at all times unless prior permission to use the airfield has
been obtained. Call RAF Weston on the Green – VHF 133·65 or UHF 255·10.
Fuel: Nil.
Tel: 01993-842551 Ext 7551 Brize Norton; or 01869-343246 Aerodrome.
       01869-343265 Gliding Club or 0836-773210 Launch Point.

49 POLZEATH (Roserrow Golf and Country Club)
                     N50 33·72 W004 54·02   131 ft. AMSL
1 nm SE of Polzeath, 8·5 nm NE of RAF St. Mawgan.   O.S. Sheet 200/947776
Grass strip 11/29 700 x 60m set in 400 acres of ground.
Helipad also available with specific landing area marked.

continued

49 POLZEATH (Roserrow Golf and Country Club) - continued
Remarks: Operated by Roserrow Golf and Country Club, Roserrow, St. Minver, Wadebridge, Cornwall PL27 6QT. Available daylight hours only.
Light aircraft welcome at all times on PPR and at pilot's own risk.
Windsock or flag displayed.
18 hole Golf Course, Tennis Courts, 20m indoor swimming pool, sauna, steam room, spa, fitness suite and beauty therapy.
Accommodation: Luxury homes on site.
Restaurant: Brasserie with sea views, open all day and evening.
Taxi/Car Hire: By arrangement. **Landing Fee:** £12.00; overnight parking: £5.00.
Fuel: Nil (nearest Bodmin) **Tel:** 01208-863000. **Fax:** 01208-863002.

50 PRIORY FARM (Tibenham)   N52 27·02 E001 06·90   188 ft AMSL
7 nm S of Wymondham, 1nm W of Tibenham airfield.   **Op hrs:** 1000-2000.
Grass strip 01/19 650 x 25m, LDA 500m.
Remarks: Operated by Mr. Bob Sage, Priory Farm, Tibenham, Norwich, Norfolk NR1 6NY. PPR. Join overhead at 500' aal. Circuits at 500' aal, LH on Rwy 01, RH on Rwy 19. Buildings on approach to Rwy 01. Possible windshear touchdown point opposite the windsock. Windsock located at southern end.
Stay clear of intensive gliding at Tibenham 1 nm to East and also avoid overflying the village 0·5nm NE.
Hangarage: Overnight possible. **Landing Fee:** Nil.
Fuel: 100LL.   **Tel/Fax:** 01379-677334.

51 REDLANDS (Swindon)   N51 33·30 W001 41·33   320 ft. AMSL
1 nm E of Swindon.   **CPT 114·35 288 18·5**
Two Grass Strips 06/24 407 x 11 m; 17/35 274 x 13 m.
Op hrs: PPR. SR-SS, except Sun 1000-2000.
Remarks: Owned and operated by Mr J and S Smith, Redlands Farm, Wanborough, Swindon. Unlicensed Microlight Airfield. Microlights ONLY. Pilots use the airfield at their own risk. Arrivals/Departures from/to the North via the two barns located N of the airfield. Inbound aircraft at 1500 ft aal. Outbound aircraft climb out over the barns to railway line before turning. Overhead joins at 1500 ft aal. Circuits at 500' aal; LH on 06 and 35, RH on 17 and 24. Observe signal square, windsock displayed. Electric fence on north side of 06/24, and west side of 17/35.
Avoid overflying all local habitation.
All aircraft must have a Third Party Liability Insurance.
Landing Fee: £3.50.   **Hangarage:** Limited.   **Restaurant:** Tea/Coffee available.
Fuel: Garage within 2 miles.   **Tel:** 01793-791014

52 REDNAL (Shropshire)   N52 50·52 W002 55·92
270 ft. AMSL
4 nm SE of Oswestry
Asphalt Rwy 04/22, 700 x 40 m.
Remarks: The home of the Classic & Vintage Aeroplane Company operated by Roger Reeves, Moss House, Malpas, Cheshire SY14 7JJ. Unlicensed airfield where PPR is always necessary. All movements at pilot's own risk.
All circuits to the East of the airfield at 1000 ft aal, with standard overhead join at 1500 ft aal. Avoid overflying local villages. Windsock displayed at West end of small hangar located near to 22 threshold.
Caution: Power cables 0·5 nm out from Rwy 22 threshold at right angles to approach and trees at Rwy 22 threshold.
Radio 118·175 A/G - Not always manned.
Landing Fee: Nil.   **Customs:** On request.
Restaurant: 2 miles.   **Hotel:** 3 miles.   **Taxi:** 01691-656149.
Fuel: Nil.   **Tel:** 01691-610507 Airfield; 01948-860111 Office. **Fax:** 01948-860222

53 RHIGOS   N51 44·57 W003 35·08   780ft AMSL
8 nm SW of Merthyr Tydfil.   **Op hrs:** Strictly PPR.
Grass strip 09/27, 550m.
Remarks: Operated by the Vale of Neath Gliding Club. PPR. Airfield not suitable for
light aircraft in strong North or South winds. Circuits LH on 27, RH on 09.
Avoid overflying Rhigos village to the East. Primary activity is gliding, beware of
launch cables. Caution required after rain, due to soft surface.
Airfield slopes down East to West. Sheep may be present on movement area.
Fuel: Nil.   **Tel:** 01685-811023

54 ROSSENDALE (Lumb)   N53 43·35 W002 15·17   925ft AMSL
3·5 nm S of Burnley. 500m W of B6238.   **POL 112·10 265 5·5**
Grass strip 12/30, 400x18m
Remarks: Operated by S. Walmsley Esq., Middle Bank Top Farm,
Lumb-in-Rossendale, Lancs. PPR. Strip is situated beneath Manchester TMA (Base
3500ft). Light aircraft welcome at pilot's own risk. Advise telephone call for briefing if
not familiar with the strip.
Caution: Strip liable to be soft during wet winter periods. Uphill gradient towards
NW. Recommend landing Rwy 30 unless strong winds from South to East. Strip is
surrounded by high ground rising to 1500ft amsl 2nm to NE. Power cables 1nm to
NE. No landing fees.
Fuel: Nil   **Tel:** Rossendale 01706-216564

55 ST. NEOTS (Honeydon)   N52 13·02 W000 21·10   170 ft AMSL
7 nm NNE of Bedford. 1 nm SE of Staughton Airfield.
Grass field E/W 640m. NE/SW 678m. NW/SE 678m.
Remarks: Operated by B. Spencer- Thomas, The Chestnuts, Honeydon, Bedford
Mk44 2LR. Light aircraft accepted on prior permission only and at pilot's own risk.
Rough surface, uncut grass grazed by sheep.
Windsock (not always erected). No landing fees.
Fuel: Nil.   **Tel:** 01234-376393.

56 SEIGHFORD   N52 49·67 W002 12·20   320 ft. AMSL
2·5 nm NW of Stafford.
Concrete Rwy 13/31, 500 x 50m.   **Op hrs:** SR – SS
Remarks: Operated by W. O. Brown, Clanford Hall, Seighford, Staffs. Strictly PPR.
Use at pilot's own risk and full insurance is imperative. Circuits at 1000' aal,
RH on 13, LH on 31. Intensive glider activity at weekends, a telephone call is
necessary for a detailed Briefing before the journey.
Avoid overflying local villages and stud farm 0·5 nm to left of approach to Rwy 31.
Windsock displayed. **Landing Fee:** Nil.
Car Hire: Eurocar, Stafford.   **Taxi:** Available on request.
Fuel: Nil.   **Tel:** 01785-282 237

57 SKEGNESS – Withdrawn.

58 SPANHOE – See entry at page 467.

59 STRATHAVEN   N55 40·80 W004 06·33   847 ft AMSL
1·3 nm W of Strathaven.
Grass strip 10/28, 730 x 90m.
Remarks: Operated by Strathclyde Gliding Club. Grass strip marked by white flush
slabs. Strictly PPR and at pilot's own risk as parts of the grass strip are very bumpy.
Glider flying at weekends and Wednesday evenings. "STRATHAVEN" in white letters
on red hangar roof. Windsock on S side only.
Beware grazing cattle when no glider flying in progress. Obstructions, HT wires and
trees 35 ft. high approximately 90 m obliquely from E boundary fence.
Landing only with club permission.
Visiting aircraft welcome on prior permission and provided they comply with the
appropriate circuit pattern.
Caution: Winch cables in use, do not join overhead.
Landing Fee: £2.00.
Fuel: Nil.   **Tel:** 01357-520235 Airfield or 0141 339 4130.

60 STRUBBY   N53 18·60 E000 10·57   47ft. AMSL
4nm SW of Mablethorpe.
Rwy 08/26 Tarmac/Con 850 x 46 m.#
Remarks: Operated by C. V. Stubbs & Sons, and Strubby Gliding Club. PPR.
A/D utilises the western section of old RAF airfield. The only usable section of
runway is the western end of 08/26; all other sections of runways are unusable.
Glider operations, winching and aerotows take place on the runway in use; beware of
cables!!
 # Note. The grass extension to Rwy 26 is unsuitable for powered aircraft.
Landing Fee: £10.00.
Hangarage & Maintenance: Limited.
Radio: Strubby Base 130·10. A/G (Gliding Club).
NDB 'SBY' 330·0 (On A/D).
Fuel: Nil.   **Tel:** 01507-450294

61 SUDBURY (Waits Farm)   N5202·05 E00038·07   200 ft. AMSL
3·5 nm W of Sudbury.   **Op hrs:** PPR
Grass strip 07/25, 520 x 18m.
Remarks: Operated by R. Teverson Esq., Waits Farm, Belchamp Walter, Sudbury.
PPR and at pilot's own risk. 1 in 60 gradient uphill on Rwy 07.
Circuits at 800 ft aal.
Do not fly near occasional traffic, especially horses, on public road near the approach
to Rwy 07. Avoid overflying villages to North and East of the airfield.
Windsock usually displayed.
Fuel: Nil.   **Tel:** 01787-373975

62 SUTTON MEADOWS   N52 23·02 E000 03·90   8 ft AMSL
5 nm W of Ely.   **Op hrs:** PPR. SR-SS.
3 Grass strips 01/19, 470m; 06/24 480m; 10/28 490m; short grass, runways not
always marked out.
Remarks: Operated by Peter B. Robinson, Argents Farm House, 114 High Street,
Sutton, Ely, Cambs. PPR. Site operated as a microlight training and club centre.
Power lines, 20 ft high to the East and South. Join overhead at 800' aal.
Circuits at 500' aal, left or right hand. Avoid overflying local habitation.
Landing Fee: £2.00 (PPR), (£5.00 without PPR). Nil for reciprocal.
Radio: Occasionally 129·825.
Fuel: Nil.
Tel: 01353-778446 Proprietor, 01487-843311 Cambs. Microlight Club,
    01487-842360 Pegasus Flight Training.

63 SWINDON (Draycott)   N51 29·75 W001 44·62   525 ft AMSL
5 nm S of Swindon. 2 nm ESE of Wroughton Airfield. **CPT 114·35 275 19**
Grass Rwy 18/36, 535 x 30m (LDA 36 – 384m)   **Op hrs:** PPR. HJ.
Remarks: Operated by Draycott Flight Centre, Chiseldon, Swindon, Wilts.
Airfield situated within Lyneham CTR — inbound aircraft contact Lyneham App on
123·40; outbound – contact Lyneham App immediately after take-off.
Airfield restricted to radio equipped aeroplanes with MTWA less than 5,000lbs.
No Circuits.
Landing Fee: £5.00   **Hangarage:** Available
Fuel: Nil.   **Tel:** 07831-237955

64 TEMPLE BRUER   N53 04·60 W000 30·77   240ft AMSL
2·5 nm NNW of RAF Cranwell   **GAM 112·80 135 20**
Grass Strip 08/26, 550 x 37m   **Op hrs:** 0800-SS
Remarks: Operated by D.A. Porter. Unlicensed airfield situated within the Cranwell
MATZ., contact Cranwell App 119·375 or Waddington App 127·35.
Light aircraft welcome on prior permission and at pilot's own risk.
Circuits LH at 500ft aal.
Power cables 400m from threshold on approach to Rwy 26, and road with raised
surface crosses 26 threshold.
Caution: Windshear on approach to Rwy 26 with NW winds. Gliders operating from
Cranwell North (2 nm to S) at weekends and summer evenings.
Landing Fee: Singles £5.00; Twins £10.00.
Fuel: Nil.   **Tel:** 01522-810840

65 THIRSK (Sutton Bank)   N54 13·63 W001 12·82   920 ft. AMSL
5 nm E of Thirsk.
Two grass strips E/W 549 m. NE/SW 732 m.
Remarks: Operated by Yorkshire Gliding Club. Will accept light aircraft, at pilot's own
risk, on prior permission from resident instructor or C.F.I. so that briefing on weather
and circuit can be given.
Turbulence in strong wind conditions necessitates steep approach. Care should be
taken not to approach over steep S and W cliffs with insufficient airspeed to
overcome local down-draughts.
Windsocks on Clubhouse building.
Caution: Some areas of airfield may be soft.
Landing Fee: Nil. **Radio:** 130·40 A/G (Glider operations only).
Fuel: Nil.   **Tel:** 01845- 597237

66 THORNBOROUGH GROUNDS   N52 01·02 W000 58·10   270 ft AMSL
2 nm ENE of Buckingham.
Grass strip 05/23, 500 m.
Remarks: Operated by Christopher M. Moore, Thornborough Grounds, Bourton,
Buckingham MK18 2 AB. PPR. Unprepared grass strip comprising two linked river
meadows. Wet at times.
Livestock graze on strip during much of the year.
Visiting aircraft accepted with prior permission and at pilot's sole risk.
Caution: Pylons and power lines on both approaches.
Landing Fee: Voluntary.
Fuel: Nil.   **Tel:** 01280-81 2170. **Fax:** 01280 81 2064

67 THURROCK   N51 32·28 E000 22·00   30ft AMSL
5 nm SW of Basildon   **LAM 115·60 134 10·5**
Grass strip 09/27, 650m.   **Op hrs:** SR-SS daily.
Remarks: Operated by Thurrock Leisure Ltd. Unlicensed airfield. Airfield not always manned. Visiting aircraft welcome at pilot's own risk.
No windsock but windmill on site gives indication of wind direction.
Please avoid overflying villages in vicinity of airfield.
Landing Fee: Nil.
Parking: Available.   **Hangarage:** Available.   **Maintenance:** M3 approved
Fuel: 100LL.   **Tel:** 01375-891165

68 TIBENHAM   N52 27·40 E001 09·25   186 ft. AMSL
12 nm SW of Norwich.
Op hrs: PPR. WINTER: Wed, Thur & weekends; SUMMER: Seven days a week.
Three tarmac runways, 08/26, 700 x 46 m; 03/21, 914 x 46 m; 15/33, 914 x 46 m;
20 acre grass central triangle and 20 acre grass around windsock.
Remarks: Gliding site operated by Norfolk Gliding Club. Aerotow and winchlaunching, cables to 3000 ft. Exercise caution when landing because of separate rope dragging circuits by Tug Aircraft.
Please book in and out, all arrivals & departures must be recorded.
Landing Fee: Nil, but £6.00 day membership fee.
Radio: c/s Tibenham Radio 129·975 A/G (Powered aircraft). 130·10 A/G (Gliders).
Fuel: Available.   **Tel:** 01379 677 207.

69 UPPER HARFORD   N5153·32 W00149·28   750 ft. AMSL
3 nm W of Bourton-on-the-Water   **Op hrs:** Strictly PPR.
Grass runway 08/26, 640 x 21 m
Remarks: Operated by Mike Jones Esq., Upper Harford House, Upper Harford, Bourton-on-the-Water, Glos GL54 3BY.
Fuel: Nil.   **Tel/Fax:** 01451-821455

70 WEYBOURNE (Muckleburgh)   N52 56·83 E001 07·32   30 ft AMSL
3 nm West of Sheringham.
2 Grass Runways, 16/34, 610 x 40 m, 03/21 370 x 32 m.
Caution: UP gradient on Rwys 16 and 21.
Remarks: Operated by Muckleburgh Estates on an ex-RAF historic site, it was a WW II AA training school using catapult launched Tiger Moth "Queen Bees" as targets. Also operating from this site were Westerland Wallace, Henleys and Miles Magisters. It was the smallest WW II runway used by the RAF!
The site now houses Britain's largest private military collection, with some 15 working tanks and over 3500 individual exhibits.
Open the second week in February until the end of October annually from 1000-1700. No landing fee if admission is taken to the Museum,
Adults £4, OAP's £3.50, Children £2.50 – if no entry required, landing is £4 plus £1 for each passenger.
All pilots are required to book in and out in the flight record at the caravan.
Use of the airfield is entirely at the pilot's own risk, and all pilot's must carry adequate Third party insurance cover; the Collection and/or Muckleburgh Estates accept no responsibility whatsoever for pilots and/or passengers in its use.
Pilots are requested to avoid overflying the villages of KELLING and WEYBOURNE and to keep a sharp lookout for model aircraft which may be operating at the airfield, and circle the airfield once before landing. Windsock displayed.
Licensed restaurant and full toilet facilities available in the Museum.
Fuel: Nil.   **Tel:** 01263-588210/608 Museum Office. 822228 Taxi
                           Website: www.muckleburgh.fsnet.co.uk

71 WHITCHURCH (Tilstock)   N52 55·93 W002 38·83   301 ft. AMSL

2 nm S of Whitchurch (Shropshire).

Concrete runway 15/33, 600 x 30m.   **Op hrs:** PPR. Closed on Sundays

Remarks: Operated by R. T. Matson Esq., Twemlows Hall, Whitchurch, Shropshire.
Intensive parachuting activity up to FL150.

Please avoid overflying the area unless with prior permission or in direct radio
contact.

Light aircraft welcome at all times with prior notification and at pilot's own risk. Care
must be taken.

Runway is east of A41 and is in reasonable condition but often has a muck heap at
one end.

Airfield closed occasionally for special one day events.

Owing to the proximity to RAF Shawbury and RAF Ternhill the following arrival and
departure procedures have been agreed with Shawbury SATCO:

ARRIVALS:

Contact Shawbury APP 120·775 when 20 nm from Tilstock. Shawbury will provide
LARS or FIS and radar vectoring if required.

DEPARTURES:

• Notify Shawbury ATC by telephone at least 10 mins prior to take-off (01939-250351
Ext 7232). Announce "Tilstock departure" and give flight details.

• When airborne remain VMC and contact Shawbury Radar 120·775, climbing not
above 1000 ft (Tilstock QFE) until in contact with Radar or well clear of the extended
centreline of Shawbury Rwy 19.

• After initial contact, or if no contact, turn either right from Rwy 33, or left from Rwy
15 onto heading 050°M. Remain VMC if possible, and continue climb. Thereafter,
turn onto desired track as agreed with Shawbury Radar or abeam AUDLEM.

• Evenings, weekends & PHs when Shawbury is engaged in limited flying and LARS
is not available, departing aircraft should free call Shawbury TWR on 120·775 when
airborne, for flight information on Shawbury and Ternhill activity.

Radio: Tilstock Radio 122·075 A/G. Shawbury App 120·775.

Fuel: Available.

Tel: 01948-663239 R.T. Matson. 01948-841111 The Parachute Centre

72 WIGTOWN (Baldoon)   N54 50·95 W004 27·03   23 ft. AMSL

6 nm S of Newton Stewart.

One concrete runway 06/24, 446x18m (30m starter extension at each end)

Remarks: Operated by A.H. Sprout Esq. Unlicensed airfield.

Will accept light aircraft on prior permission and at pilot's own risk.

Care must be taken to ensure that runways are clear of sheep.

High ground 109 ft aal, 300 m NW of Rwy 06 threshold.

Mast 143 ft aal 142°T/3 nm.

Fuel: Nil.   **Tel:** 01988-42215.

73 WING FARM (Warminster)   N51 09·83 W002 12·62   420 ft. AMSL
2 nm SSW of Warminster.   **Op hrs:** PPR.
Grass strip 09/27, 500 x 26 m.
Remarks: Operated by E.W.B. Trollope, Wing Farm, Longbridge Deverill,
Warminster, Wilts. BA12 7DD. Light aircraft welcome at pilot's own risk.
All visiting aircraft must carry third party insurance cover.
Grass strip 500 x 26 m between white 'T' threshold markers. Runway gradient 1·5%
UP on Rwy 27.
Locating landmark – SHEARWATER LAKE, surrounded by pine woods, 1 nm N of the strip.
Wind 'T' at the west end. Max take-off ground run limited to 350 m, runway so
marked.
Parking at east end. All movements confined to the strip and parking area. Long term
parking available.
Landing Fee: Light aircraft £4, Microlights £2.
OvernightParking: Light aircraft £2, Microlights £1.
Warning: Glider site 2·5 nm SSW of the airfield, cables up to 2000' agl.
Maintenance: Airbourne Composites. Prop. Tim Dews. Tel: 01985-840981.
Fuel: Petrol Stn nearby.   **Tel:** Briefing and PPR from 01985-840401

74 WOOBURN (Hedsor Golf Course)   N51 34·67 W000 44·40   327 ft. AMSL
2 nm S of Beaconsfield, 2 nm E of Bourne End.
Grass Runways, 01/19 640 x 12 m, 06/24 400x 8 m.   **Op hrs:** PPR
Remarks: Operated by Meadowbank Construction Ltd., Sheepcote Farmhouse,
Wooburn Common, Bucks HP10 0JS.
Airfield situated within the London Control Zone, contact Heathrow Director 119·90.
Strip is suitable for STOL operations only. Cross-wind landings not recommended.
Prior inspection of the ground and surrounds recommended.
Warnings: Trees approximately 80 ft high to the north, east and south of the strip.
Field divided by hedges and ditches.Landing fee by arrangement.
Fuel: Nil   **Tel:** 01628-521419, then call 01628-851285 with ETA.

75 YEARBY   N54 35·02 W00104·03   30 ft. AMSL
2 nm S of Redcar.   **NEW 114·25 147 35**
Grass strip 07/25, 635 x 50m.
Remarks: Operated by J. A. Towers, Turners Arms, Yearby, Redcar, Cleveland.
Visiting aircraft accepted on prior permission and at pilot's own risk.
Airfield situated on SE boundary of Teesside CTA, contact Teesside App 118·85.
Do not overfly I.C.I. Industrial Complex 1·5 nm NW of airfield.
Fly all circuits to the South avoiding built-up areas in vicinity of airfield.
Windsock on hangar by arrangement.
Warning: Power cables 450 m to the east of landing strip.
Home base of Acro Engines & Airframes Ltd.
Fuel: Nil.   **Tel:** 01642-470322 Acro Engines
                                              01642-485419 J. Towers
                                      01642 484340 Farm Office (ansaphone)

GOVERNMENT AERODROMES.

The following government aerodromes are additional to those already incorporated in the Guide. Use of these aerodromes is strictly PPR.

BARKSTON HEATH   **EGYE**   N52 57·74 W000 33·70   367 ft AMSL
Rwy: 06/24 1831 m Asphalt. **Lighting:** 06 & 24 — Ap Thr Rwy PAPI
Rwy: 11/29 1282 m Asphalt. **Lighting:** 11 & 29 — Ap Thr Rwy PAPI
IBcn: 'BA' Red   **Op hrs:** PPR. Mon-Fri 0830-1700.
Remarks: Operated by MoD(RAF). Satellite aerodrome for RAF Cranwell. High intensity flying training. Light aircraft operate within the ATZ SR–SS at weekends and PHs. Aerobatic practices may take place overhead the aerodrome at weekends and Hols. Unified ATS with Cranwell. Circuits RH on 24. Owing to the proximity of adjacent aerodromes radar patterns, all aircraft on Instrument Approaches may be subject to "RIS", "FIS" or Procedural service. Avoid overflying local villages.
Cranwell App 119·375. Barkston **TWR** 120·425
Fuel: Nil   **Tel:** 01400-261201 Ext 5200

BOSCOMBE DOWN   **EGDM**   N51 09·13 W001 44·84   407 ft. AMSL
Rwy: 05/23 3212 m Asphalt/Concrete.   **Lighting:** Ap Thr Rwy PAPI
Rwy: 17/35 2109 m Asphalt/Concrete.   **Lighting:** Ap Rwy PAPI
Op hrs: PPR. Mon-Thu 0830-1700, Fri 0830-1600.
Remarks: Operated by MoD(PE). All visiting aircraft to call at 20 nm. Light aircraft and helicopter flying in daylight outside Op hrs. All missed approaches will be AS DIRECTED BY RADAR. No deadside. Helicopters operate south of runway up to 500 ft QFE. Light aircraft operate to parallel section of northern taxiway from non-standard 800 ft northerly circuit. Aerodrome active daylight hours outside of aerodrome hours.
Caution: After dark, up to 2359 Mon-Fri, MATZ may contain unlit aircraft, and also aerodrome and obstruction lights may be extinguished during flying.
Boscombe **ZONE** 126·70 (LARS/MATZ). **TWR/GND** 130·75.
TACAN 'BDN' 108·20 N51 08·93 W001 45·15. **ILS** Rwy 23 (235°M) 'BD' 111·70.
Fuel: 100LL, Avtur   **Tel:** 01980-663051/2 PPR Ops

CHIVENOR   **EGDC**   N51 05·23 W004 09·02   27 ft. AMSL
Rwy: 10/28 1833 m Asphalt. **Lighting:** 10 & 28 — Ap Rwy.
Op hrs: Visiting aircraft strictly PPR (24hrs).
Remarks: Operated by MoD(RAF). Helicopter activity H24. Powered gliders operate weekends and PHs HJ, Freq 130·20 A.C. Base.
Chivenor Radio 130·20 **A/G. ILS Rwy 28** (278°M) (QFU 276°M) 'CV' 108·10.
Fuel: Avtur - Limited quantities.   **Tel:** 01271-813662 Ext 7220 Daylight hours only.

COLERNE   **EGUO**   N51 26·45 W002 16·80   593 ft. AMSL
Rwy: 07/25 1664 m Asphalt. **Lighting:** Nil
Rwy: 01/19 1095 m Asphalt. **Lighting:** Nil   **Op hrs:** HO. Civ PPR.
Remarks: Operated by MoD(RAF). Ab initio pilot training. Local topography causes circuit turbulence irrespective of wind speed and direction. Trees up to 594 ft amsl within approach area to Rwy 25. Lyneham CTR overlaps edge of ATZ.
Colerne **TWR** 122·10
Fuel: 100LL   **Tel:** 01225-745338.

CONINGSBY **EGXC** N53 05·58 W000 09·96 25 ft. AMSL
Rwy: 08/26 2743 m Asphalt/Concrete. Arrester cables, normally both UP.
Lighting: Ap Thr Rwy PAPI 3°
IBcn: 'CY' Red **Op hrs**: PPR. Mon-Fri 0800-1700.
Remarks: Operated by MoD(RAF). Civil traffic strictly PPR. Runway has concrete ends extending in 200 m from threshold. Circuits RH on 08. Rwy traffic severely restricted when Rwy 08 in use.
Coningsby **APP** 120·8 (LARS/MATZ). **TWR** 119·975.
TACAN 'CGY' 111·10 (On A/D) N53 05·46 W000 10·14.
ILS Rwy 26 (256°M) 'CY' 110·70.
Fuel: 100LL, Avtur. **Tel:** 01526-342581 Ext 2061/2

COTTESMORE **EGXJ** N52 44·14 W000 38·93 461 ft AMSL
Rwy: 05/23 2744 m Concrete/Asphalt. Arrester gear 396 m from each end of Rwy.
Lighting: 05 & 23 Ap Thr Rwy PAPI 3°. **IBcn.** 'CM' Red.
Op hrs: PPR 24 hrs. Mon-Fri 0800-1700.
Remarks: Operated by MoD(RAF). CMATZ with Wittering. If not under radar control inbound aircraft are to contact Cottesmore App 130·20. Circuits RH on Rwy 23. Avoid overflying local villages within 10 nm of Cottesmore. Visiting aircraft are not to arrive before 0830 hrs. **Caution:** Bird hazard.
Cottesmore **APP** 130·20 (LARS/MATZ); **TWR** 122·10.
TACAN 'CTM' 112·30 (On A/D) N52 42·12 W000 39·04.
ILS Rwy 23 (226°M) 'CM' 110·30
Fuel: Avtur. **Tel:** 01572-812241 Ext 7270

FAIRFORD **EGVA** N51 41·93 W001 47·40 286 ft. AMSL
Rwy: 09/27 3047 m Asphalt/Concrete
Lighting: 09 & 27 Ap Thr Rwy PAPI **Op hrs:** HO (see below)
Remarks: Operated by USAF. Aerodrome in limited service status, not available as a weather alternative. USAF ATC and base ops on stand by status 0630-1530 Mon-Fri. Airport and runway remain closed unless opened by NOTAM.
Brize Radar 134·30.
Fuel: Avtur **Tel:** 01285-714805 USAF Mildenhall

KINLOSS **EGQK** N57 38·96 W003 33·64 22 ft. AMSL
Rwy: 08/26 2311 m Asphalt/Concrete. Arrester gear 498 m from 08 threshold and 704 m from 26 threshold. **Lighting:** 09 & 27: Ap Thr Rwy PAPI
IBcn 'KS' Red **Op hrs:** H24. PPR.
Remarks: Operated by MoD(RAF). Unified Approach Control by Lossiemouth. Mandatory that inbound aircraft call Lossie APP, high/medium level at 50 nm and low level at 20 nm. Rwy 26 procedures – do not descend below 2500 ft on final approch until advised by ATC. Glider activity SR–SS, Sat, Sun & PHs. During Sep to April geese may be encountered within 10 nm of aerodrome.
Lossie **APP** 119·35 (LARS/MATZ). Kinloss **TWR** 122·10.
NDB 'KS' 370·0 N57 39·03 W003 35·23.
TACAN 'KSS' 109·80 N57 39·56 W003 32·11. **ILS Rwy 26** (260°M) 'KS' 109·70
Fuel: 100LL, Avtur. **Tel:** 01309-672161 Ext 7608 Ops.

LAKENHEATH   **EGUL**   N52 24·56   E000 33·66   32 ft. AMSL
Rwy: 06/24 2743 m Asphalt/Concrete. Arrester cables 365 & 762 m in from each end.
Lighting: 06 & 24: Ap Thr Rwy PAPI.
Op hrs: PPR. Mon-Thu 0600-2000; Fri 0800-2000; Sat, Sun & PHs 24 hrs PNR.
Remarks: Operated by USAF. All arrivals/departures to file IFR Flight Plans.
Jet aircraft avoid overflying towns N, E & W of aerodrome. Circuits RH on Rwy 24.
Lakenheath **APP** 128·90 (MATZ). **TWR** 122·10.
TACAN 'LKH' 110·20 N52 24·39 E000 32·48.
ILS Rwy 06 (060°M) 'I-LAK' 109·90. **ILS Rwy 24** (240°M) 'I-LKH' 109·90.
Fuel: Avtur   **Tel:** 01638-524186/522439 Base Ops

LLANBEDR   **EGOD**   N52 48·70   W004 07·41   30 ft AMSL
Rwy: 18/36 2286 m Asphalt; RAF Type B Barrier on 18 & 36.
Rwy: 05/23 1319 m Asphalt.
Rwy: 16/34 1282 m Asphalt; RAF Type A Barrier on 34.
Lighting: 18 & 36 – Ap Thr Rwy PAPI.
Op hrs: PPR. Mon-Thu 0900-1200 & 1300-1630; Fri 0900-1200.
Remarks: Operated by MoD(PE). Civil aircraft PPR; pilots to contact Operations Ext
3022. Visiting/transit aircraft not under control of London Mil are to contact APP at 25
nm, or 10 mins prior to ETA abeam. Unmanned target aircraft operating and main run-
way obstructed for long periods. Activity may continue during periods of aerodrome clo-
sure or withdrawal of ATS. Aircraft in transit are requested to avoid the aerodrome by 3
nm and 7,000 ft. **Caution:** Risk of bird strikes.
Warning: Easterly winds produce severe low level turbulence and rotor streaming.
Pilots should be extremely cautious if ATC indicates wind in excess of 10 kts between
045° and 135°M.
LLanbedr **APP/TWR/RAD** 122·50
Fuel: 100LL, Avtur.   **Tel:** 01341-243248 ATC   Ext 3022 Ops.

MARHAM   **EGYM**   N52 38·90   E000 33·03   75 ft AMSL
Rwy: 06/24 2786 m Asphalt/Concrete. Arrester cables 640 m from 06 Threshold and
488 m from 24 Threshold. Type B Barrier at both ends; zero over-run.
Rwy: 01/19 1800 m Concrete.
Lighting: 06 & 24 – Ap Thr Rwy PAPI
Op hrs: Mon-Thu 0800-2359, 0800-1800 Frid.
Remarks: Operated by MoD(RAF). Civil aircraft PPR. Inbound aircraft are to contact
Marham Director at 20 nm. RH circuits on 06 and 19. Glider activity outside normal
operating hours. **Caution:** Risk of Bird strike.
APP/Director 124·15 (LARS) **TWR** 122·10.
TACAN 'MAM' 108·70 N52 38·49 E000 33·18. **ILS Rwy 24** (240°M) 'MR' 110·10
Fuel: Avtur.   **Tel:** 01760-337261

MERRYFIELD   N50 57·75   W002 56·14   146 ft AMSL
Rwy: 09/27 1831 m Asphalt   Portable Rwy Lighting.
Rwy: 03/21 1294 m Asphalt.
Rwy: 16/34 1129 m Asphalt
Op hrs: PPR from Yeovilton Ops. ATZ Mon-Fri 0700-1700.
Remarks: Operated by MoD(Navy). Satellite aerodrome for Yeovilton. Civil aircraft on
prior permission from Yeovilton Ops Tel: 01935-840551 Ext 5497/5498. Intense heli-
copter activity within radius of 3 nm of aerodrome. Variable helicopter circuits, no dead-
side. Glider activity outside normal operating hours.
Merryfield **TWR** 122·10
Fuel: Nil   **Tel:** 01460-52018

MILDENHALL   EGUN   N52 21·65 E000 29·30   33 ft. AMSL
Rwy: 11/29 2810 m Asphalt/Concrete. **Lighting:** 11 & 29 – Ap Thr Rwy PAPI
Op hrs: HO (ATZ H24). 24 hrs PPR.
Remarks: Operated by USAF. All movements under IFR. Flight Plan addressees to include EGXHZGZX. Inbound aircraft to contact Lakenheath App 5 mins from CMATZ boundary.
Lakenheath **APP** 128·90. Mildenhall **TWR** 122·55
TACAN 'MLD' 115·90 N52 21·80 E00029·29.
ILS Rwy 11 (107°M) 'I-MIL' 108·10. **ILS Rwy 29** (287°M) 'I-MLD' 108·10.
Fuel: Avtur.   **Tel:** 01638-542251 Base Ops

NETHERAVON   EGDN   N51 14·83 W001 45·25   455 ft. AMSL
Rwy: 04/22 640 m Natural Surface.   **Lighting:** Rwy only
Rwy: 11/29 1092 m Natural Surface.   **Lighting:** Nil.   **IBcn.** 'NV' Red
Op hrs: PPR. Mon-Fri 0800-1700.
Remarks: Operated by MoD(Army). Inbound aircraft to call Salisbury Plain 122·75 at least 10 nm from airfield. Circuits RH on 04 and 29. All aircraft to call for start-up clearance. Parachuting Area A/G Station c/s DZ Radio 128·30 outside operating hrs.
ATIS Netheravon Information 128·30. Salisbury Plain 122·75 **A/G.**
Fuel: Avtur   **Tel:** 01980-678289

PREDANNACK   EGDO   N50 00·07 W005 13·85   295 ft AMSL
Rwy: 05/23 1814 m Asphalt.   **Rwy:** 01/19 * 1405 m Asphalt
Rwy: 10/28 * 1309 m Asphalt   **Rwy:** 13/31 * 916 m Asphalt
* Light aircraft only, surface not maintained to pavement standard.
Op hrs: Mon-Fri as required by Culdrose. PPR Culdrose.
Remarks: Operated by MoD(Navy). Satellite of Culdrose. Intense helicopter activity. Culdrose QFE is used as the approach and landing datum pressure setting.
Gliding and model aircraft activity outside normal Op hrs. Non standard markings on all runways.
Culdrose **APP** 134·05, Predannack **TWR** 122·10. Predannack Alpha Charlie Base 129·975 **Glider Ops.**
Fuel: Nil   **Tel:** 01326-574121 Ext. 2417 (PPR)

SCAMPTON   EGXP   N53 18·45 W000 32·95   202 ft AMSL
Rwy: 05/23 2740 m Asphalt   **Lighting:** Ap Rwy PAPI 2·5°
Op hrs: Contact Cranwell Operations 01400-261201 Ext 7377.   **I Bn** 'SA' Red
Remarks: Aerodrome is located at the centre of Restricted Area EG R313, circle radius 5 nm, up to 9500 ft amsl. Circuits RH on Rwy 23.
Waddington Zone 127·35
Fuel: Nil   **Tel:** 01400-261201 Ext 7377 Cranwell Ops.
                                        01522-731369 ATC.

TERNHILL   EGOE   N52 52·27 W002 32·01   272 ft. AMSL
Rwys: 05/23 980 m Asphalt; 10/28 948 m Asphalt; 17/35 720 m Grass
Op hrs: As required by Shawbury. PPR. **No fixed wing aircraft accepted.**
Remarks: Operated by MoD(RAF). Relief Landing Ground for RAF Shawbury. Variable circuits. Landing direction 17/35 indicated by broken white line (helicopters only). Minimum height of 50 ft crossing road adjacent to 23 and 28 thresholds. Thresholds have non standard markings, runways have non standard white hollow diamond markings, Powered glider activity up to 3,000 ft, outside normal Op hrs.
Shawbury Zone 120·775. **TWR** 122·10.
Fuel: Nil.   **Tel:** (Shawbury) 01939-250351 Ext. 7227

UPAVON   **EGDJ**   N51 17·17 W001 46·92   575 ft. AMSL

Large grass area with hard taxiway around the perimeter. Southern section of taxiway not available to fixed wing or rotary aircraft. Landing and take-off at pilot's discretion. Approach from the North within the sector 290°– 040°(T). ATC is manned only for certain pre-notified movements. Advisory information may be given by non ATC qualified personnel. Additional information may be obtained from Salisbury Operations   Tel: 01980-674710/674730. During daylight hours call Salisbury Ops 122·75, 5 mins before ETA and pass aircraft type, ETA and intentions. Unlit Radio Mast 52 ft agl., 65 ft. W of TWR. Glider activity during daylight hours.

Salisbury Ops 122·75

Fuel: Nil   **Tel:** 01980-615238/615066

WITTERING   **EGXT**   N52 36·75 W000 28·60   273 ft. AMSL

Rwy: 08/26 2758 m Asphalt. **Lighting:** 08 & 26 – Ap Thr Rwy PAPI. **IBcn** 'WJ' Red Type A Barrier – over-run 130 ft on 08 and 142 ft on 26.

Op hrs: PPR. Mon-Fri 0800-1700 LMT

Remarks: Operated by MoD(RAF). Unified ATS by Cottesmore. Hovering and variable circuits in operation at all times. Harrier cross circuits flown at 1,500 ft.

If not under ATCRU control inbound aircraft to contact Base App 130·20. Transit aircraft contact Cottesmore APP at least 10 nm from CMATZ boundary. Sibson Airfield 4 nm to the SE, circuits at 600 ft (Wittering QFE). Overflight below 1,000 ft (QFE) by fixed wing aircraft, of the domestic site to the SE and the fenced compounds SW of aerodrome, is forbidden.

Cottesmore **APP** 130·20 (MATZ/LARS), Wittering **TWR** 118·15.

TACAN 'WIT' 117·60 N52 36·48 W000 29·92.

Fuel: Avtur   **Tel:** 01780-783838 Ext 7090/1

HELIPADS

It is important to note that all landing sites listed below are available only with PRIOR PERMISSION (PPR). It is also advisable to check the site elevation before departure.

H1 ABERDEEN (Culter Helipad) – See page 597.

H1a ALCESTER (Arrow Mill Hotel & Rest'ant)   N52 12·17 W001 52·87   150 ft AMSL
6 nm W of Stratford upon Avon, west side of River Arrow. O.S. Sheet 150/084561
Grass landing area between Hotel and river. 'H' displayed. Adequate space for several helicopters.
Remarks: Operated by Denis Woodhams, Arrow Mill Hotel and Restaurant, Arrow, Nr Alcester, Warwickshire, B49 5NL. Converted water mill situated in 50 rural acres with 18 ensuite bedrooms, meeting rooms, restaurant and bar meals.
All helicopters made especially welcome, no landing fees.
Coarse and fly fishing, clay pigeon shooting.
Fuel: 100LL, Jet A1 available nearby.   **Tel:** 01789-762419 **Fax:** 01789-765170.

H2 ALTON BRIDGE HOTEL   N52 58·80 W001 53·65   260 ft. AMSL
0·5 nm S of Alton Towers. W side of bridge, S of river.
Landing area 1·0 acre field to N of hotel. 'H' displayed.
Local landmark: Alton Castle with 3 spires to SE of the pad.
Remarks: Operated by Mr. David Ford, Alton Bridge Hotel, Station Road, Alton, Staffordshire. ST10 4BX. PPR. 17th Century Hotel, Closest Hotel to Alton Towers. Excellent reputation for cuisine and en suite bedrooms. Overhead cable along S side of landing area. Approach from West or East.
Landing Fee: £30.00 (incl VAT). No landing fee for Hotel residents. Price includes transport to Alton Towers.
Fuel: Nil.   **Tel:** 01538-702338. **Fax:** 01538-703303

H3 ANDOVER (Apsley Estate)   N51 12·83 W001 23·67   360 ft AMSL
3·5 nm E of Andover.   O.S. Sheet 185/426466
10 acre grass field.
Remarks: Operated by Apsley Shooting Grounds Company Ltd. Apsley Estate, Nr. Andover, Hants. SP11 6NA. PPR. Helipad located on North side of the B3400, 100m East of course of a disused railway.
Fuel: Nil.   **Tel:** 01264-62403.

H4 ARRAN Heliport   N55 34·58 W005 08·02   10 ft. AMSL
300m E of Brodick Pier.   **Op hrs:** Daylight hours only.
Bitmac helipad 25m diameter, 'H' displayed.
Remarks: Operated by North Ayrshire Council. Unlicensed. PPR. All take-off and approach manouevres to be carried out over the sea to N of pad. 10 ft transition over rock foreshore to landing pad. Construction site up to 17 ft immediately S of pad, Fuel tanks 33 ft high 60 nm S of pad, shipping using pier 300 m W of pad. High ground in arc SE to N; mainly Holy Island 1100 ft amsl 148°T/3·5 nm, A'Chruach 1700 ft amsl 245°T/2·8 nm and Goat Fell 2900 ft amsl 325°T/3·5 nm. Aircraft must keep 100 m clear of shipping using the pier 300m W of the pad.
Please book Arr/Dep times by phone (01770-600450) office hours: Mon-Thur 0900-1645, Fri 0900-1630.
Landing Fee: £4.88 per 0·5 tonne (MTWA) or part thereof (minimum charge £9.75).
Fuel: Nil.   **Tel:** 01770-600450.

H5 ARUNDEL (Stakis Avisford Park Hotel) N50 51·03 W000 37·08 70 ft. AMSL
2 nm W of Arundel and bounded by A27 and B2132 roads.
Grass landing pad in front of hotel, 'H' displayed.
Remarks: Operated by Stakis Avisford Park Hotel, Yapton Lane,Walberton, Arundel,
West Sussex. By prior arrangement only.
Landing Fee: £30.00 (No landing fee for hotel residents as this is now chargeable).
Fuel: Nil.   **Tel:** 01243-551215. **Fax:** 01243-552481.

H6 ASHBOURNE (Rodsley) N52 57·53 W001 41·94 400 ft. AMSL
2 nm ESE of Darley Moor Airfield (Hang Gliding)   O.S. Sheet 128/SK 203402
2·5 nm S of disused Ashbourne Airfield.   **TNT 115·70 192 5·8**
Remarks: Operated by Richard McLachlan, French Horn Cottage, Rodsley,
Ashbourne, Derby DE6 3AL. Visiting helicopters welcome on prior permission (to
move cattle) and at at pilot's own risk. Field slopes near the house, therefore lower
part near hedge preferred. Helipad marked and Windsock displayed. No landing fee.
Warning: Power lines running up centre of field behing house.
Fuel: Nil.   Tel: 01335-330452. Email: richard@foxfield.demon.co.uk
                          Map and details also at http://www.foxfield.demon.co.uk

H7 ASTON ABBOTTS (Church Farm) N51 53·34 W000 45·89 325 ft.
AMSL
5 nm N of Aylesbury, 1 nm S of Wing disused airfield.
Landing area in field adjacent to Windsock and Barn.
Remarks: Operated by Flackwell Electronics, Dave and Alison Lewis Church Farm,
Aston Abbotts, Aylesbury, Bucks. HP22 4NB. Approach from the north, helipad in
sight of the village church. Power cables on the NE boundary.
Helicopter parking for 'The Old Masters Restaurant' opposite.
No landing fees. Hangarage for R22 available.
Fuel: Nil.   **Tel/Fax:** 01296-682126.

H8 ASTON CLINTON (The Bell Inn) N5147·03 W00043·10 315 ft. AMSL
3 nm E of Aylesbury on the S side of the A41 road and 0·5 nm N of Halton airfield.
Landing area hard standing on West car park.
Remarks: Operated by the Bell Inn (Aston Clinton) Ltd., Aston Clinton, Bucks.,
HP22 5HP. Please phone in advance. Situated within Halton ATZ, contact Halton on
130·425. Landing area surrounded by 60 ft. high trees.
No landing fee.
Fuel: Nil.   **Tel:** 01296-630252 (10 lines). **Fax:** 01296-631250
                                                       Telex: 83252 BELLIN.

H9 AYLESBURY (Hartwell House Hotel) N51 48·45 W000 50·97 300 ft. AMSL
1·5 nm SW of Aylesbury. 200 m N of A418.   O.S. 165/796124.
Grass landing pad adjacent to hotel.
Remarks: Operated by Historic House Hotels Ltd. Hartwell House, Oxford Road,
Aylesbury, Bucks. HP17 8NL. Please call hotel in advance. Use at pilot's own risk.
Landing fee £50.00 (no charge to hotel residential guests) All approaches from the
North avoiding all domestic properties. No Arrivals/Departures before 0930 and no
Arrivals after 1900 hrs.
Fuel: Nil.   **Tel:** 01296-747444. **Fax:** 747450

H10 BAGSHOT (Pennyhill Park Hotel) N51 21·03 W000 42·08 325 ft. AMSL
Open grass area to SE of main hotel building, edge of golf course, 150m from hotel.
Remarks: Operated by Pennyhill Park Hotel, College Ride, Bagshot, Surrey.
Fuel: Nil.   **Tel:** 01276-471774.

H11 BANCHORY (Raemoir House Hotel)   N57 05·20 W002 30·10 320 ft. AMSL
2 nm N of Banchory.   OS. Sheet 38/697994.   **ADN 114·30 218 15**
Grass area 30m square, S of hotel.
Remarks: Operated by the Raemoir House Hotel, Banchory, Grampian, AB31 4ED.
Pad slopes down N to S. 100 ft tree on perimeter. Use at pilots' own risk. Windsock
displayed. No landing fee.
Fuel: Nil.   **Tel:** 01330-824884. **Fax:** 01330-822171.

H12 BARNET (West Lodge Park Hotel)   N51 41·03 W000 09·10 263 ft. AMSL
2 nm SE of Potters Bar.   O.S. Sheet 166/276985.
100 x 100 ft. grass area in hotel grounds at Cockfosters Road, Hadley Wood.
Remarks: Operated by Beale's Hotels Ltd. Telephone prior to arrival. Trees in
vicinity of pad. Wind sock displayed. No landing fees.
Fuel: Nil.   **Tel:** 0208-440-8311.

H13 BARNSTAPLE (Halmpstone Manor) N51 02·23 W004 00·37   400 ft AMSL
2·5 nm SE of Barnstaple.   O.S. Sheet 180/595283
Grass area at front of Manor House.
Remarks: Operated by Jane and Charles Stanbury. Halmpstone Manor Country
House & Restaurant, Bishops Tawton, Barnstaple, Devon EX32 0EA. Visiting helis
welcome on prior permission. Power cables running WNW/ESE 450 m NE of site.
Fuel: Nil.   **Tel:** 01271-830321. **Fax:** 01271-830826.

H14 BARRASFORD (Elwood)   N55 03·32 W002 08·28   265 ft AMSL
15 nm WNW of Newcastle Airport   **NEW 114·25 280 15**
6 nm NW of Corbridge.   O.S. Sheet 87/914735
Two Pads on corner of grass field, W of village of Barrasford adjacent to the River
Tyne (North). 'H' and windsock displayed behind Coach House.
Remarks: Operated by International Aero Factors. Elwood, Barrasford, Hexham,
Northumberland NE48 4RN. Private helipad. Visiting helicopters welcome on prior
notification, and at pilot's own risk. Avoid overflying village & Elwood. Recommend
contact Newcastle App 124·375 for traffic information. Weather info available on site.
Taxi and car hire by arrangement. Accommodation &   food available H24. Security
by CCTV surveillance and Digital Movement
Detection. Overnight parking free.   **Radio:** c/s Elwood Radio 123·175 A/G.
email elwood@northumbria.com URL http:www.northumbria.com/business/elwood.htm
Fuel: 100LL, Jet A1.   **Tel:** 01434-681837. **Fax:** 01434-681026.

H15 BASLOW (Cavendish Hotel)   N53 14·68 W001 36·77   400 ft. AMSL
7 nm W of Chesterfield. 1 nm N of Chatsworth House.   O.S. Sheet 119/256721
50 m S of Hotel. 500m E of River Derwent.Helipad is a 20 metre square walled grass
paddock 50 m S of Hotel, 'H' displayed.
Remarks: Operated by Cavendish Aviation Ltd., Baslow, Derbyshire. DE45 1SP.
24 hours PPR. Avoid overflying local villages. Recommended approach from SE.
Fuel: Nil.   **Tel:** 01246-582311. **Fax:** 01246-582312

H16 BEACONSFIELD (Bellhouse Hotel)   N51 35·70 W000 35·80   250 ft. AMSL
1 nm E of Junction 2 M40.   O.S. Sheet 175/973894
Large tarmac car park.
Remarks: Operated by The Bellhouse Hotel, Oxford Road, Beaconsfield, Bucks.
Power cables running N/S 600 m E of hotel. Only twin-engined helicopters will be
accepted.
Fuel: Nil.   **Tel:** Gerrards Cross 01753-887211.

H17 BEDFORD (Woodlands Manor Hotel)   N52 09·60 W000 29·27 100 ft. AMSL
1·8 nm NNW of Bedford.   O.S. Sheet 153/036523.
Grass area on West side of hotel.
Remarks: Operated by Woodlands Manor Hotel, Green Lane, Clapham, Beds. PPR.
Site located on southern edge of disused Bedford airfield.
Fuel: Nil.   **Tel:** 01234-363281. **Fax:** 01234-272390.

H18 BETWS-Y-COED (Waterloo Hotel)   N53 05·02 W003 48·08   75 ft. AMSL
South of village adjacent to Waterloo Bridge over River Conwy.
Grass field between river and road opposite hotel.
Remarks: Operated by Waterloo Maton. Helicopters welcome at all times by
arrangement but at pilot's own risk. Contact Reception or Duty Manager
Fuel: Nil.   **Tel:** 01690-710411. **Fax:** 01690-710666

H19 BIDEFORD (LAKE-Lomas Helicopters) N51 01·93 W004 14·57 270 ft AMSL
6 nm SW of RAF Chivenor. 2 nm W of Bideford.   O.S. Sheet 180/422283
Concrete helipad on West side of hangar. Windsock displayed. Parking available.
Main operating base of Lomas Helicopters and also site for Lundy Island shuttle.
Remarks: Operated by Lomas Helicopters, Lake Heliport, Abbotsham, Bideford,
North Devon, EX39 5BQ. Private Heliport.
Visiting aircraft welcome on prior permission.
Avoid overflying the stud to the North on take-off and landing.
Landing Fee: Nil.
Radio: Lomas Operations 122·95 A/G.
Fuel: Avtur. Avgas occasionally.   **Tel:** 01237-421054.
                                                            Fax: 01237-424060.

H20 BIRKENHEAD (Bowler Hat Hotel)   N53 22·83 W003 03·05   160 ft AMSL
1 nm NE of Junction 3 – M53.   O.S. Sheet 108/301877.   **WAL 114·10 109 3·2**
Grass landing area 40 m square.
Remarks: Operated by The Bowler Hat Hotel. Visiting helicopters welcome on prior
permission. Site located within Liverpool CTR, entry via Neston or Seaforth VRPs,
obtain ATC clearance from Liverpool App 119·85. Approach should be made from the
West via the cricket ground at rear of hotel. Restricted Area R311, 5 nm to SSE.
Fuel: Nil   **Tel:** 0151-652-4931. **Fax:** 0151-653-8127.

H21 BIRMINGHAM (Moor Hall Hotel)   N52 34·02 W001 48·08   300 ft. AMSL
6·5 nm NE of Centre of Birmingham.
Grass area at rear of hotel, "H" displayed on request.
Remarks: Operated by Moor Hall Hotel, Sutton Coldfield, Birmingham. Helicopters
welcome by arrangement at pilot's own risk. Care must be taken.
Fuel: Nil.   **Tel:** 0121 308 3751. **Fax:** 0121 308 8974

H22 BLACKBURN (Northcote Manor Hotel) N53 48·52 W002 26·88 300 ft AMSL
2·5 nm NNE of Blackburn.
Open grass field to E of hotel adjacent to A59.
Remarks: Operated by Sandshow Limited, Northcote Manor, Langho, Blackburn,
Lancs. BB6 8BE. Visiting helicopters welcome on prior permission from Craig
Bancroft or Nigel Haworth. Hotel is on NW side of roundabout at A59/A666 junction.
Fuel: Nil   **Tel:** 01254-240555. **Fax:** 01254-246568.

H23 BLACKPOOL (Springfield House Hotel) N53 56·02 W002 56·08   Sea Level
6 nm NE of Blackpool, adjacent to Pilling Village.   **Op hrs**: 0900-1800.
Large grass area, 'H' displayed adjacent to Hotel.
Remarks: Operated by Springfield House Hotel, Wheel Lane, Pilling PR3 6HL. Best
approach from north or east. Visiting helicopters welcome on prior permission and at
pilot's own risk. Avoid flying over Hotel and adjoining houses and buildings.
Fuel: Nil.   **Tel:** 01253-790301. **Fax:** 01253-790907.

H24 BLAGDON MANOR (Country Hotel)   N50 44·82 W004 18·65   600 ft. AMSL
4 nm SSE of Holsworthy, West Devon.   O.S. Sheet 190/369970.
Large grass area to E of Manor. 'H' displayed on request.
Remarks: Operated by Tim and Gill Casey, Blagdon Manor, Ashwater, Devon,
EX21 5DF. Visiting helicopters welcome on prior permission and at pilot's own risk.
Trees to North of area, approach from South preferred.
Fuel: Nil   **Tel:** 01409-211224. **Fax:** 01409-211634

H25 BLATHERWYCKE   N52 32·95 W000 34·12   250 ft. AMSL
5 nm SSW of RAF Wittering.   **DTY 116·40 050 30**
17 acre grass field to West of house.
Remarks: Operated by David George Esq., The Old Rectory, Blatherwycke,
PE8 6YW. Visiting helicopters welcome on prior permission and at pilot's own risk.
Contact Cottesmore App 130·20.
Fuel: Nil.   **Tel:** 01780-450367 **Fax:** 01780-450346.

H26 BLYTH Helipark   N55 08·00 W001 32·92   25 ft. AMSL.
7 nm NE of Newcastle Airport   **NEW 114·25 047 7·6**
3 acre field with concrete landing pad, standard 'H' marking.   **Op hrs:** HJ
Remarks: Operated by Fergusons (Blyth) Ltd. Site located within Newcastle
CTR/CTA Obtain ATC clearance from Newcastle App 124·375 at 25 nm range.
4 metre transition over river bank to landing pad. Factories to South of site 10m high.
Power cables 194 ft amsl., in arc 1500 m from site, from 240° to 045°. Power Station
chimneys 585 ft amsl., 045°/1 nm. Overnight hangarage by arrangement.
Fuel: Jet A1.   **Tel:** 01670-540540 or 353761.
                                       Fax: 01670-540272. **Telex:** 538114.

H27 BOLTON (Last Drop Hotel)   N53 37·37 W002 25·30   650 ft. AMSL
3 nm N of Bolton.   OS Sheet 109/722141.
Half acre grass area SW of Hotel. ('H' displayed).
Remarks: Operated by MacDonald Hotels plc. Trees to South of landing area. Clear
approach from NW. landing fees.
Landing Fee: £50.00
Fuel: Nil.   **Tel:** 01204-591131.

H28 BOURNEMOUTH (Royal Bath Hotel)   N50 43·03 W001 52·08 75 ft. AMSL
Almost opposite the pier.   O.S. Sheet 195/091909
Grass area 100 x 50m.
Remarks: Operated by The Royal Bath Hotel, Bath Road, Bournemouth.
Twin-engined Helicopters only accepted. App/Dep over the sea. Helipad floodlit
throughout the night and in secure area. Situated within Solent CTA/Bournemouth
CTR, obtain ATC clearance from Solent App on 120·225 for handover to
Bournemouth App 119·625.
Fuel: Nil.   **Tel:** 01202-555555. **Fax:** 554158

H29 BRAUNTON (Saunton Sands Hotel)   N51 07·03 W004 13·07 160 ft. AMSL
3 nm NW of Chivenor Disused Aerodrome.   O.S. Sheet 180/446378.
Grass pad 23 x 21m, white fencing on N and E sides.
Remarks: Operated by Saunton Sands Hotel. Nr. Braunton, N. Devon. EX33 1LQ.
Approach from S. Tree to NW of pad adjacent to power cables N of area.
Windsock 50 m S of pad next to tennis court.
Fuel: Nil   **Tel:** 01271-890212. **Fax:** 890145.

H30 BRISTOL (Frenchay Hospital)   N51 29·77 W002 31·54   160 ft. AMSL
0·5 nm S of Junction 1 M32.   O.S. Sheet 172/636776
Grass landing area with concrete hardstanding, 'H' and windsock displayed
Remarks: Operated by Frenchay Healthcare NHS Trust, Frenchay Hospital, Bristol,
BS16 1LE. Non-emergency flights may be granted permission on prior application.
Landing Fees: £50.00 for all non-emergency flights.
Radio: Frenchay Radio 122·375 A/G.
Fuel: Nil   **Tel:** 0117 970 1212. **Fax:** 0117 957 2335

H31 BROADWAY (The Lygon Arms)   N52 02·02 W001 52·08   200 ft. AMSL
14 nm S of Stratford-on-Avon, 6 nm SE of Evesham on A44 road.
80 ft. x 40 ft. grass area.
Remarks: Operated by The Lygon Arms.
Fuel: Nil.   **Tel:** 01386-852255. **Fax:** 01386-858611

H32 BROMSGROVE (Grafton Manor Hotel) N52 19·18 W002 05·42 260 ft. AMSL
2 nm W of Bromsgrove.
3 acre pad in 6 acre field, 100m S of hotel.
Remarks: Operated by Grafton Manor Hotel. Bromsgrove, Worcester. B61 7HA.
Clear approaches for a radius of 100 m, but trees to the S and telephone cables
along nearby lane.
Fuel: Nil   **Tel:** 01527-579007.

H33 BUDE (The Old Wainhouse Inn).   N50 44·03 W004 35·07   600 ft. AMSL
12 nm SSW of Bude, at Wainhouse Corner.
Two acre paddock and Inn car park, adjacent to A39.
Remarks: Operated by Mr. John Watson Wyse, The Old Wainhouse Inn,
St. Gennys, Bude. Cornwall
Fuel: Nil. (Available at Bodmin Aerodrome – 30 nm)   **Tel & Fax:** 018403-711.

H34 BURY (Bolholt Country Park Hotel) N53 36·12 W002 19·67   280 ft. AMSL
1 nm E of Bury centre.   **Op hrs:** HJ closed Saturdays.
Grass area 46 m square.
Remarks: Operated by Bolholt Country Park Hotel. Visiting helicopters welcome on
prior permission and at pilot's own risk. Site is located beneath the Manchester TMA.
Lamposts along western edge of landing area. Helicopter crews are offered guest
membership to the Stables Leisure Club. No landing fee
Fuel: Nil   **Tel:** 0161-764 5239. **Fax:** 0161-763 1789

H35 CAMBRIDGE (Quy Mill Hotel)   N52 12·52 E000 14·40   50 ft. AMSL
1·5 nm E of Cambridge Airport.
Large field east side of hotel, white 'H' displayed.
Remarks: Operated by Cambridge Quy Mill Hotel, Newmarket Road, Quy,
Cambridge. Country House Hotel, 21 bedrooms, set in 11 acres close to Newmarket
Racecourse. Helipad available for hotel use only, on prior permission. Buildings and
trees to the South and West. Site is situated within Cambridge Airport ATZ, contact
Cambridge App 123·60 when within 10 nm.
Fuel: Nil   **Tel:** 01223-293383. **Fax:** 293770

H36 CAMBRIDGE (Cambridgeshire Moat House) N52 15·02 E000 01·90 40 ft. AMSL
5 nm NW of Cambridge.
Grass landing area with white 'H' adjacent to hotel.
Remarks: Operated by Cambridgeshire Moat House, Bar Hill, Cambridge.
Windsock displayed.
Fuel: Nil. Available at Cambridge Airport.   **Tel:** 01954-249988

H37 CARDIFF (Miskin Manor Hotel)   N51 30·82 W003 21·73   161 ft. AMSL
Hotel immediately north side of junction 34 on M4.
Large paddock to south of Hotel. 'H' displayed.
Remarks: Operated by Mr. Colin Rosenberg, Miskin Manor Hotel, Miskin, Nr. Cardiff,
Glamorgan CF72 8ND. Helipad for patrons, PPR. All flights to contact Cardiff App
125·85 due close proximity of Cardiff CTR/CTA. ATIS 119·47. Approach from south
over the motorway. Restaurant, leisure club and onward travel facilities are available.
Landing Fees: Nil
Fuel: Nil   **Tel:** 01443-224204
                                                                     Fax: 01443-237606

H38 CARDIFF/Tremorfa Foreshore Heliport.   **EGFC**
                              N51 28·05 W003 08·25   40 ft. AMSL
2 nm SE of Cardiff Central Area on waterfront.   **Op hrs:** Mon-Fri 0900-1700 & ¢.
300X40 m Grass runway oriented 020°/200° M. Aiming Point 'H' at each end.
70x44 m Concrete Apron.
Manoeuvring area over the sea NE to SW.
Lighting: App, Thr, FATO, PAPI 3°.
Remarks: Operated by Veritair on behalf of Cardiff County Council, Highway &
Transportation Services Dept. County Hall, Atlantic Wharf, Cardiff CF10 4LZ. PPR.
Unlicensed heliport. Inbound and outbound aircraft to contact Cardiff App 125·85.
Security fence surrounding site 6ft agl.
Avoid overflight of fuel storage tanks starboard side on Rwy 20 climbout.
Landing Fees: £6.50 per 500 kg plus VAT. Max weight 20,000 kg.
Hangarage: By arrangement.
Radio: c/s Tremorfa Heliport Radio 120·65 A/G. Cardiff App 125·85.
Fuel: Jet A1   **Tel:** 029-2046 5880.
                                                                     Fax: 029-2048 7506.

H39 CARR GATE (Wakefield)   N53 42·67 W001 32·45   260 ft. AMSL
2 nm NW of Wakefield.   O.S. Sheet 104/305239
Asphalt Helipad. 500 m SSW of Junc 41/M1.
Remarks: Operated by West Yorks Police, Air Support Unit, Cardigan House,
Carr Gate, Wakefield. WF2 0QD. Normally available to police helicopters only.
Situated beneath Leeds Bradford CTA (base 2500' ALT) and 2·5 nm South of the
CTR. Obtain ATC clearance from Leeds App 123·75.
Power cables running E/W 400 m to N (700' plus), and running NE/SW
900 m (250') to SE.
Fuel: Jet A1.   **Tel:** 01924-293130.

H40 CASTLE COMBE (Manor House Hotel) N51 29·60 W002 13·88. 260 ft AMSL
4 nm WSW of Junction 17 – M4.   O.S. Sheet 173/839772.
Hotel front lawn, 'H' displayed.
Remarks: Operated by The Manor House Hotel, Castle Combe, Nr. Chippenham,
Wilts. SN14 7HR.
Fuel: Nil.   **Tel:** 01249-782206.

H41 CHELTENHAM (Racecourse)   N51 55·09 W002 03·31   213 ft. AMSL
1 nm N of Cheltenham.
Grass Rwy 05/23, 400 x 30 m. Standard markings displayed.
Remarks: Operated by Helicopter and Aviation Services Ltd on behalf of The
Racecourse Authorities, Racecourse, Prestbury Park, Cheltenham. Helicopters are
welcome on race days, strictly PPR and at pilot's own risk. Land only 1100 hrs to half
hour before first race. Take-off 30 minutes after last race or by permission of Clerk of
the Course. Pilots are to pay particular attention to those rules which govern flying in
the vicinity of crowds. Pilots approaching/departing the aerodrome should avoid
overflying the Grandstand, paddock, stables, caravan park and the new housing
development to the SE of Rwy. High ground rises to 1083 ft amsl to the East of A/D
Trees up to 40 ft aal cross final approach to Rwy 05, 250 m from threshold.
Note: Gloucestershire Aerodrome is 3 nm to the SW of racecourse. Pilots are to
avoid the ATZ of this aerodrome.
Fuel: Nil.   **Tel:** 01279-680291.
                                                  Fax: 01279-680159.

H42 CHELTENHAM (The Greenway Hotel) N51 51·60 W002 06·98 265 ft. AMSL
2·7nm SE of Gloucestershire Airport.   O.S. Sheet 163/919179.
Grass pad in large walled garden behind hotel building.
Remarks: Operated by Mr. D. A. White. The Greenway Hotel, Shurdington,
Cheltenham. GL51 5UG. A Country House hotel in the Cotswold.
Fuel: Nil   **Tel:** 01242-862352.
                                                  Fax: 01242-862780

H43 CHELTENHAM (Ullenwood Court)   N51 51·20 W002 05·42   790ft AMSL
3·5 nm SE of Gloucestershire Airport.   O.S. Sheet 163/941171
Unobstructed approach to grass area with white markers on SW side of private drive.
Remarks: Operated by M.J. Cuttell. Ullenwood Court, Ullenwood, Nr. Cheltenham,
Glos. GL53 9QS. Prior permission must be obtained by telephone. Approach and
departure from/to the South only, to avoid livestock to the North of property.
Windsock on Southern boundary. Car may be available.
Fuel: Nil   **Tel:** 01242-236770.
                                                  Fax: 01242-254680.

H44 CHESTER (Mollington Banastre Hotel) N53 13·02 W002 53·08 30 ft. AMSL
2 nm NW of Chester Station on S side of A540 road.
Large grass landing area.
Remarks: Operated by Mollington Banastre Hotel, Parkgate Road, Chester.
Power cables 50ft high running E–W 100 m South of landing area.
Restricted Area R311, 2nm NNW of Chester.
Fuel: Nil.   **Tel:** 01244-851471. **Fax:** 851165.

H45 CHESTER (Crabwall Manor Hotel)   N53 13·22 W002 55·58   60 ft AMSL
2 nm NNW of Chester City centre. O.S. Sheet 117/385694   **WAL 114·10 150 12·5**
Landing area 100 m SE of Hotel, grass parkland, 'H' displayed.
Remarks: Operated by Crabwall Manor Hotel, Mollington, Chester. CH1 6NE.
Site located 1 nm S of southern boundary of Liverpool CTR and beneath Manchester
TMA (base 2500'); contact Liverpool App 119.85. Hawarden Aerodrome 3 nm to SW.
Restricted Area R311, 2 nm NNW of Chester. Visitors welcome on prior notification
and at pilot's own risk. Daylight hours only. Power cables 400 m to the South and
1200 m to the West.
Fuel: Nil.   **Tel:** 01244-851666. **Fax:** 01244-851400

H46 CHESTER (Racecourse)   N53 11·20 W002 53·92   40 ft. AMSL
3 nm E of Hawarden Airfield.   O.S. Sheet 117/401660
Helipad at SW corner of racecourse. (Race days only).
Remarks: Operated by Chester Race Company Ltd, The Racecourse, Chester
CH1 2LY. PPR and at pilot's own risk.
Do not overfly the stands, public enclosures or paddock area.
60 ft obstruction to North of pad. Congested areas to North and East of racecourse.
Restricted Area R311, 2 nm NNW of Chester.
Fuel: Nil.   **Tel:** 01244-323170. 01244-344971.

H47 CHESTER (Beechmoor Nurseries)   N53 11·32 W002 51·35   60 ft. AMSL
1 nm SE of City Centre. Adjacent to Park and Ride.   O.S. Sheet 117/431658
Grass pad 200 x 80 m.
Remarks: Operated by Beechmore Nurseries. Available during daylight hours only
and at pilot's own risk. Site located beneath Manchester CTA, base 2500'. Congested
area to North and West. Approach from open area to South and East. Restricted
area R311, 2 nm NNW of Chester. Hawarden aerodrome 5 nm to West.
Fuel: Nil   **Tel:** 01244-336922

H48 CHILBOLTON (Stonefield Park) — see under Airfield section.

H49 CLANDON (Onslow Arms Inn)   N51 15·73 W000 30·22   210 ft. AMSL
3 nm E of Guildford town centre.   O.S. Sheet 186/047525
Asphalt landing area.
Remarks: Operated by Mr. A. J. Peck, West Clandon, Nr Guildford, Surrey
GU4 7TE. Gourmet 16th century Inn. Bar and New Carvery Snack Bar.
Fuel: Nil   **Tel:** 01483-222447. **Fax:** 01483-211126.

H50 CLANVILLE (The Red Lion Country Inn)
3 nm NW of Andover.   N51 14·35 W001 32·85   360 ft AMSL
Grass area 50 x 35 m, 'H' displayed.
Remarks: Operated by David and Jennifer North, The Red Lion Country Inn,
Clanville, Andover, Hants. Visiting helicopters welcome without prior arrangement, at
pilot's own risk. Trees and property to the North of landing area. Open access from
South and West. Full range of Conference facilities plus restaurant and bars.
No landing fees.
Fuel: Nil.   **Tel:** 01264-771007. **Fax:** 771111

H51 CLOVELLY (Hoops Inn & Hotel)   N50 59·00 W004 23·00   710 ft. AMSL
2 nm SE of Clovelly, close to A39 road.
200 ft square, short grass pad set in a 6 acre grass field. 'H' displayed. Slight down
slope east to west. Key feature is the short cut grass runways used for occasional
large model aircraft flying, easily seen from the air.
The Hotel is a long thatched white building.
Remarks: Operated by Hoops Inn and Hotel, Horns Cross, Clovelly, Bideford,
N. Devon EX39 5DL. Best approach is from the north coast. RAF Chivenor is
located 11 nm NE of the pad.
Fuel: Nil.   **Tel:** 01237-451222. **Fax:** 01237-451247.

H52 COBHAM (Hilton National Hotel)   N51 20·03 W000 27·10   100 ft. AMSL
2 nm W of Cobham on the West side of the A3 road.
Grass area stepped down from Hotel, level with main road. White H and windsock.
Remarks: Operated by Hilton National Hotel, Seven Hills Road, South Cobham,
Surrey. KT11 1EW. Use restricted to hotel guests and patrons. 1 hour PNR in order
to ensure that landing area is clear as there is now a Golf Range in the grounds.
High tension cables cross main approach from SE which overflies the A3.
Landing fee: £20.00 (incl VAT)
Fuel: Nil.   **Tel:** 01932-864471. **Fax:** 01932-868017.

H53 COLWYN BAY (The Colwyn Bay Hotel) N53 17·52 W003 40·95 250 ft AMSL
1·5 nm E of Colwyn Bay Pier on headland adjacent to A55 road.
23 m diameter pad in tarmac carpark marked with yellow 'H'.
Also adjacent half acre grass field.
Remarks: Operated by Cambrian Hotels , Penmaenhead, Colwyn Bay. Telephone
lines and trees alongside main road. All approaches from seaward.
Windsock displayed.
Fuel: Nil.   **Tel:** 01492-516555 Manager: Richard Scott
                                                                    Fax: 01492-515565.

H54 CORNHILL-ON-TWEED (Tillmouth Park Hotel)
                                        N55 41·00 W002 11·10   160 ft. AMSL
2·5 nm SE of Coldstream.   **Op hrs:** By arrangement
Landing Area: Good lawn turf.
Remarks: Operated by Tillmouth Park Hotel, Cornhill-on-Tweed, Coldstream,
Northumberland. Residential hotel. Shooting, fishing, sports, etc. Helicopters
welcomed at all times by arrangement, but at pilot's own risk. No landing fees.
Fuel: Nil.   **Tel:** 01890-882255. Manager Mr. C.K. Carroll.

H55 CRICKLADE (Cricklade Hotel & Country Club)
                                        N51 38·20 W001 52·47   350 ft. AMSL
0·75 nm SW of Cricklade.   O.S. Sheet 163/088931
Hard surface pad, white 'H' and windsock displayed.
Remarks: Operated by Cricklade Hotel & Country Club. Helipad situated within
Fairford MATZ, contact Brize Radar 134·30. Hotel building 50 m N of landing pad,
clear approaches from all other directions. Landings facing South impracticable due
to adjacent raised lawn. Visiting helicopters welcome on PPR.
Hotel facilities include: golf course, tennis court, snooker room, indoor pool and
a la carte restaurant.
Fuel: Nil.   **Tel:** 01793-750751. **Fax:** 01793-751767.

H56 CRICK (Forte Posthouse)   N52 24.02 W001 02.10   375 ft. AMSL
4 nm E of Rugby, just off M1 (Exit 18) and 3 miles S of M6 junction.
40 ft. diameter circle of mown grass in large field.
Remarks: Operated by Forte Hotels, Crick, Northants, Rugby.
Use restricted to hotel guests and patrons. Radio masts 1·5 nm west of pad. (Masts
up to 980 ft. high in an area 1·5 x 0·75 nm). Windsock displayed.
Fuel: Nil.   **Tel:** Crick 01788-822101.

H57 CROMER (Northrepps) — see under airfield entry.

H58 CROYDON (Selsdon Park Hotel)   N51 20·03 W000 03·10   495 ft. AMSL
4 nm SE of Croydon centre, adjacent to Sanderstead village. Large grass area
adjacent to hotel.
Remarks: Operated by The Selsdon Park Hotel Ltd., Sanderstead, Surrey, CR2
8YA. Trees in vicinity of landing area. Best approach over golf course.
Fuel: Nil.   **Tel:** 020-8657-8811. **Fax:** 020-8651-6171.

H59 CUCKFIELD (Hilton Park Hotel)   N50 59·87 W000 08·10   260 ft. AMSL
1 nm SW of Haywards Heath Rly Station. (400m S of A272) O.S. Sheet 198/312237
Landing area on old tennis courts adjacent to hotel.
Remarks: Operated by Mr. & Mrs. Knox, Hilton Park Hotel, Cuckfield Sussex.
Approach and take-off in southern sector, 30 ft. trees on East and West sides and
hotel on North side. Landing area can be marked on request. **Landing Fee:** £25.
Fuel: Nil.   **Tel:** 01444-454555.

H60 DEANSHANGER (Kingfisher Country Club)
4·5 nm NE of Buckingham   N52 02·45 W000 52·45   250 ft. AMSL
Large grass area with clear approaches and displayed windsock, capable of handling
twin-rotor helicopters.
Remarks: Operated by Kingfisher Country Club Ltd. Buckingham Road,
Deanshanger, Milton Kenyes MK19 6DG. Lakeside Golf Course, Trout and Course
Fishing, Corporate and Conference Facilities. Bar and Restaurant. Ideal venue for
Wedding Receptions. Helicopters welcome at all times by prior arrangement.
Fuel: Nil   **Tel:** 01908-562332. **Fax:** 01908-260857

H61 DEVIZES   N51 21·45 W001 59·35   430 ft. AMSL
Northern outskirts of town, N of canal.   O.S. Sheet 173/011620
Concrete helipad adjacent to Police H.Q.
Remarks: Operated by the Wiltshire Constabulary. Normally available to police
helicopters only. Lyneham CTR/CTA 2 nm to the North (Lyneham Zone 123·40).
Danger Areas D123, D124 & D125 4 nm to the South (DACS from Salisbury Plain
Control 122·75). Power cables 1 nm to N and 2 nm to W.
Fuel: Jet A1.   **Tel:** 01380-722341 (ask for Air Support Unit)

H62 DEVONSHIRE   N53 58·52 W001 53·37   360 ft. AMSL
Junction of A59 and B6160.   O.S. Sheet 104/071532
Concrete helipad, 12 ft diameter.   **Op hrs:** 30 min PNR, 0600-2300.
Remarks: Operated by Devonshire Arms Hotel. Situated beneath Leeds Bradford
CTA (base 3000'). Leeds App 123·75. Surrounded by high ground, up to 1500'
within 5 nm. No landing fees. Visiting helicopters welcome on prior permission and at
pilot's own risk.
Fuel: Nil.   **Tel:** 01756-710441. **Fax:** 01756-710564.

H63 DISEWORTH (Langley Priory)   N52 48·40 W001 21·52   220 ft. AMSL
1·5 nm SW of East Midlands Airport.
Large grass area between house and lake. 'H' by arrangement.
Remarks: Operated by J. B. Wagstaff Esq., Langley Priory, Diseworth, Derbyshire.
DE74 2QQ. Visiting helicopters welcome on prior permission and at pilot's own risk.
Situated within East Midlands CTR/CTA (Class 'D' Controlled Airspace).
Inbound: Obtain ATC clearance from East Midlands App 119·65 before entering
controlled airspace. Best approach from E across parkland and lake.
Outbound: Obtain start-up and departure clearance from East Midlands Twr 124·00.
Fuel: Nil.   **Tel:** 01332-811063. **Fax:** 850362.

H64 DONINGTON PARK (Racing Circuit)   N52 49·85 W001 22·58 298 ft. AMSL
1 nm W of East Midlands Airport.
Large grass field adjacent to Competitors entrance.
Remarks: Operated by Donington Park Racing Ltd. PPR. Unlicensed helipad
situated within East Midlands CTR/CTA (Class 'D' Controlled Airspace). Use of the
helipad is subject to prior permission and is at pilot's own risk. All movements must
be confined to the Eastern side of helipad. Do not overfly property adjacent to the
western boundary.
Inbound: obtain ATC clearance from East Midlands App 119·65 before entering
controlled airspace.
Outbound: Obtain start-up and departure clearance from East Midlands Twr 124·00.
Caution: Fence 0·5 m high surrounding alighting area with trees on the western side.
Fuel: Nil.   **Tel:** 01332–810048. **Fax:** 01332-850422.

H65 DORNOCH (The Royal Golf Hotel/Golf Club)
                                    N57 52·88 W004 01·08   0 ft. AMSL
NE of Dornoch.
Grass area next to the Clubhouse. H displayed.
Remarks: Operated by The Royal Golf Hotel and Royal Dornoch Golf Club, The 1st
Tee, Dornoch, Sutherland, Scotland IV25 3LG. Caution: Flying golf balls.
Contact Inverness App 122·60 inbound/outbound.
Fuel: Nil.   **Tel:** 01862-810283/810219. **Fax:** 01862-810923.

H66 DOVEDALE (The Izaak Walton Hotel)   N53 03·35 W001 47·52 500 ft. AMSL
3 nm NNW of Ashbourne.   O.S. Sheet 119/143508.   **TNT 115·70 277 4·2**
Grass landing pad 100x70 ft.
Remarks: Operated by The Izaak Walton Hotel. Dovedale, Nr. Ashbourne, Derby-
shire. DE6 2AY. Visiting helicopters welcome on prior permission and at pilot's own
risk. Minimum safety services available. Trees on perimeter, best approach from
East.
Fuel: Nil   **Tel:** 01335-350555. **Fax:** 01335-350539.

H67 DROITWICH   N52 17·05 W002 10·88   100 ft. AMSL
1·5 nm NW of town centre.
80 x 80 ft square concrete pad. H and Windsock displayed.
Remarks: Operated by Rotorspan Limited, The Heliport Droitwich, Worcs.
Approach/Departure SSW. Power cables NNW.
Hangarage: Available. **Maintenance:** Available.
Fuel: Nil.   **Tel:** 01905-774831. **Fax:** 01905-794657

H68 DROITWICH SPA (Chateau Impney)   N52 17·02 W002 08·08 700 ft. AMSL
1 nm N of town on E side of A38, immediately N of junction with A442.
Grass lawn area in front of hotel.
Remarks: Operated by Chateau Impney, Droitwich Spa, Worcs. The hotel has 65
acres of parkland containing many trees. Please telephone and ask for Duty
Manager. Free taxi service to the Raven Hotel and the Worcestershire Brine Baths
Hotel, for hotel residents only.
Fuel: Nil.   **Tel:** Droitwich 01905-774411. **Fax:** 772371.

H69 EAST GRINSTEAD (Felbridge Hotel)   N51 08·42 W000 02·20 325 ft. AMSL
1 nm NW of East Grinstead. At junction of A22/A264.   O.S. Sheet 187/373397.
7 acre grass field.
Remarks: Operated by Jarvis Hotels, East Grinstead, Sussex. Helipad situated
within Gatwick CTR (Class 'D' Controlled Airspace), clearance to be obtained from
Gatwick Director 126·825. High tension wires to NE of field.
No landing fees.
Fuel: Nil.   **Tel:** East Grinstead 01342-326992.

H70 EAST GRINSTEAD (Hammerwood Park) N51 07·53 E000 03·48 260 ft AMSL
2·5nm E of East Grinstead.   O.S. Sheet 187/442388.
Grass area in front of Stately Home. 'H' and Windsock displayed.
Remarks: Operated by David Pinnegar. Visitors welcome on prior permission. Site
situated within the Gatwick CTR (Class 'D' Controlled Airspace), clearance to be
obtained from Gatwick Director 126·825.
Luxury overnight accommodation available.
Fuel: Nil   **Tel:** 01342-850594. **Fax:** 01342-850864.

H71 EDINBURGH (Leith Heliport)   N55 58·87 W003 10·95   15 ft. AMSL
5 nm ENE of EDINBURGH/Turnhouse Airport.
Tarmac landing pad 24 m diameter within 1 acre clear area.
Remarks: Operated by Forth Ports plc. Unlicensed Heliport. Procedures governing
the use of the Heliport available from the Harbour Master's Dept. Written confirmation
of compliance required prior to approval being given. Situated within Edinburgh CTR
(Class 'D' Controlled Airspace), obtain clearance from Edinburgh App 121·20 before
entering controlled airspace.
Approach and take-off manoeuvres to be carried out over the water 3 nm to the E.
Mast 505ft amsl 1·3 nm S; high ground 822ft amsl, 2·4 nm SE.
Parking available. Customs available. Landing fee will be charged.
Radio: Leith Radio 156·60. Edinburgh App 121·20.
Fuel: Jet A1   **Tel:** 0131-554 3661. **Fax:** 0131-553 5428.

H72 ENFIELD (Royal Chace Hotel)   N51 40·03 W000 06·10   195 ft. AMSL
Junc 24 – M25. 1 nm NW of stone church spire landmark and on the A1005 North of
Enfield.
50 ft. diameter asphalt pad, 'H' and windsock displayed.
Remarks: Operated by the Royal Chace Hotel, The Ridgeway, Enfield.
92 en-suite bedrooms, 9 conference rooms, Gallery á la carte restaurant and 'Kings'
Pub (open for food and bar). No landing fees.
Fuel: Nil.   **Tel:** 020-8366-6500. **Fax:** 020-8367-7191.

H73 ESKDALE (Bower House Inn)   N54 23·33 W000 320·58   140 ft. AMSL
6 nm SW of Scafell Pikes.   O.S. Sheet 89/131002
Grass area 30x30m.
Remarks: Operated by D.J. & B.E. Connor. Bower House Inn, Eskdale, Lake
District, Cumbria. CA19 1TD. PPR. Located in mountainous area, best approach
from West or from South via River Irt. No landing fees.
Fuel: Nil.   **Tel:** 01946-723244. **Fax:** 01946-723308

H74 EVESHAM (Twyford Farm)   N52 07·02 W001 56·08   170 ft. AMSL
1·2 nm NE of Evesham Rly. Station.   O.S. Sheet 150/046465.
Grass area 50 x 40m, 250m W of river.
Remarks: Operated by W. D. Fisher & Son Ltd., Twyford Farm, Evesham, Worc.
WR11 4TP. PPR. Garden Centre. Farm buildings, plus various shops, telephone
wires and fruit trees on Western boundary. Power pylons 300 m to the East.
Landing Fee: £15.00 by prior arrangement.
Fuel: Nil.   **Tel:** 01386-446108.

H75 EXETER (Exeter Court Hotel)   N50 39·03 W003 32·07   220 ft. AMSL
On A38 at Kennford, just South of Exeter.
100 ft. diameter pad.
Remarks: Operated by the Exeter Court Hotel. 63 luxury bedrooms, conference
rooms and restaurant. No landing fee.
Fuel: Nil.   **Tel:** 01392-832121. **Fax:** 01392-833590.

H76 EXETER (Middlemoor)   N50 43·25 W003 28·40   147 ft AMSL
Exeter, 0·75 nm SW of Junc 29/M5.   O.S. Sheet 192/959922.
Concrete helipad (illuminated) .
Remarks: Operated by Devon & Cornwall Constabulary. PPR. Normally available to
police helicopters only. Situated within Exeter Airport ATZ, 2 nm from Rwy 08
Threshold, 400 m South of extended centreline.
Inbound: Obtain clearance from Exeter App 128·15.
Outbound: Obtain start-up and departure clearance from Exeter Twr 119·80.
Radio Mast (lit) 135' agl, 50 m south of helipad. Field immediately North of pad is
12 ft above pad elevation, surrounded by trees and 10 ft wire chain link fence.
Police H.Q. buildings 50 ft agl (approx) to west and south of pad.
Fuel: Jet A1.   **Tel:** 01392-452392 (ask for Air Support Unit).

H77 GIBBON BRIDGE   N5352·52 W00233·38   295 ft. AMSL
3nm NNE of Spade Mill Resr. (Longridge).   **POL 112·10 302 17·7**
Concrete pad 9x10m, 60m NW of tennis court.   O.S. Sheet 102/637424
Remarks. Operated by Gibbon Bridge Country House & Restaurant. Nr. Chipping,
Preston. PR2 2TQ. PPR.The landing pad is sited in the gardens at the rear of the
premises. There are two good clear flight paths but there is a tree 30 metres to SW.
Fuel: Nil   **Tel:** 01995-61456. **Fax:** 61277.

H78 GLASGOW (Clyde Heliport)   N5551·75 W00417·75   10 ft. AMSL
At the Scottish Exhibition and Conference Centre.   **Op hrs:** PPR. 0800-1800 daily
Firm grass surface 31 x 42m. 'H' displayed. Adjacent parking Spots, Spots 1, 2, and
3 each 12 m diameter.
Remarks: Operated by Bond Air Services, Clyde Heliport, Glasgow. G3 8QQ.
Private licensed heliport. PPR. Situated within Glasgow CTR (Class 'D' Controlled
Airspace). Obtain ATC clearance from Glasgow App 119·10.
All approaches and departures to be over the River Clyde to the West or the East,
maintaining contact with Glasgow Approach on 119·10. Noise sensitive area, noise
abatement procedures in force. Briefing sheet available from Licensee.
Obstacles within 0·5 nm: To the East, a windsock on corner of hanger 30 ft amsl.,
Clock tower 55 ft amsl to the North of pad and a large Hotel North side of river, 400m
East of pad. Hangarage by prior arrangement. **Landing Fee:** £50.00.
Fuel: Jet A1.   **Tel:** 0141-226-4261

H79 GLENISLA   N5649·02 W00319·30   1200 ft. AMSL
13·5 nm N of Blairgowrie.   O.S Sheet 43/11957030   **PTH 110·40 011 22·5**
Grass area north side of confluence of River Isla and Glencally Burn, 'H' displayed.
Remarks: Operated by Robert Pooley Esq., Pooleys Limited, Elstree Aerodrome,
Elstree, Herts WD6 3AW. Prior permission from 0181-207-3749 or from Forter Castle.
Trees and buildings to SE and E of site. Forter Castle 3 nm to South of helipad.
Warning: Power cables (30 ft.) on north and west sides of helipad. Mountainous
region, high ground up to 3500 ft amsl in surrounding area.
Fuel: Nil   **Tel:** 0181-207-3749; 0157-582-305 Castle

H80 GLOUCESTER (Hatherley Manor Hotel) N5154·27 W00212·28   40 ft. AMSL
1·5 nm WNW of Gloucestershire Airport.   O.S. Sheet 162/858227.
2 acre grass paddock to the West of hotel building.
Remarks. Operated by Hatherley Manor Hotel, Down Hatherley Lane, Gloucester.
GL2 9QA. PPR. Site situated within Gloucestershire ATZ, contact Gloster App 125·65.
Caution: Trees adjacent to grass paddock.
Fuel: Nil.   **Tel:** 01452-730217. **Fax:** 731032.

H 81 GOAT GAP INN (Newby Moor) N5407·58 W00226·55   550 ft. AMSL
1·6 nm SE of Ingleton on A65.   O.S. Sheet 98/713703.
3·5 acre field W side of Inn car park. 'H' displayed.
Remarks: Operated by M. K. & G. J. Willis. Visiting helicopters welcome on prior
permission and at pilot's own risk. Aviation enthusiasts and hoteliers especially
welcome. Accommodation by arrangement. Excellent location for shooting, fishing,
golf, caving and walking. **Warnings:** Low flying military aircraft Mon-Fri. Telegraph
wires to the N of field, trees to the E between helipad and Inn.
Fuel: Nil.   **Tel:** 01524-241230.

H82 GOODWOOD RACECOURSE N5054·03 W00044·38 EGKG 510 ft. AMSL
5 nm NNE of Chichester.   **MID 114·00 211 10. SAM 113·35 103 23**
Heli Rwy 16/34, 500 x 30m, white 'H' in centre of Rwy. FATO 160°/340°
Heli Rwy 05/23, 240 x 30m, white 'H' in centre of Rwy. FATO 050°/230°
Remarks: Operated by Helicopter and Aviation Services Ltd., on behalf of
Goodwood Racecourse Authorities. Unlicensed heliport. Strictly PPR.
Chichester/Goodwood A/D 2 nm to SW. 40 ft high observation platform located in
NW segment. Trees on N and E boundaries and site is enclosed by 4 ft high
racecourse fence. All operators are required to produce an Insurance Indemnity in
advance of landing, forms available from Helicopter and Aviation Services. Heli
movements not permitted from 20 mins prior to first race to 20 mins after last race.
Pilots to call 'Trundle Radio' on 130·50 ten minutes before ETA.
Fuel: Normally available when Heliport licensed. other times from Goodwood A/D.
Tel: 01279-680291; 01243-530003 On Race days. **Fax:** 01279-680159.

H83 GREAT YARMOUTH (North Denes) — see page 598.

H84 GUILDFORD (Loseley Park)   N51 13·03 W000 36·30   198 ft. AMSL
1·5 nm SW of Guildford.   O.S. Sheet 186 975474.   **MID 114·00 009 9·8**
Grass landing area to north side of large country house.
Remarks: Operated by Loseley Park Estate. Visiting helicopters welcome on prior
permission. Arrival and departure times must be agreed prior to arrival. Large trees in
the vicinity, best approach from the North. Avoid overflight of livestock and local
habitation. No landing fee if Loseley Park is final destination.
Fuel: Nil   **Tel:** 01483-304440 Estate Office. **Fax:** 01483-302036

H85 HAILSHAM (Boship Hotel)   N50 52·63 E000 13·88   55 ft. AMSL
6·5 nm NNW of Eastbourne. (Roundabout A22/A267).   O.S. Sheet 199/571111.
Grass field 300 x 150m.   **Op hrs:** Summer: 08-2000, Winter: 09-1630.
Remarks: Operated by Grenville Helicopters.Unlicensed heliport. Boship Hotel,
Hailsham, Sussex. BN27 4AT. Windsock displayed. Visiting helicopters welcome on
prior permission and at pilot's own risk. Aviation enthusiasts and hoteliers especially
welcome. Accommodation by arrangement. No landing fees.
Warning: Microlight and light aircraft operating from a grass strip 04/22, 335 m which
is located to the south of the helicopter field. This airstrip is owned by Mr. Adrian Cox
and it is _not available_ for GA use.
Refreshments: Hotel Restaurant and Bar — RAC 3 star.
Local Car Hire: 01323-440622. **Local Taxis:** 01323-841869
Fuel: Nil.   **Tel:** 01323-844826 (Day),503403 (Evenings) **Fax:** 01323-843945

H86 HARLOW   N51 46·03 E000 05·90   206 ft. AMSL
SE of Roundabout at SE end of town centre.
2 x 300 sq. ft. concrete pads with 18,000 sq. ft. grass area surrounding pads
Remarks: Operated by Harlow District Council. Approach paths restricted to 1 in 7 in
SW and NE and 1 in 4 in NW and SE. Street lighting standards close to and under
NW and NE approaches. Wood close to and under SE approach.
Landing fee may be charged.
Fuel: Nil.   **Tel:** 01279-446171/72

H87 HARROGATE (Birk Crag)   N53 59·27 W001 34·42   450 ft. AMSL
1nm W of Harrogate town centre.   O.S. Sheet 104/281547.
4 acre grass area, well drained.
Remarks: Operated by J.J. Thomas, Crag House, Crag Lane, Birk Crag, Harrogate.
HG3 1QA. Visiting helicopters welcome on prior permission. Landing pad marked.
NE boundary of Leeds CTR/CTA 1·5nm to SW. Clearance from Leeds App 123·75.
Fuel: Nil   **Tel:** 01423–565638. **Fax:** 01423–843945

H88 HASLEMERE (Lythe Hill Hotel)   N51 04·95 W000 41·02   510 ft. AMSL
1·5 nm E of Haslemere, S of B2131.   O.S. Sheet 186/924 324.
Tarmac helipad.
Remarks: Operated by Lythe Hill Hotel, Haslemere, Surrey. GU27 3BQ.
Pond and floodlit tennis court near landing site, windsock on North side.
Fuel: Nil.   **Tel:** 01428-651251. **Fax:** 01428-644131

H89 HASTINGS (Castleham Helipad)   N50 52·72 E000 31·95   280 ft. AMSL
2·4 nm NW of Hastings Pier.   O.S Sheet 199/783120.
Grass area within playing field immediately SE of major road.
Remarks: Operated by Borough of Hastings. PPR (3 hrs notice requested). Day use
only. Adjacent paved car-park and grass playing field. Small tree belt to the SE.
Windsock displayed on request.
Fuel: Nil.   **Tel:** 01424-783313 (weekdays only)
                                        Fax: 01424-783208 (weekdays only)

H90 HAYES (Heliport)   N51 30·40 W000 26·47   125 ft. AMSL
2 nm N of London/Heathrow Airport.   **Op hrs:** Strictly PPR. Restricted use.
Concrete landing pad 130m x 21m. surrounded by grass, on South bank of Grand
Union Canal. Windsock on East end of main hangar.
Lighting: Hazard lighting on fence and hangars.
Hangarage & Maint: By arrangement. **Parking:** Limited. **Car Hire:** On request.
Remarks: Operated by McAlpine Helicopters Ltd/Operational Support Services Ltd.
Use is subject to PPR and helicopters must be able to communicate with London
Approach control and Royal Air Force Northolt by Radio. Approach and take-off within
Northern Sector (W to NE) avoiding Stockley Park. On Departure, climb to standard
H9 Route altitude as soon as possible.
Radio: c/s Macline (Hayes) 123·65. Heathrow Radar 119·90
          Northolt App 126·45
Fuel: Jet A1.   **Tel:** 020-8848-9647 Ops. **Fax:** 020-8569-3230.

H91 HENLLYS HALL HOTEL   N53 16·77 W004 05·98   180 ft AMSL
4 nm NE of Menai Bridge
Grass area, 42 m x 21 m between the Hotel and the woodland. Daylight use only.
Remarks: Operated by Clive Rowe-Evans, Isle of Anglesey, North Wales. LL58 8HU.
Hotel set in forty acres of woodland.
Fuel: Nil.   **Tel:** 01248-810412.
                                                    Fax: 01248-811511.

H92 HETHERSETT (Park Farm Hotel)   N52 35·45 E001 10·22   140 ft. AMSL
5 nm SW of Norwich City Centre.   O.S. Sheet 144/151036.
Grass area East side of hotel, 'H' & windsock displayed.
Remarks: Operated by the Park Farm Hotel & Restaurant. PPR.
Site is located 200 metres North of Hethersett disused airfield.
Fuel: Nil.   **Tel:** 01603-810264. **Fax:** 01603-812104.

H93 HILCOTE (Heliport)   N53 06·43 W001 19·57   450 ft. AMSL
3 nm SW of Sutton in Ashfield. 0·4 nm N of Junction 28 (M1).
Two concrete landing pads, one in front of hangar, one on grassed area.
Remarks: Operated by Auto Alloys (Group). PPR. Two windsocks displayed.
Eight 90 ft container tanks on southern boundary. Best app/dep in W to NNW sector.
Car Hire: Maun Motors, Mansfield 511599.
Radio: Company frequency 122·95.   **Tel:** 01773-811525. **Fax:** 580034

H94 HOCKLEY HEATH (Nuthurst Grange Hotel)
0·5 nm N of Junc 16 - M40   N52 20·42 W001 46·75   400 ft. AMSL
2·5 nm S of Junction 4 - M42.
Grass pad 30x16 m in front of hotel building.   O.S. Sheet 139/152713
Remarks: Operated by Nuthurst Grange Country House Hotel & Restaurant.
Hockley Heath, Warwickshire. B94 5NL. Situated within the Birmingham Control
Zone, ATC clearance must be obtained from Birmingham App 118·05.
Windsock displayed. No landing fees.
Fuel: Nil   **Tel:** 01564-783972. **Fax:** 01564-783919

H95 HULL (Hesslewood Hall)   N53 43·22 W000 27·43   98 ft. AMSL
3·5 nm E of Brough Aerodrome.   O.S. Sheet 106/018259. **OTR 113·90 282 12·7**
800m NW of North Tower of Humber Bridge 533 ft amsl.
10 acre lawns in front of main Hall, 'H' displayed.
Remarks: Operated by Brooklands Property Holdings Limited. Hesslewood Hall,
Hessle, E. Yorks. Visiting helicopters welcome on prior permission and at pilot's own
risk.
No landing fees.
Fuel: Nil   **Tel:** 01482-646060. **Fax:** 01482-643939

H96 HULL (Rowley Manor Hotel)   N53 46·68 W000 31·17   350 ft. AMSL
3·5 nm NNE of Brough Aerodrome. O.S.Sheet 106/975326   **OTR 113·90 293 16**
Stepped lawns adjacent to hotel.
Remarks: Operated by Rowley Manor Hotel. Little Weighton, Nr. Hull, Humberside.
HU20 3XR. PPR. Power cables (200 ft +) 500 m to the South running SW/NE, and
1 nm to the North running E/W. No landing fees.
Fuel: Nil   **Tel:** 01482-3848248.

H97 HUSBANDS BOSWORTH   N52 25·95 W001 02·35   505 ft. AMSL
7 nm NE of Rugby.   O.S. Sheet 141/654820
Concrete helipad 500 m South of Husbands Bosworth Aerodrome.
Remarks: Operated by East Midlands Air Support Unit, Sulby Road, Near Welford,
Northants. NN6 6EZ. Normally available to police helicopters only. Helipad located
within Gliding Club circuit, good lookout essential.
"Husbands Bosworth Launch Control" – blind calls on 129·975.
Fuel: Jet A1.   **Tel:** 01858-881155. **Fax:** 01858-881166

H98 HYTHE (Imperial Hotel)   N51 04·03 E001 04·90   5 ft. AMSL
Largest building on sea front.   O.S. Sheet. 189/169345
Lawn 80 x 65m.
Remarks: Operated by Hotel Imperial (Hythe) Ltd. Princes Parade, Hythe, Kent.
Hotel flags in lieu of windsock. Danger Area D141 is 1 nm to SW. Visiting helicopters
welcome on prior permission and at pilot's own risk.
Landing Fee: £25.00
Fuel: Nil.   **Tel:** 01303-267441.
          Fax: 01303-264610.

H99 ILKLEY MOOR (Cow & Calf Hotel)   N53 55·02 W001 47·58   800 ft. AMSL
6 nm WNW of Leeds/Bradford Airport.   O.S. Sheet 104/134446.
Large field 100m N of Hotel. White 'H' displayed.
Remarks: Operated by the Cow & Calf Hotel, Ilkley Moor, W. Yorks. LS29 8BT. Site
is for private use of hotel and restaurant patrons. Grass surface is well drained and
suitable for all types of helicopter. Low wires on N and W boundaries of field.
Site is situated within the Leeds Bradford CTR/CTA, contact Leeds App 123·75.
Fuel: Nil.   **Tel:** 01943-607335. **Fax:** 01943-816022.

H100 KENILWORTH (Riverside Hotel)   N52 19·02 W001 32·08   170 ft. AMSL
2 nm SE of Kenilworth.
Hard core area SW of car park with additional grass area.
Remarks: Operated by Riverside Hotel, Chesford Bridge, Kenilworth, Warwickshire.
CV8 2LN. Will accept visiting helicopters on PPR and at pilot's own risk. No landing
fees.
Fuel: Nil   **Tel:** 01926-858153

H101 KETTERING (Burton Latimer)   N52 22·02 W000 42·10 180 ft. AMSL
2nm SE of Kettering, adjacent to railway line.
40ft concrete square.
Remarks: Operated by Weetabix Ltd., Burton Latimer, Kettering, Northants
NN15 5JR. PPR from Sir Richard George. **Caution:** Telephone lines and 30ft high
lighting poles on railway edge. Approach directions – 150°/330°. All operations at
pilot's own risk.
Fuel: At Sywell A/D, 4 nm SW.   **Tel:** 01536-722181. **Fax:** 01536-726148.

H102 KINGSBRIDGE (Buckland-Tout-Saints-Hotel)
2 nm N of Kingsbridge.   N50 18·03 W003 44·75   350 ft. AMSL
1acre lawn on S side of hotel.   O.S. Sheet 202/758462.
Remarks: Operated by Buckland-Tout-Saints-Hotel, Goveton, Kingsbridge, Devon.
Wooded area on eastern boundary of site. Approach/Dep in SE sector.
Avoid flying over houses adjacent to the site.
Fuel: Nil.   **Tel:** Kingsbridge 01548-853055.
                                                    Fax: 01548-856261

H103 KINGS LYNN (Congham Hall Hotel)   N52 46·65 E000 32·30 50 ft. AMSL
5 nm ENE of Kings Lynn.   O.S. Sheet 132/712228.
2 acre grass paddock or lawns in front of hotel, according to season.
Remarks: Operated by Congham Hall Country House Hotel & Restaurant, Grimston,
Kings Lynn, Norfolk. PE32 1AH. Both landing areas surrounded by high trees.
Landing Fee: £25.00 (no charge to guests/patrons).
Fuel: Nil   **Tel:** 01485-600250.
                                                    Fax: 01485-601191

H104 KNEBWORTH   N51 53·03 W000 12·73   300 ft. AMSL
200 m SW of A1(M) Junction – Stevenage South.   O.S. Sheet 166/235224.
150 m x 110 m field with 50ft dia. asphalt pad. Windsock W of pad.
Remarks: Operated by Matra BAe Dynamics (UK) Limited . Strictly PPR. Site
situated within Luton CTR, contact Luton App 129.55. Best approach 180°/ 360°T.
30 ft trees surround the site. Motorway Junction lights 40 ft high. 100 ft mast E of
site.150 ft chimney NE of site. Power cables running N/S 200 metres W of site.
Fuel: Nil   **Tel:** 01438-752104 or 753233. **Telex:** 825125/6.

H105 LAKE VYRNWY HOTEL   N52 46·17 W003 26·62   1000 ft. AMSL
South eastern edge of Lake Vyrnwy.   O.S. Sheet 125/022198.
                    WPL 323·0 313 14. **WPL 115·95** 313 **14**
Large levelled area to the North of hotel, white 'H' displayed.
Remarks: Operated by Market Glen Ltd. Llanwddyn, Montgomeryshire, Mid Wales.
SY10 0LY. Visiting Helicopters accepted at pilot's own risk.
Surrounded by high ground up to 2200 ft within 5 nm.
Fuel: Nil. (Welshpool A/D 14 nm to SE).   **Tel:** 01691-73692.
                                        Fax: 01691-73259.

H106 LAMBERHURST   N51 06·03 E000 22·90   200 ft. AMSL
5 nm ESE of Tunbridge Wells. NW side of Lamberhurst.   O.S. Sheet 188/673368.
Circular concrete pad.
Remarks: Operated by K. McAlpine. The Priory, Lamberhurst, Kent. Will accept
visiting helicopters on PPR and at pilot's own risk. Contact Mr. McAlpine or
Miss Hibling.
Fuel: Nil.   **Tel:** 01892-890734.

H107 LANGBANK (Gleddoch House)   N55 55·00 W004 48·08   125 ft. AMSL
1nm above Langbank in the Clyde valley.
Landing area on open site of golf course beside the Club building.
Remarks: Operated by Gleddoch Hotels Ltd, Gleddoch House, Langbank,
Renfrewshire. Landing pad bordered on one side by 50 ft trees.
Fuel: Nil.   **Tel:** Langbank 01475-540711. **Fax:** 01475-540201.

H108 LEEDS (Hilton National Hotel, Garforth) N53 47·02 W001 24·10 170 ft AMSL
Just E of Leeds at junction of A63 and A642.   O.S. Sheet 104/393323
100ft diameter landing pad.
Remarks: Operated by Ladbroke Hotels & Holidays. Leeds CTR/CTA 2 nm to the
West. Windsock displayed. **Landing Fee:** £35.00.
Fuel: Nil.   **Tel:** 0113-2866556. **Fax:** 0113-2866556.

H109 LEEDS HELIPORT (Heli-Jet Aviation)
0·75 nm N of Leeds Bradford Airport.   N53 53·12 W001 39·48   650 ft. AMSL
O.S. Sheet 104/222426.   **Op hrs:** Strictly PPR. 0900-1900.
Concrete pad 100 x 30 m, three helipads, adjacent to A658.
Remarks: Operated by Heli-Jet Aviation. Situated within Leeds/ Bradford CTR/CTA
(Class 'D' Controlled Airspace). Obtain ATC clearance, specifying landing at CONEY
PARK, from Leeds App 123·75 prior to entering controlled airspace.
Make approach to 'H' in centre of 12 acre field directly adjoining helipad to NW.
Best approach from N or E avoiding farm complex.
Small trees around field boundary, 50 ft trees on SW boundary.
Intensive helicopter operations.
Landing Fee: Nil, if prior permission granted and fuel is uplifted.
Radio: Heli-Jet Ops 129·75 A/G.
Fuel: 100LL, Jet A1. (Rotors running).   **Tel:** 0113-2500588, 0467-843930 Ops H24
                                        Fax: 0113-2508161
H110 LIPHOOK (Old Thorns Golf Course & Hotel)   100 ft. AMSL
1·5 nm W of town centre.   N51 04·83 W000 49·98   O.S. Sheet 186/820315
Large grass area NE of Clubhouse. Concrete landing pad marked with 'H'
Remarks: Operated by the General Manager, Old Thorns Golf Course, Hotel and
Restaurants, Liphook. Visiting helis welcome on PPR and at pilot's own risk.
Best approach from SW or NE. Avoid D130/1 to the North of Hotel.
Caution: Power cables to the East, D130 to North.
Fuel: Nil.   **Tel:** 01428-724555 **Fax:** 01428-725322

H 111 LISKEARD Heliport   N50 24·53 W004 23·90   100 ft. AMSL
3 nm SE of Liskeard. S side of A38(T).   O.S. Sheet 201/300600.
Asphalt/concrete pad 106x46m.
Remarks: Operated by Castle Air. Site lies in steep sided valley. Approaches should
be made from N or S. Power cables span the valley 0·5nm N and S of site.
Land on asphalt pad to S of hangar unless otherwise directed.
Windsock on hangar roof.
Landing Fee: Nil.   **Radio:** Castle Operations 129·90 A/G.
Fuel: Jet A1.   **Tel:** Widegates 01503-240543. **Fax:** 01503-240747

H112 LLANDISSILIO (Nantyffin Motel)   N51 51·35 W004 43·82   250 ft. AMSL
9·5 nm ENE of Haverfordwest.   O.S. Sheet 158/122208.
5 acre grass area N side of motel (1nm N of Clynderwen).
Remarks: Operated by H. J. & M. M. Thomas. Nantyffin Motel, Llandissilio,
Clynderwen, Pembrokeshire. SA66 7SU. Low power cables on Eastern boundary.
Fuel: Nil.   **Tel:** 01437-563329/423.

H113 LONDON (Gatwick)   N51 09·03 W000 11·10   194 ft. AMSL
An alighting pad for day operations only is situated at the junction of Twy 4 and
Twy 8. Parking as directed by ATC. (See LONDON/Gatwick Airport page).

H114 LONDON (Heathrow Airport)   N51 28·03 W000 27·10   80 ft. AMSL
A Helicopter Aiming Point is located a tNE end of Block 97. ('H' displayed).
This aiming point is unlit and is available throughout operational hours.
Helicopter movements are at all times subject to PPR; application should be made to
the Manager, Airport Co-ordination Ltd, Tel: 020-8749 4871.
LONDON/Heathrow - Helicopter Operations - see page 613.
Radio: Heathrow App 119·90 (Helis/Special VFR) or 119·725. TWR 118·70, 118·50.
                    Tel: 020-8749 4871- Manager, Airport Co-ordination Ltd.

H115 LONDON AIRPORT (Holiday Inn Hotel) N51 29·90 W000 27·22   82 ft AMSL
1 nm N of Heathrow Airport.
300m N of junction 4 (M4) (Airport Spur).   **Op hrs:** PPR. Mon-Sat 0730-2000.
Grass area (50 ft. dia.) NE side of hotel on golf course. 'H' displayed, windsock O/R.
Remarks: Operated by Holiday Inn Hotel for patrons on prior arrangement only.
Limited daily landings. Closed Sundays and Public Holidays.
Coach service to airport (Hotel Hoppa) all four terminals – small fee.
Landing Fee: £50.00
Fuel: Nil.   **Tel:** 01895-445555. **Fax:** 01895-445122

H116 LONDON (Westland Heliport) — see page 599.

H117 MAIDSTONE (Great Danes Hotel)   N51 15·03 E000 37·90   200 ft. AMSL
3 nm E of Maidstone.   O.S. Sheet 188/827541.
Concrete square between hotel and lake.
Remarks: Operated by Great Danes Hotel (Jarvis Hotels), Hollingbourne,
Maidstone, Kent. Eastern junction M20/A20. Will accept patrons only in visiting
helicopters on PPR and at pilot's own risk. Daylight hours only, specific permission
required for evening and night landings. Care must be taken. No landing fees.
Fuel: Nil.   **Tel:** 01622-30022.

H118 MARCHAM (The Ark Restaurant)   N51 40·03 W001 22·08   220 ft. AMSL
3 nm W of Abingdon on the A338 Wantage and Frilford Heath Road.
Tarmac area sufficient for light helicopters.
Remarks: Operated by Mr. V. P. Latto. Trees on E side of landing area. Site is within
the Benson MATZ. Contact Benson App 120·90.
Fuel: Nil.   **Tel:** Frilford Heath 01865-391911

H119 MARKET BOSWORTH (Bosworth Hall Hotel)
6·5 nm NNE of Nuneaton.   N52 37·58 W001 23·93   400 ft. AMSL
Large Lawn (80x40 m) on S side of hotel.   O.S. Sheet 140/408032.
Remarks: Operated by Bosworth Hall Hotel, Market Bosworth, Nr Nuneaton,
Warwickshire. CV13 0LP. Prior notification of landing required. Helipad situated 2 nm
outside the SW boundary of East Midlands CTA (base 2500' ALT). Approach from
South avoiding overflying local habitation.
Landing Fee: £35.00.
Fuel: Nil.   **Tel:** 01455-291919. **Fax:** 292442

H120 MARKET RASEN (Racecourse)   N53 22·02 W000 18·10   95 ft. AMSL
1 nm E of Market Rasen.
Grass pad 50 x 20m.
Remarks: Operated by Market Rasen Racecourse Ltd. Legsby Road, Market Rasen,
Lincs. Helicopters accepted on PPR and at pilots own risk.
Wooded area to the east, power cables (40 ft) to the west. Windsock displayed.
No landing fees. Helipad <u>must not be used</u> during racing, unless with prior permission.
Fuel: Nil.   **Tel:** 01673-843434. **Fax:** 01673-844532.

H121 MILTON KEYNES (Central) N52 02·65 W000 44·80   360 ft. AMSL
E end of Milton Keynes City Centre. 5 nm WSW of Cranfield Airport
Concrete pad 33·5 x 33·5 ft. (Red 'H' on white background). (O.S. Sheet 152/863394)
Remarks: Operated by Milton Transport Management Ltd. Strictly PPR (24 hrs).
Contact Cranfield App 122·85. Unattended parking not advised. Pilots please refer to
Helipad Information Sheets (available from MTM) for obstacles, best approaches etc.
Fuel: Nil.   **Tel:** 01908-690463
                                        609078 Ansaphone outside office hours

H122 NAIRN (The Golf View Hotel)   N57 34·98 W003 53·58   20 ft. AMSL
Northern edge of Nairn town.
30x30 m square, short grass pad.
Remarks: Operated by The Golf View Hotel and Leisure Club, Seabank Road, Nairn
by Inverness, Scotland IV12 4HD. Caution: 2 m high stone wall to east, 1·5 m stone
wall to the north. Contact Inverness App 122·60 inbound/outbound.
Fuel: Nil.   **Tel:** 01667-452301. **Fax:** 01667-455267.

H123 NAIRN (The Newton Hotel)   N57 34·88 W003 52·88   20 ft. AMSL
NW of Nairn town, 200 m from shore.
Two Heli Pads: 1. 35x22 m;   2. 100 x 100m. Flat grass area.
Remarks: Operated by The Newton Hotel, Inverness Road, Nairn by Inverness,
Scotland IV12 4RX. Trees 30m high to the east and west. Helipad 1 surrounded by
gravel (would cause problems to parked vehicles when dry).
Contact Inverness App 122·60 inbound/outbound.
Fuel: Nil.   **Tel:** 01667-453144. **Fax:** 01667-454026.

H124 NANTWICH (Rookery Hall)   N53 05·85 W002 30·25   40 ft. AMSL
2·5 nm N of Nantwich town centre.   OS. Sheet 118/661558.
Grass area on parkland.
Remarks: Operated by Rookery Hall Hotel, Worleston, Nr. Nantwich, Cheshire.
CW5 6DQ. Available during daylight hours only. Prior notification required.
Power cables to N of pad.
Fuel: Nil.   **Tel:** Nantwich 01270-610016.

H125 NEASHAM (Newbus Arms Hotel)   N54 28·82 W001 30·42 100 ft. AMSL
3 nm SW of Teesside Airport.   O.S. Sheet 93/320097.
Grass field adjacent to hotel
Remarks: Operated by The Newbus Arms Hotel. Neasham, Darlington, Durham.
DL2 1PE. Visiting helicopters welcome on prior permission and at pilot's own risk.
Situated within Teesside CTR/CTA (Class 'D' Controlled Airspace), 2·6 nm from Rwy
05 threshold, 0·6 nm North of extended centreline.
Inbound: Obtain ATC clearance from Teesside App 118·85.
Outbound: Obtain start-up and departure clearance from Teesside Twr 119·80.
Fuel: Nil.   **Tel:** 01325-721071 **Fax:** 721770

H126 NEWBURY (Jarvis Elcot Park Hotel) N51 25·10 W001 25·82 400 ft. AMSL
4 nm WNW of Newbury.   O.S. Sheet 174/398693.
Grass area to South of Hotel.
Remarks: Operated by Elcot Park Hotel. Elcot, Nr. Newbury, Berkshire, RG20 8NJ.
Visitors welcome but prior notification is essential as cattle may occupy fields
adjoining the hotel.
Fuel: Nil.   **Tel:** Kintbury 01488-658100. **Fax:** 01488-658288.

H127 NEWBY BRIDGE (Swan Hotel)   N54 16·25 W002 57·75   100 ft. AMSL
Southern end of Lake Windermere.
Pad at W end of 2 acre grass field behind hotel.
Remarks: Operated by the Swan Hotel, Newby Bridge, Cumbria. LA12 8NB.
Slight gradient on field. Best approach/departure from/to NE. Prior notification of
landing required. Landing fee may be charged if no prior notification received.
Fuel: Nil   **Tel:** 015395-31681. **Fax:** 015395-31917.

H128 NEWCASTLE-UPON-TYNE (Europa Hotel)
                                  N55 01·00 W001 29·10 260 ft AMSL
Alongside junction of A1058 and A19, one mile North of The Tunnel.
Remarks: Operated by Queens Moat Houses PLC. Situated within Newcastle CTR/
CTA (Class 'D' Controlled Airspace), obtain ATC clearance from Newcastle App
124.375. Car park bay marked 'H'. Helicopters welcomed by arrangement at pilot's
own risk. Care must be taken to avoid standard lamps.
Fuel: Nil.   **Tel:** 0191-202 9955. **Fax:** 0191-263 4172

H129 NEWCASTLE-UPON-TYNE (Newcastle City Heliport)
N54 58·00 W001 38·00   80 ft. AMSL

1 nm west of Tyne Bridge on north bank of river Tyne.
A 6 acre heliport with parking for 50 helicopters or more and 150 cars.
Remarks: Operated by MB Air Limited. Strictly PPR. Situated within Newcastle
CTR/ CTA (Class 'D' Controlled Airspace), obtain ATC clearance from Newcastle App
124·375. Final approach to the site must be made from the south. Aim for the centre
of grassed area.
No over flying the northern boundary. Parking on upper asphalt area as directed.
Windsock displayed. Landing Fee on application. Hangarage available on request.
Hotels and Restaurants available nearby.
Fuel: Jet A1.   **Tel:** 0191-256 8000 or 0421- 611474.

H130 NEWCASTLE-UPON-TYNE (Swallow Gosforth Park Hotel)
N55 02·23 W001 37·10   270 ft. AMSL

2·6 nm E of Newcastle Airport, Western edge of racecourse.
200 x 300 ft. tarmac area on rear car park, marked with 'H'.
Remarks: Operated by the Swallow Gosforth Park Hotel, High Gosforth Park,
Newcastle-upon-Tyne. NE3 5HN. Prior permission essential so that landing area can
be sectioned off. Situated within Newcastle CTR/CTA (Class 'D' Airspace), obtain
ATC clearance from Newcastle APP 124·375. Trees near landing area.
Fuel: Nil.   **Tel:** 0191-2364111.

H131 NEW MILTON (Chewton Glen Hotel)   N50 45·03 W001 40·08 30 ft. AMSL
On SW outskirts of New Milton on N side of A337 road to Bournemouth.

O.S. Sheet 195/226942.
Large field, 'H' displayed, path to hotel on NE side (next to Car Park).
Remarks: Operated by Mr. M. Skan. PPR is essential.
Situated within Solent CTA (Class 'D'), obtain ATC clearance from Solent App
120·225. High trees on SE and NW sides of lawn.
All approaches & departures from/to NE (noise abatement) direct to landing position
on S side of Hotel. No landing fees.
Fuel: Nil.   **Tel:** 01425-275341. **Fax:** 272310.

H132 NEWPORT IOW (Swainston Manor Hotel)
3·3 nm W of Newport.   N50 41·37 W001 22·50   150 ft. AMSL
Concrete pads on Grass Lawn to N of Hotel.   O.S. Sheet 196/441879.
Remarks: Operated by Mr. F. C. Woodward, Swainston Manor Hotel.
PPR essential as cattle may occupy fields to N of Hotel.
Windsock displayed. **Landing Fee:** £7.50 plus VAT.
Caution: Radio Mast 941 ft. amsl 0·7 nm SSE of helipad.
Fuel: Nil.   **Tel:** Newport 01983-521121.

H133 NEWTON ABBOT (Passage House Hotel) N5032·03 W00334·07 5 ft. AMSL
0·6 nm East of Newton Abbot Racecourse.   O.S. Sheet 192/724880
Large lawn in front of Hotel.
Remarks: Operated by Passage House Hotel, Hackney lane, Newton Abbot, Devon
PQ12 3QH. 24 hrs PPR. Trees NE corner of pad. Gravel car park SW corner of pad.
Contact Exeter App 128·15
Fuel: Nil   **Tel:** 01626-55515. **Fax:** 01626-63336.

H134 NEWTON AYCLIFFE (Blacksmiths Arms)   N54 36·57 W001 32·50
1·3 nm E of Newton Aycliffe, 0·4 nm W of A1(M) between Junc 59 & 60. 295ft. AMSL
Grass field 114 x 70m with a slight slope towards north.   O.S. Sheet 93/297239
Remarks: Operated by Pat and John Cook, Blacksmiths Arms, Preston Le Skern,
Nr Newton Aycliffe, Co Durham DL5 6JH. Visitors welcome, but strictly PPR.
Warning: Power lines on the southern edge of the field and also some surrounding
trees on field extremities.
Fuel: Nil.   **Tel:** 01325-314873. **Fax:** 01325-307417.

H135 NORTHALLERTON   N54 24·98 W001 18·42   235 ft. AMSL
6 nm NE of Northallerton (on A19 York–Cleveland).   O.S. Sheet 93/447025.
Grass paddock near farmhouse.
Remarks: Operated by Trenholme Farm, Ingleby Arncliffe, Northallerton, N Yorks.
Contact Mr. S. W. Hutchinson. Visiting helicopters welcome on prior permission and
at pilot's own risk. Facility open to E.M.S. Helicopters at any time.
Caution: Power cables running N/S on West side of A19.
Best approach in sector 010°– 190°. **Hangarage:** Available.
Fuel: Nil.   **Tel:** 01642-370137. **Fax:** 370024.

H136 NORTHAMPTON (Swallow Hotel)   N52 13·35 W000 52·67   200 ft. AMSL
1 nm SE of city centre (A45).   O.S. Sheet 152/768590.
Large grass area between hotel and lake. Large 'H' on grass landing pad.
Remarks: Operated by the General Manager. Swallow Hotel, Northampton,
NN4 7HW. Visiting helicopters welcome on prior permission and at pilot's own risk.
Power cables 0·7 nm to the NE. Mast 417' agl 622' amsl 302°/1·6 nm.
Direct access to Champagne Table restaurant and hotel's Management Centre.
Ideal for Silverstone shuttle.
No landing fees.
Fuel: Nil   **Tel:** 01604-768700. **Fax:** 769011

H137 NORTHAMPTON (Broomhill Hotel)   N52 19·32 W000 57·70   395 ft AMSL
5 nm NNE of Northampton.   O.S. Sheet 152/709697.
Grass landing pad 20x40 m.
Remarks: Operated by the J. A. Kelly Esq., Broomhill Hotel, Holdenby Road,
Spratton, Northants. NN6 8LD. Site surrounded by trees to the North, South and
East. Approach from North, South or West to open fields and hover taxi to 'H'.
Ideally situated for Silverstone Motor Racing Circuit.
Fuel: Nil.   **Tel:** 01604-845959. **Fax:** 01604-845834

H138 NORTH WALTHAM (Wheatsheaf Hotel) N5112·45 W00111·42 420 ft AMSL
3·5 nm SW of Basingstoke.   O.S. Sheet 185/569455.   **CPT 114·35 182 17**
Grass area 20 x10 metres, adjacent to hotel. North side of A4 at Junction 8, M3.
Remarks: Operated by Mr. A. Vanesch, Wheatsheaf Hotel, North Waltham,
Basingstoke,Hants. RG25 2BB. Power cables 200 m to NE of site.
Popham Airfield 2 nm to WSW. Accommodation & Food available.
No landing fee if hotel facilities are used, otherwise £3.00.
Fuel: Nil.   **Tel:** 01256-398282. **Fax:** 01256-398253.

H139 NORTHWICH (Vale Royal Abbey)   N53 13·47 W002 32·58   110 ft. AMSL
2·7 nm NNW of Winsford Rly Sta.   O.S Sheet 118/639699.
Hard surface pad to East of Abbey. (700m W of railway).
Remarks: Operated by Mr. C. B. Hertzog. Visitors welcome on PPR.
Situated in the Manchester CTR, within the Special Low-Level Route.
Manchester APP/RAD 119·40.   Windsock displayed.
Fuel: Nil   **Tel:** 01606-889313/882131.

H140 OCKHAM (Black Swan PH & Restaurant)
                                    N51 18·30 W000 26·80   120 ft. AMSL
SE edge of Wisley disused aerodrome, 300 m E of Ockham VOR.
Grass area 75 x 55 m.
Remarks: Operated by Mr. Dennis Read, Black Swan Public House and Restaurant,
Ockham, Surrey. Situated 2nm South of London CTR and beneath London TMA
(base 2500' Alt). Available on prior permission, daylight hours only.
60 ft trees on western boundary.
Fuel: Nil.   **Tel:** 01932-862364.

H141 OLD STONE TROUGH HOTEL (THE) N53 53·65 W002 08·77 510 ft. AMSL
7 nm NNE of Burnley.   O.S. Sheet 103/900441   **POL 112·10 355 9·2**
Grass area 20 x 20 m, large grass surface, well drained and suitable for all types
of helicopters.
Remarks: Operated by The Old Stone Trough Hotel, Kelbrook, Nr Colne,
Lancashire.Site is for private use of Hotel and Restaurant patrons. Will acccept
visiting helicopters on PPR, at pilot's own risk and during daylight only.
Hotel flags in lieu of wind sock. East/West approach is recommended.
No landing fees. Car hire or taxi services available through Hotel reception.
Fuel: Nil.   **Tel:** 01282-844844. **Fax:** 01282-844428.

H142 OTTERY ST. MARY (Salston Manor Hotel)
1 nm SW of Ottery St. Mary.   N50 44·67 W003 17·73   165 ft. AMSL
 2 acre grass field.
Remarks: Operated by Beginlink Ltd., Ottery St. Mary, Devon. EX11 1RQ.
Windsock displayed. No landing fees.
Overnight accommodation & full Hotel services available.
Sidmouth 6 miles, Exeter 12 miles.
Fuel: Nil.   **Tel/Fax:** 01404-815581

H143 PARK HALL HOTEL (Spinkhill) N53 18·25 W001 18·48   390 ft AMSL
1 nm NNW of Junction 30 – M1.   **GAM 112·80 281 13**
Grass area 30 x 18 metres
Remarks: Operated by Tony and Jan Clark, Park Hall Hotel, Spinkhill, Sheffield,
S31 9YD. Visiting helicopters always welcome on prior permission and at pilot's own
risk. High trees on perimeter, best approach from South East. Minimum safety
services available.
Fuel: Nil   **Tel:** 01246-434897. **Fax:** 01246-436282

H144 PENRITH (Riverside Farm) N54 37·43 W002 57·27   900 ft. AMSL
7 nm WSW of Penrith .   O. S. Sheet 90/387260
Grass paddock S of farm buildings.
Remarks: Operated by Riverside Farm, Troutbeck, Penrith, Cumbria. Contact
Mr. S. W. Hutchinson. Visiting helicopters welcome on prior permission and at pilot's
own risk. Facility open to E.M.S. Helicopters at anytime.
Best approach arc 170° through 080°. Avoid the area 0·5 nm South of farm.
Caution: Low electric power line runs N/S 20 m South of Farmhouse.
Fuel: Nil.   **Tel:** 01642-370137. **Fax:** 370024

H145 PENZANCE (Heliport)   N50 07·68 W005 31·12   17 ft. AMSL
0·6 nm NE of Penzance.
Op hrs: SUMMER: Mon-Sat 0630-1900. WINTER: Mon-Fri 0730-1730, Sat 0730-1230.
Manoeuvring area: Grass strip 09/27, 379 x 45m. Lighting by arrangement.
Asphalt landing pad in centre of strip 30 x 30m.
Remarks: Operated by British International , The Heliport,
Eastern Green, Penzance. Use subject to PPR from BIH. Anemometer mast 80 ft aal
110 m NNE of pad. Windsock on hanger 40 ft aal, 23 m north of strip.
Fence 6 ft aal along W and S boundaries. Lighting post 26 ft aal, 40 ft amsl, adjacent
to southern edge of site. NDB mast 50 ft aal, 160 m NE of pad.
Within 4 nm of heliport: High ground up to 765 ft amsl from east through north to
south south west of heliport.
Landing Fees: Helis £30.00. Overnight Parking £15.00.
Radio: 118·10 A/G. NDB 'PH' 333·0
Fuel: Avtur, Jet A1
Tel: 01736-364296/7. **Fax:** 01736-364293.

H146 PETERHEAD (Longside)   EGPS   N57 30·98 W001 52·10 150 ft. AMSL
2 nm W of Peterhead   **Op hrs:** PPR. Mon-Fri 0730-1800, Sat. & Sun ¢.
Tarmac Rwy 10/28, 610 x 46m (helicopters only). Main helipad tarmac 25 m diameter.
Lighting: Floods on main helipad. Thr, Rwy on Rwy 10/28. IBn 'LS' Gn.
Remarks: Operated by Scotia Helicopter Services. Intensive helicopter flying.
(contact Aberdeen Radar 120·40 or 121·25).
Chimney 590' 3·4 nm to SE. A/D situated in Low Flying Area, Military traffic advised
by Highland Radar, Aberdeen ATC and Longside.
Customs: PNR (Helis from/to UK Continental shelf only).
Radio: A/G. 130·575, c/s 'Longside'. NDB 'LNS' 339·0 N57 31 W001 52.
Fuel: Jet Al.   **Tel:** 01779-838420 Ops; 838376 Switchboard. **Fax:** 01779-838708

H147 PITLOCHRY (Atholl Palace Hotel)   N56 42·00 W003 43·08   400 ft. AMSL
0·5 nm NW of Pitlochry.
Defined area of car park to SW of hotel.
Remarks: Operated by Atholl Palace Hotel, Pitlochry, Perthshire.
Windsock displayed.
Fuel: Nil.   **Tel:** 01796-472400

H148 POLZEATH (Roserrow Golf and Country Club - See Entry under Private
Airfield.

H149 PLYMOUTH (Drakes View)   N50 20·78 W004 06·97   350 ft. AMSL
4 nm S of Plymouth Airport.   O.S. Sheet 201/494519   **BHD 112·70 269 24**
Grass area 50 x 20 m. White concrete 'H' displayed. Avoid touch down on the 'H'.
Op hrs: PPR. Daylight hours only.
Remarks: Operated by Mr. T. Palmer. T.P. Air Helicopter Club. "The White House"
Drakes View, Staddon Heights, Plymouth. Visitors welcome on prior permission and
at pilot's own risk. Site is situated within Danger Area D009; DAAIS available from
Plymouth Military 121·25 or London Info 124·75. Contact Plymouth App 133·55 for
traffic information.
Warning: Two very high Radio Masts 350 m to South of helipad.
No landing fees, overnight parking free to members.
Fuel: Nil.   **Tel:** 01752-482722. **Fax:** 01752-482744

H150 PRESTBURY (Cheshire)   N53 17·35 W002 10·75   500 ft. AMSL

3 nm SE of Wimslow.   O.S. Sheet 118/881768.
Grass area (2 acres).
Remarks: Operated by Roger Reeves, Withinlee Brow, Mottram-St-Andrew,
Cheshire. Visiting pilots welcome at all times on request by phone. Landing area
surrounded by trees on N, W and E boundaries, and low level power cables on S
boundary adjacent to road. Windsock displayed on N end of outbuildings adjacent to
house. Site located within Manchester CTR (Class 'D') requiring SVFR and
compliance with published entry/exit procedures. No landing fees. Car available.
Fuel: Nil.   **Tel:** 01625-827827 or 820070. **Fax:** 01625-820050

H151 PRINCETHORPE (Woodhouse Hotel) N52 19·97 W001 25·87 250 ft. AMSL
2·5 nm SE of Coventry Airfield. (At SE corner of Birmingham CTA).
Small field 60 x 30m.   **Op hrs:** SR-SS. PPR
Remarks: Operated by The Woodhouse at Princethorpe. Desmond and Julia
Grundy. Hotel & restaurant. Situated on SE boundary of Birmingham CTA (Class 'D').
Obtain ATC clearance from Birmingham App 118·05.
No landing fees.
Fuel: Nil.   **Tel:** Marton 01926-632303 or 632131.

H152 RAINHAM (Coldharbour Point)   N51 29·20 E000 28·47   15 ft. AMSL
2 nm S of Rainham on N bank of Thames.   O.S. Sheet 177/523789.
Concrete pad. 'H' displayed, 400m E of Coldharbour Beacon.
Remarks: Operated by Freightmaster Services Ltd. Freightmaster Estate, Ferry
Lane Rainham, Essex. RM13 9DA. PPR essential.
Danger Area D135 (SFC to 1,000 ft.) 0·5nm to NE. No landing fees.
Fuel: Avtur (prior arrangement only).   **Tel:** 01708-555422. **Fax:** 01708-520460.

H153 READING (Pincents Manor)   N51 26·55 W001 03·88   200 ft. AMSL
3 nm W of Reading Town Centre. 600m N of Junction 12, M4.
Landing pad on W side of Hotel.   O.S. Sheet 175/652722
Remarks: Operated by Pincents Manor Restaurant. PPR. Hotel and restaurant
available. Helicopters welcome by arrangement, at pilot's own risk. No landing fees.
Do not approach from E sector.
Fuel: Nil.   **Tel:** 01734-323511.

H154 ROTHERHAM (Maltby)   N53 25·02 W001 12·10   380 ft. AMSL
1 nm E of Maltby.
Hard standing (white 'H')
Remarks: Operated by Aven Industrial Park Ltd. Aven Works, Maltby, Rotherham,
Yorks. Helicopters are welcome by arrangement and at pilot's own risk. Care must be
taken. Proof of adequate insurance cover must be produced when applying for
landing permission.
Fuel: Nil.   **Tel:** 01709-790763. **Fax:** 818020.

H155 ROYAL BATH AND WEST OF ENGLAND SHOWGROUND HELIPAD
N51 08·90 W002 13·38   O.S. Sheet 183/635389.   300 ft. AMSL
3 nm S of Shepton Mallet.
Level grass area.
Remarks: Operated by Royal Bath and West of England Society. The Showground,
Shepton Mallet, Somerset BA4 6QN. Use subject to PPR and written permission
and at pilot's own risk. Exemption to Rule 5 (1) of the Rules of The Air Regulations
1996 required from Civil Aviation Authority. Avoid flying over the Showground.
Approach to 'H' and park South of 'H'. Maps of landing area on application to Royal
Bath and West of England Society.
Fuel: Bristol Airport 15 nm.   **Tel:** 01749-822200. **Fax:** 01749-823169

H156 RUSHDEN (Lakeside)   N52 18·02 W000 37·10   150 ft AMSL
2 nm E of Wellingborough.   O.S. Sheet 152/937 678.
3 acres of grass.
Remarks: Operated by Lakeside Country Club, Northampton Road, Rushden,
Northants. Wires on N and W sides of landing area.
Accommodation available. Ample parking and restaurant.
Landing Fee: £15.00, free to Hotel & Restaurant customers
Fuel: Nil.   **Tel:** 01933-53808.
                                            Fax: 01933-413214.

H157 SCARBOROUGH (Willy Howe)   N54 08·12 W000 23·00   130 ft. AMSL
9 nm S of Scarborough   **OTR 113·90 344 28**
Site of disused airfield, helipad has 3° **down** slope to the west.
Remarks: Operated by P. J. Botterill Esq., East Yorks Light Avaition, Willy Howe
Farm, Wold Newton, Driffield, Yorks YO25 0HW. Helicopters welcome on prior
permission and at pilot's own risk. All approaches from the north avoiding all
domestic properties in the vicinity. Full details given on phoning for PPR.
Car available by prior arrangement. *Ganton Golf Course, one of the best, just 8 miles.*
Radio: Linton App 129·15; Willy Howe Radio 130·125.
Fuel: Nil.
Tel: 01262-470207 (best time to phone is evening, day before flight).
Fax: 01262-470326

H158 SHEFFIELD (Shirecliffe)   N53 23·98 W001 28·32   440 ft AMSL
1·5 nm N of City Centre.   O.S. Sheet 110/352895
Tarmac pad 22 m square. 'H' displayed.
Remarks: Operated by Sheffield City Council, Direcr Services, Olive Grove Road,
Sheffield. S2 3GE. Helipad Manager – Peter Jackson. Strictly PPR, 30 minutes in
emergency, 24 hrs others. Permission required under Rule 5(1) of the Rules of The Air
Regulations 1991. Site surrounded by public playing fields. App/Dep to/from the NW
along railway line and contact Sheffield Information 128·525. No unattended parking.
No security.   **Landing Fee:** £25.00.
Fuel: Nil.   **Tel:** 0114-2736525

H159 SHREWSBURY (Albright Hussey Hotel)
                                    N52 45·20 W002 44·42   280 ft. AMSL
2·5 nm North of Shrewsbury on A528.
Lawn in front of the Hotel.
Remarks: Operated by Albright Hussey Hotel, Ellesmere Road, Shrewsbury,
Shropshire SY4 3AF. First recorded in the Domesday Book as 'Elbretone', today's
Albright Hussey retains all the charm and character of its history. Restaurant and
Garden facilities are available. Call before departure to give ETA. Telegraph cables in
adjacent fields.
Fuel: Nil   **Tel:** 01939-290571/523
                                                  Fax: 01939-291143

H160 SILVERSTONE (Heliport) – See under Airfield entry.

H161 SLOUGH (Upton Court Park)   N51 30·03 W000 35·10   65 ft AMSL
1·2 nm E of Junction 6 (M4), NE corner of Park. (Grid Ref. 984790).
Grass area 60 x 60 metres.
Remarks: Operated by Sports & Leisure Dept. Slough Borough Council. Contact Ian
Taylor, Senior Client Manager. Use restricted to visits by prior arrangement. Helipad is
located within the London CTR. Heli Route H2 crosses the B416, 2 nm N of Helipad.
Fuel: Nil   **Tel:** 01753-875513

H162 SOLENT Heliport   N50 58·34 W001 14·97   190 ft AMSL
2 nm NW of Bishops Waltham VRP (SAM 113·35 079 3·8).
Grass landing area adjacent to windsock.
Remarks: Operated by Solent Helicopters. Licensed Heliport. Strictly PPR.
Situated within the Solent CTA/Southampton CTR. Obtain ATC clearance from Solent
Approach 120·225.
Fuel: Nil.   **Tel:** 01489-860686

H163 SOUTH BURLINGHAM (Church Farm)   N52 37·13 E001 30·02   70 ft AMSL
7 nm E of Norwich City Centre (0·5 nm S of railway).   **CLN 114·55 021 47·4**
Grass landing area 2 acres. 'H' and windsock displayed.
Op hrs: PPR. SR – SS.
Remarks: Operated by M. J. Flynn. Church Farm, South Burlingham, Norfolk.
NR13 4EU. Site is located next to large tiled Barn in open country opposite church.
Visiting helicopters welcome on prior permission and at pilot's own risk.
Visitors should phone for briefing. No landing fees.
Contact Norwich App 119·35 or Coltishall App 125·90 for traffic information.
Accommodation: Available on the farm.
Fuel: Nil.   **Tel:** 01493-751110.

H164 SOUTH MILFORD (Forte Posthouse)   N53 45·02 W001 15·10 175 ft AMSL
2 nm NNW of Ferry Bridge Power Station on A1 road at fork with A63.
Clay/grass standing 46 x 61m. In wet weather, triangular standing 46 x 58 x 79m.
Remarks: Operated by Forte Posthouse Hotel, Junction A1/A63, South Milford,
Leeds. LS25 5LF. Will accept visiting helicopters on PPR and at pilot's own risk.
Care must be taken. Surrounded by trees, gap from West over pylons.
Caution: Radio mast 140ft agl in wooded area adjacent to landing pad.
Fuel: Nil.   **Tel:** 01977-682711. **Fax:** 01977-685462

H165 SOUTHPORT (Birkdale Sands)   N53 38·77 W003 01·58   Sea Level
1 nm SW of Southport Pier.
Sand area 906 x 197m.
Remarks: Owned by Sefton Borough Council. Operated by Beach Aviation Ltd.
Available on prior permission and at pilot's own risk when state of sands and tides
permit.
Fuel: Nil.   **Tel:** 01704-547811. 01772-613897 Outside hours.

H166 STON EASTON   N51 16·90 W002 32·43   460 ft. AMSL
2 nm W of Radstock.   O.S. Sheet 183/625539   **BRI 380·0 137 8·8**
Lawn 60 x 53 metres, house on one side otherwise surrounded by fields.
Remarks: Operated by Ston Easton Park Hotel. Manager David Jennings.
Helicopters welcome on prior permission. Bristol Airport 9 nm to NW.
Recommend contact Bristol App for traffic information and possible radar assistance.
No landing fees.
Fuel. Nil   **Tel:** 01761-241631. **Fax:** 01761-241377.

H167 STORRINGTON (Little Thakeham Hotel)
1·2 nm NE of Storrington.   N50 55·72 W000 25·37   200 ft. AMSL
Large grass area South of hotel.   OS. Sheet 198/109156
Remarks: Operated by Tim and Pauline Ractliff, Little Thakeham Hotel, Merrywood
Lane, Storrington, West Sussex
Fuel: Nil. (Shoreham 7·5 nm SE).   **Tel:** 01903-744416.

H168 STRATFORD-UPON-AVON (Billesley Manor Hotel)
3 nm WNW of Stratford-upon-Avon.   N52 12·52 W001 47·25   250 ft. AMSL
3 acres lawned area on S side of hotel.   O.S. Sheet 151/148567
Remarks: Operated by Billesley Manor Hotel, Stratford-upon-Avon, Warwicks.
B49 6NF. Best approach from South. Avoid landing on croquet lawn.
Fuel: Nil.   **Tel:** 01789-279955. **Fax:** 01789-764145.

H169 STRATFORD-UPON-AVON (Welcombe Hotel)
O.S. Sheet 151/210568.　　　　　　　N52 12·55 W001 41·65　　　　245 ft. AMSL
NNE of town to the N of the A439 road. Obelisk identifies hotel.
60 x 60 ft. flat lawn surrounded by a larger area of uneven grass surface.
Surrounded by 18-hole golf course.
Remarks: Operated by the Welcombe Hotel. Tall trees on NE side.
No landing fees.
Fuel: Nil.　　　　　　　　**Tel:** 01789-295252 **Fax:** 01789-414666 **Telex:** 31347

H170 STRATFORD-UPON-AVON (Moat House International)
O.S. Sheet 151/206550.　　　　　　　N52 11·57 W001 41·98　　　　123 ft. AMSL
On East side of town adjacent to River Avon, public ammenities area between canal
and river.
Grassed area 50 x 40 m, 'H' displayed. Tree adjacent to landing area.
Remarks: Operated by Queens Moat Houses, Stratford-upon-Avon.
Approaches liable to flooding in wet weather. Recommend site visit prior to use.
Fuel: Nil　　　　　　　　**Tel:** Stratford-upon-Avon 01789-414411.

H171 STRETTON (Dovecliff Hall Hotel) N52 51·68 W001 37·43　　165 ft. AMSL
2 nm NNE of Burton-on-Trent.　　　　　　　　　O.S. Sheet 128/259274.
Grass landing pad 50 x 30 m adjacent hotel.
Remarks: Operated by Mr. N. O. Hine. Dovecliff Hall Hotel, Dovecliff Road, Stretton,
Burton-on-Trent, Staffs. DE13 0DJ. Site is situated beneath East Midlands CTA (base
1500' ALT). East Midlands App 119·65.
Visiting helicopters welcome on prior permission and at pilot's own risk.
Fuel: Nil　　　　　　　　**Tel:** 01283-531818. **Fax:** 01283-516546

H172 STUDLEY PRIORY HOTEL　　N5148·40 W00108·38　　　310 ft. AMSL
5 nm NE of Oxford City Centre.　　　　　　　　O.S. Sheet 164/598121.
5 acre paddock adjacent to hotel.
Remarks: Operated by the Studley Priory Hotel. Horton-cum-Studley, Oxford.
OX33 1AZ. Helicopters welcome on prior permission.
Fuel: Nil.　　　　　　　　**Tel:** Stanton St. John 01865-351203 or 351254.

H 173 SUNDERLAND (Nissan Heliport)　　N54 55·00 W001 28·10　138 ft. AMSL
W outskirts of Sunderland.　　　　　　　　　O.S. Sheet 88/336580.
Asphalt pad 40x30m, within smaller test track (white 'H' displayed)
Remarks: Operated by Nissan Motor Manufacturing (UK) Ltd. Unlicensed heliport
situated 4 nm S of Newcastle CTR/ CTA (Class 'D' Controlled Airspace). Use strictly
by prior permission. Visiting pilots should contact Newcastle App 124·375 at 25 nm
range and immediately after take-off on departure. ATC clearance must be obtained
if intending to enter controlled airspace. Approach/Dep to/from the South.
Fuel: Nil.　　　　　　　　**Tel:** 0191-4150000

H174 SWINDON (The Post House Hotel)　　N51 32·03 W001 44·0　410 ft. AMSL.
2nm SE of Swindon centre.
Grass area 180 x 60m.
Remarks: Operated by the Trust House Forte (UK) Ltd. Site is situated just North of
COATE WATER and is on the western boundary of Lyneham CTR (Class 'D' airspace).
Fuel: Nil.　　　　　　　　**Tel:** Swindon 01793- 24601

H175 TEWKESBURY (Puckrup Hall Hotel)   N52 01·67 W002 09·85   100 ft. AMSL
2 nm N of Tewkesbury.   O.S. Sheet 150/888365.   **HON 113·65 230 27·2**
Grass area E side of hotel building, 800m south of Junction1 – M50.
Remarks: Operated by Puckrup Hall Hotel. Puckrup, Tewkesbury. Gl20 6EL.
Visiting helicopters welcome on prior permision. No landing fees.
Fuel: Nil   **Tel:** 01684-296200. **Fax:** 01684-850788.

H176 THORNTON HALL HOTEL   N53 19·02 W003 02·88   150ft AMSL
9 nm NW of Chester.   O.S. Sheet 108/301803   **WAL 114·10 153 5·5**
Grass helipad at rear of Hotel.
Remarks: Operated by Thornton Hall Hotel, Thornton Hough, Wirral, Merseyside.
L63 1JF. Proprietor: Mr. C. D. Thompson. Helicopters welcome on prior permission.
Helipad situated within Liverpool CTR, 2 nm NE of NESTON VRP. ATC clearance
must be obtained from Liverpool App 119·85. Restricted Area R311 2 nm NNW of
Chester. Power cables running NW–SE, 250m to West of site. No landing fees.
Fuel: Nil.   **Tel:** 0151-336-3938/3939/3930.

H177 TONBRIDGE (Dene Park)   N51 13·73 E000 15·95   280 ft. AMSL
2 nm N of Tonbridge.   O.S. Sheet 188/598503.
Grass area 36 x 14 metres.
Remarks: Operated by Dene Park Estates Ltd. Use is strictly by prior permission
from the operator. Gatwick CTA 3 nm to the west.
Buildings on North and West side of helipad, woodland to the South.
Fuel: Nil   **Tel:** 01732-770899.

H178 TRESCO (Heliport)   N49 56·75 W006 19·88   12 ft. AMSL
0·75 nm N of Southern tip of Tresco Island, Isles of Scilly.
Landing area 30 x 30m Grass/Heather, standard 'H'.
Manoeuvring area E/W 362 x 46 m designated by white inlaid markers.
Op hrs: Daylight hours only. PPR.
Remarks: Operated by Tresco Estates. PPR. Line of trees 50m to North and parallel
to strip, 30ft. agl. Great Rocks 100m to SE, 40ft. agl.
Mast (L) 1·5nm to SE, 411ft. amsl. Avoid overflying bird nesting site 500m to SE.
Radio: c/s Tresco Radio 130·25 A/G.
Landing Fee: £50.00 unless holidaying on Tresco.
Fuel: Nil.   **Tel:** 01720-422970. Mobile 0831-108083.
                                      Fax: 01720-422870.

H179 TORQUAY (Torbay, Devon)   N50 23·03 W003 33·07   180 ft. AMSL
400 yards SE of Churston railway station, midway on Paignton to Brixham main road.
Large grass area centre of Go-Kart circuit. 'H' displayed.
Remarks: Operated by Commercial Go-Karts Ltd. Available year round.
Staff on duty Easter to September, 10 a.m. to 9 p.m. Free landings at pilot's own risk.
Nightstops permitted.
Fuel: MOGAS.   **Tel:** 01803-845592 (office). 842779 (circuit).
                                    Fax: 01803-845594.

H180 ULLAPOOL (Mercury Motor Inn)   N57 52·98 W00 510·08   50 ft. AMSL.
On A835 just North of Ullapool village.
100 ft. diameter grass landing pad.
Remarks: Operated by Mount Charlotte Thistle Hotels.
Fuel: Nil.   **Tel:** Ullapool 01854-612314. **Fax:** 01854-612158.

H181 ULLSWATER (The Ullswater Hotel)   N54 32·65 W002 56·68   500 ft. AMSL
Southern end of Lake Ullswater.   O.S. Sheet 90/388170.
120 ft grass square in front of hotel. Two landing pads.
Remarks: Operated by Ullswater Hotel Ltd, Glenridding, Penrith, Cumbria.
Site surrounded by high ground up to 3116' amsl to the SW; 2800' amsl to the South
and 2154' amsl to the East. Best approach from NE following lake to Head of
Ullswater Lake. Visiting helicopters welcome on prior permission and at pilot's own
risk. Facilities open to E.M.S. Helicopters at any time.
Car Hire: Available by arrangement.
Fuel: Nil.   **Tel:** 017684-82444. **Fax:** 82303.

H182 WALSALL (Bescot Stadium)   N52 34·02 W001 58·90   370 ft. AMSL
0·7 nm E of Junction 9/M6.   **HON 113·65 324 17·3**
Asphalt landing pad 220 x 60 m (car park).
Op hrs: SR–SS.
Remarks: Operated by Mr. R. Whalley. Walsall Football Club Ltd. Site is situated
beneath Birmingham CTA (base 1500' ALT); Birmingham CTR 3 nm to the SE.
ATC clearance must be obtained from Birmingham App 118·05 before entering
controlled airspace.
Visiting helicopters welcome on prior permission and at pilot's own risk.
Full range of Conference, Function and Meeting Rooms available.
Restaurant and licensed bar facilities available.
No landing fees where stadium facilities being used.
Fuel: Nil.   **Tel:** 01922-22791. **Fax:** 01922-613202.

H183 WASHINGTON (The Forte Post House Hotel)
                              N54 53·00 W001 33·10   249 ft. AMSL
4 nm WSW of Nissan Car factory. Alongside A1(M), 6 nm S of Newcastle.
50 x 50 ft grass area between Hotel and motorway,
Remarks: Operated by Forte Hotels, Emerson, District 5, Washington,
Tyne and Wear. Helicopters welcomed at pilot's own risk. Liability for damage to the
buildings or grounds at the hotel also rests with the pilot.
Proof of adequate insurance cover required, £25 million as at 01/11/95.
318 ft high building 1 nm to NE. 332 ft high monument to East.
Care must be taken to avoid power cables to North and small trees surrounding the
landing area. No landing fees.
Fuel: Nil.   **Tel:** Washington 0191-4162264.
                                                             Fax: 0191-4153371.

H184 WELLESBOURNE (Walton Hall Hotel & Country Club)
                              N52 10·02 W001 35·08   158 ft. AMSL
2 nm S of Wellesbourne, 6 nm E of Stratford-upon-Avon.
Grass area (0·5 acre) in front of hotel.
Remarks: Operated by Walton Hall Members Ltd., Walton, Wellesbourne, Warwicks,
CV35 9HU. Full conference and function facilities, extensive leisure centre.
Licensed bars & restaurants.
Fuel: Nil.   **Tel:** 01789-842424.

H185 WESTBURY-sub-MENDIP   N51 13·83 W002 43·4   290 ft. AMSL
3 nm W of Wells, Somerset. 9nm S of Bristol Airport.
Grass strip 11/29, 540 x 20m. Helicopters and fixed wing.
Remarks: Operated by John Lloyd & Sons, Westbury-sub-Mendip, Somerset.
PPR. Light aircraft and helicopters welcome at pilot's own risk.
Circuits LH on 29, RH on 11. Windsock on north side near hangar.
Power cables on south side.
Landing strip on site of disused railway line.
Maintenance: Fixed & rotary wing (CAA approved) by Somerset Helicopters
Ltd.
Car Hire & Accommodation: Available by arrangement.
Fuel: Nil.   **Tel:** 01749-870713 (office hours), 870647 (other times)

H186 WEST MEON, PETERSFIELD (The West Meon Hut)
                                    N51 01·90 W001 04·28   360 ft. AMSL
5·7 nm WNW of Petersfield. Junction of A32 and A272. O.S. Sheet 185/650262
3 acres of grass N and E of Pub.
Remarks: Operated by John Ruckley, The West Meon Hut, West Meon,
Petersfield, Hants. Windsock displayed.
Fuel: Nil.   **Tel:** 0173 086 291.

H187 WESTON (Hawkstone Park Leisure Ltd)
                                    N52 51·02 W002 38·0   395 ft. AMSL
4 nm N of RAF Shawbury.
Grass landing area, 70ft. diameter.
Remarks: Operated by Hawkstone Park Leisure Ltd., Weston-under-Redcastle,
Nr. Shrewsbury, Shropshire, SY4 5UY. Approach over golf course. Site is
situated within Shawbury MATZ, contact Shawbury App on 120·77.
Windsock displayed.
Fuel: Nil.   **Tel:** 01939-200611. **Fax:** 01939-200311

H188 WESTON-SUPER-MARE (Intl. Helicopter Museum)
                                    N51 20·33 W002 55·97   17 ft. AMSL
SE corner of Weston Aerodrome.
Op hrs: 1000-1600 daily (O/T by arrangement)
1 acre grass landing area N side of main buildings, W of Museum.
Remarks: Operated by the International Helicopter Museum. Main aerodrome
temporarily closed. PPR.
Variable circuits. Avoid overflying Caravan Park on East side.
Occasional Westland test flying from site at SW corner of A/D (129·50).
Two metre fence surrounds the landing area. Flags/Windsock adjacent main
road.
Landing Fee: Nil, but Museum entry charge of £3.00 per person.
Restaurant: Hot and Cold snack facilities available.
Car Hire: Uphill Motor Co. 01934-626623.
Taxis: Apple Cabs 01934-418647.   ARC Taxis 01934-627694.
Fuel: Nil.   **Tel:** 01934-635227 or 822524. **Fax:** 01934-822400.

H189 WHITBY (Larpool Hall Hotel)   N54 28·18 W000 36·77   197 ft. AMSL
1 nm SSE of Whitby, on ridge overlooking Esk valley. Disused railway viaduct to
NW.
Landing area in front of hotel.
Remarks: Operated by Mr & Mrs K. Robinson, Larpool Hall Country House
Hotel, Larpool Lane, Whitby, North Yorhshire YO22 4ND.
PPR and at pilot's own risk.
Fuel: Nil   **Tel:** 01947-602737. **Fax:** 01947-820204.

H190 WICKEN (Wicken Country Hotel)   N52 02·85 W000 55·10 300 ft. AMSL
4 nm NE of Buckingham.   O.S. Sheet 152/743395.
Lawn 70 x 25m, adjacent to hotel.
Remarks: Operated by Wicken Country Hotel, MK19 6BX.
Restaurant: Japanese.   **Accommodation:** Available.
Fuel: Nil.   **Tel:** Wicken 01908-571239.

H191 WINCHESTER (Lainston House Hotel) N51 04·95 W001 22·18 350 ft. AMSL
2·5 nm NW of Winchester Cathedral   O.S. Sheet 185/446316.
Extensive lawned areas, preferred helipad E of house on terraces.
Remarks: Operated by Lainston House Hotel, Sparsholt, Hants. SO21 2LT. PPR.
Situated beneath Solent CTA (1500'— 3500' ALT), Southampton CTR 1·5 nm to SE.
Obtain ATC clearance from Solent App 120·225 before entering controlled airspace.
Fuel: Nil   **Tel:** 01962-863588.

H192 WOKING (Knaphill Manor)   N51 20·23 W000 36·50   80 ft AMSL
2 nm WSW of Fairoaks Aerodrome. O.S. Sheet 175/972603.
                                         OCK 115·30 292 5·9
Level grass area 40 x 40m.   **MID 114·00 009 16·6**
Remarks: Operated by Mrs. T. R. Leeper. Knaphill Manor, Woking, Surrey.
Available during daylight hours on prior permission. Site is located within Fairoaks
ATZ on the southern boundary of London CTR. Contact Fairoaks Information 123·425.
Site 400 m North of the extended centreline of Fairoaks 06 runway.
Helipad surrounded by trees, best approach from S –SW. Land to the side of
ornamental rectangular pond. No landing fees for ferrying guests, others £10.00.
Fuel: Nil.   **Tel:** 01276-857962. **Fax:** 01276-855503

H193 YARM (Crathorne Hall Hotel)   N54 27·68 W001 18·80   150 ft. AMSL
4·7 nm SE of Tees-side Airport.
Extensive lawns adjacent to hotel.
Remarks: Operated by Virgin Hotels Ltd., Crathorne Hall Hotel, Yarm, N. Yorks.
TS15 0AR. Contact Sales Manager — Patrick Jones.
Fuel: Nil.   **Tel:** 01642-700398. **Fax:** 01642-700814.

H194 YORK (Middlethorpe Hall Hotel)   N5355·80 W00105·60   20 ft. AMSL
2 nm S of York Minster.   O.S. Sheet 105/599486.
Grass helipad 96 m S of Hall, 200 m E of racecourse, 45 m N of A64 (York by-pass).
Remarks: Operated by Historic House Hotels Ltd., Middlethorpe Hall, Bishopthorpe
Road, York. YO2 1QB. Helipad available to Resident guests only.
Fuel: Nil.   **Tel:** 01904-641241.

N57 07·00 W002 19·02	**ABERDEEN (Culter Helipad)**	300 ft. AMSL

5·5 nm SW of Aberdeen Airport.	**ADN 114·30 194 11**

No Radio. Recommend contact Aberdeen APP 120·40.

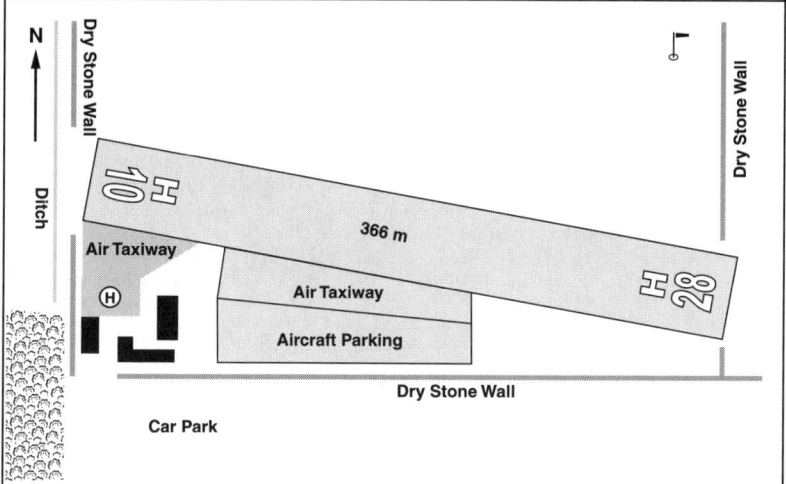

Rwy	Dim(m)	Surface	FATO(m)	Lighting
10/28	210x36	Grass	366	Nil

Op hrs: Strictly PPR.

Landing Fee: On Application.	**Customs:** By Arrangement
Hangarage: By Arrangement	**Maintenance:** By Arrangement.

Remarks: Operated by HJS Helicopters, Culter Helipad, Lower Baads, Anguston, Peterculter, Aberdeen AB14 0PR. Licensed Helipad day use only.

Helipad situated within the Aberdeen (Dyce) CTR (Class 'D' Controlled Airspace - see page 2). Contact Aberdeen APP 120·40 for Traffic information.

Circuits LH on Rwy 10, RH on Rwy 28.

Noise Abatement: Rwy 28 departures immediate right turn to avoid housing. Avoid overflying housing development of '*Hillcrest*' 0·3nm SE of the Helipad.

Caution: Power cables on North and East sides.

Restaurant: Light refreshments available.

Accommodation and Car Hire: Available by arrangement.

Fuel: 100LL by arrangement. MasterCard/Visa/Switch/Delta and Maestro.	**Tel:** 01224-739111. 01224-314038 - Out of hours. **Fax:** 01224-739222.

Robert Pooley ©

N52 38·10 E001 43·40	**GREAT YARMOUTH (North Denes)**	6 ft AMSL

1·5 nm N of Great Yarmouth.	**CLN 114·55 028 52**

c/s North Denes APP/TWR 123·40 Mon-Fri 0700-1900. Other times **A/G.**
NDB 'ND' 417·0 (On A/D).

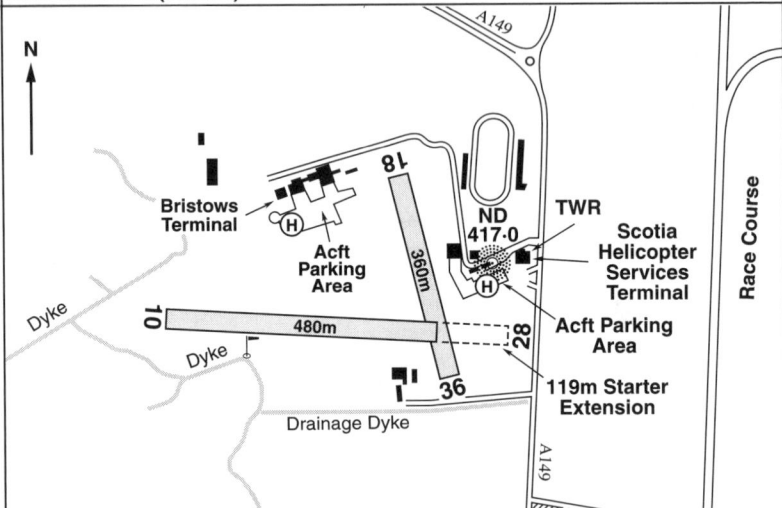

Rwy	Dim(m)	Surface	TORA(m)	LDA(m)	Lighting
10/28	480x32	Grass	10-535	10-625	Rwy †
			28-600	28-530	Rwy †
18/36	360 approx.	Grass	Unlicensed		Nil
	Concrete helicopter alighting area.				
† White runway edge lighting only.					

Op hrs: PPR. Mon-Fri 0730-1830, Sat & Sun 0800-1700.

Landing Fees: £6.45 per tonne (£20.00 minimum charge) plus charges for ATC,
Passenger Handling & Security, Freight and Parking — details on application

Hangarage: Limited.	**Maintenance:** Nil.	**Customs:** 2 hrs PNR.

Remarks: Operated by Scotia Helicopter Services. Caution in circuit – intensive
helicopter operations. Heliport on E side of A/D. Prior permission must be sought by
telephone before departure. Visiting helicopters to call North Denes Office for parking
instructions on 122·375. Avoid overflying Caister and Great Yarmouth.
HT Pylons 238' aal 244' amsl 175°/2·5 nm.
Water Tower 254' aal 260' amsl 348°/1·2 nm.

Airfield closed to fixed wing aircraft.

Restaurant: Dining facility in Terminal Building

Car Hire: Europcar. 01493-857818 (Within Terminal)

Taxi: At Terminal and on request

Fuel: Jet A1.	**Tel:** 01493-851500 Heliport. **Fax:** 01493-843757.

| N51 28·20 W000 10·77 | **LONDON (Westland Heliport)** | 18 ft AMSL |

3 nm SW of Westminster Bridge.

BIG 115·10 322 11·3

c/s Battersea. TWR 122·90.

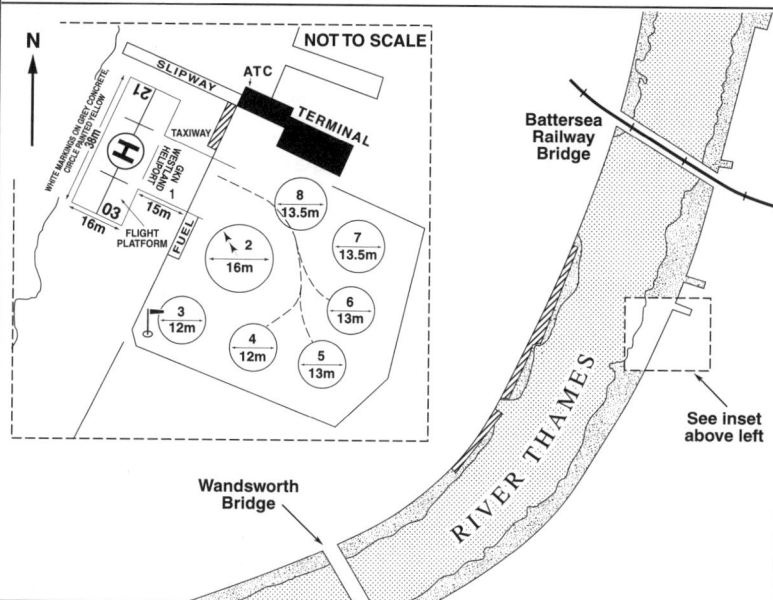

Rwy	Dim(m)	Surface	FATO	Lighting
–	38x16	Concrete	027°/207°	Full night flying facilities available.

Op hrs: Mon-Fri 0800-1730 early/late extensions, weekends & PHs by arrangement.

| **Landing Fee:** On application | **Customs:** 24 hrs PNR |
| **Hangarage:** Nil | **Maintenance:** Nil |

Remarks: Operated by GKN Westland Aerospace Ltd.

Use is subject to PPR and strict adherence to 'Arrangements and Conditions of use' (available on request).

Non-standard circuit pattern. Circuit height 1000 ft amsl.

Flying training not permitted. All pilots must have conducted a familiarisation with an appropriate qualified pilot.

No manoeuvres other than actual approach and take-off may be carried out below 500 ft agl.

Aircraft must not overfly shipping that is within 100 m of the Flight Platform.

Aircraft start-up and close down is subject to ATC approval.

Pilots must be familiar with helicopter marshalling signals.

Restaurant: Drinks only available. **Car Hire and Taxis:** By arrangement.

| **Fuel:** Jet A1. | **Tel:** 020-7228-0181. **Fax:** 020-7924 1022 ATC |

Robert Pooley ©

NON-IFR HELICOPTER FLIGHTS IN THE
LONDON CTR and LONDON CITY CTR

General

Non-IFR helicopter flying in the London CTR is normally restricted to flight at or below specified altitudes along defined routes. These routes have been selected to provide maximum safety by avoiding built up areas as much as possible.

Route details are listed at page 602 and the route structure is illustrated at page 612.

The precise routes are overprinted on the 1: 50,000 Map entitled – Helicopter Routes in the London Control Zone (available from Pooleys, Elstree Aerodrome). The illustration also shows the Specified Area of central London over which flight by single-engined helicopters is virtually prohibited except along the River Thames because of the requirement to be able to land clear of the area in the event of engine failure. All non-IFR helicopter flying in the London CTR is subject to Special VFR clearance. In addition, permission in writing from the CAA is required for flight within the Specified Area by single-engined helicopters.

H7, H9 (Hayes to Gutteridge) and H10 (Gutteridge to Kew Bridge) routes are not available to single-engined helicopters at night.

Procedures

Non-IFR flights in the London CTR are not permitted unless helicopters can remain in a flight visibility of at least 1 km, except when crossing over, taking off from or landing at Heathrow, when the reported visibility at Heathrow must be at least 2 km. Non-IFR helicopters must remain clear of cloud and in sight of surface.

Altimeter setting — will be LONDON/Heathrow QNH. Maximum altitudes (normally 1000ft.) are shown under route details. Special VFR clearances will be issued in the form "not above ..... feet" except for flights along routes H10 between Perivale Golf Course and Chiswick Bridge where the Standard Operating Altitude is 1200ft. These altitudes must be maintained accurately in order to ensure adequate terrain clearance and separation from fixed wing traffic approaching Rwy 27R at Heathrow.

Pilots should fly the precise routes as depicted on the latest edition of the 1: 50,000 Map entitled Helicopter Routes in the London Control Zone. 'Corner cutting' is to be avoided. In order to obtain sufficient lateral separation from opposite direction traffic, pilots may temporarily deviate to the right of the route. When flying along the River Thames, pilots should fly over that part of the river bed lying between normal high water marks but not so near the banks as to become a nuisance on account of noise. When deviating from the river, for reason of lateral separation, single engined helicopters must at all times be able to return to the river in the event of engine failure, in order to alight clear of the Specified Area.

Noise — On all routes, in order to minimise noise nuisance, pilots should maintain the maximum altitude compatible with their ATC clearance and with the prevailing cloud conditions. They are reminded of the requirement to comply with Rule 5(1)(e) of the Rules of the Air Regulations 1996 which precludes flight closer than 500 ft to any person, vessel, vehicle or structure. Wherever possible the overflight of hospitals and schools should be avoided. Formation flying by civil helicopters within the London CTR is not permitted.

ATC Clearance

(a) During the hours of operation of Thames Radar/ Heathrow Radar, pilots must obtain a Special VFR clearance. Thames Radar provides the control service for all SVFR flights within the London CTR east of LONON/Westland Heliport; Heathrow provides a similar service to the west of the Heliport. Pilots are requested to contact ATC three minutes before reaching the Zone Boundary, giving details of callsign, route, ETA at Zone entry point and destination.

(b) Outside the hours of operation of Thames Radar/Heathrow Radar clearance for Special VFR flights within the London CTR must be obtained from Heathrow Director (LATCC(TC)).

(c) When the destination is LONDON/Heathrow, the Special VFR clearance, for entry into the Zone, will include routeing and other instructions.

Holding. Non-IFR helicopters, particularly those using Heathrow or the routes close to it, may be required to hold at any of the locations on the route, shown under Reporting/ Holding Points and on the illustration at page 612.

Communications. Non-IFR helicopters operating within the London CTR must be able to communicate with LONDON/Heathrow Approach and Tower, Westland Heliport (Battersea Twr) and Northolt Approach (126·45), as appropriate.

Loss of Communications Procedures. In the event of communications failure in a helicopter operating in accordance with these procedures, the pilot is to adopt the procedure detailed at ENR 1.2 except as described below:
(i) If a SVFR clearance has been received to transit the CTR along a Helicopter Route, continue the flight in accordance with the clearance.
(ii) Where an intermediate clearance limit has been given (or clearance issued for only a part of the requested transit), proceed to the specified clearance limit and hold for 3 minutes. Then proceed via the requested Helicopter Route at the published maximum altitude for the route.
(iii) If no onward clearance has been received before reaching, or when holding at, Sipson or Bedfont, **reverse track and leave the CTR** via H10/Cookham if approaching Sipson or H9 if approaching Bedfont. **Do not attempt to cross London Heathrow Airport.**
(iv) Between Sipson and Bedfont:
    (a) If the landing runway has been crossed, cross the departure runway downwind of the threshold, exercising extreme caution with regard to possible landing traffic; and **leave the CTR via H10/Cookham or H9** as appropriate.
    (b) If the departure runway has been crossed, with instructions given to hold at the dual taxiways or fuel farm, **reverse track** to cross the departure runway downwind of the threshold, exercising extreme caution with regard to the possibility of landing traffic, and **leave the CTR via H10/Cookham or H9** as appropriate.
(v) If landing at London Heathrow Airport, and having crossed the runways if necessary as detailed above, proceed to land at the helicopter aiming point by day or at 27L threshold by night (then vacate 27L and await vehicle escort).

Separation between non-IFR helicopters. Separation may be decided between helicopters on the Helicopter Routes, on the basis that pilots of helicopters will be asked by ATC to maintain visual separation from other helicopter traffic, provided that:
(i) the visibility at Heathrow is 6 km or more and helicopters can operate clear of cloud and in sight of surface and remain in a flight visibility of at least 6 km;
(ii) there is agreement between the helicopters concerned;
(iii) the current route structure, the altitudes applicable and communication procedures are adhered to;
(iv) appropriate traffic information is passed to the helicopter pilots. (Normally for this purpose it will only be necessary for ATC to pass general traffic information eg....."Two helicopters westbound along H2 at 1000 ft in the vicinity of Southall — acknowledge").

Helicopter Operations at LONDON (Heathrow) — see page 613

HELICOPTER ROUTES IN THE LONDON CTR and LONDON/ CITY CTR

Abbreviations:

▲ — Compulsory Reporting Point   Δ — On Request Reporting Point   H — Holding Point

Map references are to the 1: 50 000 Ordance Survey Map of Great Britain.

Note: Pilots are to be at the lower altitude on arrival at the point at which the lower altitude applies.

Route	Significant Points National Grid & Lat/Long	Description of Refernce	Maximum Altitude (LONDON/Heathrow QNH)		Holding Point	Remarks
H2	Δ Iver TQ 035 826 N51 31·95 W000 30·52	Delaford Park			H	
	Δ West Drayton TQ 052 784 N51 29·65 W000 29·15	M4 Motorway Crossing of River Coln (1·25 nm west of Airport Spur)	1000 ft			**Note**
	▲ Airport Spur TQ 075 786 N51 29·73 W000 27·25	Junction of M4 Motorway and Motorway Spur to London Heathrow			H	

Note: Unless otherwise cleared by ATC, pilots are not to fly South of the M4 between West Drayton and Airport Spur.

Route	Significant Points National Grid & Lat/Long	Description of Refrence	Maximum Altitude (LONDON/Heathrow QNH)			Holding Point	Remarks
H3	▲ Bagshot Mast SU 908 619 N51 20·95 W000 41·95	Intersection of London Control Zone/ M3 Motorway				H	Note 1
		M3 Motorway Junction 3	1500 ft				
	△ Thorpe TQ 018 679 N51 24·03 W000 32·27	M3 Motorway south of Thorpe Green (M25 intersection)	1000 ft			H	
	▲ Sunbury Lock TQ 112 683 N51 24·15 W000 24·27	Midway between Sunbury Lock and the middle of Knight reservoir		800 ft		H	Note 2
	△ Teddigton TQ 170 714 N51 25·78 W000 19·10	Weir on River Thames (M25 intersection)			1000 ft	H	
	▲ Barnes TQ 234 765 N51 28·45 W000 13·42	North edge of Richmond Park River Thames at Barn Elms Park					
	▲ Westland Heliport TQ 266 762 N51 28·20 W000 10·77	Westland Heliport				H	

Note 1. When LONDON (Heathrow) Rwy 23 is in use, the H3 route from Bagshot Mast to its intersection with H9 route (Sunbury Lock Reporting Point), will not be available to helicopters.

Note 2. Route 3 will normally be closed whenever Easterly operations are taking place at Heathrow Airport. Helicopter pilots are recommended to obtain Heathrow runway information on the ATIS 123·90 before contacting Heathrow Radar on 119·90, or Westland Heliport on 122·90. Notwithstanding the above, special arrangements for the use of Route H3 in connection with certain events may be made. Such arrangements will be promulgated by NOTAM.

603

Route	Significant Points National Grid & Lat /Long	Description of Reference	Maximum Altitude (LONDON/Heathrow QNH)	Holding Point	Remarks
H4	▲ Isle-of-Dogs TQ 381 781 N51 29·03 W000 00·70	Specified Area Boundary crossing River Thames			Note 1
	△ London Bridge TQ 330 805 N51 30·45 W000 05·07	London Bridge (road bridge)	2000 ft		Note 2 Note 3
	▲ Vauxhall Bridge TQ 302 782 N51 29·25 W000 07·60	CTR Boundary crossing River Thames			
	▲ Chelsea Bridge TQ 286 778 N51 29·03 W000 09·00	Chelsea Bridge Road	1500 ft		
	▲ Westland Heliport TQ 266 762 N51 28·20 W000 10·77	Westland Heliport		H	Note 4

Note 1. The sector of Route H4, Isle-of-Dogs – Vauxhall Bridge, is established and notified for the purposes of Rule 5(2)(a) of the Rules of the Air Regulations 1996.

Note 2. Captive passenger carrying balloons up to 36 metres in diameter operate from sites adjacent to H4 at Tower Bridge and Vauxhall Bridge to the south and at Hyde Park to the north, by day only, to a maximum height of 400 ft agl.

Note 3. Ferris Wheel: The London Eye Ferris Wheel (464 ft amsl) lies within the boundary of H4 at Jubilee Gardens (N51 30·20 W000 07·18) between London Bridge and Vauxhall Bridge. Pilots are reminded of the application of Rule 5 (1) (e).

Note 4. There are no Holding Points on H4 East of Westland Heliport. The nearest Holding Point is at Greenwich Marshes, outside the 'Specified Area'.

604

1 DEC 00

Route	Significant Points National Grid & Lat /Long	Description of Refernce	Maximum Altitude (LONDON/Heathrow QNH)		Holding Point	Remarks
H5	▲ Northwood TQ 071 906 N51 36·20 W000 27·32	Zone Boundary midway between Harefield and Northwood	2000 ft **(Note 2)**		H	**Note 1**
	△ Uxbridge Common TQ 062 855 N51 33·53 W000 28·22	Roundabout on A40 road North of Uxbridge Common			H	

Note 1. On H5 between Northwood and Airport Spur, pilots may be required to communicate with Northolt Approach 126·45.

Note 2 When LONDON(Heathrow) Runway 23 is in use, the maximum altitude between Uxbridge Common and Northwood will be 1000 ft London (Heathrow) QNH.

Route	Significant Points National Grid & Lat /Long	Description of Refernce	Maximum Altitude (LONDON/Heathrow QNH)	Holding Point	Remarks
H7	◀ Banstead TQ 243 614 N51 20·23 W000 13·02	Golf course Northwest of town	2000 ft	H	
	△ Morden TQ 229 672 N51 23·45 W000 14·12	Sutton/Epsom railway	1500 ft		
	△ Caesar's Camp TQ 220 711 N51 25·53 W000 14·77	Cemetary Northeast of Gas Works	1000 ft	H	
	◀ Barnes TQ 234 765 N51 28·45 W000 13·42	Golf course Southwest corner of Wimbledon Common			
	◀ Westland Heliport TQ 266 762 N51 28·20 W000 10·77	River Thames at Barn Elms Park		H	
		Westland Heliport			

1 DEC 00

Route	Significant Points National Grid & Lat /Long	Description of Refernce	Maximum Altitude (LONDON/Heathrow QNH)	Holding Point	Remarks
H9	◄ Oxshott West TQ 101 609 N51 20·23 W000 25·20	Intersection of London Control Zone/ A3 Trunk Road	2000 ft	H	
	△ Esher Common TQ 136 621 N51 20·85 W000 22·17	A3 Trunk Road West of A3/A244 Intersection			
	OR				
	◄ Oxshott East TQ 160 611 N51 20·23 W000 20·11	Princes Coverts	2000 ft	H	
	△ Arbrook TQ 149 624 N51 20·97 W000 21·00	Intersection of A3 Trunk Road/ Railway Line			
	△ Esher Common TQ 136 621 N51 20·85 W000 22·17	A3 Trunk Road West of A3/A244 Intersection	1500 ft		
	THEN	London/Woking railway			
	◄ Sunbury Lock TQ 112 683 N51 24·15 W000 24·27	Midway between Sunbury Lock and the middle of Knight reservoir	800 ft	H	

Continued on next page

Robert Pooley ©

607

Route	Significant Points National Grid & Lat /Long	Description of Reference	Maximum Altitude (LONDON/Heathrow QNH)	Holding Point	Remarks
H9	△ Feltham TQ 095 726 N51 26·50 W000 25·55	Open space south of Railway Line	800 ft	H	Note 4
	△ Bedfont TQ 088 745 N51 27·53 W000 26·17	East of Terminal Four, South of A30		H	Note 4
	△ Sipson TQ 076 772 N51 29·00 W000 27·10	Open space Northeast of the Junction Motorway Spur and Main Road A4 at North perimeter of London(Heathrow)		H	
	◄ Airport Spur TQ 075 786 N51 29·73 W000 27·25	Junction of M4 Motorway and Motorway Spur to London (Heathrow)	1000 ft	H	
	△ Hayes TQ 149 624 N51 30·70 W000 26·60	Gravel pits at Goulds Green	1500 ft (Note 1)	H	Note 2
	△ Gutteridge TQ 097 845 N51 32·90 W000 25·12	A40, South of Northolt Aerodrome Runway Intersection	2000 ft (Note 1	H	Note 3
	◄ Northwood TQ 071 906 N51 36·20 W000 27·32	Zone Boundary midway between Harefield and Northwood		H	

1 DEC 00

Route	Significant Points National Grid & Lat /Long	Description of Refernce	Maximum Altitude (LONDON/Heathrow QNH)	Holding Point	Remarks
H9					

Note 1. When LONDON (Heathrow) Rwy 23 is in use, the maximum altitude between Hayes and Northwood will be 1000 ft LONDON (Heathrow) QNH.

Note 2. Between Northwood and Airport Spur, pilots may be required to communicate with Northolt Approach 126·45.

Note 3. The holding manoeuvre is to be carried out to the south of the Northolt aerodrome boundary.

Note 4. Helicopters will be held at Bedfont during daylight hours when the reported weather condition are equal to or better than 6 km visibility and 1000 ft lowest reported cloud and will be held at Feltham at all other times.

Warning: Rwy 27L missed approach procedure requires a left turn at 1000 ft aal. Pilots holding at Bedfont must remain in visual contact with aircraft on final approach to Rwy 27L.

Route	Significant Points National Grid & Lat /Long	Description of Reference	Maximum Altitude (LONDON/Heathrow QNH)		Holding Point	Remarks
H10 (Note 6)		CTR Boundary	2000 ft			
	◀ Cookham SU 898 857 N51 33·75 W000 42·37	Bridge over River Thames North of Cookham			H	
	△ Iver TQ 035 826 N51 31·95 W000 30·52	Delaford Park	1500 ft **(Note 1)**		H	
	△ Uxbridge Common TQ 062 855 N51 33·53 W000 28·22	Roundabout on A40 road North of Uxbridge Common			H	**Note 2**
	△ Gutteridge TQ 097 845 N51 32·90 W000 25·12	A40, South of Northolt Aerodrome Runway Intersection			H	**Note 3**
	△ Perivale TQ 170 828 N51 31·93 W000 18·87	On A40, North of Golf course divided by River Brent	1200 ft **(Note 5)**		H	**Note 4**
	△ Brentford TQ 186 791 N51 29·85 W000 17·52	Gunnersbury Park North of Chiswick Fly-over			H	

Continued on next page

610

Route	Significant Points National Grid & Lat /Long	Description of Reference	Maximum Altitude (LONDON/Heathrow QNH)	Holding Point	Remarks
H10	△ Kew Bridge TQ 190 778 N51 29·23 W000 17·27	North edge of Gunnesbury Park		H	
		Bridge across River Thames at NE corner of Gardens and Common	750 ft (Note 5)		
		Chiswick Bridge			
	▲ Barnes TQ 234 765 N51 28·45 W000 13·42	River Thames at Barn Elms Park	1000 ft		
	▲ Westland Heliport TQ 266 762 N51 28·20 W000 10·77	Westland Heliport		H	

Note 1. When LONDON (Heathrow) Rwy 23 is in use, the maximum altitude between Iver and Gutteridge will be 1000 ft LONDON (Heathrow) QNH, and the route between Gutteridge and Kew Bridge will not normally be available.

Note 2. Between Iver and Perivale, pilots may be required to communicate with Northolt Approach 126·45.

Note 3. The holding manoeuvre is to be carried out to the south of the Northolt aerodrome boundary.

Note 4. The holding manoeuvre is to be contained to the West of Perivale.

Note 5. This is the Standard Operating Altitude for this segment of the route (Perivale to Chiswick Bridge).

Note 6. Due to conflict with departure procedures, severe delays can be expected by helicopters requiring Helicopter Route H10 when LONDON (Heathrow) Runways 09 are in use.

Robert Pooley ©

611

HELICOPTER ROUTES IN THE LONDON CTR
and LONDON CITY CTR

LEGEND

Helicopter Routes	▬ ▬ ▬
Specified Areas	(grey area)
Heliport	Ⓗ
Reporting Point - Compulsory	◀
Reporting Point - On request	◁
Reporting Point - Where holding may be required	◀Ⓗ / ◁Ⓗ

LONDON (Heathrow) — HELICOPTER OPERATIONS

Procedures for Helicopter Operations at LONDON/Heathrow Airport

1.   General Requirements

1.1   In order to facilitate the expiditious transit of LONDON/Heathrow by helicopters operating under SVFR clearance, procedures have been devised based on ATC's ability in certain circumstances, to reduce standard separations by visual reference to traffic operating in the immediate vicinity of the airport.

1.2   Procedures based on visual separation will only be applied when:
   (a) the Heathrow reported weather conditions are equal to or better than 6 km visibility and 1000ft lowest reported cloud base.
   (b) it is during daylight hours.

1.3   Fixed-wing operations are aligned on westerly Runways 27L/27R or on easterly runways when 09R is in use for departure and/or 09L is in use for landing.

> **Note:** Visual procedures have not been devised for the few occasions when Runway 23 is in use, when 09R is in use for landing, or when 09L is in use for departures. In all other circumstances, standard separation will be applied.

1.4   Helicopter operations are to commence at Feltham, Bedfont or Sipson as appropriate. Helicopters holding at Feltham or Sipson are separated for both ATC and wake vortex purposes from fixed wing aircraft landing on, departing from or carrying out missed approach to, runways 27L/27R, 09L/09R, 23.

1.5   Helicopter may be held at Bedfont only when the conditions detailed in paragraph 1.2 exist and are separated for wake vortex purposes and visual separation only.

Pilots must remain in visual contact with aircraft on approach to Rwy 27L and are warned that the missed approach procedure to Rwy 27L requires a left turn at 1000 ft aal.

1.6   Helicopters are to transit the airport at not less than 800ft (Heathrow QNH).

1.7   SVFR Helicopter operations are not permitted at Heathrow when the reported visibility is less than 2 km.

1.8   Loss of communications procedure for helicopters overflying or landing at London Heathrow Airport are detailed at page 601.

2.   Visual Procedures

2.1   Crossing Runway 27L/27R

2.1.1   Unless otherwise instructed, helicopter pilots are to ensure that the departure runway, as advised by ATC, is crossed downwind of the threshold.

2.1.2   Clearance to commence crossing the landing runway will not be issued until such time as a suitable gap in the landing stream exists. ATC will then pass traffic information pertaining to the fixed-wing landing aircraft after which the crossing is to be effected, and having issued the clearance to cross behind that aircraft, will expect the helicopter to execute the manoeuvre as expeditiously as possible.

2.1.3   Where the departure runway is crossed first, holding prior to crossing the landing runway will be permitted between the two main runways. This operation is to be contained between the departure runway threshold and a line drawn east-west through the Dual-Taxiways (see illustration at page 615); under no circumstances is the helicopter to transgress this line until a clearance to cross the landing stream has been received.

continued

2.2 Crossing Runway 09L/09R

2.2.1 Crossing of these runways will only be permitted when Rwy 09L is in use for landing and/or Rwy 09R is in use for departure.

2.2.2 In order to provide both ATC and wake vortex separation from departing fixed wing traffic, the crossing route is as follows:
Feltham – Bedfont – Duke of Northumberland River – West of Rwy 09R threshold – Fuel Farm – (direct or as instructed by ATC) – Sipson; and vice versa (see illustration overleaf).

However, whilst the helicopter is in transit between Bedfont and Rwy 09R threshold, ATC will pass traffic information, in respect of this movement in relation to fixed wing departures from Rwy 09R.

2.2.3 Clearance to commence crossing the landing runway will not be issued until a suitable gap in the landing stream exists. ATC will then pass traffic information pertaining to the fixed wing landing aircraft after which the crossing is to be effected, and having issued the clearance to cross behind that aircraft, will expect the helicopter to execute the manoeuvre as expeditiously as possible.

2.2.4 Where Rwy 09R is crossed first, holding prior to crossing Rwy 09L will be permitted between Rwy 09R threshold and a line drawn east-west through the southern edge of the Fuel Farm (see illustration overleaf). Under no circumstances is the helicopter to transgress this line until clearance to cross the landing stream has been received.

Note: The holding manoeuvre (paras 2.1.3 & 2.2.4) must be executed in an orbit and not in the hover.

3.   Landing and Departure Procedures

3.1   During the hours of daylight, a helicopter landing at/departing from London/Heathrow will normally be effected from/to either holding area at Sipson or that at Bedfont or Feltham if appropriate from/to the helicopter aiming point located at eastern end of Block 111 and marked with a conventional 'H' (see illustration overleaf). Caution must be exercised when using this aiming point which is a live taxiway.

3.2   During the hours of darkness a helicopter landing at/departing from Heathrow will normally be effected from/to the holding area at SIPSON or BEDFONT to use Rwy 09R/27L as directed by ATC.

3.3   In circumstances as detailed in para 1.2 visual separation will be applied whilst the helicopter is in transit between the holding area and the helicopter aiming point. In all other circumstances, standard separation will be applied.

3.4   Vortex wake separation will be applied in respect of landing/departing helicopters and fixed wing operations on the adjacent runway.

LONDON/Heathrow
HELICOPTER CROSSING OPERATIONS

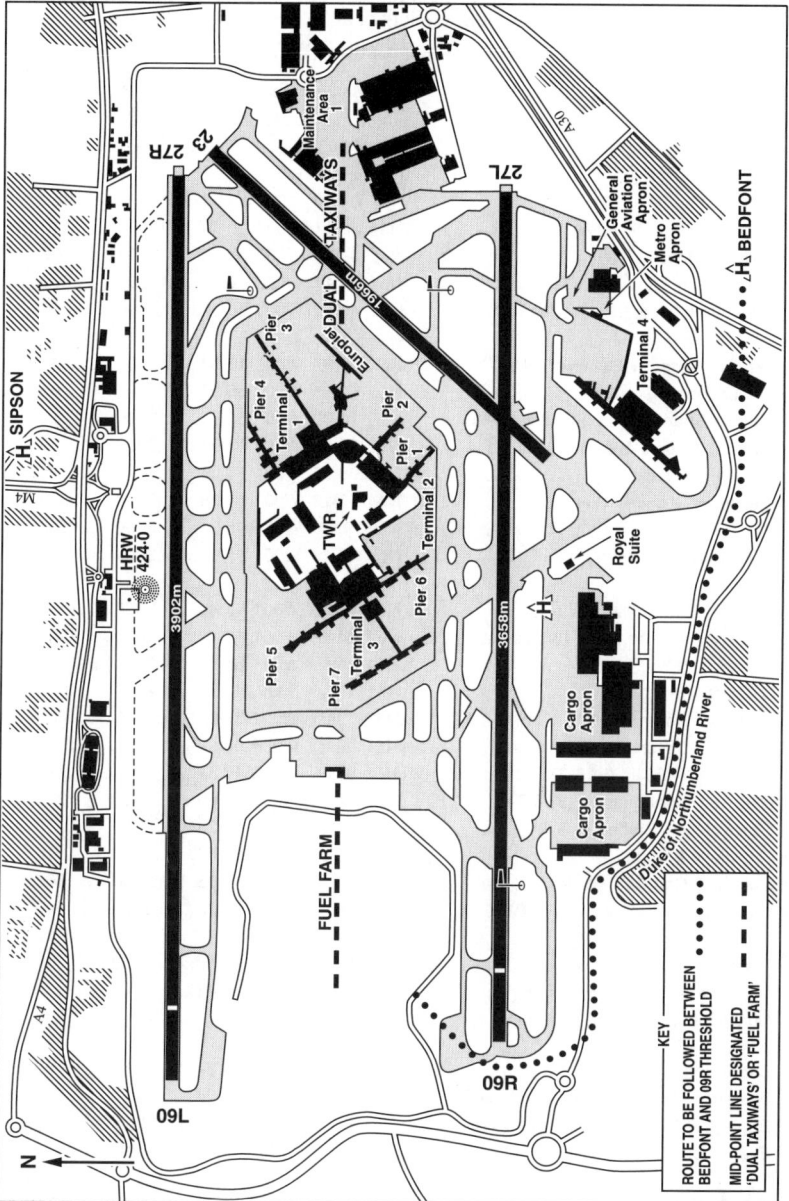

KEY

• • • • ROUTE TO BE FOLLOWED BETWEEN BEDFONT AND 09R THRESHOLD

- - - MID-POINT LINE DESIGNATED 'DUAL TAXIWAYS' OR 'FUEL FARM'

Robert Pooley ©

615

1 DEC 00

GLIDER LAUNCHING SITES

Gliders may be launched by towing aircraft, or by winch and cable or ground tow up to a height of 2000 ft. At a few sites a height of 2000 ft may be exceeded.

(T) Aerotow/Motor glider   **(W)** Winch.

Site	Co-ordinates	Op Ht ft agl	Site Elev ft amsl
Aberporth, Dyfed **(W)**	N50 06·77 W004 33·40	2000	425
Abingdon, Oxon **(T)**	N51 41·25 W001 18·97	—	261
Aboyne, Grampian **(T)**	N57 04·50 W002 50·08	—	460
Andreas, Isle of Man **(W)**	N54 22·17 W004 25·40	2000	110
Arbroath, Tayside **(W)**	N56 34·92 W002 37·27	2000	160
Aston Down, Glos **(W & T)**	N51 42·47 W002 07·83	3000	600
Aylesbury/Thame, Bucks **(W)**	N51 46·55 W000 56·42	2000	289
Barrow/Walney Is, Cumbria **(W & T)**	N54 07·87 W003 15·82	2000	47
Bembridge, Isle of Wight **(T)**	N50 40·68 W001 06·55	—	55
Benone Strand, Co Londonderry **(W)**	N55 10·00 W006 51·55	2000	SL
Bicester, Oxon **(W & T)**	N51 54·97 W001 07·93	3000	267
Bidford, Warwicks **(T)**	N52 08·05 W001 51·05	—	135
Bleesehall, Kendall **(W)**	N54 17·12 W002 41·08	2000	330
Brent Tor, Devon **(W)**	N50 35·28 W004 08·83	2000	820
Burn, N Yorks **(W & T)**	N53 44·75 W001 05·07	2000	20
Camphill, Derby **(W)**	N53 18·30 W001 43·88	2000	1350
Carlton Moor, Cleveland **(W)**	N54 24·48 W001 12·10	2000	1200
Catterick, N Yorks **(W)**	N54 21·83 W001 36·92	2000	183
Challock, Kent **(W & T)**	N51 12·50 E000 49·75	2000	600
Chipping, Lancs **(W)**	N53 53·02 W002 37·23	3000	600
Chivenor, Devon **(T)**	N51 05·23 W004 08·02	—	27
Cosford, West Mid **(W & T)**	N52 38·40 W002 18·33	3000	271
Cranwell (North), Lincs **(W & T)**	N53 02·52 W000 29·60	3000	220
Cross Hayes, Staffs **(W & T)**	N52 47·67 W001 49·23	2000	320
Crowland, Lincs **(T)**	N52 42·55 W000 08·57	—	10
Culdrose, Cornwall **(W & T)**	N50 05·17 W005 15·35	2000	267
Currock Hill, Northumberland **(W & T)**	N54 56·03 W001 50·72	2000	800
Dishforth, N Yorks **(W & T)**	N54 08·43 W001 25·10	3000	117
Drumshade, Kirriemuir, Angus **(W)**	N56 38·63 W003 01·43	2000	230
Dunstable, Beds **(W & T)**	N51 52·00 W000 32·90	2000	500
Eaglescott, Devon **(W & T)**	N50 55·70 W003 59·37	2000	655
Easterton Nr Elgin, Grampian **(W & T)**	N57 35·13 W003 18·68	2000	361
Edge Hill/Shennington, Oxon **(W & T)**	N52 05·12 W001 28·47	2500	642
Eyers Field, Gallows Hill, Dorset **(W)**	N50 42·55 W002 13·17	2000	205

GLIDER LAUNCHING SITES

Site	Co-ordinates	Op Ht ft agl	Site Elev ft amsl
Falgunzeon, Dumfries (W)	N54 56·63 W003 44·40	2000	600
Feshiebridge, Highlands (W & T)	N57 06·22 W003 53·50	2000	860
Gransden Lodge, Cambridge (W&T)	N52 10·68 W000 06·88	3000	254
Hafforty Bennett (W)	N53 12·42 W003 44·83	1500	1214
Halesland, Avon (W & T)	N51 15·73 W002 43·93	2000	870
Halton, Bucks (W & T)	N51 47·55 W000 44·27	2000	370
Henlow, Beds (T)	N52 01·17 W000 18·10	—	170
Hinton-in-the-Hedges, Oxon (W & T)	N52 01·75 W001 12·48	2000	500
Hullavington, Wilts (W)	N51 31·78 W002 08·23	2000	343
Husbands Bosworth, Leics (W & T)	N52 26·43 W001 02·63	3000	505
Jurby, I. O. Man (T)	N54 21·23 W004 31·13	—	89
Keevil, Wilts (W & T)	N51 18·83 W002 06·72	3000	200
Kenley, Surrey (W)	N51 18·33 W000 05·62	1700	566
Kinloss, Grampian (W & T)	N57 38·97 W003 33·63	3000	22
Kirknewton, Lothian (W)	N55 52·45 W003 24·08	2000	652
Kirton-in-Lindsey, Lincs (W & T)	N53 27·75 W000 34·60	2000	203
Lasham, Hants (W & T)	N51 11·20 W001 01·92	3000	618
Lee-on-Solent, Hants (W & T)	N50 48·92 W001 12·42	2000	32
Linton-on-Ouse, N Yorks (T)	N54 02·93 W001 15·17	—	53
Little Rissington, Glos (W & T)	N51 52·05 W001 41·72	3000	730
Llewenie Park, Clwyd (W & T)	N53 12·65 W003 23·20	2000	200
Long Mynd, Shropshire (W & T)	N52 31·13 W002 52·55	3000	1411
Lyveden, Northants (W)	N52 27·97 W000 34.50	2000	279
Manby (W)	N53 21·50 E000 04·98	2000	60
Marham, Norfolk (W & T)	N52 38·90 E000 33·03	3000	75
Merryfield (W)	N50 57·48 W002 56·23	2000	146
Middle Wallop, Hants (W & T)	N51 08·97 W001 34·22	2000	297
Milfield, Northumberland (T)	N55 35·23 W002 05·17	2000	150
Newton, Notts (T)	N52 57·98 W000 59·37	—	182
North Hill, Devon (W & T)	N50 51·12 W003 16·65	2000	921
North Weald, Essex (W & T)	N51 43·30 E000 09·25	2000	321
Nympsfield, Glos (W & T)	N51 42·85 W002 17·02	3000	700
Oban/North Connell, Strathclyde (W & T)	N56 27·67 W005 24·17	2000	20
Odiham, Hants (W & T)	N51 14·05 W000 56·57	2500	405

GLIDER LAUNCHING SITES

Site	Co-ordinates	Op Ht ft agl	Site Elev ft amsl
Parham, W Sussex **(W & T)**	N50 55·53 W000 28·47	2000	110
Perranporth, Cornwall **(W & T)**	N50 19·78 W005 10·65	2000	330
Pocklington, Humberside **(W & T)**	N53 55·68 W000 47·85	2000	87
Portmoak, Tayside **(W & T)**	N56 11·35 W003 19·75	2000	360
Predannack, Cornwall **(W)**	N50 00·10 W005 13·92	2000	295
Rattlesden, Suffolk **(W & T)**	N52 10·02 E000 52·27	2000	305
Retford/Gamston, Notts **(W)**	N53 16·83 W000 57·08	2000	87
Rhigos, Powys **(W)**	N51 44·57 W003 35·08	2000	780
Ridgewell, Essex **(W & T)**	N52 02·70 E000 33·70	2000	273
Ringmer, Kitsons Field, Sussex **(W & T)**	N50 54·38 E000 06·30	2500	72
Rivar Hill, Wilts **(W)**	N51 20·63 W001 32·58	3000	730
Rothwell Lodge Farm, Northants **(W)**	N52 24·60 W000 47·50	2000	400
Sackville Lodge, Risely, Beds **(W)**	N52 15·85 W000 29·08	2000	250
St. Athan, S Glam **(W)**	N51 24·28 W003 26·15	2000	163
Saltby, Leics **(W & T)**	N52 49·78 W000 42·75	2000 *	480

* 2000' Mon-Fri; 3000' Sat & Sun.

Site	Co-ordinates	Op Ht ft agl	Site Elev ft amsl
Samlesbury, Lancs **(T)**	N53 46·43 W002 33·98	—	269
Sandhill Farm, Wilts **(W & T)**	N51 36·23 W001 40·50	2000	350
Sealand, Cheshire **(W)**	N53 13·15 W003 00·92	2000	15
Seighford, Staffs **(W & T)**	N52 49·67 W002 12·20	2000	321
Shobdon, Hereford **(T)**	N52 14·48 W002 52·88	—	328
Sleap, Shropshire **(T)**	N52 50·03 W002 46·30	—	275
Snitterfield, Warwicks **(W)**	N52 14·10 W001 43·17	2000	375
Spilsted Farm, Stream Lane, Sedlescombe, Sussex **(W)**	N50 56·22 E000 31·15	2000	160
Stowe Maries, Cold Norton, Chelmsford **(W)**	N51 40·35 E000 38·72	2000	200
Strathaven, Tayside **(W & T)**	N55 40·80 W004 06·33	2000	847
Strubby, Lincs **(W & T)**	N53 18·60 E000 10·57	2000	47
Sutton Bank, N Yorks **(W & T)**	N54 13·63 W001 12·82	2000	920
Syerston, Notts **(W & T)**	N53 01·35 W000 54·78	3000	224
Talgarth, Powys **(T)**	N51 58·80 W003 12·25	—	970
Templeton, Dyfed **(W)**	N51 45·82 W004 45·28	2000	370
Ternhill, Shropshire **(T)**	N52 52·27 W002 32·00	—	272
The Park, Kingston Deverill, Wilts **(W)**	N51 07·70 W002 14·75	3000	697
Tibenham, Norfolk **(W & T)**	N52 27·40 E001 09·25	3000	186
Turweston, Northants **(W)**	N52 02·45 W001 05·73	2000	448
Upavon, Wilts **(W & T)**	N51 17·20 W001 47·00	2000	575
Upwood, Cambs **(W)**	N52 26·20 W000 08·60	2000	75

GLIDER LAUNCHING SITES

Site	Co-ordinates	Op Ht ft agl	Site Elev ft amsl
Usk, Gwent **(W & T)**	N51 43·10 W002 51·02	2000	80
Waldershare Park, Kent **(W)**	N51 10·33 E001 16·60	2000	375
Wattisham, Suffolk **(W & T)**	N52 07·65 E000 57·37	3000	284
Watton, Norfolk **(W)**	N52 33·73 E000 51·75	2000	207
Weston-on-the-Green, Oxon **(W)**	N51 52·82 W001 13·18	3000	282
Wethersfield, Essex **(W)**	N51 58·45 E000 30·23	2000	321
Winthorpe, Notts **(W & T)**	N53 05·73 W000 46·27	2000	60
Wormingford, Essex **(W & T)**	N51 56·50 E000 47·38	3000	236
Wycombe Air Park, Bucks **(T)**	N51 36·70 W000 48·50	—	520
Yeovilton, Somerset **(W & T)**	N51 00·57 W002 38·33	2000	75
York/RufforthN Yorks **(W &T)**	N53 56·85 W001 11·27	2000	165

AIR CADET ORGANISATION VOLUNTEER GLIDING SCHOOLS

Note: Callsigns are normally 'Location' followed by Alpha Charlie Base

Location	Co-ordinates	VGS No	Frequency	Remarks
Aberporth	N52 06·75 W004 33·33	636	—	Call Aberporth 122·15, if no reply call VGS 129·975.
Abingdon	N51 41·25 W001 18·97	612	—	Call Benson App 120·90, if no reply call VGS 122·10, c/s Abingdon Radio
Arbroath	N56 34·92 W002 37·27	662	129·975	
Catterick	N54 21·83 W001 36·92	645	124·40	Leeming Zone 127·75, Dishforth Radio 130·10.
Chivenor	N51 05·23 W004 09·02	624	130·20	SAR Helicopters c/s Chivenor Radio 130·20.
Cosford	N52 38·40 W002 18·33	633	—	Call Cosford Twr 118·925, if no reply call VGS 129·975.
Halton	N51 47·55 W000 44·27	613	130·425	
Henlow	N52 01·17 W000 18·10	616	121·10	
Hullavington	N51 31·78 W002 08·23	621 & 625	129·975	2 x VGS operating mirror circuits.
Kenley	N51 18·33 W002 05·62	615	129·975	Surrey Hills Gliding School operate most days mid week.
Kinloss	N57 38·96 W003 33·64	663	122·10	Call Kinloss Twr 122·10.
Kirknewton	N55 52·45 W003 24·08	661	130·40	Call Edinburgh App 130·40, VGS operates inside Edinburgh CTR.
Linton-on-Ouse	N54 02·95 W001 15·17	642	129·15	Call Linton App 129·15.
Little Rissington	N51 52·05 W001 41·72	637	129·975	
Manston	N51 20·52 E001 20·77	617	119·275	Call Manston Twr 119·275.
Predannack	N50 00·07 W005 13·85	626	—	Call Culdrose App 134·05, if no reply call VGS 129·975.
St. Athan	N51 24·29 W003 26·15	634	—	Call St. Athan Twr 122·10, if no reply call VGS 124·10. See Entry for Cardiff.
Samlesbury	N53 46·43 W002 33·98	635	—	Call Warton App 124·45, if no reply call VGS 129·975.
Sealand	N53 13·15 W003 00·92	631	—	Call Hawarden App 123·35, if no reply call VGS 129·975.
Syerston	N53 01·33 W000 54·69	ACCGS	125·425	c/s Syerston Radio.
		643 & 644	125·425	c/s Syerston Alpha Charlie Base.
Ternhill	N52 52·27 W002 32·01	632	129·975	c/s Ternhill Base.
Upavon	N51 17·17 W001 46·92	622	—	Call Salisbury Ops 122·75, if no reply call VGS 129·975.
Watton	N52 33·73 W000 51·75	611	129·975	
Wethersfield	N51 58·45 E000 30·23	614	129·975	

VGS = Volunteer Gliding School.   ACCGS = Air Cadets Central Gliding School

HANG GLIDING and PARASCENDING WINCH/AUTO-TOW LAUNCH SITES

Site	Co-ordinates	Op Ht ft agl	Site Elev ft amsl
Ansford Park Farm, Somerset . . . . .N51 05·98	W002 30·50	2000	330
Bradwell Moor, Derbyshire . . . . .N53 19·22	W001 47·12	2000	1500
Bristol, Hengrove Park, Avon . . . . .N51 24·83	W002 34·03	800	200
Brunton, Northumberland . . . . .N55 31·48	W001 40·58	2000	100
Chedworth (A/D), Glos . . . . .N51 48·75	W001 56·60	2000	790
Church Fenton, N Yorks (A/D) . . . . .N53 50·00	W001 11·77	2000	29
Coltishall, Norfolk (A/D) . . . . .N52 45·28	E001 21·45	2500	66
Cravens Gorse, Charlton Abbots, Glos . . . . .N51 54·87	W001 55·47	1000	886
Darley Moor, Derbyshire . . . . .N52 58·68	W001 44·58	2000	600
Devils Dyke, Saddlescombe Farm,W Sussex .N50 52·55	W000 13·05	2000	666
East Kirkby, Lincs (A/D) . . . . .N53 08·18	E000 00·33	2000	50
Great Fransham, Norfolk . . . . .N52 41·52	E000 48·95	2000	210
Hamble, Hamps . . . . .N50 52·07	W001 19·33	1500	65
Hampton Beach, Herne Bay, Kent . . . . .N51 22·37	E001 05·87	1000	0
Hook Green, Kent .N51 25·38	E000 10·83	900	160
Huxham Green, Somerset . . . . .N51 07·57	W002 35·83	1500	160
Kennel Farm, Warmlington, Surrey . . . . . . .N51 18·82	W000 02·48	500	590
Looe Bay, Cornwall . . . . .N50 21·08	W004 27·10	2000	0
Manchester/Barton (A/D) . . . . .N53 28·28	W002 23·35	1000	73
Manor Farm, Drayton St Leonard, Oxon . . . .N51 40·33	W001 08·27	1500	180
Mendip Forest, Somerset . . . . .N51 17·30	W002 43·45	1500	800
Mendlesham, Suffolk . . . . .N52 13·70	E001 07·48	2000	221
Metfield, Suffolk . . . . .N52 21·85	E001 23·50	2000	182
Middle Wallop, Hants (A/D) . . . . .N51 08·97	W001 34·22	2000	297
Monks Field, Shadoxhurst, Kent . . . . .N51 06·57	E000 50·07	2000	140
North Luffenham, Leics. (A/D) . . . . .N52 37·90	W000 36·45	1500	352
North Weald, Essex (A/D) . . . . .N51 43·30	E000 09·25	2000	321
Nostell Priory, W Yorks . . . . .N53 39·00	W001 23·00	1000	149
Parham, Framlingham, Suffolk . . . . .N52 11·77	E001 24·30	2000	120
Romney Street, Kent . . . . .N51 20·00	E000 13·33	1000	560

HANG GLIDING and PARASCENDING WINCH/AUTO-TOW LAUNCH SITES

Site	Co-ordinates		Op Ht ft agl	Site Elev ft amsl
Sculthorpe, Norfolk (A/D)	N52 50·82	E000 45·80	3000	214
South Ambersham, W Sussex	N50 58·58	W000 41·03	1000	80
South Cerney, Glos (A/D)	N51 41·25	W001 55·25	2000	360
Spitalgate, Lincs (A/D)	N52 53·98	W000 35·78	2000	420
Strathclyde Loch, Strathclyde	N55 47·58	W004 01·82	500	60
Thorney Island, W Sussex (A/D)	N50 48·97	W000 55·18	2000	18
Tilstock, Shropshire	N52 55·85	W002 38·78	2000	301
Topcliffe N Yorks (A/D)	N54 12·33	W001 22·92	2000	92
Truleigh Manor, W Sussex	N50 53·93	W000 15·57	2000	132
Ubley, Avon	N51 18·33	W002 41·23	2000	855
Upottery, Devon (A/D)	N50 53·08	W003 09·35	2000	835
Wanstead Flats, Forest Gate, London	N51 33·80	E000 01·80	800	50
Wheaton Aston, Staffs	N52 43·95	W002 14·13	1000	350

CAPTIVE and FREE FLIGHT MANNED BALLOON LAUNCH SITES

Flights by captive passenger carrying balloons take place at the following sites:

Site	Co-ordinates	Op hrs	Op ht up to
Longleat House, Wiltshire	N51 11·48 W002 16·65	Daylight hrs	500 ft agl/860 ft amsl
Hyde Park, London	N51 30·17 W000 10·22	Daylight hrs	400 ft agl
Tower Bridge, London	N51 30·30 W000 04·68	Daylight hrs	400 ft agl
Vauxhall, London	N51 29·25 W000 07·23	Daylight hrs	400 ft agl
Bristol High Point, Bristol	N51 27·38 W002 35·23	Daylight hrs	500 ft agl

---

Frequent launchings of manned balloons take place at or near:

Site	Co-ordinates
Ashton Court, Bristol, Avon	N51 26·65 W002 38·42
Marsh Benham, Newbury, Berks	N51 23·17 W001 38·87, several sites in or around Newbury.
Bath, Avon	Several sites in or around Bath.

MICROLIGHT SITES

Site	Co-ordinates		Site Elev ft amsl
Andreas (Isle of Man)	N54 22·17	W004 25·40	110
Arclid (Nr Sandbach)	N53 08·47	W002 19·00	262
Bagby (Thisrk)	N54 12·67	W001 17·40	160
Belle Vue	N50 58·48	W004 05·40	675
Bracklesham Bay, Chichester	N50 45·23	W000 49·83	5
Bucknall	N53 11·98	W000 15·27	50
Carltonmoor, Nr Ashmore, Derbyshire	N53 02·02	W001 49·98	990
Catton, Walton-on-Trent, Derbyshire	N52 43·67	W001 40·10	230
Chatteris (Mount Pleasant)	N52 29·02	E000 06·40	5
Chiltern Park	N51 33·03	W001 06·08	180
Chirk	N52 56·82	W003 02·72	448
Clench Common, Wilts	N51 23·23	W001 44·18	623
Coldharbour Farm, New Ramney, Kent	N50 59·53	E000 51·70	10
Colemore Common, Petersfield, Hants	N51 03·63	W001 00·58	610
Cromer (Northrepps)	N52 54·17	E001 19·72	165
Davidstow Moor, N Cornwall (A/D)	N50 38·25	W004 37·13	970
Deenethorpe (A/D)	N52 30·37	W000 35·35	328
Dunkeswell (A/D)	N50 51·60	W003 14·08	850
Eaglescott (A/D)	N50 55·70	W003 59·37	655
East Fortune	N56 00·05	W002 44·07	120
Enstone, Nr Chipping Norton, Oxon (A/D)	N51 55·77	W001 25·92	550
Eshott, Northumberland (A/D)	N55 16·90	W001 42·65	197
Farthing Corner (Stoneacre Farm) (A/D)	N51 19·83	E000 36·07	420
Finmere	N51 59·12	W001 03·38	395
Full Sutton, Humberside (A/D)	N53 58·83	W000 51·85	86
Glidden Farm, Portsmouth, Hants	N50 56·05	W001 03·30	450
Graveley, Herts	N51 56·47	W000 12·20	395
Great Orton	N54 52·55	W003 04·63	234
Halton (A/D)	N51 47·52	W000 44·12	370
Halwell, South Devon	N50 21·92	W003 42·58	623
Haverfordwest, Dyfed (A/D)	N51 50·02	W004 57·63	152
Hoghton (Higher Barn Farm)	N53 44·42	W002 35·08	329
Hougham (Glebe Farm)	N53 00·37	W000 41·23	120
Hunsdon	N51 48·18	E000 03·65	254
Husthwaite (Baxby)	N54 09·42	W001 13·90	132
Ince	N53 31·97	W003 01·65	10
Insch (A/D)	N57 18·62	W002 38·70	500
Jurby (Isle of Man)	N54 21·23	W004 31·13	89
Kirkbride, Cumbria	N54 52·93	W003 12·33	38
Long Marston	N52 08·42	W001 45·22	154

MICROLIGHT SITES

Site	Co-ordinates	Site Elev ft amsl
Manton	N51 25·72 W001 46·45	610
Meikle Endovie, Nr Aberdeen	N57 13·82 W002 40·05	475
Middleton Sands, Lancs	N54 00·58 W002 54·58	17
Milson	N52 21·68 W002 32·75	500
Misk Hill	N53 03·18 W001 14·92	581
Monmouth (Yew Tree Farm)	N51 54·02 W002 46·03	650
Montrose, Angus	N56 43·85 W002 27·07	25
Movenis (McMasters Farm)	N54 59·25 W006 38·88	180
Newton Peveril	N50 47·63 W002 06·05	9
Oakley	N51 47·08 W001 04·47	249
Oban, North Connel (A/D)	N56 27·67 W005 24·17	20
Old Sarum, Wilts (A/D)	N51 05·93 W001 47·05	285
Otherton	N52 42·52 W002 05·68	340
Oxton	N53 02·68 W001 00·10	273
Packington	N52 42·97 W001 28·28	320
Pilling Sands, Lancs	N53 56·52 W002 56·13	17
Plaistows Farm, Chiswell Green	N51 43·68 W000 22·78	395
Popham, Hants (A/D)	N51 11·67 W001 14·17	550
Pound Green, Worcs	N52 24·23 W002 21·25	360
Redlands, Nr Swindon	N51 33·33 W001 41·42	320
Roddige	N52 42·68 W001 44·58	171
Rogart, (Rovie Farm), Sutherland	N57 59·43 W004 10·32	33
Rufforth – see YORK/Rufforth		
Saddington	N52 30·65 W001 01·03	460
Sandy, Beds	N52 07·73 W000 18·58	80
St. Michaels, Lancs	N53 51·10 W002 47·58	30
Shobdon, Herefordshire (A/D)	N52 14·48 W002 52·88	328
Stoke (Isle of Grain), Kent	N51 27·03 E000 38·23	10
Sutton Meadows/Meadowlands, Suffolk	N52 23·10 E000 03·60	3
Swanton Morley	N52 43·72 E000 57·82	155
Swinford	N52 25·60 W001 09·62	492
Tarn Farm (Cockerham)·	N53 56·05 W002 50·63	15
Thorness Bay, I·O·W·	N50 44·25 W001 21·82	10
Water Eaton, Fairford, Glos	N51 38·43 W001 47·08	270
Waverton	N53 10·07 W002 47·30	115
Weston Zoyland	N51 06·30 W002 54·18	33
Wombleton, N Yorks (A/D)	N54 14·02 W000 58·13	120
Wyton	N52 21·42 W000 06·47	135
Yatesbury	N51 26·03 W001 54·08	525
YORK/Rufforth, N Yorks (A/D)	N53 56·85 W001 11·27	65

FREE-FALL PARACHUTING SITES

Regular free-fall parachuting up to FL150 takes place at the sites listed below. Some Government and licensed aerodromes where regular parachuting occurs are included in the lists but parachuting may also take place during daylight hours at any Government or licensed aerodrome. Night parachuting may take place at any of the sites listed below, as notified by NOTAM. Listing of a site does not imply any right to a parachutist to use that site.

Note. Parachutists may be expected within the airspace contained in a circle radius 1·5 nm or 2 nm of the dropping zone.

Location	Co-ordinates of Dropping Zone	Vertical Limit
Abingdon, Oxon (AD)	N51 41·25 W001 18·97	FL85 with RAF Benson ATC permission. FL150 with London ACC permission.
Ballykelly, Co. Londonderry (AD)	N55 03·67 W007 00·80	FL150
Ballyrogan, Co. Londonderry	N54 59·50 W006 45·55	FL150
Boscombe Down, Wilts (AD)	N51 09·00 W001 45·00	FL150 With Boscombe Down ATC permission.
Bridlington, Yorks	N54 07·22 W000 14·18	FL150
Brize Norton, Oxon (AD)	N51 45·27 W001 34·35	FL150 With Brize Norton ATC permission·
Brunton, Northumberland (AD)	N55 31·47 W001 40·45	FL150
Cark, Lancs (AD)	N54 09·77 W002 57·62	FL145
Carlisle (AD)	N54 56·25 W002 48·55	FL 95
Chalgrove, Oxon (AD)	N51 40·53 W001 04·98	ALT 5500 ft
Chatteris, Cambs (AD)	N52 29·32 E000 05·20	FL150
Cockerham, Lancs (AD)	N54 57·73 W002 50·12	FL95

1 DEC 00

Location	Co-ordinates of Dropping Zone	Vertical Limit
Dunkeswell, Devon (AD)	N5051·63 W003 14·10	FL150
Eaglescott, N. Devon (AD)	N50 55·73 W003 59·77	FL150
Errol, Tayside (AD)	N56 24·30 W003 10·92	ALT 5500. Drops above ALT 5500 with Scottish ACC permission.
Henlow, Beds (AD)	N52 01·22 W000 18·20	ALT 3500. Drops above ALT 3500 With Luton ATC permission.
Hibaldstow, Humberside (AD)	N53 29·93 W000 30·80	FL150 With Humberside ATC permission for all drops.
Hinton- in -the Hedges, Banbury (AD)	N52 01·60 W001 12·27	FL65.Drops above FL150 With London ACC permission.
Keevil	N51 18·85 W002 06·62	FL150
Kingsmuir, Fife (AD)	N56 16·07 W002 45·05	FL150
Langar, Nottinghamshire (AD)	N52 53·63 W000 54·27	FL150
Lashenden/ Headcorn, Kent (AD)	N51 09·42 E000 39·03	ALT 3500. Drops above FL150 With London ACC permission.
Lewknor, Oxon	N51 40·25 W000 58·82	ALT 5000. Drops above FL150 With London ACC permission.
Middle Wallop, Hants (AD)	N51 09·03 W001 34·08	FL150
Movenis, Co Londonderry. (AD)	N54 59·25 W006 38·88	FL150
Netheravon, Wilts (AD)	N51 14·38 W001 46·25	FL150
Old Buckenham, Norfolk (AD)	N52 29·30 E001 03·05	FL150

Location	Co-ordinates of Dropping Zone	Vertical Limit
Pembray	N51 42·88 W004 18·70	FL140
PETERBOROUGH/Sibson (AD)	N52 33·58 W000 23·77	FL150
Peterlee, Co. Durham	N54 46·10 W001 23·00	FL150
Redlands, Wilts	N51 33·87 W001 42·08	FL65
Rendcombe, Glos	N51 46·93 W001 57·13	FL150
Saint Merryn, Cornwall (AD)	N50 30·33 W004 58·47	FL150
South Cerney, Cirencester (AD)	N51 41·23 W001 55·32	FL150 With Brize Norton ATC permission for all drops prior to take-off.
Strathallan, Tayside (AD)	N56 19·50 W003 44·92	ALT 5000. Drops above ALT 5000 with Scottish ACC permission.
Thornhill, Stirling	N56 08·93 W004 11·15	ALT 4000. Drops above ALT 4000 with Scottish ACC permission.
Tilstock, Salop (AD)	N52 55·85 W002 39·08	FL150
Topcliffe, N. Yorks (AD)	N54 12·33 W001 22·92	FL150
Weston on the Green, Oxon (AD)	N51 52·77 W001 13·33 [Radius 2 nm]	FL85. Drops above FL150 With London ACC permission

THE PREVENTION OF TERRORISM (TEMPORARY PROVISIONS) ACT
(AIP GEN 1.2)

Under the terms of the Act, all aircraft, whether privately or commercially operated and whether or not they are carrying passengers, coming to Great Britain from the Republic of Ireland, Northern Ireland, the Isle of Man or the Channel Islands or going from Great Britain to any of those places, must, on exit from or entry to Great Britain, land at an airport designated in the Act. Similar controls apply in respect of all aircraft leaving or entering Northern Ireland when flying to or from Great Britain, the Republic of Ireland, the Isle of Man or the Channel Islands.

The purpose of these requirements is to enable the police to exercise their powers under the Actr to carry out security checks on people entering or leaving Great Britain or Northern Ireland. To this end captains of aircraft affected by the Act must obtain clearance from the examining police officer before take-off from and after landing at an **airport designated** in the Act and must comply with the requirements of the examining officer in respect of any examination of the captain, or of passengers or crew where carried. Arrangements governing scheduled flights are well established. Designated Airports are listed below.

If a pilot or an aircraft operator wishes to make a flight to or from a **non-designated airport** without an intermediate landing at a designated airport he must seek prior permission from the Chief Constable in whose area the non-designated airport is located (in Greater London, the Commissioner of Police). Permissions should be sought as far in advance as possible of the flight being made. Addresses of Chief Constables are listed overleaf.

Requirements for Civil Helicopters — Pilots in command of civil helicopters flying into Northern Ireland are required to notify the **Royal Ulster Constabulary Force Control & Information Centre – Belfast 028-9065 0222 Ext 22430,** of the point and time for the Northern Ireland coastline, in addition to the usual security arrangements for the destination. Any amendment to the crossing point/time must be advised to Aldergrove Approach on 120·90 who will advise the RUC on behalf of the pilot.

DESIGNATED AIRPORTS
Great Britain

Aberdeen	Edinburgh	LONDON/Stansted
Biggin Hill	Exeter	Lydd
Birmingham	Glasgow	Manchester
Blackpool	Gloucestershire	Manston
Bournemouth	Humberside	Newcastle
Bristol	Leeds Bradford	Norwich
Cambridge	Liverpool	Plymouth
Cardiff	LONDON/City	Prestwick
Carlisle	LONDON/Gatwick	Southampton
Coventry	LONDON/Heathrow	Southend
East Midlands	London/Luton	Teesside

Although **Filton** is not Designated Airport under the Act, the same facility will be made available if application is made, during office hours, at least 24 hours prior to the flight, Tel: 01272-699094 or 36262.

Northern Ireland:
BELFAST/Aldergrove   BELFAST/City

Isle of Man and Channel Islands:
I.O.M/Ronaldsway   Alderney   Guernsey   Jersey

LIST OF POLICE FORCES
ENGLAND AND WALES

Constabularies (unless POLICE in title)	Addresses	Telephone Number
Avon and Somerset	PO Box 37,Valley Road, Portishead, Bristol BS20 8QJ	01275-818181
Bedfordshire Police	Woburn Road, Kempston, Bedford MK43 9AX	01234–841212
Cambridgeshire	Hinchingbrooke Park, Huntingdon PE18 8NP	01480–456111
Cheshire	Castle Esplanade, Chester CH1 2PP	01244–350000
Cleveland	PO Box 70, Ladgate Lane, Middlesbrough TS8 9EH	01642–326326
Cumbria	Carleton Hall, Penrith, Cumbria CA10 2AU	01768–891999
Derbyshire	Butterley Hall, Ripley, Derbyshire DE5 3RS	01773–570100
Devon and Cornwall	Middlemoor, Exeter, Devon EX2 7HQ	0870-5777444
Dorset Police	Winfrith, Dorchester, Dorset DT2 8DZ	01929–462727
Durham	Aykley Heads, Durham DH1 5TT	0191-386-4929
Dyfed-Powys Police	PO Box 99,Llangunnor Carmarthen SA31 2PF	01267–236444
Essex Police	PO Box 2, Springfield, Chelmsford, Essex. CM2 6DA	01245–491491
Gloucestershire	Holland House Lansdown Road, Cheltenham, Glos. GL51 6QH	0242–521321
Greater Manchester Police	PO Box 22, Chester House, Boyer Street, Manchester M16 0RE	0161–872–5050
Gwent	Croesyceiliog, Cwmbran, Gwent NP44 2XJ	01633–838111
Hampshire	West Hill, Winchester Hants SO22 5DB	01962–841500
Hertfordshire Welwyn Garden City	Stanborough Road, Herts AL8 6XF	01707–354200
Humberside Police	Queens Gardens, Kingston-upon-Hull Humberside HU1 3DJ	01482–326111
Kent	Sutton Road, Maidstone Kent ME15 9BZ	01622–690690

Lancashire	P.O. Box 77, Hutton, Near Preston Lancs PR4 5SB	01772–614444
Leicestershire	P.O. Box 999 Leicester LE99 1AZ	0116–2222222
Lincolnshire Police	P.O Box 999, Lincoln LN5 7PH	01522–532222
London Metropolitan Police	New Scotland Yard, London SW1H 0BG	020–7230–1212
London, City of	26 Old Jewry, London EC2R 8DJ	020-7601-2222
Merseyside Police	PO Box 59, Liverpool L69 1JD	0151–709–6010
Norfolk	Martineau Lane, Norwich, Norfolk. NR1 2DJ	01603–768769
Northamptonshire Police	Wootton Hall, Northampton NN4 0JQ	01604–700700
Northumbria Police	Ponteland Newcastle-upon-Tyne NE20 0BL	01661–872555
North Wales Police	Glan-Y-Don, Colwyn Bay, Clwyd LL29 8AW	01492-517171
North Yorkshire Police	Newby Wiske Hall, Northallerton, N Yorkshire DL7 9HA	01609–783131
Nottinghamshire	Sherwood Lodge, Arnold, Nottingham NG5 8PP	0115–9670999
South Wales	Bridgend, Glamorgan CF31 3SU	01656–55555
South Yorkshire Police	Snig Hill, Sheffield South Yorkshire, S3 8LY	0114–2768522
Staffordshire Police	Cannock Road, Stafford ST17 0QG	01785–257717
Suffolk	Martlesham Heath, Ipswich, Suffolk. IP5 7QS	01473–613500
Surrey	Mount Browne, Sandy Lane, Guildford, Surrey GU3 1HG	01483–571212
Sussex Police	Malling House, Lewes, East Sussex BN7 2DZ	01273-475432
Thames Valley Police	Oxford Road, Kidlington, Oxford. OX5 2NX	01865–846000
Warwickshire	PO Box 4, Leek Wootton, Warwick CV35 7QB	01926–415000
West Mercia	Hindlip Hall, Hindlip, P.O. Box 55, Worcester WR3 8SP	01905–723000

Constabularies (unless POLICE in title)	Addresses	Telephone Number
West Midlands Police	PO Box 52, Lloyd House, Colmore Circus, Queensway, Birmingham, B4 6NQ	0121–626–5000
West Yorkshire Police	PO Box 9, Wakefield West Yorks WF1 3QP	01924–375222
Wiltshire	London Road, Devizes, Wiltshire SN10 2DN	01380–722341

SCOTLAND

Central Scotland Police	Randolphfield, Stirling FK8 2HD	01786–456000
Dumfries and Galloway	Loreburn Street, Dumfries DG1 1HP	01387–2521125/6
Fife	Detriot Road, Glenrothes, Fife KY6 2J	01592–418888
Grampian Police	Queen Street, Aberdeen AB9 1BA	01224–639111
Lothian and Borders Police	Fettes Avenue, Edinburgh EH4 1RB	0131–311 3131
Northern	Perth Road, Inverness IV2 3SY	01463–715555
Strathclyde Police	173 Pitt Street, Glasgow G2 4JS	0141–5322000
Tayside Police	PO Box 59, West Bell Street, Dundee DD1 9JU	01382–223200

NORTHERN IRELAND

Royal Ulster Constabulary	'Brooklyn', Knock Road, Belfast BT5 6LE	028-9065 0222

ISLE OF MAN AND CHANNEL ISLANDS

Isle of Man	Glencrutchery Road, Douglas IM2 4RG	01624–631212
Jersey Police	Po Box 789, St. Helier, Jersey JE4 8ZA	01534–612612
Guernsey Police	Police HQ, Hospital Lane, St. Peter Port, Guernsey, Channel Islands GY1 2QN	01481–725111

ALDERNEY

Alderney, Channel Islands, is within the jurisdiction of Guernsey and communications in respect of this Island should be addressed to the Guernsey Police.

GOVERNMENT AERODROMES
TELEPHONE NUMBERS

ABERPORTH	MOD/PE	Aberporth 01239-813090
BARKSTON HEATH	RAF	Loveden 01400-261201
BENSON	RAF	Wallingford 01491-837766
BOSCOMBE DOWN	MOD/PE	Amesbury 01980-66 + Ext
BRIZE NORTON	RAF	Carterton 01993-842551
CHIVENOR	RAF	Braunton 01271-813662
CHURCH FENTON	RAF	York 01347-848261
COLERNE	RAF	Bath 01225-745338
COLTISHALL	RAF	Norwich 01603-737361
CONINGSBY	RAF	Coningsby 01526-342581
COSFORD	RAF	Wolverhampton 01902-377582
COTTESMORE	RAF	Oakham 01572-812241
CRANWELL	RAF	Cranwell 01400-261201
CULDROSE	RN	Helston 01326-574121
DISHFORTH	RAF	Richmond 01748-832521
FAIRFORD	RAF	Mildenhall 01285-714805
FARNBOROUGH	DPA	Aldershot 01252-52 + Ext
HALTON	RAF	Wendover 01296-623535
HENLOW	RAF	Hitchin 01462-851515
HONINGTON	RAF	Honington 01359-269561
KINLOSS	RAF	Forres 01309-672161
LAKENHEATH	USAF	Newmarket 01638-524186
LECONFIELD	RAF	Hornsea 01964-550424
LEEMING	RAF	Bedale 01677-423041
LEUCHARS	RAF	Leuchars 01334-839471
LINTON-ON-OUSE	RAF	Linton-on-Ouse 01347-848261
LLANBEDR	MOD/PE	Llanbedr 01341-243248
LOSSIEMOUTH	RAF	Lossiemouth 01343-812121
LYNEHAM	RAF	Bradenstoke 01249-890381
MARHAM	RAF	Narborough 01760-337261

GOVERNMENT AERODROMES
TELEPHONE NUMBERS

MERRYFIELD ....RN ....Illminster 01460-52018

MIDDLE WALLOP..........................ARMY ....Andover 01980-674380

MILDENHALL.................................USAF................Mildenhall 01638-54-2251

MONA ....RAF ....Holyhead 01407-762241

NETHERAVON ....ARMY ....Stonehenge 01980-678289

NORTHOLT....................................RAF 020-8845-2300

ODIHAM..RAF ....Odiham 01256-702134

PLYMOUTH MILITARY RADAR ....NAVY..................Plymouth 01752-557809

PREDANNACK ....NAVY ....Helston 01326-574121

PRESTWICK..................................NAVY ....Prestwick 01292-475000

ST. ATHAN ....RAF ....St. Athan 01446-798282

ST. MAWGAN................................RAF ....Newquay 01637-872201

SCAMPTON...................................RAF ....Cranwell 01400-261201

SHAWBURY....................................RAF ....Shawbury 01939-250351

TERNHILL......................................RAF ....Shawbury 01939-250351

TOPCLIFFE ....RAF ....Richmond 01748-875340

UPAVON ....ARMY ....Stonehenge 01980-615238

VALLEY...RAF ....Holyhead 01407-762241

WADDINGTON ....RAF ....Lincoln 01522-720271

WATTISHAM..................................ARMY 01449-728234

WEST FREUGH.............................MOD/PE ....Stranraer 01776-702501

WITTERING ....RAF ....Stamford 01780-783838

WOODVALE...................................RAF ....Formby 01704-872287

WYTON..RAF ....Huntingdon 01480-52451

YEOVILTON ....RN ....Ilchester 01935-840551

ICAO Location Indicators — DECODE

EGAA	Belfast (Aldergrove)	EGDH	HQ 38 Group (MOD)
EGAB	Enniskillen (St Angelo)	EGDL	Lyneham
EGAC	Belfast (City)	EGDM	Boscombe Down
EGAD	Newtownards	EGDN	Netheravon
EGAE	Londonderry (Eglinton)	EGDO	Predannack
EGAL	Langford Lodge	EGDP	Portland (Air Station)
		EGDR	Culdrose
EGBB	Birmingham Airport	EGDS	HQ SPTA
EGBC	Cheltenham Racecourse	EGDX	St. Athan
EGBD	Derby	EGDY	Yeovilton
EGBE	Coventry		
EGBG	Leicester	EGEC	Campbeltown
EGBJ	Gloucestershire	EGED	Eday
EGBK	Northampton (Sywell)	EGEF	Fair Isle
EGBL	Long Marston	EGEG	Glasgow City Heliport
EGBM	Tatenhill	EGEH	Whalsay
EGBN	Nottingham	EGEN	North Ronaldsay
EGBO	Wolverhampton	EGEP	Papa Westray
EGBP	Kemble	EGER	Stronsay
EGBS	Shobdon	EGES	Sanday
EGBT	Turweston	EGET	Lerwick (Tingwall)
EGBV	Silverstone	EGEW	Westray
EGBW	Wellesbourne Mountford		
		EGFC	Cardiff (Tremorfa Heliport)
EGCB	Manchester (Barton)	EGFE	Haverfordwest
EGCC	Manchester Airport	EGFF	Cardiff
EGCD	Woodford	EGFH	Swansea
EGCE	Wrexham (Borras)	EGFP	Pembrey
EGCF	Sandtoft		
EGCG	Strubby Heliport	EGGA	London (Civil Aviation Authority HQ)
EGCH	Holyhead		
EGCJ	Sherburn-in-Elmet	EGGC	London (Dept of Environment, Transport & Regions (UK)) Directorate
EGCK	Caernarfon		
EGCL	Fenland		
EGCO	Southport Birkdale Sands		
EGCP	Thorne	EGGD	Bristol Airport
EGCS	Sturgate	EGGF	UK Airprox Board
EGCT	Tilstock	EGGG	UK AFTN Common ICAO Data Interchange Network Centre
EGCV	Sleap		
EGCW	Welshpool		
		EGGN	UK NOTAM Office (NOF)
EGDB	Mountwise	EGGO	London Area
EGDC	Chivenor	EGGP	Liverpool Airport
EGDG	St. Mawgan		

ICAO Location Indicators — DECODE	
EGGR London/Gatwick Safety Regulation Group (Aviation House)	EGLC London (City Airport)
	EGLD Denham
	EGLF Farnborough
EGGW London (Luton)	EGLG Panshanger
EGGX Shanwick OACC	EGLI Isleworth
EGGY U.K. MOTNE Centre	EGLJ Chalgrove
	EGLK Blackbushe
EGHA Compton Abbas	EGLL London (Heathrow)
EGHB Maypole	EGLM White Waltham
EGHC Lands End (St. Just)	EGLS Old Sarum
EGHD Plymouth	EGLT Ascot Racecourse
EGHE Scilly Isles (St. Mary's)	EGLW London (Westland heliport)
EGHF Lee-on-Solent	
EGHG Yeovil	EGMA Fowlmere
EGHH Bournemouth	EGMC Southend
EGHI Southampton	EGMD Lydd
EGHJ Bembridge	EGMF Farthing Corner
EGHK Penzance Heliport	EGMH Manston
EGHL Lasham	EGMJ Little Gransden
EGHN Sandown (I.O.W)	
EGHO Thruxton	EGNA Hucknall
EGHP Popham	EGNB Brough
EGHR Chichester (Goodwood)	EGNC Carlisle
EGHS Henstridge	EGNE Retford (Gamston)
EGHT Tresco Heliport	EGNF Netherthorpe
EGHU Eaglescott	EGNG Bagby
EGHY Truro	EGNH Blackpool
	EGNI Skegness
EGJA Alderney	EGNJ Humberside
EGJB Guernsey	EGNL Barrow (Walney Island)
EGJJ Jersey	EGNM Leeds Bradford
	EGNO Warton
EGKA Shoreham	EGNR Hawarden
EGKB Biggin Hill	EGNS Isle of Man (Ronaldsway)
EGKD Albourne	EGNT Newcastle
EGKE Challock	EHNU Full Sutton
EGKG Goodwood Racecourse	EGNV Teesside
EGKH Lashenden (Headcorn)	EGNW Wickenby
EGKK London (Gatwick)	EGNX East Midlands
EGKL Deanland (Lewes)	EGNY Beverley/Linley Hill
EGKR Redhill	
	EGOD Llanbedr
EGLA Bodmin	EGOE Ternhill
EGLB Brooklands	EGOG HQ Northern Ireland (MOD)

EGOM	Spadeadam	EGRA	Glasgow Weather Centre
EGOP	Pembrey (MOD)	EGRB	London Weather Centre
EGOS	Shawbury	EGRC	Manchester Weather Centre
EGOV	Valley	EGRD	Bristol Weather Centre
EGOW	Woodvale	EGRE	Malvern (MET)
EGOY	West Freugh	EGRG	Cardiff Weather Centre
		EGRH	High Wycombe (MET)
EGPA	Kirkwall	EGRI	Southampton Weather
EGPB	Sumburgh		Centre
EGPC	Wick	EGRN	Norwich Weather Centre
EGPD	Aberdeen (Dyce)	EGRO	Birmingham Weather Centre
EGPE	Inverness (Dalcross)	EGRR	Bracknell (MET)
EGPF	Glasgow	EGRT	Newcastle Weather Centre
EGPG	Cumbernauld	EGRW	Nottingham Weather Centre
EGPH	Edinburgh	EGRY	Leeds Weather Centre
EGPI	Islay		
EGPJ	Fife (Glenrothes)	EGSA	Shipdham
EGPK	Prestwick	EGSB	Bedford (Castle Mill)
EGPL	Benbecula	EGSC	Cambridge
EGPM	Scatsta	EGSD	Great Yarmouth (North
EGPN	Dundee		Denes)
EGPO	Stornoway	EGSF	Peterborough (Conington)
EGPQ	Edinburgh (CAA Office	EGSG	Stapleford
	for Scotland)	EGSH	Norwich
EGPR	Barra	EHSI	Marshland, Wisbech
EGPS	Peterhead (Longside)	EGSJ	Seething
EGPT	Perth (Scone)	EGSK	Hethel
EGPU	Tiree	EGSL	Andrewsfield
EGPW	Unst	EGSM	Beccles
EGPX	Scottish ATCC (Civil)	EGSN	Bourn (Cambs)
		EGSO	Crowfield
EGQA	Tain (MOD)	EGSP	Peterborough (Sibson)
EGQB	Ballykelly	EGSQ	Clacton
EGQC	Garvie Island (MOD)	EGSR	Earls Colne
EGQD	Lisburn	EGSS	London (Stansted)
EGQK	Kinloss	EGST	Elmsett
EGQL	Leuchars	EGSU	Duxford
EGQM	Boulmer (MOD)	EGSV	Old Buckenham
EGQN	Buchan (MOD)	EGSW	Newmarket Racecourse
EGQO	Rosehearty (MOD)	EGSX	North Weald
EGQP	UK MCC	EGSY	Sheffield City
EGQQ	Scottish ACC (Mil)		
EGQS	Lossiemouth	EGTA	Aylesbury (Thame)
		EGTB	Wycombe Air Park (Booker)

EGTC	Cranfield		EGXD	Dishforth
EGTE	Exeter		EGXE	Leeming
EGTF	Fairoaks		EGXG	Church Fenton
EGTG	Filton		EGXH	Honington
EGTK	Oxford (Kidlington)		EGXJ	Cottesmore
EGTO	Rochester		EGXM	Benbecula (MOD)
EGTP	Perranporth		EGXO	Faslane (MOD)
EGTR	Elstree		EGXP	Scampton
EGTT	London ATCC (Civil)		EGXS	Donna Nook (MOD)
EGTU	Dunkeswell		EGXT	Wittering
EGTW	Oaksey Park		EGXU	Linton-on-Ouse
			EXXV	Leconfield
EGUB	Benson		EGXW	Waddington
EGUC	Aberporth		EGXZ	Topcliffe
EGUH	High Wycombe (MOD)		EGYB	Brampton (MOD)
EGUJ	Neatishead (MOD)		EGYC	Coltishall
EGUL	Lakenheath		EGYD	Cranwell
EGUN	Mildenhall		EGYE	Barkston Heath
EGUO	Colerne		EGYH	Holbeach Range (MOD)
EGUU	Uxbridge (HQ MATO)		EGYM	Marham
EGUW	Wattisham		EGYP	Mount Pleasant
EGUY	Wyton		EGYW	Wainfleet (MOD)
			EGYY	HM Ships (All)
EGVA	Fairford			
EGVC	1 AIDU (RAF Northolt)			
EGVE	Plymouth (Military)			
EGVF	Portsmouth/Fleetlands			
EGVH	Hereford			
EGVN	Brize Norton			
EGVO	Odiham			
EGVP	Middle Wallop			
EGVV	Swanwick ACC (Military)			
EGWB	MOD UK Air			
EGWC	Cosford			
EGWD	West Drayton ATCC (Military)			
EGWE	Henlow			
EGWI	MOD UK Navy			
EGWN	Halton			
EGWR	Croughton (MOD)			
EGWS	Bentley Priory			
EGWU	Northolt			
EGWX	Northwood (MOD)			
EGXA	Northolt (RN NAIC)			
EGXC	Coningsby			

AVIATION ADDRESSES

Aeronautical Information Service,
NATS. AIS Central Office, First Floor, Control Tower Bldg,
Heathrow Airport, Hounslow, Middlesex. TW6 1JJ.
Tel: 020-8745 3456

Air Accidents Investigation Branch
Defence Research Agency
Farnborough, Hampshire GU14 6TD.
Tel: 01252-510 300. Fax: 01252-376 999.
e-mail: aaib-dot@dircon.co.uk
Web: http:/www. open.gov.uk/aaib/aaibhome.htm

Air-Britain (Historians) Ltd
General Enquires: 1 Rose Cottages, 179 Penn Road, HAzelmere,
Bucks HP15 7NE.

Air League,The
Broadway House, Tothill Street, London SW1H 9NS
Tel: 020-7222 8463. Fax: 020-7222 8462.
e-mail: exec@airleague.co.uk   Web: http://www.airleague.co.uk

Airport Operators Association (AOA)
3 Birdcage Walk, London SW1H 9JJ.
Tel: 020-7222 2249. Fax: 020-7976 7405.

Aircraft Owners and Pilots Association (AOPA UK.)
50a Cambridge Street, London, SW1V 4QQ.
Tel: 020-7834 5631. Fax: 020-7834 8623.
e-mail: aopa@easynet.co.uk   Web: http://www.aopa.co.uk

Aircraft Owners and Pilots Association (AOPA Ireland)
c/o Ms Catherine Leech, Loughlinstown Road, Celbridge, Co. Kildare.
Calling from UK - Tel: 00 353 1 490 8598. Fax: 00 353 1 490 8598

British Aerobatic Association (BAeA)
White Waltham Airfield, near Maidenhead, Berkshire,
SL6 3NJ.   Tel: 01455-617 211.
e-mail: info@aerobatics.org.uk   Web: http://www.aerobatics.org.uk

British Air Line Pilots Association (BALPA)
81 New Road, Harlington, Hayes, Middx UB3 5BG
Tel: 020-7476 4000 Fax: 020-7476 4077.
e-mail: balpa@balpa.org.uk   Web: http://www.balpa.org.uk

British Airports Authority,
Gatwick Airport. Tel: 01293-517755.

British Aviation Preservation Council (BAPC)
Secretary: Mr. Nick Forder, c/o Museum of Science and Industry,
Liverpool Road, Castlefield, Manchester M3 4FP.
Tel: 0161- 832 2244. Fax: 0161- 834 5135.

British Association of Balloon Operators (BBAC)
Cross Lanes Farm, Walcote, Nr Alcestor
Warks B49 6NA. Tel/Fax: 01789-488 100.
e-mail: babo@ukballoons.com

British Balloon and Airship Club (BBAC)
Wellington House, Lower Icknield Way, Longwick,
Nr. Princes Risborough, Bucks HP27 9RZ.
Tel: 01604-870 025.
e-mail: info@bbac.org.uk   Web: http://www.bbac.org.uk

British Gliding Association (BGA)
Kimberley House, Vaughan Way, Leicester, LE1 4SE.
Tel: 0116-253 1051. Fax: 0116-251 5939.
e-mail: bga@gliding.co.uk   Web: http://www.gliding.co.uk

British Hang Gliding & Paragliding Association (BHPA)
The old School Room, Loughborough Road, Liecester, LE4 5PJ.
Tel. 0116-261 1322. Fax: 0116-261 1323.
e-mail: office@bhpa.co.uk   Web: http://www.bhpa.co.uk

British Helicopter Advisory Board (BHAB)
Graham Suite, West Entrance, Fairoaks Airport, Chobham,
Woking, Surrey GU24 8HX. Tel: 01276-856 100. Fax: 01276- 856 126.
Web: http://www.bhab.demon.co.uk

British Microlight Aircraft Association (BMAA),
The Bullring, Deddington, Oxon OX15 0TT.
Tel: 01869-338 888.   Fax: 01869-337 116.
e-mail: general@bmaa.org   Web: http://www.avnet.co.uk/bmaa

British Parachute Association (BPA)
5 Wharf Way, Glen Parva, Leicester, LE2 9TE.
Tel: 0116-278 5271. Fax: 0116-247 7662.
e-mail: skydive@bpa.org.uk   Web: http://www.bpa.org.uk/index1.htm

British Women Pilots' Association (BWPA)
Brooklands Museum, Brooklands Road, Weybridge,
Surrey KT13 0QN. Tel: 01342-892 739.
e-mail: enquiries@bwpa.demon.co.uk   Web: http://www.bwpa.demon.co.uk

Business Aircraft Users Association (BAUA),
Crossmount House, Kinloch Rannoch, Perth PH16 5QF Scotland.
Tel: 01882-632 252. Fax: 01882-632 454.

Civil Aviation Authority (Headquaters)
CAA House, 45-59 Kingsway, London. WC2B 6TE
Tel: 020-7379 7311.   Web: http://www.caa.co.uk

Civil Aviation Safety Regulation Group
Ground Floor, Aviation House, South Area,
London Gatwick Airport, West Sussex RH6 0YR.
Tel: 01293-567 171 (Switchboard), 01293-573 700 (Licensing)
01293-573 685 (Medical Appointments)

CAA Publications and Charts
From
Westward Documedia Limited, 37 Windsor Street,
Cheltenham, Glos GL52 2DG.
Tel: 01242-235 151. Fax: 01242-584 139.

Flying Farmers Association (FFA)
Ox House, Shobdon, Leominster, Herefordshire HR6 9LT
Tel: 01568-708 351. Fax: 01568-708 177.

General Aviation Manufacturers and Traders Association (GAMTA)
19 Church Street, Brill, Aylesbury, Bucks HP18 9TG.
Tel: 01844-238 020. Fax: 01844-238 087.
e-mail: GAMTA@Compuserve.com

General Aviation Safety Council (GASCO)
Rochester Airport, Chatham, Kent ME5 9SD.
Tel: 01634-816 620   e-mail: info@gen-av-safety.demon.co.uk

Guild of Air Pilots and Air Navigators (GAPAN)
Cobham House, 291 Gray's Inn Road, London WC1X 8QF
Tel: 020-7837 3323. Fax: 020-7833 3190

Guild of Air Traffic Control Officers (GATCO)
24 The Greenwood, Guildford, Surrey GU1 2 ND,
Tel: 01483- 578 347. Fax: 01483- 578 347.
e-mail: gatcocaf@msn.com   Web: http://www.gatco.org

Helicopter Club of Great Britain (HCGB)
Ryelands House, Aynho, Banbury, Oxon OX17 3AT
Tel: 01869-810 646. Fax: 01869-810 755.

Popular Flying Association (PFA)
Terminal Building, Shoreham Airport, Shoreham-on-Sea,
West Sussex BN43 5FF.
Tel: 01273-461 616. Fax: 01273-463 390.
e-mail: office@pfa.org.uk   Web: http://www.pfa.org.uk

Royal Aero Club of the United Kingdom (RAeC)
Kimberley House, Vaughan Way, Leicester LE1 4SG
Tel: 0116-253 1051. Fax: 0116-251 5939.
e-mail: bgahg@aol.com

Royal Aeronautical Society
4 Hamilton Place, London, W1. Tel: 020-7499-3515.

Royal Air Force Club
128 Piccadilly, London, W1V 0PY.
Tel: 020-7499-3456. Fax: 020-7355 1516.
e-mail: admin@rafclub.org.uk. Web: http://www.rafclub.org.uk

Royal Institute of Navigation (RIN)
1 Kensington Gore, London, SW7 2AT.
Tel: 020-7591 3130. Fax: 020-7591 3131.
e-mail: rindir@atlas.co.uk   Web: http:/www.rin.org.uk

Society of British Aerospace Companies (SBAC)
Duxbury House, 60 Petty France, Victoria, London SW1H 9EU.
Tel: 020-7227 1000. Fax: 020-7227 1067.
e-mai: post@sbac.co.uk   Web: http://www.sbac.co.uk

The United Kingdom Association of Professional Engineers
Hayes Court, West Common Road, Hayes, Bromley, Kent BR2 7AU
Tel: 020-8462 7755.   Fax: 020-8315 8234.

CONVERSION TABLES

			AVGAS		AVTUR	
Imp Gals	US Galls	Litres	Lbs	Kgs	Lbs	Kgs
1	1·2	4·55	7·2	3·3	7·9	3·6
2	2·4	9·1	14·4	6·6	15·8	7·2
3	3·6	13·6	21·6	9·9	23·7	10·8
4	4·8	18·2	28·4	13·2	31·6	14·4
5	6·0	22·8	36	16·5	39·5	18
6	7·2	27·2	43·2	19·8	47·4	21·6
7	8·4	31·8	50·9	23·1	55·3	25·2
8	9·6	36·4	57·6	26·4	63·2	28·8
9	10·8	40·9	64	29·7	71·1	32·4
10	12	45·5	72	33	79	36
20	24	91	144	66	158	72
30	36	136	216	99	237	108
40	48	182	288	132	316	144
50	60	228	360	165	395	180
60	72	272	432	198	474	216
70	84	318	504	231	553	252
80	96	364	576	264	632	288
90	108	409	648	297	711	324
100	120	455	720	330	790	360
110	132	500	792	363	869	396
120	144	544	864	396	948	432
130	156	591	936	429	1027	468
140	168	636	1008	462	1106	504
150	180	680	1080	495	1185	540
160	192	728	1152	528	1264	576
170	204	773	1224	561	1343	612
180	216	818	1296	594	1422	648
190	228	864	1368	627	1501	684
200	240	910	1440	660	1580	720
300	360	1360	2160	990	2370	1080
400	480	1820	2880	1320	3160	1440
500	600	2280	3600	1650	3950	1800

1 DEC 00

DISTANCE CONVERSION
Nautical Miles to Statute Miles and Kilometres

Nautical Miles	Statute Miles	Kilometres
1	1·15	1·85
2	2·3	3·71
3	3·46	5·56
4	4·61	7·41
5	5·76	9·27
6	6·91	11·12
7	8·06	12·97
8	9·21	14·83
9	10·36	16·68
10	11·52	18·53
20	23·03	37·06
30	34·55	55·60
40	46·06	74·12
50	57·58	92·66
60	69·10	111·19
70	80·61	129·72
80	92·13	148·26
90	103·46	166·79
100	115·2	185·32
200	230·4	370·64
300	345·5	555·96
400	460·6	741·28
500	575·8	926·60
600	691·0	1111·92
700	806·1	1297·24
800	921·3	1482·56
900	1036·4	1667·88
1000	1151·6	1853·2

DISTANCE CONVERSION
Kilometres to Nautical Miles and Statute Miles

Kilometres	Nautical Miles	Statute Miles
1	0·54	0·62
2	1·08	1·24
3	1·62	1·86
4	2·16	2·49
5	2·70	3·11
6	3·24	3·73
7	3·78	4·35
8	4·32	4·97
9	4·86	5·59
10	5·40	6·21
20	10·79	12·43
30	16·19	18·64
40	21·58	24·86
50	26·98	31·07
60	32·38	37·28
70	37·77	43·50
80	43·17	49·71
90	48·56	55·93
100	53·96	62·14
200	107·92	124·28
300	161·88	186·42
400	215·84	248·56
500	269·80	310·70
600	323·76	372·84
700	377·72	434·98
800	431·68	497·12
900	485·64	559·26
1000	539·6	621·40

DISTANCE CONVERSION
Statute Miles to Nautical Miles and Kilometres

Statute Miles	Nautical Miles	Kilometres
1	0·87	1·61
2	1·74	3·22
3	2·61	4·83
4	3·47	6·44
5	4·34	8·05
6	5·21	9·66
7	6·08	11·27
8	6·95	12·88
9	7·82	14·49
10	8·68	16·09
20	17·37	32·19
30	26·05	48·28
40	34·74	64·38
50	43·42	80·47
60	52·14	96·56
70	60·79	112·66
80	69·47	128·75
90	78·16	144·85
100	86·84	160·94
200	173·7	321·88
300	260·5	482·82
400	347·4	643·76
500	434·2	804·70
600	521·0	965·64
700	607·9	1126·6
800	694·7	1287·5
900	781·6	1488·5
1000	868·4	1609·4

ALTITUDE CONVERSION
Feet (ft.) to Metres (m.)

ft.	m.	ft.	m.	ft.	m.	ft.	m.
1	0·30	43	13·11	85	25·91	10,000	3,048·0
2	0·61	44	13·41	86	26·21	10,500	3,200·4
3	0·91	45	13·72	87	26·52	11,000	3,352·8
4	1·22	46	14·02	88	26·82	11,500	3,505·2
5	1·52	47	14·33	89	27·13	12,000	3,657·6
6	1·83	48	14·63	90	27·43	12,500	3,810·0
7	2·13	49	14·94	91	27·74	13,000	3,962·4
8	2·44	50	15·24	92	28·04	13,500	4,114·8
9	2·74	51	15·54	93	28·35	14,000	4,267·2
10	3·05	52	15·85	94	28·65	14,500	4,419·6
11	3·35	53	16·15	95	28·96	15,000	4,572·0
12	3·66	54	16·46	96	29·26	15,500	4,724·4
13	3·96	55	16·76	97	29·57	16,000	4,876·8
14	4·27	56	17·07	98	29·87	16,500	5,029·2
15	4·57	57	17·37	99	30·18	17,000	5,181·6
16	4·88	58	17·68	100	30·48	17,500	5,334·0
17	5·18	59	17·98	200	60·96	18,000	5,486·4
18	5·49	60	18·29	300	91·44	18,500	5,638·8
19	5·79	61	18·59	400	121·92	19,000	5,791·2
20	6·10	62	18·90	500	152·40	19,500	5,943·6
21	6·40	63	19·20	600	182·88	20,000	6,096·0
22	6·71	64	19·51	700	213·36	20,500	6,248·4
23	7·01	65	19·81	800	243·84	21,000	6,400·8
24	7·32	66	20·12	900	274·32	21,500	6,553·2
25	7·62	67	20·42	1,000	304·80	22,000	6,705·6
26	7·92	68	20·73	1,500	457·20	22,500	6,858·0
27	8·23	69	21·03	2,000	609·60	23,000	7,010·4
28	8·53	70	21·34	2,500	762·00	23,500	7,162·8
29	8·84	71	21·64	3,000	914·40	24,000	7,315·2
30	9·14	72	21·95	3,500	1,066·80	24,500	7,467·6
31	9·45	73	22·25	4,000	1,219·20	25,000	7,620·0
32	9,75	74	22·56	4,500	1,371·60	25,500	7,772·4
33	10·06	75	22·86	5,000	1,524·00	26,000	7,924·8
34	10·36	76	23·16	5,500	1,676·40	26,500	8,077·2
35	10·67	77	23·47	6,000	1,828·80	27,000	8,229·6
36	10·97	78	23·77	6,500	1,981·20	27,500	8,382·0
37	11·28	79	24·08	7,000	2,133·60	28,000	8,534·4
38	11·58	80	24·38	7,500	2,286·00	28,500	8,686·8
39	11·89	81	24·69	8,000	2,438·40	29,000	8,839·2
40	12·19	82	24·99	8,500	2,590·80	29,500	8,991·6
41	12·50	83	25·30	9,000	2,743·20	30,000	9,144·0
42	12·80	84	25·60	9,500	2,895·60		

ALTITUDE CONVERSION

Metres (m.) to Feet (ft.)

m.	ft.	m.	ft.	m.	ft.	m.	ft.
1	3·28	43	141·08	85	278·86	2,800	9,186·3
2	6·56	44	144·36	86	282·15	2,900	9,514·4
3	9·84	45	147·64	87	285·43	3,000	9,842·5
4	13·12	46	150·92	88	288·71	3,100	10,170·6
5	16·41	47	154·20	89	291·99	3,200	10,498·7
6	19·68	48	157·48	90	295·27	3,300	10,826·7
7	22·97	49	160·76	91	298·56	3,400	11,154·8
8	26·25	50	164·04	92	301·84	3,500	11,482·9
9	29·53	51	167·32	93	305·12	3,600	11,811·0
10	32·81	52	170·60	94	308·40	3,700	12,139·1
11	36·09	53	173·88	95	311·68	3,800	12,467·2
12	39·37	54	177·16	96	314·96	3,900	12,795·2
13	42·65	55	180·45	97	318·24	4,000	13,123·3
14	45·93	56	183·73	98	321·52	4,100	13,451·4
15	49·21	57	187·01	99	324·80	4,200	13,779·5
16	52·49	58	190·29	100	328·08	4,300	14,107·6
17	55·77	59	193·57	200	656·20	4,400	14,435·7
18	59·05	60	196·85	300	984·30	4,500	14,763·7
19	62·34	61	200·13	400	1,312·30	4,600	15,091·8
20	65·62	62	203·41	500	1,640·40	4,700	15,419·9
21	68·90	63	206·69	600	1,968·50	4,800	15,748·0
22	72·18	64	209·97	700	2,296·60	4,900	16,076·1
23	75·46	65	213·25	800	2,624·70	5,000	16,404·2
24	78·74	66	216·53	900	2,952·70	5,100	16,732·2
25	82·02	67	219·82	1,000	3,280·80	5,200	17,060·3
26	85·30	68	223·10	1,100	3,608·90	5,300	17,388·4
27	88·58	69	226·38	1,200	3,937·00	5,400	17,716·5
28	91·86	70	229·66	1,300	4,265·10	5,500	18,044·6
29	95·14	71	232·94	1,400	4,593·20	5,600	18,372·7
30	98·42	72	236·22	1,500	4,921·20	5,700	18,700·7
31	101·71	73	239·50	1,600	5,249·30	5,800	19,028·8
32	104·99	74	242·78	1,700	5,577·40	5,900	19,356·9
33	108·27	75	246·06	1,800	5,905·50	6,000	19,685·0
34	111·55	76	249·34	1,900	6,233·60	6,100	20,013·1
35	114·83	77	252·62	2,000	6,561·70	6,200	20,341·2
36	118·11	78	255·90	2,100	6,889·70	6,300	20,669·2
37	121·39	79	259·19	2,200	7,217·80	6,400	20,997·3
38	124·67	80	262·47	2,300	7,545·90	6,500	21,325·4
39	127·95	81	265·75	2,400	7,874·00	7,000	22,965·8
40	131·23	82	269·03	2,500	8,202·10	8,000	26,246·7
41	134·51	83	272·31	2,600	8,530·20	9,000	29,527·5
42	137·79	84	275·59	2,700	8,858·20	10,000	32,808·4

WEIGHT CONVERSION
Pounds (lb.) to Kilograms (Kg.)

lb.	kg.	lb.	kg.	lb.	kg.
1	0·45	41	18·60	81	36·74
2	0·91	42	19·05	82	37·20
3	1·36	43	19·51	83	37·65
4	1·81	44	19·96	84	38·10
5	2·27	45	20·41	85	39·56
6	2·72	46	20·87	86	39·01
7	3·18	47	21·32	87	38·46
8	3·63	48	21·77	88	39·92
9	4·08	49	22·23	89	40·37
10	4·54	50	22·68	90	40·82
11	4·99	51	23·13	91	41·28
12	5·44	52	23·59	92	41·73
13	5·90	53	24·04	93	42·19
14	6·35	54	24·49	94	42·64
15	6·80	55	24·95	95	43·09
16	7·26	56	25·40	96	43·55
17	7·71	57	25·86	97	44·00
18	8·17	58	26·31	98	44·45
19	8·62	59	26·76	99	44·91
20	9·07	60	27·22	100	45·40
21	9·53	61	27·67	112	50·80
22	9·98	62	28·12	200	90·70
23	10·43	63	28·58	300	136·10
24	10·89	64	29·03	400	181·40
25	11·34	65	29·48	500	226·80
26	11·79	66	29·94	600	272·20
27	12·25	67	30·39	700	317·50
28	12·70	68	30·84	800	362·90
29	13·15	69	31·30	900	408·20
30	13·61	70	31·75	1,000	453·60
31	14·06	71	32·31	2,000	907·20
32	14·52	72	32·66	2,240	1,016·10
33	14·97	73	33·11	3,000	1,360·80
34	15·42	74	33·57	4,000	1,814·40
35	15·88	75	34·02	5,000	2,268·00
36	16·33	76	34·47	6,000	2,721·60
37	16·78	77	34·93	7,000	3,175·20
38	17·24	78	35·38	8,000	3,628·80
39	17·69	79	35·83	9,000	4,082·40
40	18·14	80	36·29	10,000	4,536·00

14 lb. = 1 stone
2,000 lb. = 1 short ton

112 lb. = 1 hundredweight (cwt.)
2,240 lb. = 1 long ton

1 DEC 00

WEIGHT CONVERSION
Kilograms (Kg.) to Pounds (lb.)

kg.	lb.	kg.	lb.	kg.	lb.
1	2.20	41	90.39	81	178.57
2	4.41	42	92.59	82	180.78
3	6.61	43	94.80	83	182.98
4	8.82	44	97.00	84	185.19
5	11.02	45	99.21	85	187.39
6	13.23	46	101.41	86	189.60
7	15.43	47	103.62	87	191.80
8	17.64	48	105.82	88	194.01
9	19.84	49	108.03	89	196.21
10	22.05	50	110.23	90	198.41
11	24.25	51	112.44	91	200.62
12	26.46	52	114.64	92	202.82
13	28.66	53	116.84	93	205.03
14	30.86	54	119.05	94	207.23
15	33.07	55	121.25	95	209.44
16	35.27	56	123.46	96	211.64
17	37.48	57	125.66	97	213.85
18	39.68	58	127.87	98	216.05
19	41.89	59	130.07	99	218.26
20	44.09	60	132.28	100	220.50
21	46.30	61	134.48	200	440.90
22	48.50	62	136.69	300	661.40
23	50.71	63	138.89	400	881.80
24	50.91	64	141.09	500	1,102.30
25	55.12	65	143.30	600	1,322.80
26	57.32	66	145.60	700	1,543.20
27	59.52	67	147.71	800	1,763.70
28	61.73	68	149.91	900	1,984.10
29	63.93	69	152.12	1,000	2,204.60
30	66.14	70	154.32	2,000	4,409.20
31	68.34	71	156.53	3,000	6,613.80
32	70.55	72	158.73	4,000	8,818.40
33	72.75	73	160.94	5,000	11,023.00
34	74.96	74	163.14	6,000	13,227.60
35	77.16	75	165.35	7,000	15,432.20
36	79.37	76	166.55	8,000	17,636.80
37	81.57	77	169.75	9,000	19,841.40
38	83.78	78	171.96	10,000	22,046.00
39	85.98	79	174.16		
40	88.18	80	176.37		

1,000 kg. = 1 Metric Ton

BAROMETRIC PRESSURE CONVERSION

Inches	Milibars	Inches	Milibars	Inches	Milibars
28·00	948·2	28·50	965·1	29·00	982·1
28·01	948·5	28·51	965·5	29·01	982·4
28·02	948·9	28·52	965·8	29·02	982·7
28·03	949·2	28·53	966·1	29·03	983·1
28·04	949·5	28·54	966·5	29·04	983·4
28·05	949·9	28·55	966·8	29·05	983·7
28·06	950·2	28·56	967·2	29·06	984·1
28·07	950·6	28·57	967·5	29·07	984·4
28·08	950·9	28·58	967·8	29·08	984·8
28·09	951·2	28·59	968·2	29·09	985·1
28·10	951·6	28·60	968·5	29·10	985·4
28·11	951·9	28·61	968·8	29·11	985·8
28·12	952·3	28·62	969·2	29·12	986·1
28·13	952·6	28·63	969·5	29·13	986·5
28·14	952·9	28·64	969·9	29·14	986·8
28·15	953·3	28·65	970·2	29·15	987·1
28·16	953·6	28·66	970·5	29·16	987·5
28·17	953·9	28·67	970·9	29·17	987·8
28·18	954·3	28·68	971·2	29·18	988·2
28·19	954·6	28·69	971·6	29·19	988·5
28·20	955·0	28·70	971·9	29·20	988·8
28·21	955·3	28·71	972·2	29·21	989·2
28·22	955·6	28·72	972·6	29·22	989·5
28·23	956·0	28·73	972·9	29·23	989·8
28·24	956·3	28·74	973·2	29·24	990·2
28·25	956·7	28·75	973·6	29·25	990·5
28·26	957·0	28·76	973·9	29·26	990·9
28·27	957·3	28·77	974·3	29·27	991·2
28·28	957·7	28·78	974·6	29·28	991·5
28·29	958·0	28·79	974·9	29·29	991·9
28·30	958·3	28·80	975·3	29·30	992·2
28·31	958·7	28·81	975·6	29·31	992·6
28·32	959·0	28·82	976·0	29·32	992·9
28·33	959·4	28·83	976·3	29·33	993·2
28·34	959·7	28·84	976·6	29·34	993·6
28·35	960·0	28·85	977·0	29·35	993·9
28·36	960·4	28·86	977·3	29·36	994·2
28·37	960·7	28·87	977·7	29·37	994·6
28·38	961·1	28·88	978·0	29·38	994·9
28·39	961·4	28·89	978·3	29·39	995·3
28·40	961·7	28·90	978·7	29·40	995·6
28·41	962·1	28·91	979·0	29·41	995·9
28·42	962·4	28·92	979·3	29·42	996·3
28·43	962·8	28·93	979·7	29·43	996·6
28·44	963·1	28·94	980·0	29·44	997·0
29·45	963·4	28·95	980·4	29·45	997·3
28·46	963·8	28·96	980·7	29·46	997·6
28·47	964·1	28·97	981·0	29·47	998·0
28·48	964·4	28·98	981·4	29·48	998·3
28·49	964·8	28·99	981·7	29·49	998·6

BAROMETRIC PRESSURE CONVERSION

Inches	Milibars	Inches	Milibars	Inches	Milibars
29·50	999·0	30·00	1,015·9	30·50	1,032·9
29·51	999·3	30·01	1,016·3	30·51	1,033·2
29·52	999·7	30·02	1,016·6	30·52	1,033·5
29·53	1,000·0	30·03	1,016·9	30·53	1,033·9
29·54	1,000·4	30·04	1,017·3	30·54	1,034·2
29·55	1,000·7	30·05	1,017·6	30·55	1,034·5
29·56	1,001·0	30·06	1,018·0	30·56	1,034·9
29·57	1,001·4	30·07	1,018·3	30·57	1,035·2
29·58	1,001·7	30·08	1,018·6	30·58	1,035·5
29·59	1,002·0	30·09	1,019·0	30·59	1,035·9
29·60	1,002·4	30·10	1,019·3	30·60	1,036·2
29·61	1,002·7	30·11	1,019·6	30·61	1,036·6
29·62	1,003·1	30·12	1,020·0	30·62	1,036·9
29·63	1,003·4	30·13	1,020·3	30·63	1,037·3
29·64	1,003·7	30·14	1,020·7	30·64	1,037·6
29·65	1,004·1	30·15	1,021·0	30·65	1,037·9
29·66	1,004·4	30·16	1,021·3	30·66	1,038·3
29·67	1,004·7	30·17	1,021·7	30·67	1,038·6
29·68	1,005·1	30·18	1,022·0	30·68	1,038·9
29·69	1,005·4	30·19	1,022·4	30·69	1,039·3
29·70	1,005·8	30·20	1,022·7	30·70	1,039·6
29·71	1,006·1	30·21	1,023·0	30·71	1,040·0
29·72	1,006·4	30·22	1,023·4	30·72	1,040·3
29·73	1,006·8	30·23	1,023·7	30·73	1,040·6
29·74	1,007·1	30·24	1,024·0	30·74	1,041·0
29·75	1,007·5	30·25	1,024·4	30·75	1,041·3
29·76	1,007·8	30·26	1,024·7	30·76	1,041·7
29·77	1,008·1	30·27	1,025·1	30·77	1,042·0
29·78	1,008·5	30·28	1,025·4	30·78	1,042·3
29·79	1,008·8	30·29	1,025·7	30·79	1,042·7
29·80	1,009·1	30·30	1,026·1	30·80	1,043·0
29·81	1,009·5	30·31	1,026·4	30·81	1,043·3
29·82	1,009·8	30·32	1,026·7	30·82	1,043·7
29·83	1,010·2	30·33	1,027·1	30·83	1,044·0
29·84	1,010·5	30·34	1,027·4	30·84	1,044·4
29·85	1,010·8	30·35	1,027·8	30·85	1,044·7
29·86	1,011·2	30·36	1,028·1	30·86	1,045·0
29·87	1,011·5	30·37	1,028·4	30·87	1,045·4
29·88	1,011·9	30·38	1,028·8	30·88	1,045·7
29·89	1,012·2	30·39	1,029·1	30·89	1,046·1
29·90	1,012·5	30·40	1,029·5	30·90	1,046·4
29·91	1,012·9	30·41	1,029·8	30·91	1,046·7
29·92	1,013·2	30·42	1,030·1	30·92	1,047·1
29·93	1,013·5	30·43	1,030·5	30·93	1,047·4
29·94	1,013·9	30·44	1,030·8	30·94	1,047·8
29·95	1,014·2	30·45	1,031·2	30·95	1,048·1
29·96	1,014·6	30·46	1,031·5	30·96	1,048·4
29·97	1,014·9	30·47	1,031·8	30·97	1,048·8
29·98	1,015·2	30·48	1,032·2	30·98	1,049·1
29·99	1,015·6	30·49	1,032·5	30·99	1,049·5

WIND COMPONENT TABLES

CROSSWIND

ANGLE BETWEEN WIND DIRECTION AND RUNWAY HEADING

		10°	20°	30°	40°	50°	60°	70°	80°
W	5	1	2	2	3	4	4	4	5
I N	10	2	3	5	6	7	8	9	9
D S	15	3	5	7	9	11	13	14	14
P	20	3	7	10	13	15	17	18	19
E E	25	4	8	12	16	19	22	23	24
D	30	5	10	15	19	23	26	28	29
K	35	6	12	17	22	26	30	32	34
N	40	7	14	20	25	30	35	37	39
O T	45	8	15	22	29	34	39	42	44
S	50	9	17	25	32	38	43	47	49

HEADWIND

ANGLE BETWEEN WIND DIRECTION AND RUNWAY HEADING

		10°	20°	30°	40°	50°	60°	70°	80°
W	5	5	4	4	4	3	2	2	1
I N	10	9	9	8	7	6	5	3	2
D S	15	14	14	13	11	9	7	5	3
P	20	19	18	17	15	13	10	7	3
E E	25	24	23	22	19	16	12	8	4
D	30	29	28	26	23	19	15	10	5
K	35	34	32	30	26	22	17	12	6
N	40	39	37	35	30	25	20	14	7
O T	45	44	42	39	34	29	22	15	8
S	50	49	47	43	38	32	25	17	9

DME AND TACAN
FREQUENCY/CHANNEL PAIRING TABLES

X CHANNELS

MHz	·00	·10	·20	·30	·40	·50	·60	·70	·80	·90
108	17	18	19	20	21	22	23	24	25	26
109	27	28	29	30	31	32	33	34	35	36
110	37	38	39	40	41	42	43	44	45	46
111	47	48	49	50	51	52	53	54	55	56
112	57	58	59	70	71	72	73	74	75	76
113	77	78	79	80	81	82	83	84	85	86
114	87	88	89	90	91	92	93	94	95	96
115	97	98	99	100	101	102	103	104	105	106
116	107	108	109	110	111	112	113	114	115	116
117	117	118	119	120	121	122	123	124	125	126
133	—	—	—	60	61	62	63	64	65	66
134	67	68	69	—	1	2	3	4	5	6
135	7	8	9	10	11	12	13	14	15	16

Y CHANNELS

MHz	·05	·15	·25	·35	·45	·55	·65	·75	·85	·95
108	17	18	19	20	21	22	23	24	25	26
109	27	28	29	30	31	32	33	34	35	36
110	37	38	39	40	41	42	43	44	45	46
111	47	48	49	50	51	52	53	54	55	56
112	57	58	59	70	71	72	73	74	75	76
113	77	78	79	80	81	82	83	84	85	86
114	87	88	89	90	91	92	93	94	95	96
115	97	98	99	100	101	102	103	104	105	106
116	107	108	109	110	111	112	113	114	115	116
117	117	118	119	120	121	122	123	124	125	126

SUNRISE – SUNSET TABLES

All times are Local, allowances have been made for British Summer Time — 25 March to 27 October 2001

Date	Jersey	London	Cardiff	Manchester	Belfast (AA)	Teesside	Glasgow	Inverness	Date
Jan 1	0803 1622	0807 1604	0818 1615	0824 1602	0847 1610	0827 1552	0847 1555	0857 1542	Jan 1
6	0802 1628	0805 1611	0816 1622	0822 1609	0844 1618	0824 1600	0844 1604	0854 1551	6
12	0759 1636	0801 1620	0812 1632	0817 1619	0840 1628	0820 1609	0839 1614	0848 1602	12
18	0754 1645	0756 1630	0807 1642	0811 1629	0833 1639	0813 1620	0832 1625	0839 1615	18
24	0748 1655	0749 1640	0800 1652	0803 1640	0824 1650	0804 1632	0823 1638	0829 1628	24
30	0740 1705	0740 1651	0751 1702	0754 1651	0814 1702	0755 1644	0812 1650	0818 1642	30
Feb 5	0731 1715	0730 1702	0742 1713	0743 1703	0803 1715	0743 1656	0800 1704	0805 1656	Feb 5
11	0721 1725	0719 1713	0731 1724	0731 1715	0751 1727	0731 1709	0747 1717	0751 1710	11
17	0710 1735	0708 1723	0719 1735	0719 1727	0738 1740	0718 1721	0733 1730	0736 1724	17
23	0659 1744	0656 1734	0707 1746	0706 1738	0724 1752	0705 1733	0719 1743	0721 1738	23
Mar 1	0647 1754	0643 1745	0654 1756	0652 1750	0710 1804	0650 1745	0704 1755	0706 1751	Mar 1
7	0635 1804	0630 1755	0641 1807	0638 1801	0655 1816	0636 1757	0649 1808	0649 1805	7
13	0622 1813	0616 1806	0628 1817	0624 1812	0640 1828	0621 1809	0633 1820	0632 1818	13
19	0610 1822	0602 1816	0614 1827	0609 1823	0625 1839	0606 1820	0618 1833	0616 1831	19
25	0657 1932	0649 1926	0700 1937	0655 1934	0710 1951	0651 1932	0702 1945	0659 1945	25
31	0644 1941	0635 1936	0647 1947	0640 1945	0655 2003	0636 1943	0646 1957	0642 1958	31
Apr 6	0632 1950	0622 1946	0633 1957	0626 1956	0640 2014	0621 1955	0631 2009	0626 2011	Apr 6
12	0619 1959	0609 1956	0620 2007	0612 2007	0625 2026	0606 2006	0615 2021	0610 2024	12
18	0608 2008	0556 2006	0607 2017	0558 2018	0611 2037	0552 2017	0600 2033	0554 2037	18
24	0556 2017	0544 2016	0555 2027	0545 2029	0557 2049	0538 2029	0546 2046	0538 2050	24
30	0546 2026	0532 2026	0544 2037	0533 2039	0544 2100	0525 2040	0532 2058	0524 2103	30
May 6	0536 2035	0521 2035	0533 2047	0521 2050	0532 2111	0513 2051	0519 2109	0510 2116	May 6
12	0527 2043	0512 2045	0523 2056	0511 2100	0521 2122	0502 2102	0507 2121	0457 2129	12
18	0519 2051	0503 2054	0515 2105	0502 2110	0511 2132	0452 2112	0457 2132	0445 2141	18
24	0513 2058	0456 2102	0508 2113	0454 2118	0502 2141	0444 2121	0448 2142	0435 2152	24
30	0508 2105	0450 2109	0502 2120	0447 2126	0455 2150	0437 2130	0440 2151	0427 2201	30
Jun 5	0504 2110	0446 2115	0458 2126	0443 2132	0450 2156	0432 2136	0435 2158	0421 2209	Jun 5
11	0503 2114	0444 2119	0456 2130	0440 2137	0448 2201	0429 2141	0432 2203	0417 2215	11
17	0502 2117	0444 2122	0456 2133	0440 2140	0447 2204	0429 2144	0431 2206	0416 2218	17

Date									Date
Jun 23	0417 2219	0432 2207	0430 2145	0448 2205	0441 2141	0457 2134	0445 2123	0504 2118	Jun 23
29	0421 2217	0436 2205	0434 2144	0452 2204	0445 2140	0500 2133	0448 2122	0507 2117	29
Jul 5	0428 2213	0442 2201	0439 2140	0457 2200	0450 2137	0505 2130	0453 2114	0511 2115	Jul 5
11	0436 2206	0450 2155	0446 2135	0505 2155	0456 2131	0511 2125	0459 2114	0517 2111	11
17	0446 2157	0459 2147	0455 2127	0513 2147	0504 2124	0518 2119	0506 2108	0523 2105	17
23	0457 2146	0509 2138	0504 2118	0522 2138	0513 2116	0526 2111	0514 2100	0531 2058	23
29	0509 2134	0519 2127	0514 2108	0532 2128	0523 2106	0535 2102	0523 2051	0539 2050	29
Aug 4	0521 2121	0531 2114	0524 2056	0543 2116	0533 2055	0544 2052	0532 2041	0547 2041	Aug 4
10	0534 2106	0542 2101	0535 2044	0554 2104	0543 2043	0553 2041	0542 2030	0555 2030	10
16	0546 2051	0554 2047	0546 2031	0605 2050	0553 2031	0603 2030	0551 2018	0604 2019	16
22	0559 2036	0606 2032	0557 2017	0616 2036	0604 2017	0612 2017	0601 2006	0612 2008	22
28	0612 2020	0617 2017	0608 2002	0627 2022	0614 2003	0622 2004	0610 1953	0621 1956	28
Sep 3	0624 2003	0629 2002	0619 1948	0638 2007	0624 1949	0631 1951	0620 1939	0630 1943	Sep 3
9	0637 1947	0641 1946	0630 1933	0649 1952	0635 1935	0641 1937	0629 1926	0638 1931	9
15	0649 1930	0652 1930	0641 1917	0700 1937	0645 1920	0650 1923	0639 1912	0647 1918	15
21	0702 1913	0704 1914	0652 1902	0711 1921	0656 1905	0700 1910	0649 1858	0656 1905	21
27	0715 1856	0716 1859	0703 1847	0722 1906	0706 1851	0710 1856	0658 1844	0704 1852	27
Oct 3	0727 1840	0727 1843	0714 1832	0734 1851	0717 1836	0720 1842	0708 1831	0713 1839	Oct 3
9	0740 1823	0740 1828	0726 1817	0745 1836	0728 1822	0729 1829	0718 1817	0722 1827	9
16	0754 1808	0752 1813	0737 1803	0757 1822	0739 1809	0740 1816	0728 1804	0732 1815	16
22	0807 1752	0804 1758	0749 1749	0808 1808	0750 1755	0750 1804	0739 1752	0741 1803	22
28	0721 1637	0717 1644	0701 1636	0720 1655	0701 1643	0700 1652	0649 1640	0651 1653	28
Nov 3	0734 1623	0730 1631	0713 1624	0733 1643	0713 1631	0711 1641	0700 1630	0700 1643	Nov 3
9	0748 1611	0742 1619	0725 1613	0745 1631	0724 1621	0721 1632	0710 1620	0710 1634	9
15	0801 1559	0755 1609	0737 1603	0756 1621	0735 1611	0732 1623	0721 1611	0720 1626	15
21	0814 1549	0807 1600	0748 1554	0808 1613	0746 1603	0742 1616	0731 1604	0729 1620	21
27	0826 1540	0818 1552	0758 1548	0818 1606	0756 1557	0751 1610	0740 1558	0737 1615	27
Dec 3	0837 1534	0828 1547	0808 1543	0828 1601	0805 1552	0759 1606	0748 1553	0745 1611	Dec 3
9	0846 1531	0836 1544	0816 1540	0836 1558	0812 1550	0807 1605	0755 1553	0752 1610	9
15	0853 1530	0842 1543	0822 1540	0842 1558	0818 1550	0812 1605	0801 1553	0757 1610	15
21	0857 1532	0846 1545	0826 1542	0846 1600	0822 1552	0816 1607	0805 1555	0801 1613	21
27	0858 1536	0848 1550	0827 1546	0847 1604	0824 1556	0818 1611	0807 1559	0803 1617	27

AAL	Above Aerodrome Level	CHAPI	Carrier Helicopter Approach Path Indicator
ABn	Aerodrome Beacon	C/O or CO	Commanding Officer
ACC	Area Control Centre	c/s	Call-sign
A/C	Aircraft	CTA	Control Area
A/D	Aerodrome	Ctl	Control
ADR	Advisory Route	CTR	Control Zone
AFIS	Aerodrome Flight Information Service	(D)	Day
AFTN	Aeronautical Fixed Telecommunication Network	DH	Decision Height
AG	Arrester Gear	DERA	Defence Experimental Research Agency
AGL	Above Ground Level	Dir.	Director
A/G	Air/Ground communication station	DME	Distance Measuring Equipment
AIAA	Area of Intense Aerial Activity	DPA.	Defence Research Agency
AIC	Aeronautical Information Circular	E	East
AIP	Aeronautical Information Publication	EET	Estimated Elapsed Time
AOA	Aerodrome Owners Association	Elev.	Elevation
Ap	Approach (Lighting)	ETA	Estimated Time of Arrival
APAPI	Abbreviated Precision Approach Path Indicators	ETD	Estimated Time of Departure
		FAT	Final Approach Track
APP	Approach Control	FBU	Flight Briefing Unit
ATC	Air Traffic Control	FIC	Flight Information Centre
ACC	Area Control Centre or Area Control	FIR	Flight Information Region
		FIS	Flight Information Service
ATIS	Automatic Terminal Information Service	FL	Flight Level
		Freq.	Frequency
ATSU	Air Traffic Service Unit	ft.	Feet
AVGAS	Aviation Gasoline	GCA	Ground Controlled Approach System
AVTUR	Aviation Turbine Fuel		
Awy	Airway	GMC	Ground Movement Control
BAA	British Airports Authority	GMP	Ground Movement Planning
BAUA	Business Aircraft Users Association	GMT	Greenwich Mean Time (UTC)
		Gn	Green
Bdry	Boundary	H+	Hour plus....... minutes past the hour
BCPL	Basic Commercial Pilot's License	H24	Continuous operation
C	Twr/Ops./Flight Office	HF	High frequency
¢	By arrangement	HJ	Sunrise to Sunset
CAA	Civil Aviation Authority	Hmr.	Homer
CAS	Controlled Airspace		

ABBREVIATIONS

HN................................Sunset to Sunrise	METAR ....Aviation Routine Weather
HO ....Hours of operational requirement	Report (in aeronautical meteorological
Hold....................................Holding Point	code)
HP ....Holding Point	MHz ....Megahertz
HTA....................Helicopter Training Area	Mil. ....Military
HX ....No specific working hours	MKR. ....Marker Beacon
hr/s..Hour/s	MM....................................Middle Marker
IAP.........Instrument Approach Procedure	MTWA ....Maximum Total Weight
IAS ....Indicated Air Speed	Authorised
IBn...........................Identification Beacon	(N) ....Night
ICAO ....International Civil Aviation	N ....North
Organisation	NATS ....National Air Traffic Services
IFR.......................Instrument Flight Rules	NDB ....Non-directional Radio Beacon
ILS ....Instrument Landing System	NM,nm ....Nautical Miles
IMC ....Instrument Meteorological	NOTAM ....Notice to Airman
Conditions	A notice containing information
Info. ....Information	concerning the establishment,
ISWL.............Isolated Single Wheel Load	condition or change in any
JB...Jet Barrier	aeronautical facility, service,
kHz ....Kilohertz	procedure or hazard, the timely
kt...knots	knowledge of which is essential to
lbs....................................Pounds (weight)	personnel concerned with flight
Lctr. ....Locator Beacon (NDB)	operations
LDA ....Landing Distance Available	OCH ....Obstacle Clearance Height
LFA ....Local Flying Area	O/H ....Overhead
LITAS ....Low Intensity Two Colour	Op hrs ....Operation Hours
Approach Slope System	OPMET Operational Meteorological
LLZ..Localizer	(Information)
m ....metres	OM ....Outer Marker
M or Mag ....Magnetic	O/R..On Request
MARAS ....Middle Airspace Radar	O/T..Other Times
Advisory Service	P................................Primary Frequency
MATZ......Military Aerodrome Traffic Zone	PAPI.................Precision Approach Path
MDH ....Minimum Descent Height	Indicators
MEDA ....Military Emergency	PPL ....Private Pilot's License
Diversion Aerodrome	PAR ....Precision Approach Radar
Met..........................Meteorological Office	PN...Prior Notice
	PNR ....Prior Notice Required
	PPR ....Prior Permission Required

ABBREVIATIONS

QFE ....Atmospheric pressure at aerodrome elevation (or at runway threshold)	VFR ....Visual Flight Rules
QFU ....Runway orientation (° Mag)	VHF ....Very High Frequency
QNH ....Altimeter sub-scale setting to obtain elevation when on ground	VMC.....Visual Meteorological Conditions
R...Red or Radial	VOLMET........Meteorological Information for aircraft in flight
RAD ....Radar	VOR VHF Omnidirectional Radio Range
RCL.........................Runway Centre Line	VORTAC ....Very High Frequency Omni Range and Tactical Air Navigation
REIL............Runway End Identifier Lights	VRP Visual Reference Point
R/T or RTF ....Radio Telephone	W ....West
RVR......................Runway Visual Range	Wh. ....White
Rwy ....Runway	
S ....South	
S ....Secondary Frequency	
SAL.............Supplementary App Lighting	
Sctr. ....Sector	
SAR ....Search and Rescue	
SFC ....Surface	
SR...Sunrise	
SRA...........Surveillance Radar Approach	
SS ....Sunset	
SSR ....Secondary Surveillance Radar	
SVFR.............Special Visual Flight Rules	
TACAN..................Tactical Air Navigation Aid (UHF)	
TAF..........................Aerodrome Forecast	
Tel..Telephone	
Thr/Thld. ....Threshold	
TMA ....Terminal Control Area	
TORA ....Take-off Run Available	
TVOR ....Terminal VOR	
TWR ....Tower	
UFN ....Until Further Notice	
UTC............Co-ordinated Universal Time	
VAD..............Visual Approach/Departure	
VASIS ....Visual Approach Slope Indicator System	
VDF ....VHF Direction Finding	

PHONETIC ALPHABET
AND
MORSE CODE

A ....Alpha ....• —
B ....Bravo ....— • • •
C ....Charlie ....— • — •
D ....Delta..............— • •
E ....Echo...............•
F ....Foxtrot ....• • — •
G ....Golf ....— — •
H ....Hotel ....• • • •
I ......India ....• •
J .....Juliet ....• — — —
K ....Kilo.................— • —
L .....Lima ....• — • •
M ....Mike ....— —
N ....November ......— •
O ....Oscar ....— — —
P .....Papa..............• — — •
Q ....Quebec ....— — • —
R ....Romeo ....• — •
S .....Sierra ....• • •
T .....Tango ....—
U ....Uniform..........• • —
V .....Victor ....• • • —
W ....Whisky...........• — —
X .....X-ray ....— • • —
Y .....Yankee ....— • — —
Z .....Zulu ....— — • •

N51 23·03 W001 10·35	**BRIMPTON (Wasing Lower Farm)**	210 ft AMSL
5·5 nm ESE of Newbury	**SAM 113·35 018 27.**	**MID 114·00 318 29**
		CPT 114·35 168 6

c/s Brimpton Radio 135·125 A/G.

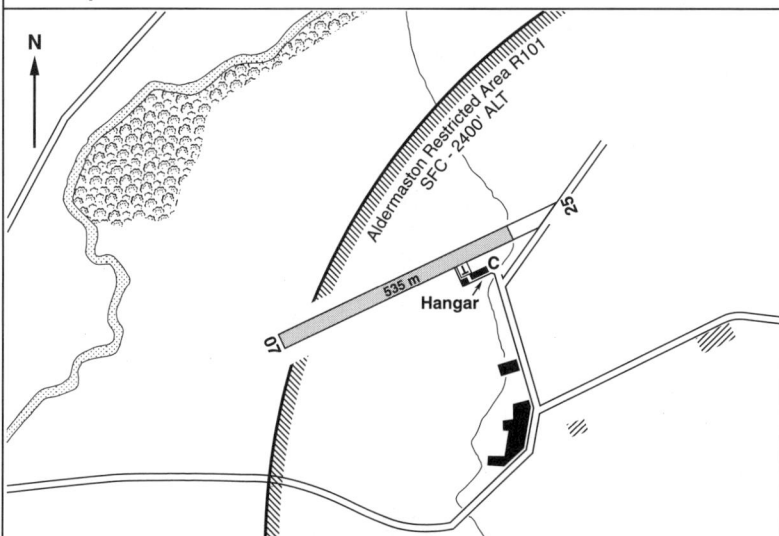

Rwy	Dim(m)	Surface	TORA(m)	LDA(m)	Lighting
07/25	535x25	Grass	Unlicensed		Nil

Additional 100 m available for take-off Rwy 25.

Op hrs: Strictly PPR by telephone, Alan House Tel: 01635-863433, 0836-775557.

Landing Fee: Singles £4.00; Twins £6.00.

Maintenance: Limited.	**Hangarage:** Nil.	**Customs:** Nil.

Remarks: Operated by Alan House Esq, Sylmar Aviation & Services Ltd., Kennet House, 77-79 Bath Road, Thatcham, Berks RG18 3BD. Unlicensed airfield.
Strictly PPR, aircraft landing without PPR will incur a doubled landing fee.

Warning: Airfield is situated just within the NW edge of the Aldermaston Restricted Area - R101, and operates under a Special Exemption.
All approaches to the airfield must be from the North. Flying South of the airfield below 2400 ft agl prohibited.

Circuits at 800ft QFE, LH on Rwy 07, RH on Rwy 25.

Avoid overflying the villages of Brimpton, Aldermaston, Woolhampton and all local habitation close to the circuit.

Restaurant: Light snacks available in the clubhouse.

Taxis: Tadley Taxis 01734-816600.

Fuel: Nil	**Tel:** 01635-863433 Operator
	01635-866088 Sylmar Aviation
	0118-971 3822 Club, when manned

Robert Pooley ©

135

| N51 22·97 W002 43·15 | **BRISTOL AIRPORT** | 622 ft AMSL |

| 7 nm SW of Bristol. | BCN 117·45 141 29 |

c/s Bristol. APP 128·55. TWR 133·85. RAD 124·35 (when directed).
VDF 128·55.   ATIS 126·025.
NDB 'BRI' 380·0 (On A/D).
ILS/DME Rwy 09 (093°M) I-BON 110·15. ILS/DME Rwy 27 (273°M) I-BTS 110·15.

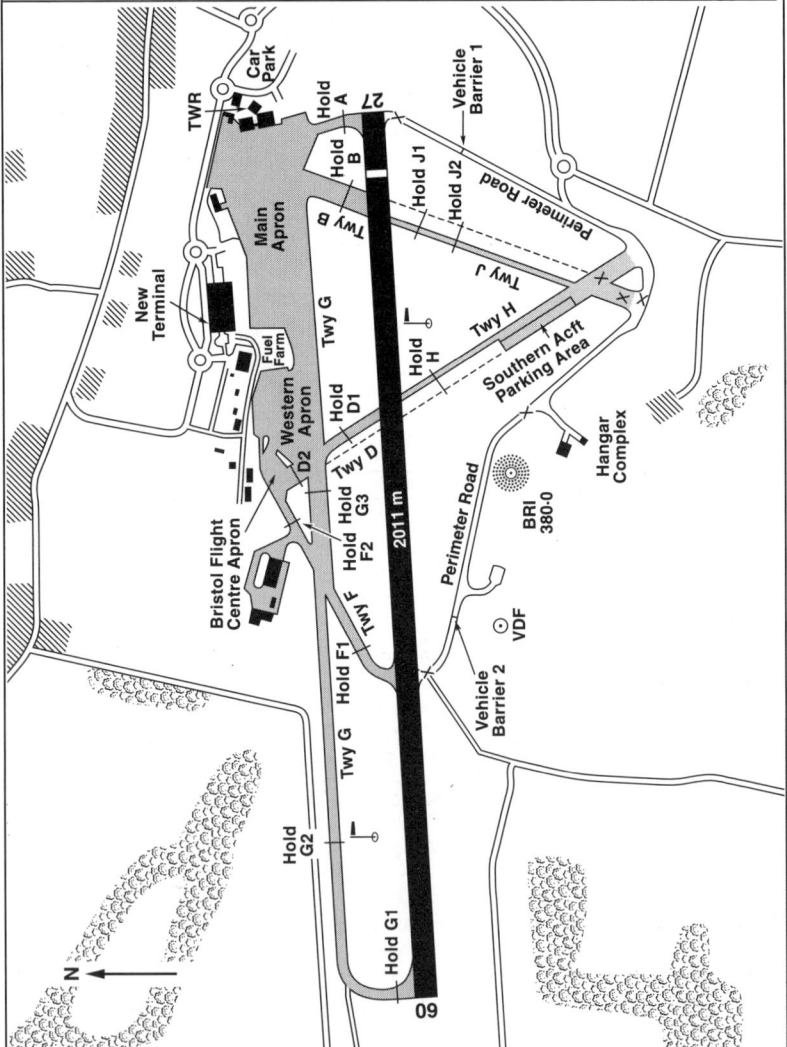

Robert Pooley ©

N50 58·05 W002 09·22	**COMPTON ABBAS**	810 ft AMSL
3 nm S of Shaftesbury.		SAM 113·35 277 30·5

**c/s Compton Radio 122·70 A/G. Radar Service available Mon-Fri from
Boscombe Down 126·70, or Yeovilton 127·35.   NDB 'COM' 349·5 (On A/D).**

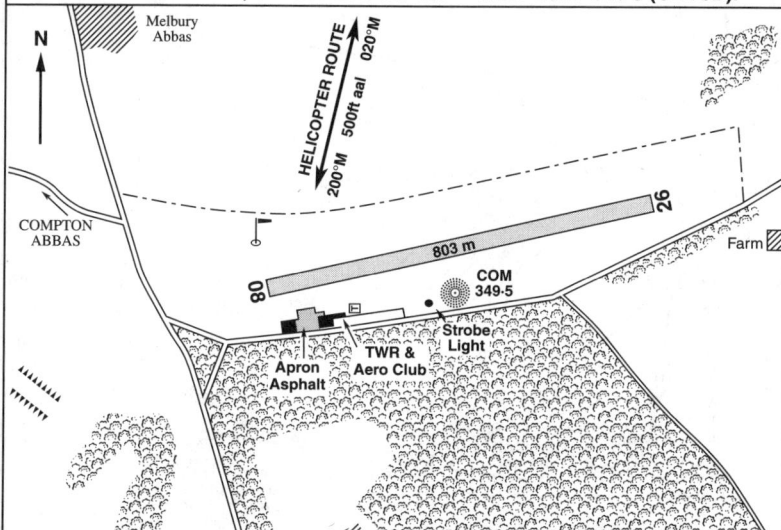

Rwy	Dim(m)	Surface	TORA(m)	LDA(m)	Lighting
08/26	803x30	Grass	08-803	08-803	Nil.
			26-803	26-803	Nil.

Op hrs: 0900-SS daily.

Landing Fee: £7.00	**Customs:** 24hrs PNR.
Hangarage: Available.	**Maintenance :** Available

Remarks: Operated by Compton Abbas Airfield Ltd, Ashmore, Salisbury, Wilts SP5 5AP

Circuits at 800 ft aal – LH on Rwy 08, RH on Rwy 26.

The high intensity white flashing strobe light operates continuously during airfield operational hours.

Due to the visual screening effect of tall trees to the south of the airfield,
it is recommended that first time visitors approach from a northerly direction, i.e
Shaftesbury – Comton Abbas is 150°M/ 3 nm.

Noise Abatement Procedures - See overleaf.

Warning: Expect turbulance and windshear with southerly winds above 10 kt.

Restaurant & Bar: Highly acclaimed restaurant and bar open 0930-SS all year. Group fly-ins and corporate days catered for.

Taxis: Readily available.

| **Fuel:** 100LL. Cash, cheque and most credit cards accepted. | **Tel:** 01747-811767
Fax: 01747-811161 |
|---|---|

Robert Pooley ©

COMPTON ABBAS
Noise Abatement Procedures

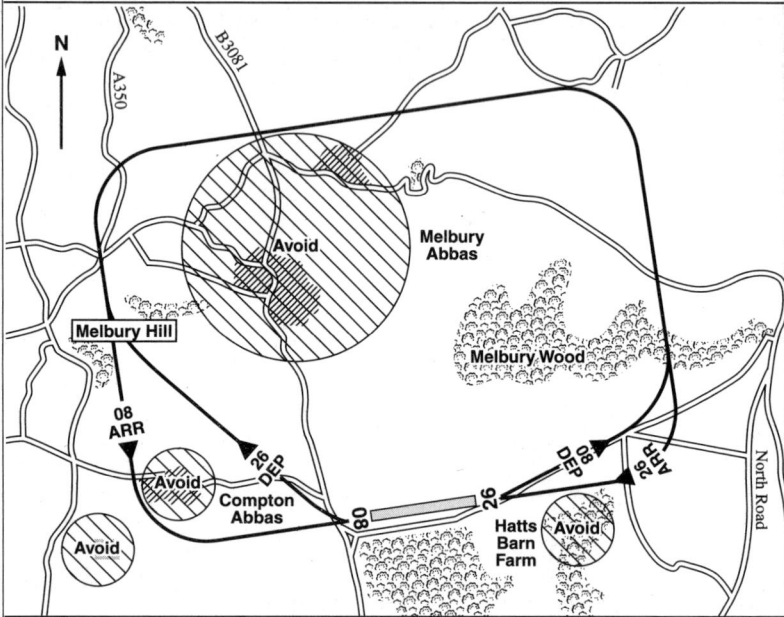

The airfield operates in an area of outstanding natural beauty, and to maintain the existing good relationship with the community, please observe good airmanship and avoid overflying hamlets and villages in close proximity to the airfield.

Arrivals:

Rwy 08 - A normal approach, but please avoid getting low on fianl approach or using excessive power settings when overflying Compton Village.

Rwy 26 - A normal approach.

Departures:

Rwy 08 - As soon as practicable, on passing the end of the runway, turn left in order to avoid overflying Hatts Barn Farmhouse.

Rwy 26 - As soon as practicable, on passing the end of the runway, turn right in order to cross the top of the Melbury Hill. Avoid overflying any part of Compton Abbas village.

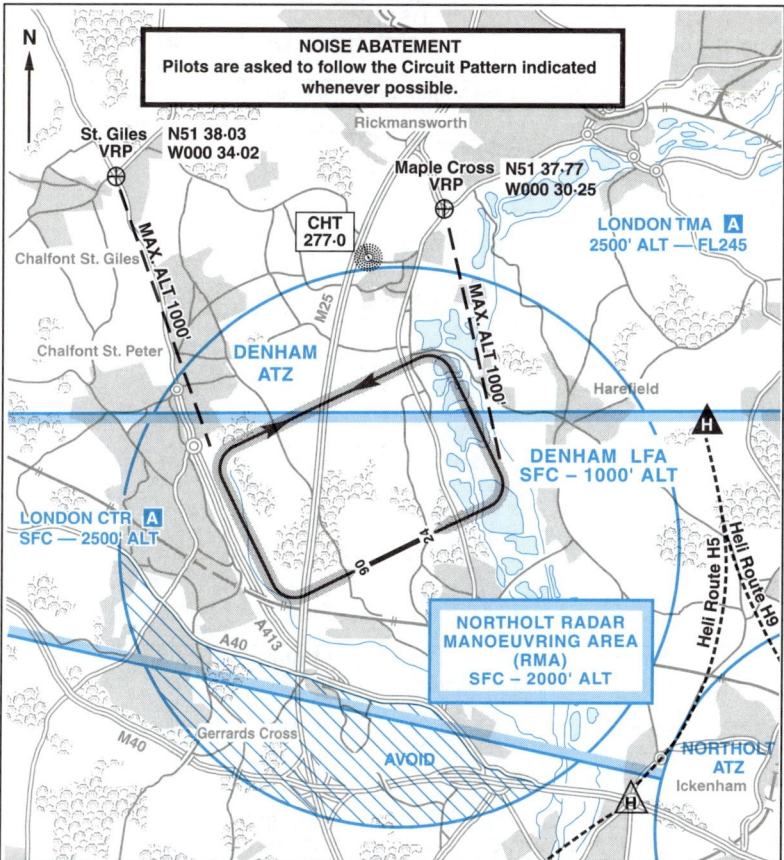

NOISE ABATEMENT
Pilots are asked to follow the Circuit Pattern indicated whenever possible.

N

St. Giles VRP N51 38-03 W000 34-02

Rickmansworth

Maple Cross VRP N51 37-77 W000 30-25

Chalfont St. Giles

MAX. ALT. 1000'

CHT 277·0

Chalfont St. Peter

DENHAM ATZ

LONDON TMA A
2500' ALT — FL245

MAX. ALT. 1000'

Harefield

DENHAM LFA
SFC – 1000' ALT

Heli Route H5
Heli Route H9

LONDON CTR A
SFC – 2500' ALT

24

06

NORTHOLT RADAR MANOEUVRING AREA (RMA)
SFC – 2000' ALT

M25

M40

Gerrards Cross

A40

A413

AVOID

NORTHOLT ATZ
Ickenham

H

H

Procedures: There is no overhead joining procedure. Circuit joining will be made directly to base leg, via Chalfont St. Giles for Rwy 06 and via Maple Cross for Rwy 24. Inbound aircraft must establish radio contact with Denham Radio at 10 nm range and then report at St. Giles for landing Rwy 06 and at Maple Cross for landing Rwy 24.

Within the Denham Local Flying Area (LFA), flights without compliance with IFR requirements may take place subject to the following conditions:

1. Aircraft to remain below cloud and in sight of surface.

2. Maximum altitude 1000 ft QNH, with a minimum flight visibility of 3 km.

3. The area to the South of the A40 is to be avoided at all times.

Note: Pilots of aircraft flying in the LFA are responsible for providing their own separation from other aircraft operating in the relevant airspace. Joing aircraft should give way to circuit traffic.

Northolt traffic in the Northolt Radar Manoeuvring Area (RMA) will cross Denham ATZ not below 1500 ft QNH but may be below this altitude in the Northolt ATZ which extends to within 0·1 nm of the edge of DenhamATZ at its closest point. Aircraft wishing to make use of the Northolt RMA when en route to or from Denham are to contact Northolt ATC for clearance.

N52 51·58 W001 37·05	**DERBY**	175 ft AMSL
6 nm SW of Derby	TNT 115·70 175 12.	HON 113·65 010 30
		DTY 116·40 343 45

Derby Radio 118·35 A/G.　East Midlands APP 119·65.

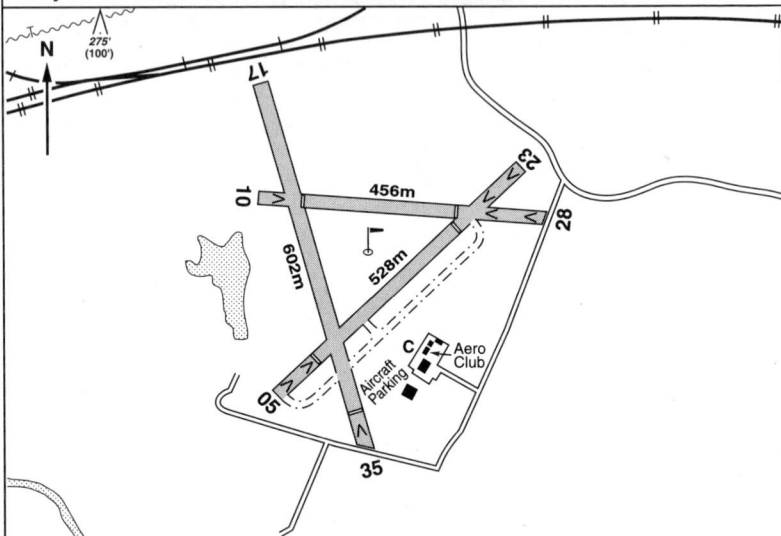

Rwy	Dim(m)	Surface	TORA(m)	LDA(m)	Lighting
05/23	528x20	Grass	05-356	05-430	Nil
			23-445	23-341	Nil
10/28	456x20	Grass	10-276	10-315	Nil
			28-300	28-291	Nil
17/35	602x20	Grass	17-525	(Take-off only)	Nil
			(Landing Only) 35-540		Nil

Op hrs: WINTER: PPR. Mon-Sat 0900-SS, Sun & PHs 0930-SS.
　　　　　SUMMER: PPR. Mon-Sat 0900-1700, Sun & PHs 0930-1700.

Landing Fee: £5.　**Customs:** Nil.　**Hangarage:** Ltd.　**Maintenance:** Available

Remarks: Operated by Derby Aero Club. Licensed aerodrome situated beneath East Midlands CTA (1500' – FL55). Special procedures applicable to all flights must be obtained by telephone from Derby Aero Club when arranging prior permission.
Non radio aircraft **not** accepted. Aerodrome not licensed for public transport flights.
Circuits: LH on 05 & 10; RH on 23 & 28, all at 1000' aal; LH on 17, RH on 35, both at 800' aal. No runway designators. Displaced landing thresholds marked by black/white or red/white wing bars. Avoid overflying local villages.
No overhead joins due to proximity of East Midlands CTA (base 1500').
Caution: Power cables 100' aal immediately North of A/D. An early 'Go around' decision vital in the event of missed approach to Rwy 35. Power cables 30' aal on approach to Rwy 28. Possible turbulence from trees on final approach to Rwy 23. These trees also shield aircraft low on final approach from those at the 23 hold.
Chimney 100' aal, 275' amsl, 010°/800 m.

Restaurant: Club facilities.　**Taxi/ Car Hire:** By arrangement.

Fuel: 100LL	**Tel:**01283-733803	**Fax:** 01283-734829

Robert Pooley ©

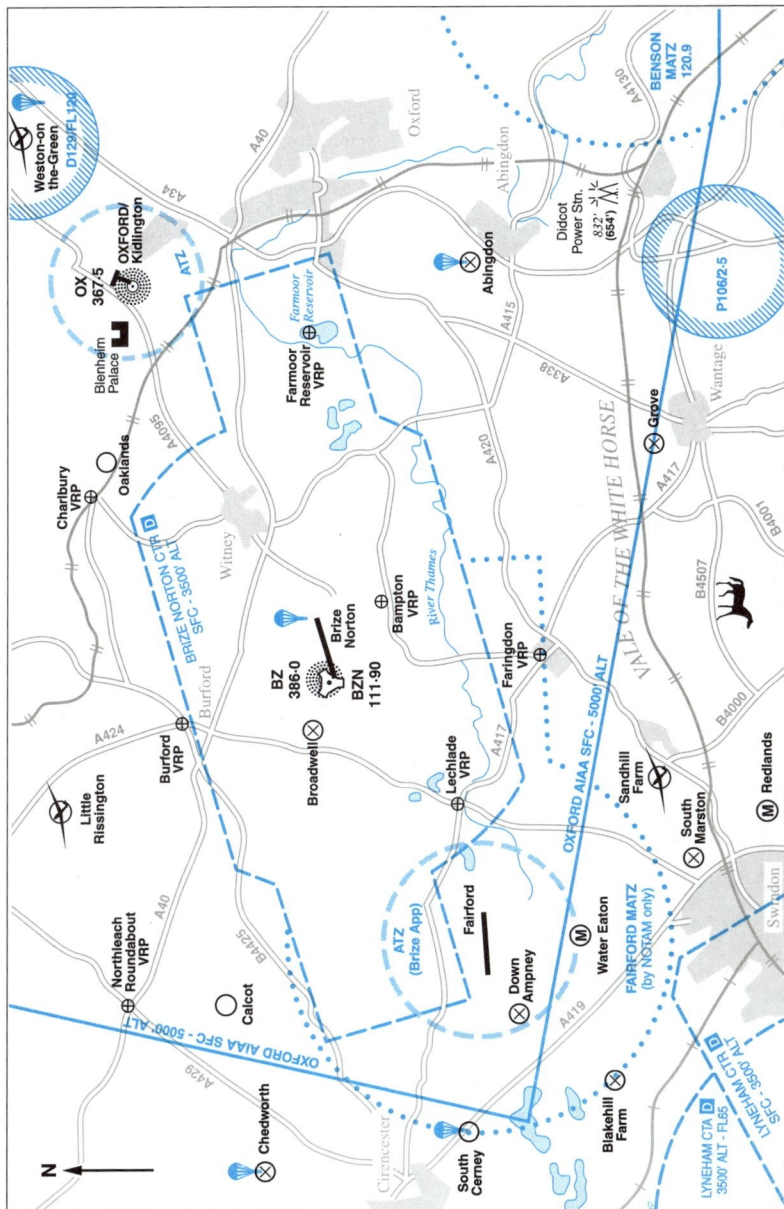

BRIZE NORTON
CTR and VRPs

1 DEC 00

Weston-on-the-Green D129/FL120

OXFORD/Kidlington
OX 367·5
ATZ

Blenheim Palace

BENSON MATZ 120·9

Oxford

Abingdon

Didcot Power Stn. 832' (654')

P106/2·5

A34 A40 A4130 A415 A338 A420

Farmoor Reservoir VRP

Charlbury VRP
Oaklands
Witney

Wantage

Grove

VALE OF THE WHITE HORSE

BRIZE NORTON CTR SFC - 3500' ALT
BZ 386·0
Brize Norton
BZN 111·90

Bampton VRP
River Thames
Faringdon VRP

OXFORD AIAA SFC - 5000' ALT

B4507

Burford VRP
Broadwell
Lechlade VRP

Sandhill Farm

South Marston

Redlands

A424 A417 A425 A419 B4000 B4001

Little Rissington

ATZ (Brize App)

Fairford

Down Ampney

Water Eaton

FAIRFORD MATZ (by NOTAM only)

Swindon

Northleach Roundabout VRP
Calcot

OXFORD AIAA SFC - 5000' ALT

A40 A429 A429

Chedworth

South Cerney

Cirencester

Blakehill Farm

LYNEHAM CTA 3500' ALT - FL65

LYNEHAM CTR SFC - 3500' ALT

N

Robert Pooley ©

143

Intentionally Blank

TEESSIDE
CTR/CTA and VRPs

1 DEC 00

TEESSIDE CTA 1 **D**
1000' - 6000' ALT

TEESSIDE CTR 1 **E**
SFC - 1000' ALT

TEESSIDE CTA 4 **D**
3000' - 6000' ALT

VALE OF YORK AIAA
SFC - FL200

Redcar

Yearby

Redcar VRP ⊕ ○

Hartlepool VRP ⊕

Hartlepool

Stokesley VRP ⊕ ○

Carlton Moor ⊗

2297 (1050)

TOPCLIFFE MATZ

Eaglescliffe

Teesside

Yarm

A19

A135

Crookfoot Reservoir

A689

A177

Fishburn ○

Sedgefield Racecourse VRP ⊕

TEESSIDE CTR 2 **D**
SFC - 6000' ALT

TD 347·5

A66

Teesside

Middleton St George

Northallerton VRP ⊕

Croft ○

A1(M)

GVS 3/3 ○

Darlington

TEESSIDE CTA 2 **D**
1200' - 6000' ALT

Junction A1(M) / A66 VRP ⊕

A1(M)

LEEMING MATZ

Catterick ⊗

A1

A1

TEESSIDE CTA 3 **D**
1500' - 6000' ALT

River Tes

N

Robert Pooley ©

487

Intentionally Blank

SOLENT CTA/BOURNEMOUTH and SOUTHAMPTON CTRs and VRPs

1 DEC 00

Intentionally Blank

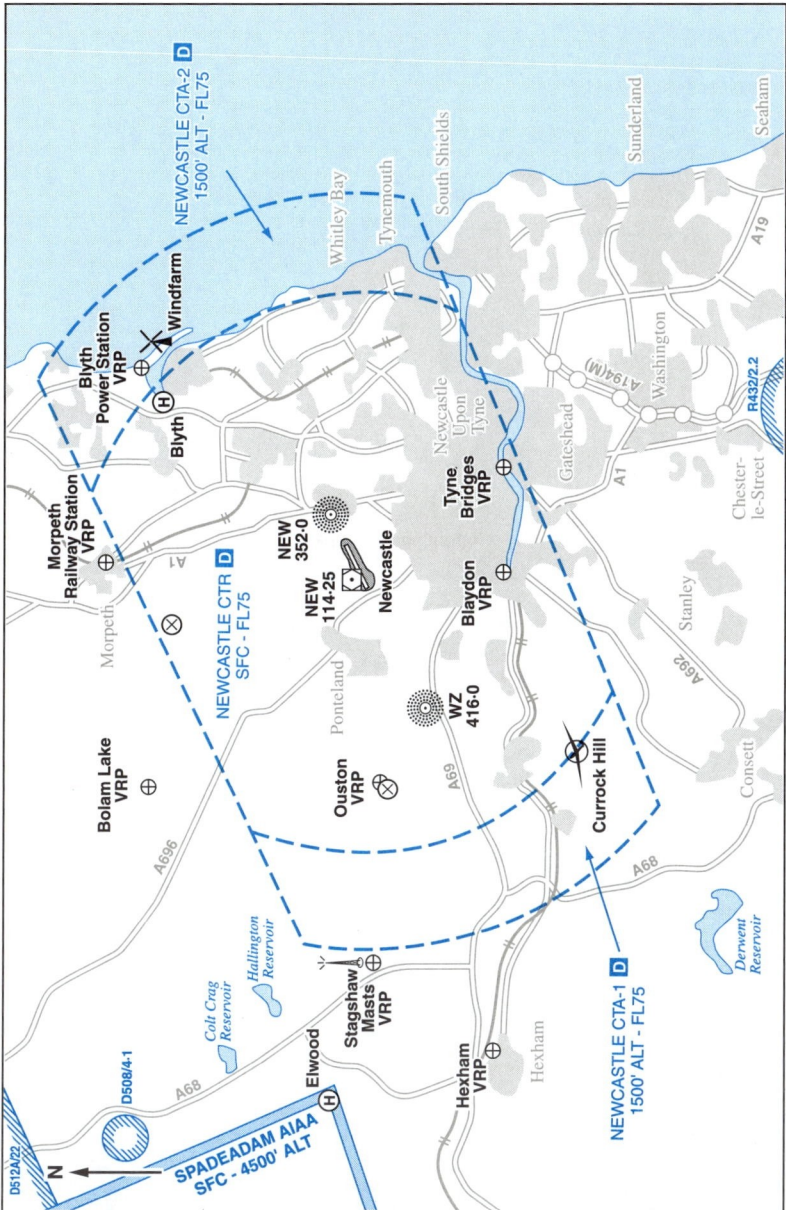

NEWCASTLE CTA-2 D
1500' ALT - FL75

Seaham

Sunderland

A19

Whitley Bay

Tynemouth

South Shields

Windfarm

Blyth Power Station VRP

Blyth (H)

Washington

A194(M)

R432/2.2

Morpeth Railway Station VRP

A1

Newcastle Upon Tyne

Gateshead

Chester-le-Street

NEWCASTLE CTR D
SFC - FL75

NEW 352·0

Newcastle

NEW 114·25

Tyne Bridges VRP

Blaydon VRP

A1

Stanley

A692

Consett

Morpeth

Ponteland

WZ 416·0

Bolam Lake VRP

Ouston VRP

A69

Currock Hill

NEWCASTLE CTA-1 D
1500' ALT - FL75

A68

Derwent Reservoir

Hallington Reservoir

Colt Crag Reservoir

Stagshaw Masts VRP

Hexham VRP

Hexham

A696

Elwood (H)

D508/4·1

A68

D512A/22

N

SPADEADAM AIAA
SFC - 4500' ALT

Intentionally Blank

MANCHESTER CTR/CTA
ENTRY/EXIT LANES AND VRPS

1 DEC 00

Robert Pooley ©

359

Intentionally Blank

Robert Pooley ©

347

Intentionally Blank

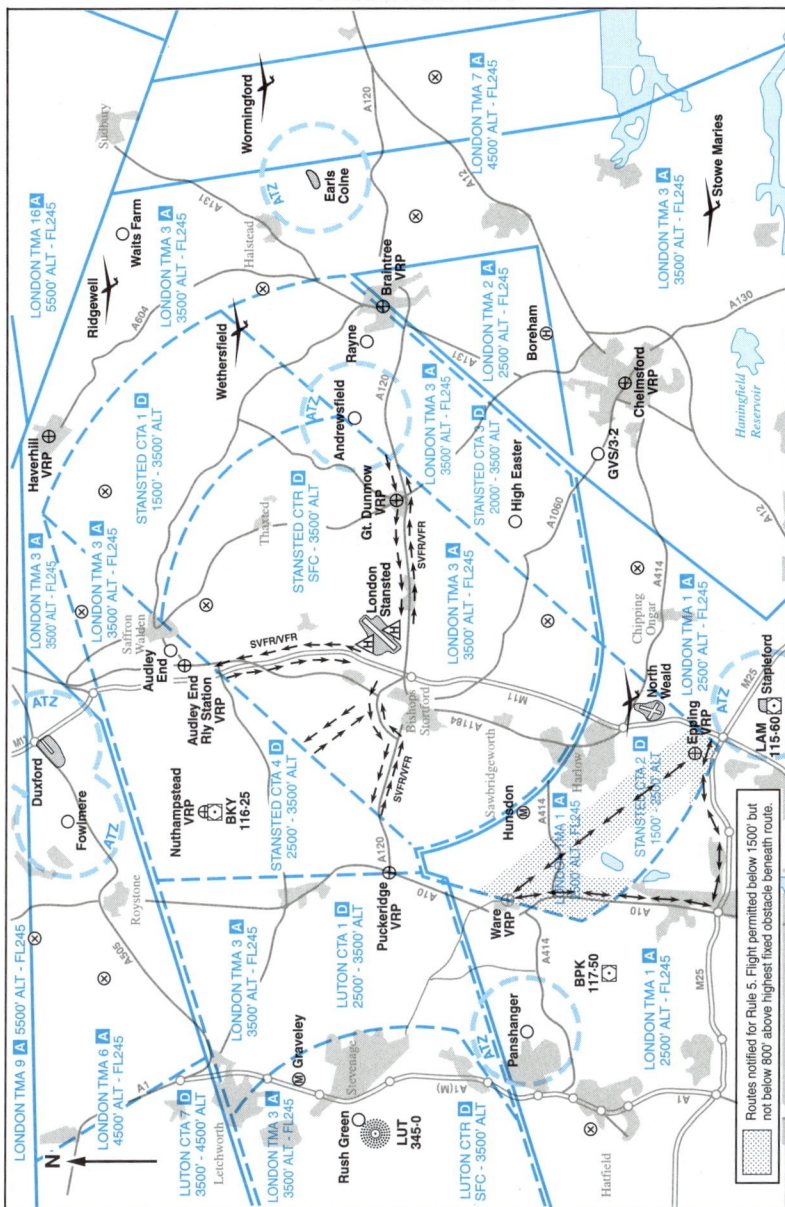

LONDON (Stansted) CTR/CTA and VRPs

Intentionally Blank

LONDON (Luton) CTR/CTA
ENTRY/EXIT LANES and VRPs

1 DEC 00

Robert Pooley ©

333

Intentionally Blank

LEEDS BRADFORD CTR/CTA and VRPs

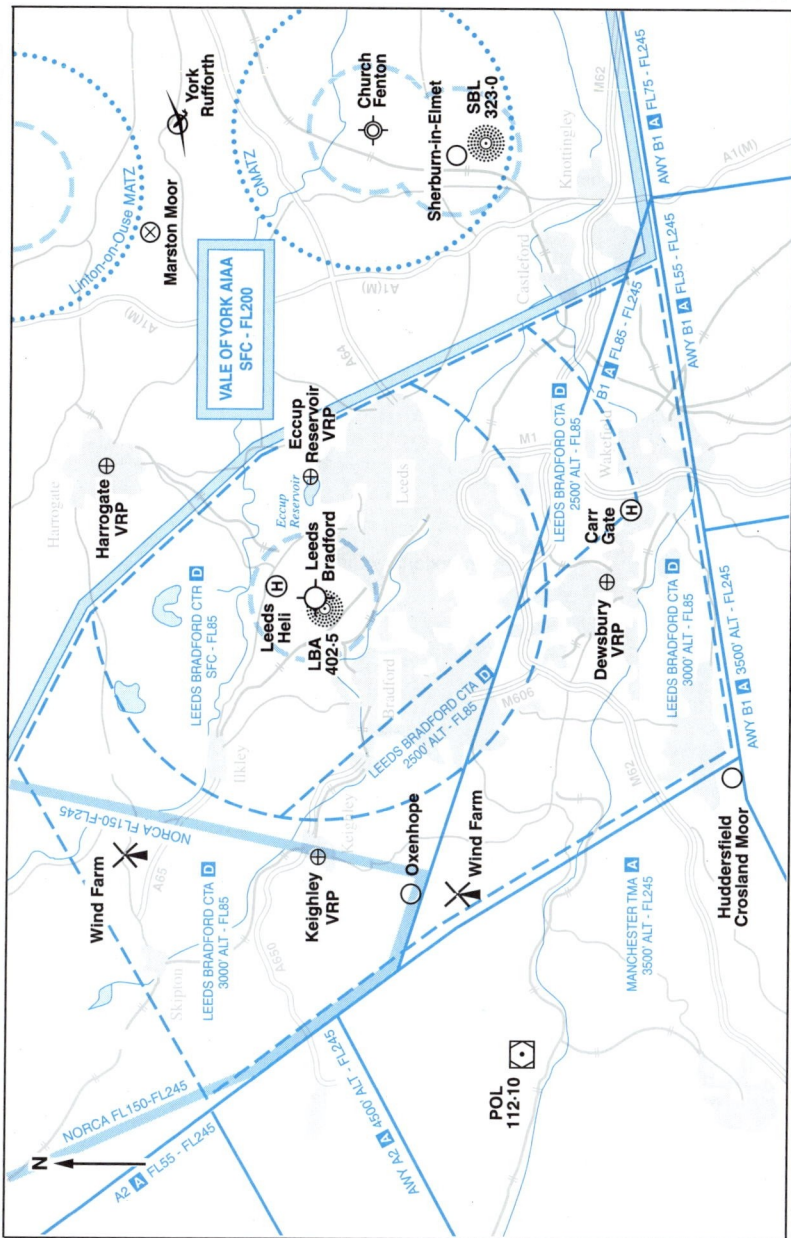

York Rufforth

Church Fenton

SBL
323·0

Sherburn-in-Elmet

Lintonon-Ouse MATZ

Marston Moor

CMATZ

Castleford

Knottingley

A1(M)

A1(M)

AWY B1 A FL75 - FL245

AWY B1 A FL55 - FL245

VALE OF YORK AIAA
SFC - FL200

A64

A(M)

M1

B1 A FL85 - FL245

LEEDS BRADFORD CTA D
2500 ALT - FL85

Ecup
Reservoir
VRP

Ecup
Reservoir

Harrogate
VRP

Harrogate

Leeds

Wakefield

LEEDS BRADFORD CTR D
SFC - FL85

Leeds
Heli

Leeds
Bradford

Carr
Gate

LBA
402·5

Dewsbury
VRP

LEEDS BRADFORD CTA D
3000 ALT - FL85

Ilkley

Bradford

M606

LEEDS BRADFORD CTA D
2500 ALT - FL85

M62

AWY B1 A 3500 ALT - FL245

NORCA FL150-FL245

Wind Farm

A65

Oxenhope

Wind Farm

Huddersfield
Crosland Moor

Keighley
VRP

Keighley

A650

LEEDS BRADFORD CTA D
3000 ALT - FL85

Skipton

MANCHESTER TMA A
3500 ALT - FL245

AWY B1 A 3500 ALT - FL245

NORCA FL150-FL245

POL
112·10

AWY A2 A 4500 ALT - FL245

N

A2 A FL55 - FL245

Robert Pooley ©

305

Intentionally Blank

ELSTREE – Fixed Wing
Noise Abatement and Circuit Patterns

1 DEC 00

Intentionally Blank

BRISTOL and CARDIFF CTRs/CTAs
VFR Routes and VRPs

1 DEC 00

A46 (T)

BATH

Charmey Down ⊗

Bath VRP ⊕

BRISTOL M4

SHEPTON MALLET

Hanham VRP ⊕

R 152/1·7

CTA D
FL65
1500' ALT

Clutton Hill ○

Radstock VRP ⊕

Old Severn Bridge (Northern)

OF
325·0

Filton

Balloons

A(T)

Chew Valley Lake

Chew Valley VRP ⊕

Franklyns Field

M5

R Avon

BRI
380·0

Mendip TV Mast

WELLS

BRISTOL CTR D
SFC — FL65

Bristol

Burrington Lake

A368

New Severn Bridge (Southern)

Portishead

Clevedon VRP ⊕

East Nailsea VRP ⊕

Churchill VRP ⊕

Weston

Cheddar Reservoir VRP ⊕

Westbury-sub-Mendip

YEOVILTON NORTH AIAA
2000' — 5000' ALT

G1 A Base FL75

NEWPORT

MOUTH OF THE SEVERN

D121/0·5

Weston-Super-Mare VRP ⊕

M5

A38

BRIDGEWATER

R Parrett

CTA D
FL65
1500' ALT

Cardiff Heliport

Cardiff Docks VRP ⊕

PENARTH

Flat Holm Lighthouse VRP ⊕

CARDIFF CTA 2 D
FL55
1500' ALT

CARDIFF CTA 1 D 1000' ALT
FL55

A39

BURNHAM-ON-SEA

CARDIFF

Wenvoe TV Mast VRP ⊕

VFR WENVOE (OUT)

VFR WENVOE (IN)

VFR EAST

BARRY

CARDIFF CTR D
SFC — FL55

BRISTOL CHANNEL

D119/5
When notified

WATCHET

A358

CAERPHILLY

Cardiff

VFR SOUTH

CARDIFF CTR

CDF
388·5

PONTYPRIDD

VFR ST HILARY

Cowbridge VRP ⊕

St. Hilary TV Mast VRP ⊕

Llandow

St. Athan

Nash South VRP ⊕

BASE FL55

A39

Junc 36 VRP ⊕

CARDIFF CTA 3 D
8000' ALT — FL55

Nash Point Lighthouse VRP ⊕

St. Athan Local Flying Zone

BASE FL55

A25 A

BASE FL65

A4064

M4

N

Cardiff VFR Routes

Robert Pooley ©

139

Intentionally Blank

BELFAST TMA, BELFAST CTR & BELFAST CITY CTR/CTA
and VRPs

1 DEC 00

Robert Pooley ©

Intentionally Blank

EDINBURGH CTR
ENTRY/EXIT LANES and VRPs

1 DEC 00

East Fortune (M)

SCOTTISH TMA [D] 6000' ALT - FL245 [E] "1500' - 6000' ALT

SCOTTISH TMA [D] 5600' ALT - FL245

SCOTTISH TMA [D] 6000' ALT - FL245 [E] "2500' - 6000' ALT

Earlsferry

Methil

Glenrothes

Kirkcaldy Harbour VRP

Musselburgh Racecourse VRP

Dalkeith VRP
Dalkeith

MOORFOOT HILLS

A7

A703

Gladhouse Reservoir

Portmore Loch

Loch Leven
Portmoak
Fife
GO 402.0

Loch Ore

Burntisland
Inchkeith

Leith

Arthurs Seat VRP

Edinburgh

Hillend Ski Slope VRP

Penicuik VRP

A701

A70

Kelty VRP Entry / Exit
Cowdenbeath

Inverkeithing

Forth Road Bridge North Tower VRP
Queensferry

EDN 341.0

A90

A8

Harlaw Reservoir

Harperrig Reservoir

Kirknewton
Kirknewton VRP

West Water Reservoir

West Linton VRP

Dunfermline

Rosyth

R603/2

Philipstoun VRP

Linlithgow

Kirkliston VRP

M9

UW 368.0

Livingston

Cobbinshaw Reservoir

Cobbinshaw Reservoir VRP

A70

PENTLAND HILLS

SCOTTISH TMA [D] 4500' ALT - FL245

SCOTTISH TMA [D] 6000' ALT - FL245 [E] 4000' - 6000' ALT

Grangemouth

Bo'ness

Bathgate VRP

EDINBURGH CTR [D] SFC - 6000' ALT

SCOTTISH TMA [D] 6000' ALT - FL245

SCOTTISH TMA [D] 6000' ALT - FL245 [E] "1500' - 6000' ALT

"Lower limits of TMA are as shown or 700ft agl whichever is higher

OCHIL HILLS

Alloa

Stirling

M9

Falkirk

Polmont VRP Entry / Exit

M9

M876

M80

GVS / 3.7

Armadale

M8

Whitburn

Cumbernauld

River Clyde

R504/2-8

Motherwell

M74

Hamilton

KILSYTH HILLS

Baillieston VRP

SCOTTISH TMA [D] 6000' ALT - FL245 [E] "2500' - 6000' ALT

Hillend Roughrig Reservoir

Airdrie

M73

M8

Strathaven

N

Robert Pooley ©

213

Intentionally Blank

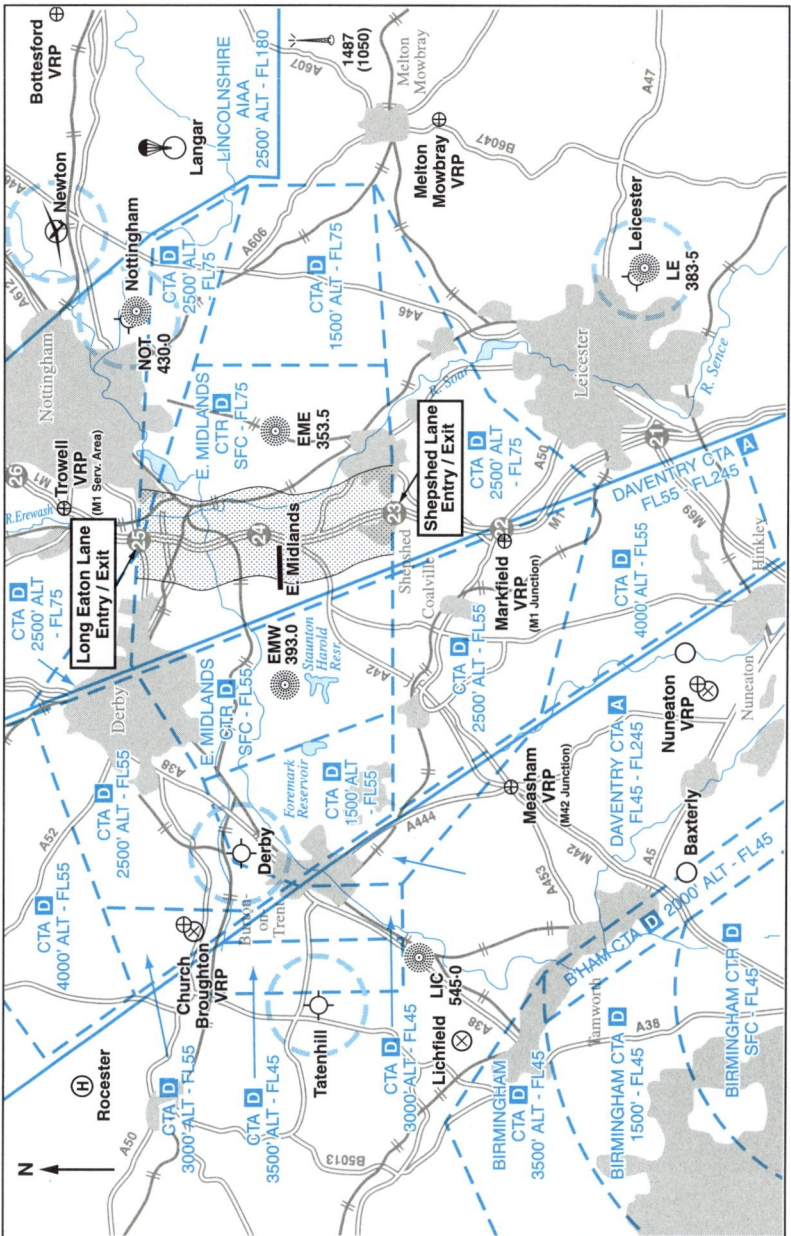

EAST MIDLANDS CTR/CTA ENTRY/EXIT LANES and VRPs — 1 DEC 00

Robert Pooley ©

207

Intentionally Blank